PRUSSIA

Berlin

Posen

Warsaw

POLAND

Dresden

SAXONY

Prague

Olmütz

AUSTRIAN

Munich

Vienna

Buda

Pest

EMPIRE

Vlágos

AUSTRIAN

Agram

Temesvár

Venice

Bologna

PAPAL STATES

Rome

NEAPOLITAN

Naples

THE TWO SICILIES

Palermo

NEAPOLITAN

Serbia

Wallachia

Bucharest

Moldavia

Jassy

RUSSIAN

RUSSIAN

OTTOMAN

EMPIRE

IONIAN ISLANDS

GREECE

N.G.

outbreaks

Abdication of a monarch

Counter-revolutionary interventions

Border of German Confederation

Revolutionary Spring

CHRISTOPHER CLARK

Revolutionary Spring

Fighting for a New World, 1848–1849

ALLEN LANE
an imprint of
PENGUIN BOOKS

ALLEN LANE

UK | USA | Canada | Ireland | Australia
India | New Zealand | South Africa

Allen Lane is part of the Penguin Random House group of companies whose
addresses can be found at global.penguinrandomhouse.com

First published 2023
001

Copyright © Christopher Clark, 2023

The moral right of the author has been asserted

Set in 10.2/13.87pt Sabon LT Std
Typeset by Jouve (UK), Milton Keynes
Printed and bound in Great Britain by Clays Ltd, Elcograf S.p.A.

The authorized representative in the EEA is Penguin Random House Ireland,
Morrison Chambers, 32 Nassau Street, Dublin D02 YH68

A CIP catalogue record for this book is available from the British Library

ISBN: 978-0-241-34766-9

For Kristina

Mehiläinen maasta nousi,
simasiipi mättähältä;
jopa lenti löyhytteli,
pienin siivin siuotteli.
Lenti kuun keheä myöten,
päivän päärmettä samosi

Contents

List of Illustrations

Photographic acknowledgements are shown where applicable.

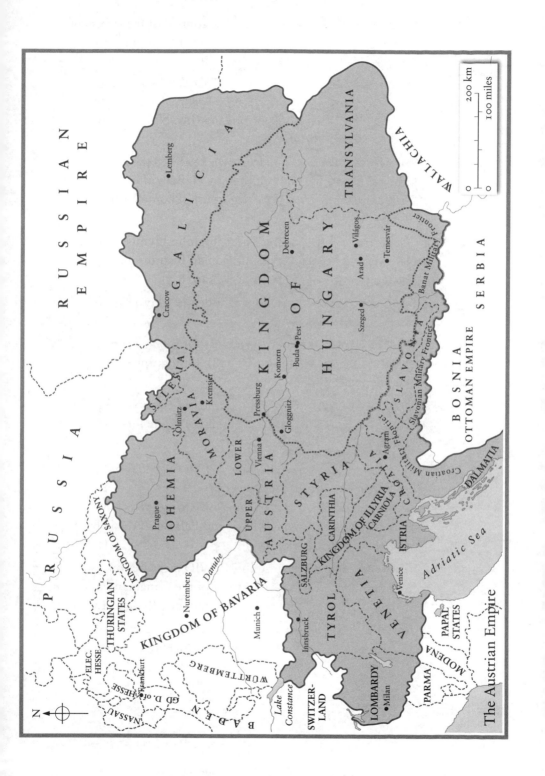

RUSSIAN EMPIRE

PRUSSIA

GALICIA

Lemberg •

TRANSYLVANIA

WALLACHIA

Cracow •

KINGDOM OF HUNGARY

Debrecen •

Világos •
Arad •
Temesvár •

Banat Military Frontier

SERBIA

Szeged •

Buda • Pest

SILESIA

KINGDOM OF SAXONY

Pressburg •
Komorn •

MORAVIA

Olmütz •
Kremsier •

Gloggnitz •

SLAVONIA

Slavonian Military Frontier

BOSNIA

OTTOMAN EMPIRE

LOWER

Vienna •

AUSTRIA

BOHEMIA

Prague •

UPPER

STYRIA

CROATIA

Agram •

Croatian Military Frontier

THURINGIAN STATES

NASSAU

ELEC. HESSE

GD. D. of HESSE

Frankfurt •

Nuremberg •

Danube

KINGDOM OF BAVARIA

SALZBURG

CARINTHIA

KINGDOM OF ILLYRIA

CARNIOLA

ISTRIA

DALMATIA

Adriatic Sea

WÜRTTEMBERG

Munich •

Innsbruck •

TYROL

VENETIA

Venice •

BADEN

SWITZER-LAND

Lake Constance

LOMBARDY

Milan •

PARMA

MODENA

PAPAL STATES

The Austrian Empire

N

200 km

100 miles

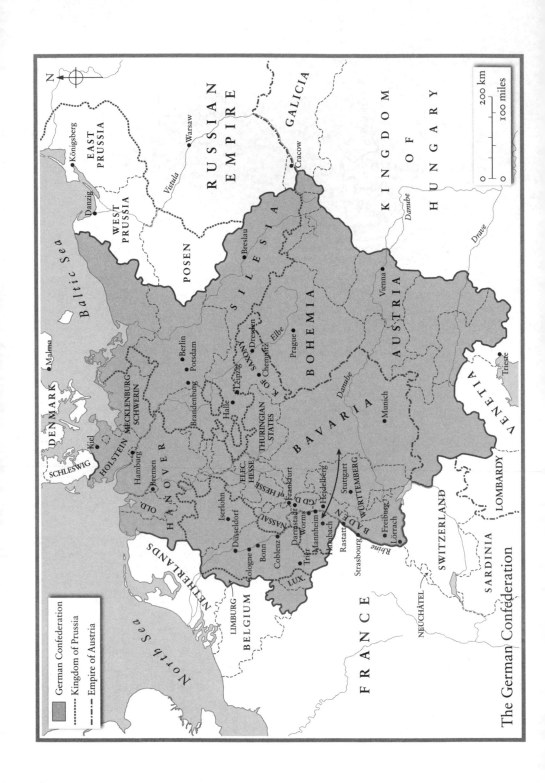

The German Confederation

The Italian States

The Danubian Principalities

N

PRUSSIA   RUSSIA

⊙ Prague
                    Cracow
                      ⊙   ⊙ Lemberg
                                                    (Lviv)
Brünn ⊙
(Brno)
        Pressburg
        (Bratislava)
Vienna ⊙ ⊙
            Buda
                 ⊙ ⊙   ⊙ Debrecen   ⊙ Iaşi
Pákozd 09.1848 ✕ Pest
                                                            MOLDAVIA
                                        ⊙ Kolozsvár (Cluj)
                                  Világos
⊙ Agram (Zagreb)   ⊙   Blaj ⊙   ⊙ Segesvár
                                                   (Sighişoara)
                          ✕ Temesvár 08.1849
                          (Timişoara)
              ✕ Újvidék 06.1849
              Novi Sad
                                            WALLACHIA
                                          Bucharest ⊙

OTTOMAN   EMPIRE

▢ Austrian Empire	Military campaign of:
— Boundary of Hungary	→ Croats 1848
⊙ Centre of revolution	⇢ Austrians 1849
✕ Battle with date	→ Russians 1849

0   200 km
0   100 miles

The Hungarian Independence War

Introduction

In their combination of intensity and geographical extent, the 1848 revolutions were unique – at least in European history. Neither the great French Revolution of 1789, nor the July Revolution of 1830, nor the Paris Commune of 1870, nor the Russian revolutions of 1905 and 1917 sparked a comparable transcontinental cascade. 1989 looks like a better comparator, but there is still controversy as to whether these uprisings can be characterized as 'revolutions'. In 1848, by contrast, parallel political tumults broke out across the entire continent, from Switzerland and Portugal to Wallachia and Moldavia, from Norway, Denmark and Sweden to Palermo and the Ionian Islands. This was the only truly European revolution that there has ever been.

But it was also in some respects a global upheaval, or at least a European upheaval with a global dimension. The news of revolution in Paris had a profound impact on the French Caribbean, and the measures adopted by London to avoid revolution on the British mainland triggered protests and uprisings across the British imperial periphery. In the young nations of Latin America, too, the European revolutions galvanized liberal and radical political elites. Even in far-off Australia, the February Revolution created political waves – though it was not until 19 June 1848 that the news of the February events reached Sydney in the Colony of New South Wales – a reminder of what the Australian historian Geoffrey Blainey once mournfully described as 'the tyranny of distance'.

The revolutions involved a vast panorama of charismatic and gifted actors, from Giuseppe Garibaldi to Marie d'Agoult, author (under a male pseudonym) of the best contemporary history of the revolutions in France, from the French socialist Louis Blanc to the leader of the Hungarian national movement, Lajos Kossuth; from the brilliant conservative

liberal social theorist, historian and politician Alexis-Charles-Henri
Clérel de Tocqueville to the Wallachian soldier, journalist and agrarian
radical Nicolae Bălcescu. From the young patriot poet Sándor Petőfi,
whose recitation of a new national song for the Hungarians electrified
the revolutionary crowds in Budapest, to the troubled priest Félicité de
Lamennais, whose ultimately unsuccessful struggle to reconcile his faith
with his politics made him one of the most famous thinkers in the pre-
1848 world; from the writer George Sand, who composed 'revolutionary
bulletins' for the Provisional Government in Paris, to the Roman popular tribune Angelo Brunetti, known affectionately as Ciceruacchio, or
'Chubby', a true man of the people, who did much to shape the unfolding of the Roman revolution of 1848–9. Not to mention the countless
women who sold broadsheets and newspapers in the streets of the European cities or fought at the barricades (they are very prominent in the
visual depiction of these revolutions). For politically sentient Europeans, 1848 was an all-encompassing moment of shared experience. It
turned everyone into contemporaries, branding them with memories
that would last as long as life itself.

These revolutions were experienced as *European* upheavals – the evidence for this is superabundant; but they were nationalized in retrospect.[1]
The historians and memory managers of the European nations absorbed
them into specific national stories. The supposed failure of the German
revolutions was sucked into the national narrative known as the *Sonderweg*, or 'special path', where it helped to power a thesis about Germany's
aberrant road into modernity, a road that culminated in the disaster of
the Hitler dictatorship. Something similar happened in Italy, where the
failure of revolution in 1848 was seen as pre-programming an authoritarian drift into the new Italian kingdom and thereby paving the road
to the March on Rome in 1922 and the fascist seizure of power that
followed. In France, the failure of 1848 was seen as ushering in the
Bonapartist interlude of the Second Empire, which in turn anticipated
the future triumph of Gaullism. In other words, focusing on the supposed failure of 1848 also had the consequence of allowing these stories
to be channelled into a plurality of parallel, nation-state-focused narratives. Nothing demonstrates better than these connected upheavals and
their fragmentation in modern memory the immense power of the
nation-state as a way of framing the historical record – we are still feeling that power today.

There were three phases to the events of 1848. In February and March, upheaval spread like a brush fire across the continent, leaping from city to city and starting numerous spot-fires in towns and villages in-between. The Austrian Chancellor, Metternich, fled from Vienna, the Prussian army was withdrawn from Berlin, the kings of Piedmont–Sardinia, Denmark and Naples issued constitutions – it all seemed so easy. This was the Tahrir Square moment: one could be forgiven for thinking that the movement encompassed the entirety of society; the euphoria of unanimity was intoxicating; 'I had to go out into the winter cold and walk and walk until I had worn myself out', one German radical wrote, 'just to calm my blood and slow down the beating of my heart, which was in a state of unprecedented and baffled agitation and felt as if it were about to blow a hole in my chest.'[2] In Milan, complete strangers embraced each other in the streets. These were the spring days of 1848.

Yet the divisions within the upheaval (already latent in the first hours of conflict) soon became glaringly apparent: by May, radical demonstrators were attempting to storm and overthrow the National Assembly created by the February Revolution in Paris, while, in Vienna, Austrian democrats protested at the slowness of liberal reforms and established a Committee of Public Safety. In June, there were violent clashes between the liberal (or in France republican) leaderships and radical crowds on the streets of the larger cities. In Paris, this culminated in the brutality and bloodshed of the 'June Days', which killed at least 3,000 insurgents. This was the long hot summer of 1848, gleefully diagnosed by Marx as the moment at which the revolution lost its innocence and the sweet (but deceptive) unanimity of spring made way for the bitter struggle between classes.

The autumn of 1848 offered a more complex picture. In September, October and November, counter-revolution unfolded in Berlin, Prague, Vienna and Wallachia. Parliaments were shut down, insurgents were arrested and sentenced, troops returned en masse to the streets of the cities. But, at the same time, a second-phase, radical revolt dominated by democrats and social republicans of various kinds broke out in the central and southern German states (especially Saxony Baden and Württemberg), in western and southern France, and in Rome, where the radicals, after the flight of the Pope on 24 November, eventually declared a Roman Republic. In the south of Germany, this second-wave upheaval was only extinguished in the summer of 1849, when Prussian troops finally captured the fortress of Rastatt in Baden, last stronghold of the radical insurgency. Shortly afterwards in August 1849, French troops crushed the Roman republic and restored the papacy, much to the chagrin of those who had once revered France as the patroness of revolution across the continent. At about the same time, the bitter war over the future of the Kingdom of Hungary was brought to an end, as Austrian and Russian troops occupied the country. By the end of the summer of 1849, the revolutions were largely over.

These grim and often very violent days of reckoning mean, among other things, that the narrative of these upheavals lacks a moment of redemptive closure. It was precisely the stigma of failure that put me off the 1848 revolutions when I first encountered them at school. Complexity and failure are an unattractive combination.

Why, then, should we make the effort today of reflecting on 1848? First, the 1848 revolutions were in fact *not* a failure: in many countries they produced swift and lasting constitutional change and post-1848 Europe was or became a very different place. It is more interesting to think of this continental uprising as the particle collision chamber at the centre of the European nineteenth century. People, groups and ideas flew into it, crashed together, fused or fragmented, and emerged in showers of new entities whose trails can be traced through the decades that followed. Political movements and ideas, from socialism and democratic radicalism to liberalism, nationalism, corporatism and conservatism, were tested in this chamber; all were changed, with profound consequences for the modern history of Europe. The revolutions also produced – notwithstanding the persistence of 'failure' as a way of thinking about them – a profound transformation in political and administrative practices across the continent, a European 'revolution in government'.

Second, the questions that the insurgents of 1848 asked have not lost their power. There are exceptions, obviously: we no longer wrack our brains over the temporal power of the papacy or the 'Schleswig-Holstein question'. But we do still worry about what happens when demands for political or economic liberty conflict with demands for social rights. Freedom of the press was all very well, the radicals of 1848 never tired of saying, but what was the point of a high-minded newspaper if you were too hungry to read it? The problem was captured by German radicals in the playful juxtaposition of the 'freedom to read' (*Pressefreiheit*) with the 'freedom to feed' (*Fressefreiheit*).

The spectre of 'pauperization' had loomed over the 1840s. How was it possible that even people in full-time work could scarcely manage to feed themselves? Entire sectors of manufacture – weavers were the most prominent example – appeared to be engulfed by this predicament. But what did this tide of immiseration mean? Was the gaping inequality between rich and poor simply a divinely ordained feature of man's estate, as conservatives claimed, was it a symptom of backwardness and overregulation, as liberals argued, or was it something generated by the political and economic system in its current incarnation, as the radicals insisted? Conservatives looked to charitable amelioration and liberals to economic deregulation and industrial growth, but radicals were less sanguine: to them, it seemed that the entire economic order was founded upon the exploitation by the stronger of the weaker. These questions have not faded away. The problem of the 'working poor' is today one of the burning issues of social policy. And the relationship between capitalism and social inequality is still under scrutiny.

Particularly difficult was the question of labour. What if work itself became a scarce commodity? The downturn in the business cycle in the winter and spring of 1847–8 had pushed many thousands of men and women out of work. Did citizens have the right to demand that, if necessary, labour be apportioned to them, as something essential to a dignified existence? It was the effort to answer this question that produced the controversial 'National Workshops' in Paris and their many analogues in other parts of Europe. But it was never going to be easy to persuade hard-working farmers in the Limousin to pay extra in tax to fund work creation schemes for men they regarded as Parisian layabouts. On the other hand, it was the sudden closure of these workshops, which poured 100,000 unemployed men back onto the streets of the capital, that triggered the violence of the Paris June Days of 1848.

The Düsseldorf artist Johann Peter Hasenclever captured the same issue in his canvas *Workers before the City Council*. Painted in 1849 and widely exhibited in a number of versions, it shows a delegation of labourers whose work creation scheme – which involved excavating various arms of the River Rhine – had just been shut down in the autumn of 1848 for lack of funds. They present a petition of protest to the city fathers of Düsseldorf in an opulent council chamber. Through a large window, an orator can be seen in the square outside addressing a raging crowd. Karl Marx loved this painting for its stark depiction of what he

Johann Peter Hasenclever, *Workers before the City Council* (1849). Workers laid off after the closure of a public works programme on the River Rhine petition their town council for a resumption of the works in the autumn of 1848. The council reacts with consternation. Through the window, a demagogue can be seen addressing an aroused crowd. The painting relates to an event that took place in Düsseldorf, but the architecture in the background is not specific to the city and hints at a more general urban predicament.

saw as a conflict between classes. At the end of a long piece for the *New York Tribune*, he praised the artist for conveying with 'dramatic vitality' in one image a state of affairs that a progressive writer could only hope to analyse over many pages of print.[3] Questions about social rights, poverty and the right to work tore the revolutions apart during the summer of 1848. They cannot be said to have lost any of their urgency.

As a non-linear, convulsive, intermittently violent and transformative 'unfinished revolution', 1848 remains an interesting study for present-day readers. In 2010–11, many journalists and historians noticed the uncanny resemblance between the untidy sequence of upheavals that are sometimes called the 'Arab Spring' and the revolutions of 1848, also known as the 'springtime of the peoples'. Like the upheavals in the Arab states, they were diverse, geographically dispersed and yet connected. The single most striking feature of the 1848 revolutions was their simultaneity – this was a puzzle to contemporaries and has remained one to historians ever since. It was also one of the most enigmatic features of the Arab events of 2010–11, which had deep local roots, but were clearly also interlinked. In a lot of ways, Cairo's Tahrir Square was not like the Piazza San Marco in Venice; the *Vossische Zeitung* was not Facebook – but they are alike enough to trigger larger connecting thoughts. The important point is a general one: in their swarming multitudinousness, in the unpredictable interaction of so many forces, the tumults of the mid nineteenth century resembled the chaotic upheavals of our own day, in which clearly defined endpoints are hard to come by.

The revolution of 1848 was a revolution of assemblies: the Constituent Assembly in Paris, which made way for the single-chamber legislature known as the Assemblée Nationale; the Prussian Constituent Assembly or Nationalversammlung in Berlin, elected under new laws created for the purpose; the Frankfurt parliament, convoked in the elegant circular chamber of St Paul's Church in the city of Frankfurt. The Hungarian Diet was a very old body, but in the course of the Hungarian revolutions of 1848 a new national Diet convened in the city of Pest. The revolutionary insurgents of Naples, Piedmont–Sardinia, Tuscany and the Papal States all established new parliamentary bodies. The revolutionaries of Sicily, seeking to break away from the rule of Naples, founded their own all-Sicilian parliament, which in April 1848 deposed the Bourbon king in Naples, Ferdinand II.

But the assemblies were merely one theatre of action. By the summer of 1848, they were coming under pressure, not just from the monarchical executives in many states, but also from a range of competing agencies of more radical colour: networks of clubs and 'committees', for example, or radical counter-assemblies such as the General Crafts and Manufacturing Congress founded in Frankfurt in July 1848 to represent those workers in the skilled trades whose interests were not catered for in the liberal- and middle-class-dominated National Assembly. Even this body split after five days into two separate congresses, because it proved impossible to bridge the divide between masters and journeymen.

Liberals revered parliaments and they looked with fastidious anxiety upon the clubs and assemblies of the radicals, which seemed to them to parody the sublime procedural culture of properly elected and constituted chambers. Even more alarming, from the perspective of 'chamber liberals', was the prospect of organized demonstrations prepared to intervene directly in the affairs of parliaments. Exactly this happened in Paris on 15 May 1848, when a crowd broke into the lightly guarded chamber of the National Assembly, disrupted the proceedings, read out a petition and then marched off to the Hôtel de Ville to proclaim an 'insurrectionary government' to be headed by noted radical personalities. The tension between parliamentary and other forms of representation – between representative and direct forms of democracy – is another feature of 1848 that resonates with today's political scene, in which parliaments face a fall in public esteem and a diverse array of competing non- or extra-parliamentary groups has emerged, using social media, and organizing around issues that may not command the attention of professional politicians.

1848 wasn't just a story of revolutionaries. Twentieth- and twenty-first-century historians of liberal instincts have naturally been drawn to the cause of those whose demands – for freedom of association, speech and the press, for constitutions, regular elections and parliaments – have entered the repertoire of modern liberal democracy. But while I share this affinity for newspaper-reading, coffee-drinking liberals and radicals, it seems to me that an account that views events only from an insurgent or liberal standpoint will miss an essential part of the drama and meaning of these revolutions. They were a complex encounter between old and new powers, in which the old ones did as much to shape the shorter- and longer-term outcomes of the revolutions as the new. Even this correction falls short, because the 'old powers' that survived the revolution were themselves transformed by it, though generally not in ways

8

that most historians have found interesting. The future Prussian Minister-President and German statesman Otto von Bismarck was still a small player in 1848, but the revolution enabled him to fuse his personal destiny with the future of his country. Throughout his life he continued to acknowledge 1848 as a rupture between one epoch and another, as a moment of transformation without which his own career would have been unthinkable. The papacy of Pius IX was profoundly altered by the revolutions, as was the Catholic Church and its relationship with the modern world. Today's Catholic Church is in many respects the fruit of that moment. Napoleon III did not think of himself as the crusher of revolution, but as the restorer of order. He spoke of the need not to block, but to channel, the forces unleashed by the revolution, to establish the state as the vanguard of material progress.

This was an upheaval in which the lines between revolution and counter-revolution were and are sometimes hard to draw. Many 1848ers died or suffered exile and imprisonment for their convictions, but many others crossed the floor, making their peace with post-revolutionary administrations that had themselves been transformed or chastened by the revolutionary shock. Thus began a long march through the institutions. More than a third of the prefects (regional police officials) of post-1848 Bonapartist France were ex-radicals; so was the Austrian Minister of the Interior from July 1849, Alexander von Bach, whose name had once stood on the lists of suspect democrats kept by the Vienna police department. Counter-revolutionaries were as often as not – in their own eyes – the executors, rather than the gravediggers, of the revolution. Understanding that enables us to see more clearly how this revolution changed Europe.

In memory, the revolutions (at least for many former participants) took on a stark emotional chiaroscuro: the bright euphoria of the early days, and then the frustration, bitterness and melancholy that came when the 'iron net of counter-revolution' (as the Berliner Fanny Lewald put it) descended on the insurgent cities. Euphoria and disappointment were part of this story, but so was fear. Soldiers feared angry townspeople almost as much as the latter feared them. The sudden panics of crowds confronted by troops produced unpredictable stampedes that can be seen in every insurgent city. 'Since 25 February [1848]', wrote Émile Thomas, architect of the National Workshops in Paris and later a zealous Bonapartist, 'we have been governed under the influence of fear, that evil counsellor that paralyses all good intentions.'[4]

Liberal leaders feared they might be unable to control the social energies released by the revolution. People of humbler social standing feared that a conspiracy was underway to stitch up the revolution, reverse its achievements and plunge them for ever into poverty and helplessness. Urban middle-class residents winced when uncouth figures from the suburbs poured in through the city gates now shorn of their military posts. They feared for their property, and sometimes for their lives. In Palermo, there was a rough, diverse and potentially ungovernable social undercurrent to the uprising in the city. The early leaders of the Palermo revolution were stolid and predictable dignitaries. But as Ferdinando Malvica, author of an unpublished contemporary chronicle of the Palermitan revolution, pointed out, the streets soon also filled with the armed *maestranze* (craftsmen's corporations) and, more disturbingly, with squads from the surrounding country: these, he wrote, were 'ferocious men, almost devoid of human feeling, as bloodthirsty as they were boorish, ugly people [by whom] the beautiful civic capital of Sicily found itself surrounded, infernal tribes peopled only by creatures in whom nothing was human but their sunburnt countenances'.[5] Without the driving force and supposed menace exercised by such people, the risings of 1848 could never have succeeded; and yet a pervasive fear of the lower orders also paralysed the revolution in its later stages, making it easier to play different interests off against each other, to woo liberals into the arms of the established authorities, and to isolate radicals as enemies of the social order. On the other hand, the subsiding of fear could trigger rushes of euphoric emotion, as happened in many European cities during the spring days, when citizens suddenly lost or overcame their fear of the security forces or of the secret police.

Specific displays of emotion could be developed as articulations of revolutionary sensibility and some of these convey the distinctiveness of 1848 as a moment of middle-class revolt. On his way to his execution by a firing squad outside Vienna early on the morning of 9 November 1848, the radical parliamentary deputy Robert Blum was seen – according to several of the poems and songs that commemorate his death – to shed a single tear. When an officer remarked: 'Don't be afraid, it will all be over in an instant', Blum brushed off the effort to comfort him and, drawing himself up to his full (but not very great) height, retorted: 'This tear is not the tear of the parliamentary deputy of the German nation Robert Blum. This is the tear of the father and husband.'

Blum's tear entered radical legend. The 'Song of Robert Blum' sung across the southern German states well into the twentieth century includes a reference to this moment of private grief amidst the public ritual of a political execution: 'The tear for one's wife and children', it solemnly intones, 'does not dishonour a man.' The tear lived on in memory because it identified Blum as a man of middle-class attachments and values, a private man who had entered public life. This was politics in a bourgeois key. (To this day, *erschossen wie Robert Blum*, 'as shot as Robert Blum', is a proverbial expression in parts of southern Germany.)

Counter-revolutionaries had emotions too, of course. At the end of an extraordinary speech to the United Diet in Berlin, in which Otto von Bismarck reluctantly declared that he now accepted the revolution as an irreversible historical fact and the new liberal ministry as 'the government of the future', he left the podium sobbing violently. These tears, unlike Blum's, were emphatically public, both in their performative character and in their causation. The cry *Berliner Schweine!* ('Berlin pigs!') uttered by rural peasant army recruits from backwoods Brandenburg as they beat suspected barricade fighters in the capital with clubs and iron rods during the March days tell us something (though certainly not everything) about the feelings country youths brought to the tasks of urban counter-insurgency. Vengefulness and anger were important to the brutality of Austrian generals like Haynau, who appeared to delight in the death sentences and executions he meted out to defeated Hungarian insurgents.

The book opens with the precarious social world of pre-1848 Europe, an era in which the great majority of the population was pressed and flexed by rapid change. The link between social distress and political upheaval was deep, if not direct. And economically motivated protest and the spectacle of extreme social distress gave off a polarizing political energy, helping to shape the allegiances of those who would make or inherit the revolutions of 1848. The political universe in which the revolutions broke out (chapter 2) was not structured by hard-and-fast commitments and solid partisan identities. The Europeans of this era charted highly idiosyncratic journeys across an archipelago of arguments and chains of thought. They were in motion, and they remained so during and after the mid-century revolutions. The political conflicts of the 1830s and 1840s (chapter 3) were fought out along many fault lines. There was no binary cleavage, but a plethora of fractures running in every direction. This remained a feature of the revolutions themselves, which appear at first glance remarkably chaotic and opaque – in that respect they resemble the conflicts that compel our attention today.

Chapters 4–6 zero in on the revolutions themselves: did revolutionaries make them, or was it the other way around? The upheavals began with scenes of often magnificent drama. An account of their inception must make sense both of their great strength and of the structural and psychosocial vulnerabilities that would later be their undoing. Chapter 5 reflects on the parallel processing that took place across the chief theatres of unrest: the transformation of cities into circuitry humming with political emotion, the solemn burial of the revolutionary dead, the creation of new governments, chambers and constitutions, often under conditions of extreme uncertainty. The revolutionaries of 1848 thought of themselves as the bringers and enablers of 'emancipation', but what did this mean for those who hoped to achieve emancipation through them? Following the paths of the enslaved Africans of the French Empire, of politically active women, Jews and the 'gypsy slaves' of the Romanian lands is one way to measure the extent and limitations of what was achieved in 1848.

Chapters 7 and 8 examine the declining arc of the revolutions, focusing first on the gradual ebbing of revolutionary energies, the diffusion of effort and the secession from common enterprises that was a feature of the summer and autumn of 1848. Then comes that long sequence of increasingly violent policing actions that bring the revolutions to an end. Making sense of this part of the story involves understanding not just the weaknesses that made it possible to check the momentum of the revolutions but also the roots of counter-revolutionary success, which lay partly in latent advantages inherited from the past, and partly in the lessons learned from watching the revolutions unfold. Among many other things, the closing phase reveals how much better the counter-revolutionaries were at collaborating internationally than their opponents. The course of the 1848 revolutions, it turns out, was shaped as much by the relations between states as by the civil tumults within them. Chapter 9 tracks away in space and time from the epicentres of the upheaval. Across North and South America, south Asia and the Pacific rim, the ripples generated by the European mid-century revolutions passed into complex societies, polarizing or clarifying political debates, reminding everyone of the malleability and fragility of all political structures. But the further we get geographically from Europe, the less suitable the metaphor of 'impact' becomes – the diffusion of content becomes less important than selective readings from afar, driven by local processes of political differentiation and conflict. On the European continent, by contrast, the legacy of 1848 was deep and lasting. To see this clearly, we must follow the people, ideas and intellectual styles of the mid nineteenth century into the revolutions of 1848 and back out again.

Europeans, like all humans, are talkative, and there has never been a more garrulous revolution than 1848. It generated a truly astonishing volume of personal testimony. I have tried throughout to listen to these disparate voices and to think about what clues they can give us to the deeper meaning of what was going on around them. But garrulousness is not always communicative, and it is important also to reflect on those situations in which the people of 1848 talked *at* rather than *to* each other. Speeches could be exciting and empty at the same time. Liberals and radicals spoke at length in front of rural people about the virtue and necessity of the revolutionary struggle, but with very meagre results. Liberals found ways of misconstruing or simply of not hearing the demands of radicals. Information circulated in a haze of rumour and fake news, much as it does today, and fear made people listen to some voices and ideas and shut their ears to others.

One of the striking things about these revolutions is the intensity of historical awareness among so many of the key actors. This was one important difference between 1848 and its great eighteenth-century predecessor: 1789 had been a total surprise, whereas contemporaries of the mid-century revolutions read them against the template of the great original. And they did so in a world in which the concept of *history* had acquired tremendous semantic weight. For them, much more than for the men and women of 1789, history was happening in the present. Its movements could be detected in every twist and turn of the revolution's development. Astonishing numbers of them wrote memoirs or historical treatises bristling with footnotes.

For some, this tendency to retrospection made of the events of 1848 a miserable parody of the great French original: the most eloquent exponent of this view was Marx. But for others the relationship was the other way around. It was not that the epic energy of 1789 had wasted away into caricature, but rather that the historical awareness made possible by the first revolution had accumulated, deepened and propagated itself more widely, saturating the events of 1848 with meaning. The Chilean writer, journalist, historian and politician Benjamin Vicuña Mackenna captured the latter intimation when he wrote in his memoirs:

> The French revolution of 1848 produced a powerful echo in Chile. For us poor colonials living on the shores of the Pacific Ocean, its predecessor in 1789, so celebrated in history, had been but a flash of light in our darkness. Half a century later, however, its twin had every mark of brilliant radiance. We had seen it coming, we studied it, we understood it, we admired it.[6]

I

Social questions

This chapter contains scenes of economic precarity, ambient anxiety, nutritional crisis and ultraviolence. It hovers over the societies of pre-1848 Europe, focusing on areas of pressure, displacement, blockage and conflict. Social discontent does not 'cause' revolutions – if it did, revolutions would be much more common. Nevertheless, the material distress of mid-nineteenth-century Europeans was the indispensable backdrop to the processes of political polarization that made the revolutions possible. It was central to the motivation of many participants in urban tumults. As important as the reality and quantity of suffering were the ways in which this era saw and tabulated social dysfunction. The 'Social Question' that preoccupied mid-nineteenth-century Europeans was a constellation of real-world problems, but it was also a way of seeing. The chapter opens with scenes from the lives of the poor and the not-so-poor and reflects on the mechanisms that alienated social groups from each other and pushed them over the boundary between subsistence and crisis. It explores the techniques employed by those who made things with their hands (weavers, in particular) to ameliorate their condition through the focused application of protest and violence. It closes with the political and social convulsion of 1846, when an abortive political uprising in Galicia was engulfed from below by a violent social upheaval – an episode rich in dark lessons for the people of 1848.

THE POLITICS OF DESCRIPTION

If you want to know how the poorest of our workers live, go to the rue des Fumiers, which is occupied almost exclusively by this class. Lower your head and enter one of the sewers that open onto the street; step into a subterranean passage where the air is as humid and cold as in a cave. You will feel your feet slipping on the filthy ground, you will fear falling into the mire. On every side as you pass you will find dark, frigid rooms whose walls ooze dirty water, lit only by the feeble light from a tiny window too badly made to be properly fastened. Push open the flimsy door and enter, if the fetid air does not make you recoil. But take care, because the dirty, uneven ground is caked with muck and neither paved nor properly tiled. Here are three or four mouldy, rickety beds, tied together with string and covered in threadbare rags that are seldom washed. And the cupboards? No need. In a home like this one, there is nothing to put in them. A spinning wheel and a loom complete the furnishings.

Thus two doctors, Ange Guépin and Eugène Bonamy, described the poorest street of their city in the year 1836.[1] The setting was not Paris or Lyons, but Nantes, a provincial town on the River Loire in the Upper Brittany region of western France. Nantes was no teeming metropolis: nearly 76,000 people lived there in 1836, together with an overwhelmingly male transient population of around 10,700 itinerant labourers, sailors, travellers and garrison troops, numbers that placed it outside the list of Europe's forty most populous cities. The city was still struggling to overcome the shock of the Revolutionary and Napoleonic Wars. These geopolitical disruptions had ruined the Atlantic Trade (especially in enslaved African people) that had enriched eighteenth-century Nantes, lining some of its best streets with the fine houses of prosperous slavers.[2] Its population had fallen during the wars, and despite a commercial revival after 1815 growth remained sluggish, partly because the French Atlantic seaboard never fully recovered from the impact of the British blockade, partly because the environment for textile production became more competitive and partly because an accumulation of silt in the Loire now prevented larger vessels from reaching the town's wharves. In 1837, the city's external trade was still less than it had been in 1790.[3] A statistical survey carried out by the mayor in 1838 revealed an industrial life dominated by quite small enterprises: 25 cotton mills employing 1,327 workers, 12 construction yards employing 565 workers, 38 woollen cloth, fustian and soft-goods factories, 9 copper and iron foundries, 13 small sugar refineries employing 310 workers, 5 conserve plants with 290 workers, and 38 tanneries with 193 workers.[4] Far more numerous were those who worked outside the factories and foundries, taking in piecework, laundering, working on building sites or as servants of various kinds.

Yet this relatively modest town exhibited in microcosm extreme variations in the quality of human life and it was these that drew the attention
of Guépin and Bonamy, physicians and public health experts with a keen
social conscience. In a vast work of statistical description, the two doctors
brought the city of Nantes to life before the eyes of the reader – its streets,
quays, factories and squares, its schools, clubs, libraries, fountains, prisons
and hospitals. But the most compelling passages of commentary can be
found in a chapter towards the end of the book on the 'Modes of Existence of the Diverse Classes of Nantes Society'. Here the emphasis was on
the variety of social destinies. The authors discerned eight 'classes' in the
city – this was not quite the dialectical triad that would dominate socialism after Marx. The first class consisted simply of 'the wealthy'. Then
came the four ranks of the bourgeoisie: the 'high bourgeoisie', the 'prosperous bourgeoisie', 'the distressed bourgeoisie' and the 'poor bourgeoisie'.
At the bottom of the pyramid were three classes of workers: the 'well-off',
the 'poor' and the 'miserable'.[5]

The holistic, sociological quality of the observations is striking. The
authors move beyond characterizing the economic conditions of each
group towards an appraisal of styles, practices, awareness and values.
'The wealthy', they find, tend to have few children (the average is two)
and to occupy apartments comprising between ten and fifteen rooms lit
by between twelve and fifteen tall and wide windows. The life of the
occupants is sweetened by 'a thousand little comforts that one might
regard as indispensable, were an enormous part of the population not
denied them'.

Immense efforts are expended in support of the seasonal balls that
the next stratum, the high bourgeoisie, holds for its daughters. Entire
apartments are cleared to make space for the dancers. A daybed is
installed in the attic for grandpa. Hairdressers go mad during the ball
season; they are besieged like doctors during an epidemic (both Guépin
and Bonamy had played a prominent role in fighting the cholera epidemic that ravaged Nantes in 1832, killing 800 residents). Whether the
night of revels that followed was really worth all the effort expended
was doubtful, at least in the estimation of the authors. For the truth was
that a great ball at Nantes was 'a throng where you sweat endlessly,
breathe stale air and assuredly diminish your prospect of longevity'.
And on the following morning, if the temperature was cold, one found
in the joints of the windows 'pieces of horribly dirty ice'. 'The vapour

which, in condensing, has formed these chunks of ice was last night the atmosphere where 300 guests breathed.'[6]

Whereas the high bourgeois maintained their own horses and carriages, the members of a 'comfortably off' bourgeois household (stratum 3) were content to travel across town on the omnibus. The paterfamilias was a loyal subscriber to his reading club, but he was also forever anxious, because 'he always knows that frugality and work will be required to cover all his expenses'. The need for economy ruled out the flamboyance exhibited by the two uppermost strata, though the children of this class mixed more easily with their social betters than their parents could.

Particularly deserving of sympathy were the 'distressed bourgeois' (*bourgeois gênés*: stratum 4). These were the employees, the professors, clerks, shopkeepers, 'the lower order of artists': together they formed 'one of the least happy classes', because their contacts with a wealthier class drew them into expenses beyond their means. These families, the authors wrote, can only sustain themselves by means of the strictest economy. The 'poor bourgeois' (stratum 5) occupied a paradoxical place in the social fabric: with about 1,000–1,800 francs per annum to spend, they earned little more than the better-off workers occupying the next class and could afford only two or three rooms, no servants and a patchy education for their children. These were the clerks, cashiers and lesser academics whose lot is 'survival for the present and anxiety for the future'. But what was poverty for them was abundant wealth for the 'comfortably off workers' (stratum 6), who could live 'without a care for the future' on a smaller income (their revenues ranged from 600 to 1,000 francs). This was the class of the printers, masons, carpenters and cabinetmakers, 'the class of good workers, generally honest, devoted to their friends, personable, tidy indoors, raising with solicitude a numerous family'. Their work was long and hard, but they laboured with courage and even joy. They derived a sense of accomplishment from the fact that their families were clothed and fed; when they returned home in the evening, they found 'fire in the winter, and food sufficient to replenish their strength'. These were the happiest of the city's inhabitants, because it was among them that means and aspirations were most perfectly aligned.[7]

At the bottom of the pyramid, beneath a shadowy class of 'poor workers' living on between 500 and 600 francs (stratum 7), were those who subsisted in a condition of 'extreme misery' (stratum 8). The life of these people was different in every respect from that of the better-off worker, not just because their income (at 300 francs per annum) was so meagre, but because they lacked the myriad intangible comforts and compensations that sweetened the day of their more prosperous fellows: there was no true rest after work, no favour in return for work well done, 'no smile to follow a sigh'. The material and moral pleasures and the sense of accomplishment that buoyed up the masons and cabinetmakers had no place in the life of the most wretched. 'For them, living means not dying.' These people lived in the foul-smelling basements of the rue des Fumiers and other streets like it, the rue de la Bastille or the rue du Marchix, for example. It was here that they worked fourteen-hour days by the light of a resin candle for a wage of between fifteen and twenty sous.[8]

Again and again the authors reached for statistics, not just because these could be used to situate their descriptions on a plinth of indisputable fact and thereby lift them away from mere political assertion, but also because numbers were sometimes more eloquent than mere words. Here are the expenses incurred by a household subsisting on 300 francs a year:

> Whatever we can say of this miserable sector of society, the detail of its expenditures will be more eloquent; here is the detail:
>
> Rent...25 fr.
> Laundry..12
> Fuel (wood and peat)...........................35
> Light...15
> Repair of broken furniture.....................3
> Change of domicile (at least once a year)...2
> Footwear...12
> Clothing...0
>   (they dress in old clothes that people
>   give them)
> Doctor...0
> Pharmacist..0
>   (The sisters of charity bring them
>   medications on doctor's orders)
>   _____
>
>   ....104 fr.

These outgoings left a poor household with an income of 196 francs per annum to cover all other needs. And, of that, 150 francs had to be spent on bread, so that 46 francs remained (per year!) to buy salt, butter, cabbages and potatoes. 'If you bear in mind that a certain amount is also spent at the bar, you will see that despite the pounds of bread dispensed from time to time by charity, the existence of these families is horrific.'[9]

Nowhere was the grip of numbers on the men, women and children of the city more obvious than in the mortality rates of the various quarters. On the quai Duguay-Trouin, a well-off street with large houses, Guépin and Bonamy found a rate of one death per seventy-eight residents per year. But on the rue des Fumiers, the epicentre of poverty in the city and situated *in the same quarter* near the Chaussée Madeleine, they recorded one death per seventeen inhabitants per year. To put the same discrepancy in more drastic terms: the authors found that whereas the residents of the rue Duquesclin died on average at the age of 59.2, the average age of the dead on the rue des Fumiers was 31.16.

During the 1830s and 1840s, a wave of such reports swept Europe. The authors had visited the factories and walked in the quarters of the poorest city dwellers. Their books and pamphlets reflected an esteem for precise observation and quantification. In 1832, James Kay, a medicine graduate from the University of Edinburgh, had published a short study of the Manchester cotton workers. Here, too, there was a discussion of death rates among weavers, and numerical tables showing the distribution of damp dwellings, unpaved streets and open cesspools in the poorest districts. And there were reflections on the drabness and squalor of daily life for working paupers. Life was tough for the cotton workers, Kay wrote, but conditions were particularly bad for the mainly Irish handloom weavers, because the introduction of the power loom had depressed the value of their labour. Their dwellings contained at most one or two chairs and a rickety table, some rudimentary cooking equipment and 'one or two beds, loathsome with filth'. A whole family might sleep together in a single bed, heaped together under a pile of dirty straw and a cover fashioned of old sacking. There were damp, stinking single-roomed cellars in which as many as sixteen people from more than one family were crowded together.[10]

Louis-René Villermé's *Tableau de l'état physique et moral des ouvriers employés dans les manufactures de coton, de laine et de soie* (1840) was the result of years spent studying the textile workers of the Haut-Rhin, Seine-Inférieure, the Aisne, Nord, the Somme, the Rhône and the Canton of Zurich in Switzerland. A pioneering advocate of hygienic reform and an early exponent of social epidemiology, Villermé was interested in the impact of industrialization on the health and quality of life of the labouring classes. His book, commissioned by the Academy of Moral and Political Sciences in Paris, was a work of laborious classification founded on the scrupulous analysis of data gathered through meticulous observation. Villermé was interested in the length of the working day, the time spent consuming meals, the distance travelled to work, the manner and amount of remuneration. Villermé had been to the places and watched the people he described, patiently following his subjects through their long work day, acknowledging what he described as 'the rigorous duty to describe the facts just as I have seen them'.[11] Watching Alsatian cotton workers approaching their factory in the morning and leaving again in the evening, Villermé observed 'a multitude of pale, skinny women walking barefoot through the mud'. Running along with them was a flock of 'young children no less dirty, no less haggard and covered with rags greasy with oil that has fallen on them from the machines as they worked'. These children had no satchels to carry their provisions in; 'they simply hold in their hands or hide under their shirts the piece of bread that has to nourish them until the time comes for them to return to their homes'.[12]

Like Guépin and Bonamy, Villermé had stepped into the workers' dwellings, dark rooms where two families slept, each in one corner, on straw thrown to the floor and held in by two planks, covered only by rags and a filthy quilt. He, too, saw and described the meagre cooking ware and the sticks of furniture. And he noted the exorbitant rents that were exacted for such marginal dwellings, rents that tempted speculators to build more and more tenements, in the certainty that poverty would soon fill them with residents. The link between income and life expectancy did not escape him. In the department of the Haut-Rhin, where eastern France borders Switzerland, the poverty was so profound, Villermé reported, that it had a drastic impact on the length of human life: whereas in the families of merchants, businessmen and factory directors one half of the children could be expected to reach the age of twenty-nine, half of the children of weavers and cotton spinners had already died before they reached the age of two. 'What does this tell us', Villermé asked, his empathy contending with something more censorious, 'about the lack of care, the negligence on the part of parents, about their privations, about their suffering?'[13]

Count Carlo Ilarione Petitti di Roreto, author of a study of the impact of factory labour on children, was a senior official in the service of the Kingdom of Piedmont and Sardinia and one of the most eminent Piedmontese liberals of his era. Petitti made it clear from the outset that he appreciated the value and necessity of child labour in factories. Children were small and nimble, they could be used for rejoining, winding or reeling torn or wayward threads; they could scramble under machines to make running adjustments without disrupting the rhythm of production (hence the spots of grease observed by Villermé on the clothes of the children leaving Alsatian cotton works); they excelled at numerous tasks requiring small fingers and quick reflexes. They were cheaper than adults and thus crucial to keeping costs down. And they supplemented the family income of the poorest working parents.

The use of children for such work had steadily increased. Children were now beginning work as young as seven and eight and their numbers had risen to the point where they accounted for as much as half of the workers employed in such plants. Petitti noted that the factory-owner had a transparent interest in maximizing output and minimizing costs and was thus likely to demand the greatest possible effort, even from his youngest employees. Impoverished parents had an interest in reducing the burden of the upkeep of their offspring and were thus drawn to place their child in work at the earliest opportunity. All the relevant stakeholders, it appeared (except for the children themselves), had an interest in this system of exploitation, and the results were pitiable. Exhausted by ceaseless labour and deprived of adequate sleep, these small proletarians constantly nodded off into dreams of 'running and jumping', until a harsh voice called them back to their tasks. If they resisted, they were beaten or deprived of their food.[14]

The younger the age at which labour commenced, the greater the danger that specific types of work would produce characteristic illnesses and deformities in adults. Observing the weavers of Lyons, one of Europe's great silk-weaving centres, Philibert Patissier noted signs of a generic debility that appeared to be related to the nature of their work and that manifested itself not just in their appearance and levels of vitality but also in their mood and attitude. In addition to a pale complexion, weavers exhibited limbs that were 'feeble or puffy with lymphatic fluid, soft flesh lacking in vitality, [and] smaller than average stature'. There was 'a certain air of simplicity and silliness in their countenance; their accent in conversation is singularly slow and flat'. Their bodies were so deformed by rickets and poor comportment that they could be recognized from a distance 'by the irregular development of the skeleton [and] their uncertain and entirely graceless gait'.[15]

Such was the power of the workshop over the constitution of the people who worked there, Patissier wrote, that young people arriving from the countryside near Lyons to embrace this profession soon lost their freshness and plumpness: 'varicose engorgement of the legs and several illnesses of the scrofulous type soon signal the revolution that has taken place in them'.[16] The problem was compounded by the appalling living conditions in the poorest areas of Lyons, where dark and foul lanes were lined by jumbles of poorly constructed and airless houses filled to overflowing with 'a great number of individuals of both sexes and all ages'. Relations among workers who lived in this manner were so intimate that 'libertinism' inevitably took hold among them 'long before their organs have acquired the necessary strength and development to support it. The habit of masturbation begins so early among these artisans that one can scarcely fix the age at which they begin to cultivate it.'[17]

In 1843, when Bettina von Arnim published a book of essays under the title *This Book Belongs to the King* criticizing the Prussian state for neglecting the masses of its poorest subjects, she appended a report on the slums of Berlin that she had commissioned from Heinrich Grunholzer, a 23-year-old Swiss student. Her decision was an unusual one for this sophisticated writer, novelist and composer. Whereas the social critique in the rest of the text was encoded in picaresque meandering dialogues with an oracular female figure, Arnim opted not to work Grunholzer's notes into a text of her own, but to publish them raw, as if to affirm 'the primacy of social fact over the process of literary production'.[18] Since the end of the Napoleonic Wars, the population of the Prussian capital had risen from 197,000 to nearly 400,000. Many of the poorest immigrants – wage labourers and artisans for the most part – settled in a densely populated slum area on the northern outskirts of the city. It was here that Grunholzer recorded his observations for Arnim's book. He spent four weeks combing through tenements and interviewing their occupants. He recorded his impressions in a spare prose that was paced out in short, informal sentences, and integrated the brutal statistics that governed the lives of the poorest families in the city. Passages of dialogue were woven into the narrative, and the frequent use of the present tense suggested notes scribbled *in situ*.[19]

Friedrich Engels's study of the 'condition of the working class in England', published in 1845, was, among other things, a work of social and cultural observation – the first phrase of the subtitle '*Nach eigner Anschauung*' (According to my own observations) made that clear. Engels, too, was a painstaking itemizer and classifier of objects and phenomena and he saw and described many of the same things that Kay, Villermé, Wolff, Grunholzer, Pettiti, Patissier, Guépin and Bonamy had seen before him. He noted the proximity of the poorest and wealthiest districts. In St Giles, London, not far from Regent Street and Trafalgar Square, he found a 'knot of streets' full of three- and four-storey tenements, dirty inside and out. But this was nothing compared to the dwellings in the courtyards and lanes *between* the streets, a maze of rotting rubbish heaps, unglazed windows and broken door frames, where the poorest of the poor cowered in filth and dank darkness. And Engels, like Villermé and many others, was struck by the fact that even these hovels commanded exorbitant rents. He marvelled at how 'the poverty of these wretches, in which no thief would hope to find anything of value', was 'lawfully exploited by the property-owning classes!'[20]

For all their differences, then, these works exhibited a certain family resemblance. They directed upon their subject matter a period eye that delighted in numbers, tabulation and precise description. New trends in statistical reasoning made it easier to mediate between the abstractions of 'large numbers' and averages on the one hand, and the behaviour of individuals on the other, which could now be seen as emblematic of broader social phenomena. The presiding influence on this statistical turn was the Belgian astronomer, statistician and sociologist Adolphe Quetelet, 'the one-man band of nineteenth-century statistics', whose foundational essay on 'social physics' (1835) showed that only the study of large datasets could elucidate the law-like forces governing human social behaviour. The measurement of correlations based on large datasets allowed the exposure of provocative causal claims, about the effect, for example, of income on mortality. Once this paradigm shift in social understanding had taken place, there was no going back. Guépin's stinging observation 'it seems that the less tax you pay, the earlier you die' bore the mark of this new statistical awareness.[21]

There was a literary dimension to social description. The writers of the Social Question seemed to be charting an undiscovered world, a world that lay, as the German radical Wilhelm Wolff put it in a widely read article on the slums of Breslau, like an 'open book' before the walls of the city, but was invisible to most of its better-off inhabitants.[22] It was an untranscendent, metonymic world, where physical proximity mattered – the perverse adjacency of the richest and poorest districts, the wriggling of dirty children under rags and the promiscuous intimacy of adult bodies in unwashed beds, the huddle of workers at factory gates, the dangerous closeness of the ill to the well. The eye of the reader was always drawn across space, tracking from one object to the next: a smashed window, a two-legged table, a broken bowl, rags, a dirty make-shift bed. But the other senses were also engaged: the stickiness of damp walls, the screams of restive infants, the smell of human waste.[23]

There was doubtless an element of voyeuristic pleasure in the consumption of such texts by bourgeois readers. So seductive was the genre that it overleapt the boundaries of expert treatises and official reports to colonize fiction. The most prominent example – itself an important influence on the burgeoning practice of social thick description – was Eugène Sue's remarkable blockbusting ten-volume novel of the Parisian underworld, *Les Mystères de Paris*, which appeared in instalments during 1842–3 and was widely imitated across Europe. The characters who peopled Sue's book were larger-than-life absurdities, but the world in which they moved was precisely that space of labyrinthine streets drowning in mire that we encounter in the literature of industrialism and urban poverty:

> The murky-coloured houses, which were lighted within by a few panes of glass in the worm-eaten casements, overhung each other so closely that the eaves of each almost touched its opposite neighbour, so narrow were the streets. Dark and noisome alleys led to staircases still more black and foul, and so perpendicular that they could hardly be ascended by the help of a cord fixed to the dank and humid walls by holdfasts of iron.[24]

Sue's work was widely imitated across Europe.[25] If readers were prepared to lose themselves in Sue's colourful demi-monde, Wilhelm Wolff declared, then they should take all the more interest in the *real* 'mystères de Breslau' before their own doorstep. August Brass, author of *Mysteries of Berlin* (1844), noted with disapproval that Sue's German translators had turned the 'mysteries' of his title into 'secrets' (*Geheimnisse*). But this was a mistake, he protested, because the life of the poor was not about secrets; it was about mysteries 'that take place every day before our very eyes'. Anyone could observe the distress and desperation of the under-world in the Prussian capital, Brass wrote, if they merely 'took the trouble to cast off the comfortable veil of selfish complacency' and direct their gaze outside their customary circles onto 'the life of our brothers'.[26] Eugène Buret, author of a substantial study of the 'misery of the working classes in England and France' (1840), put it succinctly:

> Poverty is the unknown. The nations in whose heart the mortal germs are most actively developing scarcely suspect the evil which is working within them; like a sick person who mistakes fever for a sign of vitality, they delude themselves with the solidity of a prosperity that is only apparent, they shut their ears on purpose to the inner sufferings they feel.[27]

This was the literature of what came to be known as the Social Question. It was a literature in which official reports, publicly commissioned enquiries, prize-winning essays, journalism and genre fiction merged and interacted, embedded in a mid-nineteenth-century European 'culture of enquiry'.[28] It was a question posed for the most part in the third person: what should be done about *them*? (Ange Guépin was highly unusual in directing the same inquisitive gaze upon his wealthy and middle-class fellow citizens as upon the most wretched.) The Social Question was in fact a bundle of many questions about public health and the danger of contagion, occupational illness, the loss of social cohesion, the impact of industrialization, crime, sexual morality, urban housing, population growth, unemployment, child labour, the potentially corrosive effects of economic competition, the impact of the city on the lives and attitude of its inhabitants, and the supposed decline in religion.

How the questions were prioritized and posed and how they were answered depended on the politics driving the enquiry. For Friedrich Engels, the narrative hinged on the exploitation of one class by another. If his workers with their bent backs and unsteady gaits looked like vet-erans, that was because they were indeed, in his eyes, the walking wounded of a 'social war' waged by those who, directly or indirectly, controlled the means of production against property-less masses who had nothing to sell but the strength of their arms. It was precisely the concentration of industrial capital in the hands of one class that had given rise to the proletariat, he observed. And in the antagonism between the proletariat and its exploiters, Engels believed, lay the seeds of a future revolutionary transformation. Because the rage of the 'entire working class from Glasgow to London against the rich' must in the not-too-distant future – 'one can almost measure it' – break out in a revolution, 'compared with which the first French Revolution and the year 1794 [the apogee of the Jacobin Terror] will seem like a child's game'.[29]

These scenarios of future upheaval held no appeal for Guépin and Bonamy. In the foreword to their study of Nantes, the two men stated explicitly that the purpose of their researches had been to discover 'what we must improve in order to ... enable us to reach the future without having to pass through a new Jacquerie or through a '93 [i.e. the inception of the Jacobin Terror]'.[30] Guépin, who spent his entire life in Nantes, was first and foremost a doctor and a social hygienist who saw himself as a student of the city's 'physiology'. The key to healing the rift in society lay, he believed, in reform based on the activism of associations. In the autumn of 1830, after the political revolution of that year, he founded the Société Industrielle de Nantes to help unemployed workers. With donations from the government and wealthy patrons, the society was able to acquire a building with a library and a clinic and funding to support a range of mutual aid activities.[31] His deep belief in science and in association as a tool of social reform placed him for a time in the vicinity of the elitist utopian Henri Comte de Saint-Simon (1760–1825). The chief task of modern science, Saint-Simon had proclaimed, lay in establishing an integrated 'physiology' that would observe and interpret all social and moral phenomena through the lens of a Newtonian general system. To the practitioners of such a science would fall the task of divining and managing the needs of a future society. It was precisely this feature of Saint-Simon's thought that appealed to Guépin, who would later describe himself as completing and continuing the sage's work.[32] The Saint-Simonian template implied a gradual and peaceful transition towards technocracy, not the all-transforming violent upheaval imagined by Engels. The carriers of transformation would not be enraged proletarians, but an 'industrial class' of hygienists, engineers, planners and managers.[33]

The treatises, essays and pamphlets on the Social Question were animated by a moralizing energy, by the 'grafting of morality onto economics'.[34] How this energy was focused varied from case to case. Engels made no attempt to conceal his disgust at an urban bourgeoisie that completely neglected the poor in good times, but then, when cholera was in town, 'suddenly remembered' the filthy streets of the slum districts and, 'seized with terror' lest the homes of the poor become a source of contagion, ordered chaotic and ill-considered sanitation measures.[35] Ramón de la Sagra, writing in Madrid, blamed 'the misfortune of certain classes' on 'the immorality and degradation of governments', the imprudence of certain direct taxes, the paucity of elementary education, the neglect of the moral and religious instruction of the masses and the tendency to imbue the young with 'unlimited desires and unrealistic hopes'.[36]

By contrast, Honoré Frégier, author of a study of the 'dangerous classes of the populations of the great cities' (1840), focused his indignation chiefly on the poor themselves, who were seen as co-authors of their own fate. Frégier was an administrative official, a departmental head in the Prefecture of the Seine, with privileged access to police archives. His chief concern was the link between poverty and crime, and he offered his treatise as a handbook for those officials entrusted with 'guaranteeing the inner order of this great city, along with the safety of its inhabitants and of their properties'. The fundamental root of most crime, he argued, lay in paupers' propensity to worsen their condition through vice and idleness. Frégier's male urban worker was a shrewd, mischievous fellow, mouthy and sly, easily tempted away from work by the offer of a drink with his *compagnons*.[37] And this was where the true 'social danger' of poverty lay, because 'from the moment that the worker, surrendered to his depraved passions, ceases to work, he becomes an enemy of society'.[38]

Those who passed in this way from indolence to vice entered the ranks of the 'depraved class': 'the players, the vice girls, their lovers and pimps, the brothel madams, the vagabonds, the fraudsters, the crooks, the rogues and thieves, the she-thieves and the receivers of stolen goods' – here again the voluptuous pleasure of lists. The danger posed by this milieu was not that of sedition, which was 'a rare accident in civil life' (a noteworthy assertion from the citizen of a city that had witnessed two transformative revolutions within living memory), but the chronic illness of vice itself, which ate like acid into the fibres of civilization. The solution was emphatically not to change or dismantle the industrial system, but rather to reintroduce patriarchal relations of

Illustration to the article 'Poverty and Communism', from the *Illustrierte Zeitung*, 1 November 1843. Many of the stock elements can be seen here: the pathetic furniture, wretched clothing, caterwauling children and general disorder. By placing a bottle of spirits in the hand of the male householder, this image suggests, like many contemporary accounts of poverty, that the poor are themselves partly responsible for their plight.

deference and protection between the factory-owner and his employees. 'My spirit', he wrote, 'is not offended by great industrial property and my concern is solely to develop and extend the patronage of the rich over the poor by means that honour the generosity of the former without debasing the character of the latter.'[39]

Eugène Buret's *On the Misery of the Working Classes in England and France*, published in 1840, two years after Frégier's treatise, could hardly have been more different. Buret had been working as a journalist when the Academy of Moral and Political Sciences in Paris announced an essay prize (2,500 francs) in 1837. Candidates were invited to 'establish what poverty consists of and by what signs it manifests itself in in various countries'. Buret's prize-winning essay touched all the usual bases: exorbitant rents, beds of 'wet and stinking straw', broken windows, rooms without light and the 'stale nauseating odour, with some sharp notes' of neglected humans.[40] But unlike Frégier's treatise, Buret's was a critique of the industrial system, not of the workers who served it. To blame the poor for their degradation was a fundamental misunderstanding, he argued, because 'in our view, the moral condition of the working classes is the result, the direct consequence of their physical condition'. Only an observer who possessed 'perfect knowledge' of the 'facts that constitute physical misery' would be in a position both to understand the moral condition of the poor and to look beyond the 'feeling of disgust and contempt inspired by their degradation and their vices'.[41]

Poverty was not an accidental feature of modern industrial systems, Buret argued, but rather their inevitable consequence; it was not a threat *to* civilization, as Frégier had suggested, it was 'a phenomenon *of* civilisation'.[42] Buret's chief inspiration here was the Swiss political economist Jean Charles Léonard de Sismondi, who had argued in his *New Principles of Political Economy* (1819) that the unchecked competition characteristic of modern manufacturing economies tended to lead to overproduction, while at the same time pushing down wages and thus depressing consumer demand. By this reading, low wages were not a boon to industry, but a burden on the economy as a whole.[43]

The Social Question thrived on the meticulous observation of real circumstances, but at times it could take on the quality of a moral panic. Nowhere was this more evident than when male commentators focused on the condition of working women. As vessels of endangered purity on the one hand and incubators of dissolution and vice on the other, they were emotionally charged emblems, overdetermined by latent anxieties about the stability of the gender order and the intrusion of 'conflicting drives and desires'.[44] The foremost trigger of moral panic was the supposedly intimate connection between working women and prostitution. Ramón de la Sagra, who had spent the mid 1830s in Paris before returning to Spain (with trunks full of books on the Social Question), saw 'the laws of nature and of social morality disturbed and contradicted' by the growing employment of women and children in workshops. This was the spinal cord of social disorder, of poverty and of modern demoralization and the reason for the growth in prostitution and illegitimate births in the large manufacturing centres and cities.[45] Eugène Buret cited a passage in Parent-Duchâtelet's famous study on Parisian prostitution (1837) reporting that female sex workers were almost exclusively the children of day workers, domestic servants, artisans and poor factory workers, a finding that suggested a systematic correlation between modern industrialism and the sex trade.[46]

Acknowledging a causal correlation between industrialism and prostitution opened the possibility that female sex workers were themselves products of the gross asymmetries of wealth and power that were characteristic of modern industrial capitalism. And the inequalities were even grosser for women than for men, since women were usually paid at a lower rate, on the assumption both that their work was less valuable and that their income was or ought to be a mere addition to the wage of a male breadwinner.[47] In many factories, the hours were so long, the wages so poor and the work so hard, Friedrich Engels noted, that women 'preferred to throw themselves into the arms of prostitution, rather than put up with this tyranny'.[48] For Ange Guépin, a feminist, the truly galling thing about prostitution was the way it was sustained by those very middle-class men who claimed to despise it. They needed prostitutes in order to safeguard the honour of their daughters, Guépin wrote, 'just as they need military substitutes so that their sons can avoid conscription'.[49]

Nearly all commentators acknowledged that the prostitution of the streets and brothels was just one aspect of the sex trade. Of the 18,000 domestic servants in Berlin, Ernst Dronke estimated, at least 5,000 were engaged in, if not open prostitution, then secret fornication in return for favours of some kind. Then there were the 'grisettes', young working women who lived or just slept with middle-class students, courtesans who were 'kept' by a man in an apartment placed at their disposal; and, most pitiable of all, girls who might be as young as thirteen or fourteen trafficked by procuresses into the hands of better-off Berliners, seduced by the dream of wearing fine clothes and drinking champagne. For a few years, Dronke wrote, they might be seen strolling with a friend (usually a young woman in the same situation) down the best streets of the city, where they could pass for women of the respectable classes. But their good fortune was short-lived:

> One may well ask what happens in the end to these lost creatures? When their beauty and youth have faded, they slip out of the public eye whose attention they had once found it so easy to attract. Those who have extracted from the desperation of these unhappy women the possession of their beauty and youth are the ones least likely to know anything about how their story ends. . . . Most of them go into a decline that the reader will forgive us for not describing. They end up in a position where the police press their ownership rights upon them, handing them like miserable outlaws from station to station, all the way to death.

From this perspective, prostitution was the symptom of a society 'completely corrupted in its organization'.[50] The morbid intimacy between female labour and sexual exploitation reverberated in radical manifestos and pamphlets. 'Bread or Revolution! That should be your battle cry!' intoned an anonymous flysheet circulating in Frankfurt in the summer of 1847. 'You build beautiful bed frames and soft beds [for the rich idler], so that your daughters can fall prey to his lust for whores.'[51]

'The world is the totality of facts, not of things' – thus the second sentence of Wittgenstein's *Tractatus Logico-Philosophicus*.[52] With their tables, numbers and meticulous descriptions, the treatises and fictions of the Social Question belong to the moment when such a thought became possible. The enquiry into social conditions was the place where new statistical techniques, ideas about the modern city as a historically distinctive form of existence, observational sociology and the repertoire of literary practices later known as realism fused and interacted, producing new forms of knowledge. The 'reality effect' of this new diction should not distract us from the gaps and elisions in its field of vision. A monumental study of the city of Paris has shown how older kaleidoscopic images of Paris as a 'multi-coloured city' composed of numerous 'islands' of productive and cultural activity made way during the 1830s and 1840s for a picture painted more starkly in lights and shadows. The working-class spaces of the city slid 'more and more into dark shades' that offered an effective foil to the lights of the new, bright spaces of bourgeois consumption, the *galeries parisiennes*. In focusing their attention on slum dwellings, dirt and contagion, especially after the shock of the cholera pandemic of 1832, the middle-class diagnosticians of social malaise often missed the signs of vitality and change in working-class areas, such as the thickening of commercial and manufacturing networks in the city centre, or the emergence 'from below' of new forms of labour organization.[53]

The energies generated around the Social Question fed back into politics. The arguments advanced by Engels in *The Condition of the Working Classes* went on to shape the *Communist Manifesto*, jointly authored with Karl Marx. Engels's book remained an important empirical resource for Marx and 'the foundational document of what was to become the Marxian socialist tradition'.[54] In one of the best-known tracts of the era, *The Organization of Labour* (1840), the socialist Louis Blanc cited at length Ange Guépin's findings on the average life expectancy of the social strata of Nantes to argue that modern industrial and commercial competition was 'a system of extermination for the people'. The only road out of the impasse lay in the state-managed affiliation of workers in 'social workshops' whose inner life and mutual relations would be cooperative rather than competitive.[55] For Ramón de la Sagra, pioneering Spanish exponent of 'social economy', the chronic struggle between the rich and the poor, 'always destructive of the principle of social order', raised doubts about the costs of industrial progress, unless it were guided by the principles of a disciplined 'social physics'. How a way would be found to suffuse all arms of government with the spirit of an enlightened science remained unclear.[56]

PRECARITY AND CRISIS

Poverty was nothing new. But the 'pauperism' of the early to mid nineteenth century differed from traditional forms of poverty. The abstractness of the neologism captured what was seen as the systematic quality of the phenomenon. It was collective and structural, rather than dependent upon individual contingencies, such as sickness, bereavement, injury or crop failures. It was permanent rather than seasonal. And it showed signs of engulfing social groups whose position had previously been relatively secure, such as artisans (especially apprentices and journeymen) and smallholding peasants.

We can see traces of this immiseration almost everywhere we look in pre-1848 Europe. The Bologna special census of 1841 reported that of the 70,000 persons who lived in the city, 10,000 were 'permanent beggars', while a further 30,000 lived in poverty and often required public assistance.[57] Between 1829 and 1834, more than 100 craftsmen were arrested each year for begging in the city of Bremen.[58] A statistical survey of the 1840s suggested that between 50 and 60 per cent of the Prussian population were living on a subsistence minimum.

The plight of the urban poor was richly documented, as we have seen, in the literature of the Social Question. But the crowding of workers into filthy urban streets was often a sign that things were even worse in the countryside. In the 1830s, the cottiers of the more isolated and mountainous parts of County Fermanagh in the north of Ireland lived in 'wretched huts', officially described as 'generally unfit for human habitation'.[59] Travelling through the Veneto (the hinterland of Venice) in 1841, the Briton Samuel Laing was struck by the poverty of the people: 'It is impressive', he wrote, 'to see those who raise silk – the most costly material of human clothing – going about their work barefoot, and in rags.'[60] The peasants of the region subsisted on food that lacked nutritional value, eking out their existences in flimsy, dirty houses. Chronic disease and indebtedness were rife. The supply of work was uncertain, dependence on the harvest absolute.[61] A similar picture emerges for the rural districts of Lombardy. Here, too, there was a decline in living standards from around the turn of the century. Malaria was endemic in low-lying areas and sharecroppers lived in airless cottages with dirt floors, subsisting mainly on maize. Overdependence on maize, a cheap grain preferred by the poor, gave rise to pellagra, a disease of malnutrition whose symptoms are dermatitis, diarrhoea and dementia. So stark were the nutritional differences between social strata that the middle classes – lawyers and other professionals, merchants, businessmen and property-owners – were on average 2.85 cm taller than textile workers, coachmen and barbers.[62] In Germany, too, the first half of the nineteenth century saw a downturn in average heights, particularly marked for those born in the late 1830s, that is, for children raised during the repeated subsistence crises of the following decade.[63]

Contemporaries differed on the reasons for this decline. Conservatives tended to blame the 'decorporation' of modern society, by which they usually meant the abolition or weakening of guilds and the termination during the Revolutionary and Napoleonic eras of the system of reciprocal rights and duties associated with feudal land tenure. Friedrich Engels blamed the capitalist industrial economy and its exploitative logic. Carlo Petitti pointed to the increasing employment of women and children: unguilded and accustomed to lower wages, they drove down the remuneration of all workers. For Louis Blanc the root of poverty could be traced to the ubiquitous competition between rival enterprises: 'I insist, competition produces misery: it's a fact proven by the figures.'[64]

None of these claims can be accepted without reservations, but all captured parts of the truth. Decorporation was clearly part of the story: in Barcelona, the legal disappearance of the old guilds enabled the rapid growth of the artisan sector but also exposed it to processes of 'proletarianization'.[65] The integration of the Irish economy with industrializing Britain dealt a devastating blow to Irish domestic industry – here competition was clearly a factor in immiseration, as it was for the Bohemian textile industry, which struggled in the 1840s to deal with the influx of cheaper British wares.[66] Studies of some regions of France have suggested that rural districts marked by overcrowding could have a depressive effect on industrial wages in neighbouring areas.[67] On the other hand, workers were often right to be wary when factory-owners invoked 'competition' as a reason for holding down wages.[68]

That industrialization as such 'caused' poverty is doubtful: in a classic study of European poverty in the early-modern period, Wilhelm Abel showed long ago that the deepening of modern poverty across Europe predated the onset of industrialization; the poor were getting poorer, even before the machines arrived and there is evidence to suggest that under-industrialization may have worsened the impact of subsistence crises.[69] But studies of the most industrialized parts of early-nineteenth-century Britain have suggested that new methods of production gave rise to the emergence of a non-specialized, mobile labour force whose 'structural vulnerability' made it more likely that they would experience the most wretched poverty at certain points in their lives.[70] And there is evidence to suggest, conversely, that the survival in some regions of guilds may have had a positive impact on nutritional standards. In other words: traditional forms of labour association could under some conditions safeguard living standards in ways that more dynamic industrial and commercial environments could not.[71]

Mass impoverishment unfolded against the background of accelerated demographic growth – was this the root of the problem? Between 1818 and 1850, the population of the Italian states increased from 17 to 24 million; in the German states (excluding the Austrian Empire), the population rose from 22 to 33 million; in France the figure rose from 26 to 36 million between the turn of the century and the revolutions of 1848. Moreover, the growth in population was especially marked in rural areas. In the Kingdom of Prussia, the population increased by 56 per cent from 10.3 million in 1816 to 15.9 million in 1846, but the percentage of the population living in cities rose only from 26 to 28 per cent, meaning that the brunt of growth was felt in the countryside. In the city and province of Bologna, the population of the province grew at an impressive rate in the years 1800–1848, while that of the city stagnated. The extreme case was Ireland, whose population grew at between two and three times the rates prevailing in north-western Europe, producing a population density in rural districts that was unrivalled across the continent.[72]

Yet as soon as we search for a *direct* relationship between population density and poverty, we run into problems. A major study of pre-famine Ireland showed that the lowest per capita incomes were not necessarily to be found in the most densely populated areas.[73] Nor can it generally be said that the social crises of this era were the result of a 'Malthusian trap', where the needs of the population exceeded the available supply of agricultural produce. Over the period between the beginning of the century and the 1848 revolutions, an increase in the amount of land under cultivation and improvements in agricultural productivity roughly doubled the food supply across the European lands. In other words, high as the rate of population growth might have been by historical standards, it was outstripped by growth in the food supply. And therein lay a part of the problem: in Ireland, the deepening dependence on the potato (32 per cent of arable land was used for its cultivation) helped to sustain a rate of population growth disproportionate to the needs of an otherwise stagnant economy. Similar effects can be observed in Spain, where the increased production of food thanks to expanded cultivation and liberal reforms to the structure of land tenure helped to sustain high population growth around Madrid and on the north-eastern littoral.[74] And the growth in the food supply was reflected in prices. Viewed through the lens of long-term trends, the years from 1815 to around 1850 were a period of falling average grain prices. The problem, then, was not the raw collision of human numbers and physical resources. It was rather that food supplies – notwithstanding the generally positive trend in production – remained vulnerable to natural catastrophes. Poor harvests, cattle epidemics and crop diseases could still turn the surplus into a drastic shortfall, generating price peaks that could push large numbers of people into subsistence crisis.

Unbalanced growth swelled the ranks of the most precarious social strata. In the rural districts of western German Minden-Ravensberg in the Prussian Province of Westphalia, the ratio of families living from the wages of hired labour to landowning peasants at the beginning of the century was 149/100; by 1846, the ratio had risen to 310/100. Such families earned an increasingly marginal living from a combination of agrarian labour and various forms of domestic piecework from merchants who dealt with supra-regional markets. Rural labourers of this kind spent most of their income just on bread; they were extremely vulnerable not only to rises in the cost of grains, but also to fluctuations in the business cycle which could depress demand for the goods – especially textiles – they helped to manufacture.[75]

In central Italy, too, the growing pressure on scarce land tipped the demographic balance away from traditional sharecropping to various forms of landless waged labour. Sharecropping (*mezzadria*) had been a hard way of life, but it had at least offered a stable domicile and a relatively nourishing and reliable diet. Day labourers (*braccianti*), by contrast, worked for daily wages and drifted from job to job. These were the humblest members of the agricultural system. Excluded from marrying into the sharecropping caste, they created a rural proletariat which was widely feared as a source of crime and disorder.[76] And the same imbalances can be observed in the manufacturing sector: whereas the population of Prussia rose by 56 per cent over the period 1816–46, the figure for the number of master artisans over the same period was 70 per cent. Much more dramatic – and problematic – was the rise (156 per cent) in the number of assistants and apprentices. Population growth in early-nineteenth-century Nuremberg stoked tensions between masters and journeymen in the metalworking trade. Masters complained that the journeymen flowing into the city from the small towns and villages of the region were 'overfilling' their trades and crowding the market. Journeymen, for their part, complained that the access to craft licences was far too restricted.[77] In an economy composed of increasingly large numbers of precarious existences, a period of adverse weather could trigger large movements of hungry people, many of whom made their way towards towns in search of work or charity. In 1828, as grain prices rose, Bologna began to fill with unemployed *braccianti* from the countryside; the city, in the words of one senior official, was so full of rural vagabonds that an order was issued to the province forbidding peasants to leave their villages. The order was futile, because the means for controlling such movements did not exist.[78]

What made the experience of precarity and dearth potentially threatening to public order was the fact that those who suffered did not see scarcity or immiseration as 'natural' or divinely ordained in the sense theorized by Thomas Malthus, but rather as caused by fluctuations in the power relations between human beings. These fluctuations could occur at the micro level in specific productive centres, or they could play out through political and legal changes that might be regional or national in scope. Skilled workers might be tolerant of low wages, but they became restive when they felt that managers were exploiting discretionary powers over them. The complex and poorly monitored process, so easily open to manipulation and abuse, by which merchants appraised the quality and value of the finished fabric delivered by master weavers was a constant source of tension in the Lyons silk and the Silesian linen industries, for example – the result was a tug of war between two unevenly matched groups.[79] There were repeated conflicts in Barcelona between workers and textile bosses over the practice of charging workers for spare parts.[80] The construction workers of the city of Nantes were remunerated under a complicated payments system that was eminently open to conflicting interpretations and abuse by subcontractors, especially when work was suspended on account of bad weather or other disruptions. In the summer of 1836, frustrations over capricious wage calculations culminated in a strike by the city's construction workers. The workers undertook on their honour not to work for any master who had not conceded their demands. Those who had obtained satisfaction would each pay fifty frames per day to the ones who were still on strike; those who had broken the strike would pay a fine of five francs to their

striking comrades. These measures were effective, in that most contractors swiftly backed down and accepted the demand for a more
transparent fixed tariff. But since some refused, the strike and agitation
continued. When the authorities arrested the leaders for 'unlawful coalition', their colleagues gathered en masse to stone the gendarmes and
troops escorting them from the courthouse. The unrest subsided after a
general wage agreement was finally reached.[81]

Labour protests of this kind were circumscribed challenges to local
systems of labour discipline and control. When larger structures of
socio-political power were in flux, legal arrangements that had seemed
permanent and immutable became vulnerable to waves of protest that
transcended regional and national boundaries. The ownership and
exploitation of land was at the forefront of social conflict in early-
nineteenth-century Europe, precisely because the normative framework
around it was changing. During the Revolutionary and Napoleonic
era, the confiscation of lands held in feudal tenure by ecclesiastical
bodies and great seigneurial landowners and their resale to private
buyers laid the foundations for generations of conflict. Across Andalusia in southern Spain, there were rent strikes, lawsuits and violent land
occupations in the 1820s and 1830s, as smallholders fought to reclaim
fields 'usurped' by local landowners.[82] In the province of Ciudad Real,
about 100 miles to the south of Madrid, a conflict broke out in the
1840s over the payment of feudal rents on common lands that had
once been collected by the Order of Calatrava, a Castilian chivalric
order dating back to the twelfth century. The fundamental problem
here was that the abolition of feudalism had resolved the question of
who owned the land but not the question of who had the right to
its use.[83]

Wherever traditional 'feudal' usage systems were replaced by more
homogeneous forms of commercial ownership and exploitation, communities responded with protests, law suits, illegal occupations and
attacks on enforcing officials. At stake were the many kinds of traditional usage rights that had granted local communities access to the
water, wood and pasturage on common lands. In the 1820s, the residents of Ullà near Girona in Catalonia demanded the return into
communal use of the lands known as the Forest of the March House,
recently acquired by a great local landowner. When the provincial
authorities pointed out that these lands were now private property and

refused to act, a popular revolt broke out. There were invasions, land occupations and armed confrontations.[84]

These were local tumults focused on local grievances, but that did not mean that they were 'primitive' or apolitical. In the 1820s, the small leaseholders of El Coronil and Los Morales in the province of Seville conducted a remarkably coordinated campaign in support of their rent strike, collecting what for them were huge sums of money in order to pay for legal representation against the local duke. Zealous local priests with rhetorical skills helped them to raise their objections to the level of legal and ideological coherence. The efforts of the landlord's steward to enforce payments were in vain; 'I have fallen out with all of these residents', he reported. 'Since they all pursue the same objective, I believe that this is a general conspiracy.'[85]

In Sicily, too, new laws allowed estate-owners to claim 'unfettered private property' and set aside the rights and obligations associated with the traditional feudal tenure, including the *usi civici* that accorded peasants valuable rights to the pasturage, firewood and water on land held by the lordship. The government in Naples was aware of the problem and regulations issued in 1817, 1839 and 1841 stipulated that when commons passed into private ownership, peasants were entitled to compensation (in the form of land drawn from the commons) for the loss of traditional usage rights, so long as they could 'establish a custom of ancestral usage'. But the reality was that in many areas there were no archives or records to establish usage and no adequate means of enforcing the law. Common lands were simply seized and placed under the custody of intimidators and armed rent-a-thugs. Once that happened, the Bourbon authorities tended to see possession as tantamount to title.[86] How difficult it could be to extract justice from the system is illustrated by the case of the village of Salaparuta in south-western Sicily. In 1829, the village sued the prince of Villafranca, on the grounds that he had illegally usurped a piece of previously common woodland. Furious at the presumption of the local rustics, the prince had the wood burned down. Not until 1842 was there a ruling against him by the regional authorities. The prince appealed and it was not until 1896 that the appeal court ruled in the villagers' favour. The remains of the disputed wood were returned to the village in 1903, by which time the instigators of the original appeal had been dead for several generations.[87]

In France, policy on common lands tended to be gradualist and more sensitive to the huge variety of local usage rights, though here, too, there was a general tendency towards the partition, leasing, sale and cultivation of commons, a trend that tended to benefit middling peasants and smallholders. That there was no general selling-off of the communal lands was due to the vehement opposition of the communes.[88] But if conflicts over arable land were relatively rare in post-1815 France, forestry rights remained highly contentious, especially after the introduction of the new forestry code of 1827. Whereas previous governments had tolerated various forms of collective usage right, the code sought to abolish them. The grazing of sheep and goats was henceforth forbidden (an exception was made for pigs, who needed the acorns), the cultivation of plots in the forest was severely restricted and punishments were prescribed for those found gathering fallen wood, which now counted as the private property of the owner.

Among the protests triggered by these measures was the 'War of the Girls' (*Guerre des Demoiselles*) that broke out in the Pyrenean mountain *arrondissements* of the department of the Ariège between 1829 and 1831, in which peasant men donned female garb in order to resist efforts by the authorities and private entrepreneurs (especially Catalan foundry-owners) to deny them their customary rights to collect firewood and building materials and to pasture their animals on the forest. With their loose white shirts untucked and bound at the waist with coloured sashes, and their faces daubed with thick red and black paint or with masks of cloth or paper, the *Demoiselles* fired their guns in the air, threatening and sometimes attacking the forest guards whose task it was to keep them out of the woodlands. The outlandish clothing (often supplemented with Napoleonic hats and other memorabilia from the wars) served as a disguise, but also as a symbolic attribute linking the protestors with the female forest spirits of peasant lore known as *demoiselles* or as *dames blanches*.[89] So unpopular was the new code that the Prefect of the Hautes-Alpes found it impossible to find local men willing to serve as village mayors – no one wanted to serve as the scapegoat for a policy that was so widely resented.[90] There were similar tensions in the Rhineland after the Prussian government issued a new law stipulating punishments for the 'theft' of wood from forests subject to various forms of traditional usage right. In the district of Trier alone there were 37,328 verdicts in cases of wood theft between 1824 and 1829 and more than 14,000 in cases of 'other forest-related offences'.[91]

These episodes suggest a conflict between rapacious landowners, or aggressive state authorities, on the one hand, and heroic peasant defenders fighting for their ancient rights on the other. But the transition from commons to privatized land did not take place everywhere, and the protagonists of change differed from region to region. In the Corbières, an area within the Languedoc-Roussillon region of France, it was the smallholding peasants who drove the process of economic transformation, seizing and dividing portions of common land, often without authorization of any kind, and absorbing them into a form of agriculture dominated by market-oriented viticulture, in an example of what Florence Gauthier has called the 'peasant road to capitalism'.[92]

The conflicts triggered by such changes were not just social, but also environmental in character, because the advent of the 'liberal' model of private property entailed the promotion of a new mode of resource management oriented towards the market. Agricultural uses of the soil tended to be privileged over the other mixed forms of usage (pasturage, foraging, forestry). The traditional 'agrosilvopastoral' system of open fields and communal use was swept away. It was a clash between different visions of agroecosystem management.[93] The ecological consequences of intensified cutting in the French forests in the aftermath of the Forestry Code of 1827 were profound: deforestation caused major flooding along the Rhone river in 1843 and there were massive inundations in deforested areas of the Alpine departments in the later 1850s.[94] Woodland was not the only resource that was degraded in this way. In the Liri river valley between the Appenines and the Tyrrhenian Sea on the northern margins of the Kingdom of the Two Sicilies, the abolition of the old feudal system and the privatization of the waters opened the way to the helter-skelter construction of paper and textiles mills. Bitter conflicts broke out between claimants to water usage rights, as rivals destroyed each other's dams or built illegal mills on each other's property. And in the process the ecology of the valley was transformed. The excessive construction of waterworks along the river and the deforestation of the slopes above gave rise to intensified flooding, with devastating inundations in 1825 and 1833. The anticipated industrial take-off never took place. 'The unregulated freedom of individual "owners" over the water brought "ruin to all".'[95]

Workers mobilized spontaneously against 'strangers' they perceived as rivals for scarce resources. In 1843, unemployed textile workers in the industrial town of Brünn (Brno), capital of Moravia, attacked groups of rural weavers on their way home with piecework from the city's factories, wrongly claiming that these weavers had taken their jobs.[96] In rural Andalusia, the 'workers from elsewhere' were the most marginal of those who worked the land, *pegujaleros* with tiny parcels of stony soil that barely sufficed for them to feel that they were not merely labourers. They migrated during the year, descending from the mountain ranges into the valleys in search of work because they could not support their families from their own plots. In March 1825, the captain general of Seville reported a violent protest in the town of La Algaba (whose Arabic name meant 'the forest'). The day labourers of the area had attacked the Cordoban and Granadan workers, who, 'harassed by calamity and misery with the shortage of rain in their provinces, arrived in considerable numbers to be employed in the mowing'. Their arrival, the locals argued, had pushed wages down to 'such a tiny amount' that the local workers would be unable to 'unburden themselves of the hardships of winter'.[97] The mere fact of shared misery did not suffice to generate solidarity among the most wretched.

An overview of Europe in the decades before the 1848 revolutions reveals a panorama of social conflicts driven by competition over every conceivable resource in a world marked by scarcity and low rates of productivity growth. Citizens resentful of the tax on tobacco burned down warehouses full of the precious leaves; peasants foraging for wood took pot shots at forestry officials; fishermen from neighbouring towns skirmished over fishing rights. There were attacks on tax collectors and customs offices. In the very stagnant and overregulated economies of central and southern Italy, John Davis has written, the system of allotting vending licences for tobacco, salt, playing cards, lottery tickets and other royal monopoly wares became a pretext for extortion at every transaction level, simply because screwing the customer over was the easiest way to maximize revenues. Many of the direct taxes levied from the subjects of the Neapolitan monarchy were in fact illicit duties imposed by corrupt officials or local extortion rackets. The cost of such dysfunctionality was not just further immiseration and the depression of demand, but also anger and conflict at every point in the supply chain.[98]

These fragile, inelastic systems were periodically shaken by short-term disruptions to the food supply. In 1829, a sudden rise in the price of wheat triggered cascades of riots and grain seizures. In Montmorillon, a market town in central-western France, crowds of angry townsfolk insulted and beat millers, grain merchants and even the town's mayor. The merchants were forced to accept a lower price for their product. When the local gendarmes drew their sabres, the protesters broke into the workshop of an edge-tool maker and seized scythes, knives and pitchforks. Only with the arrival of fifty horse *chasseurs* did the trouble subside.[99] Tumults of this kind proliferated at great speed across immense arcs of countryside, projecting the sense of a collective popular outrage. And in some areas the waves of unrest returned every time the prices pushed back up, striking fear into the better-off social strata. In the late 1830s, poor harvests again triggered waves of food riots, concentrated around the Atlantic ports of Brest, Nantes and La Rochelle, export depots for grain on its way to England. South of the Loire river, there were numerous *entraves*, or grain seizures, mostly on waterways leading to the Loire. In France, as in Germany and elsewhere, riots tended to take place in areas where grain was in transit from or through areas experiencing shortages and price surges.[100] The sight of the poorest massing in towns with pitchforks in their hands or aprons full of paving stones struck fear into those who had an interest in the liberal economic order of open markets and freely disposable property. 'I am not at all confident', wrote the Public Prosecutor of the commune of Ferté Bernard in north-western France in the autumn of 1831, 'as to the movements and disorders that this coming winter will bring to our appallingly wretched population.'[101]

Worse was to come in 1845–7, when a composite agrarian and industrial crisis swept across the continent. In around 1840, spores of *Phytophthora infestans* had reached Europe from America. This fungus propagates extremely quickly and, dispersed by wind and mist, can infect an entire field of potatoes in a few hours. The leaves turn black and rot, and if there is rain the infection is swiftly carried to the roots and to the potatoes themselves. In the unusually wet summer of 1845, *P. infestans* ran riot. The effect was intensified by the fact that the fungus struck hardest in the clay soil areas where edible (as opposed to factory, or fodder) potatoes were grown. The impact on the Dutch harvest of 1845 was devastating. From an average per hectare yield of 179.3 hectolitres over the years 1842–4, the Netherlands crop fell to 44.5 hectolitres, and the situation was even worse than these figures suggest, because most of the potatoes lifted in 1846 were factory potatoes; very few of these were winter potatoes suitable for storage, the early varieties being much less prone to disease because they reached maturity before *P. infestans* got to work in the middle of July each year.[102] The following year brought a degree of relief for the Netherlands: the drought in August and September of 1846 slowed the progress of the blight, there being no rain to proliferate the spores to the tubers in the ground.

In Ireland, exactly the opposite happened: whereas the blight had destroyed about half of the crop in 1845, the entire crop failed in the following year. The estimated total number of famine deaths in the Netherlands was 60,000; in Ireland, over an eighth of the population (about 1.1 million of a population of 8.3 million) perished as a direct consequence of the famine and the diseases that thrived in its wake. It was 'the greatest natural demographic disaster of modern European history'.[103] It was also an ecological event, in the sense that the damage done by the blight to the potato was permanent; the crop never recovered. The problem here was not industrialization as such, because Ireland and the Netherlands were both 'under-industrialized' by contemporary western European standards. Belgium and Scotland, which were both more industrial and more commercialized in their agriculture, weathered the potato shock far better than the Netherlands, even though the damage to crops was comparable. In other words, it was not the shift to more capitalist forms of production that generated vulnerability, but overdependence on a vulnerable commodity (how vulnerable it was, no one had guessed), exacerbated in Ireland's case by poor management of the crisis, once famine tightened its grip on the country.

Just as the blight was getting to work, there were failures at other points in the food economy. The very drought that helped to arrest the progress of the blight in northern Europe in 1846 in turn damaged grain crops, especially wheat and rye, the staple grain of the poorer classes. The French wheat crop fell from 62 million hundredweight in 1844 to 40 million in 1846. An attack of rye rust accounted for nearly half the northern European crop in 1846. And since the potato crisis had emptied food stores, the reserves that would otherwise have cushioned the impact of the shortfall were depleted. Then came the winter of 1846–7, which was unusually long and severe. In the spring of 1847, price shocks proliferated across all the substitute products, from wheat and rye to buckwheat, oats, barley and beans, making it harder for the poor to compensate for the loss of potatoes, which had now in any case become unaffordable. In the French departments to the north of the Loire River, the price of wheat rose from 20 francs per hectolitre in 1845 to 24 in 1846 and 39 in May

1847, as the hunger season (*la soudure* – the period when the old harvest was largely used up and the new one not yet in) approached.

As the price shocks triggered by the shortages proliferated across the European economies, depressing demand for manufactured goods, a lapse in investor confidence gave rise to a liquidity crunch in the commercial sector. It is easy to think of the period before the 'take-off into sustained growth' of the 1850s as an era of 'agrarian economies' in which everything depended upon the food supply. But the balance was shifting. In France, to be sure, 80 per cent of the population still lived in the countryside. But whereas the proportion of GDP accounted for by agricultural products fell from 45 per cent in 1820 to 34 per cent in 1850, the figure for industrial (i.e. manufactured) products rose from 37 to 43 per cent. And much of this manufacturing was dispersed and rural. The valleys of the Alps and Upper Silesia bristled with little spinning and weaving factories. As the population density of rural areas grew, so did the pressure on people in the countryside to find something to do other than work the soil.[104]

Wherever they worked, the people who made things for other people to buy were acutely vulnerable both to disruptions in their own supply chains and to fluctuations in demand. The rising cost of bread, a staple that most poorer households found it impossible to substitute for, suppressed the demand for other goods, eating into the receipts of workshops and factories and thus driving more people out of work. The resulting reverse-multiplier effect led to a drastic contraction of industrial production.[105] In the city of Roubaix, a major centre of wool-spinning, 30 per cent of workers were unemployed by February 1847 and 60 per cent by the middle of May. Many factories closed or laid people off and slowed down, while managers, unable to keep financing themselves, applied to the commercial banks for loans on stocks, only to find themselves falling foul of the general scarcity of credit.[106] The situation for industry was worsened by two successive shortfalls (in 1845–6 and 1846–7) in the American cotton crop. With cotton imports falling, the price of raw cotton shot up by about 50 per cent in 1845–7, further depressing home consumption at a time when the price shock in foodstuffs was also cutting into demand. The first to feel the pain were the Lancashire cotton mills, where there was heavy unemployment and short-time working, but the symptoms quickly proliferated across all the cotton manufactures of Europe.

This overlayering of an international commercial-industrial crisis with food shortages and grain price shocks is important, because it closed the scissors around the landless or virtually landless rural poor who, unable to feed themselves and their children from their own gardens, lived on income from various forms of piecework – weaving or spinning, for example. They faced the double jeopardy of high food prices and a decline in piece-rates, a fall in the quantity of orders, or even unemployment. As one observer in the Grand Duchy of Luxembourg noted, the living conditions of working-class families or families of the lower artisan strata resisted precise quantification, because 'when the flow of work dries up and foodstuffs get dearer, their revenues no longer suffice even for a miserable existence and their destinies fall into the hands of chance and charity'.[107]

The effect on the lower strata of the population was immediate and severe. The church records of Lyons show that of the 13,752 people who died in the years 1845–7, 10,274 had nothing at all to bequeath to their descendants. In Friesland, with a population of 245,000, there were 34,859 persons in receipt of poor relief in 1844 and 47,482 in 1847; in the city of Liège, the number of persons receiving emergency assistance rocketed from under 8,000 to nearly 17,000 between mid 1847 and mid 1848.[108] Under such conditions, the number of residents officially classified as poor in German towns could swell to two thirds or even three quarters of the population.[109] Food riots broke out across swathes of Europe. There was serious rioting in Leyden, the Hague, Delft and Haarlem in the autumn of 1845, where fears of the coming winter were stirred by the collapse of the potato crop and the rise in prices. One historian has counted 158 food riots for Prussia alone in the panic-filled *soudure* of April–May 1847. And the numbers involved were much higher that this total suggests: in all, around 100,000 citizens took an active part in the *c.*200 riots recorded for the spring of 1847. The rioting took a range of forms. In East Prussia, home to many landless rural labourers, looting or begging parties formed 'food marches' numbering hundreds and armed with sacks and baskets.[110] These were the *Büdner*, *Häusler* and *Einlieger*, the most precarious existences of the German agrarian world, analogous in this respect to the *pegujaleros* who came from the Andalusian mountains in spring, desperate for work. Across Europe, vagabondage and mendicancy shot up. In May 1847, one report from North Brabant in the Netherlands described 'many and among them fairly well-to-do people in the country' living on 'the herbs of the field, on stinging nettles, wild elder and such'; the poor had scoured the countryside so energetically for these plants that they had become scarce.[111] In Ireland, the sudden displacement of huge numbers of people in search of work and food did much to spread epidemics. Exhausted people unable to wash themselves or change their clothes easily became infested with the lice that carried typhus, one of the great killers of the famine years.

The bleakest evidence of the suffering inflicted by the straitened conditions of the crisis years is simply the demographic record. The catastrophic impact of the potato shock on Ireland and the high death toll in the Netherlands have already been mentioned, but we see elevated death rates almost everywhere across the continent. In the German states, the death rate for 1847 was 8.8 per cent above the norm, while in Austria the excess was 48 per cent. France was less hard hit, but even here there was a modest rise in deaths to 5.3 per cent above the average.[112] This was the apogee of the 'pauperism' that had haunted the literature of the Social Question for decades.

Disasters of this kind can sometimes seem like natural events, analogous to seismic instability or extreme weather. But hunger, as Amartya Sen has observed, is a political phenomenon, not a natural one.[113] And the European subsistence crisis was eminently political, both in the sense that its effects were shaped by structures that expressed the power relations between different social groups, and in the sense that it forced local and regional officials to make decisions under pressure. We can see this more clearly if we examine the case of a Spanish town that succeeded in evading the worst effects of the 1846 grain crisis.

By the early autumn of 1846, it was clear that the results of the harvest had been very poor in southern Spain. In the city of Jerez de la Frontera not far from Cadiz in the south-west of the country, wheat prices were already starting to surge in September, although the harvest was scarcely in. This was highly unusual: in normal years, the city balanced its grain exports with imports from the small towns of the provincial interior, hedging against fluctuations in demand. But this year the shortages were everywhere and could not be hedged against. The first to respond to the looming emergency were the speculators and grain traders, who sallied out onto the roads to buy up the grain that the muleteers were bringing to Jerez from the surrounding countryside. As the price continued to climb, anxiety spread across the city and many of the lesser towns of the region. When the provincial administration ordered an enquiry into the state of the city's grain reserves, they received an alarming reply. The

Commercial Council reported that the current stock was at about half the level needed to cope with the population's needs until the next harvest. From the Patriotic Economic Society, an association of philanthropically inclined local notables, came a forthright warning: it was essential, they insisted, that the authorities put the nutritional needs of the population above the commercial interests of the agrarian sector, even if this meant doing short-term damage to that very small portion of society that lived from the commercial speculation in staple goods.

While these exchanges were underway, panic was breaking out in the city. On 23 February 1847, a local baker spoke before the city council, declaring that he had not been able to buy sufficient wheat to make up his dough and would thus be unable to supply his retailers for the coming Saturday. This, he argued, was a consequence of all the sellers having got together and agreed not to sell in order to push up the price. For the moment, the authorities continued to trust in the market and ordered local officials to prevent any efforts to block or disrupt the trade in grain. But, at the same time, they summoned grain suppliers to the City Hall in order to ascertain which merchants currently held stocks of wheat. The grain merchants were told to keep their warehouses and granaries open for business and warned of the responsibility they would incur if their non-compliance triggered 'a major alteration of public order in the city'. Merchants and growers were ordered to produce statements detailing the precise amount of grain they had in storage. When they responded with gross understatements of their actual holdings, they were ordered to re-submit and threatened with hefty fines for under-reporting.

None of these measures succeeded in halting the upward journey of the bread price, which continued to rise into March 1847. At eight in the evening on 11 March, the city council met in extraordinary session and agreed to convene twelve of the most important bakers in the city. At eleven o'clock that night, the bakers appeared and the mayor asked them to consider lowering the price of their bread in order to make their product accessible to the popular classes of the city. The bakers baulked at this assault on their profit margins, but when more than thirty-six bakers convened on the following day, it was agreed that the city's bakeries would sell 1,140 loaves of bread daily at an agreed discount price (the number was later raised to 6,000 loaves as the crisis deepened). A subsidy for each loaf, payable by the city, would cover a portion of their losses. In this way, the town of Jerez de la Frontera and its bakers shared the burden of the emergency measures enacted to meet the shortfall in supply. This arrangement remained in place until the end of May, when the prices began to fall and tension eased.

In the context of mid-nineteenth-century Spain, this was an unusually deep and adventurous exercise in administrative interventionism. Municipal authorities with liberal economic instincts prized free markets. They were generally loath to curtail the rights of property-owners to buy and sell their goods as and when they wished, even though in this case the grain speculators, with their cartel-like behaviour, were scarcely shining examples of free-market governance. Yet, as a way of keeping a major social upheaval at bay, the pragmatic deal struck in Jerez de le Frontera worked. Prices fell again in June, in anticipation of the better harvest.[114] The bakers of Jerez were wise to collaborate in these manoeuvres: in other parts of Europe, bakers were among the chief targets of rioting crowds. Of the forty-five shops attacked and ransacked by rioters in Berlin during the 'potato revolution' of 21–23 April 1847, nearly thirty were bakeries.[115]

How the authorities handled the challenge of such tumults varied from place to place. In Prussia, three decades of economically liberal governance disposed the government not to intervene in the crisis, beyond a few cosmetic measures intended to build public confidence; instead, they placed their faith in strong and effective repression. But there were many initiatives at local level, just as in Jerez de la Frontera. In a number of Rhenish (i.e. also Prussian) commercial and manufacturing towns – Cologne, Barmen, Elberfeld, Solingen, Krefeld – local middle-class elites took the lead in organizing and financing ameliorative measures, initiatives that reinforced the claim of the better-off bourgeoisie to social and political leadership. In Danzig, too, private money was forthcoming to fund discounted potato sales and soup kitchens. Things went less well in Berlin, because the Prussian authorities there were wary of ceding any kind of initiative to the bourgeois elites in the city, with the result, for example, that their requests for preventive measures and a civil militia were rejected out of hand. Faced with the choice between an empowered middle class policing its own neighbourhood and relatively disorganized food riots, the authorities 'preferred the riot'.[116]

In France, too, there were hunger riots in Buzançais, Lisieux and le Mans, and these events were extensively pored over in the press. But bread distributions were organized by the authorities without major problems in most of the country. In Belgium, parliament voted an exceptional credit for poor relief, enabling the formation of charity committees in almost every locality, and government work creation programmes focused mainly on the improvement of local roads helped many unemployed men to make it through the worst months. In the relatively industrialized region of Wallonia, the presence of factories that were still employing large numbers (albeit on very low wages) also helped to mute the worst effects of the food shortages, it being an advantage that the cycles of grain shortage and industrial crisis were only contingently linked and thus not fully synchronized.[117]

If things were so much worse in Ireland, this was not because the British government failed entirely to intervene. When the potato blight struck in 1845, the Peel government responded immediately, buying maize from the United States for sale in Ireland, expanding the existing programme of public works and cutting tariffs in 1846 in order to ease the import of grain (similar tariff reforms were enacted in Sweden, Belgium, the Netherlands and Piedmont–Sardinia[118]). But the controversy stirred by such interventionist measures brought down Peel and his government. His successor as Prime Minister, Lord Russell, was a strong adherent to liberal laissez-faire principles and thus opposed to state intervention in society or the workings of the market. Russell's Chancellor of the Exchequer, Sir Charles Wood, was a laissez-faire evangelical who saw in the famine a work of divine judgement and a trigger of salutary structural change that should best be left to play itself out.[119] The measures adopted in 1845–6 were largely abandoned in the following year. The public works programme was shut down. The remarkably successful network of soup kitchens established in February 1847, analogous to the charity committees established in many continental towns, was wound up again in October. Against the background of anxiety about the financial burdens of famine relief and widespread 'famine fatigue' in Britain, the disaster was allowed to grind on, until it consumed an eighth of the Irish population and drove further hundreds of thousands to leave the country, among them the emigrants to rural New South Wales from whom I am descended.

WEAVERS

At about seven o'clock in the morning of Monday, 21 November 1831, 400 silk weavers formed up in orderly groups in the Croix-Rousse, a suburb of the city of Lyons. Their plan was to march down the Grande Côte towards the centre of town and insist that their employers, the town's silk merchants, accept as binding a minimum wage agreed with the city's authorities a few days before. A small unit of fifty National Guardsmen despatched to stop them were greeted with a hail of thrown stones, surrounded and disarmed. Emotions were already running high: only with difficulty did Pierre Charnier, a master weaver and one of the key orchestrators of the protest, succeed in preventing a group of enraged protestors from lynching Police Commissioner Toussaint. Re-forming in groups of four with their arms interlocked, the weavers resumed their progress down the Grande Côte, where they were met by the Grenadiers of the First Legion of the National Guard. Among the Guardsmen were a number of the silk manufacturers who employed the insurgent weavers. Shots were fired. Several weavers fell, gravely wounded; an officer was struck in the thigh by a bullet. Pushed back by the weavers, the Guardsmen broke into a disorderly retreat, while the weavers ascended in haste to call the population of the Croix-Rousse to arms. Huge barricades appeared at the entrance to the Grande-Rue and the weavers unfurled their flag, a finely made thing (they were weavers, after all). On it were embroidered words that would reverberate into the twentieth century: *Vivre en travaillant, mourir en combattant* (Live working or die fighting).

This was the opening scene of the *révolte des canuts*, the uprising of the silk weavers of Lyons (known colloquially as *canuts*) in November–December 1831. Over the next few days, the weavers attacked and captured the fortified police barracks at Bon-Pasteur, broke into the arsenal to commandeer weapons and harried various units of the National Guard and the army. The battle for the city cost 600 casualties. By the morning of 23 November, the mayor and the commanding general in the city had both fled. In its inception, the upheaval resembled other social protests of the period. The revolution of the previous year in Paris, exacerbated by a cholera epidemic in the capital, revolutions in Latin America and a banking crisis in the United States had disrupted the trade cycle in silk, leading to a fall in orders, prices and wages. The master weavers demanded a minimum piece tariff. The merchants refused to pay it, even though a general tariff had been agreed and recommended by the municipality.[120] The weavers went on strike and demanded justice.

A more remarkable feature of the Lyons uprising is the sophistication of the organizational culture behind it. In 1827, a group of master weavers had formed a Mutual Aid Society (Société du Devoir Mutuel) founded on an elaborate cellular structure of small 'companies', each consisting of no more than twenty master weavers (to avoid falling foul of Article 291 of the French penal code of 1810) and headed by a 'syndic' assisted by two 'secretaries'. The syndics reported to a 'central office' consisting of a director, two deputy directors, a secretary and a treasurer. The syndics meeting together with the five members of the 'central office' constituted a 'grand council'.[121] This 'free-masonry of the workers', as its chief instigator, the weaver Pierre Charnier, would later call it, was more than just an instrument for distributing aid; it was an attempt to offset the asymmetrical historical effects of the commercial liberty inaugurated during the French Revolution and prized by the property-owning classes of Europe. The Le Chapelier Law of 1791 had not just abolished the old guilds, but had also denied citizens the right to strike or associate in pursuit of 'their pretended common interests'. And yet it remained legal for factory-owners and merchants to engage in cartel-like behaviour or to form organizations such as the chambers of commerce.[122]

The animating principle behind Charnier's panoptical system of cells reporting to a central office was 'association', a word whose mid-nineteenth-century charisma is hard to recapture today (though perhaps less so in France, where until 2017 there was still a minister 'pour la vie associative'). Only through association would the working masses overcome the structural weakness of the individual. The idea possessed a special appeal for the master weavers, who were not gathered together in open-plan factories, but owned their own looms and worked in their own workshops, supported by an entourage of apprentices, journeymen, subcontractors, female specialists and assistants of varying ranks, ages and social statuses. Without a robust organization, it was easy for the merchants to play the masters off against each other. United through their association, the weavers would command the respect they were owed:

In association we will be able to find all the consolations for our ills. We will learn that a man who is poor in wealth is not necessarily poor in quality. When we have become suffused with our dignity as men, the other inhabitants of this city, whose glory and wealth we have unstintingly fashioned for many years, will cease to use the term 'canut' in a derisive or insulting way.[123]

In 1831, the Mutual Aid Society of the master weavers was joined by a Society of Silkworkers (Société des ferrandiniers) representing the workers, or *compagnons*. These bodies enabled the collective processing of common experiences, collective bargaining, the enforcement of collective agreements and the building of collective strategies. This ability to collaborate is itself noteworthy. The masters were small-scale entrepreneurs, owners of the means of production, who often rented out one or more of their looms to journeyman weavers, who might themselves hire assistants. Most of the *compagnons*, by contrast, were proletarians who had nothing to invest but their labour. Yet the 8,000-odd masters and the 20,000-odd *compagnons* of the city succeeded for the most part in working together. The reason for this success probably lay in the intimate geography of Lyonnais weaving: the *compagnons* often lodged with their masters; quarters like the Faubourg Croix-Rousse were densely packed with weaving households: of the 16,449 inhabitants of the Croix-Rousse in 1832, over 10,000 were weavers or their dependants.[124]

The Lyons uprising of 1831 might look at first glance like the purely 'social' or 'industrial' provincial counterpart to the political revolution of 1830 in Paris. This was certainly how the novelist and poet Marceline Desbordes-Valmore, who was in the city when the first insurrection broke out, saw it: 'Politics plays no part in this immense revolt', she wrote to a friend in Bordeaux on 29 November 1831. 'It is an uprising of hunger. Throwing themselves before the bullets, the women shouted "Kill us! Then we will no longer be hungry!" Three or four cries of *Vive la République!* were heard, but the workers and the people always responded: "No! We are fighting for bread and for work." '[125] It was not unusual for middle-class commentators to raise such tumults to the status of tragedy by insisting upon a purely social motivation, innocent of politics. But the Lyon weavers were not, generally speaking, starvelings of the kind depicted in the slum descriptions of the social hygienists, and their world was saturated with politics. The tradition of concerted protest by workers in the city dated back into the eighteenth century, and the weavers had long memories.[126]

On the eve of the uprising, Lyons was already attracting the interest of radical intellectuals. A delegation of radicals visited the city in May 1831, drawing huge crowds to their public lectures. The most sensational, by Jean Reynaud, a Lyonnais by birth who would later serve in one of the Parisian revolutionary governments of 1848, was a 'sermon' on the subject of property: 'Behold', Reynaud told his audience, 'the glory [of property] is passing and its reign expires.'[127] In June, two new republican newspapers opened in the city, *La Sentinelle nationale*, edited by Joseph Beuf (who would later be fined and arrested for sedition) and Adolphe Granier's *La Glaneuse* (The Gleaner). *La Glaneuse*, a wickedly funny satirical journal printed on pink paper, relentlessly mocked the pretensions of the new French monarchy established in 1830 through an assortment of genres: vignettes, short stories, jokes, mock recipes and advertisements. But after the uprising of 21 November, a solemn editorial piece put the ironic banter on hold to bewail the dead and to hail the victory of the weavers over the forces of 'order': 'Our sympathies, let's say it out loud! . . . are with the most numerous and the poorest class; today and always we shall be its defenders; today and always we shall claim on its behalf the sacred rights of justice, of humanity!'[128]

The well-intentioned condescension of this claim to speak 'on behalf of' a subaltern class was entirely absent from *L'Écho de la Fabrique*, a remarkable journal founded in October 1831, whose columns reflected a view of the world from within the milieu of the weavers, or at least of the master weavers. The founding cohort of shareholders in the paper included thirty-one master weavers and its columns were full of news items about industrial negotiations, arbitration proceedings and the meetings held by weavers themselves. Its purpose, openly avowed in the prospectus, was to combat the 'greed and egoism' of the bosses (*chefs de commerce*), curb abuses of the system and 'establish an equilibrium which, without damaging the general interests of the employers, will bring about an improvement in the fortunes of those who are dependent upon them'. *L'Écho* was to be a venue in which a working community made itself audible in new ways – weavers from across the Lyons community were invited to submit material they deemed newsworthy to the editors.[129] The alienated, third-person perspective of the 'Social Question' made way for a new lexicon, shaped in an eclectic way by Saint-Simonianism and later by the socialism of Charles Fourier, but also by the lived experience of its subjects, a language capable both of articulating and of normalizing the emotional textures of a workers' movement and of endowing the conflict between the Lyonnais weavers and their employers with ethical and political legitimacy.[130]

The retaking of Lyons in 1831 turned out to be surprisingly blood-less. Stupefied by this insurrection in the second city of France only a year after the revolution that had installed him on the throne, the new king, Louis Philippe, ordered that the army should proceed firmly but avoid capital executions. On 3 December, 20,000 soldiers entered the city under the command of General Jean-de-Dieu Soult, a veteran of the Napoleonic wars. There were numerous arrests, only a few of which led to prosecutions, and all of these ended in acquittals.

The story might have ended there, but three years later the silk work-ers of Lyons rose again, this time under rather different circumstances. The market for silk had recovered and there had been a surge in silk workers' piece-rates. The merchants, who feared a further downturn, tried to trim their wage bills. Protests over a reduction in the wages of the workers in plush (*péluche*) escalated, triggering a strike across the sector. The spring of 1834 brought renewed clashes and arrests; when the police found a letter full of supposedly seditious phrases written by one of the more radical *canuts*, there was a crackdown. In April there was a fully fledged uprising; during the 'bloody week' that followed, bar-ricades appeared across the city to hinder the army's progress. The workers stormed the Bon-Pasteur barracks (as they had in 1831) and the Arsenal; they transformed the various districts of the city into fortified camps. At the core of the uprising were about 3,000 insurgents, but large numbers of other residents also took part. The wife and daughters of the bookseller Jean Caussidière, for example, prepared cartridges and food and brought them to the fighters at the barricades. In the districts domi-nated by weavers, an eye-witness reported, the attitude adopted to the troops by non-combatant residents was one of 'hostile neutrality'.[131]

This time, the government's response was brutal. Adolphe Thiers, Minister of the Interior, withdrew the troops from the town, surrounded it and then took it back piece by piece, making liberal use of artillery

This image of the *Horrible Massacre at Lyons* in 1834, the work of an anonymous local engraver, captures the intimate, close-range quality of violence in the small spaces of inner cities. More than 300 were killed and nearly 600 wounded in this bitter conflict over wages and the right of workers to associate and strike.

and massacring many workers and innocent bystanders in the process, a technique he would in old age use again in crushing the Paris Commune of 1871. Cannon were used to clear squares. The use of explosive charges to blow open the doors of buildings started fires in several quarters. One man who had taken refuge in a chimney was deliberately burned alive. The son of Jean Caussidière was killed in the fighting and his body repeatedly mutilated by the troops with bayonets (after the outbreak of revolution in 1848, the other son, Marc Caussidière, a republican leader in nearby Saint-Étienne, would briefly serve as Prefect of the Paris Police). Learning from their opponents, the soldiers climbed onto the roofs of buildings and engaged the insurgents in a 'battle of the chimneys'. Estimates of total casualties range from 200 to 600, but 350 is a good guess. Contemporary visual depictions bring home the savagery of fighting at the closest quarters in small squares surrounded by tall buildings. When troops and insurgents clashed on and around barricades, battle soon gave way to massacre.

Jean-Baptiste Monfalcon, doctor, journalist and librarian, and a son of the city, noted a crucial difference between the first and second revolt: 'At first truly industrial, [the revolt] became bit by bit industrial *and* political, and the misfortune of the times would have it that it finally took on an almost exclusively party-political character.' In November 1831, Monfalcon wrote, the workers had risen over the matter of a 'poorly posed and poorly understood' question of salary. But in April 1834 it was no longer just a matter of tariffs: the workers, 'guided by political parties in open revolt against power, raised barricades in the name of republican opinion'.[132]

There is something to be said for this view. Things certainly changed between the first and second revolt. After 1831, republican agents gradually infiltrated the working population of Lyons; there was a sharpening of republican political rhetoric in the journals and Lyons became a centre of republican activism in eastern France. During the second revolt, republican leaflets were distributed in the city and posted on buildings. These argued that the revolt was no longer about workplace grievances, but about challenging the authority of the Orleanist monarchy. Propagating political ideas was relatively easy in this milieu, because about three quarters of the male silk-weavers in Lyons were literate. The masters needed good reading skills in order to be able to scrutinize the contracts they signed with the merchants. The children of weavers (including many *compagnons*) attended the free primary schools in the suburbs, and many of their parents took evening and Sunday classes at the same schools, acquiring the skills that they needed to sustain a network of reading clubs and library societies.[133]

On the other hand, although republicans led the resistance of April 1834 in a few locations, most of the rebel forces were locally recruited and commanded (often rather chaotically) by members of the mutual societies or simply by weavers or other workers. Of the 108 people arrested after the fighting in the city's fifth arrondissement, only five were listed as republicans. The weavers, for their part, continued to operate within their traditional moral economy: they were motivated more by traditional assumptions about what was fair than by the theories or prescriptions of any political grouping. Republican agitators tried hard to channel the activism of the weavers into political action, but the weavers were generally reluctant to follow their prompting.[134] At their trial in Paris, the Lyonnais weavers among the accused insurgents refused to cooperate with the efforts of the republicans also facing prosecution to turn the trial into a platform for a political repudiation of the July Monarchy.[135] The republican accused, for their part, rarely referred directly to the *canuts*, and when they did it was in the stereotypical terms of the Social Question. Here is the republican Charles Lagrange, explaining why he and his colleagues were so keen on the principle of association:

> [We have] seen in our unfortunate city 15,000 women working from five in the morning until midnight without earning enough for the necessities of life. Many of them are without fathers, brothers, or husbands, and have been forced to deliver themselves into corruption in order to survive . . . Yes, we have seen all that, and that is why we have said to the proletarians: Associez-vous![136]

But the weavers did not think of or describe themselves as 'proletarians', nor did they need the prompting of men like Lagrange to understand the value of association. And no weaver would have claimed in front of the Court of Peers that the young women of his community were prostitutes. In short: the politics of republicanism and the politics of worker activism were converging in 1834, but they had not intertwined.

The 1834 insurrection lasted only a few days, but its impact reverberated across the cultural networks of France. By July 1835, when the massive trial of accused rebels was drawing to a close in Paris, litho-graphed portraits of the most outspoken Lyonnais defendants were on sale in the bookshops and on the stalls along the banks of the Seine. The 'fine drama' of the 'two great events' (Stendhal) resurfaces in the essays, letters and novels of the canonical male literary stars of the era, from Lamartine to Balzac, Victor Hugo, Chateaubriand and Alfred de Vigny. Félicité Robert de Lamennais, the radical priest whose *Paroles d'un croy-ant* (Words of a Believer), published in 1833, was already on its way to becoming one of the most famous books in the world, dedicated a pas-sionate pamphlet to the weavers, whose trial before the Court of Peers he denounced as the betrayal of the liberty promised by the revolution of 1830. Was it for this, he asked, that the people had chased away the Bour-bons? 'The people', Lamennais warned, had at last acquired 'an awareness and a feeling for their rights'; there would henceforth be no rest for those who failed to understand the fullness of what this meant.[137] For George Sand, who dressed as a man to join the spectators in the Court of Peers, the trial was a political awakening. The lawyers defending the accused were a line-up of left-wing luminaries: Ledru-Rollin and Garnier-Pagès would both later serve in the Provisional Government of February 1848; Armand Barbès was an habitué of the revolutionary underground who would play an important role on the far left in 1848, as would the trial advocate and sometime leftist deputy Michel de Bourges, whose affair with George Sand began after they met at the trial.[138] Lyons secured a unique and lasting place in the historical imaginary of the far left, from Blanqui, Marx, Engels and Fourier to Paul Lafargue, the revolutionary journalist, literary critic activist and co-founder of the French Workers' Party (Parti Ouvrier Français). In the 1880s, Lafargue would teach the cadres of his party that the revolutions of 1789, 1830 and 1848 paled into insignificance alongside the great social revolt of the Lyonnais weavers.[139]

One of the most powerful contemporary expressions of the emotional resonance of these events is a poem by Marceline Desbordes-Valmore, composed shortly after the second insurrection. By situating the action of her poem in the immediate aftermath of the repressions, Desbordes-Valmore hides the politics of the insurrection from view. Her weavers are not activists, but blood-stained victims of repression. Their advocates, an unnamed woman and a female chorus in the manner of Greek civic drama, make no specific accusations, but there is a radical energy in the language. To say that 'the murderer makes himself king' is not quite the same as saying that the king is a murderer, but the inference offers itself. Desbordes-Valmore depicts the violence of counter-insurgency as a brutal inversion of moral order that makes a mockery of the Church's promise of spiritual comfort.

> On a dark Day in Lyons
>
> THE WOMAN
> There is no money left for burying our dead.
> The priest has come about the funeral fee,
> And here the flattened corpses, gouged by shot,
> await a winding sheet, a cross, remorse.
> The murderer makes himself king. . . .
> Like crushed flowers, God gathers
> Women and children . . .
> Death, the hired guard, who stands astride the road,
> Is a soldier. He shoots and frees
> The rebel witness; tomorrow will not hear his voice.
>
> THE WOMEN
> Let's take our black ribbons and weep all our tears
> They've forbidden us to move our murdered ones:
> They've simply piled up their pale remains.
> God! Bless them all, they were all unarmed!
>
> 4 April 1834

The reference to dead women and children is striking; it does seem that whereas there were no women among the persons arrested at the end of the fighting in April 1834, and none in the dock during the *procès monstre* that followed, women and children were quite numerous among the civilian dead (a precise count does not exist). This may simply mean that whereas women tended to withdraw from protesting crowds when the violence started, both they and their children found it difficult to escape the effects of artillery shot and the fires started by explosions. Desbordes-Valmore did not witness the second insurrection, but she had witnessed, at the age of fifteen, the 1802 insurrection of Guadeloupe, triggered by

Napoleon's decision to reimpose slavery in the island, eight years after its abolition in 1794. In Pointe-à-Pitre, where she was lodging with her mother, who was dying of yellow fever, she saw captured former slaves thrown into 'an iron cage'. One of the central figures in *Sarah*, the novel she published in 1821, was a formerly enslaved male refugee by the name of Arsène, who figures as an ersatz 'mother' to the eponymous white heroine. The violence of colonial repression reverberated in the poet's depiction of indiscriminate slaughter in 1834.[140]

For those who sympathized with the silk merchants, the experience of insurrection brought home the fragility even of a well-resourced bourgeois existence. On 22 November 1831, the day after fighting had broken out, the doctor and journalist Jean-Baptiste Monfalcon volunteered to carry a prefectoral proclamation to the headquarters of the insurgents at the top of the Croix-Rousse hill. As he walked up the Grande Côte, he was struck by the silence: 'no sound of a loom, no human sound can be heard in this street, ordinarily so crowded and so noisy'. But before he had finished his ascent up the Croix-Rousse, Monfalcon found himself surrounded. Forty men, armed with a few bad rifles, encircled him, swearing and tearing away his rifle, his sabre, the epaulettes he wore as an officer of the National Guard. Then the punches began to rain in. The proclamation he had volunteered to carry was grabbed from his hands and trampled underfoot:

> . . . from all sides I hear cries of vengeance: 'he's a merchant; let him pay for the others . . .' strong hands seize me by the neck and drag me to the gutter, and I realise how this violent scene is likely to end, when, over the shouts, I hear these words: 'don't kill him, he's my doctor, let him go'. It is the voice of a lame silk worker who is not my patient, but whom I know quite well.

The helpful acquaintance persuaded the angry silk weavers to inspect their victim's rifle; finding that it had not recently been fired, they let him go. Monfalcon remained preoccupied by this episode throughout the rest of his life; it was a physical memory that refused to leave him.[141] Himself the son of a master weaver, Montfalcon had secured an excellent education and was well known in the city for his charitable medical work among the poorer weaving families. He was a respected contributor to the literature on the Social Question with an interest in statistical analysis and social hygiene that was typical for his time – Patissier included an essay by Monfalcon on the characteristic maladies of silk weavers in his famous compendium on occupational illness. On the afternoon of 21 April, the doctor had tended the wounded from the first day's fighting – this was where he had encountered the man who would save his life on the following day. His account of his brush with death, first published in a newspaper and then, after many iterations, twenty years later in his memoirs, carried a complex message. It was an edifying fable about the redemptive impact of social engagement. But Monfalcon's description of a respected man of the bourgeoisie cowering under a hail of punches as the attributes of his rank are torn from him and he is dragged like a heifer to be killed over a gutter also carried more urgent messages about the preciousness and indispensability of civic order.

The riots that broke out in Brno in May 1843 never acquired the mythic status of the Lyons insurrections, but they too disturbed one of the great regional hearts of textile production. Brno was the 'Manchester of Moravia', the home of some the most prestigious textile brands of Central Europe – Offermann, Schöller, Peschina, Skene, Haupt and a host of lesser enterprises serving niche markets in Vienna, Pest and Milan.[142] A spike in food prices during the winter and spring of 1842/3 had depressed demand for textile goods, just as mild temperatures pushed down the demand for winter garments, leaving manufacturers with a backlog of unsold merchandise. The result was a wave of bankruptcies and dismissals. Brno was acutely sensitive to such fluctuations – of just over 45,000 people who lived in the city and its suburb at the time, about 8,000 were weavers, of whom over 2,600, about a third, were reported to have been laid off by the late spring of 1843. But there was less evidence here of an awareness of common economic interests. Rather than pressuring the bosses, the unemployed weavers turned on their fellows still in work, ambushing, for example, groups of weavers making their way home to the mountain villages of Rájec, Račice and Zábrdovice with packs of cotton to be processed. These workers were neither foreigners nor newcomers; they had been working for the Brno factories for many years without ever facing this kind of hostility. Whereas sinking wages generated indignation and fear for the future, unemployment tended to have a deadening, diffusing effect on the political awareness of workers.[143] The only upside for the dismissed weavers of Brno was that their bad news came at the beginning of summer, leaving them with the hope they might find less lucrative temporary agricultural work, or labouring jobs on the Brno–Svitavy railway, which was still under construction.

The riots that raged through the textile districts of Prague in the following year suggest a higher level of organization. The trouble started on 16 June 1844 when the managers of the Porges calico works announced wage cuts. Workers left their stations and sent a delegation to the management demanding not only that the current wage be sustained, but also that the owners abstain from putting their new block-printing machines, known as 'perrotines', into operation. The managers refused to meet either demand, and passed the names of the delegates to the police, who arrested six of them during the night. A rapid escalation followed. Workers descended on the Porges works and destroyed several of the new machines. A wave of machine-breaking spread across the city. After they had been denied access to various venues, the strikers established a headquarters in the Perštýn district of Prague, in front of a lodging house for workers from out of town. For a week, virtually every factory in Prague was on strike. On 24 June, after consultations between the Provincial Governor's office, the commander of the military garrison, General Windischgrätz, and the mayor of Prague, Josef Müller, troops and police moved in and 525 strikers were arrested.

A striking feature of these protests was the absence of women. Women made up a large part of the workforce in the textile sector, there were many exclusively female specialisms and women were no less threatened by the advent of the 'perrotines' than the men were. Yet among the 525 strikers arrested on 24 June there was not one woman. The argument that women shunned or were afraid of violent confrontations doesn't work, because eyewitness reports describe how, after the men had been arrested and taken to the courthouse at the livestock market (*Dobytčí Trh*), 'the women gathered and went from house to house, taking rebels with them. Each of them put stones in their aprons and after they had smashed the factory windows, the crowd reached the Livestock Market and began to throw stones at the soldiers.'[144] Several of them were arrested, including their leader, a certain Josefina Müllerová, and others were driven away with bayonets.

So it was not fear or an aversion to violence or the need to see to domestic duties that kept the women away from protests and demonstrations. More important was the masculine character of associational life among the Prague weavers. Like their Lyonnais counterparts, the Prague textile workers had built a network of mutual aid societies that provided cover in case of injury, sickness, death or unemployment. But these were men-only societies, whose statutes usually forbade women workers to join. Women's societies were in any case forbidden by law in the Austrian Empire, as in most continental states. And this meant, in turn, that when the strike broke out, support was provided only for male printing workers and not, for example, for the female cutters, whose work was also disrupted by the disturbances. The only women entitled to receive strike support under the statutes of most of the mutual aid societies were 'the wives of imprisoned men'. Women were thus shut out, not only from equal participation in the pecuniary benefits of association, but also from the deeper cultural advantages, the quarterly meetings with their elaborate protocols, the discussions, the votes, a rich schooling in collective action. For the working women of Prague, as for many of their English counterparts, then, the refinement of working-class associational culture brought new forms of gender inequality and segregation.[145]

An enormous policing effort was invested in ending the unrest and in tracking down and capturing escaped strikers. The labour protests of 1844 'elicited the most significant police and military activity in Central Europe since the end of the Napoleonic Wars'. Needless to say, the workers did not succeed in preventing the installation of the perrotines. Attacks on machines were extremely common in these years across Central Europe and so were petitions and demands of the kind submitted by the Prague strikers to their management. Yet they never succeeded in halting or even significantly slowing technological change.[146] On the other hand, there was some small progress on wages. Most of the Prague employers quietly raised their rates after the strikes to avoid further trouble and the Provincial Government issued guidelines for the future internal management of relations between workers and managers that assigned at least some minimal rights to labour.[147]

The aftershocks of the Prague events were still rumbling across northern Bohemia when the Silesian textile district around Peterswaldau and Langenbielau became the scene of the bloodiest upheaval in Prussia before the revolutions of 1848. The trouble began on 4 July 1844, when a crowd of angry weavers attacked the headquarters of Zwanziger Brothers, a substantial textile firm in Peterswaldau. The firm was regarded in the locality as an inconsiderate employer that had exploited the region's oversupply of labour to depress wages and degrade working conditions. 'The Zwanziger Brothers are hangmen', a popular local song declared. 'Their servants are the knaves. / Instead of protecting their workers, / They crush us down like slaves.'[148]

Having broken into the main residence, the weavers smashed everything they could lay their hands on, from mirrors, tiled ovens and gilt mirrors to chandeliers and costly porcelain. They tore to shreds all the books, bonds, promissory notes, records and papers they could find, then stormed through an adjacent complex of stores, rolling presses, packing rooms, sheds and warehouses, smashing everything as they went. The work of destruction continued until nightfall, bands of weavers making their way to the scene from outlying villages. On the next morning, some weavers returned to demolish the few structures that remained intact, including the roof. The entire complex would probably have been torched, had someone not pointed out that this would entitle the owners to compensation through their fire insurance.

Armed with axes, pitchforks and stones, the weavers, by now some 3,000 in number, marched out of Peterswaldau and found their way to the house of the Dierig family in Langenbielau. Here, they were told by frightened company clerks that a cash payment (five silver groschen) had been promised to any weaver who agreed not to attack the firm's buildings. In the meantime, two companies of infantry under the command of a Major Rosenberger had arrived from Schweidnitz to restore order; these formed up in the square before the Dierig house. All the ingredients of the disaster that followed were now in place. Fearing that the Dierig house was about to be attacked, Rosenberger gave the order to fire. After three salvos, eleven lay dead on the ground; they included a woman and a child who had been with the crowd, but also several bystanders, including a little girl who had been on her way to a sewing lesson and a woman looking on from her doorway some 200 paces away. The defiance and rage of the crowd now knew no bounds. The troops were driven away by a desperate charge and during the night the weavers rampaged through the Dierig house and its attached buildings, destroying 80,000 thalers' worth of goods, furnishings, books and papers.

Early on the following morning, troop reinforcements, complete with artillery pieces, arrived in Langenbielau and the crowd of those who remained in or around the Dierig buildings was quickly dispersed. There was some further rioting in nearby Friedrichsgrund, and also in Breslau, where a crowd of artisans attacked the houses of Jewish merchants, but the troops stationed in the city managed to prevent any further tumults. About fifty persons were arrested in connection with the unrest; of these eighteen were sentenced to terms of imprisonment with hard labour and corporal punishment (twenty-four lashes).[149]

Low wages were a key trigger here, as in Lyons and Prague; so was the shortfall in orders, as at Brno. But the crisis of the Silesian weavers had been deepening for some time, as the *Times* reported on 18 July:

> For a long period the distress among the handloom linen weavers has been dreadful. This has now extended itself to the cotton spinners, and the description of the appearance of these work-people – the formerly simple, peaceful, industrious, and happy inhabitants of the Silesian valleys – is heartrending. Pale, consumptive, weak-eyed men, languidly gliding down from the mountains, staff in hand, clad in their blue linen jackets, and bearing wearily the bundle of linen to the master's, which they have woven at 1s. 6d. the 120 ells, is the picture of the linen weavers.[150]

We are dealing here with a very different environment from the silk-working districts of Lyons. These were workers in linen and cotton, not silk, less securely linked to international markets and more vulnerable than their Lyonnais colleagues both to machine-produced textiles from England and to the vicissitudes of geopolitics (the eastward Silesian trade across the border with the Russian Empire had recently been shut down). There was no Société du Devoir Mutuel, no *Écho de la Fabrique*, and there were no networks of republicans striving to politicize the weavers or to coordinate their revolt. This was something rawer and more provincial.

What is truly astonishing about the Silesian events is their resonance in public life and intellectual discourse across the Prussian lands. Even before the revolt itself, attention was fixed on the textile districts of Silesia. There were collections for the Silesians in the textile towns of the Rhineland. During March, the poet and radical literary scholar Karl Grün toured from town to town holding popular lectures on Shakespeare, the proceeds from which were sent via the provincial government to help the weavers of the Liegnitz district. During May, on the eve of the uprising, Alexander Schneer, an official in the provincial administration

Carl Wilhelm Hübner, *The Silesian Weavers* (1844). This painting attracted large crowds when it was shown in Cologne, Berlin and other German cities. Hübner does not focus on the violence of the uprising itself, but on the social tensions at its root. He depicts a wealthy merchant turning down a bolt of cloth presented by a desperate family of weavers. Transactions of this type, in which processes of appraisal and evaluation exposed gross inequalities of power, were at the centre of many instances of social violence.

and a member of the Breslau Association, walked from house to house in some of the most affected areas, meticulously documenting the circumstances of weaver families. In this sympathetic cultural environment, it is hardly surprising that contemporaries viewed the uprising of June 1844 not as an inadmissible tumult, but as the inevitable expression of an underlying social malaise.

Despite the best efforts of the censors, the news of the revolt and its suppression spread across the kingdom within days. From Königsberg and Berlin to Bielefeld, Trier, Aachen, Cologne, Elberfeld and Düsseldorf, there were extensive press commentaries and public discussion. There was a flowering of radical weaver-poems, among them Heinrich Heine's apocalyptic incantation of 1844, *The Weavers' Song*, in which the poet invokes the misery and futile rage of a life of endless work on a starvation wage: 'The crack of the loom and the shuttle's flight; / We weave all day and we weave all night. / Germany, we're weaving your coffin-sheet; / Still weaving, ever weaving!'

For radicals in particular, subsistence riots provided the opportunity to focus and sharpen their arguments. Some Left Hegelians argued, like the 'social conservatives', that the responsibility for arresting the polarization of society must lie with the state as the custodian of the general interest. The Silesian events of 1844 prompted the writer Friedrich Wilhelm Wolff to elaborate and refine his socialist analysis of the crisis. Whereas his report of 1843 on the Breslau slums was structured around loose binary oppositions such as 'rich' and 'poor', 'these people' and 'the rich man', or 'a day-labourer' and 'the independent bourgeoisie', his detailed article on the Silesian uprising, written seven months later, was far more theoretically ambitious. Here 'the proletariat' is opposed to 'the monopoly of capital', 'those who produce' to 'those who consume' and 'the labouring classes of the people' to the domain of 'private ownership'.[151]

The debate between Arnold Ruge and Karl Marx over the meaning of the Silesian revolt provides a further illustration of the same process. In a rueful piece for *Vorwärts!*, the journal of the German émigré radicals in Paris, Ruge argued that the weavers' uprising had been a mere hunger riot that posed no serious threat to the political authorities in Prussia. Karl Marx responded to his former friend's reflections with two long articles in which he put the contrary case, arguing, with what almost sounds like Prussian patriotic pride, that neither the English nor the French 'worker uprisings' had been as 'theoretical and conscious in character' as the Silesian revolt. Only 'the Prussian', Marx announced, had adopted 'the correct point of view'. In burning the company books of the Zwanzigers and the Dierigs, he suggested, the weavers had directed their rage at the 'titles of property' and thereby struck a blow not only at the industrialist himself, but against the system of finance capital that underpinned him.[152] This dispute, which ultimately turned on the issue of the conditions under which an oppressed population can be successfully revolutionized, marked an irrevocable parting of the ways for the two men.

Neither in Silesia nor in Prague, Brno or even Lyons did the politics of the radical left bond easily with the activism of the weavers. But the bitter social conflict over resources gave off a negative energy that quickened the pace of political differentiation. Echoes of the Silesian troubles would ring into the late nineteenth century. Gerhart Hauptmann's five-act drama *Die Weber* (The Weavers, 1892), one of the classics of German naturalism, evoked the insurrection in such a vivid and compelling way that its performance was initially forbidden by the Berlin police authorities. Among those touched by Hauptmann's drama was the artist Käthe Kollwitz, whose preoccupation with this theme produced the unforgettable print series *Ein Weberaufstand*. To this day, her drawings of gaunt, hollow-eyed weavers locked in a futile struggle against an oppressive system frame public memory of what happened in 1844.

GALICIA, 1846

Nowhere in pre-1848 Europe did socially motivated resentment blend with political conflict to more destructive effect than in Galicia in the Austrian Empire. On the evening of 18/19 February 1846, an extraordinary encounter took place in front of the inn at Lisia Góra, about seven kilometres north of Tarnów, one of the principal towns of western Galicia. Polish patriots had gathered to launch an insurrection against the Austrian authorities. Among them were delegates of the Polish National Government in Parisian exile, including Count Franciszek Wiesiołowski and other distinguished figures, members of the Polish landowning nobility, along with officials from their estates, and members of the Polish clergy and professional class. All were armed in preparation for an uprising whose purpose was to seize control of Galicia and the Free City of Cracow, establish a national executive council and work from there towards the restoration of an independent Polish state. But Poland was a heavily agrarian society and the conspirators understood that they would need the support of the peasantry if their enterprise were to succeed. Peasants from many nearby villages had been summoned to appear before the inn with their weapons in hand: scythes, pitchforks, flails and pickaxes. A priest by the name of Morgenstern, who was party to the plot, addressed the peasants, urging them to join forces with the Polish lords. Then Count Wiesiołowski spoke. He promised the peasants that the rewards for their participation would be generous indeed: all their feudal burdens would be lifted; there would be no further labour services; the hated Crown monopoly on salt and tobacco would be abolished. Armed with their scythes and flails, the peasants should join the march on Tarnów and help to found a new Poland.

After Wiesiołowski had finished, a village official by the name of Stelmach, who had been standing with the peasants, spoke up against Wiesiołowski, reminding the peasants of the good things the Austrian government had done for them and begging them to remain loyal to their emperor. Emboldened by this appeal, another peasant spoke up, warning the crowd that 'if you follow the lords, they will harness you and use you just as you use your horses and oxen'. There was a pause in which everything seemed to hang in the balance. Then one of the insurgent noblemen lowered his gun and shot the peasant who had just spoken. The intention was to intimidate the gathering, but the effect was the opposite: the peasants now furiously attacked the insurgents. The landlords fired off their pistols and hunting guns but 'in hand-to-hand fighting it was the peasants with their scythes, the terrifying weapon of the Polish rustic, who had the decisive advantage'. There were fatalities on both sides. The insurgents left forty men, most of them gravely wounded, in the hands of the peasants and the rest fled from the scene. Among the prisoners were Counts Wiesiołowski, Romer and Stojowski. They were all tightly bound and confined overnight in the inn. An Austrian squadron from Tarnów picked them up on the following morning.[153]

Scenes like this played out across western Galicia over the following days and nights. On the same day at Olesno, not far from Tarnów, Count Karol Kotarski, a popular local landlord and a relatively late recruit to the conspiracy, met with other insurgents and assembled his peasants under arms, planted the Polish flag in the ground before them and promised them freedom from labour services, land of their own to do with as they pleased and social equality. Here, too, the peasants were unimpressed. They replied that they wished Kotarski no ill, but had no intention of fighting against their good Emperor Ferdinand. Kotarski withdrew to prepare for the departure that evening for the assembly point in Klikowa. But the mood among the peasants became more hostile and they began to gather around the estate house. Kotarski appeared again, accompanied by his priest, who also urged the peasants to join the insurrection. But the peasants shouted the priest down, demanding that the landlord be conveyed to the Austrian district headquarters, since he was now in effect a rebel. The situation began to get out of hand. When the peasants attempted to grab the landlord, shots were fired, the peasants made use of their scythes and in the bloody struggle that followed Kotarski, the priest, the *Mandatar* (a senior estate administrator) and two other unnamed persons were killed. The remaining Olesno conspirators, most of them wounded, were caught by the peasants, tied up and taken to Tarnów in wagons on the following morning.

The Galician uprising of 1846 was one the bloodiest episodes of civil strife to occur in Europe between the end of the Napoleonic Wars and the Revolutions of 1848. It was in fact not one uprising, but two. The first was an attempted national uprising of the Polish elites in the province and in the neighbouring Free City of Cracow; the second was the wave of peasant counter-insurrectionary violence that stopped the first uprising in its tracks.

Galicia was the name given to the southern portion of the old Polish state that had fallen to the Austrians during the partitions of 1772, 1793 and 1795, when the kingdom was annexed by its neighbours, Prussia, Austria and Russia. It amounted to about 18 per cent of the former Polish kingdom but contained around 32 per cent of the Polish population. Situated along the mountainous border between the Austrian and Russian empires, Galicia was exceptionally ethnically diverse, even by the standards of the Habsburg lands. There were scattered communities of Jews, Germans, Armenians, Czechs, Slovaks and Roma, along with an array of highland cultures occupying pockets of transcarpathian mountain terrain: the Lemkos, Boykos and Hutsuls, who spoke (and speak) dialects of Ukrainian, and communities of Gorals, speaking high-lander dialects of Polish that are close to Ukrainian. But the dominant nationalities of Galicia were the Poles in the west (which today belongs to Poland) and the Ukrainians of the eastern districts around Lemberg/ Lviv (today part of Ukraine).

For some years, Galicia had seen intensified political activity by Polish nationalist networks. Many of the refugees who had fled the Russian partition area after the failed uprising of 1830–31 wound up in Galicia, where they hoped to create a hub for irredentist activity across the Russian border. Efforts by the Austrian authorities to move them on were only partially successful, because the refugees blended easily into the Polish estate milieu and could easily acquire from patriot priests fake baptismal papers attesting their Galician identity. From the early 1840s, Austrian police situation reports from the Galician districts consistently registered high levels of revolutionary activity among the Polish land-owning aristocracy and their supporters. The province was awash with nationalist pamphlets and books that were smuggled across the borders along numerous secret routes. In 1845, the authorities launched an enquiry into the activities of a certain Eduard Rylski from Gorczków, the son of an estate-owner who was urging the peasants in his district to rise up against the Austrian government. The investigation revealed that Rylski had been promising the peasants that driving out the 'Germans' was the key to liberation from the *robot* (labour services) and abolition of the salt and tobacco duties.[154] It was a cannily framed appeal, but estate-owning noblemen who promised to liberate the peasants faced a credibility deficit: the Polish nobility themselves were the chief guarantors and beneficiaries of the feudal system of which the *robot* was an integral part. Salt and tobacco were one thing – they were monopolies of the Austrian Crown. But why should the peasants believe Polish noblemen who promised to do away with the system that defined them as a privileged corporation within their own society?

The Polish irredentist movement, led by exiles in Paris, was itself divided on whether the future Polish uprising should be purely national and political in character or whether it should not incorporate a dimension of social transformation. The aristocratic, conservative or moderate wing of the Emigration favoured, generally speaking, the former prospect: restore the ancient fatherland first, through international diplomacy

if possible, and see to issues of domestic governance later. The democratic wing favoured a revolutionary social approach: the restoration of
the fatherland should be intertwined with a process of encompassing
social emancipation that would secure the legitimacy of the process in
the eyes of the humblest Poles.[155] Throughout the 1830s and 1840s, the
tension between democratic-revolutionary and aristocratic visions of
the Polish national future remained a problem for the Polish irredentists
operating in Galica. The first version was pleasing to the landlords, but
had little to offer peasants on servile tenures. The second was potentially attractive to social subalterns, but repellent to many members of
the traditional landed elites.

The Galician countryside had not been spared any of the problems
that afflicted European agrarian society. Here, as in so many other
regions, the growth in population had reinforced the imbalances in a
social fabric ever more polarized between a very few prosperous peasants and a growing stratum of marginals just scraping by on a
combination of small-plot cultivation and labour on the estates. There
was a certain amount of rural weaving and craftsmanship, but it was
mainly for local consumption: peasant manufactures were not traded
through export-oriented mercantile networks but bought directly by
the lordships of the estates, whose monopsony, or buyers' monopoly,
encouraged them to set low prices. The interpenetration of the estate
economy with capitalist market structures was less advanced here than,
for example, in the Prussian manorial economy. So the problem here
was neither industrialization nor commercialization but lack of access
to economic opportunities outside the nexus of the landed estates. As
consumers, too, the peasants on many estates were partially cut off
from the outside world; they were obliged, for example, to purchase set
quantities of the beer and spirits produced by the estate using locally
harvested grain.

As a result, relatively little of the prosperity generated by Galician
agriculture trickled down to those who actually worked the land. One
mark of the deepening poverty of the Galician peasants was their growing dependence on the potato. By 1845, when the blight struck across
Europe, four times as much arable land was used for potato cultivation
in Galicia as for wheat and rye together.[156] In the winter of 1845–6, the
growing hunger in the countryside triggered, here as in many other
parts of Europe, relief efforts by the authorities; cheap bread was

supplied to the larger towns along with other foodstuffs, measures that helped, incidentally, to reinforce the loyalty of the peasants to the Austrian authorities.

In an agrarian society marked by such deep inequalities, it was always going to be difficult for a cohort of Polish estate-owners to persuade their subjects to throw in their lot with an aristocratic national uprising against the Austrian Empire, all the more so as the low level of literacy (only 20 per cent of children attended school in the province) made it difficult for diaspora organizations to propagandize among the peasants.[157] The instructions issued by the insurgent commanders stated that the peasants were to be raised using speeches and sermons, they were to be assured that the objective of the uprising was not a restoration of the old Poland but the creation of a new one on a 'completely free and humane foundation'.[158] The landowners promised the relief of 'feudal burdens', to be sure, but if, their peasants might well ask, they were so keen on fraternal equality between lord and peasant, why had these changes not been introduced before? On a number of the insurgent estates, protracted legal disputes between peasants and estate managements were still running in 1846 over the abuse of labour service requirements and other local quarrels. There was nothing unusual about this – we see such disputes everywhere in the Europe of that time – but in this setting they were disruptive to the logic of a Polish national movement grounded in the assumption of a community of sentiment and solidarity among all Poles. Peasants in many parts of the continent petitioned higher authorities for relief from the alleged abuses of local elites, but in Galicia such issues of arbitration had a complicating effect, since they placed the Austrian judicial authorities in the position not of oppressors, but of mediators and guarantors. The situation was further complicated in the eastern districts of Galicia by the fact that the peasants who worked the estates were not for the most part Poles, but Ukrainians whose clergy and religious rites set them apart from the Polish landowning class. For them, the idea of a Polish national insurrection had (even) less appeal than for their Polish counterparts further to the west. Even a superbly well-managed Polish insurrection would thus have faced serious obstacles in trying to raise Galicia against the Austrian Empire. And this uprising was dogged with bad luck from the start.

The centre of preparations for the uprising was not in Galicia itself but in the exile community, and specifically in the circles of the 'Polish

Democratic Society', founded in Paris in the wake of the failed uprising of 1830–31. The Society appointed the writer and military theorist Ludwik Mierosławski leader and commander of operations in Galicia. Elaborate plans were forged, not just for the institutions of the future Polish state, but also for its foreign, trade and social policy, though the details of how the future Polish authorities would handle social questions remained hazy, the planners being overwhelmingly concerned with the military preparations for their venture. The uprising would begin in Galicia and the Free City of Cracow, but would then expand to encompass all three partition areas.

Mierosławski was confident that a swift and well-coordinated armed uprising by the nobility alone would suffice to achieve the key objectives. But on 15 February a paralysing blow struck the conspiracy: the commander and his associates were arrested by the Prussian police in the city of Posen, where the conspirators had gathered to make last-minute arrangements. Along with the key coordinators, Mierosławski's secret papers also fell into the hands of the police, including lurid instructions concerning the killing of 'oppressors' in each locality in the first hours of the planned insurrection, the liquidation of occupation troops using a combination of 'trickery and the Sicilian vesper' and the establishment of provisional authorities wielding dictatorial powers. Even more galling was the fact that the information that had enabled the Prussian police to swoop on the committee came from Polish landowning circles nervous about the prospects of revolutionary upheaval.[159] This ill omen would overshadow the uprising throughout its brief course.

Perhaps surprisingly, the insurrection went ahead anyway. Only in Cracow did the insurgents succeed briefly in displacing the established authorities. Here, where the dream of a Polish national restoration commanded deeper social support, they were for a time the unchallenged rulers of the twenty-three square miles of the Free City. The Cracow uprising was only definitively broken after the battle at Gdów, when an Austrian force commanded by Colonel Ludwig von Benedek (and supported by a large formation of peasant volunteers) destroyed the largest insurgent band still operating in the area. In Galicia itself, as we have seen, the insurrection was impeded from the start by the peasantry.

What shocked contemporaries most about the events of those days was the extremity of the violence. On 19 February, according to one account based on eyewitness sources, 'Tarnów, the district capital, presented a picture with scarcely any parallel in history.'[160] Sleds and carts converged on the town, surrounded by peasants armed with scythes, pikes, flails, pitchforks and guns, filled with the disfigured bodies of noblemen, officials and stewards, swimming in their own blood. Having defeated the insurgents as they mobilized, the peasants, now armed in many cases with rifles taken from the dead, sought out suspects in their own houses. If, as sometimes happened, the now terrified insurgents or suspected insurgents sought to defend themselves by, for example, firing on the attackers from windows, the peasants stormed the house or set it on fire, sometimes killing all the men, women and children inside. This violence continued for several days. Some bodies were brought into Tarnów; others were simply tipped into ditches outside the cemeteries and buried without ceremony. Flaying, mutilation in front of family members and theatrical decapitations all figure in the atrocity lore of the massacres.

The priest Karol Antoniewicz, who was on a six-month missionary assignment to three Galician districts when the uprising broke out, walked for many days through scenes of devastation and trauma, astonished at the indiscriminateness of the savagery. He found manor houses in which everything had been either stolen or smashed. When he approached the ruins of a house and asked: 'Where is the owner', the locals would reply: 'He died under the flails.' Particularly shocking were the reports of murdered priests and the sight of desecrated churches. The very people who had been such good churchgoers had become 'pillagers of churches', 'they broke and desecrated the crosses before which, a month earlier, they had knelt'. The entire 'patriarchal social order' had been destroyed.[161] It did not occur to Antoniewicz that the insurgents, by enlisting the Galician Polish clergy as emissaries and propagandists, had themselves placed his colleagues in danger.

Particularly terrible was the lot of the Bogusz family. Stanislaus Bogusz, the 87-year-old owner of the estate at Rzendzianowice, was slain in his estate house. His sons Wiktoryn, who was ill, and Nicodem, who was almost completely paralysed, were both flailed to death in front of their wives and children. His grandson Vladimir, fourteen years of age, had his throat cut. Another son, Titus, was thrown from the attic of the estate house onto the cobblestones of the courtyard below and died of his injuries. Stanislaus junior, who was forty-six, was captured by peasants in Jaworce and taken to the magistrate at Pilzno. But another peasant band forced the mayor to hand him over, tore off his clothes and, when he tried to run away, beat him so badly with their flails that 'the brain protruded'.[162] When the peasants caught up with another group of four men from the estate, including Victor, another Bogusz brother, and a local teacher by the name of Adam Pochorecki, they beat them for some time and then cut their throats.[163]

Once things had gone so badly wrong around Tarnów, orders went out to all the other area commanders not to act, but to stand by and await further instructions. But not all these orders got through. The one for Count Sikorski, local insurrectionary commander in Sambor (now Sambir in Ukraine), was intercepted when the courier carrying it was arrested and passed to the police at Lemberg (Polish Lwów; now Lviv in Ukraine). Meanwhile, Sikorski went ahead without waiting for news of success or failure elsewhere. On the evening of 20 February, the usual sequence was initiated: the peasants of the six villages of the estate at Horoźana to the south-east of Lemberg were told to appear on the following morning with their scythes, threshing flails, pitchforks and pickaxes. About sixty conspirators, many of whom had arrived that morning by carriage, took their positions on a wooden tribune that had been built in front of the gate to the main courtyard. The peasants of the various villages formed up in their respective contingents before the tribune in a large semicircle. In front of each village contingent stood the village magistrate and the aldermen. According to one account, Sikorski mounted the tribune, raised the Polish flag on it and held a flaming speech in which he addressed his audience as 'brother Poles'. It was not a good start. Shouts were heard from the peasants: 'We are Ruthenes! We are Ruthenes!' According to another report, it was the *Mandatar*, Czaplicki, who spoke, raising his right hand to the sky to swear that he was telling truth, and then announcing that, as of this day, all payments of services and taxes were abolished, that tobacco and salt would now be cheap and that all of them, lords and peasants alike, were henceforth free and brothers, but that they must first arm themselves with their lords and drive out the Emperor and the 'Germans', who had so oppressed the peasants.[164]

At this point, the village magistrate, a Ruthene by the name of Dmytro Kuchar, spoke up. It would not go as the official wished, he declared. There would be no driving out of the Emperor, because that would merely bring back the days of the Polish Confederation, when everybody wanted to be king and every Polish nobleman could mistreat his peasants with impunity. A fight broke out. The conspirators managed to barricade themselves inside the courtyard. The peasants set fire to the gates and when the conspirators broke out en masse, they met with the same fate as so many of their fellows across the country, cut down by scythes and shattered by the flails. The dead and the almost dead were piled onto wagons and carted off to Lemberg.[165] Sikorski met a particularly sad and dramatic end: he managed with a friend to escape. When they saw that they had no chance of outrunning their pursuers, they turned their guns on each other. It was the same underlying logic as in the western districts, with the added spice of ethnic difference. But violence of this kind was otherwise unusual in the eastern districts, where the uprising was for the most part simply disarmed without bloodshed.

The brutality of the Galician events, the intensity of so many clinched, intimate massacres, shocked contemporaries and still takes one's breath away. Estimates of the total number of deaths range from 500 to 3,000; the best-founded estimates are around 1,000 dead. About 500 estate houses were destroyed. One account, written fifty years later by a nobleman who had lived through these events as a four-year-old child, captured the lasting resonance of the trauma. 'There are emotions so powerful', he wrote, 'that they move a child's soul, an experience so enormous that it is like a threshold to the development of your identity.'[166]

A consensus has never been reached on what exactly happened and why. The surviving records, which stem either from the relatives or advocates of the victims or from the Austrian authorities, offer highly polarized versions of the events. Both in contemporary press coverage and in the historiography, perceptions were fractured along the faultline between opposed national and ideological positions. Those who affirmed the legitimacy of the Austrian Empire and the political order it represented tended to focus on the recklessness of the insurrectionaries. How could they have risked launching an uprising that could only succeed with the support of a population who for the most part distrusted or hated the insurgent elite? For nationally minded Poles and those who affirmed the rectitude of their cause, the legitimacy of the insurrection was beyond question (though there were uncomfortable debates within the Emigration about its timing and planning). Almost every element of the narrative is contested.[167] Austrian accounts stressed the oppressive behaviour of the Polish landlords. Polish ones argue that the antagonism between peasants and lords was deliberately fomented by the Austrians.[168] In Austrian accounts, the killers are resentful peasants; in

Polish ones they are 'off-duty imperial soldiers', criminals and 'vagabonds of the great roads' – a lumpenproletariat alienated from its Polish
calling.[169] In Austrian accounts, the counter-insurgency figured as a
spontaneous loyal response to the uprising, in Polish and pro-Polish
ones as a murderous assault planned by the perpetrators and the Austrian authorities in advance of the uprising.

The belief that the Austrian authorities offered to pay the members of
peasant bands in money and salt for the severed heads of captured Polish
insurgents struck deep roots in Polish public memory. The legend is beautifully evoked in Jan Nepomucen Lewicki's painting *Galician Massacre*
(*Rzeź galicyjska*), in which we see peasants queueing respectfully at an
Austrian military post clutching by their hair the severed heads of Polish
noblemen, while an officer distributes cash and salt, and piles of crockery
looted from the estate houses accumulate under a table. In fact, there is
no evidence whatsoever in the documents for a 'Judas bounty' on insurgent heads. Nor can any be found for the claim repeated in some early
Polish accounts that the Austrians paid only 5 złoty for living insurgents,
but 10 złoty for dead ones.[170] On the other hand, there is little doubt that
the Austrians, having made, despite their excellent advance intelligence,
rather inadequate security preparations for such an uprising, let things
take their course for a few days, once they saw that the situation on the
ground was evolving in their favour – even Clemens von Metternich, the
Emperor's most powerful minister, was critical of their sluggishness.[171] It
is also true that in two localities low-level officials who were short of
police and troops offered rewards for the delivery of (living) insurgents to
the authorities. In any case, once it got underway, the violence soon forfeited any political pretext, acquiring a momentum of its own as murderous
bands went after the landowners and their property, whether they had
been active in the insurgency or not.

The simultaneity of two mutually antagonistic uprisings creates difficulties of interpretation. The Polish uprising can easily be situated in
the context of that long sequence of heroic failed insurrections that
punctuated the struggle of the Poles for an independent national existence. It was driven in part by an emancipatory, modernizing agenda, at
least on the part of some of the émigrés involved in planning it. Does
this mean that the peasant uprising was a counter-revolution? Or was it
an agrarian revolt against feudalism? After all, most landowners were
unenthusiastic about the prospect of a socially radical uprising, and

Jan Nepomucen Lewicki, *Galician Massacre*. In this atmospheric illustration of the Galician massacres by a Polish artist, the presence of the Habsburg eagle signals the government's involvement in sponsoring the violence. Austrian officers pay peasants with salt and cash for the severed heads of Polish noblemen, while looted silver from the country houses of the Polish nobility accumulates in piles around a table. Another Austrian official scrupulously records it all – from the silverware and the severed heads to the outpayments for services rendered – in a ledger. None of this actually happened, but Lewicki's powerful image captures the key elements of the Polish elite memory of 1846 in Galicia.

peasant leaders like Jakub Szela saw in a Polish insurrection the unhappy prospect of a restored and rampant feudalism. Szela's reputation, too, is sundered along national and ideological lines. In the eyes of the Austrians, he was an upstanding peasant driven to violence by years of abuse at the hands of his lords (the Bogusz family!). In the eyes of the surviving Bogusz and of the national memory of the Polish gentry tradition, he figures as a vexatious litigant and Austrian lackey who became a cold-blooded murderer when the opportunity arose to settle scores with his social superiors. But the peasants of the Tarnów district remembered him as a 'peasant king' who dared to defy the masters, and for some Polish and Marxist western historians of the Cold War era Szela was a peasant revolutionary.

However we read this short, sharp spasm of Central European ultra-violence, it exemplifies the multi-vectoral, diffuse quality of social upheaval. The estate-owner's national dream might turn out to be the peasant's feudal nightmare. Political and social grievances might fail to align. Upheavals could converge and magnify each other, or they could cancel each other out. Both situations would arise during the revolutions of 1848. The many-sidedness of the world, Marx commented in one of his essays of 1842 on forestry law, was a function of the one-sidedness of each of its countless constituent parts.[172]

Galicia was also a reminder of the risks that would arise if any political leadership failed to take the inhabitants of the countryside into account. 'A new era has dawned', Metternich crowed in a letter of March 1846 to Field Marshal Radetzky, the Austrian supreme commander in Italy. 'The democrats have mistaken their base; a democracy without the people is a chimera.'[173] Metternich's era was coming to an end, but Prince Felix Schwarzenberg, who would play a central role in the restructuring of the Austrian system after the political earthquakes of 1848–9, made a visit to the scenes of the violence and drew his own conclusions. One emblematic incident particularly captured his attention. At Pilsno, he claimed to have encountered a group of armed Galician peasants and asked them what they were up to. They replied (in Polish): 'We have brought in some Poles.' Schwarzenberg was puzzled: 'What does that mean, "Poles"? What are *you* then?' 'We are not Poles', the peasants replied. 'We are imperial peasants.' 'So who are the Poles then?' Schwarzenberg asked. 'Oh, the Poles!' they replied. 'That's the lords, the administrators, the clerks, the professors; but we are peasants, imperial peasants!'[174] Whether Schwarzenberg really took part in the conversation or merely heard about it from someone else, and whether it happened at all, is of secondary interest; his anecdote captures something about the Austrian understanding of what had happened. Among other things, the replies of the 'imperial peasants' at Pilsno seemed to suggest that the poorest and most downtrodden, for all their legitimate grievances, might actually be a resource on whom conservatives, or at least people with an interest in the maintenance or restoration of order, could draw in times of emergency. If the empire was more deeply anchored in popular sentiment than the Polish national movement, then this was reassuring news for the defenders of Imperial authority. Schwarzenberg would remember his 'lesson' (which, like so many 'lessons from history', merely confirmed the wishful intuitions of the learner) during and after the revolutions of 1848–9.

Some Polish activists discerned the same problem. Writing on the eve of the uprising in Galicia, the exiled democrat and philosopher Henryk Kamieński observed that the enserfed Polish peasants knew no 'motherland', because, for them, Poland was not a mother, but a ferocious stepmother.[175] The Polish poet, geographer and revolutionary Wincenty Pol had fought bravely in the insurrection of 1830–31 and was living in Krosno, about twenty-seven miles south-east of Tarnów, when the trouble broke out. He was badly beaten by peasants and lost his manuscripts and papers when the manor house he was sheltering in was burned to the ground. He might well have been killed, had the Austrians not removed him from danger. For him, 1846 was a trauma that permanently destroyed his belief in the peasantry and in democratic ways of achieving political change. Others learned meaner and narrower lessons: for the priest Karol Antoniewicz, it was clear that the chief culprits were 'the Jews', who, 'like spiders, had wrapped the poor peasants in their web of immoral behaviour'.[176] Hungarian opposition leaders learned their Galician 'lessons' too: only after the Galician events did they rally to Lajos Kossuth's proposal that the wholesale emancipation of the Hungarian peasantry be adopted as a matter of anti-Habsburg policy.[177] The prospect of the rural masses repudiating in similar fashion the leadership of the patriotic Magyar landowning class was too horrific to contemplate. Amongst the national-minded Croatian nobles and intellectuals, the Galician shock heightened awareness of the agrarian question and the threat posed by it to Croat ethnic cohesion.[178]

Largely forgotten in the West, the Galician events left deep traces in Eastern and East-Central European memory, resonating in the histories, memoirs and fictions of Austrian, Polish and Ukrainian writers and historians.[179] One of the strangest echoes can be found in Leopold von Sacher-Masoch's novel *Graf Donski. Eine galizische Geschichte*, an account of the Galician events that was published in two slightly different editions in 1858 and 1864. Sacher-Masoch, famed author of *Venus in Furs* and non-consenting eponym for the phenomenon known as 'masochism' (the psychiatrist Richard von Krafft-Ebing adopted the name without consulting the novelist), was also the son of the identically named Leopold von Sacher-Masoch, Commissioner of the Imperial Police at Lemberg during the uprising of 1846. The father is believed to be the author of a granular and in many respects authentic but also controversial account of the uprising published anonymously in Prague in 1863 under the title *Polnische Revolutionen. Erinnerungen aus Galizien*. The supposition is plausible because the account bears the imprint of police documents and administrative knowledge. But the close attention to cruelty and suffering in the father's memoir is unusual and they resurface in the son's even stranger novel.

At the centre of the novel is Count Donski, a dashing Polish insurrectionary. On the morning of 19 February, the day the uprising is to begin, he makes steamy love to Wanda, wife of a prince and daughter of the insurgent leader Rozminski, in one of the bedrooms of the manor house at 'Howozany' (presumably a play on Horoźana) where the insurgents are assembling. There follows the generic scene, familiar from the Austrian accounts, where the peasants assemble under arms before the insurgents. The estate administrator opens with the standard address:

> You probably think you've been summoned to a hunt; well, it will be a hunt, but of a different kind. We are going to hunt those German bears and wolves who have been oppressing us. The Emperor is a fine fellow, but his officials are bloodsuckers. We are not Austrians, we are Poles. You, too, are Poles! . . . Children, I give you the *robot* [i.e. the abolition of labour dues] and free salt and tobacco!

When the peasants remain silent, Count Donski loses his temper. 'You ungrateful dogs!' he bellows. 'So you don't want kindness and indulgence.

You prefer the stick! Enough with words, we'll whip this rabble if they don't come along quietly.'

After a few further provocations, the 'gentle giant Onufry', a towering Ruthene with powerful limbs and a placid temperament, pushes forward to the front of the gathering and addresses the administrator: 'I am a peasant, but I have a memory.' He reminds everyone present of the occasion many years ago when His Lordship convened a gathering like this. The peasant women were told to gather in the middle and ordered to bend over and pull up their dresses. The men were ordered to identify their wives by their bottoms. Anyone who failed to do so was to be given fifty strokes of the cane. Onufry's speech ends with a passionate injunction to the peasants to abstain from the insurrection. A shot is fired by one of the noblemen, Onufry's scythe flashes and the administrator's head is 'split asunder'. Scenes of extraordinary brutality follow. At the centre of attention is Wanda. Sitting astride her horse, she is suddenly surrounded by Ukrainians. A scythe strikes her mount from behind and the animal rears up in terror. Wanda falls from the saddle, her foot caught in the stirrup:

> Donski heard her scream, heard her weep in mortal terror . . . The nearer Donski got to her, the more wildly did her horse leap forward, dragging the princess with it. She tried to push the ground away, but her hands were torn, the flesh hung down from them in rags, she had to let go, the beautiful head sank down. Blood was already oozing from her breast, it stained the snow, now Donski saw the pretty little head – he still fancied he could feel her lips on his cheek – shattering on the stones and ice, the blood and brain were already splattering over the dark, unfastened hair and the Konfederatka [a Polish patriotic cap] that still hung by its band from the torn and bloodstained neck.

Having temporarily chased away the rampaging rustics, Donski and his people manage to get Wanda into the house. Amazingly, she is still alive. Blood streams forth from between the lips that he has 'observed, not so long ago, with kiss-hungry eyes'. He rips open her top to let her breathe, whereupon 'the white bosom of the princess comes forth fetchingly'. Things seem to be looking up. But the appearance of new 'streams of blood' reveals that all is not well. Undaunted, Donski grabs a linen napkin, dips it in water and uses it to 'push the brain gently back into the wound and close it with the wet cloth'. This unorthodox manoeuvre is surprisingly effective, as least for a moment. Wanda's eyes snap open, she reaches feverishly for Donski with the blood-soaked tatters of her hands, kisses him, smiles seraphically and dies.[180]

Reading these passages, one can see why Kraft-Ebing adopted their author as the patron saint of a sexual pathology. Yet, as we have seen, the cinematic violence of this writing does not set it apart from other recollections. The scene, for example, where Wanda's brain protrudes resembles a memorable moment in the recollections of the Polish nobleman Ludowik Dębicki. Dębicki, who was four years old when the uprising took place, described how, 'with one blow of an axe', a peasant 'cut the skull [of a young man] so that the brain jumped out onto the roof of the barn'. Horrified, the man's sister attempted to 'wipe her brother's face of blood and brain' while, improbably, some peasants brought water to 'wake him up'.[181] And Sacher-Masoch's novel has other interesting features. Among the most noteworthy is a fractured, multi-perspectival narrative in which the various parties – Polish lords, Polish and Ukrainian peasants – are all brought to life in the light of their own aspirations, values and awareness of the past. All are portrayed both as worthy of sympathy and as flawed. Perhaps this was Sacher-Masoch's way of working around the problem of how to recall past episodes of violent conflict in a society that was still trying, officially at least, to cohere. His horrified, sexualized delight in violence is harder to interpret, though it is perhaps pertinent that a truly multi-perspectival understanding of the situations in which violence breaks out must involve imaginatively situating yourself both in the role of the perpetrator and in that of the victim of violent acts. At the core of Sacher-Masoch junior's feeling for the violence of Galicia in 1846 was something experienced and remembered. In an autobiographical fragment published in 1879, he recalled what he had seen as a ten-year-old child:

> I shall never forget the horrific scenes of 1846. . . . I saw the insurgents, some dead, some wounded, arriving [in Lemberg] on an overcast day in February escorted by armed peasants; they lay on small, miserable carts, the blood ran down out of the straw and the dogs licked it up.[182]

CONCLUSIONS

In 1845, the radical German democrat and social welfare activist Dr Otto Lüning, a physician, like Ange Guépin, who worked among the poor, published a 'political panorama' of the previous year:

> These workers' tumults are too widespread to be attributed to the agitations of malicious individuals. There were uprisings in Breslau, in Bohemia, in Silesia, in Berlin, in Magdeburg; is this proliferation not a sign that the cause of the problem lies deep in the condition of our society?[183]

Lüning was not alone in feeling that the protests and insurrections of his time were symptoms of an underlying malaise – as we have seen, this was one of the *idées reçues* of liberal and radical social commentary across Europe. In 1845, when Lüning wrote these words, things were about to get much worse. In 1844, the first, industrial wave of the composite crisis had just broken across the textile factories. Further trouble would follow in 1846–7 as potato and grain shocks rippled across the continent, refracting through national, regional and local power structures to produce subsistence crises in various orders of magnitude, from small, to middle-sized to catastrophic.

It is tempting to see these troubles as a crescendo of instability that crested in the revolutions of 1848. But the linkage between social tumult and revolutionary upheaval was less direct than this metaphor would suggest. The troubles in Galicia began with the political aspirations of the Polish regional nobility, not the grievances of the peasantry, whose anger exploded in the counter-insurrectionary violence of the massacres. The protests and tumults of the pre-revolutionary decade were indeed, as Otto Lüning suggested, the symptoms of chronic illness. They were more like gout or rheumatism than cardiac arrest – intermittent, perforated by periods of quiescence. And, like gout, they afflicted specific parts of the body: during the first half of the nineteenth century, for example, there were relatively few agrarian protests in the German and Bohemian lands of the Austrian Empire, because conditions there were relatively good. In most of continental Europe, the subsistence crisis of the 1840s was over by the time the revolutions broke, thanks to the excellent grain harvest of 1847. Food rioters were in any case not the heralds of revolution. Their protests were not radical in a political sense. They tended to follow a conventional social script, reflecting the moral economy of their communities. They might mount pragmatic attempts to regain control of the food supply, like the Irish protestors who, without stealing anything for themselves, tried to prevent transports of food bound for export from leaving their country. Or they might be intent on reminding the authorities of their traditional obligations to provide for afflicted subjects. Rioters did not act as members of a class, revolutionary or otherwise, but as the representatives of local communities whose right to justice had been denied.

As for the forest skirmishes and land battles that were so widespread in pre-1848 Europe, these were often (though not always) rearguard actions against the more homogeneous and spatially delimited forms of ownership that would become characteristic of 'modern' society. The protests and revolts of the weavers (and other workers) were sometimes sophisticated in their organization, but they remained sporadic responses to emergencies and never coalesced into an oppositional movement. The processes of change that dislodged or displaced so many precarious people were European in scope, but conflicts over resources unfolded within a smaller compass, uncoordinated, shaped by dominant personalities and local bottlenecks. The narrow focus, the political myopia, of much social protest was a cause of deep frustration to some observers. In an anonymous pamphlet of 1847 excoriating the government of the Bourbon dynasty in Naples, the Neapolitan liberal Luigi Settembrini complained that the poorest part of the population focused its rage 'on those who oppress it from close quarters', and thus failed to see that 'all are oppressed and that the source of all these evils is the government'.[184]

However common they became, riots were the exceptions that proved a larger rule, namely that impoverishment and the loss of remunerative labour were more likely to render people 'speechless' and inactive than to drive them to concerted action.[185] This helps to explain why the geography of hunger in 1845–7 and the geography of revolution in 1848–9 were so different. Were there a direct link between dearth and revolution, we would expect the hungriest areas to be the most active in 1848. But the opposite is the case. In the extreme case of Ireland, the famine ground on through the revolutionary year, sapping political energies and muting the impact of events happening in the rest of Europe. The hungriest parts of the Netherlands remained largely quiescent during the revolutionary crisis. And those areas that had suffered want and malnutrition for years, like the Silesian valleys, tended to remain passive when the revolutions broke out; in Prussia, some of the hottest centres of revolutionary activism and violence were towns where there were no food riots at all during the hungry years. Over the great expanse of human history, it is the meekness of the poorest that is surely the surprising thing, not their readiness to challenge the conditions that impoverish them. 'It is a profound and repeated finding', one recent study of insurrectionary violence concluded, 'that the mere facts of poverty and inequality or even increases in these conditions, do not lead to political . . . violence.'[186] These observations matter, because they remind us that revolutions are political events, processes in which politics enjoys a certain autonomy. They are not simply the necessary consequence of the accumulating pressure of distress and resentment within a social system.[187]

There is thus no *direct* causal nexus between the social distress of these decades and the outbreak of revolution in 1848. But this emphatically does not mean that the panorama of riots and protests we have examined was irrelevant to the inception and course of the revolutions. Even if they were often spontaneous or apolitical in motivation, social conflicts could be highly political in their effect. Disputes over forest rights could trigger processes of political reasoning and clarification. When a group of rural communities in the Rhineland sued the Prussian authorities in 1827 for denying them their traditional pasturage and wood-collecting rights to a local forest, the advocate selected to represent them was none other than Heinrich Marx of Trier, the father of Karl. It was a complex case, in which an array of prior usage rights had to be weighed up against the homogeneous 'bourgeois' form of ownership enshrined in the new forestry code. Karl Marx was only nine when his father agreed to take on the case, but the suit dragged on until 1845, by which time Marx junior had already written several articles on wood theft for the *Rheinische Zeitung*. In these he critiqued the Rhenish forest code for one-sidedly privileging one form of entitlement (the law of possession) over another (the customary right to usage). The 'small, wooden, spiritless and selfish soul of interest' had triumphed over the hybrid forms of possession that had allowed persons of various classes to benefit from the same common resources.[188] In his *Critique of Political Economy* (1859), Marx would recall that his early engagement with

Rhenish forestry law provided him with a first opportunity to immerse himself in economic questions.[189]

The demands made sporadically across Europe by weavers, peasants, journeymen and apprentice artisans, and hunger rioters were heard once again in 1848, and not just in the streets and on barricades, but in the congresses organized by artisans and in countless lesser flare-ups. In every capital city where revolution raged, calls for political reform – parliaments, constitutions, franchise extensions, freedom of the press and of association – jostled for attention with demands for minimum wages, price controls on essential commodities, the organization of labour and recognition of the right to work. The attacks on bakeries that had flared up in Berlin in 1846 took off again in 1848. Across the Rhineland, conflicts that had been simmering for years came back to the boil. In Sicily, there was a resurgence of rural violence; bands of peasants who called themselves 'comunisti', because they were defending the rights of their communes over common lands, coordinated large campaigns of illegal occupation, invading forests or enclosed fields with their livestock, destroying tax and land records, and burning municipal treasuries to the ground. A mood of 'class revenge' pervaded the countryside.[190] In Spain, the most politically active areas in 1848 were the north-eastern districts where textile workers had been actively involved in protests. In Nuremberg, the discontented journeymen metalworkers of the city who had taken part in violent protests in 1830–32 not only renewed their earlier calls for a relaxation of restrictions on access to masterships in 1848, but also provided the manpower for the Worker's Association, founded in May of that year at the prompting of middle-class radicals. In June 1849, six journeymen and apprentice metalworkers were arrested for secretly arming members of the Association with long-handled scythes in preparation for a revolutionary uprising. And, in the Pyrenean forests of France, 1848 saw the dramatic culmination of the 'War of the Girls', in which entire rural communities fought pitched battles with the troops sent to support the foresters.[191]

Not all of this turbulence was revolutionary, in the sense of affirming the objectives pursued by liberal or radical intellectuals. Some of it was antagonistic to the interests of the revolutionary elites. At the heart of the Guerra dels Matiners that shook northern Spain in 1846–9 was a Catalan uprising triggered in part by the confiscation of Church lands and changes in the regime of land ownership that deprived peasants of their traditional usage rights, charcoal burning, firewood and grazing. The targets were the modernizing, centralizing policy of Ramón María de Narváez and his *moderado* regime in Madrid; in some localities, there were attacks on the well-to-do, whom the insurgents identified as 'liberals'.[192] Similar motives drove the 'Revolution of Maria Fonte' that broke out in 1846, when the peasants of northern Portugal, initially led mainly by women, unleashed an insurrection against the liberal regime of António da Costa Cabral.[193] The battles of the French forests, fought in the name of ancient rights, shook the new republic created by the February Revolution in Paris; the liberal worthies of Palermo who formed a new provisional government in the early spring of 1848 had little or no sympathy for the counter-usurpations of rural 'comunisti'. Attacks on Jewish merchants, a feature of the German social unrest of the 1840s that resurfaced during 1848, clearly did nothing to further the revolutionary cause. But revolutions are never just about the dreams of revolutionaries. They unlock all the tensions and resentments building within a society, not just the progressive ones.

When the collapse of order facilitated the expression of grievances, violence was often the result. And once violence began, processes of swift escalation became possible. A food riot might broaden from a bid to secure sustenance to a more general assault on 'symbols of wealth and places of luxury and local and state power'.[194] Or it might take on anarchical and opportunistic forms. A food riot in the Prussian weaving town of Schwiebus in April 1847 began with the pulling down of sacks of potatoes and peas, but soon broadened out into a general rebellion, in which nearly a quarter of the residents took part.[195] When the British envoy Viscount Ponsonby reported from Vienna in November 1848 that bands of armed working men had tried to break into and pillage the home of his next-door neighbour, Count Stephen Zichy, was he reporting a political protest or an act of wanton theft?[196] Did the terrible violence in western Galicia in 1846 express a combination of justified objections to arbitrary exactions and loyalty to the Austrian order threatened by the uprising, or was it, as some claimed, just a mindless rampage perpetrated by thugs and 'vagabonds of the great roads'?

The line between violence and politics was and is not easy to draw. During the 'London riots' of 2011, the media reacted with shock to the spectacle of looters carrying televisions out of ruined shops. Was this the articulation of some sort of politics, or was it simply greed, the desire for 'stuff', disinhibited by the general collapse of order? If the rioters had been organized, the blogger Rhys Williams observed, if they had demanded something from the state, if they had focused their anger, 'we would be closer to calling it revolution than criminal damage'. The looters were clearly expressing something: a negation, a lack, but they were doing so in a way that seemed brutish and inarticulate, because

> . . . to be part of the conversation, to 'protest' rather than riot, you have to have coherent dreams, versed in the language of the political land. You need to have a coherent idea of what should change and how. You need organization. And you need to believe you will be listened to, that it will make a damned bit of difference.[197]

But if they were not understood or respected, the authors of social violence were at least feared, and this too was important. It was above all the fear generated by armed bands of militant artisans that thrust liberal and radical leaders into positions of real responsibility. It was the same fear that disposed the authorities to cede power to new movements and to permit the formation of urban civil guards – armed formations of uniformed tax-payers who patrolled the streets of the better-off neighbourhoods. The same sense of dread also explains why liberals so easily gravitated back towards the traditional authorities when the spectre of further popular violence loomed. The fear was mostly reactive, but it could work pre-emptively too, as when agile liberal ministers in Sardinia–Piedmont, the Netherlands or Denmark managed to elicit transformative changes in anticipation of a future insurrectionary challenge. The fear of subaltern violence shaped the unfolding of revolution throughout its course. It was not an exogenous factor, pressing in on the revolution from outside, it was part of the revolution itself.

2

Conjectures of order*

'Everything important was said before 1848'

Carl Schmitt[1]

When the Belgian radical Zoé Gatti de Gamond surveyed the Europe of her time in 1839, she found everywhere signs of flux and disturbance. 'Spirits in every class', she wrote, 'have surrendered to doubt, anxiety and discomfort.' All forms of belief were enfeebled, all forms of authority shaken, social bonds had reached breaking point. The political horizon was dark. Neither nations nor governments knew where they were going. There was a sense of being 'on the eve of bloody wars and internal strife'.[2] In this world of disruption and dissolution, Europeans built constellations of ideas and imagined better ways of conducting the affairs of persons and nations. Some embraced the processes of change already making themselves felt in the contemporary world, others looked back to an idealized past or forward to a still unborn future.

We are accustomed to thinking of modern political ideologies as an array of programmes extending from conservative positions on the right, via a range of liberal formations in the centre to radical and socialist (or communist) programmes on the left. But this menu of options had scarcely begun to come into focus in the years before the 1848 revolutions. There existed the folk memory of the partisan formations of the Paris assembly of the early 1790s, but the terms 'liberalism', 'socialism' and 'conservatism' were only just making their way into circulation and

* I borrow this title from the magnificent two-volume study of social and political thought in the American South by my late friend and colleague Michael O'Brien, *Conjectures of Order. Intellectual Life and the American South, 1810–1860* (2 vols., Chapel Hill, 2004).

had not acquired stable meanings – they designated fuzzy and not always logically coherent constellations of arguments and claims. In continental Europe, there were no political parties capable of disciplining their members or binding them to commonly agreed positions, just loose networks and factions of the like-minded. And there were no doctrinally authoritative 'ideologies' but rather an archipelago of texts and personalities across which Europeans plotted quite idiosyncratic courses: even those who aligned themselves with a specific thinker or writer, like Zoé Gatti de Gamond, who thought of herself as a follower of the French sage Charles Fourier, admixed his arguments with ideas from other sources.

Under these conditions, the great intellectual formations of the day were bound to be amorphous and protean, always changing and regrouping. And this meant that political arguments could be infiltrated in unpredictable ways by economic discourses, patriotic claims and the language of religious belief. Arguments about how to structure the relationship between executives and legislatures could not easily be separated from questions about the location of doctrinal authority within an ecclesiastical body, or the rights attaching to membership of a nation. And political positions of all kinds were still deeply embedded in specific ways of remembering the past, even if these historical resonances were usually not 'memories' rising unbidden to the surface of consciousness, but rhetorical tools designed to endow the claims of the present with depth and legitimacy, to make them feel less like new-fangled inventions and more like the fulfilment of time-honoured tasks. In some ways the fluxy, non-linear and hazy quality of intellectual life in the 1830s and 1840s resembles the simmering confusion of our own time. They belonged to a world that had not yet encountered the great disciplining identities of modern politics; we belong to one in which those identities are swiftly dissolving.

IT'S A MAN'S WORLD

'There still exists', wrote the Parisian journalist Claire Démar in 1833, 'a monstrous power, a species of divine law which stands, imposing and severe on its ancient pedestal with a word of command on its lips, amidst the smoking rubble of so many ruined powers.' The centuries had flung their waves at this colossus without ever tearing it down. The power Démar referred to was not monarchy, religion or capital. It was 'the power of the father', in which were anchored all the forms of inequality that blighted the existence of humans.[3] The power of the father, Démar argued, was unique in its extent and depth, because it was woven into the processes by which humans were socialized and disciplined in childhood and youth. It was the power by which fathers deformed their sons, beating their 'bruised limbs' with blows to bring them into subordination. It was the power that men wielded over women when they took control of their property, demanded sexual satisfaction, or misused and dishonoured them with impunity. It was hard to imagine a world not under the sway of this power, because its effects were so ubiquitous: it could be seen in the great learned academies, in the laws and law-making bodies, in armies, ministries, factories and diplomatic corps, in polite sociability and rude taverns, and in the protocols of physical intimacy.

It was one thing to imagine the abolition of feudalism, aristocratic privilege or the special jurisdictions of guilds, as had been accomplished during the French Revolution; even the abolition of slavery, that ancient deformity, had begun to seem feasible – the Slavery Abolition Act was signed in Britain on 28 August 1833, only a few weeks after Claire Démar had penned her manifesto. But the power of men over women remained intact. Imagining its termination meant envisioning a fundamentally different world, a world without paternity, a world without inheritable property or entitlement by blood, a world in which marriage had been either abolished or transformed beyond recognition.

Marriage, Démar believed, lay at the heart of the problem. It was the cellular matrix on which all other structures of domination were built, and it was the narrow chamber in which women experienced patriarchy as bondage at first hand. The marriage bond, 'absurd in its absolutism',[4] was at once constitutionally anomalous and socially normal. In the France of the July Monarchy, notwithstanding the recent revolution, the authority of men over women was soldered into every marriage by the law itself: a statute in the Napoleonic Civil Code stated outright under the rubric 'the duties of spouses' that 'the woman owes obedience to her husband'. Everything about marriage was unequal. In entering matrimony, women forfeited control of their own property. If they fell out with the prevailing standards of sexual morality by committing adultery, their husbands (who did the same with impunity) could expel them from their homes and deny them access to their children. Since the right to end a marriage unilaterally through divorce on the grounds of incompatibility did not exist, women had no recourse against husbands who humiliated, mistreated or neglected them. Under the terms of such a union, women were doomed to be the 'playthings' and 'slaves' of men.[5] Nurtured in the image of such a parental relationship, Démar argued, the children of unequal and unfree unions were themselves condemned to be unfree.

If marriage was unequal, it was also misaligned with the spiritual and libidinal character of human beings, who were not designed by their creator for permanent unions. The entire armoury of emotions and moral values around marriage was the fruit of this mismatch between culture and nature. Marital love (here Démar recalled a remark by Germaine de Staël) was little more than 'a twofold egoism'.[6] The jealousy that poisoned many marriages arose from 'an odious sensation of egoism and personality'. 'Fidelity', Démar wrote, 'has almost always rested exclusively on fear and the inability to do better or otherwise!' The expectation of female constancy, policed with great rigour in bourgeois society, was a form of enserfment: 'It is by the law of *inconstancy* that women shall be set free.'[7]

In a future society founded on sexual equality, men and women would bond with each other under radically different auspices. Unions of the sexes would rest upon 'the broadest and best-established sympathies', tested by means of 'a more or less extended [period of experimental] cohabitation'.[8] The new women of the future would enter freely into unions of indefinite duration and terminate them when it suited them. In the course of this recalibration of sexual relations, the 'certitude' and 'presumption' of the patriarchal order would make way for a new dispensation animated by 'exploration' and 'mystery'.[9] And the consequence, Démar observed, would be a revolution, but one much deeper and longer than the shallow perturbations of July 1830, 'for the revolution in conjugal mores does not happen at the corner of two streets on the public square during three days of gorgeous sunshine, but rather takes place at all hours, in all places, in the boxes at the opera, at winter social gatherings and summer promenades, during the long nights . . .'[10] Out of these changes would flow an all-embracing process of emancipation, Démar proposed, though she was vague on how exactly the causation might work.[11] 'The liberation of the proletarians, of the poorest and most numerous class, is only possible', she wrote, 'through the liberation of our sex.' In the longer term, the consequences would encompass the 'emancipation of all, slaves, proletarians and children big and small'.[12]

Today, nearly two centuries later, these words have not lost their radical edge. The equating of women's legal and social inferiority with slavery was not new. In her *Reflections Upon Marriage* (1696), the English philosopher and advocate of equal education for women Mary Astell had posed the leading question: 'If all men are born free, how is it that all women are born slaves?'[13] But to connect the emancipation of women with the liberation of sexual appetite, to impugn sexual fidelity as a form of oppression masquerading as virtue, to strip marriage of its theological and moral scaffolding and to harness the project of liberation to a vast experiment in behavioural re-engineering was shocking and unusual, even in the radical circles she frequented. Démar had called her essay *My Law of the Future*, and she was aware of the chasm that separated the world she knew from the one in which such transformations might be possible: 'The hour is not come, the world is not ready', she wrote. The light of the future lay beyond the horizon, the present was a world of 'nocturnal shadows', a 'chaos of thought' in which 'our wishes, our words, our acts collide with each other in confusion'. The only comfort was the thought of being the first to have 'uttered a cry of freedom' amidst the 'insults, outrage, [and] loathing raised up against us even by those [women] to whose happiness we have dedicated ourselves!'[14] The polarity between present and future was too much for Démar, who committed suicide on 8 August 1833, only days after committing her essay to paper, at the age of thirty-two or thirty-four (her date of birth is uncertain). The radical journalist and seamstress Suzanne Voilquin, who published *My Law of the Future*, added a posthumous 'historical note' in which she declared her friend's farewell tract to be 'the strongest, the most energetic [cry of liberty] that has ever been hurled into the world by the voice of a woman'.[15]

Démar's was an unusually combative but not an isolated voice. Her close friend Suzanne Voilquin was one of the editors of a newspaper known variously as *La Femme nouvelle*, *L'Apostolat des femmes* and *La Tribune des Femmes*, in which authors, all of them women and most of them working class, signed only with their first names, to avoid the patriarchal implications of the patronymic, which the radical seamstress Jeanne Deroin described as the 'branding iron that imprints the initials of the master on the forehead of the slave'.[16] In the early 1830s,

MA LOI

D'AVENIR,

PAR

CLAIRE DEMAR. — 1833.

OUVRAGE POSTHUME,

PUBLIÉ PAR SUZANNE.

PARIS,

AU BUREAU DE LA TRIBUNE DES FEMMES,
rue des Juifs, n. 21,

ET CHEZ TOUS LES MARCHANDS DE NOUVEAUTÉS.

——

1834.

Claire Démar, *Ma loi d'avenir* (1834). Nearly 200 years after its appearance, Démar's essay has not lost its radical edge.

Suzanne Voilquin, pencil drawing by Philippe-Joseph Machereau (1833). Best known today as the founder and editor of *Tribune des Femmes*, Voilquin combined literary activism through journalism with social activism across many fronts, and hoped to show other women how they could live more autonomous lives.

many radically dissenting figures had begun to take an interest in questions of sexual inequality. The Saint-Simonian movement, whose numbers were growing in Paris and the French provinces, metamorphosed from a political formation focused on reform into a quasi-religious body 'preaching' a new gospel of social transformation, in which the liberation of sexual energies would play a central role.

The intellectual legacy of Claude Henri de Rouvroy, comte de Saint-Simon, who had died in 1825, was not straightforward: in his early works he had celebrated technical innovation and foreseen the benefits of a Europe united under a single legal and institutional order; later he proposed a future society in which progress would be secured not by violent upheavals, but by the unleashing of science and industry as a moral power comparable with that of the medieval Church. His last work, *The New Christianity*, placed Christian brotherly love at the heart of a perfected social order. The sage's followers differed after his death on how to interpret and communicate his ideas, and the movement began to fragment. Some of the followers turned to industry and commerce, others focused on political reform. But the most successful in terms of charisma and public resonance was the sometime banker, wine merchant and Carbonaro, Prosper Enfantin, who fused a selection of Saint-Simonian teachings with a gospel of socio-moral reform centred on the liberalization of divorce and the improvement of legal rights for women. Enfantin's wing of the movement soon acquired sect-like attributes, including a unique blue costume featuring a white vest that could only be laced up from the back, to remind each member of his or her dependence on the help of others. Enfantin came to be known as the 'sublime Father' of the Saint-Simonian 'church'. For a time, he pursued the notion of uniting himself with a 'female messiah' who would bear him a saviour. In 1832 and 1833, when he was arrested and charged with immorality, illegal assembly and gross financial misconduct, he asked that two of his female associates, Aglae Saint-Hilaire and Cécile Fournel, be permitted to defend him in court – the request was refused.[17]

One of the inspirations for the reorientation of the Saint-Simonians towards sexual equality was Charles Fourier, who viewed capitalism and marriage as 'the two principal sources of contemporary suffering'. The subordination of women to men was not one among many forms of discrimination, it was inequality's primordial paradigm. Only when this knot was unravelled would an encompassing process of social reform become possible. Fourier sketched out the implications of this idea in a futurist cosmology focused on the advent of an 'age of harmony' rooted in the liberation of human passions. Fourier imagined the woman of the future liberated from 'conjugal slavery' to enjoy a range of different 'levels of amorous union' with husbands, 'congenitors' and 'favourites'. The woman of the future might have two children with her husband and one with her congenitor – favourites were for non-procreative sexual play. Husbands, congenitors and favourites could be promoted and demoted from one rank to another as she saw fit (and vice versa).[18]

Like some other radical women, Démar drew inspiration from the Saint-Simonian movement in its Fourierist phase. But the differences are as significant as the commonalities. Démar situated her scenario of emancipation in a distant future – this was the era in which the term 'Utopia' ceased to denote an impossible place in the present and came to denote a possible place in the future. And, like Fourier, Démar was interested in a social order more closely aligned with the promptings of human nature. But, in every other respect, her vision was quite different. She, like the women activists of her network, was interested in women's emancipation; Fourier was interested in *sexual* emancipation, which was and is not the same thing.[19] What mattered to her was the inequality between the sexes; Fourier was less interested in equality than in 'harmony'; he continued to describe women as 'the fair sex' and 'the weaker sex'. His vision of sexual emancipation involved not just the liberation of desire but the gratification of 'needs'. Involuntary celibacy would be banished. Every man and woman would receive a 'sexual minimum wage'. The special needs of the physically deformed and the elderly would be met by cadres of nobles dispensing 'sexual philanthropy'. There was something almost bossy and controlling in Fourier's insistence on pleasure: in the 'phalansteries' – the intentional communities whose task would be to realize his vision – Fourier imagined 'Courts of Love' scheduling orgies to be held during the hours of daylight, for the sake of transparency and openness. There was not too much room here for the vision of personal autonomy in which Démar's 'law of the future' was rooted.

Fourier's life was marked by a divide between the dullness of his quotidian existence as a cashier in a small commercial firm and the hallucinatory radiance of his written oeuvre. He does not appear ever to have succeeded in establishing a satisfying sexual liaison with an actual woman – a hopeful overture to a promiscuous niece produced a brusque rebuff. By contrast, Démar, like many radical women contemporaries, wrote with the authority of personal experience. The freeing of amorous pleasure from convention and pecuniary interest was something that had to be lived and tested in the flesh. 'It is I who speak', she wrote, 'who have rested voluntarily, only for an hour, in the arms of a man, and this hour erected a barrier of satiety between him and me, and this hour . . . was long enough for him to recede once again in my eyes into the monotonous indifferent mass . . .'[20]

Fourier imagined the future as the triumph of his own 'system': 'I alone', he wrote in his *Theory of the Four Movements* (1808), 'have conquered twenty centuries of political idiocy and it is to me alone that present and future generations will owe the commencement of their immense happiness.'[21] Démar possessed no such certainty: for her, emancipation would come not as the implementation of a system, but through a dissonant chorus of disinhibited female voices, some of which would be strident, angry and harsh. Above all, Démar was not a man speculating on the needs of women but a woman speaking of her own experience and that of her female contemporaries: 'And I, woman, I shall speak.'[22] *Who* was speaking was as important as what was being said.

For Démar's friend Suzanne Voilquin the entry into a politically engaged life began in 1830 with the Saint-Simonians in Paris. Voilquin's faith in the Catholicism of her childhood was faltering and, like many radical activists, she was disheartened by what she saw as the banality and emptiness of the July days and their aftermath. The encounter with the Saint-Simonians was a turning point. Friends who refused to follow her into this new milieu were forgotten. Gatherings for the sake of mere pleasure were abandoned. Never had the life of an individual been more completely transformed: 'We gave ourselves body and soul to this new family, whose social, economic and religious principles were ours from that very moment.'[23] But what first attracted Voilquin to the gospel propagated by Enfantin was, as she later put it, 'the notion of a progress that is without limits and, like God, eternal':

As soon as I understood, as soon as I appreciated the fundamental idea of our liberty and of our religious future in those words of Father Enfantin: 'God, Father and Mother of all men and all women', I experienced it as a dazzlement. It gave me immense joy to find in myself the freedom of thought, heart and action that sprang from these sacred formulae.[24]

We find such moments of dazzlement in the early lives of many radical women. Jeanne Deroin recalled how 'amidst the debris, embroiled in the darkness, there escaped a beam of light, Saint Simonism appeared!' But these encounters with light should not be misconstrued as pledges of self-subordination to a charismatic male sage. Jeanne Deroin did not need the Saint-Simonians in order to become a passionate advocate for women's rights. Her conversion to that cause dated back to the indignation she had felt as an adolescent on reading a passage relating to marriage in the French Civil Code: 'The husband must protect his wife, a wife owes obedience to her husband.' From that moment she had devoted herself to a demanding programme of self-education in order, as she put it, 'to take an active part in the fight . . . against the monstrous abuse which dishonoured humankind'.[25] By the time she came to the Saint-Simonians, the ideas that would sustain her activism in 1848 and the decades that followed were already in place.[26]

The radical women, in other words, charted their paths through other people's thoughts as eclectically as their male contemporaries. Several women who were attracted to the emancipationist gospel of 'Father Enfantin' seceded from the 'church' when it became clear that the senior Saint-Simonian men had no intention of granting women an equal place in the uppermost ranks of their hierarchy. Among the secessionists were some of the journalists (including Deroin) who wrote for the *Tribune des femmes*. Calling themselves 'new women', they pledged themselves to a separate path: 'It is now up to us', wrote Joséphine Félicité in the *Tribune*, 'to work for our liberty by ourselves; it is up to us to work for it without the help of our masters.'[27]

Central to the feminist activism of these years was a sharp awareness of the limits of what had been achieved by the July Revolution of 1830. The monthly *Gazette des Femmes*, which opened in 1836, did not concern itself with female autonomy and self-emancipation, but with the rights and duties of women 'under the constitution of 1830 and French law'. The objective was to expose the hypocrisy of a regime that loudly adulated the principle of political equality but denied it in practice to half of the country's residents. The journal did not deny that constitutional progress had occurred in modern France; it was just that the improvements achieved in 1814 and 1830 had brought men out of tyranny, but not women, and thereby revealed the arbitrariness of the new order. 'Over the last 50 years', one article declared, an 'immense revolution' had 'completely changed the face of our society', yet 'in all this social upheaval we have achieved nothing'. How, the journal asked, could one reconcile Article 1 of the revised Charter of 1830 – 'the French are equal before the law whatever may be their titles and ranks' – with Article 213 of the Civil Code (book 1, title 6, chapter 6) – 'the husband owes protection to his wife, the wife owes obedience to her husband'.[28] Why should women be punished for adultery when adultery by men was permitted, and indeed encouraged by the government's policy of licensing brothels?[29] Why were the female sex workers of Paris subjected to harrassment and humiliating 'internal examinations' by the police, whereas their male counterparts, whose very existence was denied by the authorities but who numbered at least 3,000, were left in peace?[30]

In issue after issue, the *Gazette* targeted those laws that betrayed the principles the constitution claimed to be upholding. Why was there still a law (Art. 214 of the Code Civil) obliging a woman to 'live with her husband and to follow him everywhere where he judges it suitable to reside?'[31] If the French were 'equal before the law', why were women not permitted to become jurors? Why were they excluded from membership of the Institut de France?[32] The passages in the constitution referring to 'les français' should be amended to include 'les françaises' – if the government refused to acknowledge that the subjects of His Majesty the king of the French included both Frenchwomen and Frenchmen, would this not mean that half of the population was already – legally – living in a republic?[33] Women should be admitted to the study of medicine, law, arts and sciences.[34] And so the articles continued from month to month, counting off the many ways in which the machinery of political progress remained unresponsive to the claims of women and exposing with forensic irony the double standards on which liberal patriarchy was built. If the emphasis on personal experience that was so central to many contemporary women activists was absent here, this was doubtless because the editor, named as Marie or Madeleine Poutras de Mauchamps, was rather oddly a male republican journalist by the name of Frédéric Herbinot de Mauchamps. Herbinot's female companion, the former domestic servant Marie-Madeleine Poutret or Poutras fronted as editor, but she was probably illiterate and it is unclear whether she played a significant role in shaping the journal's content.[35]

Herbinot's interest in the condition of women was unusual, but not unique. The literature of the Social Question, though written mostly by men, often drew attention to the particular disadvantages and suffering of working women, though it rarely advocated specific rights or legal reforms. Ange Guépin, a physician – we met him in chapter one as a cartographer of Nantes society – and an enthusiast for the ideas of Saint-Simon, commented at length on the frustration of girls in wealthy and bourgeois households who were condemned to idleness and ignorance while their brothers entered business or skipped off to enjoy the broad horizons of tertiary education. The truncation of opportunity for young women, he remarked, was 'one of the most powerful causes of their neuroses: catalepsy, hysteria, somnambulism, all maladies that appear to be the manifestation of an intimate, mystical life independent, to a certain extent, of exterior agents'.[36] In Spain, too, there were male Saint-Simonians who dreamed of the day when the chains weighing on their 'brother men and unhappy women' would be broken, emancipating both sexes 'from the slaveries that press upon us'.[37] One attentive foreign observer of debate on this matter was the British radical John Stuart Mill. Mill began reflecting on the Saint-Simonian critique of marriage in the early 1830s; in February 1849, he wrote to his literary collaborator and future wife, Harriet Taylor, that he thought Fourier to be 'perfectly right about women, both as to equality and marriage'; in 1859, this chain of thought would bear fruit in the essay 'On the Subjection of Women'.[38]

The association of female 'emancipation' with sexual licence alarmed many women and furnished many men with an easy means of discrediting feminist arguments. In an article she wrote for a Moravian newspaper, the Czech writer Božena Němcová lamented the neglect of female education, which had left women straggling 'far behind the age, behind the banner of freedom and culture', but she confessed to a friend that she blushed at the thought that she might be accused of demanding the 'emancipation of women'.[39] Zoé Gatti de Gamond had entered political life as an intermediary among the leading male figures of the Belgian radical opposition before the 1830 revolution. She was a keen reader of Fourier, but she rejected the behavioural radicalism of 'sexual emancipation' as repellent and likely to stir scandal.[40] Her exposition of Fourier's social science, *Fourier et son système* (1838), later published in Spanish and Catalan, made no mention of the sage's more fanciful reflections on the liberation of sexual appetites.[41] It was *men* who had saddled 'women's emancipation' with connotations of sexual licence, the young Leipzig-based writer Louise Otto observed in 1843. Only this could explain why, in an era when 'emancipation' was the charismatic slogan of the day, women, alone among social groups, were denied its promise. In an essay of 1847, Otto circumvented the problem by speaking instead of 'the participation of women in the life of the state'.[42]

The radical writers and activists of this era did more than argue; they fashioned new kinds of political self. Mathilde Anneke's journey away from the Westphalian Catholic milieu of her childhood towards a political radicalism that encompassed sexual equality began with the trauma of a divorce from a violent and abusive husband. The pregnant twenty-year-old was named by the court as the guilty party and denied any right to financial support for having 'maliciously' abandoned her spouse. With the outcome of her divorce proceedings, she later wrote, she 'came to consciousness' and recognized 'that the condition of women is an absurd one, equivalent to the debasement of humanity'.[43] Flora Tristan's narrative self-fashioning also began with escape from a failed relationship. In 1838, she produced a sensational memoir, *Peregrinations of a Pariah*, which focused on the social isolation of a woman who had fled her marriage with a man she could neither love nor respect and travelled to Peru (she was of Franco-Peruvian heritage) in the forlorn hope of recovering her inheritance. Like the slaves of the United States, the Jews of the Roman ghetto and the chattel serfs of Russia, she wrote, women everywhere existed in a condition of servitude.[44] In the face of such ubiquitous oppression, the only course of action was to break open the reign of privacy that concealed the painful consequences of this servitude within myriad individual biographies and prevented it from becoming visible as a form of systematic oppression.[45] Tristan intended to set an example to her peers by naming the people who were the authors of her misfortunes: 'I shall name individuals belonging to various classes of society with whom circumstance brought me into contact: they all still exist; I shall make them known by their actions and their words.'[46] Exposing this nexus meant using the most private forms of experience as the currency of political communication, a source of authority for a new kind of voice.

Some radical women created a field of sociability that lay largely outside the ambit of male authority. A study of Flora Tristan's correspondence reveals a predominantly female network of friends and associates: socialists like Eugénie Niboyet and Pauline Roland, working-class activists like Eugénie Soudet, writers like the poet Marceline Desbordes-Valmore and the novelist George Sand, and Olympe Chodzko, an important figure in the Polish Emigration in Paris.[47] Mathilde Anneke cultivated a long sequence of deep female friendships and eventually turned to women as her 'primary partners in life and love'. There were celebrated intellectual role models from the past, like Germaine de Staël, and women who embodied female autonomy in an eloquent and powerful way, like George Sand, whose charismatic persona defied the conventional boundaries of gender. She was, as one (male) writer observed, 'by turns a capricious young man of eighteen years, a very pretty woman of 25–30; a child of eighteen who smokes and takes snuff with panache, [and] a grande dame whose wit and unexpectedness astonish and humiliate you'. She would never be a woman and she would never be a man: she would 'live calm and serene on the boundary that separates the two opposed camps; queen among men and king among [women]'.[48] Her novels – she wrote nearly sixty of them – infiltrated the imaginations of contemporaries. The Russian revolutionary Alexander Herzen was so gripped by them that he mentally filed his friends and acquaintances under the names of her characters.[49]

Radical women found ways of describing each other that bypassed conventions focused on beauty and desirability. In a note remembering her dead friend Claire Démar, Suzanne Voilquin evoked her 'handsome hands and feet, her face tired-looking but agreeably regular, her physiognomy and gaze proud, if a little hard ... her speech abundant and agile, but brusque and halting'.[50] We might compare this cameo with a portrait of Flora Tristan by Herbinot de Mauchamps: 'you need to have seen this woman ... one cannot help but admire the ardour of her large dark eyes, the ebony of that free floating hair and the brown skin that colours and reddens at the slightest emotion, in order to understand all the suffering of a woman ... whom society shuns like a pariah'.[51] The second portrait invites us to let our gaze fall on the alluring surface of a body, the first evokes the person who looks at us from inside a face.

The issues raised by the call for sexual equality reverberated in contemporary women's fiction. Virginia, the eponymous heroine of a novel published in 1845 by Aurélie de Soubiran, travelled alone, smoked constantly, wore men's clothing and lived openly with her lover in Rome.[52] The novels of Clara Mundt, who published under the pseudonym Louise Mühlbach, are more restrained, but they are full of female characters who have no intention of trading their freedom for the chains of marriage, 'whose weight one can only know when one is bound by them'.[53]

At the centre of George Sand's *Indiana*, published in 1832, was the eponymous heroine, trapped in a dysfunctional marriage to a much older man, for whom liberty could only be achieved through flight and adultery. The novels and autobiographical writings (there was no clear dividing line between the two) of Hortense Allart, a single mother of two sons, celebrated women who had become independent of men and defined themselves through friendship, amorous attachments and intellectual vitality.[54]

Like the other European political movements of this era, the advocacy for women's autonomy remained ideologically diffuse. Radical women, like their male counterparts, gravitated to a range of political positions. There remained a tension between civil-legal and behavioural forms of change; it was there because sexual inequality was made of many different things. Civil and political rights were obviously important. So was the determination of men not to cede a privilege that they took to be a feature of the natural order – this is why the Cadiz radical Margarita López Morla urged her readers to acquaint their husbands, 'the male companions of our lives', with arguments for a fairer apportioning of power.[55] But some of the disabilities that hampered women were anchored in their own formation as subjects, through education (or the lack of it), or simply through interaction with parents and male contemporaries. '. . . only through the rebirth of the self will you bring about the rebirth of your spiritual and moral freedom', declared the prophetic figure in Ida Frick's 1845 feminist fantasy, *Slavery and Freedom of Women*.[56] 'Our highest right, our highest consecration', wrote the Berlin-based poet Louise Aston in 1846 after her expulsion from the city on charges of immorality, was 'the right of free personality, in which all our power and belief reside, the right to develop our own innermost essence, unconfined by any external influence'.[57] Fiction by women was important, Aston wrote, precisely because it could explore that inner world where the seeds of a new future would have to be sown.[58]

Most importantly of all, radical women exposed the constructed and contingent quality of the gender order. Sexual inequality was the consequence of social organization, not of biological necessity. In identifying something so fundamental to the functioning and self-understanding of modern bourgeois society, the radical women dug deeper into the toolbox of modern social existence than their male contemporaries. But who was listening? Of all the structures of inequality addressed by the dissenting movements of the early and mid nineteenth century, sexual inequality was the most resistant to change. Women across western Europe would return to the fight during the revolutions of 1848, demanding access to new assemblies, claiming their civil rights, forming political clubs and publishing newspapers. Deroin, Anneke and many others would open newspapers, agitate, organize and propose political candidacies. But even as the censorship offices shut down, new parliaments ratified new constitutions and feudal land tenures were abolished, the fortified architecture of women's civil and political inferiority held firm. Like African American women in the early-twentieth-century ghettos of American cities, the dissenting women of the 1830 and 1840s had to navigate a world in which asymmetrical macrostructures distorted emotions and behaviour, and freedom was a hard-won personal experience, not a political fact; they embarked on 'wayward lives and beautiful experiments'.[59] The prospects of success were poor, but, as Suzanne Voilquin wrote: 'in a time of moral revolution, as in a time of political revolution, you must dare'.[60]

PARTISANS OF LIBERTY

What was liberalism in early-nineteenth-century Europe? We can only hope to formulate a brief answer to this question if we agree not to be too fastidious about definitions. One monumental study of how the terms 'liberal' and 'liberalism' evolved in Germany, France, Italy and England between 1789 and 1870 revealed a multiplicity of 'liberalisms' that responded in different ways to changing historical conditions, interacted with each other and exchanged ideas, but ultimately resisted convergence.[61] Another important study perceptively mapped the early-nineteenth-century 'liberal international', exposing not a stable doctrine but a dense network of activists, journalists, politicians and writers across which ideas were circulated and recombined.[62] The term 'liberal' dated back to Roman antiquity, when it referred to the generous, public-spirited behaviour of a praiseworthy citizen. Only during the Revolutionary and Napoleonic Wars did it come to refer to a specific form of politics.[63] The 'semantic sprawl' that accreted around the word 'liberal' was a mark of its success in infiltrating nineteenth-century public discourses, but it also makes the quest for conceptual clarity virtually impossible.[64]

Yet there *were* people who called themselves liberals or claimed to discern in 'liberal principles' the foundation for a new politics. Among the earliest were those who, shaken by the vibrations of the Great Disruption of the Revolutionary and Napoleonic era, repudiated the corporate privilege and towering hierarchies of the old regime, but also the authoritarianism of both Jacobin terror and Napoleonic rule. To trace a middle path between these extremes was not easy. It meant affirming the value of the French Revolution, but rejecting the 'erroneous' turn to state terror; it meant rejecting privileges of birth, but affirming the privilege of wealth (which for liberals was not a privilege, because wealth, unlike birth, can be earned); it meant demanding political equality without insisting on social equality; it meant embracing representation while rejecting democracy; it meant affirming the principle of popular sovereignty, but also limiting that sovereignty, lest it come to endanger liberty.

To embrace liberal principles, the Swiss political theorist Germaine de Staël wrote in 1797, meant combining the liberty of republics with the calm of monarchies: there could be, she wrote, 'no repose without conciliation, no tranquillity without toleration, no party which, when it has destroyed its enemies, can satisfy its enthusiastic followers'.[65] This passion for conciliation explains one of the most curious features of liberals, namely the conviction that their politics was not an 'ideology', in the sense of an all-embracing vision or theory, but a set of 'basic cultural postulates', a kit for managing the mediation of conflicting interests. In this sense it was a kind of metapolitics, a set of procedures, amiable in its openness to all-comers, but also vulnerable to the charge that it was empty and lacked positive content.[66]

It would remain a signature of nineteenth-century European liberal movements that they liked the revolution of 1789 but abhorred the revolution of 1793. Differentiations of this kind became part of the texture of liberal thought – they help to explain the vulnerability of liberal politics in periods of political polarization that favoured simple, easily explained solutions. Liberals were liable to be misrepresented by their critics on both left and right: to the adherents of the old order they looked like revolutionaries, exponents of anarchy; to leftist critics they looked like the narrow partisans of a propertied interest, no less oppressive than the 'feudal' elites they claimed to be replacing. This meant that they were forever having to disentangle themselves from definitions minted by their opponents. When the Lima lawyer and writer Manuel Lorenzo de

Vidaurre was accused by the Peruvian viceroy of colluding as a 'liberal' in an uprising at Cuzco in 1814, he replied: if a liberal was someone who sought with 'invented systems' to introduce 'disorder and anarchy', then he absolutely rejected the application of that label to his own person. But if, on the other hand, the word denoted 'a man who seeks the security of property, of life and of honour under the protection of the laws', then he was prepared to accept that he was indeed a liberal.[67]

In an essay delivered at the Paris Athenaeum in 1819, the Swiss-French political theorist Benjamin Constant provided one of the most influential early outlines of a liberal politics. Drawing on themes from the writings of Germaine de Staël, whose protégé and lover he had been for many years, Constant proposed that the French Revolution had created the conditions for a fundamentally new kind of politics founded on the defence of a liberty grounded in the rights of individuals. This new liberty, Constant proposed, was 'the right to be subjected only to the laws, and to be neither arrested, detained, put to death or maltreated in any way by the arbitrary will of one or more individuals'. It was the right of everyone to express their opinion, choose and practise a profession, associate, profess a creed, move freely and dispose of property. And to these civil rights Constant added a crucial political one: 'It is the right of everyone to exercise some influence on the administration of the government, either by electing all or particular officials, or through representations.'[68] This idea of liberty entered the bloodstream of nineteenth-century European liberalism, though it is interesting to note that the term 'liberalism' did not emerge in France or Switzerland, but in Spain, where it reflected the political turbulence generated by the proclamation of the constitution of Cadiz. In July 1813, an anonymous author writing for the newspaper El Sensato, published in Santiago de Compostela, defined 'liberalism' as 'a system founded in ignorance, invented in Cadiz in 1812, absurd, antisocial, anti-monarchical, anti-Catholic and deadly to the national honour'.[69]

The outlines of much of liberalism's future can already be discerned in these early articulations. Applied across national boundaries, the right to dispose freely of property implied the freedom of trade, an ideal drawn from eighteenth-century political economy and extolled by many nineteenth-century liberals. In a world criss-crossed by tariff boundaries and customs posts, this commitment to the free movement of capital and goods could seem utopian. The primacy of law and especially of constitutions, the most important laws of all, was another abiding theme. Liberals were the exponents of representative government. They aspired to speak for the people. But by 'the people' they generally meant a small portion of educated male taxpayers. The assembly in which representatives met should not be a shrivelled portrait of the entire population[70]; it should embody the most meritorious and deserving elements of the nation. Liberals were emphatically not democrats; they believed in a limited franchise. They justified this both by referring back to the anarchy unleashed during the most violent years of the French Revolution and forward to a society in which the growth of wealth and the improvement of education would mean that a steadily growing portion of the population would qualify for and enter the political life of the state.

Liberals prided themselves on the untheoretical character of their politics, its orientation towards practical realities. Francisco Martínez de la Rosa was one of the most prominent liberal politicians of mid-nineteenth-century Spain. He had been banished from the country when Ferdinand VII returned in 1814 and served as head of government during the *Trienio liberal* – the three years that followed the Riego revolution of 1820. When the constitutional government collapsed in 1823, he became, like many others, an exile in Paris, where he admired from close quarters the burgeoning French liberal movement that came into power in 1830. He was one of the many exiled liberals who returned to Spain when Ferdinand died and an amnesty was declared. As Prime Minister he drafted a new fundamental law, the *Estatuto Real* or Royal Statute – a short-lived constitution that was abandoned in the following year, when he fell from power. The Estatuto was conceived as an instrument with which to restore equilibrium in Spain by means of parliamentary government. The preamble, written by Martínez de la Rosa himself, declared that re-convoking the Cortes, disbanded since 1823, was the only way to 'silence unjust pretensions' and 'disarm' the country's parties. Like many of his fellow European liberals, he envisaged a limited franchise that would enable the 'classes and individuals that have a great stake in the common heritage of society' to wield 'some influence in important matters'. And this meant that the integration of the 'middling classes' (*clases medias*) into politics was essential.[71]

In a famous treatise, *The Spirit of the Century* (*El Espíritu del Siglo*), whose first volume appeared in 1835, Martínez de la Rosa observed that the defenders of absolute monarchy and the exponents of democracy were in fact quite similar. Whereas the former flattered the monarch, the latter flattered the masses, denying them nothing. Both derived the legitimacy of their claims from remote and abstract authorities. Absolutists appealed to a 'divine right' for which there was no empirical support, or to privileges inherited from times immemorial. The self-styled defenders of popular liberty cited theories grounded in an imaginary 'state of nature'. Both ways of proceeding were equally absurd, Martínez de la Rosa argued, and their fundamentalism meant that they would never converge; it would never be possible to find common ground between them. A politics oriented towards the advantages of society, he wrote, 'must consist neither in *ancient privileges* nor in *primitive rights*, but in *actual interests*'. It must be founded not on how things once had been or might one day become, but on 'the current state of nations and of men, such as they are'.[72] Here again was that metapolitical claim to offer a politics of equilibrium whose content would only be determined when the forces at work in society were brought into dialogue with each other.

But if liberals agreed in principle on many of these themes, there was room nonetheless for a wide range of conflicting positions. The very idea of 'limits', so central to liberal thinking, implied processes of calibration and adjudication that were likely to prove contentious. Even if liberals agreed on a 'limited franchise', disputes over where to set the threshold could be bitter. This was a question where the discourse of political rights threatened to become entangled with the language of social needs. How respectful would an assembly full of hungry proletarians be of the sanctity of property? All liberals favoured representative government, but what form should the representative body take? Martínez de la Rosa insisted on the re-convocation of the Cortes, but he did not want the unicameral parliament of Cadiz; he wanted a bicameral structure, in which the upper house, stocked with aristocrats and senior clergy, would form a barrier to the 'violent urges of the popular classes'; he sought to replace the broad but indirect suffrage of the Cadiz constitution with a much smaller electorate defined by an exigent fiscal franchise. These policies earned him the contempt of more radical liberals, who denounced him as a traitor to the cause – a fate that would befall many moderate liberals in 1848. And it wasn't just his politics: his biddable, slightly feline modus operandi earned him the homophobic soubriquet *Rosita la pastelera* (Rosie the cake-maker), a cake-maker being someone who patches up compromises.[73] To fall between the stools, to be denounced on the right as a revolutionary and on the left as a servile dealmaker, was one of the generic predicaments of the mid-nineteenth-century liberal.

Liberals were painfully aware of the moral panic around the Social Question, but they tended to prioritize political over social solutions. The moderate Piedmontese liberal Massimo d'Azeglio acknowledged that social inequality could weigh painfully on some individuals, but it was just 'one of so many evils to which humanity is condemned'. England, he noted, possessed the most unequal society in the world and yet was among the most politically stable. The reason lay in the English 'spirit of legality', a 'tacit and universal consensus in favour of respecting the established laws'. The laws were respected because they gave everyone, regardless of status, access to prompt justice and thus to a share of dignity. 'Men adapt themselves to material suffering with little difficulty when they do not feel despised.'[74] Not all liberals backed away from the problem of inequality. How they handled it depended on other commitments: protectionist liberals were more likely to advocate for interventionist state measures to secure the welfare of the lowest social strata; free-traders more likely to see the withdrawal of the state from all regulatory commitments and the 'unleashing' of entrepreneurial energies as the key to a general solution.[75]

To reconcile the tranquillity of monarchies with the liberty of republics, it was necessary to limit the power of the sovereign, but here again the question of where to place the limit was difficult to resolve, especially under the crisis conditions that tended to prevail at those moments when such questions were suddenly up for grabs. The task of balancing the power of the sovereign with that of new and inexperienced legislatures was a source of bitter division among liberals in 1848.

Religion was another apple of discord. Liberals tended to be sceptical of the Catholic Church because they viewed its theology and institutional culture as theocratic, arbitrary and inimical to liberty. This was a gendered hostility. In the institutions of the female religious and the celibacy of priests entrusted with hearing the confessions of married women, liberals saw the inversion of their own emphatically masculine vision of political order as dominated by male, tax-paying householders with unbound consciences. And the more liberals were divided by questions around the franchise, monarchical sovereignty, civil–military relations and the many other balancing tasks that confronted them, the more anticlericalism came to serve as a liberal cultural code, a form of feeling that all liberals supposedly had in common. This was an antipathy with an eventful future: with time, the struggle between secularizing liberal movements and Catholics determined to defend the authority and independence of the Church would become one of the central dividing lines in European politics. The first victims of this polarization were naturally the liberal Catholics, especially numerous in France and Italy, whose often vivid attachment to their faith jarred with the knee-jerk anticlericalism of other liberal luminaries.[76]

Liberals liked markets. In an era when markets are dominated by mighty global entities like Google and Amazon, it is hard to recapture the subversive magic that still attached to the idea of the market in this era. Markets were not manorial or feudal, they did not represent royal power, they were not ecclesiastical. They were a space of exchange in which individuals could operate – in theory at least – on a more or less level playing field, outside the prescriptions of an arbitrary authority.[77] But how free should 'free trade' be? Prussian and other North German liberals, with their eyes on grain exports to Britain or the commercial traffic of the German port cities, tended for obvious reasons to favour freedom of trade. Liberals affiliated with industrial interests in the German south and especially in Baden were more likely to favour protectionist arrangements. On issues like this, liberalism, for all the universalism of its language, exhibited strong regional variations.[78]

Most liberals wanted to differentiate: the Italian liberal economist and statesman Antonio Scialoja, for example, was an enthusiast in principle for free trade, but argued that, in practice, allowances had to be made for the conditions obtaining in different countries. In a country 'united and vast', adopting freedom of trade would simply mean 'lowering barriers', whereas in a 'region divided and subdivided' (like Italy), it would take the form of 'a solid bond of economic unity among the several powers, that is, a customs union'.[79] The German customs union pursued with such determination by Prussia in the 1820s and 1830s was the hobby-horse of liberal figures in the Prussian administration. Some liberals mixed free trade and protection, advocating policies specific to particular sectors. Political economy was one of the areas in which the evolution of liberalism intersected with the rise of nationalist ideas. Whereas the moderate Hungarian liberal István Széchenyi sponsored infrastructure projects designed to open Hungary to trade with the wider world, the more radical Hungarian liberals around Lajos Kossuth founded the Védegylet (Defence Association) in 1844, a protectionist lobby group whose goal was to persuade members to wear and use only products manufactured in the Kingdom of Hungary.[80]

In France, the pendulum swung from protectionism to free trade and back again. The years following the defeat of 1814–15 remained under the imprint of the protectionist Napoleonic 'system'. Only from around 1825 did free-trade arguments begin to propagate, powered by the influence of liberal economists around Jean-Baptiste Say and, from 1830, by the global free-trade propagandizing of the English radical John Bowring.[81] But, from around 1840, the climate changed as 'the nation' became the dominant framework within which economic interests were argued for and theorized. Free trade came to be seen as the instrument of a specifically British national interest, an association that knocked some of the cosmopolitan varnish off the vision of an unrestricted flow of goods and capital between countries. By the 1840s, protectionist positions charged with nationalist emotion dominated French politics – advocates spoke of 'the defence of national labour' (*travail national*).[82] And these French ideas were taken up and blended with ideas drawn from Alexander Hamilton and the emerging 'American School' by the German political economist Friedrich List, a south-German liberal who argued both for a national German free-trade zone and for the protection of German industry against foreign competition. List's arguments in turn were taken up by the Hungarian liberals around Kossuth.

Liberals were deeply implicated in the revolutions of this era. But they were reluctant revolutionaries. In Paris in 1830, liberals resolved to resist the illegal emergency ordinances of the Bourbon government, which they regarded as unconstitutional, but it was an uprising by the population of the capital that swept away the Bourbon monarchy; the liberals had to be nimble to stay abreast of the changing situation and they did everything in their power to put the lid back onto the social upheaval once their own demands had been met. Liberals loved constitutions because while they constrained arbitrary monarchical power, they were also one way of capturing the impetus of revolution in ropes of law. As the people of the 'middle way', liberals often felt they faced an unhappy choice between one evil and another. A moderate liberal newspaper in Valencia captured their dilemma in a convoluted observation: 'if, God forbid, . . . a long series of errors should lead us to the terrible dilemma of having to choose between revolution and despotism, we have suffered too much from the errors of the latter to reject the former.'[83] Many liberals would have been almost as comfortable with this sentence if the two key terms in it were reversed. Ambivalence was their thing.

RADICALS

To the left of the liberals were a range of quite diverse formations including democrats and socialists and sometimes grouped together as 'radicals', a term even less sharply delineated than 'liberals'. Generally speaking, radicals wanted universal suffrage. They wanted the franchise to include even the poorest working men (very few male radicals spoke up for the enfranchisement of women). Radicals were less interested in gradual legal reform and more interested in direct action. Their attitude to the traditional holders of power was more confrontational and less patient. They might be as concerned with social rights (minimum wages, price controls on staple foods, the right to work) as with political rights (freedom of the press or the kinds of liberties guaranteed in liberal constitutions). But the divide between 'political' and 'social' reform was not clear-cut; franchise expansion, for example, sat athwart the boundary, because it involved a change to the constitution whose consequences were social, in the sense that broadening the franchise necessarily brought new social strata into the political nation.

Radicals worried about the structure of labour markets and about what should be done when labour itself became a scarce commodity – a problem that weighed heavily on the revolutionaries of 1848. Whereas liberals saw economic competition as a force tending to optimize productivity, radicals viewed it as socially toxic. For Louis Blanc it was the root of all social evil, nothing less than 'a system of extermination'.[84] Some radicals saw competition as an impediment to the emergence of the kind of class consciousness that workers would need to lobby effectively for their interests. In *The Workers' Union* (1843), Flora Tristan urged workers to overcome their sectional, sexual and social rivalries, and work in unison, not just for the sake of securing material benefits, but also in order to 'constitute the working class' – this was five years before the appearance of the *Communist Manifesto*.[85]

Whereas liberals were likely to see wealth as gradually expanding and improving, in the longer run, the lot of everyone, radicals were more interested in how wealth was distributed. They were much more likely to see the concentration of wealth (or capital) as founded on a zero-sum relationship with poverty. To them, it seemed that the rich person was rich *because* the poor person was poor. And it must be said that the social crises of the years around 1830 and the later 1840s lent plausibility and urgency to this outlook. The metaphors of Georg Büchner's pamphlet *The Hessian Courier* (1834) bound the rich together with the poor in a skein of metaphorical equations: the sweat of the workers became ointment for the faces of the rich, the wealth on display in their houses was pillage from the dwellings of the poor. The relationship between the two was unmediated, exploitative, parasitic. The same grim logic animated the text of a flysheet that circulated in and around the city of Frankfurt in 1847, when grain prices and hunger riots were surging:

> Proletarians! Bread or revolution! That should be your battle cry. . . . You build palaces, so that the idler can indulge his piggish greed, you make castles for his boxes of treasure, so that he can lock up in them the money he gets for exploiting you; you build beautiful bed frames and soft beds so that your daughters can fall prey to his lust for whores, everything is for him, nothing remains for you but hunger . . .[86]

Texts like this suggested a predatory intimacy between the richest and the poorest and a manichean social order that opposed powerless workers and wealthy idlers – a commonplace in radical rhetoric. The reference to the prostituting of the daughters of the poor was not fanciful, it reflected the observation, widely made in the literature of the Social Question, that the daughters of poor workers made up the majority of female sex workers in the larger towns. 'What is money?' the German Communist August Becker asked his readers. 'Money . . . is silver-plated, stolen, stored-up work. Now do you understand what you are paid with! Foul swindle! [You are paid] with your own work! . . . They suck out your bone marrow and pay you for it with your own sweat.' Workers, Becker concluded, sold their bodies and souls, and were paid for these with 'their own stolen shadows'. Society could be divided vertically into those who produced things and those who did not, 'from the Rothschilds to the woman who sells fruit, from the finance minister to the man in the pawn shop, from the general to the private, from the baron to the domestic servant' – there was an affinity here with Saint-Simon's distinction between the 'industrials' and the 'idlers' of all classes.[87]

For radicals on the far left, the idea of harmony held a special attraction: they yearned to redesign society in a way that would render social and political conflict otiose. The politics they dreamed of was to be participatory, but not individualistic.[88] The German utopian radical Wilhelm Weitling called his opus magnum of 1842 *Guarantees of Harmony and Freedom*.[89] Étienne Cabet, founder of the Icarian movement, hoped by means of workers' cooperatives to overcome the antagonist logic of capitalism.[90] The matrix metaphor of his vision was a pastoral feast at which Icarians of all social stations enjoyed fine food in a beautiful setting: a Poussin landscape peopled by characters from a Frans Hals painting. Charles Fourier's theory of social transformation was a 'calculus of harmony'.[91] Alexander Herzen believed that socialism had inherited 'Christianity's original promise of universal brotherhood and love'.[92] Liberals, by contrast, presumed the inescapability of conflict: since interests were bound to collide in complex societies, the aim of a good political order was not to suppress or supersede them, but to manage their mediation. The constitutions so prized by liberals were in essence peace treaties designed to manage the relations among structurally antagonistic groups. And this in turn explains the liberal preoccupation with 'moderateness', seen as the temperamental key to any politics focused on securing compromises rather than engineering definitive solutions. Mazzini's preference for duties, which unified people, over rights, which supposedly divided them, marks him out (along with his insistence on democracy and his appetite for violent insurrection) as a radical rather than a liberal.

There were endless variations across this radical spectrum. Alphonse de Lamartine and Louis Blanc, for example, were both radicals, in that they were both democrats who favoured universal male suffrage. That placed them outside the camp of the liberals who supported either the current French franchise or a somewhat enlarged version of it. Both Blanc and Lamartine prided themselves on integrating the critical perspectives of the 'Social Question' into their politics; when Lamartine entered politics as a deputy in 1833, he affiliated himself with a loose group of deputies whom he called the 'social party' (*parti social*); Blanc's *Organization of Labour* made extensive reference to the contemporary literature of critical social observation. But when it came to the question of how to structure labour markets, the two men differed fundamentally. Blanc proposed a system in which the government would replace merchant capitalists as 'the supreme regulator of production'. State-sponsored enterprises overseen by the authorities and run by elected worker chiefs would be so successful and attractive to workers and investors alike, Blanc argued, that they would soon drive out the old private sector and secure the victory of the 'principle of association' over the 'principle of competition'.[93]

Lamartine found this idea repellent. If the organization of labour meant 'seizing, in the name of the state, the property and the sovereignty of industries and of labour', he wrote in 1844, then this programme was 'nothing else than the [principle of the Jacobin] Convention applied to the field of labour'. The liberty of industry in a setting marked by rapid change had no doubt given rise to 'difficulties and inconveniences', but this was an argument for regulating it, not suppressing it altogether. Why should the economic tyranny of a worker state be any better than the political tyranny of a despotic monarchy?

> . . . arbitrary [rule] does not change in nature when it is displaced, and . . .
> if the arbitrary rule of kings and aristocrats is insolent, the arbitrary rule
> of the people is odious. . . . Let us stop . . . agitating these empty ideas
> before the eyes and ears of the masses! They are only sonorous because
> there is nothing inside them except for wind and tempests.

The only possible 'organisation of labour' in a free country, Lamartine concluded, was 'liberty rewarding itself by competition, skill and morality!'[94] This was a trenchant rejoinder to Blanc's famous tract. Lamartine and Blanc would both serve in the Provisional Government established in February 1848 and differences over how to handle the labour question would play a central role in the unfolding of the revolution in Paris.

No form of leftist politics attracted more intellectual attention than 'socialism'. Before the ascendancy of Marx and Engels, the term did not refer to a specific theory, but to a diverse biotope of speculative writings and reformist movements. In 1841, when the young north-German scholar Lorenz von Stein travelled to Paris to study the socialist movements incubating there, he found that the term still lacked 'a fixed technical definition'. Some applied it to all movements concerned with the improvement of social conditions, others used it for the followers of specific thinkers, such as Charles Fourier.[95] The great disciplining and narrowing of socialism that would take place during the ascendancy of Marxism still lay some distance in the future. Whereas Louis Blanc imagined a labour force overseen and protected by the public authority, Fourier had virtually nothing to say about the state. Fourier (who, oddly enough, often used the word 'liberal' to describe his designs[96]) imagined a society in which authority was displaced by the intricate orchestration of libidinous appetites and work became indistinguishable from pleasure. Once human needs had been harmonized with social duties, he implied, the application of coercion would become entirely unnecessary. Wilhelm Weitling imagined a future so harmonious and controlled that persons who tried to 'evade the regulations established for the benefit of all' would be regarded not as evil or wrong but as sick, and 'cured' rather than punished.

The followers of Saint-Simon imagined that the authority to shape public life would fall into the hands of a corps of enlightened engineers, industrialists, intellectuals and scientists; little was said about the place of the state under this new dispensation. Whereas the Fourierists and some of the Saint-Simonians pressed for the emancipation of women (though they differed on what this might mean), the German radical Wilhelm Weitling insisted that women must remain excluded from offices entrusted with 'steering the administration of society' for as long as men continued to outperform women in 'useful sciences, inventions and talents'.[97] Politics, the Hungarian radical Sándor Petőfi believed, was men's business: '[the women] should cook in the kitchen and weed in the garden, but should trust men to do the work in the stables'.[98] Neither on this issue nor on any other was there a socialist consensus. Louis Blanc dismissed as 'impractical' the libidinism of Fourier and Saint-Simonian calls for the 'abolition of the family'.[99] The Saint-Simonian brothers Pierre and Jules Leroux adopted quite different programmes: for Pierre, universal suffrage under a republic was the defining issue, for Jules it was the cultivation of associations among workers.[100] Wilhelm Weitling mocked Fourier for imagining that his system of 'association' would suffice to achieve social harmony.[101] If by 'socialist' one meant 'the negation of property and the family', the radical priest Félicité de Lamennais wrote in 1848, 'then the answer is no; I am not a socialist. But if by socialism one understands instead the principle of association . . . the answer is yes; I am a socialist.'[102] Guépin took the Saint-Simonians to task for imagining that the movement's leadership, rather than the masses of the people, would initiate a great social transformation.[103]

Karl Marx dismissed most of the socialists of his time as utopian dreamers. But in the 1840s Karl Marx's was just one voice among many, distinctive for the fact that Marx rejected the quest for harmony and instead embraced social conflict, by which he meant the conflict between classes, as the necessary engine of progress.

For all its diffuseness and diversity, socialism merited close and urgent study, the political theorist Lorenz von Stein insisted, not because of the intrinsic merit of its ideas, but because the rise of socialist movements was symptomatic of something profoundly important. It was a signal that 'society' had arrived as the subject and driver of political thought and action. The 'social' could now be grasped as an autonomous category, irreducible to politics. And this was important, Stein suggested, because it showed that 'the age of purely political movements was over'. Future change would be driven by social forces, not by political ones. For the moment, he observed, socialism was still a predominantly French phenomenon; in France, he wrote, it possessed 'folkloric status'. But since 'no deep-seated movement in a European nation belongs to it alone' the spread of socialism across the continent could confidently be predicted, as other societies experienced the social changes that made its ascendancy possible; most importantly, the emergence of a hard-working but desperately poor proletariat, conscious of its collective existence as a class.[104] By reading socialism diagnostically, rather than affirming or decrying its principles, Stein was able to separate the intellectual substance of socialism from the fear of upheaval that suffused mainstream commentaries on it. Socialism was not the answer to, but rather the symptom of, the problem of social distress. The answer to the challenge posed by socialism, Stein concluded, was not infiltration and police repression, but a new 'science of society' that would be able to guide the state in devising strategies of social pacification.[105] This was an idea whose future still lay out of sight, beyond the mountain ranges of the mid-century revolutions.

CONSERVATIVES

Who were the 'conservatives' at the other end of the spectrum? An obvious answer might be that they were the ones who endorsed and identified with the current state of things. But it wasn't so straightforward. As often as not, conservatives found themselves in opposition to the state authority. In Prussia, for example, conservative political circles opposed the reforming measures of government officials. The renowned Berlin jurist Friedrich Carl von Savigny is generally reckoned among the conservatives of his era, yet he rejected the notion that law sprang from a sovereign will, or from the authority of the state. Its true source, he argued, was to be found in the 'consciousness of the people' (*Bewußtsein des Volkes*).[106] The 'current state of things' could always change, leaving former partisans of the status quo stranded under a new dispensation. In the Grand Duchy of Baden, conservative nobles rejected the constitution offered by the Grand Duke in 1819 and boycotted the parliament. In France, a 'legitimist' opposition emerged under the July Monarchy that remained attached to the idea of a Bourbon restoration under a returned Charles X and then, after his death in 1836, under his son 'Louis XIX', while the liberals who had co-opted the revolution became the pillars of the new order and thus, in a sense, the new conservatives. The oppositional status of some conservatives could give rise to odd transitional convergences between conservatives and radicals. In the spring of 1848, for example, the Spanish absolutist paper *La Esperanza* joined French radicals in celebrating the overthrow of the July Monarchy, on the grounds that this secular and liberal monarchy was 'scarcely different from a republic'.[107]

For the Swiss jurist Karl Ludwig von Haller, one of the most influential early exponents of conservative political theory, the revolution in France was an evil whose roots lay in the idea of the social contract that had taken root in western political thought since Thomas Hobbes. The social contract theory posited that the existence of sovereignties was connected to the emergence of humans from an anarchic state of nature characterized by high levels of ambient violence. In order to secure their safety, the argument went, humans agreed with each other to exchange a part of their individual freedom for a measure of collective security by ceding power to a prince who was charged with keeping the peace and protecting the land. In doing this, they left the realm of nature and entered the world of sovereignty and security. The problem with this claim, Haller argued, was partly that it could not be specified historically: when was this 'contract' drawn up and what exactly were its terms? Who, Haller asked, empowered the drafters to take on this great responsibility and where was the contract archived? How were the possible risks of such an arrangement measured and dealt with? This line of argument exposed a more general feature of early conservative argumentation, namely a preference for concrete and 'historical' exemplification over the elaboration of 'philosophical' systems.

But even if one agreed to accept the social contract as a kind of legal fiction, its logic was still troubling to conservatives, because it implied that the existence of political power reflected an artificial and unnatural state of affairs, and that since the power of the prince was something contractually delegated to him by the people, that power could also be withdrawn unilaterally by them. This, Haller argued, was the error that had given rise to the revolution in France. In its place, he proposed that the authority of some humans over others was a feature of the natural order that required no social contract. Fathers had always wielded authority over children, not because infants came together to sign a 'contract' ceding power to them, but because authority over children was a natural attribute of paternity as ordained by the divine creator (an argument that connects in interesting ways with Claire Démar's denunciation of 'the law of the father'). The inequality among human beings was a natural and necessary feature of the primordial human condition, which in reality had never been suspended in the manner imagined by Hobbes. Political power was rooted in the fact of 'natural superiority'. Hobbes's 'state of nature', in which humans fought bitterly over every resource and life was 'nasty, brutish and short', was not just a fiction, it was an impious refusal to acknowledge divine providence. Its nefarious present-day effects could be seen in the idea of 'popular sovereignty', the denial of royal authority and the modish interest in popular representation and constitutions.[108] It is worth noting that conservatives were not the only ones to reject the notion that the state of nature had been a condition of anarchy – the Spanish liberal Martínez de la Rosa did the same and so did the Danish-German liberal Friedrich Christoph Dahlmann, on the grounds that even in their most primordial condition humans had possessed reason and formed state-like structures.[109] The difference was that whereas Martínez and Dahlmann found *reason* in the state of nature, Haller found *power*.

Not all conservatives went to battle against the social contract, but common to many of them was an esteem for what they saw as the natural order. For Joseph de Maistre, a philosopher and jurist and a subject of the House of Savoy, which ruled in Sardinia and Piedmont, that order was divinely ordained. All humans were attached to the throne of the

Supreme Being by a supple chain 'that restrains us without enslaving us'. In seeking to establish their own liberty by means of revolutions, humans created complex catastrophes that ultimately diminished their freedom to act. The servants of God became the slaves of history. Robespierre had never intended, de Maistre claimed, to found the revolutionary government or to establish the Terror – he and his comrades had been 'drawn imperceptibly' to these things by 'circumstances'. And scarcely had these 'mediocrities' been thrust into positions of immense power, but they were themselves swept away and destroyed by a process that it was beyond the capacity of any individual or group to control. The revolution was thus ultimately a providential instrument of instruction whose purpose was to illustrate what happened when men trusted their pride and attempted to seize 'liberty' on their own terms. From this it followed that proper constitutions were not written documents generated by a process of deliberation, but natural states of affairs that had matured slowly under the hand of God. Naturally evolved systems required no written constitution, because they embodied rights whose value was self-evident. Viewed in this light, written constitutions were no more than a symptom of instability.[110]

For the Prussian publicist Adam Müller, the fundamental error of the French Revolution lay in the 'chimera of an absolute state, an absolute law, [and] an absolute reason'. In chasing this dream, he argued, men traduced the true character of inherited order, which was particularistic, devolved and non-standardized. The reality was that political territories were composed of innumerable subsidiary entities that were state-like in their capacity for autonomy. The male householder (*Hausvater*) stood at the head of a state, in the form of a family, but in this role he was also a member of a concentric array of 'states': a community, a corporation or guild, a city, a princely territory. Who needed 'rights' in a world where so many different forms of autonomy existed? That this naturally evolved condition derived from divine authority was obvious to anyone who contemplated it with an unbiased mind. And the composite, nested character of this order also gave the lie to the myth of the 'social contract', for the reality was that states encompassed an endless multiplicity of contracts. The republic 'one and indivisible' established by the revolution was thus an act of violence against both nature and God. In destroying the special privileges of guilds, cities, manorial lordships and provinces, the revolution and its fellow travellers had killed real liberties and replaced them with fictional ones. They were like taxidermists who stole the living organs of their victims and then stuffed their cadavers with the lifeless snippets of imaginary rights. Rather than pushing forward into the nightmare of a universal state that was the graveyard of particular liberties, the political authorities should look back for inspiration to a world that had not yet been spoiled by 300 years of speculative modern philosophy.[111]

Common to these arguments, for all the variations in emphasis, was a preference for 'natural' social relations based on paternalistic and localized structures of authority over the levelling, homogenizing thrust both of bureaucratic modernization and of liberal constitutionalism. And this explains both the affinity of many European nobles to conservative positions and their ambivalence towards political authority. In Prussia, where the nobility emerged from the era of wartime reforms with its privileges and political standing diminished, conservative noblemen railed in the immediate post-war years against the new 'administrative despotism, which eats up everything like vermin'.[112] For the conservatives of Hungary, it was axiomatic that political authority must remain in the hands of the landowning nobility. A measure of gradual change was permissible, but only if the privileges of the old elites were left intact. Hierarchy and stratification, they argued, were inherent in all social organization.[113] To the 'naturalness' of traditional social order, they opposed the 'arbitrary power' of constitutions and imposed legal orders (such as the Code Napoléon). Conservatism in this vein was often indistinguishable from the special pleading of the agrarian elite.

The preference for historically inherited particular liberties over postulated universal freedoms also expressed itself in support for devolved political structures that were felt to be better at safeguarding local autonomy. In Spain, the opposition to liberal innovations was deeply intertwined with the attachment of regions and towns to their traditional 'liberties'. In the context of the First Carlist War, a conflict that raged in north-eastern Spain from 1833 until 1840, hostility to liberal 'centralization' was one of the threads connecting an otherwise diverse array of regional movements. Here, conservatism was pitted against liberalism's unitary vision of the nation; it was not a case of freedom versus despotism, but of two different kinds of 'liberty' in contention with each other. There was an analogous tension between the federal, devolved vision of Italian governance urged by Vincenzo Gioberti and the unitary national vision of a future Italy espoused by Mazzini.[114] In Switzerland, too, conservatives tended to be protective of the rights and independence of the cantons, while liberals sought to strengthen the federal authority – in 1847, the tension between the two would trigger a war.

There was a geopolitical dimension to this conservative preference for devolved solutions. The constitution pressed upon the Swiss by the victorious powers in 1815 came to be resented by liberals and radicals, precisely because it kept the centre weak and siphoned power out to the cantons, in many of which traditional elites still ruled the roost. This made a coordinated 'national' process of reform virtually impossible. The same applied to the German Confederation established after the Napoleonic Wars, which was organized around a weak assembly of princely envoys in Frankfurt, leaving the lion's share of power in the hands of the individual governments, some of which, like Prussia, remained without constitutions or parliaments until 1848. Italy, divided into seven states, not including Austrian-ruled Lombardy and Venetia, lacked a confederal body of any kind. The Austrian statesman Clemens von Metternich, the foremost architect of these arrangements, was drawn to them because they seemed to him to embody the best hope of future European stability. Weak confederal arrangements were far more conducive to international moderation than strong nation-states – Metternich was able at low cost and risk to intervene in the affairs of Germany, Switzerland and Italy to an extent that would have been unthinkable in France. The steadiness – in theory at least – of these weak confederal orders held great charm in the eyes of a statesman for whom the warfare and turbulence of the Great Disruption had been an induction into both politics and adulthood.

One thing politicians and writers at the conservative end of the political spectrum had in common was a sense of the fragility of the existing political order in the face of the forces ranged against it. In a febrile essay on the July Revolution of 1830, the Prussian legal historian and member of the Supreme Censorship Committee Karl Wilhelm Lancizolle observed that the 'bloody sun of the July Days had reinvigorated and fertilized the filth of political chatter and writing'. However good the intentions behind the proposed innovations of the constitutional movement might be, Lancizolle declared, it remained 'a work of darkness, a broad doorway into destruction and confusion'.[115] It does not seem to have occurred to Lancizolle to ask himself why, if the conservative order was both divinely ordained and 'natural', it appeared so vulnerable to challenge.

The contagiousness of revolutionary upheaval was particularly alarming. The 'magic words' from Paris in 1830 had sufficed to stir the world into dangerous motion.[116] Lancizolle noted that once constitutional regimes were established, they appeared to develop an unstoppable dynamic, born of the inner contradictions of their politics. Liberals, he scoffed, claimed to anchor sovereignty in 'the people'. And yet they were only willing to grant real political citizenship to 'a risibly small portion' of the actual population. This elitist arrangement sat uncomfortably, he thought, with the fact that liberals usually owed their speedy ascent into power to the rampaging of 'armed masses'. These observations suggested to Lancizolle that the liberal experiment would not prove sustainable in the longer term. Lacking a legitimating logic of their own, the rickety constitutional structures of liberalism would soon be swept away by the very social forces that had made their ascendancy possible.[117] This was a hostile, but not a stupid, diagnosis; it placed Lancizolle, oddly enough, in the close vicinity of the far left.

Underlying Lancizolle's analysis was a distinction between 'political' and 'social' revolution that became increasingly important in the last decades before 1848. After the collapse of the constitutional regime in 1823, the more pragmatic Spanish conservatives came to see that 'the only alternative to a *social* revolution was a broad programme of *political* reforms'. And after the 1830 revolutions, the bifurcation of the concept 'revolution' into political and social variants gradually became a commonplace in European political discourse. For many radicals, this was a hopeful thought, suggesting that political revolutions might merely be the preamble to deeper 'social' upheavals. Some conservatives, on the other hand, used the distinction to oppose even moderate concessions, on the grounds that the process of political reform, whether revolutionary or not, would always be unfinished business. It was impossible, by this reading, to pull out individual threads of the traditional order without ultimately unravelling the entire social fabric. From this thought, it was a small step to the notion that the revolution begun in 1789 had never actually come to an end: it haunted Europe in the guise of a ubiquitous 'spirit of destruction'.[118]

For Lancizolle, liberalism was in essence an insult to God, because it 'demanded and expected' from 'human wit and human action' those benefits and goods which 'the Almighty alone ... reserves the right to grant'.[119] Conservatives often connected revolution with the sin of pride, whose primordial exemplar was Satan, the angel who rebelled against God. Revolutionaries, Leopold von Gerlach reasoned, were people who failed to acknowledge the sinfulness of humanity and the divine origin of those authorities set in place by God to bind the flesh.[120] For the Castilian Catholic political theorist Juan Donoso Cortés, the battle was already lost: history (meaning the Enlightenment, the French Revolution, the French invasion of Spain, the 1820 revolution and so on) had estranged the world from the harmonious social order ordained by God. Paganism was triumphant in religion, philosophy and politics. To counter the excesses of this history, tactical responses were called for that must make concessions to the corrupt world of adversarial politics. But how one might achieve the transition from this tactical struggle over lost ground to the wholesale restoration of Catholic social order was unclear; Donoso Cortés never found an answer to this question.[121]

RELIGION

In the autumn of 1832, a year after the collapse of the November Uprising of the Poles in the Russian partition zone, the Polish novelist and poet Adam Mickiewicz published a volume containing two tracts expressing the grief of a Polish patriot in exile. Mickiewicz could simply have retold the story of the three Partitions, recounted the history of the recent uprising and insisted that the Polish struggle for freedom was not over. But he did something quite different. Adopting the language of scripture, he invented a sacred history in which the sufferings and bondage of the Polish nation were woven into the narrative of a journey towards salvation.

The Books of the Polish Nation opened, like the Gospel of St John, with the phrase 'In the beginning' and cantered off down the annals of history from the Roman Empire to the appearance of Christ and the rise of the European kings. The worst among these were the sovereigns of Prussia, Russia and Austria, who formed a 'satanic trinity' and erected a pernicious idol called *self-interest*. Every nation in Europe bowed down before this blasphemous thing except Poland. And Poland said: 'Whoever he be that comes to me, he shall be free and equal, because I am *freedom*.' In their hatred of liberty, the satanic trio resolved to do away with Poland. And so the Polish nation was crucified and carried into the tomb. But its soul was not dead and its re-establishment, now imminent, would herald the end of days: 'after the resurrection of the Polish nation shall all warfare among Christians come to an end'.[122]

Reading this text by one of Poland's most celebrated modern poets is like encountering a selection of familiar biblical and historical situations in a dream: the chronology has been scrambled; the names and the personalities have been altered; the quotations sound familiar but are all askew; you feel that you are reading scripture, but you know that you are not. Religion is flowing through this text, but it is not the religion Europeans learned from their priests. It is a prophetic re-inscription of religious truth. The ark of redemption is repositioned over the holy history of Poland, the Christ among nations, much as the Book of Mormon, transcribed and published by Joseph Smith only two years earlier in 1830, harnesses the diction and prophetic sweep of scripture to an American revelation.[123]

In the early nineteenth century, religion passed like a spiritual power surge across Europe, threatening on occasion to burn out the grid. It energized the European archipelago of political commitments, generating endless new combinations. The new combinations were possible because the shocks of the Great Disruption had shaken religion partly loose from the institutions of theological and ecclesiastical authority, allowing it to flow out into the world. The waning of ecclesiastical authority went hand in hand with an expansion of religious feeling. The consequence was a loss of certainty and a proliferation of possibilities. In his introduction to the French edition of Mickiewicz's book, the liberal Catholic publicist Charles Comte de Montalembert observed that exile was about more than spatial displacement; it might also refer to those who found themselves psychologically shut out from religious certainty. 'Modern society', he declared, contained 'more exiles than one might think', souls that found themselves 'banished, after hard struggles, from their youthful enthusiasm, from their old faith . . .'[124]

Whatever forms it took, religious sentiment was different from political or social intuitions, in that it tended to embed human enterprise within the largest possible cosmological frame. It connected specific political claims with arguments about the journey of humankind through the ages. Towards the end of his *Guarantees of Harmony and Freedom* (1842), the German radical Wilhelm Weitling moved into prophetic mode. A new messiah, he promised, was coming to realize the socialist teachings of Christ. He would 'destroy the rotten edifice of the old social order', descending 'from the heights of wealth into the abysses of poverty', walking among the masses of the 'miserable and despised' and mixing his tears with theirs. The world would recognize 'a greater messiah than the first'.[125]

Heightening the claim-making power of politics in this way had a potentially polarizing effect, because religious arguments so often attached political issues to questions of collective salvation and perdition. It made a difference whether persons of conservative temperament viewed revolutionaries as misguided individuals, or whether they saw them as satanic rebels against God. The growth of culturally conservative Catholic revivals in western Europe filled liberal Protestants with fastidious horror because it suggested that the world-historical wheels of Protestant revelation were being thrown into reverse. For Catholic conservatives repelled by the secularizing impacts of the French Revolution or the July Revolution of 1830, liberal anti-clericals were godless, hell-bound rascals, bastard offspring of a perverted reason with whom there could be no pacts or compromises. From Spain to Prussia, Switzerland and France, the rhetorical battles between contending parties were fought with religious language. And as they passed further from the orbit of ecclesiastical authority, religious intuitions ceased to be doctrinal and became what Harold Bloom called 'spilled poetry', enablers of imagination, bridges between historically grounded reasoning and faith in a transcendent order.[126] This flowing together of religious and political intuitions was not a new thing: the histories of early-modern Britain and early colonial America are full of it. What makes this mid-nineteenth-century European panorama distinctive is the fact that the proliferation of new forms of politicized (or even secularized) religiosity coincided with a boom in the power of the traditional Churches to mobilize the faithful.

One of the things Montalembert most admired about Mickiewicz's *Books of the Polish Nation* was the spiritual radiance of the language. In France, Montalembert believed, the language of the Bible had never been stabilized by a canonical national translation of Scripture that could hold its own with the King James and the Luther Bibles, meaning that there was no French counterpart to the 'biblical and popular' prose of Mickiewicz.[127] As if to prove his friend Montalembert wrong, the priest and political theorist Félicité de Lamennais, who had contributed a 'Hymn for Poland' to the French edition of Mickiewicz, published in the following year a text that would become a global literary sensation. Lamennais had grown up in Brittany, where his family had sheltered priests who refused to swear an oath to the Civil Constitution of the Clergy. He hated Napoleon for subordinating the Catholic Church to the French state. His early published works adopted a papalist perspective, denouncing state interference in Church affairs and urging Catholics to look to the Pope for authority and protection. He first achieved renown in 1817 with a major work on the problem of religious indifference, in which he wrote that the ills of modern society were rooted not in heresy but in the triumph of private reason over collective, institutional and inherited forms of religious wisdom. At this point in his life, Lamennais looked very much like a conservative. He was closely associated with the circle around the Comte de Villèle, one of Charles X's most powerful ministers. In 1826, he endeared himself to the Curia with an essay defending papal infallibility.[128] He was offered a cardinalcy by Pope Leo XII but did not accept it.

Then something changed. Lamennais was deeply affected by the French and Belgian revolutions of 1830. In October of that year, he started up a newspaper, *L'Avenir*, which called for an enlarged suffrage, the complete separation of Church and state, and the universal freedom of conscience, instruction, assembly and the press. Like many Europeans, Lamennais was thrilled by the Polish uprising, dismayed by its failure and shocked by the papacy's condemnation of the insurrection. And then, in the encyclical *Mirari Vos* (1832), the Curia condemned (without mentioning Lamennais by name) the ideas endorsed in *L'Avenir*. Asked to affirm his adhesion to the new directive, Lamennais refused; in December 1832, he renounced his ecclesiastical functions and ceased to profess loyalty to the Church.

Paroles d'un croyant (Words of a Believer), which appeared a few months later, is an extraordinary book. It is composed in the language of prayer and revelation; indeed, it establishes precisely the kind of 'biblical and popular' prose, whose absence from France Montalembert had so recently lamented. Lamennais, who had read and warmly admired the galleys of Montalembert's translation of Mickiewicz, adopted the same collage-like, multi-genre format.[129] Like the premonition of a Walt Whitman poem, *Paroles d'un croyant* cuts from scene to scene adopting a range of voices and dictions, priestly, political, prophetic and divine. We encounter smoke, mud, bees, blood, talking rocks, menacing shadows, mysteries and visions, but also graceful parables celebrating human generosity and the plenitude of creation. There are kindly benedictions and quirky reworkings of scripture. For Lamennais as for the Polish poet, the wielders of political authority are the playthings of Satan, their hubris is the misfortune of nations. And there are dark premonitions of revolution: 'I see the people rise in tumult; I see kings grow pale beneath their diadems.' The book describes a condition of universal alienation. The people of modern society are 'strangers in the world' because economic competition has placed them in an antagonistic relation with each other.[130]

The thunder from Rome was not long in coming. The encyclical *Singulari nos*, promulgated on 25 June 1834, focused entirely on the 'Errors of Lamennais'. 'We have learned', wrote Gregory XVI, 'of [this] pamphlet . . ., for it has been printed by this man and disseminated everywhere. . . . Though small in size, it is enormous in wickedness.' Lamennais, the Pope noted, 'cloaked Catholic teaching in enticing verbal artifice, in order ultimately to oppose it and overthrow it'. By way of a 'new and wicked idea', he 'transposes the power of princes . . . to the power of Satan':

> Acting as if he were sent and inspired by God, he speaks in the name of the Trinity and then uses Scripture as a pretext for releasing the people from the law of obedience. He twists the words of holy Scripture in a bold and cunning manner in order to firmly establish his depraved ravings.[131]

If you filter out the fury, this is not a bad analysis of what is going on in Lamennais's text. Gregory XVI's outrage was in part a function of the book's prodigious success. *Paroles d'un croyant* was a unique publishing sensation. There were numerous editions and translations. Queues formed in front of reading rooms; people paid by the hour to read it; students congregated in the Jardin du Luxembourg to hear it declaimed. Montalembert wrote to the author from Vienna to say: 'I never open a newspaper without seeing your name on the front page.'[132]

Lamennais was a recalcitrant figure, hard to classify: a fervent defender of ecclesiastical autonomy and papal authority who had suddenly crashed through the safety barriers of official Catholicism, he was intellectually hypermobile and moody, sometimes neurotic.[133] Yet his book spoke to contemporary preoccupations like no other. Unlike Mickiewicz's patriot catechism, *Paroles d'un croyant* purported to speak to and for the entirety of humanity (not just for the Poles). It was attuned to the ambient pain of the Social Question in a way that the work of Mickiewicz, who had nothing to say about social issues, was not. The celebrated critic Charles Sainte-Beuve noted that when Lamennais used the word 'liberty', it was not 'sonorous and hollow', but suffused with 'a precise intelligence on the miseries of the poor and the iniquities to which they are subject'.[134] Above all, *Paroles d'un croyant* charted the journey of someone who had found new ways of connecting religious sentiment with the worldly calculus of politics.

Left-wing politics in France was suffused with popular religiosity. And this is perhaps surprising, given that the Montagnard left of the 1790s had foresworn Catholic and in many cases even Christian belief altogether. The roots of the realignment doubtless lie in the movement of religious revival that followed the revolutionary assault on the old French Church, a revival that struck deep popular roots and was in many areas only partly under clerical control. By the 1830s, the poles had been reversed: left-wing intellectuals and radical craftsmen and workers drew on the language and imagery of popular Catholicism in opposing the July Monarchy, whose liberal-conservative elite adopted a sharply secular tone (this remains a feature of the French Republic to this day). The religiosity of the left was not ecclesiastical, and it had nothing to do with the authority of bishops and priests. It was a work of bricolage made possible by the fact that key thinkers on the left had begun to separate 'true' or 'original' Christianity from the practices and personnel of the mere institutional Church. Saint-Simon argued in his later writing for a 'New Christianity', stripped of the millennial accretions of Church authority. The Fourierist Victor Considerant preached that 2,000 years of Christian theologizing had merely obscured Christ's message, which was 'a doctrine of love and charity'. Whereas Jesus had been a liberator, Considerant declared in a lecture of 1835, institutional Christianity was 'a religion of slaves, fashioned by slaves', emitting doctrines that were 'fatal to humanity'. Contempt for the hierarchy coexisted with an exalted appeal to Christ as the 'embodiment of love', whose teachings anticipated the best features of modern social thought.[135]

We find this weaving together of Christ-belief with reformist or socialist arguments right across the left of the political spectrum. For

Étienne Cabet, communism was simply 'Christianity in practice', a theme enthusiastically taken up in the journals run by his followers. 'The task of our epoch', Louis Blanc proclaimed, 'is to breathe life back into religious sentiment, to combat the insolence of scepticism.'[136] These messages succeeded for the left because they corresponded with the religiosity of a great many Catholics of humble status who, according to reports from the parochial clergy, still professed strong religious sentiments, but shaped them in accordance, as one priest put it, with 'their own whims'. A priest from Bayasse, about halfway between Cannes and Grenoble, reported that 'ordinary people' in his area 'exercised a kind of popular sovereignty with respect to religion: they, and not the priest, decided which beliefs and rituals were important'.[137]

What these observations suggest is that religious sentiment had got unstuck from religious authority. And this phenomenon was not confined to the French left. The Swiss liberal theorist Benjamin Constant proposed an analogous disconnection when he observed in his *On Religion* that whereas various forms of institutional religion had proved inimical to liberty in Europe, 'religious sentiment' (*le sentiment religieux*) as such was favourable to it. A liberal constitutional order needed the forms of trust, solidarity and social cohesion that religious sentiment provided. Conversely, the absence of religious feeling altogether tended to 'favour the pretentions of tyranny'.[138] The crucial distinction was between 'free religions' and 'sacerdotal' or priestly ones. The former adapted nimbly to the progress of human intelligence; the latter, hobbled by immutable dogmas, wound up at war with reason and could retain their hold on the minds of citizens only through coercion and manipulation.[139]

Nineteenth-century Italians pulled energetically at the threads binding religious sentiment to ecclesiastical authority.[140] For the Italian patriot in exile Giuseppe Mazzini, religion was the intangible force that gave citizens 'the strength to translate ideals into action'; without it there could be no national emancipation. Mazzini subscribed to the intense but institutionally disembodied form of religious commitment recommended by Constant as conducive to the pursuit of liberty. Mazzini's religiosity was emphatically not the 'sacerdotal' kind: in an open letter to Pope Pius IX dated 8 September 1847, he urged the pontiff to cast aside the trappings of temporal and ecclesiastical authority and refashion himself as a 'priest of love'. This gesture appeared insolent and fatuous to ecclesiastically loyal Catholics, but it made sense to the adherents of a religion that came, as Mazzini put it, not from 'kings and the privileged classes', but directly from God, whose 'spirit descended upon the many, gathered together in His name'. 'The people', Mazzini declared, 'has suffered for centuries upon the cross and God will bless it with a faith.' If the Pope failed to embrace this new faith and to unify Italy, he would 'fall by the wayside, abandoned by God and by men'.[141] The letter made no concessions whatsoever to the Pope's understanding of his role; instead it offered a utopian vista in which traditional religious attachments had been swept away and God, the people and the nation had been 'fused' into a 'sacred trinity'.[142] There was no reply from Rome.

Protestants, too, experienced this disjuncture. On the estates of noblemen in the east-Elbian provinces of Prussia – Gerlachs, Thaddens, Senfft von Pilsachs, Kleist-Retzows, Belows, Oertzens and others – the defence of noble autonomy and privilege was imbued with the fervent evangelicalism of the Pietist movement. In these conservative circles, we find a similar decoupling of faith from the structures of ecclesiastical authority, muted by the political and social conservatism of the Protestant landowning elite. What counted on the estates of the awakened was the visceral experience of spiritual rebirth, not the supposedly anodyne rituals of the state Church with its rationalist clergy. Christians of this type preferred Bible-reading circles and 'conventicles' to church services; the pietist noblemen who led them were joined by circles of pious artisans, labourers and peasants who knelt in fields to hear sermons from Pentecostal shepherds.[143]

This is not to say that the institutional religion of the traditional Churches was dead or even dying. The contrary was true: for the Catholic Church, this was an era of revival and transformation on a grand scale. The Church, as we have seen, had been one of the chief targets of Revolutionary and Napoleonic government measures and statecraft. The ecclesiastical principalities of the old Reich had been dissolved and absorbed into new or enlarged secular states, some with a Protestant majority. The revival of religion among the mass of the Catholic faithful and the tightening of clerical control over popular religious life characteristic of the Restoration era have to be seen against this background. Catholic revival reflected a larger trend away from rationalism towards a greater emphasis on emotion, mystery and revelation – in this sense at least, Catholic and Protestant revival were cut from the same cloth. But it also offered a means of compensating for the Church's traumatic loss of material resources and political clout. Whereas the Protestant awakening was dominated by lay initiatives, Catholic revivalism tended to be clerically led, even if the surges of activism driving it often came bubbling up from below. There was a dramatic growth in popular pilgrimages – the most famous occurred in 1844, when half a million Catholics converged on the city of Trier in the Prussian Rhineland, home to 20,000 residents, for a rare public showing of the garment believed to have been the robe Christ wore on the way to his crucifixion. What struck contemporary observers was the high level of clerical discipline: the untidy, festive mobs of the traditional early modern pilgrimage were replaced by ordered groups under the supervision of priests.[144]

In many Catholic regions, revival went together with an increasingly ultramontane orientation. Ultramontanes – the young Lamennais was one of them – were those who argued that the strict subordination of the Church to papal authority was the best way of protecting it from state interference (the Pope being south of the Alps and thus *ultra montes* or 'beyond the mountains'). They perceived the Church as a strictly centralized but international body. Until around 1830, Catholic conservatives were concerned above all with 'inner' religious renewal; thereafter the focus of their activity shifted to strengthening ties with Rome. By definition, the rise of ultramontanism led to increasing tension between Catholies and the state authority. In Bavaria, a dispute broke out in 1831 over the education of children in Catholic–Protestant mixed marriages. The ultramontanes went onto the offensive, and liberal publicists, Catholic and Protestant alike, depicted the debate as a struggle between the forces of darkness and light. Six years later, a much more serious fight broke out over the same issue in Prussia, in the course of which the authorities arrested and imprisoned the ultramontane archbishop of Cologne.

Such conflicts helped to accelerate the emergence of an increasingly confident and aggressive 'political Catholicism'. The *Historisch-Politischen Blätter für das katholische Deutschland*, founded by Joseph Görres in Munich in 1837, became one of the chief organs of this tendency. It favoured the political consolidation of the traditional corporate social bodies and the return to a Habsburg-led German Reich. For Görres, a skilful polemicist, the Trier pilgrimage was a this-worldly revelation. Half a million people set in motion by 'a handful of lamb's wool': what better evidence could there be that the light of Christ's incarnation was still glowing in the souls of the faithful, like the afterimages on a retina? The spectacle, grandiose and mysterious in its own right, of Catholics converging in hundreds of thousands upon a small Rhenish town, revealed that there was more to 'the world of 1844' than Europe's 'philosophers and bold thinkers' seemed capable of understanding. No other political or social movement – whether liberal, patriotic or radical – had anything to compare with this momentous demonstration of commitment.[145]

The potency of this message was not lost on Protestants or on Catholic radicals. The 'German-Catholic' movement, founded in Leipzig in 1845, called for a severing of ties with Rome and a movement of enlightened spiritual renewal that would abandon traditional dogma and create the foundation for a German, Catholic–Protestant, 'national Church'. Within two years, the movement acquired 250 congregations with a total membership of some 60,000, of whom about 40,000 were radical Catholics and 20,000 converts from Protestantism. There were close ties with Germany's leading political radicals. Among the foremost supporters was the Leipzig-based radical Robert Blum, who used his *Vaterlandsblätter* to combine anti-Roman polemic with attacks on bureaucracy, police and censorship. Another was Gustav von Struve, who would help to lead radical uprisings in Baden in the spring and autumn of 1848.

The connection between religious critique and political radicalism was just as clear in the case of the Protestant movement known as the 'Friends of Light' (*Lichtfreunde*). Like the German-Catholics, the Friends of Light combined rationalist theology with a presbyterial-democratic organizational culture in which authority was devolved onto the individual congregation and its elected elders. The movement was particularly successful in attracting poor urban and rural artisans, especially in Saxony, the most industrialized state in the German Confederation.[146] Both the Friends of Light and the German-Catholics were concentrated among social strata and in areas which later became centres of radical democratic activity: Silesia, Saxony, Electoral Hesse, Baden, Vienna. Located halfway between sect and party, these movements offer dramatic evidence of the intimate relationship between religion and politics in the decades before 1848.

Everywhere we look in the Europe of the 1830s and 1840s, we find a flowing together of religious feeling and political commitment. Catholic priests made up a quarter of the members of the Pest Conservative Club in 1847.[147] In Spain, expropriations of ecclesiastical property by liberal regimes periodically reinforced the appeal of conservative counter-movements suffused with an especially trenchant brand of Catholic illiberal royalism.[148] In the Canton Zurich, a culture war broke out in 1840 between liberal and conservative Protestants over a controversial professorial appointment to the Faculty of Theology at the city's university. In Hungary, Metternich believed, the Protestant minority was one of the key drivers of the radical challenge to (Catholic) Habsburg royal authority.[149] These and countless other analogous cases reveal the many ways in which religious sentiments and commitments could become intertwined with political mobilization and the formation of opinion. They also remind us that this was not in any straightforward sense an era of secularization, but rather one in which religious revival and secularizing initiatives inadvertently shaped and reinforced each other.[150]

The conjunctions between variations in political orientation and divergent understandings of scripture have been mapped out in exquisite detail for the Protestant Britain of this era.[151] A cartography of such conjunctions for the whole of Europe does not exist. But there is nothing to stop us imagining a colour-coded, animated digital map, in which the variations of religious sentiment over time (from the improvisations of 'free religion' to the Catholic Wessenbergians, liberals, Gallicans, Jansenists, ultramontanes; from the Protestant rationalists, neo-pietists, orthodox, Calvinists, presbyterialists, unionists and separatists to the Jewish reformers) might be correlated with emergent forms of political commitment. Straightforward patterns would be hard to discern amidst an opalescence of hiatus, differentiation and flux.

PATRIOTS AND NATIONS

'For me', the Moldavian liberal lawyer and statesman Mihail Kogălniceanu declared in 1843, 'the battle of Răsboieni [where an Ottoman army defeated a Moldavian army in 1476] is more interesting than the battle of Thermopylae.'[152] Early- to mid-nineteenth-century nationalism was above all a feeling, rather than a set of principles or arguments. That feeling could manifest itself in a specific relationship with the past. National memory was about making some things feel near and others remote. The extraordinarily rich epic song culture of the Serbs preserved the memory of the long Serbian struggle against alien rule that had commenced with the defeat of the Serbs at the hands of the Turks at Kosovo Field on 28 June 1389. Around it twined a chronicle peopled not only by shining heroes who had united the Serbs in their times of trouble, but also by treacherous villains who had withheld their support from the common cause or had betrayed the Serbs to their enemies.[153] Silvio Pellico's journey into the Italian patriot activism that would earn him a long spell in an Austrian prison began in a youthful encounter with the works of the romantic poet Ugo Foscolo, and in particular with Foscolo's poem '*Dei sepulcri*', which imagined the Italy of his time as a ruined graveyard of the illustrious dead, a country bereft of everything except the memory of a glorious past. Pellico was so stunned by this poem that for a time he saw the words *Dei sepulcri* on the cover of every book. Foscolo's elegy became the lens through which he saw his own country. 'What a magnificent city this Venice is', he wrote to his brother in 1820. 'But beyond the respect that it inspires by virtue of the memory of the power and energy that it once had, the spectacle of a sublime but ruined edifice is always painful.'[154] *Rabok voltunk mostanáig* – 'we were slaves until now' intones the second strophe of Sándor Petőfi's 'Nemzeti dal', the 'national song' adopted by the Hungarian revolutionary movement in 1848. 'Our ancestors, who lived and died free, cannot find peace in a slave land.'[155]

In 1842, the Sicilian scholar Michele Amari published a history of the Sicilian Vespers (1282–1302), a war of dynastic succession that began with a violent insurrection by the Sicilians against the then French rulers of the island. Amari reshaped the narrative in a way that heightened its present-day flair. Whereas the Wars had often been told as a dynastic transition beginning with a noble conspiracy, Amari focused his account on the Sicilian people, casting them as the principal actors. As he studied the Vespers more closely, he wrote in the preface to the first edition, they appeared to him 'in a nobler light'; 'the traces of treachery and conspiracy faded away' and he began to appreciate 'the social and moral force called into being by the revolution'. Under Amari's pen, the Vespers looked less like a well-planned plot and more like 'an outbreak occasioned by . . . the social and political condition of a people neither used, nor inclined, to endure a foreign and tyrannical yoke'.[156]

In Amari's often fanciful retelling, the people grew, the grandees shrank and the War of the Vespers became a handbook in popular insurgency. Amari had hoped that 'five and a half centuries of antiquity' would suffice to put the censors off the trail, but he underestimated the

Neapolitan authorities. His book was banned, the three censors who had initially passed it were sacked, journals that had dared to publish reviews were shut down and Amari's Sicilian publisher, condemned on trumped-up charges, was exiled to the island of Ponza, where he soon died. Invited to attend an 'interview' in Naples, Amari had the good sense to flee to Paris, where he published the book in a second edition and became a literary celebrity.[157]

The choice of history as a genre enabled Amari to achieve effects that would have been denied, for example, to a novel, a play or an epic poem. He chose history because he believed that the consciousness of a nation was stored in its knowledge of its own past.[158] History released contemporaries from the tyranny of the present, implicitly posting a question mark over the present order of things. Simply charting the course of a 'successful' revolution in the past could endow a fresh quest for change with legitimacy. In a world that cherished tradition, it suggested that even insurrection could be old and deep, while monarchy might be contingent and shallow. Amari's retelling of the Sicilian Vespers plinthed the present on a new past, levering the modern chronicle of Bourbon Sicily out of the *longue durée* of the island's history. Independence and parliamentary monarchy 'had already lasted in Sicily for seven centuries', Amari wrote, 'when the House of Bourbon stole it from the present generation'.[159] The Bourbons were recent alien growths on a long native history, no more legitimate than the doomed French interlopers of the thirteenth century.

Patriotic historians often re-sculpted the past in this way. There was no single template: the Italian *Risorgimento* fed on a variety of meta-historical myths, focusing respectively on the pre-historical Etruscans, the ancient Romans, the medieval communes and so on.[160] In all of them, a shadowy era of decline and ruin lay between the present and the shining landscapes of the past. In Mihail Kogălniceanu's *History of Wallachia*, published in 1837, the resentment of the patriot was focused not on the Ottoman overlords of the principality, but on their local proxies, the Greek-speaking Phanariot elites, who were the 'true masters of Wallachia'. It was they, a race of 'degenerated Greeks', who had despoiled the inhabitants, imposing a despotism 'more potent than the Great Wall of China' and corrupting the once pristine morals of the Wallachians.[161] History could perform ideological work precisely because it was more than a chronicle of past events: it proposed a certain modern relationship with the past, allowing some moments to swim into focus as relevant and others to recede into the distance.

Historical precedent was important, because this was a world imprinted by a romantic preference for continuity and temporal depth. In 1845, Icelandic patriots fretting at the rule of the Danish Crown convened a pop-up parliament in Reykjavík, calling it the Alþingi, after the island's medieval assembly.[162] For patriots, the nation was emphatically not a new invention, but something inherited from the past, something unique but not arbitrary. Mihály Vörösmarty's epic *The Flight of Zalán* (1825) recalled in vivid, magisterial hexameters the conquest of Hungary by King Árpád. Mimicking the narrative structures of Virgil's Aeneid, *The Flight of Zalán* endowed the drama of the Hungarian past with sublime grandeur.[163] But assembling an image of this inherited past was itself a task involving collation, invention and improvisation. This was the tension at the heart of all nationalist projects, and it is reflected in the literature of nationalism, which has tended to fall into rival constructivist and primordialist camps. Primordialists hold that nationalism predates the modern era and arises from the deep facts of ethnic and cultural specificity; constructivists maintain that nationalism is a phenomenon of more recent vintage whose emergence is in large part the consequence of processes of modernization, and particularly of mass communication and popular literacy.

We need not adjudicate between these options since they both offer valuable insights. Modern nationalisms did not simply invent themselves out of nothing – they drew on histories and traditions; on the other hand, the intensity and social depth of modern nationalism marked a new point of departure. The Hungarian national costume that became popular in the 1840s drew on ancient antecedents, but was largely the invention (or re-invention) of the tailors of Pest using locally produced materials and catering to the patriotic turn in taste.[164] The 'old-German costume' affected by the patriotic gymnasts and fraternity students of Germany was loosely modelled on German Renaissance styles, but was in fact an exercise in modern retro design popularized by the patriot publicist Friedrich Ludwig Jahn during the wars against Napoleon.[165] In 1848, a special commission was established at Slovanská Lípa to enable a team of artists to invent a Bohemian costume, not by faithfully imitating a specific folk costume, but by abstracting from different folk elements to create a national style.[166]

The emotional timbre of patriotism also accounts for its reactive character, its tendency to surge and ebb in response to historical pressures. German nationalism as a mass phenomenon tended to erupt in response to perceived threats (especially from France) and then to subside again – an example was the 'Rhine Crisis' of 1840, prompted by a tactless and unhelpful suggestion from the French minister Adolphe Thiers that the river be repurposed as France's border to the east, a measure that would have involved the annexation of 32,000 square kilometres of German territory.[167] The issue was sensitive because it awakened memories of the 1790s, when French armies had crossed the Rhine and indeed annexed territories on both banks. A storm of patriotic outrage crossed Germany, prompting poets and poetasters to compose 'Rhine songs'. The most famous of them was the 'Rheinlied', composed by the lawyer and writer Nikolaus Becker. Becker's other poetical works have been forgotten, but his 'Rheinlied' has been set to music over 200 times:

> They shall not ever have it
> Our free and German Rhine
> Though they like greedy ravens
> Cry out: it's mine, it's mine!
>
> As long as it meanders
> In its flowing dress of green,
> As long as on its gentle waves
> A rowing boat is seen.
>
> They shall not ever have it
> Our free and German Rhine
> As long as hearts take comfort
> In its sweet and fiery wine.
>
> [etc.][168]

In the manner of a 1990s battle-rapper, the poet, novelist and Parisian dandy Alfred de Musset replied to Becker's ditty with these back-handed parodic stanzas:

> We once did have your German Rhine.
> We put it in a glass.
> And does a song as anodyne

As yours erase the bloodstained sign
Of Frenchmen's hoofprints on your arse?

We once did have your German Rhine
And if your history you've forgot,
Ask your young girls – for they have not.
It was they who entertained us
With your undistinguished wine.

[etc.][169]

The memory of the 1790s, when the French republic broke out across the river and annexed German territories along the western periphery of the Holy Roman Empire, was still alive in these stanzas. In February 1848, the first reaction of the Prussian government in Berlin to the proclamation of a 'Second Republic' in Paris was not to start arresting suspected democrats, but rather to cancel the spring and summer leaves of troops serving in the federal garrison in Koblenz on the Rhine, not far from the French border.

This hostility to alien rule was one of the most transferable themes of early-nineteenth-century nationalism. Europeans identified passionately with the Greek independence struggle against the Ottoman Empire. In the Polish Clubs of Germany, France and Italy, liberal and radical politics blended with enthusiasm for the Polish effort to shake off Russian rule. In Ivan Turgenev's *On the Eve*, the sight of an Austrian officer in Venice – 'his moustaches, his cap, his whole appearance' – fills the novel's hero, a Bulgarian who has himself escaped persecution by the Ottoman rulers of his homeland, with seething rage.[170] Throughout the 1820s and 1830s, freedom fighters rushed from front to front, supporting first the Italians, then the Spaniards, then the Greeks and then the Poles – some of them survived to fight in the patriot legions of 1848.

This inter-patriotic solidarity found expression in the preoccupation with the suffering of patriots languishing in foreign jails. At a dinner in Paris in 1832, Count Charles de Montalembert described the conversation:

At Wolkonskaya's place. Curious details on Austrian and Russian cruelties. The former even worse than the latter. Appalling history of Count Gonfalonieri [sic], detained at Spielberg near Brno in Moravia in *carcere duro*, attached to a chain so short that he can neither lie down nor walk, receiving 100 blows of the cane on every anniversary of his condemnation to death.[171]

Even if they were not true in every detail (the anniversary beatings were an invention, for example), such rumoured horrors were part of the currency of patriot solidarity. This was the milieu that responded so ecstatically to the prison memoirs of the Lombard patriot, dramatist and newspaper editor Silvio Pellico. By the mid 1830s, Pellico's *Le mie prigioni* (My Prisons), published in 1832, was one of the most widely discussed books in the world. It went through 165 editions in France alone.[172] Pellico had been swept up in the Italian political unrest of 1820, arrested and interrogated, and had spent nine years in various prisons, including the former convent of Santa Margarita in Milan, the Piombi, a prison in the Doge's palace in Venice, and the Spielberg itself. Lamennais was 'ravished' by Pellico's narrative of his years in confinement and Montalembert, who read *Le mie prigioni* as soon as it appeared, could not recall 'ever having read any book that so aroused my admiration, my sympathy, my indignation'. As a 'revelation' of the 'most execrable tyranny that has ever stained the earth', Pellico's book seemed to Montalembert 'the most remarkable that has appeared in this century'. Reading of the 'horrific moral and physical tortures that the satanic genius of despotism has invented' produced 'shudders of rage that boil one's blood'.[173]

Others observed the penal vigour of the Austrian administration from closer at hand. In Karlovac, now in central Croatia, 21-year-old Dragojla Jarnević, who would later become an important Croat writer and educator, witnessed the arrival of a transport of nearly 400 prisoners from Italy, patriots from Lombardy and Venetia who had been arrested for their role in the uprisings of 1831 and were on their way to prison in Hungary. They rode six by six in carriages surrounded by soldiers with rifles. 'Their feet are in chains', she wrote in her diary, 'and the chains are pulled under the carriages from one to the other; they are chained together in pairs, and with the lower shackles they are all chained together.' The men were 'young, beautiful' and their faces struck her as happy, despite their plight. 'It is a sad sight for any patriot', she wrote, 'when one sees how the love of family and home are suppressed by a cruel hand.' Virtually the entire population of the town turned out to watch these exotic rebels, who were housed during their stay in a large barn just outside the town where hay was kept for the imperial horses. It was hot and the young Italians were dressed in long shirts that reached down to their heels. The guards stood around the barn, but the main door was wide open, and they could be seen 'climbing, sitting, singing, laughing, and most of them were standing at the door smiling at the spectators, especially at the women, so for a person of better upbringing it was better to be no nearer than fifty steps if she does not wish to be ashamed'.[174]

Nationalist discourses presented the nation as something inherited from the past, but for many Europeans, especially in central and eastern Europe, the nation was something that still had to be learned and understood. Patriotism began with the gathering of knowledge about music, literature, art, folklore and other forms of expression.[175] The periodicals that sustained patriotic subcultures in many parts of Europe published poems, short stories, folkloric notes and historical essays, but also articles about cooking, horticulture and agronomy. *The Nymph of the Dniestr*, published in Lemberg (Lviv, Lwów) in 1836 by three Ukrainian-speaking students, was a rich miscellany of Galician folk songs, Ukrainian poetry and prose, samples of lyrical and heroic poetry from a fifteenth-century manuscript, and Ukrainian translations of Serbian folk poetry. An essay by one of the editors, Markiian Shashkevych, praised the beauty of the Ukrainian vernacular tradition and provided an overview of contemporary studies on the literature and folklore of Russian-ruled central and eastern Ukraine.

Polymaths like the Moldavian patriot Gheorghe Asachi, who did much to lay the foundations for modern Romanian as a medium of literature and higher education and published the first political and literary journal in the Romanian language, were important because they connected so many ways of knowing the nation, from science and cartography to poetry and the visual arts. Only through instruction in the lore of the homeland, Asachi wrote in the first issue of his journal *Albina Românească* (The Romanian Bee) in 1829, would his compatriots acquire the 'moral wealth' that sustains 'a strong and happy nation'.[176] The *Guide to Prague* published in 1847 by the Czech patriot Karel Vladislav Zap, the first Czech-language guidebook to the city, urged the author's compatriots to walk the streets of their capital city, reading the history of the Czechs in its squares, monuments and buildings. The knowledge patriots acquired by this means was not merely propositional, but tactile and immersive.[177]

At the heart of many patriotic cultural initiatives was a passion for the unification and refinement of language. 'The only real boundary of a people is language', Ernst Moritz Arndt had written.[178] The Francophobe founder of modern German gymnastics, Friedrich Ludwig Jahn, was also the author of a lexicon of synonyms, whose purpose was to show that the High German idiom could be enriched by the admixture of words harvested from the Germanic tribal dialects; the consolidation of a national literary language, he argued, need not alienate the speaker from the authenticity of popular German speech, and replenishing the language from this source was infinitely better than borrowing from the inferior languages of foreigners.[179] The editor of the Iaşi-based journal *Dacia literară* hoped to refine Romanian letters to the point where Romanian literature would 'proudly count itself among the literatures of Europe'.[180] The 'Illyrian' patriots around Ljudevit Gaj worked in the 1840s to cleanse Croatian speech and writing of foreign loanwords: the word *štampa* (press, from the Italian *stampa*) was to make way for the south-Slav substitute *tisak*.[181] In Hungary, linguistic nationalism was infused with the fear that Magyars and their language would be unable to hold their own against confident Slavic cultures within and around the kingdom. To prevent this, the patriot Lajos Kossuth warned, the Hungarians must insist that Magyar be the language of the administration, the legislature and the executive, but also of government, justice, public security, taxation and business. Any compromise would risk national extinction.[182]

The quest for linguistic integrity did not have to be ethnically exclusive: the assimilationist language policies of the French Revolution were intended to promote republican citizenship, and a nation conceived as a linguistic community was always, in theory at least, open to 'new speakers, listeners and readers'.[183] Patriots confident in the superiority of their own national civilization sometimes expected the members of other groups to merge with them through a process of linguistic assimilation, seeing this not as an imposition but as the conferral of a benefit; in the lands of the Habsburg monarchy, this view was popular among progressive Magyar and German nationalists.[184] And some patriots espoused multilingualism, like those Spanish educationalists of the 'liberal triennium' (1820–23) who aspired to set the relationship between Castilian and Catalan on an equitable basis.[185]

For many patriots, language was above all a tool for the acquisition of an enlarged and more refined civil culture. In the Burghers' Club

(Měšťanská beseda), founded in 1846, the Czech patriots of Prague acquired a venue in which the growing Czech middle class could gather for polite conversation and entertainments on an equal footing with their German contemporaries.[186] The Mihailean Academy, inaugurated in Iaşi, Moldavia, in June 1835, and the Hungarian Academy of the Sciences in Pest, which opened as a learned society in 1831 and as an academy in 1845, served the exchange of ideas and the propagation of knowledge across a wide range of subjects, from history, philosophy and law to chemistry, agronomy and architecture. The approach was holistic and universalist – the members met in joint session for discussions that crossed disciplinary boundaries. Even when they discussed a specific field of scientific knowledge, the Hungarian academicians busied themselves with the collection of dialectal words and technical terms, the screening and recoining of terminology and the standardization of literary language.[187]

The same preoccupation with linguistic upgrading drove the work of the Matice česká, established in 1831 on the initiative of a group of Czech patriots around the historian František Palacky to elevate the Czech language as a medium for scientific communication. The Matice generated a stupendous output in lexicons and dictionaries, establishing itself as the flagship publisher of scholarly works in Czech. In all three cases, patriots were pushing back against another language of high culture whose dominance had stunted the evolution of the vernacular – German in the case of the Czechs, German and Latin for the Hungarians, Greek in the case of the Moldavians.[188] Yet the causal link between linguistic refinement and national awareness was not always direct. The first periodical published in the 'Alpine Slav', or Slovene, language appeared in 1843 in Ljubljana, where it reached about 500 readers; its purpose was to propagate knowledge of the latest agricultural techniques, not to work towards the liberation of a 'Slovenian nation'.[189]

Even if most patriots were more interested in cultural integrity than in political independence, exalting the nation carried a radical ideological charge. It did not necessarily propose, but it did imply, a kind of popular sovereignty, since the nation was something that resided in peoples, not in dynasties. It had the power – potentially – to transform rule by a foreign Crown from an inherited fact into a scandal and an abomination. Its mental maps were at variance with the political geography of the continent. Poles carried in their heads a map of the early-modern

Polish–Lithuanian Commonwealth, a vast territory that extended almost all the way from the Baltic to the Black Sea; Germans dreamed of a national union that would bring together the thirty-nine states of the German Confederation; Ukrainians began to embrace the idea of a homeland that connected Habsburg eastern Galicia with the Russian-ruled areas of eastern Ukraine; for Hungarians, 'Hungary' meant all the lands of the Holy Crown of St Stephen. By contrast, a booklet on 'Magyarism in Hungary', published in 1834 by a Slovak Protestant clergyman, divided Hungary into distinct ethnic zones: 'Ruthenia' ('Ukrainia'), 'Magyaria', 'Valachia', Croatia and so on.[190] Croatian patriots dreamed of founding an 'Illyrian' union of peoples out of the Habsburg possessions on the Adriatic Sea. The potential for conflict between these visions would only become fully apparent when the revolutions broke out.

For some patriots, ethnic 'purity' was an indispensable goal. It was not enough to despise the foreigner, the patriot activist and gymnastic guru Friedrich Ludwig Jahn argued, one must also deny him access to the ethnic substance of the nation. 'The purer a people, the better', Jahn wrote in 1810. 'The more mixed it is, the more it resembles a criminal gang.'[191] Jahn's appeal to purity rings harshly in our ears, because of what we know of the horrific future of this idea, particularly in Germany. But there were also enthusiasts for national unity who explicitly renounced the appeal to a homogeneous ethnic essence. 'Only bankrupt nations speak constantly of their ancestors', the Moldavian patriot, Mihail Kogălniceanu wrote in 1843. Nations, he argued, were composite entities – indeed that was the key to their strength: the Greeks had only succumbed to the Romans because 'they wanted to be Plateans, Thebans, Athenians, Spartans, and not Hellenes', just as 'our ancestors wanted to be Transylvanians, Muntenians, Banatians, Moldovans'.[192] In a treatise of 1835, the liberal German historian Friedrich Christoph Dahlmann drew on the same idea: Pelasgians, Thracians, Achaians and Ionians had blended together to form the lively nation of ancient Attica, and as a composite of Britons, Romans, Saxons, Danes and Normans, the British nation showed that a 'mixed people' – such as the Germans – was perfectly capable of achieving national vitality. With time, Dahlmann suggested, the importance of blood kinship receded in the history of nations, making way for an identity grounded in a shared location and the growth of education.[193] For the Palermo-born historian and orientalist Michele Amari, the cultural power of the Sicilian nation lay precisely in its 'Mediterranean' amalgam of Islamic, Caucasian and Jewish elements.[194]

As a form of committed behaviour, patriotism was more inclusive than either liberalism or the various forms of radicalism, because it embraced – theoretically at least – every member of the linguistic or cultural community, including women. Mothers mattered because they were charged with the education of the young. National allegories tended to work with female figures. Male patriots used journals to recruit women: in 1822, the Hungarian patriot Károly Kisfaludy founded *Aurora*, a literary yearbook for women bound in red, pink or white leather.[195] And even if women remained excluded from the political engine-rooms of patriotic mobilization – the clubs, newspaper offices, academies and political associations – opportunities opened for wealthy women to align themselves with national sentiment by participating in conspicuous forms of consumption, like the famous Zichy sisters, two aristocratic Hungarian women renowned for the exquisitely patriotic outfits – made entirely from locally sourced fabrics – they wore during the ball season.[196] Among the patriot women of Prague, there was tremendous interest in the national costume worn by the Polish wife of the Czech patriot Karel Vladislav Zap; her attire, like that of another Prague 'Slavic' wife, the Croat Josipa Kubínová, was an inspiration for the adoption of Czech women's national costume in the city.[197]

Almost everywhere in Europe, the 1830s and 1840s saw a deepening of patriotic networks. When the interdiction on the German gymnastics movement was finally lifted in 1842, the membership grew at an impressive rate – there were 90,000 gymnasts in 300 clubs by 1847. In February 1843, an Illyrian patriot described with delight how the patriotism of the Illyrians was 'moving forward and evolving', despite an official prohibition of the word 'Illyrian'. 'Two days ago', she wrote, 'a beautiful ball was held in the shooting range in Zagreb and all our patriots were in national clothes; there was a folk dance, singing, talking, everything was unusually beautiful. Thank God! At least our enemies [she was referring to the Hungarians] will see that our nation . . . has not perished.'[198] In the city of Pest, balls and galas became a way of showcasing Magyar national culture. At the 1846 Carnival Ball of the Pesti Kör, a reading and social club, everyone was in Hungarian national costume. The dances were all Hungarian except for one waltz and two Polish dances – offered in honour of the insurrection of the Polish nobility in Galicia. Everyone spoke

Hungarian, even those who were more comfortable speaking German. All of this was by design. The invitations had stipulated that 'the language of conversation, as well as the material and cut of dress' were to be Hungarian. Two Hungarian men who failed to read their invitations properly and turned up in tails were shamed into leaving, while the one foreigner who turned up in tails was allowed to stay on because he knew no better.[199]

Something similar happened in the 1840s among the Czechs of Prague. The membership of the Matice česká grew continuously down to the eve of the revolutions, the middle classes coming to dominate an enterprise that had initially been driven by gentry notables.[200] The Society for the Promotion of Industry in Bohemia boomed after 1843, when its statutes were altered to allow middle-class aspirants to join. In 1844, Czech patriots founded the secret society Český Repeal, named after the Irish association that Daniel O'Connell had established in 1830 to campaign for a repeal of the 1800 Acts of Union. The Prague Citizens' Club, founded for men of the Czech-speaking bourgeoisie in the following year, became an echo chamber for Czech patriot opinion, and from 1846 Karel Havlíček used his newspaper *Pražské Noviny* to promote Czech interests without attracting the attention of the Austrian censors.[201]

Even in the Grand Duchy of Finland, a politically quiescent province of the Russian Empire, there were signs of a quickening of national feeling. 'Vårtland' (Our Land; Finnish *Maamme*), the poem that would become the Finnish national anthem, was written in 1846 by Johan Ludwig Runeberg, headmaster of Borgå Lyceum in Porvoo. It was the prologue to Runeberg's edition of thirty-five heroic ballads focused on the Finnish war of 1808–9, the one that had resulted in the ceding by Sweden of Finland to Russia. Runeberg was not a radical; he was a conservative moderate patriot loyal to the Russian authorities and keen to avoid provoking repressions. This poem was meant to appease the patriotic ardour of the students without putting them in the service of an insurgent project. Runeberg's text avoids trouble by speaking of the land of the Finns in the future tense: 'Thy blossom in the bud laid low / yet ripened shall upspring.' 'See! From our love once more shall grow / Thy light, thy joy, thy hope, thy glow.' The closing lines drive the point home: 'Clearer yet one day shall ring / The song our land shall sing.' The text is sensibly imprecise about the extent and location of the national territory, referring merely to 'our native North' and 'our own fore-fathers' earth'. Set to a score by the German-born music lecturer Friedrich Pacius, 'Our Land' premiered in 1848, at a stately public performance by the choir of the University of Helsinki. On 13 May, Flora Day, a university spring festival marking the end of the academic year, the song was performed again on the Kumtähti Park, this time by the students themselves in the presence of a patriotic flag made especially for the occasion that displayed the Finnish armorial lion with a crown of laurels on a white field, making no reference to the insignia of the Russian Empire. After a patriotic speech that ended with a toast to Finland by the chairman of the student body, the several hundred students present gave a rousing rendition of 'Our Land'.

In a few rare cases, we can trace the gradual intensification of patriotic awareness in a specific individual. In the diary she kept throughout the pre-March years, the poet, essayist and educator Dragojla Jarnević of Karlovac, born in 1812 to a prosperous German-speaking Croatian mercantile family, intermittently revisited the question of what it meant to be a Croat. By the age of eighteen, she recalled, she had noticed that the Croats enjoyed 'a low level of education' and were 'simple-minded by nature'. It was impossible to find a suitable husband among them, because the only educated men were lawyers, who tended to be domineering and cruel, or priests.[202] 'Oh, I wish I had been born among people who are not as narrow-minded as Croats!' she wrote (in German) in 1836, when she was twenty-three years old.[203] Later that year, she heard for the first time of a new movement, 'Illyrianism', which aspired to refine the language and culture of the Croats and other South Slavs. Following the promptings of the political activist Ljudevit Gaj, who had urged all 'good patriots' to unite the 'Illyrian states' (a reference to the old eastern Adriatic provinces of the Roman Empire) through the cultivation of a shared literary language, a group of students at the Catholic theological seminary in Zagreb had founded an Illyrian National Society. Jarnević was unmoved: 'I don't care, let them write as they please, I don't lean towards Croatian anyway, because whoever visits this house speaks German, so they would look at me strangely if I spoke in Croatian.'[204] But the question of language refused to go away. On an afternoon in October 1837, her brother Josip brought some friends to the house, and they discussed whether it was better to call oneself a Croat or an Illyrian. Her poor spoken Croatian was now a cause of embarrassment:

'I just don't get along with that Illyrian or Croatian language, so there was a lot of laughter today when the young men forced me to speak [it].'[205] In May 1838, she recorded her frustration at not being able to write the language as comfortably as she could write in German.

By the autumn of 1838, something had changed. Jarnević now spoke Croatian whenever Vranić and Neralić, friends of her brother, came to visit. She still felt she was too old (at the age of twenty-five) to learn it properly. But in the summer of 1839 we find that her relationship with the language has evolved further: 'I gladly agreed to Trnski's visit because I will have the opportunity to speak Croatian. Oh, how my heart was full of the sweetness, after a long time, of speaking my mother tongue.' Ivan Trnski was a writer, patriot and advocate of the Illyrian movement; the fact Jarnević was in love with him was a further spur to her efforts. Trnski did not reciprocate her love, but he praised her for her efforts with 'Croatian or, as it is now called, Illyrian', and helped her to improve by reading together with her.[206] Travelling abroad helped to sharpen her patriotism. While staying in Graz, she passed a tower (quite possibly the city's ancient clocktower) to which other travellers had attached messages. Reading the inscriptions, she found one in Croatian:

Oh, how strange it was around my heart! Since I had said goodbye to Croatia I hadn't thought much about it, but now, how unspeakably I was touched by these lines in Croatian. They started like this: May my every brother be healthy, etc. I just remember that with these lines he intended to greet everyone who should understand his words and signed himself as an Illyrian from Croatia. I quickly took out a pen and put together some kind of answer, but I haven't written it down here because I didn't note it down on paper for myself. But I do remember that I wrote that there is an Illyrian woman here who understands these lines, and that she sends him a greeting, and I signed myself 'an Illyrian woman from Karlovac'.[207]

By 1840, she was working hard on Croatian poetic works for an Illyrian journal and had acquired a sense that her nation could benefit from her contribution as a writer, that her work had a public utility, an important thought to a woman who bitterly resented the sexual segregation that kept her out of public life. She took more and more delight in the company of other patriots and began to follow the politics of the Croatian Diet, where, by 1842, a struggle was under way with the

Hungarian authorities over the official status of the Croatian language. She had become one of those patriots who felt the victories and setbacks of the nation as if they were her own. And her attachment to the cause was tightly coupled with a bitter antipathy to the Magyars, whose plans to consolidate their cultural hold via language over the Slav areas under their control she saw as an existential threat. 'We must boldly despise every danger in order to prove to these stupid, evil Hungarians that we are not afraid of them and that we stand firm on the foundation of patriotism.'[208] On 8 April 1843 came a definitive oath of loyalty: 'I am only interested in the homeland, and I dedicate my strength and love to it.'[209]

As this emotional and intellectual journey shows, patriotism was open to the participation of women in a way that liberalism and radicalism were not. It is worth reflecting on what Dragojla Jarnević gained from the efforts she invested in improving her Croatian: the company and conversation of other patriots, a widening of horizons, the exciting sense that something was at stake, and connectedness with a great project that transcended the small world of a provincial town. The cause of the nation, she wrote, 'interested [her] soul' and drew her out of herself. 'My soul sensed that there was more to life than a needle and cooking and drove me to go out looking for it and to enjoy it.'[210]

'Whoever denies his national character or blasphemes the national community is the hereditary enemy, sworn to conspire with vice and madness against the Fatherland as an offender against sovereignty and a traitor.'[211] As this characteristically swivel-eyed fulmination of 1833 from the demagogue Friedrich Ludwig Jahn reminds us, national chauvinism was forever doing battle with scepticism and indifference. Nationalism projected a holistic social vision: its lore and its fictions thronged with peasants, fishermen and forest folk, and 'national costumes' riffed on traditional rural and regional styles. Yet it remained in this period, for the most part, the preserve of a cultural elite. 'For the moment', wrote Jakob Friedrich Fries, professor of philosophy, in 1816, 'German patriotism is and must be a matter for educated people and less for the general masses.'[212] In *The Village Notary*, an important novel of social observation, the liberal Hungarian writer József Eötvös acknowledged this link between social status and national identity. Peasants, observes one character, were 'things to be despised'. They were born in this place, 'and yet they have no rights, no property, and no country!' Why should one expect them to feel an attachment to a nation that despised them?[213] The noble-led Polish insurrection that broke out in Austrian Galicia in 1846 ended with catastrophe, because the peasants feared and resented their feudal masters more than they did the Austrians. We have seen that in Galicia some Polish-speaking peasants regarded the noble landowners, their estate managers, clerks and clergy as 'Poles', while they described themselves as 'imperial peasants'. The patriotic insurrections orchestrated in the Italian states by Mazzini flopped in part because popular interest in them was virtually non-existent in the areas where they were supposed to take place.

National feeling vacillated, and because it needed the ecosystem of books, newspapers and other print media to propagate itself, it was still largely confined to those literate and urban circles with a stake in the refinement of national culture. These circles tended to be small: the single most important vehicle for Romanian patriot opinion in the Hungarian province of Transylvania, where about two million Romanian-speakers lived, was the *Gazeta de Transilvania*, published in the city of Blaj. It counted 250 subscribers. Even if we imagine that there were ten or twenty readers for every subscriber, that still leaves us with a very tiny patriotic cosmos. In relatively backward and poor Dalmatia, a province of the Austrian Empire in which the people of the rural hinterland spoke a range of south-Slav dialects and the small urban population spoke Italian, attachment to the composite 'Dalmatian nation' trumped ethnic alignments, and local elites looked to Vienna to deliver economic and cultural stimulus.[214]

Once you moved away from the larger towns, the intensity of interest died away fast. 'There is no public spirit here, no spirit at all', one despondent Hungarian patriot reported from Nyitra County (now in western Slovakia).[215] In 1843, when the young noblewoman Klara Lövei spent time in the Hungarian city of Pressburg/Poszony (today Slovakian Bratislava) working as a nanny for the family of one of the delegates at the Hungarian National Diet then meeting in the city, she was shocked by the absence of national awareness among the women of the town. 'Few women are interested in the affairs of the homeland', she wrote, 'and many cannot grasp the questions of the day' – this was at the height of the Hungarian patriotic revival.[216] In the predominantly Italian-speaking population of Trieste, Italian nationalism was weak and Habsburg loyalism strong, whereas the opposite was the case in

Venice and Lombardy.[217] Italian patriots frequently lamented the difficulty of getting Italians to collaborate with each other beyond the
boundaries of their cities and regions. The Sicilian intellectuals – Francesco
Renda, Niccolò Palmeri, Giovanni Evangelista di Blasi and Rosario
Gregorio – who used history to exalt 'love for the country and the
nation' (di Blasi) were referring to the Sicilian nation, not the Italian
one.[218] The composer Đuro (also known as György) Arnold, a prolific
composer of religious and secular music, published a hymnal in the
Croatian Ikavian dialect, in the hope that this would encourage and
refine religious life among the 'Illyrians' (i.e. Croatian-speakers) of the
western Vojvodina in the Hungarian–South Slav borderlands. But he
also wrote requiems, passions, litanies, psalms and other works with
Magyar texts for Hungarian and Transylvanian musicians and published works on musical themes in German. He appears to have spoken
Hungarian and German well and to have been proficient in Croatian.
He never showed any interest in adopting any one of these languages as
an identity and was clearly 'comfortable in the multicultural and multi-
lingual surrounding of the [Habsburg] monarchy'.[219]

National feeling was not a hard-and-fast identity inherited from the
past, and nor was it something invented by newspaper editors and pam-
phleteers. It was an evolving field of awareness, a form of affiliation that
had to live alongside others: religious commitments, regional and
dynastic attachments, political visions. Under certain circumstances –
during wars and war scares, for example, or during a revolution – it
might rise to become the dominant form of belonging. But for many
Europeans it was religion, social or corporate status, politics, city or
region that shaped and focused national belonging, not the other way
around. The power of the national idea to mobilize and divide Europeans would only become fully apparent after the outbreak of revolution
in 1848.

FREE AND UNFREE

Politically active Europeans often reached for the idea of slavery when
they denounced the unfreedom of their contemporaries. For Claire
Démar and Flora Tristan, women were the slaves of men. Jeanne Deroin
compared the use of the patronymic surname by married women to the

slave-owner's branding iron.[220] For Joseph de Maistre, revolutionaries were not freedom fighters, but the slaves of history. Victor Considerant denounced Christianity as a 'religion of slaves'; Charles Fourier accused the Catholic Church of enslaving women and looked forward to a distant era in which women would have been liberated from their 'conjugal slavery'.[221] In his play *Giovanni da Procida*, a flamboyant evocation of the Sicilian Vespers, the Tuscan patriot Giovanni Battista Nicolini depicted a country despoiled by foreign rulers and 'bathed in the sweat of the slave'.[222] A proclamation printed by the insurgents of Bologna in February 1831 described the Italians in the Papal States as 'slaves, wretched under the despotism of priests' and their compatriots under Austrian rule as 'the slaves of foreigners, who enrich themselves by despoiling you and render you daily more miserable'.[223] 'Yes, because I have experienced slavery', Ludwig Börne wrote in 1832, in reference to the discrimination he had faced as a Jew, 'I understand freedom better than you do.'[224] It was the fate of the Poles who remained on the soil of their fatherland, wrote Adam Mickiewicz, to 'bear slavery with patience'.[225] Referring to the uprising of the weavers in Lyons in January 1834, a local radical declared that the nations of Europe would soon join in this insurrection, 'which will at last deliver the old world from the chains of slavery'.[226] 'The comparison of the proletariat with ancient slavery', wrote the Saint-Simonian socialist Pierre Leroux, 'has been entirely vindicated.'[227] In short, slavery had become one of the root metaphors of western political philosophy and language, a powerful trope for 'the forces that debased the human spirit'.[228]

What is striking about these references to slavery, which turn up everywhere, once you look for them, is that they do not refer, even implicitly, to the real phenomenon of slavery in the world of the early nineteenth century. For many of the critical writers of this period, slavery remained either a metaphor, or the phenomenon of a bygone age, or a theoretical abstraction. Even as they spoke of the idea, they seemed to avert their eyes from the thing. In his *Guarantees of Harmony and Freedom* (1842), the German radical Wilhelm Weitling reflected at length on slavery. It was, he argued, the darkest and most sordid consequence of the idea of property. It had first become possible in a remote past before history began. Humans reached out to grasp the beasts in the field, uttering with their blasphemous mouths the word 'mine'. Then they reached for the soil and its products, saying *this is my property*. And then at last they laid their hands on their fellows, degrading them to mere things that could be bought and sold.

Yet chattel slavery, the ownership of human beings by human beings, Weitling argued, was merely the prelude to something much worse: the modern slavery of money. In 'earlier times', he wrote, slaves were forced to work with the whip. The slave was an 'exploited, exchanged or inherited possession'. But he retained an intrinsic value. 'In those days, every owner had an interest in not overworking his slave, because he feared he might otherwise become sick and die.' All this changed with the 'introduction of money': after that, 'the condition of slavery developed in a way that was different from before':

> [Today's slaves] are worked to the blood to extract the full advantage from their strength, and if they become sick, old or weak, then they are hounded out of the workshop, the factory and the house so that there is no longer any need to feed them, and then they stand outside in great numbers and crowd into the caves of the martyrs. . . . The ugly external appearance [of the new slavery] was hidden under the shadow of contracts and laws. And in more recent times, [the old form of] slavery has been partially abolished, at least in name, whereas the condition [of the slave] continues in what is in many respects an even worse degree.[229]

It was as if Weitling only spoke of slavery in order not to speak of it. The word was employed to bring home the oppressiveness of modern economic systems and the constraints they imposed on the poorest Europeans, an effect Weitling could only achieve by pushing the practice of chattel slavery into a remote past and playing it down as the lesser evil. Weitling was not unusual in this. Hegel, a thinker of incalculably greater sophistication, importance and reach than Weitling, 'spoke surprisingly frequently of slaves'.[230] A recent re-reading of Hegel's reflections on the 'struggle to the death' between lord and bondsman has suggested that Hegel did not draw this idea exclusively from Aristotle or from studying the history of ancient Rome, but also from reading in the German press about the massive insurrection of the enslaved that unfolded in Haiti between 1791 and 1804, culminating in the victory of the insurgents, the self-emancipation of the Haitians and the foundation of a new state under unprecedented circumstances. This was the true context for Hegel's exploration of the dialectic of lordship and bondage, a concept central not just to the philosophy of freedom set out in the pages of his *Phenomenology of the Spirit*, but to the subsequent development of European philosophy, from Marx to Nietzsche and beyond. Yet the curious fact remains that Hegel thought *with* Haiti rather than writing *about* it. The Haitian context was present, but it was 'written in invisible ink'.[231]

This tendency to reach for the idea of slavery without plugging it into its contemporary context is odd, because the first half of the nineteenth century witnessed an unprecedented expansion in the use of enslaved people by the continental European colonial powers. It is well known that after 1807 Britain waged an international campaign against the trade in slaves – in which it had itself once played the dominant role. Denmark and the United States followed suit, relinquishing the traffic in enslaved humans (though not the use of slaves as such), but other states such as Spain, Portugal, France and the Netherlands resisted British pressure to end a form of commerce that they continued to view as both lucrative and legitimate. There were repeated formal interdictions of the slave trade by France, Portugal and Spain, but the traffic in captives continued. Of the three million people who left Africa as slaves after British abolition, perhaps two thirds were trafficked illegally.[232] And the *use* of slaves continued unabated in the colonies of the continental European powers. In December 1839, encouraged by the British, Pope Gregory XVI, in many other respects a deeply conservative figure, issued the apostolic letter *In supremo apostolatus* unequivocally condemning the trade in slaves and ordering all faithful Catholics to desist immediately, on pain of excommunication, from 'subjecting to slavery, unjustly persecuting, or despoiling of their goods Indians, negroes or other classes of human beings'.[233] But no one was listening. London's hope that the Pope's emphatic condemnation would nudge Spain and Portugal into enforcing their own laws against the traffic proved illusory.

The reason lay partly in the fact that abolitionism was British. Patriot activists and newspapers in Portugal, for example, tended to take the view that the suppression of slaving was an British strategy that would harm their country's interests. Inasmuch as the Portuguese were willing to join in suppressing the South Atlantic slave trade in the 1830s and 1840s, this was not because they had been convinced by the principle, but because they were concerned lest Brazil, which had become independent in 1822 and was a major consumer of African slaves, suck excessive numbers of slaves out of Portuguese Angola, and thereby prevent Lisbon from transforming Angola into a slave-based sugar economy capable of making up for what Portugal had lost through the departure of Brazil.[234] The problem was not that slaving interests opposed abolition (though they did) or that the financial means to compensate slave-based industries were lacking (though they were); it was simply that informed domestic opinion (especially on the *Setembrista* left) was opposed to abolition on grounds of national interest.[235] In Portugal, as in Spain, anti-slavery groups tended to be small elite formations with little support in the wider public and very modest political influence. There was no continental counterpart to the British movement for abolition, with its waves of petitions, abolitionist tracts and mass meetings, underwritten by the fervour of Anglophone evangelical Protestantism.[236]

Victor Schoelcher, who published the abolitionist tract *De l'esclavage des noirs* in 1833 after his return to Paris from a journey to Mexico, Cuba and the southern United States, knew all too well how difficult it was to overcome the inertia of a society that was aware of the iniquity of slavery but not sufficiently alarmed to act against it. The arguments against this institution, he wrote, were so well rehearsed and of such long standing that it was impossible to come up with new points that might catch the attention of the public. Europeans were easily roused to indignation by this or that narrative of injustice or atrocity, but their sympathy and interest quickly waned. In a compelling passage near the beginning of the book, Schoelcher reflected on the ease with which European visitors to the colonies were seduced into partisanship for slavery. On arriving in a slaving country, he wrote, you are surrounded entirely by the warmth, hospitality and anecdotes of the whites. The whole of the (white) society around you forms a 'league' dedicated to educating you in the virtue and necessity of captive labour. You begin blushing at the naivety of your opinions, your earlier ideas seem to have no traction in the world you now find yourself in.

> You are soon converted, for your initial doubts were weakly sustained, and your isolation is enough to ensure that you are unable to push back the forces that surround you, especially in a country where your generous principles are regarded by the kind of people you are likely to frequent as prejudices subversive of all social order.[237]

Having acknowledged in this way the psychological power of slavery as a form of society, Schoelcher spent the rest of the book refuting the chief claims of the slavers: black men and women were no less capable than their white counterparts; it was slavery itself that made the enslaved resigned and dull-witted, because it robbed them of dignity and initiative; free agriculture was more productive, because it allowed a fuller unfolding of energy and enterprise; the interest of the master in preserving his human property did not, contrary to a widely held opinion, provide sufficient protection against cruelty; the mortality among enslaved people was much worse than that among European proletarians; the claim that slaves were better off than 'our peasants' was an absurdity, as was the claim that they were 'happy with their lot' and would not willingly exchange it for liberty.[238] The entire book was a sequence of skirmishes against the *idées reçues* of a slaving culture. It was time, Schoelcher argued, for 'vain theories' to give way to a fact-based analysis of how slavery worked and a reasoned commitment to doing away with it. And yet he was not, at this point, in favour of immediate emancipation. He preferred a staged emergence from unfreedom into liberty via a kind of apprenticeship for freedom, an idea he borrowed from the British. And although he deplored the use of corporal punishment on the plantations, in 1833 he was still against outlawing the use of the whip, the ubiquitous instrument of slave discipline, whose suspension, he believed, might open the way to disorder.[239] He would later cast aside these reservations.

At around the same time as Schoelcher's tract appeared, Cyrille Bissette, a 'free man of colour' from Martinique, began publishing the abolitionist periodical the *Revue des Colonies*. Bissette, a merchant and a sometime slaveholder, had fallen foul of the French authorities on the island in 1823 for his involvement in the distribution of a polemical tract denouncing the discrimination by whites against free people of colour in the colony. Having been branded on the shoulder, imprisoned and stripped of his property, he was exiled along with 140 other Martiniquais of colour from the French Antilles and made his way to Paris, by now a thoroughly radicalized abolitionist who saw free people of colour and enslaved black Afro-Caribbeans as sharing common interests.[240] *Revue des Colonies*, which appeared monthly from 1834 until 1842, offered a miscellany of materials typical of the campaigning periodicals of this era: poetry and short stories, the texts of official edicts and proclamations relating to the abolition of the slave trade, detailed legal case studies, discussions of the Haitian revolution, and abolitionist petitions.[241] Bissette was an energetic seeker-out of contemporary black writers from across the world of African diaspora. He serialized a short story by Ignace Nau called 'Isalina: un scène créole', one of the first pieces of Haitian fiction, and 'Le Mulâtre' by the New Orleans-born, Paris-based playwright Victor Séjour, today regarded as the first surviving fictional work by an African American.[242]

At the heart of Bissette's advocacy was the tension between theory and practice, a theme to which he frequently returned. Slavery, he wrote, 'was at the same time a fact and a principle' – defeating the fact and extirpating the principle were different tasks. 'The colonies', he declared in his preface to the inaugural issue of the journal, 'know the great principles of philanthropy only in theory; of liberty in action, [they know] nothing.'[243] It might sometimes be necessary to report on specific case studies in tedious detail, because 'the liberating mission of the *Revue* must draw its power not merely from theories, but also from facts'. For the abolitionist working in Europe, the primary task was thus to connect the theoretical meanings of slavery with the contemporary social effects of slavery in practice, no easy feat in a metropolitan society that had become accustomed to filing them under separate forms of awareness.[244]

French abolitionism never acquired the social depth of the British equivalent. The British petition campaigns reached their peak with 1.5 million signatures in 1833 – the British Abolition of Slavery Act was passed in the following year.[245] There were periodic attempts to garner wider support for an abolitionist campaign in France, but the response was disappointing: a petition drive in Paris and Lyons in 1844 produced fewer than 9,000 signatures. The interdiction of slavery remained, for the most part, the concern of a small cultural elite. Bissette's *Revue des Colonies* was taken by 250 subscribers. Yet there were signs that a gradualist form of abolitionism was gaining ground within the political class. In 1835, encouraged by the passage of the British Abolition of Slavery Act, the matter was brought to the French Chamber of Deputies. Parliamentary reports expressed general support. A government commission produced two plans for gradual emancipation, neither of which was adopted. In 1844, the Minister for the Navy and Colonies, Admiral Mackau, proposed a parliamentary bill that envisaged a phased process of emancipation that would compensate the slave-owners and allow the enslaved to purchase their own liberty over a period of time. But the

Mackau laws, despite their generous concessions to slave-owners' interests, were blocked in the colonies and never went fully into effect.[246]

By the later 1840s, a broader abolitionist front was beginning to emerge. *Le Journal des débats*, *Le Constitutionnel* and *Le National* all backed it, and so, in the later 1840s, did the Catholic ultramontane newspaper *L'Univers*, hugely influential among the clergy, and the new radical paper *La Réforme*. A second petition drive in 1846–7 secured 12,395 signatures, still modest, but an improvement on the campaign of 1844. In the eighteen months before the outbreak of the revolutions, more than 200 pamphlets and brochures appeared denouncing slavery, many of them by Schoelcher himself, who wrote tirelessly for *Le Siècle*, the *Courrier français*, the *Revue indépendante*, the *Journal des Économistes*, *L'Atelier* and, above all, *La Réforme*, of which he was one of the co-founders.[247] Over the years, Schoelcher had shed his gradualism and become the untiring advocate of an immediate and total emancipation. Yet this slow and steady accumulation of anti-slavery sentiment might have continued for years without producing significant political effects. In the conclusion to the book of essays he published in 1847, Schoelcher expressed frustration at the glacial slowness of progress: 'There is no doubt that the cause of abolition is won in France, we hear it every day; it is just a matter of time, everyone says. But people have been saying this for a quarter of a century and still the slaves are in their chains.'[248] At that point, a totally unexpected discontinuity intervened: in February 1848, a revolution picked up the most determined advocates of abolition and deposited them close to the levers of political power. The metaphor and the thing, the readiness to argue and the power to act, would be suddenly conjoined, with far-reaching consequences.

PLACES IN HISTORY

Pity the feeble reed that pretends to block the course of the foaming swift torrent!! Pity the microscopic insect whose tiny dart hopes to strike the heart of the fiery lion through its broad flanks[.] The torrent rushes on its course towards the ocean; the lion towards its prey, the principle towards its final consequence: but what, I ask you, will become of the reed, the insect and the barriers, the futile charters and transactions?[249]

In this enigmatic passage from her *Law of the Future*, Claire Démar invoked a sense of history's violent motion. In his prison memoirs, the insurrectionary socialist Martin Bernard expressed the same intuition. The 'imprudent restrictions' imposed by the great, their vain efforts to return to 'a past that is already no more than a phantom', were of no consequence to history's larger narrative: 'Woe betide them who try to block the chariot of progress! They will be broken beneath its wheels!' Bernard was so confident of the unstoppability of the chariot that he could even find it in himself to feel a certain sympathy with counter-revolutionaries, because history showed that they hastened the onward march of progress 'as surely as those who dedicated themselves to assuring its triumph'.[250]

These were voices from the French radical left, but we find the same sense of irreversible motion among radicals, liberals and conservatives across Europe. The Italian patriots Francesco Saverio Salfi, Decio Valentini and Fedele Bono acknowledged that the French Revolution was more than an event – it was part of a world-historical process whose transformative impact was still unfolding in Italy, where a process of regeneration was underway.[251] The proliferation of early-nineteenth-century European constitutions – from Naples to Cadiz, Paris, Baden, Bavaria, Piedmont-Sardinia, Portugal and Brussels – nourished liberal confidence in the ultimate victory of the liberal constitutional order. 'A constitution', wrote the Polish liberal Franciszek Grzymała in an essay of 1820 for the periodical *Orzeł Biały* (White Eagle), soon to be shut down by the Russian authorities, 'is the foreseen future'. The power of constitutions as a political instrument, Grzymała argued, lay in their plurivocal, balanced quality. They were nothing less than a 'peace treaty between all estates, parties, classes and even antagonisms'.[252]

Liberals across Europe saw in this moderating quality of constitutions a prize of immense value. The motto of the Neapolitan journal *The Friend of the Constitution* was 'moderation and constancy'. Above all, moderate constitutionalism offered the assurance that history would not repeat itself, that humans could learn from errors and excesses of the past. In the early 1820s, attention focused on a cascade of revolutions in Spain, Portugal, the Kingdom of the Two Sicilies and Piedmont. Common to all four was the adoption by the insurgents of the 'Spanish constitution', the constitution drafted at Cadiz during the Peninsular War. The liberal regimes soon succumbed to international interventions – the last to do so was the liberal government in Spain, which collapsed in 1823 after a French armed intervention. For the Portuguese liberal Almeida Garrett, these revolutions, however short-lived, demonstrated the power of a new 'system of southern liberty' (*liberdade meridional*) animated by a self-consciously 'moderate' form of politics. The 'serene' and 'magnetic' force of liberal constitutionalism, Almeida argued, represented an unequivocal advance over the 'destructive' and 'abrasive' 'detonations' of the late-eighteenth-century revolutions, particularly in France.[253]

Conservatives tended to be sceptical of the notion that liberals had 'learned' from the mistakes of an earlier era. In their eyes, the spectacle of liberal revolution evoked memories of the radicalization that had dragged Revolutionary France into the ultraviolence of the Jacobin dictatorship. Speaking in the Chamber of Deputies, the writer and historian François-René de Chateaubriand, then Minister of Foreign Affairs, pointed to the instability of the constitutional regime in Spain and issued a stark warning: 'Revolutionary France gave birth to a [Jacobin] Convention; why should revolutionary Spain not produce one of its own?' Conservatives tended to gravitate towards a view of history as trapped within cyclical and repetitive structures. The French ultra-conservative newspaper *Le Quotidien*, which also favoured an intervention against the Spanish constitutional regime, captured this view neatly in 1823: 'revolutions turn in the same circle, they use the same language and they all arrive at the same result'.[254] Liberals, on the other hand, insisted that they were embarked on a journey into a better future.

No one was more acutely aware of this ambient pressure for change than those who claimed to be resisting it. To the conservative Prussian nobleman Leopold von Gerlach, writing in 1843, it seemed that nothing and no one was capable of holding steady against 'the always freshly blowing wind of the Zeitgeist' – even his supposedly conservative best friends seemed always to be seeking an accommodation with faddish liberal ideas.[255] In the 1810s and 1820s, *duch czasu* (the spirit of the age) was one of the buzzwords of Polish liberalism. It was a codeword for those forces that were driving all the societies of Europe along a convergent path into modernity. For the Polish reformer Bonawentura Niemojowski, the spirit of the age, 'like the ancient sphinx, devoured all those who did not guess its meaning'.[256] In his *Spirit of the Century* (1835), the Spanish liberal Francisco Martínez de la Rosa spoke of his own age as an era of reform, 'the little-known brother of insurrection'.

Reform was important, he argued, because it was the only means by which 'political and civil relations' could be adjusted in order to absorb 'great movements in the social order'.[257] Addressing a gathering of German ministers who had convened to discuss police measures against radical and liberal groups, the Austrian statesman Clemens von Metternich evoked the threat to order in words that conveyed the same intuition of irreversible motion: 'If a rescuing dam is not built to contain the streaming flood, then we could soon see even the shadow of monarchical power dissolve . . .'[258]

Wherever they positioned themselves on the spectrum of political options, Europeans had to address and make sense of this current of change. In doing so, they embarked on long journeys, weaving mutable webs of ideas and commitments from the many chains of speculative thought unfolding across Europe in the 1830s and 1840s. It was the Saint-Simonians who inducted the socialist insurrectionary Martin Bernard into politics. He was not interested in the call to sexual equality that 'bedazzled' Suzanne Voilquin, but in the idea of 'association', a 'deep word', in which, for a time, he found his 'compass'.[259] But he later dropped the Saint-Simonians and studied Robespierre through the writings of Buonarroti. Félicité Lamennais began as a defender of the rights of the Church against Revolutionary and Napoleonic authoritarianism, but he later passed through a sequence of liberal commitments and ultimately fused what remained of his Christian spirituality with a form of socialist evangelism. He had started out as an opponent of the French Revolution and ended by affirming its value. At the core of these permutations was a preoccupation with the need to restore cohesion in a society that seemed to be fracturing into an infinity of alienated individuals.[260]

We find the same flux in the writings of the Italian patriot in exile Giuseppe Mazzini. In 1832, Mazzini was still acclaiming the Jacobin phase of the French Revolution for heralding the programme of the 'great social revolution' that was supposedly on the horizon. But in 1833–4, his social radicalism waned, and he adopted a more volontarist and spiritualist conception of revolution, denouncing state terror and abjuring any profound mutation of the property base of society.[261] When Karl Marx first immersed himself in the work of Hegel in 1837, it unleashed a revelatory shock akin to a religious conversion. 'For some days', he told his father in November 1837, his excitement made him 'quite incapable of thinking'; he 'ran about madly in the garden by the dirty water of the Spree' and found himself overpowered by the desire to embrace every street corner loafer in Berlin.[262] But Marx later abandoned the idealism of Hegel; in assembling his own materialist vision of history, he became one of the most voracious and brilliant consumers, assimilators and recombiners of other people's ideas that the world has ever seen.[263]

Even Donoso Cortés, later raised up as the very emblem of eloquent conservative intransigence in the Iberian mode, entered Spanish political life as an ambivalent liberal – his conversion to a more conservative stance came after the radical uprising at La Granja in August 1836.[264] And the career of the Dutch liberal Johan Rudolf Thorbecke was marked by a journey in the other direction: he began adult life as a romantic conservative, hostile to constitutional experiments; the only legitimate source of law, he argued in an essay of 1824, was 'the history of what [had] gone before'; any higher standard was 'an illusion'. Yet, by the early 1840s, Thorbecke had metamorphosed into an advanced liberal and a partisan of radical constitutional reform who would play a key role in the transformations of 1848.[265]

In an analysis of the political journalism of Alexis de Tocqueville, Roger Boesche noticed an incongruous pleating together of themes that seemed drawn from the 'conservatism' of Chateaubriand, the 'liberalism' of Constant and the 'radical republicanism' of Jules Michelet. Boesche interpreted this heterogeneity as an index of Tocqueville's 'unusual' liberalism.[266] But everyone was 'unusual' in the world of the 1830s and 1840s. These meandering intellectual journeys across the nineteenth century were not confined to the cultural elites. The philosopher Pierre-Simon Ballanche, an esoteric figure whose own thinking underwent numerous evolutions, reported in the 1830s that he had made the acquaintance of a foreman (maître ouvrier) who had gathered around him a small circle of fellow workers for philosophical discussions. 'He had begun with Saint-Simonianism; he soon dropped that and began to profess the political economy of Fourier; but he quickly understood that a political economy founded on material well-being alone was insufficient; now he has begun to study my work and has been seized by a real enthusiasm for my doctrines . . .'[267]

Everything and everyone was in motion. Perhaps this is always true. But there are periods whose signature is stabilization, when previously unstable formations cohere and coalesce and boundaries swim into sharper focus: the 'Carolingian Renaissance', the rise of territorial states in the 13th–14th centuries, the age of 'confessionalization', the ascendancy of the modern nation-state, the Cold War. And there are periods marked by flux and transition, where the direction of travel is harder to discern, when disparate forms of identity and commitment become unpredictably enmeshed with each other. Our own age is one. This, too, is part of the fascination of those decades.

3

Confrontation

GLORIOUS DAYS: PARIS IN JULY

On the morning of Monday, 26 July 1830, Parisians woke up to extraordinary news: King Charles X had imposed muzzling orders on the press, dissolved the new parliament before it had even convened, shrunk the Chamber of Deputies to almost half of its current size and altered the electoral law. These measures had not been submitted to parliament but were imposed unilaterally in the form of ordinances countersigned by the king's ministers. Large masses of troops were concentrating around Paris. It seemed that the government intended by means of a coup d'état to break permanently the power of a liberal opposition which, only a few weeks before, had secured an impressive victory in national elections.

On that Monday, the 22-year-old Swiss poet Juste Olivier was approaching the end of a six-month sojourn in Paris. He had come in the hope of acquainting himself with the city's literary scene before taking up a professorial post at a college in Lausanne. Olivier, who kept a diary, was stunned by this 'great and terrible news'. It was hard to imagine that the liberal opposition, its confidence enlarged by a momentous victory in the June elections, would back down. But there was no reason to suppose that the most intransigently conservative ministry of recent French history would back down either. 'Where will this lead France?' Olivier wondered. 'And where will France lead the world?' When he went to enquire about an edition of poems he was publishing, his printer, 'a sensible, peace-loving chap who is fond of order and work' was in an unusual state of agitation. 'They want a second revolution!' the man exclaimed, adding, with a printer's choice of metaphor: 'And we will give it to them – corrected, revised and enlarged!'[1] That evening, as Olivier walked with a friend down the rue Saint-Honoré towards the boulevard des

Capucines, the people in the street ahead suddenly turned and surged back, though it was impossible to see why. Shop-owners ran out to close their premises. Fearing lest he be caught up in a brawl, Olivier and his friend leapt into an omnibus, which appeared to be operating as usual. The vehicle passed safely along its route through thick crowds.

On the following morning, 27 July, Olivier spoke with Jean, the bell-boy at his hotel. Jean had fresh news, because he had spent the previous evening pulling up cobblestones, cutting trenches in the streets to block the horses of the gendarmes, and detaching doors to build barricades. There was going to be serious trouble, he told the poet, because if parliament were to be closed, the factories and workshops would shut down soon after, throwing thousands out of work: 'No chambers, no workshops!' Olivier was sceptical, but in fact Jean was quite right about the impact of political disturbances on workers in the city. The forced closure of the newspapers and their printing houses immediately pushed setters and compositors, folders, and book-stitchers onto the streets. Liberty of the press was not just a political standard; it was also an economic fact. And those who were no longer needed in the print houses were soon joined by the clerks and assistants from shops whose owners had boarded up their premises to avoid the trouble brewing in the capital.

The pace of events picked up. At 9.30 in the morning, a friend, Henri Ladame, arrived at Olivier's apartment with further news of the previous day's events: although things had been quiet in the streets around Olivier's hotel, there had apparently been serious fighting at the Palais-Royal. The owners and editors of the main liberal journals had met at the offices of the *National* and jointly signed a statement protesting at the government's measures. *Le National* had issued an announcement that it intended to keep publishing, come wind or weather. People were hiding their fresh newspapers to avoid confiscation. Parliamentary deputies had gathered at the house of a long-serving colleague, where they had declared that they would not yield and that they still regarded themselves as the legitimate representatives of France.

Like an image buffering fitfully over third-rate wifi, a picture was building of something much more concerted than an urban riot. Yet the area around Olivier's hotel was still quiet. That evening, he met friends at an almost-empty restaurant near the place du Palais-Royal. After dinner, they walked down the rue Richelieu towards the rue Saint-Honoré, which appeared to be the scene of a major tumult. Here, two brigades of cavalry were charging the crowds from either end of the street, shooting, sabring and crushing citizens. Olivier and his friends could not see what was happening; but they watched from a distance how the masses of people surged in waves back and forth, advancing and fleeing by turns. Safely back in his rooms, he saw from the window of his apartment how the crowds on the quai de la Mégisserie rippled and dispersed as squadrons of cavalry pursued them. From every direction he could hear cries: *Long live the constitution! Down with the ministers!* intermingled with gunshots and the uproar of unseen crowds. Peace soon returned to the streets around his hotel, but the shouts and gunshots continued beyond midnight.[2]

On Wednesday, 28 July, the pace of events was so intense that Olivier composed separate diary entries at eight, ten and ten-thirty in the morning, and then at one o'clock, two o'clock, half past four, five, six, seven, half past seven, a quarter to eight and nine in the evening. Serious clashes were now being reported in many parts of the city centre. A crowd of people carrying pikes and clubs had been seen crossing the Pont Neuf. A group of bourgeois and workers had fired on a troop of mounted police, killing five of them. In his apartment, which was now like a box at the opera, Olivier found it increasingly difficult to reconcile keeping his diary with his need to see for himself what was going on:

> 'There they are! There they are!' cried a boy. 'Oh goodness! The crowd has turned up!' says Ladame, who is standing at the window. I leave my writing desk and I see a crowd of people who move down the street and disappear like smoke.

It is a feature of urban tumults that commotion is often interspersed with moments of incongruous normality: on the quai de la Ferraille, the carriages rolled back and forth, seemingly oblivious to the tumult. The markets were still open and full of customers. Behind the surging crowds could be seen Parisians bearing stepladders, in the hope of raising themselves high enough to see what was going on. During a hiatus in the commotion, Olivier was struck by the sight of a young dandy with pistols slung from an elegant belt and a rifle on his shoulder making his way languidly to the scene of the fight – he seemed more concerned with his own appearance than with the drama that lay ahead.

Yet there were also moments of sheer terror in which normality was entirely suspended. By six in the evening on Wednesday, the volleys of gun and cannon fire around Olivier's apartment were deafening. For the first time, he saw corpses carried away from the fighting. It belatedly occurred to him that the dinner he had been planning to attend that night – a glittering literary gathering at which Victor Hugo was expected – would not be taking place. Writing his diary was now no longer a distraction; it was a refuge. 'It is impossible', he wrote, 'to record everything in this journal, which I am writing to occupy my mind and keep a cool head.'[3]

Only around noon on Thursday, 29 July, did Olivier and Ladame learn that the formation of a provincial government had been announced under the leadership of prominent liberals and that the National Guard was reconstituting itself in readiness to take control of the city back from the king's army. At last, they felt able to leave the apartment and walk through the streets. The ground was crunchy with bullets and shell fragments and the air heavy with the nauseating odour of corpses ripening in the warm sunshine. Next to the Louvre towards the Seine, Olivier saw the bodies of three dead soldiers stretched out beside each other. The face of one of them was already black, but another was remarkably well preserved, his head, 'lightly inclined, rested on the grass. He looked serious and gentle.' Drawing closer, Olivier noted the name on the shirt badge of the third body. It was 'Lutz'. 'These are Swiss', someone in the crowd remarked.[4] This encounter with a dead compatriot was the closest Olivier came to the carnage of those days.

While the Swiss poet watched the events from his apartment window, the young wheel-fitter Jean-Baptiste Baudry was in the thick of the fight. In a letter he wrote to his parents in the village of Sainte-Hermeline in the Vendée on 11 August, Baudry reassured them that he was alive and well and described the events in which he had taken part. On Tuesday, 27 July 1830, he recalled, a 'certain number of armed men bearing the tricolour flag' and chanting *Long live the constitution! Down with the Bourbons!* and *Down with the ministers!* had swept through town, entering the boutiques, inns and workshops and inviting everyone to join them in confronting the garrison that was 'marching in all the streets of Paris to maintain good order'. While others made their way to the rue Saint-Honoré, the Hôtel de Ville or the porte Saint-Denis, Baudry had gone early in the morning to the Faubourg Saint-Antoine, a working-class district of the capital. On the way, the group he was with swelled from 800 men to more than 25,000. Among those who joined their ranks was his old friend Ouvrard, who happened to see him from his window and came to fight at Baudry's side, 'despite the tears of his wife and his little daughter'.

In the Faubourg Saint-Antoine, Baudry, Ouvrard and their fellow insurgents soon found themselves face to face with a regiment of the line, supported by infantry of the Royal Guards, a regiment of lancers, a regiment of cuirassiers, gendarmes and a battery of artillery from Vincennes, all commanded by Auguste Frédéric Louis Viesse de Marmont, Duc of Ragusa. An aide-de-camp appeared and invited them to lay down their arms or prepare 'to bite the dust', but they replied that they were not afraid of dying; the aide-de-camp had merely to chant *Long live the constitution!* and *Down with the king!* and they would retire immediately. Furious at this affront, the aide-de-camp gave the order to fire. The battle that followed lasted from ten o'clock in the morning until just after six in the evening. Despite heavy losses, the insurgents succeeded not only in holding their positions, but also in driving their opponents back with bayonet charges. One thousand men were detached to take control of the soldiers' powder magazine. By the time cuirassiers arrived to take back the magazine, the rebels had taken two pieces of cannon and deployed them at the end of the Pont d'Austerlitz, where they drove the troops back three times with gun and artillery fire – fifteen years after the end of the Napoleonic Wars, it was still easy to find men with the training to load and fire field guns. Having secured the magazine, they marched to the place de Grève in front of the Hôtel de Ville to support the insurgents fighting there.[5] At midnight, when the battle came to an end, the insurgents remained in control of the square.

But alas! What a piteous sight. It was hardly possible to take a single step on the place de Grève without stepping on a corpse, even though they had already loaded five boats full of them. ... The whole of the night from Wednesday to Thursday was a time of alarms for us. At the slightest noise we were called to arms. The dark hours were used to take stones up into the apartments from the first to the very last storey [so that they could be thrown down at the troops if the need arose], and all the lanterns were smashed to pieces and the trees of the boulevards were all cut down to make barricades to prevent the cavalry from passing though. Eventually in all the streets and on all the boulevards and the quays there were barricades everywhere and it would have been very difficult for the garrison to retake the positions it had lost.[6]

There was further bitter fighting around the Tuileries and the Palais-Royal on Thursday, but the insurgents won the day, bayonetting their opponents without mercy (especially the hated Swiss guards of the king, one of whom was the Lutz encountered by Olivier next to the Louvre). After a relatively quiet Friday, Baudry joined a detachment that marched out of the city in pursuit of the fleeing Charles X. At the château de Saint Cloud to the west of Paris, they drove away the Royal Guards, seized their cannon and entered the château, only to find that the king had recently left for Rambouillet. 'But we had the pleasure of finding his dinner', wrote Baudry, 'which we ate with no further ado, and it did us more good than it did him.'[7]

'Those poor people!' exclaimed Countess Marie d'Agoult when she first heard the dull thud of cannon fire at around 5 p.m. on Tuesday, 27 July. Whereas Olivier and Baudry were supportive of the opposition to the recent government measures, the mood among the people around d'Agoult, who published her memoirs under the pseudonym Daniel Stern and would later write an outstanding contemporary history of the 1848 revolution in France, was ambivalent. The friends visiting her were shocked: 'Poor people, madame? But these are wicked people who want to sack and pillage everything!'[8] Like Olivier, d'Agoult subsisted during the days of fighting on a diet of rumour: 'Our friends, our neighbours, our staff, all frightened, entered and left, each with his or her own sinister piece of news.' With the press largely silenced, her conversations with family and friends were full of questions: 'Where was the king? Where was Prince Polignac [the Prime Minister]? What was the Minister of War up to?'[9]

D'Agoult, who was heavily pregnant, was suffering from the summer heat. There was talk of moving her away from the troubles in Paris to Brussels, which was still at peace, but her brother insisted that the journey would bring more risks than benefits. The house where she lived with her mother was on the rue de Beaune, just across the river from the Louvre and the Palais-Royal. On 29 July, the fighting intensified and drew nearer. Columns of workers and students could be seen streaming along the quays towards the Louvre and the Tuileries. D'Agoult was forbidden by her relatives to go out onto the terrace. But watching from a window on the second storey, she could see an extraordinary spectacle unfold: soldiers fleeing in disarray across the gardens of the Tuileries. It dawned on her that the monarchy of Charles X was collapsing. The

Jean-Victor Schnetz, *The Battle for the Hôtel de Ville, 28 July 1830* (1830).
Many of the stock themes of the barricade paintings of 1848 can already be
seen in this image by the successful academic painter Jean-Victor Schnetz: the
view from behind the barricade, the presence of diverse social ranks and types,
the presence of the tricolour, the use of chiaroscuro to heighten the drama, and
the attention to urban architectural detail. One interesting difference: the red
flag flanks the tricolour, but it is embroidered with the words 'Long live the
constitution [*Charte*]' and thus does not imply a radical social challenge to the
liberal revolution. The revolutions of 1830 exhibited the connectivity and
cascading proliferation effects of the 1848 revolutions, but on a smaller
geographical scale.

next day, 30 July, brought a cascade of news: the Duke of Ragusa had been replaced by the Crown Prince as commander of the troops in the capital; King Charles had left the Palace of Saint-Cloud for an unknown destination; the Duke of Orleans had been appointed Lieutenant-General of the kingdom; King Charles had abdicated; his son the Crown Prince had abdicated. Placards appeared across the city urging the nation to confer the Crown on the Duke of Orleans.[10] After seventy-two hours of bitter fighting that would come to be known to French history as 'the three glorious days', the July Revolution was over. About 800 civilians and 200 soldiers died in the fighting; 4,000 civilians and 800 soldiers were wounded. In the process, the insurgents had constructed 4,000 barricades across the city.[11]

A LIBERAL REVOLUTION

Unlike the great French Revolution of 1789, and the revolutions of the early 1820s in Spain, the Kingdom of the Two Sicilies and the Kingdom of Sardinia-Piedmont, the July Revolution of 1830 took place within a constitutional political order. It was precisely the breach of constitutional discipline by the government that triggered the revolt. The *Charte* granted by Louis XVIII in 1814 had established a parliament whose deputies were regularly elected – albeit under an extremely restrictive franchise – only 0.3 per cent of the population was eligible to vote. In March 1830, the liberal majority in the chamber clashed with Louis's successor, Charles X, sparking a crisis. Of a total of 430 deputies, 221 liberals adopted a statement announcing that the king's government no longer enjoyed the support of the people. Charles responded swiftly, dissolving the chamber, announcing new elections to be held in June and working with a group of loyal officials to manipulate the public mood in the hope of producing a more conservative chamber. The king hoped that the news of the French expedition to Algeria would rally patriotic feeling behind the monarchy and collapse support for the liberal opposition. But the expedition was delayed by a storm and French troops did not penetrate the city of Algiers until 5 July, too late for the news of victory (which took five days to reach Paris) to have much effect on the election result.[12] The new chamber was even more liberal than the old: the opposition now controlled 274 mandates.

It was Charles X's decision to break with the constitution and reset the political order that doomed the Bourbon monarchy in France. The ordinances of 25 July 1830 triggered outrage, but they also ensured that the defence of the constitution, and of the rule of law more generally, would be at the heart of the resulting insurrection. When twelve journalists met at eleven in the morning on 26 July to discuss the steps to be taken in the face of the government's measures, they convened at the offices of André Dupin, legal counsel to the editors of the *Constitutionnel*. At almost the same time, a larger meeting took place at the offices of the *National*. Here, too, legal advice was crucial: present among the journalists of the *National*, the *Constitutionnel*, the *Journal de Paris* and the *Courrier français* was the famous trial advocate Mérilhou, who had won his spurs in a series of press freedom cases related to coverage of the 1820 revolution in Spain. The offices of the *National* became the unofficial headquarters of the opposition and, by shuttling back and forth and briefing all the key players, Mérilhou helped the deputies and the key judicial bodies to arrive at a consensus on the illegality of the ordinances.[13]

The joint declaration signed on 27 July by forty-three 'managers and editors of the papers currently operating in Paris' anchored their protest in the government's breach of law: 'The rule of law is suspended', they announced; 'that of force has begun. In the situation we find ourselves in, obedience ceases to be a duty.' Since the first group of citizens summoned to obey the new ordinances were the journalists, who faced the prospect of illegal censorship measures, they would have to be 'the first to set the example of resistance to an authority which has stripped itself of its legal character'. The next group to resist must be the deputies elected in the recent elections, but now illegally deprived of their mandates. Their right to convene and to represent France remained undiminished. 'France implores them not to forget that.'[14]

This was in some ways a rather narrowly conceived gesture of protest, calibrated very precisely to the nature of the provocation offered by the government. The declaration that obedience was no longer a duty *sounded* radical, but the authors of this declaration were referring not to the laws as such, which remained in force, but to the *ordinances* – hence the special salience of the two groups, journalists and deputies, whose rights had been directly affected by them, and of the lawyers, whose expertise was crucial to building a case against the government. Article 8 of the French constitution, the authors noted, obliged citizens 'to behave in conformity with *the laws*; it does not say "with the ordinances"'.

Yet the liberal notables who formulated this protest were soon joined by a wave of insurgent workers without whose support they could never have overthrown the regime. The reasons for this are not immediately obvious. The liberals themselves were initially ambivalent about the prospect of a popular uprising, even if they were quick to embrace it once it became a reality.[15] But why should shoemakers, sugar refinery workers, carpenters, foundrymen and weavers have risked their lives for the rights of a chamber whose members they were not entitled to elect? Why should they have taken up arms on behalf of newspapers many of them did not read? In an account of these years that became a bestseller in 1840s France, the socialist Louis Blanc argued that the common people were simply swept into the revolution by the liberal leaders. 'Precipitated into a movement that they could not understand', the 'men of the people' had 'yielded bit by bit to the action of that fluid that is given off by every strong agitation' and 'imitated' the bourgeois revolutionaries.[16]

But there is reason to believe that the attachment to liberal ideas may have been socially deeper than this analysis suggests. Most of the printing workers were highly literate and many of them regularly read the papers they worked for.[17] For them, the suppression of the newspapers was an existential threat; they were among the first to go out onto the streets in July 1830. And there was no shortage of venues in which liberal intellectuals could fraternize with interested workers. At the Conservatoire des arts et métiers, a free school had opened in the 1820s at which liberal activists gave lectures that were heard by 'the foremen and workers of Paris'. This was not a radical or republican milieu – most speakers did not, for example, espouse universal male suffrage – but it was openly anticlerical and critical of the government. Police observers noted that the workers who came to such events often congregated afterwards at liberal cafés and reading rooms. And workers who were drawn to this subculture had no difficulty in laying their hands on affordable reading material. There was a market in cheap literary and political texts – anticlerical and antiroyalist chronicles and other items catering to liberal tastes could be had for as little as ten sous a copy (the average Parisian worker earned between twenty and a hundred sous a day). In Paris and in many other towns, anticlericalism was something that connected liberals with urban workers. Popular tumults against the Jesuits or missionary orders often coincided with liberal anticlerical campaigns in the press or in booklets that might sell for as little as five sous.[18] And even if doctrinaire liberals used the word 'liberty' in a rather austere sense, many workers associated it with the amelioration of social conditions and access to secure and dignified labour. Finally, there was the fact that the king himself, by barricading himself behind unpopular and discredited ministers and adopting a policy of outright provocation, had stirred an almost unanimous opposition to his government. 'It was the entire nation', the writer and socialite Adèle d'Osmond recalled. 'I say *entire*, because, in those early days not a single voice, not even in the ambit of those who followed Charles X in his flight [from Paris], spoke up to justify the policies that had precipitated him into that abyss; never did a sovereign fall in the face of such unanimous sentiment.'[19]

Whatever the motives for worker militancy in 1830, the role played by 'men of the people' left a deep impression on observers. In many parts of the city, the insurgents had proved more than equal to the forces mustered by the regime. Hastily improvised barricades impeded the efforts of cavalry to attack strongpoints, but barricades were also thrown up behind advancing troops, in order to trap them in areas where they could be fired on by snipers or bombarded with stones, tiles and other missiles from the rooftops and the windows of the upper storeys.[20] In the aftermath of the violence, the liberal press did everything possible to dispel the notion that the militancy of the workers posed a threat to the high ideals of liberal revolution. The newspapers that appeared during and just after the unrest were full of vignettes about the selfless dedication of the workers engaged in the fight. It was said that Parisian workers had forced would-be looters to throw pillaged furniture and books into the Seine, saying 'Are we thieves?' Rumours circulated of a young worker who risked his life protecting a wounded Swiss guard from the rage of the crowd. On 31 July, the columns of *Le Constitutionnel* were packed with anecdotes broadcasting the saintly self-restraint of the insurgents. A group of workers had broken into one of the barracks of the gendarmerie looking for powder and guns. Finding a chest with money and bank notes in it, they said: 'That's not what we're after', shut the chest again and left. Other 'decent workers' (*braves ouvriers*) had risked their lives to bring precious objects from the Tuileries Palace to the Hôtel de Ville, where they would be safe. 'We may have changed our government', said one of them, but 'we have not changed our consciences.'[21] *Le Corsaire* reported the praiseworthy conduct of the crowd during the sacking of the Tuileries Palace.[22] And we find the same insistence on the virtuous conduct of the insurgents in eye-witness accounts: 'One cannot too much admire', wrote Juste Olivier on 30 July, 'the care that the people took not to pillage anything, not to appropriate anything, with the exception of a few bottles of royal wine. They even shot several individuals who were carrying objects away.'[23]

These rumours and anecdotes shaped contemporary awareness of what had happened. The liberal press organs were unanimous in crediting the mobilized workers for the victory against absolutism. Liberal press commentary folded the armed workers into a reassuring panorama of civic unanimity. 'The people did everything', intoned the editors of *Le Constitutionnel*. 'And by this word *people*, forever respectable, we mean the entirety of the citizenry, from the richest to the poorest.'[24] The monarchy of Louis Philippe became the first regime in history to acknowledge publicly that it owed its existence to a worker insurgency. Countless contemporary lithographs disseminated images of 'women and children, top-hatted bourgeois gentlemen and shirt-sleeved labourers, Napoleonic veterans and students of the École Polytechnique' defending together 'the embodiment of their collective resistance: the barricade'.[25]

By a royal ordinance of 13 December 1830, pensions were awarded to the widows and orphans of those who had perished in the fighting, the orphaned sisters of fallen brothers and even to the elderly parents of fallen insurgents of the 'glorious days'; arrangements were made to ensure that the children of such fallen patriots would be educated in suitable institutions, and that fighters who were permanently incapacited by amputations or illness, or whose injuries had affected their earning capacity, were granted an indemnity commensurate with their disability. A monument was to be raised to the struggle and sacrifice of the three glorious days – the July Column that stands today in the place de la Bastille.[26] Two official decorations were created to honour those who had played a role in the fighting: the 'July Cross' for people who had distinguished themselves by their devotion to the cause of liberty, and the 'July Medal' for acts of courage during the days of the revolution. The great majority of these awards went to Parisians, but there were provincial awards too: 68 of the 1,789 July Crosses went to citizens of the city of Nantes, and 65 of the 3,763 July Medals also went to citizens of Nantes, among them the doctor Ange Guépin, Saint-Simonian expert on the health of his city, the stove-fitter Michel Rocher, the carpenter Chapé and many other 'men of the people'. The *Nantais* stonemason Tessier, who kept order after a deadly clash between troops and insurgents on 30 July, received the Légion d'Honneur.[27] It remained to be seen how successful these efforts to co-opt insurgent workers into the origin myth of the new regime would be in the longer term.

To those who took part in it, this felt like a very French revolution, triggered by a specifically French crisis. But it was also a 'European media event'.[28] Contemporaries remarked on the 'roaring speed' with which the news of the Paris events raced from city to city. By 3 August, the Tübingen-based *Allgemeine Zeitung* was already citing reports from trade courier dispatches that fighting had broken out on Paris, though it was not until three days later that a fuller account of the revolutionary events was possible, based on letters from correspondents and articles in the Paris press. Like many other Europeans, the poet Heinrich Heine was taking the waters when the revolution broke out. The news reached him on the island of Heligoland just off the German North Sea coast. Years later, he recalled the excitement with which, on 10 August 1830, he opened the thick package of newspapers that had just reached him from the mainland. 'Sunbeams wrapped in printed paper' flew into his brain and set his thoughts burning. He tried dipping his head into the sea, but it didn't help: 'No water can extinguish this Greek fire.' All the guests seemed affected by the same 'Parisian sunstroke'. Even the 'poor old Heligolanders' were rejoicing, though they had only an 'instinctual grasp' of the events. The fisherman who ferried Heine across to a little sandbar said to him laughing: 'The poor people have won the day!'[29]

Even the Russian survivors of the Decembrist revolts of 1825, exiled with their families in far-off Siberia, had learned through letters of the revolutionary events by the end of August. Their wild rejoicing puzzled their guards, uneducated men who knew nothing of European politics. From Lugano to Quedlinburg to Copenhagen, publishers across Europe rushed to get eyewitness accounts, panoramas, sketches and pocket histories into print.[30]

Already in 1830, we can discern that cascading of political upheaval that would be such a striking feature of the revolutions of 1848. Just weeks after the July events in Paris, unrest erupted in Brussels, Namur, Liège and other towns in the southern Netherlands, followed by a fully fledged revolution that overturned Dutch rule in the southern

Netherlands and brought an independent Belgian kingdom into being with its own liberal constitution. Between the autumn of 1830 and the summer of 1831 further uprisings broke out across Switzerland and the German and Italian states, and a major insurrection took place in the Russian-controlled Kingdom of Poland. These were (except for the massive, doomed insurrection of the Poles against Russian rule) relatively circumscribed and short-lived upheavals. In their geographical range they fell far short of the continental revolution of 1848. But they demonstrated the fragility of the European elites and the susceptibility of the continent's societies to revolutionary contagion. Europe would spend the next eighteen years digesting the implications of 1830.

UNFINISHED BUSINESS

Once upon a time, there was a paving stone in one of the streets of Paris. No one knew where it had come from. Some said it had been brought across the sea from the new American republic. Others claimed it was a native French cobble that had formed part of one of the walls of the Bastille prison until 14 July 1789. Whatever its origin, on 27 June 1830, when a revolution broke out in Paris, it was settled down comfortably among many other stones paving the place Saint-Germain-l'Auxerrois. In the morning, it heard tell of illegal ordinances issued by the government. People cried: 'Long live the constitution!' Until that point, the stone was in a condition of perfect tranquillity. But now it felt an iron spike scratching its head. It turned to see what was up and imagine its surprise when it beheld a face with lively eyes under a pair of thick brows. It was the face of a man of the people. In vain did our stone try to wriggle back into its hole, for it was now in the power of a pair of vigorous hands and found itself planted atop a barricade. The noise of the gunfire was horrific, and every so often the paving stone felt the weight of a new victim fall upon it. There's no point in telling you what the stone experienced – its memoirs are due to appear shortly in the best bookshops. On the evening of 29 July, calm returned. A family of kings fled to Cherbourg and from there to Scotland. Our paving stone was now transferred to the front of the Palace of the Tuileries, where a new family of kings had taken up residence. Today everyone has forgotten the old paving stone of the people's barricade. And now they are going to put it into one of the dykes that the ministers are building around the royal palace. Once the paving stone protected the people against a king. Today it protects a king against the people.

This 'story of a paving stone' appeared in *La Glaneuse*, a left-republican Lyons newspaper, on 29 November 1831.[31] Fables of this kind were fashionable at the time. In 1833, the free-styling poet Eugène de Pradel, moderately renowned in Paris for improvising intricate poetic combinations around words proposed by his audience, published a short story under exactly the same title in a famous literary anthology. De Pradel related the recollections of a loquacious stone that had witnessed a tragic love affair in a Parisian garden and subsequently found itself pressed into service as a weapon during the fighting of the Glorious Days.[32] In the anonymous 'Memoirs of a Looking-Glass', a talkative mirror told of how it had once reflected the countenance of Napoleon, been discarded by the returning Bourbons because of the carved imperial eagle crowning its frame, and thence made its way down the tiers of the social structure through the apartment of a *grisette* who entertained male companions and then into the drab room of a simple artisan.[33]

Because the experiences of such non-human protagonists occupied a larger timeframe than a single human life, they offered the enjoyable fiction of an innocent, radically non-participant eye on the spectacle of historical change. Story and history could seamlessly merge. The story of the stone in *La Glaneuse* proposed that history had stopped in its course. Far from inaugurating a new and better era, the revolution of 1830 had merely installed a new iteration of monarchy, no less remote from the interests of the people than its predecessor. *La Glaneuse* was a tiny operation, run on a shoestring and serving a small audience of provincial republicans.[34] After repeated battles with the censors and a spell in prison for the editor, it shut down in 1834. But the story of the paving stone that defended the Bastille and then became a weapon of the people, only to wind up embedded in another royalist rampart, captured the enraged frustration that defined the politics of political dissent after 1830.

To be sure, the 1830 revolution brought changes, both symbolic and substantial. The new king did not inherit his office – he was elected by the two chambers (albeit with many absentees). The tricolour of the revolution replaced the old royal standard. France now enjoyed the benefits of a new franchise with twice as many electors, though the proportion of citizens entitled to vote rose only from 0.3 to 0.5 per cent of the population, an increase from 140,000 to 241,000 of a population of around twenty-six million. The privileged constitutional status of the Catholic Church was downscaled: whereas the *Charte* of 1814 had identified Catholicism as the official state religion, the revised version described it merely as 'the religion preferred by the majority of the French'. Whereas the kings of the Restoration had sworn an oath to the constitution as part of the coronation ritual, the new monarch did so 'in the presence of the two united chambers' (Art. 65). Article 14 curtailed the sovereign's power to override the laws. Elections were extended to the general councils of districts (*arrondissements*) and municipalities, which had hitherto been appointed by the authorities.

These were not trivial achievements, but they were very *liberal* achievements. The still strongly plutocratic national franchise, the heightened ritual eminence of the constitution, the mildly anticlerical correction to Catholic privilege and the incremental quality of the whole project, embodied not in a new constitution, but in a *Charte révisée*, breathed the spirit of moderate liberalism and the educated, propertied class whose worldview it expressed. The new settlement had little to offer those whose disquiet with the old regime was centred on social demands. This was a problem, because there was at first no relief from the economic crisis that had helped to bring the revolution about, and the early 1830s, still overshadowed by disruptions in the food supply, witnessed intense strike activity, especially in the capital, where there were eighty-nine strikes in the years 1830–33. Barely a year had elapsed before the Lyons uprising of 1831 foregrounded the social grievances of those who remained excluded from the formal political life of the new regime. This was the context for the story of the stone in *La Glaneuse*: the journal's editor, Adolphe Granier, was a member of the Provisional General Staff of the Lyons insurrection and his employees fought alongside the insurgents.

SOCIAL REVOLUTIONARIES

The July Revolution of 1830 marked the spectacular triumph of the *juste milieu* politics of the most moderate liberals, but it also inaugurated a new form of political opposition centred on a growing republican movement. This was in some ways a surprising development, because the term republic, recalling the First French Republic of 1792–1804, was still strongly associated in French memory with state terrorism and continental war; after 1815, enthusiasm for it had survived mainly underground in fragile and exiguous secret associations and networks.[35] It was the July Revolution that breathed new life into the republican idea. Founded on 30 July 1830, the republican 'Society of the Friends of the People' was led by activists who had played a key role in the insurrection. The scientist and public health reformer François-Vincent Raspail, a pioneer of the cell theory in biology, had been wounded attacking the barracks of Sèvre-Babylone; the revolutionary socialist Louis-Auguste Blanqui had been among those who stormed the Palais de Justice; Godefroy Cavaignac, the son of a regicide Montagnard (left-wing) member of the convention of 1793 who had fled France at the Bourbon Restoration, had helped to plant the tricolour flag on top of the Louvre. Although the number of members was modest (perhaps 300), the Society also ran a journal; its meetings in the rue Montmartre usually attracted between 1,200 and 1,500 interested fellow travellers; the print-runs of its brochures could be as high as 8,000. Carbonari, freemasons, neo-Jacobins and Saint-Simonians gravitated towards the Society, gathering and exchanging ideas. This was not a proletarian milieu: the second-wave republicans were medics, merchants, students and literary people. Their horizons were international and cosmopolitan. The Society mounted protests in support of the Polish struggle against Russia and helped to find lodgings for Polish refugees, some of whom became members. 'To support the emancipation of peoples against the efforts of tyrants', a Society manifesto of October 1831 declared, 'is a sacred duty for a free nation.'[36]

The republican opposition was not unanimously committed to direct action against the Orleanist regime. As republicanism grew, it acquired a broad palette of political flavours ranging from moderate and liberal groups to the socialist left. Some left-republicans favoured mounting an armed assault on the authorities, but there were socialist republicans who, like Louis Blanc, renounced conspiracy and violence. Nevertheless, the clashes between the government and the hard core of its most implacable enemies had a spectacular quality that impressed itself upon public awareness. Three insurrections that shook Paris during the 1830s revealed both the structural weakness and the increasing radicalism of the far left.

On 5 June 1832, at the Parisian funeral of a popular general, a veteran of the Napoleonic Wars known for his ties with the political opposition, clashes with the police flared into an insurrection that quickly spread from the Faubourg Saint-Antoine to the central district near the rues Saint-Denis and Saint-Martin. The insurgents broke into gun shops, disarmed guard posts and constructed barricades across the narrow streets of the medieval heart of the city. In less than two hours, the Prefect of Police later recalled, they seized 4,000 rifles and other munitions and occupied nearly half of the city.[37] The army, the National Guard and the Municipal Guard were called in until the point was reached where the government's forces numbered nearly 60,000 men. Fighting went on all night, the city echoing with the thud of artillery barrages. About twenty-four hours after the uprising had begun, the last barricades were shelled to fine rubble and the streets fell silent. The insurgents had suffered around 800 casualties in dead and wounded.[38] This was the historical episode that would inspire the climactic barricade scenes in Victor Hugo's *Les Misérables*. Two days later, when Heinrich Heine visited the morgue where the bodies of the killed had been taken to be identified by friends and relatives, he found people forming long queues, as if they were waiting outside the Opéra to see Meyerbeer's *Robert le Diable*.

The government mounted vigorous attacks on the Society of the Friends of the People, fining and arresting key members, shutting down the meetings in the rue Montmartre and prosecuting the leaders for breaches of the Law on Associations. The trial that followed the insurrection of 1832 shed light on a left-republican milieu in which the relatively mellow, bourgeois figures of 1830 were already making way for (mainly skilled) workers with a preference for direct action. When the Society of Friends of the People collapsed in the aftermath of the unrest, a new association, known as the Society of the Rights of Man and the Citizen took its place as the leading republican formation.

It was the efforts of the government to crush this network that triggered a further insurrection in April 1834. Protests had erupted in the streets of Paris in response to new laws limiting the freedom of association and expression. Excited by reports of the second weavers' insurrection in Lyons, and confident that they enjoyed the support of progressive elements of the population, the Society of the Rights of Man launched an uprising in the capital. This was a different kind of venture: not spontaneous in the manner of 1830 or 1832, but planned in advance. Barricades went up across the Right Bank between the rue Saint-Martin and the rue du Temple and around the Sorbonne on the Left Bank of the river. This time, the police response was swifter and better organized. By evening, the insurgent groups around the Sorbonne had been dispersed. At dawn on the following day, the National and Municipal Guard closed in on the barricaded areas of the Right Bank, engaging the insurgents in the streets and flushing them out of residential buildings, a process attended by at least two sprees of indiscriminate killing.

On the rue Transnonain in the Saint-Martin area, members of the 35th Battalion of the National Guard entered a building believed to be the source of shots that had killed an officer and the troops gunned down or bayonetted a dozen occupants over several floors. The artist Honoré Daumier memorialized this event, which occurred just three blocks from his home, in a monumental lithograph. Entitled *Rue Transnonain, le 15 avril 1834*, it depicts a working-class family massacred during the raid. This was not an action scene; Daumier chose to depict the moment of eerie calm after the violence; terror exists only in the traces it has left, in dishevelled corpses, murky bloodstains and an overturned chair. It is the viewer who must reconstruct in her own mind the horrors that have just transpired.

When the leaders of this group disappeared in their turn into jail and the movement went underground, a new and yet more radical body emerged, the Society of Seasons, led by three men of the hard left: Louis-Auguste Blanqui, Armand Barbès and Martin Bernard. The emphasis was now less on the removal of monarchy, which was taken for granted, and more on an all-encompassing agenda of revolutionary social transformation, to be achieved through collaboration with cadres of armed worker activists.[39] The insurrection they launched on Sunday, 12 May 1839, went wrong from the start. Around 400 activists attacked gunshops, confiscating weapons, taking control of guard posts and attacking the prefecture of police. Driven away by troops and National and Municipal Guardsmen, who were quick to move to the centre of the insurgent-controlled area, they broke up and barricaded themselves into several streets on the Right Bank. There were short, savage bursts of violence as insurgents and security forces fought it out in various locations with a range of weapons, including swords and axes. By eleven in the evening, the barricades had been reduced and the insurgents killed, arrested or dispersed. The casualties were much lower than in 1832: there were twenty-eight deaths among the soldiers and guards, and sixty-six civilians were killed, of whom twenty-seven were bystanders – among them was the eighteen-year-old

Honoré Daumier, *Rue Transnonain, 15 April 1834*. In this haunting image, Daumier depicts a working-class family massacred during reprisals that followed an attempted insurrection in the capital. The artist focuses not on the events, but on their aftermath. This was a work of imagination – Daumier did not personally enter the room – but the date included in the title announced that it was also the image of a historical event. Unlike so many of Daumier's prints, *Rue Transnonain* does not elicit laughter or ridicule, but silence and horror.

shawlmaker Minette Wolff, who was killed by a stray bullet as she rushed to get inside her house.[40]

The first analysis of the political vision that animated the insurrection of 1839 was conducted by the investigators and lawyers who assisted in the prosecution of the surviving rebels before the Court of Peers. An exhaustive search of the clothes, dwellings and hiding places of the dead, the captured and their suspected contacts turned up numerous notebooks and planning documents, on the basis of which it was possible to construct an image of the inner life of the Society of Seasons. At the lowest level, members were formed into a group of seven known as a 'week', whose chief was called 'Sunday'. Four weeks meeting together were known as a 'month', led by an officer known as a 'July' and three of these in joint session composed a 'season', commanded by a leader known as a 'Spring'. When four seasons came together, they formed a 'year', led by a 'revolutionary agent'. The aim was twofold: by ensuring that each cell remained ignorant of the doings of the others, the Society hoped to prevent its cadres from being infiltrated by police informers, and by operating in small units it hoped to evade the strictures of the Law on Associations. These hermetic structures recalled the cellular hierarchies of the Carbonari.

Tellingly, the chief counsel for the prosecution of a number of the accused was none other than Joseph Mérilhou. This fascinating figure had been a high-ranking member of the French Carbonari, a brilliant defender of prosecuted journals under Charles X and the foremost legal adviser to the liberal insurgents of the Glorious Days of July 1830. Now the scourge of the Bourbons had become a pillar of the July establishment. 'As you can see', Mérilhou told the court, 'it's not simply a political revolution [the plotters] have in view, it's a social revolution; it's property that they want to revise, modify and transfer.'[41] Far from representing a progressive vision, Mérilhou insisted, the politics of the conspiracy was a journey back into the year 1793, the year of the Jacobin dictatorship and the Great Terror. In this way, Mérilhou ousted the far left from the progressive historicity of the moderate liberals.[42]

The activists of the Society of the Seasons had increasingly isolated themselves from the rest of French political society, which, for the most part, viewed such schemes with horror. The secretive inner structure of the Society also helped to cut the movement off from the popular classes.[43] But the insurrectionist republicans remained connected with the European exile networks. The transmission of leftist ideas in a range of variations can be tracked across the activist diaspora.[44] Heinrich Heine was struck by the sight of the national flags of the German, Italian and Polish exile communities alongside the French tricolour.[45] Among the insurgents killed during the 1839 insurrection was an exiled Italian hatter by the name of Ferrari, and the captive insurgents who later stood trial included a certain Florentz-Rudolph-Augustus Austen, known as 'Austen le Polonais', a 23-year-old Polish bootmaker from the city of Danzig who had fought in the November Uprising of 1831. Austen, whose only previous indictment in France was on a charge of beggary, claimed under interrogation to have been 'forced' to help the insurrectionaries. When it was pointed out to him in court that his numerous injuries, including bullet, sword and bayonet wounds, demonstrated beyond doubt that he had been involved in the fighting, he replied that he had been 'forced under repeated blows to accept cartridges'. The court did not believe him, and he wound up in the same dank French prison as the insurgent leaders, Louis Auguste Blanqui, Armand Barbès and Martin Bernard.

Joseph Mérilhou was right to point up the social isolation of these militants of the left. In a sense, their insistence on conspiracy was born precisely of the insight that they lacked the means to raise the masses against the prevailing order. Captured documents revealed that they anticipated installing a 'dictatorial power' invested in the 'smallest possible number of men' whose task would be to 'direct the revolutionary movement', excite the masses to enthusiasm and 'suppress those of its enemies whom the whirlwind of popular indignation had not already devoured in the heat of combat'.[46] This dictatorship would be legitimated by the fact that it was wielded not in the name of the exploiters of commerce, industry and agriculture, but of those proletarians who possessed nothing but the strength of their arms.[47]

How these activists embodied and performed the idea of revolutionary commitment was as significant as the content of their ideas. Rather than attempting to evade punishment, 'like vulgar culprits who must blush at their acts and intentions', the accused insurgents resolved to choose defenders who shared their political views – deputies, lawyers, journalists or men of letters – regardless of whether they were listed on the roll of advocates (tableau des avocats). The aim was to use the court not to evade punishment, but as a means of 'glorifying their cause and doctrines'.[48]

When he stood trial for his part in the insurrection of 1832, Louis-Auguste Blanqui refused to play the role assigned to him by the court: 'I am not standing before judges, but in the presence of enemies. As a result, there would be no point in defending myself.'[49] A number of the leading insurgents of 1839 refused to answer questions, both in police custody and before the Court of Peers. When asked why he persisted in remaining silent, Armand Barbès replied: 'Because between us and you there can be no true justice. I do not wish to play a role in the drama which is going to unfold here. You are the men of royalty and I am a soldier in the cause of equality. . . . There are only questions of force.'[50] It is the ontological radicalism of this response that is striking: in answering thus, Barbès collapsed the normative claim and the procedural grandeur of the Court into an expression of mere violence by the regime of 'the exploiters'. For the moment, this understanding of political order as the raw interplay of force was a speciality of the left; only after the revolutions of 1848 would it infiltrate liberal and conservative discourses.

In defying the political and ethical norms of 'bourgeois' society, the activists of the left invented a new kind of political self. We can see this more clearly if we compare two prison narratives of the era. What struck readers about Silvio Pellico's memoir, *Le mie prigioni* (1832), which became a classic (see chapter 2) and is still read by Italian children in high school today, was the modesty, simplicity and homiletic intensity of the writing. Nowhere did Pellico express anger or vengefulness towards those who had ensnared, betrayed, interrogated or punished him. The book focused on the writer's often labile and exalted emotional state – the sorrowful paternal love he felt for a deaf-mute waif raised by warders; his tearful happiness when he saw the handkerchief of another imprisoned patriot waving from a cell window; the anguished reflections on family and friends; the letter he wrote to a comrade in another cell using a small shard of glass wetted in his own blood; the desperate reaching towards the presence of God in the darkness and solitude of his cell; the cruelties and suffocating tedium of prison routine.[51] Politics, on the other hand, was completely evacuated from the narrative.[52] And this was essential to the book's success. If the book had simply been 'an ordinary invective against Austrian oppression, conceived and executed in the usual perfervid manner of Italian partisanship', a reviewer for the *Foreign Quarterly Review* observed, 'it would have been forgotten in a fortnight'; Pellico's 'calm, classical and moving picture of suffering insinuates itself irresistibly into the heart and will long maintain its hold on the memory'.[53]

In the prison memoir he completed in 1851, Martin Bernard, one of the three leaders of the insurrection of 12 May 1839, adopted a different approach. Born in 1808 and thus nineteen years Pellico's junior, Bernard, the younger son of a printer in Montbrison, central France, traced an emblematic journey across the early-nineteenth-century political spectrum. As an adolescent he longed to fight for Greece; in the later 1820s he devoured the journals, brochures and pamphlets of the liberal opposition. The 1830 revolution marked a turning point: he missed the action and elation of the Glorious Days, but when he returned to Paris in the following year, he was horrified at how the 'principles of the revolution' were being 'betrayed'. A cohort of 'shameless mountebanks' (*éhontés bateleurs*) had taken control of the country and were exploiting the victory. The liberals remained 'obsessed with the suffrage, the sovereignty of the people'. Bernard's thoughts, by contrast, turned towards 'critique of the social organisation'.[54] His quest for a theoretical foundation on which to develop his social critique led him first to the Saint-Simonians, then to Charles Fourier, and eventually back to Robespierre and the pursuit of 'democratic and social fraternity which was the goal of our fathers and will be the conquest of our century'.[55]

For his role in the insurrection of May 1839, Bernard would remain incarcerated in the fortress at Mont Saint-Michel, nearly a mile off the coast of Normandy, until his unexpected liberation at the outbreak of revolution in 1848. The challenges he faced in the dungeons there – boredom, isolation, cold, damp, foul air, untreated illnesses – were those that Pellico had known. But the emotional texture of his memoir could hardly have been more different.[56] For the 'touching elegy' and the soft, plangent masculinity that had animated the Italian's memoirs, Bernard substituted a posture of haughty, unbending defiance. Cautioned by the director of the prison that any infraction of the code of silence would result in solitary confinement in a tiny cell remote from the other prisoners, Bernard warned him: 'Be on your guard, sir. . . . The time will come . . . when you will be asked to give an account of how you applied these orders.'[57] Whereas Pellico was always seeking out the humanity of his warders, Bernard treated them as the nerveless tools of a regime of power, neither good nor evil in themselves, small human wheels in a large repressive apparatus.

These differences, Bernard believed, derived from the divergent ideological stances of the two men. Pellico and his fellow Italian patriots had been imprisoned for indulging 'vague, wishful fantasies of national independence and liberalism, the flickering light of eternal rights'. Bernard and his fellow insurgents, by contrast, had been 'retempered in the faith of the immortal vanquished of Thermidor [i.e. of Robespierre and the Jacobins]'. They had acted in the name of an 'idea that must regenerate the world'. It was only natural that Pellico should respond to setbacks with wistful resignation and Bernard with an implacable 'disdain' – one of the key words of his narrative. But this was not the haughty disdain of an eighteenth-century nobleman – it was a posture of self-mastery that sprang directly from his faith in the 'sacred doctrine of equality', a doctrine whose triumph was both inevitable and imminent.[58] By the later 1840s, this temperamental difference was coming to be seen as the behavioural marker of a new form of leftist politics: the enthusiastic and demonstrative politics of the old-school *exaltado*, one German newspaper noted in January 1848, was much less dangerous than the 'cold and tranquil' communist who proceeded directly towards his objective.[59]

Not everyone at Mont Saint-Michel was tough enough to live up to Bernard's ideal of stoical revolutionary masculinity. The younger men among the prisoners of 1839 chafed at the constraints of prison routine. Noël Martin, who was not yet twenty, broke the rules by shouting to the other prisoners and then resisted his guards as they led him to be chained and manacled. In the ensuing fracas he was stabbed, then kicked and beaten and thrown into solitary confinement, chained and covered in blood and bruises. It had always been difficult to communicate with the Polish radical known as 'Austen' because he spoke a curious Franco-Polish patois, a trait that had amused his judges in Paris. Austen had not observed the code of silence before the Court of Peers, trying instead to talk himself out of trouble with implausible excuses. Once in prison, he fell into a 'strange mutism', breaking his silence only to complain of imaginary things. Only after he wounded himself with a knife in his cell did the prison authorities concede that he might be mentally ill. 'Austen le Polonais' was transferred to solitary confinement and eventually moved to the asylum at Pontorson. The news shocked the radical prisoners more than his death would have done, Bernard recalled, because they all remembered:

the noble nature of this child of Poland, his tall and slender stature with the long blonde hair, the pale and dreamy countenance with the straight and regular lines; the blue eyes at one moment suffused with melancholy, at another with a singular martial ardour. We remembered his heroism on the barricade at Grenétat, where he fell pierced with twenty bayonet blows . . .[60]

THE CULT OF CLANDESTINITY

For some of those of those caught up in the political upheavals of these years, the conspiracy – as a form of political action – acquired an almost sacred status. The Pisan writer and conspirator Filippo Giuseppe Maria Ludovico Buonarroti (1761–1837), a fervent adherent to the doctrine of Jacobinism, came to wield a unique influence over insurrectionary political thinking in the 1820s and 1830s. During a long sojourn in France, Buonarroti had taken part in the 'Conspiracy of the Equals' (1796), a failed putsch against the French Directory, whose leader, François-Noël Babeuf, had intended to establish a republic designed along Jacobin lines. In 1828, Buonarroti, who was now sixty-seven and living in Brussels, published a book about the insurrection, describing in detail the meticulous planning that had preceded it and praising the Jacobin terror and the constitution of 1793. The book had a deep influence on the radical exile networks, and especially on the Italians.[61] The emotional taproot feeding Buonarroti's activism was a profound admiration for Maximilien Robespierre, whom he had met and got to know in 1793, at the height of the Terror. For Buonarroti, the purpose of the seizure of power by violent means was not political reform, but a complete social and economic reordering in the name of equality. His book was important, because at a time when the early popular histories of the French Revolution – Thiers, Guizot, Mignet – praised the moderation of the constitutional monarchy of 1789–92 and deplored the extremism of the Jacobins, Buonarroti placed Robespierre at centre stage, acclaiming him as 'the emancipator of mankind', 'the oppressed man's consolation and the oppressor's scourge'.[62] Babeuf, the executed putschist of 1796, was held up as a shining exemplar of the dedicated insurrectionary.

Buonarroti was involved throughout his life in underground networks that connected him directly or indirectly with virtually every significant

European dissenting activist between 1796 and his death in 1837. For this lifelong revolutionary, clandestinity was a way of life. After years of imprisonment and deportation to Geneva in 1806, he became a senior member of the Loge des Amis Sincères, which had been suppressed by the Genevan authorities and re-emerged under the obscure Pythagorean name 'Triangle'. And *within* this lodge, he reshaped a secret branch of the Philadelphians (a Masonic network associated with conspiratorial revolutionary activity) into a new society, to which he gave the name 'Sublimes Maîtres Parfaits' and whose objective was the republicaniza-tion of the whole of Europe. The Supreme Masters were a masonry within masonry, operating under the camouflage of the Masonic net-works. It was sometimes expedient, Buonarroti wrote, for members of secret societies to hide inside other associational structures, even if these were officially prohibited.[63] Like other networks of its type, the SMP were esoterically hierarchical: the lowest grade was called 'the Church' and was headed by a 'Sage'. The middle grade was called 'the Synod' and its members were known as the 'Sublime Elect'. 'Territorial Dea-cons' supervised the Churches, which received instructions via 'Mobile Deacons' from the 'Great Firmament' at the apex of the organization. Only once you reached the highest grade were you initiated into the socialist credo, according to which the evils of society had all sprung from the private ownership of property. Under the transformed social order of the new Republic, a programme of 1820 declared, the state would be the sole proprietor: 'Like a mother, it will afford to each of its members equal education, food and labour.' This, the Masters of the Grand Firmament declared, was 'the only regeneration aimed at by the philosophers. This is the only rebuilding of Jerusalem.'[64]

It is difficult to measure the impact of networks like these. The idea that the real motors of history might lie hidden within webs of conspir-ators enthralled contemporaries and has lost none of its attraction for restless minds. The conspirators themselves and the prosecutors who pursued them were especially prone to overrate the efficacy of such net-works. But the clandestinity of the Buonarrotian groups makes it virtually impossible to quantify or assess their membership, or even to determine which parts of them existed in the real world and which did so only in Buonarroti's head. When the secret societies mounted actual operations, these were often poorly managed: in 1823, Buonarroti dam-aged his own reputation when he sent a garrulous and impulsive young

Frenchman by the name of Alexandre Andryane from Geneva into Austrian-controlled Lombardy with a writing case full of 'statutes, diplomas and ciphers' relating to the secret networks. After various indiscretions, the papers were captured. Andryane was arrested. The débâcle cost him and a brace of incriminated Lombard patriots long years in prison.[65]

Rather than appraising radical networks of this type in terms of the (minimal) impact of their activities on the existing structures of authority, we should perhaps think of them as structures that – at least in dissenting circles – could sustain and replenish a certain compensatory emotion, valuable to those who felt stranded in the world of the 1820s and 1830s. Buonarroti did not just *expound* his politics; in his remarkable fidelity to the Jacobin past and the regretless ardour of his lifelong commitment, he embodied it too. When the Carbonaro Joachim Paul de Prati visited Buonarroti in 1830, he found 'a man of seventy, with silver hair floating over his most prepossessing countenance, with a Prometheus-like energy, bidding defiance to the powers of the earth'.[66]

Among those who read and were impressed by Buonarroti was the enigmatic and prodigiously gifted young Hessian dramatist Georg Büchner, who inferred from his reading of the Italian communist sage that neither a liberal reform of the existing social order nor the peaceful conciliation of material interests would suffice to redeem humankind.[67] There remained only the revolution from below, unleashed by conspiratorial means. In the summer of 1834, Büchner published an uncompromisingly radical pamphlet under the title *Hessian Courier*. In eight pages of incantatory prose, Büchner and his collaborator, the pastor Friedrich Ludwig Weidig, who redacted the harshest passages of the text before publication, painted a dark picture of the relationship between the peasants of Hesse-Darmstadt and the prosperous landowners and functionaries who controlled the country. The populace was their flock; they were 'its shepherds, its milkers and knackers', they 'wrapped themselves in the skins of the peasants. The 'plunder of the poor' was in their houses. 'The tears of widows and orphans [was] the grease on their faces'. 'You pay them six million florins in tax, so that they can govern you, which is to say: make you feed them and rob you of your human and civil rights. Behold the harvest of your sweat.' The pamphlet closed with an unequivocal call for violent insurrection:

Filippo Buonarroti, portrait by Philippe Auguste Jeanron. Buonarroti's *History of Babeuf's Conspiracy of Equals* (1828) became a talismanic text for revolutionaries of the hard left. It revived interest in Robespierre and the policies of the Jacobin regime of 1793–4. This accomplished journalist and agitator embodied a new social type: the lifelong, full-time conspiratorial revolutionary who gave everything to the struggle.

He who raises his sword against the people will perish by the sword of the people. . . . You have dug in the earth all your long lives; now dig a grave for your tyrants. You have built fortified castles; now tear them down and build a house of freedom.[68]

The readers of these words were instructed not to rise immediately, but to stay alert and wait for a signal from 'messengers of the Lord', who would give the order to rise up when the moment was ripe.

There was no insurrectionary network behind this venture, just a small circle of eloquent and imaginative men, and there was no reason whatsoever for believing that the largely illiterate peasantry of Hesse-Darmstadt would follow such heralds of freedom into the dangers of an insurrectionary struggle. But this was the stuff that the nightmares of prosecutors and interior ministers were made of. Like so many of the radical conspiracies of these years, this one was betrayed in advance to the police by a spy. The authors and their associates were hunted down as soon as the pamphlet had appeared. Georg Büchner hid and then fled across the border to France and Zurich, where he would die of typhus in 1837, at the age of twenty-three. But his friend and collaborator was less fortunate. Weidig had already been arrested once in 1833 for his involvement in preparing the great liberal festival at Hambach (see p. 211). After publication of the *Hessian Courier*, he was arrested again. The defence offered by his brother-in-law Theodor Reh, a Darmstadt attorney-at law and liberal activist who would later serve as a deputy in the German revolutionary parliament of 1848, was in vain. After two years of mistreatment in the detention centre (*Arresthaus*) at Darmstadt, Weidig committed suicide.[69]

The *Hessian Courier* – leaving aside the enduring power of its language – was a study in political futility. Even Buonarroti had warned of the difficulty of 'convincing the multitude' of the value of revolutionary innovations – hence his insistence on the need for a revolutionary dictatorship.[70] The men around Georg Büchner possessed neither the means of persuasion nor the means of coercion. They were in communication with dissenting intellectual networks in Germany, France and Switzerland, but there were no revolutionary cadres on hand to seize control of the levers of power.[71] The authors of the *Courier* couldn't even agree with each other – Büchner was so offended by Weidig's alterations to his original text – intended to mute its radicalism! – that he subsequently refused to be associated with it. Nothing remained but the eloquent dream of a mass uprising sanctioned by justice and God, and the martyrdom of poor Weidig, whose name would reverberate for years across the radical networks.

Lives of this kind were propelled by a political commitment that was new in its scope and intensity. Louis Auguste Blanqui, lifelong revolutionary and orchestrator of clandestine networks, who joined his friends Barbès and Martin Bernard in the dungeons of Mont Saint-Michel after the failed Parisian uprising of 1839, embodied the type of the absolute activist. Born in 1805, Blanqui was twenty-two when he took part in his first armed protest, and he took part in every major Parisian insurrection, except for the February Revolution and the Commune of 1871 (for which he had a good excuse: he was already in jail outside Paris when they broke out). Blanqui never gave up, because, for him, the work of revolution would not be finished until the bourgeois social order lay in ruins. 'You have confiscated the rifles of July, yes', he told the *Cour d'assises* at the trial of the Parisian insurgents of 1832, 'but the bullets have been fired. Every bullet of the workers of Paris is on its way around the world. They are constantly finding their targets and they will continue to do so until not a single enemy of liberty and of the felicity of the people remains standing.'[72] By 1881, when he died at the age of seventy-six, he had spent a total of thirty-three years in the prisons of the monarchy, the empire and the Republic.

Blanqui's political vision, like Buonarroti's, was anchored in a devout attachment to the Jacobin experiment of 1792–4, though Blanqui did not share Buonarroti's admiration for Robespierre, whom he saw as a an enemy of the 'revolutionary spirit'.[73] A successful insurrection, as Blanqui imagined it, would secure power by means of a dictatorship: all laws would be suspended while the dictator, supported by a compact band of 'friends of the people' tended to the necessary public services. The duration of this dictatorship was to be indefinite and Blanqui had little to say about what would come thereafter.[74] It all looked very much like a reincarnation of the Committee of Public Safety of 1793, an institution of which Blanqui, unlike Buonarroti, had no personal experience; he knew it only through books like Buonarroti's *Conspiracy of the Equals*. It was an interesting feature of the activists of this generation that the grip of the revolutionary era on their imaginations was no less for the fact that they had not experienced it directly. Blanqui longed throughout his life to return to 'that imagined place where revolutions are born'.[75] His longing for that past was ostentatious, theatrical and performative. He affected tattered dress to signify his solidarity with the poorest of his fellow citizens and made repeated pilgrimages with his disciples to the graves of republican martyrs.

Revolutionaries of this type would play a limited role in the events of 1848, but they haunted the imaginations of conservatives, moderate liberals and police chiefs. More important was the paradigm of the entirely politicized personality that they came to represent. This was not just about the readiness to embrace martyrdom when the moment came. It was about a political commitment that was as long as life itself, a commitment that trumped all personal ties and individual pleasures. The Leipzig radical Robert Blum, not an authoritarian socialist of the Blanqui type, but a passionate supporter of parliamentary democracy and social justice who played a significant role in the events of 1848, felt acutely the tension between political calling and private attachment. In 1838, he had fallen in love with a young woman, who returned his affection. He warned his future wife that the seriousness of his temperament would allow him only a fleeting acquaintance with the 'flowering of love, the sweet, champagne intoxication of feeling and sensuality'. Eugénie was not discouraged and remained committed to the relationship. Marriage was only possible, Blum explained to his sister, if his wife understood that however happy he might be in his domestic life, he would leave her and his children as soon as a higher duty called him. Even the certainty of his loved ones' impending destitution would not keep him for one moment 'from dedicating my life to a great cause, my Fatherland'.[76]

APOSTLES OF NATIONAL INSURRECTION

In Italy, as in France, armed insurrections became more common after the watershed of 1830–31. The key figure in this transition was the Italian patriot in exile Giuseppe Mazzini (1805–72). More than any other individual, Mazzini came to preside over the European irredentist milieu of the 1830s and 1840s. For many years, he was the most wanted man in continental Europe. He remains an uncomfortable figure, difficult to situate precisely in the turbulence of those years. He was the most prominent of the Italian nationalists, yet he spent much of his life in exile, first in France, then in Switzerland and then in London, which became his home. Like the great Polish patriot Czartoryski, he ran a vast network of associations and movements dedicated to the liberation and political unification of his country. But whereas Czartoryski ran his affairs from the splendour of the Hotel Lambert, which he owned, Mazzini scribbled away for years in a cramped London bedsit. He was selfless to a fault. Such money as he earned from writing or received from his mother as an allowance tended to wind up in the hands of penniless Italian refugees or was swallowed up by the school he founded for Italian orphans. Mazzini was a passionate champion of Italian national self-determination but also the prophet of a democratic Europe of liberated nations – the notion that the emancipation of nations might give rise to conflicts between them does not appear to have troubled him, mainly because he believed that true democracies were likely to be natural allies.[77] He was a sublimely gifted founder of organizations and movements; his Giovine Italia (Young Italy) and his Giovine Europa (Young Europe) were widely admired and imitated across the world. By the 1860s, he was an 'icon' for radical liberals and democratic nationalists across Europe, Asia and the Americas. His productivity on paper and in print was astonishing: the official edition of his articles, manifestos, pamphlets, books and correspondence runs to no fewer than one hundred large volumes. Yet the political impact of his networks remains difficult to quantify.[78]

Like Gandhi, Mazzini embodied his politics: austerity and self-denial were inscribed in the gaunt face and the painful thinness of the body. 'He gave himself up as a martyr and sacrifice to his aims for Italy' wrote his friend and admirer Thomas Carlyle, who did more than anyone to fashion Mazzini's reputation in England. '[Mazzini] lived almost in squalor; his health was poor from the first, but he took no care of it. He used to smoke a great deal, and drink coffee with bread crumbled in it, but hardly gave any attention to his food.' The black attire he affected heightened the priestly mystique of his person. A 'more beautiful person I never beheld, with his soft flashing eyes, and face full of intelligence', gushed Carlyle.[79] The American journalist and critic Margaret Fuller described him as 'by far the most beauteous man' she had ever seen.[80]

But while Mazzini could be luminous at the dinner table and in the company of small groups, he was a poor orator and found it difficult to make an impression on a crowd. He possessed the 'charisma of the coterie', sufficient to mobilize a hard core of supporters, but he lacked

Daguerrotype of Mazzini, 1850s. Gaunt and pale, Mazzini embodied a politics of renunciation and risk. He invested everything he had in the struggle for an independent Italian republic.

the 'charisma of the masses' that would accumulate around Garibaldi.[81] His power to forge movements and goad enthusiasts to acts of sacrificial courage had less to do with the authority of his person than with the power of his printed words. Mazzini's writings for the patriot movement constantly recycled key symbolic terms: 'nationality', 'republic', 'duties', 'belief', 'mission', 'apostolate', 'association', 'humanity'.[82] 'Now, we need the masses', Mazzini wrote to a follower in Paris in the autumn of 1831.

> We need to find a word that may have the power to make armies of men decide to fight for a long time, desperately. Men that will be willing to bury themselves under the ruins of their own cities. Men who will follow us, believing that we will guide them to the best place for them.[83]

In the 1820s, young Mazzini had passed through some of the same patriot networks as the much older Buonarroti. At the age of twenty-two, he joined the Carbonari in Tuscany, and in around 1830 he became a member of the Apofasimeni, a clandestine militia with which Buonarroti was also affiliated. The group used Carbonari-stye induction rituals and an esoteric hierarchy, and cultivated a mood of sacrificial devotion – the Greek name meant 'those who are condemned to death'.[84] But by the early 1830s, with the failure of the central Italian uprisings, Mazzini distanced himself from Buonarroti, and the two men came to represent quite opposed approaches to the problem of revolution. For Buonarroti, equality had always been the first and last goal. He imagined a future dictatorship that would employ violence to impose equality as the crucial precondition for the emancipation of humankind.[85]

Mazzini's vision of the future, as it evolved in the early 1830s, could not have been more different: his republic, he wrote to a friend in July 1833, was 'based on the people'. But 'people' was not, for Mazzini, a social category, or at least not one that included some members of the nation and excluded others. He had no intention of exalting one class or dissolving another. 'By people, I mean the aggregate of all classes – for all people I want freedom, progress, improvement. However, I never ask: what is your name, and your rank?'[86] Mazzini's struggle was in essence not social, but moral. The *people* that constituted the nation was a community of elevated sentiment, something akin to a religious congregation. He understood the nation as 'faith, an idea of strength'. For Mazzini, the politically unified republic was the sacred goal. For

Buonarroti, the republic was merely a waystation on the road to a profound social transformation.[87]

Yet Mazzini's rejection of social revolution did not imply a renunciation of violence. In the 1830s, Mazzini became Europe's most notorious orchestrator of armed insurrections. In 1833, a failed attempt to stage a military uprising in Turin led to harsh reprisals: twelve of the captured plotters were executed and one of Mazzini's closest friends, Jacopo Ruffini, committed suicide in a Genoese dungeon after weeks of interrogations. Mazzini was tried and sentenced to death in absentia. Undeterred, he mounted a military incursion into Savoy (then one of the territories of Piedmont-Sardinia) in 1834. Some 200 Polish, Swiss, French and German volunteers (but not Mazzini himself) gathered on the Swiss side of the border under the command of the tireless Franco-Italian General and Carbonaro Gerolamo Ramorino, who had led a unit of international volunteers in Poland, then returned via Austrian Galicia to Paris and raised volunteers to fight for liberty in Portugal. But this was not Ramorino's finest hour. The venture collapsed before it had got properly underway. Among the first to defect was Ramorino himself; the Savoy government learned of the plot even before it started and Ramorino left the scene under compromising circumstances. The few conspirators who made it across the border were swiftly rounded up by the Savoyard police.

Mazzini was not discouraged by this fiasco. In the following years, there were further uprisings in various parts of the peninsula, all of them failures. The most notorious – and the most damaging to Mazzini's reputation – was the landing of the Bandiera brothers on the coast of Calabria in 1844. Attilio and Emilio Bandiera were Italian officers in the Austrian navy who had been converted by Mazzini to the national cause. Having tried and failed to trigger a mutiny against the Austrians, they fled to the island of Corfu, then under British control. Learning – probably from Mazzini – that the people of the Neapolitan mainland would rise en masse at the appearance of a determined leader, they resolved to make a landing near Cotrone (today Crotone), march to the nearby city of Cosenza gathering volunteers along the way, liberate all the political prisoners they could find and issue a proclamation of independence. Once again, everything went awry from the start. Only nineteen men could be found who were willing to join the venture. There was no support whatsoever from the locals in or around Cotrone. The young men were quickly rounded up by Neapolitan gendarmes. Two were shot in the process of capture and a further nine were subsequently executed, including Attilio and Emilio, who died with splendid dignity, bantering with the firing squad and expiring with the words 'Long live Italy!' on their lips.

Mazzini subsequently denied that he had played any role in planning the Bandiera expedition, insisting that 'those who know me know that I would never organise an expedition without sharing myself in some way or other the risks of those who might compose it'. That wasn't quite the whole truth, since in practice Mazzini repeatedly urged others into the fray without himself joining the fight. And it soon became clear that whether or not he had actually planned the Bandiera fiasco, he had been deeply involved in it – this emerged beyond doubt when a scandal broke out over the revelation that the British government had illegally opened his correspondence and leaked details from it to the Austrian authorities, who were thereby warned in advance of the timing and location of the landing.[88] In any case, Mazzini made no secret of the fact that violent insurrection was at the heart of his political programme. It was not merely the means by which a rising patriot movement should seize power; it was also a consciousness-raising experience, essential to the forging of the nation. 'Education and insurrection', he wrote in the *Manifesto for Young Italy*, were to be adopted simultaneously as mutually sustaining aims. 'Education must ever be directed to teach by example, word, and pen the necessity of insurrection. Insurrection, whenever it can be realized, must be so conducted as to render it a means of national education.'

The appropriate technique for such an insurrection, Mazzini believed, was 'warfare with bands', meaning the mobilization of partisan irregulars. This was the only means of compensating for the lack of a regular army; it could be conducted with varying numbers; it was the surest way of inducting civilians into the armed struggle and it offered a means of 'consecrating every foot of the native soil by the memory of some warlike deed'.[89] In his preference for warfare with bands, Mazzini was channelling the writings of Carlo Bianco di St Jorioz, a former officer in the Piedmontese army who had been sentenced to death for his role in the 1821 uprising, had escaped to Spain and had fought for the Riego constitutional regime alongside commanders who had become well versed in partisan warfare against the armies of Napoleon. Mazzini knew Bianco well: he was one of the founders of the Apofasimeni and Mazzini had offered him the command of the military incursion into Savoy of 1834.

Bianco's treatise on partisan warfare, *On the National Insurrection-ary War by Bands*, published in 1830, drew deeply on his Iberian experience.[90] Bianco imagined an entire nation rising as one man, dagger in hand, against the 'barbarous Goth' (code for the Austrians), waging a forever war in which each defeat would trigger a resurgence and the Italians, having withdrawn to mountain fastnesses to rearm and prepare themselves, would pour like rivers into the lowlands and fall 'with stubborn fury' upon the 'exhausted and famished adversary', purging every last trace of the 'infamous swarm' of intruders from the soil of the peninsula. These visions were painted in a declamatory *Risorgimento* Italian style full of tight, drum-like rhythms and sonorous rhetorical flourishes.[91]

For Mazzini (though possibly not for Bianco) the ultimate victory was less important than the struggle itself. 'If one insurrection fails', he wrote, 'the third or fourth will be successful. If failure is repeated, what matter? The people must be taught not resignation but steadfastness. They must learn how to rise and be defeated and rise again a thousand times, without being discouraged.'[92] The Milanese Carbonaro and republican Carlo Cattaneo put it well: Mazzini 'considered disasters victories, provided that one fought'.[93] Disasters mattered because they supplied the movement with the blood of martyrs. And martyrs mattered, because the most implacable foe of the Italian nationalist movement was the inertia, resignation, cynicism, egoism and narrow municipalism of the Italians themselves. Extraordinary sacrifices would be needed to sow the seeds of faith in such flinty hearts. The Italians, Mazzini wrote to his lover Giuditta Sidoli in 1835, were 'the vilest race, the most reluctant to act, in the world . . . if you could see the satanic smile I have on my lips for them!'[94] It was Italy that had captured Mazzini's heart, not Italians.[95]

As a conspirator and orchestrator of insurrections, Mazzini was a failure. But as a promulgator and propagandist of the democratic national idea, he was without parallel. His patriot cadres may not have succeeded in overthrowing absolutist regimes, but they were a superb instrument for the 'elaboration and diffusion of homogeneous ideas'.[96] His achievements as a publicist were stupendous: as the founder, director, editor, correspondent and printer of a cumulative total of twenty newspapers, he deployed minimal resources to global effect, doing more than any other individual to establish the language, symbology and secular theology of the Italian patriot movement. As a builder of networks, too, he wielded immense influence, establishing a web of Young Italy movements that spanned Europe and the Atlantic. It was, above all, thanks to Mazzini that an idea of Italy that had once led a dreamy life confined to romantic poetry and fiction acquired traction as a political principle. Mazzini has sometimes been contrasted with the great freedom fighter Garibaldi, as if the two represented opposed forms of political commitment, an austere activism of ideas and words on one hand, and a flesh-and-blood activism of armed struggle and physical risk on the other. And yet the two were interdependent: Garibaldi was converted to the patriot cause and sustained in it by Mazzinians, and it was Mazzini and his Young Italy affiliates worldwide who wove around Garibaldi the myth of virtuous Italian heroism that would establish him as the charismatic embodiment of the Italian movement.[97]

Mazzini worked heroically to overcome the structural and psychological disadvantages of an expatriate life. There were many others who gave up the struggle altogether, despaired or lost their mental health. The passionate exponent of 'warfare by bands', Bianco di St Jorioz, lost heart and gassed himself in Brussels in 1843. Mazzini kept at it, but his life's work was disfigured nonetheless by the predicament of long exile. Having dedicated himself to the service of a country of whose inner affairs he had less and less first-hand knowledge, Mazzini embraced a national vision that was democratic in principle but lacked social texture. 'A country', he wrote, 'is a fellowship of free and equal men bound together in brotherly accord of labour towards a single end. You must make it and maintain it as such.' A country was not an 'aggregation', it was an 'association' that could thrive only if all the individuals constituting it were free to unfold their 'powers and faculties'. Unless there were a 'common principle accepted, recognized and developed by all', there could be no country. In the final analysis, a country was 'the sentiment of love' that bound its members together. 'Caste, privilege and inequality' could have no place in such an organism.[98] This was an attractive vision, but it lacked granularity. How should inequality be banished, given Mazzini's reluctance to embrace a social revolution or to think about mechanisms of redistribution? How would the opposed material interests and ideological orientations that characterize complex societies be reconciled? Was it feasible to imagine that such exalted collective emotional states could be sustained over the longer term?

Mazzini had nothing but ridicule and contempt for the 'little mediocrities' of *juste milieu* Italian liberalism – the wistful resignation of those who wept over Pellico's prison memoirs, the diplomats who looked to foreign powers for the liberation of Italy, the gradualist exponents of 'homeopathic' progress, who believed they were regenerating Italy by opening kindergartens, convening scientific conferences or campaigning for the construction of railways.[99] But while the Italian (and European) liberals found it hard to resolve questions around the power of the sovereign, the use of armed force and the menace of social upheaval, some of them did at least model political change in a complex way that made space for a range of potentially opposed interests, all of which were in possession of certain rights. By contrast, Mazzini imagined an undivided national community in which all were 'subject in common obedience to a general faith and in the obligation of duty'. Duties were important to Mazzini because they united people. Rights were problematic because they divided them. The revolutions of the past, he believed, had been founded on a theory of rights; this was why they had ended in chaos. It was time to leave the French Revolution in the eighteenth century and seek a new kind of unity. Small wonder, then, that the Italian fascists of the twentieth century saw in Mazzini a 'slightly inconsistent but quite definite precursor'.[100] Theirs was a distorted and selective memory of the nineteenth-century statesman-exile: Mazzini's cosmopolitanism, his passionate advocacy of democracy and universal suffrage for men and women, and his belief that free nations were part of a plan for the emancipation of humankind had to be forgotten. But Mazzini's hostility to individualism, his cult of heroes and martyrs, his investment in collective states of emotion as the key to political cohesion and his almost theocratic vision of the nation as a union of souls slotted comfortably into any totalitarian programme.

Whether or not he succeeded in his own terms, Mazzini, too, exemplified the absolute activism of his era. His fight for the Italian cause went on day and night. There was no resource within his reach that Mazzini was not prepared to invest in. The partisan and freedom fighter Giuseppe Garibaldi was Mazzini's physical and temperamental opposite, but shared his deep commitment to the patriot cause, if not his single-mindedness. Garibaldi entered adult life as a merchant seaman and his conversion to the national struggle probably dated back to his contacts with Mazzinians in the Black Sea port of Taganrog. In 1833–4, he became involved in an uprising orchestrated by Mazzini in Piedmont. When this venture failed, Garibaldi was condemned to death in absentia by the Piedmontese authorities. He fled initially to Marseilles, where he lived under an assumed name, working again as a merchant seaman on routes that took him to Odessa and Tunis, always remaining in touch with the Italian diasporal networks. In the summer of 1835, he moved to Rio de Janeiro for reasons that remain unclear.

Once in Rio, Garibaldi contacted a vibrant network of exiles, some of whom were Mazzinians. He worked for a time in his old trade before entering the service of the rebel Rio Grande Republic, which was then fighting a war of independence with the Brazilian Empire. Garibaldi's Latin American years are reminiscent of early-twentieth-century schoolboy fiction: there were shipwrecks, perilous journeys up rivers, ordeals of imprisonment and torture, narrow escapes, failed business ventures and years of fighting in the complex wars of the Rio Grande region, not to mention elopement with Anita, the spirited eighteen-year-old wife of a Brazilian shoemaker.

The Rio Grande region was full of Italian exiles and migrants; Montevideo, where the Garibaldis moved in 1841, was home to 6,000 of them. From 1843, Garibaldi commanded an 'Italian Legion' of some 600 volunteers. The legion was dogged by a reputation for unreliability until February 1846, when Garibaldi and his men defeated a numerically superior enemy force of conservative 'Whites' (*Blancos*) of the Uruguayan National Party at San Antonio del Salto. It was a turning point: from this moment onwards, Garibaldi was world-famous, his exploits celebrated in print across the Mazzinian networks and taken up by the liberal media on both sides of the Atlantic. Like its Polish antecedent, the Italian Legion became a focus of hope and pride among patriots. Its sporadic involvement in the convoluted struggle known as the Uruguayan Civil War or the *Guerra Grande* (1839–51) was reframed as freedom-fighting legend. In the process, Garibaldi forged political partnerships of great value. None was more important than his relationship with Ana Maria de Jesus Ribeiro da Silva, known as Anita, a fearless comrade-in-arms and an outstanding horsewoman, who helped initiate Garibaldi into the *gaucho* (cowboy) culture of the Uruguayan and Argentinian plains. The refashioning of Garibaldi into a *gaucho*, a 'mounted nomad' who knew no master and was the antithesis of bourgeois society, endowed him with a unique hold on the romantic political imagination of the 1840s.[101] Anita would bear him four children and fight at his side until her death in 1849 at the age of only twenty-eight.

The decades before the European revolutions of 1848–9 throng with these highly mobile characters whose lives unfolded as journeys from struggle to struggle and risk to risk. Many of the older ones were veterans of the Napoleonic Wars who belonged to what has been called 'the Grande Armée of liberty'.[102] The ex-Napoleonic cohort dwindled somewhat after the 1830 revolutions, because many French veterans now made their peace with the July Monarchy. But others remained active: an example is the indefatigable Pole Józef Bem (born in 1794), a veteran of the Napoleonic armies who had won the Légion d'honneur for gallantry in the French campaign of 1813, fought in the Polish uprising of November 1830 and travelled to Portugal to fight for the liberal cause. After the outbreak of revolution in 1848, he would command a small Hungarian army with distinction in the war for independence from Austria.

In the 1830s, the depleted ranks of the old soldiers were replenished by a new generation of politicized fighters and activists. Francesco Anzani, who became one of Garibaldi's closest associates in Montevideo, had fought in the Greek Independence War, then in the Glorious Days of Paris in 1830, then in the ill-fated June insurrection of 1832, after which, having worn out his welcome with the July Monarchy, he travelled, like Józef Bem and the Italian Carbonaro Gerolamo Ramorino, to Portugal to fight for the liberals against the government of Dom Miguel, before joining the fight against the Carlists in Spain. After a spell of imprisonment in an Austrian jail in Milan, Anzani travelled to the Rio Grande, where Garibaldi entrusted him with the command of the Italian Legion. Anzani belonged to that generation of 'drops of burning blood', born 'in the bosom of war' whom Alfred de Musset described in 1836 as 'sons of the [Napoleonic] Empire and grandsons of the revolution'.[103]

POLITICAL FERMENT IN GERMANY

The July Revolution in Paris triggered a protracted political crisis across the German states. In Saxony, Braunschweig, Hesse-Darmstadt and Electoral Hesse there were major episodes of Paris-inspired civil unrest. In Braunschweig, there was open rebellion; the ducal residence was set on fire on 7 September and the widely hated duke forced to flee. Although these tumults had little to do with high politics – more important was the failure of respective administrations to meet social needs following the poor harvests of 1829–30 – they had lasting political consequences. Constitutions were subsequently granted in all four states. Hanover, too, which remained relatively quiet in 1830, subsequently received a new liberal constitution. The Hanoverian constitution of 1833 reinforced the powers of the 'Estates Assembly', made modest extensions to the franchise and subjected ministers to a degree of responsibility. Factional politics in the parliaments became more confrontational. Across the states of the German Confederation there was an unprecedented flood of political pamphlets and a proliferation of new dissenting organizations.

Of these organizations, the most important was the Patriotic Club in Support of the Free Press ('Press Club'), which emerged in 1832 to coordinate protests against the illiberal policies of the Bavarian government. Members were distributed across 116 auxiliary associations in Bavaria and neighbouring states. Whereas the printed propaganda of the Press Club tended to focus on constitutional issues and to reflect the worldview of the commercial and academic *Bürgertum,* the speeches of individual agitators often focused on social issues and adopted a more radical tone. Press Club agitation culminated in a political festival at the ruined castle of Hambach near Neustadt. The *Hambacher Fest* attracted at least 20,000 participants; the 'festival' format was chosen because, like the banquets beloved of French liberals and radicals, festivals lay outside the direct remit of the censorship authorities. And here, too, the internal tensions within the opposition were manifest; the radicalism of some of the speeches far exceeded the intentions of the organizers. This did not escape the notice of the Austrian Chancellor, Clemens von Metternich, whose spies were watching the proceedings closely. What interested Metternich was the growth of the radical fringe on the left of the liberal movement. 'Liberalism has given way to radicalism', he remarked in a letter to the Austrian ambassador in Berlin.[104]

This was a simplification. What the German upheavals revealed was a bewildering complexity in the dynamics of protest. Electoral Hesse is a case in point. Here, the upheaval of 1830 was marked by simultaneous but completely uncoordinated protests from diverse social strata. A gathering of guild superintendents convened on 2 September to formulate a petition listing their numerous grievances. Four days later, the

bakers of Kassel refused to continue baking unless there was an immediate suspension of the bread tax. When the news of the proposed
bakers' strike got out, crowds destroyed twelve bakeries in the inner
city. A contemporary reported that the people involved were 'louts, day
labourers, apprentice boys and women of the lowest class'.[105] The middle classes were only marginally involved. Concerned that these excesses
would trigger an all-out attack on property, the government ordered
that the city's marksmen's club, a stolidly bourgeois body, should be
mobilized, reinforced with politically reliable volunteers and put to
work patrolling the streets. The ministers feared the 'dangerous classes'
of the city, but, like so many of their mid-nineteenth-century contemporaries, they also worried lest malcontents from the villages in the
surrounding countryside, unsettled by the partial failure of the 1830
harvest, pour into Kassel and wreak havoc.

As happened in many other places, the liberal elite used the threat of
general unrest to extract concessions from the government. On 15 September, the elector received a delegation composed of twenty
representatives of the municipal administration armed with a petition
demanding political reforms, including a constitution. It was a signal
moment. The liberal Mayor Schomburg of Kassel introduced the petition with a brief address in which he emphasized the 'feelings of a
general emergency' that had seized the burghers of the city and warned
that a plebeian uprising was likely if the reforms requested were not
swiftly granted: 'God preserve this country from the horrors of anarchy
and the rage of the people!' When the Elector agreed to accept the petition and appeared moved to tears by the occasion, jubilation filled the
room and the square outside. Recalling this moment of elation, the liberal lawyer Friedrich Hahn, a member of the delegation, succinctly
captured the liberal attitude to popular tumult: 'not a single eye
remained dry; as if by a magic spell the revolution had been suffocated'.[106] As these words suggest, many liberals saw urban unrest both
as an opportunity and as a threat – they would do so again in 1848.

Operating through the institutions of the German Confederation and
in cooperation with the German sovereigns, Chancellor Metternich
pushed through new decrees forbidding 'festivals' and large assemblies
and tightening censorship controls. At a series of Viennese conferences
held in 1834 and attended by ministers of the German member states, he
coordinated the introduction of further policing measures designed to

support the governments in their efforts to suppress oppositional political networks. A 'Central Investigative Office' was set up in Frankfurt to
continue and expand the work of the investigative body founded in
Mainz after the murder of Kotzebue by the radical Karl Sand in 1819.
Metternich also established his own extra-territorial intelligence bureau,
known as the 'Mainz Central Police' or the 'Mainz Intelligence Agency'.
This was a more clandestine body. Its main purpose was to coordinate
political espionage and policing at the courts of Berlin, Wiesbaden, Darmstadt and Vienna. It was 'the first institutionally independent, centralized
secret service, organized as a state authority, on German soil'.[107] It built
up a dragnet of spies, agents and informers that covered the entire Confederation, with external offices (also running agents) in Zurich and Paris.
It generated immense amounts of reporting on suspect persons, associations and events. The aim was to observe expatriate and refugee networks,
infiltrate conspiratorial circles and crush insurrections before they had
passed beyond the planning stage. This was an ominous exercise in adaptive learning in which state agents mimicked and shadowed non-state
actors, forming underground structures that resembled the dissident networks. Only by acting like their opponents could the Austrian police and
their affiliates across German Europe hope to master the challenge posed
by them.[108]

Emboldened by these measures, several German states launched
crackdowns in the hope of regaining the ground they had lost through
concessions. In the Electorate of Hesse, the government clashed with the
liberal majority in the parliament over demands for a new press law,
and the country entered a period of intensified constitutional conflict
that culminated in a period of constitutional paralysis.[109] In the Kingdom of Hanover, too, there was a frontal assault on the principles of
liberal governance. The death of William IV and the ascent of Queen
Victoria to the British throne in 1837 brought the personal union
between Britain and Hanover to an end, because Hanoverian dynastic
law did not permit the succession of a woman. The new monarch was
Ernst August, a son of George III of England who had served with the
Hanoverian and British armies during the early wars of coalition against
Napoleon and later with the King's German Legion. Ernst August, who
had opposed the emancipation of Catholics in Britain, was already
known as a man of deeply illiberal views when he came to the Hanoverian throne in 1837. One of his first acts in office was to suspend the

moderately liberal constitution of 1833, on the dubious grounds that he and his relatives had not been consulted when the constitution was adopted. This produced the odd situation that one of the most reactionary sovereigns of German Europe was a British prince.

The focal point of Hanoverian political dissent was the university town of Göttingen. Seven Göttingen professors, including the famous Brothers Grimm, Jacob and Wilhelm, and the historians Friedrich Christoph Dahlmann and Georg Gottfried Gervinus, signed a joint letter of protest addressed to the President (Rektor) of their university. The protest letter simply pointed out that the signatories had taken their oath of office on the constitution of 1833 and that they objected on these grounds to its unilateral suspension. It was framed, in other words, as a procedural complaint. But the press got hold of it and there was intense interest across the German states. The new king was furious and ordered the dismissal of the seven and their banishment from the Kingdom of Hanover. Their case became a cause célèbre across the states of the German Confederation. Today, the 'Göttingen Seven' are crucial to the online identity of the city's university, where they figure as academic folk heroes who spoke truth to power. At the time, they were almost isolated within their institution, most of their colleagues taking the view that professors should stick to their books and keep their noses out of politics.

Despite many frustrations and setbacks, the German representative assemblies remained important theatres of political dispute. In Hesse-Darmstadt, a long contest between the opposition and the reactionary Grand Duke Ludwig II during the early and mid 1830s resulted in the emergence of a liberal faction under the able leadership of Ludwig von Gagern; he and his party were to win an impressive victory in the parliamentary elections of September 1847. In 1843, liberal deputies in the parliament of the Grand Duchy of Baden, who had previously taken their seats as assigned by lots, began to sit together, thereby declaring their willingness to work together under a single programme. The vote of no confidence passed by the lower chamber in the same year did not result in a change of government, but it represented a further milestone in the development of parliamentary politics in Germany.

The provincial Diets of the Kingdom of Prussia, a state with no constitution, were retrograde bodies, even by the standards of their time.[110] Yet even these rudimentary organs of representation became focal points of political change. Tentatively at first and later more emphatically, the

Diets sought to expand the role assigned to them.[111] They also began to channel political pressures from a broader, politically literate public. The signatories to a submission of 1843 from the East Prussian town of Insterburg (today Chernyakhovsk) included not just merchants and communal officials but carpenters, stonemasons, locksmiths, bakers, belt-makers, a furrier, a glassblower, a bookbinder, a butcher, a soap-maker and others. This diverse group requested not just a National Assembly and public proceedings, but also a 'different mode of representation' that would give less weight to landed property.[112] In the Prussian Rhineland, too, the provincial Diet became a focal point for liberal mobilization.[113] Slowly but surely, this energizing commerce around the Diets expanded their political pretensions.

The growth of activism around the Diets reflected a process of politicization that extended deep into the social fabric. In the Rhineland, the 1840s saw dramatic growth in the popular consumption of newspapers. Rates of literacy were high in Prussia by continental standards, and even those who could not read for themselves could hear newspapers being read aloud in taverns. Beyond the newspapers, and far more popular with the general public, were 'people's calendars' (*Volkskalender*), a traditional, cheap, mass-distributed print format that offered a mixture of news, fiction, anecdotes and practical advice and catered to a range of different political preferences.[114] Even the traditional commerce in popular printed prophecy (a precursor of today's horoscope columns) acquired a sharper political edge in the 1840s.[115] Song was an even more ubiquitous medium for the articulation of political dissent. In the Rhineland, where memories of the French Revolution were especially vivid, the records of the local police are full of references to the singing of forbidden 'liberty songs', including endless updated variations on the 'Marseillaise' and the 'Ça ira'. Liberty songs recalled the life and deeds of the radical assassin Karl Sand, celebrated the virtuous struggles of the Greeks or the Poles against Ottoman and Russian tyranny, and commemorated moments of public insurrection against illegitimate authority. From the 1830s, carnivals and other popular traditional festivities such as maypole ceremonies and charivaris also tended increasingly to carry a (dissenting) political message.[116] No fair or public festivity was complete, moreover, without travelling ballad-singers (*Bänkelsänger*), whose songs were often irreverently political in content. Even the 'peep-show men', travelling performers who exhibited trompe-l'oeil scenes inside small viewing boxes, were adept at weaving witty political critiques into their commentaries, so that even ostensibly harmless landscape views became pretexts for satire – they resembled those 'smoothtalkers' of Aimé Césaire's Belgian Congo, itinerant traders who peppered their sales patter with anti-colonial political innuendo.[117]

Across the kingdom, there was a dramatic sharpening and refinement of critical politics. The radical physician Johann Jacoby was a member of a group of like-minded friends who met for political discussions at Siegel's Café in Königsberg. His pamphlet *Four Questions, Answered by an East Prussian*, published in 1841, demanded 'lawful participation in the affairs of state', not as a concession or favour, but as an 'inalienable right'. Jacoby was subsequently arraigned on charges of treason but acquitted after a chain of trials by an appeals court; in the process he became one of the most celebrated figures of the Prussian opposition movement. By contrast with the genteel circle around Theodor von Schön, the liberal governor of the *Land* of East Prussia, Jacoby represented the more impatient activism of the urban professional classes. Like Ange Guépin and Eugène Bonamy of Nantes, he was a physician and a specialist in public health who helped the authorities to handle the horrific cholera epidemic of 1831. It was the French revolution of 1830 that brought him into politics; at that time he began a journey from moderate liberal commitments towards increasingly radical social-republican positions.

In his many links with liberals and radicals across Germany, Jacoby exemplified the thickening of dissident networks that was such a salient feature of the last years before 1848. In the early 1840s, he contributed to Robert Blum's radical Leipzig-based journal *Vorwärts!* and the *German–French Yearbooks* edited by Karl Marx and Arnold Ruge. In 1847, he made a long journey across the map of German radicalism, travelling first to Berlin and then to Saxony (where he met with Blum), south Germany, Switzerland, Cologne and Brussels.[118] Radicalized intellectuals of this type found a forum in the new political associations that proliferated across the major Prussian cities – the *Ressource* in Breslau, the Citizens' Club in Magdeburg and the Thursday Society in Königsberg, which was a more formally constituted version of the Siegel's Café group.[119] But political participation could unfold in many other contexts as well – in the Cathedral Building Society of Cologne, for example, which became an important meeting place for liberals and radicals or at the lectures given by visiting speakers in the wine gardens of the city of Halle.[120]

These hitherto fragmented liberal and radical movements gradually coalesced into loose trans-territorial coalitions. The 'Hallgarten Circle' of political activists from Prussia, Baden, Hesse, Württemberg, Nassau and Saxony had been meeting since the early 1830s at the vineyard of the liberal deputy Adam von Itzstein, leader of the opposition in the lower chamber of the Baden assembly. The tone of discussion had initially reflected the moderate preferences of the host, but in the 1840s, under the influence of the indefatigable Leipzig-based democrat Robert Blum, the circle acquired a more radical character. In September 1847, radicals and left-liberals from a number of German states (including several members of the Hallgarten Circle) met at a guesthouse in Offenburg (Baden), where they formulated thirteen demands that were subsequently approved by a public assembly numbering more than 500 participants. A month later, eighteen prominent liberal politicians from Prussia, Nassau, Württemberg, Baden and Hesse-Darmstadt – moderate deputies of the various diets and chambers – congregated at the Half-Moon guesthouse in the Hessian town of Heppenheim, where they too, after long debate, drew up a political programme.

Both gatherings brought together men who would play a major role in the revolutions of 1848. The programmes they produced reflected the divergent outlooks of the radical and moderate wings of German political dissent. The manifesto of the Offenburgers demanded freedom of the press and association and a 'democratic military constitution' on the grounds that 'only the armed citizen trained in the use of weapons can protect the state'. Other items on the wishlist included a progressive income tax, democratic representation at the level of the German Confederation and an end to the arbitrary harassment of citizens by the police. Article 10 was a call for labour protection: 'We demand that the imbalance between labour and capital be redressed. It is the duty of society to raise and protect labour.'[121]

By contrast, the Heppenheimer gathering – according to a summary composed and published shortly after the meeting by one of its members, the Baden liberal Karl Mathy – focused mainly on the need for political reforms in the spheres of communication, justice, military expenditures and the measures required to expedite the creation of a German nation-state. The tone was restrained and pragmatic, as one would expect of politicians used to working towards incremental change in close collaboration with the authorities.[122] Social issues received attention, but they were viewed with less urgency. The assembly, Mathy reported, gave 'time and attention to the means for combating impoverishment and suffering', but agreed that 'such important and sweeping subjects' were too complex to be resolved in haste.[123]

In an autobiographical sketch published after his death, Robert Blum, who was born in Cologne in 1807, recalled his childhood in the tiny house on the Fischmarkt as a time of bitter need. His father made an exiguous living as a cooper. After the father's death in 1815, the mother took in work as a seamstress. Robert helped with sewing and darning and took care of the smaller children. The mother's remarriage to a Rhine boatman, a traumatized veteran of the Napoleonic Wars who was struggling with alcoholism, brought little relief. During the famine years 1816–17, his stepfather's daily earnings were not sufficient even to purchase the bread that the family needed to survive.

It was an emphatically Catholic milieu. Cologne Cathedral was a stone's throw from the house. Blum was taught by priests and served as an altar boy in his parish church, earning pocket money he took home to his mother. His relations with the many priests he encountered as a child were ambivalent. With some he formed warm and affirming relationships. It was the priests of his parish who first spotted the boy's special intellectual ability. But there were also early and formative clashes. When Blum used the confessional to share his personal doubts about the theology of the Holy Trinity, the confessor shrank back 'as if a snake were hissing at him' and reported the boy's remarks to his colleagues.[124] Challenged by an improvised priestly tribunal, Blum remained defiant. As an adult, Blum would reject the Church entirely. Since the family was unable to afford the fees required for the Gymnasium, Blum left school at fourteen and looked for an apprenticeship. After two abortive arrangements with disreputable masters, Blum spent several miserable years performing mainly menial tasks for a master bronze-worker. By 1827, he was working for the lantern manufacturer Johann Wilhelm Schmitz, a post that brought him the opportunity to travel across Germany as a salesman and customer service manager. But the general direction of his life was still unclear and at the age of twenty-three, when Schmitz's lantern business collapsed, Blum was still drifting.

The breakthrough came with a post at the Cologne City Theatre under Friedrich Sebald Ringelhardt. Blum would remain in Ringelhardt's employment, first in Cologne and later in Leipzig, until 1847. He learned quickly on the job, advancing from a range of assistant roles to become the indispensable administrator and chief accountant of Ringelhardt's small but complex operation. The meagre salary sufficed to establish a modest household, first with Adelheid Mey in 1837, who died following a miscarriage after only 102 days of marriage, and then with Jenny Günther, the sister of a close friend.

For a man whose means had never been commensurate with his talents, the theatre offered many opportunities. Though important to the bourgeoisie, the theatre was not bourgeois: this was a world where social status and background mattered less than commitment and flair. Negotiating contracts, managing a troupe of actors of varying pay grades and distinction, balancing creative aspirations with the need to maximize ticket sales, liaising with the municipal authorities and wooing critics (or attacking them in print for harsh reviews): this world of small margins and large egos demanded political and diplomatic skills of a high order. Most importantly, Blum now found himself among people who believed in the importance and power of words.

In his youth, Blum had already acquired the habits of a passionate autodidact. Every spare minute was spent poring over books. Blum was known for his ability to read while walking through town, somehow avoiding obstacles without lowering his text (accidents did happen, but they were rare). And during the 1830s and 1840s he constantly honed his literary skills. His poems, with a few exceptions, were technically proficient but not first-rate; the dramas were overwrought epic canvases ill-suited to the stage. By contrast, the political writings reveal a man whose grip on the great issues of his day was steadily tightening.

Like his contemporaries, Blum made it up as he went along, sharing and borrowing ideas from a widening circle of like-minded friends. In the process, he moved from moderate to more radical and democratic positions. A constitutional monarchist in the early 1830s, he was a tentative republican by the time the revolutions of 1848 broke out. The 'Social Question', a term that captured the moral panic around poverty and extreme social inequality, was at first marginal to his interests, perhaps because, unlike many influential commentators on poverty, Blum had himself grown up with and in it. But in the 1840s questions of social justice became more central to his worldview.

Blum's role in the political networks of the era provided opportunities to sharpen his arguments and clarify his own position. He was one of the leading voices of the Hallgarten Circle. He was also one of the most important writers for the *Sächsische Vaterlandsblätter*, a thrice-weekly radical journal that had been campaigning for freedom of the press and soliciting donations for the victims of political persecution since 1840. From 1843, he edited the political almanach *Vorwärts!*, which attracted contributions from some of the biggest names in the radical milieu, including Johann Jacoby of Königsberg. In December 1845, he founded the Leipzig Society for the Cultivation of Oratory (*Redeübungsverein*). This was a cover organization for radical discussions, but the name was not entirely meaningless; Blum assigned great importance to oratory, which he saw as intertwined with the quest for political liberty: 'The evidence of history shows that oratory', he observed in an entry for the *Theater-Lexikon*, 'flourishes only under a free political constitution and declines with it.' The exercise of this skill called for a clear understanding, good judgement, a lively spirit, 'a strong, pleasant-sounding voice and the highest dignity when presenting an address'.[125] With these words, Blum could have been describing himself.

In the same year (1845), Blum became one of the early exponents of German-Catholicism, a vehemently anti-papal and anticlerical movement that had sprung up in the Rhineland to denounce and drive back the new culture of ultramontane mass piety exemplified by the Trier pilgrimage of 1844. Blum founded a branch of the German-Catholics in Leipzig, a provocative step in a kingdom where the royal house was Catholic and the population almost entirely Protestant. In Saxony, as in other German regions, the German-Catholics became a quasi-religious outlet for political dissent, attracting many lower-middle-class Catholics in the industrial areas and serving as a bridge between bourgeois and plebeian dissenting groups.[126]

Blum's political thinking turned on a constellation of concepts, 'freedom', 'progress', 'justice', values that, to a striking degree, he saw as mutually reinforcing. The central linking concept was 'unity'. Only a unified people could struggle successfully for freedom; only a unified nation could secure rights and justice internationally. Yet without a measure of social and legal equality, unity was impossible. In a brief essay on 'unity',

Blum observed that the pursuit of 'unity' was inseparable from the quest for freedom, because the fact of disunity within and among nations always resulted from the policy of 'divide and rule' practised by the powerful. The sundering of nations into 'estates, confessions, income groups, guilds and a thousand other splinters' enabled reactionary governments to bind individual segments of society to themselves while preventing them from coalescing and thereby maintaining them in a condition of impotence.[127] All of this suggested that the quest for unity must also be a quest for democracy, since unity was incompatible with the division of society into active and passive citizens. Like almost all his radical contemporaries, Blum confined this dream of political unity and enfranchisement to men, though he often expressed respect for the cultural and intellectual achievements of women.

On 13 August 1845, Robert Blum caught the morning train from Dresden, where he had been seeing to some theatre business, to Leipzig, where he lived. He found the city in a state of uproar. A group of friends met him at the station and explained what had happened: on the previous evening, clashes between troops and citizens had left eight dead and four wounded. The city was on the brink of an insurrection. Blum was Leipzig's most prominent radical, and his judgement and personal integrity were widely respected. His intervention would be crucial to resolving the crisis. The events of that day marked an inflection point in Blum's life.

The trouble in Leipzig had started on the day before (12 August) with the arrival of Prince Johann, brother of the king of Saxony, in the city. Political tensions had been increasing across the Kingdom of Saxony since 1843, when King Frederick August II had appointed the hardliner Julius Traugott von Könneritz as his Chief Minister, inaugurating a conservative crackdown. The authorities had stepped up the surveillance and disruption of radical networks, especially of the German-Catholics. In the evening, as the prince and his entourage dined with officers and the city's dignitaries in the Hôtel de Prusse, crowds gathered on the Roßplatz in front of the hotel. Stones shattered hotel windows.

The dignitaries were unsure of how to respond. A request for backup was sent, first to the headquarters of the city's Civic Guard and to the local garrison, where reserve troops of the Royal Saxon Army were stationed. When contingents of both forces arrived at the same time, the

Civic Guardsmen were told by a military commander that they were no longer needed and could go away. This was an insult to the militia that represented the tax-paying, law-abiding burghers of the city, and by extension an affront to municipal autonomy, but it was also a serious tactical error, because whereas the Civic Guardsmen were used to handling tumults of this kind in a supple and (relatively) commensurate way, the garrison troops were not.

In the mêlée that followed, the officers lost their nerve and the order to shoot was given. Most of the dead were found to have been shot in the back as they fled the approaching soldiers. Among the casualties was Gotthelf Heinrich Nordmann, a print corrector who had stepped out of his front door to see what was going on and was struck by a bullet in the chest, leaving a widow and five orphans in the house behind him.

On the following day, radical students summoned a mass meeting in front of the Schützenhaus, the clubhouse of the Leipzig shooting association, a large building on the edge of the inner city. Blum rushed to the scene, where his arrival caused huge excitement. For Blum, this was a completely new experience. He had often given toasts and addressed gatherings of like-minded friends. But he had never stood in front of a crowd of strangers that suddenly fell silent, hungry to hear what he had to say. And what he had to say was in some ways rather surprising. Blum did not goad his listeners to a higher pitch of outrage; he urged calm and restraint. 'Stay within the confines of the law!' he told the crowd.[128] Rather than engaging in futile acts of revenge, the citizens should focus on communicating their demands to the authorities. He proposed that they form a procession and relocate to City Hall for discussions with the municipal authorities.

This was a shrewd move. City governments in the German states were responsible to assemblies of elected representatives and thus more open to critical opinion than the local emissaries of central government. In 1848, they would serve as waystations to revolution in many European cities. In almost complete silence, a procession of 10,000 walked past the railway station south-westwards onto Goethestraße and then along the Grimmaische Straße to the Marktplatz, where the City Hall stood. A delegation formed, of which Blum was naturally a member. And once the delegation entered the council chamber, it was Blum who took the floor and formulated the surprisingly moderate and practical demands of the aroused citizenry: the dead must be buried with due

Robert Blum addresses the crowd in Leipzig, 1845. For Blum, this first appearance before an aroused crowd was a turning point in his political evolution.

solemnity; the safety of the city must be entrusted to the Civic Guard alone; the army must be removed from the city and the garrison changed; there must be a detailed public investigation of the events of 12 August. Blum stuck to this pragmatic and moderate script over the days that followed, even at the funeral of the fallen, where he delivered a eulogy that combined the expression of public anguish and political determination with notable restraint.

The authorities quickly recovered their nerve: a sham investigation concluded in a blanket exoneration of the military and an official reproof to the City Council for being so slow to act against the troublemakers; the meetings in front of the Schützenhaus were forbidden; key activists, including two of the other speakers at the funeral, were arrested. The flurry of petitions from Leipzig citizens demanding freedom of the press and association, new electoral laws and official toleration of German-Catholicism was roundly ignored. Julius Traugott von Könneritz, who was Minister of Justice as well as Chief Minister, even announced in the Saxon parliament, without any factual foundation whatsoever, that the Leipzig riot had been part of a premeditated attempt to launch a revolution planned 'weeks in advance'.[129] Fearing the suspension of commercial privileges, the city councillors signed a letter grovelling before the government and begging the sovereign not to withdraw his favour – only one conservative councillor withheld his signature, because his law-abiding neighbour happened to be among the slain of 12 August.

Blum remained free, not because he had won official approval, but because it was impossible to pin anything on him. He had not been in the city when the tumult occurred, and he had not escalated the situation but had striven publicly to maintain calm and order. 'The content of his speeches may be provocative and damaging', one baffled police spy reported to the Austrians. 'But his every word is "law" and "order"' and 'he constantly warns against every kind of extreme, refusing to countenance any remark that directly insults the government.'[130] Blum took no pleasure in his escape from official sanction. In a letter to his friend Johann Jacoby, he expressed regret and self-disgust. Surely his radical critics were right to say that he had played too softly on the pianoforte of History when the circumstances called for loud music. In his defence he could only say that the human material around him – meaning the stolid, sleepy citizens of Leipzig – seemed to rule out any other option than to proceed with great caution, however much it might grate on his nerves.[131]

But the deeper meaning of the Leipzig events was not lost on him. The writer Louise Otto, advocate for the improvement of women's social standing, was there when Blum spoke. She heard the 'sonorous voice' address the crowd. There was nothing 'demonic' or 'cruel' about Blum's public persona, she later recalled. It was rather that 'his prudence amidst all the excitement and the conviction of his words and reasoning worked a kind of magic on the aroused masses that no one has achieved before or since'.[132] For a moment, one man – an intelligent, hyperactive autodidact from a very modest background – had held a city's fortunes in his hands. After the watershed of August 1845, Blum began to throw himself with ever more energy into his political work. At the end of the year, he was elected to a seat in the city parliament – this was his initiation into the club-like atmosphere of the Leipzig commercial, professional and academic elite and his first experience of chamber politics. In the summer of 1847, finding it harder to balance the demands of his political work with his day job as theatre secretary, he resigned from the theatre post, with the intention of establishing an independent radical publishing house.

It was a bold move. The family had next to no savings; city representatives were not paid, and his wife and children had hitherto lived on Blum's meagre income from his theatre work; the chances of making a profit through the publication of works catering exclusively to radical spirits appeared rather slim. One of the first fruits of the new publishing business was a 'Christmas album' for 1847 celebrating 'Progressives of the Present' (*Die Fortschrittsmänner der Gegenwart*) and addressed to the 'freethinking men and women of Germany'. Readers could browse through six accessible portraits of male liberal and radical worthies, from the decidedly moderate Johann Adam von Itzstein, convenor and host of the Hallgarten Circle, to the Königsberg radical Johann Jacoby and, more surprisingly, the xenophobic nationalist and anti-Semite Ernst Moritz Arndt, who was celebrated here not for his xenophobia, Blum insisted, but for his steadfast support of the cause of German unity.[133]

The salient features of Blum's political talent were already on display: rhetorical skill; a resounding voice that could be heard from a distance (crucial in an era before the advent of artificial voice amplification); the personal charisma of a 'man of the people' whose short, stocky figure inspired confidence in people of modest station; a reputation for

Robert Blum, portrait by August Hunger (between 1845 and 1848). With his sonorous voice, stocky figure and unpretentious manner, Blum could win the trust of a crowd like few other revolutionary leaders of 1848.

probity and dependability; a preference for pragmatic and moderate over extremist solutions and the ability to traverse between very different communicative environments – the square and the chamber. The Leipzig moment was short-lived, as moments usually are, but it was a foretaste of the alchemy of revolution that would ultimately consume Blum's life.

SWISS CULTURE WARS

In Switzerland, as in the German states, the unrest of 1830 produced a flurry of new constitutions. A gap opened between the governments of the more liberal (and mainly Protestant) cantons and the Swiss Diet, a weak confederal body constituted under terms imposed by the Vienna Congress of 1815. An attempt to reform the central government in 1832 was blocked by the conservative (and mainly Catholic) cantons, but tensions continued to flare around the question of constitutional reform, and these became intertwined with longstanding religious divides.

In the canton of Aargau, relations between the mainly Calvinist government and the Catholic areas of the canton hit a rough patch after 1835, when the authorities shut down monastic schools and ordered convents to stop accepting novices. In 1841, having failed to block liberal reforms by means of a referendum, the conservatives mounted an insurrection, supported by convents and other religious establishments in Aargau and the neighbouring cantons. When the government sent troops to arrest the leaders of the uprising on 10 January 1841, an enraged crowd released the captives and imprisoned the men sent to arrest them. On the following day there was a clash in Vilmergen, a sleepy town in the south-east of the canton, in which two soldiers and seven insurgents were killed. Having restored order, the cantonal authorities resolved to suppress all the monastic houses within the borders of the canton, prompting further uproar. The canton of Lucerne to the south appealed against this measure to the federal Diet, on the grounds that the Swiss federal constitution forbade state interference with established religious houses. Wrangling over this question dragged on into the mid 1840s. Cases like this one revealed a deepening of religious tensions, not just in Switzerland, but across the continent.

In Aargau, the canton had polarized around the divide between liberal (mainly Calvinist) Protestants and Catholics. In the canton of Zurich to the east, the faultline ran between conservative and liberal Protestants. The trouble here started in 1839 when the radical government of the canton nominated the liberal German theologian David Friedrich Strauss to the chair of theology at the city's university. Strauss was already world-famous as the author of *The Life of Jesus, Critically Examined*, which had appeared in 1835–6, when its author was twenty-seven years old. Rather than reading the gospels as revelations of divine truth, Strauss analysed them in context as historical documents and concluded that the miracles recorded in them were in fact 'myths', by which he meant not falsehoods, but forms of language used by Christ's contemporaries to exalt him. In Strauss's reading, myth became a tool for subjecting gospel revelation to historical critique, by embedding Jesus in the semantic and folkloric world of Second Temple Judaism. It is difficult today to imagine the anger and outrage stirred by this book among conservative Christians – the reception in the Islamic world of Salman Rushdie's *Satanic Verses*, though much more violent, conveys a sense of the book's impact. Strauss was sacked within weeks of the book's publication from his post at the Tübingen seminary, and theologians across the German faculties vied with each other to condemn it.[134]

The news that Strauss was to be appointed to the chair at Zurich triggered a wave of protests from the pulpits of Protestant churches across the region. 'Councils of religion' were formed throughout the canton; these 'committees of faith', as they were soon called, became insurrectionary organizations. On Sunday, 10 March 1839, a petition demanding that the appointment be annulled was drawn up by the central 'committee of faith' in the capital and was presented to the electors of every parish. The petition declared that, in appointing Strauss, the city authorities had breached the cantonal constitution: 'There are moments in the life of states', the petitioners declared, 'when the legal authorities exceed their powers and the people rise up and punish these infractions!' Amidst frenzied campaigning, 39,225 electors – virtually the entire enfranchised population – voted for the petition; only 1,048 voted against.[135] Alarmed by the depth of the backlash, the executive Great Council in Zurich rescinded its offer of a professorial chair and pensioned Strauss off instead.

But the unrest continued to grow. To the chagrin of the faith committee, which now resembled a kind of government-in-waiting, the defenders of Strauss on the Great Council refused to resign their offices.[136] The religious questions raised by the appointment fused with issues around liberty, popular sovereignty and the limits of government authority. Preacher-agitators whipped rural parishes into a frenzy against the capital. Led by clergymen and singing hymns, columns of armed men marched on Zurich and drove out the members of the executive council. Johannes Jakob Hegetschweiler, a widely admired physician renowned for his publications on alpine vegetation, was shot in the head as he tried to mediate between the council and the insurgents; he died three days later.[137] The *Züriputsch*, as the event came to be known, marked the entry of the Swiss-German word *Putsch*, meaning a blow or a collision, into the modern political lexicon.[138]

Something rather similar took place in the very Catholic and Alpine canton of the Valais. Geography was crucial here, where the key faultline ran between the sparsely populated conservative districts of the Upper Valais and the much more liberal (though also Catholic) districts of the Lower Valais, which extends to the wine-growing districts of the Rhône river. Tension over the adoption of a more liberal constitution inevitably became entwined with religious commitments, because the Valaisian constitution of 1815 not only assigned a preponderant political influence to the less populous north but also placed the cantonal Diet under the presidency of the Bishop of Sion, the canton's most senior clergyman. The imbalance was corrected to some extent by the liberal constitution of 1839, secured after long campaigning by the southerners, but the Church continued to enjoy contentious privileges and immunities.

In the Valais as in so many other places, the fight over the constitution was flanked by a broader process of ideological polarization. When the 'priest-ridden cowherds' of the north, as Friedrich Engels called them, refused to accept the new liberal constitution of 1839 and formed an illegal counter-government under clerical control, liberal troops marched north to depose the secessionists by force. Martin Disteli's engraving of the Battle of St Leonard on 1 April 1840 shows Upper and Lower Valaisians firing on each other at close range in a steep Alpine setting thick with streams and trees and overlooked by a church. The southerners were victorious and the northerners were forced to accept the new constitution. But the battle over ecclesiastical privileges and immunities continued. The state councillor Maurice Barman, a moderate liberal, tried to mediate between north and south, but he was outflanked on the left by the radicals of Young Switzerland, a movement founded in 1835 to press for democratization and oppose the pretensions of the Church. A civil war broke out; this time, the north invaded the south. When Young Swiss volunteer riflemen met Upper Valaisian forces in May 1844, the result was a crushing defeat for the liberals. Sixty men were killed. The canton passed under conservative clerical control and many leading liberals fled into exile.[139]

As these conflicts revealed, religion had the power to deepen and widen the abyss between opposed interests. When the things that one group held most sacred were viewed with contempt by another, conversation between the two became impossible. The Zurich physician and Alpine botanist Hegetwschweiler had understood this. Born in the quiet village of Rifferschweil at the foot of the Albis, a chain of wooded hills, Hegetschweiler had become an educated man without ever distancing himself from the pious rural world of his childhood. As a physician at the beds of the sick and dying, he had witnessed every day the strength that believers draw from faith, even in moments of extreme suffering. He had warned the anticlerical radicals on the Great Council against pressing ahead with the appointment of Strauss, on the grounds that the offence this caused would never be forgiven. And when radical militiamen and armed protesters exchanged fire in the streets outside the council chamber, he was the first to run to the scene, in the forlorn hope that his standing with the people would allow him to mediate between the warring parties.

THE RADICALIZATION OF HUNGARY

In Hungary, the Diet, which met between 1802 and 1848 in the city of Pressburg (today Bratislava in Slovakia – it met in what is today the city's University Library), was the most important political forum. This was an ancient institution. It possessed medieval antecedents and had been meeting (with some interruptions) since 1527, though the Diet of 1825 was the first to be convened since 1811–12. The Diet was a representative assembly of sorts, though one in which the Magyar landed nobility and gentry were hugely preponderant – peasants, proletarians, and the Slavic minorities and the Romanians of Transylvania were not represented. The delegates of the Lower Table, chosen by the electoral committees of the respective counties, were not politicians tasked with engaging in debate, but envoys bearing the instructions of their respective County Assemblies, which usually focused on specific grievances, such as unsanctioned taxes or troop levies or the dispensing of royal patronage. This made it unlikely that the Diet would mutate into a parliament of the modern type. And yet, as with the provincial diets of Prussia and Denmark, this antiquated institution became an important forum for the articulation of political dissent. From the Diet of 1825–7 onwards, Austrian spies watching the proceedings noticed the emergence of a new oppositional grouping around the eloquent and widely travelled nobleman Count István Széchenyi.

In the first of a series of political tracts, *Hitel* (On Credit), published in 1831, Széchenyi set out a sweeping critique of Hungarian political economy. A stagnant rural economy, poor infrastructure and outmoded institutions condemned Hungarians to a life in backwardness and poverty. As remedies, Széchenyi proposed improved education and transparency, a national bank, export premiums and, above all, adequate legal protections for the provision of credit. Credit was not just a means of facilitating investment, it was part of a virtuous system based on trust and probity.[140] It was time for the old rural elites, composed of conservative landowning debtors, to overcome their traditional distrust of political economy, banks and paper money, and create space for a new elite of creditors, financiers and merchants.[141] Nothing stood still in the world, Széchenyi wrote; why should Hungary alone remain motionless? Széchenyi was a conciliator and a coalition-builder. He preferred moderate, feasible objectives to delusional bids for perfection. 'The past is not within our power', he wrote. 'But we are masters of the future.'[142]

This was a voice at the most irenic end of the reformist spectrum, gradualist, respectful of traditional authority, keen to keep all stakeholders inside the conversation. Széchenyi resembled those later Polish exponents of 'organic work' who responded to the failure of repeated uprisings with a politically low-volume programme of constructive, patriotic engagement. Széchenyi and his allies wanted agricultural improvement, savings banks and credit facilities, modern communications. They did not seek independence or blame Austria for Hungarian conditions. But Széchenyi's mild proposals stood little chance of succeeding. In a Hungary ruled by the Habsburg dynasty, a programme of moderate reform needed the support of the Austrian government. This support was not forthcoming. Metternich knew Széchenyi socially – both men were members of the Habsburg high aristocracy – but the Austrian shunned him as an insurrectionary and refused to collaborate with him. This was a major blunder: Széchenyi embodied the best shot the Austrians would get before 1848 at a non-revolutionary path of change.[143]

Széchenyi was soon outflanked by liberals adopting more emphatic positions. In Hungary, as elsewhere, the frustration of moderate reform strengthened the case for a more radical approach. Wealthy, confident, physically imposing, eloquent in Magyar, politically Anglophile and endowed with a sociable, attractive and passionate personality, the Transylvanian nobleman Baron Miklós Wesselényi pushed dietal debate away from the politics of grievance towards the principled articulation of a dissenting political stance. He travelled across the country, addressing the county assemblies and encouraging them to communicate and coordinate with each other. Despite an Austrian prohibition, he used a lithographic press to publish the debates of the Diet and even presented his little printing press to the chamber, to the acclamation of the delegates.[144] By these and other means, he 'turned the excitement and unfixed purposes of the people to a single point'.[145] Wesselényi called for the release of all peasants from servile tenures, the equality of all before the law, taxation for all, freedom of the press and ministerial responsibility.

His demands were not novelties, Wesselényi insisted, merely 'a restoration of the ancient noble democratic constitution'.[146] His close associate, the lawyer Dénes Kemény denied that they were 'liberals'; nor did they 'oppose' the government; they merely sought the fair application of the existing laws.[147] In reality, Wesselényi's style of dissenting politics did represent a radical departure from the gradualism of Széchenyi, because it sought to establish the Diet as a national forum and a driver of reform. The Austrians understood this: in 1835, they arraigned him on trumped-up charges of treason. The investigation and trial dragged on for years, during which Wesselényi added further to his fame by rescuing large numbers of victims from a flood at Pest in 1838. By 1839, when he finally disappeared into a three-year prison sentence, he was a Hungarian cause célèbre.

Nothing the Austrians did seemed to work. Jailing Wesselényi broke his health and pushed him out of public life (at least until his triumphant return to the political stage in 1848). But it did not dent his popularity, and other yet more outspoken leaders emerged to take his place. The

Austrians tried hounding, arresting and jailing the younger, more radical figures who could be seen politicking at the diets, but this merely raised the political temperature further. Using favours and intimidation to dissuade the county assemblies from electing liberals to the Lower Table of the Diet did succeed in a few cases, but also discredited the monarchy and deepened the alienation of the Hungarian political class from Vienna. And as the style of politics became more adversarial, the political society of the kingdom began to sunder along ideological lines. The social activity around meetings of the Diet had always been segregated by status, but spectators at the 1839 Diet noticed for the first time liberal and conservative delegates, aristocrats and commoners alike, walking and lunching in separate groups.[148]

This fracturing of the Hungarian political world was in part a function of socio-economic change. A divide had opened between the aristocracy and the lower nobility or gentry, driven in part by a transformation in lifestyles. The first half of the nineteenth century was an era of rising fortunes for the Hungarian landed nobility. The demand for agricultural exports was high. But the gains were partly offset by a sharp rise in expectations. Noble families that had once been content to live in log cabins now insisted on houses made of stone or brick. Noble delegates attending meetings of the Diet had once slummed it in tents, roasting their own meat over an open fire; now they needed apartments in which they could receive guests. Sugar, coffee, tableware, watches and imported textiles became essential attributes of elite life. For the wealthiest aristocrats, the income from huge estates and new distilleries or factories sufficed to carry the costs with ease. But many of the gentry saw their much smaller incomes eaten away by the need to maintain standards. Even as revenues were rising globally for people of their social type, they felt pinched and downwardly mobile. They were getting (slightly) richer but feeling considerably poorer.[149] People of this type were less likely to be impressed by arguments grounded in the 'ancient liberties' of the Magyar aristocracy.

It is striking how many of the new generation of Hungarian liberal activists, though men of noble lineage, were in serious financial difficulties. Baron Joseph Eötvös, a highly accomplished writer who would be swept into political office by the revolutions of 1848, was always short of cash; at one point he was reduced to couch-surfing in friends' houses because he was unable to afford a place of his own. The poet and lawyer

Bertalan Szemere, descendant of an ancient family who would become prime minister in the aftermath of the revolutions, 'lived in oppressive and melancholy poverty'. And meeting expenses was perennially difficult for Lajos Kossuth, the man who came to dominate Hungarian oppositional politics in the 1840s.[150]

Like Széchenyi and Wesselényi, Kossuth understood that an effective oppositional strategy would have to intervene in the public sphere, transcending the political demarcations of the country to build a head of steam behind liberal patriotic reforms. When the government shut down the lithographic printing of dietal debates, Kossuth continued to circulate samizdat reports of the proceedings. By the autumn of 1833, he had dispatched to fee-paying subscribers across the country seventy handwritten copies of his Parliamentary Reports, in which he heightened and embellished the speeches of liberals and reformers. (Conservative speeches were either ignored or 'spiced with venomous comment'.) Even after the Diet of 1836 closed, he continued to write despatches known as the Municipal Reports from the county assemblies. The dull title notwithstanding, these texts were even more risqué than their predecessors: they attacked corrupt officials, lauded patriots and denounced conservative opponents.[151] Like Wesselényi, Kossuth was arrested, tried and sentenced to four years in prison. And, like Wesselényi, he became a cause célèbre of the kind that every dissenting movement needs. From the 'Göttingen Seven' to radical Parisian cartoonists and Italian patriots in Austrian dungeons – harassed, exiled or imprisoned political activists helped to focus political commitments.

Astonishingly, the Austrians allowed Kossuth, on his departure from jail in 1841, to edit a new political newspaper. Since the printer who proposed to go into business with him was an agent of the Austrian police, it seems that Metternich was behind this venture. Why Metternich should have taken this risk is unclear. Perhaps he hoped that the publication of a newspaper would absorb Kossuth's energy and talents and make it easier for the authorities to track the evolution of the opposition. Perhaps he thought Kossuth's intemperate tone and radicalism would alienate the *juste milieu* of Hungarian liberal opinion and thus split the reformist bloc – this was not an unreasonable hope: Kossuth was an abrasive and impulsive figure who was loathed by many Hungarian moderates, and a moderate–conservative grouping was emerging around Count Aurél Dessewffy that looked likely to mute Kossuth's impact.[152] Perhaps Metternich simply felt politically strong enough in 1841 to manage and contain the further fermentation of dissent. His political field of reference was geopolitical and European. He believed that his ability to manage domestic challenges depended on the international standing of his empire. Relations with Guizot's France were improving. If push came to shove, he could call on his allies Prussia and Russia. And if the radicals in Hungary got out of hand, he remained confident that it would be possible to mobilize the peasants and the non-Magyar nationalities against the cabals of restive magnates.[153]

Whatever the reasons for Metternich's unexpected magnanimity, the appearance of Kossuth's newspaper *Pesti Hírlap* (Pest Journal) electrified Hungarian opinion. In searing editorials, Kossuth laid into the obsolete political and social structures of the country and insisted on accountability and *glasnost* in government: 'we need transparency; out into the sunshine, gentlemen, sunshine will remedy our problems'.[154] At the same time, he published letters from correspondents across the country, establishing *Pesti Hírlap* as a national clearing house for critical opinion, the place where a sense of Hungarian political community could grow. The paper had 4,700 subscribers and is reckoned to have had around 100,000 readers.[155] Kossuth's rise was not unopposed. In 1845, Széchenyi published a polemical tract under the title *Á Kelet népe* (People of the East), in which he denounced both Kossuth's social 'radicalism' and his Magyar nationalism, which risked alienating the non-Hungarian nationalities in the kingdom.[156] In 1846, a 'Conservative Party', secretly sponsored by Metternich, emerged in Budapest; its manifesto attacked the 'blind imitation of foreign examples' and exalted the kingdom's 'ancient constitution', in an attempt to wrest one of the key words of liberal discourse from the hands of the opposition.[157]

But it was now too late to stop Kossuth. *Á Kelet népe* failed to attract much attention and did nothing to diminish Kossuth's ascendancy in national opinion. While the conservatives foundered, Kossuth oversaw in June 1847 the formulation of a declaration setting out the demands of the liberal patriots: the administrative unification of the Kingdom of Hungary, a bill of rights, economic and social reform, freedom of the press and religion, an extension of the franchise, a Hungarian Cabinet responsible to a new National Assembly, and the abolition of peasant servitude – the last point seemed especially urgent in the aftermath of the Galician horrors of 1846. The Austrian authorities forbade the publication of the declaration, but clandestine editions soon circulated across the country. The Diet elections of October aroused wider popular interest than ever before, electrifying the conversation of patriots who met in the cafés and clubs of Pest and Pressburg. There were mass banquets and parades, and when the polls opened on 18 October 1847, Kossuth's supporters marched to vote in closed ranks adorned with red, white and green feathers in reference to the Hungarian tricolour. There were rapturous victory celebrations when Kossuth was elected to a seat. A showdown of some kind between the government and the opposition in the Diet seemed imminent. The excitement belied the fact that of the very small and male dietal electorate of the county of Pest – 14,000 noblemen in a county with 600,000 inhabitants – fewer than 5,000 had bothered to vote.[158]

ECLIPSE OF A BOURGEOIS MONARCHY

By the early 1840s, the French government was starting to look fragile. In the chamber of 1842, the government commanded the support of 185 conservative and twenty-five 'doctrinaire' liberal deputies. Against them were ranged two formidable blocs, the 'left-centre' and the 'dynastic left', led by two energetic lawyers, Adolphe Thiers and Odilon Barrot, each commanding 100 mandates, plus a raggle-taggle group of around twenty-five legitimist ultra-conservatives and crypto-republicans. The most important chink in the government's armour was the one that had also bedevilled the constitutional monarchy of Charles X: no matter how solidly the government was situated within the confines of the 'political nation', that nation remained extremely small, thanks to the extremely restrictive franchise. Yet King Louis Philippe and his ministers refused to countenance electoral reform and adopted a policy of constitutional inertia that would come to be the regime's greatest liability.

The politician who, more than any other, presided over and defended this policy was the foreign minister and effective head of government, François Guizot, who dominated the political life of the Orleanist monarchy from October 1840 until the outbreak of revolution in 1848. Guizot, a person of prodigious intellect, talent and energy, is one of those mid-nineteenth-century figures who explode every one of the categories we would like to place them in. He was an indefatigable writer of political and literary essays and especially of histories – particularly of England – whose scholarly productivity flagged only slightly during the years when he was the most important politician in France. His early essays on the history of European and French civilization were admired across Europe. He was a powerful advocate of educational reform and of history as a discipline anchored in rigorous source work. He was a distinguished interpreter, editor and translator of Shakespeare. An austere Calvinist in his spirituality and temperament, he was also capable, when he saw the need, of unscrupulous political manoeuvring. He was a liberal with conservative instincts. Respected but never popular, Guizot lived eighty-seven years and wrote seventy books, many of them substantial, multi-volume works.

Like everyone of his generation – he was born two years before the outbreak of the French Revolution – Guizot was deeply marked by the turbulence of the Revolutionary and Napoleonic era.[159] He was six years old when his father was decapitated on the scaffold at Nîmes on 8 April 1794, and the memory of this episode shaped his politics in later life, imprinting him with a deep abhorrence of extremism and political violence. He remained a determined opponent of the death penalty and always pursued a politics of moderation that sought to steer clear both of revolutionary insurrections and of counter-revolutionary reprisal by tracing a middle path between absolutism and popular government. At the end of the Napoleonic Wars, he aligned himself with the monarchy of Louis XVIII and the 1814 *Charte*, but he was repelled by the reactionary crackdown that followed the murder of the Duc de Berry and eventually became one of the leading lights of the liberal opposition to Charles X. In March 1830, as member for Lisieux, Guizot delivered a speech to the Chamber of Deputies in which he called for greater political freedom. It was the acclamation of this address by a majority of deputies that triggered the dissolution of the chamber by the king, the first in a train of events that would culminate in the revolution of 1830.

After 1830, Guizot remained a defender of the elitist limited monarchy established under the *Charte révisée*. He had always believed that 'popular sovereignty' was a false and illiberal concept favoured by those who preferred insurrection and turbulence to order and justice. If the authority of the monarchical state were to serve liberal ends – meaning: the protection of liberties – then it could not, Guizot argued, be derived from the people. Rather, authority should be wielded by a well-educated and trained governing class, whose elevated awareness of the public interest would overcome the despotism of special interests. The aristocracy of merit that would perform this task had nothing to do with the hereditary nobility of the Old Regime; it must rather be a class whose education and wealth marked them out as possessing the 'capacity' to govern.[160] Underlying these arguments was a lively vein of fear, fear that universal suffrage might unleash anarchy, a fear grounded not just in Guizot's memories of 1794 but also in the historical awareness of a French Protestant. Being Calvinist in France implied a deep memory of violent persecution by the Catholic majority. This was not some ancient fear left over from the reign of Louis XIV. The area around Nîmes, where Guizot was born, had seen intense interdenominational violence during the 'White Terror' of 1815 and again in 1830.[161]

Whatever his underlying motivations, Guizot embodied the ambivalent pathos of those political actors who hope to arrest the process of change at what seems in their eyes to be the optimal moment. Those who called for an extension of the franchise, he told the Chamber of Deputies in a speech of 1843, should bear in mind that the struggle for the 'conquest of rights' was now over in France. The task for the present was to 'make use of those rights'. His advice to those who aspired to enter the political nation was: 'inform yourselves, enrich yourselves, improve the material and moral condition of France; these are the true innovations; this is what will satisfy the ardour of the movement, the need for progress that characterizes this nation'.[162] Torn from its context, the phrase 'enrich yourselves' would later be hurled in Guizot's face by those who denounced his government as a class regime run by and for the property-owning bourgeoisie.

Despite these structural weaknesses, the 1840s were a period of consolidation for the July Monarchy. The threat from the far left that had produced such spectacular explosions in the 1830s receded. The insurrectionary networks remained socially isolated; many of their leaders now languished in jail. On the right, too, it seemed that the monarchy's enemies were running out of steam. The influence of the legitimist ultra-conservatives who favoured a Bourbon restoration was waning. Something similar had happened to the Bonapartism that had driven so many violent local uprisings in the later 1810s and 1820s. The myth of Napoleon continued to grow under the July Monarchy, but it shed its association with insurrectionary protest. Adulating Napoleon no longer meant rejecting the monarchy, it signified pride in a resurgent France. The July regime strove with some success to attach the prestige of the dead emperor to itself. The Vendôme column, erected in 1806–10 by Napoleon I to commemorate the victory at Austerlitz, was restored in 1833. When the Palace of Versailles opened as a museum in 1837, the displays included a room full of imperial paintings, including portraits of the emperor.[163]

In December 1840, the 'return of the ashes' (*retour des cendres*) became the occasion for the greatest set piece of the Orleanist regime, a funeral procession of breathtaking solemnity and opulence. The body of Napoleon, which had not in fact been cremated, but remained astonishingly well preserved inside its airtight coffin, was transferred back from St Helena and transported through the streets of Paris to the Dôme des Invalides on a thirteen-ton catafalque drawn by sixteen black horses caparisoned in cloth of gold. The event was orchestrated by the king and his senior minister, Adolphe Thiers (who was no longer in office by the time the procession took place), in the hope of consolidating the patriotic standing of the regime. The divisive political legacy of the empire was airbrushed out of the picture; Napoleon now stood for the abstract idea of a strong and unified France.[164] Although a group of students used the occasion to sing the 'Marseillaise' and chant 'Down with Guizot', the event passed off peacefully. The fears of those deputies who had refused to vote in favour of the transfer, lest the reappearance even of a dead Napoleon provoke a national insurrection, were shown to be unfounded. Guizot, who had stayed out of sight all day, was relieved. 'It was pure spectacle', he wrote to a friend in London. 'Napoleon and a million Frenchmen came into contact . . ., and there was no spark.'[165]

And this in turn helps to explain why two attempts by the dead emperor's exiled nephew, Louis Napoleon, to seize power by means of an insurrection, were such a miserable failure. In 1836, Louis Napoleon, who had been living in Switzerland, turned up at Strasbourg in the uniform of an artillery officer, won the support of a local regiment in the manner of Napoleon I during the 'Hundred Days' and seized control of the prefecture. The garrison commander alerted the authorities, a loyal regiment arrived, the mutineers were surrounded and Louis Napoleon fled back into Switzerland, then to America and later via Europe to England. The second attempt was even more farcical: in August 1840, hoping to capitalize on the wave of sympathy unleashed by the announcement that the French government intended to repatriate the remains of his uncle, Louis Napoleon gathered a contingent of armed men, much as the Bandiera brothers would do in Calabria three years later, sailed across the Channel in a hired boat and tried to seize the port of Boulogne.[166] After a short exchange of fire in the course of which one of the conspirators fell into the water and drowned, another was wounded and yet another shot dead, the remaining would-be putschists were simply arrested. Louis Napoleon was tried and sentenced to life imprisonment in the Fortress of Ham. Asked in the Court of Peers what his profession was, he replied, to the amusement of the gallery: 'French prince in exile.' The press heaped ridicule on the enterprise. 'We would be laughing with contempt at these acts of folly, if blood had not been shed', declared the *Constitutionnel*. 'You don't execute madmen', commented the *Journal des Débats*, 'but you do lock them up.'[167] Louis Napoleon remained a captive until 1846 when, disguising himself as a carpenter, he shouldered a pile of lumber, ambled out of the fortress, and escaped to England. If proof were needed that popular attachment to the memory of Napoleon did not equate with the threat of a Bonapartist insurgency, this was surely it.

While some of the old threats receded, the Guizot regime benefited from a spell of clement economic weather. The 1840s saw – at least until 1846 – robust economic growth. Under the framework established by the Railway Law of June 1842, the state financed 900 miles of new track, creating tens of thousands of new jobs and a boom in the mining, metallurgical and chemical industries. And the Guizot administration proved adept, within the narrow confines of the French 'legal nation', at playing the system to the government's advantage. The opposition deputies in the chamber were, for the most part, loyal to the regime, even if they were critical of specific policies. And the government could build majorities by buying the support of independent deputies from poor rural constituencies or securing the election of salaried officials in the pay of the state.[168] Periodic diplomatic triumphs, such as Guizot's success in promoting a French candidate as husband for the Queen of Spain in 1846, could trigger waves of patriotic enthusiasm.

The picture was less rosy outside the boundaries of the legal nation. The political press had played a central role in the July Revolution, channelling the decision to resist the 'ordinances' and helping to bed down the new order once the insurrection was over. Editorial offices had doubled as insurrectionary headquarters. Thus began the era of a 'civilization of the journal' in which newspapers articulated and organized public opinion to an extent that has become unimaginable in our time.[169] As the new regime settled in, however, an oppositional press of a new type began to wage a war of words and images against the government.[170] A growing corps of full-time journalists generated some work of lasting distinction, but also a barrage of partisan denunciation characterized by 'insult, calumny, tendentious reporting and simplistic, skewed judgements of complex issues'.[171] Images were at least as important to this war as written arguments. None was more devastating to the dignity of the new royal house than the cartoonist Philipon's famous likening of the king's head to a pear, an exercise in physical ridicule that rapidly metastasized across the political print of the July Monarchy. This amiable, rotund fruit became part of a 'caricatural jargon or code' that, whenever it was invoked, turned all those who recognized it into conspirators against the constitutional regime.[172] A good example is an image by Charles-Joseph Traviès published in Philipon's journal *La Caricature* in 1832. Entitled 'Crock of Shit' (*Pot de mélasse*), it shows a large black cast-iron pot wearing a sash emblazoned with the word *mélasse* (meaning molasses, slang for excrement), on top of which teeters an almost featureless pear. In the background, a crowd representing a variety of French social types gawks disgustedly at the puzzling contraption.[173]

The government did what it could to clip the wings of the critical press. Police harassment of the journals was commonplace. Newspaper offices were searched after every public disturbance, their editors taken to court and saddled with heavy fines and prison sentences. The editors of *Quotidienne*, the *Gazette de France*, the *Tribune* and the *National* were confined so often in the prison of Sainte-Pélagie that special quarters were kept for them there. The press laws of September 1835 created a list of new offences to make prosecutions easier. Some newspapers, like the *National*, survived with the help of loyal subscribers and patrons; others collapsed, like the *Tribune*, which by the time it closed in May 1835 had undergone 111 lawsuits and been fined a total of 157,630 francs. More than thirty provincial papers were killed off by the new press laws of 1835.[174]

Yet there was little the government could do to stem the tide of mockery. Trials and draconian penalties merely underscored the importance of the press. Philipon, the most brilliant and impertinent of the cartoonists, used his trial to demonstrate before the court with pen and paper how the king's face could be transformed into a pear in just four steps. He wanted to make the point that in removing the king's sideburns and facial features, in stripping him down to a piece of fruit, he had abstracted his image from the monarch's person to the principle of power that he represented. 'Is the king designated in our drawings by his name, by his titles, or by his insignia?', Philipon asked the court. 'Not at all! You must therefore believe me when I say it's power I'm representing by a sign, by a resemblance that can just as well belong to a mason as to a king; but it's not the king.' If the courts found him guilty, they would have to prosecute all drawings of fruit.[175] This prank made Philipon for a time one of the most celebrated men in Paris. To be successful, 'representation does not have to convince, it has only to occur'.[176]

The laws enacted to protect the king against hostile or insulting images and commentary merely diverted the flow of invective away from the sovereign towards the ministers, conservative deputies in the chamber and prominent figures in bourgeois society. Even Daumier's lampoons of bourgeois life, which ridiculed the vanity and self-serving hypocrisy of middle-class families, were not politically innocent, since they alluded indirectly to the 'bourgeois' character of the Orleanist monarchy, in which the king and his family featured as the embodiments of a social order founded on the greed and venality of selfish family networks. In this way, the in fact rather virtuous and sentimental private life of the French royal family was turned against it as an index of corruption.[177]

What all of this meant was that the Orleanist regime remained on the defensive in the face of an overwhelmingly hostile press. It was also less and less visible because the rising frequency and seriousness of assassination attempts had led to a drastic reduction in public appearances. Guizot continued to prosecute newspapers whenever he could – there was a flurry of such cases in 1847, when the police uncovered the operations of a few secret societies – but this merely fed the anger of the journalists. It was an example of what can happen when a political regime gets bogged down in perpetual skirmishes with the media. In 1847, the American minister in Paris was struck by the contrast between the 'fire' pouring forth from the press on 'all public measures' and the apparent contentment of the prosperous classes of Paris.[178]

Political banquets were another means by which ideas and emotions circulated outside the narrow walls of the franchise. Banquets had always performed both a social and a political function in France. They were crucial to the sociability of corporations, extended families, communities (religious and secular) and professions. And royal banquets had long been part of the repertoire of representational power, allowing monarchs to perform their metaphorical role as nourishers of the people. But their function changed after the end of the Napoleonic Wars. From 1818 onwards, liberals began using banquets to critique the policies adopted by the governments of Charles X. Funded by subscriptions paid by the electors, they were used to prepare elections or congratulate opposition deputies on important speeches. They became the means by which the evolving milieu of the liberal opposition manifested itself in visible social form. And they were important because they took place in public and thereby advertised the liberals' rejection of clandestinity and their commitment to legal and transparent forms of political communication. In this sense, they were the polar opposite of the shadowy gatherings of Buonarroti's 'sublime perfect masters'. Meticulously organized, from the order of speakers to the decorations and the content of toasts and menus, the banquets were not an insurrectionary device, but a cohesion-building tool.

Once they had been hoisted into power by the revolution, the liberals stepped up their banqueting, though they were now celebrating the powers that be. But new oppositional groups, disappointed with the limits of what had been achieved, soon began to orchestrate their own banquets. While the 'dynastic opposition' ran banquets of the liberal type – well-behaved and dominated by enfranchised notables – the republicans invented the 'democratic banquet', open to all and with cheaper subscriptions accessible to the lower middling classes or even to workers. These gatherings sometimes ran to thousands of guests; there were long political speeches and playful manipulations of the standard iconography, such as the breaking accidentally-on-purpose of a bust of the king overlooking the diners. In 1840, a banqueting campaign in support of an extension of the franchise gathered more than 20,000 guests across the country. Whereas the early liberal banquets had functioned as a kind of addendum to the chamber, a form of sociability that unfolded within the boundaries of the tiny electoral franchise, their more radical successors aimed to expand the horizons of the political nation. In 1847, the failure of bills proposing franchise reform triggered a national campaign of protest banquets whose purpose was not just to demand franchise reform, but to show that France was ready for it by highlighting the political commitment of those excluded from participation in the electoral process.[179]

These events were not the work of a single organizing executive; on the contrary, they sprang from local initiatives and reflected the diversity of opposition politics across the country. There was no agreed programme of reform and the speakers at banquets often articulated a range of positions, from polite criticisms of specific policies, to demands for the amelioration of the condition of the working classes, to the coded expression of republican sentiments, as at Damville in October 1847, where one speaker declared that 'in the state of affairs we are in, the chief remedy is a large and radical electoral reform. This is the key to all other political and social reforms.'[180] Even in its most extended form, this enlarged political nation remained a predominantly masculine space. There were rare occasions before 1848 when women made an appearance at banquets, but they were mostly confined to the margins. At the reformist banquet of Chalon in December 1847, the ladies of the town, who, according to a local paper, had 'braved the cold, damp and rain to honour this important demonstration with their presence' were permitted to take their places in a 'reserved area' located beyond the tables of the diners. The men attending the Lamartine Banquet in July 1847 marvelled at the 'beauty' and 'elegance' of the women, wives and relatives of the male subscribers, who sat in 'galleries' reserved for them on the edge of the banqueting area, wearing the elaborate regional costumes of the Bresse and the Maconnais.[181]

There was not a great deal the government could do to stop a banqueting campaign. The organizers went to great pains to avoid public order offences and there was much ostentatious lip service to monarchist flourishes, such as the loyal toast. Banquets fell outside the remit of the legislation used to police and suppress political associations – this was part of their charm in the eyes of opposition activists. They did not involve incitements to violence or other illegal acts. They were widely dispersed: the 1847 campaign encompassed major gatherings in over thirty *départements*. They were such an organically embedded social practice that ministers, many of whom had themselves previously attended and spoken at such events, were reluctant to act against them. Yet by 1847 a radicalizing momentum was unmistakeable. At a banquet in Mâcon in July 1847, the usually mild-mannered Lamartine, elated by the success of his *Histoire des Girondins*, denounced the July Monarchy as a corrupt 'regency of the bourgeoisie' and warned that if it continued to disappoint the hopes of the people, it would succumb to a 'revolution of contempt'.[182] At a banquet in Limoges on 2 January 1848, there were toasts to 'the sovereignty of the people', 'the organization of labour', 'the problem of the proletariat', 'universal suffrage', 'Jesus Christ' and 'the people' and across all banquets toasts focused on social issues outside the purview of chamber liberalism were becoming more frequent.[183] The Guizot ministry was under increasing pressure to shut the campaign down, at least in Paris. The attempt to do so in February 1848 would trigger a revolution.

TRIUMPH OF THE MODERATES: ITALY

Looking back over a long career in public life, the Bolognese economist and statesman Marco Minghetti discerned a sea change around 1840 in the expectations of politically active people in the Italian states. Most young people, he wrote, already embraced the idea of a 'great and free fatherland'. But experience had shown that conspiracies, political sects and half-cocked insurrections produced 'no useful effect'. They merely embittered the incumbent regimes, prevented civic improvements, hampered the growth of civic wealth and threw many families into poverty. Mazzini's 'mystical announcements' and his calls for 'uprisings and massacres', composed in the safety of far-off London, began to jar on patriotic ears. All of this, Minghetti wrote, suggested that 'the time had come to try a new way, a road more serious, practical and safe'.[184]

The publicist who came more than any other to exemplify this turn towards a moderate politics of gradual reform was Vincenzo Gioberti, a liberal Catholic clergyman trained at the University of Turin. Ordained in 1825, Gioberti had served for a time as chaplain at the court of King Charles Albert, became involved with patriot circles, was arrested on suspicion of conspiracy, and was briefly jailed and exiled in 1833. After a short spell in Paris, he moved to Belgium, where he worked at a private school and produced the treatise that came to define his historical role, *On the Moral and Civil Primacy of the Italians* (1843). Wordy and ponderous, this book, which ran to over 1,100 pages in two volumes, was one of the bestsellers of the pre-revolutionary decades. Eight editions appeared over five years and some 80,000 copies were sold, though the true readership was much larger. It was read throughout the Italian peninsula.

Gioberti flattered the vanity of patriots. Italy, he claimed, was the 'creator, conserver and restorer of European civilisation' and 'refinement' (*incivilimento*).[185] Only from the 'Italic genius', Gioberti wrote, could the human race receive the catalogue of civil benefits necessary to a well-tempered political order.[186] But Italy was more than an excellent nation, worthy of emulation – it was the chosen instrument of divine providence. Its uniqueness was embodied in the special role of the papacy. Eighteen centuries of history had forged an indissoluble bond between the nation and the Holy See and it was Italy's deep attachment to Catholicism that would regenerate and unify the nation, not by means of a revolution, but through a peace mediated by the Pope among the princes and the peoples of the peninsula.[187] Not the people, but the Pope-King would be the agent of Italy's revival, made possible by the establishment of a federal union of the Italian states.[188]

Why was the book such a huge success? The answer must lie in the self-consciously muted tone and substance of the book. 'Equity', 'tolerance', 'moderation', 'moderateness', 'temperateness' (*equità, tolleranza, moderazione, moderanza, temperanza*) were all key words, flanked by the Giobertian adjectives 'wise', 'sensible', 'judicious', 'impartial' (*saggio, assennato, giudizioso, imparziale*). Gioberti wanted neither parliamentary nor absolutist government; the authorities should be advised by a consultative assembly without law-making powers and informed by public discussion and debate; only this moderate solution would keep both princely despotism and popular anarchy at bay.[189] Gioberti's arguments appealed to Italians because they conjoined ideas that had previously seemed irreconcilable: the universal authority of the papacy and the national movement of the Italians; Catholic faith and political modernity; sovereign power and respect for public opinion; the historical memory of the Italian elites with the Catholic religious awareness of the masses.[190] In the sometimes somnolent cadences of Gioberti's prose, the dilemmas of modern life seemed to dissolve in a promise of tranquillity. It wasn't passionate or exciting, but to some it seemed preferable to the exalted activism of Mazzini and the dangerous enterprises of the insurrectionaries and the secret societies.[191]

Was Gioberti a liberal? It was a defining feature of liberal political thought that it presumed the inevitability of conflicts of many kinds and imagined politics as a way of mediating among opposed interests. Gioberti was not attracted to this vision. Nature, he argued, was not in itself conflictual. It was part of a harmonious created whole. Politics should strive to reflect that innate existential equilibrium. The problem with Hegelian and all other forms of dialectical thought, Gioberti argued, was that they assigned to conflict a constitutive role in human affairs: progress had to be the fruit of mutual negation. If this were true, all political life must consist of a violent oscillation between extremes.[192] For Gioberti, moderation was not the fruit of conflict, it was the constitutive precondition for a politics that sought the good of all in the manner extolled by Aristotle.[193] The task of politics was not to balance between opposed interests, but to prevent the emergence of potentially destabilizing oppositions in the first place. This was the apotheosis of moderation; it placed harmony and social peace above liberty.

In the early 1840s, Gioberti and his book became the focal point for Italian 'moderate opinion', especially in the northern territory of Piedmont, ruled by the House of Savoy. Moderates of the Giobertian type combined the 'timid advocacy of "negative" liberties' with the appeal to patriotic virtue.[194] Like Gioberti, the Piedmontese nobleman and Italian patriot Cesare Balbo argued for 'intermediary bodies without representation' in the form of consultative assemblies lacking any legislative power.[195] Another leading Piedmontese moderate, Massimo d'Azeglio, published a powerful survey of economic and social oppression in the Papal States in 1846, but the treatise he published in the following year on the emancipation of Italy had nothing to say about constitutions. D'Azeglio's solution to the misery of the masses was not representation, but better government: 'administrative uniformity, economic liberalisation and reforms fostering the rule of law'.[196] We see similar efforts in the neighbouring Papal States. Prominent moderate figures gathered around the Agricultural Society of Bologna and the weekly journal *Il Felsineo*, which ranged across many topics but took a special interest in the social problems of the region: unemployment, vagabondage, poverty and crime. The contributors, mostly well-heeled local worthies, proposed improvements to education and training, the regeneration of the traditional sharecropping system known as *mezzadria* and infrastructural investment as ways of mopping up the surfeit of unemployed young males who were seen as posing a threat to social peace. The real significance of this reformist activism lay less in the proposals themselves than in the readiness of a growing portion of the elite to view itself as a political actor with responsibilities for public safety and welfare.[197]

Although contemporaries sometimes spoke of a 'moderate party', there was never an agreed manifesto or policy programme. Anxiety about crime and threats to social stability from below were a common theme, but like followers of the other 'parties' of this era, the moderates disagreed with each other on many issues and never formed a single organization. Moderatism remained an attitude, but it was one that commanded increasingly wide support within the wealthiest social strata. Its currency reflected the emergence of a composite elite in which pragmatic and progressive figures from the northern Italian aristocracy blended with elements of the industrial, financial and cultural bourgeoisie. It was well adapted to conditions in Austrian-ruled Lombardy-Venetia because it was more concerned with capacity-building than with mounting doomed frontal challenges to the existing structure of power. In Venice, for example, reformers focused instead on establishing an association that would promote agriculture, manufacturing and commercial activity. The larger aim was to create an associative network that could 'bring the leading groups of Venetian society together into a common front'. These efforts brought together prominent activists, like the young Venetian lawyer Daniele Manin, wealthy Venetians of patrician stock, literary pretensions and expertise – criminologists, statisticians, scholars of science – the kind of people who had gathered around *Il Felsineo* in Bologna.[198]

Moderatism's centre of gravity within the wealthiest strata raised questions about its social depth. But for all its fragilities and limitations, the moderate turn in Italian liberalism was important. It connected the most conservative of the Italian liberals with the status quo politics of Guizot's France and the authoritarian liberalism of the Spanish *moderados* under Ramón María Narváez. Its charisma would be tarnished during the revolutions of 1848, which brought more-radical politicians and ideas to the fore. Yet we should not underestimate the futurity of this kind of limited politics. It operated from a centre ground across which disparate elements of a political nation defined by wealth and education could join hands. It proceeded from the current balance of political power in the societies of the peninsula, rather than from an idealized or imagined state of affairs. It was elitist, technocratic, modernizing and unashamedly counter-revolutionary. In these ways, it prefigured the reformist centrism that would dominate the political life of most European states after the mid-century revolutions.

THE ROCK OF ORDER

Against the challenges mounted by liberal and radical activists, the European authorities deployed sanctions ranging from military interventions to prosecutions, the covert sponsorship of government-friendly organizations and newspapers, and networks of spies and informants. The European security culture that emerged after 1815 deepened after 1830 as police forces collaborated internationally to track suspects who had left their own jurisdictions.[199] We have seen that police forces learned to engage with conspiratorial and underground networks through a process of adaptive mimicry, infiltrating local cells and collating information across their own transnational networks. They became accomplished at rooting out conspiratorial groups and disrupting radical networks – that is what they were good at. But whether any of this police activity delayed a revolution is highly doubtful. The revolutions that broke out in 1848 were not the fruit of long-laid plans and conspiracies, but of massive societal protests driven by a combination of political dissent and severe economic dislocation. Conservatives did their best to uncover foreign professional agitators among the fallen and wounded of March 1848, but none could be found.[200] The interest of the police in underground networks was understandable, given that these groups defined themselves as planners and authors of insurrection, but the effort to break them up distracted the authorities from the more pressing task of inoculating the existing social and political order against upheaval through far-reaching social, political and economic reforms.

In Paris, the police prepared for a new iteration of the insurrections of 1832, 1834 and 1839. According to mobilization plans drawn up after the 1832 insurrection, troops were to be confined to barracks in the event of trouble. If major acts of violence were reported, one National Guard battalion and one army battalion were to concentrate at each of seven assembly points, all of them situated in major open areas in the city. Guards from isolated posts were instructed to withdraw to these assembly points in order to avoid being captured. Once the centre or centres of the insurrection were identified, units would converge on the source of trouble and contain it. The swift suppression of the insurrections of 1834 and 1839 seemed to demonstrate the effectiveness of the new system against a conspiratorially organized, secret-society-driven insurgency. On the other hand, the French capital – along with every other European capital city except London – remained completely unprepared for the massive political demonstrations that would usher in the revolutions of 1848.[201] The insurrectionaries of this era were thus less important for their techniques or political objectives than for the fact that they unwittingly drew the gaze of the authorities away from the real threat.

More than any other statesman, it was Clemens von Metternich who came to embody the defence of the post-war European order. Metternich had helped to install the devolved constitutional settlements in Switzerland and Germany. He was at the forefront of the intensification of international political policing that took place, especially after 1830. His position at the hub of a vast network of police officers, agents and spies made him one of the best-informed men of Europe. Metternich's strategy of counter-revolutionary containment was not rooted in a cosmic vision of the clash between God and the devil, but in his experiences of the Great Disruption and in a youthful, epiphanic encounter with Edmund Burke's *Reflections on the Revolution in France*. For Metternich, Burke seemed to propose a middle path between the hard-line royalism of the French émigrés, whose absolutism Metternich found abhorrent, and the radical authoritarianism of the Jacobins. Metternich could live with change, provided it was slow, continuous and always reconcilable with 'order'. Viewed in this light he was less a continental reactionary than a British conservative Whig. 'If I were not what I am', he wrote to his friend Princess Lieven, 'I would like to be an Englishman. If I could neither be the one nor the other, I would rather be nothing at all.'[202]

The young Metternich had witnessed with his own eyes how some of his teachers, amiable figures steeped in the rationalism of the late Enlightenment, aligned themselves with the violence of the revolution. He had spent his young adulthood in the borderlands – Strasbourg, Mainz and Brussels – where the European impact of the revolution was first and most intensely felt. As the revolutionary armies spilled across the borders of France into western Germany, he had witnessed the swift destruction of the intricate devolved structures of the old Holy Roman

Empire of the German nation, which his family had served for generations. It was not just a political but also a financial disaster: most of the
family's Rhenish possessions were lost, leaving them dependent on the
income from the Bohemian estate of Königswart. Metternich was an
attentive reader of pamphlets and constitutions. He understood the
power of ideas and of the networks that propagate them. He watched
the Jacobin Club in Mainz evolve from a reading circle to an engine of
social revolution. And he saw how the revolution had transformed the
traditional order of war. In an anonymous pamphlet of 1794, Metternich described the consequences: 'Old men and children, willing or
unwilling, timid or brave, all fought in the same ranks. Peoples attacked
armies and small forces had to resist enormous masses. Thousands fell
on one side, and thousands replaced them; hundreds fell on the other,
and their places remained empty.'[203]

Deeply impressed by the ambient instability of his early years,
Metternich came to see in the quest for an all-embracing system of
tranquillity the central meaning of his life. For him, peace meant more
than the mere absence of war. The vortex of violence he had witnessed
showed that peace was vulnerable unless it was founded on robust
structures and principles – in short, on a European order. But this order
had to be of a special kind, capable of connecting the arrangements
regulating the interaction *between* states with factors ensuring a stable
social and political order *within* them. Hence Metternich's support for
interventions against the constitutional uprisings of the early 1820s and
1830s in Spain and Italy and for the intensified surveillance, infiltration
and suppression of radical and liberal networks. When his friend and
former employee Alexander von Hübner came to visit the 86-year-old
former statesman late in May 1859, only a week before his death, Metternich summed up his own career in politics with the words: 'I was
always a rock of order.'[204]

In a sympathetic reflection on Metternich's political thought, Henry
Kissinger, an admirer, exposed what he called 'the conservative dilemma'.
Conservatism is the fruit of instability, Kissinger observed, because in a
society that was still cohesive 'it would occur to no one to be a conservative'. It thus falls to the conservative to defend, in times of change,
what had once been taken for granted. And – here is the rub – 'the act
of defence introduces rigidity'. The deeper the fissure becomes between
the defenders of order and the partisans of change, the greater becomes

the 'temptation to dogmatism' until, at some point, no further communication is possible between the contenders, because they no longer speak the same language. 'Stability and reform, liberty and authority, come to appear as antithetical, and political contests turn doctrinal instead of empirical.'[205]

For all his undeniable gifts, Metternich is a textbook case of this rigidifying effect. He remained flexible and pragmatic in international affairs: he accepted and eventually supported the establishment of a Greek nation-state forged by revolution on formerly Ottoman soil. He acquiesced in the emergence of the Belgian nation-state after the revolutions of 1830 and argued against an international intervention against it. But within the area in which he wielded more direct control – the German states, Italy and his own Austrian Empire – he found it increasingly difficult to distinguish between radicals and reformers. This mistake led him, for example, to shun collaboration with the moderate and conciliatory Hungarian patriot István Széchenyi, the only ally who could potentially have slowed the ascendancy of the more intransigent Lajos Kossuth. 'Liberalism is doing fine', he quipped in a letter to Dorothea Princess Lieven. 'It is raining Sands.'[206] This was a reference to Karl Sand, a German fraternity student notorious for his assassination of the dramatist August von Kotzebue in 1819. But Karl Sand was no liberal; he was a mentally unstable fanatic who hankered after the exaltation of the wars against Napoleon and was psychically unable to resituate himself in the present. Perhaps something similar happened to Metternich. Whereas the years 1813–15 occupy more than a third of his published memoirs, composed from notes and diaries in the 1850s, the thirty-three years from 1815 until 1848 take up less than 10 per cent of the text. As his finest biographer, Wolfram Siemann, puts it: Metternich 'never managed to shake off the past when designing the future'.[207] The brilliance and agility Metternich had shown in managing the forces contending for control of the continent deserted him when he turned to the forces now awakening in European society.

'Out of the storms of our time, a party has emerged whose boldness has escalated to the point of arrogance', Metternich told a gathering of representatives of the thirty-nine states of the German Confederation in Vienna in 1834. 'If a rescuing dam is not built to contain the streaming flood, then we could soon see even the shadow of monarchical power dissolve . . .'[208] The metaphor of the dam captured the intuition of irreversible movement.

Something had been set in motion that had the destructive force of a great river in flood and the task of the conservative statesman was to contain it. In 1848, the metaphorical dam would break. For Otto von Bismarck, the dominant statesman of post-revolutionary Central Europe and in some ways Metternich's later-nineteenth-century Prussian analogue, it would no longer be a question of building dams, but of steering one's boat on the turbulent river of history.

CRACKS IN THE DAM

Little was known of Giovanni Maria Mastai-Ferretti when he acceded to the papal throne after a hurried two-day conclave on 16 June 1846, but he profited from general relief at the death of his predecessor, the stern and reactionary Gregory XVI. The old pope had died at the age of eighty; the new man, who adopted the name Pius IX, was forty-eight years old with a warm personality, an attractive countenance and a cheerful, winning manner. Whereas Gregory had opened his reign in 1831 with a wave of violent repressions, Pius's first act in office was a blanket amnesty to the political prisoners languishing in the jails of the Papal States.

The response took everyone, including the Pope, by surprise. When the amnesty was made known, it unleashed a wave of euphoria in the city. Crowds formed in the summer twilight, chanting 'Viva Pio Nono!' Contemporary witnesses speak variously of joy, delirium and intoxication. It was, one clerical observer recalled, as if a ray of divine love had suddenly descended on the town. There were extraordinary scenes on the Piazza del Quirinale, the square in front of the papal palace. Thousands of Romans converged hoping for blessing, and at around 10.30 in the evening the Pope appeared at the balcony of the palace with his hands raised in greeting, to deafening cheers and then silence as the people fell en masse to their knees to receive his blessing. 'To describe the explosion of universal jubilation', an eyewitness recalled, 'is not just difficult, it is absolutely impossible. – Everyone looks up towards this most beloved sight; all cry out in choked voices, blocked, because impeded by abundant tears of tenderness.'[209] A few hours later, at around one in the morning, an even bigger crowd assembled in the square, and for the second time that night the Pope bestowed his blessing on his people.

This was papal government in a new key: charismatic and eloquent. The American journalist Margaret Fuller, to whom we owe the most evocative and insightful eyewitness accounts of Roman events, was riding with a friend on the Campagna when she happened to see the Pope on foot, taking exercise, walking quickly in 'simple white drapery' and accompanied only by two young priests in spotless purple: 'all busts and engravings of him are caricatures', she wrote; 'it is a magnetic sweetness, a lambent light that plays over his features, and of which only great genius or a soul tender as his own would form an adequate image'.[210] And it was quickly apparent that the Pope was warming to his role, that he 'liked to please', as one observer put it.[211] Reformist initiatives brought further waves of adulation. There were judicial and prison reforms; a committee was appointed to consider the construction of railways (something Gregory XVI had refused to countenance); tariffs on staple grains were reduced to alleviate the social distress of the poor; plans were announced for gas lighting in the capital (another of Gregory's pet hates); censorship restrictions were relaxed; laymen joined priests in key administrative and deliberative organs; a civil guard manned by Roman taxpayers was created to keep order in the city. On 1 October 1847, the Pope announced that Rome was in future to be ruled by two bodies: a deliberative municipal council of one hundred members, only four of whom were to be clergymen, and a senate to consist of nine members elected by the municipal council – this concession in particular was greeted with loud rejoicings: on 3 October, a great demonstration of thanks was held, attended by about 4,000 of the Civic Guard. Stirred by the rise of nationalist sentiment in the city, Pius IX even became, in January 1848, the first pope ever to pronounce the words 'God bless Italy!' in public.

There was something volatile in this new and intense relationship between the pope and the population of Rome. Did he really have a choice about whether to bestow his blessing when thousands of citizens gathered in the square in front of his palace in the middle of the night? Over the summer months, the clamorous expressions of popular enthusiasm for the Pope began to grate on the nerves of well-to-do citizens, who feared that they might serve as a cover for crimes against property or even for political upheavals.[212] And this was indeed the core of the problem, because the enthusiasm for Pius IX soon acquired political connotations. The cry 'Long Live Pius IX!' soon morphed into: 'Long live Pius IX, king of Italy!' and to this was soon added 'Death to the Austrians!', or even 'Death to the Pope's evil advisers!' What if, as actually happened on the evening of Tuesday, 7 September 1847, crowds who had converged on the residence of the Tuscan legation to cheer Duke Leopold II of Tuscany, subsequently made their way to the Piedmontese legation to cheer Charles Albert, the king of Piedmont-Sardinia, and then, with their spirits fired up, marched into the Piazza Venezia, where the legation of the Austrians was situated? As the foreign overlords of Lombardy and Venetia and the conservative Catholic hegemon on the Italian peninsula, the Austrians were objects of obsessive hatred for Italian liberals, patriots and democrats of every stripe. The sight of Roman crowds chanting 'Death to the Austrians' and 'Long Live Italian Unity!' rang alarm bells in Vienna.[213] 'The revolution has seized upon the person of Pius IX as its flag', wrote Metternich in the summer of 1847.[214]

From Pius IX's perspective, these were profoundly unsettling developments. There were quite narrow limits to the reforms the Pope was willing to concede. He was a moderate with a progressive reputation, but not a liberal. How could the divinely appointed monarch of what was in essence a theocracy share real power over the great affairs of state with laymen and popular assemblies? There could be no question of the Pope's supporting a campaign of any kind against the Austrians, on whose support and regional clout his security depended. He was not immune to the patriotic emotion of his fellow Italians, but the dream of a *politically* united Italy was, in his eyes, a chimera and perilous trap. And as the liberals and radicals in Rome became more confident and articulate, his misgivings deepened. 'God bless Italy!' he cried to a crowd outside his palace on 10 January 1848. But then he added: 'Do not ask of me that which I cannot, I must not, I wish not to do.' 'The Italians', Margaret Fuller wrote in May 1847, 'deliver themselves, with all the vivacity of their temperament, to perpetual hurras, vivas, rockets and torchlit processions. I often think how grave and sad the Pope must feel, as he sits alone and hears all this noise of expectation.'[215]

The raucous lovefest in Rome unfolded against a background of rising political tension across Europe. As the harvest failures of 1846/7 pushed up grain prices, hunger riots were reported from across Spain, Germany, Italy and France. In Prussia alone, 158 food riots – marketplace riots, attacks on stores and shops, transportation blockades – took place during April/May 1847, when prices were at their highest. There was a surge of banditry and petty crime in the Italian states, striking fear into the hearts of the middle classes. Contemporaries noted a hardening of political discourse. In France, as we have seen, the toasts and speeches given at banquets acquired a more radical edge. In the summer of 1847, the moderate journal *Il Felsineo* noted the influx from neighbouring Tuscany of new and 'pernicious' communist doctrines.[216]

Disquieted by the liberal patriotic cult around Pius IX, the Austrians reinforced their troops in the garrison city of Ferrara on the northern border of the Papal States: on 17 July 1847, the Austrian generals Nugent and d'Aspre entered the city with 800 soldiers under fluttering flags and fixed bayonets. Although the Austrians possessed longstanding treaty rights in respect of Ferrara, the reinforcement had a dramatic effect. The agitation around the Pope reached a new pitch of intensity, liberal and radical opinion throughout Italy linked the news of Austrian troop movements with (unfounded) rumours of a reactionary conspiracy to bring down Pius IX. The mood of agitation and outrage deepened. The radical Tuscan newspaper *Il Popolo* reported in September 1847 that the peasants of the Valdichiana, an alluvial river valley that passes through the provinces of Arezzo and Siena, were fully apprised of the situation, they talked 'only of the Pope and of the Germans' [i.e. the Austrians]: 'for them the only notion is the Pope, and by this they understand, or rather replace, every other idea. The claim that if the Pope were to ask for it, they would drop everything to come and defend him against the Germans, is on everybody's lips.'[217]

The Italian sovereigns responded to this tide of political emotion in different ways. In Tuscany, long known for the relative mildness of its governance, the Grand Duke moved closer to the reformist elites, issuing decrees easing the censorship of the press and enlarging the consultative state council. In Piedmont, King Charles Albert vacillated, surfing the wave of anti-Austrian feeling but offering, for the moment, only minimal concessions to the reformers. Impatience at the resulting deadlock pushed the moderates back towards an accommodation with the radicals: they no longer sought partial adjustments but a major recalibration of the kingdom's administration and institutional landscape, including the demand for a constitution. In the south, Ferdinand II, king of the Two Sicilies, tried a different approach. He shuffled his ministers and offered crowd-pleasing windfalls to the poorest strata, such as the abolition of the hated duty on milled grains, while holding back on substantial reform. But unlike his Piedmontese colleague, the Bourbon Neapolitan monarch was neither willing nor able to offer himself as a plausible partisan of the national idea, which he regarded as a noxious utopia.[218]

In 1847, as the harvest crisis began to bite into the kingdom's economy, the Neapolitan man of letters Luigi Settembrini published an anonymous clandestinely printed pamphlet bitterly attacking the monarchy and its servants. Settembrini had grown up in a milieu saturated with radical and patriotic activism. He was the son of a lawyer who had played a role in the Neapolitan revolution of 1799. During the constitutional revolution of 1820–21, seven-year-old Luigi had often accompanied his father to meetings of the Carbonari. In 1834, he had joined Mazzini's Giovine Italia, together with an even more secretive sect called Figliuoli della Giovine Italia (Sons of Young Italy), which emulated the Illuminati and cultivated a democratic and neo-Jacobin sensibility. In the following year he secured a professorial position at the Liceo in Catanzaro, one of the four high schools of the Kingdom of the Two Sicilies, all the while remaining an active participant in the radical underground. Betrayed by a priest in May 1839, he was arrested and imprisoned for three years. Unable to resume his professorship after his release in 1842, he eked out a living as a private teacher. He took a sympathetic interest for a time in the arguments of Gioberti, but soon rejected them as impractical fantasies. In the summer of 1847, he wrote the swingeing attack on the Neapolitan regime for which he is best remembered today, at least in Italy.

The *Protesta del Popolo delle Due Sicilie* (Protest of the People of the Two Sicilies) was a searing indictment of virtually every feature of the Bourbon monarchy. The country's government, Settembrini wrote, was 'an enormous pyramid', whose base was made up of 'cops and priests' and whose summit was the king, the 'biggest and most disgusting worm' in the pile (interestingly enough, Büchner and Weidig had used the same metaphor for Grand Duke Ludwig II of Hesse-Darmstadt). 'From the usher to the minister, from the common soldier to the general, from the gendarme to the Minister of Police, from the parish priest to the king's confessor', every officeholder of this kingdom was 'a ruthless and crazed despot toward those who are his subordinates, and a servile slave towards his superiors'.

For 26 years the two Sicilies have been crushed by a government whose stupidity and cruelty can hardly be described ... The ministers who compose the entire government are vicious or stupid. ... This is the country where the science of economics was born and where even today many distinguished men write learned treatises, and yet its administration is placed in the hands of idiots and thieves. ... In a kingdom so beautiful and fertile that could nourish twice as many inhabitants as it possesses, bread often runs short, men are often found dead from starvation; grain often has to be brought from Odessa, from Egypt and from countries that are called barbarous. If you ask the ministers: Do you know how much grain there is? Do you know how much the kingdom needs? They know nothing. ... All are oppressed and the source of all these evils is the government.[219]

This was strong stuff, even by the standards of an age rich in denunciatory rhetoric. Unlike the mild and oblique critiques of the northern moderates, Settembrini's indictment left no space for negotiation or compromise (how do you negotiate with a worm?). *Protesta del Popolo* was a literary sensation in the kingdom and throughout the Italian peninsula. A copy of it was thrown by an enthusiast into the carriage of King Ferdinand II of the Two Sicilies while he was visiting Palermo.[220] A Neapolitan liberal estimated that more than 1,000 copies were in circulation on the mainland; everyone in Naples and across the provinces was talking about it. Many copies were hunted down and destroyed by police, but the precious few that escaped were 'read by everyone, whether friends or enemies of the government'. Liberal activists and printers were arrested on suspicion of having written it or played a part in its production.[221] A French translation helped to darken the (already poor) reputation of the Neapolitan Bourbons in the eyes of continental liberal opinion. Fearing that he would be identified as the author, arrested and sentenced to death, Settembrini fled to Malta on 3 January 1848. He would return only a few weeks later, when the revolution that had broken out in Palermo reached the Neapolitan mainland.

By the mid 1840s, the Prussian political system, too, seemed to be living on borrowed time. This was not just a matter of rising popular expectations, but of financial necessity. Under the terms of the State Indebtedness Law of 17 January 1820, the Prussian government was prevented from raising state loans unless these could be cleared through a 'national estates assembly'. During the 1820s and 1830s, successive Prussian finance ministers had avoided trouble by raising loans indirectly through the nominally independent Seehandlung, a state bank, and keeping overall borrowing to a minimum. But this could not continue for ever. The king, Frederick William IV, was a passionate railway enthusiast at a time when the economic, military and strategic importance of the revolution in transport technology was becoming increasingly apparent.[222] Since this was an area too important to be left to the private sector, it was clear that the Prussian state would soon have to extend its reach and face infrastructural expenditures it could not cover without raising substantial loans. And this it could only do if it convened a 'national estates assembly'. The king was reluctant, but he had no choice: no assembly, no railway.

The 'United Diet' as the new composite body was called, was controversial even before it met. There was a small chorus of moderate conservative enthusiasts, but they were drowned out by the roar of liberal and radical critique. Most liberals felt that the new assembly fell far short of their legitimate expectations. 'We asked you for bread and you gave us a stone!' thundered the Silesian liberal Heinrich Simon in a polemical essay published – to avoid the Prussian censors – in Saxon Leipzig.[223] If the Patent was offensive to liberals, it also alarmed hard-line conservatives, who saw it opening the door to a full-blown constitutional settlement. And at the same time the announcement of the United Diet also triggered a further expansion of political expectations.

On Sunday, 11 April 1847 – a cold, grey, rainy Berlin day – a crowd of provincial delegates numbering over 600 were herded into the White Hall of the royal palace for the inaugural ceremony of the United Diet. The king's opening speech, delivered without notes over more than half an hour, was a warning shot. The king was in no mood for compromise. 'There is no power on earth', he announced, 'that can succeed in making me transform the natural relationship between prince and people ... into a conventional constitutional relationship, and I will never allow a written piece of paper to come between the Lord God in Heaven and this land.' The speech closed with a reminder that the Diet was no legislative parliament. It had been convened for a specific purpose, namely, to approve new taxes and a state loan, but its future depended upon the will and judgement of the king. Its task was emphatically not to 'represent opinions'. He would only reconvene the Diet, he told the deputies, if he considered it 'good and useful, and if this Diet offers me proof that I can do so without injuring the rights of the Crown'.[224]

In the event, the deliberations of the Diet were to prove the ultra-conservatives right. For the first time, Prussian liberals of every stripe found themselves performing together on the same stage. They mounted a campaign to transform the Diet into a proper legislature. If the government refused, they insisted, the Diet would not approve the government's spending plans. The importance of this experience in a state where the press and political networks were still fragmented along regional lines can scarcely be overstated. It fired liberals with a sense of confidence and purpose; it also taught them a first lesson in the virtues of political cooperation and compromise. As one conservative ruefully observed, the liberals regularly worked 'late into the night' coordinating their strategy for key political debates.[225] By this means they succeeded in retaining the initiative in much chamber debate.

The conservatives, by contrast, were a shambles. Throughout much of the proceedings they seemed on the defensive, reduced to reacting to liberal proposals and provocations. As the champions of provincial diversity and local autonomy, they found it harder to work together on an 'all-Prussian' plane. For many conservative noblemen, their politics was inextricably bound up with their elite corporate status – this made it difficult to establish a common platform with potential allies of more humble station (Hungarian conservatives faced the same problem). Whereas the liberals could agree on certain broad principles (constitutionalism, representation, freedom of the press), the conservatives seemed worlds away from a clearly defined joint platform, beyond a vague intuition that gradual evolution on the basis of tradition was preferable to radical change.[226] The conservatives lacked leadership and were slow to form partisan factions. 'One defeat follows another', Leopold von Gerlach remarked on 7 May, after four weeks of sessions.[227] The liberal deputy Adolphe Crémieux noticed the same asymmetry in Paris in mid February 1848: 'the [opposition] movement in Paris is magnificent, the camp of the conservatives is in disarray'.[228]

In purely constitutional terms, the Prussian United Diet was a non-event. It was not permitted to transform itself into a parliamentary legislature. Before it was adjourned on 26 June 1847, it rejected the government's request for a state loan to finance the eastern railway, declaring that it would only cooperate when the king granted it the right to meet at regular intervals. 'In money matters', the liberal entrepreneur and deputy David Hansemann famously quipped, 'geniality has its limits.' Yet in terms of political culture the United Diet was of enormous importance. Unlike its provincial predecessors, it was a public body whose proceedings were recorded and published, so that the debates in the chamber resounded across the political landscape of the kingdom. The Diet demonstrated in the most conclusive way the exhaustion of the monarch's strategy of containment. It also signalled the imminence – the inevitability – of real constitutional change. How exactly that change would be brought about, however, remained unclear.

THE AVALANCHE

By the mid 1840s, the conflicts unfolding in the Swiss cantons had started to fuse into an all-Swiss crisis. In 1845, the Catholic government of Lucerne announced the passage of a decree readmitting the Jesuits, who were hated throughout Protestant Switzerland, and directing them to take control of the cantonal education system. To forestall possible unrest, the government detained liberal leaders, stirring further outrage and triggering waves of refugees into the neighbouring cantons. 'It was and is unheard of in the history of our fatherland', a liberal eyewitness declared, 'that such a great number should have been forced to leave their homes and flee from such a small country [the canton of Lucerne] on account of their political opinions.'[229] Twice, the liberals in neighbouring Aargau mounted abortive armed raids into Lucerne. On the second occasion, in the spring of 1845, over 4,000 men marched on the city, led by the radical Bern lawyer Ulrich Ochsenbein. The liberals hoped that they would be welcomed by the population there as 'liberators from the tyranny of the Catholic populists'.[230] But the Lucerners repulsed both raids with the assistance of allied troops drawn from the neighbouring conservative cantons of Zug, Uri and Unterwalden. The chasm between the progressive and the Catholic camps deepened. While liberals in the progressive cantons pushed through amendments to their constitutions, the Catholic cantons pulled more closely together and formed the Sonderbund, or Special League, a fully fledged military alliance with provision for a central military authority.[231]

The liberals in the federal diet responded in the following year by proposing that the Sonderbund be declared illegal under the federal constitution (whether it was or not depended on whether you viewed Switzerland as a genuine federation or simply a confederacy of quasi-independent states). In January 1847, the presidency of the Diet (*Vorort*) had passed to Bern, a strongly liberal canton whose government was headed by the very Ulrich Ochsenbein who had commanded the volunteer brigades in the raid on Lucerne. The Diet resolved to act against the Sonderbund and decreed the formation of a federal army. About the likely outcome there could be little doubt: the progressive cantons commanded three times the population and nine times the resources of their conservative opponents.

The war that followed lasted twenty-five days, took ninety-three lives and left 510 wounded on both sides, though it would have been much deadlier, had the federal command not pursued a policy of humane restraint.[232] The most lethal confrontation was the Battle of Gisikon in the Reuss Valley in the canton of Lucerne. The troops of the Sonderbund had dug in on elevated ground above the River Reuss and a Colonel Ziegler of the Federal Army led three successive assaults on their positions, until, after two hours of bitter fighting, the Sonderbund troops ceded their emplacements and retreated. Thirty-seven men were killed and about 100 wounded. This was not just the longest and bloodiest battle of the war, but also the last pitched battle ever to be fought by the Swiss Army and the first in world history to see the use of purpose-designed ambulances, in the form of wagons operated by nurses and volunteers from Zurich, to treat the wounded on the battlefield.

Contemporaries were in no doubt as to the significance of this conflict. For Ulrich Ochsenbein, a passionate, Protestant man of strong opinions, the raid on Lucerne was nothing less than a world-historical stand-off between Jesuitical servitude and 'a people struggling for its mental and physical freedom'.[233] In Paris and Vienna, the Swiss crisis was seen – not least by the statesmen – as a 'test case in the struggle between revolution and reaction in central Europe'. The Swiss troubles should not be understood in isolation, the French envoy in Berlin wrote to Guizot, but rather as one aspect of 'the revolutionary question in general'.[234] Metternich and Guizot hoped to prevent the success of the liberal movement in Switzerland from infecting neighbouring territories and both supported the Catholic cantons, though mutual distrust prevented an armed intervention. Official press reporting in France depicted the

war as a struggle in defence of suppressed cantonal and religious liberties. Prussia, too, was implicated in the Swiss upheaval. King Frederick
William IV of Prussia was the sovereign of Neufchâtel, one of the cantons of the Swiss confederation. Prussia was formally neutral in the
conflict, but the king's sympathies were firmly on the side of the Sonderbund and against the liberal cantons struggling to create a new Swiss
state.

There was nothing anybody could do to prevent enthusiasm for the
Swiss liberals from spreading into France and south-western Germany.
In the autumn and winter of 1847–8, there were toasts to 'Swiss liberty'
by the radical speakers at French banquets. Across south Germany and
the Rhineland, there were spontaneous demonstrations and open letters
with lists of signatories expressing solidarity with the federal cause.
Donations for the widows and orphans of fallen federal troops poured
in from the German Confederation, France, Belgium and England.[235]
Italian patriots arrived from Austrian-controlled Milan.

German radicals came to see the events in Switzerland as the opening
chapter of the revolutions of the following year. 'In the highlands were
fired the very first shots, / In the highlands against the priests!' sang Ferdinand von Freiligrath, radical bard of the German revolution. In
Freiligrath's poem, the Sonderbund war is an 'avalanche of rage' that,
once in motion, rolls across Europe, from Sicily to France, Lombardy and
the German states.[236] In Baden and Württemberg, volunteers – most of
them radicals – signed up to fight for the liberal cause in Switzerland.
Among the officers of the federal forces was the German radical Johann
Philipp Becker. Born in 1809 at Frankenthal in the Palatinate, Becker had
been imprisoned for his role in political agitation after the 1830 revolutions and settled in Switzerland with his wife and children in 1837. He
continued to be politically active as a radical democrat, though he also
made a solid living from a range of business ventures, including part-
ownership of a cigar factory. He was appointed adjutant of Ochsenbein's
division of the Federal Army in the autumn of 1847 and fought bravely
against the Sonderbund, acquiring military experience that would serve
him well during the German revolutionary upheavals of 1848 and 1849.

European opinion distilled the Swiss crisis into a binary clash between
Protestants who were also liberal and conservatives who were also
Catholic. The reality, in this small but highly diverse country, was much
more complex. There were Catholics and Protestants on both sides.

The canton of Ticino, though Catholic, did not join the Sonderbund. Catholic and Protestant liberals alike distrusted and feared the neo-Jacobin radicals in their own religious camp. Both the commander-in-chief of the Sonderbund, General Johann Ulrich von Salis-Soglio from the Grisons, and the commander of the federal troops, General Guillaume Henri Dufour, were conservative Protestants. The officers serving on the federal side included conservative Protestants sceptical of the liberals in Bern, and the officers of the Sonderbund included individuals of liberal convictions. And on both sides officers and men believed that they were fighting for 'liberty' against 'tyranny' (no one fought under the banner of servitude!).[237] The image of a binary stand-off between progress and reaction endowed this small war with a disproportionate European resonance, building solidarities and mobilizing spirits. But it also masked a multitude of lesser conflicts that cut in different directions across the embattled cantons: town vs country, the mountains vs the lowlands, liberals vs radicals, Catholic cantonal particularists vs papalist ultramontanes, conservative vs liberal Protestants. Had the Swiss war lasted longer, these fractures might have widened, undermining the cohesion of the two parties, and the Austrians might well have mounted an armed intervention in support of the Sonderbund, tipping the balance in the other direction. European liberals and radicals saw and drew inspiration from the triumph of 'liberty' over 'reaction', but they missed the many fissures and instabilities. On this occasion, as on so many before and since, victory was a poor teacher.

4

Detonations

I PREDICT A RIOT

Early in January 1848, printed notices appeared on walls across Palermo announcing that a revolution would take place on 12 January under cover of celebrations for the king's birthday. It was a puzzling apparition: why would the leaders of a still secret conspiracy choose to give the authorities advanced warning of their plan? Over the following days, the troops of the city's garrison were held in a state of high alert. From dawn on the appointed day, patrols went out from the citadel at the mouth of the harbour to observe the city. There was no sign of trouble. But from the early afternoon, large crowds of people indeed began to congregate in various locations, at the Porta S. Antonio, the Casa professa, the Peperito and La Flora. When troops were sent to disperse them, fighting broke out. From the upper windows of apartment buildings, citizens began raining stones, pieces of wood and tiles down on the soldiers. By nightfall, the insurrection was in control of much of Palermo and the numbers of the insurgents, though small, were steadily growing – from the towns and villages in the mountainous areas around the capital, squads of armed men began to flow into the city.

As with all the revolts that would launch revolutions across Europe that spring, an element of happenstance attached to the moment of combustion. The note posted across the city announcing the revolt was signed off in the name of a 'revolutionary committee', but the ascription was fictitious and it is doubtful whether a real conspiracy or plan existed.[1] The true author of the poster was Francesco Bagnasco, a veteran of the revolution of 1820, who became personally convinced that the leading citizens of Palermo were ready to confront the tyrant, and that the announcement of a revolt would suffice to bring one about.[2]

His assessment proved correct. When the heralded day arrived, there was in fact no planned insurrection; it was rather that the anticipation of one brought curious crowds into the centre of the capital whose presence was itself enough to supply the occasion for more general unrest, once a possibly accidental shot fired by a sentry had triggered a clash between citizens and troops.[3] Alphonse de Lamartine noticed something similar in his account of the opening scenes of the Parisian revolution that would break out six weeks later: 'Curious and inoffensive crowds', he noted, 'continually moved along the boulevards, gathering numbers as they went; other crowds streamed from the suburbs of Paris; they appeared, however, rather to observe what was passing than to meditate any act. The event seems to have been engendered by the curiosity that attended it.'[4]

The Palermo uprising of 12 January was no bolt out of the blue. The island, one contemporary observed, had been in a continuous state of political agitation since the revolution of 1820.[5] There had been repeated uprisings. In 1837, when a cholera epidemic swept across Sicily, it was widely believed that the Bourbon administration in Naples had poisoned the island. A number of suspected Bourbon agents were murdered. By the summer of 1847, the Neapolitan regime was permanently on the defensive. King Ferdinand II, a Spanish Bourbon with an Austrian wife, remained deaf to the entreaties of his Prime Minister, Pietracatella, that he must 'do something and soon', issue a law liberating the press and involve 'men of talent' in the government of his provinces.[6] Instead he focused on cultivating the principal institutions that kept him in power, namely the army and the Church. He curried favour with the populace by touring the provinces, lightening the tax on milled grains (especially hated by the poorest strata) and occasionally replacing the most unpopular ministers. On 11 August 1847, Ferdinand II published an edict reminding his subjects of the efforts he had made to lighten the tax burden and reduce public debt. But his kingdom had already crossed that mysterious threshold where the promise of incremental reform fails before the implacable logic of 'too little too late'. Once this point is passed, concessions no longer mollify but only embolden the political opposition.

Early in the afternoon of 1 September 1847, a few handfuls of men, armed for the most part with antiquated hunting rifles, converged from

the village of S. Leone, and from the suburbs of Boccetta, Zaera and Por-
talegni on the centre of the Sicilian city of Messina at the north-eastern
end of the island. They were a mixed crowd: of around ninety-seven
insurgents, twelve were students. The rest included brokers, shoemakers, professors, umbrella-makers; a shopkeeper, a sea captain, several
kinds of clerk, a hatter, a player from the royal band, a clergyman, a
spinner, a tailor, a goldsmith, a silversmith, an architect, a hairdresser
and a gunsmith. Two were of modestly noble lineage and two, known
by the nicknames 'Bicchireddu' (Small Glass) and 'Tre Naschi' (Three
Noses) were men of the city's labouring class.[7] The outcome was foreseeable: the band was swiftly crushed and the revolt was over by dusk,
only a few hours after it had begun.

In retrospect, the Messina revolt seems doomed from the beginning:
there was no clear political leadership, organization or plan, and little
evidence of solidarity on the part of the Messinese citizenry, who
retreated to their homes when the trouble started. The general insurrection envisaged by the insurgents did not materialize: Palermo, Cosenza
and Cantanzaro remained quiet; only Reggio Calabria rose up.[8] But for
those who remained attached to the traditional authorities, there were
plenty of ominous signs. The presence alongside bourgeois worthies of
artisans and men of the poorest social strata reflected the impact of an
economic downturn that had begun in the agrarian sector, but was now
gnawing away at business and manufacturing. The Messinese insurgents
marched waving Italian tricolour flags – evidence that the patriotic rhetoric of liberal local journals such as *Il Maurolico* and the *Spettatore
Zancleo* had left its mark on the populace of a city with relatively high
literacy levels, thanks, ironically, to the educational reforms of the Bourbon era.[9] And the cries of *Viva Pio Nono!* hinted at the deepening
connectedness of the political tumult unfolding in dispersed locations on
the Italian peninsula. Ferdinand II had expressly announced that he had
no intention of following the Pope's example and ordered that any manifestations in support of the reforming pontiff be suppressed forthwith.
But these efforts to disconnect the political life of his kingdom from the
ferment of the Italian peninsula were completely ineffective.

Throughout the autumn and winter of 1847–8, the Kingdom of the
Two Sicilies remained in a state of seething anticipation. In a despatch
filed on 7 September 1847, Prince Felix von Schwarzenberg, the Austrian envoy in Naples, reported that the 'revolutionary movement . . .

agitating the entire kingdom' was marked by 'two distinct tendencies'. The people of the city of Naples and of the mainland provinces, he wrote, wanted 'active and regular government' by means of a constitutional and representative system. In Sicily, by contrast, the general wish was for independence: 'the hatred towards Naples and the Neapolitans is the most vivid sentiment harboured by each individual. . . . they have not forgotten in Sicily the era when England, as it were, forced King Ferdinand to sanction a constitution.'[10]

The British peer Ernest Augustus, Earl of Mount Edgcumbe, who arrived in Palermo on 10 November 1847 in the hope of improving his failing health, noted in his memoirs that rumours of an impending public disturbance were circulating continuously in the capital. Everyone he spoke to in the city – most of his contacts were members of the Palermitan aristocracy – agreed that the discontent was 'extreme and universal'.[11] At the end of November 1847, news of the victory of the liberal cantons in the Swiss Civil War triggered new demonstrations and disorders in both Naples and Palermo.[12] On 27 November, 'men and women raised bursts of applause for the king, for Pius IX, for Italy and above all for the independence of Sicily'. On the following day, the same shouts were heard in the Flora gardens, and that evening a tricolour flag appeared in the theatre. On 30 November, a large crowd gathered on the Piazza della Madrice to listen to a priest, who, having planted a tricolour flag in the hand of the statue of Santa Rosalia, delivered a homily on liberty. 'The multitude continued to grow', one witness reported, 'and once the sermon was finished and the flag withdrawn from the statue, they set off in a riot towards the police station.' But once the troops appeared the crowd swiftly dispersed, leaving the flag on the cobblestones.[13]

Individually, these tumults were easy to master – collectively, they suggested an irreversible momentum. Piecemeal reforms, intimidating troop movements, waves of pre-emptive arrests, the dismissal of unpopular ministers: nothing seemed to make any difference. And the noises from central and northern Italy were not reassuring. It was the ascendancy of Pius IX, the putative protagonist of 'new destinies for Italy and Europe', that moved Francesco Bagnasco to print and post his placard 'announcing' an insurrection. At the end of December 1847, sixty-six prominent Piedmontese and Roman liberals signed a public letter to Ferdinand II, urging him to mimic 'the policy of Pius IX, Leopold [of

Tuscany] and Charles Albert [of Piedmont-Sardinia]' and thereby align himself with 'an Italian policy, the policy of Providence'. Widely reprinted in the liberal press, the letter exposed the unstable dynamics of a peninsula on which some states appeared already to have embarked on the road to reform, while others had not.

In the words he chose for the 'proclamation' of 9 January, Francesco Bagnasco spoke to the impatience of a political elite that no longer believed in the possibility of reform:

> Sicilians! The time of useless prayers has passed. The protests, the pleas, the peaceful demonstrations were useless. Ferdinand II viewed it all with contempt; and as for us, a free people reduced to chains and misery, will it take us yet longer to regain our legitimate rights? To arms, children of Sicily, to arms! The strength of all is omnipotent: the union of peoples is the downfall of kings. On 12 January, at dawn, the glorious epoch of universal regeneration will begin.[14]

The strangest thing about the uprising that began on the evening of 12 January is that it was ultimately successful. The early protests were small, chaotic and easily dispersed. The authorities were prepared; indeed, they were better prepared than the insurrectionaries themselves. Across the city there were secure premises where soldiers could shelter from hostile crowds, including a well-fortified complex on the Quay, easily supplied by ship. In the forts there were elevated positions from which the troops could direct artillery fire onto streets and houses where insurgents might be gathering. From the water off the Porta Felice, a Neapolitan war steamer could align itself with the Via Toledo (now Via Vittorio Emanuele, though the old name is still in use), the broad thoroughfare that has cut the city in half since its foundation by the Phoenicians, and fire shells or grapeshot down its length to prevent insurgents from forming large crowds. And reinforcements from Naples were within easy reach. On the morning of 16 January, nine Neapolitan war steamers disembarked 6,000 fresh royal troops, including a battalion of artillery, to join the 4,000 already in Palermo. At this point, the Earl of Mount Edgcumbe later recalled, 'it was impossible for any reasonable man to suppose that the revolutionists retained a chance of success'.[15]

Yet by 4 February the government's troops had largely withdrawn from the city; on the following day, a Te Deum was held to celebrate the victory

of the insurgents. How was this possible? Part of the reason lay in the relative friendlessness of the Bourbon regime in Sicily, and especially in
Palermo. 'In a country where the masses languish in bitter poverty and the
upper classes are all aligned against the regime', Schwarzenberg reported
from Naples on 13 January 1848, 'the government is weak, controlling
only a few garrisoned strongpoints.'[16] The two great streets that cut across
the centre of Palermo were easy to control with cavalry and artillery, but
they also divided the city into four great mazes of twisting lanes, where
fleeing insurgents were safe and troops were vulnerable. Even the Neapolitan gunboats that cruised about in the waters off the quay lobbing shells
into the city were not invincible. On 24 January, one of these boats positioned itself opposite the opening to a long narrow street that crossed one
of the central avenues of the city and began firing occasional shells up it,
until, that is, some insurgents managed to seize an elderly field gun, roll it
down to the shore and fire it at the boat. 'This species of reciprocity was
evidently beyond its calculation', Edgcumbe observed, 'for instantly on the
first ball passing it, without even losing the time turning would have taken,
it commenced retreating backwards, the men at the sweeps redoubling
their exertions as other shots passed it.'[17]

A more fundamental factor in the insurgent victory was the irresolu-
tion of the regime itself and of its troops. When bands of poorly armed
rebels attacked soldiers, the generals responded by agreeing to pull back
the men and to concentrate on defending the most important objects –
the financial administration, the Royal Palace, the Police Station, the
Tribunals and so on. And this meant that the crowd could focus first on
one prestigious building and then another, driving the guards away with
rifle fire and even shells fired from looted cannon. Particularly disheart-
ening for the royal forces was the constant influx from the countryside
of *squadre*, bands of men prepared to fight alongside the insurgents.
Even after the reinforcements arrived from Naples, the regime remained
cautious and hesitant. As early as 16 January, the new commander of
the incoming troops, Roberto de Sauget, concluded that the game was
up for the regime in Sicily. His reports to Naples argued against trying
to surround and starve the city. Rather than seizing the initiative, de
Sauget sat tight in the Castello near the Quay, sending detachments of
troops to bring provisions and munitions to the troops encamped in the
Royal Palace and the Financial Administration and a few other places
where royal forces were still holding out. These relief parties were

routinely shot at and pelted with stones and tiles as they hurried to and from their destinations, so that, as one witness on the Neapolitan side noted, 'the feeding of some cost the lives of others'.[18]

The reasons for this hesitancy may have been political rather than military: de Sauget, though a senior military servant of the Bourbon regime, was known to be a moderate liberal who favoured constitutionalism. During the revolution of 1820–21, he had served as chief of staff under Florestano Pepe, the general sent by revolutionary Naples to bring Sicily back under the control of the constitutional regime. At that time, he had published a pamphlet on the Sicilian Question in which he affirmed his adherence to the revolutionary government and argued for concessions to the Sicilian rebels. These affinities muted the ardour he brought to the task of pacification – that was certainly the view of those pro-Bourbon conservatives who later blamed him for the failure of the Neapolitan intervention in January 1848.[19] But to make de Sauget responsible for the collapse of the regime on the island would be to miss the point. The Bourbon monarch was as irresolute as his general. Schwarzenberg was shocked by the swiftness with which the Neapolitan court gave up the fight. The king, he observed, was weak and fearful, and his advisers were no better; the consternation triggered by the crisis had fed 'the pusillanimity of some ministers and the liberalism of others'. Nobody in the king's entourage sought to 'revive the flagging courage of their master'; instead they all spoke of 'the urgent necessity of saving the monarchy by satisfying the demands of the age and avoiding even greater misfortunes'.[20] Samuel Gross, the Swiss guard who commanded the troops garrisoned in the Castello, received orders from the king to avoid firing shells into the city and focus solely on defending his fortress and the Financial Administration. And the king's own brother, Don Luigi, who had travelled to Sicily with the intervention force, urged the government on his return not to keep fighting but to accept the demands of the insurgent Sicilians, even if this meant separating the insular administration altogether from that of the mainland.[21] Here, as in so many European capitals in that year, the collapse of the regime's confidence in itself preceded and facilitated the revolution raised against it.

The activism of the consular corps in Palermo and the presence of foreign warships in the waters off the city were a further reason for caution. In Palermo, the royal artillery was ordered to cease its cannonades of the city, for fear that shells might strike the consular residences. The consuls made regular representations to royal headquarters, insisting that the troops avoid measures that would endanger civilian lives and property. The British consul played a crucial mediating role in negotiations between the revolutionary Provisional Committee and the Neapolitan forces encamped in the city. The same happened in Messina, where an insurrection broke out in the last week of January. Here, the consuls were able to extract from General Domenico Cardamone a promise to desist from the shelling of civilian areas. When Cardamone retracted his promise and shelling recommenced, a delegation of consuls, led by Captain Codrington of the British warship *Thetis* and Captain Ingle of the US warship *Princeton*, presented themselves at the general's residence and upbraided him for breaking his word. When Cardamone protested that he had his orders, the French consul, placing his sword across his knee, told the general that if his own sovereign had ordered him to commit such a monstrous crime, he would have broken his sword, and thrown it at his Majesty's feet.[22]

The presence of these powerful foreigners is one of the most interesting features of the Sicilian revolution. The consuls, as a collectivity, represented a kind of moral tribunal: their protest letter to Cardamone was framed 'in the name of an indignant Europe'.[23] The British consul and even prominent English, American and other expatriates found that doors opened to them wherever they went; they could inspect royal fortifications, visit insurgent trenches and pass through barricades without being seized or molested.[24] Even more important were the war steamers of the foreign powers. These floating chunks of extra-territorial sovereignty provided spaces of encounter, negotiation and refuge that could not be found on land. In Messina, a deputation from the city's revolutionary Provisional Committee, accompanied by the consuls, repeatedly met to discuss ceasefires and other arrangements with Neapolitan military commanders on board Captain Codrington's boat, the *Thetis*. These were often quite emotional encounters, at which the revolutionary delegates and the Neapolitan officers were seen 'kissing and bedewing each other with tears of joy in the Italian fashion'.[25] But gunboats were also projections of geopolitical force with the potential to endow the revolution with international legitimacy. On 22 February, for example, following the seizure of a number of forts and an arsenal by the insurgents, the American vessel *Princeton* 'draped out her rigging and fired a salute with all her guns'. The Americans insisted that they were merely celebrating

General Washington's birthday, but British observers concluded that the republican sympathies of the American mariners had got the better of their discretion: 'I am pretty sure', Matthew Babington wrote, that 'they are by no means sorry to kill two birds with one stone.'[26]

The past masters in the art of killing many birds with few stones were the British, the dominant naval power in the Mediterranean. At one point, ten English ships of war under the command of Admiral Sir William Parker were drawn up before Naples. When the Neapolitans complained that their expedition against Sicily was being hindered, Lord Napier, the British Chargé d'Affaires at Naples, denounced the complaints as calumny, insisting that the ships in the bay were not drawn up in battle array. (One wonders how the British government would have responded if a Neapolitan fleet had reacted in the same way to a naval expedition to Ireland.) Throughout the violent first phase of the revolution, British ships and personnel in the waters off Palermo and Messina mounted repeated armed mediations, sanctioned by London. At the same time, English agents supplied the insurgents with weapons. Already on 18 January 1848, a notice signed by Ruggiero Settimo, a member of the Provisional Government, thanked 'an English gentleman, who wishes to remain unknown' for placing at the disposal of the Committee 'all the military munitions on his boat'.[27] In his 'military history' of the Palermitan uprising, the anonymous author, who was probably an officer in the king's service, sourly described bands of insurgents attacking the police station, the Tribunals and the Financial Administration with rifles and high-explosive artillery, 'all provided by the English', while the bells sounded the alarm from all the church towers.[28] This propensity to intervention was woven from diverse strands. The memory of the 'English' constitution drawn up under the supervision of Admiral Bentinck in 1812, when Britain was the custodian of Sicilian independence from the 'French' Kingdom of Naples, ruled by Napoleon's brother-in-law Joachim Murat, was one of them. By the rather sinuous reasoning of British diplomacy, the constitution of 1812 remained in force, since it had never been modified or abolished and had never 'ceased to exist by its own consent'.[29] 'If there be any moral obligation resting upon England', Palmerston's special envoy, Lord Minto, informed Lord Napier in Naples, 'it must be in support of the constitution of 1812, imposed upon Sicily by British influence and authority.'[30]

Humanitarian objectives were offered as public justifications for

intervention, but the pursuit of strategic advantage was a more fundamental motive. Lord Palmerston, the British Foreign Secretary, made it
clear from the outset that he favoured the Sicilian cause (notwithstanding
the annual subsidy that the British government had been paying to the
court of Naples for decades). He worked behind the scenes to manage the
choice of a new sovereign for the island from among the Italian princes.
But, at the same time, he warned of the instabilities that might result from
full Sicilian independence. If it were entirely severed from Naples, he told
his ambassador there, 'it would run the risk of becoming an object of
contest and of sinking at last into the condition of satellite to some one of
the more powerful States of Europe'.[31] Duty and interest were in
alignment.

For the Americans, too, the events of 1848 presented geopolitical
opportunities. In March 1848, Commodore George C. Read, Commander
of the American Mediterranean Squadron, took advantage of the political ferment in the Kingdom of Piedmont-Sardinia to request base rights
at La Spezia on the Ligurian coast. Aware that the presence of American
warships might prove useful in the event of a conflict with Austria, the
government in Turin immediately approved the request on the most generous terms. Encouraged, Read made a similar request to the newly
formed government of insurgent Sicily and acquired base rights in the
harbour of Syracuse on the island's Ionian coast. These forays triggered a
flurry of American interest in the idea that proffering 'political philanthropy' in the name of liberty to republican regimes in Mediterranean
Europe might serve as a means of augmenting American power.[32] In Sicily, as in many parts of Europe, political tumult became caught up, as we
shall see, in the gears of the relations among states, with profound implications for the course and outcome of the revolutions.

No one was more sensitive to these geopolitical entanglements than
the Austrians, who depended more than any of the other great powers
on the fragile machinery of the 'European concert'. Prince Schwarzenberg was disgusted by the openness of the British meddling in the affairs
of the Neapolitan monarchy; there could no longer be any doubt as to the
'interest' Britain had in seeing the insurrection triumph in Sicily.[33] The
decision by the insurgent Provisional Government to 'place itself in
the hands of England and France', Schwarzenberg wrote, was 'the grav-
est and the most unforgiveable of the blunders into which its blindness
had led it'.[34] For the moment, Metternich remained unperturbed. He had

long expected this crisis, he told his ambassador, affecting the calm of the statesman who has seen it all before. The only means of resolving the Sicilian question lay in 'an agreement among the great courts' and he was already at work on preparation for a joint démarche with Berlin, St Petersburg and Paris. The British could not be relied upon, that was clear. But 'the French government will march, I think it is safe to say, in step with us'.[35] Had Guizot remained in power, Metternich's prediction would doubtless have been borne out. But ten days after he signed this letter Paris rose in revolution.

Like many places in 1848, insurgent Palermo witnessed a rapid escalation of violence. After early clashes with the troops and police, fighting spread swiftly across the city. Barricades were thrown up, prisons broken open and their inmates released, tax collectors and policemen killed. In the early days, when the troops still risked sorties into the cities, they were easily pinned down by sharpshooters firing from the windows of apartments. On 29 January, when two companies of soldiers left the Saracenic Gate to engage a barricade on the Strada Austria, many were killed by gunfire (the insurgents claimed thirty-five military dead, the military command conceded nineteen).[36] The shelling of cities was in fact not especially deadly, but its indiscriminate quality attracted moral outrage. In Messina, its victims included 'four poor boys, who were huddled together in a hovel at the upper part of the town and were all killed by a shell which burst among them'.[37] In retaliation, sharpshooters picked off the guards manning the fortified buildings. There were also many episodes of surprising restraint, in which the insurgents captured and released soldiers, or allowed fortified buildings to be evacuated without molesting the departing occupants, though a distinction was generally made between the troops of the king (and their families), on the one hand, and the local police agents (*sbirri*) on the other, who were often butchered or shot on capture. The Earl of Mount Edgcumbe was shocked to see people in such good spirits dragging about the corpses of slain policemen and 'permitting their children to join in the disgusting mutilation of them as in a sport'.[38] Such was the ferocity and popularity of the insurrection across the island that after a few weeks only the forts of the port town of Messina remained under the monarchy's control.

There was nothing particularly new in this parallelism of political upheaval and a protean, plebeian violence. In notes he had made on the Sicilian rebellion of 1820, the writer Domenico Scinà described how, as the uprising broke out, the hills surrounding the city were dotted with torches and fires; it was, he recalled, 'the peasants who were coming down to help the people'; the prisons were broken open; the *sbirri* were chased, disarmed and massacred; the garrisons were attacked and taken, soldiers were lynched. Only after hundreds had died, and with some difficulty, did a 'supreme revolutionary council' take control, composed of noblemen who had already been members of the Sicilian parliament of 1812.[39] We find similar language in the contemporary account of Ferdinando Malvica, a literary scholar of anti-Neapolitan sympathies who served from 1834 in the public administration of the Kingdom of the Two Sicilies. Malvica was a moderate figure who tried where possible to mute the excesses of Neapolitan policing. In 1848, he returned to Palermo, where he compiled the notes that later became an unpublished manuscript, the *Storia della rivoluzione di Sicilia negli anni 1848 e '49*. The early weeks of the revolution, Malvica wrote, saw the swift emergence of a Palermitan opposition leadership: Giuseppe La Masa, Baron Rosalino Pilo, the priest Vito Ragone, the veteran Ruggiero Settimo, the lawyer Paolo Paternostro, and many other liberal and patriotic worthies. But the streets were filled by men of a different sort: the armed *maestranze* (craftsmen's corporations) and the *squadre* from the surrounding country:

> ferocious men, almost devoid of human feeling, as bloodthirsty as they were boorish, an ugly people [by whom] the beautiful civic capital of Sicily found itself surrounded, infernal tribes peopled by men whose only human characteristic was their sunburned countenance.[40]

If the social strife was deeper and wider in 1848, this was because the first half of the nineteenth century had witnessed structural changes that deepened social tensions on the island. Here, as in so many regions of Europe, changes in the pattern of landholding were at the heart of the trouble. The land reform measures of the Bourbon government after 1815 abolished the remaining economic and judicial jurisdictions of the old, landed nobility, created a freer market in land, and did away with commons and mixed-usage rights. The aim was to break the power monopoly of the old nobility and create a new stakeholding middle class loyal to the Bourbon regime. What in fact happened was that, between the end of the Napoleonic Wars and the 1840s, former rent-collectors began to purchase large tracts of the noble estates. And this emergent landholding class, having profited from the break-up and sale of common land, even acquired the plots allocated to peasants as compensation for the land enclosures, using its access to legal expertise to secure a strategic advantage over peasant aspirants. This resulted both in a marked deterioration in the condition of most peasants and in the disinhibition of peasant violence, because whereas peasants had formerly been bound by debt and dependency to the old landowning class, they were now both less secure and less deferential to the new landowning elites. And once the violence of the peasants was unleashed, it was very difficult to contain. Violence against landowners and armed occupations of common lands were a major feature of the 1848 revolutions in the Sicilian countryside.[41]

For the elite strata caught up in the Sicilian uprisings, including those who were sympathetic, the experience of such turbulence was always edged with fear. When Matthew and Hannah Babington walked into the streets of Messina at the end of January, they passed through a 'motley group' armed with guns, pistols, pikes, drawn swords and large knives. Taking fright, Hannah dragged her husband into a shop to buy a revolutionary cockade. He was displeased to be paraded through the streets wearing an emblem which 'has throughout my life been an abhorrence, having been from my earliest years associated with the horrors of the French Revolution'.[42] It was the Earl of Edgcumbe's view that the Palermitan gentry only joined in the revolution 'when the mob became more to be feared than the government'.[43] In the memoirs he wrote of the Palermo revolution, Francesco Crispi, Secretary of the insurrectionary committee and later a member of the new Sicilian parliament, accused the moderate liberals of 'fearing the victory of the people more than that of the Bourbon troops'.[44] Similar observations would echo across Europe during the year of revolutions. And, of course, no one was immune to the terror of shell bursts and the cannonballs that thudded through walls and partitions into bedrooms and kitchens. The consuls flew their respective national flags from their residences in the vain hope that this would deter artillerymen from targeting them. The poorer native Sicilians nailed images of their favourite saints or of the Virgin to their doors. When the bombardment was especially intense, the expatriate community in Palermo and Messina fled to the safety of the foreign boats – in an era when so much personal wealth was tied up in the contents of warehouses, simply fleeing the country was not an option.

There was fear on the other side too. The Neapolitan commander Roberto de Sauget reported that his troops were 'immensely discouraged and tired' and not up to the extraordinary stresses of a war in which one could discern no enemies but only windows, walls and gutters belching smoke, in streets that were home to a hostile citizenry 'supported and incited by strangers'.[45] When the royal forces were ordered to ship out of Palermo, the captains of the Neapolitan boats refused to send their launches to pick up the men, because they feared that the citizens would attack them – British boats were brought in to transfer them instead. The embarkation under General de Sauget was a picture of ignominious haste. In a hurry to get away and lacking sufficient launches to make the transfer, de Sauget ordered that the horses should be killed. Very few of the cavalrymen had the heart to do it; most simply unharnessed their animals and abandoned them, weeping. 'And so,' an eyewitness recalled, 'one saw dead horses, and others gasping [their last]; and those that had been left alive neighing, many of them throwing themselves into the sea towards the ships and following them until, exhausted, overcome, they disappeared beneath the waves. This was the miserable close of an unmemorable withdrawal.'[46]

The news from Sicily alone was enough to bring crowds out onto the streets of Naples. The liberals and radicals of the urban cafés were there, along with large crowds of *lazzaroni*, turbulent people of the slum districts who were feeling the bite of the economic crisis. When news reached the capital of a peasant uprising in the province of Cilento, panic gripped the government. Following a pattern that had been seen in many places during the unrest of 1830–31, the liberals of the city's upper strata saw their opportunity and stepped up the pressure on Ferdinand II, arguing that only political reforms would resolve the crisis. A cascade of concessions followed: the liberal leader Carlo Poerio was released from prison to general jubilation. On 27 January a massive demonstration – too large to be dispersed by troops – took place in the capital. With his grip on Sicily loosening and his forces at home depleted by the Sicilian war, Ferdinand II at last backed down and promised a constitution.

'NOUVELLES DIVERSES'

In one of the appendices to a classic study of the barricades of mid-nineteenth-century Europe, the American historian Mark Traugott asked an interesting question: 'Did the Wave of Revolutionism in 1848 Originate in Paris or Palermo?' His own research, he went on to say, had uncovered no evidence that 'Parisians active during the February Days made reference to or had in mind the previous month's events in Palermo'. From this he concluded that 'the insurrection's direct influence was largely confined to the Italian-speaking world'.[47]

Before we turn to the relationship between Palermo and Paris, it is worth reflecting for a moment on the assumptions built into the metaphor of the 'wave', which is ubiquitous in the literature on the revolutions of 1848. In physics, and mathematics, a wave is a 'propagating dynamic disturbance'. It is certainly true that when we map the disturbances of 1848 chronologically onto the space of the European continent, they appear to disperse outwards, like the concentric ripples set in motion by a stone flung into water. But waves travel through both space and time. We can visualize the revolutions as propagating outwards across space from nodal points of high instability – Palermo, Rome, Paris, Vienna, Berlin. Or we could think in terms of the propagation of instability *over time*, the accumulation of conflict. The first option encourages us to think about where the revolutions 'began', where they diffused *from*. The second allows us to imagine a plurality of cumulative instabilities evolving over weeks, month or years in many locations. We need to think along both axes in order to make sense of what happened in 1848. Revolutions did not, for the most part, cause each other, as the aligned pieces in a domino effect cause their neighbours to fall. But they were not mutually independent either, because they were cognate, rooted in the same interconnected economic space, unfolding within kindred cultural and political orders, and precipitated by processes of socio-political and ideational change that had always been transnationally connected.[48] When revolution broke out in 1848, synchronous propagation effects interacted with evolving conditions of instability.

In Paris, those who would take control during the revolution of 1848 were acutely aware of what was happening in the rest of Europe. If we examine the day-to-day news coverage in *La Réforme*, a radical republican Parisian daily, during the last months before the outbreak of the revolution in Paris, we find not just stories focused on the political ferment in France, but also thoughtful reports on disturbances elsewhere in Europe. *La Réforme* is an especially interesting source, because its editors and contributors included key participants in the February Revolution. The founding editor, Alexandre Ledru-Rollin, a supporter of universal suffrage and a champion of the working classes, became Minister of the Interior in the Provisional Government established after the February Revolution. The socialist Louis Blanc, celebrated expert on the Social Question, who also joined the Provisional Government, was a sometime editor and contributor; so was the former Carbonaro and insurgent of 1832 and 1834 Étienne Arago, who fought on the barricades during the February Revolution; having occupied the postal administration building during the fighting of February 1848, Arago became the Director of Postal Services. Another collaborator was the journalist Félix Pyat, who served as a revolutionary commissar of the Provisional Government and later as a leftist deputy in the Constituent Assembly.

In short: *La Réforme* articulated the outlook of some of those most actively involved in the February events and their aftermath. And what is striking, if one reads this newspaper during the last weeks before the outbreak of the revolution, is the European horizon of the reporting. From 23 January 1848, when the first article on the Palermitan insurrection appears, there is not a single issue without a substantial account of the latest news from Sicily. The tone is gloating, exultant. Despite 'the most heroic efforts', the editors note, the 'first insurrection' (in Messina) had failed, for lack of unity among the insurgent factions. But now the situation was different: 'it's no longer Messina or Reggio, Palermo or Syracuse that are pushing against the monster, the Bourbon of Naples; it's Sicily with all of its cities, all of its villages'. In the same issue, we read of a further insurrections elsewhere. These events are not perceived as random dysfunctions in an otherwise tranquil Europe, but as parts of a connected phenomenon. 'The working classes are no happier in Spain than they are in France, Belgium, or in England – everywhere, the same misery prevails, everywhere wages are insufficient, everywhere the same menacing symptoms manifest themselves.'[49] The issue of 26 January contained extensive reporting on Sicily and Naples and a serialized excerpt from Settembrini's *Protest of the Neapolitan People*, but also pieces from the Italian press about the situation in Switzerland following the victory of the Federal Army over the cantons of the Sonderbund, and a story on a mutiny among miners employed in the construction of a tunnel at Neustadt in the Bavarian Palatinate.[50]

To be sure, these reports recognized that the events in Italy, Switzerland, Germany and elsewhere were embedded in specific circumstances. But, for the writers of La Réforme, it was clear that the challenge to authority would not stop short at the political borders of France. There was no fundamental distinction to be drawn between 'advanced' and 'backward' countries; Europeans participated in a shared political culture. When a pro-Guizot deputy claimed in a speech to the chamber that backward Italy possessed no political parties and was thus irrelevant to the advanced political life of France, the editors of La Réforme were having none of it: 'Italy, like France, like Germany, carries in its breast all the germs, all the parties; it nourishes all the hopes and seeks all of the solutions. If you doubt it, study and observe the polemics, still so young but so strong, in her journals.'[51] On 5 February, the journal reported that the radicals of the Hungarian Diet had for the first time begun to speak on behalf of all the lands of the empire, a sign that it was becoming the spearhead of an irreversible process of political change. 'Everywhere', people were 'tired of the systematic tutelage and enslavement of the spirit'; they sensed the need to 'take a more active part in the interests of the state and of the nation'.[52] It was inconceivable that this transformation would leave the institutions of old Europe unscathed. After the 'vibrations of the Neapolitan drama', and the upheavals in Turin, Florence and Rome, the monarchies of the continent were 'gasping for breath'; the swift triumph of the Swiss republic in the aftermath of the Sonderbund War had 'profoundly ulcerated' the conservative post-Vienna consensus in Europe.[53] Public interest in these foreign tumults was intense. On 29 January, when Lamartine was scheduled to address the chamber on the Italian question, the galleries filled up long before the opening of the session; ladies, foreigners and people from the provinces were seen quarrelling over the seats; the chamber, too, was fuller than usual. Curious onlookers crowded the entrances to the Palais Bourbon, despite the rain and slush underfoot.[54]

The truly astonishing thing, the editors of La Réforme declared, was the complacency of the French leadership, which seemed to think that it was somehow immune to such perils. For the moment, the French government had opted to align itself with the old order, in the hope of 'burying' the incipient revolutions. For how long would the French people tolerate this refusal to swim with the current of history? 'In France we are talking; in Sicily they are fighting', intoned a leader article of 1 February. 'Here, fear takes the floor, and down there the revolution takes action. Like cowards, we issue commentaries on the treaties of 1815, while Italy tears them to pieces!' Whether they were constitutional, consultative or absolutist in type, all the European governments faced the same imminent calamity: the 'social war' was gnawing equally at the entrails of them all. 'Sleep on, senators of the 3 per cent! Sleep on your money boxes; it won't be long before you are woken again!'[55]

It may seem unsurprising that a leftist journal should have joined up the crises confronting Europe in the winter of 1847–8 in this way. For Marx and Engels, too, the spectre of communism haunted *Europe*, not just the most authoritarian states. That connective view of the continent, one might argue, was the consequence of a philosophy of history that saw Europe as a conflicted society, rather than as an array of dynastic, national and imperial silos. But the socialists and radicals were not alone. Alexis de Tocqueville, liberal of conservative temperament, academician and representative of the town of Valognes in Normandy, expressed similar intimations of catastrophe in a speech to the chamber on 27 January 1848, embedding them in the same panorama of European upheaval:

> Do you [he is addressing the ministers of the government] not feel, by some intuitive instinct which is not capable of analysis, but which is undeniable, that the earth is quaking once again in Europe? Do you not feel . . . what shall I say? . . . as if a gale of revolution were in the air? This gale, no one knows where it springs from, whence it blows, nor, believe me, whom it will carry with it . . . Can you say today that you are certain of tomorrow? Do you know what may happen in France a year from now, or even a month or a day from now? You do not know; but what you must know is that the tempest is looming on the horizon, that it is coming towards us. Will you allow it to take you by surprise?[56]

This was a plea for emergency reform, not a gleeful evocation of impending doom. The editors of *La Réforme* were not impressed. M. de Tocqueville, they remarked, 'speaks like a prim and severe Quaker; he discourses in the manner of preachers; his indignation wears a ruff and a short coat; he is the spirit of correct virtue encased in the pride of a pedantic and conventional man'. They mocked the naivety of his presumption that it was still possible for the leopard of the July Monarchy to change its spots – could he not see that the ministers of the government were 'fatally ensnared' in a moribund structure, the 'servants of a forced situation'?[57] But on one thing Tocqueville and *La Réforme* agreed: the notion that France with its distinctive national institutions might simply ride out the storm was delusional. The revolution that could already be seen on the European horizon would soon be in the streets of Paris.

In other words, episodes of conflict and political dysfunction abroad were not observed piecemeal, as isolated, contingent mishaps, but as parts of an interconnected disorder.[58] We find the same tendency elsewhere in Europe. In February 1848, the Spanish radical newspaper *El Clamor público* reported extensively on events in Switzerland, the Kingdom of the Two Sicilies, Piedmont, Lombardy, the Papal States and France, displaying a clear preference for the liberal cause. The *Clamor* did not see Spain as a kingdom apart, but as a nation deeply implicated in the political fortunes of the continent and in danger of being left behind by the latest wave of political transformations.[59] On 22 February 1848, in a piece entitled 'The People and Their Oppressors', *El Eco del Comercio* depicted a European panorama of upheaval: the Spanish monarch and her *moderado* ministers must act before it was too late.[60] *El Siglo* provided detailed coverage of the French banqueting movement and published the new constitution granted by the king of the Two Sicilies after the revolution in Naples.[61] These were all papers of the liberal and radical left, with a vested interest, one might say, in hailing foreign tumults. But we find the same pattern of attention in the more conservative *El Heraldo*, close to the *moderado* regime. Here, too, there was reporting on the events in Switzerland and Sicily, on new demands from the Hungarian Diet that were inspired by the reforms recently conceded in the Papal States; throughout February there was very detailed reporting on all the theatres of unrest in Italy.[62]

In the Netherlands, the *Algemeen Handelsblad* observed that Ferdinand II of the Two Sicilies would not be in such a pickle if he had pre-empted the revolution with timely reforms, adding that 'this might give some pause to princes and politicians outside Naples too'.[63] Already in November and December 1847, newspapers in Berlin were following closely the events in Switzerland while drawing attention to the fact that King Frederick William IV's role as the sovereign prince of Neufchâtel made him a stakeholder on the 'Jesuit' side of the struggle – in these months, attacks on 'Jesuitism' in Switzerland and elsewhere were read as a veiled attack on the Prussian monarchy.[64] Attentive readers of the *Vossische Zeitung*, a moderate liberal Berlin daily, on 17 January 1848 could scarcely have missed the broader pattern: a motion by the lower chamber in Karlsruhe (Baden) demanding full freedom of the press; ratification of the new Swiss constitution in various cantons; in Electoral Hesse the dismissal of trumped-up charges against a famous liberal politician and opposition deputy; a tax boycott in Milan, disturbances in Parma, Naples and Genoa; reform banquets in Paris; a rebellious public mood in Rome, where the government was 'trying to deflect the elements of fermentation in every manner and at any cost, so as to defer for as long as possible the explosion that threatens'.[65] Every issue revealed a similar panorama of political spot-fires, upheavals and signs of impending storm.[66] Even in Helsinki in the Russian Empire, where the news from the insurgent capitals took about a month to get through, the Finnish-language *Suometar* provided coverage of the events as interconnected tumults, leaving readers in no doubt as to the editor's sympathies with the insurgents.[67]

The essential point is that weeks before the February Revolution in Paris, the (mainly urban) readers of European newspapers were well informed about the advancing frontier of political unrest and in a good position to recognize its trans-European character. And this was true even of papers on the European 'periphery'. On 10 February, *Curierul Românesc*, the biweekly Bucharest newspaper edited by the moderate liberal Ion Heliade Rădulescu, opened with reports of disturbances in Livorno and Milan and (belated) news of a popular petition signed by 10,000 people in Palermo in December.[68] A week later, a long article reported the Palermitan events of 12 January: on the day set aside for celebrating the king's birthday, the editors wrote, a 'popular revolution' (*revoluție popolului*) had broken out. Other pieces reported disturbances in the other Italian states and a circular from the king of Bavaria to his officials announcing the abolition of censorship.[69] On 2 March, a piece based on correspondence from Genoa noted that the movements in the Kingdom of the Two Sicilies were now reverberating across Italy; in Florence and Pisa, the word 'constitution' had become 'a rallying cry of the people'. And then came a sharp departure from the paper's usual tone of apolitical detachment: 'The Two Sicilies are demonstrating that if the people demand their true rights, they can have all of them.'[70]

Only a small minority of the most richly endowed papers could afford to run their own correspondents; most coverage was pieced together from private correspondence and copy filleted and translated from local papers in newsworthy locations or from authoritative titles like the London *Times* or the Augsburg *Allgemeine Zeitung. Curierul Româ-nesc* sourced many of its stories from the *Gazeta de Transilvania*, published within the Kingdom of Hungary, which also reported on political developments in France, Rome, Piedmont, Tuscany, Lombardy, Venetia and Switzerland.[71] But the provenance of news stories was of secondary importance – what mattered was that they enabled Europeans to feel that they belonged to a shared present, a present in which history was awakening to rough life. In that interconnected setting, the question of whether the 'wave' of revolutions 'began' in Palermo or Paris loses much of its importance.

The eyes of the Austrian Chancellor, Clemens von Metternich, and François Guizot, Minister of Foreign Affairs and, from 18 September 1847, Prime Minister of France, were also fixed on this European horizon. To Metternich, it seemed that the upheavals across Europe, though at different stages of maturation, were following the same script. 'If I may compare the revolution with a book', he observed on 23 February, 'I would say that we are still at the preface, whereas France has already reached the final pages.'[72] The Europe of Metternich and Guizot was not the transnational, radical networked world of insurgencies and social movements, but the connected fabric of the 1815 settlement, a post-Napoleonic 'security culture', an international web woven together out of laws and treaties.[73] Both men followed closely the upheavals in Switzerland and Italy, though their information came from diplomatic correspondence in the first instance, rather than from newspapers. For Guizot, the disturbances in the south were not arguments for reform. In a moment of continental flux and uncertainty, he believed, sudden concessions would merely give rise to further instability. The France of the doctrinaire liberals would only survive this wave of continental turbulence if the government stood firm until the ship of state could be manoeuvred into calmer waters.

A REVOLUTION IN FEBRUARY

If Guizot and the ministers remained complacent, this was in part because their ascendancy still seemed secure. The elections of 1846 had enlarged the pro-government majority in the chamber, whose members represented the wealthiest 3 per cent of the French population. In 1847, a majority of deputies rejected two moderate proposals for franchise reform. The opposition responded by launching a cycle of political banquets focused on the suffrage question. The sequence was meant to culminate on 22 February in a banquet hosted by local legions of the National Guard in the restless 12th district of Paris. But on 14 January the government announced that it would prohibit the final banquet.

The news of the prohibition triggered consternation among the members of the National Guard who had taken on the task of organizing the banquet. When they appealed for support to the opposition deputies of the chamber, they were told that they must tone the event down if they hoped to circumvent the prohibition. In order to achieve this, the opposition deputies imposed certain conditions. The banquet must be placed under the supervision of a committee composed mainly of deputies and members of the Electoral Commission of the Seine, who, unlike the original organizers (petit-bourgeois Guardsmen), had the right to vote. The relatively modest price of the subscription ticket must be raised to shut out undesirable elements. (This decision created awkwardness, because hundreds of tickets had already been delivered and it would now be necessary either to refund them or to exchange them for new ones that were more expensive.) The name 'Banquet of the 12th District' could be retained, but the location must be changed from the unruly 12th district to the steadier and more salubrious Champs Élysées.[74]

Here, already, were the key ingredients of the turbulence that would initiate the February Revolution and sweep away the last French monarchy. Wrestling control over the banquet of the 12th district out of the hands of the local legions of the National Guard, almost none of whom were enfranchised, had an alienating effect on many other Guard regiments, especially in the more restive areas of the capital. And, at the same time, republicans involved in the planning decided that a call should go out to members of the National Guard, students and workers to flank and support the deputies on their way to the banquet, which was thereby transformed into the mere centrepiece of a much larger public manifestation. The news that the government continued to withhold permission for the banquet prompted a heated debate in the chamber. For many days, the deputies discussed the 'reformist banquets' and the legality of the government's efforts to suppress them.[75] Did citizens possess a fundamental *right* to hold banquets? Did a right to suppress them exist on the part of the government? The Minister of the Interior, Charles Marie Tanneguy, Comte Duchâtel, and the Keeper of the Seals, Michel Hébert, were quick to point out that the revised *Charte* of 1830 made no reference to the right to assemble, to which a parliamentary wag made the droll objection that the *Charte* did not refer to the right to breathe either, and yet no one proposed granting the government the power to forbid respiration.[76] One of the most interesting and widely noted interventions was a speech by the radical opposition deputy Alexandre Ledru-Rollin, in which he argued that whether or not the *Charte* of 1830 acknowledged the right to assemble, there existed 'a solemn and foundational text that protects the liberty of assembly and considers its use as one of the duties of the citizen'. He was referring to the constitution of 1791, which explicitly guaranteed to citizens 'the right to assemble without arms'.[77]

Ledru-Rollin could make this argument in part because the absence of clear stipulations defining the right to assemble created a lacuna in the legal fabric through which it was possible, as it were, to peer back into a more remote past. But his argument also spoke to a reverence for particular constitutions that, as we have seen, was not unusual in early-nineteenth-century Europe – the 1812 constitution of Cadiz, known affectionately to its adherents as 'The Sacred One' (*la sagrada*) and 'The Pretty Girl' (*la bonita niña*), had attracted similar veneration across Europe and Latin America, and there were plenty of Spanish radicals who argued after the deposition of the liberal regime in 1823 that, since its abrogation by the king was unsanctioned and illegal, it simply remained in force. In 1848, the British government and some Sicilians took a similar view of the Sicilian constitution of 1812, which, in their eyes, had never been legally revoked and whose continuing validity justified British intervention in support of the Sicilian uprising. The Poles revered their enlightened constitution of 1791 and held even the imposed constitutions of 1807 and 1815 in a degree of respect. The doctrinaire liberals close to Guizot had their own constitutional idol: the *Charte* of

1814, in the revised version of 14 August 1830. The numinous presence of past and present constitutions, including many that stemmed from the era of the Revolutionary and Napoleonic Wars, is one of the distinctive features of the European revolutions of this era.

Even if the government felt itself to be on firm legal ground in arguing that it was permissible to disallow an assembly deemed to pose a danger to public order, the political dimension of the question was much harder to resolve. We have seen that banqueting enjoyed a special status in France as a form of sociability with deep customary roots. The right to assemble and dine together was important to the sociable life of the professions and the schools of the great universities. The government's prohibition of the annual typographers' banquet of 1847 had stirred resentment, as did the cancellation of the academic Banquet of the Schools, just at the time (January 1848) when the lectures of the charismatic radical historian Jules Michelet, himself the son of a printer, were cancelled at the Collège de France. And as the 'democratic banquets' articulated increasingly radical demands, the social resonance of political banqueting deepened. More and more convenors opened their doors (and tailored their prices) to the popular classes excluded from the French franchise. By 1847, women, too, were starting to take part, and not just as decorative marginal additions to the main event. Whereas in 1838 the Fourierist leader Victor Considerant had refused Flora Tristan entry to the banquet marking the sage's first posthumous birthday, the banquet convened in 1847 to toast Fourier, Poland and the emancipation of women was distinguished by the presence of over one hundred women of diverse social rank, some of them accompanied by children.[78]

These changes broke open the high wall separating the small political and the much larger social nation. The electoral franchise looked increasingly grotesque and outlandish. The fundamental flaw of the July Monarchy, Alphonse de Lamartine declared to the chamber on 11 February, in a speech acclaimed even by his critics on the radical left for striking a new and uncompromising tone, lay in the fact that 'the system' established in 1830 had 'refused to replace a narrow oligarchy with the vast democracy promised by the constitution, that it changed hands without changing actions'.[79] Only against this background does it become clear how the debate over the right to assemble at banquets could acquire such explosive power, the power not just to stir indignation and even rage, but also to bring together diverse social groups, from the oppositional deputies of the liberal and radical elite, to radical women, students, typographers, guildsmen and National Guardsmen. The editors of *La Réforme* could not know how imminent the revolution was, but they saw clearly on 14 February that the struggle over the banquet for the 12th district had created a new political situation. The stand-off between the ministers and the opposition had reached an impasse. Now there were only two options. Either the opposition would withdraw, or it would 'go to the utmost lengths'. If the former happened, the opposition would 'forever be lost in the eyes of public opinion'. If the latter happened, 'far-reaching consequences' were to be expected. 'So this is a crisis, a true crisis of the state that is opening up before our eyes!'[80]

The government continued to insist on the prohibition, even after the changes recommended by the opposition deputies. A period of uncertainty followed. The banquet, though proscribed, was still scheduled to take place, and so was the parade/demonstration that had been planned to honour the banqueters as they processed to their venue. The mood of crisis deepened. 'The focus here is on the coming banquet', declared an impressively clairvoyant leader article in *La Réforme*. 'And it feels as if revolution is absolutely imminent and the orchestration of this banquet will be intertwined with it.'[81] For some weeks, the government had been preparing for the worst. Already on 11 February, General Sébastiani, commander of the First Military Division, had ordered that extra supplies of biscuit, firewood and rice be stored in the barracks of each Parisian regiment. Orders to stockpile horse fodder, picks and hatchets (for pulling down barricades), rifled-musket rounds and demolition bombs (also for barricades) followed. These measures were not lost on the radicals: 'We only meet', *La Réforme* announced on 14 February, 'to count the bombs, and the litres of powder and brandy, the bundles of axes and the boxes of cartridges that are supposedly being distributed to the barracks . . .'[82]

Only late on 21 January did the military command learn that the liberal leaders had cancelled the banquet. The order to prepare for a major insurrection was rescinded and the troops returned to the stations they occupied for minor disturbances. But it was too late to prevent the crowds from forming on the next day to see or join a parade whose purpose no longer existed. Shortly before midday on 22 February, large crowds began to flow together at various points along the Left Bank, thickening as they traversed the bridges across the Seine towards the place de la Madeleine and the place de la Concorde. Some were clearly ignorant of the cancellation; others, like the men and women who had gathered in the centre of Palermo only six weeks before, were simply curious and wanted to see what was up. As the news spread that there would be no banquet or parade, there was a souring of the mood. Efforts to disperse the people gathered in front of the Madeleine and on the place de la Concorde proved fruitless: the crowds were simply too vast. Only at around 5 p.m. did the drums begin to roll throughout the city at the assembly points of the National Guard, the signal for mobilization. But the response was disappointing: most guards stayed at home or simply mingled with the crowds. A second call to duty on the following morning (23 February) revealed the depth of the alienation that had taken hold among the guards. Some National Guard commanders, rather than reporting for duty, went to the homes of opposition deputies to ask them for instructions.[83] Even among the minority who responded, discipline was poor, the Guardsmen preferring to fraternize with the demonstrators or to interpose themselves between units of Municipal Guards, a widely feared corps whose loyalty to the monarchy remained strong, and the insurgent crowds. 'The shopkeepers', the journalist Philippe Faure observed, in reference to the petit-bourgeois status of many Guardsmen, 'have no desire to fight for Louis Philippe.'[84] It was one thing for the Army and the Municipals to suppress an insurrection without the help of the National Guard and very much another to pacify the capital city in the face of actual resistance from the Guardsmen.[85] The troops were dispersed to assembly points across the city, poised to deal with emergent 'trouble spots'; the crowds formed in even greater numbers after a night of cold rain. But it was now virtually impossible for the army command to send or receive messages or supplies, the crowds were too dense and hostile. Confusion deepened.

Throughout the growing agitation, Guizot remained confident that he could still make the 1830 system work. He and his government flatly ignored the calls for franchise reform and continued to plan for the future. On the afternoon of 22 February, a correspondent for *La Réforme* found the chamber deep in discussion of a law relating to the Bank of Bordeaux. Outside: smashed streetlamps, barricades, troops and streets thick with people; inside: the meticulous, clause-by-clause discussion of a banking law. Guizot appeared sombre, but not a word was said by or to the chamber about the situation evolving in the capital. It was not that no one knew what was going on – from time to time, deputies would run across the chamber to the benches, bringing the latest news of events in the city. It was rather that the government remained on a kind of auto-pilot that often comes into play in regimes on the verge of extinction, locked in a trance-like illusion of normality and determined to press ahead regardless. For all his subtlety and sophistication as a politician and a man of letters, Guizot was completely unable to register the mean-ing of the disaster that was about to sweep the doctrinaire liberals from power. Until the day of his death he would continue to think of himself as the inerrant defender of liberal constitutional principles, which, in a devastatingly narrow way, he was. He had always believed that reality would eventually catch up with his theory.[86] When the king withdrew his support from his Prime Minister on the following afternoon (23 Febru-ary) Guizot resigned immediately. His last contribution to the crisis – late on the night of 23/24 February – was to urge the monarch to put down the insurrection with all necessary force.

'The events carry us away; they rush like a hurricane', the editors of *La Réforme* wrote. They hoped that their readers would understand that 'amid this incessant action, all cut through by episodes and the adventures that the people have set in motion by their powerful agita-tion', it would be impossible to publish all the details of a convulsion that had 'thrown the entirety of Paris' onto the streets and squares. On 23 February fighting flared up across much of the city centre, from the porte Saint-Denis and the rue de Cléry to the rue neuve Saint-Eustache, the rue Montmartre and the rue Vieille-du-Temple. Barricades sprang up, were dismantled by the troops and then rebuilt as soon as the troops withdrew. In the streets between the boulevards and the quays, there were barricades every fifteen paces, transforming the neighbourhoods into a honeycomb of insurgent cells.[87]

As the space of the city became more fragmented, the narratives of eyewitnesses broke down into pieces containing less and less time; synop-sis made way for shards of information: a citizen walking alone along a street was stabbed twice in the arm for no apparent reason by a mounted Municipal Guardsman who happened to be galloping by; at half past one in the afternoon, another man who was minding his own business on the corner of rue Saint-Honoré and the rue Neuve-du-Luxembourg, was struck from behind with a bayonet in the left shoulder by a Municipal Guardsman. 'The violence was such that the bayonet protruded from the front of his chest and the poor fellow was killed on the spot.' There was a decisive escalation that evening on the boulevard des Capucines. Here, three companies of regular army infantry had formed up in front of Guizot's Ministry of Foreign Affairs, screened from the populace by a body of National Guard. But the Guardsmen were called away to deal with a disturbance somewhere else, leaving the troops confronting the crowd. At between 8 and 9 p.m., masses of jubilant citizens interspersed with defecting National Guardsmen pushed towards the ministry, as if to gain entry. As the troops pushed back against the jostling Parisians and the bodies swayed first this way and then that, an unknown person discharged a firearm, probably by accident. The panicked infantrymen reacted by firing several volleys without notice into the crowd, killing fifty-two persons and wounding seventy-four.

The effect was transformative. With astonishing speed, the news of the deadly clash on the boulevard des Capucines rippled across the city. Amélie Crémieux had walked out onto the streets that evening with her mother, a phlegmatic lady who had already witnessed two French revolutions. Troops were nowhere to be seen; a spontaneous general illumination had lit up the streets like a theatre set. 'Paris was superb to see. We were still on the boulevards when we heard the echo of the volley of shots that has enraged the people. We saw with what swiftness the news spread; as we traced our route back home, we found that everyone already knew what had happened. We saw the ferment, the anger . . .'[88] New barricades – 1,500 in all – went up across the city, the initiative passed from the chamber to the street, barracks that had been abandoned by troops were stormed and looted, railway lines sabotaged to prevent the arrival of more troops. A violent randomness had burst into the lives of the citizenry. Parisians were passing into a time out of control, too diffused and multifarious to be captured in narrative. 'It is impossible to write anything; the facts carry us away; let us leave chronicles for later.'[89]

When the sun rose on 24 February, the army remained strung out across its 'trouble spots'. Most units were cut off from headquarters and running short of supplies. More and more National Guardsmen were seen fraternizing with the insurgents. Efforts by the army command to regain control of the capital failed: the units sent to secure strategic posts found themselves drowned in crowds, their weapons pulled from their hands by the demonstrators. The political picture remained unclear. Count Louis-Mathieu Molé, appointed by the king to succeed Guizot as

Prime Minister, failed to form a government; the king tried replacing him first with Adolphe Thiers, a popular deputy of the centre-left, and then with Odilon Barrot, a democrat who had demanded electoral reform as the only way to avoid a revolution. But the time for last-minute substitutions had passed. Despairing, Louis Philippe, king of the French, abdicated and fled from Paris. On the following day, the front page of *La Réforme* was emblazoned with a stirring proclamation from the Provisional Government. A 'retrograde and oligarchic old government', the new government announced, had just been overturned by 'the heroism of the People of Paris'. The old government had already fled the country, 'leaving behind it a trail of blood that must rule out its ever returning to power'. These words could have appeared in any one of the liberal journals of 1830, but then came the hint at a definitive break with the past: 'The blood of the people has flowed, as it did in July [1830]; but this time, this generous blood will not be betrayed.'

As the events of February revealed, the military and police authorities of Paris – like so many of their counterparts across Europe – had spent the last eighteen years preparing for the wrong revolution. The counter-insurgency plans of the Parisian authorities had focused on a tightly organized and well-planned uprising of the kind that had broken out in 1832, 1834 and 1839. What happened was something more inchoate, multifocal, socially deep, something anchored not in seditious conspiracy, but in the waning of respect and trust and in the emergence, unexpectedly, of a cause – the right to assemble – capable of bringing together heterogeneous disaffected elements, at least temporarily. The most important legacy of the conspiratorial insurrectionists was thus to have distracted the attention of the authorities from the real task at hand, which was to recalibrate the processes of government in such a way as to meet and channel the expectations of an increasingly politicized and critically aware society. Had the French government dared to do this, the term *juste milieu* (happy medium, judicious moderation), adopted in self-description by the doctrinaire liberals, might have come to signify the broad and diverse centre of French political society, with left-insurrectionist and legitimist elements banished to the fringes of the system. Instead, it came to mean the middle in a purely mathematical sense: a point supposedly equidistant from the hard left and the hard right, encased within the ramparts of the franchise, a franchise that excluded many of those who were expected to rally to the monarchy in a moment of crisis.

There were many reasons why the most crucial actors in that pre-revolutionary moment found it impossible to choose the road of reform. One of them was that the revolution of July 1830, repudiated by the republicans, remained a sacred moment of inception for the Orleans monarchy and the moderate liberals who served it; it seemed to exempt them from the duty to countenance further transformations. Another was that the prospect of franchise expansion raised old and formidable questions about what would happen when less prosperous citizens, people of the 'covetous classes', entered the citadel of politics. Under-lying the confident bluster of Guizot's 'enrich yourselves' was a visceral fear of the popular classes who had done so much to secure the July Monarchy and had received so little from it. 'We have said it: the gov-ernment is afraid', wrote *La Réforme* on 16 February, as the controversy over the banqueting movement intensified. 'It makes no secret of the fact; it admits it for the first time since 1830.'[90] The resulting deadlock in the official thinking of the constitutional monarchy could only be broken by the brute force of a major upheaval.

The accumulation of pressures around the suffrage question draws our attention to a plane of causation that is sometimes lost from view when we think of revolutions as the consequences of remote causes (economic cycles, the distillation and refinement of ideas) and proxim-ate events (the appearance of a poster announcing an insurrection, the accidental discharge of a bullet, a massacre that transforms the emo-tional chemistry of a city). Between the remote and the proximate is an intermediate plane of causation: the accumulation of political tension, the hardening of language, the collapse of consensus and the exhaustion of compromise, the emergence of tripwire issues – a political dynamic that lives neither in years nor in hours, but in months and weeks.[91]

This is the 'time of politics', and it belongs to the rhythm of all the revolutionary crises of 1848. In Prussia, as we have seen, the deadlock between the Berlin government and the newly convoked United Diet of 1847 produced a new situation. Across the German states, the same year witnessed an intensification of opposition and a proliferation of political banquets. In Hungary, the opposition in the Diet produced, for the first time ever, a comprehensive political programme; the authorities forbade its publication but could not prevent clandestine versions of it from circulating across the country. In the states of the Italian peninsula, the enthusiasm for Pius IX merged, as we have seen, with liberal and radical agitation. And in some countries, scandals and moral panics – an unpopular royal mistress in Bavaria, the conviction of two French ministers for corruption in the summer of 1847, campaigns against the Jesuits – fed the outrage. Everywhere, causes crystallized – the right to assemble, a tobacco boycott, a new and unpopular tax, the imprisonment of a celebrated activist or the prohibition of a well-known pamphlet – that could bring together diverse constituencies, while personalities appeared who seemed to capture the prevailing mood. And throughout much of Europe, as we have seen, these pressures accumulated against the background of a wave of economic disruption that had begun and subsided in the agrarian sector but was still eating away at commerce and urban manufacturing in many European cities.

'We are standing at a turning point in Europe's fortunes', the Prussian officer and diplomat Joseph von Radowitz wrote to his wife from Berlin on 28 February 1848. 'What began with Switzerland and advanced through Italy is now entering its European phase.'[92] The February events in Paris did not start the revolutionary sequence that shook Europe in 1848, but they inaugurated a period of heightened momentum and complexity. From the beginning of March 1848, it becomes impossible to trace the revolutions as a linear sequence from one theatre of turbulence to the next. We enter the fission phase, in which almost-simultaneous detonations create complex feedback loops. Reports of political upheaval from Cologne, Mannheim, Darmstadt, Nassau, Munich, Dresden, Vienna, Pest, Berlin, Milan and Venice and elsewhere fuse into an all-engulfing crisis. The narrative bursts its banks, the historian despairs and 'meanwhile' becomes the adverb of first resort.[93]

WE ARE DEAD

On 10 March 1848, a statement in the official section of the *Wiener Zeitung* set out the Austrian government's view of the recent events in Paris. 'His Majesty regards the change of government which has taken place in France as a domestic concern of that country.' Austria had no intention of intervening in French domestic affairs, the anonymous author declared, but if the new government in Paris threatened in any way the territories of the Austrian Empire or of the German Confederation, 'then His Majesty the Emperor will repulse such a breach of the peace with all the means that Providence has endowed him with'.

This must have made strange reading for burghers who sat poring over the paper in the cafés of the Austrian capital. For weeks, news had been trickling in about the growing turmoil in Italy – the revolution in Palermo, the concession of a constitution in Naples, the ferment in Rome, Bologna, Tuscany, Venice and Milan. The non-official section of the very same issue of the *Wiener Zeitung* was full of political storm warnings: in Cologne, a crowd had forced its way into the municipal council, presenting the representatives with 'demands of the people' (a list of the demands followed). In Munich, a deputation of citizens had presented a request to the king; when this was refused, an armed crowd had forced the authorities to back down and concede. In Nassau, the duke had just announced that all 'popular demands' were to be fulfilled. The 'usually peaceful' city of Darmstadt in Hessen presented 'a picture of the greatest agitation'.[94] And amidst the noise from within and beyond the borders of the Habsburg monarchy, this breathtakingly placid announcement from the Hofburg: the Parisian events were a distant storm in a French teacup; Vienna remained the enforcer of the European order; the Emperor counted on the unity and loyalty of his faithful subjects.

In reality, the city of Vienna was already in a state of ferment. Surging food prices, the collapse of confidence in commercial and industrial enterprises, a run on the banks and a squeeze on credit had produced panic. On 29 February, a mysterious poster, reminiscent of the proclamation of the previous month in Palermo, appeared at the city's Carinthian Gate: 'In one month, Prince Metternich will fall. Long live constitutional Austria!'[95] On 4 March, the radical physician Ludwig von Löhner drew up the programme of a newly founded 'Progressive Party in Austria', urging the citizens of the Austrian lands to rise up and build a new Austria with their own hands on the ruins of the old.[96] Letters from concerned citizens reached the most senior officials of the Habsburg administration warning of an impending crisis and proposing a range of remedies: a constitution for the Habsburg lands and for the empire as a whole, meritocracy and transparency in official appointments, freedom of the press and the abolition of censorship.[97] On 3 March, thirty-three members of the oppositional faction in the Lower Austrian Diet submitted a memorandum to the body responsible for overseeing the Diet's business, in which they warned of the perils facing the monarchy if the creaking machinery of the bureaucratic state was not immediately overhauled.[98]

Six days later, a large group of prominent citizens of the city gathered at the apartments of the radical physician Dr Alexander Bach to sign a petition to the Diet commending a familiar list of reforms: the full publication of the state finances, establishment of a full-blown parliament with regular meetings and budgetary and legislative powers; a press law instead of censorship; a judicial system open to public scrutiny; and the establishment of a modern system of local and municipal representation, among other things. This text was adopted as a petition by the Legal-Political Reading Club, an association of reform-minded officials, lawyers and professors and soon attracted 3,000 signatures. The fact that Dr Bach himself solemnly paraded it through Vienna on horseback in order to present it at the Landhaus, where the Diet would soon be convening, did nothing to diminish its resonance.[99] On 12 March, thousands of students gathered on the square in front of the university with the intention of asking the monarch to let them take part in the deliberations of the Diet, and that afternoon a petition signed by 30,000 Viennese citizens was presented to the emperor. As so often in revolutionary situations, there was a sudden proliferation of voices, of individuals, groups and institutions claiming the right to shape the process of change.

And as the voices demanding change grew in volume and number, news reached Vienna of the extraordinary address the patriot leader Lajos Kossuth had delivered to the Hungarian Diet on 3 March. In it, Kossuth blamed the Habsburg administration for all the ills of the monarchy and set out a list of demands: a separate administration for Hungary; the abolition of 'feudal' obligations on the land (with compensation for landowners); the abolition of tax exemptions for the nobility; extension of the franchise to the urban middle classes and the independent landowning peasants; a Hungarian Cabinet responsible to a Hungarian parliament. These measures were to be flanked by analogous reforms in the Austrian part of the monarchy. Habsburg absolutism, he declared, was 'the pestilential air which . . . dulls our nerves and paralyses our spirit. . . . The dynasty must choose between its own welfare and the preservation of a rotten system.'[100] A German translation of the speech was forwarded to the Legal-Political Reading Club and clandestinely distributed across the capital. It fell, one eyewitness recalled, 'like a kindling spark into the already agitated minds of the Viennese'.[101]

Kossuth's last point was important, because it suggested that he intended to renew the monarchy, not to destroy it. In general, these early articulations of revolutionary protest were framed not as calls to destroy the existing structure of power, but as warnings whose purpose was to save the system from the consequences of its custodians' errors. Protests of bourgeois provenance tended, even before the revolution had got underway, to point to the untold horrors that would result if timely reforms were not enacted to appease the 'discontented masses'. They were about claiming power for the propertied classes while protecting their property and preventing further radicalization. Even Löhner's manifesto, by some margin the most radical of these early days, studiously avoided the word 'revolution', renounced violence and expressed the ambition to 'rescue the state, the empire and the emperor' by re-establishing the bonds of trust between the monarchy and its subjects. In Vienna, as in many other places, it was the ministers who attracted the ire of the reformers, not the monarch or the institution he embodied. This was partly a function of popular affection for Emperor Ferdinand, a clueless and incompetent ruler but a hugely amiable man with a warm wit and a gift for connecting with ordinary people. But the Viennese had other reasons to pin their hopes on the monarch: it was well known in the streets of the capital that the key figures at the imperial court were divided on how to proceed and that there were some who felt that the time had come to drop the unpopular police minister, Sedlnitzky, and the foreign minister and Chancellor, Prince Metternich, who was seen by the liberal and radical intelligentsia as the longstanding incarnation of the worst features of the Austrian system.

By the time the Lower Austrian Diet finally convened on 13 March, there was intense excitement. The students, who had by now taken control of the university, had organized a demonstration outside the Landhaus, where they were joined by artisans celebrating their traditional 'blue Monday' off. The crowds surrounding the building were so dense that it was difficult to get into the courtyard. While the members of the Diet began their deliberations inside the building, the people outside delivered speeches of their own. The first to clamber up onto the ledge of a fountain and speak was a 32-year-old physician from Buda by the name of Adolf Fischhof, who gave stirring expression to the hopes of the crowd, speaking of liberty and religious equality, though very few could actually hear his words above the din of the cheering – the canonical version that later emerged of the speech he gave (demanding freedom of the press, trial by jury, a parliamentary assembly and unity among the peoples of the monarchy) was probably largely invented. Yet for Fischhof, this was a pivotal moment, a first step onto the political stage, comparable with Robert Blum's debut in front of the Leipzig Schützenhaus, and an especially momentous step for a Jewish subject of the Austrian Empire. For the politically active Jews of the European states, as we shall see, 1848 was a moment of tremendous promise and opportunity, as well as of danger.[102] After Fischhof, everyone wanted to have a go. 'Pale with terror at their own daring', as the American Chargé d'Affaires at the Court of Vienna later recalled, the speakers rehearsed the usual demands.[103] A Tyrolean with a booming voice climbed up and read out, amidst deafening cheers, a German translation of Kossuth's speech to the Hungarian Diet while copies were passed out among the crowd.

Carl Wilhelm Ritter von Borkowski, eighteen years old, had travelled from his hometown of Czernowitz, today Chernivtsi in western Ukraine, to study at the Polytechnic Institute in Vienna. He felt how the air was shaken by the noise of the crowd after each speech. Just as in Leipzig a delegation had materialized out of the crowd and entered the city parliament; a 'committee' of students and medics now formed outside the Landhaus and entered the Diet chamber to convey their demands to the representatives inside. Among them was Dr Adolf Fischhof. Panicking, the Diet in turn sent a small delegation to the Court with a letter calling for reforms.

In a letter to his parents in Czernowitz, Borkowski described what happened next: tired of waiting for a reply from the authorities, the crowd began smashing the windows and then the furniture of the Landhaus. When the city's commanding general, Archduke Albrecht, approached with his men, they were 'pelted with stones, pieces of wood and other such [missiles]'. Having coolly ordered his troops to halt, the general issued the command to fire.[104] Among the five people killed, four were struck by bullets; the other was an elderly woman who was trampled by the people around her fleeing to safety. The four included the vinegar-maker Fürst, who was on his way to see a customer when he was caught up in the commotion around the Landhaus, and an eighteen-year-old Jewish Polytechnik student by the name of Heinrich Spitzer, a young man

An orator addresses the crowd outside the Lower Austrian Diet on 13 March 1848. Outside the relatively sedate world of the diets and chambers, the ability to address crowds and capture their attention could be central to effective political leadership.

of extraordinary talent and promise. Two further male corpses could not be identified but 'appeared to belong to persons of the working class'.[105] There was more shooting and bayoneting as soldiers pursued fleeing citizens down side streets and lanes. In all, twenty-nine people were killed.

Towards evening, violence broke out beyond the city walls in the Viennese suburbs, where bands of workers attacked factories and tore gas pipes out of the ground, starting fires whose reflected glare was visible across the city. Piped gas, a recent innovation, proved a novel vulnerability in cities torn by revolution. In the extramural districts of Fünfhaus and Sechshaus, the police headquarters was stormed, four factories were destroyed and then burned to the ground, two churches plundered, and all the gas lamps smashed. A crowd of 200 people attacked the Zappert finishing factory (*Appreturfabrik*), an establishment that employed 180 workers, breaking not just the machines but also any furniture, carriages and objects of value they could lay their hands on. The boilers of steam engines were hammered to pieces. The Consumption Tax Office on the Mariahilfer Linie (today Europaplatz) to the west of the old city was also sacked. This building, seat of the administration that collected this hated tax, had already come under attack in 1830.[106]

As these events show, the working-class suburban violence of March 1848 focused on more than one type of target. Machines were destroyed if they seemed to pose a threat to jobs, in a manner that recalled the protests of Central European textile workers in the 1840s. Like the Silesian weavers of 1844, the crowds singled out the premises of enterprises that were viewed as bad employers – factory-owners known for integrating a measure of paternalist assistance into their management practice were spared. Administrative buildings were also sacked, especially if they were associated with policing, or with levies like the consumption tax, which was seen as especially burdensome to the poorest, because it raised the prices of staple foodstuffs. One of the earliest administrative responses to the disturbances in the suburbs was thus the abolition or reduction of the taxes on key staples such as potatoes, milk and grain-based products 'for the benefit of the poorer classes of the population'.[107]

A complex picture began to emerge. In the inner city, working women and men who succeeded in making it past the guard posts at the gates demonstrated or fought alongside burghers and students against the Imperial troops. On 21 March, the journal *Der Humorist* listed the names of thirty-six persons known to have been killed in the fighting in the old city during the March days. They included journeyman shoemakers, ribbon-makers, turners, smiths, bakers and carpenters, a hosiery weaver, domestic servants, a washerwoman, a housemaid, two day labourers and a stonemason, but also a professor's wife, a factory accountant and a surgeon.[108] Just as in Berlin, people of the more modest social strata dominated among the killed. These deaths were quickly folded into the narrative of struggle and sacrifice that sealed the swift success of the revolution. But the same did not apply to those who fought outside the city walls in the name of social grievances. Carl von Borkowski's first task as a member of the Academic Legion was to join his patrol and march southwards out of the city through the Erdberg district onto the Simmeringer Heide, an area of open land, where they dug in and waited for the arrival of a 'band of plunder-hungry riff-raff' about 180 strong carrying 'torches of pitch and all the requisites for arson and sack'. After protracted hand-to-hand fighting, in which several were killed and wounded on both sides, the students took the remaining 'riff-raff' prisoner. There were similar clashes at many places on the city's periphery.[109]

Hardly had the authorities agreed to devolve responsibility for the maintenance of law and order, than the armed citizenry of the newly formed National Guard and Academic Legion found themselves called upon to suppress pockets of violent proletarian protest. Far from seeing these protests as a component of the political revolution to which they were themselves committed, they viewed them as perverse and degrading expressions of criminality devoid of any political content and forfeiting any right to the solidarity of observers. Recalling the 'unforgettable springtime of the Austrian imperial state' in 1848, the National Guardsman Matthias Kneisel described the fighting between armed students of the Legion and marauding workers in the districts of Fünfhaus and Sechshaus to the west-southwest of the old city. The 'young people', he wrote, showed great courage and sagacity in clearing the houses occupied by plunderers. The 'most determined of them were thrown downstairs and received their just portion of blows with rifle butt and the flat of the sabre. Amongst all this riff-raff, it was unfortunately the plundering, drunken females who presented the most horrifying spectacle, festooned with rags, bloodthirsty, stumbling and drunk on brandy, loaded up with stolen goods, they were all rounded up.'

The revolutionary city and the rebellious suburb seemed to be entirely separate worlds. 'Exhausted, befouled and deeply depressed by the horrific scenes they had experienced', students and National Guardsmen who had spent many hours manning pickets in front of factories or the houses of their owners would return into the 'joyfully decorated and jubilant city'.[110] Matthias Kneisel described an encounter between a group of workers and a female factory-owner. 'What do you people want?' she asked them. They replied: 'You can see it in our faces! We have nothing to live from, for weeks there has been no work; need drives us to desperation, we have come to destroy all the machines that are guilty of our ruin!' And yet years of accumulated agonizing over the Social Question had done little, it seemed, to kindle the sympathy of bourgeois observers for proletarian protests driven by the direst kind of need. On the contrary: Kneisel's account of the pacification of the suburbs took delight in the lethal violence meted out en masse to workers.[111] Nowhere else in those March days were the simultaneity and separateness of political and social revolt as starkly on display as in Vienna.

'Is it true that you are leaving tomorrow?' The question, posed by an Esterházy countess in a spirit of faux-naive malice that must be common at courts, took Melanie von Metternich by surprise. Why was she asking? 'Well', the countess explained, 'Louis Széchény [brother of the famous Hungarian reformer] just told us that we should buy candles for an illumination tomorrow because you will be sent away.' Reporting on this conversation in her diary, Melanie reflected that, as a senior courtier of long standing, Louis Széchény must know what he was talking about.[112] Central Vienna was and is a small, almost intimate, space. Only 300 yards from the portico of the Landhaus was the window of Chancellor Metternich's study, from which the noise of the crowd in the courtyard was clearly audible. At seventy-four, Metternich himself was too deaf to make out the words, but a secretary took notes for him. He was now the most unpopular man in Vienna.

Metternich, though hugely influential, had never wielded the single-handed power attributed to him by liberal opinion. There was no 'Metternich system', but rather a plurality of power centres that manoeuvred into and out of alignment with each other. Since March 1835, the incapacity of Emperor Ferdinand, who suffered from hydrocephalus and experienced up to twenty epileptic seizures a day, had deepened the fissiparity of the executive structure. The *Staatskonferenz*, an inner circle of Habsburg clan members and ministers that acted as a kind of regency government on behalf of the emperor, entrenched the confusion. And to make matters worse, the government was paralysed for long periods during Ferdinand's reign by the bitter rivalry between the two most powerful ministers, Metternich (foreign affairs) and Anton, Count Kolowrat (interior and finance). The Austrian diplomat Count Joseph Alexander von Hübner, who visited Metternich on 26 February 1848, noted that the intrigues of the Chancellor's enemies at court had already pushed him onto the defensive: 'The prince is isolated and paralysed; in a word, powerless.'[113]

As the March crisis of 1848 deepened, the many players in this hive-like structure fell into two camps, one favouring political concessions and the other preferring to hold fast and steer through the storm. Metternich was in the latter camp. Whereas he had always looked warmly, in theory at least, on reform, in the sense of political change initiated and overseen by the legitimate authority, he viscerally disliked the idea of concessions under the pressure of a revolutionary tumult. Count Hübner was with Metternich at the beginning of March, shortly after he received the news of the proclamation of a republic in Paris. 'Everyone says we must do something', Metternich remarked. 'Well, of course, but what? . . . To these good people I say: we must make everything anew, but such reconstructions cannot be improvised.'[114] There was a certain logic in this: the more dysfunctional the system became, the more time would be needed to repair it. And this meant that as the events speeded up, Metternich's politics slowed down. But it was already much too late for 'reform' in this sense and the Chancellor's dismissal was now among the concessions demanded by the aroused populace of Vienna. As if this were not enough, his old enemy Kolowrat was scheming behind the scenes, building a coalition at court to winkle him out of office.

The tipping point was reached on the evening of 13 March. At a uniquely uncomfortable meeting of the *Staatskonferenz*, Metternich was pressured into resigning. On his return to the residence on the Ballhausplatz, Princess Melanie greeted her husband with stoical gaiety: 'Are we completely dead?' 'Yes, my dear', Metternich replied. 'We are dead.'[115] The Metternichs fled the capital immediately, the Chancellor travelling with false identity papers under the name of Friedrich Mayern, a merchant from Graz. The destination was London. There was a fortnight's pause before taking the boat from Rotterdam, while the party waited out the results of a Chartist mass demonstration on Kennington Common in London, planned for 10 April 1848.

Asked how he went bankrupt, Bill Gorton, a character in Hemingway's novel *The Sun Also Rises*, replies: 'Two ways: gradually and then suddenly.' Revolutions, too, as we have seen, have this dual speed setting. First, the medium-term accumulation of pressures and grievances and then the helter-skelter of concessions as a regime buckles and new centres of power emerge. Vienna, like so many other theatres of revolution, experienced a vertiginous acceleration: 'Three days have passed, richer in events than three centuries', wrote the journalist Moritz Saphir, editor of *Der Humorist*, on 15 March. 'What was scarcely conceivable yesterday is reality today and history tomorrow!'[116]

The news of Metternich's departure on 13 March was met with general euphoria. But the city walls were still bristling with cannon, the Hofburg was surrounded by a thick cordon of troops and field guns could be seen pointing down the most populous streets. To the joy of the students, the government agreed to the formation of an armed 'Academic Legion', tasked with keeping order and protecting property and commanded by none other than Adolf Fischhof. The Legion soon numbered 30,000 men. But the arming of this new militia progressed very slowly, the atmosphere remained tense and the agitation 'grew from hour to hour'. On 14 March came two further announcements: freedom of the press (with the abolition of censorship) and the establishment of a National Guard. Members of the Diet and patrols manned by armed students and citizens spread the news through every part of the city. Improvised flags appeared bearing various legends: 'freedom of the press', 'National Guard', 'Order and Safety'. People adorned themselves with white sashes and 'peace cockades'.

Not all the news was good. The announcement that Field Marshal Prince Alfred zu Windischgrätz, an elderly but energetic counter-revolutionary, had been appointed military and civil commandant of the capital stirred fears that a crackdown might be imminent. These were further fuelled by the text of a public statement signed by the prince and urging the citizens of the city to 'remain obedient to the public measures required for the establishment and maintenance of peace and security' and warning them that 'insults of any kind to the Imperial and Royal troops' would not be tolerated.[117] If the troops continued to control the streets of the capital, one might ask, what was the point of the National Guard? The announcement that the 'Estates committees' (*ständische Ausschüsse*) of the German, Slav and Italian provinces of the empire were soon to be jointly convened aroused interest but also suspicion. Was this how the authorities intended to pacify the people? By granting them a 'joint committee' composed from elements of the empire's retrograde diets, while denying them a constitution and a proper parliament? That was the solution Frederick William IV had reached for in Berlin in 1847; the time had surely passed for such half-measures.

SHALL WE BE SLAVES?

It was on 15 March that the Viennese revolution passed the point of no return, not because events in the capital had got out of hand, but because this was the day on which the crisis of authority unfolding in Vienna fused with the crisis that had been deepening in Hungary since the previous autumn. In Pest and Pressburg (seat of the Diet), Kossuth's speech of 3 March had triggered an upward spiral of political expectations. Showing a sound tactical instinct in this highly dynamic situation, Kossuth turned to the Pest branch of the Party of Opposition, a body, as we have seen, that had coalesced in the previous year, and asked them to work his speech up into a statement to be presented as a popular petition to the authorities. The Pest branch delegated the task in turn to the Society of Ten, a group of café-haunting radicals who called themselves Young Hungary in the Mazzinian manner. In short: Kossuth upped the ante by pushing the political initiative to the left.

The dominant personality in the Society of Ten was the 25-year-old lyricist Sándor Petőfi, an ardent patriot and a man of passionate political convictions who knew and loved the peasant world of the Hungarian steppe, hated the caste spirit of the magnate nobility and was unfamiliar with the still largely German-speaking milieu of skilled crafts and manufacturing in the capital city. Petőfi and his friends produced a document appreciably more radical than Kossuth's speech. It was not a statement, but a list of twelve demands, including freedom of the press, a separate Hungarian government situated in Buda-Pest and responsible to an elected parliament, a National Guard, trial by jury, a national bank, a Hungarian national army, the removal of all 'foreign' Habsburg troops,

an amnesty for political prisoners and union with Transylvania, hitherto administered as a separate Habsburg possession. Yet even this very
advanced menu of demands made no reference to the needs of the urban
working class or the landless peasantry.

On 14 March, the news of the revolution unfolding in Vienna reached
Buda-Pest, triggering a further escalation. That night, radicals gathered
in the Café Pilvax. Amidst passionate discussions, it was resolved that it
was now too late to circulate the twelve demands for signature and then
present them as a petition to the Diet; direct action was called for and it
must take place immediately. On the morning of 15 March, Sándor
Petőfi turned up with the 'National Song' he had composed over the last
few days. There was a reading of this poem in the café. Petőfi's friend
Mór Jókai read out the Twelve Demands and the group processed
through the streets of Pest at the head of a steadily swelling crowd, stopping off at various progressive locations for further readings and
speeches – a girls' school, the university's law school. There were 2,000
of them by the time they reached Lajos Landerer's printing house. Here
copies of the twelve demands were printed in haste and distributed to the
crowd. Next stop was the newly opened National Museum, where Petőfi
recited his National Song before a crowd that now numbered around
10,000. The plebiscitary energy of the text was perfectly suited to the
occasion: 'Arise Magyar, your country calls! Now or never, our time
demands it! Shall we be slaves? Shall we be free?' In the refrain, Hungarian patriots make a vow before God – strongly reminiscent of the text of
'Rule, Britannia' – that they shall never be slaves again – 'Esküszünk,
hogy rabok tovább / Nem leszünk!' It was the dreamscape of European
national memory: a remote past radiant with freedom and glory, an
intervening era of humiliation and 'slavery', and the present exalted as
the moment of transformation through committed action.

With the crowd still growing and in an increasingly delirious mood,
they marched, like so many of the revolutionary crowds of that year, to
City Hall, where the 100-man municipal council was in session. Ordered
to ratify the Twelve Demands, the deputy mayor, Lipót Rottenbiller,
made an interesting reply: 'We should not let history later blame us for
having kept Pest behind other European movements.'[118] The city's seal
was attached to a copy of the Twelve Demands. In the process of the
discussions, a 'Committee of Public Safety' emerged, tasked with coordinating the political management of the twin cities and consisting of

four radicals from the Petőfi circle (incuding Petőfi himself), six liberals from Pest City Council and three noblemen, allies of Kossuth. Having passed the initiative out to the far left like a football to escalate the crisis, the Kossuth party were now reclaiming control. Leaving City Hall, the crowd flowed through the streets of Pest and across the Danube towards Buda, seat of the Vice-Regal Council. The plan was to present the Twelve Demands and insist on the liberation of the city's sole political prisoner, Mihály Táncsics, serving a jail sentence for sedition. A spokesman for the Committee of Public Safety, still unused to this new role, addressed the grandees of the Vice-Regal Council 'stammering in all humility', as Petőfi later recalled, 'and trembling like a pupil before his teacher'.[119] But the councillors were as nervous as the petitioners and immediately offered concessions, and it is easy to see why: a crowd of perhaps 20,000 now surrounded the castle, from whose balconies a sea of people could be seen filling the gardens – in a city whose residents on both sides of the river counted 145,000, these were unprecedented scenes. The mainly Italian troops of the castle garrison had greeted the demonstrators with cheers and were clearly not to be relied upon. The garrison was instructed not to interfere with the political changes taking place in the city, censorship was abolished and Táncsicz was immediately released.

On the morning of the same day, 15 March, a 150-strong delegation of Hungarian representatives made its way on two Danube steamers to Vienna. Arriving in the Austrian capital at around 2 p.m., the 'Argonauts', as the Viennese called them, because they arrived by boat, found the city much deeper in the grip of revolution than the news of the previous day had led them to expect. It was immediately clear that the people controlled the streets, and that the authority of the Habsburg regime was deeply shaken.[120] At around 11 a.m., the emperor had himself ridden out with his brother and his eldest nephew, Franz Joseph, into the aroused streets of the city, where the crowds greeted the imperial trio with 'indescribable jubilation'. The sight of a city transformed into a sea of human faces had a twofold effect on the people around the emperor. On the one hand, it was a reminder that if the government did not act fast, it might soon be facing an all-out insurrection. On the other hand, the thunderous cheering showed that the imperial-royal capital of the House of Habsburg was far from exhausted. The revolution was a denunciation of certain policies and ministers, not of the monarchy as such. And if this was the case, there was still plenty of room for man-oeuvre if one played one's cards right. (In exactly three days' time, the king of Prussia would be forced to make similar calculations.)

At around 4 p.m. came the sensational announcement, delivered by an imperial herald in front of the palace, that delegates would soon be summoned from all of Austria to discuss the constitution that the sover-eign had just decided to grant. A statement signed by the emperor declared that he had taken this step 'out of love for my people', adding: 'I am all the happier to do so for the fact that I was able in your midst to assure myself of your loyalty to the sovereign House.'[121] The news of the promised constitution became known just as Kossuth and a part of the Hungarian delegation were making their way towards the palace through streets thick with cheering crowds and detachments of the National Guard. 'It was a gripping moment', the editors of the *Wiener Zeitung* reported. 'People embraced each other, shook hands, joy radiated from every eye, there was no limit to the celebrations. The brotherhood of all the nations that are united under Austria's sceptre was irrevocably sealed.'[122] Among the Viennese students, there was excitement that morn-ing at the news that armed contingents of Hungarian and Bohemian academic youth were on their way from Pressburg, Prague and Olmütz; they, too, Carl Borkowski told his parents, were welcomed by the citi-zens of Vienna with 'incredible jubilation'.[123] This was the moment of revolutionary fusion, sublime in its apparent unanimity.

Surprised at how quickly the Austrian government had ceded ground, the Hungarian delegation decided to step up the pressure. Difficult dis-cussions among the three leading delegates, Kossuth, Széchenyi and Batthyány, produced a new policy focused on the more or less immediate establishment of Hungary as a separately governed entity within the Habsburg imperial monarchy: a national Hungarian government was to be formed forthwith and Batthyány was to be appointed its Prime Minister – this went some way beyond the Twelve Demands that received the seal of the municipal government in Pest at around the same time. It was agreed on the afternoon of 15 March that instead of presenting demands to the Austrian court in the manner of petitioners, the Hungar-ian delegation should draft the text of a rescript that the king (meaning the emperor of Austria, who was also, by virtue of the personal union of the Habsburg Crowns, the king of Hungary) should be asked to sign.

Presenting a policy document for signature to the monarch was a dramatic departure from the usual course; the Hungarian delegation were in effect claiming the right to behave like the Cabinet ministers of a constitutional monarchy. During an official reception at court for the Hungarians on the afternoon of 16 March, a 'painful scene' unfolded. Emperor Ferdinand, exhausted and confused by the commotion of recent days, gave way to a bout of anxiety and, turning to Archduke Stephen, the Hungarian viceroy, raised his hands as if in prayer and pleaded with him in Viennese dialect: 'I' pitt di', nimm mir meinen Thron nit!' – I beg you, please don't take my throne away! There was both pathos and menace in this encounter: on the one hand, it revealed the human fragility at the heart of the Habsburg imperial system; on the other, it was a reminder that the real power to shape the future of the monarchy did not lie with the man who sat on the throne, but with the opaque web of archdukes, archduchesses, ministers, generals, officials and courtiers around him.[124]

The Austrian government baulked at both the form and the content of the Hungarian demands: a rescript was signed and handed back to the Hungarians on 17 March, but it was not the rescript the Hungarians had presented. There was no undertaking on the part of the king to approve without delay legislation passed by the Hungarian parliament, and no reference to the appointment of Batthyány. Instead, the Habsburg state conference assigned enhanced powers to the Hungarian vice-regent, Archduke Stephen, who was now instructed to act as the 'alter ego' of the emperor himself. It wasn't quite the arrangement the Argonauts had wanted, but it satisfied the need to preserve the formal structure of Habsburg governance while granting the Hungarians the wriggle room they needed to further develop their position. Kossuth's party lost no time in securing the appointment of Batthyány as Prime Minister from Archduke Stephen. Batthyány accepted the post and embarked on a journey into revolutionary Hungarian politics that would end with his execution in October 1849 by an Austrian firing squad.

When they arrived back in Pressburg in the early evening of 17 March, the delegates were besieged by cheering crowds. 'My friend', Széchenyi wrote to his secretary that night, 'we lived through miracles! Act One of the drama was a magnificent success! I am full of the greatest expectations.' But the irresistable euphoria of the moment belied a deep unease about the course events had taken. Széchenyi, as we have seen, had always disapproved of the abrasiveness of Kossuth's style and

Széchenyi (*left*) and Kossuth were brilliantly gifted and energetic patriots who adopted very different approaches to the liberation of Hungary. Széchenyi was the man of gradualist reform and incremental improvements, Kossuth the gambler prepared to risk everything for maximum gains. The tension between them outlived the revolution.

the radicalism of his objectives. He would have preferred a more gradual path, more sparing of the dignity of the imperial-royal house and less likely to trigger the antagonism of the other nationalities in the kingdom of Hungary. To Széchenyi, it seemed that Kossuth and he embodied two quite distinct forms of political temporality. Széchenyi was the man of compound interest at 10 per cent per annum, a politician who looked to incremental gain and sustainability over the longer term; Kossuth, by contrast, was a catastrophist, a gambler, the man who, at the decisive moment, risked winning or losing everything. For the moment, it looked very much as if Kossuth's approach had won out: 'My policy was certain . . . but slow', Széchenyi told his secretary. 'Kossuth staked everything on one card and has already won more than my policy could have produced over perhaps 20 years!' But it was still unclear whether Kossuth's course would prove sustainable in the longer term. That night – we know this from his diaries – Széchenyi was plagued by nightmares: he found himself on a sinking ship in heavy seas while the world around him descended into darkness.[125]

The Hungaro-Austrian upheaval of mid March 1848 was more than a political event; it was a grandiose piece of theatre. When Sandor Petőfi led the crowds through Pest on 15 March, he was dressed for the occasion in a black silk attila with silver buttons, a raked felt cap with an ostrich feather, the Hungarian jacket favoured by the gentry, tightly tailored trousers and tufted evening shoes.[126] As the patriots approached the river, the famous actress Lujza Farkas Szathmáry of the National Theatre could be seen waving an enormous Hungarian tricolour and directing the crowd to cross the pontoon bridge and ascend the steep streets on the other side.[127] Széchenyi and his fellow Argonauts turned up in Vienna wearing tight red trousers, a short red velvet coat lined with fur and braided with gold, a black velvet dolman (a heavily embroidered jacket cut tightly to the waist), yellow spurred boots and a yellow cap with a tuft – not to mention richly ornamented scabbards and knee-high boots with tinkling spurs.[128] Petőfi's wife, Júlia Szendrey, was already well known for wearing clothes in the Hungarian national colours.[129] Carl Borkowski was moved by the sight of detachments of Hungarian law students, 'extremely tasteful in their Hungarian national costume', and later by the German students who streamed in from the provinces dressed in the Old German costume of the student fraternities.[130] At a student congress in Eisenach, the German radical Carl Schurz was amazed by the uniforms of the Viennese Academic Legion: 'black felt hats with ostrich plumes, blue coats with black shining buttons, tricolored, black-red-gold sashes, bright steel-handled swords, light-gray trousers, and silver-gray cloaks lined with scarlet'; they looked to him like a 'troop of knights of old'. And this meant, among other things, that 'all competition with the Viennese for the favors of the fair sex was in vain'.[131] In Karlovac, the Croatian teacher and patriot Dragojla Jarnević delighted in the sight of forty Croatian delegates setting out to present their demands in Vienna, 'wearing red hats and surkas', the folk costumes worn by Croatian adherents of the Illyrian movement in the 1830s and 1840s.[132]

Everywhere in Europe, town squares, clubs and cafés provided the backdrop for theatrical performances by students, tribunes of the people, or orators with a thespian gift, such as the Mazzinian actor Gustavo Modena in Venice.[133] Stage fright, too, was part of the experience of revolution. Because people didn't necessarily already have public voices, they often had to find them.[134] Adolf Fischhof and his fellow orators in the courtyard of the Landhaus were ashen-faced when they spoke their first words to the throng; the delegates to the Vice-Regal Council stuttered as they spoke their words before the representative of the House of Habsburg. The theatrical quality of revolution called for theatrical forms of speech. Virtually all the memoirs of the early days of the revolutions describe the extraordinary sight of illuminated cities, a candle shining in every window, evoking the nocturnal brilliance of a stage set.

The heightening of gesture and expression that so often characterized revolutionary situations aroused ambivalent responses in contemporaries. Alexis de Tocqueville and Gustave Flaubert, fastidious personalities, easily disgusted, winced at the inauthentic mummery and play-acting of insurgents gauchely inhabiting unfamiliar roles. The radical Berlin law student Paul Boerner smiled wryly at the hyperbole of some of those who stood on tables to address meetings. But, for the participants in revolution, theatricality was important. It endowed events with an epic mood and drove them forward. It allowed people to inhabit more fully moments of collective emotion, to shed inhibitions, to merge their private selves with a public cause. It offered the spectacle of an improvised pageantry that made it possible to experience the present as the unfolding of history.

SOLDIERS OUT!

On 28 February, an extra edition of Berlin's *Vossische Zeitung* featured a 'telegraphic despatch' reporting that King Louis Philippe had abdicated. In view of the 'current state of France and of Europe', the editors declared, 'this turn of events – so sudden, so violent and so utterly unexpected – appears more extraordinary, perhaps more momentous in its consequences than even the July Revolution [of 1830]'.[135] As the news from Paris broke in the Prussian capital, Berliners poured onto the streets in search of information and discussion. 'The excitement was incredible', one witness recalled. 'From the highest classes of bourgeois society right down to the pubs of the proletarians, it was as if people had received an electric shock.'[136] For the law student Paul Boerner, it was impossible to remain cooped up in his room:

> I had to go out into the winter cold and walk and walk until I had worn myself out, just to calm my blood and slow down the beating of my heart, which was in a state of unprecedented and baffled agitation and felt as if it were about to blow a hole in my chest.'[137]

Reading clubs, coffee houses and public establishments of all kinds were crammed to bursting. 'Whoever managed to get his hands on a new paper had to climb onto a chair and read the contents aloud.'[138] The excitement grew as word arrived of events closer to home – large demonstrations in Mannheim, Heidelberg, Cologne and other German cities, the concession of political reforms and civil liberties by King Ludwig I of Bavaria, the dismissal of conservative ministers in Saxony, Baden, Württemberg, Hanover and Hesse.

One important focal point for debate and protest, here as in so many cities, was the Municipal Assembly, where elected members of the burgher elite regularly met to discuss the affairs of the city. This body had been a channel for liberal reformist demands for some time: already in the winter of 1846/7, left-liberals and moderates in the assembly had passed resolutions calling for freedom of the press and religious equality for dissenting sectarian groups such as the 'Friends of Light' and the German-Catholics, and even demanding the 'complete emancipation of the Jews'.[139] After 9 March, when a crowd forced its way into the Berlin

City Hall, the usually rather stolid assembly began to mutate into a protest rally.

There were also daily political meetings at the 'Tents', an area of the Tiergarten just outside the Brandenburg Gate reserved for outdoor refreshments and entertainments. These had begun as informal gatherings, but they soon took on the contours of an improvised parliament, with voting procedures, resolutions and elected delegations, a classical example of the public meeting democracy' that unfolded across the German cities in 1848.[140] Among those who dared to speak for the first time in front of an expectant crowd was the radical student Paul Boerner. It didn't go especially well. There was a dense crowd of craftsmen, students, commercial employees and literary people, and the discussion was extremely lively. At first Boerner could neither see nor hear anything. With a thudding heart he raised his hand and asked to speak. But his throat seemed to have been laced shut. He thought better of it and withdrew. Once he had gathered his courage, he made a second attempt and mounted the wooden stage:

> Now I was standing on high; in front me was a dark knot of people that made me feel anxious. I had forgotten everything I wanted to say! Eventually I managed to get started, referring as usual to 'thirty-three years of shameful servitude'. This was greeted with loud applause. Then I wanted to explain that we should conquer our freedom for ourselves; hardly had I got going with the words: 'we don't want to be free with the help of France', but the crowd took me for an opponent of the February Revolution and a general concert of hissing and laughter forced me to renounce, for today at least, my quest for oratorical fame.[141]

It was not long before the Municipal Assembly and the Tents began to work together; on 11 March, the assembly discussed a draft petition from the Tents demanding a long list of political, legal and constitutional reforms. By 13 March, the gathering at the Tents, now numbering over 20,000, had begun to hear speeches from workers and artisans whose chief concern was not legal and constitutional reform, but the economic needs of the working populace. An assembly of workers at one corner of the crowd formed a separate assembly and drew up a petition of its own pressing for new laws to protect the workers against 'capitalists and usurers' and asking the king to establish a Ministry of

Labour. Distinct political and social interests were already crystallizing within the mobilized crowd of the city.

Alarmed at the growing 'determination and insolence' of the crowds circulating in the streets, the Chief of Police, Julius von Minutoli, ordered new troops into the city on 13 March. That night, several civilians were killed in clashes around the Palace precinct. Boerner was on his way from the Tents into the city centre. Seeing that the streets were filling with crowds and soldiers, he went with a friend to the Café Volpi on the Stechbahn to watch the situation unfold. It was here that he witnessed for the first time in his life an assault by soldiers on unarmed civilians. Without warning, a squadron of cuirassier guards suddenly attacked a crowd of people returning from the Tents:

> I couldn't bear to watch, I had to step back from the window when I saw them striking even the women with the palasch [a long, straight, single-edged sword]. . . . I could not free myself from the thought of the terrified screaming of the people, the wounded women, a boy cut down in front of our eyes . . . A hundred times I asked myself: how is it possible that our compatriots can behave in this way?

Public outrage at these excesses, which continued through 14, 15 and 16 March, soon pervaded 'every class of the population'.[142]

The crowd and the soldiery were now collective antagonists in a struggle for control of the city's space. Over the next few days, crowds flowed through the city in the early evenings. They were, in Manzoni's memorable simile, like 'clouds still scattered and scudding about a clear sky, making everyone look up and say that the weather has not yet settled'.[143] The crowd was afraid of the troops, but also drawn to them. It cajoled, persuaded and taunted them. The troops had their own elaborate rituals. When confronted by unruly subjects, they were required to read out the riot act of 1835 three times, before giving three warning signals with the drum or the trumpet, after which the order to attack would be given. Since many of the men in the crowd had themselves served in the military, these signals were almost universally recognized and understood. The reading of the riot act was generally greeted with whistling and jeers. The beating of the drum, which signalled an imminent advance or charge, had a stronger deterrent effect but this was generally temporary. On several occasions during the struggles in Berlin, crowds forced troops standing guard to run through their warning routines over and over again by provoking them, then melting away when the drum was sounded, then reappearing to start the game again.[144]

So poisonous was the mood in the city that men in uniform walking alone or in small groups were in serious danger. The liberal writer and diarist Karl August Varnhagen von Ense watched from his first-floor window on 15 March as three officers walked slowly along the footpath of a street adjoining his house followed by a shouting crowd of about 200 boys and youths.

> I saw how stones struck them, how a raised staff crashed down on one man's back, but they did not flinch, they did not turn, they walked as far as the corner, turned into the Wallstrasse and took refuge in an administrative building, whose armed guards scared the tormentors away.

The three men were later rescued by a troop detachment and escorted to the safety of the city arsenal.[145]

The military and political leadership in Berlin, as in so many other cities, found it difficult to agree on how to proceed. The mild and intelligent General von Pfuel, Governor of Berlin with responsibility for all troops stationed in and around the capital, favoured a mix of tact and political concessions. By contrast, the king's younger brother, Prince William, urged the monarch to order an all-out attack on the insurgents. General von Prittwitz, commander of the King's Lifeguards and a hardline supporter of Prince William, later recalled the chaotic atmosphere that reigned at the court. The king, Prittwitz claimed, was buffeted about by the conflicting advice of a throng of advisers and well-wishers. The tipping point came with the news (breaking in Berlin on 15 March) that Chancellor Metternich had fallen following two days of revolutionary upheaval in Vienna. If Paris was the signal that resonated with the democrats and radicals, it was the news from Vienna that did most to shake the confidence of the court in Berlin. Deferential as ever to Austria, the ministers and advisers around the king read this as an omen and resolved to offer further political concessions. On 17 March, the king agreed to publish royal patents announcing the abolition of censorship and the introduction of a constitutional system in the Kingdom of Prussia.

But the moment had passed for piecemeal reforms; the initiative was already slipping away from the government. Plans had been laid for an afternoon rally to take place on the following day, 18 March, in the Palace Square. On that morning, the authorities broadcast the news of the latest concessions across the city. Municipal deputies were seen dancing on the streets with members of the public. The city government ordered the illumination of the city that evening as a token of its gratitude.[146] But it was too late to stop the planned demonstration: from around noon, streams of people began to converge upon the Schlossplatz, including prosperous burghers and 'protection officers' (unarmed officials recruited from the middle classes and appointed to mediate between troops and crowds), but also many artisans and workers from the slum areas outside the city boundaries. As the news of the government's decisions circulated, parts of the crowd became festive, euphoric. The air was filled with the din of cheering. The crowd, ever more densely packed in the warm sunlit square, wanted to see the king.

The mood inside the palace was light-hearted. When Police Chief Minutoli arrived at around one in the afternoon to warn the king that he believed a major upheaval was still imminent, he was met with indulgent smiles. The king thanked him for his work and added: 'There is one thing I should say, my dear Minutoli, and that is that you always see things too negatively!' Hearing the applause and cheering from the square, the king and his entourage made their way in the direction of the crowd. 'We're off to collect our hurrah', quipped General von Pfuel.[147] At last the monarch stepped out onto a stone balcony overlooking the square, where he was greeted with frenetic ovations. Then Prime Minister von Bodelschwingh stepped forward to make an announcement:

> The king wishes freedom of the press to prevail! The king wishes that the United Diet be called immediately! The king wishes that a constitution on the most liberal basis should encompass all the German lands! The king wishes that there should be a German national flag! The king wishes that all customs turnpikes should fall! The king wishes that Prussia should place itself at the head of the movement!

Most of the crowd could hear neither the king nor his minister, but printed copies of his latest announcements were being passed through the throng and the wild cheering around the balcony soon spread across the square in a wave of elation.

Not everyone was elated. Witnesses noted that the people at the front of the crowd and closest to the palace hailed from the wealthier social strata – top hats and dark suits could be seen everywhere. This was the area where people could be seen embracing each other, 'congratulating each other on these wonderful achievements'. Further back, the mood was less jolly. The areas where the adjoining streets opened onto the Schlossplatz were thick with 'proletarians and workers, who said, when they saw the joyful faces around them: "all of this is of no use for us poor people!"'[148] A dark cloud now appeared on the crowd's horizon: under the arches of the palace gates and in the courtyards behind them, lines of troops could be seen moving slowly into the square. There was some panic on the edges of the crowd, where people feared to be pushed up against the soldiers. The chanting began: 'Soldiers out! Soldiers out!' The situation in the square seemed about to slip out of control. At this point – it was at around two in the afternoon – the king transferred the command over the troops in the capital from Pfuel to the more hawkish Prittwitz and ordered that the square be cleared immediately by troops and 'an end be put to the scandalous situation prevailing there'. Bloodshed was to be avoided: the cavalry should advance at marching pace without drawing swords.[149] A scene of utter confusion followed. A squadron of dragoons pushed slowly forwards into the crowd but failed to disperse it. Controlling the men was difficult, because the noise was so intense that no orders could be heard. Some of the horses took fright and began to pace backwards. Two men fell when their mounts lost their footing on the cobbles. Only when the dragoons raised their sabres and made to charge did the crowd flee the centre of the square.

Since substantial crowds were still concentrated on the eastern edge of the palace precinct between the Langenbrücke and the Breite Straße, a small contingent of grenadiers was sent to clear them. It was during this action that two weapons were accidentally discharged. Grenadier Kühn's musket caught on the handle of his sabre; warrant officer Hettgen's gun went off when a demonstrator struck it on the hammer with a stick. Neither shot caused an injury, but the crowd, thinking with its ears, was convinced that the troops had begun to shoot civilians. Word of this outrage passed swiftly through the city. The rather surreal attempt of the palace to correct this misinformation by employing two civilians to walk the streets with a massive linen banner bearing the words: 'A Misunderstanding! The king has the best intentions!' was predictably futile.

Barricades sprang up across Berlin, improvised from materials to

Fighting between insurgents and troops on the Breite Straße, Berlin, March 1848.

hand. If these closely resembled their counterparts in Paris and else-where, this was not, Paul Boerner noted, because 'Polish or French emissaries' had been at work, but because the structure and material texture of the city imposed certain solutions: 'we instinctively found out the right way to do it'. As in Palermo, and Paris, every conceivable material was put to use, including carriages, which provided an excel-lent core for fortified walls. Footmen quickly got wise to this, and throughout that year carriages could be seen prudently hurtling out of the city centre whenever a crowd gathered.[150] These makeshift barriers became the focal points of the fighting, which followed a similar pattern across the city: infantry advancing on a barricade came under fire from the windows of buildings in the vicinity. Tiles and stones rained down from the roofs. The houses were entered and 'cleared' by troops. Barri-cades were demolished with artillery shot or dismantled by troops, sometimes with the aid of prisoners taken during the fight. Varnhagen von Ense described how the defenders of a barricade near his house responded to the sound of approaching troops: 'The fighters were instantly ready. You could hear them whispering, and upon the order of a youthful sonorous voice: "Gentlemen, to the roofs!" each went to his post.'[151] But the resolution of the insurgents could not compensate for the shortage of weaponry: the gunshops were opened and emptied but turned out to contain relatively few firearms. Houses were meticulously searched for privately owned weapons. Yet only a small minority of the barricade fighters had firearms during the first phase of the uprising; the rest had to make do with pitchforks, axes or planks of wood.[152]

The social geography of the struggle added a dimension of complex-ity: whereas the barricades were built and manned for the most part by artisans and workers of various kinds, the surrounding houses were mostly in middle-class hands. Houses, Paul Boerner observed, were the insurgents' best defence, even better than barricades. But 'the houses belong to the bourgeois'. 'It is therefore only possible to fight on the streets with success if the Philistines [of the bourgeoisie] support the struggle.' An implicit division of labour emerged: to the 'youth and men of labour' fell the tasks involving 'physical violence'; the task of the bourgeoisie was to offer 'passive' support by allowing the worker insur-gents to enter their buildings unhindered, stockpile arms and missiles, and to use the windows of their apartments as positions from which guns could be fired or stones thrown.[153]

A Private Schadewinkel who took part in the storming of a barricade in the Breite Straße later recalled his role in the action. After the man beside him had been killed by a shot to the head, Schadewinkel joined a handful of soldiers who broke into a building where protestors had been seen. Fired with murderous rage, the men charged up stairways and into apartments, 'cutting down anyone who resisted'. 'I am unable to give any precise account of events inside the house', Schadewinkel declared. 'I was in a state of agitation such as I have never been in before.'[154] Here, as in many parts of Berlin, innocent bystanders and the half-involved were killed along with the combatants. Paul Boerner fled into a first-floor apartment after the shelling of his barricade. His host, a man of the prosperous middle classes, was terrified at the sudden appearance of the young man, but his wife insisted that they hide him under the cover of a four-poster bed in the guest room. Boerner lay curled up in the darkness, listening to the boots of the officers and floorboards creaking as they searched the apartment for insurgents, overcome with the feeling that he was too young to die. He was lucky to escape with his life.[155] Others were less fortunate. Two young men who had run into a second-floor apartment on the Spittelmarktstraße and hidden themselves with their rifles behind the sofa were dragged out and beaten with rifle butts by the pursuing troops. Their commander, a Captain Pannewitz, ordered that they be shot on the spot. 'This order was immediately carried out by a soldier, who pressed the barrel of his rifle onto the temple of a still very young and personable youth and shattered his head, to the extent that the wall and a wall mirror were completely splattered by the brain.' The other captive was shot a moment later.[156]

Notwithstanding the brutality of the repression, it proved harder to take control of the city than the commanders had imagined. At around midnight on 18 March, when General Prittwitz, the new commander-in-chief of the counter-insurrectionary forces, reported to Frederick William IV in the palace, he had to acknowledge that while his troops controlled the area between the River Spree, the Neue Friedrichstraße and the Spittelmarkt, a further advance was currently impossible. Prittwitz proposed that the city be evacuated, encircled and bombarded into submission. The king responded to this grim news with an almost other-worldly calm. Having thanked the general, he returned to his desk, where Prittwitz observed 'the elaborately comfortable way in which His Majesty pulled a furry foot-muff over his feet after taking off his boots and stockings, in order, as it seemed, to begin writing another lengthy document'.[157] The document in question was the address 'To My Dear Berliners', published in the small hours of the following day, in which the king appealed to the residents of Berlin: 'Return to peace, clear the barricades that still stand . . ., and I give you my Royal Word that all streets and squares will be cleared of troops, and the military occupation reduced to a few necessary buildings.'[158] The order to pull the troops out of the city was given on the next day shortly after noon. The king had placed himself in the hands of the revolution.

This was a momentous decision and a controversial one. The forced 'withdrawal' from Berlin was the most vexing challenge the Prussian army had faced since its defeat at the hands of Napoleon in 1806. Had the king simply lost his nerve? This was certainly the view taken by the hawks within the military.[159] Prince William of Prussia, whose preference for hard measures had earned him the sobriquet 'the shrapnel prince', was the most furious hawk of all. Having heard the news of the withdrawal, he marched up to his elder brother and spat out the words: 'I have always known that you were a babbler, but not that you are a coward! One can no longer serve you with honour' before flinging his sword at the king's feet. With tears of rage in his eyes, the king is said to have replied: 'This is just too bad! You can't stay here. You will have to go!' William, by now the most hated figure in the city, was at length persuaded to leave Berlin in disguise and cool down in London.[160]

The king, though profoundly shaken, manoeuvred shrewdly through these events. The early departure of the troops prevented further blood-shed. This was an important consideration, given the ferocity of the fighting during the night of 18/19 March. With a toll of over 300 dead protesters and around 100 dead soldiers and officers, Berlin saw some of the bloodiest urban fighting of the German March revolution. By contrast, the death toll for the March days in Vienna was around fifty.[161] Frederick William's decision preserved Berlin from artillery bombard-ment, a fate that was visited upon several European cities during that year. Most importantly of all, the king's actions after 18 March allowed him to emerge from the tumult with his reputation untarnished by the violent confrontations in the capital, and to capitalize on the still strong royalist attachments of the great majority of Berliners.[162] On 21 March, six days after Emperor Ferdinand and his nephew Franz Joseph had done the same in Vienna, Frederick William would ride out unguarded into the streets of Berlin, cheered wildly by the crowds.

Similar scenes, in which crowds relieved at the success of the revolution embraced their humbled sovereigns, unfolded in many of the German states. When Prince Nikolaus, the sixteen-year-old son of the Duke of Nassau, who was currently away in Berlin, walked out into an angry gathering of armed citizens to assure them that his father loved them and would grant their wishes when he returned, he, too, was greeted with delirious cheers. 'This miraculous blending of the old loyalty with the unconditional demand for a new freedom shines as a bright, conciliatory glow over the great drama of our March Days', the liberal Nassau-based journalist Wilhelm Heinrich Riehl recalled. 'Only later would it darken.'[163]

THE FIVE DAYS OF MILAN

On 18 February 1848, Count Joseph Alexander von Hübner, Chargé d'Affaires at the Austrian legation in Leipzig, received a despatch from Prince Metternich summoning him to Vienna. Only when he arrived in the capital did he learn the reason: the Prince intended to deploy him as a kind of roving Austrian ambassador to the Italian courts. His mission would be to reassure the Italian states of Austria's support and to help them coordinate their efforts against revolution. During his brief sojourn in the capital, Hübner read the incoming despatches and was able to acquaint himself with the situation in France and Italy. By 28 February, he had concluded that the game was lost. 'Revolution cannot be stopped by diplomatic notes and journal articles', he wrote in his diary. 'Do you stop a locomotive with a wand?'[164]

Leaving Vienna on 2 March, Hübner travelled by train as far as the foot of the Semmering, proceeding from there on post horses – it took him seventy-four hours to reach Milan. He was shocked to find that the Austrian governor, Count Spaur, was on the point of leaving. 'This seems the worst possible time for a holiday', he wrote in his diary. 'His temporary replacement, . . . Count O'Donell, has absolutely nothing to tell me on the situation.'[165] The departure soon after of the viceroy was another depressing signal. In the evenings, Hübner took part in the usual round of cultural outings. At the Scala opera house, he noted the

Italian and Austrian ladies mingling in their elegant attire, but also saw how the first two rows of the orchestra seats, reserved for Austrian officers in their splendid mess uniforms, formed two solid white lines, a privilege that dated back to 1815. How was it possible, he wondered, 'with the storm grumbling over our heads, to be as genial as we are?'[166]

In conversations with the most senior Austrian functionaries and officers, Hübner gained a sense of how the situation in Milan had evolved. Over the past six to eight months, there had been a marked change in attitudes, Field Marshal Radetzky's adjutant-general told him. The native civil service, once so loyal and dedicated to their work, fell nowadays into two categories, the 'terrorized' and the 'traitors'. Hostile demonstrations prepared by 'invisible hands' had become more frequent. Clashes over a tobacco boycott organized by radical patriots at the beginning of the year had further embittered the mood. Hoping to deprive the Austrian authorities of the income generated by the tobacco monopoly, the patriots had urged the Milanese to join them in abstaining from smoking. Many troops of the Austrian army continued to smoke ostentatiously on the streets, some strutting through the evening crowds with cigarettes stuck in each corner of their mouths. They were attacked by the populace, a fight ensued, the soldiers drew their sabres. Several civilians were killed. A delegation led by the city's mayor, Gabrio Casati, had protested to the Austrians, who refused, however, to forbid their troops to smoke in public. The fighting and protests eventually subsided, but the mood remained tense. Everyone seemed to be waiting for something to happen. And the balance of authority had shifted: 'The chiefs of the Italian party are obeyed and the imperial authorities are not, for the truth is that they no longer have any grip on the population.'[167]

On 17 March, news reached Hübner of the latest events in Vienna: crowds had smashed the windows of Prince Metternich's residence; a student demonstration had demanded the liberties claimed by 'the revolutionaries in Germany'; the government had announced major concessions. But why was there no letter with instructions from Metternich, or from anyone else, for that matter? In this sophisticated Italian city of 200,000 people, it was easy for an Austrian envoy to feel isolated. The weather was as sombre as the mood: a fine, cold rain fell without interruption. When he walked out in the evening with a friend, he found that the streets around the Piazza del Duomo, normally so animated, were virtually empty. Here and there, little groups could be seen whispering with each other, 'but they dispersed as we approached'. The organ grinders were still plying their trade in front of the cafés, but there was nobody listening to them. That night, Hübner felt overwhelmed by gloom. It didn't help that he was lodging in the cavernous apartments of the departed viceroy. But what troubled him most was 'the uncertainty in which I am left by Prince Metternich, if he is still Chancellor, which I doubt'. 'The fear of violence and total upheaval weighed on me like a nightmare and chased away sleep . . .'[168]

While Hübner tossed and turned in his bed, the leaders of the Milanese liberal opposition gathered to discuss how to respond to the rapidly changing situation in Vienna. It was agreed that on the following day the mayor, Gabrio Casati, should lead a peaceful demonstration in support of various demands: the abolition of the old police regime, the creation of a Civic Guard and of a provisional Lombard government. For Casati, this was an exquisitely difficult balancing act. He was not immune to patriotic emotions, but for many years he had worked closely with the Austrians and he had an excellent relationship with them. Nothing better illustrates his divided loyalties than the educational choices he made for his two sons: one was sent to serve as an artillery officer in the Piedmontese army and the other to study law at the University of Innsbruck. Casati assured the Austrian governor, O'Donnell, that the event would be peaceful and succeeded in persuading him not to bring out the garrison. Determined not to be caught off guard, Field Marshal Radetzky ordered extra artillery to the city and increased the posts on the city walls.

In the café where Hübner took breakfast on the following morning, 18 March, a man posted a news sheet and left in a hurry. Several people left their tables to study it in silence, exchanging glances, 'like people who understand each other without words'. He wondered why they were behaving in this un-Italian way. When they had gone, Hübner read it himself: it reported that the emperor had abolished censorship and announced the forthcoming convocation of all the estates of the Austrian lands. But there was still no clue as to why this 'change in the system' had taken place. It was an uncomfortable situation for a special envoy to be in. Returning to his rooms, he found an Austrian officer, the young Count Thun, waiting for him and they smoked a cigar together.

Across the city, everyone seemed to feel that a major incident was imminent, though no one knew what form it would take. The city was in the grip of a conspiracy without conspirators; the uprising owed its inception, the patriot Enrico Dandolo later recalled, 'much more to the unanimity of the combatants than to any preconceived plan of action'.[169] Passing through the streets, the young republican Carlo Osio saw faces marked by 'a rage mixed with terror and an irrepressible longing for vengeance'. The shops suddenly closed for business and locked their shutters; the doors of the houses were secured: 'There was a mute swirling of whispers, a sudden bustle, a universal commotion.' Osio rushed to his home, armed himself with pistols, a dagger and an iron-shod club, and made his way with a company of friends towards the Porta Orientale, and then, in the wake of surging crowds, towards the government palace, where he saw the first shots fired by insurgents at the troops guarding the building, the opening salvo in what would become known as the 'Five Days of Milan'.[170] The first Austrian officer to fall into the hands of the Milanese insurgents was Count Thun, who, still unaware of what was happening in the city, was surrounded by armed men shortly after he left Hübner's apartment, arrested and taken immediately to prison.

For Carlo Osio, a fully fledged insurrection against the Austrians couldn't come soon enough. His fellow republican, the sometime Carbonaro Carlo Cattaneo, was more equivocal. The experience of the people of Lombardy, Cattaneo argued, was quite different from that of France: whereas France had merely been defeated in 1814, Lombardy had been *conquered*. 'The foreign occupation in France was just a contingent and transitory event; the occupation of Italy was rendered permanent by the treaties of Vienna', which assigned Lombardy and Venetia to Austria for ever.[171] And what did a state of permanent occupation mean? It meant the stunting of intellectual life over more than a generation, the filtering of news and information, the extraction of revenues on a grand scale and the denial of respect. Above all, it meant powerlessness:

> Our core problem was that in order to have independence, we needed to fight, and in order to fight, we needed to have an army. But ... the Army had not existed for thirty-four years. The soldiers recruited from our midst formed good regiments, but they were dispersed for the greater part across garrisons on the extreme peripheries of the empire, in Hungary, in Galicia, the Vorarlberg, in Prague; their officers were mostly Germans and Slavs.[172]

For Cattaneo, this meant a popular insurrection was out of the question. It would be tantamount to surrendering cities and towns full of family homes to sack and pillage. Cattaneo was impatient with those monarchist patriots who spoke of encouraging King Charles Albert in Piedmont to drive the Austrians out of Lombardy and annex it to his own kingdom. What was the point of exchanging one monarch for another? To Cattaneo, it seemed that the pro-Albertine patriots were not interested in resolving 'the problem of the revolution, but only the problem of war'. Those who called for the conquest of Lombardy by Piedmont failed to see that it was the lamentable governance of the *Italian* princes that enabled the Austrians to rule their Italian possessions with such ease. Italy was not the captive of Austria, but of the 'retrograde ideas of its own princes'.[173]

Cattaneo witnessed the profound excitement that gripped the city in the first two months of 1848. 'One day it was Palermo that was rising, then Naples, Florence, and Turin ... Then came the thunderbolt from Paris.' But he also saw how the impact of these real events was amplified by an electric current of rumour: there was talk, for example, of 60,000 rifles, sent by the king of Piedmont to the Lombard frontier, and then of 40,000 rifles due to arrive in Milan itself; military units were supposedly on their way to help the city. Cattaneo remained sceptical. On the morning of 18 March, as the streets were filling with insurgents, two friends came to him in a state of euphoria at the thought that the moment had come to strike down the tyrant. Cattaneo tried to dampen their ardour: with which forces, he asked, did they intend to attack the imperial garrison, a force that was prepared for war and might even deliberately have provoked the current unrest in order to seize the initiative? Exactly how many men did they have? His friends responded sheepishly that they had rounded up only a few dozen armed men, but more would surely be forthcoming soon, because 40,000 rifles were on their way from Piedmont. Had they seen these rifles, Cattaneo asked. 'We haven't seen them', they replied, 'but we know that the directing committee expect to receive them from Piedmont.' But where was this directing committee, Cattaneo asked, did it really exist? 'Without doubt, everyone knows it, everyone is talking about it.' 'Well, my friends', Cattaneo replied, 'you'll see soon enough that there are neither rifles nor a directing committee.'[174] As it turned out, the executive body that emerged around Mayor Casati in the course of that day was merely an extension of the municipal administration, a body composed mainly of conservative civil servants with a track record of loyal service to the Austrians. Here, as in so many other places, it was the revolution that made revolutionaries, not the other way around.

None of this diminishes the bitterness and cruelty of the fighting that followed, or the courage of many of those who took part in it. Having warned against a premature insurrection, Cattaneo suppressed his doubts and took charge of the 'council of war' entrusted with coordinating the insurgent campaign, which initially consisted of completely uncoordinated pockets of activity dispersed across the city. The fighting was often hand to hand. In order to overcome their lack of firearms and ammunition, groups of young Milanese would crouch behind doors or in side streets, leap onto isolated troops and seize their rifles. At San Francesco di Paola, a baroque church on what is today the Via Alessandro Manzoni, a forward sentinel was disarmed and killed with his own rifle in the presence of an entire battalion by a young man who had leapt on him from behind a barricade in a small side street. Captured guns and ammunition were husbanded with great care by the insurgents. Only men who were practised in their use were allowed to fire them. The insurgents took care to fire only at close range, for fear of wasting bullets; 'at our headquarters, powder was distributed in pinches, like tobacco'. The munitions problem largely disappeared once the insurgents secured control of the city's barracks and arms stores.[175] To Cattaneo, Osio and other Milanese observers, the insurgents were heroes fighting against overwhelming odds. Austrian witnesses were more alert to the vulnerability of their own forces: Hübner watched as a squadron of Hungarian hussars cantered out of the Via del Pesce under heavy fire from roofs and basement windows. A little later, a detachment of Croats appeared, the men 'pale, calm and resolute', with their fingers resting on the triggers of their rifles, the officers with drawn sabres. As they approached the narrow part of the street, the troops were exposed to 'an infernal fire'. They returned fire from the street, 'but what can bullets achieve against an enemy who is invisible and hidden behind walls?'[176]

Everyone pitched in: astronomers and opticians of Milan took up positions in the observatories and on the clock towers to discern the movements of the enemy outside the city walls. To save time, they attached their reports to a metal ring and sent them whizzing down ziplines to the ground, where they were picked up and taken to headquarters by the boys of a college of orphans, who now formed an improvised military postal service. Messages requesting help were sent out into the countryside under small balloons – they sailed up, shrinking to hopeful dots, and sailed out across the country, well beyond the range of the Austrian troops taking pot shots at them from the ground. Some made it as far as Piedmont and the Swiss border. And they seem to have worked, because the towns of the hinterland soon began rising in their turn, capturing or driving out their small garrisons. Squadrons of auxiliaries were seen descending from the hills towards the besieged city, including 500 men from the Italian-speaking canton of Ticino of Switzerland.[177] This was Milan's repayment for the service of Lombard freedom fighters in the Sonderbund War of the previous year.

On the night of 21/22 March, an offer arrived from Turin: Charles Albert would march into Lombardy and engage the Austrians, but only if he received an official request to do so from the Milanese. Cattaneo was opposed to this idea. He rightly saw that the Piedmontese monarch's objective was to annex Lombardy and possibly also Venetia. What would then become of the republican movement in Milan? But he agreed to a compromise: Milan would frame an appeal for assistance, but to 'all the princes and all the peoples of Italy', not to Piedmont alone. Discussions of what *political* form the new Lombard or Italian entity took would be postponed until after the 'victory'. In fact, Radetzky had already decided to withdraw his forces from the city. On 23 March, the Milanese woke up to the news that they had already left. Having burned their dead, the Austrian army had stolen away in silence to the safety of the 'Quadrilateral', a system of impregnable fortresses at Verona, Peschiera, Mantua and Legnano. This was at best a strategic retreat, rather than a defeat, but for the moment no one was worrying about that, especially after the news arrived that the king of Piedmont had at last crossed the River Ticino and entered Lombard territory.

The scenes of euphoria that followed resembled those in other European cities: the Milanese 'ran through the streets shedding tears of joy', strangers embraced like brothers and 'men of grave demeanour' were seen 'leaping and singing in the public thoroughfares'. People abandoned their houses and wandered about aimlessly 'as if they were seeking to inhale under the open sky that blessed air of liberty'. The exchanging of stories began as participants in the struggle pointed out to their friends the places where they had fought. The narratives would later diverge, as the heroes of the Five Days fashioned memoirs denouncing each other for misrepresenting the facts and bigging up their own roles. But, for now, harmony reigned. 'On that day', Enrico Dandolo wrote, 'all were included in the bond of brotherhood, and scarcely a being, however hardened in selfishness and hatred, could resist the influence of such universal joy and affection.'[178]

THE DOGS THAT DIDN'T BARK

When we remember the spring of 1848, images of insurgent barricades and urban bonfires come to mind. But in some places political transformations took place without a major insurgency. The Netherlands are a good example. In 1847, the ingredients for a major upheaval were accumulating. Frustration with the authoritarian monarchical constitution of 1815 was growing. The franchise was both indirect and narrow: in Amsterdam, of a total population of 215,297 (1845) only 6,000 had the right to vote and only 1,259 were eligible to elect deputies to the lower chamber. The upper chamber consisted exclusively of members appointed for life by the monarch. 'In the Netherlands, too', the Dutch historian Piet de Rooy observes, 'all of the conditions were satisfied for the unleashing of a rebellion: a hungry population and an increasingly radical middle class. Here, too, there were processions and demonstrations that demanded lower taxes, cheaper food and more democracy.'[179]

In the mid 1840s, a liberal group emerged under the leadership of the university professor Johan Rudolf Thorbecke, a man who had entered adult life as a romantic conservative but moved during the early 1840s towards an advanced liberalism that favoured radical constitutional reform.[180] But Willem II, king since October 1840, remained opposed to concessions, as did his conservative consort, Anna Pavlovna of Russia, the daughter of Tsar Paul I. In October 1847, the king agreed in principle to certain very limited reforms, but these fell far short of the liberal faction's demands. And political deadlock coincided with a deepening economic crisis: there had been riots and other disturbances in the aftermath of the potato crop failure in 1846 and 1847 and in the spring of 1848, as the downturn triggered by the agrarian crisis bit into manufacturing and commerce, there were numerous bankruptcies and business failures.[181]

In February 1848, as the news from Paris reached Brussels and The Hague, the liberals hoped that the king would panic and back down. But the contrary happened: in early March, enquiries by his intelligence services and by networks of police informers suggested that there was no reason to fear an uprising. Emboldened by these reports, the king declared during a public dinner on 11 March that 'Revolution does not stand a chance in the Netherlands.'[182] The Cabinet, too, a body of conservative loyalists, remained confident in the tranquillity of the country, concluding that the state of public opinion was such that the king could 'do no wrong'. And yet, in the middle of the month the king suddenly caved in, summoned the president of the lower chamber for a discussion, announced the necessity of major constitutional reform without consulting his ministers and invited Thorbecke and the liberal parliamentarian Donker Curtsius to sit on a newly established Constitutional Committee. There were gasps of horror from the Cabinet ministers, who resigned en masse. Conservative deputies lamented that the king had surrendered without cause to the 'extrême gauche', ignoring the advice of his councillors and reinventing himself as a 'roi des Halles', a king of the masses.[183]

Why did the monarch behave like this? The news from France, though it galvanized the liberal opposition, did not impress him much. Far more important were two letters he received on 9 March from his daughter Sophie, daughter-in-law of Carl Friedrich, Grand Duke of Sachsen-Weimar-Eisenach, whose court in the small city of Weimar had been shaken by repeated tumults. Carl Friedrich had responded by acceding to the demands of the liberals: long-serving conservative ministers were dismissed and replaced by more progressive figures who soon got busy curtailing the power of the monarch. At around the same time, there were reports from Joan Hodshon, colonel of the Amsterdam Militia, who warned of rising tension in Amsterdam; soon even the director of police in The Hague, Abraham Ampt, who had earlier talked down the threat of social unrest, joined the chorus of those warning that serious trouble would result if the government did not make major concessions.[184]

The king was also under a lot of personal strain. He was crushed by the news of the death of his eldest son on 20 February 1848 in Portugal, after a long and mysterious illness. For some years, he had been under pressure from petty criminals, journalists and professional intriguers threatening to publish documents relating to the Dutch king's political intrigues against the post-1830 administrations in Brussels, intrigues that now looked extremely embarrassing. By the spring of 1848, the two dominant figures in these machinations were Adriaan van Bevervoorde and Regnerus van Andringa de Kempenaer, noblemen whose fortunes were in an advanced state of disrepair. These two had fallen into the unsavoury habit, whenever they were short of money, which was nearly all of the time, of offering to 'protect' the king against black-mailers, which is to say, other blackmailers than themselves. They were in a particularly strong position in February 1848, because a German fraudster and extortionist by the name of Petrus Janssen had surfaced with documents detailing the king's homosexual liaisons. Bevervoorde and Andringa managed to get Janssen to return to Germany, a service for which they were handsomely paid. At the same time, they leaked a few juicy scraps to other scandal writers, so that they too came forward for hush money, from which the king's 'protectors' extracted further healthy commissions. Buying off the blackmailers cost the king over 10,000 guilders and ultimately destroyed his peace of mind.

For van Bevervoorde, it wasn't just about the money. In 1845–7, like many others, he had migrated from the liberal to the radical political milieu; in November 1847, he was present at the foundation in Brussels of the Association Démocratique, of which Karl Marx was the chair-man. He ran three small newspapers, in which he defended press freedom and advocated measures against unemployment and poverty. On 8 March, he was received at the palace, where he urged the king to part ways with his conservative ministers and present himself as a reformer. In this way, the threat of personal exposure became inter-twined with the pressure to concede liberal demands. By the time Willem II backed down and asked Thorbecke to form a committee charged with constitutional and other reforms, he appears to have been close to a nervous breakdown.[185]

It is impossible to know whether a revolution might have broken out if these highly contingent events had not placed the House of Orange on the path towards far-reaching reforms and political renewal. Once the danger had passed, Dutch liberals, like their British counterparts, tended to congratulate themselves on the superiority of their liberal political and social order. 'While in several countries the blood of citizens has flowed and every step brings scenes of disorder and anarchy', one deputy told the Second Chamber in August, 'we were fortunate in bringing about our social reform with circumspection and through mutual consultation; the Netherlands remained calm, respect for the law continued to reign every-where.'[186] But there were also well-informed contemporaries who felt that the king's timely response had saved the day. In other countries, the dep-uty Nicolaas van Heloma remarked in a speech to the Second Chamber on 28 March, kings were still trembling on their thrones, but in the Netherlands 'our king is greeted with cheers of joy, because He, knowing the needs and interests of the inhabitants of the Netherlands, accommodated, of his own volition, their just and fair wishes'.[187] 'See the ravaged cities go up in flames, hear the scream of murder, it's as if the Middle Ages have returned!' Johannes Kneppelhout declared in a pamphlet published in April 1848. In the Netherlands, on the other hand, 'the prince has touched the people with his sceptre in good time, understood the moment, provided for the need of the times, averted the storms.'[188] The king's decision to launch a liberal constitution 'took the sting out of the rebellion'.[189] This is not to say that the protests ceased altogether, but rather that the policy change initiated by the monarch prevented them from posing a threat to the stability of the system.[190]

The Dutch events show how important the behaviour of a monarch could be, even one as fretful and mercurial as Willem II. They show how quickly the power to shape political outcomes could accrue to liberal activists who had previously found it impossible to get past ministers and officials. They show, too, how the fear of social tumult could amplify the resonance of liberal demands. And they remind us of how diversely structured the connectedness of the European revolutions was. For Dutch liberals and radicals, the Paris revolution of February was an epoch-making event; for the king and his ministers much less so, because they saw France as a case *sui generis*. It was the news from Weimar that really moved Willem II, not the fall of Guizot. The same diversity of response can be observed in Berlin, where it was above all the February Revolution that stirred the radicals, but the events in Vienna and the German states that impressed the king and the people around him. The Netherlands did not 'avoid' a revolution in 1848; rather, it successfully absorbed and translated the revolutionary crisis sweeping Europe. As the Dutch envoy to Brussels sagely remarked: 'it is better to pre-empt than to be pre-empted'.[191]

In other countries, too, pre-emptive initiatives helped to fend off the threat of revolution. In Piedmont, King Charles Albert announced a constitution on 9 February and published it on 4 March. Grand Duke Leopold of Tuscany saved his throne by granting one on 11 February. The situation was different in Belgium, where the recent revolution of 1830–31 had already endowed the new nation with a constitution that was widely admired. Doctrinaire liberals easily controlled the government, most of whose key personnel were veterans of the 1830

revolution and thus figures with a special claim on the nation's gratitude. But here, too, the potential for a revolutionary upheaval existed.
The socio-economic crisis that helped to trigger upheavals in many
other countries was also present in Belgium, especially in the Flemish
countryside, where hunger and mass unemployment were still a problem in spring 1848. There were numerous demands for radical social
reform and no shortage of radical associations, newspapers or networks. And the franchise was extremely narrow, comprising the 1.1 per
cent of the population who met a stringent fiscal requirement, a constituency composed of rich landowners, clergymen and university grad-
uates.[192] There were thus many parallels with the situation in France,
and these included the sense, widespread among radicals, that the birth
of the Belgian state in 1830–31 was a betrayed revolution, whose social
potential had deliberately been suppressed and squandered.

If a fully fledged revolution never broke out in Belgium, this was
partly because the country was so stringently policed. As soon as the
news of the February Revolution in Paris became known, orders went
out to governors and mayors across the country to be vigilant in the
maintenance of order; the army was swiftly purged of any officers
deemed to pose a risk to its political cohesion. Reservists and soldiers on
leave were called up; an expanded gendarmerie kept a close watch on
potential trouble spots; a well-run state security service with a far-flung
network of spies and informants kept information flowing in on suspect
persons and groups.[193] A contingent of radical Walloon workers travelled from Paris by train, intending to spread the good word in Brussels,
but in an episode reminiscent of a Buster Keaton movie, their carriages
were decoupled from the rest of the train and rolled onto a branch line.
Surrounded by Belgian troops, the men and women aboard the train
were disembarked, disarmed and interrogated. Numerous foreigners
were deported, including Karl and Jenny Marx, who were pushed over
the border into France along with around forty other politically active
Germans. The Brussels City Council protested at this high-handed
behaviour, but the government ignored them, as it ignored the protests
and complaints of the native radical movement.

These repressions were flanked by measures designed to mute the resonance of radical demands among the poorest strata. The doctrinaire
liberals who ran the Belgian state knew very well from personal experience the threat posed to public order by stagnation and unemployment.

Under the agile leadership of the liberal Minister of the Interior, Charles Rogier, the government launched a programme of counter-cyclical invest-ment in railway expansion and other infrastructural projects and work creation programmes directed particularly at the areas of Flanders worst hit by recession. Unlike the French Provisional Government, the Belgian ministers did not raise controversial taxes in order to meet these expenses, but rather a forced loan to the value of twenty-seven million francs cali-brated to the various income categories. The loan was not exactly popular, but it did not attract the bitter resentment stirred by the French 'forty-five-centimes tax', to which I return below. And at the same time Rogier isolated the radicals politically by offering an extension of the franchise, a policy dear to the hearts of left-liberals and moderate radicals. In this way, they 'mowed the grass around the feet of the radicals'.[194]

It is worth noting this proactive and somewhat aggressive management of the revolutionary threat, because it takes us beyond the presumption, often recycled in the older literature, that those countries in north-western Europe that escaped revolution in 1848 did so because the appetite of their populations for political and social reform was already sated. Nowhere was this view more entrenched than in nineteenth-century Brit-ain. 'If we ask why this country has scarcely felt the shock under which all Europe now reels', the *Times* of London declared on 21 March 1848, 'The first and most obvious answer is that this nation is already reaping the fruits of a harvest which continental Europe is only beginning to sow.' Englishmen already possessed 'those things which other nations are every-where demanding'.[195] Britons rejoiced in the tranquillity of their country during the continental troubles and generally saw it as a cause for self-congratulation and evidence – if any more such were needed – of the inferiority of the European states and the people who ran and lived in them. This rather glib appraisal reverberated for over a century in the Brit-ish historiography.[196]

Yet there is reason to suppose that Britain came closer to a revolution-ary crisis than all this cheerful condescension would suggest. Chartism, the largest dissenting formation in British politics, was a very diffuse phenomenon, drawing together disparate strands of protest, such as ten-sions over land management, hostility to the Poor Law and resentment of a Stamp Tax that priced newspapers beyond the reach of most working people. Religious themes, such as temperance activism and Nonconformist hostility to Anglican privilege, were woven in as well. The Chartists created distinctive rhetorical and sartorial styles – Feargus O'Connor was famous for delivering speeches in a red liberty cap.[197] But all of this can also be said, as we have seen, of dissenting politics in the European states. The obsession with the suffrage was shared by many European reformers and the manifold links between Chartism and the continental radical movements do not suggest a deep schism in political outlooks.[198] Like radical movements elsewhere, Chartism tended to peak at moments when socio-economic distress surged: the early 1830s, the early 1840s and 1847–8.

If Britain escaped a major insurrection in 1848, this was not because Chartism was intrinsically weak. On the contrary: the movement succeeded better than any of its continental counterparts in integrating dissenting opinion and bringing it to the attention of a broad public. The National Charter Association launched in Manchester in July 1840, with its 50,000 members and over 400 branches, had no continental counterpart; nor did the immense readerships of the most influential Chartist papers. British conservative and liberal contemporaries often contrasted the Chartists with European radicals. The Chartist, they proposed, was, for all his faults, an Englishman and a good fellow who would rather get home to tea with his wife than set fire to some other fellow's house. He had nothing in common with raving, red-eyed revolutionaries of the continental type. Observations of this kind filled the pages of the British middle-class press during the months of revolution. They doubtless brought comfort to those who made or heard them, but they reflect a fundamental misunderstanding of the vast majority of those who took part in the protests that triggered revolution in mainland Europe. The continental upheavals were not brought about by cohesive fronts composed of 'revolutionaries'. The contrary was true: those who already saw themselves and were known by each other and others as revolutionaries tended to play a very marginal role in the events of 1848. The revolutionaries of 1848 were not the authors of revolution, but people who had been precipitated into positions of responsibility by the sudden collapse of authority.

It may well be that the early emergence of Chartism as the 'most significant working-class political movement of the nineteenth century' enabled the more agile figures in British governments to respond in good time with reforms that undermined the movement's appeal. The great suffrage reform enacted in 1832 had an ambivalent impact in this sense, because the £10 occupational franchise clarified and hardened the economic divide between those who were represented in parliament – about 10 per cent of the population – and those who were not. More important were the economic reforms of the 1840s: the taxing of upper-middle-class incomes in 1842, the suppression of financial speculation by means of the Bank Charter Act of 1844 and, most importantly, the assault on the landlords' grain monopoly through the repeal of the Corn Laws in 1846.[199] These reforms, all the work of Sir Robert Peel, provided the kind of carefully dosed counter-revolutionary prophylaxis that was lacking in almost all of the continental states, where the political pressure of a mass movement comparable with Chartism was lacking. Peel's innovations would be widely imitated by the European administrations as they re-emerged from the revolutionary crisis of 1848–9.

Most important of all, however, were the vigour and scale of British policing. In the autumn of 1843, following a wave of industrial disruption, the authorities arrested 15,000 activists. The 150,000 Chartists who met at Kennington Common on 10 April 1848, causing the anxious Metternichs to delay their departure from Rotterdam, were faced down by 4,000 police, 12,000 troops held in reserve and 85,000 club-wielding volunteer constables. The number of special constables may have been much higher – some contemporaries were convinced that they outnumbered the demonstrators.[200] It is easy to smile at the 'pantomime farce' of the special constables, and to contrast them with the heavy-handed deployment of mounted cuirassiers in Paris or Berlin. But nowhere else in Europe did a government succeed in mobilizing such an impressive body in its own defence. The Ultra-Tory blowhard Charles Sibthorpe MP was surely neither alone nor wrong in presuming that if the Chartists had shown more fight, 'they would have got the damnedest hiding mortal man ever received'.[201] The specials may have included some eccentric figures, but they also included the future Emperor Napoleon III, still in English exile, who signed up as an enthusiast of 'order'. Once the immediate danger had passed and the news of the 'June Days' in Paris had turned middle-class opinion against the Chartists, the government initiated a crackdown, arresting and prosecuting many key activists. By September 1848, the British historian Boyd Hilton has written, 'the movement was dead, but it had been killed by the strong arm of the state, not died from its own inanition'.[202] And this observation applies *a fortiori* to Ireland, notoriously riot-prone, which was five times as heavily policed as rural England. In 1848, the combined effects of famine, the weeding out of agitators through arrests and transportations, and determined policing on the ground sufficed to remove the potential for a major rebellion.

The success of British efforts at containment was not lost on the continental administrations. The Prussians were so impressed that they sent the former president of police in Berlin, Julius von Minutoli, to Britain in the summer of 1848 to look at its policing structures. Minutoli spent a month studying administration and procedures in London, before making a journey to observe provincial policing in Edinburgh, Glasgow, Liverpool and Dublin. The Berlin government was especially interested in Ireland, and Minutoli sent back a detailed account of the relatively new Irish Constabulary (1836), a military police force under civilian political control. His reports fed into the planning of a reformed police force for Berlin in the following year.[203] So it would seem that in the domain of policing, at least, Britain was not a model of relaxed liberality but of vigour and forcefulness.

Like almost everything else in nineteenth-century Britain, counter-revolutionary policy had an imperial dimension. Britain protected itself against upheaval by adopting policies that pacified home populations but heightened tensions on the imperial periphery.[204] The transportation en masse of potential troublemakers from England and Ireland triggered protests in Australia and the Cape Colony. To keep sugar cheap, the British government abandoned the system of tariff walls known as imperial preference, exposing colonial planters in Jamaica and British Guyana to competition from outside the British Empire and giving rise to protests, riots and political paralysis. In Ceylon, the introduction of new taxes to cut costs without burdening British middle-class taxpayers triggered the emergence of a protest movement that soon encompassed around 60,000 people. I will return to these 'global' impacts. But for the moment it is worth noting that this franchising out of political contention to the periphery puts paid to the myth that there was no 'British 1848'.

In Spain, rebellions broke out that closely followed the European pattern, provoking a response from the authorities that was unique in its swiftness and repressive energy. Here, as in France, it was the doctrinaire liberals – known in Spain as Moderates – who ruled the roost, easily controlling a parliament elected by 0.8 per cent of the population. Radical and democratic critics saw the Moderate regime as a tawdry Spanish imitation of Guizot's government in Paris, though the Spanish Prime Minister, Ramón María Narváez, was a much more intemperate and authoritarian figure than his French counterpart. Urged by advisers to cultivate a 'good press', he famously quipped that the only way to do that was to execute all the journalists. Many years later, when he was asked on his deathbed to forgive his enemies, he would reply: 'My enemies? I have none. I have had them all shot.'[205] When news of the Paris revolution became known, Narváez immediately reached for emergency legislation suppressing the individual rights and freedom guaranteed by the constitution and permitting the government to raise emergency funds to cover the cost of military operations against insurgents. The exceptional powers law, ratified on 13 March, established a legal dictatorship in which Narváez could arrest, imprison and deport with impunity his progressive and democratic opponents.[206]

Although the progressives and democrats controlled only 47 and 6 respectively of the 349 seats in the Cortes, they had built up a robust extra-parliamentary network of radical literary and debating societies, clubs, academies and newspapers. At least two hubs of radical sociability doubled as depots for the stockpiling of weapons.[207] The news from Paris divided this progressive milieu. The more moderate gravitated towards legality and the Narváez government. The more radical held up the February Revolution as an example worthy of emulation. And the most radical of all sent emissaries to Paris, one of the hubs of the Spanish leftist diaspora, in the hope of securing French support. On 26 March, at a meeting between Spanish democrats and Lamartine, now the French foreign minister, Lamartine poured cold water on their hopes, declaring that France would 'impose its desires and its interests on no one'.[208]

The uprising launched in Madrid on 26 March displayed all the marks of haste and poor planning. The two conspiratorial groups involved, one military and one civilian, had only agreed to join forces four days earlier. Like so many secret conspiracies, this one was not entirely secret: rumours of an impending insurrection reached the authorities, and the troops were mobilized ahead of time. Subversive elements in the army were arrested or transferred, as in Belgium, and the guard contingents at key locations were reinforced. Indeed, the government's measures were so intimidating that the leaders of the insurrection decided to call it off. But it was too late: the more radical elements, excited by the latest news from Vienna and Berlin, pressed ahead and took to the streets at the appointed hour. Barricades went up in parts of Madrid. Government troops took some time to get to the trouble spots. There was violent resistance and bitter fighting until around eleven o'clock in the evening, when the two remaining pockets of insurgents trapped in the streets of San Geronimo and del Príncipe were arrested and taken away. Around 200 were killed in the fighting, more than in Vienna and fewer than in Berlin.

On the following day, a state of siege was declared: radical debating societies and several oppositional newspapers were shut down. A further insurrection took place on 7 May, only a few days after the end of the state of siege. This time, the revolt stemmed mainly from disaffected elements of the military: two battalions of the Regiment of Spain, supported by around one hundred middle-class civilians, took control of the Plaza Mayor and the adjacent streets at three o'clock in the morning. After some hours they were dislodged and captured in fighting that cost 35–40 lives. In the aftermath, eight soldiers and five civilians were executed, 1,500 suspected insurgents arrested and some 800 deported, mainly to the Philippines. Hundreds of other progressives and radicals left the city or fled into exile. Despite these setbacks, further uprisings occurred on 28 and 30 March in Barcelona and Valencia. In May, following the second Madrid uprising, the cycle resumed, with uprisings in Seville, Murcia, Cartagena, Zaragoza, Galicia, Algeciras, Ceuta and other locations. All of these were severely repressed.[209] In the north of the country, there was a wave of student protests, starting on 29 March in Barcelona, where the students locked themselves into the university, and reaching Valencia on 3 May. For the city of Zaragoza, eighty of whose young men had published a letter congratulating the French Provisional Government on its victory over the Orleanist monarchy, the effects of the repressions were lasting. The traditional civic festival of the Cinco de Marzo was abolished, for fear that it would serve as a pretext for protests; censorship was rampant, 'the population was infected with the breath of the secret police'; for years, a professor at the university recalled, the citizens of Zaragoza were treated as a 'people of helots, as a tribe of savages'.[210]

As these episodes show, Spain took part in the movement of protest and upheaval that unsettled Europe in 1848–9. It was not the Iberian special case sometimes conjured in the literature, shut off by the Pyrennees and enclosed in a cycle of civil strife that insulated it from the political life of the continent. Its insurgencies revealed the familiar European spectrum of aspirations. The repressions launched by the Moderate regime were unusually swift and decisive, but in all other respects 'the scenes experienced in Madrid scarcely differed in their actors, rituals or discourse from those that we see in the streets of Paris or Berlin'.[211]

THE END OF THE BEGINNING

The commonalities are striking. The same words rang out everywhere: constitution, liberty, freedom of the press, association and assembly, civil (or national) guard, franchise reform. This was the liberal vernacular of nineteenth-century Europe, the fruit of decades of transnational conversation. None of these revolutions – with the possible exception of the unsuccessful uprisings in Madrid – was the consequence of conspiratorial planning. None was under the control of any single group. The 'revolutionaries' of 1848 were not the executors of a plan, but improvisers for whom the present was an exposed frontier. They shared a strong sense of their location in a specific epoch, the age – in Paul Boerner's histrionic characterization – of 'servitude' inaugurated by the Vienna Settlement of 1815. The swiftness of the victory was astonishing and the euphoria that followed completely understandable. But an infinity of problems remained, tasks that would press with varying urgency on the different theatres of revolution. How should one conduct negotiations with monarchs who remained on their respective thrones and continued to control armed forces? This was an especially pressing question in the Habsburg lands, Prussia, and many of the German and Italian states, where affection for the monarch or respect for the institution he represented remained strong within the population. Who should see to public order in places where the police structures had been dismantled or replaced by enthusiastic amateurs? How could the 'political revolution' beloved of urban liberals be reconciled with the calls for 'social revolution' emanating from radicals, or from the workers of restless industrial suburbs? How far should franchise extension extend? Where would the money for post-revolutionary government come from? How could insurrections that were emphatically local in focus be merged to sustain larger regional or national efforts? When should a policy of compromise yield to one of armed confrontation?

Of course, one mustn't push this observation too far: all governments face insoluble problems – that is what government is for. It is in the nature of political problems that they cannot be 'solved'; this is precisely how they differ from the problems of physics and mathematics. Nevertheless, disagreements on these and many other questions drove fine fracture lines into the embryonic structures emerging from the upheavals. For the first time in their lives, people who had thought and talked for many years about the great issues of the day were expected to solve them. This has never been an easy transition.

As it became clear that the Neapolitan forces were retreating from the city of Palermo, a mood of euphoria took hold. The Swiss commander of the garrison troops, Colonel Samuel Gross, was hugged and kissed by the crowd as he made his way down to the quay at the head of his men. The Earl of Mount Edgcumbe was amused and slightly disgusted to see the 'gigantic' colonel lowering his 'weather-beaten face to the level of ordinary men, that he might be kissed by dirty, whiskered mouths'. At the service of thanksgiving in the cathedral on 5 February, the city's gentry, the literati, political leaders and clergy rubbed shoulders with crowds of armed men from the countryside firing off their muskets in token of joy, and well-dressed ladies were seen 'shaking hands that had apparently never touched water'.[212]

But even after the last Neapolitan troops had left Palermo for the mainland, many uncertainties remained. The citadel at Messina, easily supplied by sea, was still under Neapolitan control. And the better-off families were already streaming out of the major cities to alternative country residences or to the houses of relatives, taking their money with them. The Crown treasury had been removed to Naples and cash soon ran short. It was not at all clear how the new administration would succeed in making citizens pay taxes whose avoidance had become second nature under the Bourbons. The furious attacks on the *sbirri* had left the island without a police force, and since the army, too, had left, this raised ominous questions about law and order. The answer of the Provisional Government, as of so many insurgent authorities across Europe in that year, was the creation of a National Guard – a security militia that admitted only the better-off citizens and whose chief task was the protection of property. But how would these armed and uniformed taxpayers, whose role in the administration grew steadily more important, get on with the 'wild men' of the *squadre*, who saw themselves as the true warriors of the revolution and who also expected to be paid for their services? The challenges facing the new Sicily, the Earl of Mount Edgcumbe reflected in his journal, 'cannot but impress the mind looking at the future, with much fear and little hope'.[213]

5

Regime change

In the euphoria of the first hours of success, it was easy for the revolutionaries of 1848 to forget how much remained to be done. When governments collapsed or gave way under the pressure of popular uprisings, those who intended to step into positions of power faced formidable tasks of consolidation. They had to secure control of the public spaces in which the revolution had germinated. Acts of rebellion had to be retrospectively sanctioned and reframed as the sublime inauguration of a new political order – in many cities, this need was met through elaborate rituals to honour those who had died during the fighting of the spring days. New leaderships had to emerge, and these had to secure executive power, or a share in it, either by forming a provisional government of some kind or by acquiring places in the existing political structure. They had to secure some acceptable means of policing public space. The commitment to representative government shared by all the revolutionaries of 1848 meant that the new authorities had to convene elected chambers. And these assemblies were entrusted with establishing a lasting legal framework – a constitution – that could channel the energy of revolution into a stable and durable political order. The parallel processing of these tasks, which involved a combination of brute force, public ritual, protracted negotiation and the arduous bedding down of a new normative order, was at the heart of the revolutionary process in 1848.

REVOLUTIONARY SPACE

Ya, ya al-midan. Kont fen men zaman?
Haddet el-soor, nawart el-noor
Lamet hawalek sha'b maksoor

'Oh square, oh square. Where have you been all this time? You broke down the wall, you turned on the light. You gathered around you a broken people.' The song 'Ya al-Midan', performed by the band Cairokee and featuring Aida El-Ayoubi, was one of the viral soundtracks of the Egyptian revolution of February 2011. Tahrir Square was the cradle of the revolt that toppled the dictator Hosni Mubarak in that year. It was the place where the diverse currents of the uprising flowed together and became visible as a movement. The square, the song goes on to say, is the place where the distance between people is abolished and where collective emotions are awakened. It is not an empty space, but a field of energy, 'a square like the tide – some ride it, others are pulled along'.[1] It is hard to think of a text that better articulates the importance of urban space to the experience of revolution.

In 1848, the euphoria of revolution resonated in the streets and squares of cities: the Landhaus courtyard or the universitätsplatz in Vienna, the Schlossplatz in Berlin, the place de l'Hôtel de Ville in Paris, the Piazza del Quirinale in Rome, in Pest the Theatre Square or the Herrengasse in front of Café Pilvax.[2] These were places where people became part of something larger than themselves. Crowds flowed like blood through arteries down the ordinary streets of the inner cities. The emotions that became possible in such shared environments formed a commons on which everyone could draw. 'I could have embraced the entire world', Paul Boerner wrote. 'The scales had fallen from my eyes and around me I saw a new and unknown world! I heard the heartbeat of people, I recognized their thoughts . . .'[3]

The city came to life as the exoskeleton of a sentient being, as if its built structures were themselves taking part in the events. When the writer Fanny Lewald arrived in Paris on 12 March, two weeks after the February events, she was astonished by the constant singing. As she walked through the city, she saw 'groups of thirty to forty men, almost all workers', singing the 'Marseillaise' and an old Girondist song, set to a martial tune, that celebrated death in battle for one's country. Cries of *Vive la République!* rang out every few minutes. The singing and chanting kept her awake at night. The horse-drawn vehicles had largely disappeared, but pedestrians were everywhere and everyone seemed 'set upon asserting themselves, expressing their meaning without reservation'.[4] Pest was so alive with the elan of the March revolution, one observer wrote, that one almost expected the Danube to join in the festivities.[5] When Heinrich Brockhaus visited Frankfurt on 6 April 1848, he found 'a truly lovely sight, everything was cheerfully decorated, not a single house without a flag and flowers, flags on all the church towers, the whole city in motion, everywhere people were cheering and giving salutes'.[6] The Neapolitan liberal Francesco Michitelli remembered the illuminations in Naples on the night of 10 February when the king published the new constitution: 'From the largest palace to the smallest dwelling of the vastness of Naples, one could see only lights.' The finance ministry in Via Toledo was 'a mass of light'; in the Piazza Mercato, an enormous, illuminated canvas depicted the king in the act of swearing an oath to the constitution.[7] An eyewitness report in the *Illustrierte Zeitung* described a similar evening scene in Pest: the town was illuminated, the public buildings all wore the same 'uniform of light', cafés and tobacconists stayed open late so that they could illuminate their windows. Even in the windows of the most modest dwellings, candles and lamps could be seen burning. It may not have been as visually impressive as past official illuminations in honour of dynastic personnel, but the fact that this was an initiative by the city itself made it especially stirring.[8] Walking down to the Graben in Vienna, the novelist Adalbert Stifter was pleased to see flags hung from the windows, houses decorated, newspapers with unfamiliar titles for sale on the streets, and cheerful crowds flowing along the thoroughfares: 'I will never forget this beaming expression of a deeply exhilarated, manly spirit, freed from all fears.'[9] It was almost as if, the Hessian writer Heinrich König recalled of his native Kassel, 'the city lay under a different sky [and] a different air flowed into the rooms where [people] lived'.

People didn't just congregate or walk in these spaces, they inhabited them in a new way: 'How briskly people walked about, necks straight, glances radiant and how loudly they laughed!'[10] The absence of troops was one reason for this disinhibited mood. 'Throughout this day in Paris', Alexis de Tocqueville recalled of 25 February, 'I never saw one of the former agents of authority: not a soldier or a gendarme or a policeman; even the National Guard had vanished.' Not everyone experienced this withdrawal of the traditional guardians of public order as a liberation. Noting the bands of armed workers guarding public buildings, Tocqueville observed that it was 'an extraordinary and terrible thing to see the whole of this huge city, full of so many riches, . . . in the sole hands of those who owned nothing'.[11] The city, one might say, had been turned inside out.

Those whose idea of order had disciplined and controlled public space now watched anxiously from the private spaces of houses and apartments, while those who had once had most to fear from the security forces felt comfortable and in command on the streets and squares.

It was in these spaces that the transformations triggered by the revolutions became visible and audible. The suspension or relaxation of censorship opened the door to a flood of new papers, pamphlets and flysheets that could be seen on sale all over the city. 'As soon as you find yourself on the street', Fanny Lewald wrote, 'you are surrounded by newspaper vendors – men, women and children. "*La Presse! La Presse! Journal du Soir*, second edition! – *Le Moniteur du Soir*, sir! – Look here, ladies! *La Voix des Femmes*! Buy *La Voix des Femmes*! – Buy *La Presse*, gentlemen! *La Liberté*! *La Liberté* for one sou, sir! The real *La République*! Crimes of that villain Louis Philippe and his villainous ministers! *Le Chant de la Liberté*! *La Voix du Peuple*!" are the mingled cries swirling and sounding around you.'[12] As Lewald suggested, it wasn't just the sudden profusion of new titles, it was also the people selling them, many of them women, applying the skills of the marketplace to the sale of news and ideas. In Vienna, the 'Flysheet-woman' (*Flugschriftenweib*) became one of the stock figures of the city's life during the revolutionary year, renowned for her rebellious, irreverent demeanour and her gift for savage repartee.[13]

The new authorities recognized the importance of certain spaces, renaming them as memorial sites within weeks of the uprisings. In Pest, Hatvani Street, the address of the Landerer & Heckenast printing house where the 'twelve demands' were printed on the morning of 15 March and distributed to a cheering crowd, was renamed 'Freedom of the Press Street', City Hall Square was renamed 'Freedom Square' and the Café Pilvax, where Sándor Petőfi had penned his National Song and fortified himself with coffee, received the glorious name 'Revolution Hall'.[14] In Vienna, Fleischmarkt, Schönlaterngasse and Rotenturmstraße were all renamed Barrikadenstraße (Barricade Street), the Michaelerplatz in the centre of town received the name Konstitutionsplatz (Constitution Square); other odonymic novelties included Unity Square, Freedom Lane, March Street, Students' Street, Reconciliation Street and People's Square and most of these names referred to locations associated with key events during and after the March revolution.[15] On 6 April 1848, the provisional authorities in

Carlo Canella, *The Five Days of Milan: Barricade near Porta Tosa, March 21, 1848* (1848). Milanese insurgents fought hard for control of the Porta Tosa, which was later renamed the Porta Vittoria. The painting was based on a sketch made by the artist, who lived on the Corso di Porta Tosa, as the events were unfolding. Note the presence of women and children.

Milan issued a decree announcing that the Porta Tosa, scene of bitter fighting between Milanese insurgents and Austrian troops, should be renamed Porta Vittoria, on account of its having been 'the first to be conquered by the courage of the people'.[16]

The cafés frequented by radicals and liberals became part of the energized space of the revolutionary city. In Rome, the cafés were hubs of political sociability: demonstrations began when people left the cafés; this was where people found out what was happening and resolved on collective responses; if you needed to round up supporters, this was where you went. In Paris, the café Tortoni, the café Anglais, the Café de Paris, the café Riche and, most importantly, the café Divan, were frequented by journalists from all of the best-known papers: this was where press campaigns were coordinated. For the predominantly male habitués of this milieu, the cafés were an intermediate point between the genteel world of the salons, where women presided, and the uncurated life of the streets and squares.[17] In Vienna, Milan, Venice, Berlin and many other cities, cafés were a place where newspapers were read and discussed. In February and March 1848, Paul Boerner went every day to the Café Stehely, well known for its literary pretensions and its excellent assortment of German and foreign newspapers. Boerner succeeded in gaining access to the 'red room', an inner sanctum open only to trusted initiates, where political discussions took place every afternoon at 4 p.m. under the moderation of Dr Adolf Rutenberg, formerly editor of the *Rheinische Zeitung* in Cologne (his successor in this post was Karl Marx). As the situation in the Prussian capital became tense in the early weeks of 1848, the crowds of patrons grew:

> The rooms were no longer big enough for the masses that came pushing in to hear the latest news. The stock of newspapers was no longer sufficient, because no one wanted to wait for them, even for a minute. So a kind of podium was improvised, and it was Dr Rutenberg with his fine, powerful voice, who read out the newspapers, throwing caution to the winds and adding his own explanations and comments.[18]

When one crowd of patrons had its fill of news and discussion, another took its place. These were the synapses of the city. They were especially important for those groups that lacked other venues for conviviality and discussion. The French laws restricting *compagnonnages* and journeyman's fraternities, for example, forced Parisian workers to use cafés in the working-class districts as organizational centres. While many trades shut down in the festival atmosphere of March 1848, the cafés remained open and full to bursting and the new government rewarded the Parisian cafés for their part in the recent events by restructuring the indirect tax on alcoholic beverages at the end of March in order to reduce the duty on drinks consumed in bars. 'Unlike other small shopkeepers', the owners of working-class cafés 'saw repression, not revolution, as bad for business'.[19]

In Naples, the Caffè Europa became the haven of the moderate liberals, especially after 16 February, when a banquet was held there for better-off citizens and members of the Neapolitan nobility in honour of the new constitution. It was at the Caffè Europa that one could find the kind of people who had their hair done at Paolucci's, the coiffeur favoured by Neapolitan high society. At the Caffè Buono, on the other hand, one found the mainly Calabrian radical leaders and democratically inclined students from the provinces: in short, people who favoured rejecting or substantially reforming the constitution proffered by the monarch.[20] The presiding spirit here was Saverio Vollaro, 'small, thin, but a true demon, always jumping onto the tables, haranguing his companions and forever dragging them to the strangest street demonstrations'.[21]

Both of these venues were on the Via Toledo, and to walk from one end to the other of this splendid thoroughfare was to journey through a universe of groups and small crowds gathered in front of shops and cafés, or around the stands where newspapers and flysheets were sold and read aloud, often passing journalists and well-known political personalities, or ministers on their way to or from an audience with the king.[22] For a more rarefied radical ambience, there was the Caffè delle Belle Arti, tucked in beside the Academy of the same name in the historical heart of the city. It was here that the young Hegelians of Naples gathered to discuss philosophical questions under the watchful eyes of the Bourbon police, who recorded the names of everyone seen entering the premises.[23] No one better understood the nexus between revolutionary activism and these spaces of political conviviality than the counter-revolutionary police agents tasked – after the Neapolitan revolution was over – with compiling lists of suspected subversives. In addition to registering all of those who had taken part in major demonstrations or held radical speeches, they drew up lists of people deemed guilty of 'conspiratorial comportment in a public place' or of 'meddling in the seditious conventicles of certain cafés in the capital'.[24]

The composite space, partly public and partly commercial, of the revolutionized city thus performed a twofold function. Cafés, hostelries and other hospitable venues could be engines of differentiation, heightening the camaraderie and cohesion within particular occupational or social milieus, or helping to sift the like-minded into factions. At the same time, the streets and squares became, in moments of revolutionary upheaval, spaces of de-differentiation, in which the distance between strangers and between different social strata was temporarily reduced. Contemporary visual representations of street life during the revolutions emphasize the intimacy among people of diverse stations, and the presence of women, who are seen selling newspapers, running from oncoming troops, tending to the wounded, waving flags, preparing lead shot behind a barricade or even fighting alongside male insurgents.

The streets also harboured a reservoir of observers and bystanders who were not necessarily politically committed but could easily be drawn into taking part in demonstrations and protests. Their involvement could make the difference between a highly focused local protest and an oceanic movement of people. On the evening of 12 February, several small flocks of citizens set out from the Caffè Buono behind Vollaro and made their way along the street that led towards the ministerial buildings chanting 'Peace with Sicily!' and 'Down with the ministry!' and pelting mud at the residences of unpopular ministers. Giovanni La Cecilia, who was there, watched the protest unfold: 'I accompanied these demonstrators, and from a few hundred at the beginning they grew, thanks to the addition of stickybeaks and simpletons, to many thousands.'[25] Throughout Europe, stickybeaks and simpletons were crucial to the fluid mechanics of crowd behaviour.

'We are spatial beings', the historian Karl Schlögel has written. He added that this can be a problem for historians, because 'a space cannot be told'.[26] Spaces were where the intoxicating simultaneity of the revolution was lived. Contemporaries understood intuitively their fundamental importance. For evidence of this, we need look no further than the effort dedicated to the pacification and erasure of revolutionized streetscapes by the counter-revolutionary authorities that emerged in the aftermath of the revolutions' collapse. Nowhere was this process more aggressive than in Paris, where the immense restructuring project launched by

Baron Haussmann resulted in a profound 'disarticulation' of urban popular space and the 'gutting' (*éventrement*), as Haussmann himself put it, of the city's ancient centre, 'the neighbourhood of uprisings and barricades'.[27] The streets renamed by the revolutionary authorities in Vienna all returned to their original condition after 1848 and the police authorities were vigilant in the prevention of memorial enactments of any kind. In Berlin, the post-revolutionary governments went to great lengths to prevent even small groups from congregating at symbolic locations in a manner that might serve the purpose of commemoration, including at the Friedrichshain cemetery, where many of the 'March fallen' were buried.[28] And in Cairo, too, the regime of General Abdel Fattah al-Sisi has since made every effort to cleanse Tahrir Square of associations with the uprising of 2011. The song 'Ya al-Midan' is banned from official media. An ancient granite obelisk has appeared at the centre, bearing an inscription commemorating the advent of the military dictatorship in 2013. Around it stand four enormous ram-headed, sandstone sphinxes relocated from the Karnak temple complex in Luxor, 300 miles to the south.[29] The square is heavily guarded by plainclothes security forces, even small gatherings are immediately dispersed and the streets connecting it with the city's neighbourhoods are routinely closed on the anniversaries of the 2011 events.

HONOUR YOUR DEAD

At ten o'clock in the morning of Saturday, 4 March, the Madeleine church in Paris became the scene of a remarkable public ceremony in honour of those who had died in the fighting of 22–24 February. The church was decked out in mourning black. An inscription above the main entrance read: 'To the citizens who died for liberty.' From the Madeleine to the place de la Bastille, the lamps and trees that lined the streets were hung with long flags in the national tricolour and two enormous banners had been suspended from the statue of the genius of liberty at the top of the July Column, one black but spangled with silver stars, the other in the national colours. Around the column stood twenty funereal tripods of the ancient type burning with green and blue flames, and overlooking the square was a purpose-built platform draped in the national colours and reserved for the members of the Provisional Government.

The service began when a funeral float as high as a three-storey building, topped with a statue representing the republic and covered in branches of oak and laurel, approached the entrance of the Madeleine. After the service, the float made its way from the square in front of the church towards the place de la Bastille, followed by a fleet of hearses carrying the bodies of the dead and a troop of grieving relatives. Behind these an immense cortège formed, consisting, according to the editors of *La Réforme*, of 200,000 citizens – in all, the crowds ran to half a million people. Representatives of every conceivable profession were there, from the firemen to the postal workers, students of Saint-Cyr and the École Polytechnique, the heroes of July 1830 organized into fourteen companies, each with its own flag, the association of bookbinders, railway workers, pupils at the schools of Paris, house painters, musicians, tinsmiths, the staffs of the great courts and tribunals, judges and academicians, teachers, printers, typographers, market porters, copper smelters, journalists, the standard-bearing 'wounded of the three days' and many more.

It was a moment of carefully orchestrated public emotion. As the last hearse approached the July Column in the place de la Bastille, there was an uncomfortable misunderstanding: the grieving relatives of the deceased, who until this point had been following the coffins, mistakenly occupied the places in the columbarium reserved for the Provisional Government. When the National Guard proved unable to dislodge them, the secretary-general of the new government approached them and spoke these words:

> Family feelings, as sacred as they are, must give way today to the larger feelings of the country. The relatives you have lost, the children you are weeping for, who died for the Republic, are above all children of the Republic. . . . Leave to us, leave to the Provisional Government, the pious mission of expressing at once the anguish of private pain and the profound emotion of public recognition and public pain.[30]

Funeral processions for fallen insurgents took place everywhere that month, but this was the most elaborate of them all. Everything about it was freighted with symbolic charge. Of all the churches in nineteenth-century Paris, the Madeleine was the least church-like; originally commissioned by Napoleon to serve as a 'Temple to the Glory of the

Great Army', it was a stringently neo-classical structure modelled on the Roman *Maison Carrée* in Nîmes. Overlooking the place de la Bastille, where the procession came to an end, was the Colonne de Juillet, a monument in the form of a forty-seven-metre Corinthian column executed in cast bronze and commemorating the 'Three Glorious Days' of 1830. The route between the Madeleine and the place de la Bastille had already been used in 1840 when, under the scrupulous management of Charles de Rémusat, then interior minister, the remains of 615 victims of the July Revolution were processed along the same route and deposited in the columbarium under the foundation, to the accompaniment of a funeral symphony composed for the occasion by Hector Berlioz.[31] It was a commemorative act, but also an aggressive statement on behalf of the July Monarchy and the signal of a revival of official confidence after the difficult 1830s.[32] In choosing the same route, the revolutionary authorities of 1848 invested the same spectacular space with new meaning. The funeral float was even larger and more impressive, and whereas the king and the Prime Minister had stayed away from the 1840 event for fear of assassination attempts, the new Provisional Government in its entirety was present and prominently visible for the interment of the victims of February 1848.

The funereal pomp of 4 March 1848 was necessary because it signalled the advent not just of a new government, but of a new form of state. A royal ordinance of 1816 ruled that the right to signal appreciation of services rendered to the state and to assign rewards to those deemed worthy of them fell exclusively to the king.[33] Against that background, the procession of 4 March announced in the clearest possible way that one form of sovereignty had been replaced by another. 'THEY DIED FOR THE REPUBLIC', declared the enormous banner suspended at the front of the funeral float. The oaks and laurels, the burning tripods and the emphatic neo-classicism of the architectural setting all invoked republican antiquity. The music chosen for the service in the Madeleine (the Cherubini funeral march, Rameau's 'Chorus', the prayer of Moses from Rossini's *Mosè in Egitto*) was beautiful and solemn but not religious enough to distract from the republican message of the event.

In the ordinary life of states, people who challenge the authorities and die as a result in clashes with the security forces are treated as rebels or criminals. An alchemical transformation is required to turn them into something else: martyrs for a new political order, the lamented 'children' of a new state. In achieving this, the new authorities in Paris made a paradoxical claim: to die in the uprising of 22–24 February meant rendering service to a state that had not existed when the uprising took place, or, more precisely, to a political idea that had only now begun to take shape as a state. In this way, the Provisional Government turned insurgents into revolutionaries. And in legitimizing them, it legitimized itself.

In every city where citizens perished in the fighting, there were efforts to honour the dead in a manner commensurate with their sacrifice. But the logic of public bereavement differed from place to place. In Paris, the revolution resulted in the replacement of one regime by another. The same applied in a different sense to those places, like Milan for example, that were liberated from 'foreign' control by an insurrection. In Milan, 220 named dead citizens (of whom twenty-four were women) and a further seventy-six who could not be identified (of whom five were women) were buried in the midst of an elaborate ceremonial that opened with a requiem mass in the city's magnificent cathedral attended by the entire Provisional Government, all the municipal notables, representatives of nearby cities, and foreign consuls and envoys. Outside the cathedral on the Piazza del Duomo stood an improvised monument consisting of a pedestal surmounted by a Lombard lance, symbol of kingship among the medieval Lombards, surrounded by statuettes and vases bearing shrubs of funereal cypress.[34] Inscribed on the sides of the pedestal, a kind of stunted obelisk, were patriotic commendations of the dead and their victorious struggle against the 'barbarian' overlords.[35]

In Berlin, the process began with an improvised but extremely dramatic spectacle. In the early afternoon of 19 March, the corpses of insurgents were gathered from the places where the fighting had been fiercest and draped on delivery carts or pieces of wood serving as stretchers. Many of the bodies were in horrific condition. Their clothes were folded back so that the wounds could be seen. At many locations, processions formed and the bodies of the fallen were slowly walked towards the Schlossplatz – though it was later impossible to reconstruct how this concerted action came about.[36] Paul Boerner joined one of these improvised funeral processions. Three years later, when he came to recall it in writing, the memory was still as vivid as if the event had taken place only a few days before. The group he was with had gathered five corpses from the Friedrichstraße. They lay half naked on their wooden boards, until women covered them in sprigs of greenery. Flowers were thrown down from the windows as they passed. A 'ragged little lad' ran along with them sobbing: the corpse at the front, with a grey beard and a bullet hole in the forehead, had been to his father. The boy had stayed with the body in the hours since the fighting and still refused to be separated from it. With every step, the cortège grew in number.[37]

As they passed the Army headquarters (*Kommandantur*), the few soldiers still on guard were forced to pay their last respects to the dead. Near the Schlossplatz, processions from various parts of the inner city merged and the bodies were brought together and laid on the ground in front of the palace. Minute by minute new processions arrived with their grim cargo: a man carrying the body of his fifteen-year-old son, a worker whose face had been blown away by a cartridge, a widow killed in the fighting and now surrounded by her children. The mourners gathered in silence until someone shouted: 'The king must come, he should see the bodies!'[38]

Inside the palace, blank panic had broken out. With pale faces, ministers of the newly appointed government stepped out into the sight of the crowd. They tried to speak but were drowned out by voices crying 'The king! The king!'[39] Only when the bearers picked up the corpses and made to bring them into the palace itself did the king appear with the ashen-faced queen, who was finding it difficult to remain upright. The king happened to be wearing his military cap; 'Hat off!' roared an elderly man near the front of the crowd. The monarch doffed his cap and bowed his head, repeating the gesture several times. 'The one thing missing now is the guillotine', murmured Queen Elisabeth, who was 'white with horror'. The king, who was only a few paces away from the crowd, appeared 'pale and almost shivering', although one middle-class eyewitness reported seeing tears of pity on the faces of the royal couple.[40] The air was thick with tension until some men in the crowd began singing the choral 'Jesus meine Zuversicht' (Jesus I Trust in Thee):

> It was [Paul Boerner recalled] as if the passion of the outraged mass was dissolved in these tender notes of pain. . . . When they were reminded of the pious dreams of their childhoods, when the memory of their loved ones came upon them, so heartfelt and soft, the strong arms grew weak and the mute angry corpses were lowered to the ground. Everyone joined in. Where a moment ago the wildest emotion had found expression, the tones of the old church song now resounded. Under their protection, the king greeted the crowd once more and withdrew with his wife.[41]

For Paul Boerner, this spectacular and improvised display, a masterpiece of revolutionary choreography, was a manifestation of 'the deep and grandiose poetry that slumbers in the hearts of the men of labour'. It is easy to see what he meant. Amongst all the drama of those days across the cities of Europe, this confrontation between an angry, grieving people and a humiliated king stands out. It was 'a scene', one unnamed middle-class observer noted, 'that excelled in its tragic pathos' anything ever seen in the 'dramas of ancient and romantic art'. This commentator, clearly an educated and well-informed person, went on to compare the events in Berlin favourably with the recent revolution in Paris. Whereas the Parisian revolutionaries had dragged the king's throne out of the Tuileries Palace and broken and burned it, their Berlin counterparts had merely broken the heart of their king, purging it in a 'purifying fire from which he emerged reborn for his own and the people's salvation'.[42]

Strip away the evangelical pathos and this is not a bad characterization of the contrast. The French had chased their king into exile and destroyed the attributes of his majesty. The Berliners had merely humbled their king; the hymn they sang expressed grief, but also announced the possibility of forgiveness. And in bringing their dead to the door of their king, the Berliners showed how deeply imbued they were with the mental habits of monarchy, how reluctant they were to place the sovereign outside the horizons of their moral economy. As for the king, this was beyond doubt a traumatic moment, a living nightmare whose grip on his imagination never weakened.[43] But he was quick to recover his composure and the shock was soon replaced by a vengeful determination to restore his authority and humiliate the authors of a revolution that, in his mind, seemed a satanic rebellion against an office ordained by God. Only two days later, on 21 March, Frederick William IV would take the extraordinary step of riding virtually unguarded through the streets of the capital, draped in the German tricolour and declaring to loud applauses that he intended to place himself 'at the head of the movement' to found a united German fatherland.

It was the Berlin city authorities, not the government, that took responsibility for the arrangement of a public funeral on 22 March. The planning was contentious from the start. A committee consisting of conservative members of the city council and the Municipal Assembly initially intended to bury the civilian dead together with the soldiers who had perished in the same battles, as a gesture of reconciliation. But this idea triggered sharp objections, not just from the democratic and liberal left, but also from representatives of the military, who wished at any cost to avoid giving the impression that the army accepted the insurgency as legitimate.[44] The plan was dropped, and the ceremony of 22 March focused exclusively on the civilians killed by troops. On that morning, 183 coffins were loaded onto a purpose-built multi-tiered structure in front of the Neue Kirche on the Gendarmenplatz in the centre of Berlin. A funeral service followed, during which representatives of the city's faith communities held short addresses before the wall of coffins. The liberal clergyman Karl Leopold Adolf Sydow, preacher at the Neue Kirche, spoke for the Protestants, Joseph Nepomuk Ruland of St Hedwig's spoke for the Catholics and Rabbi Dr Michael Sachs, a scholar of the Jewish religious poetry of medieval Spain, for the Jewish community. Whereas Sydow and Ruland emphasized conciliation and the redemptive power of German national unity, Sachs struck a different note: it was not death as such that joined the dead together as equals, he observed, but 'the power of an idea' that could 'tear down all the ramparts and divisions that separate humans from themselves and from each other'.[45] The conquest of political liberty merged here with the specifically Jewish dream of an emancipated humanity.

The coffins were loaded onto carts and the procession moved slowly towards the Friedrichshain cemetery. Behind them followed a cortège running to perhaps 100,000 in which, as in Paris, many occupational groups walked in closed ranks, watched by an audience estimated to have encompassed 200,000 people. It took about ninety minutes to complete the route; the people at the back were only just getting started when those at the front arrived at the destination – around three hours had passed by the time the various contingents took their places at Friedrichshain.[46] A piquant detail: the cortège included a group of barricade fighters dressed in exactly the clothes they had worn on the night of 18/19 March. This was a theatrical touch whose heightening and authenticating effect on the spectacle was lost on no one. But it signified something else as well: the self-historicizing temperament of mid-nineteenth-century people. The revolution had only just begun and already it was possible to re-enact it. This was what it meant to apprehend the present as the unfolding of history, and it helps to explain the swiftness with which so many participants in these events were able to recycle their experiences into historical narratives. Already on 1 April 1848, less than a week after the Milanese insurrection, it was possible to read in the *Gazzetta di Milano* a review of a book by the citizen and eyewitness Ignazio Cantù entitled *The Last Five Days of the Austrians in Milan. Accounts and Reminiscences*.[47]

Like its Parisian counterpart, the Berlin procession was an elaborate performance of unanimity. And yet, even as the crowd gathered around the open graves at Friedrichshain, there were hints at the fault lines that would later help to pull the revolution apart. It was Sydow who delivered the main funeral address, and he used the occasion to frame the recent violence as a kind of catharsis. 'A steamy, unhealthy cloud had come to rest between the king and his loyal people', he said, referring to the miasmatical infection theory still popular in mid-century medicine. But now this cloud had vanished and 'the word of harmony' had been found: 'into our hearts the inexpressible blessing of trust has returned'.[48] After Sydow had finished, Bishop Dr Neander pronounced a blessing, the delegations lowered their flags, the marksmen's club fired the salute and the ceremony might have concluded at this point, were it not for the chairman of the Democratic Club, Dr Georg Jung, who now delivered a speech of his own, despite the efforts of several members of the organizing committee to prevent it.

For Jung, whose words were heard in total silence by the crowd, the events of 18/19 March were not a passing storm that clears the air, but a legacy and a challenge to the living. Words of reconciliation, of peace, had been spoken, he told the crowd. And yes, it was right to forgive and to forget. The call for 'raw vengeance that demands blood for blood' would have to give way. But – and here was the rub – the living would only be able to atone for the dead if they took on and fought to achieve the cause for which the deceased had died. Peace was good, but not a shameful peace that robbed the victors of the spoils and cheated the dead of the expiation of their blood. The reason for the atrocities, Jung suggested, lay precisely in the nature of the authority in whose service the troops had fought, 'a dark power that issued inalterable orders from an inaccessible height' and demanded a 'blind, unswerving obedience'. If the living stepped back from the struggle against this power, then the enemy would creep up on them in a moment of exhaustion, 'and your slavery or your struggle will begin anew'. To Sydow's cycle of sorrow, forgiveness and reconciliation, Jung opposed the imperative of historical progress through the continuing struggle for rights and liberty.[49]

In Vienna, too, the carrying of the fallen of 13 March to their graves was an occasion of great solemnity and drama. Four days later, to the beat of muffled drums and a band playing 'Beethoven's Funeral March' (presumably the Marcia funebre of the Eroica), a cortège walked to the Scottish Gate (Schottentor) in the north-western wall of the old city and onwards to the Schmelzer Cemetery, a journey of some two hours. The students of all faculties and from the Technical College were formed up in yearly cohorts, all wearing black sashes and armbands. Professors, clergymen, National Guardsmen and the representatives of corporations and professions passed easily through dense crowds of onlookers that opened to let them pass, 'as once the waves of the Red Sea parted before the Israelites'.[50] At the head of the procession, a student held aloft a plaque inscribed with the words: 'Fallen for the Fatherland'. The plaque was framed by a wreath of oak leaves and the ends of the white ribbons attached to it were held by six little girls dressed in white. Black ribbons waved from the windows as the procession passed.[51] At the cemetery, the coffins were lowered into a single grave.

To the astonishment of many who were present, the first clergyman invited to speak over the open grave was the reform Rabbi Isaac Noah Mannheimer, present because two of the dead, Leo Spitzer and Bernard Herschmann, were of the Jewish faith. He was followed by the Catholic chaplain of the students' Academic Legion and various other dignitaries. This was an entirely unheard-of and unique procedure – it would not be repeated for the Jews and Christians who fell in the much deadlier fighting of the Viennese counter-revolution in October. In fighting and dying 'for their Fatherland', Mannheimer declared, the fallen had died the 'death of the just', which was the greatest possible moral good. And to this he added a striking reflection: their cause *would have been* just, even if it were not, as he put it, 'victorious in this hour'. It was an interesting twist on the martyrology of the Parisian ceremony, which tended to merge the sacrifice of the dead with the victory of the Republic. By contrast, Mannheimer separated the sacrifice and death of the fallen from the political flux of the moment. Most remarkable to contemporary ears was the inclusiveness of the language:

> I pray for them and for their Christian brothers, because they are all equally dear and precious to us and to my heart; they are human souls, formed in Your [God's] image and likeness, who sanctified Your name on earth. And so with all the strength of my soul I pray for them, [that they may find] a light-filled place in Your heavenly kingdom.

The eulogy closed with a plea to his Christian audience to remember this common humanity and this common struggle when the time came to apportion the rewards of victory: 'You are free men. . . . Accept us too as free men and may God bless you!'[52]

In the address that followed, Anton Füster, a Catholic priest, but also a member of the university's Faculty of Philosophy, stressed the unique and sublime character of the current moment. There were hours in human affairs, he declared, when spirit triumphed over matter. The dead lying in their open grave were proof that such an hour had struck. The fallen had died 'the most beautiful death, death for the Fatherland'. They had died for ideas: truth, law, liberty and love, four daughters of one heavenly father. They were fallen fighters, but they were also victors whose fame would never fade.

Füster's speech, unlike Mannheimer's, scarcely mentioned God, except in his role as the unnamed father of truth, law, liberty and love.[53] This may have been because he was addressing the gathering in the name of the philosophical faculty, rather than of his Church. It was the university that had invited him to speak, not his superiors within the hierarchy, who gave him a cold reception when he went to inform them of the fact. Was he not aware, the director of the Archiepiscopal Chancellery asked him, that it was illegal in Austria to hold speeches over graves? Was the director not aware, Füster retorted, that a revolution had just taken place? He could speak if he must, the director replied, but not in his clerical habit. To which Füster replied that it would be indecent to change his clothes in front of thousands of people and, besides, it would convey the impression that the Church condemned the revolution. Clergymen, answered the director, ought to stay out of politics, they ought to stand above movements of all kinds, to which Füster replied that whereas it was easy in the comfort and splendour of an archiepiscopal palace to sit back and see to one's own precious needs (*sich um das eigene liebe Ich zu kümmern*), leading people, fighting at their side and averting the worst excesses was another matter entirely. Told that he could see the archbishop if he returned in an hour or two, Füster replied that he would not return, he was needed at the university and hadn't the time for 'unnecessary walks'.[54]

As this exchange makes clear, Füster's relations with his clerical line managers were not especially warm and he appeared completely uninterested in working towards their improvement. He was an example of that fascinating and not especially common species of 1848: the radical priest. Across Europe, the Catholic hierarchy tended to keep its distance from the revolutionary movements, whose clerical adherents tended to come from the lowest ranks. In the Kingdom of the Two Sicilies, the high clergy firmly supported the Bourbon monarchy, but there were areas where parish priests were active in support of the revolution. The same phenomenon was observed in Wallachia, where many local orthodox priests favoured the revolution, while their superiors opposed it.[55] As a teacher of philosophy at the University of Vienna, Füster was already known for his promotion of democratic ideas. After the revolution broke out, he became a passionate defender of the student movement. As chaplain of the Academic Legion, he took part in the barricade fighting that broke out in May when the government tried to shut the legion down.

Füster, in other words, was a very different figure from Sydow, the steady-handed, moderate liberal clergyman who would oversee the burial ceremony in Berlin. Sydow was a former chaplain to the Prussian court and the preacher of the Neue Kirche: his presence embedded the event in the official ecclesiastical landscape of the city. Füster was a more combative and controversial figure, only loosely linked to his hierarchy and already affiliated with the radical wing of the revolution. In Prussia, moreover, whether he wished it or not, the king was central to dramaturgy of the revolution, both on the traumatic afternoon of 18 March and on the following day, when the corpses were gathered, and again as the cortège passed the Schlossplatz on 22 March, where his head could be seen 'like a white dot' nodding before the dead as the hearses passed; in Vienna, by contrast, the emperor was nowhere to be seen. Military were seen posted on the city walls, their helmets glinting in the sunshine, but it was not clear whether they were there to pay their respects or to prevent possible excesses (of which there were none). Whereas the Berlin ceremonial was organized at the behest of the city authorities, the Vienna procession bore the imprint of the emergent student movement, whose activism and centrality to the insurgency were a distinctive feature of the Vienna revolution. And the scale was smaller, partly because the fighting had been less intense (the Viennese would more than make up for that in October), and partly because not all of those who had 'fallen' were carried to their graves on that day.

In a powerful article for the liberal-constitutional *Die Gegenwart* (The Present) a writer signing as 'Falke' drew attention to the small number of coffins. Where were the others who had died? Why weren't their coffins being carried out to the cemetery? The answer, Falke observed, lay in the fact that some of the missing dead were suburban proletarians who upon learning of the uprising had committed arson and plunder outside the city walls. Hunger and misery had rendered them insensitive to the higher meaning of liberty. For them, the revolution was their hour of vengeance for the 'years of suffering they had been made to bear'. But what of those workers who perished in the centre of town fighting alongside students, hopelessly outnumbered and outgunned by the military – why had they been left mouldering in the morgue? Why hadn't all the fallen been buried together? In the light of the deep emotions awakened by the ceremony, it seemed tasteless to raise such questions, the writer remarked; perhaps the years to come would bring forth answers.[56] In Vienna, as in Berlin, the effort to honour the dead revealed fine fault lines in revolutions that had scarcely begun.

ESTABLISH A GOVERNMENT

We think of a revolution as a process that replaces one government with another. The 'July Monarchy' makes way for the 'Second Republic'. Seen on a Wikipedia timeline, the transition looks automatic and self-explanatory, as if one were driving over the border between France and Spain. But the reality in Paris was quite different. In the moment when the revolution was accomplished, the new form of state did not yet exist, even embryonically. There was no cohort of future ministers waiting in the wings and no provisional authority formed in advance to oversee the process of demolition and installation. More importantly, the procedures that might govern the emergence of such an authority did not exist; a revolution that unfolded under agreed rules of succession would be no revolution at all. In short, the February Revolution was not a 'transition', but rather a hiatus, in which the future was suddenly blown open.[57] From this it follows that the emergence of a provisional authority is a more mysterious process, and one more worthy of our attention, than the metaphor of transition suggests.

It was easy enough for anyone to propose a list of provisional ministers. But who had the authority to do such a thing? For the moment, the people itself was in power. But who could be said to represent the people in the absence of an electoral process? To these and other questions, the Paris revolutionaries of February 1848 found interesting answers. Early on 24 February, while the fighting was still ongoing, committees formed at the editorial offices of *Le National* and *La Réforme*. Surrounding both premises were crowds of insurgents and National Guardsmen.

Mediating between the two newspaper committees was the Alsatian leftist lawyer and former deputy Édouard Martin, who, learning that the people at *Le National* had drawn up a list of provincial ministers, went to find the socialist Louis Blanc and accompanied him to the offices of *La Réforme*, where he urged the staff – the editor, Ferdinand Flocon, was still out on the streets somewhere – to draw up an alternative list. Only after a tug of war between the two papers were the radicals Flocon, Ledru-Rollin and Louis Blanc added to the list.[58] The process of public ratification was equally chaotic: the list was read to the National Guards of the 2nd Legion for their acclamation, mainly because they happened to be in the streets nearby. A revised version was proposed and acclaimed an hour or so later at the Chamber of Deputies, now largely abandoned by the deputies and heaving with Guardsmen and insurgents and then, sometime later, at the Hôtel de Ville, the ancestral backdrop for French revolutions. Emil Regnault, who would head the office of the provisional Minister of the Interior in Paris (and later write his own history of the Provisional Government), described:

> an immense Babel where all the sounds of the human voice collided with each other – cries of joy, groans, bursts of laughter, songs of triumph, surges of enthusiasm, menacing addresses, inarticulate endearments – it was all as naïve as the delirium of a child and as terrible as the frenzy of a giant.[59]

In this energetic space still vibrating with the revolution, a final version of the Provisional Government list received its public imprimatur.

The most curious of the radical names was the machinist known as 'Albert the worker'. Albert was a habitué of the insurrectionary secret societies of the 1830s and 1840s. He had never attracted the attention of the left-wing press before and he had never held an office of any kind, elected or otherwise. In the account she wrote of these events, Marie d'Agoult, writing under the pseudonym Daniel Stern, recalled the circumstances surrounding the machinist's sudden elevation. M. Albert, she observed, must have owed the abrupt ovation that carried him into power to 'some mark of courage or simply to some happily chosen word', because in the days that followed no one could otherwise explain why he should have been preferred to 'so many others more competent and better known'. Yet she conceded that there was a consequential logic to this unprecedented procedure. Despite his 'vexing mediocrity', she wrote, the nomination of a worker to the Provisional Government was a 'historical fact whose meaning and character should not be misunderstood'. 'It is a sign of the emancipation . . . of the working class; it marks the hour of transition from the political revolution to the social revolution.'[60] The publicity generated by the new government over the following weeks never omitted to mention the humble social origin of 'Mr Albert, who is himself a worker'.

This media-driven process of political regeneration seems less odd when we recall that something similar had happened in 1830. At that time, it was the leading liberal journals, and most importantly *Le National*, which had focused and led the political revolution, announcing that they had no intention of accepting the unconstitutional ordinances of Charles X. *Le National* had played a key role in guiding the people of Paris back out of the vacuum of revolution into the new normal of the July Monarchy. That this journal should be joined by the more radical *La Réforme* in 1848 was a sign of a leftward shift in the political culture of the capital. But the papers could only take on this role because they were already important switchboards for liberal and radical opinion. This was what it meant to live in a 'civilization of the journal'.

The Provisional Government that resulted from this curious process was not a government at all, but a 'revolutionary authority' drawn from the groups and networks capable of wielding influence in the hiatus of 24 February.[61] Its members ranged from the moderate liberals around *Le National* (Marrast, Marie, Garnier-Pagès, François Arago), to the radicals around *La Réforme* (Ledru-Rollin, Flocon), to the socialists (Blanc, Albert). And it was sociologically diverse: radical journalists, chamber deputies, a socialist writer, a worker. Lamartine was there because of his eloquence and popularity. The lawyer Jacques Charles Dupont de l'Eure, who would turn eighty-one on 27 February, was a seasoned parliamentarian who had sat on the Council of Five Hundred, the lower house of the French Directory, in 1798–9; he was the only member of the group who bridged the huge interval between First and Second French

Republics. Over the weeks that followed, the steadily deepening hostility between Louis Blanc and his moderate republican colleagues would undermine the government's unity and capacity to act.[62]

Around the new government, other officeholders materialized in a similarly haphazard way: Marc Caussidière, whose brother had perished in the fighting at Lyons in 1834, simply took possession on his own initiative of the prefecture of police; Étienne Arago, the more radical brother of François, did the same with the postal service – both were subsequently acknowledged in official announcements by the new government. The abolitionist Victor Schoelcher, one of the founders of *La Réforme*, was appointed Under-Secretary of State for the Colonies and tasked with heading a commission that would prepare a general decree of emancipation for the enslaved people of the French colonies. Potential obstructions to the monopoly of legitimate power were removed: the Chamber of Peers was forbidden to convene; the Chamber of Deputies was dissolved; ministerial posts were parcelled out to trusted officeholders (not all of whom were members of the government); and from 26 February every announcement carried an official header: 'République française. Liberté, Égalité, Fraternité'. And yet the Provisional Government continued throughout its tenure to operate from the Hôtel de Ville, the symbolic theatre of the revolution, rather than taking up residence in a building more fitting to its national calling.[63] It was not the old regime, and it was not the new regime; it was a thing sprung from the revolution itself, embodying the tensions and contradictions of that moment.

In the city of Milan, where the revolution took the form of an uprising against a foreign government, the formation of a provisional authority took place under quite different auspices. But here, too, as in Paris, the question arose of how to legitimate the new authority. Mayor Gabrio Casati and his associates found an ingenious answer. The sequence of official announcements published on the first page of the first edition of the new *Gazzetta di Milano*, the organ of the provisional authority, opened on 23 March with three announcements issued five days earlier (18 March) by the Austrian vice-governor, Count O'Donnell. Sensing that the situation in the city was no longer under his control, the vice-governor authorized the municipality to arm the Civic Guard, shut down the Directorate of Police and transferred responsibility for public order to the municipal authorities. The decrees that emanated from the provisional leadership during the insurrection all derived the authority to act from this transfer of responsibility.[64] In this way, the fiction was created that the Austrians themselves had laid the foundation for the authority that oversaw their expulsion from the city.

All the same, the emergence of the new government was a remarkable achievement. Casati handled with tact and skill the political divisions that opened during the fighting between his executive committee and the 'council of war' dominated by the radical Carlo Cattaneo; on 31 March, Cattaneo resigned, and the council of war was absorbed into the new government. Over the days following the flight of the Austrians, Casati extended the Provisional Government's control across Lombardy, inviting the major cities of the provinces to send envoys to serve in the Milanese government.

In a mordant, almost contemporary analysis of the situation that faced the city after the flight of the Austrians, the writer and journalist Cristina Trivulzio di Belgioioso reflected on the way in which the Milanese provisional authority had emerged. Reading in the black and white letters of printed announcements the names of the new provisional ministers, it was easy to get the impression, Belgioioso wrote, that some kind of popular election must have assigned the sovereign power to this small band of men. 'Nothing could be more mistaken: while the noise of cannons, rifles, alarm bells and military drums filled the air, while death stalked our streets, . . . most of the men we have just named made their way to the Marino Palace, shared out the roles and assigned to themselves portions of power.'

This rather arbitrary procedure, Belgioioso suggested, had not produced a government in which posts were well matched with experience, qualifications and aptitude. The new director of police, Angelo Fava, was a former physician from Padua who had moved to Milan in 1840. He was a man of patriotic feeling, but he had no policing experience whatsoever and owed his appointment as president of the Public Security Committee and later as chief of police mainly to the fact that he was close to the group around Gabrio Casati. Fava was a man of wit, Belgioioso wrote, but he was also vain, superficial and flighty; 'never did a post demand a rarer mix of penetration, agility and firmness; never was there a man less suited to occupy it than the new director of Milanese police'.[65]

A far more serious problem was that the men of the government and the envoys delegated to it by the larger Lombard cities represented a range of very disparate political positions. Casati and Count Vitaliano Borromeo, a celebrated agronomist and sponsor of scientific research, were men of conservative, monarchist temperament; so was Francesco della Torre Rezzonico, the delegate from Como. Cesare Correnti, by contrast, was a longstanding opponent of Austrian rule and a republican with close links to the wider patriot networks of the peninsula: in 1844, he had published an anonymous tract condemning the Austrians for suffocating the national liberty of the Italians and stifling the country's economic progress. Marquis Guerrieri, the delegate from Mantua, was another well-known republican. The result of these appointments, Belgioioso argued, was a government composed of two factions embodying radically divergent visions of the future, whose mutual distrust would paralyse the management of public affairs during the months that followed the insurrection. We find similarly acerbic portraits of the new leaders in Ferdinando Malvica's unpublished chronicle of the Sicilian revolution.[66] Belgioioso and Malvica knew too much about the people they were describing to be impressed by their sudden elevation. To see people you have known for many years catapulted into positions of power can be an ambivalent experience.

The structure of the uprising against the Austrians in Venice was quite different. In Milan, Mayor Casati and his committee managed to stay in control of the process and to impose themselves on rival factions. In Venice, there was no such organ of control and the insurrection unfolded along several parallel paths. The leading patriot in the city was the republican lawyer Daniele Manin, freshly out of jail after a conviction for sedition. Manin busied himself planning an uprising against the Austrians, much to the horror of the municipal congregation, whose members had no desire to see Habsburg rule come to an end and no intention of ceding power over the city to a popular tribune. After a clash on Piazza San Marco on the morning of 18 March, during which troops fired on a crowd, killing eight people, Manin succeeded in persuading the Austrian authorities to grant the city the right to establish a Civic Guard – precisely the concession that the Austrian vice-governor Count O'Donnell made to the Milanese on the same day.

Manin hoped that the Civic Guard would perform a double role. It would shield middle-class property against the threat of plebeian violence, but, should the opportunity arise, this body of armed citizens might also be used against the Austrians.[67] But it remained unclear how he would muster the forces required to expel the substantial garrisons of the Austrians. On the evening of 21 March, when he informed his closest political friends that he intended to raise an insurrection on the following day, they were sceptical of his plans; Angelo Mengaldo, commander of the new Civic Guard, refused to commit his forces to such a hare-brained enterprise.

On the morning of 22 March, before Manin could start an insurrection, a mutiny broke out in the boatyards of the Venetian arsenal. Here, local grievances were in play. The 800-odd workmen of the boatyards, known as *arsenalotti*, had repeatedly demanded a pay rise from their chief supervisor, a notoriously merciless Croat by the name of Captain Marinovic. Marinovic's habitual reply to such demands was: 'forse la prossima settimana' – 'perhaps next week'. Amidst surging grain prices, tensions in the boatyards rose in early March. On 18 March, the *arsenalotti* learned that they would be barred from the newly instituted Civic Guard. This was unsurprising, given that the guard had been instituted precisely to protect the propertied classes against aroused proletarians. On 21 March, when the men of the boatyards petitioned the commander of the guard to admit them to its ranks, resentment over wages and the Civic Guard reached boiling point. When Marinovic turned up to work on the following morning, he was the wrong man in the wrong place at the wrong time. A group of *arsenalotti* chased him through the yards and up a tower, mortally wounded him with a knife, and dragged him down the stairs by his feet. Still barely alive, he asked for a priest, to which his tormentors replied: 'perhaps next week'.[68]

Hearing the news of what had happened, Manin rushed to the Arsenal and took control of the situation. That he was accepted in this role is an indication of his communicative skills, though it probably helped that he could pose as the man who would shield the workers against Austrian reprisals. Civic Guards hurried to the spot to prevent Austrian garrison troops from gaining access to the boatyards. When the Austrians turned up and gave the order to fire on the insurgents, the troops, most of whom were Italian peasants from the Venetian hinterland, refused to fire and overpowered their officers. From this moment, the days of the Austrians in Venice were numbered. Manin succeeded in having the weapons depots opened, so that the populace could arm themselves. Recognizing that they had irreversibly lost control of the city, the Austrians slipped away with no further fuss.

The Austrians in the city were beaten, but there was still no interim government. A power struggle broke out between the largely conservative municipal congregation, led by Mayor Giovanni Correr (Gabrio Casati's Venetian counterpart) and the insurgent leaders around Manin. On the evening of 22 March, hoping to wrest back control of the city, the congregation announced a new government under the premiership of the moderate liberal lawyer Gian Francesco Avesani. But a group of influential citizens met in the Café Florian on Piazza San Marco on the following day to protest at the exclusion of Manin and demand the resignation of Avesani. Fearing further unrest, Avesani and the congregation caved in. On the afternoon of 23 March, Manin was proclaimed President of the Venetian Republic. A list of the members of his government was read out and acclaimed by the crowd.

The composition of Manin's new government reflected an effort to bring together as broad a range of milieus and interests as possible. Most of the ministers were solid bourgeois with a variety of professional expertise, but the Minister of the Interior was the not especially patriotic or popular nobleman Carlo Trolli, who had been working closely with the Austrians for years – his appointment was presumably intended to mollify the pro-Austrian aristocracy in the city. At the other end of the social spectrum was the tailor Angelo Toffoli, Minister Without Portfolio, chosen, Manin later explained, 'for his influence among the lower classes, as a symbol of democracy'. This was Manin's effort to acknowledge the role played in his success by the city's proletariat and to capture the enigmatic charm of 'Albert the worker'. In reality, Signore Toffoli was no 'workman' at all, but a master craftsman and small entrepreneur with an atelier employing several men. Most of these appointees were well suited to their respective jobs. But, like their Milanese counterparts, they lacked political cohesion. Their unity would soon begin to fray under the pressure of governing a new and volatile political entity.

In Paris, Milan and Venice, provisional governments emerged in the hiatus created by the collapse or local withdrawal of a regime. The situation was quite different in countries where the structures of the pre-revolutionary sovereignty remained in place. Here, leading dissenters, known in many states as 'March ministers', took their place alongside establishment figures. A complex struggle for power usually followed. At its heart was a contest between old and new ideas and people, a context that unfolded in a field of tension between radical pressures from below, manifested in democratic clubs and street-based mobilizations, and the still-sovereign monarch, who might or might not be prepared to accept certain limitations on his power.

The Kingdom of the Two Sicilies experienced both patterns. In Palermo, as in Milan and Venice, the provisional regime emerged from the process of the insurrection itself: 'The authority of the government having altogether ceased to be recognized in the city', one observer reported, 'the insurrection naturally assumed a sort of regular organization.'[69] On 14 January, the new authorities announced the formation of four committees responsible for food supply, war and munitions, finance, and a 'fourth committee', responsible for collating and publishing relevant information, chaired by the retired lawyer Ruggiero Settimo.[70] From 18 January, communications from the royal Neapolitan authorities to the Praetor of the city were redirected to the committees, which henceforth took responsibility for diplomatic communications with Naples and with mediating personnel, such as the foreign consuls or envoys of the great powers. On 23 January, Settimo was elected 'General President' of the committees, and two days later he began signing off as 'President of the General Committee'.[71] An announcement issued on that day urged the 'reputable and honest citizens' who had emerged as the leaders of the insurrections in the other Sicilian cities to form themselves into committees and send envoys to the Palermitan General Committee (Milan and Venice would follow a similar procedure). By working together, the delegates of the insurrection across the island would be able to institute a 'general parliament' capable of 'converting the needs, the preferences, the opinions of all into stable and durable laws'.[72]

A Palermitan 'government' born out of the spirit of insurrection still needed to establish an administration for the island as a whole. Caution was called for here, because the memory of the disastrous revolution of 1821 was still vivid. At that time, Palermitan efforts to impose the authority of the capital on the rest of the island had triggered a civil war and the cities of eastern Sicily had sided with Naples against Palermo. The leaders of 1848 had learned their lesson and were determined not to repeat the error. The seven jurisdictions of the island, with their authorities and tribunals, would be left intact and the regional and municipal administrations would remain 'as free and as independent as possible'. Only in this way, Ruggiero Settimo declared, could one learn from the mistakes of the past: 'Sicilians, our past misfortunes have at least bequeathed us a profitable and salutary lesson for the future.'[73]

A very different picture emerged on the Neapolitan mainland. Here, the news from Sicily created a wave of unrest, including massive demonstrations. On 29 January, King Ferdinand II became the first Italian monarch that year to promise his subjects a constitution. Published on 10 February, it was closely modelled on the revised French *Charte* of 1830. In retrospect, this seems a strange decision. The tiny French franchise was already the subject, as we have seen, of extremely bitter political controversy in Paris, and just two weeks later it would be jettisoned along with the entire facade of French doctrinaire liberalism. In addition to offering a version of the *Charte*, the Neapolitan monarch opened the executive structure to several prominent liberal personalities, including Carlo Poerio, who had only just left prison, where he had been confined for political offences.

These were short-term fixes. When the news from Paris reached Naples, enthusiasm for the Neapolitan version of the old French constitution cooled fast and the calls for democratization resumed. As for the liberal ministers now in government, they were pressed into an awkward and unworkable cohabitation with colleagues inherited from the absolute regime, such as the Duke of Serracapriola, who remained Chair of the Council of Ministers. The liberals found it impossible to impart a new direction to the policies of the executive, which persevered in its Sicilian counter-revolutionary war, dragged its heels over administrative reform and rejected calls for franchise reform. And as the liberals lost their traction in government, the progressive and radical elements that had initially supported the liberal compromise pushed back into open opposition, creating a fissure between those who accepted and those who rejected the constitution offered by the king. On 1 March, the mixed government resigned, making way for a more thoroughly liberal ministry. But it remained exceedingly difficult to operate in the power triangle between the monarchy and his apparatus, the bourgeois and aristocratic liberal elites, and a network of progressive and radical activists skilled in mobilizing elements of the urban populace.

In Prussia, as in Naples, the monarch remained the hub of the power structure. On 21 March, King Frederick William IV issued a proclamation demanding 'truly constitutional charters, with responsibility of ministers' for all German states (which was a bit rich, given that several of the lesser German states had possessed constitutions for decades). On 24 March, when eighteen Rhenish cities petitioned the king to dismiss his unpopular Prime Minister, the king obliged almost immediately, ordering that a new Cabinet be sworn into office under the two prominent Rhenish liberal bankers, Gottfried Ludolf Camphausen (as the new Prime Minister) and David Hansemann (as finance minister).

It was a good start: the king's responsiveness to the Rhenish liberal elites signalled a shift in the Prussian kingdom's centre of political gravity from the conservative rural plains east of the River Elbe to the prosperous and progressive industrial and commercial centres of the Rhineland. Camphausen and Hansemann were intelligent, determined and capable men, moderate liberals who understood the complexities of the post-March situation in Prussia and were willing to craft compromises. Like many of their fellows across Europe, they were beneficiaries of the revolution, but not revolutionaries. From the beginning, the new ministers saw it as their task both to constitutionalize and to stabilize the Prussian monarchy; by taking political responsibility for the policy adopted by the government, they would protect the Crown against the effects of further political instability. The leaders of the old opposition had become the pillars of the new monarchy.[74] Far from weakening the position of the king, they assured the monarch in a letter of 30 March, this arrangement would enable him to 'take decisions in inviolable serenity, raised above the surging agitations of the moment'.[75] It looked good on paper. But what if the king refused to float serenely above the 'surging agitations'? What if the new parliament challenged the pact between the ministers and the monarch? Beyond the Crown–government–parliament triangle there was the city of Berlin with its strong radical-democratic movement, and a partly radicalized proletariat hungry for genuine social reform and resentful of the liberals and their Civic Guard of prosperous taxpayers. And beyond Berlin there were other Prussian cities with strong liberal and radical elites: Breslau, Cologne, Königsberg and many others. Like their counterparts elsewhere, the March ministers in Berlin would soon find themselves ground between parliament, public opinion and royal power.

Vienna followed a trajectory of its own, quite unlike the revolutions in Paris and Berlin. Here, the old sovereignty was neither vanquished nor pressed into an alliance with a portion of the liberal elite. There was neither a provisional government nor a March ministry, because the cogs of the revolution never meshed with the apparatus of imperial government. Instead, a revolution increasingly dominated by radical students and democrats gradually secured control over the city of Vienna in a process over which the Habsburg authorities had little control. But, at the same time, the monarchical executive took the initiative, proposing (on 25 April) a constitution of the Belgian type and calling elections for an Austrian constituent assembly under a restricted property franchise. The democratic political opposition in Vienna rejected this constitution, and the protests that followed were of such scale and energy that the government was ready by 15 May to concede the formation of a Cadiz-style unicameral national assembly that would draft a definitive constitution.

The Principality of Wallachia, a semi-autonomous entity under Ottoman suzerainty and a Russian 'protectorate', followed a highly distinctive itinerary into and out of revolution. Here, it is possible to trace the emergence of a group that planned for and to some extent coordinated in advance a revolutionary transition. The group that would form the germ cell of the revolution was woven together of several strands. For some years a society known as the Frăția (Brotherhood) had cultivated a culture of masonic secrecy and ritual in the manner of the Carbonari. At the end of February 1848, young Wallachians and Moldavians studying in Paris began gathering at night to discuss how to propagate the revolution to their homelands. All of the Wallachians flocked back to Bucharest in March and April, bringing the elan of the February Revolution with them.[76] And even before they had returned, the news of the Parisian revolution broke in the Wallachian capital in the third week of March, stirring deep agitation, especially among the youth of the wealthiest families.[77] It was reported that boys at the city's *gymnasium* were talking politics between their lessons, that young people were addressing each other as 'citizen' in the streets, and that anonymous posters had appeared overnight demanding the abolition of gentry privileges, the formation of a Civic Guard and freedom of the press.[78] In Iași, capital of the neighbouring principality of Moldavia, the news from France caused a great commotion. The Prussian consul in the city, Emil von Richthofen, noted that the deep attachment of the Romanian elites to France amplified the local resonance of signals from Paris: 'the Boyars [landowning gentry] here love to imitate everything French and they like to call their country *La France orientale*'.[79]

On 22 May, a group of insurrectionaries, including the returned students Dumitru and Ion Brătianu, gathered to form a 'revolutionary committee' in Bucharest. The aim was to overthrow the regime imposed by the Imperial Russian authorities, personified in the current ruling prince (*hospodar*) Gheorghe Bibescu. The members busied themselves recruiting activist cells among the workers of the city, commissioning banners and tricolour Romanian cockades and stockpiling arms in the monasteries of sympathetic clergymen. By mid June, after some wrangling over specific policies, the group had drawn up a twenty-two-point programme outlining a transformation of the political order: the peasants were to be granted land (their boyar gentry landowners would be compensated); all would be equal before the law; taxation would be based on income; privileges of rank and title were to be abolished; all children of both sexes would be granted free access to education; and freedom of speech, the press and association were to be guaranteed. On 21 June, the programme was read out by a member of the committee and distributed to an audience of peasants, clergymen and soldiers in the tiny hamlet of Islaz in the south-western corner of the country. Within days a revolution had broken out in the capital. A Romanian tricolour flag in blue, yellow and red was unfurled in the Lipscani commercial quarter of Bucharest, the 'Proclamation of Islaz', as it would become known, was read aloud and passed through the streets thronged with men and women sporting cockades and waving copies of the proclamation. The crowds converged on the palace of Prince Gheorghe Bibescu, hospodar of Wallachia.

The timing was auspicious. Only two days before, three young Boyars who appear not to have been affiliated with the revolutionary committee had pulled alongside Bibescu's carriage as he took his evening ride and fired their pistols at him before racing off into the night. None of the three bullets struck their intended victim, but one tore through Bibescu's epaulette. Efforts to track the perpetrators down were fruitless – the young men had fled the city. Shaken, the prince asked his militia forces on the morning of 23 June to renew their oath of allegiance. He was told that his men remained loyal but would not under any circumstances agree to shed the blood of their fellow Wallachians. News of this fact spread across the city, emboldening the citizenry. At around 4 p.m., the churches on Dealul Mitropoliei began sounding the tocsin – an effect generated by striking the tongue repeatedly against only one side of the bell. By around ten in the evening, Bibescu was ready to concede. He signed a copy of the Islaz proclamation, now in the process of metamorphosing into a draft 'constitution' and agreed to appoint a government of new ministers imposed on him by the revolutionary leaders. The revolutionaries had hoped that he would remain in place as a stabilizing presence, to provide a 'legal framework for change'.[80] But on 25 June Bibescu resigned, packed his bags and fled into Habsburg Transylvanian exile. Wallachia was now in the hands of a revolutionary government.

On the list of provisional ministers were Ion Heliade Rădulescu, editor of *Curierul Românesc*, which had done so much to bring the news of the European revolutions of 1848 to Bucharest, the Wallachian general Christian Tell, known as the 'sword of the revolution' because he raised his troops in its support, Gheorghe Magheru, who had fought under Tudor Vladimirescu in the Wallachian uprising of 1821, and Ştefan Golescu, a patriot activist and major in the Wallachian army. Among the secretaries were Ion Brătianu, recently returned from his studies in Paris, Constantin Alexandru Rosetti, a businessman, writer, journalist, bookseller and one of the presiding spirits of the Frăţia, and Nicolae Bălcescu, an expert on the agrarian question – it was he who had pressed for the inclusion of land reform in the programme that became the Islaz constitution. Golescu, Rosetti, Brătianu, Rădulescu and Bălcescu had all been members of the revolutionary committee; and many of the new ministers were affiliated with the Frăţia network of Wallachian patriots. Tell, Golescu and Magheru were all army officers.

The Wallachian events followed an untypical sequence. As we have seen, it was different elsewhere: almost none of the people who emerged as leaders from the upheavals elsewhere in Europe were revolutionaries before the act. Daniele Manin was unusual in having planned to launch an insurrection, but his conversion to radicalism was recent and the uprising did not break out at his bidding. Most of the new leadership cadres in Europe were men who had not previously countenanced revolution or had cautioned against it. They were not the authors but the inheritors of revolution. As Élias Regnault put it: 'the circumstances dominated the men'.[81]

Yet in Wallachia it *was* the revolutionaries who produced the revolution, not the other way around. The smallness and the tightly knit texture of the Wallachian patriot elite was part of the reason for this. Bucharest, with around 100,000 inhabitants, was an intimate world, especially for the most privileged strata (the figures for Venice, Milan, Berlin and Paris were *c*.123,000, *c*.160,000, *c*.440,000 and *c*.1,000,000 respectively). The men who led the revolution knew each other from a range of shared contexts – kinship links, journalism, military service, study in Paris, the Frăţia and so on – and their relatives knew each other too. It was not difficult to coordinate planning in such a milieu. For months, moreover, the news of revolutions abroad had been trickling into Bucharest. This meant that the Wallachian activists with their fran-cophile instincts could model their seizure of power on European antecedents in a way that would not have been possible in March. The news of foreign tumults helped to build social support for a challenge to the traditional princely power structure and focused the discontent brewing in the Wallachian countryside. Finally, there were echoes from the past. The Wallachian revolution may have resembled its European analogues ideologically, but the prominence of military figures and the compact social structure of the insurrectionary leadership was reminis-cent of the *pronunciamento*-based revolutions of 1820–21. Then, as at Islaz in June 1848, the revolution had begun with men in a peripheral location reading aloud a revolutionary manifesto amidst flags and offic-ers on horses. The Wallachian revolution was not – or at least not primarily – a societal upheaval: it was a bid by one sector of the elite to secure control of the executive structure.

Across Europe, the journeys from upheaval and conflict to the quasi-stabilization of a post-insurrectionary order reveal an extraordinary diversity of forms. In Paris, two newspapers channelled the process of political regeneration in a situation of total hiatus; in Palermo, Milan and Venice, provisional authorities fruited hermaphroditically from insurrectionary movements; in Naples and Berlin, processes of co-option and partial displacement produced hybrid governments; in Vienna, the revolution rolled, as it were, past and around the structures of power. Only in Islaz and Bucharest did plans laid in advance bear fruit in a revolutionary upheaval. The differences were not merely con-tingent; they expressed the political biodiversity of nineteenth-century European cities and states. In 1848, substantial portions of urban soci-ety, in a moment of collective disinhibition, overleapt the boundaries of political compliance, permeating some state structures and damaging or washing away others. And, in this state of disequilibrium, elite political groups in each epicentre of upheaval imposed their diverse characters on the process of restabilization.

By whatever routes these new structures came into existence, they were all fragile. They were tied to societal coalitions that lacked leader-ship or cohesion. The men who entered provisional government were for the most part poorly prepared for the tasks awaiting them. They had never had the opportunity to form a common view of how to proceed once in power and quickly fell into factions. They remained beholden to the social strata that had placed them in power and prey to uncertainties about their own status.[82] In the longer term they had to come to terms with the unpredictability of politics under a drastically expanded franchise, the turbulence of parliaments in which partisan strife was not yet muted by custom, and the difficulty of synchronizing the slow politics of the chamber with the fast politics of clubs and streets. Some of them would face, and fail to master, the problem of financing a new political order at a time when capital was in hiding or in flight and tax revenues were depressed by the disruption to commerce and trade. Most importantly, the question of power remained unsolved. In Palermo, Vienna and Milan, there remained the danger that the old authorities, only temporarily absent, would return and reimpose themselves. In Naples, Berlin and Vienna, the durability of the revolution's achievements depended on the dubious good will of monarchs who still commanded armies. In Wallachia, where the Ottoman and Russian Empires exercised a complicated dual control, the new leadership faced the daunting prospect of a foreign intervention.

ELECT A PARLIAMENT

On 25 March 1848, the Sicilian parliament opened in Palermo. Tapestries, tricolour flags and festoons of flowers adorned the shops, windows and terraces of the capital city. Giuseppe La Farina, who was there as an elected deputy for the city of Messina, remembered the fine weather. It was, he wrote, one of those beautiful days of the Sicilian spring when the sky is filled with light and the air suffused with sweet smells. All the way down the Càssaro to the Church of San Domenico, seat of the new assembly, national and municipal guards and revolutionary militias (*squadre*) lined the street. 'It was a fine and moving thing', La Farina wrote, 'to see these proud men of the mountains in their poor and rough clothes', exulting in the resurrection of ancient liberties so recently 'repurchased with their blood'. The General Committee, led by President Ruggiero Settimo, walked slowly in triumphal procession down the entire length of the Càssaro: the streets in all directions were choked with people, the houses packed with women and children waving flags and ribbons and throwing flowers and garlands. Around midday, the notables of the city gathered at San Domenico. The peers of the Upper House were there, along with the elected deputies, the senate, the senior officers of the new Sicilian army and navy, the archbishops, bishops and abbots, and the foreign consuls, with the notable absence of the Austrian and the Russian.

The bell of San Domenico that had once summoned the people to take part in an insurgency now announced the arrival of the General Committee. Mounting a purpose-built tribunal inside the church, Ruggiero Settimo delivered a brief address. The 'supreme reason' of public security and the sovereign will of the people had rendered the 'dictatorship' wielded by the General Committee during the revolution 'as legitimate as any government in the world'. Before dissolving itself, the committee, in a final act of that legitimate dictatorship, would place its own power into the hands of the parliament. The president's address closed with an appeal to the parliament to begin their deliberations by drafting a law on how the executive power should be exercised under the current conditions. 'May God bless and inspire the votes of the parliament and may he look kindly on the land of Sicily and conjoin it with the great destinies of a free, independent and united Italian nation!' An 'immense applause' greeted these words. The Cardinal Archbishop blessed the gathering, a battery of cannon thundered in salute, and across the city the bells began tolling as citizens everywhere embraced, 'weeping with joy and excitement'.[83]

In his artful account, La Farina blended the details of memory with political reflections on the place of a parliament in the revolutionary process. The rough men of the *squadre*, whose appearance in the city had alarmed prosperous Palermitans, had become pillars of good order. The bell that had once called citizens to fight for their rights now rang in the name of fraternity and peace. Cannon that had been used to fire upon the bastions of liberty now saluted the revolution. A fearsome dictatorial power, claimed in the name of a civil emergency, was meekly placed in the hands of legislators. This was a template for the transition from insurgency to orderly government.

Parliaments and other representative bodies sprang up in great numbers in 1848. They did so under a bewildering variety of circumstances and in a wide range of forms. In Piedmont, Prussia and the Austrian Empire, unprecedented new parliaments of the modern type, with

First session of the National Constituent Assembly in Paris on 4 May 1848. Drawing and engraving by Charles Ficot and Jules Gaildreau.

elections and broad suffrages, based on the votes of individuals rather than on corporate bodies, emerged for the first time. In Denmark, the king and his ministers ordered the election and convocation of a 'constitution-giving assembly' (*Grundlovgivende Rigsforsamling*) to finalize the content of a new framing law. The German national parliament that convened in Frankfurt was an entity without precedent, convened to oversee a political union of the German states. It owed its origin to a meeting of fifty-one political activists in the city of Heidelberg who called for an all-German convention drawn from the existing parliaments and municipal assemblies of the German states.[84] In France, the old bicameral parliament of the July Monarchy was replaced by a new assembly elected on a much broader franchise. In Hungary, the national Diet gave birth of its own initiative to a modern parliament by abolishing its corporate internal voting procedure, passing a new electoral law and then dissolving itself. The picture was particularly complex in the Austrian Empire: some of the old corporate diets – the Moravian, the Styrian, the Carinthian, the Tyrolean and the Upper Austrian – were modestly reformed to do service as parliament-like bodies capable of defending regional interests. Others, such as the Bohemian and Galician diets, tried to do the same but were obstructed by the Austrian authorities and never met at all.[85] And, at the same time, the Habsburg authorities conceded the convocation of a new Reichstag in Vienna, so that for a time six parliament-like bodies (not including the Hungarian) were operating in parallel. In the mainland portion of the Kingdom of the Two Sicilies, elections were held in April 1848 under the terms of a constitution decreed by Ferdinand II, but the chamber was dissolved on the day after its convocation following rancorous disputes over the content of the constitution. New elections were held in June after the revolutions were over, but again the chamber was dissolved almost as soon it had been convened and then repeatedly postponed before being dissolved again in March 1849.

This transcontinental spawning of new parliamentary bodies reflected the ascendancy of a liberal vision of politics – polyvocal, conflictual and deliberative. But many questions remained unanswered. Jurisdictions overlapped. In the Frankfurt parliament, for example: the problem arose that many of the ministers appointed to oversee the implementation of the assembly's resolutions were also the employees of particular German states. Should this conflict of interest not disqualify them from office?[86] The Czechs were told in April that the question of the unification of the lands of the Czech Crown (Bohemia, Moravia and Czech Silesia) could not be resolved by the forthcoming Bohemian Diet but must be deferred until the central Reichstag was convened in Vienna.[87] Who had the right to issue a law compensating landowners for the abolition of feudal dues in Moravia? On 19 June 1848, the Moravian Diet presented such a law, but it was turned down in Vienna by the interior minister, Pillersdorf, because he intended to reserve this decision for resolution by the Reichstag.[88] Conflicting national or institutional commitments could create confusion. The catchment of the 'German parliament' established at Frankfurt, for example, included the multi-ethnic Austrian and Bohemian lands of the Austrian Empire, but when the pre-parliamentary committee invited the Prague-based Czech politician František Palacký to take part, Palacký sent a famous letter respectfully declining the offer. The invitation was a great honour, he wrote, but as a non-German member of a German national assembly he would be obliged, should he join such an assembly, either to deny his feelings and 'play the hypocrite' or 'contradict loudly at the first opportunity that offered itself'.[89] A request from delegates of the Croatian Diet and the Hungarian National Assembly to be officially received and heard by the Austrian Reichstag was refused after heated discussion by majority vote.[90] On 15 July, the National Assembly in Frankfurt was surprised to learn that the Imperial Caretaker Archduke Johann, a prince of the Habsburg family and the interim chief of the newly created German 'imperial administration', intended to travel back to Vienna in order to open the Austrian Reichstag.[91]

Parliaments could even manoeuvre or be manoeuvred against each other. The Ukrainian National Assembly (Holovna rada ruska) that convened on 2 May 1848 was established with the support of Count Franz Stadion as a counterweight to the nationalist agitation of the Poles, whose National Council (Rada narodowa) he had dissolved just a week before.[92] When the new Hungarian government applied pressure on Vienna to lever the Croat leader, Ban Josip Jelačić, out of power, Jelačić responded by bringing forward the convocation of the Croatian Diet, one of whose first acts was to invest him with dictatorial powers, an anti-Hungarian move discreetly supported in Vienna by a group of conservatives around the Minister of War, Count Baillet de Latour.[93] The Austrian deputy Franz Schuselka suspected that the truly extravagant per diems paid by the Vienna government to the deputies of the Austrian Reichstag were intended to raise it above the dignity of its German competitor.[94]

Notwithstanding these complexities, the convocation of a parliament was usually an occasion for celebration. Marie d'Agoult remembered the splendid sunshine that bathed the procession of the Provisional Government to the opening of the new assembly in a hall recently set up for the purpose in the Palais Bourbon. Unbroken applause rose from the dense crowds along the route of the cortège, from the windows and the roofs of the houses. 'This was not applause on order', she wrote. 'It was a spontaneous acknowledgement that burst forth at the sight of these first citizens of the Republic, who had come to hand over to the legal representation of the people the power they had held by its acclamation.'[95] The newly elected deputy Franz Schuselka made his way from Vienna to Frankfurt by train. 'Cheerful and brave, the cloud-belching, spark-spraying iron horse led us through the night. We hardly slept; we dreamed with open eyes the beautiful dream of the unity and greatness of Germany.' By the time the Austrian representatives reached Leipzig, the news was ahead of them; their arrival had been announced in the papers and crowds of excited people gathered at the railway station to cheer the deputies on their way.[96] The theatre manager and radical publicist Robert Blum travelled to Frankfurt in a state of sublime excitement. As his train threaded its way through towns full of tricolour flags and jubilant townsfolk, his carriage filled with political luminaries. The tributaries of radical Germany seemed to be flowing together into a great river. Among other things, Blum found that he had become a national celebrity. The spectacle of young women waving kerchiefs and throwing flowers was especially beguiling.[97]

In Vienna, as the opening of the Austrian Reichstag drew near, people 'suspended any kind of political action' because they preferred to wait on the decisions reached by the legislature.[98] 'It was touching', one witness observed, 'to see with what credulous trust the people expected all good things from the Reichstag. No one gave a single thought to the difficulties of such a gathering ... "The Reichstag will sort everything out! If only the Reichstag were in session!" was the general wish and thought.'[99] In Tuscany, where the Grand Ducal government had avoided a revolution by means of timely concessions, a constitutional catechism published in April 1848 urged electors to view the vote as a 'sacred act of popular sovereignty' and churches were set aside for polling, not just because other suitable public buildings were scarce, but because their solemn atmosphere was thought to suit the momentousness of the occasion.[100] Franz Schuselka, who had resigned his Frankfurt mandate at the end of May 1848 to take a seat in the Austrian Reichstag in Vienna, where he represented a cluster of industrial suburbs outside the walls of the old city, was moved to see the respect with which the electors regarded their prospective representatives:

> they truly and piously believe that someone who has been chosen by such a great quantity of the people must thereby be endowed with a special insight and strength of will. I began to understand with joy and humility what a high and holy calling it is to represent such a people.[101]

Yet the euphoria and the sense of promise soon wore off. As anyone who has watched them from galleries or on television will know, there is a ponderous quality to parliaments – they lack both the charisma of insurrectionary movements and the splendour of traditional authority. Franz Schuselka recalled the sense of disappointment that gripped him after his arrival in Frankfurt. 'When one sees people and things from close-up', he wrote, 'the poetic gleam deserts them and their height and greatness shrink considerably.' This was partly a matter of external appearances, he observed, for there was no denying that 'a ruler in an ermine coat still receives much more respect and obedience from European humanity than one in a black frock coat'. But there was more to it than that. He was shocked by the orderliness and stodginess of the meetings he witnessed in Frankfurt. These were extraordinary times and the deputies had only just begun their work, yet already the gathering seemed 'completely lacking in momentum or enthusiasm'. And when tempers rose, it was usually over a matter of lesser importance. On the very first day of the new parliament – shortly after the deputies had made their ceremonial entry into St Paul's Church – a bitter quarrel broke out over two points in the proposed rules of procedure.[102] Looking back at the work of the Vienna Reichstag, the former radical deputy Hans Kudlich expressed a similar exasperation at the 'pointless, unnecessary and truly pedantic consultation over the rules of procedure', which consumed the greater part of the first three months of the parliament's work.[103]

In a body like the Reichstag in Vienna, where almost nobody had any previous experience of parliamentary debate, it was difficult to secure consensus on questions of importance: 'interpolations on every conceivable subject shot like comets in irregular orbits across the firmament'. The inexperience of the Reichstag presidents made it difficult to control the agenda or prioritize issues, so that for example many hours were spent debating whether one should admit spectators with or without entry tickets and whether a particular quota of complimentary tickets should be set aside for the students of the Academic Legion.[104] But even in assemblies with substantial contingents of experienced legislators, like the Frankfurt National Assembly or the Constituent Assembly in Paris, critics were frustrated by the cumbersome quality of the proceedings. Reflecting on the Frankfurt parliament, the Austrian Franz Schuselka wondered whether the problem might not lie in the boredom that lay like an oppressive atmosphere over the city of Frankfurt, a miasma infused with the 'diplomatic coffin-stink' of the Confederal Diet that had begun residing there after the end of the Napoleonic Wars.[105] To these reflections Schuselka added a more serious thought: that the timidity of the parliament might reflect the hesitancy of men who did not believe in their own power.[106] In her history of the revolution of 1848 in France, Marie d'Agoult found exactly the same flaw in the Parisian Constituent Assembly, namely that it 'lacked an awareness of its own strength'.[107]

But perhaps the most striking feature of the new parliaments of 1848 was that they turned out, for the most part, to be predominantly conservative. In France, the proportion of the population eligible to vote leapt from less than 1 to 23.1 per cent. And yet, far from flushing out the old elites, the expanded franchise consolidated their political dominance. About a fifth of the deputies elected to the Constituent Assembly in Paris – Alexis de Tocqueville was one – had already served in the parliaments of the July Monarchy. More than a third had held official or administrative posts before 1848. In all, two thirds of the new deputies had sworn an oath of loyalty to Louis Philippe and about three quarters would have qualified for election under the restrictive fiscal franchise of the July Monarchy. Heinrich Best discerned the same pattern in the Frankfurt National Assembly: 83 per cent of the Frankfurt deputies had served as state officials, 56 per cent were still employed as public servants. And this was not a German peculiarity: we find the same trend in the expanded Netherlands parliament, where the figure was 46 per cent.

Only one in twenty of the delegates in Frankfurt and Paris had been arrested or imprisoned for political offences before 1848.[108]

Part of the reason lay in the nature of the electoral franchises of 1848, which, though expanded in varying degrees, were still not truly universal, even for the male population. Several of the converted diets of the Habsburg lands adopted hybrid franchises, in which older corporate elements were blended with the representation of new 'interests' such as cities, commerce or the universities.[109] The franchise adopted for the elections to the Austrian Reichstag stipulated that all 'independent' (*selbständige*) male workers should be allowed to vote, if they could prove their residency for the past six months. But this still excluded a great number of individuals, because most of the workers in Vienna were itinerants or migrants or people lacking papers and in no position to prove residency. And the criterion of 'independence' was applied by the Habsburg authorities in many regions to exclude journeymen, waged workers and agricultural labourers.[110] Elections to the Prussian Constituent Assembly and the Frankfurt National Assembly were broad but indirect. In Hungary, Croatia and the Italian states, deputies were elected under a direct but limited franchise that excluded between half and two thirds of adult males.

It is difficult to know how differently these elections might have unfolded if a broader franchise had been applied. Voting behaviour in rural France revealed a strong preference for established elite figures, even among those newly enfranchised electors who were voting for the first time, a reminder of how resistant social structures could be to rapid political change.[111] Alexis de Tocqueville, who had repeatedly stood for election under the July Monarchy, recalled with pleasure and a sense of vindication the affectionate demeanour of the electors of his rural constituency on the day they went to cast their votes (for Tocqueville himself) in the last week of April 1848: 'I had never had so much respect shown to me before . . .'[112] It was one thing, Franz Schuselka noted, to call for social equality and another to root out the habits of deference in a deeply unequal society: 'Those who have done away even with the frock coat in the hope of making the [worker's] smock the sole general uniform of humanity have always had to find out that the smocks do not obey when a smock is giving the orders.'[113]

But it wasn't just a matter of deference. If the parliaments returned under the expanded suffrages of 1848 were preponderantly moderate, this was also because in the late spring of 1848 most of the electors were moderate or conservative. In Pest, radical intellectuals had shaped the course of the revolution after the events of 15 March. They were strongly represented on the Committee of Public Safety that ran the city for a month. And yet very few of them succeeded in getting elected to the first representative assembly, in which the moderate government of Count Batthyány commanded an overwhelming majority. Even the charismatic Sándor Petőfi, romantic hero of 15 March and author of the National Song, failed to secure a seat.[114] The deputies elected to the Constituent Assembly in Paris, Marie d'Agoult wrote, 'brought from their provinces a loyal resolution not to affiliate themselves with any party, a very imperfect knowledge of the situation and ... the desire to spare the country ... the shock of factions and the explosion of a Civil War'; their contributions to debate in the early sessions of the chamber 'bore the imprint of prudence'.[115] Franz Schuselka noted the same tendency in the National Assembly at Frankfurt: it consisted in its 'overwhelming majority' of 'non-revolutionary characters' who hoped to achieve their objectives without any further upheavals. The concessions granted across many German states in the upheavals of March, Schuselka suggested, had created in the majority of electors 'such a mood of benevolence and credulous trust that people saw violent revolutionary measures as totally superfluous, or even condemned them, because adopting them would have seemed ungrateful towards the princes who had ceded so much'.[116] And the same pattern was seen on the Neapolitan mainland of the Kingdom of the Two Sicilies, where the elections of April 1848 produced an assembly with only twenty radical members and an emphatically moderate majority.[117]

There was deep uncertainty within these gatherings about how to manage the legacy of the uprising that had inaugurated the revolution. In many places, the new parliaments were the direct consequence of the fighting between insurgents and troops. This was the point La Farina made when he wishfully described how the rough men of the *squadre* had become protectors of the people's representatives on their peaceful procession towards the new Sicilian parliament. But the relationship between the flesh-and-blood fighting of the insurgencies and the rhetorical skirmishes of parliaments remained unresolved and a source of discomfort. Most deputies were reluctant to see parliaments as the continuation of insurgency by other means. For the liberals and moderate conservatives who dominated most of the assemblies, parliament was not the continuation of revolution, but the return to orderly political conditions, an achievement that rendered insurrection not just unnecessary but fundamentally illegitimate.

As the revolution receded into the still very recent past, its charisma and its hold over the political imagination faded fast. In Paris, conservatives used the debates of the assembly to unpick the 'principles of February', focusing their efforts, for example, on extirpating the right to work, which had once been such a central preoccupation of the 'social revolution', from successive drafts of the new constitution.[118] Already in early June, the writer Fanny Lewald noticed, the word 'revolution' seemed to have fallen out of favour; instead, people spoke of the 'occurrences' or the 'events' of March. 'Mr Camphausen [the Prime Minister] and his colleagues', she wrote, 'should regard this revolution as their *mother* and think rather of the commandment: Honour your father and your mother.'[119]

A debate in the Berlin National Assembly revealed the awkwardness of this question. On 8 June, the radical deputy Julius Berends proposed a motion to the effect that the assembly should officially record its view that 'the fighters of 18 and 19 March had done good service for the Fatherland'. Since the battles on the barricades, Berends pointed out, the revolution had been 'repeatedly scorned and diminished in various quarters' and the 'moral uprising of the people' degraded to a mere 'street mutiny'. 'The assembly itself is an outgrowth of this revolution, its very existence is the factual acknowledgement of the Revolution.' Confirming this by means of a formal statement, Berends argued, would be one way of underscoring the sovereign power vested in the assembly by the people through their revolution. Yet a narrow majority of deputies rejected this view, on the grounds that the gains made in March had been secured not through the 'great March events' alone, but also through 'negotiation with the monarch'. The Berends motion failed. The democratic newspaper *Die Lokomotive* responded with an acrid critique, accusing the National Assembly of denying its origins, 'like a badly brought up boy who does not respect his father' – an unwitting masculine echo of Lewald's feminine metaphor.[120]

For the people of the political left, this was a problem of the greatest magnitude. Many Parisian left-republicans had foreseen that swift elections were likely to consolidate the dominance of moderate and conservative interests. The novelist George Sand was among those who worried about what would happen if the elections proved to be the 'downfall', rather than the 'salvation', of the republic. She had been tasked by the Provisional Government with drafting the dispatches, known as 'Republican Bulletins', that were sent by the Minister of the Interior to the eighty-six departments of France to stimulate republican commitment in the provinces. In one of these, dated 13 April, over a week before voting began, she spoke darkly of the 'perversion' of the public will in the provinces by privileged interests and warned that if the elections did not bring about 'the triumph of social truth', then 'the people who built the barricades' would have no choice but to 'express their will a second time and adjourn the decisions of a false national representation'.[121] It was partly in response to left-republican agitation that the government agreed, on the pretext of technical difficulties, to postpone the elections by two weeks.[122]

All the same, the moderate/conservative and 'unrevolutionary' character of the new popular assemblies was a profound shock to the left. When they saw the consequences of universal suffrage, Marie d'Agoult wrote, 'the principal revolutionary chiefs' in Paris urged each other to pay no heed to them and began plotting against the assembly. In the Ministry of the Interior, 'little cabals' of radicals discussed the possibility of dissolving it on the day of its opening. It was reported in the radical press that 'universal suffrage, falsified by a thousand electoral manoeuvres, had lied to the people, that the republic had been perverted'.[123] In a newspaper article of 29 April reflecting on the election results, the radical Pierre-Joseph Proudhon announced that the Social Question had been 'postponed' indefinitely. The cause of the proletariat, pursued with such energy on the barricades of February, had been lost in the elections of April. Henceforth the bourgeoisie would determine the condition of the workers, just as they had done before. On the following day he raged against the 'mystifications of universal suffrage', a principle founded on the false presumption that the will of the people could be discerned through the counting of individual votes. Universal suffrage, Proudhon argued, was 'the surest way to make the people lie'; it turned voters from stakeholders in a shared patrimony into smallholders and privateers.[124]

In short, parts of the Parisian left responded to the success of their opponents by denying the legitimacy of the process that had produced it. Proudhon saw the irony: those who had clamoured for the enlarged suffrage now complained of losing power through a 'lottery', while those who had been sceptical about franchise reform now professed to admire 'the mechanism that has afforded them their privileges'.[125] But there was more to this panic on the left than the *mauvaise foi* of the sore loser, because the apparent failure of the elections to produce a mechanism capable of pushing ahead the process of social reform gave rise to a genuine problem. The liberals had achieved their revolution, or appeared to have done so, but the left had not. What was to be done if a revolution unexpectedly generated the conditions of its own negation? Contemporaries estimated that there were in all between 20,000 and 100,000 committed republicans in France.[126] What was to be done if the process of representing the people arrested rather than furthered the process of change, if parliament became a blocked artery at the heart of the revolutionary process? Three possible courses of action presented themselves. Radicals could continue to press their case as minority groups within the organs created by the new suffrage. Or they could pressurize governments and deputies by means of various forms of extra-parliamentary mobilization. Or they could return to the politics of insurrection, a step that might reignite the revolution, but threatened also to destroy the achievements of February and March. The struggle to resolve this question would have a profound impact on the course of the revolutions.

Whatever their defects, the parliaments represented an important space of political experience. They provided the setting for debates that were widely reported and discussed. Members of the public, women and men, crowded into the galleries. There was a lively trade in entrance tickets.[127] The expansion of the male suffrage brought new social groups into the political process, nowhere more so than in Vienna, where the members of the new Reichstag included a substantial contingent of peasants, whose exotic clothing attracted the stares of urban gawpers.[128] Not everyone leapt at the opportunity to vote – in Piedmont and the Grand Duchy of Tuscany, only around half of those who were entitled to cast a vote actually did so; in the Papal States and the Kingdom of the Two Sicilies, it was less than a third.[129] In France, on the other hand, the turnout among the enfranchised was 83.3 per cent. Electing a representative meant taking part, whether actively or passively, in election campaigns, political debates, and discussions in taverns and cafés. For those who actually entered parliament, this was a chance to combine with like-minded contemporaries and to test the relative strength of one's own group against that of other ideological coalitions.

It took time for clearly delineated parties to emerge. The Constituent Assembly in Paris initially lacked parliamentary caucuses or partisan voting discipline of any kind.[130] In the early days of the Frankfurt assembly, the liberal deputy Karl Biedermann recalled, there were clubs and gatherings, but 'sharply defined, organized parties did not yet exist'.[131] People gravitated together because they happened to come from a particular region.[132] Newly arriving deputies drifted from club to club, looking for the tone and atmosphere that suited them best. By the beginning of June, the process of differentiation had reached the point where one could speak of 'complete, constituted and organized parties'. Because an agreed nomenclature for partisan preferences did not yet exist, the clubs of the like-minded tended to be known by the places where they congregated: the Milani, the Casino, the Landsberg, the Württemberger Hof, the Augsburger Hof, the Holländischer Hof – an exception was the *Donnersberg* (Thunder Mountain) on the far left, the home of Franz Schuselka, named in honour of the *Montagne* of 1790s France. The same thing happened in Paris, where the caucuses were known for the streets or venues where they met: the Réunion de la rue de Poitiers, the Réunion du Palais National and so on.

Karl Biedermann, who visited all the Frankfurt caucuses, observed interesting patterns. In the Café Milani at the right end of the spectrum, cigars were forbidden, and meetings took place in 'elegant, comfortable surroundings observing the niceties of the finer forms of sociability'. At the Casino, the tone was less aristocratic; cigars were allowed, and the spacious premises were dominated by a green table, at which the presiding member of the committee sat, flanked by a record-keeper. As you moved leftwards across the political spectrum, the premises became more modest and the protocol more relaxed. In the Augsburger Hof and the Landsberg, members observed each other through scrolls of cigar smoke and speakers had to make themselves heard above the clatter of plates and glasses; at the Württemberger Hof, where people were pressed together in a narrow room, jackets and neckerchiefs were thrown aside on warm evenings, so that meetings looked more like a student club than a gathering of the people's elect. Biedermann noticed that charismatic leaders were more important to the cohesion of the clubs of the left and right than they were in the centrist groupings, which focused more on issues and policies. Speeches tended to be short and to the point in the centre, and long and meandering on the right and left, where there was a tendency for speakers to 'rouse and outdo each other in spirited speeches full of well-known buzzwords'.[133]

All elected assemblies are marked by the competition between opposed viewpoints – that is what they are for. Dissension was easier to absorb in settings where the legal status and political function of the parliament were clear at the outset. In several of the parliaments of 1848, however, partisan divisions were amplified by uncertainties about the status of the parliament itself and its relationship with other sources of authority. When this was the case, factional struggle had the potential to undermine the corporate self-confidence and functionality of the parliament. The Frankfurt assembly, for example, was deeply divided on the question of its own nature. For the right, the parliament was merely a delegated organ of the existing state sovereignties, an assembly under suffrage. For the left, it was the organ of a sovereign people, empowered to draw up independently a general German constitution.[134] Analogous disputes sapped the energy of the Prussian National Assembly and the Austrian Reichstag, where many uncertainties remained about the relationship between the chamber and the still-sovereign monarchy. Arguments about taxation, rights or citizenship did not endanger the cohesion of parliament – they might even enhance it. But internal disagreements over the powers and permanence of the parliament itself were a very different matter. Not all dissension is salutary.

Many contemporary observers noted the failure of the parliaments of 1848 to develop a transcendent corporate awareness of their political calling. The 'perpetual exchange of ideas and sentiments', Marie d'Agoult noted, usually brings forth a 'collective spirit' within disparate gatherings of men – the histories of religious communities, academies, municipal governments and armies were rich in examples of it. But the Paris Constituent Assembly, riven by 'anguish and contradictions', never reached the point where that 'good spirit' could come into its own.[135] For the former Sicilian Carbonaro, government functionary and monarchist Ferdinando Malvica, the Sicilian parliament was a 'bilge of vices' (*sentina di mali*), a free-for-all in which the deputies (with a few virtuous exceptions) used their mandates to secure favours. 'Most of them were appointed ministers, magistrates, directors, envoys, financial agents, commissars of the political executive, military commanders, prelates', while those who had no jobs in Palermo – because there were not enough for everybody – 'soon left their seats and returned to their own districts, where, placing themselves at the head of the administration, they began to vex their opponents, destroy their ancient enemies and become despots of their unfortunate municipalities'. As for the members of the public who sat in the galleries cheering or whistling, these were not the representatives of a free public, capable of forming its own opinions, but 'hired men', and 'friends and dependants of the ministers' bearing tickets handed out by the government. Whereas ministers were greeted with loud applause as soon as they stood up to speak, interpellations or critical comments by deputies were drowned out by shouts, whistles and other signs of disapproval, so that it was sometimes impossible to carry on.[136] For these shortcomings, Malvica, a hostile witness, blamed the venality of the new political leadership. A more sympathetic observer might have added that it takes more than a few months of parliamentary debate to erase the legacy of generations of deeply rooted clientelism.

Many of the parliaments born in 1848 were short-lived. With the resurgence of counter-revolutionary monarchical executives, parliaments were pushed from one location to another, haemorrhaging deputies as their political clout waned. After the crushing of the Vienna Uprising of October 1848, the Austrian Reichstag relocated from Vienna to the little Moravian town of Kremsier (today Kroměříž in the Czech Republic). The ministers of the Habsburg government in Vienna began from the beginning of December 1848 to stop turning up for Reichstag debates, or even for sessions at which they were supposed to answer questions related to their conduct in office, and the assembly was dissolved on 7 May 1849. On 5 November 1848, the Prussian National Assembly was ordered out of Berlin to the provincial city of Brandenburg and then dissolved one month later. The deputies who were still attending the Frankfurt parliament (many had resigned their mandates on the instructions of their home governments) were obliged to flee Frankfurt in May 1848 and relocate as a 'rump parliament' in Stuttgart, by which time only around 100 mainly left-wing deputies remained. On 18 June 1849, further meetings of the rump were prohibited on the instructions of the Württemberg Minister of Justice, Friedrich Römer, himself a former deputy in the Frankfurt assembly. Deputies who tried to take their seats were turned away by troops. The papers of the assembly were packed into boxes and carted off to Switzerland.[137]

These ignominious closing scenes should not distract us from the lasting significance of the parliaments of 1848. In those parts of Europe where nations and states were not coextensive, parliaments became a way of reflecting on the relationship between local, regional, territorial and national commitments. 'Bear in mind', the electors were told during the Constituent Assembly elections of the Roman Republic in 1849, 'that your vote will weigh not just on the destinies of your provinces but on those of the entire peninsula. These days more than ever you cannot be good Romans without being good Italians.'[138] The elections of the Italian states in 1848–9 were the 'first Italian elections' and a crucial apprenticeship in nation-building.[139] The same can be said of the elections to the Frankfurt parliament: these were the first 'German elections'.

Even if they lacked the power to resolve national questions in a geopolitical sense, parliaments provided spaces for debates that resonated widely in newspapers and pamphlets during the life of the revolution. The speeches of deputies were widely reprinted or excerpted in the principal political newspapers, especially in the electoral districts of the deputies who had spoken up on a specific issue. A genuine feedback loop emerged between the German electoral districts and the Frankfurt parliament: deputies sent articles to be printed in the local papers of their home towns, while local interest groups – workers, peasants, artisans, Catholics – regaled their deputies with proposals, requests and petitions.[140] In this way, they both refined and normalized national discourses, especially in the Italian and German states, connecting broad commitments in principle with organizational nitty-gritty. In Germany, the deliberations of the National Assembly in Frankfurt fixed 'the national parameters . . . of later political deliberation and debate': in this respect, one historian has noted, the German revolution was a success.[141] There were extensive discussions in the Economic Committee (Volkswirtschaftliche Ausschuss) of the Frankfurt assembly of the arrangements that would govern a future national telegraph network, a network that, so the deputies hoped, would provide the basis for a unitary German nation-state.[142] In the discussions of committees like this, the cultural or constitutional dream of the nation was already being displaced by a materialized vision of unity, a unity made not of feeling, language or culture, but of infrastructure, which was already beginning to acquire the nimbus of prestige it would come to enjoy after the revolution.

Reliable stenography was an important, if overlooked, aspect of this

The German National Assembly in St Paul's Church, Frankfurt (1848–9), lithograph after a drawing by Leo von Elliot. Festooned with the national colours and with an enormous portrayal of Germania by Phillipp Veit, this chamber was designed to reverberate to the great patriotic issues of the day.

public resonance. Tachygraphy – the art of swift writing – was an ancient skill and parliamentary stenography was already established in eighteenth-century Britain, but it was only in 1848 that the broad outlines of a modern parliamentary stenographic service first saw the light of day in Paris. In the Constituent Assembly of 1848, two stenographers, a 'rolling stenographer' (*sténographe rouleur*) and a reviser (*réviseur*) perched on opposite sides of the tribune. The former succeeded each other in rotation, taking stenographic notes for two minutes and then transcribing them in haste, while the reviser, working in eighteen-minute stints, collated the transcriptions of his colleagues and established the sense or meaning by 'revising' the text. The whole thing was then reassembled, verified and certified by the head of service, who was also present during the session for as long as the assembly was sitting. Once this was done, the pages of transcript were carried by a porter to the printing works of the official *Moniteur Universel*, corrected once and then signed off for printing, authorized for publication and made available to the principal press organs on the day following the session recorded.[143] This put an end to the parallel circulation in the political press of conflicting versions of the same speeches that had vexed the legislators of the July Monarchy.[144]

The director of the new stenographic service, Hyppolite Prévost, an unparalleled master of tachygraphy and the leading light of mid-nineteenth-century French stenography, insisted that good parliamentary recording should not exhibit a slavish fidelity to the spoken word but should be 'intelligent', processing the texts harvested from the chamber into a 'readable form of orality'. This was important, because whereas in London the indirect style was used to report speeches, French and German reporting aimed to capture the texture and tone of direct speech. The inclusion of interruptions and heckling could produce highly comic effects, as when a member standing in front of the tribune ridiculed a prolix orator with the words 'Don't give him any more water, he will only stop when he gets thirsty.' Parenthetical references to reactions from the chamber ('prolonged hilarity on the left', 'interruptions in the centre') enabled readers who had never set foot in a parliament to grasp something of the spatiality and atmospherics of debate.[145]

One advantage of this almost-simultaneous communication of chamber debates was that it enabled readers from outside politically active circles to become part of a process of judgement and discernment. As a deputy to the new Second Chamber in The Hague remarked during a speech of 1849 hailing the new Dutch stenographic service, 'the great advantage of a prompt and accurate communication of what has been discussed' was that it facilitated 'a reciprocal influence in the ongoing consideration of matters, between the Representation and the Nation'. Only this would enable the broader public to wield an 'indirect and moral influence' on the business of parliament and guard against the assumption, which the speaker believed was widespread in the Netherlands, that ordinary people were best advised to leave political debates and decision-making to the parliament. There was a counter-revolutionary edge to these observations: the speaker, Guillaume Groen van Prinsterer, was a doctrinaire conservative liberal who was bitterly opposed to the revolutions and to the efforts of more-radical Dutch politicians to channel them through reforms. He hoped that instantaneous reporting would empower 'the nation', relativize the significance of parliamentary debate and prevent the political press from establishing itself as an autonomous power between parliament and people.[146]

Many of the parliaments of 1848 saw the emergence of strong fractional or partisan structures, and here, too, there were apprenticeship effects. The lives of the new parliaments may have begun with flux and confusion, but caucuses and clubs soon became highly effective ways of imposing group discipline and clarifying shared positions. In Paris, disciplined structures emerged on the right and the left (the groups at the centre were more fluid). The conservative Réunion de la rue de Poitiers had begun as a loose grouping of delegates from Lot-et-Garonne, but after Adolphe Thiers became a director, it began to pull in uncommitted deputies from the right and centre, eventually providing the foundation for what would become the Party of Order.[147] By October 1848, 80 per cent of the deputies in the Frankfurt assembly belonged to one of the political clubs. 'Their activity', the liberal lawyer and deputy Robert von Mohl recalled in 1850, was 'the secret history of the parliament and in many cases the sole key to a true understanding of it'.[148] Newcomers were required to sign up to a programme and statutes. Dual memberships were not allowed. A number of the caucuses had their own newspapers and some even published their parliamentary correspondence.[149]

These organizational experiences had profound, long-term effects. Many politicians who achieved prominence at Frankfurt in 1848 resumed their careers after the counter-revolutionary reaction had subsided. In

France, the 'Party of Order' that emerged in 1848 played an important role in focusing the energies and arguments of the Bonapartism of the Second Empire. And many deputies and leaders in the Italian revolutionary parliaments resurfaced in the unification and consolidation of the new Italian kingdom after 1859. In the Czech lands, the liberal and radical activists of 1848 returned to political life as leaders of the Old and Young Czechs who shaped the nation's politics until beyond the turn of the twentieth century.[150] The 1848ers were no 'lost generation'.[151]

DRAFT A CONSTITUTION

1848 was the year of constitutions. Revolutionary France had used them as a means of giving normative legal expression to the successive political mutations of the French republic. Napoleon had deployed them as a tool of imperial statecraft. The Constituent Assembly in Cadiz used its constitution of 1812 to reclaim occupied Spain in the name of a sovereign people. By the early 1820s, constitutions had become the lingua franca of a transnational liberal movement. The revolutions of 1830 had triggered a new wave of innovations and adjustments. France amended the *Charte* of 1814. Revolutionary Belgium acquired a widely admired constitution, with a bicameral legislature, ministerial responsibility, civil rights and the separation of powers. The tinkering continued: the relatively modest Hanoverian constitution of 1833 equipped the parliament with limited budgetary oversight and opened the lower chamber to city dwellers and peasants. The Spanish constitution of 1837 drew on elements of both the Cadiz and the Belgian constitutions, expanding the franchise to 10 per cent of the male population, acknowledging civil rights and the division of powers, and placing restraints on the royal executive.

Some of these constitutions were of lasting significance: the one that established Saxony as a constitutional monarchy in 1831 was in force for eighty-seven years, until the collapse of the German Empire in 1918. The Belgian constitution of 1831 (with numerous amendments) is still in force today. Liberal contemporaries saw these achievements as milestones in humankind's long trek towards liberty. But constitutions could be withdrawn or replaced by less liberal substitutes. In Spain, the *moderados* replaced the constitution of 1837 with the more authoritarian one of 1845, which reinforced the executive power and shrank the franchise back to less than 2 per cent of the male population. Prince-Regent Frederick William of Electoral Hesse pruned back the concessions granted in 1831. The Hanoverian constitution of 1833 was unilaterally rescinded by the monarch in 1837, sparking a major crisis.

Even against this background, 1848 stands out. Every state in the grip of the revolutions issued a constitution of some kind. They are so numerous and emerged under such diverse circumstances that synopsis is difficult.[152] Some (Piedmont, Netherlands, Denmark) were issued or promised by governments to anticipate and fend off revolutions. Others (Switzerland, France, the Frankfurt assembly) were drawn up by assemblies elected for this purpose in order to stabilize the revolution, capture its energy in a relatively immobile legal framework, secure its achievements for the future and prevent further radicalization. And some constitutions (Prussia in December 1848, Austria in March 1849) were imposed after the revolutions by resurgent monarchical executives as instruments of counter-revolution. Constitutions had always been versatile, and they remained so in 1848.

But even the 'pre-emptive' constitutions issued early in the year were the consequence of revolutionary unrest. The Piedmontese constitution of 4 March 1848, for example, was not drafted in cool-headed anticipation of future trouble, but in an atmosphere of fear and emergency. In January, it was still the view of King Charles Albert and his ministers that the very idea of conceding a constitution was 'intolerable'. There were violent disturbances in Genoa, whose citizens had not forgotten their republic's annexation in 1815 by the House of Savoy. In Turin, the brilliant publicist Count Cavour and his newspaper, *Il Risorgimento*, oversaw the swift radicalization of public opinion. Then came reports on 3 February 1848 that Ferdinand II of the Two Sicilies had backed down five days before and offered his subjects a constitution.

The news from Naples threw Charles Albert into a state of 'fury and terror'. He at first declared that he would 'fight to the end' (*combattre jusqu'à l'extrémité* – the debates of the State Council in Turin were conducted in French!) to avoid a similar fate. There was talk at the court of toughing out the crisis with a combination of 'lead [bullets] and the noose'. The Council of State manoeuvred the monarch out of his intransigence by insisting that granting a constitution was now the only way to prevent something even worse. Wasn't it better, Alfieri, the Minister of Education, asked, to 'constitute public opinion in a parliament, rather than letting it persist in this state of antagonism, whose direct and immediate impact was every day shaking the monarchy to its foundations?'[153] Implicit in Alfieri's argument was the notion, pressed hard by Cavour and other newspaper editors, that a constitution would not weaken, but rather strengthen, the monarch. This was exactly the argument that the Rhenish liberal Ludolf Camphausen would make to Frederick William IV of Prussia in March 1848: that a constitutional system with responsible ministers would protect the monarchy from the vicissitudes of politics and opinion, rendering the Crown more, not less, independent. And to these arguments the ministers in Piedmont added a further consideration, rich in historical consequence. By acquiring a constitution, Charles Albert would strengthen his claim to a wider leadership among his fellow Italian princes.[154]

Known as the *Statuto Albertino* (Albertine Statute), the constitution published on 4 March was drafted at great speed. The process of redacting it took up only four meetings of the Council of State. It was not the product of a long and slow 'cultural reflection', but of a panicky process of improvisation, in which bits and pieces of the Cadiz constitution, the revised French *Charte* of 1830 and the Belgian constitution were cobbled into a text whose purpose was to integrate an element of representation without undermining the primacy of the monarchical executive. The new statute guaranteed the equality before the law of all citizens, assured freedom of religion for all existing forms of worship and guaranteed a range of civil liberties, including the right of assembly and freedom of the press. It stated explicitly (Art. 5) that the executive power was vested in the king alone and that his assent (signature) was required for the signing of bills into law. On the other hand, taxes could only be levied with the consent of both houses of parliament. The king could dissolve parliament, but if he did so, he was obliged to summon both houses again within four months. The chambers could initiate legislation, but they could not remove ministers from office by a vote of no confidence – ministers could be nominated and removed only by the king. On the other hand, a parliament could in theory boycott an unpopular minister or ministers by refusing to sign bills into law. In short, the *Statuto Albertino* was the constitutional expression of the moderate liberalism that had become so dominant in northern Italy. It was a consequence, but not the fruit of, the revolutions. It represented an effort to integrate the representative elements demanded by public opinion while retaining as much as possible of the Crown's executive primacy.

The *Statuto Albertino* was a gift from the king to his people – hence the choice of 'statute' over the word 'constitution', which might be taken to suggest a document drawn up by a constituent assembly. In France, by contrast, the new Provisional Government chose the latter path. We have seen that the composition of the new assembly was a bitter disappointment to the left. The preponderance of conservative and moderate interests was even more pronounced in the eighteen-man committee entrusted with drafting the new constitution – there was only one socialist, Victor Considerant. The objective of the drafters was not to project the revolution forward into the future, but to capture it in something cool and inert, conserve a liberal understanding of what had been achieved and thereby prevent further radicalization. This last point was important. Odilon Barrot, who was a member of the Constitutional Committee, later recalled how the 'fear of social war' left its mark on the drafting of the constitution: 'the agitation that had suffused this society, the exasperation of some, the anxiety of others, did not permit the calm, the coolness of mind required for such a task'. He could not forget, he wrote, how in the room where the commission was deliberating, the sounds of civil strife could be heard through the windows.[155]

These words suggest that there was a rift between the moderate, stabilizing intention of the constitutional commission and the turmoil that continued to unfold on the streets of Paris. 'Fraternity', the presiding motif of the radical movement, was a diffuse idea, resistant to legal codification. It expressed itself in popular calls for government intervention in areas of social provision such as labour laws for women and children, public hygiene and so on. But it remained completely unclear how the diverse needs associated with the Social Question related to constitutional questions about the form of government.[156] Was it even the business of a constitution to regulate such matters? The debate over this question focused above all on whether the constitution ought to recognize the 'right to work' as a fundamental right requiring active intervention by the state. And the to and fro of the discussions tended to reflect the political flux in the country at large. A reference to the right to work appeared in the first draft of the new French constitution but was removed under the pressure of the extreme violence of the 'June Days' in Paris. Then it was reinstated by means of an amendment proposed by Mathieu de la Drôme, a July Monarchy liberal whose politics had radicalized in the later 1840s and who now sat with the *Montagne* on the far left of the assembly. But after further controversial discussion the right to work was again removed from the final draft.[157] These tussles notwithstanding, the constitution promulgated on 4 November belonged among the most democratic in Europe: it created a unicameral legislature of the kind established during the early French republic and at Cadiz in 1812. The parliament was to be elected by all men who had reached at least twenty-one years of age. Sovereignty rested entirely in the citizenry of France, meaning that the head of state, the President of the Republic, was also to be elected by universal male suffrage. But even this constitution, a fruit of the revolution that had swept the Provisional Government into power, was no unequivocal endorsement of the 'ideas of February'. To the hallowed revolutionary principles of 'Liberty, Equality and Fraternity', the drafters, frightened by the violence of June, added 'Family, Work, Property [and] Public Order'.[158]

Even in those settings where the hot months of 1848 passed without a major revolutionary episode, the changes introduced through constitutions could be quite profound. The new Dutch constitution was a milestone. It enshrined freedom of religion, freedom of education and freedom of association.[159] It moved the centre of gravity from the king and his ministers to the electorate and the Second Chamber of parliament.[160] By introducing ministerial responsibility (*ministeriële verantwoordelijkheid*), which made the king inviolable and the ministers responsible for his actions, the new constitution did away with much of the king's personal power. At the same time, the Second Chamber gained in importance, since it now acquired the right to amend legislation along with the *recht van enquête*, the right to establish commissions of enquiry. It now set the annual budgets (with the right to amend them) and it gained more influence on colonial policy. Its members were now directly elected. Whereas the old constitution had excluded the 'people's power', Thorbecke wrote in his report on behalf of the constitutional commission, the new one aimed to absorb it 'into every vein of the state'.[161] The whole experience of election was now quite different.[162]

This is not to say that the Netherlands became a 'democracy' overnight in 1848: under the new franchise, the minimum amount of tax a male individual had to pay to acquire the right to vote was set at between twenty and 160 guilders, depending on the district. In practice, this meant that between 1850 and 1880 around 11 per cent of the male population aged twenty-three or above was able to vote in Second Chamber elections.[163] And this in turn had the perverse effect of producing a slightly smaller electorate than had existed under the old system, the difference being that this electorate now voted directly for the candidates it favoured.[164] The Second Chamber returned in the first elections under the new law was quite a different creature from its predecessor. Of the sixty-eight members elected only twenty-two had previously sat in the chamber and the bulk of the new representatives came from outside the political establishment.[165] Small wonder that during the opening session of the chamber, on 14 February 1849, the new Speaker (*voorzitter*) welcomed 'the beginning of a new age in our history'.[166]

In several countries, constitutions were promulgated more than once, and for different purposes on each occasion. In July 1848, after long and arduous deliberations, the Prussian National Assembly presented the constitutional draft known as the Charte Waldeck (Waldeck Charter) for the then chairman of the assembly, Benedikt Waldeck. This was a very radical document: in addition to granting various basic rights, it foresaw the creation of a people's army under parliamentary authority, restricted the king's right to veto decisions by parliament and stipulated that the elections for the lower chamber would take place under universal male suffrage. But the Waldeck Charter was rejected by the monarch, whose assent was needed before it could pass into law. In December 1848, the government promulgated without consultation a more authoritarian constitution that endowed the monarch with an absolute veto over parliamentary resolutions and restored his undivided personal command over the military. The universal suffrage granted in the Charte Waldeck was initially retained, along with articles guaranteeing various civil rights, but in the following year a further unilateral amendment imposed a three-class franchise that geared the system in favour of the wealthiest voters.

The picture was even more complicated in the Austrian Empire, where we encounter all three types of constitution: preventive, revolutionary and counter-revolutionary. On 25 April 1848, the government issued the 'Pillersdorf Constitution', named for the interior minister, Franz von Pillersdorf, who drafted it. This document, designed for use in the Austrian Crown Lands (and thus excluding the Italian provinces, where a civil war was still in progress, and Hungary, whose future status was uncertain), foresaw a relatively broad but indirect male franchise and endowed the monarchy with the power of absolute veto over decisions made by the parliament. This constitution was abandoned under the pressure of protests and petitions from radical groups in Vienna and the initiative passed to the new Reichstag that met first in Vienna and then, from October 1848, in Kremsier (Kroměříž). This body, a true product of the revolution, in the sense that it would never have been convened without it, produced a much more progressive document offering a more comprehensive catalogue of basic rights, a more muscular and autonomous parliament, and a weaker monarchical executive with a suspensive veto, meaning that the king's veto would lapse if the chamber kept voting in support of a specific measure. But on the very day that this constitution was published – 4 March 1849 – the imperial government issued an imposed counter-constitution of its own, largely drawn up by Count Franz Stadion, the indefatigable architect of counter-revolution in the Habsburg lands. The latter constitution cancelled out the former and the Kremsier parliament was dissolved. Here, as in Prussia, a constitution was used to kill a constitution.

Denmark hatched two constitutions in 1848–9, the first a preventive effort drawn up by councillors close to the king, the second the work of a constituent assembly elected by universal suffrage. The second one wrought a profound transformation in the political life of Denmark, which had until then been governed by an absolute monarchy. Both houses of parliament were henceforth elected under a broad franchise encompassing all reputable Danish men over thirty, with the exception of servants lacking their own households and recipients of social welfare.[167] In Hungary, it was the old-world corporately structured Diet that generated the legislative programme known as the 'April Laws' that would serve as the constitution of an increasingly autonomous Hungarian state.[168] Various of the provincial diets in the Austrian lands pressed ahead with regional constitutions of their own – in the Tyrol, the German and Italian-speaking Tyroleans refused to deliberate together and produced separate draft regional constitutions. After political unrest in Luxembourg, the Dutch king shut down the old Estates Assembly and announced elections to a constituent assembly, whose constitution was promulgated on 10 July 1848. In Wallachia, the wish list of reforms known as the 'Proclamation of Islaz' acquired constitutional status, much as the April Laws did in Hungary.

I have scarcely begun to scratch the surface of this prodigious European effort at constitution-spawning.[169] Constitutions are not most people's idea of lively bedside reading. But the constitutions of 1848 were and are much less boring than one might think. They did interesting and important things, like defining (or trying to define) the relationship between the executive power and the military (this was an especially bitter question for the deputies of the National Assembly in Berlin). In many jurisdictions, they emancipated the Jews and did away with political discrimination by creed (none of the constitutions made any gesture in the direction of the emancipation of women). The Proclamation of Islaz and the constitution of the Roman Republic were among the first such documents to abolish the death penalty. Many of the constitutions of 1848 did away with the special services and payments in kind associated with 'feudal' agrarian tenures. Almost everywhere, though to varying degrees, the constitutions broadened the franchise, deepening the purchase of politics on the population. And it wasn't just about rights and liberties. The Danish constitutional project was also about binding Schleswig more closely to the Danish state, just as the democratic counter-constitution drawn up by the Schleswig-Holstein Constituent Assembly in August–September was supposed to underscore both the autonomy and the inseparability of the two duchies.[170] The constitution drawn up by the Frankfurt parliament was not just about enshrining basic rights in law, but also about providing the legal scaffolding for a German national union that did not yet exist. The Swiss constitution of 1848, a consequence of the Sonderbund War, replaced the confederation of sovereign cantons ratified in 1815 with a new confederal state. The April Laws envisaged the political union within a Magyar state of all the 'lands of the Crown of St Stephen', including Transylvania and Croatia. The *Statuto Albertino* was intended to burnish Charles Albert's credentials as the pre-eminent Italian monarch. Constitutions continued to do many kinds of work.[171]

These were not dry, cookie-cutter statutes cribbed from a common template; they were highly idiosyncratic documents in which monarchical or republican elites spoke directly to the masses of the governed. The constitutions of 1848 had a communicative dimension that has not always received the attention it deserves. The avuncular opening passages of Austria's preventative Pillersdorf constitution explained that a constitution was necessary because 'the institutions of the state' must always reflect 'progressive developments in the cultural and intellectual life of nations'.[172] The *Statuto Albertino* opened with the voice of the monarch assuring his subjects that this new law would be 'the most certain means of redoubling the bonds of indissoluble affection' between the Crown and 'a people who have given us so many proofs of faith, obedience and love'.[173] The expository text of the Wallachian Proclamation of Islaz was composed in the hallucinatory language of Lamennais (whose *Paroles d'un croyant* was published in Romanian in 1848 in a version that had already circulated for some time in manuscript form) and addressed the nation as if it were a congregation at worship.[174] The opening line verged on the liturgical: 'In the name of the Romanian people "God is Lord and has appeared to us; blessed is he who comes in the name of the Lord".' Justifying the principle of a free press, the drafters went far beyond the standard invocations of progress and freedom:

> Truth, ideas, knowledge come from God for the general benefit of men, like the sun, like the air, like water, and are therefore universal property, and if the property of individuals must be respected, how much more sacred and untouched is universal property. To drown the truth, to extinguish the light . . . is an apostasy to God. Freedom of the press can harm none but the sons of darkness.[175]

The almost hypnotic preamble to the constitution of the French Second Republic announced that France would now 'walk more freely on the road of progress and civilization', that the Republic would assure an 'ever more equitable distribution of the burdens and advantages of society', conveying its citizens 'with no further commotion, by the continual and constant action of its institutions and laws towards an ever-higher degree of morality, enlightenment and well-being'.[176]

Some of these constitutions were short-lived. The Pillersdorf Constitution lapsed with the decision to summon a constituent Reichstag, as did the Danish draft of February–March 1848. The imposed Habsburg 'March constitution' that cancelled out the Kremsier charter of 4 March 1849 was itself suspended by the New Year's Eve Patent (*Silvesterpatent*) of 31 December 1851, which restored monarchical absolutism in the Austrian Empire. We have seen that the Waldeck Charter drawn up by the Berlin National Assembly never went into effect. Nor did the *Reichsverfassung* drafted by the Frankfurt National Assembly, which was rejected in 1849 by the resurgent monarchies of the German states. But even rejected or rescinded constitutions could live on in other forms. Many clauses from the Waldeck Charter were carried over into the imposed Prussian constitution of December 1848. The text of the Frankfurt Constitution continued to resound in the Weimar Constitution (1919) and the Basic Law of the Federal Republic (1949). Even the counter-revolutionary Austrian New Year's Patent of 1851 expressly retained certain stipulations of earlier constitutions, such as equality before the law and the abolition of feudalism.

Some of the constitutions of this era were destined to enjoy long lives. The Danish *Junigrundloven* of 5 June 1849 is still the country's constitution today and its promulgation is celebrated every year. The Dutch constitution of 11 October 1848 is viewed as the template for the *Grondwet* currently in effect in the Netherlands and the same can be said of the Swiss Confederal constitution, despite the many revisions that have occurred since. The *Statuto Albertino* performed precisely the task envisaged for it: it helped to establish Piedmont as the focal point for Italian liberal and nationalist opinion and was imposed – for better or for worse – on all the states of the peninsula in the aftermath of political unification, becoming, with some amendments, the constitution of the kingdom of Italy. In short: the constitutions of 1848 were not dead letters. They were living texts at the heart of the revolutionary and nation-building process.

There had never been a moment like this before and there has been none since. One might say that it represented the apogee of a certain kind of liberal politics. We have seen how attached liberals, who were often lawyers, were to these grandiloquent texts. They prized them as constraints on executive caprice, as commitments to correct procedure and 'peace treaties' between opposed political and social interests. In 1848, constitutions also served as a means of delegitimating radical challenges from the left. Having done away with the 'right to work', the French constitution moved the passages suggesting a commitment to social amelioration from active clauses in the body of the text to the preamble, where they provided amiable mood music but were not legally binding. Indeed, it is a mark of the success of the constitution as an instrument of state-building that its association with progressive politics

407

was diluted, that it entered more general use. And one consequence of this was that certain counterarguments ceased to be heard. Before 1848, an important strain of conservative thought had denounced written constitutions as the fruit of rebellion and mayhem, or as a satanic disruption of the mystical union between monarchs and peoples. The events of 1848 exhausted the plausibility of this view. The great majority of post-1848 conservatives embraced constitutions as an instrument for the stabilization of politics. None would deploy this instrument more brilliantly for conservative ends than Otto von Bismarck.

All of this meant that there was an ambivalence in 1848's bulk spawning of constitutions. Their ubiquity, in endless variations, revealed an unexpected emptiness. What had once been an end gradually subsided into a means. Constitutions would remain an indispensable state-building tool – witness the flurry of new constitutions after the world wars – but that extraordinary period of political struggle, from Cadiz, via Madrid, Naples, Piedmont, Lisbon and Brussels to the constituent assemblies of 1848, had come to an end. The struggle would continue, but it would no longer be a struggle for constitutions. The political scientist Lorenz von Stein, a witness to this transition, captured one of its meanings when he wrote that 1848 represented the end of the age of 'constitution' and the beginning of the age of 'administration'.[177]

6

Emancipations

'What is the task of our time?' the poet Heinrich Heine asked in 1828. 'It is emancipation. Not just the emancipation of the Irish, the Greeks, the Frankfurt Jews, the West Indians, the Blacks and oppressed peoples of that kind, but rather the emancipation of the entire world and particularly of Europe.'[1] Like the word 'history', 'emancipation', which had originally referred to the liberation of Roman slaves, passed during this era through a process of semantic inflation in which the liberation of specific groups – races, classes, nations (Heine did not mention women) – merged into a single, all-encompassing process. And once this happened, the word became a channel through which history flowed, as if there were no path into the future that did *not* pass through it. Specific 'issues of emancipation', one author noted, were 'individual components or phases' in an irreversible 'universal emancipatory process', a process that was inseparable from historical progress and the emergence of modern society.[2]

In the last years before the revolution of 1848, the idea of emancipation proliferated across newspaper articles, public addresses and parliamentary speeches. It shaped laws and constitutions. Enslaved people and their advocates, women and Jews all campaigned for their share of it.* For all of them, 1848 marked a new point of departure. But the revolution did not deliver the linear transition into liberty that the word had come to promise. The emancipatory efforts of specific groups did not merge into an all-encompassing symphony of change, and the road out of servitude, discrimination and civil disability was not linear, but faltering, tortuous and strewn with pitfalls and setbacks.

---

* The term emancipation was also used about peasants, but in a very different sense, since the unfreedom of mid-nineteenth-century peasants did not attach to their persons, but to their land and the character of their tenure. For that reason, they are discussed in a later chapter.

THE DAY OF THE ABOLITIONIST

No one can have been surprised that Victor Schoelcher, newly arrived in Paris at the beginning of March 1848 after a fact-finding journey to Senegal, was chosen to head the new 'Commission for the preparation of an act of immediate emancipation in all of the colonies of the Republic'. In 1846 and 1847, Schoelcher had published article after article in the Parisian reformist and republican press fulminating against the slave systems of Martinique, Guadeloupe, Île Bourbon and French Guyana in a language dense with detailed observations and data harvested from a far-flung network of correspondents, including many clandestine informants on the slave islands. He had reported on the frequency of suicides among the enslaved, which he viewed as acts of 'renunciation' generated by the condition of slavery itself. He had ridiculed the discrepancies between the government's ineffectual efforts at reform and the realities on the ground. Some of the articles focused on the horrific corporal punishments that were still being inflicted on enslaved Africans on the Antillean plantations or the parodic ritual performances that passed for 'justice' in the colonies; others angrily parried the relativizing canards that did the rounds at Parisian social gatherings: that the slaves were 'better off' than peasants, that they preferred to be unfree, that the sugar economy would collapse without them and so on. Slavery, Schoelcher argued, was not a 'necessary evil' whose effects could be muted by piecemeal regulation. It was an abomination that must be extirpated unconditionally. The title page of the collection of essays he published in 1847 was inscribed with the words 'The humane regulation of slavery is as impossible as the humane regulation of murder.'[3]

Schoelcher was not the only French abolitionist – there were several among the members of the Provisional Government. But already in the mid 1840s he had come to embody the movement in a way that no one else did. Arago, Ledru-Rollin, Louis Blanc, Lamartine, Tocqueville, Broglie, Agénor de Gasparin all favoured abolition in one form or another, but none of them gave themselves to it as Schoelcher did. He outlasted everyone else, because his commitment was not romantic, driven by empathetic emotion, but philosophical and unbending. A professed atheist of austere style and tastes who never married, Schoelcher brought a unique inerrancy to his pursuit of the cause. As early as 1843, the

Victor Schoelcher, portrait by Louis-Stanislas Marin-Lavigne (1848). Schoelcher was not the only French abolitionist, but none was more dedicated to the cause than he.

Martiniquais man of colour Cyrille Bissette accused him of hogging the abolition limelight.[4] After his death, he would soar in the collective memory of the Antilles, particularly in Martinique, where streets, the most beautiful library in the West Indies, a town and the Lycée Schoelcher, attended by Aimé Césaire and Frantz Fanon, are named after him.

Schoelcher poured cold water on the panegyrics of his fans (and the extravagant denunciations of his enemies), protesting that he had achieved nothing alone. 'I was merely one of the workers in the vineyard, carrying out the task that I had the honour to be entrusted with', he wrote in 1883, when he was seventy-nine years old.[5] This wasn't quite true: in March and April 1848, his intervention was decisive in pushing France towards immediate and universal emancipation. The Provisional Government was still groping its way over the uneven ground between the barricades and the materialization of a constituent assembly. The colonists' lobby in Paris was already pressuring the new Minister of the Navy and Colonies, François Arago, to delay a decision. As the new Under-Secretary of State in Arago's ministry, Schoelcher was able to derail these plans.

The Schoelcher commission was a mixed group. Armand Mestro had served for years as the ministry's Director of Colonies. François-Auguste Perrinon was a man of colour from Martinique, the commander of a naval artillery battery and a graduate of the École Polytechnique. Adolphe Gatine was an abolitionist advocate at the Council of State who had distinguished himself since 1834 by his defence of free people of colour in cases that exposed the perversity of the laws pertaining to slavery. 'Citizen Gaumont' was a worker in the clockmaking trade, the only 'proletarian' on the commission. He was there because, as editor of the *Union Ouvrière*, he had coordinated the abolitionist petition drive of 1844. He also helped to burnish the working-class credentials of a project that had an elite social profile. One of the two commission secretaries, Henri Wallon, a lecturer at the École Normale, had published an erudite three-volume history of ancient slavery with a transparently abolitionist agenda.[6]

The commission met for the first time on 6 March and convened thirty-three times over the next forty days. They conducted auditions with stakeholder groups and read out letters received. Spokesmen for the colonists of Guadeloupe, Martinique and Réunion (formally Île Bourbon – the name was changed by decree on 7 March 1848) were the first to present their views. Then there was a delegation of 'negroes and

Official portrait of Victor Petit-Frère Mazuline (1848), member of the
Constituent National Assembly of France. Mazuline, the son of enslaved parents
and himself enslaved in his youth, was about twelve when he left the island with
his 'master', a French police official, in 1802. When the revolutions of 1848
broke out, he was living free and married in Paris, where he was a well-known
frequenter of the cafés in the area around the Jardin du Luxembourg. Elected to
a place as substitute (*suppléant*), he took his seat after alleged electoral
irregularities led to the withdrawal of the abolitionist Cyril Bissette. It was said
that Mazuline's daughter, who had returned to Martinique to run a girls'
boarding school, played an important role in securing his election.

mulattos', among whom was Victor Petit-Frère Mazuline, an expatriate Martiniquais who would later become the first former enslaved man to serve as a deputy in the National Assembly. Delegates from the port cities, representing the interests of maritime commerce, also addressed the commission. The discussions ranged across many issues. Dejean Labatie, delegate of Réunion, questioned the right of the Provisional Government to 'resolve for itself the question of slavery'.[7] Schoelcher was firm on this: a government that had, by means of a revolution, destroyed one regime and inaugurated another must surely possess sufficient legitimacy to 'proclaim the liberation of the blacks'. To put it in other words: the legitimacy of the commission derived from the legitimacy of the revolution itself. As for the objection levelled by the colonists, that the liberation of slaves was irreconcilable with the government's proclaimed respect for the sanctity of property, the commission were having no truck with that: 'it repels the mind', one of them wrote, 'to see a piece of property in a man'.[8]

Timing was another problem. The colonists and the delegates from the port cities, representing the interests of maritime commerce, argued that the process should be put on pause while the commission resolved the matter of the indemnity to be paid to the slave-owners. Their strategy was to feign support for emancipation, but to slow it down with complications: the indemnity, a regime of post-emancipation labour controls, fiscal protection for the sugar produced on plantations. But the commission, pressed by Schoelcher, opted to treat abolition as a discrete executive intervention and leave the other issues to the deliberations of the Constituent Assembly. Schoelcher was hostile to the use of the term 'indemnity', because it implied a retrospective acknowledgement of a property right in human beings. 'What indemnity', he asked a delegation of colonists, 'will we give to the slaves for having been so long deprived of the possession of themselves?'[9] Pushing forward as fast as possible also seemed the best way to avoid potential disorders – on this last point the commission found themselves in partial agreement with a colonist by the name of Montlaur from Réunion, who argued that any delay would encourage the enslaved to 'hasten their liberation by violent means'.[10] On the other hand, there was some sympathy for the view – articulated by one of the deputies from Guadeloupe – that the abolition decree should not come into effect before 1 August, in order to avoid disrupting the sugar harvest.[11]

Then there was the question of the political meaning of emancipation. The working draft of Article 1 of the abolition decree stated that those who were liberated would automatically become French citizens. Did that mean that they would be entitled to vote? There was disagreement on this within the commission. Mestro and Perrinon were gradualists (as was the minister, François Arago); Perrinon favoured immediate emancipation, but not the enfranchisement of the recently liberated. The delegates of the planters of Martinique and Guadeloupe were against enfranchisement altogether.[12] But Mazuline, the freed man of Martinique and one of a delegation of 'negroes and mulattos', also expressed anxiety about opening the franchise to former slaves: 'Will they understand what they are doing?' he asked the commissioners. 'They will be influenced, they will act without knowing, they will nominate men who will not defend their interests.'[13]

As the commission sifted through the issues, it became increasingly clear that emancipation was much more than a change of legal status. In societies where the majority had until now been enslaved persons, and where the entire economy was founded on enslaved labour, it was likely to be a profound social transformation with far-reaching consequences. The enslaved workers lived in houses that belonged to the masters – who would be responsible for the upkeep of these buildings? How should the labour of the formerly enslaved be paid for? Who or what would prevent them from simply abandoning their plantations and wandering about or establishing their own plots in the highlands? Should emancipated slaves be forced into some form of association under coercive legislation? Should new laws be drafted to restrict labour mobility? On 17 March, the commission discussed the possibility of creating workshops for the colonies analogous to the ones announced on 26 February for the workers of Paris – an idea associated with Louis Blanc, a member of the Provisional Government and head of the Luxembourg Commission tasked with addressing the demands of labour after the February Revolution.[14]

Schoelcher had his way, and these ancillary questions were left to one side. The preamble to the act of abolition stated that slavery was 'an assault on human dignity' and that by 'destroying the free will' it suppressed the 'natural principles of right and duty'. The abolition of slavery and of its accoutrements, including the sale of unfree persons and the use of corporal punishment, would take effect exactly two months after the promulgation of the decree (Art. 1). 'Purified of servitude', the colonies would be represented in the National Assembly (Art. 6). The principle 'French soil frees any slave who touches it' would henceforth be extended to the colonies and possessions of the Republic (Art. 7). French nationals were henceforth forbidden (Art. 8) to 'possess, buy or sell slaves' or to participate in any way in such transactions. Any breach of this rule would incur the loss of French citizenship. The question of the indemnity was held over for discussion by the National Assembly (Art. 5). Nothing was said of the coercion of labour or of the need for new laws against vagabondage. The two-month delay was not an 'apprenticeship', but a pause to prepare for a break that, when it came, would hopefully be quick and clean. The decree of 27 April was a victory for Schoelcher's vision of an immediate and unconditional liberation.

BLACK 1848

If this is starting to sound like one of those narratives in which a fine idea, fashioned by Europeans, extends its beneficent influence across the earth's surface, then we need to shift the perspective now, and for two reasons. The first is that the process of emancipation did not diffuse in a linear way from the metropolis to the colonial periphery. The enslaved seized their freedom from the hands of the masters before the new Republic could give it to them. The second is that the act of abolition and the destruction of the slaving system proved to be very different things. Abolition took place in Paris as a clean transition from servitude to liberty. Emancipation – meaning the transition to a full and free citizenship – was a very different and far slower process. Impeded by local resistance and slowed by the ebbing of political will at the centre, it unfolded at different speeds in different locations and was not linear, but subject to setbacks and reversals.[15]

When we celebrate the achievement of Schoelcher, the writer Aimé Césaire told a French journalist in 1982, 'we must not forget the extremely important actions of the slaves themselves ... who fought for many years for their own liberty. We have erected a statue to Schoelcher, but we should also raise a statue to the unknown negro runaway.'[16] Martinique had seen slave uprisings in 1789, 1800, 1811, 1822 and 1831. These upheavals blew wind into the sails of abolitionist agitation worldwide; they weakened slavery as an institution, demoralized the colonists, hardened the enslaved population and rendered the metropolis less receptive to the arguments of the masters.[17] The enslaved even used the law to fight the system.[18] The alienation of 'free men of colour' from the white elite in Martinique undermined the fragile alliance of convenience between upperclass people of colour and the white planter class, facilitating the emergence of a cadre of local activists whose loyalty to the current system was dubious. The scar of the branding iron on Cyrille Bissette's shoulder was a reminder that not even liberty, prosperity and education could protect a free man of colour from the racism of a slaving society.[19]

The accumulation of anti-slavery sentiment and the weakening of the system that sustained it thus preceded the promulgation of the decree of 27 April 1848. In the era before transoceanic telegraphs, it took around thirty days for news to get from Paris by packet boat to Martinique. Even before the Provisional Government had begun to address the slavery question, the news of the fall of the monarchy and the establishment of a republic were read in Martinique as harbingers of imminent emancipation.[20] On 12 April, the *Journal officiel de la Martinique* and the *Courrier de la Martinique* both published the Parisian decree of 4 March stating that a commission had been formed to prepare with the greatest possible haste 'an act of emancipation to take effect immediately in all the colonies of the Republic'.[21]

By the time the Schoelcher commission's decree of 27 April 1848 reached Martinique, the enslaved residents had already taken matters into their own hands. In the second half of April, a broad wave of agitation engulfed the island. There were protests and demonstrations, clashes between crowds and troops, and mass absconding from the plantations. The general mood was such that local upsets could ignite larger conflicts. In the third week of April, for example, Léo Duchamps, the son of the proprietor of the Duchamp plantation, a diehard who had resisted all efforts at change and compromise, suddenly forbade the enslaved workers on his plantation to play their drums on Saturdays while they made manioc flour. Rattled and aggressive, Duchamp drove his point home by smashing the drum of one of his workers, a man by the name of Romain. This was an unexpected prohibition, because the playing of drums on Saturday was a very old custom, widely observed across the island. When Romain appeared on the following Saturday

(20 May) drumming on a wooden box, Duchamp discerned a provocation and called upon the mayor of the principal town, Saint-Pierre in the neighbouring district, to have Romain seized, manacled and dragged off to jail. Word got around and enslaved workers and free people of colour descended on the prison at Saint-Pierre, from plantations across the district. Unnerved, but also stirred, by the indignation of the crowd, the mayor's adjutant and chief of police, Porry-Papy, the son of a free man of colour and a freed woman of Martinique, ordered Romain's release.

Events of this kind flared up in cascades across the island.[22] By 22 May, there were major skirmishes in the main city of Saint-Pierre as enslaved people invaded the town and fought with armed white settlers. These conflicts at first produced only black casualties, but in one incident a crowd of protesters who had been shot at from a house, having failed to break into it, set the building on fire, killing thirty-two of the white colonists (including women and children) who had barricaded themselves inside it. White families in many districts now fled their plantations to take refuge on the boats. The island was in a state of general insurrection. On the afternoon of 23 May, with no definitive order from Paris yet in hand, Governor Rostoland gave in to pressure from many quarters and signed a local act of emancipation, in which he waived the two-month transition period envisaged by the government in Paris and appended to the decree an unconditional amnesty for 'any political offences committed during the period of movement through which we have just passed'.[23] The enslaved had in effect anticipated developments in Paris, seizing liberty before the decree of 27 April could be promulgated on the island.[24]

The governor of Guadeloupe followed suit a few days later, issuing an exact copy of Rostoland's proclamation on 27 May 1848, also without metropolitan sanction. And once the enslaved people of Martinique and Guadeloupe had secured their freedom, it proved impossible to sustain the authority of the slave-owners on the nearby Dutch islands of the Lesser Antilles, St Maarten, St Eustatius and Saba. The Dutch slaves simply ceased to behave as slaves, and since their 'masters' lacked any means of coercing them, the institution was unilaterally nullified.[25] This was a de facto abolition, not a legal one: only many years later would the Dutch government get around to compensating the slave-owners. Something broadly similar happened on Saint Croix, a Danish possession of the Lesser Antilles: on 2 July 1848, rebels occupied plantation buildings and raised a general alarm. On the following day, 8,000 slaves

François-Auguste Biard, *Proclamation of the Freedom of the Blacks in the Colonies* (1849). In this painting, the artist, a successful academic painter known for his arresting images of exotic people and landscapes, captures the French republican view of emancipation as an act of generosity on the part of the colonial authority, welcomed by grateful former captives.

refused to commence work and gathered instead in the town of Frederiksted to demand their liberation. The Danish governor responded much as Rostoland had done in Martinique, telling the crowd: 'Now you are free, you are hereby emancipated.'[26]

In the case of Martinique, the outward diffusion of the news of revolution intersected with an autochthonous, self-organized movement powerful enough to pre-empt metropolitan abolition. A particularly striking feature of the insurrection on Martinique was the speed with which the enslaved on plantations across the island came to each other's aid and coordinated their protests. But the impact of the upheavals on Martinique and Guadeloupe then passed sideways to the nearby possessions of another empire. Although the Dutch authorities looked favourably on emancipation in theory, they would not otherwise have freed their Antillean slaves, because they were reluctant to accept the costs of compensating slave-owners. The proposal that the Netherlands abolish slavery outright and provide former owners with a loan of ten million guilders to ease the transition was rejected by the Council of Ministers.[27] As a result of this calculus, the mainland South American Dutch possession of Surinam, for example, retained slavery until 1863. On the Dutch Antillean possessions, it was proximity to another theatre of political change that triggered events, not signals from the metropolis. On the other hand, the insurrection on Saint Croix was sparked not just by the news from Paris, but also by rumours to the effect that the king of Denmark was about to issue a decree of emancipation. Metropolitan decision-making interacted in unpredictable ways with local initiatives and island-to-island signalling to produce the cascade of events that swept across the Caribbean in 1848.

Across the French colonial empire, the impact of the decree of 27 April 1848 was refracted through heterogeneous social and political structures. Abolition meant one thing in the French Caribbean, which was a space of high-density chattel slavery fed by the importation of captive Africans. It worked out differently in Nossi-Bé and Sainte-Marie, island dependencies off the coast of Madagascar, or in Algeria, where slavery was not practised by French colonists but by the indigenous peoples. In Algeria, where the resistance to French authority had been exceptionally persistent and fierce since the invasion of 1830, Governor-General Bugeaud insisted:

It would be impossible to demand of a government like ours the vigilant surveillance required to prevent the arrival of the negroes by the desert caravans and their sale on the markets of Algeria. To achieve this, we would need more than the army of greater and lesser functionaries that you have in France and I ask: where would we go to cover our expenses?[28]

In 1848, Senegal was still very small, consisting of Saint-Louis, Gorée and a few fortified trading posts: Merinaghem in the Waalo, and Dagana, Bakel and Sénoudébou on the river. Here, it was not white Europeans who owned slaves, but the *habitants*, a mixed-race coastal trading class. Enslaved people were not worked on plantations but rented out by their owners as masons, weavers, laundresses, sailors and labourers of various kinds, skilled and unskilled.[29] They worked and even on occasion captained the boats that traded up the Senegal River with the interior. French colonial administrators in Senegal tended to support the *habitants* in arguing that the slavery of the region was completely different from the slavery of the sugar islands, that this was a relatively benign form of servitude whose abolition would do little to improve the lot of the enslaved.[30]

These objections did not prevent the enactment of the decree. On 23 August, the day set for emancipation in Senegal, the freed slaves went down to bathe together in the ocean, before processing to the French administration building and chanting praises for the French Republic. But the complications continued to multiply. Article 7 of the decree had stated that the principle 'French soil frees any slave who touches it' would henceforth be extended to all the colonies and possessions of the Republic. The commissioners in Paris had already discussed the possibility that this might trigger an influx of refugees from the neighbouring African principalities, all of which were slaving polities, or of enslaved Africans fleeing from 'chiefs in the interior'.[31] Perrinon and Schoelcher had dismissed these concerns, arguing that refugees could be welcomed as a source of labour recruitment; Article 7 was duly retained in the final version of the decree. But in 1849 Governor Baudin reported from Senegal that large numbers of enslaved people had indeed sought refuge at Saint-Louis. The neighbouring Emirate of Trarza was refusing to trade in gum arabic until its fugitives were returned. The *damel* (monarch) of the Wolof principality of Kajoor was withholding a shipment of peanuts that had already been paid for and threatening to block the export of other indispensable consumer products to the *habitants* of Saint-Louis unless something was done to modify the decree of 27 April. Since Senegal was at this time transitioning from gum arabic to peanuts as the staple product for export, these were not matters to be taken lightly.[32]

Article 8 of the abolition decree threatened French citizens in all jurisdictions, French and foreign, with the loss of their French citizenship if they continued to 'possess, buy or sell slaves' beyond a three-year transitional period from the promulgation date of the decree. This provision reflected the commission's (and especially Schoelcher's) sense that citizenship of the republic was incompatible with connivance in slavery, and that this incompatibility knew no geographical limits. 'Every Frenchman established in a foreign country', Schoelcher wrote, 'should be, as it were, a living, permanent protest against slavery.'[33] The effects of this provision were felt beyond the French colonial empire in the diasporas of Brazil, Cuba, Puerto Rico and Louisiana, a former French possession that had only been sold to the United States in 1803, where some 5,000–6,000 French citizens resided, many of whom owned slaves. Some French Louisianans had immigrated with their human property from the French Caribbean, others had married slave-owning Americans, and yet others had simply bought them, just as their American neighbours did. In a series of anguished letters to Paris, the French consul in New Orleans, Aimé Roger, expressed his alarm at this measure. Slavery was the lifeblood of the Louisiana economy – there was no other source of labour. French citizens who sold or freed their slaves would in effect be withdrawing from the state's economy, since all forms of production, whether in agriculture or in manufacturing, depended on it. The unilateral mass liberation of the French citizens' slaves would 'spread disorder and might well compromise public safety'. This was a matter of great personal awkwardness for the consul. Slavery was 'repellent to all of my sentiments as a man and a French citizen', but it so happened that his American wife had just inherited from her grandfather a 'family of Negroes' whom she employed in her domestic service.[34]

The consul's wife did eventually emancipate her enslaved family, but her example was not widely followed and the tussling between metropole and diaspora continued. The abolitionist ardour of the republican revolution of February began to cool. Schoelcher remained committed, but he was moved from his position at the Ministry for the Navy and

Colonies and became a mere deputy in the National Assembly. From 1849, successive French governments continued formally to honour the decree of April 1848, but they became more accommodating of requests for indulgence from the owners of slaves in slaving jurisdictions. In February 1851, an amendment was passed over the protests of Schoelcher and his allies extending the transition period in Article 8 from three to ten years. A new law of May 1858 formally reaffirmed the prohibition but created so many loopholes and exemptions that the measure was now largely ineffective.[35]

The abolitionists had often observed that the principle and the fact of slavery were two different things, meaning that it was possible to abolish the principle without abolishing the fact. The same must, by extension, apply to liberty, namely that it can be granted in principle without being enjoyed in fact. The experience of emancipation on the islands of the French Antilles bears out this observation. The mass flight from the plantations that the colonists had feared did not take place. The great majority of the formerly enslaved remained in their places of employment.[36] The freed workers abstained for the most part from active resistance, but they insisted on treating their traditional houses and the provision grounds where they grew vegetables for their own use as their personal property. Many of them refused to work on the estates where they had served as slaves, preferring to keep their places of work and residence separate. There was persistent friction over the supervision of field work and the keeping of regular hours, aspects of estate management that carried memories of the old ways.

The man sent to smooth the path from slavery to liberty was none other than François Perrinon, who served as 'Commissioner of Abolition' on the island from June to November 1848. Perrinon's answer to the problem of labour relations in this volatile situation was to draw up a standardized contract of association by which the owner and the workers would annually renew their commitment to collaborate in drawing revenue from the estate. The workday was set at nine hours and the workers were paid for their labour with a share of the crop commensurate with their days worked. In order to make this system stick, Perrinon proposed severe measures to drive out the 'idlers' who wanted to remain in their houses without coming to an arrangement with the proprietors. At the same time, he tried to limit private economic activity, setting a maximum size for the provision grounds and restricting the use of commons in charcoal-burning and fishing. There were parallels here with the suppression of common resources in the agricultural landscapes of early- to mid-nineteenth-century Europe (ch. 1). But the social tensions continued to accumulate as the house and the yard became the terrain of a struggle to maximize the autonomy of the worker and resist the reconstruction of the labour force pursued by the colonists. When the fieldworkers in Lamentin refused to keep working on plantation land, Perrinon had them expelled from their houses; they responded by burning down their own dwellings. In later years, under the rule of Napoleon III, even more repressive labour codes were introduced. Under Governor Gueydon, who became governor of Martinique in 1853, former slaves were bound to their plantations by the combined use of vagrancy law, a workbook system and a head tax.[37]

In Senegal, too, most freed slaves continued to work for their former masters, though some took advantage of the opportunities created by liberation – skills and entrepreneurial know-how helped to smooth the transition. At the same time, the 'free soil' principle was allowed to fall into disuse under the supervision of Governor Faidherbe – which is interesting, because Faidherbe had a track record as a radical abolitionist of the Schoelcher type. During his previous posting in Guadeloupe, he had gone down very badly with the white creoles because he was known for frequenting the houses of people of colour. If he changed his mind about Article 7, this was because the automatic liberation of fugitive slaves and the insistence on abolition now cut diametrically across the logic of French imperialism in western Africa, which aimed at extending influence over (and eventually annexing) the nearby independent African slaving states. Explaining the need for this adjustment in June 1855, the new Minister of the Navy, Ferdinand-Alphonse Hamelin, offered an appropriately sinuous rationale:

> To say to the populations that surround us that, in order to live under the protection of our flag, they must immediately renounce their captives would be tantamount to alienating them from us forever and throwing them into the arms of our enemies and would completely betray our objective of seeing to their future emancipation and the interests of civilization.[38]

In this way, the absorption of 'emancipation' into a larger civilizational imperial project became a means of perpetuating slavery. In general, it is striking that even those who were most critical of slaving (with very few exceptions) stopped short of repudiating empire or colonialism as such. Nowhere in the Europe of 1848 did the revolutions generate a serious challenge to imperialism and its dizzying asymmetries of power. On the contrary, the abolition of slavery was seen as entirely compatible with the consolidation of old and the acquisition of new imperial possessions and the exploitation of their lands and inhabitants. In France, one historian has noted, 'the germ of imperialist thought developed at the heart of the abolitionist ethic'.[39]

Slavery would not be definitively suppressed in French western Africa until the decree of 12 December 1905. For Algeria, 1848 brought both the abolition of slavery and the incorporation of the territory as a part of France – a move that some American southerners welcomed as analogous with the annexation of Texas by the United States.[40] And here, as in so many other locations, the resilience of pre-colonial custom, the resourcefulness of slave-traders and owners in working their way around the prohibition and the languid pragmatism of the French authorities, who preferred to let sleeping dogs lie, especially in the more remote areas of the interior, conspired to ensure that Algerian slaving outlived its own abolition for nearly half a century.[41]

The process of abolition was too paradoxically intertwined with the structures of local and metropolitan power in the French colonial empire to permit the clean transition from servitude to liberty that Schoelcher had hoped for. This was not a specifically French problem. Categorical abolition did not come to Spanish Cuba until 1880. But, even then, it arrived in an emphatically gradualist form, meaning that slavery was replaced in the first instance by a highly coercive system of controlled labour.[42] And in Portuguese Angola, where abolition was decreed in 1875, various forms of forced labour persisted well into the twentieth century.[43] Almost everywhere, including the postbellum United States, slavery proved a sticky, recalcitrant institution. It had grown too deeply into the fabric of social relations for its habits and attitudes to be easily eradicated. In this area, then, the Parisian February Revolution of 1848 failed to achieve its promise. The republican idea of universal citizenship already denied to women was further fractured by the social fact of racial inequality. The citizenship of the new colonial citizens remained juridically distinct from and inferior to that of their metropolitan fellows. Algeria is a case in point. The Provisional Government of 1848 endowed the white

425

French settlers there with full citizenship rights, but denied them to the native population.[44]

And yet the reform announced in Paris on 4 March and enacted in the decree of 27 April 1848 set in train a process of change that, like so many of the things begun in that eventful year, could be managed, blocked or deflected, but not reversed. Its longer-term effects can only be discerned in myriad human journeys away from the squalor of slavery. Paul Nardal was born in Martinique in 1864 to Joachim and Alexandrine, both of whom had been born enslaved at Saint-Pierre and were freed in 1848 at the age of fourteen. Paul became the first black man to win a bursary to the École des Arts et Métiers in Paris and later became the first black engineer in the Department of Public Works in Martinique, enjoying a long and illustrious career as manager in the Department of Highways and Bridges, where he left many lasting memorials to his work, including the reservoir at Éveché and the Absalon Bridge. If he never made it to the highest ranks of the administration, this was because, in a world that attached value to such differences, he was classed in his native Martinique as a 'black' rather than as a mixed-race 'man of colour'. But this devout Catholic and noted flautist worked hard on the education of the next generation of Martinican engineers and remained throughout his life passionately attached to his status as a French citizen. He was the husband of Louise Nardal, a piano teacher, and the father of Paulette Nardal, writer, feminist and luminary of the *négritude* movement. Paul died in 1960 at the age of ninety-six. Among his most prized possessions (until a fire at the family home destroyed it in 1956) was a letter congratulating him on his bursary from Victor Schoelcher.[45]

WAVING FROM WINDOWS

Berlin on the night of 18 March: we observe a barricade from behind. In the distance, shrouded in thick smoke, are raised military sabres and the horse of a cavalryman rearing up in terror. The roofs of the five-storey apartment blocks that recede into the background are fringed with tiny figures showering paving stones on troops we cannot see. The shards and splinters that fly up from the front of the barricade tell us that an artillery shell has just struck. Behind the barrier, in the foreground, a scene of frenetic activity: two men dig up and collect paving

F. G. Nordmann, *Barricade on the Corner of Kronen- and Friedrichstraße on 18 March by an Eyewitness* (1848). This dramatic but highly contrived scene compresses into one frame many features of barricade fighting: the improvised quality of the rampart, the presence of fighters of diverse social backgrounds, the bombardment of troops from the rooftops, the showers of splinters thrown up by artillery rounds. Above all, it captures something that struck many contemporary observers of the revolutions of 1848: the presence of women at the heart of the action. Here, we see a mother helping her sons to pick lead from a casement window so that it can be melted and turned into shot.

stones, another is about to throw one at the troops. Several are loading their rifles. Struck by a bullet, a man falls back clutching his throat. A fellow in a broad-brimmed hat clambers up over the broken lumber and wagon wheels to plant a German tricolour atop the barricade, while three others carry a wounded comrade off to the left. And in the centre, a scene of surreal calm: a woman and her three sons pick the lead from a casement window and melt it in order to pour balls of shot for the fighters. A screen of white smoke rises behind her, allowing the viewer to see her head inclined towards her boys in sharp outline. They look as if they are roasting marshmallows by the fireplace at home. Notwithstanding the action unfolding around them, it is they who keep drawing the viewer's attention.

The title of this image by the lithographer F. G. Nordmann suggests authenticity: *Barricade on the Corner of Kronen- and Friedrichstraße on 18 March by an Eyewitness*. But the scene as we see it is a highly composed ensemble. Whereas the barricade fighting of that night was done mainly by artisans, especially journeymen and apprentices, the lithograph shows a rich social mix: several students in soft caps recalling the 'old German costume' of Friedrich Ludwig Jahn, two figures in top hats who appear to be men of the middle classes and a few workers clearly recognizable by their blue smocks. The diverse social references and the family scene at the heart of the image are there to make an argument: that the revolution is a thing of the people that brings together both sexes and all professions and social strata.[46] Nevertheless, in placing a female figure at the centre of the action, Nordmann's lithograph conveys a feature of the revolutions that was widely remarked by contemporaries.

Women were present in virtually all the tumults that shaped the course of the revolutions of 1848. They joined food and market riots and revolutionary crowds. Women helped to build barricades or brought food and drink to the men defending them. They tended to fallen fighters, founded and wrote for newspapers, sold broadsheets, sewed flags for the National Guard, the Democratic clubs or the Students' Legion and waved them from windows. In Berlin, women brewed coffee and passed bread rolls into the streets. An extra edition of the *Berlinische Zeitung* on 20 March reported that women and daughters, including ladies of the nobility and the wives of senior officials, had been seen carrying stones in baskets and aprons up to the rooftops and steeples of the churches as well as to their own windows in the upper storeys.[47] A woman described as a 'girl' was seen by a witness mustering a large troop of workers and ordering them to build a barricade.[48] In Paris, the dressmaker Adélaïde Bettrette was burned in the face while making gunpowder for barricade fighters during the February Revolution. The purse-maker Joséphine Clabot fought armed and dressed as a man on the barricades of the working-class district of Belleville in June. Among her comrades was the 76-year-old widow and veteran of previous insurrections Anne-Marie Henry, who led a group of women on the barricade of the rue des Trois-Couronnes.[49] In Berlin, eleven women were among the dead of 18 March and there were numerous women among the dead of Milan.[50] During the June Uprising in Prague, women and girls were seen tending to the wounded and carrying arms.[51] When a conspiracy of conservative army officers threatened to bring down the revolutionary Provisional Government in Bucharest in June 1848, a 42-year-old pistol-wielding patriot by the name of Ana Ipătescu led a crowd into the Royal Palace and liberated the captured ministers. In the spring and summer of 1849, women joined the radical south-German militias that fought to turn back the counter-revolution, sometimes in a command role.[52]

Yet getting a grip on the activities of women and their impact on the course of the revolutions is difficult, not just because their participation was distributed across such a wide range of milieus and activities, but because the texts that allow us to gauge the extent of their contribution – newspaper reports, police records, and painted or engraved images – are for the most part the work of men. The visual images that survive of life inside the clubs formed by radical women, for example, often used in history books to illustrate accounts of female activism, are without exception caricatures drawn by male cartoonists. They throng with a menagerie of negative female types who nurse squalling infants or neglect unruly children, smoke, gossip or shout over each other. The images that survive of armed women mainly relate to the revolutionary Parisian female militia known as the Vésuviennes. And yet the Vésuviennes never existed; they were a fantasy that derived partly from folklore and partly from a hoax recruiting poster printed by the radical Daniel Borme in March 1848.[53] Borme's poster announced that since women were to acquire the rights of citizenship, they must also take on the military responsibilities of their male fellow citizens. To be eligible, one need merely be 'between the ages of fifteen and fifty' and 'unmarried'. The idea was picked up by the liberal press, which published images showing buxom uniformed women cuckolding their credulous husbands, smoking pipes or cigars, and sporting little beards and moustaches. Some of these depictions were erotically charged, some contemptuous; none tells us anything of substance about the actual participation of women in the violence of revolution. In Vienna, one satirical paper reported that 'free women' were being recruited to an 'Amazon Legion' in Paris, adding that since women tended to be most enraged when they were at home, it might be a good idea to bring along their husbands 'to ensure that they remain in a state of constant eruption'.[54]

If we focus instead on the utterances of mobilized women, we find that their aspirations were just as diverse and just as embedded in local networks and circumstances as those of the men around them. The first edition of *La Voix des Femmes*, a Parisian daily edited by the radical Eugénie Niboyet, contained a 'Profession of Faith' that insisted on women's right to share in the fruits of the new revolution. Employing a rhetorical technique that had been sharpened in the 1830s and 1840s (ch. 5), Niboyet prised open the contradictions of the liberal patriarchal order. Together, she wrote, a man and a woman united in matrimony surely constitute the composite 'social individual' on which the social order is built. But wouldn't the stability of this fundamental building block suffer if one allowed men to progress while one held women back? 'An abyss would soon open up between them.' And why should the right to vote be afforded to men and withheld from women? The standard reply was that a man's vote was 'complex', because he made his choice on behalf of his family. But if this was so, Niboyet asked, why did this 'complexity' suppress the separate rights of wives and daughters, and not those of sons? Democracy, a system founded on the collective choices of multitudes, was surely ill served by a franchise in which 'the least intelligent male citizen possesses the right to vote and the most intelligent female one does not'.[55] The emphasis on political rights was even stronger in a manifesto drawn up by the recently founded Society for the Emancipation of Women. Why, the authors asked, applying a familiar liberal argument, should women continue to pay taxes in whose passage into law they had had no say? Women must come together with men in drawing up laws to realize their common interest.[56]

About five weeks later, a twenty-four-point petition entitled 'Demands of the Radical Hungarian Women' appeared in the *Pesti Divatlap* (Pest Fashion Magazine), a patriotic and liberal journal that had been running since 1844 and catered mainly to prosperous and educated women of the Hungarian-speaking gentry and middle classes. This document, which claimed to have been signed by 'several hundred Hungarian women', asserted the right of women to take a larger part in public life and insisted on their importance to the revolution, but the agenda was otherwise quite different from Niboyet's 'Profession of Faith'. Article 1 demanded that Hungarian women 'comprehensively fulfil the requirements of intellectual development and know, at least in outline . . . the situation, constitution, laws, political relations, and history of Hungary and the world'. The Hungarian woman should be able to speak 'modestly as befits a female, but also sensibly on every public affair'. The Hungarian woman should always be ready to support patriotic enterprises (Arts. 2, 3 and 12) and this should include (Arts. 8 and 9) speaking only Hungarian in order to establish it as 'the reigning language of domestic and social circles'. As a mother, she should raise 'ardent, loyal Hungarian sons and daughters for the homeland' (Art. 4) and refuse to teach them any foreign languages (Art. 10) until they speak the national one 'clearly, beautifully, and fluently'. Hungarian women should not 'waste their money on foreign goods', should keep only Hungarian servants (no English or French governesses!), read only Hungarian newspapers and books, and cultivate only Hungarian fashions, sporting the national costume 'not only on holidays, but constantly in domestic circles' (Arts. 11, 14, 15, 17, 18 and 20).[57]

In this manifesto, the cause of women was almost entirely merged with that of the nation – a striking example of how nationalism could absorb other priorities. And this commitment to the nation was coupled with middle-class and gentry resentment of the old ruling elites. The ideal Hungarian woman evoked in the 'Demands' was the behavioural antipode of the aristocratic *grande dame*. 'Traitorous degenerate girls' who read only foreign papers and novels would be expelled from the circles of the new Hungarian woman, whose Hungarian clothes would be beautiful but also simple and economical: 'The aristocratic golden age of gold lace and silver flourishes has passed' (Art. 20). Her deportment would embody the gestural and emotional thrift of the middle classes, rejecting forever the flamboyance and largesse of the aristocratic lady: 'We demand that indecent flirting, affectation, stiff correctness, ostentation, shrewishness, and other weaknesses that are so opposed to the genuine character of a Hungarian woman be forever banished from our circles' (Art. 22).

The women who composed and signed this petition were radical in their cultural politics and in their repudiation of the magnate elite, but their advocacy on behalf of women *as women* was strikingly modest, even regressive. The Hungarian woman with a literary vocation who took up her pen in support of her homeland was warned not to forget 'the women's realm and responsibilities'. The document had much to say about the Hungarian woman's duties – to nation, husband, family, children, the poor, etc. – but nothing to say about her rights. There was no reference to the right to vote or to stand for election, to own and dispose of property or to be admitted to university. Formidable caveats were attached to her access to the public sphere: 'she should avoid . . . endless, pedantic politicizing' and occupy herself instead with 'matters agreeable to a woman's temper', such as the arts, literature and social life (Art. 1).

The contrasting objectives of the women of Paris and Pest are not surprising if we bear in mind the very different milieus in which women were politically active. The gender politics of the radical women around *La Voix des Femmes* in Paris was also a class politics. The editor received and published petitions from working women and the paper's leader articles repeatedly insisted on the inseparability of the workers' cause from their own.[58] In aligning the patriotism of the Hungarian woman with the expectations of the educated and propertied bourgeoisie, the activists in Pest also articulated a socially embedded politics of class. In Paris and Pest, the tendency to attach the cause of women to a not explicitly gendered transformative programme pulled female advocacy in different directions. The preference of the Pest women for duties over rights was, as we have seen, a feature of nationalist discourses more generally. In April 1848, as the elections approached, *La Voix des Femmes* published a statement entitled 'What the socialists want' and signed off by 'Jeanne Marie', who was probably Jenny d'Héricourt, vice-president of the Society for the Emancipation of Women. In it, d'Héricourt characterized socialism as a vision focused on the happiness of society as a whole and merged the call for an end to the 'slavery' of women with a palette of demands on behalf of the weakest groups – workers, children, invalids.[59]

To this one should add that the oppression of women functioned on so many levels – inferior education, exposure to violence and sexual predation, legal disabilities, moral double standards, exclusion from the franchise, wage discrimination, the cultural transmission of polarized gender norms – that it was difficult to know where to start: schooling? Marriage and divorce? Labour protection? Moral reform? The right to vote? The right to stand for election? This, too, helps to explain the very disparate viewpoints within the networks of politically engaged women. Jenny d'Héricourt, Eugénie Niboyet, Désirée Gay and Jeanne Deroin were interested in franchise reform because for them the revolutionary struggle of women – as for disenfranchised working-class men – was about the meaning of citizenship, though they were also interested in labour protection, poverty, schooling and other questions. Countess Blanka Teleki, a prominent figure in the Hungarian revolution who had opened a patriotic school for girls, believed that women should first educate themselves for participation in political life and only later seek enfranchisement – her central concern was the creation of a female elite cadre capable of supporting the nation in its struggle for independence.[60] When the women around *La Voix des Femmes* invited George Sand, whom they admired for her counter-cultural persona and her radical politics, to stand for election to the National Assembly, Sand responded in a haughty letter to the editor of *La Réforme*:

> A journal edited by ladies has announced my candidature for the National Assembly. If this joke merely wounded my vanity by imputing to me a ridiculous pretension, I would let it pass as one of those gags to which any one of us in this world can fall prey. But my silence could lead people to believe that I adhere to the principles that this journal intends to spread. I therefore ask you to receive and make known the following declaration:
>
> 1: I very much hope that no elector will waste his vote by being foolish enough to write my name on his ballot.
>
> 2: I do not have the honour of knowing any of the ladies who form clubs and edit newspapers. . . .
>
> I cannot permit that I be adopted, without my consent, as the representative of a female coterie with which I entertain not the slightest relationship, good or bad.[61]

Political emancipation would come one day, George Sand believed, but that day was still far off. To press the matter now was to indulge in 'childish games'.[62] Marie d'Agoult agreed. In her *History of the*

Revolution of 1848, she gave short shrift to the women who had become active as feminists in the wake of Saint-Simon and Fourier. In embracing the sectarian excitement of these esoteric movements, she argued, they had succumbed to the agitations of an overstimulated fancy. Some, locked in battle with their own minds – this may have been a coded reference to Claire Démar (ch. 2) – had taken their own lives. There was no sympathy here for the 'bedazzlement' that had engulfed Suzanne Voilquin when she first entered the circles around Prosper Enfantin.[63] These tensions around the question of how women should become active in their own interest were obviously not a uniquely female predicament. But the difficulty of establishing an order of priorities or a consensus on objectives impeded the efforts of activist women to renegotiate the terms of their legal and political inferiority. In the 'Age of Questions', it did not seem possible – for the moment at least – to disentangle the Woman Question from the other questions around it.[64]

The mainstream liberal press in Vienna, Berlin and Paris was full of approving reports of women embroidering flags or raising funds for charitable activities in support of the new government. And we can read everywhere in the daily newspapers of women waving ribbons and kerchiefs from windows, a picture that warmed middle-class male hearts because it reconciled female support for the revolution with decorousness and domesticity. 'As unforgettable as the momentous events of 15 March', Moritz Saphir wrote, was 'the beautiful, touching and universal involvement of the Viennese women. They waved ribbons from the windows, donated pretty flags to the National Guard, brought food and drink and always their kerchiefs were waving, and always their voices could be heard above the general hubbub.'[65]

On the other hand, women who sought to enter the public sphere as autonomous agents, whether through franchise reform, lobbying, journalism, involvement in associations, the foundation of kindergartens or simply participation in political rituals, risked encountering the scepticism, mockery or hostility of men. Conservative and republican journals alike derided the feminist socialists as mannish blue-stockings and 'divorceuses'.[66] A letter published in *La Voix des Femmes* by a certain Henriette, an artist, reported that she and her many fellow petitioners – women artists and workers of Paris – had struggled to get any publicity at all for a petition they had drawn up and sent to the Provisional

Government: 'Copies of the petition went to most of the papers, there were personal visits, entreaties, no stone was left unturned on our part. ... Every day the papers published new petitions, but alas! ours never arrived. ... The conspiracy of silence has entirely succeeded . . .'[67]

For Dragojla Jarnević, a 36-year-old schoolteacher and poet in Karlovac, capital city of the Kingdom of Croatia-Slavonia within the Austrian Empire, the revolution brought a painful sense of exclusion. 'Day by day', she wrote in her diary on 16 April, 'I regret that I am not a man, so that I can join the circles of action in which the whole of Europe is caught up; everything is politicized, small and great transactions take place, only I am not allowed.'[68] Women were excluded from active participation in the institutions that emerged from the revolutions. They were denied membership of the democratic clubs – this is one reason why some radical women established clubs of their own.[69] None of the new parliaments admitted women as deputies. The discussion of votes for women elicited guffaws and hoots from the deputies at Frankfurt and was dismissed out of hand. The admission of women as spectators was at first controversial. It was only by means of a complicated ruse that the writer Malwida von Meysenbug, a friend and the wives of a few deputies managed to smuggle themselves into St Paul's for the last public session of the pre-parliament, convened to arrange the elections for the National Assembly. The women crouched together in the pulpit, concealed by the long tricolour banners draped in front of it, peering down onto the assembly and discussing in whispers the political orientations of the speakers.[70] If most parliaments did eventually allow women to take seats in the galleries, this was because it was universally acknowledged that women belonged to and could embody the nation, even if they were excluded from the process of representing it politically. As spectators, they became the sounding board for the performances of the men, passive partners in the business of representation. They shared in the excitement and drama of the debates, but without being able to speak. Julie Pagenstecher, wife of the Wuppertal physician and moderate liberal deputy Alexander Pagenstecher, wrote to her son Carl in words that convey the tensions in the role of the female spectator: 'One really does get swept into the politics, but I take care not to say a word and don't tell a soul about what I am writing here, it always sounds too silly when women talk about it, and anyway I have to tell you something because Daddy hasn't the time [to write].'[71] Even as spectators in parliament, women were still waving from windows.

Parliaments were special places, charged with political purpose, but in other venues, too, the presence of politically or socially engaged women could trigger hostile male responses. On 21 May 1848, the Fête de la Concorde took place on the Champ de Mars in Paris. There were allegorical figures representing liberty, equality, fraternity and the friendship uniting the nations of France, Germany and Italy. The attractions included music, processions, floats and, most importantly, a troop of 500 young working women from Paris. Dressed in white and wearing crowns of oak leaves, they represented a cross-section of the predominantly female trades of the city: shawl-makers, seamstresses, fringers, corset-makers, lacemakers, porcelain painters and makers of artificial flowers. Others worked in retail or domestic service, and some stated that they were without work and living with their parents. These women had not simply been drafted by the authorities: they had applied to take part. Henriette Bécat had written to the authority tasked with organizing the festival, expressing her 'ardent desire' to be chosen along with her little sister. Joséphine Saleilles hoped to be there with two friends and wrote to the mayor begging him to 'do us the greatest favour of being able to take part in a great festival and the great joy of attending the ceremony'.[72] In his memoirs, the Paris police chief, Marc Caussidière, a man of the republican left, recalled the extreme excitement of the girls, many of whom had not slept on the night before the ceremony, 'so much importance had they attached to [it]'.

On the other hand, when workers from the women's National Workshops in the first arrondissement asked their director for banners to mark their delegation in the parade, he refused, on the grounds that 'it [was] not suitable for women to involve themselves in political festivals'. As it happened, even the 500 girls met with a very mixed response from the spectators. Among the dignitaries sitting on the tribune was the parliamentary deputy Alexis de Tocqueville. Tocqueville was clearly on edge that day: he had brought his pistol along in case there was trouble. Nothing about the festivities pleased him, but it was the 500 young women who offended him most. The majority, he noted, 'wore their virginal costumes in so virile a fashion that one could have taken them for boys dressed as girls'. Their arms appeared excessively muscular, more accustomed to hard labour than picking flowers (what had he expected?), and when one of the women, struggling with nerves, recited a poem for Alphonse Lamartine, Tocqueville recoiled at the sight of the 'large young girl' pulling 'frightful faces' as she spoke, her 'two coarse cheeks dripping in sweat'.[73] The Victorian playwright John Palgrave Simpson, who spent the early months of the revolution in Paris, also cast a fastidious eye over the 500, finding in them a poor advertisement for the famed beauty of Parisian women: 'had the famous "five hundred little girls in white" been chosen for the quality the very reverse of loveliness, they could scarcely have been better selected'.[74]

These may seem trivial observations of no larger political import, but they remind us of the hateful gaze to which women who entered public space exposed themselves, especially when they were construed as politicized subjects. The disgust felt by Tocqueville was partly political – he had no time for what he saw as pointless left-republican pageantry – but it was rooted in something deeper, something that focused his loathing not on the orchestrators of the event, but on the excited young women who had been allowed to take part in it. Even the women who sat quietly in the galleries of the Frankfurt National Assembly listening to the debates were lampooned by male journalists, who accused them of neglecting their children and families.[75] That undercurrent of ridicule and contempt, a contempt that felt instinctive and thus 'natural' to those who entertained it, was one of the most powerful weapons in the armoury of the patriarchal order. Nothing better demonstrates its power than the fact that it infiltrated the awareness of so many women, even the most politically active ones, who struggled to reconcile their activism with 'inherited notions of womanliness'.[76]

It is difficult to decide what is more striking – the tireless advocacy of the women activists or the immovability of the patriarchal structure they were challenging. Those women who pushed directly at the legal and political disabilities of women achieved remarkably little. Women were not enfranchised anywhere in Europe in 1848 – there was no women's equivalent of Schoelcher's act of abolition. In most European countries, female suffrage was withheld until 1918–19; in France, it was not granted until 1946. The oppressive French laws relating to divorce – the bête noire of radical activists since the 1830s – remained in place in France until 1884. The Napoleonic Civil Code, so crushing in its implications for married women, remained in place in the Low Countries until 1905. The underlying reason for this has often been remarked: in the emergent 'bourgeois society' of the early to mid nineteenth century, gender norms had become more, not less, polarized, meaning that the dramatic expansion of political participation that occurred in that year took men to places that the women could not reach.[77] Those women who challenged patriarchy directly found that Claire Démar had been right: it remained the most impregnable and fundamental of all the bastions of inequality.

Women succeeded better, at least in the medium term, when they worked with, rather than against, the prevailing norms and expectations of mid-nineteenth-century society. Advocacy for the education of girls and young women was less objectionable to many men (and women) because it corresponded to widespread assumptions about the role of mothers in the education of the young. The kindergarten movement founded by the radical German pedagogue Heinrich Froebel is a good example. Froebel's *Sketch of a Plan ... for Founding and Developing a German Kindergarten ... Presented to German Wives and Maidens*, first published in 1840, combined a highly innovative approach to early education with a vision of professionalized care for the young that would 'rescue the female sex from its hitherto passive and instinctive situation and, through its nurturing mission raise it to the same level as the male sex'. The plan lay dormant until 1848, when it was picked up by the new cohort of young, radical women and forty-four new kindergartens were opened.[78] Malwida von Meysenbug was drawn to the idea by its radical pedagogy, but also by the professional opportunities it offered to women: 'That only girls and women should lead the kindergarten, that Froebel wished to entrust early childhood education only to women, seemed to me a delightful thought.'[79]

Tied up with the programme of the kindergarten movement was a vision of emancipation quite different from that of the socialists around the Parisian feminist newspapers or the radical Hungarian women of Pest. 'I foresaw an entirely new age dawning for woman', Henriette Breymann wrote in 1849, 'when she will ... bring to the broader community ... the spirit of motherhood in its deepest meaning and in its most varied forms.' The aim was to improve the standing of women not by propelling them into the roles already occupied by men, but by exalting the tasks they already performed, by making them, as Breymann put it, 'mothers to society and not just to their own households'.[80]

The notion that women should receive formal training to work in this sector was a further incentive, because it promised professionalization and the systematic recognition of achievement. In 1849, an association of women in Hamburg invited Froebel to conduct a kindergarten training course for young women. Among those enrolled in the Hochschule für Frauen, a teachers' college established in the following year, was Meysenbug. 'The young girls who attended', she later recalled, 'included some outstanding personalities, real intellectuals – they showed a special gift for mathematics.'[81]

Yet even in this relatively innocuous domain of activism, women faced the hostility and condescension of men. Henriette Breymann was shocked when a schoolmaster attending a conference in Rudolstadt in 1848 objected to the idea that women should be tasked with delivering a specific pedagogical approach: 'I have a horror', he declared, 'of philosophical women!' Even Froebel was repelled by the incipient professional ambition of the women attending the teacher-training courses. In 1851, the Prussian government banned the kindergartens, and the Hamburg Senate soon followed suit by shutting down the Hochschule für Frauen. Education for girls continued to expand, but mainly under the supervision of the Churches. In France, too, there was an impressive expansion of girls' education following the Falloux Law of 1850, which made it easier for religious communities to found faith schools. Male republicans mocked the Catholic girls' schools as obscurantist and regressive, but the Catholic schools, too, were committed to the education of girls and offered professional opportunities for gifted young women, especially nuns, that remained elusive elsewhere.[82] In Portugal, too, a dramatic expansion in girls' education took place after 1848, even if a headcount in 1858 revealed that fewer than 10 per cent of the children enrolled in public schools were female.[83]

For some literary women, becoming engaged as women had less to do with challenging the hegemony of men or entering the public sphere than with creating a space in which women could listen to the voices of other women. In a poem she published in 1848, the 27-year-old Cadiz-based poet Rosa Butler y Mendieta described herself interrupted during a trance-like contemplation of nature by an angel who comes to her from God to offer her a lyre, not so that she may aspire to compete with the illustrious male virtuosos of this instrument, but so that 'in your sufferings the lyre will serve as consolation'. When the poet gently objects that the histories of Rome and Greece are still unknown to her, the angel assigns her a poetic mandate that captures precisely the boundaries set by the cultural consensus for women's literary activity: 'Sing of the heavens and of the earth, of birds and flowers; . . . / and sing of your pain, sing the impressions you have experienced.'[84] And yet the women's literary periodicals that appeared in Spain in the early 1850s – such as *Ellas*, the *Gaceta del Bello Sexo* and *La Mujer* – did not perform a withdrawal into a politically deactivated and feminized space, but rather expressed an angry and rebellious determination to celebrate the genius and heroism of women.[85]

In many of the theatres of revolution, literary women found ways in the 1850s of exploring the meaning of the tumult for them. It is noteworthy that the novels written after 1848 by women who had been politically active during the revolutions often structured their narratives around difficult choices between active participation and withdrawal into safety and decorum, choices that were sometimes embodied in intense friendships between two women – one a nervous introvert drawn back into the domestic interior, the other a person of enterprise and daring who plunges out into the streets.[86] The idea that revolution confronted the individual with choices of this kind spoke in particular to women, who felt the polarity between shelter and exposure more starkly than men. Kathinka Zitz-Halein was a former activist in the German-Catholic movement, an advocate for women's activism and the founder of the Humania Association, an organization that dispensed aid to wounded, jailed or banished revolutionaries and their families. In the poem 'Forwards and Backwards', published in 1850, Zitz-Halein captured this sense of a choice between starkly polarized options:

> Forwards! call the apostles of light
> Let us be torches of truth and right.
> Backwards! howl the men of the dark
> Hide from the brightness of the spark.
>
> Forwards we struggle and forwards we strive
> The will to action keeps us alive.
> Backwards, if safety and wealth you prefer
> Back to the darkness of things as they were.

Forwards! the eagles call as they fly
On proud wings towards the sun in the sky.
Backwards! whimper the owls as they glide
Back to the holes that they cower inside.

Forwards! History will always show
That freedom's the noblest prize we know.
Backwards! Go feed your guts, not your heads
And you will raise slaves in your children's beds.[87]

Mapping the modulations of post-revolutionary awareness across the expanse of European women's literature is a task that lies beyond the horizons of this book, but it is worth noting that for today's historians of the revolutions, women writers provide a distinctive and uniquely valuable form of contemporary understanding and witness. Of the various eyewitness accounts that survive of life in Rome during 1848 and 1849, the diaries and journalism of the American feminist Margaret Fuller stand out for their combination of astute political analysis with an imaginative sympathy for all the key actors, regardless of their political orientation. Writing as 'Daniel Stern', Marie d'Agoult produced the best contemporary history of the Revolution of 1848 in France by a long margin. It was not just elegantly written, but analytically sharp and historiographically self-aware, unfolding its story within the framework of an enquiry into the role of class antagonisms in the causation and course of the revolution. It was also far more deeply researched than any of its competitors: d'Agoult trawled through the records of parliamentary debates, reports, proclamations and petitions; she also interviewed numerous contemporaries who had played a role in events, from Louis Blanc, whom she went to see in his exile on the island of Jersey, to Ange Guépin, the medical sage of Nantes, to the sometime Minister of War General Lamoricière, from whom she extracted a map illustrating the deployment of troops against the Parisian insurgents of June 1848. D'Agoult was remarkably even-handed in her distribution of criticism, finding crucial flaws in almost every key political actor.[88] Though she made little effort to hide her prejudices, she also strove to correct for them, and her principal characters, like Fuller's, remained three-dimensional and entitled to a portion, however small, of the reader's sympathy.

Marie Catherine Sophie, Countess d'Agoult, portrait by Henri Lehmann. Under the pseudonym 'Daniel Stern', d'Agoult, the daughter of an aristocratic French émigré who had settled in Germany, wrote the best contemporary history of the 1848 revolution in France. This three-volume work is not just elegantly written, but is deeply researched and develops a sophisticated argument about the social and political forces unleashed by the revolution. D'Agoult was among those mid-century women who chose a completely autonomous life, at odds with the bourgeois morality of her time, though without embracing the emancipationist politics of feminists like Jeanne Deroin and Suzanne Voilquin. Today she is best known for her relationship with Franz Liszt, with whom she had three children. D'Agoult never married Liszt and never divorced her husband, Count d'Agoult. Cosima, her second daughter by Liszt, later married Richard Wagner.

Cristina di Belgioioso never produced an historical canvas to compare with d'Agoult's, but her journalism on the revolution in Milan and the notes that became her memoirs also exhibit an emotional and intellectual detachment that allowed her to look past political affiliations and situate the key male actors of all persuasions within a large machinery of interaction and crisis. Bettina von Arnim, novelist and commentator on the Social Question, did not take part directly in the events of 1848 in Berlin, but during that year, to the horror of her relatives, she hosted not one but two salons. The first consisted mainly of conservative and liberal establishment figures from the noble milieu in which her family socialized; the second was a 'democratic' salon frequented by people like the new French ambassador to Berlin, Emmanuel Arago (François's brother), the Russian leftist Mikhail Bakunin, the left-republican Julius Froebel (nephew of Friedrich) and the Polish democrat Julia Molińska-Woykowska. Her correspondence during the months of turmoil reveals an unflagging effort to mediate among the different camps.[89]

Elevated social status (d'Agoult, Belgioioso, von Arnim) may have helped here, or the estranged perspective of an American in Rome (Fuller). But it surely also mattered that in the eyes of women, living and writing in such a sexually segregated world, the politicians and popular tribunes of 1848 were also visible as *men*. Whereas men saw each other as republicans, reactionaries, monarchists, liars, traitors, renegades, enemies, allies, mountebanks, firebrands and communists, women could, occasionally at least, perceive them as men trapped in the rivalries and antipathies of politics.[90] In *L'Opinion des femmes*, the socialist Jeanne Deroin suggested that women viewed the events of the revolution differently from their male counterparts. Women, Deroin declared, whatever their political views, were united in seeking a 'policy of peace and labour' to replace the 'egoistic and cruel policy' that drove men to destroy each other. 'Where men see nothing but the struggle and feel nothing but hatred, women see the suffering produced by the struggle and feel the pity.'[91]

LIBERTY AND RISK

'At half past three [we learn that] the shops are closed and that the military are shooting at citizens and so on! I run the short distance back home and by 4 p.m. there are several hundred barricades in Berlin! You should have seen me carrying stones and rolling blocks. ... All of the political prisoners have been freed (even the Poles), all the [political] trials have been cancelled.' Moritz Steinschneider, who wrote these words to his Prague fiancée, Auguste Auerbach, on 20 March 1848, was no born revolutionary. He had studied Talmud in Mikulov (Moravia) and Prague before moving to Vienna and Berlin to devote himself to the study of Oriental literatures and comparative philology. With time he would earn international renown as a prodigiously learned bibliographer and orientalist.[92] Steinschneider's academic work was recondite and technically demanding, but it was not narrow. For decades, he studied the role played by Jews throughout the Middle Ages as intercultural 'interpreters', collating and analysing every conceivable scrap of documentary evidence in a great number of languages in order to reconstruct 'the cultural transfer between Jews, Muslims and Christians, between Hebrew, Arabic and Latin scholarship, between authors, readers and translators'.[93]

What elated Steinschneider – he was twenty-two at the time – about the events in Berlin was not the revolutionary upheaval as such, but the falling away of the barriers between people:

> Hundreds of soldiers and civilians have fallen or been wounded, among them a remarkable number of Jews! They are preparing a general burial and memorial and – praise be to God – there is no longer any talk of 'Jew' or 'Christian'. Within four weeks, Prussia's Jews will have to be emancipated, because the people are emancipating them already. Who is thinking of themselves now? Over these days, the Berlin mob has made tremendous cultural progress, everywhere the consequences of the most recent events are undeniable![94]

To many Jews across Europe, especially younger men like Steinschneider, it seemed as if the bell of liberty was ringing at last in 1848. Many of the constitutions drafted by revolutionary groups and assemblies affirmed or implied the civil equality of the Jews: Article 4 of the 'Twelve Demands' published by the radicals in Pest on 15 March 1848 called for 'civil and religious equality before the law'. Point 21 of the Wallachian Proclamation of Islaz, later adopted as a quasi-constitution, announced the 'emancipation of the Israelites and political rights for the compatriots of other faiths'. Article 18 of the 'Waldeck Charter' drawn up by the

Prussian National Assembly in Berlin declared that 'the enjoyment of civil and political rights [was] independent of religious confession or the participation in any religious community'. The seventh of the 'fundamental principles' that opened the constitution of the Roman Republic of 1849 stipulated that 'the exercise of civil and political rights does not depend on religious belief', and the Kremsier constitution drawn up by the Austrian Reichstag stated (Art. 14) that 'the difference in religion cannot form the basis of any difference in the rights and duties of citizens'. These provisions (except for the Proclamation of Islaz) did not refer expressly to the Jews, and Jews were not the only group affected by them, but no other minority was as widely associated with the idea of religious freedom, and none had campaigned so effectively for it.

There was thus good reason for Steinschneider's enthusiasm. Across much of continental Europe, the outbreak of revolution in 1848 brought euphoria and a sense of widening horizons to Jewish communities. Jewish men fought and died on barricades, joined demonstrations and clubs, delivered speeches, signed petitions, edited liberal and radical newspapers, volunteered for the Civil Guards and patriotic militias, and served as deputies in the newly formed parliaments. Rabbis and Christian clergymen presided, as we have seen, over mixed funerals for the fallen of Vienna and Berlin, while in Rome fraternization lunches were held for Jews and Christians in the districts adjoining the ghetto. In the Venetian Republic, 'Citizen Rabbi' Abraham Lattes became a popular celebrity after he urged the men of his community to join the Civil Guards and contribute financially to the new republic.[95]

But if the revolutions brought real and lasting relief to many communities, they also brought new dangers. In Jewish communities that were already deeply divided between traditionalists and assimilationist modernizers, the revolution sparked (sometimes violent) factional conflicts. In Galician Lemberg/Lwów/L'viv, traditionalist Jews murdered the reformist rabbi Abraham Kohn, because they feared that he would use the revolutionary upheaval to pursue his modernizing agenda.[96] In some borderland regions, the Jews were ground between the wheels of opposed national groups. The ameliorations granted by some revolutionary executives were rescinded when the authority of those executives waned. Most importantly, perhaps, the prospect of Jewish emancipation stirred popular antagonism, as parts of the Christian majority mobilized against the changes unfolding around them. In some regions, the revolutions were marked from the outset by an upsurge in violence against Jewish persons and property; among their legacies would be new and virulent forms of anti-Jewish prejudice.

Until 1848, Jews in most of central and southern Europe lived under restrictive special laws. In the Habsburg provinces of Lombardy and Venetia, they could not stand for election for the municipal assemblies, occupy civil or judicial posts, or practise the profession of pharmacist or notary, and they were still subject to a specifically Jewish jurisdiction.[97] In Habsburg Moravia, Jews were confined to specific towns, mostly market towns in the Czech-speaking south and the centre of the country, where they resided in clearly demarcated Jewish districts.[98] In Rome, capital city of the Papal States, they remained cloistered in their ghetto in the Rione Sant-Angelo on the banks of the Tiber, subject to special taxes and tributes, denied access to important social benefits, tightly controlled in their movements outside the city and obliged to take part in a humiliating annual public ceremony in which a rabbi and two community leaders knelt before city officials in the presence of numerous local and foreign guests and recited a formula expressing their humility and imploring the authorities to treat the Jews with benevolence.[99] The practice of rewarding the rabbi for this performance by kicking him in the backside had died out by the nineteenth century, but, as a delegation of ghetto leaders put it on 14 January 1847 in a letter to Pius IX, the ceremony remained 'as painful to those who offer it as it is null and insignificant to those who receive it'.[100]

The picture is further complicated, especially in the Habsburg lands, by the fact that whereas some regulations were vigilantly policed, others were honoured in the breach. In Hungary, for example, Jews were banned from most professions and from many urban centres, but this did not prevent them from settling illegally in the cities and practising proscribed professions without papers.[101] There may have been as many as 10,000 illegal Jews in Vienna by 1848. The Jews of Habsburg Galicia were excluded from the membership of all professions and guilds and forbidden to practise as apothecaries, brewers, millers or even innkeepers – the traditional calling of the Jews in the Polish lands. But the local authorities made no effort to implement this last prohibition and about 2,000 Jewish innkeepers continued to ply their trade in Austrian Poland.[102]

Jews in the states of the German Confederation were subject to a bewildering variety of local regulations. On the eve of the revolutions, the Jews of the Duchy of Nassau were still what they had been in the eighteenth century: 'Schutzjuden', or 'protected Jews', without civil rights and subject to special restrictions.[103] The situation was especially complicated in the kingdom of Prussia. Here, an edict issued in 1812 at the height of the Napoleonic wars had defined the Jews currently settled in Prussia as 'nationals and citizens'. But the edict applied only to those provinces that belonged to Prussia *in 1812*, at the time of the edict's promulgation – it was not extended into the new Saxon, Polish and Rhenish-Westphalian territories that fell to Prussia as part of the territorial resettlement of 1814–15. And this meant that after 1815 the Jews of the Prussian lands lived under more than twenty different regional jurisdictions, each with its own regulations.

More importantly, the edict postponed judgement on the question of whether positions in government service would be made available to Jewish applicants.[104] After 1815, the Prussian authorities adopted a highly restrictive approach to this issue, on the grounds that the Christian character of the Prussian people obliged them to exclude non-Christians from the administrative and political life of the state. In 1830, when the Jewish Lieutenant Meno Burg, who had served with distinction ever since joining the Grenadier Guards as a volunteer rifleman in 1812, came up for promotion to captain, the king issued a Cabinet Order stating that, in view of his accomplishments and experience of life among Prussian officers, Burg ought to have the sense to recognize the truth and redeeming power of the Christian faith and thereby 'clear away any obstacle to his promotion'.[105]

In a world in which processes of standardization and the suppression of privilege and juridical exception were already well underway, the Jews continued to embody an older order in which privileges and special jurisdictions were the norm. The great exception was France. Here the link between religion and citizenship had been severed entirely by the revolutionary constitution of 1791, which embedded Jewish entitlements in a universal endorsement of citizenship and political rights. But, even here, the momentum of this development was temporarily reversed in 1808, when Napoleon, unnerved by complaints from Christian merchants and artisans in Strasbourg, imposed harsh restrictions on the economic activities of Jews in the German-speaking eastern départements. The law of 1808 lapsed again in France after the end of the wars, but in the areas of the Rhineland that fell under Prussian and Bavarian control, it remained on the statute books for decades.

The *Charte* of 1814 guaranteed 'freedom of religion' to all the citizens of France, but it also made special provision for the Catholic Church as the official state religion. Only after the revolution of 1830 was this special status revoked; in the revised version, Catholicism was described merely as the religion 'professed by the majority of the French'. On 8 February 1831, the July Monarchy extended the state support paid to Catholic and Protestant clergy to rabbis, thus fully recognizing Jewish religious equality. One odious remnant of discrimination survived, the so-called *more judaico*, which obliged Jews to read out a humiliating text when swearing oaths before certain courts. Through the efforts of Adolphe Crémieux, who would join the Provisional Government in February 1848, the oath was finally abolished in 1846.

As even this brief overview makes clear, the journey of the Jews out of negative privilege into a form of citizenship indistinguishable from that of others had never been a straightforward process. Edicts announcing 'toleration' and 'emancipation' were not framed as the expression of universal or human rights, but as one-off concessions to a specific social group in a particular territory, concessions that could be withdrawn again or allowed to lapse. Geopolitical change could bring radical transformations in the legal environment, as happened to the Jews in those areas of western Germany and Italy that were annexed to metropolitan France during the Great Disruption and later returned to more conservative management. Only in the 1840s did momentum begin to build behind the idea of an encompassing liberation of the Jews from their disabilities. In the mid 1840s, the Prussian provincial diets began calling for the concession of full civil rights to Jews. In the session of 1839–40, the lower chamber of the Hungarian Diet voted overwhelmingly for a bill proposing that the Jews be placed on an equal footing with the non-noble populations of the country.[106] There was a loosening of legal controls in Hanover and Hamburg in 1842 and even in relatively strict Bavaria in 1847.[107] In Baden, the liberal majority in the new parliament (Landtag) of 1846 resolved by a majority of two to one to request a law of emancipation from the government.[108] In the autumn of 1847, the issue was taken up by the most important liberal papers in Tuscany – *Il corriere livornese*, *L'alba*, *La patria* and *Il popolo*. In December 1847, the Piedmontese liberal leader, Massimo d'Azeglio, published the essay

'On the Emancipation of the Jews', composed in the form of an open letter to the Pope; d'Azeglio decried the squalor of the Roman ghetto, reminded his readers that the abject condition of its inhabitants was the consequence of legal discrimination and prejudice, and insisted that Christians had a moral obligation to grant to the Jews the freedoms and opportunities that they themselves enjoyed.[109]

Jewish activists and publicists became increasingly important in the campaign for emancipation. The case of Adolphe Crémieux and his battle against the *more judaico* showed that skilful advocacy in the public sphere could on occasion bring about change for the better, and there were other Jewish spokesmen, such as Gabriel Riesser in Hamburg or Johann Jacoby in Königsberg, who spoke up in public for the cause of Jewish rights. Well-run petition campaigns by Jewish leaders helped to bring about the relaxation of anti-Jewish regulations in Bavaria in 1847, and on New Year's Day 1848 the editor of *Der Orient* noted that the Jewish press had at last come of age as an instrument for the defence of Jewish rights.[110]

But the same dynamic could work in the opposite direction, when 'Christian' interests succeeded in pressuring the authorities to withdraw Jewish entitlements or impose new restrictions, or when opinion turned against the Jews for one reason or another. This helps to explain the non-linear character of the process: whereas the lower chamber of the Hungarian Diet of 1839–40 passed a bill of Jewish emancipation (subsequently rejected by the upper chamber), an almost identical bill failed in the lower house four years later in 1843–4, partly because the deputies of the cities opposed it; in the final session before the outbreak of the revolutions (1847–8), the historic session that would produce the April Laws, Jewish emancipation was not even on the agenda.[111]

It was common for governments to reject the loosening of restrictions on the grounds that this would provoke protests from vested interests, or even stir unrest and endanger public order. In Hesse-Kassel and Hamburg, for example, the government's reluctance to dismantle guild privileges was a serious obstacle to the integration of the Jews into what was still in many respects a 'Christian economy'.[112] And this meant in turn that states were not the only agency determining the course of emancipation or the meanings of 'citizenship'. The Jews of Baden, for example, were citizens of the Grand Duchy in a statutory sense, yet they were excluded by local laws and regulations of various kinds from residence in over 80 per cent of the territory's cities.[113] In Habsburg Galicia, despite a Patent permitting Jews to settle in the whole of the province, many of the towns insisted on invoking their ancient privilege *de non tolerandis Judaeis* and refused admission to Jews.[114]

In short, the notion of emancipation as a forward-driven, unitary transformation defined teleologically by a striving for the liberation of society does as little justice to the historical experience of Jewry before and during 1848 as it does to the experience of women and enslaved Africans. The removal of Jewish legal disabilities was a drawn-out, haphazard affair that proceeded with halting steps at varying speeds in different times and places. In many jurisdictions, policymaking was based on the assumption that emancipation, far from being a 'right', was something the Jews would have to earn, as the Privy Council of Electoral Hesse put it, by leaving behind 'activities dishonourable to the citizen', such as 'brokering, peddling, personal loans and the sale of second-hand goods'.[115] Yet these were precisely the niches into which centuries of occupational restrictions had pushed the great majority of European Jews; requiring their abandonment was one sure way to delay emancipation indefinitely. The picture was further complicated by the fact that efforts to push the agenda of emancipation forward tended to trigger powerful countercurrents within the surrounding society. The journey to emancipation, Reinhard Rürup has written, was 'tortuous and thorny'; it makes more sense to think of emancipation as a multitude of meandering 'paths', rather than a road plotted out in advance to reach a specific goal.[116]

The festival of Purim fell on 20 March in 1848. This feast commemorates an episode recounted in the Book of Esther from Persia in the fourth century BCE. The Jew-hating Haman, Prime Minister to the Persian king Ahasverus, plots to exterminate the Jews of all Persia, but he is outmanoeuvred by Esther, Ahasverus's Jewish queen. Haman falls from power and is executed. After a bloody settling of accounts, Mordechai, a Jewish resident of the city of Shushan, takes Haman's place as the most powerful minister in the kingdom. The festival is a joyful one, recalling a moment of deliverance and triumph. In the mind of Moritz Steinschneider, who wrote to his fiancée Auguste on that day, the Berlin of 1848 and the Shushan of ancient times merged and the Purim story seemed full of positive portent. Things looked different to the anonymous Berlin correspondent of *Der Orient*, a Leipzig-based journal focused on Jewish life in past and present. This correspondent also made the connection with Purim as he pondered the meaning of the latest political events in Europe, but to him the messages appeared more ambivalent. A weak and vacillating king, a reactionary Jew-hating minister, a bloody revolution: how much had really changed? In France, to be sure, the left-liberal Jewish lawyer Adolphe Crémieux, a modern Mordechai, had just been appointed to the Provisional Government. And yet, at the same time, Europeans 'drunk on freedom' were celebrating that freedom by attacking and beating Jews and pillaging their property in Alsace and Baden. The Frankfurt city senate had just turned down a proposal to abolish legal discrimination against the non-Christian confessions. 'In France', the correspondent wrote, 'Mordechai occupies a ministerial post; in Germany, there are legions of Hamans!' Freedom, it seemed, was no docile handmaid, but 'a badly behaved daughter who lashes out in every direction'.[117]

At nine o'clock in the evening of 27 April 1847, Mayor Neumann of Landsberg (today Gorzów Wielkopolski) on the Warta River wrote in panic to the Provincial Government in Frankfurt an der Oder requesting military reinforcements. The city was in 'a state of complete tumult'. Since five in the afternoon, more than a thousand people of the 'labouring class', men and women and children, had been pouring through the town 'screaming for work and food'. Towards eight o'clock it seemed that the tumult might be dying down, but then the storm bell began to ring and 'the whole crowd of them' surged towards the Wallstraße, in order to empty the potato stores of Louis Boas in the cellar he rented from the merchant Itzigsohn. 'The whole mob of them are still busy with that right now', the magistrate wrote.

> It appears that the rioters intend, after satisfying their needs, to make their way to the Roßwiese, in order to destroy there a distillery belonging to Louis Boas. We urgently request: please be so kind as to order some military units to come to us by requisition of the high general command, since we lack any means whatsoever of repressing these tumults. In the meanwhile, we will try and see if we can calm down the aroused population with the help of our citizens. May Heaven grant that the liquor stores they are storming are not actually broken into.[118]

Across Europe, the price surges and food shortages of 1847 produced waves of violence (ch. 1), in which the Jews were often prominent
targets – Louis Boas and the merchant Itzigsohn of Landsberg were
both Jewish. When he encountered an angry gathering of men, women
and children waiting near a bridge, Mayor Neumann asked them what
they were after and received the reply: 'We are waiting for potato wagons that were bought by Jews. We and our families are forced to starve,
and the Jews alone are responsible for this, so it is right to punish them
severely.'[119] In Prague and other Bohemian cities, there were attacks on
Jewish textile firms in the spring and early summer of 1847. In north
Baden, officials discovered a pamphlet circulating early in April that
named the nobility and the Jews as the chief enemies of the people and
the prospective targets of violent reprisals:

1. The nobility must be destroyed;
2. The Jews must be driven out of Germany;
3. The kings, dukes and princes must go; Germany must become a free
   country like America;
4. All officials must be murdered. Then things will go well in Germany.[120]

Even before the February Revolution in Paris, then, a pattern was
emerging that linked the pressure of social distress with an anti-Jewish
sentiment that served in moments of crisis to focus anger on specific
enterprises and individuals. As the revolutions broke out in the spring
of 1848, a wave of violence unfolded across eastern France, southern
Germany and the Habsburg monarchy whose focus was unequivocally
anti-Jewish.

The trouble began in Alsace. Here, as elsewhere, there had been sporadic outbursts of anti-Jewish feeling as the effects of the poor harvest of
1846 and the collapse of the potato crop made themselves felt, but it was
the revolution in Paris that triggered an escalation. The news of the proclamation of the Republic reached Altkirch, a small town on the border
with Switzerland, early in the evening of 26 February. Within hours,
crowds attacked and plundered the houses of Jews, sometimes beating
the occupants. There was more looting on the following morning (27
February), during which the crowd broke into the synagogue, destroyed
devotional objects and defiled the interior. Further looters arrived from
the nearby villages and towns. Not until the arrival of troops, from the

garrison towns of Hüningen and Belfort, was order restored. Similar outbreaks occurred across the region, forcing the Jews in many districts to flee into neighbouring Baden and Switzerland.[121]

Troops called to the scene were shocked by the scale of the destruction. In the town of Dürmenach they found that more than one hundred houses had been sacked – the streets were full of debris of every kind. 'It looks absolutely like a village that has been taken by armed force and then retaken several times', the commander reported. Another account described the villages of Ober- and Niederhagenthal, where officials found that 'all the houses of the Jews' had been 'entirely pillaged and devastated'. Such was the boldness of the looters that, having stolen everything they could carry out of the houses, they had ordered carriages, so that they could transport it all back to their own homes.[122] In many places, the forces of order proved ineffective: garrison troops were usually dependable, if slow to act, but in some towns the National Guard extorted 'protection fees' from the Jews, in others they sided openly with the attackers. In Marmoutier, between 500 and 600 people gathered and marched to Saverne to liberate looters who had been jailed there; when they arrived, they were joined by workers who wanted to release a butcher who had been locked up for assaulting a Jew. Overwhelmed by these numbers, the gendarmes of Saverne and a contingent of sixty National Guards simply withdrew. It was not just a matter of forcing the Jews to leave their domiciles; in some cases, packs of locals gathered to waylay them on the main exit routes, beating them with wooden staves as they fled from the area. On one such occasion, a small child was so seriously injured that it died on the following day. The worst disturbances were over by the end of the first week of March, but sporadic outbreaks of looting and assault carried on into the last week of April, after which peace returned to the region.[123]

There was nothing new about Jews being blamed for price surges and food shortages – though the duration and scale (there were reports of crowds numbering up to 3,000 in some villages) were unusual. Witnesses reported the presence of some artisans and landowning peasants and the occasional fanatical priest, but the perpetrators were for the most part landless rural labouring people, the social stratum most exposed to the effects of the economic downturn. Two things made these tumults especially unsettling. First, France was a country where the process of legal emancipation had been largely accomplished. How were such scenes possible in towns where neighbours were also fellow citizens? Second, the looters were often heard crying *Vive la République!* and singing the 'Marseillaise' as they went about their work. What they meant by that is difficult to ascertain, and of course no one took the trouble to ask them. Perhaps they saw in the news from Paris the signal of a general loosening of discipline, a moment to shed inhibitions. Or perhaps revolution meant liberation from an economic distress for which they blamed the local Jews, as the poorest European Christians had done for centuries. Whatever the motivations, the violence, and particularly the flight of French Jews into neighbouring Switzerland and the Grand Duchy of Baden, were mortifying for the new government, especially as they risked giving the impression that the new management was not in control of the country. The justice minister, Crémieux, and his non-Jewish colleagues urged the authorities in Alsace to take firm action and a Jewish special commissar was sent to the region to investigate the excesses and see to the prevention of further outrages.[124]

The violence in Alsace was just the beginning of a wave of anti-Jewish rioting and unrest that swept across Europe 'from Amsterdam to Rome' during the early months of the revolution.[125] On 4 March, there were outbreaks of anti-Jewish unrest across Baden. Houses were stoned, looted or burned. On 17 March, during a torchlit procession in honour of the Hungarian revolutionary leader Lajos Kossuth in Pressburg (Hungarian Poszony; today Bratislava in Slovakia), crowds of apprentices and labourers used the event to launch an attack on the Jews, throwing their torches onto the roofs of Jewish houses and subjecting the people inside them to brutal beatings.[126] In the weeks that followed, the violence gained in extent and intensity, culminating during early April in pogroms that spread from city to city. In Székesfehérvár, a town to which Jews had only relatively recently been admitted, it was reported on 14 April that the entire Jewish population, consisting of just sixty families, had been driven out of the town.[127] On 24 April alone, ten Jews were killed and forty wounded in Pressburg/Bratislava. In Grätz (Grodzisk Wielkopolski), a town in the Prussian province of Posen, Polish townsfolk occupied houses belonging to Jews, drove out the people inside them and then threw out onto the street and destroyed everything they could find in them – including doors and window frames.[128] Similar tumults took place in Thuringia in late April and early May, including in the little town of Lengsfeld, where a band of would-be looters forced the magistrate to sign a document 'officially' permitting them to plunder the Jews of the town.[129]

These attacks were wave-like in their near-simultaneity, but also intensely local, often pivoting on key personalities (mayors, commanders, administrators and Jewish community leaders) and embedded in very different geographies and social structures. Economic motives clearly played a role. Most, though not all, of the rioters were from the poorer social strata worst pressed by the crisis that had begun in the agrarian sector in 1846 and was still gnawing at trade and manufacturing in the spring of 1848. In the towns of central Europe, Jewish merchants and artisans were seen as unwelcome competition. In many rural areas, they occupied exposed positions on the front line between the most vulnerable credit providers and the most precarious clients. In rural areas with no credit institutions, where the Jews were the only ones willing to lend to local smallholders, this was a source of potential risk, especially in periods of economic crisis, when the anxiety and rage of defaulting debtors tended to focus on creditors.[130] Jews weren't the only creditors, of course. And in some areas of Baden, after the first wave of attacks on the houses and businesses of Jews, the unrest also focused on the estates of the great landowning families, and specifically on the offices where stewards recorded the taxes and other dues owing from tenants and smallholders.[131]

Popular published critiques of contemporary economic relations, and particularly those of the left, focused inordinate attention on the Jews. In the anti-Semitic tract *Les Juifs, rois de l'époque*, published in 1845, sold out and reissued two years later, the Anglophobe Fourierist Alphonse Toussenel had argued that modern finance and commerce were controlled by an 'alien' Jewish presence that had created a modernized form of 'feudalism'.[132] In 1846, Toussenel's arguments were endorsed and popularized in an article bearing the same title by the former Saint-Simonian and self-styled 'humanitarian' Pierre Leroux.[133] So it was not just a question of economic distress, but of the frameworks on offer to make sense of it, frameworks that focused the hostility to capitalism on a small minority of its representatives. It is unlikely that the unemployed day labourers who stole bedding from Jewish homes in Hüningen had ever read Toussenel or Leroux, but the flysheets and pamphlets that appeared during these episodes of unrest suggest that arguments linking the Jews to 'feudal' capitalist 'exploitation' were ambient. This makes it easier to understand why looters and arsonists sang the 'Marseillaise' or chanted *Vive la République!* Identifying the Jews as a metonym for the dysfunctions of a society passing through crisis enabled the diversity of 'daily experiences and contacts' with actual Jewish people to be displaced by 'negative schemata and stereotypes'.[134]

One might thus say that this was one area in which the stresses generated by the general crisis of 1846–8, focused by a readily available and popular hermeneutic, spilled over directly into lawbreaking and tumult, the Jews being easier targets than wealthy and powerful Christians. But the timing of the violence suggests that political prompts were important too. In Baden, the troubles began with rumours that the parliament of the Grand Duchy was about to grant the Jews full legal equality. In some districts, the citizens only agreed to end their attacks if the local Jews renounced their communal rights and privileges. The link between emancipation and violence was so tight that in one Baden commune the Jewish residents, terrified of further reprisals, even petitioned the Landtag not to emancipate them. In Pressburg, similar rumours triggered 'bloody and deplorable persecutions'.[135] In Pest, the rioting started on 21 March, the day on which a bill proposing municipal voting rights to all the residents of cities, regardless of religion, came before the Diet.[136] In Gleiwitz (today Gliwice in Poland), the circulation of pamphlets for and against the emancipation of the Jews prompted demonstrations on 1 May.[137] In short, the violence was not simply an expression of economic pain but a political protest against a specific policy.

In Rome, the news that Pope Pius IX planned to ease the residential restrictions on the Jews had already stirred such resentment in the summer of 1847, especially in the districts adjoining the ghetto, that public lunches were organized to try to reconcile the inhabitants of the Regola and Trastevere districts with their Jewish neighbours. The main orchestrator was the wine wholesaler and popular leader of the Campo Marzio district, Angelo Brunetti, known as Ciceruacchio (a nickname meaning 'chubby' or 'chickpea'). These were impressive events, not unlike the liberal and radical banquets of France – prominent Christian and Jewish leaders gave speeches and there were elaborate performances of fraternity in which workers from the abattoirs dined with Jews, or Christian and Jewish crowds bearing torches approached each other, offered mutual greetings and then merged before processing through the ghetto into Trastevere. Pamphlets and leaflets painted the event in sympathetic colours. These efforts continued through the winter and into the spring. On 26 March 1848, the canon Ambrogio Ambrosoli delivered a homily in which he told his listeners that there must be an end to 'persecutions, quarrels, and rancour' – the Jews must not be abandoned 'in the vestibule' to nibble on 'crumbs from the banquet of civilisation'.[138] These were warm words, even if the sermon closed with the devout wish that the Jews might soon find their way into the Christian fold. On 17 April, the doors of the ghetto were lifted off their hinges and the Jews were permitted to walk about in the capital as they pleased. Fearing anti-Jewish reprisals, Ciceruacchio and a group of companions rushed to the scene and orchestrated yet another performance of brotherhood between Christians and Jews.[139]

But the opposition to emancipation kept pace with the movement for reconciliation. In January 1848, Abbot Luigi Vincenzi, a Hebrew language professor at Sapienza University, published a tract flatly rejecting the case for reform. The degraded condition of the Jews, Vincenzi argued, was not the consequence of Christian intolerance, but an illustration of 'the admirable process of divine providence'.[140] His message for the Jews of Rome was: I do not hate you or judge you. Your degraded condition is a self-inflicted consequence of your own denial of God as incarnated in Jesus Christ. For you, the only authentic form of emancipation is a sincere conversion to the Catholic religion. Appended to the main body of the essay was an attachment refuting the arguments advanced in Massimo d'Azeglio's *Emancipation of the Jews*. Against d'Azeglio's promise that the Jews, once released from their disabilities, would make excellent citizens, Vincenzi argued that they would never be loyal to Italy because the fatherland to which their religion called them was Jerusalem.[141] Freeing them from their traditional disabilities, Vincenzi argued, would merely enable them to throw aside papal authority and fulfil their never-abandoned dream of oppressing Christianity.

Vincenzi's tract was flanked by a surge in local manifestations of hostility towards the Jews: mysterious handwritten posters with touches of dialect calling on the citizens of Rome to 'massacre' (*massagrare*) the Jews, protests by fishmongers, artisans or traders who considered themselves threatened by them, but also countless uncoordinated personal attacks like the one on Beniamino Sonnino, a shopkeeper in the ghetto. On the evening of 8 July, the bricklayer Giacomo Bolognini, who owed the shopkeeper money, approached Beniamino and told him to say: 'Long live Pius

IX!' Although Sonnino obliged amiably enough, Bolognini slapped him repeatedly in the face until the shopkeeper and his brother fled.[142] In the summer and autumn of 1848, as the political mood deteriorated in the city, such episodes grew dramatically in number and tended increasingly to involve gunshots and stabbings rather than fisticuffs. Particularly disturbing was the fact that the Civic Guards often failed to act effectively against the violence, or even took part in it. Of the city's eight battalions of Guards, four – including the one that recruited from the working-class Trastevere quarter next to the ghetto – refused to recruit Jews and threatened to disband if forced to do so. When mobs beat or stabbed Jews in the ghetto, the uniforms of the 'Civics' could often be seen among them. The man who used a dagger to cut a (Jewish) star into the shoulder of Isach Sonnino during the widespread violence of 23 October 1848 was recognized on the following day when he turned up in uniform as one of a detachment of Civic Guards tasked with patrolling the ghetto.[143]

'This occasional fooling around against the Jews by dopey Germans', the Jewish novelist Berthold Auerbach told his father on 5 March 1848, 'has to be seen in its larger historical perspective. Revolting outbursts of this kind are swiftly checked by the liberals and the upheaval as a whole remains sublime and uplifting.'[144] Liberal Jewish observers who remained convinced of the essentially progressive movement of history found ways of bracketing out the bad news of plunder and pogrom. Leopold Zunz, founder of modern Judaic studies, was similarly upbeat. 'The storm of the riffraff against the Jews in certain areas', he wrote in March, 'will pass without trace like other nonsense, and liberty will remain.'[145] To be sure, these were without doubt the worst anti-Jewish excesses of modern times, one observer noted in a Viennese journal. But one should put aside for a moment the 'smoking piles of rubble', the 'shattered happiness of families' and 'the pain in one's own heart' and focus instead on the larger picture. The roots of the hostility were social rather than religious – that was surely good news. The Jews had only been targeted because rioters and looters felt that crimes against them were less likely to be punished. The perpetrators accounted only for a tiny fragment of Christian society – most people were horrified by the excesses of the violent few. And there was an upside even to the persecutions, because they confronted governments with issues of public order and thereby forced them to accelerate the process of emancipation.[146]

How many Jewish contemporaries shared this optimism? The phase of the revolution most marred by anti-Jewish violence (March–April 1848) happened also to be the one in which the expectation of an imminent emancipation seemed most justified – a state of affairs that seems less odd when we bear in mind the causal nexus between emancipation and violence. In March–April, numerous statements by prominent liberal leaders and near-unanimous decisions for emancipation in many legislatures showed that the political will was there. But, as so often in the past, reality was slow to catch up. The Austrian Pillersdorf Constitution of 25 April 1848 assured the Jews the freedom to practise their religion, but Article 27 stated expressly that the 'differences in civil and political rights attached to membership of specific religious confessions' were a matter to be resolved by the forthcoming Reichstag.

The revolutionary administration in Hungary also dragged its feet. There were grandiloquent expressions of solidarity with the Jews by Lajos Kossuth, but the charter proposing full municipal citizenship rights to the Jewish residents of cities was withdrawn, meaning that whereas many peasants now had the vote, even the wealthiest and best educated Jews did not. The new Hungarian Constituent Assembly, having voted for a gradualist emancipation requiring the Jews to pass through various qualifying steps, then omitted to pass the relevant legislation. It was not until 28 July 1849 that the Hungarian National Assembly, now meeting in Szeged, finally enacted into law the emancipation of the Jews. But, by then, the Hungarian state wrenched from the grip of Austria was on the verge of collapse and dissolution. The new law remained a dead letter.[147] Not until December 1867, in the aftermath of the dualist restructuring of the Habsburg monarchy, was an emancipation bill passed by both houses of the Hungarian parliament.

Italy presented a cheerful prospect in the short term: comprehensive emancipation laws were passed in Piedmont, Tuscany, Modena, the provisional governments of Lombardy and the Republic of Venice, and by the Roman Republic of 1849. But these changes were reversed in all the Italian states (except Piedmont) after the collapse of the revolutions. The Jews would have to wait until the wars of unification and the establishment of the kingdom of Italy in 1861. In Rome, the right to leave the ghetto was revoked after the Pope's return to the city and the Jews forced back within their ancient walls. Only in 1870, when papal Rome fell to the armies of the kingdom of Italy, was the Roman ghetto definitively abolished.

In Germany, there were the usual complexities and setbacks. There was one outstanding breakthrough: the Reich Constitution drawn up by the Frankfurt parliament proclaimed civil and citizenship rights to be independent of religious affiliation and was subsequently endorsed by twenty-nine of the lesser German states. In Prussia, Saxony and Hanover, new constitutions issued in 1849 abolished all legal disabilities. But many of these successes proved as short-lived as the revolutionary situation that had given rise to them. The 'Basic Rights' set out in the Frankfurt constitution were repealed by a reconvened version of the pre-revolutionary Confederal Assembly, rendering the official endorsement of 1849 meaningless. Some states (including Saxony and Württemberg) did move to retain equality of rights, but in others the emancipatory process was halted or even reversed. Hesse-Kassel withdrew political rights and even took measures to introduce segregated schooling. In Prussia, the revised constitution of 1850 reaffirmed (Art. 12) that civil and citizenship rights were independent of confession, but also asserted (Art. 14) that 'the Christian religion shall form the basis of all institutions of the state concerned with religious practice'. Throughout the 1850s and 1860s, this latter provision was used to exclude Jews from virtually all state employments. Only in 1866–7 and 1871, with the foundation of the North German Confederation and the German Empire, was the issue definitively resolved in favour of a comprehensive emancipation.

Even if the issue was resolved in the medium term in most jurisdictions by emancipatory legislation, the experience of revolution in 1848 was rich in sombre lessons for European Jewry. It was a reminder, if any were needed, of how easily the movement towards emancipation could be halted or reversed. The sanguine Berlin correspondent of the Viennese *Central-Organ* was wrong when he claimed that pogroms had the effect of accelerating the pace of reform. The opposite was the case: Kossuth's response to the horrors of April 1848 was to argue that the government should abandon the sponsorship of civil equality, on the grounds that it would trigger further reprisals.[148]

Commenting on the anti-Jewish unrest of 1848 in the city of Miskolc in northern Hungary, a Jewish correspondent observed that this was not 'the first time we have seen horrific phantoms rise up, enlivened with the breath of medieval prejudice and go about their terrible work'.[149] Framed in this way, the violence appeared to be the terrible remnant of a bygone era, a temporary intrusion of the past into the present. But the

Johann Jacoby (1863). The son of a Königsberg merchant, Jakoby belonged to the first generation of Jewish activists to combine the commitment to liberal and radical politics with advocacy for the emancipation of Jews from their civil disabilities.

circulation of tracts and essays, some of them very sophisticated, in which the Jews served as a metonym for capitalism and the power of money, suggested that anti-Jewish sentiment was already finding new and modern modes of articulation. Among these was the claim that what was called for was not the emancipation *of* the Jews, but emancipation *from* the Jews.

This idea had a complex pre-revolutionary genealogy. If it gained ground fast after 1848, this was in part a function of the rhetorical inflation around the word 'emancipation'. It was also a response to the conspicuous wealth of a very small number of Jews and to the visibility of Jews as the members of political clubs, elected assemblies or the occupants of ministerial posts – a feature that distinguishes 1848 from the upheavals of 1830 or 1789.[150] And this novelty was in turn only possible because in several countries the 1830s and 1840s had seen a rapid improvement in the cultural and economic standing of the Jewish minority and the emergence of an alliance between liberal leaders and the most progressive Jews.[151]

The slogan *emancipation from the Jews* was important because it placed the Jews on the wrong side of history, branding their liberation not as a victory for universal rights or an enlarged concept of citizenship, but as the triumph of a narrow interest. 'Without anyone having noticed it', the former revolutionary Richard Wagner would write in 1850, 'the "creditor of kings" has become the "king of the credulous" and we can only find the demands of this king for emancipation extremely naïve, given that we find ourselves obliged to fight for emancipation from the Jews.'[152] This idea, which offered a bridge between the political discourses of right and left, would become one of the central tropes of modern anti-Semitism.[153] By contrast, the caricatural depiction of inverted gender roles, in which, for example, a rebellious wife in trousers told her cross-dressing husband 'Slavery is abolished, now it's your turn to be a slave', remained within the realm of the farcical.

LIBERATION OF THE 'ROMA SLAVES'

In 1843, a Bucharest journal announced that the children and heirs of the deceased Serdar Nika of Bucharest were offering 200 families of 'gypsies' for sale. The men listed on the bill included locksmiths, goldsmiths, cobblers, musicians and agricultural workers. Since the families could be bought only in batches of at least five, the executors were selling them for 'one ducat less than the ordinary price'. Financial terms were available.[154]

When this sale was announced, the history of Roma slavery in the Romanian lands was entering its final chapter. By 1830, there were about 200,000 enslaved Roma in total in the two Danubian Principalities. They fell into three groups: those owned by the state, those owned by the Church and those owned by private individuals. The slaves of the state were freed by laws passed in 1843 in Wallachia and 1844 in Moldavia. The Church was obliged to give up its slaves in 1844 and 1847 in Moldavia and Wallachia respectively. However, there remained the third category of 'gypsy slaves', who were the property of private individuals – boyar or non-noble landlords, civil servants, doctors, soldiers or even foreigners who had only recently arrived in the principalities. Their exact numbers are not known because their names were not recorded in the cadastral surveys, but there were probably between 40,000 and 50,000 of them in 1848 when the Wallachian revolution broke out.[155] These privately owned Roma fell into two broad categories. *Lăieşi* slaves remained nomadic and roamed freely throughout the country practising various itinerant trades and paying their owner an annual tribute. *Vatraşi* were sedentary Roma who might serve as 'house' or 'courtyard gypsies' (*ţigani de casă, ţigani de curte*) working as domestic servants, or as 'field gypsies' (*ţigani de câmp*) employed on the owner's estate.[156]

As the abolitions of the 1840s suggest, cultural pressure for the abolition of Roma slavery had already begun to accumulate before the outbreak of the revolution. In 1831, the historian and polymath Mihail Kogălniceanu had published a widely read 'sketch' of the 'history, customs and language of the Gypsies' in which he lamented the indifference of the Europeans to the fate of the Roma: 'they [the Europeans] form philanthropic societies for the abolition of slavery in America, while on their own continent, in Europe, there are 400,000 Gypsies who are slaves and another 200,000 who live in the shadow of ignorance and barbarism'.[157] Kogălniceanu was among those progressive Moldavians who welcomed the laws emancipating the state and monastic Roma slaves. The new laws 'raise our country to the ranks of the most civilized', a leader piece in a liberal weekly declared. At a time when 'the colonies of France and many states of the North American Union [were] teeming with millions of blacks', they added, Moldavians had 'sanctified the principle that all men were born free'.[158] On 26 June, only one day after its creation, the Provisional Government in Bucharest announced the manumission of all remaining Roma slaves: 'The time of slavery is over, and the gypsies are our brothers today.'[159]

Beating and other forms of mistreatment were banned with immediate effect, and owners warned that continued abuses would entail the loss of compensation rights. Landlords were urged to follow the 'beautiful and Christian example' of those who had already freed their slaves without compensation. Those who insisted on their right to 'take money for the soul of man' were to be issued with compensation tickets, while the enslaved Roma were to receive 'liberation tickets' doubling as identity cards; they specified the date of issue, the name and age of the liberated person, and, tellingly, the name of the former owner. A text on the card stated that the person concerned was 'freed according to the principles of the constitution of the country', and henceforth entered 'the class of free inhabitants of the Romanian lands'.[160] On 10 July, a new 'Commission for the Liberation of the Slaves' opened for business. It established a release procedure, drew up a budget, arranged for the printing of forms, set a two-month deadline for the submission of supporting documents for those who wished to receive compensation, processed the incoming sub-missions, issued the corresponding certificates, communicated with the Department of Home Affairs, the police and the county administrations, and received and resolved complaints and claims.

For such a small administrative body, this was a stupendous achieve-ment. But the practical difficulties were overwhelming. Many owners in remote districts complained of the cost and difficulty of submitting the necessary documents in time to meet the deadlines. Owners who were unable to supply documents proving the existence and identity of slaves who had been in their family for generations demanded that the authori-ties send an official to verify the existence of their slaves. The commission was deluged by such a multitude of applicants for liberty that it devolved the issuing of liberty tickets to the county administrations and sub-administrations and deferred the handling of compensation applications to a later date. But by the end of July the local administrations were still waiting for their forms. Amidst the resulting confusion, dissatisfaction with the process mounted. The June abolition proclamation had set tens of thousands of people in motion in search of their liberty, creating bot-tlenecks in the capital. There were clashes between owners and enslaved people. Owners wrongly accused their former slaves of stealing or damaging their property; there were summary expulsions and punishments in contravention of the new laws. As on the French island possessions, owners invoked the ban on resettlement and vagrancy law to prevent their former slaves from leaving their employment, while the latter refused to stay, saying that they needed to 'breathe again from the mistreatment they had suffered in their bondage'. In Dolj County, the resistance among the owners was so determined that there were disorders across the region; in mid August, most of the county's Roma remained unfree.[161]

It turned out that for the Roma, as for Jews and the enslaved Africans of the Caribbean, there was a gaping difference between the proclamation of abolition and the implementation of emancipation. The same questions loomed here as for the liberated black cultivators of the sugar islands: who should compensate the former owners and how, if at all, should the processes of liberation and compensation be connected? Should emancipation be immediate and absolute or partial and gradual? What should be done to ensure the integration of former slaves into Wallachian society and more particularly to prevent them from deserting their old places of employment and wandering about? In the short term, these questions were moot, because the collapse of the revolution after the Ottoman–Russian intervention in September 1848 put an end to the entire process. A decree issued by Fuad Effendi, the new Ottoman commissioner, and Constantin Cantacuzino, the newly installed regent (*Caimacam*) of Wallachia, on 28 September 1848 stated that:

> all the decrees issued during the revolution, with regard to the Gypsies of private individuals were abolished, that the notes issued to each of those Gypsies, from 11 June until 13 September, [should] be returned and destroyed, and that the condition of the private gypsies should remain in the state it [had been] in before the events of 11 June.[162]

For the enslaved Roma of Wallachia, the revolution was over. The process of legal emancipation would resume under more auspicious circumstances in the mid 1850s.

THE TIME OF EMANCIPATION

Among those who addressed the crowd at the feast of reconciliation organized by Ciceruacchio at the Tor di Quinto on 4 July 1848 was the Mazzinian writer and journal editor Tomaso Zauli-Sajani from the city of Forlì in the Emilia-Romagna region of the Papal States. Zauli-Sajani had fled into Maltese exile after taking part in the revolution of 1831, returning to his home only after the amnesty conceded by Pope Pius IX on his accession in 1846. In his speech to an audience of Jews and Christians, Zauli-Sajani recalled the abolition of slavery in London and Paris and proposed that the equality of humankind was 'the principle of modern civilization'. But the highpoint of his address was a passage on the great Irish patriot Daniel O'Connell, who had campaigned for the British Emancipation Act of 1829, a law that admitted Irish and English Catholics to Parliament and allowed them to occupy nearly all public offices.

The reference to Daniel O'Connell was charged with emotion for Romans, because in 1847, already old and ill, O'Connell had embarked on a pilgrimage to Rome, dying en route in Genoa. His heart was cut from his body, placed in an urn and sent to the city of Rome for burial. A few weeks later, the renowned Theatine preacher Gioacchino Ventura delivered a sensational funeral oration on the Irish hero in the Roman basilica of Sant'Andrea della Valle, in which he used the figure of O'Connell to push back against the notion that the Catholic faith was in some sense incompatible with the universal struggle for emancipation.[163] How was it now possible, Zauli-Sajani asked the Catholics in his audience, that the tolerant spirit of O'Connell should find obstacles to the relief of Jewish disabilities here in Rome, of all places, in these 'good days of love, brotherhood, rebirth and the generous will of the great Father of the Faithful, of the immortal Pius IX?'[164] This was a shrewd way to frame the issue, because it connected the plight of the Jews with that of the Irish Catholics. But it also reflected Zauli-Sajani's belief that the emancipation of the Jews was just one strand of a common human task. (It is interesting to note that he did not at any point mention the emancipation of women, although his wife, Ifigenia, who had fled with him into exile, was a well-known writer of politically engaged novels.[165])

In novels, ballets, short stories, plays and operas, European culture endlessly rehearsed imaginary versions of all four emancipations. The

Hebrew slaves of Verdi's *Nabucco* (1841) were just one example of a preoccupation with the liberation of the ancient Israelites that remained present in Christian theology and political rhetoric throughout the early and mid nineteenth century, and Gotthold Ephraim Lessing's *Nathan the Wise*, centred on a sympathetic and admirable Jewish sage and arguing against prejudice and religious discrimination, had become a staple of the German stage by the 1840s.[166] There were numerous ballets – some of them huge popular successes – that featured rebellious women: from Louis Henry's *La Belle Arsène* (1818, 1823) and *Les Amazones* (1823), to Taglioni's *Die neue Amazone* (1835) and Auguste Mabille's *Nisida ou Les Amazones des Açores* (1848). In Taglioni's *La Révolte des femmes* (1833) women seized weapons, performed war dances and invited their fellows – according to the programme notes – to 'revolt against the despotism of men'.[167] The emancipation from slavery, too, kept intruding into the contemporary imagination, mostly in the form of reworkings of the Haitian revolution, from Kleist's *Die Verlobung in Santo Domingo* (1811) and Victor Hugo's *Bug-Jargal* (1820) to Julius von Heyden's *Dessalines. Ein romantisches Charakter- und Zeitgemälde* (1836), the anonymous *Améline . . . ou la révolte des noirs* (1843) and Philip Körber's *Der Negeraufstand in Hayti* (1845).[168] Ion Heliade Rădulescu's sketch 'Jupân Ion' presented the idealized portrait of a loyal gypsy retainer dedicated to the welfare of his master's children, while the poems and novellas of Cezar Bolliac and Vasile Alecsandri delighted readers with depictions of virtuous young gypsies and beautiful gypsy girls untouched by mean interests.[169] These works and many others like them allowed European cultural elites to keep chewing on emancipation without ever quite swallowing it.

The emancipations also present a common chronological structure and narrative shape. Epochs of expanding possibility alternated with periods of contraction. There was a first stirring of interest and activism in the early 1790s and a thickening and enlargement of advocacy networks around all three issues in the 1830s and 1840s, as exemplified by Cyrille Bissette's *Revue des Colonies* and the journalism of Victor Schoelcher, Suzanne Voilquin's *La Femme nouvelle* in its various iterations, Julius Fürst's *Der Orient*, and Gabriel Riesser's *Der Jude* and the works published by liberal and radical Romanian writers. We have seen that the revolutions of 1848 brought a further intensification of this public work. For Julius Fürst, editor of *Der Orient*, the process of advocacy was even more important than legal reform: 'What matters', Fürst wrote in 1851, 'is not the result, but rather the activities that gave birth to this outcome.'[170] The same general point could be made for women, whose work ultimately bore fruit in the steady, if very slow, growth of support for female emancipation within the post-1848 republican movement.[171]

And yet, for all four groups, the ebbing of the revolution brought another narrowing of horizons. Parts of the abolition decree were deactivated, restrictions on female participation in political organizations were reintroduced, edicts abolishing discrimination by creed were modified or dropped altogether. Slavery was abolished (in the French colonies), but for the formerly enslaved real autonomy and a truly equal citizenship remained a distant prospect and there was no fundamental change in French colonial and imperial policy.[172] For formerly enslaved women, moreover, abolition brought the transition from a social system in which women and men, as chattels, were interchangeable, to one in which women were subordinated to the authority of men.[173] The Jews fared well where liberal nation-building projects triumphed, but the waning of liberal energies in the 1870s and 1880s brought a new wave of popular and administrative anti-Semitism that insisted on the 'Christian' character of public institutions, and rejected the least assimilated Jews as obnoxious strangers and their most assimilated brethren as camouflaged parasites and racial aliens. Wallachia is a good example. The rights granted under the Proclamation of Islaz were withdrawn when the revolution collapsed. The first draft of the liberal Romanian constitution of 1866 – the foundational constitution of the new nation-state – provided for the naturalization of all residents, including Jews, but the Moldavin political leadership protested and the final version restricted citizenship rights to Christians. There was some piecemeal emancipation of individuals in the late 1870s, but as late as 1914 only a tiny minority of the country's Jews had been granted the status of citizens. Across Central Europe, the twentieth century would bring a wave of restrictive regulations culminating in the catastrophe of the National Socialist seizure of power in 1933. Roma emancipation was the first casualty of the counter-revolution in Wallachia – gypsies in private ownership would have to wait until 1855, when the process started up again, though the social emancipation of Roma as equal citizens arguably still remains incomplete. Women, as we have seen, achieved least of all in 1848 and would wait longest for the concession of basic political rights.

There were contemporaries who saw the various emancipatory struggles as enmeshed with each other: William Lloyd Garrison criticized
Kossuth for asking Americans to support the Hungarian struggle while
refusing to deplore the slavery of Afro-Americans. For the Prussian dissident and American exile Karl Heinzen, the fight against slavery in
America and the fight against reaction in Europe were parts of the same
struggle. In the *North Star*, the newspaper he founded in 1847, the formerly enslaved writer Frederick Douglass viewed abolitionism in the
United States and the revolutionary upheavals in Europe as different
manifestations of the same global struggle.[174]

Yet the emancipation of women, enslaved Africans, 'gypsy slaves' and
Jews never merged virtuously together in the way the nineteenth-century
inflation of the word suggested they should. The destinies of the various
groups were too deeply anchored in specific histories and social logics.
Racial or ethnic and sexual difference and the peculiar predicament of
the Jews, in which theology, eschatology, xenophobia and social anxiety
blended to create a remarkably resilient form of suspicion and hatred –
these three rationales of discrimination were not mutually reducible;
they were not functions of each other, they were separate fundaments, so
deeply built into modern European culture that they seemed primordial,
natural, ordained by God. The upheavals that opened the door to liberty
also unleashed countervailing forces: competitive resentment, xenophobia, misogyny, fear of disorder, and the zeal to discipline and control. To
acknowledge this is not to write 1848 off as a 'failure' and should not
distract from the real advances made, especially in the area of advocacy.
But the ambivalence and waywardness of the emancipation process are
a reminder of the peculiar recalcitrance of racial and sexual inequality as
domains of political action, then and now.

7

Entropy

A scene in front of the Hôtel de Ville in Paris: standing on an armchair that has been taken from the building's interior, Alphonse de Lamartine addresses the milling crowd. Around him stand the men of the Provisional Government, Dupont de l'Eure, François Arago, Ledru-Rollin, Louis Blanc, Laurent-Antoine Pagnerre, Flocon, Albert, Pierre Marie de Saint-Georges, Adolphe Crémieux, Garnier-Pagès and Armand Marrast. Smoke wafts over the scene. The space is strewn with hints at the recent fighting: a small artillery piece, the rubble of a barricade, a dead or dying horse, a wounded fighter on a makeshift stretcher who bleeds from the bandaged stump of his right hand – this is the sculptor Benaud, mortally wounded at the Château d'Eau. On a box marked 'Collection for the wounded' sits a bowl full of freshly donated coins, so this is a generous crowd, mindful of the sacrifice of those who have fought. Other narratives are woven into the hubbub: near a horde of precious objects, presumably looted from the royal palace, lies an untidy corpse. It is the body of the journeyman mason Roux, who was shot by his comrades for committing a theft during the fighting. On his bloodstained chest rests a banner inscribed with the words 'Death to Thieves'. A statuesque worker points solemnly at the dead man as if to impart a message to another onlooker, who peers at the thief in horror as if he recognized him. Others are shown pushing a cart brimful of silver and gold towards safety inside the building. A little boy hastens to pick up and replace a silver spoon that has fallen to the ground – this is the drummer boy Pierre, who beat the charge at the capture of the Château d'Eau from government troops. This is a virtuous crowd, one that punishes thieves (with death) and fastidiously abstains from pilfering – a theme inherited from depictions of worker insurgents in the 'glorious days' of 1830.

Among well over one hundred individual faces, we can make out

Henri Félix Emmanuel Philippoteaux, *Lamartine Refusing the Red Flag in Front of the Hôtel de Ville* (*c.* 1848). On this enormous canvas, Philippoteaux captures the tensions latent in the February revolution in Paris.

men of the regular army, National Guards, armed insurgents, labourers, apprentices and journeymen, prosperous bourgeois with brushed top hats, small boys and a few women. The space around Lamartine is marked off by a trio of huge tricolour flags bearing the legends 'Abolition of the Death Penalty' (words that suggest a tension with the slain thief in the foreground), 'The Organisation of Labour' (where Louis Blanc can be seen) and 'Liberty, Equality, Fraternity'. But wading slowly through the crowd from the left is a woman in a red Phrygian cap astride a white charger. She holds aloft a red flag inscribed with the words *Vive la République*. She has the grandeur of allegory, but she also represents 'Marie of Lille', a young woman who was famous for tending to the wounded under fire during the revolution and would later be awarded the Cross of the Legion of Honour. Lamartine fixes her in his gaze and raises his hand in a gesture whose meaning is deciphered by the painting's title: *Lamartine Rejecting the Red Flag in Front of the Hôtel de Ville, 25 February 1848.*[1]

Over more than eighteen square metres of canvas, Félix Philippoteaux paints a scene of great dramaturgical complexity. Strangest of all is the temporal location of the action: the jets of burning powder flaring from guns in the background suggest a revolution that is still ongoing; the scroll of paper in Lamartine's left hand – presumably the proclamation of the Republic – suggests a revolution that is already complete. And in the gap between a revolution that is already complete and one that is yet to end, Philippoteaux depicts a stand-off between two political options. A woman proposes to plant the red flag of social revolution before the Hôtel de Ville. Lamartine, his waist, like those of the provisional ministers around him, wrapped in a tricolour sash, intends to prevent it.

The mood of this scene is difficult to read. There is a willingness to act together, for the moment at least, despite the boundaries of class and occupation. But the facial expressions are too varied and the members of the crowd too embroiled in local transactions with each other to suggest a collective emotional state. The image gives us no reason to think that when the sun rises on a new day, these people will still be willing or able to act together. This chapter follows the journeys of the people of 1848 away from the common revolutionary enterprise that united them in the spring days. In the aftermath of the upheavals, everything was up for grabs. Who should assume authority? Was the revolution over when the fighting stopped, or had it just begun? How should the contradictory demands of the revolutionary movements be reconciled? Why was it so difficult to mobilize the countryside in support of revolutionary objectives? What happened to liberal and radical solidarities when colliding national movements pulled people in opposite directions? Sometimes, as in Baden in the spring of 1848, radicals broke with the liberal project and struck out on their own; and sometimes, as in Paris in the summer, moderate liberals crushed radical movements in the name of the revolution. These centripetal movements into antagonism along many fault lines resist the tools of historical narrative, which tends to require unifying themes, lines of perspective and points of convergence. But if the apparently random dispersal of newly hatched wasps and the churning of dust motes in a sunbeam manifest a deeper pattern and meaning, then the same must be true of the myriad journeys of the people of 1848.

VAGABOND SOVEREIGNTY

The observation that the revolutions of spring 1848 both united and divided people seems banal. Isn't this true of all major historical events? What was unusual about these revolutions was the speed and amplitude of the transition from unity to conflict. First, the dizzying sense of togetherness and unanimity, the oceanic immersion in a collective self; then the anxiety and distrust as fault lines appeared, like fine cracks in the surface of paint.

The French Provisional Government remained fragile after the February Revolution. The ministers lost no time in shutting down the deliberative organs of the defunct monarchy, and since the king, most of his family and many of his ministers had fled the capital, the authority of the new government seemed secure. But the streets were still full of insurgents. A dense network of radical political clubs emerged, of which the most important, both in terms of their audience and their determination to press directly on the course of the revolution, were the Central Republican Society and the Revolution Club, led respectively by Louis-Auguste Blanqui and Armand Barbès, former jailmates of the socialist Martin Bernard (ch. 3). Blanqui was even thinner and paler than he had been before the insurrection of 1839. His wife had died while he was in prison and 'he had reached the point', Victor Hugo later recalled, 'of no longer wearing a shirt. His body was clad in the garments he had worn for the past twelve years: his prison clothes – rags which he displayed in his club with gloomy pride.'[2] But the analytical prowess remained, and his 'penetrating and reflective words' still 'cut coldly, like the blade of a knife'.[3] He remained an implacable enemy of the bourgeois social order.

During the early months of the revolution, about 100,000 people took part in regular political meetings of some kind. The clubs were not sociable get-togethers: they viewed themselves as representative bodies and thus as instruments of popular sovereignty. 'We represent the Republic and the Revolution', the barricade fighter and former political detainee Charles Crousse told a large audience at the Central Republican Society, urging the members to take control of the Republic that they themselves had made. The moderate liberals who had just secured control of the Republic were 'impotent eunuchs' who would squander the Republic if they were allowed do it. 'We must save it', Crousse proposed, 'by putting ourselves in their place.'[4]

The challenge from the left revealed how far radical and moderate liberal understandings of the revolution had drifted apart. For liberals, the revolution was an accomplished event whose consequences now needed to be stabilized. For Parisian radicals, by contrast, it was a process that had only just begun. For liberals, people of the tricolour, the primary task facing the inheritors of the revolution was political reform; for radicals, people of the red flag, the revolution was social transformation, the structural amelioration of social inequality. No issue better illustrates the schism between them than the question of labour.

On 25 February, the day Lamartine 'rejected' the red flag, the machine mechanic Marche, head of a deputation of workers, walked straight from the barricades to the Hôtel de Ville and demanded, rhythmically banging the stock of his rifle on the floor, that the government immediately formalize in law the 'organisation of labour', 'the right to guaranteed work' and the creation of a fund to protect unemployed workers from the extremes of poverty. Lamartine tried to fob him off. But Marche insisted. The people, he declared, in a dig at Lamartine's literary reputation, had 'had enough of fancy talk'.[5]

This was not the moment to gainsay an armed hero of the people, and while Lamartine reasoned with Marche, three of the most left-wing members of the Provisional Government, Louis Blanc, famous for his work on the organization of labour, the radical democrat Alexandre Ledru-Rollin and Ferdinand Flocon, editor of the radical journal

La Réforme, busied themselves drafting a decree that was subsequently signed (with mixed feelings) by every member of the government. Published on 26 February, it promised to 'guarantee labour to every worker' and affirmed that 'workers must associate among themselves to enjoy the benefits of their labour'.[6] As this episode suggested, the authority dispersed when the July Monarchy fell had not yet been recaptured by a single institution; it was still a vagabond sovereignty flowing unpredictably through the mobilized population of the capital.[7]

Under these conditions, the balance of initiative could shift from one day to the next. When a crowd of workers several thousand strong filed past the Hôtel de Ville two days later to demand the creation of a Ministry of Progress that would be charged with implementing Louis Blanc's decree, the more conservative ministers refused to comply. They offered instead to create a special commission under the chairmanship of Blanc and Albert that would be tasked with preparing an economic reorganization plan for consideration by the future National Assembly. The new commission was given a splendid headquarters in the Palace of Luxembourg, but the decree establishing it said not a word about how, when or even whether its recommendations would be implemented.

In the meanwhile, the question remained of what to do about the tens of thousands of unemployed men milling about on the streets of the capital. For Louis Blanc, the remedy for sudden labour market contractions lay in a system of state-controlled cooperatives that would stop the decline in the real value of wages and put an end to the problem of unemployment. Blanc's ministerial colleagues recognized that something had to be done about this potentially combustible reserve of inactive men. But most of them were private-property liberals who recoiled, like Lamartine, from the idea of deep state intervention in the economy. In place of the system proposed by Blanc, the government announced the creation of National Workshops, to be run *not* by Louis Blanc and *not* from the Palace of Luxembourg, but under the auspices of the Minister of Public Works, Pierre Marie de Saint-Georges. 'Marie', as he was known, was a lawyer with a distinguished record as a defender of republican journals and activists under the July Monarchy, but he was also a determined opponent of socialism. The purpose of the *ateliers nationaux* was not to organize labour on a new basis, but to palliate the social crisis in the capital and neutralize indigent workers who might otherwise hang about in the radical clubs or get swept up in demonstrations and protests. There was huge interest in the workshops; within two months, 100,000 men had signed up for work there.

It looked very much as if Lamartine and the moderate liberals had outmanoeuvred the leftists within the government. They had kicked the 'organization of labour' into the long grass and used old-fashioned palliation as a means of circumventing structural reform.[8] But that was not the end of the story. The Luxembourg Commission outperformed expectations and became a 'hub of coordination' for the politicized workers of Paris. It became the place where delegates of the trades and corporations met to discuss the issues that divided and united them. It acquired parliament-like qualities: there was an executive body, selected by lots, and a 'general assembly' with separate meetings for the professions. The moderate liberals of Le National called Blanc's operations at the Luxembourg Palace a 'mere commission of enquiry'. Blanc saw it differently. In a speech of 10 March, he addressed the assembled labour delegates as 'representatives of those who produce and suffer'. On 28 March, he described the commission as an 'Assembly of Labour', an 'Estates-General of the People'.[9] The radical police chief Marc Caussidière agreed that the Luxembourg belonged at the heart of the revolutionary process: it was the work of Blanc's commission, he wrote, that gave 'a precise definition to the character of the new republic'.[10]

In Prussia, by contrast with Paris, political power remained centred on the monarchy and the ministry, with its awkward mix of old-regime figures and moderate liberals. But the revolution *forced* the government to be responsive to popular initiatives – something Prussians had never witnessed before. When the king resolved not to create a new parliament, but to reconvene the United Diet that had met in 1847, a spontaneous movement of protest spread across the Prussian provinces. Under pressure from the strong democratic movement in their city, the municipal authorities of Breslau in Silesia sent a deputation to Berlin demanding 'a popular representation based on direct elections'. If this demand were not fulfilled, they warned, there was a danger that Silesia 'would turn away from the Prussian state in order either to merge with Austria or to form a Silesian Republic'.[11] In the face of this extraordinarily bold threat, the king and his ministry backed down. The United Diet continued to meet for a time, but it was eventually shut down to make way for a Prussian National Assembly based on universal manhood suffrage.

Here, as in Paris, revolutionary clubs and associations proliferated. They were, as the *Spenersche Zeitung* put it, 'the pulse of [the city's] political life'.[12] The radical Political Club (later Democratic Club), founded on 23 March, was one of several groups to emerge from a gathering initially convened to arrange the burial of the March fallen.[13] It saw itself as a monitoring body whose purpose was to ensure that the 'ideas of March' were put into practice by the government. Attendance at public meetings increased from around 3,000 to over 20,000 people by mid May, including a growing contingent of workers. The club also hosted special sessions at which workers and journeymen discussed their demands and then passed them via deputations to the relevant authorities.[14] There was a parallel here with the 'workers' parliament' emerging at the Palace of Luxembourg. Even more popular among Berliners was the People's Club (Volksverein), which claimed to represent 'all classes, but particularly those who constitute the marrow and core of the people, the propertyless workers'. Among the stated objectives of this club was 'authentic representation of the people' – a jab at the 'false' representation on offer in the form of the United Diet.[15]

In this world of crowded meetings and heated debates, it was not at first clear which skills best enabled a man (women also sought admission but were excluded) to acquire a leading role. A strong voice that could carry across a crowd was essential: the otherwise gifted socialist Gustav Julius had to renounce his ambition to play a leading role in the Political Club because his voice was too feeble. The intelligent radical publicist Arnold Ruge had been a celebrated figure in the pre-March world but failed to make his mark on the Berlin club scene because he lacked both the sociable gifts of a 'party man' and the knack of 'impressing large meetings and leading them'. On the other hand, it was easy for meetings to fall under the sway of an untrustworthy orator with a talent for public speaking. Paul Boerner recalled a certain Herr von Brand, a sallow young man who spoke 'the finest phrases' and could combine them with such agility that 'even the soberest and smartest listeners in the room were often pulled along by the momentum of his speeches'. Brand shot 'like a meteor across the revolutionary sky', before disappearing without trace and resurfacing some months later as a police spy in Austrian service. Some speakers succumbed to a laboured theatricality. Robert Ottensoser, a leading member of the Political Club, was notorious for the tiresome repetition of pet phrases. 'I lay in chains in Spandau prison!' and 'We have made a revolution!' were two favourites. The latter phrase, uttered 'in every vocal modulation', was the 'acme of Ottensoser's eloquence'.[16]

The diffuseness of revolutionary mobilization left its mark on policing. The dominant law enforcement organization in Berlin after the departure of the army to Potsdam was the Civil Guard (Bürgerwehr). But this was a heterogeneous formation whose political outlook varied from district to district. And attached to the Civil Guard were no fewer than ten semi-autonomous flying squads (*fliegende Corps*). The students' squad, which numbered 700 by mid April, was originally run by the professors of the university. When they, predictably, proved unable to perform effectively in this role, it was run by the students. There was an armed student band for every political tendency on campus, including one for the theologians and one widely feared group known after its leader as 'Monecke's Band', whose members wore black Calabrian hats with a long red feather in honour of the south-German insurrectionist Friedrich Hecker (see below). Monecke's men were notorious for demanding 'donations' for their flying squad from terrified Berlin residents. Security at the Berlin Arsenal on Unter den Linden was in the hands of the artisans' flying squad, consisting of 450 journeymen with over 200 guns. Even the artists formed a flying squad for the purpose of guarding the galleries and museums, as did the machine-makers, the members of the Institute of Trade and the sixth-formers at the city's academic high schools.[17]

In Vienna, the new National Guard, the equivalent of the Berlin Civil Guard, took over control of the city after most of the military left. But the students were allowed to form their own 'Academic Legion'. Carl Borkowski reported to his father his deep pride in becoming a 'guard' (the lowest rank) in the Legion and the proud custodian of an enormous gun, a cumbersome hunting piece from the previous century. Relations between the National Guard and the Academic Legion were difficult. The students often felt themselves sandwiched between the senior officers of the Guard, many of whom were conservative property-owners, and the 'aroused mob' that tended to appear at protests and demonstrations. Both the students and the rank and file of the National Guard distrusted the army units that remained on guard duty in the city.

In Paris, too, the revolution complicated the urban policing scene. The hated municipal guards were disbanded, leaving the city in the hands of the National Guard, but other more radically oriented forces soon emerged, including semi-official armed groups such as the Company of February, the Company of Saint-Just and the 'Men of Lyons'. The new Prefect of Paris police, the republican Marc Caussidière, whose brother had been killed and mutilated by government troops at Lyons in 1834 and whose sisters had prepared cartridges and food for the fighting *canuts*, ran his own revolutionary police force known as the Montagnards, consisting of around 600 men distinguished for their role as barricade fighters. Joseph Sobrier, a veteran of the insurrectionary movement of the 1830s and a radical of independent means, 'borrowed' a military squad from the police and established a headquarters of his own, to the great annoyance of his bourgeois neighbours, on the fashionable rue de Rivoli. These accommodations housed not just the editorial staff of his newspaper and the administration of the Club des Clubs, but also the most important munitions depot accessible to the radical clubbists.[18] In order to visit this well-intentioned but alarming man, Marie d'Agoult wrote, visitors to his apartments had to pass through a long gauntlet of men 'armed to the teeth and demanding the password in a sinister manner'.[19]

For the moment, left-republican forces were still relatively confident and strong in Paris, while the conservative response appeared tentative. But by mid April it was clear that the tide was turning fast against the left. In a ballot conducted on 8 April to appoint officers of the National Guard in all the arrondissements of Paris, scarcely any left-republicans were elected and not a single worker made it into the upper ranks. It was worrying to left-republicans to see the revolutionary militia fall under the control of moderates and conservatives, and many rightly saw the National Guard ballot as a warning that the left would lose the national elections too. If that happened, then the hour of social and labour reform would be adjourned indefinitely. 'Turning an anxious eye towards the provinces still half submerged in shadow,' Louis Blanc wrote, 'they wondered whether their hopes were not going to be suffocated at the bottom of the ballot box.'[20]

On 16 April, a crowd of around 100,000 radical workers converged on the Champs-de-Mars and walked towards the Hôtel de Ville. The aim was to present a list of left-republican candidates for command posts in the National Guard and to demand progress on the question of labour reform. The mood was boisterous but pacific: the crowds were unarmed and chanted 'Long live the Provisional Government!' as they walked. Walking with them was Louis Blanc, a minister of the government, in the company of M. Albert, his vice-president at the Luxembourg Commission. But when they arrived at the place de la Grève in front of the Hôtel de Ville, the demonstrators found an enormous turnout of National Guards wielding fixed bayonets. Hemmed in on both sides by the dense ranks of armed men, the avant-garde of the demonstrators shuffled slowly into the square amidst the jeers and catcalls of the guards and cries of 'Down with the communists!' No one from the Provisional Government was willing to parley with the crowd or its delegates. An adjutant to the mayor appeared, but only to dismiss them brusquely. Confused and embittered, the crowd dispersed. In the hours that followed, National Guard units attacked the premises of the leading radical clubs across the capital.[21]

This may not have been an especially bloody clash, but it was of great symbolic importance for the left. After all, this demonstration had been cleared in advance with the relevant authorities. The organizers saw themselves as friends and protectors of the Provisional Government, not as would-be insurrectionaries. So why had the Guard been called out? Why had the government armed itself against its protectors? The answer lay in the maelstrom of rumour and propaganda that had agitated the city on the eve of the demonstration.[22] Reports had circulated in Paris that the clubs were preparing a violent seizure of power. There was talk of a mysterious Committee of Public Safety, to be chaired by the ultra-radical Blanqui. Louis Blanc would later argue that these rumours were not spontaneous expressions of alarm but fragments of misinformation, fake news engineered for the purpose of triggering a crisis. 'Unknown persons', Louis Blanc claimed, had run about 'in every quarter of the city' on the night before the event 'sowing lies whose effects had been perfidiously thought through'.[23] Whether there was any truth in this claim is difficult to say. In situations of polarization and heightened anxiety, people tend to regard their own fears as authentic and those of their opponents as manipulated; Blanc's account of mysterious nocturnal provocateurs was of course itself the fruit of hearsay and fear.

Particularly alarming for the left was the skill with which moderate and conservative republican propagandists were already exploiting the divisions within the Provisional Government. On the morning of 16 April, the journal *L'Assemblée Nationale*, a moderate republican organ committed to supporting the forthcoming national elections, opened with the mid nineteenth century's equivalent of a deepfake video. Heading the first page was a text purporting to be a 'manifesto' by the interior minister, Ledru-Rollin. In fact, it was a confection cobbled together from the most inflammatory phrases of the minister's bulletins. In these official communications, which emanated from Paris but were gazetted nationally, Ledru-Rollin had found an unsettling language that vacillated between cockiness and anxiety. The men of the old regime were still everywhere, he had warned. They must be winkled out of positions of power. Only true republicans could faithfully serve a republic. Vigilance was essential. 'If we march confidently on the road of the revolution, then there can be no limits to its glory and prosperity; if our ardour wanes, everything is to be feared.' 'Your powers are unlimited', he told the political commissars sent out across France to oversee the installation of the new Republic. They would bring to their task the immense might of a sovereign people. They would have to be prepared to do whatever the circumstances demanded. In pressing the case for a continuation of the revolution as a far-reaching process of transformation, Ledru-Rollin articulated a specifically radical view of the tasks ahead.

The leader article in *L'Assemblée Nationale* construed the minister's words as 'the proclamation of the new dictatorship by the new government, which they hope to inaugurate within the next three days'. But the 'manifesto' they wove together from scraps of the minister's bulletins was a fabrication. The mask had fallen, the editors declared, the enemy had shown his true face, the call to arms had sounded. 'Today, on all the walls of Paris, . . . we can read the first chapter of the proclamation of the new dictatorship.'[24]

The article caused widespread alarm, but the person most deeply affected by it was Ledru-Rollin himself. Terrified lest he be denounced as the traitorous instigator of an uprising against his own government, he ordered a massive armed callout of the National Guard against a demonstration that he had himself approved. The convoluted tussle of 15 April revealed how much ground the left-republicans had already yielded to their moderate and conservative opponents. 'Your circulars', Lamartine told the embattled interior minister, 'have harmed the Republic more than ten lost battles.'[25]

The effects of political polarization could be felt across provincial France. Throughout the spring of 1848, there were anti-tax rallies, local fights over access to forestry resources, and violent, often lethal, altercations between gendarmes and peasants in rural areas.[26] Provincial workshops for the unemployed became the focus of protests against government labour policy, and there were bitter fights over wages, attacks on overseers and police, and conflicts between local and foreign workers.[27] Far from channelling the energies of revolution into the pacific habits of modern democracy, the elections of 23 April, held under direct universal male suffrage with very high rates of participation, were marred by episodes of violence at over one hundred polling stations, in the course of which 981 people were arrested, 237 wounded and 49 killed. Poll workers, mayors and other local authority figures were physically attacked. Protesters smashed or stole ballot boxes or sheaves of counted votes. Electoral officials and groups of voters brawled with each other.[28] When they realized that the conservatives were winning in Limoges, workers invaded the prefecture armed with clubs and pikes, elbowed aside the National Guard and destroyed the official record of the electoral count. In the days that followed, the workers remained in control of the city, patrolling the streets in bands armed with axes. Only after two weeks did they stand down and cede the city to the Guard.[29]

The worst unrest of those days was seen in the Norman textile city of Rouen in the department of Seine-Inférieure. Here, as in so many other places, the left-wing list was soundly defeated. Not even Frédéric Deschamps, the radical political commissar to the department and a close associate of Ledru-Rollin, managed to secure a mandate. In front of dense crowds, bands of furious workers clashed with units of regular troops and National Guards around the town hall. During the ensuing struggles, the classical escalatory situation arose: a shot fired by accident from a window triggered panic. Barricades went up across the inner city. The insurgents spent the night of 27 April collecting firearms, digging up paving stones and carrying them up to the rooftops. Bitter fighting followed on the next day, as the military dug the insurgents out of their strongholds and used artillery to break down the barricades. In all, twenty-three insurgents were killed; many more were wounded, some very seriously; over 500 were arrested.[30]

Disappointment with the election results was part of the reason for the upheaval, but it blended for most of the insurgents with an anger born of declining living standards and extreme precarity. The textile industry in the city had been in crisis since the winter of 1847. The April election results mattered above all because they seemed to kill off any hope that a social revolution would bring lasting relief for workers. Frédéric Deschamps went to reason with the insurgents on the morning of 28 April, in the hope of getting them to stand down before the shooting started. He tried to explain to them the absurdity of their enterprise. 'Even if you were to succeed', he told them, 'what would you do then? Do you not support the current authorities?' One of them answered: 'That's true, but it's better to die by a bullet than to perish of hunger.'[31]

In Berlin, too, the middle weeks of April brought a sharpening of the political mood. There were heated discussions about the forthcoming assembly, though the issue at stake here was not, as in Paris, the timing of the elections, but the question of whether the suffrage should be direct or indirect (radicals favoured direct elections; moderates and conservatives, supported by the government, did not). This debate, like the French one over timing, was won by the moderates, with the curious result that the indirect suffrage applied in Prussia produced a rather more radical assembly than the direct one chosen by France.

Far more rancorous than the debate over the suffrage was the furore triggered by the news that the prince of Prussia was about to be summoned back from England. In the late spring of 1848, as we have seen, Prince William of Prussia, the younger brother of the king and the heir to the Prussian throne, was the most hated man in Berlin. It was said that he had refused to countenance requests from the citizenry to stand down the troops on the Schlossplatz, that it was he who had given the sign for the dragoons to charge the crowd on the afternoon of 18 March, that he had blocked all attempts at mediation between the city authorities and the king, that when the first wounded citizens were carried into the Palace courtyard, he had bellowed: 'Grenadiers, why didn't you shoot these dogs down on the spot!'[32] After a clash with his brother the king, William was persuaded to leave Berlin for London, but the demand for his abdication as Crown Prince continued to be heard across the city, and when an angry crowd gathered before his palace in order to demolish it or burn it down, armed Academic Legionaries could only save it by painting the words: 'Property of the People' on the façade.

The question of the prince's return to Prussia polarized Berlin as nothing else could. Not for the last time, the debate over a Hohenzollern Crown Prince stirred deep emotion in the population of the

Prussian capital. Radicals read the rumours of his imminent return as the signal of an impending counter-revolution. Some moderate liberals were prepared to accept his return on condition that this question of high policy be resolved by the forthcoming National Assembly, not by executive fiat. But then, on the evening of 10 May, a royal Cabinet Order appeared in the *Staatsanzeiger* announcing that the prince would soon be recalled.

When the radical student Paul Boerner looked back over the spring days in Berlin, it seemed to him that the outrage over the return of the prince marked a turning point in the revolution's history. There was heated discussion in the clubs. The walls of the city filled with placards and flysheets furiously attacking the government's plan. There were animated debates in the factories and workshops. For the first time, Boerner wrote, the entire population of Berlin seemed ready to rise and 'continue the revolution'.[33] After a mass meeting at the university, the students sent a four-man deputation to present demands to the Prime Minister. Paul Boerner, who was one of them, recalled the somewhat incongruous appearance of this group, with their ragged clothes, one of them still carrying a book under his arm. The meeting with Prime Minister Camphausen was cordial but fruitless. There was nothing to be done, the minister explained; yes, it was regrettable that the university had not been informed in advance of the decision to recall the prince; the representations of the young men would receive serious consideration, and so on.

Much more interesting than the content of the discussion is Boerner's description of Camphausen's appearance. This man of medium height, dressed simply in black, made a 'pleasing impression', Boerner wrote. There was nothing ministerial in his appearance; he looked more like a 'beleaguered schoolteacher' who was struggling to keep order in the classroom. 'Good-natured eyes, melancholy and weary, looked out from under the intelligent brow; the features of his face ... showed the endless exhaustion of this man, who seemed predestined to be betrayed and abandoned by all sides, to trust everyone and be deceived by everyone.'[34] As a portrait of what it meant to be a liberal ground between the cogs of politics in the early summer of 1848, this is hard to beat.

The protests against the Crown Prince continued. At the Tents in the Tiergarten, where the March movement had begun, speakers at a mass rally called for concerted action against what was now called 'the Reaction'. Placards appeared calling on like-minded residents to gather at

5 p.m. on Sunday, 14 May. Members of the Civil Guard and the flying squads were requested to appear 'armed and in marching formation'.[35] It was proposed that the king be confronted with a list of names for an alternative Cabinet, in which the radicals would be the ministers of Justice, Finance and Trade. A 'Defence Committee' was formed to draw up a 'war plan'. It looked for a moment as if the city were willing to defend and extend – by armed force if necessary – the accomplishments of the March revolution.

Yet even before it could be implemented, this plan was already beginning to come apart. The liberals of the Constitutional Club got cold feet and distanced themselves from the planned protest. The commission changed its mind about the armed formations and issued a new announcement begging all participants to leave their weapons at home. On the day of the demonstration, crowds filled the streets around the ministry of state. When a deputation entered the building to negotiate with Camphausen, they found that the minister was away in Potsdam consulting with the king. What should now be done? The members of the deputation discussed the options, and it was agreed that the crowd should remain in occupation of the ministry while couriers were sent to Potsdam to secure an official answer to their demands. Friedrich Wilhelm Held, one of the best-known radical orators of revolutionary Berlin, a popular speaker at the clubs and the editor of radical newspapers, was chosen to go out onto the balcony and address the people.

Then something odd happened. Instead of communicating the decision of the deputation, Held announced that the demonstration would now retrace its steps and return to the Tents. The tension in the crowd dissipated. To countermand Held's announcement was impossible – his grip on the crowd was too strong.[36] The demonstration was over; people began to drift away. Looking back, Paul Boerner felt that this was the moment when the radical movement in Berlin missed its appointment with history.[37] Over the following weeks, while the army rejoiced and conservatives came back out into the open, a sense of hopelessness began to gnaw at the democratic movement. Audience numbers at major club events fell. The momentum of change begun in March was lost.[38]

Held's about-turn on the balcony above the crowd was so baffling that Boerner suspected he was acting as an agent of the counter-revolution.[39] Was it true? Friedrich Wilhelm Held was a complicated figure. In 1841, he had published a booklet under the title *Prussia's*

Heroes, dedicated to Prince William of Prussia. The book was a bright-eyed celebration of centuries of military prowess – during the months of revolution, his enemies would occasionally brandish it during speeches to embarrass him. After a brief and unhappy spell in the army, Held got by with acting roles in various travelling provincial theatres. He published a number of radical newspapers, including the *Locomotive* of Leipzig, which was forbidden by the Saxon authorities when it reached a print run of 12,000 in 1843 (Held restarted it in Berlin after the March days). Those who knew him well found it hard to take him seriously: the overblown pathos of the speeches, the actorish mane of hair, the beard of a Germanic warrior and the broad-brimmed black hat worn at a rakish angle suggested a poseur rather than a politician of substance.[40] But the crowd loved him. Whether Held was an agent of some kind or simply changed his mind at the last moment is not important. He was a crucial link in the sequence of that day's events, a link made of capricious and changeable stuff. That a man like him should have found himself in such a position on 14 May 1848 tells us something about the absence of a cohesive radical leadership cadre.

In Vienna, too, stability remained elusive after the March upheavals. The problem was not a global loss of order. It was rather the parallel emergence of new kinds of order-making. The signs of a general mobilization of society were everywhere. Industrial protests became more frequent as trainee carpenters, masons, assistant printers, compositors, and the waiters and fireboys (*Feuerburschen*) of the Viennese coffeehouses went on strike or negotiated or petitioned for improved working conditions.[41] The choirboys of the Hofoperntheater refused to attend the church where they had singing duties unless the choirmaster gave them a portion of the annual fee he received for their services.[42] A few days later, the choirboys of another theatre marched in formation to the office of the choirmaster and demanded 'a rise in fees and a reduction in working hours', threatening that if their demands were not met, they would stop singing and would 'beat' any boy who broke their boycott.[43] The simultaneous empowerment of divergent interests produced a sharpening of tone. Press commentary became angrier and more biting. It was suddenly fashionable to send anonymous threats by post to one's political enemies or to unpopular public figures.[44] Anticlericals attacked the religious establishments of the Jesuit and Redemptorist orders – both seen as closely aligned with the conservatives at court. The crowds drove them out of town and then clashed with the National Guards sent to restore order.[45]

Among the most characteristic indices of polarization were the increasingly common cat-concerts of April and May 1848. Writing excitedly to his father on 12 May, Carl Borkowski described how they worked:

> A new technique has been brought to bear ... to force various fuddy-duddies of the old system ... to resign the offices they have misused. Pipes, drums, rattles and barrel organs [all play a role], but the main thing with these devil's symphonies are the cat-voices, which are imitated by the students with indescribable virtuosity. Not to mention the barking of dogs, the crowing of roosters, the crying of ravens and the clattering of pans. Honestly, dear Father, these cat-concerts ... are a true music of hell.[46]

Late in April, Borkowski helped to organize a cat-concert involving more than 200 people against the Prime Minister, Count Ficquelmont, for which he composed a chorale, whose text was copied and distributed to his fellow students. It included the following deathless lines: 'What Ficquelmont is up to / Nobody really knows. / He has never spared us blows! / He should abdicate today. / ... / Or into the grave we'll stow him away! / We'll stow that leathery man away!' Despite the deafening noise, there was no reaction to these antics from the Ficquelmont residence. The minister was apparently not at home – he had probably been warned in advance by a police spy. But when a terrified servant was seen closing the shutters on the first floor, paving stones shattered the windows. With some difficulty, Borkowski and his fellow students, armed members of the Academic Legion, managed to prevent a further escalation: 'we stepped forward quickly into the breach and were able to stop the mob from pushing into the interior of the house'.[47] Many of those Viennese burghers who had initially cheered the cat-orchestras as a likeable expression of youthful initiative came to see in them yet another symptom of general disorder and the waning of civility and respect. Articles in the quality press about the refreshing confidence and directness of the newly emancipated 'man of the people' made way for pieces bemoaning the disinhibition and rudeness that now seemed to mark social relations in the city.

The effects of this coarsening of the political mood could reach deep into private life. 'The Revolution', wrote the radical priest Anton Füster, 'cost me two of my best friends, the only friends I had in Vienna.' These were old and close friendships, and their loss was painful. It was politics that had destroyed them. Füster, who served as field chaplain to the Academic Legion, found some comfort for this loss in the devotion of the radical students under his pastoral care. But many of the students, too, suffered personally from the political schism in the city. In far-off Czernowitz, Carl Borkowski's parents lovingly indulged the radical adventures of their boy, but other students were less fortunate. Füster knew many who had been abandoned not just by friends and acquaintances, but also by grandparents, parents, brothers and sisters. There were students from wealthy families whose parents had disowned them and cut off financial support; they found themselves without shelter or even the means to pay for a Legionary's uniform. The bitterness and division only made sense, Füster reflected, if one remembered that the radical students were 'the bold apostles of a new religion'. Christ had said: 'I came not to send peace but a sword', and Christianity, after all, was itself a revolution: 'one of the greatest, bloodiest and most effective'.[48]

There was one important difference: whereas the political initiative gradually slipped to the right in Paris and Berlin, the opposite happened in Vienna. On 25 April, under pressure from the ministers, the Habsburg government granted the 'Pillersdorf constitution' modelled loosely on those of Belgium and Baden. It was an attempt, in the manner of Charles Albert of Piedmont-Sardinia, to fend off a further radicalization by pre-emptively meeting liberal demands. If the same framing law had been offered in early March, the tactic might have succeeded. But by the last week of April the horizons of popular expectation had advanced to the point where the Pillersdorf document seemed hopelessly obsolete. It was not the work of an elected assembly. Its tax-linked franchise excluded most of the population. Comparisons with Germany, where preparations were under way for the democratic election of a popular constituent assembly, helped to fire up the resentment. Withering commentaries appeared in the press. 'No one', the radical priest Anton Füster recalled, 'was satisfied with this imposed charter, except for the courtiers and the bureaucrats [of the Habsburg administration].'[49]

The government's refusal to back down or improve its offer set the scene for an escalatory spiral. Cat-concerts became increasingly frequent in the inner city, as crowds of students and workers singled out ministers and officials for ritual humiliation. The 'Central Committee', a body that had come together in early April to coordinate the disparate groups emerging from the March insurrection, reached for a radical measure: a 'storm petition' to be presented directly to the authorities by a massive demonstration. In it, the committee demanded the removal of the remaining regular army units (feelings were running as high against the military here as in Berlin), occupation of all military guard posts by members of the National Guard and the establishment of a security committee to oversee the administration of the city.

In the face of this growing pressure, the government made a gross blunder, triggering an abrupt radicalization. On 13 May, it ordered the dissolution of the Central Committee. Workers across the industrial sub-urbs on the outskirts of the city responded by storming factories and attacking textile block-printing machines. The Academic Legion and the National Guard formed up under arms in Stephansplatz and marched towards the Royal Palace. Shortly before midnight, it was announced that the Habsburg government had conceded all demands. The contrast with Friedrich Wilhelm Held's contemporaneous volte-face on a balcony in Berlin could scarcely be sharper. In a breathless anonymous account of these events jotted down at the time and hurried into print by a shrewd bookseller, an excited national guard expressed his elation: 'In Austria, the spirit of caste is dead. The people are happy. They cheer and shout! The city is illuminated. Long live the University of Vienna! Long live the citizens of Vienna!'[50]

There had hardly been time to take stock of the new situation when the emperor and his court took a shocking and unexpected step: on 17 May, without warning, they left the capital for the relative calm and safety of Innsbruck. This dramatic gesture of disavowal gave rise to confusion and consternation. Eight days later, the ministers followed up by ordering the closure of the university and the dissolution of the Academic Legion, but this merely triggered a further radicalization. On 26 May, National Guard and Academic Legion units took over responsibility for the defence of the city, entirely displacing the mili-tary units that remained there. Unpopular officials were dismissed. A Security Committee (*Sicherheitsausschuss*) emerged alongside the municipal government and soon established itself as the real power in Vienna. Under the presidency of Dr Fischhof, the physician who had stood up to speak in front of the Landhaus in March, the committee

Barricade at the University of Vienna on 26 May 1848. Nowhere else were radicals as successful in taking back control of the revolution as in Vienna. Student Legionaries, seen here standing on the barricade, were central to this process.

settled down to the task of managing the crisis in the city. The revolutionaries were now truly in control of Vienna.

Neither in Berlin nor in Paris did the radical wing of the revolutionary movement reclaim lost terrain in this manner. But even within the ranks of those who helped to secure this victory, there was apprehension about what might come next. In a letter he wrote to his parents on 5 June, the Academic Legionary Carl von Borkowski remembered 'the universal enthusiasm that seized each heart', but also acknowledged his own ambivalence: 'It often seems to me', he told his parents, 'that the Viennese Jacobins are gaining more and more in importance. In these days we often find ourselves thinking of the "terror and horror" of 1789.'[51]

In retrospect, we can see that the Viennese triumphs of May 1848 were less robust than they seemed. The Security Committee, an incomparably more sober and pragmatic body than its Jacobin analogue, lacked the means to raise revenues or to handle the deepening economic crisis. As in Paris, Berlin and so many other cities, an emergency public works programme was launched. By the beginning of June, it had attracted 20,000 unemployed workers from Vienna and the surrounding areas. But unemployment continued to soar, while consumer confidence dropped. The wealthier families fled the city, taking their money with them. The streets were full of domestic servants who had been dismissed from their posts without notice. Silver coinage, hoarded by those who had it, disappeared from the streets. This evaporation of silver currency was seen in many areas of protracted turbulence, from Rome to Budapest.

Yes, the court had withdrawn from the capital. That looked, in the eyes of some of the radicals, like a great victory for the revolution. In reality, it was a sign of the monarchy's strength rather than of its weakness. It was possible because Vienna was just one imperial seat in an empire of which Austria was merely a province. The Habsburg executive faced many threats during that season of turmoil – in Lombardy, Venetia, the Czech lands, Poland, Hungary and in Austria itself. But for every opponent in one place, the monarchy had friends in another. And the plurality of fronts, menacing as it seemed at times, endowed the court with a freedom of action other European sovereigns lacked. Even as they lost control of Vienna, they were able to seize the initiative in other theatres. In April, Count Stadion, Provincial Governor of Galicia, had already declared the abolition of feudal tenures – a move designed to secure the loyalty of the Galician peasantry, while Count Hartig was already busy in Italy, wooing the Lombardo-Venetians with the promise of future political reforms and a reduction in the most unpopular taxes.[52] In May, as the Viennese democrats were organizing mass demonstrations and the court was fleeing to Innsbruck, conservative Habsburg officials and soldiers were working with Croatian, Ukrainian, Slovakian, Serbian and Romanian national movements to weaken the Hungarian and Polish bids for national autonomy.

Seen in this light, the 'flight' of the court from one location to another, its capacity to operate in peripatetic mode, like the roving medieval kingship of Charlemagne, was a formidable resource and a key to survival. The loosely constellated aristocratic structure of Habsburg authority may have given the impression of fragility, but it allowed some parts of the apparatus to take the initiative while others were paralysed or under pressure. In June, while democratic elections to the new Austrian Constituent Assembly were underway, Habsburg forces commanded by Field Marshal Windischgraetz were already reimposing their authority in Prague, while the armies of Radetzky were in the process of recapturing the hinterland around Venice. For all its structural and personnel weaknesses, the Habsburg Crown remained a free agent, capable of projecting armed force and of launching a counter-revolution, even as the revolution in the capital city deepened.

RADICAL BREAKAWAY

Tucked into the south-western corner of Germany along the borders of France and Switzerland, the Grand Duchy of Baden was the first of the German states to witness serious political unrest in 1848. Since the mid forties, an oppositional party had been crystallizing in the country's Landtag, which met in the capital, Karlsruhe. Baden radicals had crossed the Swiss border to fight on the liberal side in the Sonderbund war. The victory of the liberal cantons in Switzerland galvanized the radical movement in the Grand Duchy. On 27 February 1848, electrified by the news from Paris, 4,000 people attended a mass meeting in Mannheim, where radical and liberal leaders spoke to the crowd, articulating a range of demands.[53]

One of the most charismatic and memorable figures to emerge from the revolutionary ferment of these months was the Mannheim-based lawyer and activist Friedrich Hecker. He was deeply embedded in that world of bourgeois voluntarism that shaped the lives of nearly all the political activists of this era: he had joined the Mannheim Music Society in his youth and was later a member of the establishment club 'Harmonie'.[54] In 1842, he secured election to a seat in the lower chamber of the Baden parliament. In the mid 1840s, Hecker was still working closely with the leading moderate liberals of Baden. He was one of a group of liberals who signed a letter congratulating Robert Blum on his role in the Leipzig events of August 1845. He belonged to the Hallgarten Circle, which brought together opposition luminaries from across the German states, and he contributed to various liberal journals.[55]

Like so many of his politically active contemporaries, Hecker was on an ideological journey. In 1846–7, he swerved to the left, adopting increasingly radical democratic and republican ideas. Hecker possessed all the attributes and gifts of a popular tribune: he was a 'fiery orator' whose words could carry an audience away. There was, Karl Biedermann recalled, something 'youthful and elastic' about the way he moved; his 'interesting countenance' was framed by 'long, chestnut-brown tresses'. His captivating manner alternated disarmingly between laddish crudeness and chivalry.[56] The Heidelberg university historian and sometime liberal Landtag deputy Ludwig Häusser remembered Hecker's 'youthful' and 'stormy' character, paired with argumentative gifts that only a practised lawyer can acquire. But Häusser also noted an element of flightiness and immaturity: the radical leader 'was and remained the dashing student who conducted politics in the manner of a university prank'. There was a theatrical excess in his manner, a tendency to 'the eccentric, the unusual and the baroque'.[57] And as he broke away from the liberal opposition mainstream, Hecker became one of those leaders who model a specific revolutionary style: riding boots into which loose trousers were tucked, a baggy blouse, a scarf (preferably red), the indispensable floppy, broad-brimmed hat with a feather, worn at an angle with a tricolour cockade or sash, and a large 'manly' beard. Neologisms for these items entered colloquial German: the *Heckerhut*, the *Heckerbluse*, the *Heckerbart*.[58]

At the end of March 1848, Hecker was among those chosen to represent their constituents at the German pre-parliament in Frankfurt am Main. It was immediately clear that the Hecker radicals and the liberal majority harboured fundamentally divergent understandings of what the revolution was and how it should continue. The liberal scenario ran like this: the pre-parliament, a body of elected representatives, would agree the steps required to establish a democratic German national assembly. Having done that, it would dissolve itself and transfer its authority to a 'Committee of Fifty' that would work in tandem with the old Confederal Assembly established in 1815 to oversee the implementation of the resolutions agreed by the pre-parliament. This was a model that imagined the new order emerging through cooperation with the old. Heinrich von Gagern, one of the most eloquent and authoritative liberals, captured the moderate view when he urged the pre-parliament 'not to destroy, but to build'.

By contrast, Hecker and his associates proposed a concentration of power. There must be no dissolution and no delegation to a committee: the pre-parliament in its entirety must become a permanent executive body. 'Executives of the German nation', he told the members of the assembly, 'be permanent; we expect of you nothing else but permanence.' The historical template for this demand was the French Revolution of 1789, when the Third Estate had pulled away from the Estates General, declaring itself to be the sole organ and representation of the people. Hecker's closest associate, the Bavarian surgeon and Mannheim-based lawyer Gustav Struve, distilled the views of the radical faction when he interrupted Gagern's speech with the words: 'The old authority is a corpse!'[59] And what could possibly be the point of collaborating with a corpse?

Like their colleagues in Paris and Berlin, the radicals at the pre-parliament in Frankfurt found themselves in the minority. They lost the debate over permanence by 148 to 368 votes. Tension reached a head over the issue of how to handle relations with the Confederal Assembly (Bundesversammlung), the rather musty body of princely envoys that had been meeting in Frankfurt since 1815. In its essence, this issue was about the question of how radically an administration needs to break with the past in order to qualify as unequivocally new. The assembly had laid off several individuals who had been involved with repressive episodes in the 1830s and it had formally declared its support for the March reforms underway in many parts of Germany. For the liberals, this was already enough. Keen, as ever, to avoid unnecessary ruptures, they saw the Confederal Assembly as a useful administrative holdover. But the radicals were having none of it. The assembly, they argued, should only be allowed to continue meeting on the condition that it categorically condemned its own earlier connivance in repressive laws and conducted a thorough purge of its personnel.

The Mannheim liberal Friedrich Daniel Bassermann tried to finesse the issue by proposing an amendment to the radical motion. Whereas the radicals had proposed that the Confederal Assembly be allowed to continue meeting only *after* removing all representatives of the old regime from its midst, the Bassermann amendment suggested that the Assembly continue meeting *while* it purged all representatives of the old regime. The issue now turned on the choice between the conjunctions 'after' and 'while'. To the surprise of the liberals, Hecker announced that he would leave the assembly with his associates if the Bassermann amendment were to be accepted. Taken aback by this tactic, the moderates drew together and dug in their heels. When the amendment was passed by a large majority, Hecker and Struve flounced out of the assembly with around forty like-minded deputies. They returned the next day, but the message was clear. These were activists whose support for representative politics of the liberal type was conditional – it would continue only for so long as the chamber met radical demands.

When the pre-parliament failed to elect any radicals at all to the interim 'Council of Fifty', Hecker changed course. It was now clear to him that the liberals of the pre-parliament were dangerous timewasters: they had 'entered onto the road of revolution' but lacked the courage to 'press forward to a decision in hours of danger and ruin'. Their 'chatter' (Hecker's term for parliamentary debate) would merely play into the hands of the reactionaries. Day by day, he later recalled, letters, addresses and deputations arrived urging him to launch an armed uprising in the name of a republic.

Republicanism, ubiquitous in France, was still quite rare in Germany, where attachments to the various dynasties remained robust. But it was relatively strong in Baden, thanks in part to the influence of neighbouring Switzerland and France. This did not mean that republicanism was a mass movement. 'In those days', Ludwig Häusser recalled, 'the population was still in a state of political naivety, and the question of whether one wanted a monarchy or a republic had not yet touched the masses.'[60] But the republican networks were stronger here than anywhere else in German-speaking Europe. It seemed clear – to Hecker at least – that the entire population of Baden was tensed and ready to spring. One need merely say the word and they would rally to the cause. It is a part of the power of political networks that they can come to seem all-encompassing to those who live and think within them. After the arrest of a close political associate by the police, Hecker fled Mannheim and travelled to Constance on the southern border of Baden. On 12 April 1848, he declared an insurrection in the name of a 'German republic'. As he and a small band of insurgents marched through the Grand Duchy, new volunteers joined them until there were about 1,200 men in Hecker's force, divided into riflemen, musketeers and scythe-men. There was also a small and probably not very effective artillery battery consisting of two field guns from the Thirty Years War (1618–48). Since there were no horses to be had, even for the leaders, the entire band were on foot. The Baden government in Karlsruhe responded by mobilizing the 8th Army of the Confederal military, composed of contingents from Baden, Hesse and Württemberg. A week later, Hecker's little band was roundly defeated by a more disciplined and better-armed force of about twice the size at the Battle of Kandern.

This was an experience rich in disappointments. Of those who had written letters and petitions goading the conspirators to action, many shrank back when the uprising actually broke out. In the memoirs he published of these events at the end of 1848, Hecker reasoned that most of these 'traitors' were city folk corrupted by the courtly service culture. The leading insurgents had at first found comfort in the conviction that things would go better in the little villages of the countryside, where minds and hearts were still free. But this, too, was an illusion. Hecker was shocked to find that in several places 'the women and girls turned out to be braver and more enthusiastic than the men' – some volunteers had to be bullied into service by their wives and girlfriends. In Stühlingen and other small towns, he found that liberal or conservative propagandists had turned the locals against the rebels by depicting them as if they were 'a horde of Huns', or 'not real citizens' but merely 'an evil mob'.[61] In Donaueschingen, where they had expected to find thousands of armed men ready for the fight, they found only two or three hundred – Amalie Struve, who also joined the campaign, put this down to the fact that the town was the seat of a once-sovereign princely dynasty.[62] The famous local radical Ochsenwirth of Bonndorf astonished Hecker by imploring him with tears in his eyes to abandon the enterprise.

There were some fine moments, too, when rays of sunshine broke through the April rain clouds, bathing the green hills in golden light. At moments like these, Hecker and his men felt as if they were walking through history, in a land of old chronicles and forgotten fairy tales. But there was also a lot of tramping miserably about in wet clothes through deep mud with fighters who had contracted diarrhoea from drinking bad water.[63] For some of the insurgents, it must have been a relief when the Battle of Kandern put an end to it all.

Two other forces had joined the uprising. Commanded by the social-ist poet Georg Herwegh, the 'German Democratic Legion' was a volunteer corps of around 1,000 artisans and other radical exiles from Paris and Switzerland. A further 500 volunteers served under the com-mand of Franz Sigel, a former officer of the Grand Ducal Army. But neither of these forces managed to rendezvous with Hecker before the debacle at Kandern. When Herwegh learned of Hecker's defeat, he wheeled eastwards across the country in the hope of uniting with Sigel and then attempted to withdraw to safety in Switzerland, but his force was broken up in a skirmish at Dossenbach. Franz Seraph Stirnbrand's painting of this small but brutal engagement shows men of the 6th Württemberg Infantry shooting and bayoneting a small band of scythe-wielding insurgents on the crown of a small hill while their comrades fire on fleeing volunteers. Among the latter was Herwegh, who made it to the Swiss border in an open carriage, hiding under the skirts of his wife, Emma. When he learned of the disaster at Kandern, Franz Sigel also turned east towards Schopfheim, but, like Hecker, he found the population in a hostile mood. He pressed on to Freiburg, where a few urban insurgents had set up barricades, but his force was broken up as they tried to pass the ring of Confederal troops encircling the city. It wasn't an especially lethal campaign by the standards of modern civil wars – the total insurgent dead at Kandern came to ten. Thirty were killed at Dossenbach and another twenty on the southern outskirts of Freiburg. A further eleven died in the barricade fighting as Confederal contingents retook the city. The total, allowing for those who died later as a result of wounds, probably came to around eighty. As one would expect, given the unequal forces involved, the losses were lower on the military side, at around twenty-three in all.

Militarily, the First Baden Uprising was a washout. But its transfigura-tion into a golden chapter of radical memory began as soon as the fighting was over, with the appearance of the first articles and memoirs by the

Franz Seraph Stirnbrand, *The Fight near Dossenbach*. Troops of the
Württemberg Army confront insurgents of the German Democratic Legion
under the command of the radical poet Georg Herwegh, near the little town of
Dossenbach on 27 April 1848. The Württembergers are seeing bayonetting and
shooting cornered Legionaries, while their colleagues fire on others fleeing from
the scene. The encounters between revolutionary militias and government
troops were often small in scale, but they were no less cruel for that.

principal insurgents. Hecker's memoir, published in the safety of Basel before his departure for the United States, left the reader in no doubt as to the importance of the venture. 'The first major republican uprising in Germany', Hecker announced, 'constitutes such an important and consequential moment in the history of our people, that it is the duty of the co-conspirators to convey a true account of it to posterity.'[64] Amalie Struve's account of the same events, published in Hamburg in 1850, dedicated to 'the women of Germany' and written (unlike Hecker's) in lucid, economical prose, was candid about the 'childish naivety' of the 'freedom army'. What mattered to her was its power as inspiration and model. The time would come, she wrote, when 'a free German people [would] remember with love and veneration those men who first dared to raise the banner of the republic openly against the prevailing tyranny'.[65] On this point, her prediction was sound. Hecker is still fondly remembered in the south and west of Germany, and in present-day memory his reputation overshadows the moderate revolution of his liberal contemporaries.

For Giuseppe Mazzini, as we have seen, splendid failures had always been as good as (or perhaps even better than) victories, because they refreshed the patriot movement with new waves of emotion. The fiasco of the Bandiera brothers in the Kingdom of the Two Sicilies was a case in point. The First Baden Uprising was 'Mazzinian' in this sense. But the differences are as interesting as the commonalities. Whereas it was Mazzini and his proxies who put the Bandiera brothers into service for the Italian patriot cause, the Baden insurgents were political actors and propagandists on their own behalf. They were not the emissaries of a mastermind in far-off London, but natives of the Grand Duchy. And unlike Attilio and Emilio they did not perish in front of a firing squad but escaped and lived to fight another day. Yet, like Mazzinian heroes, they remained true to the cause. Having fled to Switzerland, Amalie and Gustav Struve crossed back into Germany in September in order to launch an even less consequential uprising, the 'Struve-Putsch', which collapsed after only three days. After a spell in prison, they both joined the south-German radical struggle of the summer of 1849, a far larger and more coordinated effort, before fleeing again, first to London and then to the United States, where Amalie became a writer and a famous spokeswoman for feminism. Hecker remained a political activist in the United States and served the Union with distinction during the Civil War. In later years, he published an essay arguing against women's rights in which he observed that the bone structure, pelvic shape, cranial size and inferior 'brain mass' of women disqualified them from occupying political offices. He had apparently forgotten the role women played in his adventure – Amalie Struve in particular had ferried guns and ammunition in a borrowed carriage across difficult terrain from one rendezvous point to another, a high-risk task requiring strong nerves.[66] Franz Sigel became a major-general in the Union army, helping to recruit German-speaking immigrants, though he was less effective as a field commander. Emma Herwegh, who had served as an envoy between the volunteer corps during the insurrection, became one of the outstanding personalities of the radical diaspora – in the mid 1850s, she ran a Zurich salon frequented by many of the most brilliant dissenting intellectuals of the era – the sparkling, precarious world so brilliantly evoked in Tom Stoppard's trilogy *The Coast of Utopia*.

This was an era of radical celebrity. Amalie and Gustav Struve were already famous when the uprising broke out. As he passed through Triberg on his way to Constance to join Hecker, Gustav was surrounded by crowds of friendly strangers. In Stühlingen, Amalie, who was travelling incognito and had never been in this part of the country before, was recognized as soon as she refused to eat meat at a hostelry: apparently everyone already knew that she and her husband, as followers of the *Lebensreform* movement, were vegetarians.[67] Hecker became one of the most famous and recognizable men in Europe, his outfit imitated by would-be revolutionaries everywhere. If the leaders all emerged from the uprising as notorious personalities, this was in part because the phenomenon of celebrity was integral to the processes of political mobilization that propelled the revolution. In attempting to counter that celebrity, liberal and conservative journalists and cartoonists also focused on the individuals rather than the issues. There were numerous images of Hecker as a piratical, wild-eyed fanatic bristling with pistols – a kind of diabolical (if perversely attractive) alter ego of the sensible bourgeois householder. Depictions of Herwegh tended to focus on the fact that it was his wife, Emma, who had spirited him away from the battlefield. A widely reprinted poem depicted Georg Herwegh hiding under Emma's skirts, his head clamped between her thighs, as she drove him in a carriage towards Switzerland. In later years, fellow exiles who knew the story would annoy Herwegh by asking him if he happened to know the name of 'the man who had helped him escape to Switzerland'. 'I never thought to ask him' was Herwegh's usual reply.

The Baden story gave a human face and a concrete fabular shape to a specific form of radicalism. The memoir Hecker published in the autumn of 1848 fizzed with hatred of monarchy in all its forms. The Germans had been profoundly disfigured by this horrific institution. 'No other people of the civilized world' had 'sacrificed its happiness and its honour for so long and with such credulity and patience to the Moloch of monarchy', Hecker wrote. The plantation-owners of the West Indies, he claimed, drawing on no evidence whatsoever, 'treated their slaves with more gratitude' than the 'thirty-four clans' that reigned over the German states. The roots of the popular ambivalence and inertia the insurgents encountered among their fellow citizens lay exclusively in the paralysing influence of monarchy and its institutions. This was a vision strangely lacking in social nuance, drawn from that zero-sum discursive world in which everything the rich ate was plucked from the mouths of the poor. While the weavers of Silesia 'put grass, wild leaves and bad roots into their mouths with hands shaking from fever', 'the kitchen and cellars at [the Hohenzollern court in Berlin] swam in the saturated fragrance of fine foodstuffs and drinks'.[68] The monarch, by this reading, was the all-consuming monster, the 'disgusting worm' described by Settembrini in his pamphlet of 1847, or the verminous exploiter of Büchner and Weidig's *Hessian Courier* of 1831. Nowhere does this implacable vision find more graphic expression than in the hate speech of the 'Hecker Song', which imagines guillotines 'greased with the fat of tyrants' and the republic taking root in soil watered with gouts of princely blood. Versions of the 'Hecker Song' circulated in many variations until well into the twentieth century. An anti-Semitic version surfaced as a marching song of the SA during the 1920s and 1930s.[69]

Not all radicals were impressed by this kind of thing. Robert Blum was one of the many who were not. He had known and worked with Hecker for many years. He had met him through the radical networks. He had published Hecker's essays. His Christmas album of 1847, *Fortschrittsmänner der Gegenwart*, included a panegyrical essay by Hecker on the moderate progressive mentor of the Hallgarten Circle, Adam von Itzstein. But when Hecker threatened to leave the pre-parliament over the question of relations with the old Federal Assembly, Blum drew a line. Blum was unequivocally a radical, but he also valued the procedures and institutional culture of representative democracy. When opinions divided over the Bassermann amendment, Blum broke

Caricature of Friedrich Hecker as a piratical disturber of the peace (c. 1850).
His 'Hecker hat' set the tone for revolutionaries everywhere.

with Hecker, saying: 'I support the sharper version, but if it is defeated, I will respect the majority.' Like many radicals, Blum was frustrated by the prospect of remaining in the minority for the foreseeable future. He did his best to cultivate good relations with the radical clubs. But he refused to join those who stormed out of the chamber when they were unhappy with a result. His reluctance to burn bridges to the liberal factions earned him the contempt of the hard left. When Hecker and Struve abandoned the parliament to mount an insurrection, Blum was horrified: 'Hecker and Struve have betrayed the country in terms of law – that is the least of it', he wrote to his wife, Jenny, on 3 May 1848. 'But in launching this crazy uprising they have betrayed the People; they have blocked it in its triumphal progress; that is a disgusting crime.'[70]

TOWN AND COUNTRY

The European peasantries were the black box of the 1848 revolutions. We have seen that there was a moral panic around the topic of urban poverty. Books in the 'mysteries' genre cribbed from Eugène Sue claimed to explore the hidden world of the inner-city lanes and suburban shanty towns. But the real mystery was rural society. The countryside was where most people lived. In France, three quarters of the population lived in the country or in hamlets of fewer than 2,000 inhabitants, and the agricultural labour force accounted for about half of the population.[71] In northern, central and south-western Germany, the figure was between 50 and 59 per cent. Across most of central, southern and eastern Europe, more than seven in ten people worked the land.[72] And they did so under a dizzying array of highly diverse regimes, accretions of local custom and circumstance that defied and still defy generalization. Rural society was not a mass of 'homologous quantities' comparable with a sack of potatoes, as Marx famously put it in one of his less insightful moments, but a mosaic of highly stratified social systems marked by stark differences in wealth, status, occupational structure and power. In his relations with the poor landless agricultural labourer, the Austrian agrarian expert Hans Kudlich observed, the peasant in possession of a farm, however small, behaved like a blue-blooded aristocrat. Marriages between these vastly different castes was inconceivable and never occurred, even though the children of both strata grew up together in school, church and work.[73] Rural life was not the unchanging scenery that smiled from mid-nineteenth-century peasant genre paintings, but a field of flux in which politico-legal change, economic forces and demographic growth were always producing new tensions and precarities. No other sector of society generated such contradictory signals in 1848.

The news of revolution in the spring of 1848 triggered a wave of rural unrest. In Lombardy, during the battle for Milan, peasants followed the call of the tocsin sounding from their village churches and walked in thousands towards the capital. They flocked from the villages to help oust the Austrians from the lesser towns of provincial Lombardy. In the Veneto, too, peasants joined the National Guard in large numbers – here, by contrast with Berlin, Paris, Vienna and many provincial cities, the large number of peasant and rural artisan recruits endowed the Guard regiments with a genuinely popular character.[74] Across south-western Germany, mayors were ejected from their offices in small towns, there were cat-concerts against unpopular local officials and attacks on peddlers, 'usurers' and Jewish traders. Peasants from the villages came together to form mobs that attacked estate archives and administrative buildings or demanded concessions from administrators, such as the suspension of dues or labour services and the abrogation of hunting privileges.[75] On 26 March, the estate administrator at Gusow near Lebus in Brandenburg reported that around a hundred sharecroppers and day labourers had formed a 'band' (*Rotte*), thrown stones through the windows of his house and forced their way into his office issuing threats and demanding concessions: an increase in the daily wage, lower rents, a reduction in the price of wood and peat.[76] In the south of the Haute-Garonne, a small-scale peasant terror raged during March and April, while the hungry villagers of La Barousse in the Upper Pyrenees responded to the signals from Paris by sweeping down into the prosperous lowlands around Saint-Gaudens and pillaging the area until they were chased back into the mountains by troops.[77]

But how exactly did these manifestations of protest connect with the revolutions unfolding in the cities? If peasants in Lombardy or the Veneto joined the Guard or turned up to defend insurgent towns, did this signify support for the revolution, or was it a way of repudiating 'Austrian' institutions – taxes, monopolies and conscription – that were widely hated in the region? The violence against Jewish property cannot easily be slotted into a narrative of revolutionary 'politicization', even if those sacking the houses of Jewish citizens sometimes sang the 'Marseillaise'. The 'band' that menaced the administrator on the Gusow estate in Brandenburg was interested in rents, labour services and hunting rights – no mention was made of the constitution, elections, parliaments or freedom of the press. They also threatened to attack the homes of the better-off peasants: that night they processed to the house of a peasant proprietor (*Ganzkossäten*) by the name of Maren, who lived just outside the estate, and forced him to hand over money and a gun. As Robert von Friedeburg has observed, peasant violence and protest tended to be focused on local grievances and directed against specific allegedly culpable persons – bossy administrators, exploitative agents, peasant proprietors who were viewed as bad employers.[78]

As these examples suggest, establishing the nature of the connection between rural protest and urban revolution is not straightforward. We shouldn't exaggerate or mystify the divide between urban and rural people. The 'floating populations' of many towns, especially in central Europe, included large numbers of peasants. Peasants routinely entered towns and cities on market days – this is one of the ways in which the news of revolution was disseminated into the countryside. The characteristic institutions of the revolution quickly reproduced themselves, even in quite small rural communities. In the town of Votice in Bohemia, a community comprising 208 houses, a National Guard formed, even though the town lacked the means to provide its members with weapons – the guards marched with carved wooden guns, while the local potter made himself a rifle and a trumpet out of clay.[79]

And yet for many mid-nineteenth-century urban people, to journey into the countryside was to enter a different world and a different time. Dialectal and linguistic difference and the persistence in many regions of costumes that had become exotic in urban eyes were part of this estrangement. So was the stylized urbanity of the better-off city dwellers, which overlayered spatial demarcations with differences of class. The unevenness of transportation and communication networks meant that life slowed down sharply as soon as one left the vicinity of the larger towns.[80] But the core cause was simply the intense localness of peasant life, which manifested itself in a tendency to view politics, along with everything else, through the interests of families, clans, factions and communes. And these conflicting interests could be crosscut by emergent class antagonisms. A classic study of peasant society in eastern Westphalia showed that the cleavage within the rural population – between landowning peasants and hired labourers of various kinds – was more fraught than the conflict between 'peasants' and any other social group. Demographic growth had disproportionately swollen the numbers of the landless, producing a cruel power differential between those who controlled scarce arable resources and those 'rural proletarians' who had nothing to sell but the strength of their arms. Over the years, the landowning peasants had ensnared the landless ones in a 'quasi-feudal' system of exploitative leases.[81] Something similar happened in central Lombardy, where the emergence of a managerial class of agents and tenant farmers as middlemen between the latifundial landowners and peasant smallholders drove a turn towards more exploitative labour relations and generated new antagonisms.[82]

Local and regional histories of land management shaped grievances and demands. In some regions, such as Hanover and the eastern provinces of Prussia, where land privatization had done away with the commons, peasants demanded its restoration. In the south-German regions, conversely, where the authorities had intervened to protect, rather than distribute, commonly owned resources, the landless rural poor called for a *partitioning* of the commons, in the hope that the resulting parcels would provide a way out of poverty.[83] In Auronzo di Cadore, a commune about 120 kilometres north of Venice, villagers demanded that the local forest, which was communally owned, be divided up among the families of the village.[84] In the Kingdom of the Two Sicilies, by contrast, where the land had already been extensively privatized, rural protest tended to focus on illegal land occupations, hedge-burning and field devastations, followed by assaults on rent records and land and tax registries in the nearest provincial cities. In such cases, rural unrest could easily mutate into a generalized hostility to 'the rich'. In areas where the local landowning nobility were seen as the chief exploiters and impediments to an amelioration of conditions, peasants were more likely to look to the state as a potential ally, just as their fellows in the Ottoman Empire did.[85] We have seen how potently this assumption affected the events in Galicia in 1846. This was the default setting in the Habsburg lands, where the monarchy had historically been relatively active in pursuing agrarian reform, while the magnates had opposed it. In the summer and autumn of

1848, the Habsburg administration played masterfully on this register of expectations.

When the physicist and hydrostatics expert Giovanni Cantoni, chief secretary of the Department of Defence in the Milanese Provisional Government, cast an eye over the rural population of Lombardy in July 1848, he found little to celebrate. In the relatively dry central part of the country, the system of large multi-family farmsteads that had long enabled groups of peasant families to enjoy a secure living was falling apart. In order to maximize revenues, the landowners had subdivided their holdings, forcing tenants onto smaller, single-family plots. The practice of supplying the farmsteads with animals and tools had fallen into disuse and peasants faced higher costs. A threefold rise in taxation had eaten further into farming incomes, and because many plots were too small to be put profitably under maize, the peasant was obliged to rent extra land from the landowner, often at punishing rates.[86] The practice of handing the management of large estates over to a tenant farmer or agent had made matters much worse, Cantoni noted, because this middleman, having 'placed himself between the owner and the peasant', naturally strove to increase his own revenues through arbitrary rent hikes backed up with the threat of eviction.[87]

There was an environmental and ecological dimension to the problem: the pressure to maximize returns at the lowest level tempted peasants to cut down the thick hedges that surrounded and divided the land, leaving them chronically short of firewood and poles to support their vines. Moreover, 'the continuous clearing of the woods makes hail damage and drought more frequent, as the meteorologists have noted'.[88] Even worse off were the rural labourers of the well-irrigated areas around Milan and Lodi and along the Po valley. Cantoni described the workers in the areas where rice was cultivated in words that recall the documentary language of the Social Question:

> If we walk through the paddy fields, if we visit those damp and filthy dwellings and sit with those ... spectres animated by a languid breath of life, workers who in their prime, at the age of forty or a little older, already have their feet in the grave and the veil of death upon their earthen faces, if we observe their food, their drink, their labours and their hardships, then, after all this, we must especially curse the system of contracts that prevails among the paddy farmers.[89]

Peasants entered into complex relations of credit and debt with the owners of the land, but since all records were kept by the landlord's agents, there was no way of monitoring whether accounts were being properly handled. How were peasants supposed to know whether they were being paid fairly for produce from their plots? When the steward said he was withholding payment to offset debts accumulated over the past few years for equipment rents or house repairs, or to hold it in store for future emergencies, how could the peasant know whether these sums had been fairly recorded and added up? Especially worrying were the moral consequences for a country obliged to fight for its independence against a powerful enemy. When a government treated its poorest citizens in such a 'stepmotherly' way, how could it expect them to make sacrifices to the motherland? How should patriot leaders – like Cantoni himself – go about the task of inspiring in them a courage that they had 'forever lost'?[90]

This was an insightful and empathetic analysis of the conditions prevailing among rural workers. But it was also highly unusual. Most of the radical and liberal leaders of the western European states exhibited a yawning ignorance of rural life. In many places, the upheavals of that year removed or weakened elites whose members had a good if often condescending understanding of the countryside (because they were members of the landowning nobility) and replaced them with liberals and radicals from the world of newspapers, clubs and urban commerce or industry. Writing of France after the February Revolution, the historian George Fasel diagnosed a 'flat contradiction' between the aspirations of the new leadership and 'the society in which they lived'. Although evidence of a deep rural social crisis was mounting, the Provisional Government in Paris failed to put forward any agricultural reforms of significance, offering in their place 'trivial gestures', such as the awarding of prizes to exemplary farmers.[91] This indifference to rural conditions explains the single greatest policy error of the Provisional Government. In March, as they fished around for a means of financing the national workshops created for unemployed workers in Paris, the government decreed a surtax of 45 per cent (meaning that persons liable to tax of ten francs were now required to pay 14.5 francs).

In purely fiscal and financial terms, the 1848 surtax made sense. The February Revolution had destroyed confidence in paper assets such as bonds, shares and bank deposits, prompting a run on gold and silver that would be seen across much of Europe. Emergency measures such as the suspension of payments on maturing treasury bonds, the closure of the stock market, the forced acceptance of bank notes and restrictions on withdrawals from savings accounts helped to dampen the volatility, but private enterprise remained in the grip of a crisis, not least because bank closures made it difficult to convert letters of credit into cash. To ease this problem, the Minister of Finance in the Provisional Government, Louis-Antoine Garnier-Pagès, created on 7 March the first *comptoirs d'escompte*, or dispensers of credit notes, for Paris and other commercial hubs. By August 1849, the Comptoir National de Paris, which had opened on 19 March 1848, had facilitated 244,297 transactions, helping to ease the passage of commercial firms through the political turbulence of the revolution and its aftershocks. This was a 'revolution in banking'. It widened access to credit and created the first truly republican bank. And the finance for this bold departure from traditional practice derived largely from income raised through the 45 per cent surtax.[92]

The problem lay in the way the money was raised. The burden of the surtax fell most heavily on the masses of the peasantry. The Belgian government faced similar extraordinary expenditures, but it chose a different route, levying a forced loan to the value of twenty-seven million francs calibrated progressively to the various income categories. This was not popular, but it was much less hotly hated than France's 'forty-five centimes'.[93] Louis-Antoine Garnier-Pagès chose to tax the countryside partly because he was a fiscal conservative committed to balancing the books, but also because, like many urban liberals, he believed that while French banking, commercial and financial interests were intrinsically fragile, agricultural France, 'despite its sufferings', was 'of such inexhaustible fecundity that there [was] no disaster [it could] not recover from'.[94] The government did try to mitigate the impact on the poorest strata by inserting special exemptions, but these were ignored by many regional officials. The forty-five centimes did irreparable harm to the reputation of the new government in the countryside, indissolubly linking the revolution with taxation, the bête noire of the French peasant. The government's efforts to collect ran into concerted and violent resistance, especially in the south of the country, where army units were often needed to crush tax riots. Conservative and left-republican agitators found it easy to exploit resentment of a tax that was seen to be robbing hard-working peasants to pay doles to Parisian

loafers. In many areas of rural France, the result was a profound alienation from the new liberal political order.

We encounter the same problem in the Italian states. Antagonism to the
Austrians went deep into the society of the Veneto, meaning that the
struggle to drive 'the Germans' out of the province triggered spontaneous manifestations of solidarity among the peasant communities.
Unlike the peasants of Galicia in 1846, the peasants of the Veneto supported the insurgent patriots, not the Austrian regime. But the support
of the peasants could not be retained with patriotism alone. They
expected more from the revolution: less exploitative employment contracts, for example, a reduction in the hated Austrian taxes (especially
the salt tax and the personal tax) levied in cash from communities where
cash was always scarce, and caps on the prices of staple foodstuffs, an
issue of burning importance to the landless rural poor. The republican
government did reduce the salt tax and abolish the personal tax, to the
joy of many peasants, but this on its own did not suffice to relieve the
misery of rural communities, and there was no sign of a more concerted
effort to tackle rural social distress.

There were some who pointed to the mounting risks. Gherardo Freschi, agronomist, reforming landlord, and co-founder and director of
the Friuli Agricultural Association (1846), warned repeatedly of the danger of neglecting the problems of the countryside and urged the
republican government to regulate the price of bread by decree. The
editorials of his crusading agri-reformist journal *L'Amico del Contadino* became so intemperate that the republican authorities closed it
down at the beginning of May 1848.[95] The Venetian civil servant Fortunato Sceriman pressed the government to get active on the issue of
exploitative short-term contracts. But these isolated voices failed to
break through the prevailing indifference. And the indifference fed
through into the Manin government's management of the war against
the Austrians, which 'took practically no account of what was happening in the countryside'.[96] The revolutionary government in Milan was
even less responsive to peasant grievances than its Venetian counterpart.
Only in late June did it get around to abolishing the hated personal tax.
In both provinces, peasant enthusiasm for the revolution and even for
the struggle against the Austrians rapidly wilted. The spontaneous *levées en masse* witnessed in the early months were seen no more. By July,

the first cries of *Viva Radetzky!* – in reference to the Austrian field commander whose armies would soon restore Habsburg rule – could already be heard in the Lombard countryside.[97]

For the Hungarian government under Prime Minister Batthyány, agrarian policy was the most intractable problem of all, even thornier than questions around the franchise, minority-nationalities policy or the emancipation of the Jews. In this policy domain, the government had to balance the interests of the peasantry with those of a landowning class who composed much of the political elite, including the government itself (the new National Assembly that met from June 1848 was composed exclusively of landowners). But the Hungarian revolutionaries were neither ignorant of nor indifferent to the conditions prevailing in the countryside. Agrarian reform had been one of the central preoccupations of the Hungarian opposition since the 1820s, when a decline in the bargaining position of peasants on servile tenures triggered a 'crisis of neo-serfdom'.[98] The diets of 1836–44 had already enacted reforms securing peasant ownership rights to 'urbarial' plots, meaning plots that were farmed by peasants under hereditary tenures. Since 1840, peasants on hereditary tenures had been allowed to redeem themselves and their land by means of a one-off payment to their lords, though under terms so onerous that only 1 per cent did so.[99] Not until 1846 did the terrors of Galicia persuade liberal and radical Hungarian opposition leaders to join Lajos Kossuth in proposing that peasant emancipation be adopted as a firm policy commitment.[100] It wasn't just about fear: for the reforming liberal noblemen of the Hungarian opposition, it was impossible to imagine a 'modern' Hungary without a property-owning peasant class. And there was a tactical dimension too. The Habsburg administrations had historically been quite proactive in the sphere of agrarian reform; a Magyar elite that dragged its feet risked being outpaced by Vienna in the race to secure peasant loyalties.[101] In April 1848, the new government opened with a bold gesture, abolishing feudal labour services and most tithes, patrimonial jurisdiction and payments in kind on formerly servile peasant land. The subordinate feudal status known in the Hungarian statute books as 'rusticity' was erased.

Yet complicated questions about the type and extent of the land covered by the new laws remained unresolved. Which lands ought to count as 'urbarial', and which were merely leaseholds belonging to the lordship? Longstanding discrepancies between what the land records officially said and what people had been doing for generations created enormous potential for dispute. The new leaders were aware of the issue. On 19 April, Kossuth, as Minister of Finance in the Batthyány government, published an order clarifying several points in the new law and stating that those landowners who claimed land currently under peasant cultivation were under an obligation to prove that they remained the property of the lordship.[102] But this was an acknowledgement of the problem, rather than a solution to it. How strong did the 'proof' of ownership need to be? Where was the dividing line between obsolete 'feudal burdens' and the commercially justifiable right of landowners to require rents? Who should have title to commons land formerly enclosed by the lordship? The reforms themselves created new asymmetries. Some tithes were done away with, but the wine tithe was preserved. Some noble privileges were expunged, but others persisted, such as the noble monopoly on wine sales (finally abolished in September) and on most hunting and fishing rights. Most importantly, the blessings of April did not extend to those peasants – more than half! – who worked and lived on land personally owned by the lords: *they* were still obliged to provide the traditional goods and services. The grey areas were so numerous that the process of resolving them all would not be complete until 1896.[103] Here, as with the abolition of slavery and the relief of Jews from their civil disabilities, there was a gaping divergence between the legal act, accomplished with a stroke of the pen, and the social process of emancipation, which might extend over generations.

This helps to explain why the agrarian statutes of 1848, far from resolving the land question, triggered a wave of protests, even though the Hungarian revolutionary leadership were incomparably better attuned to the problems of rural society than their French, Lombard, Venetian or Sicilian counterparts. Peasants rebelled in Croatia in the hope of forcing the regional nobility to implement the Pest laws in the region as quickly as possible. The Serbs of southern Hungary and the Romanian-speakers of Transylvania mobilized for the same purpose, focusing their protest on the grey zones in the new legislation: the status of commons meadows and forests, recently enclosed land, vineyards, tavern licences and monopolies.[104] Here, as in so many other parts of Europe, there were calls for the return of 'usurped' land, refusal of payment and services and armed land occupations. 'In our misery, the news of the March events was for us a message from heaven', the peasants of the County of Baranya in southern

Hungary told the new government in Pest. But their petition went on to list numerous grievances relating to the implementation of the new laws.[105] Throughout late spring and early summer, tithe strikes, illegal land occupations and riots continued. In the Tisza region in the eastern part of the Hungarian plain, where cattle-raising was the main occupation of the peasantry, the rioting was almost continuous. In the county of Békés, where the revolutionary government feared that a peasant revolt was imminent, even the troops had difficulty in maintaining order.[106] On 21 June 1848, the Minister of the Interior, Bertalan Szemere, proclaimed a state of siege for the entire country. During the repressions that followed, ten ringleaders were publicly executed.[107]

If there was one administration that stood out in 1848 for its efforts to find a revolutionary solution to the Land Question, it was the Provisional Government of Wallachia. Here, as in many parts of Italy, peasants greeted the news of revolution with shows of enthusiasm. There was never any doubt that the new government would assign a high priority to agrarian reform. Among its members was the soldier, historian and journalist Nicolae Bălcescu, one of the co-founders of the secret patriotic organization Frăția. In 1846, Bălcescu published a study in the social history of landownership in which he argued that the current concentration of property in the hands of a powerful landed elite was the consequence of a centuries-long process of usurpation, principally through the forceful occupation of peasant land.[108] From this it followed that a true and just solution to the Land Question must lie in the repartitioning of the land and the restoration to the peasantry of plots in full ownership. This was not a socialist vision in a Marxian sense; it expressed an esteem for a free, smallholding yeomanry that Bălcescu shared with the Polish agrarian radicals of the 1830s, the Jeffersonian Democrats and the Prussian reformers of the Napoleonic era. Bălcescu described those who worked the land not as peasants or farmers, but as 'ploughmen' (*plugari*), a locution that aligned them with the ancient Roman ideal of the virtuous free farmer embodied in the statesman Lucius Quinctius Cincinnatus.[109] An agriculture anchored in unencumbered smallholdings, he argued, would not only be freer and more productive, but would also strengthen national cohesion: 'Those who possess land', Bălcescu wrote in 1848, 'will better defend their birthplace, are more deeply penetrated with national sentiment and will stand firmer against foreign incursion.'[110] In an environment where counter-revolution was most likely to come in the form of a Russian or Ottoman invasion, this was an important consideration.

Bălcescu's agrarian vision went too far for most of his fellow conspirators, some of whom were themselves wealthy landowners. But while the members of the Provisional Government baulked at Bălcescu's notion of usurpation, they did recognize the need to dismantle feudal property relations and to compensate peasants for generations of toil on the estates. Article 13 of the Proclamation of Islaz announced 'the emancipation of the peasants, who become owners by compensation'. The accompanying expository text exalted 'the ploughmen, the feeders of the towns, the true sons of the fatherland' who had 'borne all the hardships of the country'. It abolished forthwith the taxes in money and labour (*claca* and *iobăgie*) imposed on the peasants following the abolition of serfdom in the eighteenth century and promised them a piece of the land that they had 'redeemed over so many centuries with their sweat'. On the other hand, it also undertook to compensate the landowners for their 'generosity'. 'Like a good and just mother', the country would compensate every landowner for 'every small parcel of land' that he gave to the landless peasants, 'in keeping with the demands of justice, the voice of the Evangelist, and the beautiful heart of the Romanians'.[111]

This was to prove the most contentious of the new government's commitments. The wording of the text was both imprecise and contradictory: did the peasants possess a right or title of some kind, or did the partition depend on the 'generosity' of the landowners? Across the country, the deference and fear of punishment that kept peasants within the confines of the manorial order began to fray. Many peasants refused to perform their traditional labour obligations until they received the land they had been promised. The entire agrarian sector was thrown into crisis. Some landowning families simply left the country to wait out the turbulence. Others openly resisted the new measures, gathering in the Hotel Momolo on 1 July to denounce Article 13 as 'a clear violation of the rights of man'. The Minister of War, General Odobescu, and Colonel Salomon, a commander who was also a wealthy landowner, marched with troops on the Provisional Government's palace, but were stopped by a mass intervention on the part of the citizens of Bucharest. As soon as the alarm was sounded, people of the city came running, armed with swords and guns. A flash mob formed in the courtyard of the palace, hemming in the small force of putschists. Among them was

a 43-year-old woman by the name of Ana Ipătescu, the wife of a functionary in the treasury, who leapt up onto a carriage armed with two
pistols, exposing herself to the fire of the putschists, and goaded the
people around her not to give up the fight. An obscure figure in her time,
she would later be enshrined in Romanian popular memory. Seven
people were killed and nine wounded during this skirmish.

In order to calm the situation, the government announced the creation
of a 'Property Commission' (Comisia proprietăţii). This body would
comprise thirty-four delegates, two for each of the seventeen counties of
Wallachia, one of each pair representing the landowners and the peasants
respectively. They would deliberate on the issues in a 'mature' manner
and find 'a brotherly solution through a clear understanding among all
interested parties'.[112] Nicolae Bălcescu was probably the instigator of this
idea, though he was not asked to oversee the commission, possibly
because he was seen as too radical a figure to command consensus. The
task fell instead to the technocratic reforming agronomist Ion Ionescu de
la Brad.[113] But in his opening address Ionescu de la Brad antagonized
many of the landowners present by echoing the arguments from Bălcescu's
famous 1846 essay on the ploughmen.

The Property Commission was a unique institution in the Europe of
1848. No other government attempted to address the agrarian question
in this way. Since it was open to the public, who observed the discussions
from the galleries, it was more like a small parliament than a committee
(elections for the National Assembly had not yet been held). There were
spectacular confrontations and many fascinating debates. When a peasant objected that his onerous feudal duties amounted to 'slavery', a
landowner insisted that all duties, whether paid in cash or in kind, were
simply rents on land owned by another. The peasants pointed out that
anyone who had signed an oath to the constitution, as many landowners
had, was obliged to deliver on Article 13, meaning that it would be illegal
for the landowner to backslide on their commitment to relinquish a portion of their land. The landowners invoked the sanctity of property, but
the peasants, as James Morris observes, 'refused to recognise property as
sacred until they had some of their own'.[114] 'The whole of Europe', one
landowning delegate warned the commission, was watching the Wallachian revolution; the powers would surely withhold their sympathy and
help if they saw that 'our peaceful and public revolution . . . had commenced its work by abolishing the right of property and disorganizing

human society!'[115] One landowner broke ranks with his fellows, declaring, amidst storms of applause, that he would keep the oath he had sworn on the constitution of Islaz:

> I swore on the 21 articles of the constitution. I swore that I would give you land for your nourishment and for your livestock. . . . You were slaves, more slaves even than the Roma . . . and I enslaved you, brothers. I beat you. I disrobed you. For thirty-six years you cursed me for it! Forgive me, my brother peasants. Take back what I stole from you.

From the galleries came cries of 'Hurrah . . . God forgives you, brother! We are brothers! We will live in peace! Hurrah! Vivat! Long Live the Constitution!'[116] At moments like this, the Comisia proprietăţii resembled the truth and reconciliation commissions of recent times.

This was excellent political theatre, but after the first few sessions the landowners began to drift away to their estates on threadbare pretexts, raising doubts as to whether the commission was still quorate. Since there was little reason to suppose that further discussions would yield a workable compromise, the government decided that the issue should be placed in the hands of the forthcoming National Assembly (which never met). By the eighth and final session of the commission, only six of the seventeen landowners were still in attendance (there was one peasant absentee).[117] The failure to tackle the questions arising from the emancipation of the Wallachian peasantry undermined the popular legitimacy of the revolutionary experiment. An enquiry conducted after the revolution was suppressed in September revealed the extent of peasant rebelliousness: mass absconding, illegal pasturing, the theft of firewood from forests and orchards, and even – though this was rare – attacks on the houses of landowners.[118] Putting the disorder down by military means was out of the question, since most of the new recruits were themselves peasants. But inaction was perilous, too, since it alienated the rural elites whose support was also crucial to the success of the revolution.

No one could accuse the Wallachian revolutionary government of being unaware of the urgency of the Social Question on the land. But here, as in Italy and Hungary, the new authorities lacked the institutional grip, and above all the time, to solve the most intractable problem of European society. The complexity of the agrarian question meant that even in countries where the revolutionaries had made a good start on it, it was the post-revolutionary regimes that ultimately took on the task of clearing away what remained of 'feudalism' on the land, a process that tended to favour the landowners, including latifundial proprietors *and* independent peasants, over those very numerous rural people who merely worked the land.[119]

Many of the administrations that emerged from the revolutions of 1848 made valiant efforts to proselytize amongst the rural population, to win them over to the cause of the revolution. The Provisional Government in Paris sent revolutionary commissars to every department, tasked with explaining the revolution, and the education minister, Hippolyte Carnot, sent a fleet of emissaries out across the country to mobilize the schoolteachers in towns and villages in support of the new government. The reports sent by Commissaire Léoutre, tasked with 'revolutionizing' the department of the Meuse, to the Minister of the Interior convey a sense of how the functionaries set out to achieve their objectives. Léoutre spent the first two months of his stint travelling tirelessly across the department addressing the constituents; he met with local civil and military officials and sent 'intelligent and devoted citizens' to dispense propaganda in those localities he himself could not reach. He addressed circulars to the villages that were read aloud to gatherings of all the citizens summoned by a drum to the square in front of the *mairie* and the church.[120] In Wallachia, too, between three and five commissars were sent to every county of the Principality. Their mission statement declared that they were to act as 'priests of the constitution' and 'apostles of liberty'. The peasants should be gathered into the villages to hear readings of the constitution. The clergy should offer ceremonies of thanksgiving in the churches. This blending of religion and politics was characteristic of the Wallachian revolution, whose constitutional proclamation was saturated in the language of the gospels. But it also reflected the reality that no one could be found in most Wallachian villages except on Sunday – commissars who turned up to proselytize on other days of the week found that everyone was out in the fields.[121]

Impressive as these efforts were, they were monological, in the sense that they involved a one-way traffic in ideas and promises from the ardent emissaries of the new order to a supposedly grateful rural citizenry. When disorder continued despite this glorious dawn, the commissars tended to respond with puzzlement. Commissaire Léoutre noted that there had been 'a few disturbances' at various locations in his department. A combination of firmness, conciliation and 'a few severe sentences' to strike 'the culprits with salutary terror' had sufficed to quieten things down. But his characterization of the troubles is revealing:

> ... these disorders were not motivated by politics. Often, they were the result of divisions between communes or even families, divisions rekindled by the fermentation which any great social upheaval necessarily produces in the minds of people. The forests were also sometimes threatened, but the damage caused was of minimal importance.[122]

This brings us close to the nub of the problem. The commissars often shook their heads in frustration at the supposedly apolitical turbulence of their rural constituents. To them, the rural population appeared opaque and unresponsive. The politics of the revolution seemed to 'diffuse through them without leaving a trace'.[123] But the emissaries of revolution had failed to see that clan and communal rivalries and raging against foresters was exactly the kind of thing rural politics was made of. In order to understand that, they would have to have spent more time listening to, rather than preaching at, the people who worked the land. They would have to have been less like evangelists and more like anthropologists. Their failure to grasp the nettle of rural land reform allowed the counter-revolutionaries to regain the initiative by promising or launching reform programmes of their own.

'If you take the trouble and have the patience to enter into the peasant's train of thought', wrote the Austrian radical and Reichstag deputy Hans Kudlich, 'then it won't be difficult to connect with his rationality. It's not enough to write smart factual articles, or to go to meetings and hold speeches that are perfectly pitched for a Viennese lawyers' club. What you must do is sit yourself down with the peasants at a table and let them all hold forth.'[124] Kudlich was himself the son of peasants who lived and worked under the old feudal tenure system – his father still performed the hated *robot* on the estate of the lordship. Kudlich was studying in Vienna when the revolution broke, and he received a bayonet wound in the fighting outside the Landhaus in Vienna on 13 March. He joined the Academic Legion, was elected to the Austrian Reichstag on 24 June and took his seat there as the youngest member – he was twenty-four years old. A month later, he presented a draft bill abolishing feudal subordination and all the services and levies that went with it, from the *robot* to the tithe. The bill, which became known as the 'Kudlich-Gesetz', passed (with a few small amendments) into law on 7 September 1848, but no time remained to implement the measures envisaged by it. In October Kudlich tried, without much success, to raise the rural communities in support of the terminal struggle of the revolution in Vienna. Kudlich was that rare thing: a radical who understood the politics of the countryside. He saw more clearly than most how completely the new political leaders of 1848 had failed to connect with the issues that pressed upon the peasantry, and he was astonished by their condescending disappointment at the paucity of peasant revolutionary zeal. 'Only a radical theoretician who didn't know the peasants at all could have believed that they would rise for a revolution which after eight months in government had given no thought to their liberation!'[125]

NATIONAL QUESTIONS

In September 1847, the twenty-year-old Genoese patriot Goffredi Mameli composed a song and sent it to Turin to be set to music by the composer Michele Novaro (a fellow Genoese). The song, known variously as 'Il Canto degli Italiani' and 'Fratelli d'Italia', still serves as the country's national anthem. It is a text of hallucinatory intensity. The opening verse addresses itself to the 'brothers of Italy' – Mameli originally wrote an additional verse urging the country's young girls to sew flags and cockades, but he later suppressed it, meaning that the 'sisters' never made the final cut.[126] Italy, the song tells us, has woken up and put on the helmet of Scipio, a valiant general of ancient Rome. Then comes a question: 'Where is Victory?' As soon as Victory is found, the song continues, let her bow down to the Italians, because God created her as the slave of ancient Rome. The refrain, a call to arms, is dominated by the extraordinary declaration, uttered four times in each iteration and twenty times in all when the song is sung in full, that 'we are ready for death' (*siam' pronti alla morte*). Then comes a verse that contrasts the past with the present: Italians were once downtrodden and despised because they were disunited. But those times are over! Because the hour has struck for Italian unity and things are going to change. The third verse is composed in the language of prayer: if 'we' unite and love each other, the 'ways of the Lord' will be revealed to the nations, and with God on our side 'who can overcome us?' Verse four returns to the theme of historical precedent: the memories of Ferruccio (a sixteenth-century Florentine patriot) and Balilla (an eighteenth-century Genoese boy patriot) are still vivid and no one has forgotten the glories of Legnano in 1176 (when the Lombard League defeated the German Emperor Barbarossa) or the Sicilian Vespers of 1282 (when Palermo rose against the French). The anthem concludes with a jab at the nation's enemy. The 'Eagle of Austria' has shed its feathers – why? Because the heart of the eagle was burned when it gorged itself on the fiery blood of Italians and Poles.

This text is such a tangle of the bizarre and the conventional that it is difficult to know what to say about it, beyond noting that it sits quite comfortably amongst a family of similarly unhinged European anthems. The tight, dotted quavers in Novaro's setting and the call to arms in the refrain (*stringiamci a coorte*; let us form cohorts) recall the 'Marseillaise'. The reference to past shame and humiliation is a commonplace of nationalist song, found also in Sándor Petőfi's national song for the Hungarians. The patriots of olden days are another stock theme. The combative fifth strophe, which imagines the 'Eagle of Austria' sickening on the gore of Italians and Poles, reciprocates the acknowledgement of Italy in Wybicki's march of 1797 (still the Polish national anthem today), whose refrain opens with the words 'March, march, Dąbrowski, to Poland from the Italian land' (Wybicki was in Reggio Emilia organizing the Polish Legions for Napoleon when he wrote his song). And there are connections with the text of the Greek national song written by Dionysios Solomos in 1823, the longest anthem text in the world, with 158 strophes (of which only two are ever sung). The Greek anthem refers explicitly to the plight of Italy, alluding to the watchful eye of the Habsburg eagle, which 'feeds its wings and claws with the guts of the Italians' – this was almost certainly the inspiration for the aquiline passage in Mameli's song text. Here, too, the connection was biographical and historical as well as textual and literary: Solomos had spent the years 1808–18 in Cremona, where he met Italian patriots, wrote poetry in Italian and joined the Carbonari.[127] Connections of this kind can be found everywhere: Pacius, the composer who set the Finnish national anthem to music in 1848, was German; Runeberg, who wrote the words, was a Swede; Sándor Petőfi, writer of the Hungarian national song, who once referred to the national minorities as 'ulcers on the body of the motherland'[128], was of Serbian or Slovakian heritage (his birth certificate names him as 'Alexander Petrovics') and spoke Hungarian with a Slavic accent. For all its emphasis on the unique character and destiny of each nation, European nationalism was a thoroughly transnational phenomenon.

Nationalism presses on the story of what happened in 1848 in a way that no other concept does. These revolutions may have been experienced as pan-European upheavals, but they were nationalized in retrospect.[129] Over the century and a half that followed, the historians and memory-managers of the European nations absorbed them into specific national narratives. This makes it difficult to insert oneself imaginatively into a world before the political ascendancy of the nation, a world where national feeling was present and could be very intense, but as something quite mutable and localized, as one feeling among many. And this means that we need to steer a course between uncritical adoption of the nationalist perspective and overcorrection in the opposite direction, which would mean denying or downplaying the significance of nationally focused emotion. Balancing the analysis in this way focuses attention on the binary temporality of nationalism: for Europeans, the surge of national emotion and the rush to build national institutions could be experienced as a sudden and even shocking transformation. But that did not mean that it felt new or invented. The peculiar power of nationalism lay in the fact that it always manifested itself in the feelings of patriots as the recovery or resumption of something old, as an inheritance from the past. Nationalism could be shocking, but it was never surprising.

Long before the revolutions of 1848 broke out, it was already clear that conflict would result if national activists tried to realize their cultural projects by political means. Whether they used laws to enable or protect the use of a specific language in universities, schools or government agencies, or sought improved access to civil service posts on behalf of a specific linguistic group, or demanded a degree of regional autonomy, or a regional government of some kind, or even – at the far end of the spectrum – a new and independent nation-state, the advocates of different nations were going to wind up competing over the same terrain and institutions. The fundamental problem lay in the mismatch between the patterns of ethnic settlement on the continent of Europe and the lines on the political map. Some nations were subdivided into multiple sovereign states; others were enfolded within states controlled or dominated by others, or distributed across a plurality of states, in none of which they wielded political control. Some experienced more than one of these predicaments at the same time. The Germans were sprawled across thirty-nine German states, but they were a national minority in Danish Schleswig. There were six sovereign Italian states on the Italian peninsula in 1848, but in Lombardy, in Venetia and along the Adriatic littoral Italians lived under Austrian Habsburg rule. The Croats were spread across several provinces of the Austrian Empire, in most of which they were administered by the Hungarian authorities. The Romanians were settled across three regions, the Principalities of Wallachia and Moldavia, under joint Russian and Ottoman control, and Transylvania, which belonged to the Kingdom of Hungary. The Polish nation remained torn into three parts by the eighteenth-century partitions.

But to put the matter this way is already to flatten and simplify the issue, because it was not always clear who belonged to which nation. Was an Italian-speaking merchant with a south-Slav name who lived all his life in the Austrian province of Dalmatia on the Adriatic littoral an 'Italian', a 'Croat', an 'Austrian' or a 'Dalmatian'? An important study of nineteenth-century Dalmatia has shown that regional affiliations tended to outweigh ethnic or national ones.[130] 'We are Slavs by nature and Italians by culture', observed the Dalmatian lawyer, former Carbonaro and writer of poetry in Croatian Stjepan Ivičević.[131] Abbot Agostino Grubissich, leader of a group of Dalmatian patriots in Vienna, put the same point in a different way: 'we do not need to be either Italians or Slavs, but Dalmatians'.[132] Was the speaker of a German alpine dialect who lived in the Tyrol a 'German', or an 'Austrian' or a 'Tyrolean'? Among historians of nineteenth-century Europe, there has been a lot of recent interest in people who were 'nationally indifferent', either because they had founded mixed families, or defined themselves in terms of social status rather than culture, or felt a strong attachment to an ethnically mixed region, or shunned the polarizing rhetoric of patriotic enthusiasm: 'I am neither a Czech nor a German', wrote Count Joseph Matthias Thun in 1846, 'but a Bohemian.'[133] As a nobleman, Thun belonged to a transnational social caste that could be quite resistant to the blandishments of nationalism – many of the noble families of Bohemia were so mixed that assigning a national tag was simply impossible; 'whether a particular family was to become "Czech", "German" or "Polish" was often still in the process of being decided in the nineteenth century'.[134] But we have also seen that in Galicia in 1846 there were Polish-speaking peasants who saw their landlords as 'Poles' and themselves as 'imperial peasants'.

To abandon essentialist categories and focus instead on the language people spoke almost solves the problem, except for the fact that there were many patriots who did not speak or write their 'national language', or at least not well. Even someone determined to be a good Croat, like Dragojla Jarnević, might have to learn Croatian first. One of the key aspirations of Hungarian patriots was to wean their fellow Magyars off German and get them speaking more and better Hungarian. In parts of central and eastern Europe, as we saw in Chapter 5, patriotic movements were still working hard to construct a shared idiom of literary and scientific communication. The orthography of Romanian was still highly unstable and there was no single agreed name for Croatian, even among those who spoke it: 'ilirski', 'slovinski and 'arvatski' were all in use among patriots, who spoke a range of distinct dialects.[135] When the revolutions broke out, the first periodical in Slovenian had only just been founded. In some places, moreover, language was a less important fault line than religion – we have seen how this played out in the Swiss Civil War of 1847. In the areas of mixed Polish German settlement there were Protestant speakers of Polish dialects who identified as 'German' and Catholic speakers of German who identified as 'Poles'. When German-Catholics spoke of the nation, they imagined a sprawling commonwealth that included Catholic Austria, reminiscent of the old Holy Roman Empire of the German Nation. Protestants tended to think of a more unitary and Prussian-dominated 'lesser Germany' excluding the Habsburg lands. At festivities and demonstrations calling for manifestations of national sentiment, the two groups reached for different symbols.[136] There were similar fault lines between those Italians who sought a secular unitary republic of the Mazzinian type, those who favoured a constitutional monarchy, those who aspired to live in a secular federal republic, and those who, like Gioberti, preferred a federal or confederal state under papal tutelage. Among the German-speakers in the Tyrol, two parallel forms of identity emerged in the 1840s: one was strongly clerical-Catholic and pro-Habsburg and the other was liberal and less deferential to Vienna, but both were equally defensive of Tyrolean regional autonomy.[137]

And yet, in places where the conflict between ethnicities intersected with political tumult, nationalism became a uniquely powerful principle of mobilization. Nothing else could explain why, at the beginning of August 1848, the peasants of the hill and mountain communities of

Lombardy, who had every reason to be disappointed with the social achievements of the revolution, streamed towards Milan in their thousands to mount a last-ditch defence of the country against the Austrians.[138] In Hungary, despite the many outstanding questions around land reform and the franchise, the prospect of gathering the Magyars under a Magyar government mobilized the population as no other idea or argument could, drawing masses of townspeople and peasants into the struggle for autonomy and – in 1849 – national independence. This is one reason why the politically radical 'Society for equality' founded by newspaper editors and deputies to the National Assembly in Pest made so little headway, even though it had managed to muster 1,000 members by September 1848. The Ukrainians were very successful in creating political associations – there were about fifty of them in Austrian-ruled Galicia. But these were almost exclusively focused on consolidating Ukrainian rights and autonomy. The Polish–Ukrainian ethnic divide got in the way of efforts to extend Polish radical networks into the countryside. At the height of its appeal, nationalism could push other social and political demands down the hierarchy of needs, suppressing or at least postponing internal conflicts for the sake of the common fight. At such moments, it might ascend from the status of an approximate guiding precept to that of a first principle with an absolute claim on the individual.

Like the words 'history' and 'revolution', the word 'nation' underwent a dramatic process of semantic inflation. People used it 'with an almost universal confidence in its legitimizing power'.[139] It didn't seem to matter that it signified contradictory things. It became a word through which time flowed. The path towards a fuller form of nationhood seemed for many people the only imaginable way into the future. In a commentary published on 22 April 1848, the Helsinki-based Finnish newspaper *Suometar* captured this sense of movement and destiny. The French, the Italians, the Germans, the Magyars, the Scandinavians and the Slavs, the editor observed, all hoped, 'unimpeded by any national division, to come together in a self-united life of fellowship and thus . . . to play a part in the furtherance of civility'. This 'feeling for one's nationality' had awakened in every people 'emotions that were hitherto unknown'. 'From now on', the Finnish writer concluded, 'this is how European nations will walk into the future.'[140]

*

In Italy, the nationalist movement had always been fuelled by resentment of the presence of the Austrians in the north. The news of the March revolutions in Lombardy and Venetia provoked a mix of euphoria and Austrophobic frenzy. As the cities rose and the Habsburg troops pulled back eastwards to entrench themselves in the fortresses of the Quadrilateral, war fever gripped the peninsula. Bands of volunteers formed to assist the insurgents. Tuscany, the Papal States and the Kingdom of the Two Sicilies all sent military contingents to support the struggle against Austria. In Rome and Naples, the Habsburg insignia were torn from the Austrian legations and publicly burned. Newspapers launched fund-raising campaigns. The language of the Old Testament was summoned into service: plagues, exterminating angels, providential calamities, a time of sacrifice and judgement for a chosen people.[141] The Austrians were monsters, 'a thousand times more cruel than the Muslim'.[142] If the Italians were the children of Israel making their way out of captivity, they were also participants in a holy war of the medieval type. In the Veneto, the bands that formed to fight the Austrians were called 'crusades', a term that implied papal leadership. 'The Austrians are having to recruit criminals and bandits', a Civic Guard commander reported from the town of Spilimbergo, 'since no Christian will fight against the vessel of the redemption, blessed and guided by the immortal Pius IX.'[143] In Padua, volunteers lined up for registration in a state of almost mystical fervour. It was extraordinary, one of them observed, to see the 'incredible ardour' of these 'new crusaders who, marked with the sign of the cross on their chests in imitation of the crusaders of old, wanted to chase our oppressors across the Alps'.[144]

Attention focused on Charles Albert in Piedmont, the only Italian sovereign who was not only hostile to the Habsburgs but also possessed an armed force capable of making a meaningful contribution to the struggle. Across the country there were demonstrations in support of a Piedmontese intervention. In Genoa, there were signs that the agitation had acquired a republican edge. And then, on 23 March, came a fulminating leader article from Camillo Cavour, editor of the newspaper *Il Risorgimento*, which only weeks earlier had played such an important role in pushing the king towards the concession of a constitution. The Italian nation, Cavour argued, was de facto already at war with Austria. Italians were arming themselves for the struggle and preparing to move north. The question was thus no longer *whether* to commence hostilities, but *how* to do so: by means of a 'high' policy conceived 'in the name of humanity and of Italy' or via 'the tortuous paths of a policy of equivocation and doubt'. Under these circumstances, 'audacity [was] the true prudence' and hesitation was recklessness.

> Men like us, cool-headed men, accustomed to listening to the promptings of reason rather than to the impulses of the heart, having carefully considered every one of our words, must in good conscience declare that only one path lies open for the nation, for the king. War! Immediate war, without delay![145]

For a man like Charles Albert, the pressure was intolerable. He had hoped by means of the *Statuto Albertino* to bring public opinion over to his side. Now there was a new and even more dangerous demand. To invade Lombardy would be a frontal assault on the 'European order' of 1815, in which the Savoyard monarch, like so many of his royal colleagues, felt himself to be embedded – Piedmont, too, had after all been a beneficiary of those treaties. In 1831, Charles Albert himself had signed a secret pact with Austria in which Turin and Vienna agreed to put a joint army into the field in the event of a war with France.[146] The king was risk-averse and indecisive by temperament – the poet Giosuè Carducci would later call him the 'Italian Hamlet' (*italo Amleto*). But there were good reasons for not leaping into the breach. The army was in a poor state of readiness. There was not even a plan for a campaign in Lombardy or the Veneto and there were no serviceable campaign maps.

On the other hand, if the king did not act, he believed he might well be swept from his throne. He probably also wondered whether this might be the moment his dynasty had been waiting for, a chance to perform on a larger stage. He had long been attracted to the prospect of becoming a truly Italian and thus a truly European monarch. The lofty language of Cavour's appeal, with its invocation of a 'high' policy attuned to the destiny of Italy and of humanity spoke to that part of him. On the day after the article's appearance, 24 March 1848, he announced that he would intervene. But Hamlet was still hedging his bets: secret letters went out to the great powers assuring them that the campaign was merely a policing action to prevent the uprising in Milan from morphing into a republican revolution.

Roars of delirious applause greeted the announcement of the king's decision. But the ambivalence of the Piedmontese intervention soon became apparent. The army advanced at snail's pace across Lombardy (having no maps didn't help). There was no attempt to disrupt the Austrian withdrawal, to initiate hostilities in the Veneto or to cut the Austrian supply lines. Only as they approached Milan did it occur to the Piedmontese commanders that they might need tricolour national flags, the Milanese Provisional Government having made it clear that the banners of the House of Savoy would not be welcome in their city. A last-minute order duly went out for seventy tricolours.

The radicals around Cattaneo, who had taken charge of the fighting during the insurrection, got a cold reception from the Piedmontese monarch, who preferred the company of the local aristocracy. Charles Albert shunned the newly arriving bands of volunteers from the other Italian states, who he believed were infected with Mazzinian republicanism. When the king ordered a plebiscite to prepare the way for a fusion of Lombardy with Piedmont, it dawned on the locals that he was pursuing a dynastic and annexationist policy, rather than a truly national and Italian one. The suspicions of the other Italian sovereigns, who had been watching Charles Albert's moves with beady eyes, were vindicated. So were those of Milanese republicans like Cattaneo, who had warned against collaborating with a king, well remembering how badly such partnerships had come unstuck in 1820 and 1831.

Even without the support of the irregulars, the forces deployed by Charles Albert and his Italian allies ought to have sufficed to push the Austrians back. But the king sat tight in Lombardy, almost as if he were hoping to avoid an encounter with the Austrians. The other Italian contingents began to drift away: growing alarmed at the way he was being pulled into ever new commitments, the Pope dug in his heels and ordered his military contingent back into the Papal States. Having broken the oppositional forces of Naples in May 1848 in one of the first counter-revolutionary strikes, Ferdinand II of the Two Sicilies also recalled his troops. This was a heavy blow, because the Neapolitan contingent had fought bravely and well in the north.[147] The crumbling of the Italian coalition depressed morale and the slowness to take the initiative gave the Austrians precious time to reinforce their heavily fortified positions in the Veneto and plan for counterattacks when the moment was ripe.[148]

The Piedmontese army was well equipped (even if poor logistics ensured that this was less true at the battlefront), but they were weak in the area of command and control. Radetzky is reported to have had such a poor opinion of the Piedmontese generals that he ordered his gunners to 'spare the enemy generals – they are too useful to our side'.[149] When the Austrians finally attacked the Piedmontese army and the few remaining Italian contingents in a gruelling engagement at Custoza on 23 July, the result was a rout. Having failed to regroup effectively along the River Mincio, the Piedmontese withdrew in haste to Milan. Efforts by the city's insurgent leaders to persuade the king to remain and defend the city were fruitless – he slipped away at night as his army withdrew from the city. Over 100,000 citizens fled the city. A mood of bitterness and mutual recrimination settled over the national movement. It wasn't the end of the Italian revolution – the Venetians and the Sicilians were still holding out, and Rome was still in the grip of a process of radicalization that would culminate in the proclamation of the Roman Republic in February 1849. But Custoza did mark the end of any realistic chance that a combination of Italian forces would be able to pressure the Austrians into accepting a national solution to the Italian Question.[150]

Enrico Dandolo, who took part in the 'five days of Milan' and fought with the volunteers in the Lombard campaign of spring and summer 1848, recalled early scenes of rapturous welcome and euphoria and women waving from windows, throwing Italian tricolour cockades down onto the passing fighters. He evoked the courage and pathos of the volunteer brigades, marching through rain and mud poorly armed and grotesquely garbed in 'coats of every cut and colour', including discarded Austrian uniforms, peasant smocks and 'velvet suits' – these latter were fashionable in Milan at that time among patriots hoping to encourage native silk manufacturing, but not at all well suited to marching through impassable terrain in wet weather. Dandolo remembered the extraordinary valour of the Polish Legionaries 'grown grey in war' under their commander, Colonel Kamienski.[151] But his memoir also offered an unsparing account of the antipathies and distrust that undermined the unity of the Italian enterprise from the start.

If it proved impossible to coordinate the operations of the volunteer units effectively with the Piedmontese army, Dandolo argued, this was due to the egoism and jealousy of the individual patriot commanders, who hailed from different parts of the peninsula. Particularly harmful, in Dandolo's view, was the influence of the Mazzinians, who propagandized incessantly against the Piedmontese monarch. The hottest republicans said: 'We love the Croats better than the Piedmontese.' And yet, Dandolo argued, the Mazzinian dream of a nation in arms seizing liberty with its own hands failed miserably when it was tested on the battlefield. The cities had ejected the occupying garrisons and the volunteers had achieved great individual feats of courage, defending passes against the Austrians or harrying their lines, but they had done nothing that a regular regiment could not have done better. The persistent localism of so many Italians, their reluctance to think beyond the horizons of municipal politics, hobbled every effort to combine forces. Once the battle was won in Milan, Dandolo claimed, many of the insurgents had felt that their job was done. When the Provisional Government posted a proclamation inviting young men to enrol in the city's volunteer force and take the fight to the Austrians, only 129 armed men turned up. 'Municipal rivalries ... agitated the firmest minds, overturning all order and discipline', and the glorious formula 'the five days [of revolutionary Milan]' (*I cinq giornad*) became the slogan of a parochial municipal pride.[152]

Dandolo's was a partisan account. He was a moderate liberal and a constitutional monarchist. But the disillusioned tone of his memoir chimed with a view of the Italian events that was already widely held in Europe. When the Milanese republican and insurgent leader Carlo Cattaneo fled to Paris after the collapse of patriotic resistance in Lombardy in the summer of 1848, he found that the most influential literary and political figures were already almost universally of the view that the roots of the failure lay in the weakness of national commitment among the Italians. In Italy, they were saying, most Italians were still 'Austrian in spirit' and there was no popular foundation for liberty. The Piedmontese king had made 'heroic efforts', but these had been foiled by the 'discord, cowardice and perfidy' of the patriots. Distinguished Parisian men of letters had the effrontery to inform Cattaneo that the whole Italian movement was nothing but the hoax of a few noblemen who had oppressed and plundered the 'brown race' of Italy, indigenous to the countryside, whose only protectors had been the Austrians. To beat the Austrians, they explained, one needed to prepare everything in advance; one needed kindergartens, savings banks and railroads; one needed to wean the peasants from their lazy life of ease. In two or three generations, they assured him, the people would be mature enough for liberty. Cattaneo was enraged by such encounters: his interlocutors, who included General Cavaignac, the historians Augustin Thierry and François Mignet and the Minister of Foreign Affairs, Édouard Drouin de Lhuys, spoke of Italy as if it were a colony teeming with uncultured natives; they 'preached at [him], as they might have done to an Egyptian'.[153] If these attitudes were offensive to Cattaneo, they also suggested that French zeal for the Italian cause was likely to wane fast.

Cattaneo's own memoir of the struggle against the Austrians, written in a few frantic weeks of September 1848 and published in the following month, proposed a very different interpretation of the setbacks of that year. The Italians, Cattaneo insisted, had demonstrated their virtue and national spirit beyond doubt: who would have thought that a city like Milan would wake up one morning and drive out 20,000 Austrians, or that Venice would be 'lord of its lagoons', finding once again 'the serene constancy of ancient times'? The root of the failure was not to be found among the hardy Italians, who had given everything to the struggle, but in the perfidy of Piedmont-Sardinia, a kingdom in which the pride of Italian nationality was unknown. It was the cowardice, ambition, and duplicity of Charles Albert and his satellites that had condemned the national struggle to failure. The dream of the Piedmontese was not a national dream, Cattaneo argued, it was the dream of courtiers and sophists, the dream of the 'Italian north', of 'Upper Italy', of the 'non-Italian Italy'. Piedmont was 'a mendacious greatness' and a 'poisoned tunic'.

Cattaneo's memoir was conceived as an assault on the 'imaginary Italy' that he had found 'in the minds of foreigners'.[154] Dandolo's account was written as an angry riposte to Cattaneo. The dispute between them wasn't just about the choice between a monarchy and a republic. Cattaneo was a republican, but he was also a federalist, hostile to the unitary centralism of Mazzini. But unlike Gioberti, who was also a federalist, Cattaneo favoured a political order anchored in the autonomy of the cities, not a confederation of states or regions, because he believed that the city was the institution in which the Italian genius had always flourished most impressively.[155] The 'municipalism' that Dandolo hated was, for Cattaneo, the nation's most precious heirloom. 'The city' he wrote, 'was the 'intellectual thread' that endowed thirty centuries of Italian history with narrative coherence.[156] Even as it revealed formidable reserves of commitment and courage, the effort to mobilize 'the Italian nation' in the cause of unity exposed a deeply fractured vision of the future.

*

Across the lands of the Austrian Empire, the revolutions triggered a chain of interlocking national mobilizations. Some German-Austrian nationalists looked to the parliament emerging in Frankfurt as the key to a reorganization of German-speaking Europe. Recall the Austrian radical Schuselka, who found himself unable to sleep on the journey to Frankfurt as he dreamed 'with open eyes the dream of the unity and greatness of Germany'.[157] Polish nationalists hoped that the revolution in Prussia might provide the occasion for a renewed attempt to restore the lost Polish commonwealth. The new Hungarian administration, animated by its own national vision, intended to bring the Kingdom of Hungary under Magyar political and cultural hegemony. This last project was especially fraught because the kingdom was in fact a multi-ethnic state. The Hungarians, though the largest single group, made up only 41.4 per cent of the total population. Alongside the 4,800,000 Magyars, there were 2,240,000 Romanians, 1,740,000 Slovaks, 1,350,000 Germans, 250,000 Jews and a composite Slav population comprising 1,100,000 Ukrainians, Croats, Serbs and Slovenes. The Hungarian patriots have often been faulted for their short-sightedness in at first refusing to acknowledge the rights of the lesser nationalities, but in this respect they were no better or worse than any other European nationalist movement. And among the lesser nationalities there were national movements every bit as vocal, ambitious and well organized as the Magyars. By the end of March 1848, the Slovaks in the Kingdom of Hungary had already produced an official list of national demands that resembled those of the Hungarians, including the introduction of the Slovak language into schools, courts and the country administration.[158] Conflict was inevitable.

If we look briefly at the Croatian areas, where escalation was especially swift, we can discern some of the mechanisms and dynamics involved.[159] The geopolitical situation of the Habsburg Croats was convoluted, and its convolutions had a long history, dating back to 1102, when Croatia became part of Hungary. The Kingdom of Croatia, where a little over half a million Croatian-speakers lived, enjoyed a degree of autonomy. Its capital city, Zagreb, was the seat of a Diet dating back into the Middle Ages. But it was ruled from Pressburg (today Bratislava), the seat of the Hungarian Diet, to which the Croatian estates sent representatives. The ruler, or *ban*, of Croatia was always (until 1848) an appointee of the Habsburg ruler in his capacity as king of Hungary. More than 160,000 speakers of Croatian dialects lived outside the Kingdom of Croatia in the neighbouring inland Kingdom of Slavonia, a territory pieced together from lands conquered from the Ottomans in the eighteenth century and directly subordinate to the Kingdom of Hungary. And over 300,000 more lived in the Kingdom of Dalmatia, a territory built out of the captured former Adriatic possessions of the Venetian Empire in 1815 and ruled directly from Vienna. Others lived in Istria, further up the Adriatic coast, or in counties that were parts of Hungary proper. It was an incredibly messy, composite situation of the kind typical of Europe in the era before modern nation-states. There was a burgeoning patriotic movement among Croats, but the populations of these territories did not share a single, homogeneous 'national identity'.

To be ruled from Pressburg by Hungarians in the name of the king of Hungary, who was also the Austrian emperor, made sense for as long as Hungary remained itself entirely subordinate to Vienna. But the growth of the Magyar national movement created a new situation. From the early 1840s, there was deepening tension over Hungarian efforts to suppress the cultural expression of Illyrian patriotism. 'They oppress us on all sides', wrote an angry Dragojla Jarnević in 1843. 'We Illyrians must be given the name of our language and the freedom that our works may be printed. The Hungarians must never . . . oppress our mother tongue and impose their language on us.'[160] The twin revolutions in Vienna and Pest placed the traditional arrangements under pressure and opened the future to conflicting speculations. Hungarian patriots hoped to tighten their hold on the Croat periphery; Croat patriots intended to resist a Magyar power grab. The multiple persons of the Habsburg monarch – Austrian emperor, king of Hungary and king of Croatia (to name just three) – began to pull apart as the conflicts of interest began to mount.[161] It was a situation rich in threats and opportunities.

As soon as the news of the events in Vienna and Pest arrived in Zagreb, a group of patriots led by the Illyrian activist Ivan Kukuljević began drafting a list of thirty demands (*Zahtijevanja*) on behalf of the people.[162] A 'national assembly' was to be convened by 1 May at the latest; the Kingdoms of Croatia, Slavonia and Dalmatia were to be unified 'in accordance with the spirit of our laws and history'; the national vernacular was to be introduced as the language of schooling, church life and the governance of 'our kingdoms'; the 'national treasuries' that had been 'managed in Hungary' were to be returned to Croatian control;

the Croatian troops currently fighting for the Habsburgs in Italy were to come home immediately; the Croatian army must swear allegiance to the municipal constitution and to 'all other free peoples of the Austrian Empire, according to the principle of humanity'.

The Thirty Demands opened by affirming the loyalty of all Croats to the Habsburg dynasty, and the text repeatedly invoked ancient law and precedent. And yet in seizing the initiative in this way the patriots announced an abrupt departure. The most consequential break with tradition was the appointment of Colonel Josip Jelačić von Bužim, a man of wealth and patriotic credentials, and an experienced commander of the Habsburg troops in the region, as the new Croatian *ban*, or viceroy. Legally, this office was in the gift of the Austrian emperor, in his capacity as king of Hungary. The patriots and the Croatian Diet were thus acting *ultra vires* when they appointed their own head of state. But they insisted (in Art. 1 of the 'Demands') that the 'extraordinary position' in which the country found itself justified the establishment of a sovereignty that would return the kingdom into a condition of 'legal existence'.[163]

Looking back over the turbulence of 1848, the Illyrian educator Mijat Stojanović recalled how quickly the unanimity and connectedness of the opening phase of the revolutions gave way to the clash of conflicting interests. Some Croatian-speakers, known disparagingly as Madaroni, or 'pro-Magyars', supported the Hungarian revolution. But Stojanović belonged to the majority party of the 'Croatian-Slavonian patriots' who supported the newly appointed *ban* and intended to fight for the 'ancient municipal rights of the [Croatian] Triune Kingdom'.[164] Stojanović was a patriot, but he did not aspire to create a Croatian nation-state. He did not even call himself a Croat. He thought of himself as a resident of the Vojna Krajina, the military frontier, a historic borderland of the Habsburg monarchy that had been settled since the sixteenth century by Croatian-, Serbian-, German-, Romanian-speaking and other soldier-colonists, whose task was to fortify and defend the area as a cordon sanitaire against incursions from the Ottoman Empire. People from this region were usually known as *Grenzer* (frontiersmen), rather than by an ethnic tag. For Stojanović, the Croats proper were 'brothers', but so were the Serbs, whom he also embraced as 'brothers of one blood' (he would later pull away from this Illyrian commitment and embrace a more exclusively Croatian form of nationalism).

Stojanović described how he strove to help the people in his village confront a world in which everything was in flux and there were suddenly strategic choices to be made. When it became known how the 'Croat brothers' were preparing for war under the banner of Jelačić, he wrote, the local peasants 'began to come to me in large numbers, asking me to read them newspapers', to be instructed in 'what we should do under conditions of general disorder' and in 'how to behave in that critical and dangerous time towards the emperor, the *ban* and towards the Hungarian neighbours who saw our Slavonian region as their country . . .'[165] On 21 April (Good Friday) 1848, Stojanović explained to a gathering of villagers that the people of the military frontier had no choice but to abide by the emperor and 'to go the same path as our Croatian brothers'. Two days later, a petition was drawn up stating that the Croats of the frontier intended to join the military struggle of their 'Croat brothers' against the Hungarians.[166]

With the choice of Jelačić as *ban*, the Croatian movement acquired a new impetus. For many patriots, it was as if the nation were now incarnated in this splendidly uniformed man. Waves of emotion flowed towards him whenever he passed among the people. Mijat Stojanović recalled the occasion of his formal installation in office in Zagreb early in June 1848. Everything was cheerful, he wrote, everything had come to life. The streets of the capital were full of the fine carriages of Croatian nobles; deputies and envoys cantered on fine horses, everyone dressed in national attire, throngs of National Guardsmen, people of both sexes, diverse classes and all ages streamed into the capital from 'all over the homeland' and the neighbouring countries. 'Where can I find words strong enough to describe the enthusiasm of the people, how the ceremony was officiated, it was a rare thing – not since the time of Frankopan and Šubić [seventeenth-century patriotic noblemen, executed for their part in a conspiracy against the Habsburgs] had any *ban* been celebrated as Jelačić was.' Nowhere else in the national panorama of 1848 did patriotic feeling crystallize around a figure like Jelačić, who combined military experience, ruthlessness, personal authority, and the gravitas and independence of a wealthy nobleman.

The surge of Croat national elation feels familiar in the context of the panorama of revolution in 1848: the sense of immersion in a collective self, the presence of an emotion so intense that it is almost painful. We have seen how states of exaltation took hold in the streets of Palermo,

Naples, Paris, Berlin, Vienna and other cities. The presence of deputies and other 'representatives of the people', the melting together of diverse classes and regions, the memory of past fighters for freedom, the religious heightening of secular experience – these were all part of the common currency of revolutionary emotion. In Zagreb, they were heightened by the sense that the subject of revolution was not the individual citizen, but the nation as a common inheritance, redeemed from history. The streets were full of tricolour flags in red, white and blue; everyone was wearing cockades.

This was the national experience of 1848. It was all-encompassing and synaesthetic: the red hats and the blue surkas (folk jackets), the cockades and the bright tricolours, the music of one's own language resonating in the most solemn settings, suddenly connecting the world of childhood with that of history, public life and the political future. (Sadly, Stojanović does not divulge whether the food consumed in the streets and dining halls of Zagreb was also patriotic in character, but if it was, we could add taste and smell to the senses engaged in the pleasures of that day.) The magic of such events lay in their ability to transform consciousness while masking their novelty in a sense of continuity with a deep past.

Stojanović was himself transformed by this moment. He had initially felt himself to be an Illyrian frontiersman, rather than a 'Croat'. But his constituents in the Posavina county soon elected him to a seat in the new Zagreb parliament. It was here that he would truly acquaint himself with what it meant to belong to a nation of Croats. 'Life in Zagreb', he wrote, 'was a practical classroom for me.' 'I got to know our domestic history better', he wrote. 'I encountered the spirit of our old laws in the deliberations in parliamentary and committee sessions.' It wasn't just about the law-making: Stojanović took part in conversations with learned men, attended parties and dinners at which only Croatian was spoken, observed theatre and dance, and 'often visited the National Museum and the newly established National Reading Room'.[167] This experience of immersion produced both a deepening and a narrowing of vision. As a forgotten history swam into memory and doors opened onto a national future, other things were lost to view. The pace of emotional and intellectual change was remarkable. The *ban* would soon lead the Croats into a war against revolutionary Hungary. Jelačić would become one of the key players in the restoration of Austrian imperial fortunes. Among those things that would have to be forgotten was the solidarity, proclaimed in the Thirty Demands, with 'all other free peoples of the Austrian Empire, according to the principle of humanity'.

In sleepy, provincial Karlovac, Dragojla Jarnević was astonished to see how swiftly politics 'sprang up' in her hometown. The streets were full of citizens wearing the red hats and surkas of the Illyrian movement. Everyone 'longed for freedom.' When news arrived of the election of Jelačić, the entire city was illuminated in his honour. Music and singing rang in the streets, and 'at every moment, someone could be heard shouting *Long live!* The young men got hold of red hats and acted like members of the National Guard.'[168] The stolid apolitical journals of the 1840s, which had consisted mainly of material translated and reprinted from other sources, were now joined by twelve new Croatian-language titles, political newspapers of the modern type that handled a broad range of themes and were distributed widely across the Croatian regions.[169] For Jarnević herself, it was a sublime but also frustrating spectacle:

> as a woman, I am among the excluded and I cannot act in this profession of life . . . Day by day, I regret that I am not a man, so that I can be in the circles of action, in which the whole of Europe . . . is politicized, and in which more or less all business is conducted; only I am not allowed [to take part].[170]

Across the lands of the Austrian Empire, Slavic and Romanian groups counter-mobilized against the national claims of Hungarians, Poles or Germans. We can follow them in a cascade of mass meetings: the Croats convened one in Zagreb on 25 March, the Slovaks at Liptovský Swätý Mikuláš on 10–11 May. At Sremski Karlovci, an assembly of Serbian patriots demanded the annexation of the Hungarian regions of Srem, Banat, Bačka and Baranja into the province of Serbian Voivodina on 13 May. Each case was highly distinctive and yet they all bear a family resemblance. For the Czechs, the chief concern was those German nationalists – both in Vienna and in Frankfurt – who saw Prague as a German town and Bohemia as a German landscape. Here, as in so many other regions, the events of 1848 confronted patriots with predicaments that forced them to favour their own national struggle over another's. In April 1848, when German patriots prepared for the formation of the pre-parliament that would see to the creation of a national assembly in

Frankfurt am Main, the question arose as to which regions should be invited to send deputies. At that point, it still seemed reasonable – at least to German liberals – to suppose that Bohemian patriots might wish to take part in this great historical task. Their nationalism had not yet lost its cosmopolitan nimbus. An invitation was duly sent to the Czech philologist and historian František Palacký, author of the *History of the Czech Nation in Bohemia and Moravia*, an outstanding archivally based study that had appeared in German in 1836 and was subsequently translated into Czech.[171]

Palacký's answer of 11 April declining the invitation to take part is today among the most famous documents of the revolutionary era. The invitation itself, Palacký conceded, was moving evidence of the 'high humanity and love of justice' animating the German patriots at Frankfurt. If he felt unable to take part, this was for the simple reason that whereas the Frankfurt project existed 'to strengthen German national feeling', Palacký was not himself a German. He was 'a Bohemian of Slav descent'. And the history of Bohemia (which he knew better than any) did not justify the claim that the Slavs there were or ever had been part of a German nation. To these arguments from genealogy and history, Palacký added a strategic consideration that was also important to the Croats, the Slovaks and several other small nations: in creating a more cohesive German state, the Frankfurt patriots intended to 'weaken Austria as an independent empire', even to 'make it impossible'. But the people of Bohemia could have no interest in undermining a state 'whose maintenance, integrity and strengthening is and must be a high and important affair not only of my people, but of the whole of Europe'. Austria had long mistreated the nations under its sceptre, withholding from them the respect they deserved. Yet it remained 'Europe's shield and refuge' against the East, called into existence by 'nature and history'. The patriots of the little nations should at all costs stop short of full national independence, for an Austria partitioned into tiny national republics would merely offer 'a welcome basis for the Russian universal monarchy'. 'Truly, if the Austrian Empire had not already existed for a long time, then one would have to hurry in the interest of Europe and the interest of humanity to create it.'[172]

Nothing better demonstrated the willingness of the Slavic cultural elites to pool their resources than the Slavic Congress that convened in Prague between 2 and 12 June 1848. The 363 delegates met in three working sections, the Czecho-Slovak, the Polish–Ukrainian and the South Slav (Croats, Serbs and Slovenians). Proposed by the Hungarian Slovak philologist and ethnographer Pavol Jozef Šafárik, head of the University Library in Prague, supported by the new Croatian *ban* and organized by a committee of distinguished Czech activists, including František Palacký and Karel Zap, this was an impressive effort: many of the leading lights of central European nationalism as an advancing field of knowledge and research met each other here for the first time. There were exploratory discussions about how one might transform the Austrian Empire into a federation of autonomous peoples. In an unmistakeable signal of fealty to Vienna (or at least to the idea that Vienna represented), the Czech organizers ensured that plenary meetings took place before a huge black and yellow flag bearing the Habsburg double-headed eagle.[173]

The congress prompted furious responses from German and Magyar nationalists, who denounced it as a sinister conspiratorial operation to prepare the ground for a Russian pan-Slavist hegemony in eastern Europe. The reality was that the various delegations found it difficult to agree, even on who the enemy was. The Czechs worried about German doings at Frankfurt. The Serbs, Croats and Slovaks were more worried about the Magyars. The Ukrainians worried about the Poles. Some Poles wanted to harness Russia to a pan-Slavist project of geopolitical transformation, others remained committed to the struggle against Russia.[174] Language was a problem. The delegates went to great lengths to avoid speaking German, at least in plenary debates. As one Galician participant recalled:

> In the general sessions, each spoke in his own tongue. We pretended that we understood each other perfectly. However, when we wanted to know what was really happening, it was necessary to ask the speaker to repeat his remarks in German. The repetition took place in private, because it was impossible to admit openly that we had not understood.[175]

None of this affected the political impact of the debates, since the congress lacked any kind of enforcing power or sovereign sanction; not one of the proposals discussed there was ever officially adopted. The meetings ended when an uprising broke out in Prague on 12 June 1848. It would take the titanic effort of the war against Hungary to bring

Croats, Serbs, Slovaks and Transylvanian Romanians together into the same struggle.

There was jubilation in Berlin when King Frederick William IV announced an amnesty for the 254 Poles incarcerated for their role in the abortive uprising of 1846. The released men immediately formed a 'Polish Legion' of the National Guard, and their leader, Ludwik Mierosławski, was seen waving the German tricolour before cheering crowds. There was talk among both Polish and German radicals of the cession of the predominantly Polish areas of the province of Posen to a new Polish state and of an impending war against Russia that would allow the Germans and the Poles to solve their respective national questions in parallel.

But while Poles and Germans fraternized in Berlin, a spontaneous Polish uprising broke out in the province of Posen, showing how swiftly the transnational solidarity among ethnic groups could wilt in the face of competing claims to the same territory. In this province, secured to Prussia under the terms of the 1815 settlement, about 60 per cent of the residents were Catholic Poles, 34 per cent were mainly Protestant German-speakers and 6 per cent were Yiddish-speaking Jews. On 20 March, as the authority of the Prussian administration melted away in the Polish areas, the Poles formed a National Committee. Here, too, the emphasis was at first on inter-ethnic cooperation – at a Polish–German mixed demonstration on 21 March, German radicals wore both the German tricolour and Polish red and white cockades. The early official announcements of the Polish National Committee stressed that the Poles and the Germans were allies in a common revolutionary struggle. But the speed and widening scope of the Polish uprising created new alarms. Within a few days, the Polish National Committee had taken over Posen town hall. This famous sixteenth-century building, with its mannerist façade, elaborate loggia and a clock featuring mechanized goats that butt each other when the bells ring at noon, became the headquarters of what soon amounted to a Polish Provisional Government. Subordinate committees sprang up across the province, together with an improvised fiscal administration. As soon as Mierosławski arrived from Berlin, he established a network of militia encampments filled with recruits armed mainly with scythes and pitchforks.[176]

As the activities of the Polish National Committee expanded, the

Germans founded a National Committee of their own. Their requests for administrative offices in Posen town hall were turned down and the Polish leaders refused to accept a German proposal that the two national committees be merged. While the leaderships failed to cohere, a wave of inter-ethnic violence broke out across the province. In the heavily Polish areas, attacks on Jewish and Protestant German-speaking residents triggered the first waves of refugees. Harassed or threatened, many Prussian officials fled from their posts, to be replaced by Polish commissars who lost no time in removing all symbols of Prussian authority from the squares and public buildings and confiscating municipal treasuries. In the predominantly German-speaking areas of the west and north, German militias formed and intimidated Polish residents. In many areas, the Jews found themselves ground between the wheels of German and Polish nationalist mobilizations, though the majority either remained loyal to the Prussian Crown or gravitated for cultural reasons towards the Germans, an attitude that earned them no friends among Polish patriots.[177]

On 23 March, the town of Meseritz became the first to send a deputation to Berlin begging the king to defend his German subjects and, if the province was to be surrendered to the Poles, at least to annex Meseritz and its hinterland to the German Confederation. An order of 24 March from the king announcing a 'national reorganization' of the province merely deepened the confusion, since no one knew what 'national reorganization' would mean in practice. There were petitions for help from other localities. Some towns sent separate petitions to the king, the United Diet and the Ministry of State under Prime Minister Camphausen, because they were unsure of who was now running things in Berlin.[178] At the end of April, with clashes multiplying across the territory, the Berlin government sent in troops. Order was swiftly restored, the scythe men of Mierosławski being no match for troops of the regular army.

Nationalism was the most dispersed, emotionally intense and contagious experience of the revolutions. It flared up with extraordinary speed. It abolished or reversed the hierarchy between centre and periphery. Liminal locations like Schleswig-Holstein, the Vojvodina, Dalmatia and the province of Posen suddenly moved to the centre of attention. News from distant epicentres of conflict reverberated in great national assemblies. Nationalism stimulated new solidarities that allowed Bavarians and Neapolitans to emote on behalf of Holsteiners and Lombards.

And, almost everywhere, this kindling of solidarity within nations went hand in hand with an embitterment of the relations between them. A study of German folk lyric in Schleswig-Holstein revealed a dramatic sharpening of tone during the revolutionary year: 'Rise up, Kiel! Against Denmark's cowardly fools!' urges one song published in 1848. 'Prussian's weapons shine again, ach! so red with Danish blood' intones another.[179] The Mazzinian vision of nations marching with linked arms into a shared future was not yet dead – the Poles, after all, were still prepared to fight in Paris, Lombardy, Sicily, Hungary and Rome. Around 1,500 French volunteers fought for the Italian national cause, and we can still find Spanish and Italian volunteers in many theatres of conflict.[180] But the mechanics of solidarity and shared sentiment that had evolved in the 1830s and 1840s were now primarily deployed within the framework of individual nations.

There was a pop-up quality to the nationalist wave of 1848. Mass meetings saturated with the sounds, colours and symbols of the nation had a deep impact on those who experienced them, partly because they were so new. Obscure personalities flickered into prominence, like the minor functionary and popular tribune Eberhard Freiherr Kolbe von Schreeb, who seemed for a few weeks to embody the German 'national' struggle in Posen, and then disappeared from view again at the end of April.[181] The protest meeting of around 40,000 Romanian-speakers that took place on 15 May 1848 in charming, sleepy Transylvanian Blaj, a town with about 20,000 residents, was a completely unprecedented phenomenon.

Yet it belonged to the miraculous alchemy of nationalism that even as it inducted Europeans into new forms of solidarity manifested itself as the revelation of something inherited from the past – the struggles of the Lombard League, Moldavians locked in battle with the Ottomans at Răsboieni, Serbs fallen on the Field of Blackbirds, the Polish–Lithuanian Commonwealth, Sicilian rebels of all ages, the German 'Wars of Liberation' against Napoleon. It was as if the past conjured by patriots in the history books, operas, academic paintings, learned journals and poetry of the 1820s–40s had begun to pour into the present.

Underlying this mythical heightening of the present was the intimation that the nation was the oldest and thus the most legitimate of all things. In a petition of 19 April 1848, the Ukrainians of eastern Galicia petitioned the Habsburg court for support against the national pretensions of the Poles. The Ukrainians, too, they reminded the emperor, had once possessed 'princes of our own, descended from Vladimir'. It was true that the Poles had since then erased almost every trace of the Ukrainian nobility, 'the natural representatives' of the Ukrainian people.

> Nevertheless, the core of the nation remained – amidst all of these political and religious storms, the Ukrainian people remained firm and undaunted, always preserved its language and writing, and, having preserved the faith of its fathers and its nationality throughout all these tribulations, [the Ukrainian people] has bequeathed it to us as a priceless heirloom.[182]

This was an appeal to an imagined past, rather than to history as such, because, for the Ukrainians, history was part of the problem, not of the solution. It was history – and above all the history of Polish conquest and discrimination – that had robbed the Galician Ukrainians of their autonomy. The nation, on the other hand, was the thing that had survived *despite* history, always there, forgotten but alive, and still the subject of political rights.

> The fact that we lived for four centuries under Polish rule does not mean that we have lost our nationality, for the rights of a people never expire. The Greeks, who stood for centuries under the dominion of the Turks, have not ceased to be Greeks – they did not become Turks. Nor did the Lithuanians become Polish, although they too lived under Polish rule.[183]

On the grounds of this survival narrative, the Ukrainians now proposed that the province of Galicia be partitioned by the Austrian Crown into western Polish and eastern Ukrainian jurisdictions.

The representatives of the Galician Poles naturally rejected this proposal, and in doing so they also rejected the recursive logic of the Ukrainian case. When 'we' turned up in the Galician lands, the Poles argued, there was no one there. It was the Poles who had settled the empty lands of Galicia and it was the Poles who had built the Galician towns. What was most striking about these Ukrainian complaints, the Poles pointed out, was 'the fact that they are only now being presented'. If the Ukrainian demands really were the expression of a 'long repressed wish', then why had nothing been heard from the Ukrainians after the eighteenth-century partitions of Poland and the acquisition of Galicia by the Austrian government? Where had they been all this time? The bulk of the Polish counter-petition to Vienna was spent showing that the Ukrainian nationality was an elaborate fiction constructed by mischievous activists.[184] Like many nationalists, the Poles were primordialists when it came to their own nation and constructivists when it came to the claims of others to the same terrain.

Attacking the historical credentials of a rival national group was one way out of the impasse created by irreconcilable national claims. Another more radical option was to put aside the weighing of rights and accept that history itself, meaning armed conflict, was the only ultimate arbiter of such contests. It was an exercise in 'idiotic sentimentality', the radical democrat Wilhelm Jordan told the National Assembly in Frankfurt, 'to aspire to re-establish Poland' simply because it was sad to contemplate the story of its decline. For too long, Jordan argued, the Germans had languished in a 'dreamy state of selflessness'. They had 'raved' about the national struggles of others, even as they themselves endured a 'shameful servitude, trodden underfoot by the rest of the world'. It was time they embraced a 'healthy national egoism' (*gesunden Volksegoismus*) that assigned highest priority in all questions to the 'welfare and honour of the fatherland'. The right of the Germans vis-à-vis the Poles was not a historical or a legal or moral right: 'I say it clearly: it is none other than the right of the stronger, the right of conquest.'[185] It has often been observed that in speaking thus Jordan betrayed the generous, cosmopolitan vision of revolutionary radicalism. If we adopt the Mazzinian view, with its shining ideal-types, then this is doubtless true. But Jordan himself saw it differently: 'I wish to point out that I speak in this way not although, but because I am a democrat.'[186] His 'egoism', he told the assembly, was not the betrayal, but the expression, of Germany's national revolution.

Within a month of the outbreak of the revolutions, a crisis seethed over the future of the duchies of Schleswig and Holstein. These were predominantly agrarian principalities that straddled the frontier between German- and Danish-speaking northern Europe. The legal and constitutional status of the two duchies was defined by three awkward facts. First, a law dating back to the fifteenth century forbade their separation; second, Holstein was a member of the German Confederation whose representatives attended the Confederal Assembly in Frankfurt, but Schleswig to the north was not; third, the duchies operated under a different law of succession from that of the Kingdom of Denmark – succession through the female line was possible in the kingdom but not in the duchies. This last issue began to cause consternation in the early 1840s when it became clear that the Danish Crown Prince, the future Frederick VII, was likely to die without children. For the government in Copenhagen, the prospect loomed that Schleswig, with its large minority of Danish-speakers, might be separated for ever from the Danish state. In order to prevent this eventuality, the Crown Prince's father, Christian VIII, issued an open letter in 1846, in which he announced that Danish inheritance law would henceforth also apply to Schleswig. The letter caused a furore among nationally minded German liberals, some of whom now looked to Prussia for leadership in the face of the threat to German interests and specifically those of the Germans in Schleswig.

When he acceded to the throne on 21 January 1848, King Frederick VII raised the temperature further by announcing the imminent publication of a national Danish constitution and stating that he intended to integrate Schleswig into the Danish unitary state. A process of escalation now unfolded on both sides of the border: in Copenhagen, the Danish king found himself under pressure from the nationalist 'Eiderdane' movement. On 21 March, the new Danish government annexed Schleswig. The Germans in the south of the duchy responded by forming a revolutionary Provisional Government. Outraged by the Danish annexation, the Confederal authorities in Frankfurt voted to make Schleswig a member of the German Confederation. Acting with the official endorsement of the Confederation, the Prussians assembled a military contingent, reinforced by small units from several other northern German states, and marched into Schleswig on 23 April. The German troops quickly overran the Danish positions and pressed northward into Danish Jutland, though they failed to break the superiority of the Danish forces at sea.

In the National Assembly that began meeting in Frankfurt on 18 May 1848, the success of the Prussians and their German allies stirred an excitement verging on delirium. The representatives travelled from across the German states to take their seats in the new Constituent National Assembly, which met in the rotunda of St Paul's Church in the centre of the city of Frankfurt, an elegant, elliptical space draped in the national colours and dominated by a huge painting of *Germania* by the artist Philipp Veit. Veit's monumental allegorical work, which was painted onto canvas and suspended in front of the organ loft in the main chamber, showed a standing female figure crowned in oak leaves, a cast-off manacle at her feet; behind her, the rising sun shot darts of light through the tricolour fabric of the national flag. This was a chamber fashioned to reverberate to the news from Schleswig and Holstein. Several of the most prominent liberal deputies, Georg Beseler, Friedrich Christoph Dahlmann and the historian Johann Gustav Droysen had close personal connections with the duchies. Their pleas for concerted action on behalf of the beleaguered Germans of the northern frontier stirred powerful waves of emotion in the assembly.

What the nationalists in Frankfurt failed adequately to appreciate was that the Schleswig-Holstein question was swiftly becoming a European affair. In St Petersburg, the Russian government was alarmed to see the Prussians collaborating, as they saw it, with the forces of revolution. The Tsar, who happened to be the Prussian king's brother-in-law, threatened to send in Russian troops if Berlin did not withdraw the Prussian and allied forces from the duchies. The energetic Russian démarche in turn alarmed the British government, which feared that the Schleswig-Holstein question might serve as a pretext for the creation of a Russian protectorate over Denmark. Since the Danes controlled access to the Baltic Sea, this was a matter of strategic concern to London. In France, sympathy pivoted away from Prussia to Denmark. Paris had initially looked warmly on the German mobilization against the Danes in Schleswig, but things changed after the Prussian army marched into Posen. In his newspaper *Le Peuple Constituant*, Lamennais went onto the attack, excoriating the 'hypocrisies' of German national policy, which upheld the rights of a German population in a Danish province while suppressing those of the Polish population in a Prussian one.[187] French enthusiasm for the German insurgents soon gave way to anxiety about Prussian expansionism. Under growing international pressure from Russia, France and Britain, Berlin was ultimately forced to agree to a mutual evacuation of troops under the terms of the Armistice of Malmø, signed on 26 August 1848.[188]

The armistice came as a profound shock to the deputies in Frankfurt. The Prussians had signed it unilaterally, without even gesturing in the direction of a consultation with the parliament. Nothing could better have demonstrated the impotence of this assembly, which was headed by a provisional 'imperial government' but had no armed force of its own and no means of obliging German (let alone foreign) governments to comply with its will. In the mood of outrage that greeted the news of the armistice, a majority of the deputies voted on 5 September to block its implementation. But this was mere posturing. On 16 September, the members voted again; this time they capitulated to power-political realities and accepted the armistice.

There was unrest in Frankfurt that afternoon as the news of the vote spread. On the following day, a crowd of more than 10,000, including leftist deputies of the National Assembly, gathered on the Pfingstweide, an area of meadows outside the eastern walls of the old city. The 258 members of parliament who had voted for the armistice were denounced as 'traitors to the German people, to German freedom and honour'. There were calls for the leftist fractions to break away from the parliament and form an alternative body that would be a true representation of the nation. Towards evening, a group of hard-line radicals resolved to launch an armed uprising on the following day. Warned of what was coming, Anton Ritter von Schmerling, interior minister on the executive council of the Frankfurt National Assembly, requested military assistance. Once again, the tension between the street and the chamber was drastically exposed.

Prussian and Austrian troops entered the city early the next morning. After clashes on the Paulsplatz – directly in front of the church where the parliament met – the civilians dispersed to build barricades throughout the city centre. The assault on insurgent positions began in the afternoon. Negotiations for a ceasefire yielded no fruit because Schmerling, who knew that the army was bringing up artillery to reduce the barricades, refused to make any concessions. The shelling began and the soldiers took possession of the Old City. There were thirty dead among the insurgents; military losses came to a total of sixty-two dead and wounded. The moral impact of the defeat was amplified by the murder of two deputies in the streets of Frankfurt. Felix Prince Lichnowsky and General Hans von Auerswald, both members of the conservative 'Casino' faction and both Prussians, happened to be recognized by an enraged mob as they rode past the Friedberger Tor. The crowd pursued them, cornered Auerswald and killed him. Among the assailants was the baker's daughter Henriette Zobel, who struck at the victim with her brown umbrella. It was easy to identify her because witnesses remembered a well-dressed woman wearing a hat and scarf and carrying an umbrella. Since a post-mortem revealed that Auerswald had been killed by a bullet, it is highly unlikely that Zobel made any material contribution to his death. But, as a woman, she attracted public vilification and a correspondingly harsh sentence. After sixteen years in prison, she was released on account of the poor state of her health. Her (broken) brown umbrella can still be viewed at the Historisches Museum in Frankfurt.[189] Prince Lichnowski managed to slip away from the crowd and hide himself in a cellar, but he was later found, dragged out and wounded so seriously that he died on the same evening. Horror at these murders further isolated the left and drove many liberals to the right.

For the radical deputy Robert Blum, this was the last straw. Keeping the left united had always been difficult. Blum led the faction known as the Holländischer Hof, named, like many of the other Paulskirche factions, for the hostelry where they met to eat, drink and talk. To their left was the *Donnersberg*, a disparate group of far-left radicals who often voted against Blum and his fellow faction-members. Blum had managed to navigate his faction out of the crisis created by Hecker's insurrection in Baden. He was a partisan for German political unity, because, like many radicals, he saw the sundering of Germany into thirty-nine principalities as an intrinsically oppressive and counter-revolutionary arrangement. But then, in July 1848, his own group split over the Polish question. Blum had supported a motion calling for the 're-establishment of an independent Poland', on the grounds that the Germans could hardly in good conscience deny to a neighbouring nation a right that they claimed for themselves. He favoured a partition of the province of Posen, to be conducted after a thorough and objective study of the ethnic composition of the territory. It was in rebutting Blum's arguments that his fellow radical Wilhelm Jordan denounced the 'idiotic sentimentality' of those who betrayed their people by advocating an independent Poland. Jordan stormed out of the Holländischer Hof to found his own splinter group. The crunch came in September, when the parliament (but not the radicals) voted in favour of ratifying the Armistice of Malmø. Barricades shot up once again in the centre of Frankfurt, manned by angry proletarians. Blum had attended the meeting on the Pfingstweide, but on the following day he found himself defending the parliament against 'the people', an uncomfortable role for the famous popular tribune.

'The fragmentation of Germany', Blum wrote to his wife Jenny on 4 October, 'has not just alienated states and tribes from each other, it eats away at individuals like a malignant tumour and divides them from their comrades and from every necessary form of common enterprise.' The frustrations of life in the parliamentary minority, the parlaying among mutually hostile factions and the endless in-fighting on the left were wearing him out. 'I have never been so weary and lacking in energy as I am now.'[190] The decision to join a parliamentary delegation bound for Vienna, where a new and more radical iteration of the revolution had just broken out, was doubtless motivated in part by the sense of futility that had begun to engulf him in Frankfurt. But Blum also believed that Vienna was now the hub of the German revolution, the place where the entire project would either succeed or fail. By 17 October, when he arrived in the Austrian capital, Blum had just over three weeks to live.

'If the past imposed great efforts on us, it was at least better than the present,' Chancellor Metternich told his old friend Field Marshal Count Radetzky, in August 1847. 'You and I know how to fight against bodies, but against phantoms material force can achieve nothing, and today we are fighting phantoms everywhere.'[191] Nationalism was the most powerful and influential of the phantoms that haunted European politics in the 1840s. It sustained the extraordinary independence war of the Hungarians; it drove many of the parliamentary and constitutional experiments; it put fire into the bowels of insurgencies across central and southern Europe; it could even suppress, temporarily at least, the tension between radical and moderate revolutionary factions. But its effect on the revolutions as a whole was like that of heroin on the body and mind of an addict.

It produced states of unforgettable elation and an astonishing readiness to risk everything. But it also undermined the fellowship among revolutionary movements, creating opportunities for regimes that sought to use them against each other, as elements of the Austrian administration used Ukrainians and Croats against Hungarians and Poles. 'Through their separatism and national terrorism', the Austrian radical Carl Schuselka argued, 'the Czechs and the Magyars put weapons in the hand of the counter-revolution.'[192] It did not occur to Schuselka, who served in the Frankfurt National Assembly and the Austrian Reichstag, and whose memoirs are shot through with hostility and contempt for the Czechs, that his own perfervid pan-German nationalism was also part of the problem.

The sense of unity nationalism created was intoxicating, but it could also be deceptive. Many of the peasants who flocked to the standards of the national struggle soon drifted away again. In Germany, Protestants and Catholics, radical republicans and moderate liberals turned out not to share the same vision of the nation. Italians, too, as we have seen, were divided by their very different visions of what the Italian nation was. Nationalism forced many Europeans to choose between their identity and their politics. The American Chargé d'Affaires in Vienna quipped that in 1848 Italy and Germany could have achieved either liberalism or national unity; they tried for both and thus won neither. This was not actually true (national unity was for many reasons beyond the reach of both in 1848), but it does grasp the underlying logic of the relationship between liberal politics and national identity.[193] In September 1848, when a delegation of Magyars, deputies of the Hungarian parliament, turned up in Vienna asking for permission to address the Reichstag, there was a bitter debate over whether to allow them into the chamber. The Bohemian-German radical Ludwig von Löhner conceded the faults of the Magyars, but he reminded the deputies of the magnitude of the Hungarian achievement: in a time of general oppression, only the Magyars had found the courage to chart the way ahead under 'the modest light of a constitution'. But Löhner's appeal to revolutionary solidarity failed against the indignation of the (mainly Czech) deputies who rose in turn to denounce the oppression visited by the Magyars upon the Slavic nations. For as long as the Hungarians refused to render national justice to Slavs, their deputies would not be welcome in the Austrian assembly. National difference trumped revolutionary solidarity.[194]

Perhaps the single most dangerous feature of nationalism was that it lured revolutionaries onto terrain where they were destined never to find a firm footing, the terrain of geopolitics, on which they would always be outgunned by the powers of the old regime. This problem became critical when revolutions were suppressed by armies of intervention, but also when nationalists ceded control of their own national struggles to better-armed competitors. The Italian patriot volunteers could no more compete with the army of Piedmont than the deputies in Frankfurt with the army of Prussia. The history of the post-revolutionary decades would show that nationalism was most potent when it was yoked together with the machinery of state power.

A REVOLUTION SHUTS ITSELF DOWN

By the summer of 1848, the National Workshops established by the Provisional Government in February had become the most controversial revolutionary institution in France. They had been rushed into existence under pressure. Lamartine would later describe the decision to create them as a 'temporary expedient, terrible but necessary'.[195] They were unpopular with the independent entrepreneurs and employers of Paris, who saw them not as a machine for social pacification, but as an encouragement to labour unrest, since workers who went on strike in the private sector could always sustain themselves by seeking relief in the workshops. They were hated by the taxpayers of provincial France, who were expected to pay for them. And even if they prevented some families from starving, they were frustrating for the Paris unemployed, who entered the workshops expecting a new domain for the application of unalienated labour, but found themselves saddled with often meaningless tasks for minimal pay and bossed about by 'group leaders' recruited from the students of the École Centrale, a training institute for engineers.[196]

The National Workshops were not even popular with the man who ran them.[197] Émile Thomas was a 'firm friend of the cause of order and an implacable opponent of Louis Blanc and all his works'.[198] He spoke in his memoirs of 'that terrible, that absurd decree [of 25 March – the work of Louis Blanc] guaranteeing work to all citizens'. The mood at his headquarters on the rue Bondy often verged on panic. The entire operation was run on a shoestring, and it proved virtually impossible to reconcile the will to control indigent humans with the unpredictability of the labour markets in a city gripped by revolution. 'We found ourselves', Émile Thomas later wrote, 'plunged in a situation from which we could see no exit.'[199] Neither the centralization of the labour force nor the payment of doles to workers were principles he accepted. He only claimed 'credit', he wrote in his memoirs, 'for the establishment of that semi-military order, of those instruments of moral influence by which for almost three months I was able to maintain order in Paris . . . and to vanquish the perpetual stirrings of anarchy'.[200]

While Émile Thomas struggled to control the unemployed of Paris, the balance of political power in the city continued to slip away from the left. On 9 May, the Constituent National Assembly replaced the Provisional Government with a five-man collective presidency called the Executive Commission. The new body comprised four moderates (Garnier-Pagès, Marie de Saint-Georges, François Arago and Alphonse de Lamartine) and only one radical (Alexandre Ledru-Rollin). In an increasingly polarized assembly, the new Executive Commission and its ministers commanded the support neither of the left nor of the right of the chamber. It was also bitterly resented and distrusted by the left-republican Parisian clubs. This was important, because it meant that the new government was unable to mediate between parliament and the clubs. The gap between the two opened further when the conservative majority of the National Assembly pushed through a resolution suspending the right of the clubs to send delegations to deliver petitions to the assembly, a sans-culotte practice of 1792–4 that had resumed in February 1848.

On the morning of 15 May, around 20,000 members of the radical clubs marched from the place de la Bastille down the main boulevards towards the place de la Concorde and from there to the Palais Bourbon, where the assembly was meeting. At their head was Aloysius Huber, president of the Club des Clubs. The plan was to protest against the Prussian suppression of the Polish national insurgency underway in the province of Posen. Polish emissaries from Posen and Galicia had asked one of the deputies in the chamber to raise the Polish question at the session of 15 May, and the left-republican clubs, keen to make up the ground they had lost since the elections, chose this day to mount a large demonstration, during which they intended to present a petition in support of the Polish freedom struggle.[201] If they were frustrated by French inaction on the international front, they were also indignant at the suppression of petitioning rights and the failure of the assembly to make progress on social reform at home. The catalyst here was a proposal by Louis Blanc, presented to the chamber on the afternoon of 10 May, that a Ministry of Progress be established to take control of the Social Question. This was not the first time Blanc had made this demand, but it now came to be seen as a test of the chamber's good faith. When his proposal was shouted down by the deputies and replaced by a plan to open an 'investigation' into the problem of poverty, there was a surge of indignation in the radical press. Now, if not before, it was clear that republicanism and the commitment to social causes were different and separable things. The planning for 15 May – such as it was – took on a more insurrectionary character.[202]

The invasion of the National Assembly produced scenes of chaos that call to mind the events of 6 January 2022 in Washington DC. Around 3,000 protesters, some of whom were armed, crowded into the chamber. They observed the deputies in their seats as if they were fugitives who had at last been run to ground. Alexis de Tocqueville, who was observing the scene from his seat, heard one man in a worker's blouse point to the elderly deputy Lacordaire, sitting in his black and white Dominican habit high up on the benches of the left, and say: 'Look at that vulture there. I should love to twist his neck.' Ever ambivalent, Tocqueville was shocked by the violence of the sentiment but also impressed by the aptness of the simile, since he had to concede that Lacordaire, with his long bony neck, narrow face and glittering eyes really did resemble a bird of prey.[203]

Valentin Huber, the putative leader of the invasion, had forgotten to bring along the text on Poland that he was supposed to read aloud to the deputies, so the scientist Alexandre Raspail, struggling to make himself heard amidst the din, read out a fiery, hastily improvised substitute. Among those who stepped forward to address the chamber was Louis-Auguste Blanqui, who demanded that the Polish fatherland be restored. Alexis de Tocqueville, who was seeing him for the first time, recoiled from the sight of this untiring veteran of the radical struggle and later captured him in language saturated with the visual codes of July Monarchy caricature: 'He had sunken, withered cheeks, white lips and a sickly, malign, dirty look, like a mouldy corpse; he was wearing no visible linen; an old black frockcoat clung to his lean, emaciated limbs; he looked as if he had lived in a sewer and only just come out.'[204]

Blanqui spoke briefly of Poland until he was distracted by the people around him, who pushed him and cried: 'Rouen! Rouen! Speak of Rouen!', at which point he turned to the massacre of 28 April, blaming the assembly for the misery in which the textile workers now found themselves. Armand Barbès, who had done time with Blanqui at Mont-Saint-Michel and Doullens, followed with an address in which he stated a number of peremptory demands: the assembly must 'immediately vote the departure of an army for Poland', a tax of a billion francs on the

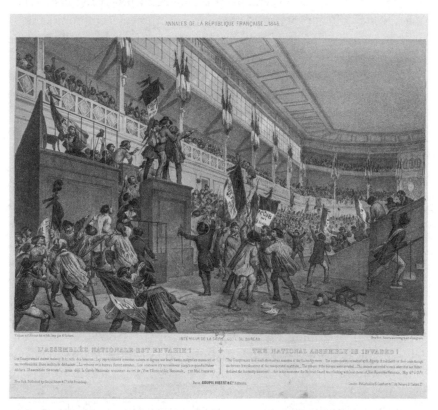

15 May 1848. The invasion of the Chamber by angry demonstrators expressed the frustration of the Parisian radicals, who felt ignored and abandoned by their representatives and by the government of the Second Republic. It supplied the pretext for a crackdown on the radical networks that culminated in the closure of the National Workshops and the violence of the June Days. Lithograph by Victor Adam and Louis-Jules Arnout (1848).

rich and the expulsion of all remaining troops from Paris – if they refused, the deputies would be declared 'traitors to the fatherland'.[205] As his address came to an end, the chamber descended into chaos, various radical leaders stepping forward to shout demands that most of those present could no longer hear.

When the National Guard arrived to eject the intruders, a crowd of between 3,000 and 4,000 demonstrators made their way to the Hôtel de Ville, where they proclaimed a new government, whose members included Louis Blanc and 'Worker Albert', Alexandre Ledru-Rollin, the communist Étienne Cabet, the republican socialist Pierre Leroux and the radical chemist and medical doctor Raspail. The demonstrators wanted to remind the chamber who was boss, they wanted the Deputies to understand that, whatever the majority they enjoyed in their respective constituencies, they were still delegates of 'the people'. There was no prior agreement among the organizers about what should happen after the invasion of the chamber. The leaders of the left were in any case divided by disagreements and personal feuds – even Barbès and Blanqui had fallen out, despite the years they had suffered together in prison. What the intruders into the chamber had in common was the desire to reclaim a piece of revolutionary sovereignty that they believed they were on the verge of losing. The demand that an army be sent to Poland was not just an expression of solidaristic emotion, but represented the aspiration to co-determine government policy in a core area of competence.

The government rallied the National Guard and lost no time in dislodging and disarming the insurgents from the Hôtel de Ville. The left-republican leaders were arrested; the prefect of police, Marc Caussidière, who had failed to act against the rebels, was sacked. So was his assistant, Sobrier, whose arms and munitions depot was seized by the authorities. Caussidière's men, still loyal to their leftist chief, barricaded themselves inside the prefecture headquarters until they were forced out after a siege. On 5 June, the National Assembly passed a law restricting public gatherings. The commandant of the National Guard, Amable de Courtais, who had refused to order his men to fire on the insurgents, was arrested, charged with treason and replaced.

Many conservative contemporaries saw in these events a providential escape from disaster. Reading the newspapers in the safety of his ancestral chateau in Aude, Alphonse d'Hautpoul, who in the winter of that year would support the presidential candidacy of Louis Napoleon, 'thanked heaven for the recent delivery of France from one of the greatest risks it has ever run'. Had Barbès succeeded, d'Hautpoul wrote, a revolutionary committee would have replaced the National Assembly and the consequences would have 'gone beyond even the horrors of 1793'. 'In every village of France, they would have proclaimed the need to kill us all in our homes.'[206] This was a rather overblown reaction to the disturbances of 15 May, which, however alarming, were extremely poorly prepared. What the invasion of the chamber really revealed was the fractiousness and disorganization of the left, not the imminence of a neo-Jacobin coup d'état. But the fear of the left, often captured in the spectre of 'communism', was itself a force to be reckoned with.[207] On 29 May, a report from the Paris prefecture suggested that the appetite was building across the better-off suburbs of the city for a showdown of some kind with the left. Police observations suggested that citizens with commercial and industrial interests 'prefer[red] a violent confrontation to letting things drag on'.[208]

The National Assembly became more hostile to the Executive Commission. Even Lamartine came under suspicion. He had played no role whatsoever in the planning of the insurrection. On 15 May, he had tried in vain to calm the situation in the assembly, before slipping away into the streets to join a National Guard unit pursuing insurgents near the Hôtel de Ville. But his closeness to Ledru-Rollin and his generally emollient attitude towards the left now earned him the contempt of the conservative majority. On 12 June, when he spoke before the assembly to warn of the threat posed by the victory of Louis Napoleon Bonaparte in a recent by-election, his voice was drowned out by hecklers accusing him of having conspired with the insurgents of 15 May. Lamartine tried as usual to outmanoeuvre his attackers with rhetoric: 'Yes, no doubt, I conspired with these men', he quipped. 'Do you know how I conspired? I conspired as a lightning rod conspires with lightning!' But this time his elaborate metaphors were lost on the audience.[209] Nothing could better illustrate how far the balance had shifted from the left to the right than the abrupt descent of this great star of the February Revolution. For George Sand, who was close to some of the radicals and had helped Ledru-Rollin draft his controversial Bulletins of the Republic, it was clear that a threshold had been passed. 'I am crushed and broken', she wrote to a friend on the day after the chamber invasion. 'The spectacle of the bourgeois reaction saddens me to the point of making me sick. Yesterday's events set us back ten years. What deplorable madness!'[210]

The moderate republicans who dominated the assembly at last felt strong enough to move openly against the National Workshops. One of the chief arguments for their establishment had been that they would keep the workers away from the sermonizing of the radical clubs and Louis Blanc's Luxembourg Commission.[211] But since it transpired that more than half of the demonstrators who had joined the march to the assembly on 15 May were National Workshop employees, this justification now lost much of its force. On 20 May, a commission of enquiry stocked with conservatives was tasked with investigating the workshops. The commissioners duly concluded, as one member put it, that they were an 'instrument of corruption', little more than a 'permanent organised strike that cost the state 170,000 francs a day'.[212]

But simply shutting the workshops down was risky, because although they were shambolic and controversial, they were also, for the moment, the best hope the government had of preserving social peace in the capital. Count Falloux, a conservative member of the commission of enquiry and one of the leaders of the chamber majority, identified a dilemma: on the one hand, closing the workshops would be dangerous unless one first found a way of reviving the economy, so that the dismissed workers would have somewhere to go; on the other hand, the workshops were now so expensive and controversial that it was hard to see economic confidence returning unless they were done away with.[213] Lamartine proposed to cushion the impact with a programme of economic reflation based on state investment in the railways – a plan that resembled the technocratic visions of the Saint-Simonians and would take time to implement.

It was the hardliners who prevailed. Frustrated by what he saw as the delaying tactics of the left-republicans, the new Minister of Public Works, Ulysse Trélat, moved to shut the workshops down. Summoned to the minister's office, Émile Thomas was told: 'You must help us to destroy what you created; what was formerly necessary has today become dangerous.'[214] When Thomas objected to this plan, pointing out that closing down the ateliers would put 100,000 disgruntled unemployed workers onto the streets, the minister stopped listening. On the night of 25 May, under cover of darkness, Thomas was hustled out of the city on the orders of the minister and taken to Bordeaux. That a minister could act in this high-handed way demonstrated the weakness of a government so divided that it was no longer capable of reining in its own members. Trélat was a medical doctor who had been decorated for his part in the fighting of 1830 and was famous in Paris for his work with poor patients during the cholera crisis of 1832. He had worked on the editorial staff of *Le National* and joined various radical secret societies, including the Carbonari, the Society of Friends of the People and the association known as Help Yourself and Heaven Will Help You. In 1834, he fell foul of the anti-sedition laws of the July Monarchy and was sentenced to three years in Clairvaux prison, from which he emerged determined to withdraw from politics and re-dedicate himself to science. And then, in 1848, as Minister of Public Works, he pushed for the suppression of the National Workshops and manhandled their director out of the capital as if he were a functionary of Louis XIV brandishing a *lettre de cachet*. Challenged on this point, Trélat would later say that he had acted not as a minister but as a medical doctor addressing an emergency.[215] Whatever the reasons for his authoritarian turn, this was someone whose politics, like everyone else's, were in motion.

Paris woke up to the news of Thomas's disappearance on the following morning and a long train of protests began. For several weeks, petitions circulated against the government. The issue came to a head on 21–22 June when the government announced that it intended to shut down the workshops altogether and either draft the unemployed into the army or transfer them for drainage work in the swamps of provincial France; failure to comply would incur the stopping of wages.

The scene was now set for the 'June Days' of Paris, a brutal showdown between the armed forces and a last-ditch worker insurgency. The June uprising may have looked like a reprise on a larger scale of the conspiratorial insurrections of 1834 and 1839, but it was much more chaotic and spontaneous than they had been. This is not surprising, given that a wave of arrests and arms seizures after 15 May had largely decapitated the Parisian left. Nevertheless, a chieftain of sorts did emerge, even if he was a gifted agitator rather than a political leader. At dawn on 23 June, a 26-year-old man by the name of Louis Pujol addressed a large crowd of protesters on the place de la Bastille. Standing before the tombs at the base of the July Column, recently replenished with the corpses of the February fallen, he demanded respect for the dead of the revolution: 'Hats off! You are standing at the tomb of the first martyrs of liberty;

down on your knees! Friends, our cause is that of our fathers; they wrote on their banners these words: "Liberty or death".'[216]

It was Pujol who sent the demonstrators back into their districts to start building barricades. The son of a tailor, Pujol had served a stint in the *Chasseurs d'Afrique*, a light-cavalry regiment deployed to Algeria. After a period in lock-up for insubordination, he was released and returned to Paris, where he joined Auguste Blanqui's club and registered for the National Workshops. On 15 May, he took part with Blanqui and Joseph Sobrier in the invasion of the chamber. Pujol's speeches were saturated with the language of heterodox popular Catholicism – the comparison between the suffering poor and the broken and bleeding body of Christ was a stock theme. At some time around the end of May, he published a pamphlet composed in the mystical language of Lamennais. It opened with the ominous words: 'People, in truth I say unto you: I am the prophet of misfortunes.' In a long sequence of psalm-like sentences addressed to the government, Pujol contrasted the suffering of the people with the arrogance of their political leaders: 'They came to you with trust, and you repulsed them with contempt. . . . They spoke in the sinister voice of hunger, and you shut your ears to their mournful complaints. . . . They spoke to you of justice, and you replied with insolent bayonets.' The pamphlet closed with an appeal to the cleansing power of revolutionary violence: 'bloody days' lay ahead, but Liberty would emerge radiant from the bosom of the revolutionary tempest, 'like the sun that brings back serenity and fruitfulness'.[217] Not much is known about what, if anything, Pujol did during the days of battle that followed. He had the eloquence to start an insurrection, but not the charisma and judgement required to lead one.

The fighting of 23–26 June was bitter, with a much higher body count than the February insurrection. About 40,000 men and women took up arms against the government and about twice that number were deployed against them. General Louis-Eugène Cavaignac, Minister of War and the man entrusted with the task of putting down the insurrection, possessed impeccable republican credentials. His father had been a regicide member of the Jacobin Convention and his brother Godefroy, who had died in 1845, had helped to plant a tricolour flag on top of the Louvre during the Glorious Days of 1830. As a captain, Cavaignac had himself been transferred to Algeria in 1832 on account of his republican political activism. There he adopted the controversial exterminatory tactics used by the French to subdue indigenous Algerians, taking part in the scorched-earth raids knowns as *razzias*, and pioneering the use of *enfumades*, in which Algerian civilians were smoked to death in caves. By 1848, the upper echelons of the French army were largely occupied by men who had experienced colonial warfare of this kind.

It was the Provisional Government that promoted him to division general in February 1848, and the Executive Committee that invited him to return to Paris as Minister of War after the 15 May assault on the assembly. On 23 June, as a new insurgency took hold in the city, he was invested with full executive powers and told he should do whatever he deemed necessary to crush the revolt. Cavaignac resolved to approach the matter as a purely military task. He took his time. No parties were sent out to parley with the insurgents, despite Marc Caussidière's offer to negotiate with the men on the barricades.[218] The troops were concentrated and then sent in with artillery batteries to destroy the rebellion with overwhelming force. The spectral presence of colonial violence hung over the streets of Paris. Supporters and critics alike perceived Cavaignac's counterinsurgency operation as an application of 'Algerian' methods, even though the techniques deployed during the June Days did not formally resemble those used by the French forces in North Africa, and the brunt of the fighting was borne by the Mobile Guard, rather than by the regular army. The atrocities ascribed to the insurgents in the media echoed earlier newspaper reports of Algerian atrocities: it was said that the insurgents had tortured and mutilated captured soldiers, that they had cut out their tongues and strung them together on cords, or impaled a child on a pike to distract the army's snipers.[219] The tools deployed in the service of 'civilization' in Algeria were now being put to use against the 'barbaric' proletarians of the capital, while Algeria, in turn, now became the place where recalcitrant workers could be 'civilized' through (forced) settlement programmes.[220]

Thousands were killed during the fighting. Prisoners were murdered on both sides and many insurgents were summarily shot on capture. The Archbishop of Paris, Monsignor Affre, was pleading for peace on the place de la Bastille when he was either struck by a spent bullet from the government side or, more probably, shot without warning by a fanatical lone-wolf insurgent.[221] Over 2,500 wounded were admitted to the hospitals – the number of those who sought help elsewhere for fear of capture is impossible to ascertain. Nearly 12,000 were arrested and sentenced to deportation. Most of them evaded this fate through releases and pardons, but a 'hard core' of 468 men were deported to Algeria.

The violence and fear of those days burned indelible memories into the minds of those who experienced them. Alexis de Tocqueville, who prided himself on his sangfroid, sent his wife away from Paris. Many of the deputies slept in the chamber, where Cavaignac had set up his headquarters. Some of them called for an evacuation of the parliament to the suburban palace of Saint-Cloud, or even further afield to Bourges.[222] People remembered the smell of powder, the sight of blood in unexpected places, and the bleak stillness of abandoned streets and squares. Victor Hugo took part in the fight against the insurgents, leading repeated assaults on the barricades under heavy fire. 'I am safe and sound, but what disasters!' he wrote to his mistress Juliette Drouet when it was all over. 'I will never forget the terrible things I've seen during the past forty hours.'[223] On the morning of 26 June, after a night of intermittent cannon fire, the radical Russian writer Alexander Herzen walked with his friend, the traveller and journalist P. V. Annenkov, towards the Champs Élysées. The cannon had fallen silent, but occasional bursts of gunfire still echoed across the city. On the place de la Concorde, a boy of about seventeen was addressing a small audience of poor women with brooms, some ragpickers and concierges from the surrounding houses:

> He and all his comrades, boys like himself, were half drunk, their faces blackened with gunpowder and their eyes bloodshot from sleepless nights . . . 'And what happened then, there's no need to describe.' After a pause he went on. 'Yes, and they fought well too, but we paid them out for our comrades! . . . I stuck my bayonet up to the hilt in five or six of them; they'll remember us', he added, trying to assume the air of a hardened criminal. The women were pale and silent; a man who looked like a concierge observed: 'Serve them right, the blackguards!' But this savage comment evoked not the slightest response. They were all of too ignorant a class to be moved to pity by the massacre or by the wretched boy whom others had turned into a murderer.[224]

Near the Madeleine, Herzen and his companion were stopped and arrested by soldiers at a checkpoint where an officer claimed to have seen Herzen 'more than once at [radical] meetings'. It was a moment of real danger: Herzen had not fought in the insurrection, but in those days many captured suspects were shot in the holding cells. The two friends were eventually released without incident, but there was one vexing detail. On his way to the police station, Herzen happened to recognize a member of the Constituent National Assembly. It was Alexis de Tocqueville. But when he begged the famous writer for help, Tocqueville bowed politely and slipped away, saying that it would be inappropriate for the 'legislative authority' to interfere with the operations of 'the executive'.[225]

Tocqueville's memoirs of 1848 make no mention of Herzen, but he, too, had vivid memories of the June Days. He recalled walking towards the scene of the fighting on 25 June, driven by a curiosity to understand 'why the combat was lasting so long'. As he approached the Château d'Eau, he found the first traces of recent fighting: 'houses pitted by cannonballs or bullets, paving stones piled up, straw mixed with blood and mud'. At the Château itself, he found government troops still engaged in a mopping-up operation against the rebels. Ahead of them stretched a long street that 'bristled with barricades all the way to the Bastille'. He recalled the terror when insurgents appeared on a nearby rooftop and began firing on the troops down below. The men around him fell into utter confusion, shooting in every direction without any idea of what they were doing. In the panic of the rout, Tocqueville was knocked down and trampled by cavalry: 'I lost my hat and came close to losing my life.'

For politically active contemporaries, the inarticulacy of the revolt was one of its most striking features. 'Deceived and beholding unabated misery at their firesides', the former chief of police Marc Caussidière wrote, '[the people] threw themselves into that insurrection of despair.'[226] The insurgents were never joined by the great personalities of the Parisian left who could have shrouded the enterprise in the language of a great cause. Even Louis Blanc refused to support them, though he did try to persuade them to stand down in the hope of avoiding further bloodshed. The lack of a clear doctrine or principle, beyond the forlorn cry 'Liberty or death!', had an unsettling effect, even on hostile observers. Why had they done it when the odds were so perilously stacked against them? And why had so many of them persisted in the struggle, even when its suicidal character was obvious? This was the question that continued to trouble thoughtful contemporaries.

Tocqueville had no sympathy with the rebels. And yet he kept returning

Barricades on the rue Saint-Maur on 25 June, before the attack by government forces, daguerrotype by Charles-François Thibault (1848). The June Days were almost over by the time this photograph was taken from a house on what is now the rue du Faubourg du Temple. Note the locked shutters and the emptiness of the street. This working-class area of eastern Paris was one of the last to fall to government troops.

in his thoughts to the idea that the insurgency had been motivated by a 'sincere belief that society was founded in injustice'. And might this not be true? After all, Tocqueville would later write in a passage reflecting on the failure of socialism in 1848, 'what we call necessary institutions are often just the institutions to which we are accustomed'.[227] Victor Hugo remained convinced that it had been necessary to crush the uprising, but an underlying sympathy with the defeated insurgents continued to nag at his peace of mind. Surely, he pondered in Les Misérables, it was possible to understand the roots of such a rebellion and to 'venerate it, even while attacking it'? His ambivalence evolved to the point where his politics pivoted away from the party of order towards the advocates of a 'democratic and social republic'.[228] The news from Paris plunged George Sand, who had withdrawn to her estate at Nohant, into despair. 'What is there to say?' she wrote to the publisher Hetzel. '[The] future looks so dark that I feel a great desire and a great need to blow my brains out.' Yet even Sand, who had stuck loyally to her left-republican friends during the turbulence of May, was starting to lose faith both in the cause of the left and in that of the French republic. 'We were not ready for the Republic', she wrote to a friend. 'The people were not with us.' And in any case, she wrote to another, 'I do not believe in the existence of a republic that starts out by killing its proletarians.'[229]

Karl Marx had no time for the melancholy equivocations of the intellectuals. He discerned in the bloodshed of the June days a grandiose moment of clarification. In an article he wrote for the *Neue Rheinische Zeitung* on 29 June, he extracted a characteristically paradoxical lesson from the violence in Paris. Yes, the workers had been 'crushed by a superior power'. But the deeper reality was that the vanquished had defeated the victors. In enacting their momentary triumph over the workers, Marx wrote, the 'moderate republican party' had murdered the very revolution it claimed to be defending, because it had annihilated the 'delusions and illusions' of February. Small wonder that the National Assembly had been 'paralysed' with stupor: its members had seen at last how their questions and answers could make blood run across the cobblestones of Paris; they looked on stunned as their dreams disappeared in the smoke of gunpowder. Did the reprisals of June mark the end of the revolutionary workers' movement, should democrats abandon the political struggle as 'meaningless, illusory, and futile'? 'Only weak, cowardly temperaments', Marx answered, could pose such a question.

> The collisions that are generated by the very conditions of bourgeois society have to work themselves out through struggle, they cannot be reasoned out of existence. The best form of state is one that does not blur social contradictions or seek arbitrarily . . . to contain them. The best form of state is one in which these contradictions play themselves out freely and thereby come to a resolution . . .[230]

This was more than an observation – it was a revelation that would continue to power Marx's thinking through *The Class Struggles in France*, *The Eighteenth Brumaire of Louis Bonaparte* and beyond.

A few leftists welcomed this diagnosis, but most radical democrats and liberals did not. How could a violent rebellion against a republic of universal suffrage be legitimate? Historians have been critical, too, pointing out that the actual character and course of the June events do not correspond to Marx's descriptions of an incipient class struggle. A study of the evidence suggests that the contending forces on both sides of the barricades were recruited from the same social strata. The combatants on both sides reflected that broad cross-section of artisanal trades that had come under such acute economic pressure in recent years. Their readiness to commit to the respective fronts in the struggle was not a function of class origins, but of organizational contexts (such as the intensive training environment of the Mobile Guards) and divergent experiences (such as the fury felt by many unemployed workers after the closure of the National Workshops).[231] George Sand came closer to the truth when she wrote that June 1848 was not a battle between 'natural enemies', but 'a conflict between two factions of *the people*'.[232]

It must be said, though, in Marx's defence, that the tallying of artisans and proletarians on both sides of the barricades slightly misses the point of his analysis. Marx had pushed hard on the notion of the conflict of classes and would do so again, but in this early reflection, written within days of the events, he was also saying something else, namely that the violence of June represented the end of something that had begun in February, the dream of a united revolutionary front under the banner of 'universal suffrage'. June had shown that the myth of February (which was in some ways a new iteration of the myth of July 1830) could only sustain itself by bracketing out the social demands that had helped to bring the revolution about. More importantly, Marx was saying, the bloodshed of the June Days revealed that the potency of the myth did not ultimately rest upon the beauty of the idea at its heart, but upon the threat of naked violence. The triumph of liberty, property and order was the triumph of one force over another. The rhetorical fireworks of Lamartine had metamorphosed into the actual cannon-fire of June. Here again was that theory of force that had first seen light within the insurgent movements of Paris and Italy. It was an idea with a lot of future in it. But for those who had once rejoiced in the idea of a truly 'popular' form of government, there was desolation in this victory of one violence over another.

IN THE HEAT OF THE CENTURY

To follow every secession from the common enterprise in 1848–9 would be like writing the history of a fire by narrating in succession the distinctive biography of each of its flames. We have seen that there is a mismatch between such phenomena and the narrative tools that historians use. By 1848, physical scientists, on the other hand, had been puzzling for many years over the problem of what happens when heat, which they were beginning to think of as a form of energy in transit, passes from one body into another, cooler and more inert than itself. In the 1820s, Sadi Carnot, son of the Lazare Carnot who had engineered the revolutionary *levées en masse* of the 1790s, published a paper on the motive power of heat. In it, he reflected on the thermodynamic principles governing the operation of an engine capable of achieving the total conversion of heat into motion, though he knew that no such engine existed; even the best steam engines of his time, he observed, managed to utilize only one-twentieth of the 'motive power of the combustible'.[233] In the 1830s and 1840s, scientists such as Clapeyron, Clausius, Thomson and Rankine continued to work over the implications of Carnot's arguments, but the emphasis shifted towards an interest in how heat was lost when such conversions from heat to motion took place.[234] In a celebrated paper published in 1850, *On the Motive Force of Heat* (*Über die bewegende Kraft der Wärme*), the Prussian scientist Rudolf Clausius observed that the operation of Carnot's heat engine was irreconcilable with the principle of the conservation of energy, according to which the total energy of a system remains constant and is conserved over time. Throughout the 1850s Clausius continued to reflect on the way heat was dissipated in the course of irreversible thermodynamic processes, and in 1865 he gave this irreversible heat loss a name: entropy.[235]

It would be vulgar to posit that these esoteric reflections on thermodynamics were in some sense a translation or reflection of experiences gained in the field of politics. That is not how the relationship between science and society works. On the other hand, we should not assume that the world of the scientists was far removed from that of the revolutionaries: the February Provisional Government in Paris included a number of distinguished scientists, and the tireless Polish freedom fighter and engineer Józef Bem was also the author of a distinguished study of steam engines.[236] After 1848, many German socialists gravitated away from philosophy towards the natural sciences, in the belief that these could better explain the human condition.[237] And one of the consequences of the revolutions, as we shall see, was an appetite for a more 'scientifically' grounded form of politics drawing less on inspiration and ideological conviction and more on systematically assembled bodies of knowledge. The conceptual handles the scientists of this era used connect so easily with other forms of experience: movement, the transfer of energy from a hot to an inert body, the dispersal of effort, the loss of cohesion.

We can find these correspondences elsewhere too. Early-nineteenth-century nerve science still pictured the human body as a system traversed instantaneously by electrical currents. But in the middle years of the century the emphasis shifted. Using new precision measurement techniques, the Prussian scientist Hermann Helmholtz showed in 1850 and 1851 that the impulses conducted along chains of nerve cells were in fact subject to an organic delay that gave rise to a 'loss of time', producing a 'latency period' between the stimulus and the response.[238] The science of the human body witnessed a shift in emphasis away from the electrical imagery of early nerve science towards a more vascular awareness of the body as a circulatory network. Whereas nervous metaphors had implied that all parts of the body could receive or 'feel' as well as send impulses simultaneously, the circulatory metaphor made room for blockages and spatial variegation in the flow of information. It focused attention on the effortful 'coordination, rather than mere connection, of the most heavily trafficked arteries with the lesser veins of the physical (or political) body'.[239]

Viewing them in this light, we might see the existential weariness of Robert Blum in September or the suicidal misery of George Sand after the June days as two individual intimations of a larger dispersal of effort,

Adolph Menzel, *Laying Out the March Dead* (1848). Menzel conceived this painting to express his passionate identification with the March events. But during the summer he lost interest in the painting and it remained unfinished. No image better captures the dissipation of revolutionary emotion during the summer of 1848.

the heat death of a revolution. We might note that despite their extreme temporal compression, the uprisings of 1848 began at different times and unfolded at different speeds, driven by very diverse local circumstances in a wide variety of dispersed settings. The resulting asynchrony generated blockages and counter-currents that militated against the convergence of revolutionary impulses across the continent. When revolution broke out in Wallachia in June 1848, triggered in part by the arrival in Bucharest of some Romanian students who had been living in Paris, the new Provisional Government sent an envoy to France in the hope of securing money and weapons, only to find that a conservative administration had now taken control in Paris that had no interest whatsoever in offering practical assistance to Wallachians. By the time the German national parliament at Frankfurt am Main finished the long work of drafting a German constitution, public sympathy for the revolution had ebbed and Prussia had seized de facto control of the German national question. In the summer of 1849, those Roman republicans who had looked to Paris for support found instead that the France of Bonaparte's presidential republic preferred to crush the Roman Republic and restore the papacy. The dynamics of connection and disconnection could become paradoxically intertwined: when the cohort of Romanian radical students in Paris decided to leave the city en masse in March in order to foment revolution at home in Bucharest, were they connecting or disconnecting the two theatres? Might it not, as one Romanian historian has suggested, have been better to leave at least *someone* in the city to manage relations with the new Provisional Government?[240]

It would be going too far to place the downward arc of the revolution under the rubric of a global loss of order, because, as we have seen, the waning of cohesion was not just the consequence of an entropy intrinsic to the process, but also the result of new and competing forms of order-making facilitated by the upheaval. The instability of the relations among them should not distract us from noticing that over the longer term some of these enterprises – liberalism, socialism, radical democracy, agrarian radicalism, social democracy, nationalism – would bring forth brilliant and terrible futures. In the shorter term, however, European political actors and thinkers would derive deep lessons from the scattering and cooling of the embers of revolution.

8

Counter-revolution

NAPLES IN SUMMER

On 29 January 1848, copies of a royal decree announcing the imminent publication of a constitution could be seen posted on every wall in central Naples. 'An infinity of gigs and carriages' and omnibuses 'full of people decorated with ribbons and waving tricolour flags' filled the streets. Among them was the coach of Lord Napier, envoy of the 'generous and liberal nation of Britain', cheered by a populace fully aware of the role Britain had played in consolidating the revolution in Palermo. On the evening of 10 February, the day on which the new constitution was formally sworn in by the monarch, the entire city was illuminated. The ministry of finance was 'a mass of light' and all the public buildings were festooned with lights and decorations. In the Piazza del Mercato hung a huge canvas depicting the king in the act of swearing an oath to the constitution. At one o'clock in the morning, a choir of sixty girls and sixty boys, accompanied by a military band, sang a hymn of gratitude to King Ferdinand. Citizens chatted and fraternized with the troops; even the *sbirri*, the hated police agents, were not spurned. 'Victims and butchers met and embraced like friends and brothers', wrote the liberal dramatist and journalist Francesco Michitelli.[1]

Among the most exotic figures observed on the streets in those days were the political offenders of the revolution of 1821, now released under a general amnesty. Some were 'men of sepulchral appearance, who had grown grey and old under life sentences', others were 'deportees with florid faces burned by the sun' condemned for long years to languish on penal islands.[2] In Naples, as in Paris, Berlin and many other cities, the 'return of the political prisoners' was a moment rich in drama, not just because these men personified both the emancipatory promise and the personal risk of revolution, but also because the sudden reappearance of the veterans of previous tumults endowed the present with historical depth and a sense of cumulative momentum.[3]

It was a sublime beginning. And yet by the middle of May it was all over. After brutal reprisals against crowds of protestors in the centre of Naples, the king shut the revolution down on the mainland and then sent an expeditionary force to wrest control of the island of Sicily from the patriots who had seized power there. He would eventually put aside both the constitution he had sworn to observe and the parliament he had sworn to convene. He would return the Kingdom of the Two Sicilies to its pre-revolutionary condition as an 'absolute monarchy'. This transit from revolution to counter-revolution was unusually compact and extreme, even by the standards of that changeful year. How was it possible? And what does the Neapolitan case reveal about the dynamics of counter-revolution across Europe?

This chapter follows the arc of counter-revolution, an arc as expansive and encompassing as that of the revolutions themselves. We begin in Naples and track the Austrian counter-insurgency operations from Prague to northern Italy and Vienna. We watch two very differently structured counter-revolutions unfold in Paris and Berlin. We visit the Ionian Islands, and Cephalonia in particular, where the British authorities handled an insular uprising with exemplary severity. Then come the 'second wave' counter-revolutions of 1849 in Rome, Saxony, Frankfurt and Baden, Moldavia, Wallachia and Hungary. The aim is not simply to chronicle the often violent suppression of the revolutions, but to reflect on the mechanisms that drove counter-revolution and the lessons contemporaries derived from it.

In Naples, as in Berlin, Vienna, Munich, the Papal States and many other principalities, the uprising did not destroy, but merely unsettled, the monarchical authority. New ministers were admitted into positions of responsibility, but they had to cohabit with old-school conservatives inherited from the old system. This made it difficult for the government to respond nimbly to the changing situation in the city. Then there was the constitution itself. We have seen that the king opted for a charter closely resembling the French *Charte révisée* of 1830. But this document now appeared obsolete – it was already mired in controversy in

France, and it would be swept away entirely by the February Revolution in Paris. The euphoria triggered by the initial announcement soon made way for scepticism, confusion and frustration.

In Naples, as in Paris, Vienna and Berlin, the uprising inaugurated a process of mobilization that, once begun, proved difficult to halt. Broadsheets pressed for an end to the Sicilian war and the recognition of the island's autonomy. There was bitter criticism of the narrowness of the new electoral franchise and the ample powers assigned to the Upper House – an assembly of peers appointed by the king. For the Neapolitan radicals, as for their colleagues elsewhere, the revolution was not an event but a process that was still unfolding, especially after the news of the Parisian February Revolution, a 'terrible spectre' that haunted the doorsteps of the royal palace, reminding the adherents of the old regime of what might happen if the government failed to stay ahead of the tide of opinion. 'Whether one wished to or not', Francesco Michitelli wrote, 'it was necessary to follow in some way the politics of the times and to yield to the universal current.'[4]

Radical leaders spoke in the clubs, the pop-up hubs of urban activism, addressed improvised assemblies and gatherings in cafés, and marshalled the demonstrations that became increasingly frequent during the second half of March.[5] In the first week of April, the political turbulence in the streets of the capital, largely started and steered by the radicals, triggered a political crisis. A cycle of street protests had culminated in a demonstration against the Austrian Embassy, in the course of which students who frequented the radical Caffè di Buono tore the imperial arms down from the façade, broke them up and burned them. On the following day, a long procession down the Via Toledo to the Royal Palace demanded that the king dismiss his government and send a military contingent to support the freedom fighters against Austria in Lombardy. On 3 April, fearful lest he lose control of the city, the monarch brought in several new radical ministers, opening a policy divide within the government itself.

The most outspoken of the new colleagues was Aurelio Saliceti, an austere figure who reminded his enemies of Robespierre.[6] The new government secured the monarch's support for a programme of constitutional reform that would strengthen the Chamber of Deputies in its relations with the upper house. On 7 April, the new Prime Minister, Carlo Troia, persuaded the king to contribute a Neapolitan contingent to the war unfolding against the Austrians in Lombardy. The Neapolitan royal navy was sent off up the Adriatic to assist in the defence of Venice.

The balance of power was shifting in the radicals' favour. They remained in the minority in the Cabinet, but their support networks in the streets and clubs and their ability to mobilize their following at short notice made them a 'functional majority'.[7] As in Vienna, there were riotous processions to the houses of unpopular ministers, at which young people performed raucous cat-concerts. Politics seemed to be taking the form of 'a permanent popular demonstration'.[8] And this activism was not confined to the capital city. Networks connected the streets of Naples with many provincial centres of Calabrian radical activity, especially after activists started filtering back from the city to their provincial homes in the spring of 1848. In April and early May, two prominent radicals proposed two different draft constitutions that resembled neither the charter recently offered by the king nor the Cadiz-inspired constitution of 1820.

Among the deepest of the cleavages that opened during these weeks was the stand-off between progressive anti-clericals and conservative defenders of the Church. In Naples, as in Vienna and many other places, the Jesuits were the canary in the mine. On 9 March, radical students gathered in the Mercatello square in front of the elite Jesuit boarding school and a deputation went in to demand that the fathers vacate the school, which also served as a residence for members of the order, and leave the city. Signs appeared on the street corners instructing the families of Neapolitans who sent their children to the school to retrieve them immediately, lest they be exposed to the 'righteous anger' of the people. Parents rushed to the school on foot and in carriages and 'it was very affecting to see those poor terrified children weeping in the arms of their trembling mothers who were making their way as best they could through a crowd of the people rejoicing and applauding what they were doing'.[9] As the crowds continued to grow, a deputation acting 'on behalf of the people' went to the house of Saliceti, recently appointed radical Minister of Justice, and demanded that a magistrate be appointed to begin drawing up an inventory of the items inside the premises. From the morning of 10 March, National Guards sealed off the perimeter of the house and prevented any of the clergy from leaving. The fathers, numbering 130 in all, were holed up overnight in a single room while the authorities confiscated the little money they could find, sealed the papers, and put the furniture and silverware into storage. On the following morning, 11 March, the liberal minister Bozzelli presented a departure order to the Jesuits, and seventeen carriages arrived from the prefecture of police to transport them under the watchful eye of the National Guard to a pier, where they were transferred onto a steamboat. In one carriage, 'a decrepit and apparently blind old Jesuit was seated, supported at the side by two others, who never stopped reciting feeble prayers, as one would do for a dying man . . .'[10]

The Neapolitan radicals were not unusual in their hostility towards the order. In a best-selling French anti-Jesuit tract of 1843, the historian Jules Michelet proposed that hatred of the order was universal. 'Take a man in the street, the first one who passes by, and ask him: "What are the Jesuits?" He will answer without hesitating: "The counter-revolution".'[11] Jesuits were to the European left what freemasons were to the right: a shadowy global conspiracy that allowed a multitude of threatening or unwelcome phenomena to be booked under one rubric and assigned to a unifying cause. Francesco Michitelli, whose history of these months described the expulsion in detail, did not doubt the justice of the anti-Jesuit measures. 'From its first foundation', he wrote, the order had wielded 'a pernicious influence on the moral and political education of the people'. They had been the masterminds of 'every famous crime committed in Asia and Europe'. In recent years, they had stirred up the 'horrors of the civil war' in Switzerland. As an authority on the matter, Michitelli pointed to Eugène Sue's novel, *Le Juif errant* (The Wandering Jew), a fanciful romance that described in vivid colours the ruses by which the Jesuit order sucked proselytes and riches from all over the world. The order, Sue declared, was an immense police network, 'infinitely more exact and better informed than has been that of any state', disposing of a huge bank of knowledge about the individuals they hope to influence, and perpetually engaged in 'dark machinations'.[12]

It was possible to hate the Jesuits and love the Church, to be sure. But in Naples many, including most of the clergy, saw the evicted Jesuits as a synecdoche for the Church as a whole. The sources that describe the crowds in the Mercatello square speak of 'radical students', and Michitelli's account of the eviction of the Jesuits relates that many of those guarding the order's residence were people of 'good character and intelligence' who wound up chatting with the fathers about their work, about 'the first Jesuits, the Institutions [of Loyola]' and so on. Grateful for these attentions, the Jesuits made them gifts of books, prints and other such things. In other words: the attackers were not a cross-section of 'the people', but a highly specific constituency of educated anticlericals who happened to have the ear of the radical ministers in the government. They were pleased to see the fathers escorted down to their steamboat. But outside the radical anticlerical bubble the picture was different. The texts of many of the petitions submitted to the authorities in the autumn and spring of 1848–9 demanding the suspension of the constitution suggested that the expulsion of the Neapolitan Jesuits was one of the initiatives that alienated popular opinion from the liberal-radical revolutionary project.[13] These were petitions from the 'continental south' – a different picture emerged in Sicily, where the Jesuits sided with the revolution.[14]

Whether the king and his 'camarilla' of military officers, personal advisers and courtiers were already planning a counter-revolution, as some liberal and radical contemporaries feared, is unclear. But there were certainly signs that a reactionary party was forming whose members were bitterly hostile to the revolution. When the city's printers mounted a peaceful demonstration on 25 April, shots were suddenly fired by troops without warning into the crowd, although the demonstrators were already complying with orders to disperse. In Pratola, near the border with the Papal States, 500 armed men marched under the banner of the Bourbon dynasty chanting 'Long live the king! Down with the constitution! Down with the gentlemen!'[15] There was a more serious outrage on 11 May when a radical priest was lured into a church by marines of the Royal Neapolitan Navy and repeatedly stabbed with bayonets. The priest was the famous Canon Pellicano, a member of Mazzini's Young Italy, spiritual leader of the liberals at Reggio Calabria and a co-architect of the abortive uprising of 2 September 1847 in Reggio and Messina. A military commission had condemned him to death, but the sentence was commuted to life imprisonment and he was deported to the penal island of Nisida, only to be released under the general amnesty in January 1848. On his return to Naples, the government had engaged him to preach in support of the new constitution, which he did with great success – prints of his portrait were seen throughout the city. It was a swift ascent for the former convict: in March, the government entrusted him with the task of establishing a committee to reform education in the kingdom. On 8 April, the new administration appointed him Undersecretary of State for Ecclesiastical Affairs. In this role, he became one of the foremost targets of hatred among adherents of the absolutist regime.

Left for dead by the marines, Pellicano survived the attack and later left Naples to convalesce in Reggio. But the assault suggested that the opponents of the revolution might be on the point of mobilizing and coming out into the open. Rumours circulated that clandestine reactionary networks had already infiltrated liberal organizations and even radical demonstrations. On the day after the attack, the liberal journal *Il Nazionale* ran three articles accusing the government of covertly fomenting disorders in order to secure the pretext for an armed crackdown. The absolutist government had 'trembled, abased itself and fallen', one of the articles declared. But now that its fear of the revolution had dissipated, it was reaching 'for all the weapons of perfidy to fight it'.[16]

In reality, there was no need for the court or anyone else to 'organize' a counter-revolution or to foment disorders – these were already implicit in the process of polarization that had taken place since 29 January, a process driven not by cabals or conspiracies, but by the general disinhibition of politics, suspicion, fear and the hardening of irreconcilable viewpoints. But even if neither side was in fact secretly preparing a strike against the other, each suspected the other of doing so. Lord Napier, the British ambassador in Naples, reported rumours of an impending counter-revolution, but also gatherings of 'Calabrese, or radicals' in the city, whose numbers 'were said to have been strengthened by the arrival of . . . partisans from that province'.[17]

'The mine was already charged with powder', wrote the liberal journalist Giuseppe Massari. 'All that was needed was a spark to ignite it. And this spark was the question of the oath [to the constitution].'[18] On 14 May 1848, the authorities published the programme of the opening of parliament, scheduled to take place on the following day. It was going to be a splendid occasion. The National Guard would be drawn up in two wings from the Royal Palace down the Via Toledo and all the way to the Church of San Lorenzo. At 11 a.m., an artillery salute would sound from the fortresses of the capital. Flanked by pages and officers in ceremonial uniforms, the royal carriage and the carriage of state would proceed amidst a din of trumpets to the entrance of San Lorenzo, where the king would be met by a deputation of representatives consisting of ten Peers and ten Deputies and conducted to his throne. In the evening, there would be 'a grand illumination at the Theatres and in the public buildings'. But there were two contentious details. Article 12 of the programme stated that when the divine service was over, the king would 'renew before the Chambers . . . the oath [he had] already given, to observe the Constitutional Charter'. And Article 13 stipulated that 'the Peers and Deputies and all the other persons present at the ceremony' would 'take the same oath'.[19]

A number of the deputies were unhappy with this formulation, saying that it effectively bound everyone to the constitution as it now stood, leaving no room for the notion that a representative government ought to have the power to amend the law when this became necessary. And what had become of the agreement of 3 April, which had promised to strengthen the Chamber of Deputies by means of constitutional reform? It seemed that the king intended to renege on the deal struck during the April crisis and to return to the position of 29 January. This was not an acceptable basis for collaboration with the Crown, and during the afternoon of 14 May and throughout the night the deputies sat in the town hall sending runners to the palace with proposals for an amendment of the oath to be sworn at the inauguration. But no agreement was reached: the king dug his heels in and refused to compromise.[20]

During the previous evening, aware of the stand-off, liberal and radical sympathizers had poured into the main streets. When the four regiments of Swiss Guards were seen exiting their quarters, alarm seized the crowd and rumours spread that the king intended to use the stalemate with the deputies as a pretext for suppressing the assembly and revoking the constitution. While citizens threw up barricades along the main thoroughfares leading to the palace, the numbers of guards and troops drawn up in the city centre increased until around 5,000 men were deployed.[21] Anxious to speak with the king, the British ambassador, Lord Napier, approached the palace at eight in the morning of 15 May: 'I found it guarded by a force of cavalry and foot, while within forty paces of its windows a great barricade closed the entrance of the Toledo, manned by the National Guard of the quarter. The issues of the smaller streets were obstructed in the same manner, the Palace was on that side blockaded, and the opposite forces surveyed each other in silence.' When he left again at nine, Napier found that the efforts of 'the insurgents' had increased; he could see 'common people' being directed or compelled by uniformed National Guards to drag timber and carriages and to raise the paving-stones. At eleven o'clock in the morning, a gunshot from somewhere in the ranks of the National Guard triggered an exchange of fire and the government went onto the offensive.

Once the fighting began, the king's forces went about their task with cool precision:

> The barricade was first cleared by two discharges of cannon, after which the Swiss took it by assault. Having surmounted the impediment, they advanced along the street in two files, firing respectively at the opposite windows by the direction of their officers, who walked in the centre. Before the next barricade was stormed, the intervening houses were cleared of combatants, and then the discharge of artillery, the attack, the assault of the houses proceeded as before. . . . The loss on the part of the insurgents cannot be ascertained. No doubt a number of innocent persons and even some women and children fell, victims to the soldiers on their first irruption into the interior of the houses.[22]

Napier estimated that 600 members of the royal forces had been wounded and about 200 killed. A study of the archival records suggests that the actual number was closer to six dead and around twenty wounded. Napier's exaggeration doubtless reflected his sympathy with the king's forces. Like most of his British diplomatic colleagues across Europe, Napier took a very dim view of insurgencies and was deeply hostile to radical popular tribunes. It seems that the reprisals took the lives of around 100 citizens and wounded about 600 more. Many of those killed and wounded were found not to have been bearing arms.[23] Giuseppe Massari, elected to a seat in parliament but not present when the disturbances took place, recalled the atrocities committed by the *soldatesca*. They 'raped and pillaged, they cut the throats of young boys and old men, they slaughtered women'. In a scene reminiscent of the fighting on the night of 18 March in Berlin, Massari described the fate of a youth by the same of Santillo, who, seeing the soldiers running up towards his rooms, leapt into bed and feigned illness in the hope of placating their anger; he was simply slaughtered in his bed. In the evening, the Toledo, the birthplace of the January revolution, was strewn with corpses.[24]

15 May 1848 in Naples. Royal Neapolitan troops take back control of the streets. Well planned and executed with terrifying precision, the Neapolitan crackdown was a turning point. From this moment onwards, the revolutions would never regain their early momentum

From this moment unfolded a long sequence of counter-revolutionary measures. The king immediately formed a new ministry almost identical to the one of 29 January. It was a sign that he hoped to arrest the revolution in the very moment of its inception, something neither the radicals nor even the liberals believed possible. Naples was placed under a state of siege. A commission was appointed to enquire into the causes of the events of 15 May. The National Guard and the parliament were dissolved and the expeditionary force to Lombardy was recalled, along with the naval squadron that had sailed for Venice. The government quickly got to work spinning the events of 15 May. Official announcements depicted 15 May as a victory over 'communists' bent on sowing anarchy. The repressions had been necessary to suffocate a 'republican' movement that was the enemy of all order. But who, Giuseppe Massari asked, were these 'republicans'? The citizens who joined the fray, most of them young men, were opponents of absolutism and corruption. The republicans, Massari concluded, existed solely in the imagination of the 'swaggering thugs' who had harvested the fruit of the carnage and who hoped to calumniate their victims by imputing to them 'concepts and designs that they never had'.[25]

For the moment, the constitution remained in force and elections were called for a new parliament. A proclamation issued on 24 May announced that the king's 'firmest and most immutable desire' was to maintain the constitution of 10 February 'pure and intact and [free of] excesses of any sort'. It would remain the 'sacred ark' on which the destiny of his people and of his Crown would stand.[26] Other statements declared that the king had been successful in 'defending the constitution'. The state of siege was raised on 15 June, the day of the elections, and the new parliament assembled on 1 July, this time 'amidst funereal silence with no external pomp'. Serracapriola, the elderly duke who had been presiding over the government when the revolution broke out, was again the President of the Council of State. In the lower chamber, liberal constitutionalists predominated. Of a total of 164 deputies, perhaps twenty supported the government.[27] There was no shortage of knowledge or talent in the new Chamber of Deputies, but the new parliament faced the hostility of the military, most of the clergy, the magistracy and the populace, not to mention the court and the government. There were daily infringements of the chamber's dignity and rights. One deputy-elect was refused the passport he needed in order to return to Naples and take up his seat; another, though elderly and infirm, was ordered to leave the kingdom within twenty-four hours. In a weird inversion of the media climate that had preceded the uprisings in many European cities, government newspapers pelted the parliament with an acid rain of ridicule, while gangs organized a kind of informal terror against the liberal and radical journals. Journals that attracted the hostile attention of the authorities were liable to be visited by uninvited guests who rubbished the offices, broke the presses and beat with clubs anyone who dared to protest.[28]

In the streets, too, the tables had turned. Gone were the liberal Guardsmen and the radical students from the Caffè di Buono. In their place, bands of soldiers and *lazzaroni* marched, chanting 'Down with the chambers! Long live the absolute king! Death to liberty!' Even the ministers were hostile: they ghosted the parliament, refusing to present laws and scarcely even turning up to take part in discussions. Key decisions, such as the massive armed expedition against Sicily, were taken without so much as a word of consultation. After two months spent slowly collapsing under the weight of its own futility, the parliament was prorogued.

The reconquest of Sicily began in the first days of September, when 24,000 Royal Neapolitan troops crossed the straits to Messina, taking control of the city after a murderous thirty-hour battle that only came to an end when the British and the French intervened to stop the carnage. An offer of partial autonomy from the king was rejected by the Sicilian government and the battle dragged on, marked by egregious looting, wanton destruction and atrocities against the Sicilian population, including numerous rapes and the killing of children and elderly people. There were frequent massacres of captured Sicilian troops. Among those resisting the Bourbon advance was the indefatigable Ludwik Mierosławski, who had fought in the Polish November uprising of 1830–31. He had helped to plan the abortive Galician uprising of 1846, for which he was arrested and sentenced to death by the Prussians. His sentence was commuted by the king to imprisonment and he was released in the spring of 1848 under the general amnesty for political prisoners. In the spring of 1848, as we have seen, Mierosławski helped to organize the Polish nationalist militias in the Prussian province of Posen. From December 1848 until April 1849, he would head the staff of the forces of the 'revolutionary Italian army' in Palermo. When that army collapsed, he went off to Baden to join the revolutionaries there mounting a final struggle against the royal armies of the German states.

He was one of those transnational fighters for liberty who remind us of the persistence, despite the rise of inter-ethnic hatreds and chauvinism, of a cosmopolitan vision of the nation as an instrument of emancipation. This was not, to be sure, a cosmopolitanism for its own sake; it reflected the entirely understandable belief of many patriotic Poles that the 'Polish Question' would remain unanswered until the political order sustaining the current system of European powers was overturned, as it eventually was, in 1917–18.

Once reinstalled as sovereign of the island, the king convoked once again the Sicilian parliament on 1 February 1849. But this parliament, like its sister in Naples, was condemned to a state of suspended animation. Treated with contempt by the royal executive and by the ministers, the deputies were condemned to irrelevance. When they voted an address to the king denouncing the current Cabinet and demanding a change of policy, the king refused even to receive the document. The business of parliament became a puppet show, the deputies debating finance bills that were irrelevant, because the ministers chose to bypass them using royal decrees. Having emptied it of any political meaning and held it up to general ridicule, the king shut the Neapolitan parliament down for good on 13 March 1849. On that day, the Minister of Commerce, Prince Torella, presented himself to the chamber and whispered a few words in the ear of the commander of the Civil Guard, who ordered his men to load their rifles. A sealed envelope was passed to the Speaker of the chamber – it was an order of dissolution. The deputies left without making a fuss. Two months later, the Sicilian parliament, too, was formally shut down. Yet the king neither formally revoked the constitution nor abolished the parliament; he preferred to preserve these institutions as mummified remnants, as if he were reluctant to be seen stepping back into the pre-constitutional past. If that was his motive, it was an unwitting testimony to the power of the liberal idea of a constitution.

The revolution was now well and truly over, but the counter-revolution was not. A wave of purges followed. Even those ministers who had acquiesced in the measures of the executive, like Bozzelli and Torella, disappeared from public life. Docile yes-men replaced them. Preventative censorship was reintroduced for all printed works. The police returned to their old abuses. Two sensational trials provided cover for a vindictive campaign against all of those who had been caught up in revolution. Many deputies and former ministers were swept into the net. Scialoja, one of the ministers of 3 April, was sentenced to eight years of seclusion, commuted to exile. The king's former Minister Plenipotentiary to Turin, Pietro Leopardi, was condemned to perpetual banishment. Others received death sentences later commuted to confinement in irons. Silvio Spaventa, editor of the liberal journal *Il Nazionale*, which had struggled to trace a middle path between the royalists and the radicals, was found guilty of conspiracy against the state and received a death sentence, subsequently commuted to life imprisonment. In all, he spent eleven years in prison. This was no comfortable fortress arrest with spacious rooms and afternoon walks on the battlements: the chains used to shackle him left permanent scars on his legs and affected his gait for the rest of his life.[29]

The impact of this dénouement was felt far beyond the boundaries of the Kingdom of the Two Sicilies. The withdrawal of the Neapolitan contingent from the forces engaged against Austria in Lombardy was a blow to the morale of the patriot forces. The Neapolitan army and navy were the largest of any Italian state. King Ferdinand II of Naples had only agreed to send them north in the hope of checking the ambition of his rival Charles Albert and he was glad of the opportunity to withdraw them.[30] 'The victory of the king on the streets of Naples', wrote the Austrian officer, Carl von Schönhals, 'was worth as much to Radetzky [the Austrian commander] as a victory on the banks of the River Po.' The withdrawal of the Neapolitan royal troops left nothing on the river but 'undisciplined hordes' of Roman volunteers who forfeited any military significance whatsoever, once the Neapolitans were no longer there to support them.[31] The effect on the morale of the national movement of 15,000 Neapolitans traipsing back down south through the Italian cities was substantial, even if it cannot be quantified. In Ancona, according to the report of a British witness, 'the mob' responded to the news of the withdrawal by tearing down and burning the coat of arms on the residence of the Neapolitan consul and a deputation was sent to head off the approaching troops and warn them that they were not welcome in the city.[32]

The withdrawal of the naval squadron sent to the aid of Venice had a similarly demoralizing effect. In 1848, the navy of the Venetian republic possessed a number of well-equipped sailing frigates, but not a single steamship, meaning that it could easily be outmanoeuvred in adverse weather. The Venetian envoys in Paris got busy trying to negotiate the sale of a steam-powered vessel, but Manin countermanded these efforts on the grounds that the Neapolitans would soon be arriving, with five steamships of their own. The Neapolitan fleet was 'welcomed and fêted by all our population', Daniele Manin told the Neapolitan envoy in the city in May 1848, because its arrival signalled the end of the Austrian blockade. All the greater, Manin wrote, was the 'profound sorrow and astonishment' occasioned by the news of its withdrawal, which 'overturned' the plans the Venetians had formed for their defence.[33]

Beyond these specific knock-on effects, the Neapolitan counter-revolution inaugurated a larger shift in contemporary awareness. In suddenly turning on the revolution and crushing it piece by piece, Charles de Mazade later recalled, Ferdinand 'helped to break the redoubtable and violent charm of the revolution'. He had made a discovery of great moment, namely that this revolution, 'once you looked it in the face, was not as formidable as people had thought'. For months, the revolution had 'strutted from capital to capital amidst the rout of governments and the uncertainties of public opinion'. This was the turning point, and it emanated not from Paris, Vienna or Berlin, but from Naples.[34] It was a turning point because it abated the fear of those who hated the revolution but had not dared to oppose it. A contemporary analysis captured this dimension succinctly when it described the events of 15 May 1848 in Naples as 'the disequilibrium of two fears' (*lo squilibrio di due paure*).[35]

Once fear was overcome, counter-revolutionaries everywhere in Europe enjoyed the inestimable advantage of being able to set the timing of their own interventions. Revolutionaries, as we have seen, had no control over the timing of revolutions. They were often as confused as their opponents by the upheavals that swept them into power. But counter-revolutionaries were reacting to a fait accompli; they could choose the moment and the manner of action. In Naples, it was the king who set the pace, reneging on earlier concessions and responding to the objections of the deputies with an escalation of armed force that made a definitive showdown all but inevitable. The Neapolitan crackdown, when it happened, did not bear the marks of panic and improvisation, but of rigorous planning and precision in execution. The king and his troops may not have planned the clash of 15 May, but they had planned *for* such a clash and were ready to act when the moment came.

Naples revealed that the counter-revolution still had cards up its sleeve. The continuing loyalty of the armed forces was one of them. But this was a card that could only be played when the broader conditions were right. The spring revolutions had shown that armed force alone was not sufficient when a society withdrew its support from the prevailing regime of power. An effective counter-revolution needed an anchorage of some kind in popular feeling. Perhaps the most striking revelation of 15 May was that the revolution and popular opinion had drifted apart. 'The lower orders took no role in this revolt', Lord Napier wrote to the Foreign Secretary, Palmerston, with lip-smacking complacency. 'It was said, on the contrary, that on the market-squares and the quays they rose and disarmed the National Guards. They paraded the streets with white flags and cries of "Long Live the King!" – they assisted the Neapolitan soldiers in the plunder of the captured houses and in securing the prisoners.'[36] Giuseppe Massari, a supporter of the revolutionary cause, observed the same alliance between the forces of the monarchy and the poorest strata of the city's population. 'The scum of the plebs crowned the work, competing with the soldiers in their filthy greed and unrestrained robbery.' 'The groans of the dying were drowned out by the obscene shouts of the soldiery and the rabble.' There were attacks on the houses of prominent liberals. Three times on that day a crowd of soldiers and *lazzaroni* descended on the house of the former minister Saliceti but failed to find him. Asked why they harboured such bitterness towards a man who had done them no ill, they supposedly replied: 'we have promised his head to the king!'[37] Whoever they were, these were not the people who, only four days earlier, had asked Saliceti to assist them in driving the Jesuits out of town.

The ebbing of the revolution was followed by a massive popular mobilization against it. Thousands of petitions and supplications poured into Naples from across the continental south, expressing allegiance to throne and altar and begging the king to revoke the constitution. The 'constitution', the petitioners declared, was a perilous thing in 'whose name alone resounds the echo of fright and terror in the hearts of all'. It was a flame leaping from tree to tree in an arid forest; it resembled, according to the provincial council of Basilicata, 'a volcano spewing flames and destructive fire'. It was, wrote the petitioners of Cercemaggiore in Molise, 'an electric spark' that had 'set fire to Europe', a 'political cholera that attacks every class, every age and every sex'. Attacks on the constitution were flanked by denunciations of the press, parliament or the 'moral illness' of liberalism.[38] Many of these documents bore hundreds of signatures. Some claimed to represent the unanimous state of opinion in their respective districts. The signatories of a petition from Pratola, where there had been demonstrations against the constitution before 15 May, claimed to be the authentic voice of 'the entire population of the district, prostrate at the foot of the Throne of Your Majesty'. Others spoke also in the name of those unable to sign: 'Many ... would have affixed their signatures, but they could not, for not knowing how to write.' The list of signatories on a petition from Avigliano closed with a note: if no further names had been added, this was because 'here ... the people are almost all illiterate'.[39]

How authentic a reflection of the real state of opinion were these petitions? Some of them were clearly coordinated by local clergy and officials; others appear to have been spontaneous expressions of adhesion to the moral order of absolute monarchy. What nobody knew in 1848–9 was that the Kingdom of the Two Sicilies had only ten years to live. In 1859–60, the Second Italian War of Unification would definitively push the Bourbons from power. Garibaldi would arrive with his thousand volunteers and sweep through the kingdom, gathering new recruits by the thousands wherever he went. The Bourbons would flee, making way for the Piedmontese (Savoyard) monarchy of a liberal and constitutional Italian nation-state. For many Neapolitan officials who had signed pro-absolutist petitions but hoped after 1859 to make their way within the new national and parliamentary order, the entire episode was suddenly a huge embarrassment. The accusation 'You begged the Bourbon to renounce the Charter!' became the rhetorical weapon of choice for those seeking to wound Neapolitan personalities now trying to make their way in the new Italian politics. Pressed to explain themselves, the accused naturally argued that there had been no alternative; resistance was impossible in an environment that forced people to choose between acquiescence and personal ruin.[40]

While opportunism and compliance under pressure were surely part of what drove the petition campaign, there are at least three reasons for supposing that there was more to it than that. The first is that the texts generated by the petitioners are sufficiently diverse and idiosyncratic to suggest that they were at least to some extent authentic reflections of local attitudes. The second is that, in the years after unification, a movement of intermittently violent resistance to the new liberal and national order took shape in the Italian south, striking deep roots into the populace. It was marked by a contempt for the institutions of the new state and by nostalgia for the extinguished monarchical order. In other words, even when the absolutist apparatus of coercion was gone, attachments to the old order persisted, at least on the Neapolitan mainland. In Sicily, the chemistry was slightly different: most people wanted anything but the Bourbons until, that is, they got the House of Savoy (i.e. Charles Albert and the Piedmontese), at which point, at least for some Sicilians, there was a softening of attitudes to the vanquished dynasty.

The third and perhaps most important reason for taking the counter-revolutionary petitions seriously is that Naples was not alone in witnessing a conservative resurgence of this kind. In Bavaria, the passage into law of a bill emancipating the kingdom's Jews triggered a wave of petitions protesting against this measure in 1849–50 (552 of them can be found in the Bavarian state archives). In these texts, antipathy to the Jews as strangers and economic competitors blended with an attachment to threatened traditional rights and hostility towards the parliamentary government introduced in 1848. Here, as in Naples, the message seemed to be that 'neither the government nor the [liberal] press controlled the people'.[41] In Prussia, too, the conservative opposition to the revolution began to organize itself as a mass movement. Already in the summer of 1848, a range of conservative associations – veterans' societies, Prussian patriotic leagues and peasants' associations proliferated across Brandenburg and Pomerania. By May 1849, over 60,000 people – artisans, peasants and shopkeepers – were enrolled in organizations of this kind.[42] In France, the presidential elections of December 1848 would reveal how resistant parts of the countryside remained to the 'charm' of revolution.

What did this mean? In an essay on the Neapolitan events published in the *Neue Rheinische Zeitung* on 1 June 1848, Friedrich Engels conceded that the alliance between the troops and what he called the 'lumpenproletariat' of Naples was the decisive factor in the revolution's defeat. But he contradicted himself in trying to account for it. The *lazzaroni*, he wrote, 'usually favoured the cause of the people'; they had only jumped ship at the last moment when they saw that the revolution was doomed. But then, at a later point in the same article, Engels changed tack, observing that the poorer strata of Naples had always been 'sanfedist' in their sympathies.[43] This was a reference to the Sanfedisti (full name: 'The Army of the Holy Faith in Our Lord Jesus Christ'), a resistance movement that had helped to bring down the Neapolitan (Parthenopean) Republic in June 1799, a satellite state of revolutionary France. The Sanfedisti had marched under the banner of the Cross, amassing a force consisting mostly of peasants, but also of bandits, clergymen and deserters, notorious for purges and atrocities.[44] Engels's first conjecture placed the emphasis on contingency and opportunist realignments. The second carried a different message: in aligning the turbulent Neapolitan lower classes of 15 May 1848 with the sanfedist tradition, Engels hinted at the possibility that the counter-revolutionary zeal of the poorest of Naples might be rooted in something deeper than instrumental calculus, an attachment to monarchy and Church that predisposed them to reject the politics on offer from urban liberals and radicals.

Conservatives tended to gravitate towards the second view. For them, the message of the conservative backlash was that if you moved beyond the cities into the small towns, villages and hamlets, you could reconnect with 'little people', whose faith and loyalties were still intact, their instincts unsullied by education or the urban press. These were the salt of the earth, magnificent in their contempt for the antics of radical urbanites. This was the 'lesson' that Metternich had claimed to learn from the failed Polish uprising of 1846 in Galicia, when he rejoiced that the democrats had 'mistaken their base' and that 'a democracy without the people [was] a chimera'.[45] In France, the conservative parliamentary notables of 1848 and 1849 celebrated their success at the polls as the popular vindication of their traditional social dominance.[46] Otto von Bismarck captured this understanding of 1848 in a passage of the memoirs he wrote after his retirement. In it, he describes what happened when the news of the revolution reached his district in rural Brandenburg. On 20 March, he recalled, the peasants of his estate had reported that some 'deputies' from nearby Tangermünde, a picturesque town on the Elbe River, had appeared in the villages on the Bismarck estate, demanding that the German tricolour be planted on the tower of the estate residence. If the locals did not comply, the intruders threatened, they would soon be back with reinforcements: 'I asked the peasants if they intended to defend themselves: they answered with a lively and unanimous "yes" and I urged them to drive those city chaps out of the village. The deed was immediately done, with the eager participation of the women.'[47]

Whether or not this encounter took place as described, its meaning is clear enough. The sturdy yeomen (and yeowomen) of the countryside would never stand for a revolution. There was, to be sure, a strong dose of wishful thinking in this diagnosis. The second-wave revolutionary mobilizations of the autumn and spring of 1848–9 in France, central Italy and central, western and south-western Germany would reveal that the countryside could be responsive to radical appeals, if these were appropriately framed.[48] At some level, conservatives understood this and responded with measures designed to shut the poorest out of the electoral process. The French law of 31 May 1850 used stringent residency and tax qualification to exclude more than three million citizens from voting, while in Prussia the 'three-class franchise' adopted in 1849 tilted the system in favour of the wealthiest male voters.[49] Nonetheless, the intuition that the people 'out there' had conservative hearts, once established, was hard to shift, perhaps because it was too attractive to relinquish. In 1866, Bismarck would shock his friends and his enemies alike by proposing that the German Confederation be reorganized around a national and democratically elected parliament. His justification for this initiative bore the marks of 1848: 'In moments of decision, the masses will always stand by the king.'[50]

THE EMPIRE STRIKES BACK

Alfred Meißner was attending a fancy-dress ball hosted by the Concordia Club of Prague late in the evening of 29 February when the news of the Parisian revolution reached the city. In their elaborate period costumes, the painters, architects, musicians and writers of Prague were a sight to behold, but the centre of attention, for the all the wrong reasons, was Ferdinand Mikowec, president of the Concordia Club. Mikowec, a German-speaker but an avowed Czech patriot, had come dressed as Lumir, the ancient Slavic god of song. His costume consisted mainly of an enormous wolfskin he had ordered from Warsaw. Under the heat of the lamps and the press of guests, it became clear that the wolfskin had not been properly cured. It began to give off a pungent and nauseating odour. Mikowec had spent the previous days smoking it over juniper berries, hanging it out in the cold winter air and dousing it in Cologne water, but it now became clear that these therapies had entirely failed. As the wolfskin resumed the process of decomposition, a space of empty floor expanded around the Slavic god of song.

Meißner was watching these antics from the box of a wealthy banker who had offered him a free seat, when he noticed a commotion around the Governor's seat on the opposite side of the theatre. 'Something important must have happened in the city', the banker remarked nervously. Just as he was asking the young man next to him to find out what was up, one of the banker's colleagues stormed into the box and passed around two letters, newly arrived from Paris. The first read: '23 February. Five o'clock in the evening. Paris has risen. Fighting in the Saint-Eustache district and on the carré Saint-Martin. The Guizot ministry has fallen.' And the second, a postscript from the same correspondent, stated simply: 'Louis Philippe has abdicated. No more Bourbons! A republican government has been formed.' Meißner read the words over and over again. 'I felt', he recalled, 'as if the hand of a demon had hoisted me up and turned me around in the air.'[51]

The revolution in Prague followed a familiar European pattern: it opened with excitement at the news of foreign tumults, public meetings and lists of demands. On 8 March, members of the Czech patriotic organization Repeal placarded the city with posters inviting citizens to attend a public meeting at the St Václav Baths on 11 March at 6 p.m. This venture was not without risk. Unauthorized public meetings were illegal in Prague, as throughout the Habsburg Empire. The location the organizers had chosen was close both to the turbulent working-class quarter of Podskalí and to two barracks housing government troops. Everyone remembered the 'terror' of 1844, when workers had rioted throughout the city, triggering a violent response from the armed forces. The prominent Czech liberal Josef František Frič stocked his household with firearms in case it might prove necessary to defend his property – not against the organs of the state, but against rampaging proletarians.[52]

The Austrian viceroy, Count Rudolf Stadion, could have banned the meeting, but chose not to, possibly because he was impressed by the news of what had happened when the authorities of the July Monarchy had banned the banquet of the 12th arrondissement in Paris.[53] Despite heavy rain, a large crowd turned up on the evening of 11 March. A famous Belgian cellist who had the misfortune to be giving a concert on the same evening found himself playing before a virtually empty hall and was obliged to pay towards the expense of hiring the venue. Of the 3,000–4,000 people who had turned up, about 800 of the better-dressed demonstrators were admitted into the baths to take part in the meeting. It was the radicals of Repeal who had set the ball rolling, but by the time the meeting of 11 March took place, moderate liberal patriots had taken control. The original radical demand list had included the 'organization of labour and wages' – a theme borrowed from Louis Blanc. But the list read out at the meeting toned down the radical content while dialling up the nationalism. There was no mention of the organization of labour, but the list now opened with a call for the union of the lands of the Czech Crown (meaning Bohemia and Moravia) under a unified administration with a single common Diet that would alternate yearly between Prague and Brno. The Czech language must henceforth play an equal role with the German.

Instability was wired into this situation from the outset. The gathering at the St Václav Baths was overwhelmingly Czech. In a city whose ruling classes were still largely German, that was potentially a problem. Proletarians were few and far between, and such as there were did not make it out of the rain and past the ushers into the meeting. There was no attempt to reach out to the restless elements of the Prague worker suburbs, even though the memory of serious urban unrest was still fresh. The city's liberal bourgeoisie, like their Viennese counterparts, viewed the unskilled labourers of the industrial suburbs as an underclass that 'must be held in check by coercion, not reform'.[54] There were also anxieties around the balance of power between moderates and radicals – many leading moderate figures, including the historian František Palacký, author of the famous letter turning down an invitation to join the Frankfurt parliament, stayed away from the early meetings, for fear that they would degenerate into a radical free-for-all. The new organs of law enforcement exhibited the same fractured structure as in many of the other theatres of revolution: the National Guard and the Academic Legion were both a mix of Germans and Czechs, an arrangement that worked well during the irenic opening phase of the revolution but became more difficult later. In addition to these bodies, Czech patriots formed their own purely Czech guard known as 'Svornost' (unity). Unlike the other National Guard units, which were predominantly middle class, Svornost encouraged aspirants from the Prague working classes – wage-earners came to make up 10 per cent of the total numbers, an unusually high figure by the standards of the National and Civic Guards founded in 1848.[55]

As in several other theatres of revolution, the management committee generated by the earliest protests soon developed executive pretensions. The 'Committee of Prague Citizens' founded on 11 March took responsibility for organizing an interim executive, putting in place the necessary preparations for the election and convocation of the new Diet. At a mass meeting on 10 April, a list was read out of the names of those who would serve on the new body. Alfred Meißner happened to be sitting in the garden next to the Václav Baths correcting the galleys of a poem about the March Revolution when he was startled to hear his own name read out to the meeting next door. 'The audience roared its approval, and so it happened that I, who had come to the Václav Baths as a solitary walker, was suddenly transformed into a member of the Bohemian National Committee.' Walking through sunlit streets full of cheering citizens and flanked by members of the National Guard, the committee members made their way across the river and up the Malá Strana to the residence of the viceroy.

Count Rudolf Stadion, Meißner recalled, was a tall aristocrat in his middling years with 'an elegant, almost foppish appearance of the English type'. He was immaculately coiffed and shaven and a pince-nez on a broad black band perched on the bridge of his shapely nose. Stadion greeted his visitors with the affable charm of an old-school Austrian nobleman. He was most delighted to see his guests, he said. They were, after all:

> men who enjoy the trust of the people – yes, this was something he wished to emphasize – it gave him the most particular pleasure – that was not putting it too strongly, indeed it was probably understating the matter – this circle of men – well, it was an admirable circle of *competent* men, *venerable* names. And he himself – placed as he was, on the one hand, in the service of the government, and having in view, on the other, the interests of the country –[56]

Stadion was cut off in the middle of these burblings by Peter Faster, the innkeeper and moderate liberal, who reminded the Count that he and his fellow delegates had not walked all the way up the hill to his residence to engage in idle chitchat. No one would blame Stadion for wishing they would go to hell, but they were here now and that was that. They had been chosen by the people to prepare the ground for the elections of a Diet elected by the entire country. There was no time to lose. And, incidentally, they would make other executive dispositions as these seemed necessary.

The Count had never been addressed by anyone in this way before. As Stadion listened in stunned silence to Faster's peroration, the pince-nez fell from its perch and swung gently at the end of its band. During the more detailed discussion that followed in a neighbouring room, he seemed unable to focus on what his visitors were saying.

> I will never ever forget the many uses he found for his foldable pince-nez. At one moment, he would observe it with statesmanly gravity, then he would pull forth a silk handkerchief and clean it, then place it again with thoughtful dignity on the bridge of his nose, before letting it drop once again. At one point, he folded it and held it closed in the immediate prox-imity of his nose but then, in his nervousness, pressed accidentally on the little spring, so that the frame sprang open and struck him hard on the side of his nose. And then, smiling mildly at this small upset, the Count let his gaze fall on the circle of men [seated around his table].[57]

Stadion resigned a few weeks later, having concluded that his position was unworkable. Over the next two months, the National Committee became the hub of political activity in Bohemia. It brought radicals and liberals together with members of the Habsburg administration, under the chairmanship of Stadion's successor as governor of Bohemia, Count Thun.

Yet the larger political situation remained volatile. The workers of Prague were feeling the same economic pressures and uncertainty as their counterparts in Paris, Vienna and Berlin, and the city never quite settled down. In Prague, as in other Bohemian and Moravian towns, cat-concerts became increasingly frequent. In the city of České Budějovice (Budweis), these became so common that a curfew was imposed from 10 p.m.[58] During the last week of May there was a fresh wave of plebeian protest; this time the mass meetings were dominated by radicals. Strikes and protest marches became more frequent, and with them attacks on bakers and Jewish merchants. Against this back-ground of ambient unrest, the news that Prince Windischgrätz, a key figure in the Habsburg military leadership, was about to return to Prague as commander of the imperial forces in Bohemia was bound to

cause outrage – everyone remembered the role he had played in putting down the textile workers' revolts in 1844. Within days of his
arrival on 20 May, evidence of increased troop activity could be seen
everywhere. Armed patrols were more frequent, especially in the
working-class areas. There were military parades, at which vivats rang
out for the general. Artillery batteries were established at prominent
positions in the city 'in order to be forearmed for all eventualities'.[59]

These dispositions coincided with a radicalization of the mood in the
city, especially among the students, who were closely networked with
the radical student movement in Vienna. Many radicals were heartened
by the sudden departure of the monarch and the court to Innsbruck on
17 May, because they misread it as a sign that the old regime was on the
verge of collapsing. The students organized two rallies on 27 and 29
May, at which speakers demanded the immediate removal of Windischgrätz. On 1 June, a new radical journal appeared in the city, the
Prague Evening Post (Pražský wečerní list), which set itself the task of
'correcting false rumours from the mouths of malicious men, hostile to
freedom, who hate our nation'.[60] The national question continued to
seethe. German commissioners sent from Frankfurt to persuade the
Germans in Bohemia to vote for representatives to the German National
Assembly were mocked and threatened in the streets and there were tit-
for-tat skirmishes between the Czech and German patriotic clubs.[61] On
11 June, posters printed in red ink appeared throughout the city,
demanding that the military hand over 2,000 rifles and 80,000 live cartridges and an entire battery of artillery to the Academic Legion, as well
as removing the batteries already installed at various points in the city.
When Windischgrätz refused most of these demands, the students
formed a makeshift 'Ministry of War'. In the lecture halls of the university, home-made bullets were handed out to the students in preparation
for a showdown with the military.

The flashpoint came on Monday, 12 June, the day after Pentecost.
The radical students had called for a rally that would take the form of a
mass, to be celebrated in front of the statue of St Václav (Wenceslas). A
huge and mainly Czech-speaking crowd formed, including more than
2,000 workers from the industrial districts. After the mass, a crowd of
protesters marched to the military headquarters nearby, where there
were clashes between troops and demonstrators. Barricades went up
across the city. For six days (12–17 June), the June Uprising raged in the

capital. It was a conflict full of bitterness for Windischgrätz: while observing a tumult in the square from her window in his residence, the prince's wife was struck and killed by a spent bullet on the first day of the fighting. She died knowing that her son, an army officer, had also been seriously wounded in the fighting.[62]

Perhaps the most surprising thing was the extent to which Windischgrätz operated independently of the government in Vienna. The political leadership – not to be confused with the court, which had left for Innsbruck – sent a two-man commission to Prague in the middle of the uprising with a view to getting the prince to treat for a cessation of hostilities. Windischgrätz initially agreed to tender his resignation, but he changed his mind when placards appeared in the streets of Prague boasting that the army had 'capitulated' to the insurgents. Infuriated by this presumption, Windischgrätz got back into the fight and stepped up the counter-insurgency campaign.

That the general could withdraw and recommit in this way demonstrates how effectively the loose constellation of powers that made up the Habsburg imperial system continued to function under the semi-acephalous conditions of the summer of 1848. Prague was bombarded into submission and capitulated on 17 June. On the following day, a state of siege was declared and the police began rounding up suspects. In all 43 insurgents were killed, of whom 12 were unskilled workers and at least 29 did manual work of some kind. We know of 63 wounded, of whom 11 were students.[63] The combatants were mostly young and male, though witnesses described the involvement of women, including a contingent of pupils from a girls' school who helped in the building of barricades.

With the insurgency defeated, Windischgrätz established a commission to go after the participants. Among those who came under suspicion were Poles and Magyars who happened to be staying in the city and the Russian anarchist Bakunin, who was in Prague at the time but appears to have played no role in the uprising. Houses were searched, letters were opened and an appeal from the authorities triggered such a flood of denunciations from citizens hoping to win favour or settle old scores that the police struggled to get through all the paperwork. The National Guards were purged and the National Committee and the Czech patriot militia Swornost were both dissolved. Similar closures were enacted in towns and villages across the country. In the small town of Votice in central Bohemia, the National Guard was shut down and ordered to surrender its banner, drum and weapons. No weapons could be surrendered, because the guards had never been provided with weapons – they had marched with wooden rifles (except for the town potter, who had made one out of clay). The banner was no longer available since it had been restored to its earlier role as the weathervane on the church steeple, and the drum could not be handed over either, since it was the municipal drum used to accompany the announcement of city ordinances.[64] This was the world of small commotions that would later give birth to the splendid Švejk, the clueless hero of Jaroslav Hašek's dark comical novel, *The Good Soldier Švejk*.

The rift between the leadership in Prague and the Pillersdorf government in Vienna remained open. The government pressed the general to lift the state of siege, but Windischgrätz and the Governor of Bohemia, Count Thun, both refused. The journalist Karel Havlíček was arrested on one day on account of an article he had written for *Národní Noviny* and then elected on the next to represent five different districts in the Constituent Reichstag, due to convene on 22 July. Seeing that support for his policy was waning, Windischgrätz agreed to lift the state of siege on 20 July. The investigatory commission was shut down and the prosecution of suspected insurgents placed in the hand of the regular courts. Between early August and mid September, nearly all the suspects were released – only those believed to be among the chief instigators of the uprising remained in detention.

As the grip of the authorities loosened, the radical movement began to revive. When Windischgrätz issued a statement on 2 August claiming that his investigative commission had uncovered a conspiracy involving a large part of the city's population, there were protest meetings, including a gathering of over 400 women, the first ever political assembly of women to take place in Prague. An article by J. Slavomil Wawra in the *Pražský wečerní list* reported on the event with a mixture of enthusiasm and condescension. At last, he wrote, the women had stepped forward to take advantage of the right of association and assembly secured through the revolution. Almost every female social type could be found there, from 'serious ladies full of dignity' to 'cute overdressed divas' dressed in Czech colours, to 'a grey-haired matron with a tearful eye'. The women took turns sharing their experiences during the violence. Some had been robbed, several had encountered the technician Schwarzer, whose ear had been cut off by an Austrian officer, others had seen soldiers drag women down the street by their hair. Wawra expressed admiration for the orderliness and candour of the proceedings, 'which could actually serve as an example for many gatherings of men', and closed on a positive note: 'We welcome with reverence and joy this phenomenon, hitherto unknown in our country, and we rejoice in the benefit to the country . . . To you, therefore, good daughters of our land, shall the nation thrice aloud offer praise and thanks!'[65]

Stirring as such demonstrations were, they could not conceal the weaknesses laid bare by the insurgency. Very few of the Germans in the city had taken part. On 5 July, sixty-seven members of the German Casino Club had even filed a petition asking for the state of siege to be continued. The rate of participation had been low. Of a population of around 100,000, only 1,500 had chosen to fight at the barricades. About 800 of these were students, but the activist students made up only around a quarter of the student body in the city. The efforts to drum up interest in the rural areas around Prague had proved almost entirely fruitless. And in the aftermath of the insurgency the increasingly aggressive monitoring of the press and the endless intrusion of spies and informants into every domain of political life cramped the ardour of many patriots. Perhaps the most dispiriting feature of the post-insurgency landscape was the continuing presence and the remarkable independence of Windischgrätz. He was hated by the Czechs of Prague and he was under pressure to send his troops to Italy, where they were needed by the Habsburg forces engaged in putting down the revolutions in Venetia and Lombardy. But he was too well connected at court to be so easily dislodged and he stayed on in the Bohemian capital. When he eventually left, this was because a new revolution had broken out in Vienna. Windischgrätz was determined to repeat there the victory he had accomplished in Prague.[66]

As the Austrian forces fought to regain the initiative in northern Italy, they benefited from the weaknesses of their Italian opponents. There were, to be sure, many episodes of extraordinary Italian courage and determination. At Curtatone near Mantua on 29 May, a small mixed force of Neapolitan and Tuscan regulars and volunteers held off an assault by a numerically superior Austrian force under Radetzky's command. This minor action relieved the pressure on nearby Piedmontese positions, paving the way to a victory over the Austrians at

Goito on the following day. But, for the most part, the Italian patriot leaders failed to coordinate the many volunteer legions and bands with each other and with the various regular units. A simple lack of armaments was another problem: of the 2,000 men who marched on the Austrian positions at Montebello and Soria on 8 April 1848, only 500–600 had firearms.

Coordinating volunteer bands with regular troops was difficult, in part because most military commanders were distrustful and intolerant of irregulars. General Zucchi, like many of his military generation a former officer in the army of the French Empire, was a case in point. He had fought in the Italian uprisings against Austria in 1821 and 1831 and been sentenced to death by an Austrian military court. After this penalty was commuted, Zucchi spent a spell in fortress confinement that only ended when he was liberated by the revolution in 1848. In other words: he was not hostile to insurgency and political activism as such. It was the indiscipline of the irregulars that worried him. Writing in his memoirs of the 150 volunteers sent by Manin to support his forces at Palmanova, Zucchi had this to say:

> These people gave themselves the title of 'crusaders', but what race of men they in fact belonged to is revealed by the following words, with which the president of the revolutionary committee at Udine warned me of their arrival. – 'Citizen General, the crusaders of Venice, who will arrive today at Palmanova, should be kept under the most rigorous surveillance, having shown themselves during their two-day sojourn [in Udine] to be the dregs of society as regards their rudeness and arrogance.'[67]

The Piedmontese commanders were even less respectful of volunteers than Zucchi. And none was more hostile than King Charles Albert, who even took steps to disband many of the units that had formed in the aftermath of the revolution's outbreak. It proved extremely difficult in practice to plait the patriotic enthusiasm of the volunteer movement together with the narrow dynastic calculus of the monarchical armies, even if they seemed to be committed to the same struggle.

It would be churlish to deny the Austrians their part in the success of the Habsburg counter-revolution. Radetzky deployed his troops with ingenuity, responding swiftly to the evolutions of the conflict by concentrating his forces at critical points in the enemy's dispositions. He made better use of intelligence than his opponents and enjoyed higher esteem and confidence among his own officers and men than the Piedmontese generals did among theirs.[68] And the Austrians proved adept at manipulating the populations of northern Italy with a blend of terror and the promise of better things. In mid April 1848, Radetzky sent two battalions to clear out the Italian volunteers encamped in and around the village of Castelnuovo, to the west of Verona, adding that the whole village should be burnt down, and its inhabitants massacred. More than one hundred children, women and men perished in the action that followed. The news of this atrocity struck terror into the insurgent local governments of the region, who feared that the Austrians had a similar fate in store for their own communities.[69] At the same time, Count Hartig, the official entrusted with the 'pacification' of the newly reconquered areas, was sent to the Veneto to reconcile the locals to Austrian rule. In mid April, he published a proclamation to the Lombardo-Venetians promising to cut the most unpopular taxes. The seizure of a major town was followed by edicts assigning greater powers to the municipalities and communal deputations of the region around it. Here, as in many parts of the Habsburg Empire and elsewhere, the concession of some key revolutionary demands was a weapon in the armoury of counter-revolution. In May, Hartig issued a statement addressed to 'the good peasantry' and declaring that the Austrians had come to 'liberate' them from the 'despotism' of agitators bent on plunging the entire region into war and famine.[70]

The socio-political tensions that undermined the cohesion of the revolution in other countries were also present in northern Italy. The truce between the republicans and the monarchists was fraying fast. But the republicans were divided too. In May 1848, the Milanese republicans around Carlo Cattaneo called for a break with the Provisional Government and for a democratically elected Lombard assembly, but when they begged Mazzini to support them, he refused.[71] In many towns, socially motivated unrest continued. In Padua, for example, coachmen mounted violent protests against a local omnibus company; tailors and hatters used violence to disrupt the market in off-the-peg suits and factory-made hats. A popular Paduan tribune emerged, comparable in some respects with Ciceruacchio in Rome. The thirty-year-old miller

Giovanni Zoia employed his own small police force, alarming some of the better-off inhabitants of the city, who complained to the authorities in Venice that he and other such pop-up folk leaders were 'despots of liberty'. Alarm at this kind of turbulence pushed many politically active people into the camp that preferred fusion with the Kingdom of Piedmont to the vagaries of life under a Venetian republic.[72] To these internal ailments we should add the exogenous shock of the Papal Allocution of 29 April 1848. In distancing himself unequivocally from the struggle against Austria, Pius IX deprived the patriotic cause of its spiritual leadership and shattered one of the generative illusions of the movement, namely the dream of an Italy federally united under the captaincy of the Pope. This in turn triggered a slow migration of Catholics away from the national cause.

The loss of cohesion and the baffling plurality of interests and visions would doubtless have dogged any effort to build a new polity in northern Italy, even if it had proved possible to eject the Austrians permanently. The underlying problem was that the early victories against the Habsburg armies had neither reversed Austria's strategic superiority in the region nor diminished the war-fighting capability of Radetzky's forces.[73] When these resources were thrown into the balance against a divided and under-resourced Italian opponent, only one ultimate outcome was possible.

The endgame in Lombardy opened with the shattering Austrian assault on the Piedmontese positions around Custoza on 24 and 25 July. Shaken, King Charles Albert fell back on Milan. It seemed at first as if he had resolved to mount a last-ditch defence there. There was outrage and dismay when it became known that on 5 August the king had asked Radetzky for an armistice under whose terms he would withdraw into Piedmont with his forces and leave Lombardy and Venetia to the Austrians. Furious patriots besieged the king's Milanese headquarters and he departed for Turin cursed by many as a coward and a traitor. Republicans like Cattaneo had warned all along that this would happen, but there are disasters so complete that even the opportunity to say 'I told you so' brings no comfort. About a third of the Milanese population chose to leave rather than witness the re-entry of the Austrians into their city. The revolution wasn't quite over yet – Daniele Manin was still holding out in Venice, and Piedmont would (in vain) wage war against

Austria in the following year. But, for the moment, the dream of emancipation from Austrian rule receded into an unforeseeable future.

In Vienna, the power-sharing arrangement established on 26 May remained in place. The National Guard and Academic Legion continued to patrol the streets; the military were hardly to be seen. Under the sage leadership of Adolf Fischhof, the Committee of Safety operated as a kind of ersatz government. The Prime Minister, the mild-mannered Baron Franz von Pillersdorf, struggled to keep up with the political demands of the radical organizations. On 8 July, after a clash with the committee, Pillersdorf resigned. His successor, the liberal Baron Anton von Doblhoff-Dier, remained in office for only ten days. His replacement was the amiable and liberally inclined former diplomat Johann Philipp von Wessenberg-Ampringen. Wessenberg-Ampringen's sudden elevation, first to foreign minister and then to Prime Minister, was a sign that the Habsburg court was running out of options. Politically, he was a sensible enough choice, but he had been in retirement since 1831. Amidst the invective showered on him by the radical press, one sympathetic biographer later remarked, the many achievements of a career that had begun in the 1790s were totally forgotten. Only profound attachment to the imperial state and its ruling house could have driven a 75-year-old old man 'to exchange the ease of a tranquil private life rich in intellectual pleasures' for the 'thorny crown' of ministerial office in times like these. And yet, for the moment, everything seemed to fall into place. Wessenberg-Ampringen was a sincere supporter of the constitutional monarchy; the ministry now included the well-known farmer democrat Dr Alexander Bach, who served as Minister of Justice. It looked as if the constitutional order might be stabilizing itself. On 22 July, the new constituent Reichstag opened in the Spanish Riding School. On 12 August, the emperor returned into residence.

Yet the potential for social upheaval remained. The emergency public works programmes created by the Committee of Safety weighed heavily on the exhausted finances of the city. It wasn't just the money that was running out: so was willingness of the property-owning moderates in the government to keep throwing public resources at the Social Question – there were analogies with the growing impatience of the French republicans with the Parisian workshops. On 18 August, the new Minister of Labour, Ernst von Schwarzer, a well-known democratic publicist, announced that the wages of the 'earthworkers' (*Erdarbeiter*), a contingent of some 20,000 men and women consigned to digging and excavation works, would be reduced by five kreutzer (the equivalent of around ninety-five eurocents) a day. This was more than an economizing measure; it was a show of strength and a ministerial disavowal of plebeian social radicalism. Alexander Bach, the justice minister, drove the point home when he declared that protests by 'anarchist and republican groups' against the pay cuts 'would not be tolerated'.[74] Here, as had happened in Paris, the governmental moderates and the radicals of the streets found themselves on opposite sides.

Three days later, the announcement that the wages of women and children would be reduced across all the public works projects triggered skirmishes and demonstrations across the inner city, in which women played a prominent role. Thousands of women workers marched to the offices of the Committee of Safety and announced that they would not leave until the pay cuts had been rescinded – this was the first political demonstration by women in Austrian history.[75] When the radical priest Anton Füster appeared before the crowd and tried to explain why the authorities had docked the wages, 'the words No! No! rang out from a thousand female throats'.[76] A well-dressed man who pushed his way uninvited into a crowd of women on the Hoher Markt and started explaining the new policy to them received 'a thorough beating' from his audience.[77]

The unrest culminated in a mass demonstration on 23 August. The workers responded to the five-kreutzer wage cuts in the language of carnival. They produced an effigy of clay and straw supposedly choking on the coins the government had saved through its wage cuts. Placing it on a bier and labelling it 'Kreutzer-Minister', they orchestrated a mock funeral procession, telling the spectators: 'He swallowed four kreutzer and choked on the fifth.'[78] When this procession, flanked by workers armed with shovels and pickaxes, reached the Praterstern in the heart of an entertainment district on the northern outskirts of the city, they found their way blocked by a large force of National Guards. After an exchange of insults, the demonstrators began a spontaneous cat-concert. Enraged, the mounted Guards, whose ardour for the revolution was in any case waning fast, spurred their horses into the crowd and lashed out with their sabres against the tightly packed women, men and children.[79] Many received sabre cuts to shoulders, backs and flanks as they fled from the scene. It was reported that a National Guardsman pursuing children who had fled from the trouble to hide at the back of an inn cut off the arm of the publican when he tried to intervene. The seriously wounded whose names are known included ten women. The *Wiener Gassenzeitung* reported 282 wounded and eighteen dead. A radical pamphlet published in Bern in the following year to raise money for German refugees claimed that 'hundreds of men and women' (an exaggeration) had been 'cut down and shot dead'.[80]

Whatever the exact numbers, for many Viennese observers, this was a revelatory shock. The participants had endowed the event with a special symbolic weight. On their way to the Praterstern, the marching workers had received the 'flags of 26 May', a reference to the second May uprising, when the men of the National Guard and the Academic Legion had taken control of the city. It was a sign that the workers intended to roll back the horizon of the revolution, that they saw it as a process, and not as an event. The Guards, for their part, captured the flags and carried them as trophies through the city.[81] A troubling detail, at least for left-radical observers: the Academic Legion stayed aloof from the unrest. Even the radical law student and co-founder of the Committee of Safety, Adolf Willner, known for his advocacy of higher wages and the ten-hour working day, had not taken the workers' side, urging them instead not to challenge the new measures. The Committee of Safety and the Academic Legion seemed to be decoupling themselves from the workers they claimed to represent.[82] The ecstatic fraternizing that had delighted Carl Borkovsky was no more. In this sense, though in a very muted register, 23 August resembled the June Days in Paris. And like their Parisian counterparts, the moderates in Vienna had no intention of relinquishing their advantage. Confident that they could handle the revolution from here on, the ministers terminated the power-sharing arrangement with the Committee of Safety. The committee duly dissolved itself, convinced that it had failed in its core task.

This was the first serious defeat. Working-class radicalism now lacked any kind of political forum. Many feared, with good reason, that an armed counter-insurgency was imminent. Looking back a year later, the refugee radical Albert Rosenfeld remembered 23 August as a 'black page in the history of our days'.[83] For the radical journal *Wiener Gassenzeitung*, it was clear that the revolution had arrived at a turning point. A dark future lay ahead. The workers would no longer allow themselves to be herded together in the streets like cattle and cut down. From now on, they would network and conspire; they would bury more than mere effigies of clay and straw. They would form a 'phalanx against property'.[84] In the skirmishes of 23 August, the more perceptive Viennese observers discerned a breach in the structure of the revolution.

The fuse of the Viennese counter-revolution was lit in the South Slav borderlands of Hungary. In March, as we have seen, General Baron Josip Jelačić had been appointed *ban* and military governor in Zagreb. It was not the Illyrian radicals known to Dragojla Jarnević who backed Jelačić, but the Croatian conservatives. They hoped that this ardent patriot would rally South Slav support against Hungary while at the same time diverting the Illyrian revolution into safe channels and avoiding social experiments. And, as we have seen, their hopes materialized. As a political leader, Jelačić became the focal point of intense patriotic emotion. The response from Vienna was ambivalent. Since the Habsburg authorities were still preoccupied at this point negotiating a settlement of some kind with the new leadership in Pest, they could hardly officially endorse the enthronement of an anti-Magyar firebrand in the southern borderlands of the Kingdom of Hungary.

A situation of almost comical complexity now arose. Official Vienna refused to acknowledge the new ban and agreed with the Magyar leaders that the military frontier remained under the authority of Pest. At the same time, conservatives around the Ministry of War in Vienna mobilized in support of Jelačić, whom they viewed as a loyal Austrian asset. The ministry in Vienna continued to issue orders to the military border, as if control over it had never been ceded to Pest. Jelačić, for his part, blankly refused to acknowledge the authority of the Hungarian government, or even to accept communications from the Hungarian Ministry of War. When the Hungarians filed a formal complaint about this insubordination, the emperor issued a statement on 7 May stipulating that all troops stationed in 'Hungary-Croatia', including the border areas, must comply with orders from the Hungarian Ministry of War. With this document in hand, the Hungarians sent their own 'royal commissioner', Lieutenant Field Marshal John Hrabowsky von Hrabova, to unseat the ban and restore the authority of the Pest government.

Jelačić was aware of these adverse signals from official Vienna, but he chose to listen instead to the assurances of Baron Franz Kulmer, the liaison man for the conservatives at court, who assured him that the Hungarian 'royal commissioner' had as yet received no royal orders and that the Hungarian king (who was also the Austrian emperor) had not officially removed any of the ban's powers. Encouraged by these messages of support, Jelačić began to concentrate his forces along the Croatian–Hungarian border on the River Drava. While the Hungarians were watching these ominous developments, an insurrection broke out among the Serbs of South Hungary, who now proclaimed the establishment of an autonomous Voivodina. Three authorities now claimed to control the border area: the Serbian Supreme Council (Glavni Odbor), the Hungarian Royal Commissioner Hrabowsky and Ban Josip Jelačić, whose control over the Illyrian radicals was still holding, but looked increasingly fragile. To complicate matters further, the emperor – now sheltering in Innsbruck – responded to renewed complaints from the Hungarian government by issuing an order on 10 June deposing Jelačić altogether from the Banship.

The situation was less hopeless for Jelačić than it seemed. The tide was turning in favour of the counter-revolution. Radetzky was well on his way to defeating the Italian insurgents in northern Italy (except in Venice), and within days of the order of 10 July Windischgrätz would crush the Pentecost Uprising in Prague. As the conservatives around the emperor regained their confidence, a cohesive 'military party' began to emerge. Baron Kulmer assured Jelačić that he was the man of the moment, even in Vienna; he was not to be put off by all the contradictory signalling – the order deposing him was null and void because it had never been countersigned by any of the ministers. These were the perplexing games one could play with the loose command structure of the Habsburg monarchy in the summer of 1848.

By early September, the confidence of the court in Vienna had revived. The pressure for an armed intervention in Hungary was mounting. Even many liberals in Vienna now felt that too much had been conceded to the Hungarians during the panic of spring 1848. It was time to claw back lost ground. On 29 August, the government announced that it was taking back centralized control of the financial and military affairs of the monarchy. The Hungarians, who had been building up a national army since the early summer, were told to desist from such preparations immediately. The order formally assigning control of the borderlands to Pest was formally countermanded: Vienna would henceforth control the military frontier directly. On 4 September, there was an order formally reinstating Jelačić in all of his offices.

The time had come to act, Baron Kulmer told Jelačić on 27 August. 'Only after you have actually crossed the Drava, will confidence in you, which is now rapidly declining, be restored. Once you have successfully invaded Hungary, you will receive imperial sanction.' Eight days later came the kind of warning one associates with an organized crime syndicate: if Jelačić did not invade immediately, the consequence might well be a reconciliation between Vienna and Pest – at Croatia's cost.[85] Anxious lest the Hungarian forces grow yet larger, and badgered by his handlers in Vienna, Jelačić took the plunge and crossed the Drava on 11 September. It was not an impressive campaign. The *ban* found it difficult to keep his troops under control and his men left a trail of robbery and murder behind them as they slogged their way through Hungary looking for a decisive showdown with Magyar national forces.

This was the situation in the last week of September: in Vienna, reports of the atrocities committed by Croat irregulars in the wake of the Jelačić army helped to power a surge in radical opposition to the Austrian intervention in Hungary.[86] Whereas German-speaking radicals in Vienna had cheered the defeat of Italians and Czechs, whom they saw as rivals and opponents in areas of mixed settlement, many of them viewed the Hungarians as allies against the Slavic nationalities. It was a striking feature of German patriotism within the Kingdom of Hungary that it tended not to mobilize against the Magyars, but to affirm a politics of 'Hungarian–German dual nationality'.[87] For once, nationalism reinforced, rather than cross-cut, trans-ethnic revolutionary solidarity. Fearing a radical backlash in the capital, the Austrian government went back to its games: Prime Minister Johann Philipp Wessenberg Ampringer new publicly denied any connection with Jelačić and his Hungarian venture. At the same time, relations between Pest and Vienna went from bad to worse: in Pest, several of the moderate, pro-conciliation ministers resigned; Széchenyi, now in the grip of a nervous breakdown, fled the city, followed by the Hungarian Palatine (the emperor's representative in Hungary).

The Habsburg court responded to these developments with an act of baffling recklessness. It appointed Count Franz Philipp Lamberg as the military commander and provisional Palatine of Hungary and sent him into the country to take up his new office, reassert control over the Hungarian administration and oversee a return to peace. Lamberg arrived in

Buda on 28 September. The timing could hardly have been worse. Lamberg had been a popular and respected figure. He was a Hungarian-born Austrian with a native command of the Hungarian language. He had worked as a journalist and writer, starting with pieces for the Hungarian press and later publishing books in both Hungarian and German, including a celebrated guide to the non-Hungarian lands of the monarchy. In 1844, he had been considered for membership of the Hungarian Academy of Sciences. But in the political heat of the revolutionary year these accomplishments counted for little. Lamberg still lacked formal accreditation when he travelled to Buda, because his appointment had not yet been countersigned by the Hungarian Prime Minister, Batthyány. It seems in retrospect an act of madness to have sent this man unprotected and burdened with a mission that was an incoherent blend of executive and diplomatic tasks to a place in which Vienna had no real leverage. And this at a time, as the people at court knew perfectly well, when the approach of the Jelačić army, covertly supported by Vienna, was stirring panic in the streets of the Hungarian capital. The Hungarian radicals denounced Lamberg as an interloper with no official standing and posters appeared in Buda calling for his execution as a traitor. On 29 September, as Lamberg tried to make his way in a fiacre across the Danube on the bridge of boats from Buda to the relative safety of Pest, he was recognized by an angry crowd, dragged from his carriage, beaten, pierced with bayonets, disembowelled and butchered in the street. Pieces of his body were carried about on the ends of scythes by a howling mob. On the very same day, 29 September, Jelačić's advance on the Hungarian capital was blocked by a swiftly improvised Hungarian national force. The policy of equivocation had run its course. The government in Vienna resolved to launch an armed intervention. The decision to order troops to the Hungarian border would trigger the last and most spectacular revolutionary outbreak in Vienna, an insurrection more potent than anything that had yet been seen in that year.

At seven in the morning of 6 October, the radical parliamentary deputy Hans Kudlich was shaken awake by his friend the law student Carl Hoffer, a member of the Student Committee. The university was in a state of uproar, Carl told him. The Richter Battalion had received marching orders for Hungary. Guards, students and members of the people were on the Danube Bridge, trying to prevent them from leaving the city. Without stopping to eat breakfast, Kudlich hurried to the scene. Walking out of the city to the north-east, he found the Jägerzeile (today the Praterstraße) full of people in excited conversation: should the military be allowed to march or not? The name of the Minister of War, Count Theodor Baillet-Latour, a hate figure in the working-class districts, was on everyone's lips. As Kudlich approached the river, the crowds thickened, but they seemed inquisitive rather than aggressive. The entrance to the bridge was blocked by a troop of dragoons. Kudlich introduced himself to their commander and was allowed to pass. Most of the bridge's boards had been torn up to prevent cavalry from crossing the river. On the bridge itself small groups of grenadiers could be seen, looking clueless and isolated. Walking northwards again towards the Zwischenbrücken district, Kudlich encountered 'a mass of about 1,000 men', most of them armed – workers, soldiers, Guards and a few students all mixed together, 'talking and gesticulating', but all resolved to prevent the departure of the troops 'at any price'.

Recognized by two of the leading student radicals, Kudlich was asked to 'say a few words' and hoisted onto a table. His message was ambivalent. Yes, the intervention in Hungary was a 'reactionary' policy. It was unjust and an act of treason against the people. But it was the Reichstag, the deputies elected by the people (of whom Kudlich was one), that must act now, not disorganized bands of the people. The 'reactionary party', Kudlich warned, had long been waiting for a pretext to 'annihilate freedom and to destroy the parliament'. It would be folly to be lured into a confrontation with the troops. People should either disperse or wait until parliament had convened and issued new instructions to the government.[88] The replies – 'The grenadiers must not pass!' 'Latour is to blame!' – did not suggest that the crowd accepted Kudlich's counsels of caution. His words revealed a confidence in the continuing importance and authority of the parliament that seems strange in retrospect but was shared by many of the more progressive deputies. As he left the scene to hurry back into the city, Kudlich begged a cavalry commander not to fire on the demonstrators. Precipitous action would unleash a 'general uprising with unpredictable consequences for the parliament, the city and possibly for the monarchy itself'. Given the time to act, parliament would mediate, and all would be well.[89]

When he reached the Reichstag at around 10 a.m., Kudlich found the doors of the chamber locked. A group of around 100 deputies had gathered nearby, and he had the opportunity to observe a paradoxical reversal of political outlooks. The most radical deputies, Löhner, Zimmer, Goldmark, Schuselka, were all deeply shocked to learn of the latest unrest and looked with horror on the prospect of a revolution in the city. By contrast, the conservative Reichstag president, Strohbach, and the Czech deputies appeared to be finding it difficult to suppress 'confident smiles of triumph', almost as if they hoped that the situation would soon slip out of control. There was now a lively debate. Löhner and various others pressed for an emergency meeting of the parliament. But Strohbach and his conservative allies refused to accept this departure from protocol, arguing that the present crisis was not a matter for the parliament, but for the ministry, for 'the executive'. When Kudlich's Silesian compatriot Hein, a conservative deputy from Troppau (today Opava in the Czech Republic) shouted: 'It's time to get serious with this university riffraff!', the two men almost came to blows. There were shouts of 'Traitor! Traitor!' as Strohbach left the room with the radical deputy Smolka trailing along to monitor his next moves.[90]

When Kudlich went with a delegation of thirty deputies to see the government, he found the same pattern: the more emollient and moderate ministers were 'downtrodden and sad', while the hardliners were confident, cheerful and ready for the next steps. When it was announced that the Reichstag intended to convene an emergency session, Minister of War Latour, offered a chipper rejoinder. He thanked the deputies for their solicitude. But there was no need to be alarmed. There had been some minor disorders, but nothing the authorities couldn't cope with. Everyone should relax. When Kudlich warned the ministers that bands of armed peasants were reported to be on their way to the city, there was a sharp retort from Minister of Justice Alexander Bach. The deputies had clearly got used to pushing the ministers around. But those days were now over: 'The executive you see before you will tolerate no interference, whether it should come from a fraction of the parliament or from the street!'

The schism between the ministers and the parliament, reminiscent of the situation in counter-revolutionary Naples, could scarcely have been more sharply expressed. It was a matter of indifference whether the parliament convened a meeting, Bach told the deputies, provided it stayed well out of the way of 'the executive'.[91] The equation of the parliament with 'the street' must have stung the deputies, coming as it did from the

former democrat Bach, a man who once had been named in police suspect lists – seven months earlier, he had ridden through town on a white
horse bearing the 'demands of the people' to the Landhaus. Bach was on
a long journey across the political landscape, a journey that would continue into the 1850s, when he became one of the presiding figures of the
post-revolutionary, neo-absolutist Habsburg regime.

By the time Kudlich rejoined the parliament, which was now in emergency session, a major escalation was underway. As the discussions
began, Prime Minister Hornbostel, a moderate, burst into the chamber:
'Gentlemen, the war ministry is in the hands of the people, [Minister of
War] Latour is in danger, [we must] rescue the Minister of War!' A delegation of the most popular deputies now made its way with a huge
white flag, fashioned out of fabric torn from the curtains in the chamber, from the Riding School to the ministry. They intended to place
Latour under the protection of the Reichstag – here again was that
hardy faith in the authority of a parliament. Their arrival at the ministry
provoked a storm of cheering from the crowds around the entrance.
Pushing forwards into the building, the delegates found a small detachment of frightened soldiers and a large crowd of armed artisans,
labourers, Guards and Legionaries. The radical deputy Borrosch climbed
onto a table and explained to the crowd what was going to happen
next. The minister would be placed under the protection of the Reichstag and taken away in due course. The people should trust the
parliament; the minister would be held to account for his actions. But
the crowd did not trust the parliament: 'He [Latour] deserves death!'
'He killed our brothers!' Despairing at their deafness to his arguments,
Borrosch reached for something more melodramatic. 'If you must have
a victim, then take this old grey head!', he cried, and flung his hat with
a passionate flourish into the crowd, as if he were throwing his own
head to a ravenous tiger. 'Today', Kudlich would later write, 'all of this
may perhaps sound rather theatrical, but at that sombre moment [Bor-
rosch's] performance made the most tremendous impression!'[92]

The delegates left the ministry persuaded that the crisis had passed, but
they were wrong. While Borrosch and his companions announced the
success of their mediation to parliament, fresh crowds, full of people who
had *not* seen him fling his hat, entered the Ministry of War. Fearing the
worst, Latour, who was still upstairs in the ministry, changed into civilian
clothes and concealed himself in an annex. His friends placed furniture

against the door and scattered papers across the floor to create the impression that the room had already been searched. Had Latour remained in this lightless cubbyhole, he might well have made it safely through the critical next few hours. He was only persuaded to come out by the arrival of yet another parliamentary delegation that turned up at the ministry with a contingent of Guards to rescue him. Among them were Fischhof, the temperate former chairman of the Committee of Safety, and Goldmark, a Hungarian-born physician and chemist and one of the leading exponents of Jewish emancipation. They explained to the minister that they could only help him if he signed a document resigning from his office; he did so, though he added the words 'pending his Majesty's consent'. Hemmed in by an escort of twenty armed National Guards and four parliamentary delegates, the 68-year-old Latour processed down the main stairs to the lobby, where the crowd was waiting. Plucking away his defenders one by one, they set upon Latour, beating him with hammers and iron pipes and piercing him with bayonets. The efforts of Fischhof and Goldmark to shield him with their own bodies were in vain and he died in their arms. Forty-three gaping wounds were later found on his corpse. The body was stripped, strung up from a lamp post outside the ministry and subjected to further indignities. The discarded clothes were torn into fragments to circulate as 'relics', and women dipped their handkerchiefs in his blood.[93] To heighten the theatricality of the spectacle, the three massive lanterns atop the post were illuminated; someone had the bright idea of scaling the structure and 'winding up' the cadaver so that it twirled slowly under the yellow light. Glancing back a year later from his Swiss exile, the former radical student Albert Rosenfeld still felt the shock of it: 'Thousands stood around the corpse – men, women, children – and not a single tear of pity; in every gaze: revenge! ... The horror is too great, we should dwell no longer on the subject!'[94]

In the years following the end of the revolution, contemporaries waged a battle of words and mutual accusations over the events of 6 October. The conservatives blamed the students of the Academic Legion, the seditious doctrines of the left-wing intellectuals, and the cabals of Jews and foreign agents. And these claims had serious consequences. Among those sentenced to death for the murder of Latour was the Jewish Reichstag deputy and member of the medical corps of the Academic Legion, Joseph Goldmark, who had wisely fled the country. This was a poor reward for Goldmark's efforts to shield Latour from the hammer

Johann Christian Schöller. The crowd gathers around the body of the Minister of War, Count Theodor Baillet de Latour, hanged by revolutionaries on the square Am Hof, 6 October 1848. This is a sanitized depiction of the lynching of Latour, who was naked and grossly mutilated by the time they hanged him from a lamp post outside the Ministry of War. Note the presence of women among the onlookers.

blows of the crowd by wrapping his arms around the victim. The verdict was only struck down in 1870, by which time Goldmark had made his fortune as a manufacturer in Brooklyn.[95] Father Anton Füster's recollections of the events were still suffused with the anger he felt for Latour, who, in his view, had done more than anyone else – with the possible exception of Alexander Bach, 'the Judas of German democracy' – to stir the Viennese working classes into a froth of outrage.[96] Some saw the murder of Latour as an assassination planned by leftist agents or the consequence of seditious agitation; others insisted that his murderers had acted without any premeditation whatsoever, in a state of blind rage: Latour was simply the 'spark' that fell into an open powder keg.[97] Hans Kudlich was enraged by the claim that the normally good-natured Viennese had been misled by intellectuals, foreign agents, atheists and Jews. The murderers of Latour, Kudlich pointed out, had been workers, not Hegelians. They had never studied David Friedrich Strauß's scandalous *Leben Jesu*. They belonged neither to the parliamentary left nor to any democratic club. There was not a single Jew or Gypsy among them, and neither Italian nor Hungarian money nor instructions from Mazzini or Kossuth could be found in their pockets. They were angry, he argued, because they understood that Latour was an implacable enemy of the revolution.[98] For the conservatives, on the other hand, and for many moderate liberals, the murder of Latour, like the lynching of Lamberg, possessed revelatory meaning: to them, it seemed to expose the satanic malevolence at the heart of the insurgency. It nourished a hunger for vengeance that would give wings to the counter-revolution.

The sun had only just gone down. Tocsin bells were ringing across the city, barricades appeared in the main thoroughfares and huge crowds streamed in from the suburbs. The focus of attention moved to the imperial arsenal. Having failed to persuade the small guard detachment inside to leave, the insurgents shelled the main door with confiscated field guns. When this failed, they dragged a heavy cannon up a nearby tower and fired on the arsenal from above. Then they tried hurling burning mattresses soaked with pitch onto the roof. As the fire took hold in part of the building, 'a bright redness coloured the sky', one student leader recalled. 'The shouting of the fighters and the din of the storm bells rang through the stillness of the night and rockets ascended from the towers of St Stephen's and the university. It was a terrifying and beautiful picture!' At around seven o'clock on the following morning, a small delegation persuaded the troops to open the door and agree the terms of a capitulation. They left soon afterwards amidst wild cheering from the crowds. The workers went in and handed out arms and ammunition. 'In an instant, 30,000 serviceable weapons passed into the hands of the people.'[99]

For the emperor and his court, the time had once again come to leave the city. At midday, a battalion from the Infantry Regiment Freiherr von Heß had been ordered to cross the Danube from the east on pontoons and make their way to the Alser Barracks to the north-west of the old city. Finding that the garrison troops had already left their stations, they went to the Schönbrunn Palace, where they received orders to escort the royal family and the court out of the city.[100] The horses were fed and watered, and the officers received refreshments from the palace refectory while trunks and carriages were packed for the imperial family's departure. They left Vienna early in the morning of 7 October, surrounded by a battery of cannon and 6,000 men, most of whom had no idea who was travelling in their midst. Only when the column stopped to rest some distance from the capital was an announcement made to the troops, who responded with deafening cheers and the waving of hats. Moved by this show of loyalty, the emperor and Archduchess Sophie showed themselves from the carriage, their faces wet with tears; the archduchess was sobbing so hard she was unable to speak. All along their six-day route they were welcomed with cheers and flaming beacons. In Krems, the emperor left his escort behind and went among the people, speaking with them in his naïve manner:

> Children, I will keep my promises. The labour duties and the tithes and all that stuff are all finished with, I've sanctioned it and signed it and that's how it will stay. Your emperor gives you his word and you should believe him, he wishes you well. But in Vienna there are some people who have it in for me and they want to seduce you and there's nothing for it: I'm going to have to send soldiers there.

The peasant crowds around him answered these words with deafening cheers.[101] Similar scenes took place at every stop along the route. When the emperor arrived six days later in Olmütz (Czech: Olomouc) in Moravia, his horses were taken out of the harness and his carriage pulled into the city by a jubilant populace. This was another of the underlying strengths of the old powers in 1848. The journey out of Vienna (or Berlin, or Paris, or Rome) seemed to lead into a world where the revolution had not yet happened. This was an optical illusion: if it had really been true, then the Habsburg court might have dispensed with its elaborate security arrangements, which included lining the route through settled areas with an espalier of heavily armed Croats and confining the local garrisons to barracks in case they contained unreliable elements. On the other hand, the enthusiasm of the peasant crowds was genuine, and their cheers were a reminder of how completely the revolution's leaders had failed to connect with the rural population.

For the next three weeks, Vienna was under the control of the most radical revolutionaries, flanked by leftist National Guard detachments from the suburbs, the students of the Academic Legion, the democratic clubs and bands of armed workers. It was a distillation of the processes of mobilization that had swept through the city since March: radical students, leftist lawyers and journalists, democratic artisans and insurgent proletarians from the industrial suburbs. It looked like a motley crowd, but it contained the seeds of a new kind of left-wing politics, in which social and political demands would flow into a coherent platform, the politics that would later be called social democracy. Of the Reichstag deputies, the centrist and conservative fractions now complied with an order from the emperor and left the capital to reconvene in Kremsier/ Kroměříž, close by Olmütz. The more conservative ministers left the city. The most radical deputies remained in Vienna, where they continued to meet, deliberate and pass resolutions in the Spanish Riding School. In a batch of defiant and unanimously supported motions, the rump Reichstag affirmed that it was and remained an 'indivisible whole' representing all of the peoples who had elected representatives to fill its seats, that it remained an 'indissoluble constituent assembly', that it would continue faithfully to do its duty under the current 'threatening circumstances', and that it remained 'the sole legal constitutional organ' of the 'union between the constitutional monarch and the sovereign people'.[102] This was a radical revolution, not a republican one.

There were now two Austrian parliaments and two Austrian executives. In the city, the Committee of Safety was reconstituted as the governing organ of the revolution. The gap that had opened within the revolution in Paris and Berlin assumed even more dramatic form here. By contrast with the Paris of June, the leaders of the right and centre absented themselves entirely from the scene. Their departure was like the ominous withdrawal of seawater along a beach before the arrival of a tsunami. Orders had already gone out from the imperial headquarters at Olmütz to both Jelačić, who was now retiring from Hungary, and to Windischgrätz, who was still in Prague: Vienna was to be their next objective. Everyone in the capital understood that a showdown was coming soon. Labourers worked in continuous shifts to reinforce the fortifications, and stores of food and munitions were built up at strategic locations. Radical groups in some of the larger Austrian cities – Graz, Linz, Salzburg, Brno – sent money, supplies and small contingents of men, but Hans Kudlich's efforts to raise the peasantry yielded predictably meagre results. It was too late to win the peasants to the cause of a revolution that, as they saw it, had done so little for them. While the radicals prepared for a bitter defence of their stronghold, others, like the bourgeois members of the city's Municipal Council (Gemeinderat), played a more equivocal game, maintaining the appearance of frenetic activity while dragging their feet over defence-related tasks and putting out feelers to the Windischgrätz army. In this way, they ensured that the council and its members would survive the coming storm unscathed.[103]

The shared knowledge of what lay ahead steeped the city in a weird calm. At night, only armed men could be seen in the streets. Behind and sometimes on top of the barricades were the campfires of the armed workers in their distinctive blouses. The city walls, too, were dotted with little fires encircled by Academic Legionaries with their Calabrian hats. The rising of the sun brought a dawn chorus of women and boys calling the names of newspapers in the silent streets. The Legionary Albert Rosenfeld described the atmosphere:

> The silent dawn of thoughts is a thing of the past. Every poetic thought, every fancy, is immediately summoned to duty, from which there is no respite, save a few hours' sleep. As soon as it wakes up, the population reaches greedily for the Reichstag report. Every eye, every thought, is focused on the Reichstag, the open heart of the whole life of the state and of the city.[104]

One hope remained for insurgent Vienna: on the evening of 10 October, two Hungarian envoys brought assurances that 30,000 Hungarian regular troops would come to the aid of the city if the Viennese could hold out for long enough. A Hungarian force did eventually arrive on 30 October, but by that time it was too late to make a difference: Vienna was already surrounded and besieged, and the Hungarians were driven off at Schwechat, today the site of the city's airport.

The battle for Vienna began in earnest on 24 October. After a first assault through the Brigittenau district to the north of the city, there was an intense artillery duel along the heavily defended Nussdorf Line to the north-west of the old city. On 27 October, Windischgrätz offered the city an ultimatum: surrender within twenty-four hours or be overrun. The offer was rejected, and a general advance began late in the morning of 28 October. The noose of siege tightened around the defenders, who pulled back from the Nussdorf Line, leaving the enemy in possession of the populous Leopoldstadt district on the northern outskirts of the old city. The editor of a Viennese paper recalled the fighting of that day. So intense were the bombardments of the besieging artillery that their reverberations could be felt in the ground. 'Flash after flash blinded the horrified eye of the observer. Explosions deafened the listening ear (we counted over one hundred cannon shots in five minutes!).'[105] On the following day, 29 October, Wenzel Messenhauser, commander-in-chief of the forces defending the city, offered a capitulation. A ceasefire was declared and the decommissioning of insurgent weapons began. But on 30 October, exhilarated by the news that a Hungarian relief army had arrived, the Student Committee and radical elements of the National Guard seized the initiative, repudiated the ceasefire and re-initiated hostilities. On 31 October the imperial troops, having shaken off the Hungarians, broke into the suburbs on all sides of the city, raining shells down on the insurgents inside the city walls. A stray cartridge pierced the roof of the Hofburg and set fire to the natural science collections there. The water used to extinguish the blaze damaged many of the books in the imperial library. The old city held out until early in the evening, at which point the troops managed to break open the gates in the fortifications and charge into the city centre. The insurgents dispersed in every direction, tossing aside their tell-tale Calabrian hats. Many of them hurried to barbers' shops to have their long hair trimmed and their 'Hecker-beards' chopped off.

Robert Blum, former bronzeworker, lantern-seller, theatre-administrator and autodidact publisher of radical essays and lexicons, arrived in the

Austrian capital on 17 October, just as the Austrian armies commanded by Windischgrätz were closing in around the outer perimeter of the city. He was there, as a radical deputy of the National Assembly in Frankfurt, to bring fraternal greetings from his fraction to the sister parliament in Vienna. And he was there because he believed that Vienna was the last chance for the German revolution. 'If Vienna does not prevail', he wrote to his wife Jenny, 'only a pile of rubble and corpses will be left'.[106] This was not, in his eyes, a journey into chaos, but a pilgrimage to what was now the heart of the revolutionary order. Vienna was not just a 'revolutionary city'; the continuing presence of the Reichstag marked it as the legitimate capital of the 'legal Austrian state'.[107] It was the monarchy that had broken the law, not the population of Vienna.

Blum was impressed by the work of the defenders and enchanted by the beauty of the city – this was the first time he had seen it; Vienna was 'fine, magnificent, the most adorable city I have ever seen'.[108] He arrived as a celebrity. He was the only one of the Frankfurt group invited to deliver an address to the Viennese rump parliament. He dined and debated with the notables of the radical intelligentsia in the Red Hedgehog, a venue favoured by the Viennese democrats. He had intended at first to leave after a few days, but soon changed his mind and resolved to remain in the city for the impending struggle. When Windischgrätz issued a proclamation on 22 October stating that Vienna was now under the control of a band of criminals, Blum replied with a bitingly eloquent piece in the leftist organ *Der Radikale* in which he stated that criminals and thugs were indeed usurping control over the capital city – in the form of Windischgrätz and his fellow commanders. Windischgrätz would remember this insult.

On 25 October, he was accepted into the Corps d'Élite of the defence force. This was a largely honorific appointment, given that Blum (now 'Captain Blum') had no combat experience whatsoever. He had been exempted from military service in Prussia on account of his very poor eyesight, the result of a childhood bout of measles. Nevertheless, he threw himself into the new role with his usual gusto, focusing mainly on the logistical questions that had preoccupied him in his work as a theatre manager. He was first assigned the task of defending the Sophienbrücke, a bridge across the Danube canal on the north-eastern perimeter, where he faced the first Army Corps under Ban Josip Jelačić. On the following day he was deployed to the Nußdorf Line in the north, where a grazing shot left a hole in his jacket. He was among those who argued for a capitulation on 29 October but changed his mind on the following day when it seemed that the Hungarians might be about to break the siege. When the battle was over and the cause was lost, he wrote to Jenny saying that he would soon be returning home.

Blum appears to have been confident that his status as a deputy of the Frankfurt Constituent National Assembly would protect him against reprisals. Instead of hiding out until the coast was clear and then stealing away, he sent a written request for permission to leave the city to an officer of the military command, Major-General Freiherr von Cordon. Cordon immediately ordered his arrest, because Blum's name, along with that of his fellow Frankfurt radical Julius Fröbel, was on a list of 'dangerous individuals' circulated by Windischgrätz had sent to Cordon. The two men were arrested in their hotel and confined in a regimental lockhouse known as the Stabsstockhaus, where they were well fed and provided with cigars and newspapers. Twice Blum protested in writing against his arrest, pointing out that as a deputy of the Frankfurt National Assembly, he possessed – or ought to possess – parliamentary immunity.

Two factors above all militated against Blum's release. First: the commander of the Viennese defence, Wenzel Messenhauser, in the hope of evading the death penalty himself, inculpated Blum, claiming (falsely) that Blum was the man who had sabotaged the capitulation agreed with Windischgrätz on 29 October and presenting himself as the heroic defender of peace against a dangerous foreign agitator. These words did not save Messenhauser from execution (he was shot on 16 November), but they worsened Blum's chances. The second adverse factor was a coincidence: it so happened that the Austrian diplomat Alexander von Hübner, who had been sent to Milan by Metternich on the eve of the March insurrection, was now in Vienna as adviser to Prince Felix von Schwarzenberg, the brother-in-law of Windischgrätz. Hübner had been stationed in Leipzig when Blum took control of the crowd there in 1845. The report he filed at that time on Blum's role in the 'August days' was suffused with condescension and malice:

Sprung from the yeast of the masses, [Blum] acquired middle-class status as a theatre-ticket-dispenser; as a scribbler and polemicist and lately as a religious apostle, he worked his way into politics to the point where he was able easily to place himself at the head of the movement [in Leipzig], which in turn promptly lost its character as a mere commotion in the streets. Thanks to Blum, the Revolt became a revolution.[109]

This was a grossly distorted and incomplete view of Blum's role in Leipzig, where he had in fact played a moderating role. It placed him on the same footing as Hecker, whose politics of direct action and contempt for parliamentary deliberation Blum had always deplored and rejected. In his memoirs, Hübner identified Blum as a dangerous 'anarchist', whose fateful influence over the masses was responsible for the lynching of the two Prussian deputies of the Frankfurt parliament during the September crisis of 1848, a claim for which there was and is not the slightest scrap of evidence (Blum had never been an anarchist and the murder of Lichnowsky and Auerswald was the consequence of popular outrage over the parliament's response to the Schleswig-Holstein crisis).[110] Hübner's account of Blum's role in Vienna was no less tendentious. He accused Blum of having addressed a crowd at the university consisting of a mixture of armed workers and 'that disgusting horde known as Amazons' (female fighters) with the words: 'We are going to have to *Latourize* 2,000 people!'[111] These were scraps of disinformation, fantasies from the armoury of the counter-revolution. In the situation of November 1848, their impact could be lethal.

After his sojourn in Italy, Hübner had been summoned back to Vienna in early October. He joined the entourage that accompanied the royal family to Olmütz. Once there, he was in daily contact with Prince Schwarzenberg, a Habsburg centralist already designated to take over as Austrian Minister-President once the smoke of the insurrection cleared. When Windischgrätz offered to release Blum and expel him from the country, in order to spare his brother-in-law the 'diplomatic inconveniences' arising from his parliamentary privilege, Schwarzenberg replied from Olmütz on 7 November that 'parliamentary privilege' had no legal standing in Austria, that the only privilege Blum deserved was the privilege of martial law. Blum was 'the most influential chief of the German anarchists'; if he were condemned and shot, 'his comrades [would] see that in Austria we do not fear them'.[112] It was almost certainly Hübner who briefed Schwarzenberg on Blum and advised him to take this line.

Blum was tried by court martial on 8 November and sentenced to death by hanging. But since no executioner was available, it was resolved to carry out the sentence 'by powder and lead'. On the morning of the following day, he was woken at 5 a.m. A priest attended him and offered confession. Blum declined but expressed his thanks and offered the clergyman a token to remember him by. It was his hairbrush – an indispensable accoutrement for a man with such thick wavy hair; in any case there was nothing else left to give away. The farewell letter scribbled to his wife Jenny as he waited to be collected from his cell remains one of the most affecting passages of nineteenth-century German prose.

> My dear, good, beloved wife, farewell! Live well for the time that is called eternal but is not. Bring up our – now only your – children to be fine people . . . Sell our few possessions with the help of our friends. God and good people will help you. Everything I feel runs away in tears, so I say again, live well dear wife! . . . Farewell! Farewell! Thousand, thousand, the last kisses from your Robert.
>
> Written in Vienna on 9 November at five in the morning, at six it will all be over.
>
> I forgot the rings: I am sending you my last kiss on the wedding ring. My seal ring is for Hans, the watch is for Richard, the diamond button for Ida, the chain for Alfred, as things to remember me by. Everything else sort out as you see fit. They are coming! Farewell! Well!

The letter became a relic, widely distributed across the radical networks, often in such carefully executed facsimiles that their owners today still believe them to be the original.[113] It entered the collective memory of the revolution because it identified Blum as a man of domestic attachments, a private man who had entered public life. If this was heroism, it was heroism in a bourgeois key. In an entry on 'The Hero' for the *Theater-Lexikon* he co-edited in 1841, Blum observed that the concept of the hero had been brought into disrepute by 'the overwrought handling of the heroic role in novels and drama'. 'If the hero is to command attention, then the idealized character of the role must be balanced with the purely human. It should never be detached entirely from the domain of human weakness and error.'[114] Blum was executed in a wooded area of the Brigittenau district, just north of the city centre. He had become the embodiment of the German revolution. There was a bleak appropriateness to the fact that he and it were extinguished together.

Windischgrätz and Schwarzenberg, the chief authors of Blum's downfall, were also the principal architects of the monarchy's renewal. Emperor

The Last Moments of Robert Blum (1848), lithograph, printed and coloured by H. Boes after Carl Steffeck. Blum was executed by firing squad on the morning of 9 November 1848. Like many contemporary images of Blum's execution, this one shows him in an open white shirt about to face death without a blindfold. He is shown here refusing the offer of priestly assistance. There is no evidence that this actually happened at the scene of his execution, but since he had turned his back on the Catholic Church to join the antipapal German-Catholic movement, the gesture captures something real.

Ferdinand remained as incompetent as ever and the two men had been lobbying for some time to have the young archduke, Franz Joseph, placed on the Habsburg throne. The current emperor's marriage was expected to remain childless. The heir to the throne was Ferdinand's younger brother, Franz Karl, but since Franz Karl was temperamentally almost as ill-equipped for the demands of the imperial office as Ferdinand, attention had focused for some time on his eldest son, Franz Joseph, the emperor's eighteen-year-old nephew. Schwarzenberg persuaded Ferdinand to abdicate and Franz Karl to waive his right to the succession in favour of his son. During the ceremony, Ferdinand, ever the most affable of men, said to the new young emperor: 'God bless you! Be good and God will protect you.'[115] Franz Joseph would occupy the Habsburg throne for nearly sixty-eight years. In 1848, he was young and inexperienced, but intelligent and determined, and he had one strategically crucial advantage over his uncle: he had made no concessions to the revolution and he had never signed an oath to abide by constitutional government.

THE IRON NET DESCENDS

After the June Days in Paris, the effort to shut down the French left continued with a vengeance. New laws tightly regulated the operations of the political clubs. The government reintroduced caution money and stamp tax regulations with a view to shutting down the cheapest newspapers and thereby 'silencing the poor', as Lamennais put it.[116] There was a purge of prominent leftists. Many leaders were arrested, including 'worker Albert', Blanqui and Raspail; Louis Blanc and the former police chief Marc Caussidière were attacked so violently that they made their way to London to avoid arrest. These were the first exiles of the Second Republic. The political centre of gravity continued to slide to the right.

On 31 July, Pierre-Joseph Proudhon presented a proposal to the Constituent National Assembly. Proudhon had for some time been making the case for the creation of an exchange bank capitalized by automatic levies on farm and property rents and tasked with providing interest-free credit – a measure he believed would go a long way towards resolving the Social Question. Proudhon, though unquestionably a radical, had played no role whatsoever in the violence of May or June. His relationship with the other factions of the left was oblique, sometimes mocking and always ironic. He did not even think of his scheme as 'socialist', but as the expression of a rigorous economic rationale capable of appealing to anyone versed in the technicalities of credit. Perhaps it is unsurprising that in an assembly dominated by moderates and conservatives he found few takers for such a bold experiment. But it is the reaction of the chamber that is telling. Proudhon's voice was completely inaudible, so loud was the jeering throughout his speech. His proposal was rejected by 600 votes to 2. To add insult to injury, the few socialists in the assembly, who included Victor Considerant and Pierre Leroux, abstained because they had their own socialist 'systems'.

This rightward shift in political sensibilities left its mark on the constitutional structure of the Republic. There was lively debate over the organization of executive power in the Republic. Should there be a president? If so, how much power should he have? What was to prevent him establishing himself as a neo-monarch or opening the door to a monarchical restoration? The left-republican deputy Félix Pyat argued that a presidential office set apart from the assembly would fatally divide the sovereignty of the Republic, which ought to be situated in the collectivity of its elected representatives. A presidency, he argued, would 'encompass, concentrate and absorb all the power, representing, personifying, embodying the people, thus turning the Republic into a veritable monarchy'.[117] By contrast, the party of order argued for a strong executive president, elected separately by the people. In-between was a group, including some leftists, that supported a presidency elected by the chamber. Among the supporters of this option was Ferdinand Flocon, whose newspaper, La Réforme, had played such an important role in the February Revolution.

Inevitably, given the state of opinion in both the Constitutional Committee and the assembly, the left lost. The Constitutional Committee and the chamber majority opted for a President elected by the people, even though it was already clear that this might result in a victory for Louis Napoleon Bonaparte, who was widely suspected of harbouring monarchical aspirations. By the end of October, Bonaparte and Cavaignac had emerged as likely frontrunners in the presidential elections scheduled for 10 December. A rallying of energies on the left produced Alexandre Ledru-Rollin as the candidate of the 'Mountain', while a group representing Cabet's Icarians and surviving fragments of the conspiratorial secret-society networks supported the 'independent socialist'

candidate, François-Vincent Raspail. A small rump of right-wing monarchists put forward the general Nicolas Anne Théodule Changarnier as
the 'legitimist' candidate. Still sublimely confident that he could rebuild
his lost popularity, Lamartine entered the fray as the 'independent liberal' candidate.

The December elections proceeded much more smoothly than the April
elections of 1848 – a hopeful sign that the mechanisms of democracy were
settling in. But the result was a huge shock, even to the winner:

Presidential Election of December 10th, 1848			
Candidate	Political Party	Popular Vote	%
Louis-Napoléon Bonaparte	Bonapartist	5,434,226	74.44
Louis-Eugène Cavaignac	Moderate Republican	1,448,107	19.65
Alexandre Auguste Ledru-Rollin	The Mountain	371,431	5.08
François-Vincent Raspail	Independent Socialist	36,964	0.49
Alphonse de Lamartine	Independent Liberal	17,914	0.28
Nicolas Anne Théodule Changarnier	Legitimist		0.06
Total			100

It was one of those outcomes that seem unlikely beforehand but are
viewed as inevitable in retrospect. Cavaignac's role in suppressing the
July insurrection had earned him the contempt of the left, and he never
succeeded in winning the confidence of the party of order, which decided
to throw in its lot with Bonaparte. Cavaignac had adopted clever tactics
in the run-up to the election, using his incumbency as interim Chief
Executive to bargain with the various conservative factions. With hind-
sight it became clear that Bonaparte's self-presentation as a mediocre
and straightforward character who would do what he was told once
installed in office had been a more effective electoral strategy.

In a national election, of course, what mattered most was the allegiance of the masses of the people. The election revealed that immense numbers of peasants, perhaps as many as four million, had chosen Bonaparte. In the most memorable of his political polemics, Marx railed at these benighted rustics, observing that they had chosen a candidate with no interest whatsoever in improving their condition. They had done this, he believed, because they lacked any awareness of their common predicament as a class. They were not politically conscious actors, but merely 'homologous quantities'. In this respect they resembled a sack of potatoes, clearly recognizable as such to all but themselves and each other.[118] The potatoes were not impressed by Cavaignac's impeccable republican credentials or by his Algerian military record; indeed, they may have chosen his rival as an act of inchoate protest against the regime currently in power. On the other hand, they did like the name 'Napoleon', a name they had heard before. It seemed to promise the return of good times.

But this was not a uniquely peasant perspective, and the votes for Bonaparte did not come from peasants alone. Only in four departments did Louis Napoleon fail to secure a relative majority; in thirty departments he secured an absolute majority and in thirty-four he obtained more than 80 per cent of all votes cast. This was a phenomenon that crossed occupational and class boundaries. For over a decade, as we saw in Chapter 3, a politically neutered version of the first Napoleon, shorn of controversy, had been ascending to the status of a national icon, a process in which successive July Monarchy governments had actively collaborated. The third Napoleon reaped the profits of this political alchemy. Cavaignac was not the only casualty. The results for Ledru-Rollin and Raspail revealed the drastic national shrinkage of the republican left as an electoral force. Changarnier's paltry few votes were a death knell for the legitimist cause, which would never recover from this blow. And Lamartine's miserable showing, at 0.28 per cent, confirmed his sudden irrelevance to the country's public life. This great celebrity of the reform banquets and the February Revolution was now officially a man of yesterday.

In Berlin, too, the energy of the revolution was dissipating fast. From April to June, there was bitter wrangling between the king and the ministers over the text of a new draft constitution – Frederick William IV later described his constitutional discussions with the Camphausen Cabinet as 'the ghastliest hours of my life'. The amended draft included (on the sovereign's insistence) revisions asserting that the monarch ruled 'by the grace of God', that he exercised exclusive control over the army and that the constitution was to be understood as an 'agreement' (*Vereinbarung*) between the king and his people, as opposed to a basic law imposed by popular will.[119] In the increasingly polarized mood of June, the chances of securing a majority in the National Assembly for the compromise draft were slim. When he failed to do so, Ludolf Camphausen resigned on 20 June and his fellow 'March minister' David Hansemann was asked to form a government. Prime Minister of the new Cabinet was the liberal East Prussian nobleman Rudolf von Auerswald, brother of the Auerswald who would be killed by a crowd in Frankfurt on 18 September. The Constitutional Committee, chaired by the respected democrat Benedikt Waldeck, hammered out a counter-proposal for the assembly's consideration. The new draft constitution limited the monarch's power to block legislation and provided for a genuinely popular national militia.[120] But this draft was as controversial as the last one. Debates over it polarized the assembly and no agreement was reached. The constitution remained in limbo.

It was the question of the relationship between the civilian and military authorities that did most to dissolve the fragile political compromise in Berlin. On 31 July, a violent clash over the arbitrary orders issued by a local army commander in the Silesian town of Schweidnitz resulted in the death of fourteen civilians. There was a wave of public anger. Julius Stein, deputy for one of the constituencies of Breslau, capital city of Prussian Silesia, presented a motion to the National Assembly proposing measures to ensure that officers and soldiers act in conformity with the constitution and 'distance themselves from reactionary tendencies'. These were diffuse formulations, but they expressed the understandably deepening alarm of the new political elites over the unbroken power of the military. If the army remained the obedient tool of interests opposed to the new order, then it might be said that the liberals and their institutions were living on sufferance, that their debates and law-making amounted to little more than a farcical performance. The Stein motion tapped a deep vein of nervousness in the assembly and was passed with a substantial majority. Sensing that the king would not yield to pressure on the military issue, the Auerswald–Hansemann government did its best to avoid a head-on collision. But the patience of the deputies soon ran out and on 7 September they passed a resolution demanding that the government implement Stein's proposals. Frederick William was predictably incandescent and talked of restoring order by force in his 'disloyal and good-for-nothing capital'. In the meantime, the controversy over the Stein proposals forced the government to resign.

The new Prime Minister was General Ernst von Pfuel, the very man who had commanded the forces in and around Berlin on the eve of 18 March. This was in some ways a good choice – Pfuel was an emollient figure whose youth had been consumed by an intense homoerotic friendship with the romantic dramatist Heinrich von Kleist. Pfuel had been a keen frequenter of the Jewish salons and was widely admired in liberal circles. But not even this mild-mannered man could mediate between an intransigent king and an obstreperous assembly, and on 1 November he, too, resigned. The news filtering in from Vienna reinflated the king's confidence. 'Here', the liberal nobleman Karl Varnhagen von Ense observed on 16 October, 'everything is on hold as we await the turn of events [in Vienna]; court and people alike feel that their cause hangs in the balance there.'[121] 'The news from Vienna gives courage to the court', Varnhagen wrote on 2 November. 'They are ready to take action.'[122]

The announcement on 2 November that Pfuel's successor would be Count Friedrich Wilhelm von Brandenburg was greeted with dismay in the liberal ranks. Brandenburg was the king's uncle and the former commander of the VI Army Corps in Breslau. He was the favoured candidate of the conservative circle around the king and the purpose behind his appointment was straightforward. His task, according to Leopold von Gerlach, would be to 'show in every possible way that the king still rules in this country and not the assembly'.[123] The deputies sent a delegation to Frederick William IV on 2 November to protest against the new appointment, but it was brusquely dismissed. In Berlin, as in Naples, the 'disequilibrium of two fears' made itself felt. The chamber felt increasingly trapped and disempowered; the king was less and less afraid and more willing to risk a confrontation.

On the foggy morning of 9 November – the day, though no one in Berlin knew it at the time – of Robert Blum's execution – Count Brandenburg presented himself before the assembly in its temporary home on the Gendarmenmarkt and announced that it would remain adjourned by royal order until 27 November, when it would meet in the provincial city of Brandenburg, about sixty kilometres west of Berlin. A few hours later, the new military commander-in-chief, General Wrangel, entered the capital at the head of 13,000 troops and rode to the Gendarmenmarkt to inform the deputies in the assembly personally that they would have to disperse. The assembly responded by calling for 'passive resistance' and announcing a tax strike.[124] On 11 November, martial law was declared, the Civil Guards were disarmed and disbanded, political clubs were closed down and prominent radical newspapers were banned. Many of the deputies did attempt to congregate in Brandenburg on 27 November, but they were soon dispersed, and the assembly was formally dissolved on 5 December. On the same day, in an astute political move that would later be cribbed by the Austrians, the Brandenburg government announced the promulgation of a new constitution.

The revolution was over in the capital, but it smouldered on in the Rhineland, where the well-organized political networks of the radicals were successful in mobilizing mass opposition to the counter-revolutionary measures of the Berlin government. There was strong support throughout the province for the tax boycott announced by the National Assembly in its dying hours. Every day for a month, the *Neue Rheinische Zeitung*, organ of the socialist left, ran the words 'No more taxes!' on its masthead. 'People's committees' and 'citizens' committees' sprang up to support the boycott in Cologne, Coblenz, Trier and other towns. Anger over the dissolution of the assembly blended with provincial hostility to Berlin, confessional resentments (among Catholics) and the discontents associated with the patterns of economic stress and deprivation common to many textile-dependent regions during the revolutionary year. In Düsseldorf, a parade by the now illegal Civil Guard culminated in a public oath to fight to the bitter end for the National Assembly and the rights of the people. The tax boycott campaign revealed the strength and social depth of the democratic movement in the Rhineland, but the loss of the assembly deprived them of a political focus. The arrival of fresh troops, coupled with the imposition of martial law in some hotspots and the swift disarmament of makeshift leftist militias, sufficed to restore order and state authority.[125] 'The state of siege has been declared', Fanny Lewald wrote in Berlin on 18 November. 'Since then, it seems as though an iron net has been spread out over us and we are denied even the sight of the heavens.'[126]

COUNTER-REVOLUTION
IN A VERY SMALL PLACE

It has often been observed that Britain escaped revolution in 1848, and that this reflected the maturity and liberality of the country's political institutions. Whether we should reckon the unrest that flickered up across the British imperial periphery among the 'revolutions of 1848' is an interesting question, to which I return in the next chapter. But there was a European uprising in 1848 that gave the British government an opportunity to demonstrate the liberality of its institutions, namely a chain of upheavals on the Ionian Islands, a dependency under the control of the British Crown.

The United States of the Ionian Islands comprised seven territories (Corfu, Paxo, Cephalonia, Ithaca, Santa Maura, Zante and Cerigo), whose total population in 1858 was 240,000. Traditionally possessions of the Republic of Venice, they were placed under the sovereign protection of King George III by the treaty of Paris in November 1815. Britain welcomed their acquisition as a means of reinforcing the dominance of the British navy in the Adriatic and the eastern Mediterranean. Since they were a protectorate rather than an imperial possession, the islands remained nominally independent, meaning that the local representative of the British Crown was not a governor but a Lord High Commissioner, who answered to the Colonial, not the Foreign, Secretary.

Since the treaty of Paris promised the Ionians a 'free constitution', the first Commissioner, Sir Thomas Maitland, issued a 'Constitutional Charter' in 1817. It provided for an elected legislative assembly and a senate with a mix of legislative and executive functions but was otherwise strikingly illiberal. The Constituent Assembly was made up entirely of Maitland's appointees and presented with a draft largely drawn up by the Commissioner himself.[127] Elections were held under a franchise of the doctrinaire July Monarchy type – only the wealthiest Ionians were eligible, meaning that around 1 per cent were entitled to vote. In an arrangement that was unusually authoritarian, even by doctrinaire standards, the Ionians were obliged to choose their representatives from the 'double lists', meaning that each constituency could choose just one person from a list of two. These (very short) lists were drawn up by a 'primary council', whose members were chosen by none other than the Lord High

Commissioner.[128] The Commissioners were thus 'benevolent despots' with powers comparable to those of a Crown Colony governor.[129] 'By the constitution of Sir T. Maitland', a senior British functionary in Corfu wrote, 'the press was more restricted, and the parliament was more submissive than in England under the Tudor princes.'[130]

But if this system endowed the Commissioners with great power, it also accentuated their dependence on the shallow social elite that voted for and sat in the assembly. And this in turn made it difficult to tackle the problems that were gnawing away at Ionian society. Of these, the most fundamental was the *colonia* system of land tenures, under which the proprietor and a cultivator in temporary occupation of the land entered a contract stipulating, along with other special conditions and limitations, that a portion of the produce be paid to the proprietor in lieu of rent. This system was further encumbered by complicated traditional credit arrangements known as *prostichio* that provided only very weak security for loans and thus discouraged lending and investment. Just as in Lombardy, where a very similar system prevailed, proprietors used advance payments to ensnare the cultivators in debt.[131] British administrators recognized the negative effects of this system, but the Commissioner's political dependency on the landed insular elites made reform virtually impossible. At the same time, the transition from the polyculture of an earlier age to a monocultural system based on olives (in Corfu) and currants (in Cephalonia and Zante) heightened the vulnerability of island society to gluts, shortfalls and disruptions in supply.

If British rule seemed a comfortable arrangement in the years when the Greek mainland was still part of the Ottoman Empire, this was less true after the Greek War of Independence (1821–9), which stirred patriotic excitement among the people of the islands. The inhabitants, Maitland reported, 'displayed the strongest sympathy in favour of the insurgents, who were of the same religious persuasion with themselves, with similar habits, language and manners'.[132] The British authorities imposed a policy of neutrality on the Ionians, monitoring the flow of refugees in order to prevent political instability. After two incidents of serious violence between islanders and Turkish refugees, the British imposed martial law and executed offenders – five on Zante and five on the tiny island of Cerigo. From Zante under martial rule it was reported that the bodies of executed Ionians were 'thrown into cages of iron, in which they are still exposed on the summits of hills, as if by way of menacing the rest of the people with a similar fate'.[133] Far from extinguishing patriotic feeling, these measures stimulated a nationalist reaction. In the 1840s, an opposition movement formed, known as the Rizospastai (Radicals), who questioned the legitimacy of British rule, invoking the principles of national self-determination and popular sovereignty.[134]

The arrival of Sir John Colborne, Lord Seaton, as High Commissioner in 1843 brought a change in substance and tone. From the beginning of his period in office, Seaton pressed for reforms, first in the financial sphere – a reduction in the duty on currants, a cut in the military contribution – and later in the constitutional and political domain – a new Charter, limited budgetary powers for the Ionian Legislative Assembly. He relaxed controls on the press. These had been especially severe in the earlier years of the British protectorate: no printing office or press was permitted in the Ionian states, except under the direct control of the Senate and the Commissioner.[135] He launched new public works projects. At the same time, Seaton began to open the British system of government to a broader segment of the native elites. He passed petitions from currant-growing landowners and other notables to London. He consulted more widely on matters of public interest. He accepted a dinner invitation from the 'Greek Casino' at Corfu, a literary society that was in fact a political club, like the Casinos of the Habsburg cities and the *circoli popolari* of Italy. Since the chairman of the Casino was the editor of the principal opposition newspaper and 'the most prominent leader of the anti-English faction', the Commissioner's attendance caused delight in some quarters and stupefaction in others. Among the stupefied was the rector of Corfu University, a rather crusty Tory by the name of Francis Bowen, who denounced Seaton as a traitor to his people. 'The conduct of Lord Seaton', Bowen, a Protestant Ascendancy Irishman, would later write, 'gave the same sort of heavy blow and great discouragement to the friends of British connexion in the Ionian Islands, as would have resulted from the Lord-Lieutenant [of Ireland]'s dining in the Conciliation Hall of Dublin.'[136]

These changes earned Seaton the gratitude and loyalty of a Reformist faction within the islander elite, but they also permitted the consolidation of a radical opposition, for whom the reforms were too little too late, and British rule an outdated institution and an impediment to union with the Greek motherland. The news of revolutions in Italy and France in 1848 brought a flurry of political clubs and newly opened newspapers 'full of the most bitter abuse of England and of Englishmen, repudiating British protection and openly advocating annexation to the Kingdom of Greece'.[137] At the same time, the price of currants dipped sharply, triggering various disturbances. In September, an uprising broke out in Cephalonia. Two crowds consisting of hundreds of peasants marched on the two principal towns of the island. The disturbance was easily put down by British troops, but worse turbulence broke out in August and September of the following year, when peasants revolted across the island. In a miniaturized version of the Galician rebellions of 1846, bands of peasants, led in some cases by known brigands, attacked and murdered several landowners. One of them, the wealthy *cavaliere* Niccolo Metaxa, was first wounded and then burned alive inside his own house. It was said that when the victim cried out to his attackers: 'What have I done to you . . . that you should kill me, have I not ever been a good patriot', he received the reply: 'Cuckold, what price will you put on the currants today?'[138]

As this exchange suggests, the violence of September 1849 was more in the manner of a Galician-style *jacquerie* than a fully fledged uprising of the Parisian or Viennese type. If the British authorities responded in this case with exemplary brutality, this is because a new Lord High Commissioner had just taken office on the islands. The handover was a study in contrasts. The departing Lord Seaton was an old-school military Tory who had served with notable valour at Waterloo. The newly arrived Sir Henry Ward was a civilian member of the most advanced liberal faction in the House of Commons. His arrival was greeted with joy by the Ionian radicals, who naturally thought that if the old Tory had been good to them, the new Whig would be even better. How wrong they were! Ward found the islands to be in a volatile mood. His first speech to the Ionian Assembly – now elected, thanks to his predecessor's reforms, on a somewhat broader franchise – met with loud cheers. But on the following day he found the assembly so hostile that he prorogued it until October. When news reached him of the disturbances in August and September, he proclaimed martial law for Cephalonia. Nearly 500 troops were deployed there to restore order. Ward himself sailed to the island and immediately took an active role in the suppression of the revolt.[139] An officer engaged in one of the disturbed areas reported that 'Sir Henry Ward personally hunted with the troops and kicked doors open and was otherwise active and excited.'[140]

There were sixty-eight courts-martial, which dealt out forty-four death sentences, twenty-one of which were carried out by hanging. Only two of those hanged had committed capital offences. Several further people were simply shot in the course of reprisals (Ward was said to have been present at the summary execution of two peasants who never made it to trial). Furthermore, and this is of special importance, a great number of people – the official number was ninety-six, but the total may have run to as many as 300 – were summarily flogged in the villages for such offences as 'creating disturbances in the guard-rooms, obstructing the soldiers, or refusing to give evidence'. These sentences were administered with the 'naval cat', also known as the cat-o'-nine tails. An unknown number were reported to have died of infections arising from the lacerations they sustained. This was a punishment hitherto unknown among the islanders, who associated it with the 'cruelties formerly exercised by the Turks'.[141] In addition to these measures, islanders reported mock executions along with 'the burning down [of] houses [and the] uprooting of vineyards and currant plantations, as a punishment upon suspected or criminated individuals'.[142] Little effort was made to distinguish between insurgents and ordinary villagers.[143] The islands took a long time to settle and there were further reprisals. At the beginning of 1851, a number of prominent figures – municipal councillors, journalists such as editor-in-chief Callinico of the *Rhigas* of Zante, three deputies from Cephalonia – Pylarinos, Zervos and Monferrato – and a fourth from Zante, François Domeneghini – were arrested in their domiciles by the police and thrown, without trial or judgement, onto the island of Cerigo. This very small island was virtually deserted at the time, save for thirty poor fishing families. There was no infrastructure for the expellees, who were obliged to eke out a living in the manner of Robinson Crusoe. Deputy Pylarinos was especially badly off because he was nearly blind when he was exiled. He lost his sight altogether during his stint there. 'The "hard confinement" of Austria', one Frenchman who visited the island observed, 'was just a game compared with the fate of the deportees on Cerigo.'[144]

In a speech to the Ionian Assembly on 10 November 1849, Sir Henry Ward explained himself: 'I had to deal not with an ordinary insurrection, in which I should have rejoiced in the opportunity, of marking the first moment of success by a large measure of grace, but with the congregated ruffianism of the community ...'[145] The Ionians were not convinced and nor were parts of the British press. The *Daily News* noted that 'twenty-one capital punishments arising out of one insurrection, in an island the total population of which does not exceed 70,000, certainly does not look like an error on the side of leniency . . .' In the 'number and severity of the punishments', the *Morning Chronicle* wrote, Ward had 'by far surpassed the rigour ascribed by political antagonists to the Austrian generals in Hungary'. He had, as the *Daily News* put it, 'aped the cruelties and rigour of Austrian and Russian commanders'.[146] And it is true that if one tallies even the twenty-one officially confirmed executions against the small population of the island (under 70,000), the intensity of the reprisals is comparable with the counter-revolutionary violence of Austria and Naples.

This small, ugly episode took place in a peripheral location, far from the cultural highways of Europe. But it is suggestive, nonetheless. Not because it was unusual: faced with an insurrection in Ceylon in 1848, the British authorities under Lord Torrington behaved in a very similar way. Much worse would happen in Jamaica after the Morant Bay Rebellion of 1865, when Edward John Eyre proclaimed martial law and presided over the killing of more than 400 and the flogging of more than 600 people (including pregnant women). But these were 'colonial' locations, places where the violence of imperialism was played out in a setting marked by stark hierarchies of race.

The United States of the Ionian Islands was not a colony. It was a European protectorate. To be sure, British administrators and visitors perceived the Ionians as 'lazy', 'idiots', 'thick', 'savages', 'orientals', 'ruffians', 'removed but one degree from donkeys'.[147] This was the vocabulary Europeans reached for when they turned their fellow Europeans into 'racial others' – remember the 'infernal races' Ferdinando Malvica saw entering his beloved Palermo during the early days of the revolution and the 'alien race' from the industrial suburbs whose presence in Vienna so unsettled Carl von Borkowski. Sir Henry Ward had never been a colonial governor. He had begun his career as a diplomat, serving in Sweden, the Hague and Spain; he had been chargé d'affaires in Mexico. Justifying his actions on Cephalonia he observed that he had 'seen a good many of the same breed in Spain and Mexico and felt satisfied that nothing but the most rigorous measures would do'.[148]

In other words, the reprisals on Cephalonia did not reflect the reimportation into Europe of an extra-European colonial practice. Sir

Henry Ward was an 'advanced liberal' with a strong attachment to classical economics. As an MP, he had opposed the Factories Act 1847, which limited the working hours of women and young persons (from thirteen to eighteen) in textile mills to ten hours a day. He was a bitter opponent of Chartism, which he viewed in terms of class conflict. He was a supporter even before the Great Famine of assisted emigration for the Irish, who he thought were too numerous for their own good. In short, he was a rather ordinary member of the British cultural and political elite. Faced with the plebeian unrest on Cephalonia, he behaved exactly as many of his continental European counterparts did when they confronted similar challenges elsewhere.

In the winter of 1850/51, William Gladstone made a visit to southern Italy, where he encountered liberal opponents of Bourbon rule. The Neapolitan liberals told him of the cruel fate suffered by the political prisoners of the Neapolitan monarchy. On his return to London, Gladstone resolved to bring up the matter with Lord Aberdeen, an old friend of Metternich who still had contacts in the Austrian government. A letter was eventually sent to Prince Schwarzenberg gently asking him to raise the matter of the prisoners with Ferdinand of the Two Sicilies. Schwarzenberg wrote back to Aberdeen, saying that he would speak to the Bourbon monarch. But he added that he saw no reason why he should be preached at by Britain on the matter of the rights of man and pointed to the measures used to crush the recent uprising on Cephalonia.[149] Oppressive regimes (and liberal regimes that have been caught out behaving oppressively) will always indulge in this kind of moral evasion and what-aboutery. But Schwarzenberg had a point. The British government did not view Ward's handling of the Cephalonian crisis as egregious or anomalous. The Lord High Commissioner to the Ionian Islands was not officially reprimanded. In May 1855, Sir Henry Ward became governor of Ceylon.

THE SECOND WAVE

On the evening of 24 November 1848, Pope Pius IX fled from the city of Rome. At 5 p.m., he changed out of his Moroccan silk slippers with crosses embroidered on their uppers, put aside the red velvet papal cap, and dressed himself in the black cassock and broad-brimmed hat of a country priest. Half an hour later, in a state of great agitation, he left the papal audience chamber in the Quirinale Palace via an internal stairway and tiptoed down to the courtyard, where a carriage was waiting for him. The French minister to the Holy See, Eugène duc d'Harcourt, remained alone in the chamber for forty-five minutes speaking in a loud voice, so that no one in the vicinity would suspect that the Pope had already left the building.

At the church of SS. Marcellin and Peter, the Pope's vehicle was met by the Bavarian ambassador, Count Karl von Spaur, who was clutching a pistol in his right hand, in case they were challenged. The fugitive was bustled into a small open carriage, and driven out of the city, his face obscured by the brim of his hat and the gathering darkness. Ten miles to the south, a larger and swifter vehicle waited to convey him to the southern border of the Papal States and into the neighbouring Kingdom of Naples. Throughout the night the party sped southwards, so swiftly indeed, that at one point they had to stop in order to let the coachman extinguish a fire that had started around the axles of Count Spaur's carriage. By the afternoon of the following day, Pius IX was safely installed in a modest house inside the walls of Gaeta. He would remain in the Kingdom of Naples until April 1850.

Pius IX's cloak and dagger flight into exile is one of the signal episodes of modern history. It confirmed the widening rift between the Catholic Church and the movements for political reform and national unification unfolding in Italy and across Europe. In the city of Rome, it marked a turning point, opening the door to the republican experiment of 1849, but also preparing the ground for the reactionary crackdown that would follow. It prefigured the collapse of the temporal sovereignty that the popes had wielded in central Italy since AD 754. And for Pius IX himself the experience of flight and exile was a trauma whose grip on his personality would tighten over the years. But its effects would also be felt further afield, as the papal Curia adjusted its outlook and its rules of public engagement to the post-revolutionary situation.

In 1848, as the revolution took hold across Europe, the weakness of the Pope's position was drastically exposed. Metternich, godfather of the Italian status quo, had been forced to flee from Vienna. Revolutionaries had seized power in Venice and Milan, forcing the Austrians to pull back their forces. The geopolitical foundations of traditional papal sovereignty appeared to be subsiding. And yet, at the same time, a wave of patriotic enthusiasm for the Pope swept through the peninsula. His name was everywhere: in the proclamations of the sovereigns, in newspaper articles, in the private letters of the volunteers who set out to fight for Italy, in patriotic sermons, in the edicts of the provisional governments. He was 'great', 'glorious', 'immortal'; he was the 'star of Italy', the 'love of all', Italians were his adoring 'children'. The Pope mutated into a new Moses, liberating his people – a people chosen by God – from the pharaonic servitude of Austria.[150] Pius IX ceased to be merely a man of history and became a man of myth, in the sense that he became a way of thinking about the world. The myth of the liberal and national pope was not a function or consequence of actions and decisions actually taken by the pontiff; nor did it result from the political position of the Curia or the indecisiveness and ambivalence of the incumbent's personality. It was not something constructed by Pius IX, or even by the people around him. It was a cultural and emotional phenomenon in its own right, a force that the Pope himself struggled to come to terms with.[151]

It became harder to plaster over the contradictions in the Pope's position. In the city of Rome, support for the struggle to drive the Austrians out of northern Italy was almost universal. It had surged in 1847, when the Austrians, noting the growing volatility of central Italy, reinforced their garrison at Ferrara on the northern border of the Papal States. When news arrived of the insurrections in Lombardy and Venetia, Roman crowds surged into the Piazza Venezia and attacked the Austrian legation, leaning ladders against the wall and tearing off the *Reichsadler*, the coat of arms bearing the image of the Austrian two-headed eagle. There was wild jubilation when a contingent of papal troops marched off to the north, supposedly to guard the borders against possible incursions. But how could the Pope commit himself to a war against Austria?

Austria was not just Europe's foremost Catholic power; it was the traditional guarantor of papal security. For Pius IX, an 'Italian' war with Austria was an appalling prospect. In his allocution of 29 April, he broke decisively with the national movement, condemning those 'enemies of the Catholic religion' who were spreading the 'calumny' that he supported the policy of opposing Austria by force of arms. There were many people, he wrote, who spoke of the Pope as if he were 'the chief author of the public commotions which have lately happened'. It was time to 'repudiate the crafty counsels ... of those who wish that the Roman

Pontiff should preside over some new Republic, to be formed of all the people of Italy'.[152] Only three days later, the Pope wrote to the Austrian emperor, begging him to pull back from 'a war which can never reconquer for your empire the minds of the Lombards and Venetians' and would bring with it 'the fatal series of calamities that always accompany war'. He was confident, he wrote, that the German nation (by which he meant in this context the Austrians), 'being honestly proud of its own nationality', would not 'engage its honour in shedding the blood of the Italian nation; but rather nobly recognise [Italy] as a sister'.[153] The two communications should be seen as two strands of the same policy. The letter opened with a reference to the allocution; having extricated himself and his reputation from the war against Austria, Pius hoped (vainly) for a reciprocal gesture of restraint from the Austrians. But whereas the letter to Emperor Ferdinand was a private communication, the allocution was reprinted all over the peninsula. It seemed to suggest that Pope favoured leaving Lombardy and Venetia in Austrian hands.

The dream of a pope who could be all things to all Italians was suddenly dead. The loss to the patriot cause was incalculable. 'His name had a real moral weight', Margaret Fuller wrote. 'It was a trumpet appeal to sentiment. It is not the same with any man that is left. There is not one that can be truly a leader in the Roman dominion, not one who has even great intellectual weight.'[154] Now the Pope stood exposed as a friend of the hated Austrians and 'the retrograde champion of the existing regimes'.[155] The news of the allocution breathed life back into the Neapolitan counter-revolution, while the withdrawal of the papal troops dealt a blow to patriot morale in the north.

By the summer of 1848, a determined and articulate liberal political leadership had emerged in the city of Rome, anchored in a network of clubs whose members included refugees from other parts of Italy. Under a new liberal constitution, elections took place for the lower house of a bicameral legislature. Committing an error that has recurred many times in modern European history, the Pope viewed the two chambers as merely advisory bodies, failing to grasp that the deputies saw themselves as embodying a new form of government that would come to displace priestly rule. The deadlock between Pope and government hardened, the mood soured further and the last embers of the love feast of 1846 were extinguished. 'Italy was so happy in loving him', wrote

Margaret Fuller, daguerrotype by John Plumbe (1846). Fuller was a perceptive critic of marriage, which she described as the 'nightmarish destiny' of most women. As a journalist and correspondent, particularly in Rome, she produced some of the most acute and evocative writing that survives on the events of 1848. On 19 July 1850, she was on her way home to the United States when she drowned in a shipwreck with her Italian husband and child off Fire Island.

Margaret Fuller in May 1848. 'But it is all over. He is the modern Lot's wife and now no more a living soul, but a cold pillar of the past.'[156]

Pius IX had been thinking for some time about escaping. Exile was a recurring theme in the history of the papal office and Pius had fled from political unrest before, in 1831, during an uprising in Spoleto, where he was archbishop. Then, too, his refuge had been the Kingdom of Naples, where he sat out the troubles while the Austrians restored order in his diocese. There was no shortage of possible destinations. To host an exiled pope was an honour worth striving for. Spain was keen to ferry him to one of the Balearic islands, and a French frigate weighed anchor off Civitavecchia in case he needed a lift to Marseilles. The British sent their new paddlewheel war steamer *Bulldog* to Italy and the Americans promised him a ship, should he want one. But it was only in November 1848 that Pius made up his mind to leave.

The trigger was the assassination of the Pope's friend and confidante Pellegrino Rossi. Pellegrino was an intriguing figure, whose biography reminds us of how European Europeans were before the ascendancy of the nation-state. Educated in Pisa and Bologna, Rossi supported the Napoleonic regime in Naples and escaped to France when it fell in 1815, taught at the Calvinist Academy of Geneva for some years, where he took Swiss citizenship, became a champion of Swiss constitutional reform, served for a time as a deputy to the Representative Council, and then accepted the chair of political economy at the Collège de France in 1833. Having taken French citizenship, he became an active supporter of François Guizot. In 1845, the Guizot government sent him on a diplomatic mission to the Papal States, with instructions to negotiate the expulsion of the Jesuits from France with the Holy See. For his successful completion of this task, Rossi was ennobled and promoted to ambassador. When the Guizot government fell, along with the French monarchy, in February 1848, Rossi's posting came to an end, but he stayed on, first as the friend and adviser of the Pope and then as the most energetic minister of the papal administration.

Focused on technical solutions and administrative reforms, Rossi represented precisely that kind of pragmatic and moderate politics that wins few friends in an environment polarized by conflict. As Minister of the Interior and Police, he pursued a moderate-liberal and gradualist programme focused on the laicization of the papal administration and the reinforcement of representative politics. These policies, together with his well-known opposition to a resumption of the war with Austria, earned him the hatred of democrats and conservative hardliners alike.

On 15 November 1848, at about one o'clock in the afternoon, Rossi arrived in a carriage at the entrance of the Chancellery Palace, where he was due to open the session of the Council of Deputies of the Papal State. With him was the acting Minister of Finance, Pietro Righetti. Righetti tried to clear a path through the crowd of shouting Civic Guards and Legionaries recently recalled from the campaign in the Veneto, but was jostled so hard that he had to walk behind the Prime Minister. A sea of angry faces surrounded Rossi, but the minister remained serene, even though he had received warnings that his position on the Austrian War exposed him to the danger of assassination. As he ascended the stairs of the palace, an assailant appeared and plunged a dagger into his neck, severing the carotid artery. As he sank to the steps in a welter of blood, the Legionaries on all sides raised their mantles to conceal the flight of the assailant.[157] The news of the minister's violent death sent the crowds of Rome into a frenzy of celebration. 'Blessed be the hand that stabbed the tyrant!' they sang, as they marched through the city, holding aloft Italian tricolour flags and a pole from which dangled the bloodstained knife of the assassin. Days of terror followed for the Pope and his closest associates. Crowds attacked the Quirinale Palace, cannon were drawn up before the entrance, and a prelate, Monsignor Palma, was shot dead in his own chamber while standing near the window. Bullets fired from the square made it into the Pope's antechamber.[158] It was time to go.

The departure of the Pope set the scene for one of the most engrossing episodes of the mid-century revolutions. Just as the revolution was dying in Paris, Berlin and Vienna, Rome witnessed a new beginning. After a period of uncertainty and tense negotiation, the Council of Ministers announced the creation of a 'provisional and supreme council of state', which would exercise all the offices of a political executive temporarily, pending the establishment of a 'constituent assembly of the Roman states'. The weak deliberative councils established under Pius IX were dissolved; in December the council of state announced that elections would take place under a direct and universal suffrage, in which all (male) citizens of twenty-one years and above were eligible to vote and all of twenty-five years and above eligible to stand for election.

A quarter of a million voters turned out, which was not too bad, given the difficulty of motivating the peasants, the ardent opposition of much of the clergy, and the vociferations and excommunications issuing from the Pope in his exile in the Kingdom of the Two Sicilies. The assembly convened for its first session on 5 February 1849 in the Chancellery Palace.

The Roman Republic declared on 9 February 1849 was a strikingly humane and restrained polity, and much was achieved during its short life. The Inquisition was abolished; the clerical monopoly in university teaching was ended; clerical censorship lapsed and dozens of new journals appeared; the protective duties that hindered trade and agriculture were swept away; the secret ecclesiastical courts lost their monopoly of justice and were replaced by a lay judiciary; taxes were adjusted to help poorer citizens; all discrimination on the basis of creed was abolished, meaning that the Jews of the Papal States were at last definitively freed of their traditional burdens. It is worth emphasizing these inconspicuous successes because the enemies of the republic were assiduous in circulating horror stories. Pius IX issued a blanket excommunication of all members of the assembly and of the hundreds of thousands who had voted for them, inaugurating a long tradition of election boycotts that would mark Italian political life well into the twentieth century. His partisans traded in tales of wanton spoliations, cruelties and outrages. And yet witnesses in the city testified to the high levels of public security, despite the lack of police.

The new constitution abolished the death penalty (it was the first constitution to do so – the second if one counts the Wallachian Proclamation of Islaz) and stipulated a general freedom of religion, though the new leaders also guaranteed to the Pope his continuing right to govern the Catholic Church. Among the eight 'fundamental principles' that opened the text, an early draft included a clause stipulating that the Catholic religion was the 'religion of the state', but this was later dropped. Principle 2 announced that 'equality, liberty and fraternity' were the guiding ideals of the new polity and Principle 3 committed the republic to the 'improvement of the moral and material conditions of all citizens', just as the French constitution did, though without stipulating precisely how this amelioration might be achieved. Freedom of the press was instituted, and provision made for secular education. Among those who drafted this document was Aurelio Saliceti, jurist and former justice minister in

Naples, who had fled into exile after the Bourbon counter-revolution. And yet even as it made these provisions for the future, the Republic struggled to secure its own material existence. Like many of the provisional polities of the mid-century revolutions, this one soon ran out of money. As the people with cash fled the capital and silver currency vanished from the streets, the Republic was forced to subsist on debased fiat coinage and inflated paper money elegantly inscribed with eagles, fasces and cannonballs.

If money was scarce, celebrity was not. On 27 January, citizens flocked to the première of Giuseppe Verdi's *The Battle of Legnano*, conducted by the composer himself, in the splendour of the Teatro Argentina. This was an opera composed throughout with a patriotic purpose, a work designed to capture and amplify the emotions of the moment. In adapting the text of Joseph Méry's play *La Bataille de Toulouse*, the librettist Salvadore Cammarano moved the action from France to medieval northern Italy, scene of the victory of the Lombard League over the invading German emperor Frederick Barbarossa at Legnano. The audience needed no tutoring to read this set piece from 1176 as an allegory for the aspirations of contemporary Italians, even if the chances of a modern Legnano seemed vanishingly slim. Verdi sustained the pathos throughout, from the opening chorus, 'Long live Italy! A sacred pact binds all her sons', to the closing chorus of freedom, 'Italy rises again robed in glory'. The entire performance drove the packed audience to a 'frenzy of enthusiasm'. At the point where the hero cries *Viva Italia!* and leaps from a balcony into the moat in order to swim to his regiment, one soldier in the audience, stirred beyond endurance, threw his sword, coat and epaulettes down onto the stage, together with all the chairs in his box and then himself.[159]

The luminaries of the worldwide Italian insurrectionary networks now descended on Rome. Giuseppe Mazzini arrived from London via France and Switzerland on 5 March 1849 – it was his first visit to the city. A unanimous vote of the newly elected assembly had already granted him honorary citizenship of the Republic. He was welcomed on arrival by delirious crowds and immediately invited, like Blum in Vienna, to address the assembly. In a stirring speech, he called on Romans to demonstrate a patriotism that was not hostile to religion. They should show the world that freedom and equality could coexist. Liberty of conscience and speech were rights to be enjoyed by everyone; there should be no intolerance or hatred of political opponents, only unity in support of national independence. Mazzini showed no interest in a government post, but when the assembly voted overwhelmingly to offer him one, he eventually agreed to serve as one of the triumvirs of the republican executive. He governed with moderation, displaying an unexpected talent for administration, and soon by default became the sole ruler in practice. He lived without ceremony in Rome, as he had in London, working unguarded from a single room and eating in a nearby restaurant.

For Mazzini, who had long hoped to displace ecclesiastical Christianity with a new form of spirituality focused on the nation, the sojourn in Rome had an ambivalent impact. The Republic, with its tolerant but emphatically secular constitution, was clearly, from his perspective, a step in the right direction. But his immersion in the spaces and behaviours of Rome also brought home the abiding moral authority of the Church over the masses of the faithful. On Easter Sunday 1849, he made his way with a friend to St Peter's, where he saw an ocean of people gathered between Bernini's curved colonnades to receive a blessing; before them rose the splendid façade of the basilica under the white immensity of Michelangelo's dome. No one had done more than Mazzini to embed national sentiment in politically active Italians, but what did the patriots have to compare with this stunning spectacle? 'This religion is strong', he remarked wistfully to his companion, the painter Nino Costa, 'and it will remain strong for a long time to come, because it is so beautiful to the eye.'[160]

Giuseppe Garibaldi arrived in the city at the end of April 1849 with a detachment of Legionaries. In the spring of 1848, Garibaldi had offered to fight for the Pope and for King Charles Albert and been rebuffed by both. He had joined the struggle for Milan before retreating into Switzerland after the Austrian victory. Having spent the autumn and winter in Nice with Anita and their three children, Garibaldi joined Mazzini in Rome. These larger-than-life personalities endowed the Republic with an almost spiritual charisma. There was an ethereal, priestly grace about the 'apostle of the revolution', as one enthusiast described Mazzini. For those of less austere taste, there was the Dolce & Gabbana extravagance of Garibaldi, who entered Rome atop a white horse wearing a red jacket with a short tail and a small black felt hat, his chestnut hair falling in tousled tresses to his broad shoulders. Never far from Garibaldi was his famous companion Andrea Aguyar, the son of enslaved parents from Uruguay, who had committed his life to the Italian revolutionary from the moment he had joined him in Montevideo. Aguyar sported a red tunic, a jauntily tilted beret, and blue trousers with green stripes. He got about on a glossy jet-black charger. When Garibaldi and Aguyar rode out together, as they often did, they never failed to cause a sensation.

If these individuals unleashed intense emotions, this was because they resonated with a romantic culture in which secular, spiritual and religious motifs were profoundly entangled. The entanglement was only possible because the bonds between religious sentiment and ecclesiastical authority had loosened. The Barnabite monk-turned-revolutionary Ugo Bassi, who encountered Garibaldi outside Rome in April 1849, described him as 'the hero most worthy of poetry of any I can ever hope to meet in my entire life'. 'Our souls', Bassi wrote, 'have been conjoined, as if we had been sisters in heaven before finding ourselves living on earth.'[161] The inchoate spirituality that had fed the cult around Pius IX now flowed towards the fiercely anticlerical adventurer Garibaldi. Bassi would remain chaplain to the Legionaries and spiritual adviser to Garibaldi until his execution by an Austrian firing squad just four months later. Like the Catholic Church, the Roman Republic had its saints and it would soon harvest its share of martyrs.

Among the patriot luminaries who gravitated to Rome was Cristina di Belgioioso. She was one of the few female European celebrities of this era, an Italian counterpart to George Sand. Belgioioso's fame had many facets. Before 1848, she was known for her involvement in the Lombard patriot movement, her glamorous Parisian exile, her generosity in supporting fellow Lombard expatriates and her progressive management of Locate, the estate she inherited between Pavia and Milan. Here she established a kindergarten and schools for the children of the villages on the estate, together with laboratories for training talented peasants and large heated rooms for communal meals in winter.[162] She was also known, like Sand, for her striking appearance, her perplexing blend of masculine and feminine 'sentiments and concerns',[163] and her amorous friendships with men (and possibly also women). In Milan she organized and financed a troop of soldiers and took part in the struggle to free the city from the Austrians. When the insurrection failed in the summer of 1848, she returned to Paris, where she published insightful analyses of the Milanese events in the *Revue des Deux Mondes*. After her arrival in Rome in the spring of

1849, Belgioioso was placed in charge of the city's military hospitals in preparation for the defence against a counter-revolutionary army of intervention. Among those she employed to assist her (possibly on Mazzini's advice) was Margaret Fuller, who took over direction of the Fate Bene Fratelli hospital on the western side of the Tiber Island.

In a letter written late in May 1849, when the battle to defend Rome was already underway, Fuller observed that the princess had received no income since leaving Milan, 'her possessions being in the grasp of Radetzky'. Yet she seemed able to operate as agilely without money as she had in her days of plenty. Belgioioso's published appeal to the women of Rome for lint and bandages was a huge success. She initiated a fundraising campaign by walking through the streets with two other veiled women begging donations from prominent citizens. This unheard-of procedure triggered a wave of gifts, including one contribution of $250 from the Americans of Rome, of which 'a handsome portion came from Mr Brown, the consul'.[164]

It is one of the oddities of the timeline of the revolutions that the counter-revolutions of autumn 1848 were followed by a further wave of revolutionary unrest that extended into the spring and summer of the following year. These second-wave tumults were different in character from the tumults of spring 1848. They were dominated by radicals rather than liberals. They were better planned and more robustly networked than the spring upheavals. They revealed what the political left had learned from the failures of spring and summer.

Many liberals felt that the election of parliaments, the concession of constitutions, the dismantling of censorship and the adoption of other political demands had largely fulfilled the objectives of the liberal programme. They were far from being 'socio-political nihilists', unaware of the socio-economic pressures on the poorest strata.[165] But most liberals were unwilling to bind political authority to the satisfaction of social demands, because they saw the social and economic lives of humans as something rooted in private relationships, a domain that must be protected against the interventions of the state. As Lamartine summed it up in his polemical exchange with Louis Blanc: 'We recognise no other possible organization of labour in a free country than liberty rewarding itself by competition, skill and morality!'[166] Liberalism had always been a politics of balance and calibration, of 'thus far and no further'. In

1848, liberals hoped to stabilize the revolution at precisely the point where they and their own politics approached satiation.

But the deepening of political participation continued on the left, even as it slowed in the liberal centre. In Germany, the most important stimulus to radical mass mobilization was the forced closure of the parliament in Prussia in November 1848. When the deputies in Berlin called for a tax boycott, there was heated debate in the Frankfurt assembly over whether to support them. The moderate-conservative majority of the Frankfurt deputies voted against it. In response, a group of deputies on the left founded the 'Central Association for the Preservation of the Accomplishments of March' (Märzverein). Once it got going, the Märzverein spread swiftly across the democratic south and west of Germany. By the end of March 1849, it encompassed 950 clubs with approximately 500,000 members.

The emergence of an increasingly numerous and ramified left-wing movement, especially in France and Germany, alarmed the liberals, who faced the prospect of being ground like wheat between the millstones of counter-revolution on the one hand and leftist mobilizations on the other. In an analysis (written in 1849) of the revolution's course in the Grand Duchy of Baden, the liberal politician Ludwig Häusser was critical. The clubs, he argued, were not just talking shops for the left, but were a 'well-organized anti-government' and a 'state within the state'.[167] Liberals disliked the way the Märzverein blended parliamentary and extra-parliamentary activism; they viewed it as an anti-parliament; they remembered the clubs of the French Revolution. Because they loved the procedural steadiness of the chamber, they hated the rowdiness and crowd-pleasing rhetoric of the clubs. The openness of the Märzverein to republican ideas was another problem, since most German liberals were constitutional monarchists to whom the word republic signified rebellion, anarchy, the terrorist rule of the mob and the dissolution of the bourgeois world.[168] Some liberals were prepared to emulate the left in using associational networks to deepen and consolidate their own platform. 'Let us learn from the enemy! He has already organized himself!' one liberal journal urged in August 1849 (referring to the radicals, not the monarchical counter-revolution!).[169] But the liberals were almost always less successful than their competitors on the left, partly because their mandarin style resonated less with the masses of the people and partly because the social catchment area for their form of politics was simply smaller.

Something similar happened in France after the disaster of the June days. A new left-republican umbrella organization emerged. Known as Republican Solidarity (Solidarité républicaine), it had grown by January 1849 to encompass 350 affiliated clubs with auxiliaries in three quarters of all French departments. The authorities promptly shut the organization down. But the mobilization continued underground, giving rise to an ever more ramified structure of secret societies with over 700 associations, to which some 100,000 people were actively committed. The emergence of such groups revealed a deep polarization in political sentiment that also shaped election results in the winter and spring of 1848–9, leaving liberals out in the cold. In Saxony, the December elections of 1848 produced a Lower House in which sixty-six of the seventy-five mandates fell to democrats.[170] In January and May 1849, elections in the Kingdom of Prussia and France revealed an erosion of the middle ground, as the mandates polarized towards left and right. The same thing happened in Württemberg during the autumn of 1848. Among the candidates elected to seats in the reformed Württemberg chamber that convened in late September was David Friedrich Strauss, the sometime *enfant terrible* of the Zurich putsch (Chapter 3). He was hostile both to the 'anarchic left' and to the 'aristocratic right' (as he called them), but found there was virtually no one in the middle with whom one could build a moderate party.[171]

One reason for this withering of the middle was that the functionality and larger purpose of liberal politics was no longer self-evident. The more frightened the liberals became of the left, the more they themselves gravitated towards the forces of order. Wherever liberals were in government, they subjected democratic political clubs, public meetings and demonstrations to police surveillance and rigorous countermeasures, while at the same time turning a blind eye to right-wing attacks on the legitimacy of the revolution. Within the revolutionary assemblies, the liberals tended increasingly to vote together with their former conservative enemies, against the deputies of the moderate and radical left.[172]

This was in some ways a marker of liberal success. If the liberals were a 'saturated power', if they had achieved what they had struggled for, why should they not align themselves with public order and the protection of the new establishment? Satisfaction and a sense of liberal accomplishment were certainly part of the motivational mix, but a deeper and more important driver of liberal behaviour was the fear of further instability. From the summer of 1848, liberals adopted an increasingly schematic and apocalyptic view of political and social conflict. They saw themselves locked in a zero-sum conflict with an enemy that represented the absolute negation of the bourgeois social order. In a series of lectures he published in 1850 on the history of the revolutions, the Berlin writer, historian and liberal-Jewish pedagogue Sigismund Stern described the impact of the Parisian June Days on the propertied classes of Europe:

> The bourgeoisie . . . was filled with terror at the thought of rule by a party that threatened to overturn society, and to destroy all the sources and means of acquiring income. And this panic fear of the bourgeoisie in the face of the spread of socialism and of communism across the whole of Europe provided important footholds enabling the counter-revolution to take root within this part of the population.[173]

Between the autumn of 1848 and the spring of 1849, the second-wave mobilization of the left became intertwined with the politics of the German question. Late in October 1848, the Frankfurt National Assembly voted to adopt a 'greater-German' (großdeutsch) solution to the national question: the Habsburg German (and Czech) lands would be included in the new German Reich; the non-German ones would be formed into a separate entity and ruled from Vienna. The chief problem with this plan was that the Austrians had no intention of accepting it. The Habsburg court was recovering its confidence fast. On 27 November 1848, Prince Felix Schwarzenberg, the new Chief Minister in Vienna, exploded the greater-German option by announcing that the Habsburg monarchy would remain a unitary and indivisible political entity. The consensus in Frankfurt now shifted in the direction of the 'lesser German' (kleindeutsch) solution favoured by a faction of moderate liberal and mainly Protestant nationalist deputies. Under the terms of the lesser-German option, Austria would be excluded from the German union, pre-eminence within which would now fall to the Kingdom of Prussia.

This option only stood a chance of succeeding if the Prussian monarch agreed to become the crowned head of a lesser-German polity. Late in November, the new Minister-President of the provisional Reich government in Frankfurt travelled to Berlin in the hope of persuading Frederick William to accept – in principle – a German-imperial crown.

The king's initial reaction was not encouraging. He spoke disparagingly of an 'invented crown of dirt and clay'. But he also kept open the possibility of an acceptance, should it be possible to secure the agreement of Austria and the other German princes. This was not much to go on, but it was enough to keep the lesser-German option afloat for the next few months. In a series of hurried debates and resolutions, the deputies in Frankfurt agreed, first, that the new Germany would be a monarchy (i.e. not a republic), second, that this monarchy would be hereditary, and third, that this role should be offered to the king of Prussia. The imperial constitution (*Reichsverfassung*) published on 28 March 1849 foresaw a German executive headed by a prince bearing the title *Kaiser*. The ministers would be responsible to a bicameral parliament endowed with the right to initiate legislation. Laws supported by both houses could be delayed by the government, but there was no absolute veto. Orders by the *Kaiser* only became valid when they were countersigned by a minister. The question of whether the Austrian lands would at some point become part of the new entity was left open.[174]

In April 1849, in one of the emblematic episodes of modern German history, a delegation from the assembly, led by the Prussian liberal Eduard von Simson, travelled to Berlin to make a formal offer. The king received them cordially and thanked them warmly for the trust that they, in the name of the German people, had placed in him. But he refused the crown, on the grounds that Prussia could accept such an office only on terms agreed with the other legitimate princes of the German states. The king's refusal was a blow to the dignity of the parliament. It announced that the national project would advance under purely monarchical, not parliamentary, auspices. And it signified a brusque rejection of the imperial constitution drawn up with such care by the deputies of the Frankfurt assembly.[175]

The German national question now floated in a kind of limbo. There was an 'imperial executive' in Frankfurt, but it had no power. There was a crown, but no one to give it to. The constitution was ratified by a scatter of thirty small and tiny states, but rejected by nearly all the big players: Prussia, Hanover, Württemberg, Bavaria, Saxony, Austria.

And so it came to pass that, in the spring of 1849, the radicals threw their weight behind a campaign to force the counter-revolutionary states to accept the imperial constitution drawn up by the Frankfurt assembly. This was in some ways a counter-intuitive development. The imperial constitution had only barely secured a majority in the Frankfurt parliament. The left wing of the radical movement had not traditionally been very interested in constitutions or the deliberative processes that shaped them. The jeering refrain of Georg Herwegh's poem 'Das Reden nimmt kein End', first published in July 1848, captured the dismissive attitude typical of these circles: 'In the parlia-parlia-parliament, the empty chit-chat never ends'. The poem closes with a strophe urging 'the people' to shut the Frankfurt parliament down. (Herwegh's ditty would enjoy a comeback among the ultraradical students of the West German 'Extra-Parliamentary Opposition' movement after 1968.)[176]

And yet, under the conditions of spring 1849, the decision to mobilize behind the imperial constitution was tactically astute. As the 'written distillation of the March revolution', the constitution was a symbol with formidable integrative power.[177] It was ennobled by the haughty contempt of the princes. It was a liberal document with some radical touches (a catalogue of rights, for example). And most of the German radicals drew a distinction between weak parliaments that met and deliberated at the pleasure of princes, and strong ones that ruled in the name of popular sovereignty. Only the latter could truly represent the nation, as a people.[178] The Reich constitution campaign thus signified a continuing commitment to the national project, as a process driven from below, by the people's assent. As the conservative princely governments dissolved their respective parliaments in a wave of counter-revolutionary crackdowns, the imperial constitution became a way of choosing between two stark alternatives: revolution and counter-revolution.

Drawing on the expanded second-wave networks of the left, the constitutional campaign developed an impressive momentum. The District Committee of the democratic associations in Würzburg managed to gather 10,000 signatures for a petition in favour of the constitution. A spring gathering of the 'people's clubs' in Reutlingen, Württemberg, brought together 20,000 people. The campaigning in the Hanoverian city of Celle was organized by a committee representing seventy-five local clubs. From mid April until July 1849, the German states were rocked once again by a cascade of insurrections from Saxony and the Prussian Rhineland to Württemberg and the Bavarian Palatinate. There were protests in all the German states whose monarchs rejected the imperial constitution.

In Prussia, there were major disturbances, especially in the heavily industrialized Rhineland, home to the oldest and densest radical networks. Radicals armed themselves, erected barricades and formed 'committees of safety' – improvised organs of local government. The most serious unrest was seen at Iserlohn in Westphalia, home to about 9,000 citizens. Iserlohn was a small industrial town with wire, pin, silk, satin and cloth manufactures, paper mills, tanning works, bronze foundries and over sixty commercial businesses. A contemporary description of the town praised the pleasing combination of bustling energy and natural beauty: 'a fragrant green garland of mountains and valleys weaves around the city, offering to the eye a welcome resting place when it turns away from the restless commotion of traffic'.[179] On 10 April 1849, a crowd stormed the city's arsenal, breaking down the doors with axes. The intruders carried out whatever they could find: helmets, guns, shirts and trousers. A woman who saw a man leave the building with a pair of newly looted boots shouted to her husband: 'Johann, you've got nothing for your feet, get some for yourself as well!' Children skipped into the streets with pistols in their hands. A 'wild-looking female' was seen at the head of a 'wild mob' striking a looted military sabre so hard on the cobble stones that the sparks flew.[180]

Having barricaded themselves into the town centre, the insurgents established a Committee of Safety. On 13 May 1849, the committee issued an uncompromising 'proclamation':

> The arsenal has been stormed; the weapons are in the hands of the People. This People, the citizens of Iserlohn, have planted the banner of German unity on their barricades; they serve an *ultimatum* to the Crown: the Ministry of Count Brandenburg must be dismissed and replaced with a Cabinet of the People, whose first act must be the unconditional acknowledgement of the German imperial constitution . . .[181]

There was no reply from the Prussian authorities. Four days later, troops stormed the city. Over a hundred insurgents were killed, most of them labourers and craftsmen.

In Saxony, King Frederick Augustus II refused to ratify the constitution, dissolved both chambers of parliament and sacked the more uncooperative among his ministers. An uprising broke out on 3 May and barricades appeared across Dresden. The king, a rump of loyal ministers and the court packed their bags and made off in a hurry to the massive fortress at Königstein. In the wake of their departure, the radicals established a revolutionary Provisional Government, led by the lawyer Samuel Tzschirner, the pre-eminent radical democrat in the lower house of the Saxon parliament. As one of the co-founders of the Democratic Fatherland Club, Tzschirner was at the heart of the second-wave radical mobilization. In the lower house of the Saxon parliament in 1848, he had transformed the democratic minority into a cohesive opposition; he continued to lead it after the December elections produced a democratic majority. In January 1849, he led a commission tasked with exploring the circumstances surrounding the 'killing' – the commission did not use the word 'execution' – of the 'Saxon citizen' Robert Blum.[182] Among Tzschirner's close collaborators in the Provisional Government was the lawyer Otto Heubner, who had served as a deputy to the Frankfurt assembly, where he first sat on the moderate left and later joined the more radical group around Blum. The impact of Blum's death on the political outlook of these prominent Saxon democrats must have been profound, even if it is difficult to quantify.

Tzschirner and Heubner were radicals of the pragmatic type, focused on prosaic matters of procedure and administration. But revolutions need poetry too. In an article published in Dresden on 8 April 1849, Richard Wagner, the *Kapellmeister* at the Saxon court, invoked the redemptive violence of revolution, channelling, in a manner reminiscent of Lamennais, the prophetic voice of the 'goddess of revolution':

> I shall destroy the existing order of things that divides united mankind into hostile nations, into powerful and weak, into privileged and deprived, into rich and poor, for its sole effect is to render us all unhappy. I shall destroy the order of things that makes millions the slaves of a few and those few the slaves of their own power. I shall destroy this order of things that divorces enjoyment from labour, makes labour a burden and enjoyment a vice . . . I shall destroy . . .[183]

And so on. Among the prominent supporters of the uprising was the architect Gottfried Semper, who, it was said, designed some of the handsomest and most elaborate barricades seen anywhere in revolutionary Europe. The Russian anarchist Mikhail Bakunin, newly arrived from Prague, was in town, and so was the communist Stephan Born, lately of Berlin. In all, the Provisional Government could count on the support of

Insurgents on the Altmarkt in Dresden on 6 May 1849. The 'second wave' uprisings of 1849 revealed that the radicals had learned much from the setbacks of the previous year: their networks were larger and better organized and their politics more focused on pragmatic forms of social amelioration. But they lacked the equipment and manpower to fend off the royal armies. It was too late to stop the counter-revolution unfolding across the continent.

about 3,000 active insurgents and an improvised militia of perhaps 5,000 men, of whom many were armed only with agricultural implements. The panic amongst the court-in-exile at Fortress Königstein soon subsided. The insurgents had failed entirely to win over the Saxon royal army. And once the army joined forces with the approaching Prussians, it was clear that the hours of the insurgency were numbered. On 9 May, after a shattering assault on the insurgent positions, the Dresden uprising collapsed. Of the roughly 3,000 people who had joined it, 250 were killed and around 400 wounded, a casualty rate of over 20 per cent.

The Dresden uprising exposed both the strengths and the weaknesses of the radical second wave. The effort to build radical associational networks had been staggeringly successful: the Dresden Fatherland Club alone counted 4,000 members. Across Saxony as a whole, 75,000 people were enrolled in 280 radical associations. The social profile of this movement was deep, an inversion of the social cross-section mobilized by the liberal associational networks. The 'working classes' were numerically dominant, with a substantial upward tail of professional and academic activists. Of the 180 persons later confined in the Waldheim penitentiary for their involvement in the May uprising, 68.3 per cent were master artisans, journeymen and labourers. Teachers, artists, lawyers and businessmen made up a further 13.3 per cent.[184] This alone was an extraordinary achievement.

On the other hand, the command structures and resources required to prevail in the face of armed force were lacking. The problem lay partly in the difficulty of recruiting armed men with the necessary training and commitment and partly also in the mismatch between the skill set and temperamental resources of self-styled revolutionaries and the real demands of crisis management and urban warfare. Bakunin was a brilliant, mischievous and captivating figure but not a gifted organizer. He spent the last few days before the Prussian assault strolling around the barricades, smoking cigars and making fun of the inadequate preparations of the defenders. His chief contribution to the defence of Dresden was to order the destruction of the fine trees that lined the Maximilians-Allee, so that they could be piled up to impede the advance of cavalry, a measure that failed to have any appreciable impact on the counter-insurgent forces. When the residents of the city wept for the loss of their 'beautiful trees', Bakunin mocked them, declaring that the 'tears of the philistine' were 'nectar for the gods'.[185] Wagner spent the night of 7 April perched on the steeple of the Kreuzkirche observing the movements of the Prussian troops and trying to avoid being shot by the enemy snipers whose bullets rang out as they struck the stone parapets. It was a sobering experience and Wagner, having been woken early next morning, as he would later claim, by a nightingale, left the city on the following day. By mid May, as we know from a letter to his wife, Wagner had concluded from these experiences that he was 'anything but a true revolutionary'. The streets and the steeples of an insurgent city were nowhere for an unarmed man. He was too attached to 'wife, child, hearth and home' and not sufficiently fond of destruction: 'people of our kind are not destined for this terrible task. . . . Thus do I bid farewell to revolution.'[186]

Only with the defeat of the second-wave revolution in the Grand Duchy of Baden did the suppressions in Germany come to an end. in April 1848, Hecker and Struve had launched their doomed republican uprising here. Struve returned to kick off a second abortive putsch in September. But these episodes pale into insignificance beside the 'May Revolution' of 1849. This time, exceptionally, it was the army that led the way. On 11 May 1849, the garrison of the Rastatt fortress mutinied, triggering a sequence of mutinies in other garrison towns. This pronunciamento-like overture mobilized the radical networks, which were deeper and thicker here – especially in the small and middling towns – than anywhere else in Germany. On 12 May, Badenese radicals organized a mass meeting at Offenburg. By the time a delegation had arrived in the capital, Karlsruhe, on 13 May to present demands, the Grand Duke and his ministers had fled the country. The radicals declared a Republic. German tricolour flags went up. There was music and feasting. The old parliament was dissolved and a new Constituent Assembly elected in great haste; it began meeting on 10 June. But time was already running out for the insurgents. The Prussians joined up with contingents from Württemberg, Nassau and Hesse. Slowly, the forces of counter-revolution closed in on the Baden Republic. On 21 June 1849, Confederal forces defeated an insurgent army at Waghäusel. These were bitter and deadly encounters: the revolutionaries formed an armed force numbering over 45,000 men, many with military training, and fought pitched battles with the enemy.

The campaign in the south ended only with the capitulation of the hungry and demoralized remainder of the revolutionary army at the

fortress of Rastatt on 23 July 1849. Under a Prussian occupation administration, three special courts were established in Freiburg, Mannheim
and Rastatt to try the leading insurgents. Staffed by Badenese lawyers and
Prussian officers and operated under Baden law, these tribunals issued
verdicts against sixty-four civilians and fifty-one military personnel. There
were thirty-one death sentences, of which twenty-seven were actually carried out over the next few weeks. Among those who stood before the
firing squad was the former watchmaker and café-owner Georg Böhning.
Böhning had left his country to fight as a volunteer in the Greek War of
Independence, where he had served as a colonel in the Swiss Legion. Böhning was a revolutionary in the Hecker style, with long hair and a bushy
beard, a broad-brimmed hat, a loose blouse and a red scarf. It was said
that he wore his hair long because some Turks in Greece had mutilated
his ears. During his court martial, Böhning insisted that he had not
rebelled against the Grand Duchy of Baden, he had merely accepted the
request of the Provisional Government – at that time the legitimate
authority in the land – that he serve in its defence. Böhning was executed
on 17 August. He declined to be attended by a priest, sauntered to the
place of execution smoking a cigar and refused to be blindfolded. Before
the shots rang out there was time for a brief improvised prayer: 'Father, I
come to you to ask for vengeance against my murderers.'[187]

The Prussian troops who manned the firing squads took no pleasure in their task. According to one eyewitness who watched them at
work inside the walls of Rastatt fortress, they returned from each execution with faces 'white as chalk'. But they obeyed their orders to a
man. Of the many resources the counter-revolution could call on, the
continuing loyalty and effectiveness of the armed forces was the most
decisive. The Prussian army had marched into Posen in May 1848 to
put down the Polish uprising there, expelled the Prussian National
Assembly from its Berlin premises in November and closed its successor in Brandenburg a few weeks later. It was called in to deal with
countless local tumults across the country. It coordinated the counter-
revolutionary campaigns in Württemberg, the Palatinate and Baden.
Yet this was an army of Prussian citizens, drawn from the very social
strata that supported the revolution. Many of them had been recalled
at short notice from leave in the summer of 1848, meaning that they
went directly from participating in the revolution to assisting in its
suppression.[188]

So it makes sense to ask why more men did not defect or refuse to serve, or form revolutionary cells within the armed forces. Some did, of course – especially in Baden. The radicals made strenuous efforts to recruit soldiers and they were sometimes successful. We have seen that large parts of the army of Baden went over to the insurgent side. But the great majority of troops remained loyal to their respective sovereigns. The motivations for their compliance varied according to local conditions and individual circumstances, but one factor stands out. This was the widespread belief among soldiers entrusted with the repression of local insurgencies that they were *protecting* the social order against the 'anarchy' and 'mayhem' of the radicals. This perspective acquired a certain plausibility from the intimidating rhetoric of many radical groups. In November 1848, the left-wing deputies of the French National Assembly renamed themselves 'the Mountain', in reference to the left-wing caucus of the Jacobin-dominated Convention, the parliament of the first French Republic. Increasingly, the red flag was seen alongside, or even instead of, the tricolour. And the closing months of the revolution saw a proliferation of symbols and enactments harking back to the great Jacobin experiment of 1792–4: Phrygian caps, liberty trees, and even toasts to Marat and Robespierre.

But these gestures belied the real direction of travel, which was towards a more mixed and politically moderate leftist programme. French second-wave radicals came to be known as 'democ-socs', meaning the exponents of a 'democratic and social republic'. The word captured the blend of franchise reform and social demands that had always been at the heart of the radical movements. But the political change they were striving for in 1849–51 was ameliorative rather than transformative: the new state would provide subsidized timber for impoverished peasants; it would establish credit institutes (recall Proudhon's exchange bank scheme); the numbers of police, officials and foresters would be reduced, allowing a reduction in taxation. Theirs was not a republic of virtue in the Robespierrian sense. Most radicals did not conspire against the order of property; they merely promised to 'guarantee prosperity to those unable to obtain it for themselves'.[189] The 'programme' of the Triumvirs of the Roman Republic put it concisely: there was to be 'no war of classes, no hostility to existing wealth, no wanton or unjust violation of the rights of property', just 'a constant disposition to ameliorate the material condition of the classes least favoured by fortune'.[190] The left was already on the path away from the romantic revolutionism of the 1840s towards a democratic republicanism focused on the social well-being of citizens.[191] The spectre of 'communism' that haunted middle-class liberals and conservatives became a way of not seeing or understanding what the radicals were actually asking for. The second-wave radicals were precisely not 'communists'; they were the ancestors of today's social democrats.

GEOPOLITICS

We think of revolutions as a form of civil tumult that takes place within states. Revolutions can have transnational effects when they trigger cascades of unrest that roll over political borders. But in focusing on the civil dimension of revolution, it is easy to lose sight of the ways in which the relations *between* states could shape their inception, evolution and consequences. Geopolitical tensions were implicated in the inception of the revolutions. International interventions (and non-interventions) shaped the revolutions' course and conclusion. And the revolutions, in turn, reshaped the geopolitical thinking of Europeans.

We have seen that the fuse of revolution was not lit in Paris, but in the continent's most politically unstable country, Switzerland. It was apparent even before the fighting started that this was a conflict of European dimensions. And not just because of the danger of transnational contagion. It was a European question because the Swiss constitution was a European construction. It was one of the curious features of the Vienna peace settlement that in addition to resolving the territorial disputes between former belligerents, it also guaranteed several strategically important constitutions. Among the additional documents appended to the Vienna Final Act of 1820 were the constitution of the new German Confederation and the Federal Treaty, the legal foundation for the new Swiss Confederacy of 1815. This intertwining of a treaty among states with regional and domestic constitutional settlements gave the peace order established at Vienna an unusually deep purchase on the political life of the continent as a whole.[192] But it also meant that the presiding powers would view internal challenges to these arrangements as a threat to 'European order' that might justify an intervention by the powers.

This is why challenges to the Swiss federal system rang alarms across

Europe in 1846–8. The militarily inferior Catholic states of the Sonder-bund only allowed it to come to a war because they were confident that the Austrians would intervene on their behalf. In January 1847, when the government of the confederation passed to radical Bern, Austria, Russia and Prussia all moved their diplomatic representations from Bern to Zurich in protest. Yet there was no military intervention. And that non-intervention was as consequential for the opening phase of the European revolutions as the counter-revolutionary interventions of 1849 were for their defeat and closure. The Swiss case reminds us that the distinction we sometimes draw between domestic and international turbulence made very little sense in a Europe in which constitutional settlements were woven into the international order.

The 'European order' was an ideological abstraction, of course. It was usually invoked when axes needed grinding. Those who appealed to 'Europe' were often pursuing the interests of their own states, but these, too, shaped the inception and early course of the revolutions. Prussia is a good example. We have seen that the political crisis there began with a financial impasse. In response to the news that the French government was building a strategic rail network whose eastern termi-nals would pose a potential threat to the security of the German Confederation, the Prussian government drew up plans of its own for a railway artery that would link the Rhineland and the French frontier with Brandenburg and East Prussia. The problem was that to finance this project, the government needed to borrow a large amount of money. And under the Prussian State Indebtedness Law of 1822, loans on this scale could only be ratified by a united all-Prussian representative assembly. This was the impasse that obliged the Prussian government to convene what became known as the United Diet of 1847 – and we have seen what an important role this body played in the processes of politi-cal escalation that made the Berlin revolution possible.

In Sicily, the presence of consuls in the island's major cities and of armed boats in the waters off Naples and Palermo endowed the local representatives of the great powers with the ability to shape the course of events during the revolution. The consuls bargained with the Nea-politan forces over the use of artillery to target specific districts; they issued complaints and even threats to the Neapolitan commanders; they proffered advice to the revolutionary Provisional Government; they passed messages back and forth between the armed adversaries.

Foreign war steamers provided pieces of floating, extra-territorial sovereignty on which the belligerent parties could meet and negotiate. The consuls spoke often of Europe, but they also pursued specific national interests. For the British, who viewed Sicily as a strategically sensitive location, the foremost concern was to prevent either the French or the Russians from capitalizing on the mayhem to secure a new foothold in the central Mediterranean – London lost interest in the island in the summer of 1848 when these threats receded from the horizon.

Geopolitics also impinged on the process of revolution because the revolutionaries themselves thought and acted geopolitically. We have seen how frustration over French policy vis-à-vis the Polish question drove the turbulence of 15 May, which set in train a sequence of effects that culminated in the June Days. In Rome, the cry *Viva Pio Nono!* soon morphed into a geopolitical slogan: *Long live Pius IX, king of Italy! Death to the Germans!* The Piedmontese envoy in Rome could hardly object to a crowd below his balcony chanting *Viva Carlo Alberto! Viva l'Italia.* But it was another matter entirely for the crowd to surge down the street and around the corner into the nearby Piazza Venezia, where the Austrian legation was, and to wake the minister and his family with threatening chants, or even to force him to move his family out of the city. It was in response to demonstrations of this kind that the Austrians reinforced their garrison at Ferrara on the northern border of the Papal States, an act that did much to escalate the upheaval unfolding in the city of Rome. From the very beginning, the movement of radical and liberal enthusiasm for reform on the streets of Rome represented a factor in international relations.

Since the Pope was not just a priest, but also the elected sovereign of a substantial Italian state commanding a small army, it was inevitable that he would be drawn into the Italian national struggle (which was also a European struggle) in one way or another. The 'multi-layered actorness' of the Holy See – as a state, a diplomatic entity and the presidency of a transnational Church[193] – ensured that the travails of the Roman Curia were always entangled with geopolitics. And this applied as much to the suppression as to the inception of the revolution there. There was intense competition among the European powers to control the terms under which the restoration of papal government should take place. Having no forces of his own to call on in his Neapolitan exile, Pius requested military intervention from Austria, France, Naples and Spain. All four agreed to despatch forces, but none was more exercised by this task than France. French Catholics – a large constituency – were likely to be supportive of efforts to restore the papacy. But liberals and radicals were not.

That France must intervene in some way was clear, Prime Minister Odilon Barrot told the French National Assembly. 'The right to maintain our legitimate influence in Italy, the desire to help ensure that the people of Rome obtain a good government founded on liberal institutions' required that France despatch forces to central Italy without delay. Swayed by this rationale, a majority of the assembly voted on 16 April 1849 to send an expeditionary force to Rome. But how was a French army intervening against the Roman Republic supposed to ensure that the consequence would be a government founded on 'liberal institutions'? This could only happen if the Pope agreed to commit himself to a liberal future. But Pius's commitment to reform had always been lukewarm, and the trauma of November had hardened his politics and his personality. Whereas his chief counsellor and political friend during the spring and summer had been the supple and worldly Pellegrino Rossi, he now fell into the orbit of the vulpine Cardinal Antonelli, a vengeful reactionary, whom Pius appointed Cardinal Secretary of State at the end of November 1848. As the exponents of a French policy that claimed to be safeguarding liberal institutions but also intended to reinstate a counter-revolutionary pope, French policymakers had to learn to live with the contradictions. But there was a limit: as the French assembly grew more suspicious of the government's intentions, the support for an intervention began to dry up. Having voted on 16 April 1849 for the expedition, the assembly voted eleven days later in favour of a resolution forbidding the French government to attack Rome.[194] This resolution came too late to make any difference.

On 24 April 1849, a French army of 10,000 men disembarked at the Roman port of Civitavecchia under the command of General Oudinot and set out for Rome, a journey that would take them six days. The mood was good, because the men believed they would be hailed as brothers and fellow strugglers for liberty by the Romans. During a meeting with Rusconi and Pescantini, deputies of the Roman National Assembly, the general assured his interlocutors that France intended no offence; the army was coming to 'secure Rome from Austro-Neapolitan invasion'. The deputies testily replied that the intervention did not 'savour much of friendship, but rather tended to excite suspicions of an intention to restore the dominion of the clergy'. But nothing could be further from his wishes, Oudinot assured the two deputies. France had no intention of interfering in the affairs of Rome; the delegates should please return immediately to the city and 'incline their fellow citizens to receive his soldiers as friends'. This message was reinforced by proclamations assuring the Roman population that France had no intention of imposing upon them a government adverse to their wishes, but was coming in the spirit of 'sympathy' for the restoration of 'order and liberty'.[195] Along the route, the men were puzzled to see copies of the text of Article 5 of the French constitution affixed to the trees: 'The French Republic respects foreign nations, as it expects others to respect its own, not initiating any war of conquest and never employing its forces against the freedom of any people.' Oudinot was confident that the occupation of the city would be over in the turn of a hand. On the eve of the assault, when he and his army were encamped on the western outskirts of Rome, a delegation arrived from the Roman National Assembly and implored the general to cancel the attack planned for the following day. If he went ahead with it, they warned, there would be serious resistance. Oudinot remained relaxed. He had been thrilled throughout the journey from Civitavecchia by the good humour and splendid appearance of his men. 'Nonsense', he replied. 'The Italians do not fight. I have ordered dinner at the Hôtel de Minerve, and I shall be there to eat it.'[196]

Oudinot's good humour was the first casualty of the next day's fighting. As they advanced towards the walls of the city, the French, who had brought neither ladders nor heavy siege cannon, came under fire from Roman artillery units atop the ramparts. Flustered, Oudinot deployed his men to the Pertusa Gate, which he intended to blow open with gunpowder. But on arriving there, they found that the gate marked on their military maps no longer existed. It had been walled up decades before. Oudinot reoriented the attack towards the Cavalleggieri gate, but came under withering fire from the walls. Regrouping again to break open the Porta Angelica, they once again came under intense fire. Among the dead were the artillery captain leading the assault and the four horses pulling the lead cannon. Oudinot never made it to dinner at the Hôtel de Minerve; that night he ate with his men on the road to Civitavecchia, burying the dead and listening to the groans of the many French wounded. It was a temporary setback. In the longer run, with reinforcements, the French army would prevail over the city's defences, though it would take sixty-four days of bitter fighting.

For the people inside the city, a period of extraordinary tension and danger followed. Women made bandages and gathered rocks to be thrown at the enemy from ramparts, boys roamed the city picking up spent cannon balls and unexploded shells. Garibaldi's headquarters was reduced to rubble by artillery fire. Margaret Fuller was at work every waking hour in her hospital on the Tiber Island. She had had no idea, she wrote to Ralph Waldo Emerson, 'how terrible gun-shot wounds and wound-fever are'; she was moved by the courage of the young men under her care, many of them student volunteers from the northern cities: one gallantly kissed his own amputated arm goodbye, another collected the pieces of bone extracted from a wound as relics of the finest days in his life. Luciano Manara, the Milanese patriot and volunteer leader, now Garibaldi's chief of staff, was killed by a shot to the chest while observing enemy positions through a telescope. The Genoese patriot Goffredo Mameli, author of the Italian national anthem and a member of Garibaldi's staff, was wounded in the thigh when the French took the city and died of wound sepsis a few days later. Garibaldi's Uruguayan companion Andrea Aguyar died when his head was struck by shrapnel from a French bomb. This was a hopeless fight, in the Mazzinian manner, designed to swell the ranks of the Italian martyrs: 'Nothing would be more welcome for me than to die for Garibaldi', Ugo Bassi told a group of Legionaries. 'Italy needs martyrs, many martyrs, before it can be free and great.'[197] On 3 July, the French army at last entered Rome. At noon on that day, as French troops moved into the Piazza del Popolo, the deputies of the Constituent Assembly met on the Capitoline Hill to hear the first (and last) reading of the constitution of the Roman Republic.

There could be no question of securing 'liberal institutions' in the conquered city. The notion that the Pope might be amenable to compromises brokered by the foreign minister of the French Republic, who happened now to be Alexis de Tocqueville, proved entirely illusory. The Pope seemed not to feel any gratitude for the role the French had played in his delivery, and he made no concessions to the French government's need to mollify liberal opinion in France. The restored papal regime was not the kind of pragmatic constitutional settlement that emerged in states like Piedmont and Prussia after 1848. It was a literal unmaking of the liberal revolution, an attempt to turn back the wheels of time. The constitution was rescinded without replacement. Liberals, radicals and suspected fellow travellers were rounded up and thrown into dungeons. The Inquisition was reinstated. The slackening of discriminatory restrictions on the Jews that had attracted such notice in the early days of the Pope's reign was reversed. The right to leave the ghetto was withdrawn and the Jews were forced back within their ancient walls. Only in 1870, when the French forces were withdrawn and papal Rome fell to the armies of the Kingdom of Italy, was the Roman ghetto definitively abolished.

In Germany, as we have seen, geopolitics erupted into the civil struggles of the revolution and infiltrated the life of parliaments. Prussia's armed intervention against Denmark over Schleswig-Holstein stirred excitement across the German states, but also prompted misgivings among the other powers. Russia and Britain were already sceptical; France turned away from Prussia to favour the Danes. And it was the growing *international* pressure on Prussia to withdraw that gave rise to the armistice of Malmø, which in turn triggered the September crisis in Frankfurt.

The 'German question' that so preoccupied the Frankfurt parliament was and always had been a European question, in which all the great powers were implicated. Through the shouting and gunfire of 1848, Frederick William IV had heard German music. But he was shrewd enough to see that a Prussian 'imperial Crown' might not go down well with the other continental powers. He spoke cordially with the Frankfurt delegates when he turned down the imperial title on 3 April 1849, but in a letter addressed to his sister Charlotte and intended for the eyes of her husband, Tsar Nicholas I, the Prussian king spoke a very different language: 'You have read my reply to the man-donkey-dog-pig-and-cat delegation from Frankfurt. It means, in simple German: "Sirs! You have not any right at all to offer me anything whatsoever. Ask, yes, you may ask, but give – NO – for in order to give, you would first of all have to be in possession of something that can be given, and this is *not the case*!"'[198]

These words were intended to dispel the Tsar's suspicion that his Prussian brother-in-law intended to exploit the current disorder to Prussia's advantage. But the truth was that Frederick William remained interested in the idea of leading a German federal state. He hoped that the lesser German kingdoms would repay him for his services to the counter-revolution by supporting his efforts to establish a Prussian-led union of German states. In the spring and summer of 1849, there were arduous negotiations with representatives of the lesser German king-doms, Bavaria, Württemberg, Hanover and Saxony. In June 1849, liberal and conservative supporters of a Prussian-led small-German union were invited to a meeting in the city of Gotha and a 'parliament' packed with docile liberals and boycotted by the radicals was convened in the following March in the city of Erfurt. But these Prussian efforts to pluck a German union out of the ashes of the revolution were a flop. The lesser German states remained suspicious of Berlin's politicking. Bavaria refused to join the union; Baden and Saxony refused to stay in it. The whole project collapsed abruptly when the adamant opposition of Vienna brought the German states to the brink of a civil war, forcing the exhausted German princes to agree on a return to the status quo ante 1848. The Habsburgs would never be able to sound the bright trumpets of German unity, but they could still play masterfully on the wheezing barrel organ of the old German Confederation. In the ears of the lesser German dynasties, this was still the more congenial music.

The more geopolitically exposed a territory was, the more international relations became entangled with the civil contestation within states. Most exposed of all were the largely Romanian-speaking principalities of Moldavia and Wallachia, which sat in the force field between the Austrian, Ottoman and Russian Empires. Since the peace of Adrianople of 1829, the principalities were under two Russian protectorates, but were also vassal states of the Ottoman Empire. There were cultural links with neighbouring Transylvania, a largely Romanian-speaking ter-ritory inside the Austrian Empire. Political life in Wallachia and Moldavia unfolded within the parameters of the Organic Regulation (Regulamentul Organic), a constitution-like charter drafted by a reform-ist Russian governor and subsequently ratified by the Ottomans. Adopted in 1831–2, the statutes established an authoritarian and elitist form of representative government that resembled the system established under Maitland on the Ionian Islands. Tensions built in the region during the 1840s: the Russians kept tweaking the statutes in an authoritarian direction, efforts that were read by the elites in the principalities as her-alding an all-out annexation. The growth in Romanian historical and national self-awareness fed a mood of impatience with Russian tutelage that would find expression in the unrest of 1848.[199] There were also ten-sions over the export of Wallachian and Moldavian grain through the

Danube river delta into the Black Sea. By the 1840s, the inland cities of Galați and Brăila, both of which are on the Sulina Channel of the Danube, were flourishing export harbours servicing the grain markets in Constantinople and London. Fearing that they would suck ever more custom away from Odessa, Russia's great Black Sea port city, the Russians, who were responsible under the terms of the Treaty of Adrianople for the physical maintenance of the Danube delta, tried to choke off traffic through the Principalities by ceasing to dredge the Sulina Channel, so that it gradually filled with silt.

These conditions imposed heavy constraints on those who hoped to challenge the traditional wielders of power in the Principalities. But they also created opportunities for dissident political leaders, who could hope, in principle at least, to exploit the margins between the Russians and the Ottomans. The Wallachian revolutionaries took great care to avoid a breach of any kind with the Ottoman authorities. In late May, a month before the revolution broke out in Bucharest, the young revolutionary Ion Ghica was sent to Istanbul with a letter setting out the wishes of a group of 'highly influential' Wallachians who were 'desirous of assuring the internal prosperity of their country under the aegis of the Ottoman Empire'.[200] The authors included most of the members of the Provisional Government that would take power a month later. In providing the Ottomans with a conciliatory rationale for an uprising that had not yet taken place, the Wallachian dissidents exploited one of the advantages of leading the only truly pre-planned revolution of 1848.

It was the Russians they were worried about, and with good reason. The Tsar had issued a manifesto in March 1848 in which he set out the Russian perspective on the current events. It stated that the Russians had no intention of intervening unless the revolutions were to threaten the internal stability of the country. This was mainly a warning to Polish emigrés not to jeopardize the tranquillity of Russian Poland. But the Russian consul in Bucharest made it clear to the Wallachian progressives that an uprising in the principality would trigger a Russian invasion.[201] When the insurrection took place on 21 June, the signals from the Russians were unequivocal. It was reported that a Russian general had already been authorized by the Tsar to invade when the moment was right.

On 8 July, seventeen days after the Wallachian insurrection, Russian forces entered Moldavia and occupied Iași in order to prevent the unrest from proliferating northwards across the border. The news of the

Russian invasion caused such alarm in Bucharest that the Provisional Government withdrew from the city for several days, temporarily throwing the future of the new regime into question. On 18 July, once it had regained its nerve and restored order in the Wallachian capital, the government published an official response stressing the peaceful and moderate character of the new administration and expressing the hope that the Tsar would accept this work of 'peaceful regeneration'. If the Tsar refused, the ministers warned that they would call upon all of Europe for help and place the Principality under the protection of the Great Powers.[202]

The Wallachian ministers got their answer a fortnight later in the form of the 'St Petersburg Manifesto' of 31 July. In this document, the Tsar made known his intention to intervene in the insurgent province. The manifesto drew a stark categorical distinction between 'great states', with which Russia might enter into treaties from time to time as one power with another, and mere territories that were not 'recognised states, but provinces pure and simple forming part of an empire, tributaries to their Sovereign, governed temporarily by their princes, whose elections have to be sanctioned'. Russia neither recognized nor claimed the right to protective intervention in the affairs of other powers. But petty states that owed their very existence to international agreements were a different matter. The insurgents in Wallachia had risen in the name of a 'pretended [Romanian] nationality, the origin of which is lost in the dark recesses of history'. But this experiment could not be allowed to succeed, because, if it did, 'all the diverse peoples of which the Ottoman Empire is composed' would soon follow suit.[203] It is hard to imagine that anyone outside Russia was deceived by this high-minded solicitude for the integrity of Russia's imperial competitor on the Black Sea.

By contrast, the Ottomans pursued a liberal and accommodating policy in Wallachia. In late July and early August, they negotiated with the revolutionaries and settled an agreement. The Provisional Government would dissolve itself, making way for a Princely Lieutenancy in which moderate liberals were dominant. There would be changes to various articles in the Proclamation of Islaz. The National Guard would be renamed the Civic Guard. The franchise would be tightened to encompass only those who could read. The radicals naturally felt that they had been sold short. But viewed against the background of what happened across Europe in the summer and autumn of 1848, this was a strikingly flexible and intelligent response from the Porte, whose local representatives, Suleiman Pasha and Emin Effendi, were reformers in the Tanzimat tradition and critics of Tsarism. With the Princely Lieutenancy, Wallachia secured for the first time a government with real international backing. It was now possible to begin consolidating a new administrative order.[204]

But the Ottoman–Wallachian compromise soon came under pressure from the Russians. They accused Suleiman Pasha of encouraging the 'demagogic party' in Bucharest and treating with rebels on a 'power-to-power' basis. The Russian ambassador, Vladimir Pavlovich Titov, lobbied hard in Constantinople, and the two reformers, Suleiman Pasha and Emin Effendi, were recalled. Suleiman was replaced by Fuad Effendi, also a man of the Tanzimat reform party, but one who hoped through reforms to neutralize separatist and nationalist tendencies by instilling a sense of 'Ottomanism' in the subject populations. His mission, according to the French consul, was to 're-establish the old order of things'.[205] When a delegation from the Princely Lieutenancy travelled to Constantinople, at the instruction of Suleiman Pasha, to present their reform programme, the government refused to receive them.

On 25 September, an Ottoman army (accompanied by the Russian General Duhamel) entered Bucharest. The Ottoman Porte, the British consul, Robert Colquhoun, reported, had 'come into the views of Russia', disavowing its earlier settlement with the Wallachians. Colquhoun was surely right in seeing Russian pressure as the key factor in triggering the intervention. Food security was another concern: the agrarian unrest triggered by the Wallachian land reform question threatened to disrupt the Ottoman grain supply. Whatever the reasoning behind it, the Russian–Ottoman intervention put an end to the Wallachian revolution. The Ottoman forces were unopposed as they approached the capital, but a battle flared up as they marched into the barracks on Dealul Spirii. For about 150 minutes, a force of 900, led by the city's firemen, engaged Fuad's army in a skirmish that cost just over 200 lives. Although it did nothing to alter the larger strategic or political picture, the 'Battle of Dealul Spirii' was captured in a famous engraving and occupies a central place in Romanian national memory of the revolutions of 1848.

Two weeks later, the Russians established an occupation of the whole of Wallachia, in which the Ottomans reluctantly acquiesced. Russia seized

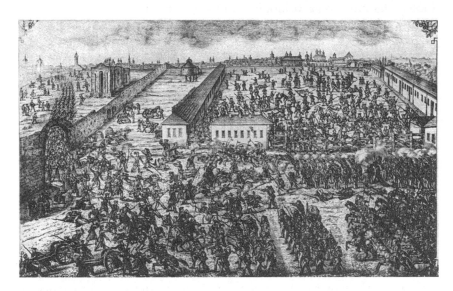

The firemen of Bucharest fight the Ottoman army on Dealul Spirii,
13 September 1848. This battle flared up as the Ottomans took control of
the city. It lasted less than three hours and claimed the lives of just over
200 people. In present-day Romanian memory, this is the best-remembered
image of the Wallachian revolution.

the revenues of the Principality, revised the commercial tariffs and prohibited the export of Wallachian produce. The Principalities were obliged
to support the Russian occupation force out of their own resources. A
credit was opened for them in St Petersburg, meaning that they soon
began to accrue a growing debt to the Russian Crown. Alarm bells rang
in London. In 1847, around half of the maize exported through Galați
and Brăila had gone to British buyers, and the Russian ban on foodstuffs
exports triggered protests from the European consuls in Bucharest.[206] The
ban was eventually dropped, but Russian measures to suppress external
trade in the region continued to generate tension with the Great Powers.
In the years after the revolutions, Romanian political exiles in London
and other European capitals would play hard on this geopolitical theme,
arguing that Russia's handling of the Principalities threatened not just the
prosperity of the region but also the peace and stability of Europe.[207]

The Hungarian struggle, first for autonomy and later for independence,
was the most violent and complexly structured conflict of the revolutions. No other theatre of operations better illustrates the multi-vectoral
character of these tumults. The Hungarian war was in fact a cluster of
mutually embedded civil wars. The core problem was that the revolution
threw open the future for *all* ethnicities, encouraging each to fight for a
larger share in whatever settlement would eventuate. We have seen that
the Austrians sought to exploit the resulting uncertainties by urging the
lesser nationalities to take up arms against the Hungarian revolutionary
government, though most of them needed no encouragement from on
high. One consequence of this policy was the invasion of Hungary by the
Jelačić army. An especially bitter struggle raged between the Magyars
and the Serbs of southern Hungary from the summer of 1848 onwards,
complicated by murderous local conflicts between the Serbs, reinforced
by ethnic comrades from across the border in Serbia proper, and the
Romanians and Germans of the Banat. Transylvania also witnessed
intense regional conflict. Here, the collapse of Habsburg authority shattered the power structures in the region into many local shards.

The loose alliance of forces that emerged in Transylvania to fight
against Kossuth and his Magyar nationalist government was a microcosm of Habsburg complexity. It comprised conservative 'Saxon'
(meaning German) burghers of the market towns, Romanian guards
from the border regiments, the Orthodox and Uniate clergy, Romanian

intellectuals of all political stripes, and – the most numerous group – Romanian peasant guerrillas. Perhaps the strangest ingredient was a contingent of ultra-conservative Hungarian magnates who preferred the multi-ethnic aristocratic world of the Habsburg monarchy to the liberal-national Hungarian state of Kossuth – a rare example of a social alignment that trumped ethnic and national affiliations. This motley coalition fought against the Hungarian armies, but it also clashed, in ever-changing combinations, with the aroused warriors of the Székely nation, a substantial population of Magyar-speakers settled inside Transylvania who declared their support for Hungary in October 1848. In many cases, ethnic tensions were amplified by social tensions. In October 1848, when an Austrian commander, Baron Anton Puchner, urged the Romanians of Transylvania to 'rise to the last man, one for all and all for one', he triggered a Galician-style free-for-all against the landowning class, in which mainly Romanian peasants hunted down and often slaughtered the Magyar nobles and officials. Several thousand were killed; hundreds more died when the Székely then descended on the affected areas to exact vengeance, wiping out entire Romanian villages.

Given the seismic instability of the social terrain in much of the Kingdom of Hungary and the many fronts on which conflicts flared up, it is astonishing that the Hungarian government managed to arm itself and hold the Austrians at bay for as long as it did. Before March 1848, the Kingdom of Hungary possessed no national army. There were Hungarian regiments, but most of them were in service elsewhere, and these units tended to remain loyal to Vienna. The Battyány government could call on about 50,000 regular soldiers, but these were scattered across the kingdom, hailed from many different units and at first lacked any sense of common purpose. Hungary had no armaments industry to speak of. Constructing a functional national army was thus a gargantuan task and the creation of a Honvéd numbering 100,000 men by December 1848 and 170,000 by June of the following year must be reckoned the single greatest achievement of the breakaway government, or, more specifically, of Kossuth, who increasingly took on personal responsibility for managing the Hungarian war effort. Arms were purchased from abroad using the bullion that Kossuth had seized from the Hungarian royal treasury when he was Minister of Finance. Captured weapons were collected and modified if necessary for Hungarian use. Of the 508 field guns deployed by the Hungarian army, 187 had been cast in brand-new specialist Hungarian foundries. In the increasingly well-armed and sometimes brilliantly commanded Hungarian army, the Austrians had at last found their match.

Three things account for the failure of the Hungarians to extract a compromise peace from the Austrians. The inter-ethnic dissension in areas of mixed settlement made it difficult to concentrate all resources on defeating the enemy. The Austrians, oddly enough, helped to resolve this problem by alienating all the non-German nationalities. The 'imposed' Austrian constitution of 4 March 1849 envisaged a central-ized and unitary model of governance, a form of empire that would no longer be multi-national, but a-national. That put paid to the dreams of regional autonomy that had animated many South Slav and Romanian patriots, many of whom now regretted throwing in their lot with the emperor. Their bitterness against Buda-Pest began to ebb.

The second factor was political dissension within the Hungarian leadership. In civil conflicts, politics and warfare tend to become closely intertwined. The war placed the leaders of the Hungarian revolution under extreme pressure. The Peace Party wanted a deal of some kind with Austria. But was such a deal possible? The Austrians were becom-ing more intransigent as they recovered their strength in the Habsburg heartland. Kossuth was on the radical wing; he pressed for a complete declaration of independence. On 13 April 1849, the National Assembly, now meeting in Debrecen because the Austrians had seized Buda-Pest, voted in favour and independence was formally declared on the follow-ing day. But there were deep tensions, both among the leaders and within the army, whose officers, after all, had sworn an oath of alle-giance to the Habsburgs as kings of Hungary.

Among those who opposed Kossuth's course was the most brilliant of the Magyar strategists and commanders, Arthur Görgey. Görgey had never thought of himself as a subordinate of the government – let alone of Kossuth – but as a peripatetic soldier-statesman acting in his own right. When he disliked the instructions he received from the govern-ment, he simply ignored them. He ran his own diplomatic communications and had no qualms about striking deals with the enemy command when it served his purposes. He had no interest in founding an independent Hungarian nation-state. What he hoped for was the return of Hungary into the empire under the terms of the 'constitution' of 1848.[208] On 5 January 1849, he made his allegiance clear by issuing a proclamation to his Corps of the Upper Danube, currently defending the approaches to Pest against an oncoming Austrian army. His army, he declared, remained 'faithful to its oath to the constitution of Hungary' and would continue to obey the legitimate Minister of War, meaning the Habsburg appointee. This was an unequivocal disavowal of Kossuth and the National Defence Committee he had created to run the war effort. But it also articulated a divergence in views of the revolution that we have seen elsewhere: for Görgey, the revolution was an event whose consequences now needed to be safeguarded; for Kossuth, it was an open-ended process extending into the future.

Kossuth was furious when he learned of the Proclamation of 5 January and he cursed the general as a traitor. But Görgey was no traitor. He was just a patriot for Hungary, rather than for Kossuth. Since his views were shared by a large part of the Hungarian officer corps, Görgey was probably the single most important factor in the continuing cohesion of the army. Kossuth hated him, but he could not get rid of him. Much as these two men loathed each other, their fractious partnership was crucial to Hungarian military success during the spring of 1849, when the Magyars recaptured Buda and Pest and secured control of a large part of the kingdom.

By the time the Hungarians were celebrating these victories, a more serious threat had appeared on the horizon. The most decisive factor in Hungary's failure to force Vienna to a compromise peace was the Russian intervention of summer 1849. On 21 May, after various informal feelers had been extended, Emperor Franz Joseph travelled to the then Russian city of Warsaw to meet with Tsar Nicholas I in person and ask his assistance in preserving 'modern society from certain ruin' and supporting the 'holy struggle of the social order against anarchy'. The meeting opened with a gesture that confirmed the geopolitical reality of the moment: Franz Joseph sank to his knees and kissed the Tsar's hand. The ultimate outcome of the Hungarian conflict was now clear. Against a combined strength of 375,000 men serving under Croatian, Austrian and Russian commands, the Hungarians could field at most 170,000. After a long sequence of extremely bitter and costly battles, the Hungarian war came to an end on 13 August 1849 when the Hungarians capitulated to the Russians at Világos (now Şiria in Romania).

Geopolitics was deeply woven into this closing episode of the central-European revolutions. Tsar Nicholas obtained French acceptance of his intervention by acquiescing in Louis Napoleon's assault on the Roman Republic. He assured Lord Palmerston that Russian troops would stay only briefly in the Principalities (a promise that, as it happens, was not fulfilled). But Palmerston also looked the other way because he wanted to preserve the Austrian Empire, partly, ironically, as a bulwark against Russia, but also as a barrier to the nation-building ambitions of the Prussian king, Frederick William IV, whose German unionist machinations were making him uneasy. For the Russians, who could ill afford this large operation, there was the additional calculation that if the Hungarian revolutionaries remained undefeated, the next theatre of national insurrection would almost certainly be Russian Poland. This was not an unreasonable apprehension. Among the most successful of the commanders on the Hungarian side was the Polish veteran General Józef Bem. Bem had fought in a command role during the siege of Vienna and managed to escape the city as it fell to Windischgrätz. In December–January, Bem rustled up an improvised army and drove the Austro-Romanian forces out of most of Transylvania. In general, it is striking to note how cosmopolitan the Hungarian war effort remained despite the national objectives for which it was waged. The thirteen heroes of the revolution executed by the Austrians in the fortress of Arad included 'a German of Austrian origin, a German-Austrian, two Hungarian-Germans, a Croat, a Serb from the Banat and two Hungarians of Armenian origin'. Not all the five 'pure' Hungarians were familiar with the Hungarian language.[209]

In the aftermath of the conflict, the tension between Britain and Russia came again to the fore, prompted not just by tension over the Danubian Principalities, but also by the Austro-Russian demand for the extradition of Hungarian and Polish revolutionaries who had found refuge in the Ottoman Empire. On this latter issue, Palmerston abandoned the equanimity of his earlier pronouncements and confronted Nicholas I directly, less because he was opposed to extradition in principle than because he detected behind the demands for it a Russian challenge to Ottoman sovereignty. Here again was a causal thread that would later be spun into the outbreak of the Crimean war.[210]

THE BIRTH OF REALISM OUT OF THE
SPIRIT OF COUNTER-REVOLUTION

If any single insight emerges from the chaotic closing phase of the revolutions, it is the following: that the transnational revolutionary networks never mustered a power capable of fending off the threat posed by the counter-revolutionary international.[211] To be sure: the revolutionaries thought of their enterprise as European in scope. Volunteers made long and dangerous journeys to fight in the cause of other nations. The Sicilians organized an international recruiting system; by 1849 foreign volunteers accounted for about 10 per cent of Sicilian fighters. In the struggle for the Roman Republic, we find French fighters engaged on both sides in a kind of displaced 'French civil war'. The radical Gabriel Aveyron, the correspondent of Proudhon and friend of poet and writer Gérard de Nerval, was killed defending Rome by a French bullet and subsequently entered the Italian national pantheon. These were sometimes purely voluntary efforts, but they occasionally enjoyed quasi-official support – the several thousand French volunteers who arrived in Marseilles at the end of May to take a boat to Italy were carrying official notes from the Parisian prefecture of police, which, at the point when they left the capital, had been in the hands of the radical Marc Caussidière. In short: there was a 'diplomacy of the peoples' that ran parallel to the relations between states.[212]

But the numbers of such volunteers were always small. Although many of them were former soldiers, they lacked the equipment and logistical support of the territorial armies. Once these latter entered the fray, the defeat of the revolutionary forces was a certainty. The Prussians intervened against the revolution in Saxony, Bavaria and Baden. The French intervened in the Papal States. The Russians intervened in Moldavia, Wallachia and Hungary. The radicals and liberals were hugely successful in creating transnational networks, but these networks were horizontal; they lacked the vertical structures and resources required to wield decisive force. The counter-revolution, by contrast, drew on the combined resources of armies whose loyalty to the traditional powers had never been seriously in question. Towers prevailed over squares. Hierarchies beat networks. Power prevailed over ideas and arguments.

Contemporaries discerned a deeper significance in this outcome. In a series of essays composed for the *Neue Rheinische Zeitung* in 1850, Marx and Engels looked back at the cascade of counter-revolutions and noted how little weight ideology – whether of the revolutionary or the reactionary kind – seemed to carry in the post-1848 political universe. The sonorous *words* of the revolutions – progress, association, moral law, freedom, equality, brotherhood, family, community – were exactly that: words. They had had no real bearing on the success or failure of the revolutions, because a 'true revolution' was 'only possible when *two factors* [came] into *conflict*: the *modern productive forces* and the *bourgeois forms of production*'. The 'various bickerings' (i.e. political debate) in which factions engaged each other were only possible because all the contending parties were securely bound within the same (bourgeois) productive system.[213] This priority of force over political ideation was a source of biting irony. The bourgeoisie had triumphed, they noted, but only by calling upon forces that it could not control. The true mother of the counter-revolution, they argued, was not a political idea, but the return of 'industrial prosperity'. In every political manoeuvre, Marx and Engels saw hands compelled by force: the leaders of the February Revolution were 'forced by the immediate pressure of the proletariat' to attach 'social institutions' to the republic. The National Guard was 'forced' to admit proletarian recruits. The Paris proletariat was 'forced' by the bourgeoisie into the June insurrection.[214]

We see a similar pattern of emphasis in the two authors' reading of contemporary developments in international relations. In an overview of European politics since 1848, Marx and Engels focused on the role Prussia had played in defeating the revolution in Germany. This kingdom, they noted, had gone to enormous pains to suppress radical forces in the southern German states and thereby rescue the lesser dynasties. The Prussians had naturally presumed – here is the irony again – that these lesser states would show their gratitude by joining the project for a Prussian-led German confederation excluding Austria. But these dreams foundered on the realities of power: 'Prussia had restored the rule of the forces of reaction everywhere, but the more these forces re-established themselves, the more the petty princes deserted Prussia to throw themselves into the arms of Austria.' Prussia pursued a German union, Austria opposed it. And behind the Austrians stood the incalculable power of the Russian Tsar. 'At the Tsar's command', Marx and Engels predicted in October 1850, 'rebellious Prussia will give way without a drop of blood being spilled.' In this analysis, it was not the manoeuvring of princely envoys or the speeches at Erfurt but the immense power of Russia that underwrote the post-revolutionary international order.[215]

A closely analogous realist reorientation can be discerned in the reasoning of Otto von Bismarck, for whom the 1850 stand-off between Prussia and Austria was a deeply instructive episode. At a conference in Olmütz on 28–29 November, the Prussians agreed to abandon their unionist project and signed a document known as the 'Punctation of Olmütz', in which they promised to work together with Austria in negotiating a reformed and restructured Confederation. These negotiations duly took place, but the promise of reform was not fulfilled; the old Confederation was reinstated, with some minor modifications, in 1851. For the German patriot enthusiasts of the unionist project, the Punctation seemed a shocking defeat, a humiliation, a stain on Prussia's honour that called out for vengeance. The liberal nationalist historian Heinrich Sybel later recalled the mood of disappointment. The Prussians, he wrote, had cheered their king as he took up the national cause against the Danes over Schleswig-Holstein. 'But now came a change: the dagger slipped from the trembling fist, and many a doughty warrior shed bitter tears into his beard. . . . From a thousand throats rang a single cry of pain . . .'[216]

By contrast, Otto von Bismarck welcomed the clarity of the new situation. In a famous speech to the Prussian parliament of 3 December 1850, Bismarck rejected the arguments of those national-minded parliamentarians who denounced Olmütz as a humiliation, adding that he did not think it lay in Prussia's interest 'to play Don Quixote all over Germany on behalf of disgruntled parliamentary celebrities'.[217] In such weighty matters, he argued, the decisions of the Prussian government should not be swayed by public emotion but by the cool and precise evaluation of the threats and exigencies of a specific moment. Here was that same move away from the din of colliding projects, arguments and ideas towards the detached evaluation of the balance of forces. 'Realities', wrote the lesser-German nationalist and historian Johann Gustav Droysen in 1851, 'began to triumph over-ideals, interests over abstractions . . . Not through "freedom", not through national resolutions would the unity of Germany be achieved. What was called for was one power against the other powers.'[218]

There was a similar reorientation in Italian political commentary, which had traditionally criticized the international system established at

Vienna in 1815 for being founded on power rather than justice. After the disasters of the summer of 1848, influential voices began to embrace the quest for power. Commenting on the Austrian victories in northern Italy, the moderate Massimo d'Azeglio observed that this 'tremendous and painful lesson' had taught the Italians something that they 'ought to have known already', namely that 'there is nothing more serious than power!'[219]

From the radical-liberal camp, too, came a reappraisal of the relationship between ideas and power, in the form of August Ludwig von Rochau's *Grundsätze der Realpolitik* (1853, 1859). The beginning of all political understanding, Rochau wrote, lay in the analysis of 'the forces that shape, support and transform the state'. The first step towards such understanding was the insight that 'the law of power wields a dominion over the life of the state that resembles that of the law of gravity over the world of bodies'.[220] Questions about who should rule, whether it should be one individual or the few or the many, belonged to the domain of philosophical speculation; 'practical politics has to proceed from the fact that only power can rule'.[221] Like the realism of Marx, Engels and Bismarck, Rochau's realism was anchored in the 1848 revolutions. It was at once an attempt to explain the failure of those revolutions and to manage the consequences of their success. In recent times, he wrote, 'a rich new growth of youthful societal forces has emerged, all of which demand acknowledgement within the life of the state, either individually or in combination'. These included national sentiment, partisan politics and the press. 'No well-conceived policy should deny them as much official acknowledgement as their power justifies.'[222] These arguments were not the same as each other: Rochau focused on cultural forces, Bismarck on military prowess, and Marx and Engels on the forces emanating from changing economic conditions. But all three were interested in superseding radical and liberal rhetoric with a pragmatics of power; all three applied this form of reasoning both to domestic and to inter-state relations.

In a book published under the title *On Force in Political Affairs* in 1826, the Italian exile and former Jacobin Luigi Angeloni Frusinate had drawn on various strands of eighteenth-century materialist philosophy to argue that 'everything is force in the matters of the universe and therefore also in our politics here on earth'.[223] 'Good', 'evil', 'justice', 'injustice', 'virtue' and 'vice', Angeloni proposed, were 'mere words without any innate or abstract existence in the human mind'. 'Natural rights', he argued, were mere dreams, since 'everything in the universe is governed by force'. Every force was 'the aggregate of other forces' and lesser forces were always subdued by greater. The study of humankind, society and politics thus had to begin with the analysis of forces.[224] We find something similar in the explanation Armand Barbès gave for refusing to reply to the questions of his judges before the Court of Peers after the Paris insurrection of 1839: 'Between us and you there can be no true justice. . . . There are only questions of force.'[225]

The point of these observations is not that Angeloni invented or prefigured an idea that Marx, Engels, Bismarck and Rochau later elaborated. It is highly likely that none of them knew Angeloni's book, an obscure publication printed at the author's own expense. They were not responding to the arguments of Angeloni, but to the mid-century counter-revolutions. The point is that the idea of an ideologically disenchanted science of forces escaped from its location on the far left (Angeloni was a close friend of the Robespierrist insurrectionary Buonarroti) to colonize the political right and centre. We have seen that people of the early and mid nineteenth century were not locked into finished worldviews but embarked on long and idiosyncratic journeys across an archipelago of arguments and chains of thought. But ideas and intellectual styles could be mobile, too, especially under conditions of political turbulence. The thread that leads us from Angeloni via Barbès to Marx, Rochau and Bismarck is the trail of a realist temperament on the move. What had once been on the margins became mainstream; what had once been esoteric became ordinary.

THE DEAD

So much had been given to the struggle. It would be wrong to end the story of the counter-revolution with a nod at the mood of disenchanted pragmatism that would preside over the following decade. The revolutionaries should have the last word. 'We are ready to die', intoned the refrain of Goffredi Mameli's 'Fratelli d'Italia'. It is easy to affirm a readiness to die. But Mameli, as it happens, really was ready to die. He was wounded in the left thigh with a bayonet on 3 July 1849 while resisting the final French assault at the Villa Corsini in Trastevere. His leg was amputated (a form of martyrdom in its own right before the age of modern anaesthesia), but he died three days later of wound sepsis, at the age of twenty-one. It had been clear since 22 June that the siege of Rome was unwinnable, that it was just a matter of days before the French would take the city. Why, the patriot fighter Enrico Dandolo asked, did Mazzini 'cause the useless slaughter to be continued for eight days longer'? The last days of the Roman Republic, Dandolo declared, were a time of 'useless perils' and 'fruitless displays of courage'. Dandolo was there, and he knew whereof he spoke.[226]

But Luciano Manara, the Milanese soldier who had helped to drive out the Austrians during the 'five days', fought with the Piedmontese army and then journeyed south to join the struggle for the Roman Republic, emphatically did not see his own death as fruitless. 'We must die to bring '48 to a serious conclusion', he declared in the last letter he managed to write before he was himself killed on 2 July by a French bullet. 'For our example to be effective, we must die!'[227] But what did it mean to bring 1848 to a 'serious conclusion' (*chiudere con serietà il quarantotto*)? Since no one, not even Manara, believed in even the slightest prospect of victory, he cannot have meant success in the military sense. The words suggest the termination of a narrative, the completion of a story. We have seen what ardent storytellers the men and women of 1848 were. If the nation was a 'melodrama', as one Italian historian has suggested,[228] so was the revolution. It was a melodrama with real characters, whose deaths on stage were both performed and real.

Consider the death of the Barnabite Garibaldian monk Ugo Bassi, captured near Ferrara and sentenced summarily to death by a vengeful Austrian officer. He walked placidly to the place of execution and knelt, praying quietly. When a soldier approached to blindfold him, he asked that a priest be allowed to do it, so that the last touch he felt would come from the hand of a colleague. Robert Blum was said to have tied his own blindfold when the Austrians executed him on the Brigittenau. The most famous of the Robert Blum songs puts into his mouth an appeal to future generations:

> He takes the blindfold and fastens it tight.
> 'O my Germany that I have fought for,
> That I have seen my life cut short for,
> Keep following liberty's light!'[229]

Whether Blum said these words or not – it seems highly unlikely – matters little: this man of the theatre stayed true to the script he had written for himself: his death was a gift to the future.

Not all of these heroes presented themselves as paragons of virtue. Among the men shot by the Prussians at Rastatt in the summer of 1849 was Ernst Elsenhans, the atheist son of a preacher, condemned for his authorship of 'treasonable' essays in one of the improvised journals that popped up towards the end of the last Baden insurrection. He remained true to his atheism as the hour of execution approached, so there was surprise when he requested a prison visit by the Protestant chaplain of the city. The Reverend Lindenmayer came to see him, intending to comfort the young man with words from the gospel. But Elsenhans merely gave him three envelopes with money inside, asking that they be delivered discretely to his three concurrent girlfriends; one of them, the condemned man said, had supported him for a time. Disappointingly, Lindenmayer then sent all three envelopes to the woman who had supported him, with a letter explaining whom the other envelopes were for, 'so that she might be comforted by knowing how unworthy her lover had been'. But this radical Lothario died with breath-taking courage, his face turned towards posterity. Elsenhans's last words, before he tied his own blindfold, were: 'It's hard to have to die just for expressing your beliefs.'[230]

Not all deaths were verbally eloquent. A Polish Legionary struck across the head by a musket ball during the fighting for Rome, his face streaming with blood, roared at the French attackers: 'Shoot lower, you bastards, shoot lower!' They did, and he sank to the ground. Sándor Petőfi, composer of the Hungarian 'National Song' and radical idol of the March Days, was killed at an unknown location, probably by Cossacks, during the Battle of Segesvár (today Sighişoara in Romania); his remains were never found. No stirring quips are recorded from the women 'cut down and shot dead' by mounted guards on the Praterstern on 23 August 1848. Ciceruacchio, hero of the Roman *popolani* and orchestrator of fraternity feasts between the Jews of the ghetto and their Christian neighbours, was captured by the Austrians together with his two sons and five Garibaldian Legionaries. The men were intercepted trying to escape into Venetian territory over a month after the fall of the Roman Republic. All eight were executed without trial. Ciceruacchio (Angelo Brunetti) was a well-known radical politician, and his elder son, Luigi, was widely known to be the murderer of Pellegrino Rossi.

They knew their chances of survival were slim if they fell into Austrian hands. But the younger boy, Lorenzo, was only thirteen years old. The father pleaded with the Croatian officer presiding over the execution to spare the child. The officer responded by ordering that the boy be shot first. Ciceruacchio was a man with a knack for finding the right phrase, but under these circumstances, even he must have been lost for words.

And around these emblematic figures lie the unmarked catacombs of the anonymous dead: the 40,000–50,000 killed during the Hungarian Independence War, about whom next to nothing is known, the thousands killed in the Transylvanian civil strife, the dead of the wars in Baden, Lombardy and the Veneto, the fallen of the June Days, the urchins struck by shrapnel in the streets of Trastevere, Messina and Palermo, the insurgents summarily shot by the castle moat in Naples, the more than one hundred children, women and elderly massacred by Radetzky's troops at Castelnuovo and countless more. To these we should add the many thousands swept away by the cholera outbreaks that spread in the wake of the counter-revolutionary armies. The fact that cholera mortalities, already elevated in the autumn of 1848, shot up in the following year suggests that counter-revolutionary military conflict, which involved armies passing across political borders, did more to spread this deadly disease than the revolution itself.[231] The Russian army of intervention in Hungary alone buried 11,028 cholera victims during its deployment. Grass has grown over them all.

9

After 1848

THE PRESENT IS A FOREIGN COUNTRY

The suppression of the European revolutions and the reprisals that followed triggered waves of forced displacements. By the end of April 1849, 15,000 Romanians, Szeklers, Germans and others had made their way from Transylvania, where the fighting was especially fierce, into Wallachia. Prince Constantin Cantacuzino, the conservative regent installed by the Ottomans after the collapse of the Wallachian revolution, ordered that a special commission be established to organize relief for these refugees. A public subscription for their benefit drew generous donations from the new political leadership, senior clergymen, prominent merchants, the Ottoman and French envoys and even Duhamel, the Russian representative in Bucharest.[1] As the war in Hungary ground to a close, entire battalions of the Hungarian Honvéd and the whole remaining strength of the Italian and Polish Legions crossed the borders into the Ottoman Empire. On 17 August, Lajos Kossuth arrived in Turkey with an entourage of some fifty individuals. By the end of October, over 5,000 refugees, most of them servicemen, were estimated to be sheltering at a camp in Ottoman Vidin, a port town on the southern bank of the Danube, in what is today north-western Bulgaria.[2]

Many of those who had simply fled the fighting tried to return as soon as peace was restored, but most of the 'political' refugees, who were known to the police and faced sanctions in their respective homelands, stayed on under the protection of the Ottoman Empire. Whereas the Russians handed many captured Hungarians over to the Austrians, the Ottomans resisted Russian and Austrian demands for the extradition of political refugees, even when the Russians hinted that their obduracy might result in a military intervention. Some of the refugees even converted to Islam and entered Ottoman service – about 300 Hungarian soldiers did so, as did the Polish commander Józef Bem, who had fought in the Polish insurgency of 1830–31, fled to Paris after the Russian victory, helped to coordinate the defence of Vienna during the Windischgrätz siege, and then commanded an army of Szeklers in the Hungarian Independence War. Bem now became Murad Pasha and accepted the governorship of Aleppo. In this role, he won a final victory against an army of Bedouin besieging the city before dying of malaria in 1850.

It is worth noting the liberality of the Ottoman response to the refugee crisis triggered by the revolutions. An Ottoman policy memorandum of 14 September 1849 reported that the terms of the Russo-Ottoman treaty of Küçük Kaynarca (1774) contained an extradition agreement in respect of persons found guilty of 'capital crimes' and noted that the Austrians and the Russians were exerting considerable pressure to return their refugees. But to comply with this demand, the memorandum continued, 'would harm the reputation of the Ottoman Empire. If we return them, they are likely to be executed or tortured and this will cast a bad light on the Ottoman authorities. Instead, they should be given shelter and protection.'[3] This advice reflected the preferences of the reformist, pro-Tanzimat elements in the administration. But the Ottomans also hoped to project an image of their empire as enlightened and progressive, by contrast with the administrations in Austria and Russia, and thereby win the sympathy of the western liberal powers, Britain and France. These manoeuvres paid off: in 1853, when Russia once again occupied the Danubian Principalities, in breach of its treaty with the Ottoman Empire, it faced the opposition of both Britain and France. Both countries saw a wave of pro-Ottoman public sentiment that owed much to Istanbul's liberal handling of the refugee question after 1848.[4]

Some of those who had been tireless fighters for liberty on various fronts continued to fight after the dust of 1848 had settled. The English-born soldier Richard Guyon, descendant of a French noble family, had fought with the liberal forces in Portugal against Dom Miguel, later entered Austrian service as an officer in the Hungarian Hussars and offered his services to the Royal Hungarian Army as soon as the revolution broke out. After distinguished service at the battles of Pákozd, Schwechat and Kapolna, he was made a general. Having escaped to Turkey when the Hungarian campaign collapsed, he entered the service of the sultan and became the governor of Damascus under the title

Kourshid Pasha without being required to change his religion. His grave can still be visited at the Haydarpaşa cemetery in Istanbul, established for British military personnel who took part in the Crimean War. The Italian republican Luigi Ghilardi had fought in Portugal and Belgium in 1830, before joining the Spanish army to fight the Carlists. When the revolutions broke out in Italy, he requested leave to fight in the Independence War against Austria. When the fighting stopped, he travelled down to Sicily to fight the Bourbon dynasty there, before moving north, like Aurelio Saliceti, to Rome, where he fought alongside Garibaldi to defend the Republic. Ghilardi fled Europe after the defeat of the Roman Republic and was seriously wounded while fighting with a liberal army in Mexico during the Second Franco-Mexican war (1861–7).[5]

More than 50,000 of those caught up in the revolutions in the Italian states are thought to have fled into exile, most of whom first chose to seek refuge in Piedmont.[6] In the aftermath of the defeat of the insurrection in Baden, 9,000 people, mainly men, fled into Switzerland. In all, it is estimated that as many as 80,000 people were obliged to leave Baden for political reasons in the 1850s.[7] Several thousand insurgents fled Saxony after the collapse of the May Uprising. In France, where the consolidation of the Bonapartist regime produced fresh waves of protests, imprisonments and deportations, around 10,000 republicans fled the country, mainly for England, Switzerland and Belgium. Those who had found a refuge in one place were often subsequently moved on, as happened for example in Piedmont, where the authorities viewed the more radical refugees as a threat to public order, and in France, where the authorities of the Second Empire harried many foreign refugees, especially Poles, into further emigration.[8] The state of Baden financed the emigration of politically compromised individuals to other jurisdictions.[9] Prussia, too, encouraged the emigration of political prisoners under partial amnesty, and the Bavarian authorities sometimes granted pardons to political offenders who were willing to emigrate to the United States.[10] So encompassing was this phenomenon that one historian has referred to an 'exiled generation' of 1848ers.[11] Seven leaders of the Young Ireland Movement, arrested by the British authorities for offences committed in the course of the political unrest in Ireland, were transported to Van Diemen's Land; others, most of them illiterate farm labourers suspected of having served 'under' prominent rebels, were rounded up and transported during the next few years.[12] In Spain, the repression that followed the uprisings of 1848 gave rise to the first wave of mass deportations to the Philippines.[13]

In theory, the sanction of exile focused on individual (male) offenders, but the reality was that it often functioned as a collective punishment for the families of those who had fallen under suspicion. When Richard Guyon, for example, fled into exile in the Ottoman Empire, the Austrians arrested his wife and children. The wife of the radical general and revolutionary leader Mór Perczel was also sent to prison, and so were the children of Lajos Kossuth, along with the children's tutor, until the Austrians released them under international pressure. During his sojourn in Buda in 1849, the British journalist and writer Charles Pridham found that the elderly mother and sister of the Hungarian leader were confined in a small dungeon in the fortress there – they were only released after British complaints to the Austrian authorities.[14] When Henriette Hajnik, wife of Pál Hajnik, the exiled former Minister of Police in the Hungarian insurgent government, applied for permission to visit him in Paris, she was provided with an exit-only passport. The confiscation of the property of proscribed exiles inevitably also affected their dependants. 'What good does it do to ruin our family?' the wife of one exile from Württemberg asked in a petition to the Ministry of Justice. If the family, rather than the individual, was the practical unit of punishment, petitioners often asked, then why not weigh the innocence of the wife and children against the alleged guilt of the offender?[15] Accompanying the Spanish deportees forced to make the long journey by ship to Cuba or the Philippines were a number of women who preferred to go into exile with their husbands.[16] Since women had to combine survival under straitened circumstances with the responsibilities of care for children and other relatives, they bore a disproportionate share of the burden of exile. While men often found it difficult to secure employment in exile, women frequently took up teaching, or needlework, or translation and other literary tasks to sustain their families.[17]

The émigrés of 1848–9 were not a compact or homogeneous group. They were also much more numerous than the Spanish refugees of the early 1820s or the Polish emigration of the 1830s. They came from every theatre of turbulence. Daniele Manin, having risked his life on many occasions during the Austrian siege of Venice, secured an honourable capitulation on the basis of a general amnesty and exile for himself and a few of his colleagues. On 24 August 1849, he boarded a French steamer and left Italy, never to return. Eight years later he died in poverty in Paris, having given everything he had to the Venetian struggle. Alexandre Ledru-Rollin and Louis Blanc both fled Paris for London in the summer of 1849 to avoid sanction for their role in protests against the policies of President Louis Napoleon Bonaparte. After a spell in prison, the feminist journalist Jeanne Deroin left Paris and travelled to London with her two youngest children, working as a teacher and embroiderer in Shepherd's Bush. The democratic lawyer and leftist Frankfurt deputy Ludwig Simon of Trier fled to Switzerland and was sentenced to death in absentia for treason. Eugénie Niboyet, the driving force behind the journal *La Voix des Femmes*, went into exile in Geneva, where she scraped by on the income from literary translations. Carl Schurz, who had fought in the revolutionary army of Baden, was trapped in the fortress at Rastatt when the Prussians captured it but managed to escape to Switzerland, before re-entering Prussia under a disguise, springing his friend, the Bonn revolutionary Gottfried Kinkel, from jail and helping him to escape to Edinburgh. Schurz himself travelled to Paris and then emigrated to the United States, where he became an important Republican politician and played a command role on the Union side in the Civil War.

The dispersal of revolutionary energies now manifested itself as a dispersal of people. With exile came the risk of isolation and the depletion of purpose. The émigrés came up with many strategies for avoiding this. For the Romanians in exile after 1848, one historian has written, 'friendship and love' within networks of solidarity were crucial weapons against the anomie of exile.[18] They founded newspapers and clubs and gathered in cafés and restaurants run by compatriots. During his Ottoman exile, Kossuth proposed to create a Hungarian 'colony' near İzmir on the grounds that 'if we scatter around in the world, we will degrade to individuals, we will lose our corporate being, we will not represent anything . . .'[19] He succeeded in purchasing a suitable spot and raising funds, but the plan was stymied by the objections of the Austrians and the Russians. Jeanne Deroin continued to support workers' cooperatives from her perch in Shepherd's Bush and maintained an extensive correspondence with feminist networks in Britain, France and the United States. The boarding school she founded for the children of French exiles collapsed for lack of money, partly because she insisted on admitting children whose parents could not afford to pay fees. The former London Chartist leader William Cuffay, the son of a naval cook and a formerly enslaved woman, convicted on dubious evidence of sedition in 1848 and transported to Tasmania, remained on the island after his pardon in 1856 and became involved once more in radical politics and trade unionism.[20]

The political rifts that had bedevilled the revolutions often grew wider in exile. Kossuth's prominence and endless self-promotion excited the anger of other exiled leaders of the Hungarian emigration. Count Kázmér Batthyány, exiled in Paris, a distant cousin of the Lajos Batthyány executed for his role in the Hungarian revolutionary government, attacked Kossuth in *The Times*, suggesting that his 'impetuous and restless temper', his 'hankering after notoriety' and 'the inherent weakness of his character' were 'the main cause of the ruin and downfall of his country'.[21] In 1852, Bertalan Szemere, formerly interior minister of the Batthyány government and Prime Minister during Kossuth's brief regency in the summer of 1849, escaped into Turkey and later emigrated to Paris. In 1853, he published a tract denouncing Kossuth as a strutting mountebank and reckless gambler who presumed to give boastful speeches at the grave of the Hungarian nation without seeming to see that it had been brought there exclusively by his own errors.[22] Among the Italian patriots, too, there was a battle of pamphlets and memoirs, as key players vied to lay the blame on Piedmont, the republicans, the volunteers or the 'municipalism' of the Italian cities. Mazzini, who had returned to London via Marseilles and Switzerland, continued to plan doomed uprisings and refused to make common cause with the Piedmontese monarchy, now under the firm control of Victor Emmanuel II and his agile minister Camillo Benso, Count Cavour. Mazzini became a bystander in the historical events that would forge the new Italian kingdom.

There were as many roads out of revolution as there were into it. And this is as true of the inner journeys of the exiles as it is of their careers. Some, like Mazzini, just kept running the same political algorithms, as if nothing had happened. Others found secure niches in the new order or withdrew into political passivity or threw themselves into commercial ventures. Lamartine soon came to terms with the authoritarian regime of Napoleon III: 'I look the other way.' He never again held political office and spent most of the 1850s writing potboiling historical works in a (vain) effort to clear his debts.[23] Some socialists abandoned the political struggle altogether, or found new causes to expound, like Moses Hess, who later re-emerged as a theorist of Zionism. To Pierre-Joseph Proudhon, the disasters of 1848 suggested that what had doomed the revolution was the concentration of power in the executive; this revelation pushed him towards a principled hostility to the state that would establish him as one of the founding fathers of anarchism.[24]

For some who had passed through the collision chamber of revolution, making sense of what had happened, absorbing the shock and repairing the damage was an all-consuming task. The fall of the Roman Republic forced Cristina, Princess di Belgioioso, into exile, first on Malta, then in Constantinople and later in a remote location about 200 kilometres from Ankara, where she remained, except for an eleven-month sojourn in Jerusalem, until 1855. The first glimpse we get of her thoughts on what she had experienced date to the autumn of 1850, when she published redacted versions of her correspondence with a friend in the Parisian newspaper *Le National*. In a letter written from Malta, she reflected on the impact of the recent events. She planned, she told her friend, to 'embrace a new kind of life', a 'new existence that would cancel out the memory of the old'. Above all, she was going to have to 'alter the course of [her] ideas and break temporarily with politics'.[25] But what did it mean to 'alter the course of [one's] ideas' after a cataclysm like the fall of the Roman Republic?

In the essays she had written for the *Revue des Deux Mondes* after her flight from Milan in the summer of 1848, Belgioioso had offered an astute high-political appraisal of the weaknesses of the revolutionary Provisional Government, focusing on factional tensions and the mismatch between the demands of the city's predicament and the skills of the men thrust suddenly into positions of responsibility for addressing it. But when, from her Maltese exile, she came to reflect on her own experience of the Roman siege of summer 1849, the pattern of emphasis was quite different. She had nothing to say – neither praise nor criticism – about the men who had administered the city during the short life of the republic. Instead, she focused entirely on the women who had worked with her in the city's hospitals. For two months, Belgioioso wrote, she had worked amidst 'the most dramatic horrors and miseries'. Her headquarters was in the temporary military hospital at the Quirinale, meaning that her lodgings were in the papal palace; indeed, she was allocated one of the cells normally occupied by the cardinals during the conclave. The local women she recruited were not easy to work with: 'At Rome the masses of the people lack the slightest varnish of civilization, you would think they had sprung just yesterday from the jungles

Princess Cristina Trivulzio di Belgioioso, portrait by Henri Lehmann (1843). A brilliant commentator on the political history of the Milanese revolution, Belgioioso administered the emergency military hospitals of the beleaguered Roman republic. When the republic collapsed, she fled into Ottoman exile and turned her attention to the improvement of women's education.

of America.' The younger women were the worst: Belgioioso had to prowl the wards with a stick in her hand like a strict governess to guard against misdemeanours of every kind, from petty theft to sexual hanky-panky with the wounded men. Where was the Roman girl, she asked, who did not have lovers? Where was the Roman woman who did not seek pleasure with another when she grew bored of her husband? But there was more to say than that.

> All this notwithstanding, these ill-bred, disinhibited girls and women think neither of their interest nor of their comfort, they forget themselves, when a noble feeling inspires them. I have seen how the most depraved and corrupted women, once they approached the bedside of a dying man, refused to leave him, neither to eat nor to sleep, for three or four days in a row and just as many nights. I have seen them take on the hardest and most disgusting tasks, bending down over gangrenous and suppurating wounds, putting up with the oaths and caprices of unfortunates exasperated by suffering and accepting everything without showing disgust or impatience. And I have seen them remain indifferent and composed as musket balls, bullets and bombs flew in over their heads and whistled in their ears, so absorbed were they by caring for these bloodstained wrecks from the field of battle.[26]

This slightly backhanded eulogy to the Roman women was a response to the calumnies of papal anti-republican propaganda. In the encyclical *Nostis et Nobiscum* of 8 December 1849, Pius IX had expressed outrage that wounded men who died in hospital during the Roman siege had been 'deprived of all the help of religion and compelled to breathe their last in the arms of a wanton prostitute'.[27] Belgioioso had responded in a sarcastic open letter to the pontiff, pointing out that all of her hospitals had been staffed with priests, and that 'not one of the victims so rightly lamented by Your Holiness died without the assistance of a priest and the comfort of the sacraments'. If the Pope was unaware of this fact, she continued, his representatives were not, 'because as soon as the Cardinals assumed the powers that Your Holiness conferred on them, all the priests who had exercised their sacred ministry in the hospitals were thrown into the prisons of the Holy Office of the Inquisition'.[28]

The princess's letter for *Le National* offered a less frontal riposte to the papal calumny, feigning a concession on the point about sexual immorality, but then inverting it in defence of the women who had served her so well – a technique she often used in her writing. The capacity of working-class women for virtue and even for heroism was beyond doubt, she wrote in her letter from Malta. 'But how much longer must they be denied any education?'[29] After the collapse of the Italian revolutions, the education of women and girls came to occupy a central place in Belgioioso's writing. The two novellas she wrote in the orientalist mode during her long exile in the Ottoman Empire focused on this issue, deploying the conventional trope of intrusion by a stranger into the harem to puncture the mystique of the genre.[30] The harem, as Belgioioso depicted it, was not a haven for sensual and witty Scheherazades, but a space of poor hygiene and ennui inhabited by uneducated and narrow-minded women. Throughout *Emina, a Kurdish Prince* and *The Two Wives of Ismaïl Bey*, she combined conventional orientalist tropes with a critique of patriarchal institutions.[31] In the essay she dedicated to 'the present condition of women and their future' in 1866, Belgioioso focused almost exclusively on education as the key to overcoming their social and legal inferiority.[32] In short: after 1849, Belgioioso, a brilliant political analyst, pivoted away from the world of adversarial conflict in which men made their names and careers and turned towards literary writing and advocacy for the education of women. This was not a withdrawal from politics, but the substitution of one form of politics for another. The cultural advancement of women was as integral to societal progress as the concession of constitutions and liberal press laws, but it was not mediated by the masculine machinery of political reform that had been so central to the revolutions of 1848.

In September 1848, as relations between Pest and Vienna approached the point of irremediable breakdown, the moderate, Kossuth-critical reformer Count István Széchenyi suffered a nervous breakdown and withdrew to Vienna. He spent the next few years in a state of deep clinical depression at the mental asylum in Döbling. By 1857, he was recovering and ready to take up his pen. The provocation that motivated him to re-enter the fray was an anonymous propaganda treatise of 1857 praising the political evolution of Austria since the counter-revolution and justifying the repressive measures of the government. Rightly suspecting that the author was the former democrat Alexander Bach, who had ascended after the revolution to become the most powerful minister in the Habsburg government, Széchenyi published his own anonymous counter-treatise, a point-by-point take-down of Bach's book and its author. The text was tightly focused on the personality and motivations of the opponent; the tone was chatty, sarcastic and mocking. To Bach's claim that Austrian policies since 1849 had reduced inequality, for example, Széchenyi replied that in Hungary they had only achieved this by reducing all inhabitants of the kingdom to the same servile status.[33] A police investigation was launched in Vienna to identify and prosecute the unknown author of the tract. Pressure mounted on Széchenyi, but he was now too fragile to handle the consequences of exposure. On 8 April 1860, he shot himself in the head.

Dr Bach vs Count Széchenyi: what an emblematic stand-off. In one corner was a shrewd and talented bourgeois who had once ridden through Vienna on a white horse with a copy of the 'people's demands' to be presented to the Lower Austrian Estates at the Landhaus. Bach owed his ascendancy to the revolution and yet emerged from it as one of the embodiments of counter-revolution. As Minister of the Interior, this former democrat curbed freedom of the press, abandoned public trials and presided over the imposition of a 'neo-absolutist' system of centralized control. In the other corner was a Hungarian nobleman who owed nothing to the revolution except the collapse of his own mental health, had been ambivalent about the uprising from the outset, and had consistently opposed the adventurism of Kossuth. Széchenyi still believed ten years later that Hungary would have been better off if the revolution had never taken place.

For the radical priest Anton Füster, who denounced Bach in his memoirs as the 'Judas of German democracy', it seemed that there was suddenly nowhere in German Europe where a radical could feel at home.[34] As he fled from Austria via Dresden through Prussia to Hamburg and on to America, he recalled the patriotic song of Ernst Moritz Arndt, 'Was ist des Teutschen Vaterland?' In this text, which had become something of an unofficial national anthem by 1848, Arndt asks a sequence of rhetorical questions: 'What is the German's fatherland? Is it Swabia or the Prussian strand? Is it the Rhine, where the vineyards lie? Or the Baltic where the gulls do cry? Oh no! no! no! His Fatherland is greater still.'

Only a year ago [Füster wrote in 1849] we were solemnly singing [this song], but now it sounds different. 'What is the German's Fatherland?' Is it Austria? No, I had to flee from there. Is it Prussia? No, I was arrested there. Is it Saxony? No, I was expelled from that country. Is it Hanover or Bavaria? No, they both published 'wanted' posters bearing my name. Is it Hamburg's free city? No, it threw me out like a capricious prince. So where *is* the German Fatherland? In England and America! Only there can the German who refuses to see his freedom and honour suffocated by Russian, Prussian and Austrian bayonets find a secure and tranquil refuge![35]

Among the torments of political exile is the spectacle of others making themselves at home and flourishing under the new order. One of the most enigmatic and powerful reflections on what it meant to live in a post-revolutionary world was the novel *Political Fashions* (Politikai Divatok) by the Hungarian writer Mór Jókai. Jókai, a lawyer by training and a writer and dramatist by vocation, had been at the heart of the oppositional cultural scene of 1840s Pest. His first substantial novel, *Working Days* (Hétköznapok) had established him as the leading new voice in Hungarian fiction. He had collaborated with Kossuth on the *Pesti Hírlap*. His closest literary friend was the patriot and poet Sándor Petőfi. In March 1848, the two men, Petőfi at twenty-five and Jókai at twenty-three, were both members of the Society of Ten, a club started by Petőfi, whose members styled themselves 'Young Hungarians' in the Mazzinian manner. Jókai was initially a moderate liberal, but he supported Kossuth's break with Vienna and was present at the surrender of the Hungarian army to the Russians at Világos (now Şiria in Romania).

In 1861, a moment of short-lived political relaxation in Habsburg Hungary, Jókai resolved to write a novel that would 'recall the struggle for freedom':

I remembered the world of 48/49 vividly: all the great, small, tragic and comic figures of that era, full of glory and horror, lived there, haunted my soul: and I was naive enough to believe that all this could be raised from the ashes, from the mist.[36]

Out of this reckoning with the past came a novel full of false starts and narrative evasions, a novel that manoeuvres around the events of 1848 rather than addressing them directly; they are present only as a pressure on the emotional texture of the language. At the centre of the narrative, though his actual appearances in the novel are highly episodic and dispersed, is the character Pusztafi, a lightly disguised rendering of Petőfi. Pusztafi's striking physical appearance – 'a tall, muscular figure, with brown loose curls, a small moustache, and a Spanish goatee' – is strongly reminiscent of the dead poet; the playful insertion of the word *puszta* into his name identifies him with the ancestral landscape of the Hungarian steppe. The novel reimagines Petőfi's fate in 1849. Instead of being killed by the Cossacks at Segesvár (today Sighişoara in Romania), Petőfi/Pusztafi escapes with a wounded friend and takes refuge in a marsh, where he lies under the surface of the dark water, breathing air through a reed, as their Cossack pursuers splash about looking for them. His friend bleeds to death at his side, but Pusztafi escapes. And this improbable episode is prefaced in the novel by an evocation of the experience of submersion as a dreamlike suspension between past and present, as if Pusztafi's escape from the Cossacks were also a journey out of historical time:

> I am like the diver who walks on the bottom of the sea. Above, perhaps, there is a storm; sky and sea embrace, the giant monsters of fable beat their wings . . .; human battle mingles its voice with the roar of the storm; the sound of cannon, the breaking of masts, the collapse of galleys . . . There is nothing down here: the diver picks up the shells in which the pearls are growing, walks among the fauna of the seabed, and perhaps, if he finds a broken anchor with a torn rope in the red forest of coral, he will find a cannon sunk in mud, or a dead man whose face is so familiar . . . [37]

Having eluded his pursuers, Pusztafi disappears altogether from the narrative, except as an unsettling presence in the memories of the other characters. It is as if he has vanished from the face of the earth. But then, nine years later, at the very end of the book, on a 'cold October morning' – a significant detail, because it recalled the Austrian execution of thirteen Hungarian rebel generals, the 'Martyrs of Arad', on 6 October 1849 – Pusztafi makes a startling reappearance, accosting his old friend Béla Lávay. The returned poet is a wreck. His hair and beard are matted and 'more white than black', his clothes soiled, his stature heavy, his brow furrowed, his face florid, 'as with one who comforts himself with strong drink'.[38] Entering his friend's apartment, he is delighted to find that there are no mirrors: 'There are many faces in the world that I would not be happy to meet; foremost among them is my own. I haven't looked in a mirror in nine years.' Pusztafi confides to his friend that he drinks to numb himself against the pain of memory: 'When a memory of the past strikes me . . ., a glass of wine down the neck and it goes to sleep'. When Béla tries to buck him up by reminding him that a man does not live for himself alone but also for his country, Pusztafi coughs violently and produces the following peroration:

> His country? Hahaha! Would you please explain what that is, a town, or a county, or the whole district of a governorate? Consider that I was born in the Vojvodina. Or do you mean a larger country than that? . . . Are you talking about my narrower country or my broader country? Because I don't know which of them I signed a promissory note to live for.

It quickly becomes clear that Pusztafi is ill equipped for life in the present. He gives voice to a sense of radical dissociation from his social environment: 'You are not the sort of people for me', he tells his friend. 'I want men who hate me, who pull their chairs away when I sit down among them, who plug their ears when I speak . . .' Did this scene convey an implicit critique of Pusztafi for failing to expatriate himself from the past? Was it a critique of the suppression of memory that came in the wake of the Austrian counter-revolution?[39] Or was it a denunciation of a society that had estranged itself from the recent past and was unable to assimilate one of its most emblematic representatives? In the manner of all good novelists, Jókai abstains from an explicit adjudication, but he puts eloquent words into the mouth of his broken hero: 'If there were the slightest trace of pride left in the people of this country', Pusztafi remarks, then 'every man would walk through the street with his head bowed low. Is it not the highest expression of human insolence that "we" are still alive?'[40] A few pages later Pusztafi walks out through a door and is never seen again. He is an exile, not because he has left his country, but because he has returned to it. His sense of radical alienation from the present is an indictment of those who have made comfortable accommodations with the 'new normal' of the post-revolutionary world. Thus Mór Jókai captured both the watershed character of the revolutions and the sense of homelessness that afflicted those who, having risked everything in 1848, outlived the collapse of their hopes.

GLOBAL 1848

What happened when the news of revolution passed beyond the margins of Europe into the wider world? The revolutions of 1848 took place before the age of the transoceanic telegraphs. The announcement that a republic had been proclaimed in France reached New York by the steamship *Cambria* on 18 March 1848, just as the revolution in Berlin was beginning. It took around thirty days for news to get from Paris by packet boat to Martinique. It was not until Monday, 19 June 1848, that the citizens of Sydney in the colony of New South Wales could read of the February Revolution four months earlier. Did these exorbitant delays make a difference to how the revolution was received and processed? Longer and more complex routes and conflicting reports from different sources made confusion more likely. In July 1848, the *Sydney Morning Herald* reported that a general European war had broken out (the story was later retracted), and in Jamaica reports that Queen Victoria had gone to the Isle of Wight mutated into rumours that she had been forced to abdicate.[41] But long distances also transformed the temporal texture of the news, which arrived in large packets of newspapers that might carry a week or a month of editions. And this meant that to readers in Kingston, Cape Town, Auckland or Sydney, the chronology of the revolutions seemed even more compressed than they did to *in situ* contemporaries. Distance attenuated the immersive euphoria of the eyewitness, offering instead a clearer view of the historical shape of events.

Yet even across great distances the report of events in Europe made a deep impression. The news from France, the *New York Herald* declared on 20 March:

> are on every tongue and palpitating in every bosom of this great metropolis. The excitement during the last two days has been most tremendous and the public feeling has expressed itself in every possible way – celebration, the hanging out of flags, speeches and congratulations of all kinds, have occupied the people for the last forty hours.[42]

On 30 May, the liberal *El Mercurio* of Valparaiso in Chile was exultant:

> The French revolution of 1848, ... led by enlightenment and sanctioned by religion, will bring to Chile true liberty, and even if the most unheard-of forces assemble to contain this spirit and this feeling which has been germinating in the land for so long, it is rising today with such freshness and vigour that nothing will be able to oppose its development.[43]

As we move away from Europe, 'impact' becomes a less pertinent metaphor. Even within Europe, we have seen that there was no straight-forward 'diffusion' of content from hubs to peripheries. Time-lags across dispersed theatres generated counter-currents that militated against a convergence of revolutionary impulses. What, one might ask, was being diffused or received when the news of revolution crossed oceans? Even those upheavals whose development was relatively closely synchronized could evolve into an antipathetic relationship with each other. This problem was especially salient in central Europe, where conflicting programmes focused on national or ethnic empowerment sometimes pitted revolutionaries against each other, obscuring the common impulses that had once shaped their respective struggles. The politically conflicted character of the revolutions confronted responders in remote locations with choices. With which strand of the revolution should they engage? With the radical revolution of democrats and socialists, or the gradualist revolution of the liberals? The fast politics of streets, clubs and rallies, or the slow politics of constitutionally elected chambers? The Hungarian struggle against Austria, or the Croat struggle against Hungary? There was no single issue at the heart of the revolutions, but rather a multitude of questions – about democracy, representation, social equality, the organization of labour, gender relations, religion, forms of state power, among many other things – and an even greater multitude of competing answers. This, too, complicates the task of tracing the revolutions' impact on the wider world.

We have seen that in Martinique and Guadeloupe, colonial possessions of France, the news of the February Revolution was read through the lens of the abolition question, and not just by the enslaved but also by the white and mixed-race elites.[44] But even here, where the case for impact appears unshakeable, the unfolding of emancipation resists linear narratives. The arrival of the news from Paris intersected with self-organized insular movements of the enslaved, who took matters into their own hands. And once this happened, processes of inter-island signalling triggered sympathetic upheavals on nearby islands under different imperial jurisdictions. And yet signals from the centre remained important. Spain, an important Caribbean stakeholder, offers a telling contrast: here there was no official decision to emancipate. The uprisings of 1848 in continental Spain were swiftly crushed by the *moderado* government under Narváez. As a result, slavery survived in the Spanish Caribbean. On the other hand, in those Latin American countries – now independent republics – that had once been Spanish colonies, the shock effect of the February Revolution in *Paris* sufficed to set in train a cascade of initiatives that by the mid 1850s had abolished what remained of slavery in Peru, Argentina, Ecuador, Colombia, Bolivia and Venezuela.[45]

When actors in remote locations responded to the tidings of revolution, they often did so because they saw in them the vindication of claims they were already making. In the United States, for example, once the initial wave of excitement had subsided, public discussion of the revolution was filtered through American partisan alignments. On 29 March, Senator William Allen (Ohio) moved that the Senate formally congratulate the French people 'upon their success in their recent efforts to consolidate liberty by imbodying [sic] its principles in a republican form of government'. There might well have been very wide support for this proposal, but on the following day when debate on Allen's resolution began, Senator John P. Hale (New Hampshire) proposed an amendment in which the French were additionally congratulated for 'manifesting the sincerity of their purpose by instituting measures for the immediate emancipation of the slaves of all the colonies of the republic'. It was this amendment that brought the pro-slavery senators into open opposition. Senator John Calhoun (South Carolina) spoke against it, conceding archly that the upheaval was 'a wonderful event – the most striking in my opinion, in history', but adding that the real test of a revolution was whether or not it continued to 'guard against violence and anarchy'; since this test had not yet been passed, 'the time [had] not yet arrived for congratulation'.[46]

The same issue would dog the Hungarian patriot Lajos Kossuth after his arrival in New York on 5 December 1851. Kossuth had come in search of American money and diplomatic support for the now militarily defunct Hungarian cause against the Austrian Empire. He was a superstar, mobbed by jubilant crowds in almost every town he visited; Indiana, Mississippi and Ohio named towns for him and his fans turned up wearing Hungarian-style fur hats and boots. But when, a few weeks after his arrival, a delegation of African Americans visited him and asked him to say a few words in support of the abolitionist cause, Kossuth refused, fearing that taking sides in such a contentious question might alienate potential high-value donors. The result of this reticence was a famous letter of rebuke in *The Liberator*, penned by its abolitionist editor, William Lloyd Garrison:

> It was natural that the uncompromising advocates of impartial liberty should look to you for at least one word of sympathy and approval, – at least an incidental expression of grief and shame at the existence of a bondage so frightful, in a land so boastful of its freedom. . . . Deplorable as it is, the relation of your countrymen to the Austrian government is incomparably more hopeful, a million times less appalling, then that of our slave population to the American government; yet you invoke for the Hungarians the sympathy of the civilized world . . .[47]

Precisely the issue that had aligned abolitionist US senators with the French Republic now drove a wedge between the anti-slavery movement and the charismatic representative of the failed Hungarian national struggle.[48] Although Kossuth remained a crowd-puller, there was deepening ambivalence about the liberal and revolutionary credentials of the Hungarian cause. A long and perceptive piece published by Francis Bowen in his *North American Review* in 1850 argued that the Hungarian struggle was not 'a republican or independence war' at all, but rather 'an attempt on the part of the Magyar untitled nobility, 600,000 in number, to preserve the ancient feudal Constitution of the state, which guaranteed their aristocratic privileges and the dominion of their race'. This, the author argued, was hardly a programme with a legitimate claim upon American sympathies.[49]

Studies of 1848 in the United States have revealed many different kinds of reception and transfer. The American feminist and abolitionist Lucretia Mott observed in August 1848 that the Seneca Indians were 'learning somewhat from the political agitations abroad and . . . are imitating the movements of France and all Europe in seeking a larger liberty . . .', and the speakers at the Seneca Falls Convention in July

1848 – the first American women's rights convention – were quite explicit in connecting their claims with events across the Atlantic.[50] The key works of the American Renaissance of the 1850s, from *The Scarlet Letter* to *Moby-Dick* and *Leaves of Grass*, were all deeply in dialogue with the recent events across the Atlantic.[51] Americans were well informed about the events in Europe and could pick and choose from the revolutionary menu. Senator John Calhoun, for example, was more impressed by the German revolutionaries in Frankfurt than by the French revolutionaries in Paris, because he admired the seriousness of their federalism and their interest in states' rights.[52] 1848 elicited many kinds of response from many parts of the American political landscape, reframing old debates, accelerating processes of political differentiation, and generating effects so diverse and dispersed that summarizing them is difficult.[53]

The exiles of 1848 were, of course, part of this story. The influx of German radical exiles after the collapse of the revolutions had a deep impact on the evolving fabric of mid-century labour organization in the United States.[54] The Polish and Hungarian refugee colonies in Istanbul were crucial to the infusion of nationalist ideas into the political culture of the city.[55] In Britain, 'democ-soc' ideas were absorbed into the radical movement, even if the antisocialist messaging of Kossuth and Mazzini, titans of public communication, tended to crowd out the low-key appeal of Louis Blanc and his vision of a state-organized labour force, while the quarrels and schisms among the exiles weakened their impact on British radicals.[56] Mathilde Franziska Anneke is an interesting case. Together with her husband Fritz, she had taken part in the Baden insurrection, acting as a mounted messenger for the insurgent forces. When the Prussians captured Rastatt in the summer of 1849, she and Fritz fled to the United States, where she established the first woman-owned feminist periodical in the country, the *Deutsche Frauen-Zeitung*, which addressed itself to the women of the then very large German-speaking population. In Anneke's case, the impact travelled in both directions across the Atlantic. Having separated from her husband, Mathilde and her life companion, Mary Booth, who had also separated from hers, returned to Europe and formed a 'bicultural writing team' advocating an agenda that encompassed both the abolition of slavery and women's rights.[57]

These intercontinental resonances were possible in part because

imperial structures, post-colonial social and cultural ties, migrant diasporas and common institutions still connected the metropolitan theatres
of revolution with numerous remote locations and societies. The British
Empire is a good example. We have seen that Britain protected itself
against upheaval by adopting policies that pacified home populations
but heightened tensions on the imperial periphery, such as the transportation of potential troublemakers to Australia and the Cape Colony, or
abandoning the sugar tariffs that protected colonial planters in Jamaica
and British Guyana from external competition.[58] In Ceylon, the introduction of new taxes to meet administrative costs without burdening
British middle-class taxpayers triggered the emergence of a protest
movement that soon encompassed around 60,000 men. Here, a new
land law, the Waste Land Ordinance of 1840, had asserted the Crown's
control over the commons, wastes and forests, enabling marginal lands
to be placed under coffee at the cost of the poorest peasants. There were
analogies here with those European rural communities disturbed by the
privatization of commons and forests.

But the intensification of cultivation in these areas required the construction of new roads.[59] At around the same time, the new head of the
Colonial Office laid out new guidelines for taxation, in which he argued
that taxation ought to favour those branches of trade and industry
'which require the direction of civilized and educated men, such as the
production of sugar and coffee', and 'so far as prudence will admit',
press 'rather upon those who are content with a mere subsistence than
upon the possessors of property and the purchasers of luxuries'.[60] Under
strict instructions to balance the colony's budgets and thus lighten the
burden on British taxpayers, Lord Torrington, the governor of Ceylon,
rushed new taxes into law, including a Road Ordinance that required the
inhabitants either to pay a road tax of three shillings per adult male or
to render labour services on the island's roads. The burden thus fell disproportionately on the poorest families, who could not afford to
commute their services. And many of these were already suffering from
the effects of the suppression of commons usage rights.[61] The consequence was a wave of rioting in the Kandyan areas of Ceylon's interior
in 1848, to which the British authorities responded with exactly the kind
of overkill that would later be seen on Cephalonia. Over 200 Kandyans
were slain in counter-insurgency actions; there were eighteen executions,
fifty-eight floggings and one hundred imprisonments and deportations.[62]

In the longer term, disruptions like this across the imperial periphery would produce constitutional adjustments that transformed the relationship between Westminster and its colonies.[63]

This franchising out of political contention to the periphery reminds us that the potential for conflict could be transmitted in many ways. The global traffic in news was part of the story. The leaders of the tax protests in Ceylon cited the overthrow of the French monarch, Louis Philippe, in February 1848 as a model worthy of emulation by those who toiled under the yoke of colonial rule; New Zealand radicals in Wellington held banquets on the French model and Henry Parkes, a campaigner for Australian franchise reform, eulogized the French leader Alphonse de Lamartine.[64] But the nexus of empire complicates the story, because these episodes of colonial turbulence were not just echoes of Europe's 1848; they were rooted in the pressures generated by British measures to pre-empt a revolution on the mainland.

In far-off New South Wales, the editors of the *Sydney Morning Herald* were quick to see the link between tranquillity in the mother country and tumult on the periphery. Why, they asked in October 1848, when they learned at last of the bloodshed of the June Days in Paris, had Britain escaped the bloodshed that had recently disfigured Paris? The answer lay in the fact that Britain possessed settler *colonies* – 'those vast outfields wherein her redundant masses may find the sustenance which they cannot find at home'.[65] The drawback of this model was that the very colonial appendages that insulated Britain against unrest also conducted the spirit of revolt outward, towards the edge of the British world. The paper returned to this theme in 1854, when an uprising broke out on the goldfields around Ballarat in the Australian colony of Victoria. A campaign by the Ballarat Reform League against heavy-handed policing and the high cost of miners' licences culminated on 3 December 1854 in an encounter between miners and mounted troops at the 'Battle of the Eureka Stockade', in which around thirty-five perished, most of them miners. The *Sydney Morning Herald* deplored the lawlessness of the Victorian diggers. But it added that upheavals of this kind were inevitable on the periphery of an empire whose solution to the problem of 'loose and disorderly populations' at the centre was to throw them at regular intervals 'off to its outskirts'.[66] Two weeks later, the newspaper developed the point in more depth. It appeared, the editors noted, 'that the bulk of the insurgents were southern Irish and foreigners'.

The leaders did not understand our British principle of moral force and Constitutional agitation ... They adopted the plan with which they were the most familiar, that of revolution and red republicanism. You will observe that the secretary of Mazzini was there, and Vern, the Hanoverian, for whom a reward of £500 is offered, was, it is said, one of the June heroes of Paris.[67]

The 'secretary of Mazzini' was Raffaello Carboni, a native of Urbino who had fought for the Roman Republic under Mazzini and Garibaldi in 1849, before fleeing to London and thence to Melbourne. Carboni's chatty, meandering book, *The Eureka Stockade*, published in 1855, became the only complete first-hand printed account of the insurrection.[68] 'Vern the Hanoverian' was Friedrich Wern, a German radical who had fled continental Europe after the revolutions and had travelled to Victoria as a ship's mate. Wern absconded from the Stockade to avoid capture and ran off into the bush. As far as I know, he was never seen again; the Victoria Government offered the huge sum of £500 as a reward for his capture, but to no avail.

There was massive public support for the arrested miners during the subsequent trials and Eureka became a focal point for groups in Australian society seeking constitutional reform. Within two years of the fighting at Ballarat, the governments of Victoria and New South Wales were forced to concede universal male suffrage, the secret ballot and a reduction in the property qualification for holders of public office. 'The mechanisms for future change had been established.'[69] But if 1848 was part of the Eureka story, its impact transmitted on this occasion through the presence of exiles and transportees, it was only a small part. A movement to secure franchise reform already existed in New South Wales and Victoria, whose intellectual substance had more to do with the rights of 'freeborn Englishmen', as expounded by John Lilburne, Richard Overton, John Milton and John Locke, than with continental radical traditions. The memory of 1848 could only play a role here because it merged temporarily with the efforts of local interests to secure local objectives.

In Peru, the news of revolution in Paris resonated with local debates over suffrage: whereas conservatives preferred to retain a tax qualification that prevented the majority from voting, liberals demanded franchise expansion. It was the latter who saw in the European revolutions an incitement to action: 'It is not possible to remain stationary when the entire world is moving', declared the liberal *El Comercio* of Lima in January 1849. 'In Europe they are tearing down thrones amidst torrents of blood . . . Should we be sleeping?'[70] Liberal journalists were cheered by the prominence of the press as an agent of political change. 'For the first time', the editors of *El Zurriago* declared, the press 'was achieving the purpose for which it was destined in this world, namely, to serve as the vehicle for the liberty of the human race.'[71] Liberal, radical and conservative arguments circulated in a Lima public sphere that had greatly increased in density and sophistication since around 1840.[72]

In Santiago de Chile, the ideas of 1848 arrived before the revolutions had even happened, in the form of a book. A cult sprang up around Lamartine's epic three-volume *Histoire des Girondins*, which arrived in Valparaiso in February 1848. A group of prominent liberals met in the offices of the newspaper *El Progreso* to read it aloud; early copies were sold for six ounces of gold apiece, enough to buy a small library; Lamartine was venerated as 'a demigod, like Moses'. His work was an epic account of the *first* French Revolution composed in the high romantic style with many fanciful inventions, but it was read as 'a prophetic book', a key to the present. Prominent members of the liberal and radical intelligentsia adopted the names of his characters as pseudonyms.[73] The extraordinary impact of Lamartine's *Girondins* reminds us that 1848 was susceptible to a historicized contemporary understanding in a way that its great predecessor had not been. It was not just that Madrid could no longer filter the information available to literate Chileans, it was the fact that a mental template existed against which to anticipate, interpret and 'understand' the mid-century revolutions as a piece of history unfolding in the present.

It is not easy to quantify intellectual excitement, and even harder to measure its impact on events and structures, but the emergence of new associations in Santiago, such as the Reform Club in 1849 and the Society for Equality in 1850, and the creation of a new campaigning periodical (*El Amigo del Pueblo*) suggest that the discussions triggered by the news of the continental revolutions concentrated and sharpened Chilean radicalism as a system of 'principles, symbols, ideas and images'. At the same time, they consolidated a liberal milieu whose members would later occupy the highest public offices of Chilean institutional life. The liberal Chile that emerged in the last three decades of the century was largely conceived in this moment.[74] A key figure in this transition was the writer and liberal politician Francisco Bilbao Barquin. Bilbao was living in Paris when the revolution broke out and returned to Chile in 1850, where he founded the Society of Equality and led an unsuccessful insurrection against the government in 1851. On the other hand, Bilbao was not a mere conduit conveying ideas from the revolutionary centre to the American periphery: during his sojourn in Paris, he had been a purveyor of Latin American republican ideas.[75] The 'waves' that crossed the Atlantic moved in both directions and generated highly diverse effects. Félix Frías, an Argentinian intellectual in exile in Paris from 1848 to 1853, was propelled in the other direction by the spectacle of revolution, which transformed him into an enemy of working-class libertarian socialism.[76] In the immediate aftermath of 1848, liberal Mexican coverage of Lajos Kossuth and his revolution tended to stress Magyar xenophobia and the oppression of non-Magyar nationalities; a decade later we find radical journalists invoking the Hungarian 1848 revolution as a model for Mexico's struggle for political freedom.[77]

Even the Brazilian Praieira Revolt of 1848–51, which combined protest over social inequalities and precarious land tenures with a language of liberal dissent that invoked European precedents, was the culmination of a feud that had been smouldering for some years between liberal and conservative patronage networks. It was concentrated in parts of the province of Pernambuco where the fall in international sugar prices and punitive British tariffs on slave-produced goods, combined with cotton blight and a prolonged drought, pushed parts of the rural population into severe distress. The rebels' demands focused almost exclusively on local grievances, and the violence of the uprising in the coastal towns owed much to resentment and hatred of the Portuguese commercial and business elites, who were attacked under the slogans 'Liberty, Equality and Fraternity'. The radical editor of the Recife journal O Progresso, Antônio Pedro de Figueiredo, welcomed the February Revolution in Paris, but he also warned that it would be a mistake to import the terms 'liberty' and 'fraternity' to Brazil, on the grounds that they could have no traction in a society so profoundly structured by highly coercive forms of clientelism.[78]

One could examine further cases of resonance across Latin America without greatly enhancing the picture that has already emerged: charismatic individuals, newspapers and printed books carried the drama and ideas of revolution to remote locations, triggering waves of euphoria and enthusiasm, but also critique and resistance. How these played out in the longer term depended upon processes of contestation already underway in the receiving location. And in differentiated public spheres the spectacle of revolution tended to trigger responses that were nuanced, selective and ambivalent. If there was intense interest in the European revolutions in the Ottoman Empire, for example, this was not simply because the government saw in them a potential threat to order, but because in the era of the Tanzimat reforms (1839–76) a complex discussion was already underway on the meanings of legal equality, political cohesion, constitutionalism and 'fraternity'.[79]

If we compare the impact of 1848 worldwide with the transformative power of the transatlantic revolutions of the axial era between the 1770s and the end of the Napoleonic Empire, then the global balance of the 1848 revolutions may appear rather modest. But this contrast is only meaningful if we exclude from view the enormous political and social impact of warfare. Between 1792 and 1815 the continent was wracked by wars in which vast conscript armies were pitted against each other, with correspondingly enormous casualties. France intervened against Britain in the American War of Independence; Britain joined with the other continental powers in attempting to contain first revolutionary and later Napoleonic France. Across the wider world, many places, from India and the Caribbean to Egypt and Java, were flexed by conflict among the great powers.

The revolutions of 1848 were not born in war. For all their cruelty, the wars sparked by the revolutions in Italy, southern Germany and Hungary were counter-revolutionary police actions that, for the most part, came to an end once 'order' had been restored. They tended to shut the revolution down, rather than to diffuse its ideology. A continental revolutionary power capable of projecting and embodying ideology by force of arms in the manner of 1790s or Napoleonic France never emerged. This is not to say that the mid nineteenth century was an era of global tranquillity: the opposite is true. This was a period of 'endemic worldwide violence', in which warfare was dispersed, decentred and mostly of low intensity. What was distinctive about these years, and so different from the previous revolutionary wave, was the lack of any 'grand design or central nervous system' linking them.[80]

And this helps to explain why the causal linkages become so much weaker once we leave the jurisdictions of the European states and their empires. It is tempting to imagine that there must have been a connection of some kind between the European revolutions of 1848 and the largest single non-European upheaval of that era, the Taiping Rebellion (1850–64) – an immense civil war between the Qing Dynasty and the millenarian movement of the Heavenly Kingdom of Peace that cost between twenty million and thirty million lives. And yet it has not so far been possible to find any evidence at all for a direct link to the mid-century upheavals in the European cities.[81] 'There is nothing to suggest', one historian has written, 'that the Taiping rebels in China had heard a word about the 1848 revolution in Europe.'[82] This is emphatically not an argument against the importance of the revolutions of 1848. But it is a reminder that there is an enormous difference between writing a history of the revolutions that is alert to global resonances and writing a global history of the year in which they happened.[83]

In 1848, the tidings of revolution had to travel in civilian clothes. They reverberated in cafés and political clubs, circulating in communicative networks that were incomparably denser, socially deeper and more sophisticated than their late-eighteenth-century predecessors. The unpredictable, many-cornered conversations that resulted were the fruit of an era of spectacular intellectual biodiversity. The processes of change that resulted were not less deep or important than after 1789 – they were just more subtle.

NEW CONSTELLATIONS

How different was the political life of the European states after the revolutions of 1848? We have seen that in many parts of Europe harsh repressions followed. Prominent revolutionary personalities fled into exile; others were deported or imprisoned. Press restrictions returned. Police forces expanded and the sphere of their responsibilities grew. Surveillance networks at home and abroad were bigger and better organized than they had been in the age of Metternich. In many of the cities that had seen turbulence in 1848, there were concerted efforts to erase the memory of insurrection from public awareness.

Yet there was no return to the pre-revolutionary *status quo ante*. Too much had changed. The most obvious novelties were the new constitutions. In states that had possessed no constitution at all before 1848, these marked a new point of departure, because they brought with them the entire apparatus of modern representative politics: parliaments, parties, election campaigns and the publication of parliamentary debates. And, almost everywhere, the advent or reform of constitutions had a stabilizing effect. The Dutch constitutional reform (*Grondwetsherziening*) of 1848 moved the centre of gravity from the king and his ministers to the electorate and the Second Chamber of parliament, establishing the foundations for the present system of parliamentary democracy in the Netherlands.[84] The Danish constitution was the most democratic of all: it stipulated that both houses of parliament were to be elected by a virtually universal male suffrage and dramatically curtailed the prerogatives of the monarchy. This was nothing short of a constitutional revolution – it transformed Denmark from an absolutist monarchy into one of the most democratic political cultures in the world. In Piedmont, the constitution (*Statuto Albertino*) granted in March 1848 proved a more dynamic and open-ended compromise than most contemporaries could have predicted. Even the imposed Prussian constitution of December 1848 was a new point of departure: it was popular with the great majority of liberals and many of the moderate conservatives.[85]

At the other end of the constitutional spectrum were Austria and France. In the Austrian Empire, the new emperor, Franz Joseph, rescinded the constitution of 1849 by means of the New Year's Eve Patent of 31 December 1851. The Patent reaffirmed the principles of the equality of all citizens before the law and the abolition of servile land tenures, but declared that the constitution of 4 March 1849 was otherwise annulled. It announced that there would henceforth be no constitution; instead, suitable laws would emerge in due course through the wisdom of 'experience' and the 'painstaking examination of all conditions'.[86] The French constitution of 14 January 1852 was a characteristically Bonapartist document devised to officialize the recent coup d'état against the Second Republic. It 'recognized, confirmed and guaranteed the principles proclaimed in 1789' and reasserted the 'sovereignty' of the people. But it also concentrated sweeping powers in the hands of the president, assisted by a Council of State under his chairmanship and control. The upper house of parliament (Senate) was a chamber of presidential appointees; the lower house could neither amend laws nor censure the actions of the ministers.[87]

In all of these states, there was a deep change in the tone and shape of politics. In the parliaments of Prussia, Piedmont and the Netherlands, a coalition of interests emerged, through which flexible conservatives and liberals could cooperate in reformist projects. In Piedmont, the first post-revolutionary elections in the winter of 1849/1850 produced an overwhelming majority of moderate liberal deputies. Of the 204 electoral colleges of the Kingdom of Piedmont-Sardinia, 123 chose moderate candidates and 38 chose candidates of the centre-left. Only 43 selected candidates of the radical left. The deputies who sat in that chamber during the first legislative period included no fewer than 96 lawyers. Under these circumstances, a parliamentary challenge from the radicals was out of the question.[88] Count Camillo di Cavour, who had once been known for his eccentrically reactionary and confrontational politics, now occupied a position on the 'centre-right' (a term that only entered circulation after 1849). His newspaper, *Il Risorgimento*, celebrated an epoch of 'press and judicial freedom, of the free and broad activity of our institutions, of a government simultaneously progressive and strong, of debate that is lively but full of ideas, serene in spirit and upright in its intentions'.[89]

In 1852, Cavour entered an alliance with the former democrat Urbano Rattazzi, who, like Cavour, had moved to the centre, but from the other direction. Having left the Democrats for the Moderate Liberals, Rattazzi became the leader of the 'centre-left'. Known as the *connubio*, or 'marriage', the ideologically flexible coalition between Cavour and Rattazzi enabled the government to secure parliamentary support for modernizing initiatives.[90] Among the forces holding this new consensus together was a shared hostility to the political ambitions of the Catholic Church. Monastic religious orders were suppressed, measures were introduced to limit the political influence of the clergy and there was a partial secularization of Church property. By this means, the kingdom set itself apart from the Papal and Bourbon south, where Catholic-reactionary forces ruled the roost after 1848.[91] Piedmont became one of the first states to experience the culture war between anticlericals and Catholics that would engulf Europe during the second half of the nineteenth century. It is a mark of the robustness of the new system that, far from endangering the post-revolutionary consensus, the feuding between ultramontane Catholics and anticlericals brought a form of conflictual stability, replacing the old antipathy between left and right with a politico-cultural cleavage that, for all its bitterness, could play itself out without destabilizing the system. The new constitutional settlement in the Netherlands had a similar system-stabilizing effect, allowing Liberals, Protestants and Catholics to skirmish over culture war issues like schooling and religious processions without undermining the post-revolutionary political order.[92]

The Kingdom of Saxony, scene of one of the most impressive 'second-wave' mobilizations of 1849, witnessed a relatively drastic counter-revolution: in July 1850, a coup d'état dissolved the Landtag elected at the end of 1849, recalled the old Diet under the unreformed constitution of 1831, suspended the laws adopted during the revolutionary months, suppressed the liberal and democratic associations, and subjected the press and all public meetings to strict controls. The opposition luminaries of 1840 largely withdrew from political life. And yet here, too, a coalition formed within the Diet between old liberals and reformist conservatives, enabling the authoritarian minister of state, Friedrich von Beust, to modernize the judiciary and the administration and to push through reformist measures such as the liquidation of seigneurial rights in the countryside. Under Beust, one historian has written, the Landtag sank to the status of a mere 'notary', charged with validating the new contract between the state and society.[93] And yet the minister's technocratic reforms, like those of many of his colleagues elsewhere, aimed to pre-empt further tumult by drawing selectively on the deactivated project of 1848.

Even within the highly authoritarian setting created by Louis Napoleon's coup d'état in France, something new emerged. The stability of the regime that would soon call itself the Second Empire depended not just upon coercion (though that was also important in the early years) but upon its ability to construct a consensus from the post-1848 remnants of moderate republicanism and constitutional monarchism. In this respect, the 'Bonapartism' of the post-revolutionary period was quite distinct from its pre-revolutionary predecessor – it was a more 'composite' entity, in which leftist elements flowed together with forces of order seeking firm government.[94] Even in Austria, where counter-revolutionary measures were especially severe, the policies adopted by the 'neo-absolutist' administrations of the 1850s reflected a new order of priorities that took account of a much broader range of social and economic interests than the policies pursued by Austrian administrations before 1848. Here, the post-revolutionary decade was 'not restorative at all, but innovative, on a broad front, with a clear and ambitious programme'.[95] The severity of the counter-revolution militated against constitutional freedoms, but the limited municipal autonomy secured in 1848 was retained, as was the emancipation of the monarchy's peasantries, which itself necessitated a major restructuring as the authorities got to work creating the monarchy's first centralized and fully standardized administration.[96]

A similar pattern can be discerned in Spain and Portugal. In mid-nineteenth-century Iberian politics, the key fault line did not run between liberals and conservatives, but between authoritarian and radical brands of liberalism. The authoritarian-liberal option was epitomized by the *moderados* of Narváez, who had responded so ruthlessly to the Spanish uprisings of 1848. Only in 1854 would an upheaval break out in Spain whose scope compared with those of 1848 in the rest of Europe.[97] The Spanish administrations that emerged after 1854 conformed to the pattern we see elsewhere in Europe. First there was the period of unstable coalition government known as the 'Bienio Progresista' (1854–6). When this collapsed in the political crisis of 1856, it was succeeded by an entirely new force in Spanish politics. Known originally as the 'parliamentary centre' and later as the Unión Liberal, it was built around a coalition of left-wing *moderados* and pragmatic radicals, supplemented by a cohort of younger political figures with 'eclectic and centrist attitudes'.[98] It developed a composite programme, in which the traditional social and constitutional conservatism of the *moderados* were juxtaposed with progressive reformist impulses (especially in the sphere of economic policy). The aim, according to a leader article in the *Época*, the organ of the Unión, was to 'establish the constitutional system in a solid way, without the exaggerations of the left, the disorders of democracy and the excesses of reaction'. It was only fitting that the new entity should find itself under attack from disaffected figures on both right and left.[99]

In neighbouring Portugal, two episodes of acute upheaval, the Revolution of Maria da Fonte in 1846 followed by the Patuleia of 1846–7, set the scene for the emergence in 1851 of a new regime under Field Marshal Saldanha. Saldanha adopted the name Regeneração (Regeneration) for his government, whose ministry was composed of a 'strange coalition' of prominent centrist figures from both camps and liberalized the old conservative constitution by incorporating some of the demands of the opposition (including direct elections and the abolition of the death penalty).[100] The political system thereby established was known as *rotativismo* because it involved the rotation of power between the two main political factions.[101] There followed a period of political stability unparalleled in Portugal between the Napoleonic invasion and the later twentieth century.[102]

In short, the precise form taken by the new political constellation varied according to constitutional conditions, but across the European states the agenda was set by a post-revolutionary rapprochement that proved capable of answering to the aspirations of the more moderate elements of the old progressives and of the more innovative and entrepreneurial elements among the old conservative elites.[103] So effective was this post-revolutionary order in controlling the middle-ground of politics that it successfully marginalized both the democratic left and the old right. In Spain, the accommodationist *resellados* of the Progressive movement joined the Unión Liberal, while the left-wing *puros* were left sulking on the margins.[104] The same fate awaited those radicals (*setembristas*) in Portugal who refused to make their peace with the new dominant coalition. In France, the radical elements of the old republicanism were marginalized as the post-revolutionary regime consolidated its popular base.[105]

The old ultra-conservatives faced the same fate. Most of the French responded to the pretensions of 'Henri V', the Bourbon pretender, or 'Louis Philippe II' with yawning indifference. In Piedmont, Prussia and Austria, the old aristocratic right – the *Hoch-* or *Altkonservativen*, or the *codini*, as they were known in northern Italy – were displaced and set aside. Cavour's 'marriage' with Ratazzi alienated and isolated the old aristocratic right of which he had once himself been an intermittent representative. In Spain, the feebleness of the Carlist rebellion of 1855 demonstrated how isolated the extreme right now was.[106] The politics of the traditional conservatism, with its pious attachment to corporatist structures, now appeared narrow, self-interested and retrograde. In abolishing what remained of the old 'feudalism', the post-revolutionary administrations broke their old pact with the landed aristocracies. It was unthinkable, the Prussian Minister-President Otto von Manteuffel pointed out to the conservative rural opponents of fiscal reform, that the Prussian state should continue to be run 'like the landed estate of a nobleman'.[107]

In Wallachia, the Princely Lieutenancy established under Suleiman Pasha was cut short by the military intervention of September. But, even here, the revolution marked a new point of departure. The Russo-Ottoman Convention of Balta Liman (1 May 1849) confirmed the arrangement established in 1831–2, under which Wallachia and Moldavia were subject at the same time to Ottoman suzerainty and a Russian protectorate. The *hospodars* (princes) were no longer elected by an oligarchical national assembly, but simply appointed by the Ottoman government for a seven-year term. It was an unpromising start, and yet the new Wallachian *hospodar*, Barbu Dimitrie Ştirbei, embarked on a reformist course, whose purpose was to soothe the tensions that had given rise to the June Revolution and close the rifts in Wallachian society. Working in close collaboration with the Ottoman authorities, the Ştirbei administration confiscated a portion of church revenues, broke up some of the larger estates, invested in infrastructure and alleriated what remained of 'feudal' burdens on the peasants. These policies were broadly aligned with the spirit of the Proclamation of Islaz – in this sense, the ideas of 1848 shaped the 'post-revolutionary reorganization' of Wallachia.[108]

THE AGE OF CIRCULATION

The programmes and rhetoric adopted by the post-revolutionary governments naturally varied from state to state in accordance with specific circumstances and traditions. But there were many common features. In the domain of economic policy there was a transition from profit- or revenue-oriented policies towards those aimed at the stimulation of medium- and long-term economic growth. This was achieved in part through permissive reforms – such as the abolition of regulations preventing the formation of joint-stock companies – whose aim was to dismantle the various old-regime laws and regulations that obstructed capital concentration and investment.[109] In January and February 1852, the Cavour government concluded commercial treaties with Belgium and Britain, and further treaties followed with Greece, the German Customs Union, the Netherlands and even Austria, inaugurating an era of free-trade economics that would last until the return of protectionism in 1887.[110] One of the beneficiaries of this wave of deregulation was Iceland, a possession of the Danish Crown. When an Icelandic National Assembly convened in 1851 to demand more autonomy, the Danes shut it down, but in 1855 they passed a law that abolished the traditional trading monopoly granted by the king to Danish merchants on the island. Iceland could now begin to enjoy the blessings of free external trade.[111]

The state was also involved in the proactive encouragement of growth. Across Europe, public spending on domestic investment surged. Governments focused on those forms of territorial infrastructural investment that – because they were likely, in the first instance, to be unprofitable – only the state could be entrusted to undertake. In Saldanha's Portugal, a new Ministry of Public Works launched a vast programme of public building financed by borrowing. In 1850, Portugal had lacked railways or telegraph connections of any kind and disposed of fifty-three steam engines in all, generating the grand total of 777 horsepower. By 1856, Portugal possessed the beginnings of a railway and telegraph network, a substantially improved road system and an array of government-sponsored credit institutes specializing in the investment needs of the farming sector.[112]

In Spain, the uprisings of 1848 triggered an almost immediate shift within the *moderado* regime towards a more proactive investment policy. A new Ministry of Commerce, Education and Public Works was founded in the autumn of 1851, whose task would be the provision of infrastructure: 'the construction of public works, roads and railways, canals, ports and lighthouses is a necessity that none will contest, because it constitutes the routes of circulation, the single open avenue to the future for our producers'.[113] These trends were further reinforced during the *Bienio Progresista* and the Unión Liberal. A Ministry of Development circular of March 1857 declared that infrastructural investment must be 'brought under a fixed system' in order to provide the 'order and unity' that were essential for profitable results.[114] In 1858, the government created an 'extraordinary budget' of two billion reales, funded by the secularization of Church properties, for 'a general plan, to be realized within eight years of refurbishment, completion and new construction of roads, canals, ports, lighthouses and other works of this kind ...'.[115] Between 1854 and 1863, thanks to consistent investment and support from the government, an electric-telegraph network was constructed that linked Madrid with all the provincial capitals, including the Balearic Islands and Ceuta in northern Africa.[116] Public investment came to constitute a higher proportion of total investment in Spain during the years of the Unión Liberal than at any time (leaving aside a brief upsurge in 1912) until the early 1930s.[117] The result was an improvement and expansion of infrastructural networks that established – for the first time – an integrated national market and made possible the gradual modernization of traditional sectors of production over the following decades.[118] Far from starving out other industrial sectors and thereby hindering growth, as some analysts have suggested, the infrastructural investments realized under the Unión Liberal broke the bottleneck in the mid-century Spanish transport system and triggered a substantial growth in national income.[119]

France must occupy a special place in any analysis of these transformations, because its new head of state personally embodied the priorities of the post-revolution like no other.[120] It is worth reflecting briefly on a strange pamphlet Louis Napoleon published in Brussels in 1839, in which he set out his vision of politics, a blueprint to which he remained absolutely faithful after the coup d'état. In *Les Idées Napoléoniennes*, whose reception in France at the time suffered from the poor reputation of its author, Louis Napoleon made it clear that he was not a conservative, but an adherent to the progressive view of history. 'Do we move', he asked, 'in a closed circle, in which light succeeds ignorance, and barbarism civilization?' The answer was a resounding negative: 'Far from us be so sad a thought ... The improvement of society marches onward, despite obstacles, without intermission; it knows no limits but those of the earth.' This was the onward rush of history that had struck awe into Martin Bernard and Claire Démar. But progress was not an impersonal commotion, like the rushing of a hurricane, Louis Napoleon wrote. It was mediated by institutions. And the most important of these was government, which was 'the beneficent motive power of all social organization'. Progress, Louis Napoleon wrote, 'never disappears, but it is often displaced ... It goes from the government to the governed. The tendency of revolutions is, always, to restore progress to the governors.' The first Napoleon, in his genius, had understood that he was not called to be the gravedigger, but to be the 'testamentary executor' of the revolution.

Without the Consulate and the empire, Louis Napoleon proposed, the French Revolution would have been 'drowned in the counter-revolution'. But the opposite had happened, 'because Napoleon planted deep in France, and introduced everywhere in Europe, the principal benefits resulting from the grand crisis of 1789'. Reactionary policies, Louis Napoleon argued, were not the negation of revolution but merely the perpetuation of its instabilities. The only salutary way out of revolution lay in channelling its energies into a 'general fusion' that did not renounce the principles of the revolution but absorbed them into a political order that was 'superior to the petty passions of parties'. In short: Louis

Napoleon gazed at his uncle and saw himself. This was more than an historical interpretation; it was a roadmap for post-revolutionary progress.

In the 1850s, these ideas would merge seamlessly with the authoritarian technocratic romanticism of the Second Empire.[121] The construction sector boomed. The railways entered a golden age. In France, total network mileage rose from 3,248 km in 1851 to 16,465 km in 1869. The insatiable demand for fuel to support the iron and steel industry drove expansion of the coalmines of the Département du Nord. This wasn't exclusively the consequence of government stimulus: the gold rushes of Victoria and California injected vast quantities of bullion into the system, helping to drive a wave of cheap credit that primed the pumps of state investment after the revolutions. But these macroeconomic factors were channelled and focused by state-sponsored institutional change. In 1852, the brothers Émile and Isaac Pereire founded the Crédit Mobilier, an investment bank designed to channel capital towards industrial projects. Its purpose was to realize the 'industrialism' elaborated by Saint-Simon, who, as we saw in Chapter 1, had argued that the creation of an industrial society based upon a hierarchy of merit and respect for productive work would ultimately resolve the problems and pressures that tended to generate upheavals and place society on a path that would combine high rates of growth and innovation with high levels of political and social stability. The Pereire Brothers were Saint-Simonians whose new banking enterprise exhibited a striking fidelity to the views they had espoused in Le Globe, organ of the Saint-Simonian movement, in 1832.[122] The influential economist and engineer and economic adviser to the emperor Michel Chevalier was another former Saint-Simonian; in 1832, Chevalier had spent six months in prison for his involvement with the journal Le Globe after the passage of a law declaring that the 'sect of the Saint-Simonians' constituted a threat to public order.

This is why the critic Sainte-Beuve called Napoleon III a 'Saint-Simon on horseback', though it is unclear whether the emperor himself had ever read the sage's works. But the providential charisma of Bonaparte should not distract us from the fact that similar reorientations took place in other states after 1848. In Prussia, there was a heightened emphasis on the right of the state to deploy public funds for the purpose of modernization.[123] Such arguments benefited from the congenial climate of contemporary German economic theory, which pivoted away from the stringently anti-statist positions of the German 'free-trade school' towards the view that the state had certain macro-economic objectives to fulfil that could not be achieved by individuals or groups within society.[124] In Piedmont, after Cavour became Minister of Finance in 1851, the government enacted measures to promote industry and agricultural credit, encourage joint-stock companies, and reduce overheads such as grain and navigation duties. By 1854, Cavour, now Prime Minister, had spent more than 200 million lire on railways alone.[125] In Hanover, Saxony, Württemberg, Piedmont and the Austrian Empire, projects sustained by heavy borrowing were launched under state supervision – tunnels through the alps, railways, canals, port facilities, schools, administrative buildings, bridges.[126] They served to bind peripheral regions to the metropolitan centres, and to legitimate state authority in a general sense, but they also constituted a new form of state patronage. Under Franz Joseph in Austria, public works became an instrument for managing the subject nationalities; in France, a railway terminus might be offered in return for a favourable vote in a plebiscite.[127] In Piedmont, the concessions offered to Genoese and other Ligurian business circles to establish shipping routes to Sardinia and the United States or to expand mining operations on Sardinia helped to strengthen bonds between the government in Turin and a traditionally obstreperous regional elite.[128]

The economic interventions of the post-revolutionary governments were distinctive not merely for their greater ambition and generosity with state resources, but also for their insistence upon the need to develop administrative measures in a uniform way and in accordance with an overarching plan. The standardized forms that play a role in all bureaucratic procedures today were still a novelty: in Spain, the Ministry of Justice, keen on collating reliable crime statistics, sent out a circular imploring the local authorities to 'fill out accurately' the forms they had received and to reply 'in uniform fashion to the questions that the form contains' – an injunction strongly suggestive of the unfamiliarity of this procedure to the functionaries obliged to carry it out.[129]

Whereas railway construction in Saxony and Württemberg before 1848 had proceeded in a more or less haphazard and fragmented way, administrators after 1848 insisted that railway policy must be focused on the creation of a unified and rational territorial network: 'The state can and must see its state railways as a whole', wrote the Saxon foreign minister, Friedrich Beust, in 1857.[130] In France, too, after 1848, the government encouraged a more coordinated approach to the laying of tracks and the framing of policy at a regional rather than a local level, drawing once again on the ideas and vocabulary of Saint-Simonianism.[131] During the business crisis of 1846–8, some prominent Prussian liberals had called upon the state to take over the administration of the kingdom's railways and unite them into 'an organic whole'.[132] In the 1850s, the Prussian finance minister, August von der Heydt, himself a liberal entrepreneur, presided over a gradual 'nationalization' of the Prussian railways, motivated by the conviction that only the state was capable of ensuring that the resulting system was rational in terms of the state as a whole – private interests alone would not suffice.[133]

These efforts to tie individual railway concessions into a larger policy framework reflected a more general shift in governmental rhetoric. The organic connectedness of economic systems was the fashionable commonplace of the era. In a letter of 15 January 1860 to his Minister of State, Achille Fould, Napoleon III expressed his conviction that 'the mediums of exchange must be increased in order for trade to flourish; that without trade, industry stagnates and maintains high prices that hamper the growth of consumption; that without a prosperous industry that ensures capital growth, even agriculture remains in its infancy'.[134]

Even if the talk of an economic 'policy' was sometimes little more than a mask for pragmatic muddling through, the new emphasis on the formulation of 'policy' as a crucial dimension of domestic administration was itself significant. It related to a growing tendency to conceptualize the state as distinct from society.[135] In Portugal, the Maria da Fonte uprising, which was provoked by government efforts to introduce a new and more efficient system of taxation, stirred panic among the political elites. The conclusion was drawn that the government must henceforth do more than just appeal to 'order' and instead provide the population with prior knowledge not only of the intentions of the government, but also of what it planned to do to realize them. From this moment onwards, we see the swift diffusion of the concept of a political 'programme'.[136] The quest to commit governments to a more or less coherent and binding programme generated structural reforms designed to increase transparency and streamline decision-making processes.[137]

These policies were a direct consequence of the revolutions. They were only possible because conservative political groups that had previously opposed or resisted them had been pushed away from the centre of power.[138] In Prussia, the major public expenditures of the 1850s would have been impossible without the 1848 constitution. By establishing the first all-Prussian parliament, the revolution enabled the government to escape the shackles of the State Indebtedness Law, which had limited public spending before 1848. As one deputy of the Prussian Landtag declared in March 1849, the government's requests for the sums needed to develop the country had in the past been 'stingily refused'. But now, he added, 'we stand at the government's side and will always approve the funds required for improved transport and for the support of commerce, industry and agriculture . . .'[139] Neither the new income tax introduced in 1851 (whose legitimacy was perceived as deriving from the new territorial suffrage) nor the reform of the old land tax in 1861 (which redressed the traditional fiscal imbalance in favour of the more industrial and commercial western provinces) would have been possible before 1848.[140]

MATERIAL PROGRESS

A corollary of these developments was the growing prestige of ministries of finance and of the men who led them. As Europeans relaxed into this world of big projects and stopped asking anxiously where the money was coming from, public trust flowed towards the makers of the new order. In Piedmont, his intermittent control of the finance ministry was pivotal to Cavour's exercise of power, and his role in shaping infrastructural and economic policy completely transformed his reputation, enthroning him as an expert and a practical man, 'herald of the serious and industrious modernity that beckoned as the future of the new Piedmont'.[141] The Spanish finance minister, Manuel Alonso Martínez, exercised a dominating influence in the Cabinets of the Bienio Progresista, and in Portugal the former revolutionary and sometime Minister of Finance and Public Works, António Maria de Fontes Pereira de Melo, became the most prominent representative of the Regeneração. The term *fontismo*, still in use today, was coined to denote the dramatic expansion of government investment and promotion that took place after 1851.[142]

Economic policy came to occupy a central place in the efforts of the various post-revolutionary regimes to legitimate themselves in the eyes of the public. The use of 'developmentalist' arguments as such was not new, nor was the concept of unitary transport networks or the employment of circulatory metaphors;[143] what was distinctive about the post-revolutionary era was the prominent place such topoi now occupied in government propaganda. Again, it is France that provides the most extravagant example: Napoleon III's appeals to the French public consistently foregrounded the economic achievements of the regime and sought to legitimate it in terms not of a higher moral order, but of the material betterment of the French.[144] For the Murillo and O'Donnell governments in Spain, the 'appeal to material interests' became a recurrent theme. Official statements on economic policy were couched in a celebratory language that promised all things to all people. In the minutes of the Spanish Council of Ministers during the Bienio Progresista, we find the following effusion: '[our objective is] to open the springs of civilization, to bring them to our country by means of those mighty vehicles [i.e. steam trains] that constitute the glory of modern civilization, to reinforce our political unity by facilitating communication among all the provinces; to bestow movement and value upon our products'.[145] The financial and economic managers of this era were elevated to the status of gurus, technocratic saviours entrusted with the redemption of humanity. In the sessions of the Conseil Général of the Département du Nord of 1858, there is a 'Report on Domestic Water Transport' in which we find entirely characteristic panegyrics to the planners and engineers:

> Let us honour the men to whom the State has entrusted the task of securing the benefits that that this admirable creation of the human spirit [i.e. the steam engine] promises us; [and let us hope] that their activity, that their intelligence will be generously remunerated . . .[146]

What underlay this emphasis on material achievement was the belief – highly characteristic for the post-1848 era – that material 'progress' (the word was often used in this connection) would ultimately do away with the need for the ideologized, confrontational politics of the old regime. It was time, one radical Portuguese journal observed, 'to close the abyss of civil wars'. The new age did not call for amendments, 'philosophical constitutions' or 'republics of whatever colour', but rather for the physical improvement of the country.[147] In Spain, it was the Fomento, the Ministry of Development, that took responsibility in

1851 for creating a commission tasked with 'harmonizing the reciprocal interests of the factory-owners and textile-workers of Barcelona' – conceptualizing 'the economy' as a network of interdependencies encouraged legislators to believe that sage government provision could bridge the social divide.[148] 'Peace, order and contentment reign throughout the country', Marshal Saldanha told Queen Maria II in the summer of 1854. 'The people renounce politics in order to busy themselves with their own affairs'; the country was so prosperous, he told another correspondent, that it was 'beyond the power of any individual or party to disturb the public tranquillity'.[149]

A report of 1856 by the French Ministry of Agriculture, Commerce and Public Works made the link between economic growth and political quietude explicit: at the time of the February Revolution, it pointed out, there had been 3,600 km of railways in France. But the three years of political turmoil that followed had seen total stagnation – not a single track had been laid. Only since the Bonapartist seizure of power had there been a surge in construction of an asset which 'in our modern civilization has become an essential condition of prosperity, indeed for the very existence of a country'.[150]

In other words, the post-revolutionary settlement went beyond 'counter-revolutionary inoculation'. It was not just about investing in material progress as a means of muting the forces of revolution; more and more it was the other way around: political peace was valued for the sake of prosperity and progress. It was in large part thanks to the becalmed political situation that the post-revolutionary states were prepared to invest a greater volume of financial resources in infrastructure.[151] Material progress itself came to constitute the ultimate public and political good. The resulting reordering of priorities can be seen in the grand historicism of the post-1848 railway stations, which aligned these connective hubs with the destiny of the nation, and in the 'economization' of political discourses.[152] The improvement of infrastructure, Fontes argued, would bring more than revenues; it promised to build the 'arteries and veins for circulation' that would bring languishing nations back to life.[153] In the late 1860s, Napoleon III began sketching out notes for a novel he planned to write. At its centre was a character by the name of M. Benoît, who had left France in 1847 and returned in 1868. He is astonished by the changes wrought since the revolution. He notes the political tranquillity and the absence of demonstrations and riots, but he also marvels at the infrastructural novelties, the telegraphs, railways and the welfare measures that have raised living standards among the poorest strata. The novel was never finished. These notes tell us nothing about the objective character of the post-revolutionary order, but they do tell us something about how the emperor hoped to be remembered.[154]

In a world that had begun to think of 'the economy' as an autonomous living entity and of progress as a quantifiable material transformation, the collation of consistent statistical data acquired a heightened importance.[155] The emergent technology of national statistics – many of whose most prominent exponents had long been active in the cause of political and social reform – in turn became a platform for the co-option by the post-revolutionary state of reformist forces within civil society.[156] In Germany, the practitioners of 'statistics as an autonomous science' had tended to be progressives, and the new statistical bureaus established after the revolution became important agents of administrative modernization.[157] In Spain, too, the ministers of the Unión Liberal insisted on the formation of a new statistical administration, on the grounds that without the 'investigation and knowledge of the fiscal and moral conditions of a nation' no government would be able to facilitate the 'germination of the seeds of prosperity' or remove 'the obstacles that oppose the progress and well-being of peoples'. Previous regimes had collated statistics, of course, but these fell short because they consisted of data collected 'in isolation' and therefore lacked the 'connection and unity' essential for sound statistical analysis.[158] The coalition Cabinets of the Unión Liberal facilitated a merger of conservative and progressive statistical approaches: whereas the *moderados* had tended to see statistics as an instrument of societal control and centralization, the *progresistas* saw it as an instrument for supporting the state's progressive intervention in the economy – the former preferred to place statistics within the remit of the Ministry of the Interior, the latter in the Ministry of Development. In 1861, the two tendencies merged in the Junta General de Estadística – a structure that would remain in place until 1945.[159]

In France, the responsibilities of the Statistique Générale de la France (founded in 1833) were greatly expanded in 1852 to allow for the integrated compilation of national data on an independent basis. And here, as in Spain, the long-standing rivalry between the official 'administrative statisticians' and the progressive, extra-governmental circles of 'social investigators' and 'moral statisticians' was resolved by the foundation, in

1860, of the Statistical Society of Paris, a voluntarist grouping that sought and obtained official endorsement from the Ministry of Trade.[160] This is not to suggest that the preoccupation with statistics was something new – the European statistical movement was well underway by the 1830s, when the Italian poet Giacomo Leopardi (1798–1837) complained that his era was an 'age of statistics'.[161] And we have seen how central the 'moral mathematics' of the Belgian mathematician Quetelet was to progressive commentary on the Social Question (it was far more prominent in the works of left-wing analysts such as Louis Blanc, Ange Guépin and Eugène Buret than in the conservative tracts of writers like Honoré Frégier). The networks across which statistical techniques and knowledge were traded were already in place when the revolutions broke out.[162] What was distinctive about the 1850s was the transformation in the relationship between statistics and the state. This period witnessed – across much of the European continent at least – the transition from a purely governmental to a civil-society-based statistical regime in which assumptions that had gained ground within reformist circles before the revolution could be brought to bear directly upon government. The resulting administrative effects reached deep into regional and local management structures in the form of demands for information.

THE POST-REVOLUTIONARY CITY

The management of urban space was one area in which the challenge posed by revolutionary upheaval, the new emphasis on infrastructural improvement and a readiness to embrace substantial programmes of public spending combined to generate closely analogous initiatives across the capital cities of the European states. Paris, Berlin and Vienna had all seen street fighting and the erection of barricades in 1848, and the same occurred in Madrid in 1848 and 1854. All four cities saw substantial programmes of improvement during the 1850s. The best-known case is Paris, where the local prefect, Baron Haussmann, launched a massive programme to restructure the centre of the old city, extend and modernize its sewerage system and provide it with clean running water. A central concern was the perceived need to clear away the obstacles posed by the old inner city to the circulation of persons and goods – 'circulation' was as resonant a concept to the urban planners as it was to liberal economic theorists.[163] Madrid witnessed a restructuring programme that displayed many similar features – the laying down of broad avenues, the clearance of slums, the clarification and embellishment of key junctions (the Plaza del Sol being the best-known example), the standardization of building regulations and the first halting efforts at the construction of salubrious working-class housing. The most ambitious project of these years was the construction of a system of dams, syphons, aqueducts and reservoirs to bring clean fresh water to the city. Launched in 1851 and upgraded after financial difficulties in 1855 with the help of a huge public loan, this innovation transformed the prospects of the city, sweeping away one of the most important obstacles to its expansion. Here, as in Paris, the rationalization of the inner structure of the city went hand in hand with municipal expansion. The expansion of the outer borders of Madrid was promoted above all as a means of bringing the largely improvised and under-serviced new quarters on the city's periphery under the control of the municipal authorities: of imposing order, in other words, upon a process of spontaneous expansion that was already well underway. Urban planners aimed to create a rational and hygienic urban civic space, characterized by a salubrious blend of air and light, harmoniously proportioned apartment houses, parks and tree-lined avenues, as well as the various other necessities of city life – marketplaces, slaughterhouses, hospitals and prisons.[164] Madrid may never have achieved the level of dramatic transformation that reshaped the city of Paris, but the enhanced prominence and political voice of urban planners testified to a new sensitivity on the part of the state authority to the needs of the city as a living system. What was distinctive about the projects of planners such as Mesonero and Castro in Madrid was a 'global conception of the city' that aimed to heighten its 'socio-spacial homogeneity' while at the same time accommodating the exigencies of the urban class structure.[165] In Haussmann's writings, one finds, similarly, a 'global and systematic approach to the urban problem and a conception of the totality of methods appropriate to its treatment'.[166]

In Berlin, too, there were efforts to impose a new and coordinated approach to urban space, and here, too, the prime mover was not a mayor or municipal official, but a policeman: Karl Ludwig von Hinckeldey. Like Haussmann, Hinckeldey demonstrates the intimacy between counter-revolution and urban reform. During the revolution, Hinckeldey had overseen the expansion and professionalization of civilian policing in the city and was hated by the populace for his robust handling of protests and demonstrations. He was one of the security advisers in whom Frederick William IV, unnerved by the revolution, placed a special trust.[167] But he was also an innovator who 'dragged Berlin single-handedly into modernity'. He installed a modern fire service and a network of soup kitchens for the poorest social strata; public baths and washhouses opened in the poorest areas; he oversaw the establishment of a refuge for unemployed female domestic servants, a notoriously vulnerable social group. In 1852, he had an English engineering firm build waterworks to supply the city with clean drinking water. For the first time in 300 years, Berlin acquired a uniform building code.

Nothing in Hinckeldey's biography is more emblematic than the manner of his death. In 1855, at the urging of the king, Hinckeldey ordered his men to shut down the Berlin 'Jockey Club', a private gambling den run from an expensive suite in the Hôtel du Nord by the young aristocratic tearaway Hans von Rochow-Plessow. On the night of 22 June 1855, Hinckeldey's police raided Rochow's rooms and arrested the young men in attendance, releasing them soon after. Outraged that a civilian like Hinckeldey should have dared to disrupt the private entertainments of young noblemen, Rochow paid the police chief a visit and demanded an explanation. Hinckeldey pointed out, correctly, that the king had authorized the raid. The matter might have ended there, except that the king refused to confirm in public that he had indeed been the instigator of the raid. Hinckeldey and his family suddenly found themselves shunned by court society. Tension grew between the aristocratic army and the emphatically bourgeois police and there were frequent altercations between the two on the streets of Berlin.

Seeing that Hinckeldey had been abandoned and was vulnerable, Rochow raised the ante by accusing him publicly of lying to cover his own back. Under the unyielding honour code of those days, as binding for the bourgeoisie as for the nobility, Hinckeldey had no other way of preserving his public standing but to challenge Rochow to a duel. The problem was that whereas Hinckeldey was profoundly myopic and 'scarcely knew how to fire a pistol', Rochow was a crack shot who could put a bullet into the centre of an ace of spades from twenty metres away. The outcome, when the two men met on 10 March 1856 in the Jungfernheide, a charming area of forest and heathland in the north of Berlin, was inevitable. Hinckeldey's bullet went wide. Rochow's bullet struck the police chief in the chest and killed him on the spot. The truly extraordinary thing was the public response. The man once resented for the firmness of his discipline was now a folk hero. A public subscription was launched to raise funds for his widow and her seven children. Tens of thousands of Berliners turned up to follow his coffin to the cemetery, in what was seen as a massive demonstration by the middle classes 'against the Junkers and the *Kreuzzeitung*' (the newspaper favoured by the conservative nobility). The king burst into a 'frightful weeping and wailing' at the news of Hinckeldey's death, though his crocodile tears probably had more to do with the feeling that he was himself being blamed for what had happened: 'The public regards me as *the one* who sacrificed my beloved Hinckeldey to myself, as though I were a Moloch!' It was yet another lesson – if more were needed – in the perfidy of kings. More importantly, it demonstrated the difference between political reaction (Rochow was a know-nothing reactionary of the old school) and the protean politics of the post-revolution.[168]

Vienna was not subjected to the kind of structural reform that transformed Paris, but here, too, there was debate about how to respond to recent events. Should the ring of fortifications that surrounded and enclosed the inner city be maintained or dismantled?[169] On this issue, the lessons of the revolution were difficult to read. During the upheavals of 1848, the insurgents had themselves scaled the fortifications and used them as firing positions against the troops deployed to restore order within the city. The military leadership, whose authority in security matters was paramount during the immediate post-revolutionary years, took the view that the walls offered an indispensable line of defence against a potential uprising in the working-class areas outside the inner city, and argued that the early-modern line of fortification should in fact be further extended and strengthened. Only in 1857 was the debate resolved in favour of those who preferred to dismantle the walls and use the resulting space for the construction of a broad ring road flanked by representative buildings, green areas and high-quality housing.[170] The result was the laying out of the spacious Ringstraße that still runs around the inner city of Vienna.

The desire for a more ordered urban setting was not in itself a product of the revolutions. In Paris and Madrid, the improvement of the urban fabric had been a theme of public discussion for much of the first half of the century and there had been calls to open up the inner city of Vienna for at least fifty years. But the revolutions changed things. They further reinforced the association between overcrowding, poor sanitation, disease and political upheaval.[171] And a further consequence of this concern was the increasing involvement in urban management of extra- or semi-governmental committees of hygiene experts, whose advisory role was now formalized under new legislation – this happened in many European cities after 1848.[172] In this domain, as in various other 'technical' spheres of administration, governments drew increasingly on the expertise accumulated within the progressive circles of civil society. And, in these circles, technical expertise was often suffused even before 1848 with ideas from the left.[173] In Vienna, as in Berlin, Paris and elsewhere, the revolution shifted the balance of power between the state and the municipal authorities, enabling the former to override the entrenched opposition of municipal elites to major public expenditure.[174]

One of the most striking features of the paradigm shift in urban planning that followed the revolutions was the absorption of the Social Question into administrative practice. Karl von Hinckeldey was obsessively interested in statistics. He collected tables on population growth, mortality rates, causes of death, the cost of apartments, average food and market prices, the volume of poor relief and much else.[175] Under his supervision, the way of seeing and mapping the environment that had evolved in the treatises and pamphlets of the Social Question became a tool of urban policing. In France, too, the revolution pushed the issues raised by the Social Question into high politics. In 1849, Armand de Melun, a deputy of the National Assembly and head of the Society for Charitable Economy, proposed a law against 'insalubrious housing', whose purpose was to empower public authorities to enforce housing quality standards on new-builds. The new law, enacted on 13 April 1850, saddled landowners with legal responsibility for ensuring that certain health standards were met and foresaw draconian fines if they failed to comply. Those who persistently fell short faced the expropriation of their properties. For the first time, the legal instruments designed to support infrastructural projects (such as the clearances required for railway lines and junctions) were applied to the development of inner cities. And the effects of these changes were felt far beyond Paris – in Strasbourg, the city council created a housing commission to oversee the local application of the new law. The commission produced a report, much of whose text could have been drawn from the pages of Louis Blanc, Ange Guépin, Eugène Buret, August Braß or Friedrich Engels:

> The state of the [city's] small streets and housing is a veritable calamity . . . Men and women, mostly in rags, bear on their features the imprint of misery, and their children, with few exceptions, are rickety, scruffy, scabby, of a livid and filthy pallor that bears witness to their parents' unhappy existence.'[176]

What does it mean when the language and arguments associated with a specific critical and dissenting subculture enter the repertory of the state authority? One could read this convergence as a process of co-option and neutralization, the injection of just enough deactivated virus from oppositional discourses to immunize the system against further commotions. Or one could see it as a victory for the progressive sages of the Social Question, as the story of how an idea conquered a portion of the high ground of the state. Or one could simply concede that both claims can be true at the same time. Whichever view one takes, the prominence of experts in the new administrations is striking. There were echoes here of that cohort of savants and specialized functionaries who had fanned out across Europe in the Napoleonic era applying the laws and norms of the empire to newly annexed territories. Like their Napoleonic predecessors, the experts of the 1850s were agents of post-revolutionary stabilization. They carried ideas and practices incubated within progressive civil-society groups into the heart of government.

FROM CENSORSHIP TO PUBLIC RELATIONS

Censorship – in the sense of the vetting of printed material for political content prior to publication – had been an important instrument of government power in the Restoration era and the call for its abolition was one of the central themes of liberal and radical dissent before 1848. Across Europe, the provisional governments abandoned the old censorship regimes and enshrined the freedom of the press in laws and constitutions. Many of the permissive press laws issued in 1848 did not survive the reimposition of 'order'. But this did not imply – in most states – a return to pre-March conditions. A substantial component of the liberal programme thus survived the debacle of the revolution.[177]

The focus of press policy in most countries shifted from the cumbersome pre-censorship of printed material to the confiscation of material deemed to be seditious or dangerous to public peace. This was an important shift because it brought governmental measures into the open. Newspapers and journals could only be penalized after they had begun to circulate, after the 'damage', as it were, had been done. At the same time, differences between the police authorities, the judiciary and responsible ministers as to what constituted an illegal printed utterance meant that efforts by the former to deploy repressive measures to the full were often thwarted.[178]

In France, the coup d'état of Louis Napoleon in December 1851 was followed by severe measures against the oppositional press; many journalists were arrested, and a number of journals simply disappeared. The republican press in the provinces virtually vanished altogether and only eleven newspapers remained in operation in Paris.[179] Small wonder that the conservative Prussian Minister-President, Otto von Manteuffel, contrasted the high-handedness of French policy with the relative liberty enjoyed by press organs in Prussia.[180] But the severity of the new legislation should not be exaggerated. Once the new regime had established itself, the suspension of journals, though permitted in theory, became very rare in practice. Far more common were official police warnings to dissenting editors, but even these became much less frequent from the summer of 1853, with the accession of Persigny and later of Billault to the Ministry of the Interior.[181] More importantly, perhaps, the overall circulation of newspapers as a whole went up sharply as these were sold at lower prices (subsidized by advertising) in the railway stations rapidly proliferating across the country.[182] In France, as in Spain, Prussia, the Netherlands and a number of the lesser German states, the expansion of political print and of the politicized reading public proved irreversible.[183]

Governments dealt with this expansion by adopting a more supple and consistent approach to the business of shaping public attitudes. On 23 December 1850, the coordination of press policy in Prussia was for the first time given a secure institutional basis in the Central Agency for Press Affairs (Zentralstelle für Presseangelegenheiten). The Agency's responsibilities included the administration of funds set aside for the purpose of subsidizing the press, the supervision of subsidized newspapers, and the cultivation of 'relationships' with domestic and foreign papers, in the hope that this would inaugurate 'an organic exchange between all arms of the state and the press'.[184] The new agency thus oversaw the transition from a system based on censorship to one based on news and information management.

Analogous changes can be observed in many of the other continental states. In the more authoritarian climate of the early Bonapartist regime in France, the interior minister, Persigny, argued that repressive measures ought to be supplemented by 'energetic intervention on the part of the administration in favour of good social principles', and added that such intervention could best be accomplished by means of 'publications and pamphlets encouraged and, if need be, financed by the administration'.[185] The advent of the new regime brought a more proactive and coordinated approach to the management of public opinion. As Pierre Latour-Dumoulin, founder and chief of the new Directorate for Publications (Direction générale de la Librairie) observed in a report to the emperor in 1856, official warnings and prosecutions had a negative effect on public opinion. It was preferable to 'prevent the excesses of newspapers in order not to have to repress them' and to 'temper the rigours of the law by moderating its enforcement'.[186] A survey of press policy elsewhere in Europe reveals many parallels.[187] Even the non-governmental press was very substantially penetrated by government sponsorship – throughout the states of the German Confederation almost all major newspapers accepted material from journalists and correspondents in the pay of the various government press offices.[188]

The Catholic Church, too, responded to the upheavals of 1848 by reframing its relationship with the press and the public. It was only after the revolutions, under the pressure of the dramatic expansion in political print, that the papacy developed a broad-circulation press organ of its own. Several factors converged here. From the beginning of his reign, Pius IX was more flexible – if not more positive – in his attitude to the press than his predecessor had been, and there were tentative moves in the direction of a more relaxed press regime within the Papal States. The situation of acute instability created by the Italian war brought home the need to correct potentially damaging misperceptions of his political intentions – late in April 1848, Pius IX issued an allocution to the cardinals urging them to refute rumours to the effect that he was encouraging the Catholics of Lombardy and Venetia to rise up against the Austrians. This was followed, as we have seen, by a formal repudiation of 'all the newspaper articles that want the Pope to be president of a new republic of all the Italians'. And later, during his exile in Gaeta, the pontiff issued a personal statement urging the bishops – for the first time – to defend 'the truth' through the press.

When Carlo Curci, a young Neapolitan Jesuit undergoing training in Rome, proposed that a moderately priced vernacular journal of broad cultural interest be founded to assist the Curia in combating directly the spread of revolutionary ideas, the Pope was receptive. The proposal was opposed by Curci's superior, the Jesuit General P. Roothaan, who had also been pressing for a new journal, but envisaged a much less accessible organ devoted to erudite subject matter and published in Latin. Pius IX preferred Curci's option and even offered to take on the costs of the first issue. The result was the foundation in April 1850 of *Civiltà Cattolica*. Initially published in Naples, the paper was moved to Rome six months later, where it soon boasted a print run of over 12,000. Considerable effort was invested to maximize the new journal's public impact: some 120,000 programmes and 4,000 manifestos were distributed, and the first issue was widely announced in the Catholic press.[189]

It would be going too far to say that these developments signalled the emergence of a modern papal 'publicity policy'. The pontiff's own views on the press remained deeply equivocal. It is clear nonetheless that the existence after 1848 of *Civiltà Cattolica* provided the Pope with a potent means of influencing public opinion. On 1 June 1867, the journal ran a leading article entitled 'A New Tribute to Saint Peter', which argued that, having rendered up their tribute of gold (the Peter's Pence) and blood (the Zouave volunteer movement), Catholics should now offer the tribute of intellect (*tributo dell'intelletto*). This was to take the form of an oath to expound faithfully and if necessary to the point of martyrdom the infallibility of papal ex-cathedra pronouncements. The article had a remarkable impact, especially in France, where flysheets bearing oaths to infallibility were distributed on the streets, and parish priests were pressed to add their signatures to petitions collected by laymen.[190]

The larger point that emerges from these observations is simply that whereas the Pope appears to have learnt little if anything from the revolutions about how to run his states, which remained in a condition of political stagnation, he did extract important lessons in how to lead his Church. History dealt harshly with the papal monarchy. In 1860, with the region already in open revolt against papal rule, the armies of Piedmont-Sardinia conquered the eastern two thirds of the Papal States and absorbed them into the Kingdom of Italy proclaimed in the following year. Europe looked on and shrugged its shoulders. A rump territory around Rome (Lazio) remained under papal control, but this, too, would be taken, along with the city of Rome itself, by the Italians in 1870. The Pope lost his temporal domains, save for the forty-four hectares of the Vatican. Like other states that failed to digest the meaning of the revolutions of 1848 – Hanover and Naples, for example – the Papal States were expunged, unmourned, from the map of Europe.[191]

But even as his temporal domain shrivelled, Pius IX, not as monarch but as priest and spiritual leader, presided over a remarkable revival of Catholic moral authority across Europe and the wider world. *Civiltà Cattolica*, still in operation today, was an important part of that story. His decision, in 1854, to raise the Immaculate Conception of Mary to the status of Catholic doctrine followed extensive enquiries into the condition of popular Catholic piety worldwide and reflected his sensitivity to the devotional culture of more-humble Catholics. His charismatic gifts remained undiminished, and he continued to receive and address delegations of pilgrims and admirers, whose numbers swiftly increased in the era of steamships and railways. He became the first pope ever to see an edition of his own speeches printed for general consumption. His image, endlessly reproduced in cheap colour lithographs, could be seen in millions of Catholic dwellings. Between 1861 and 1870, more than 7,000 young Catholic men from nearly twenty countries, but principally from Belgium, France and the Netherlands, joined the volunteer army known as the *Zouaves* in order to defend the Papal States against revolution from within and invasion from without.[192] This pope was a polarizing figure, to be sure: in the Syllabus of Errors of 1864, he aligned the Church with a trenchant rejection of the liberal version of modernity. But his success in galvanizing Catholic opinion and building a transnational community of sympathy whose depth and extent exceeded anything achieved by his predecessors can scarcely be denied.

*

Amidst all the post-revolutionary convergence, we should note one important exception. While the states of western Europe – and the papacy – looked for new ways of managing information and shaping public opinion, the Russia of Nicholas I entered what Russian historians have called the 'Epoch of Censorship Terror'. This transition was not entirely the consequence of 1848: it began in 1847, when the Moscow authorities detected the first signs of an awakening of Ukrainian national feeling in the western provinces of the empire.[193] But the news of the revolutions stirred deep alarm within the regime. Count Vladimir Zotov learned of the Paris events in mid March from an acquaintance who had heard it from his brother. That evening, he sauntered up to the St Petersburg police official Trubecheev in a theatre during the intermission and remarked: 'Ah, the French! What have they done!' He was shocked by the response.

> Trubecheev, his facial expression visibly altered, replied, almost whispering: 'Please, not a word of this to anyone, not to me, not to any of your other acquaintances ... the police have orders to report to the Third Section [responsible for domestic security] anyone who speaks of the revolution. We were told to arrest even those who merely talk about the details.'[194]

In the years that followed, an enlarged censorship apparatus intensified the surveillance of newspapers and journals and especially books and leaflets (*lubki*) for poorer people. The censors were hyper-responsive to anything even remotely suggestive of social grievances, such as a hint at undeserved riches in a fictional story or a poem called 'Blacksmiths' in a collection of folk songs. When rumours circulated about the imminent closure of the universities, a protegé of the Minister of Education wrote, with his patron's support, a painstakingly patriotic and ingratiating piece pointing out that universities turned students into loyal subjects of the tsar and ought thus to remain open. Nicholas was furious and ordered that such pieces also be banned in future.[195] It was an era of 'terror', the populist writer Gleb Uspenskii would later recall: 'One could not move, one could not even dream; it was dangerous to give any sign of thought . . .; you were required to show that you were scared, trembling, even when there was no real ground for it.'[196]

The small circles that embodied Russian political opinion processed the revolutions in complicated ways. Slavophile conservatives saw in the 'sanguinary chaos' of 1848 confirmation that Russia had nothing to learn from a morally corrupt West dominated by a rapacious and violent bourgeoisie. The revolutions were a rebellion against Christ, rooted in the 'debauchery of will', in ugly contrast with the spirit of 'humility and obedience, strength and greatness', that prevailed in Russia.[197] Not for the last time, the reign of 'the West' as vanguard and model was declared to be at an end. Among Russian radicals, too, the failure of the leftist projects of 1848 produced a mood of disenchantment and contempt for Western-style liberals and socialists. In December 1852, Alexander Herzen recalled how on the eve of his departure from Russia he had longed for 'breadth, depth, open struggle and free speech'; since then, he wrote, he had experienced only 'the loss of all hopes'; and 'indescribable moral disintegration'. Out of this mood of alienation came the notion that Russia itself would one day show the world the road to socialist redemption.[198]

CONCLUSIONS

In 1856, the Victorian essayist Walter Bagehot published an essay on the British statesman Sir Robert Peel, who had died in 1850. The essay was ostensibly a review of Peel's memoirs, but Bagehot had nothing to say about these and may not even have read them. What interested him was Peel as a personality type characteristic of the modern era in politics. Bagehot built his portrait around a contrast between Peel and his contemporary Lord Byron, with whom Peel had attended Harrow school. Two men could scarcely be more different, Bagehot suggested, than Peel and Byron. The mind of Byron, Bagehot wrote, acquired an understanding of the world through moments of 'intense, striking effort': there was a 'single bright spark of light'; an image was burned on the memory; there was no need for a second effort. The style was 'dashing, free, incisive'. Peel's mind, Bagehot wrote, was the exact opposite. His opinions resembled 'the daily accumulating insensible deposits of a rich alluvial soil'. Over time, grain by grain, a 'mould of wise experience' propagated upon the 'still, extended intellect'. Whereas Byron's thoughts carried the imprint of his unique individuality, Peel's possessed 'no particular stamp'. They might have been anyone's ideas, because they derived from 'the general diffused stock of observations' that were to be found in the modern world. 'Like a science', Peel's ideas were 'credible or incredible to all men equally'.

There was more to this than a droll study in personal contrasts. For Bagehot, the bland, un-Byronic seriousness of Peel was emblematic of a larger historical shift in the nature of politics. The politics of the present – Bagehot was writing in 1856! – was no longer about *what* was to be done, but about *how* it was to be done. The legislative activity of modern statesmen was for the most part a matter of mere 'administrative regulation'. It did not prescribe 'what our institutions shall be, but in what manner existing institutions shall work and operate'. And this was the moment made for a man like Peel, whose skills were those of a political manager, not those of a political architect. In a world where leadership meant administration, the steady accumulation and processing of data mattered more than thundering speeches and flashes of inspiration. 'The aristocratic refinement, the nice embellishment, of the old time were as alien to [Peel] as the detail and dryness of the new era were suitable.'[199]

Robert Peel died at the age of sixty-two in 1850, but he was well known to the statesmen who inherited power in Europe after the revolutions of 1848. He was remembered as a conservative who had dared to embrace liberal and radical policies. His support, over howls of protest from the old Tories, for Catholic emancipation (1829) and his decision to join with Whigs and Radicals in repealing the Corn Laws (1846) were seen in Europe as plotting a new political path, pragmatic and flexible. In his biography of Peel, published in 1856, François Guizot praised 'an essentially practical spirit, consulting the facts at every step'.[200] In a speech to the Piedmontese parliament in March 1850, Cavour pointed to the 'luminous example' of Peel, who had attacked the privileges of the great grandees of his own party, offending the greater part of his friends and exposing himself to accusations of 'apostasy and betrayal'. His courageous stance, Cavour argued, had preserved Britain from the 'socialist commotions that were then agitating all Europe'.[201] Peel had shown 'in the most splendid manner', Cavour wrote in *Il Risorgimento*, how it was possible to rebuild the 'political and economic system of a people' in a way that was 'both conservative and reformist', 'both energetic and moderate'. Peel had 'marked out the path that alone, in our belief, can save the present generation from the dangers that lie ahead'.[202] In a speech to the Spanish Cortes in 1854, the progressive deputy for Segovia,

Benito Alejo de Gaminde, observed that Peel had understood how to 'kill political questions' by assigning to economic ones the great importance they deserved. 'Let us aspire, gentlemen, to achieve the same.'[203] In Britain, Peel was seen by many as a vacillating opportunist, but his continental admirers saw him as the embodiment of inerrant principles: Peel, 'one of the greatest English statesmen', had often been abandoned by his party comrades, Peter V, the young king of Portugal, observed in a letter to Prince Albert in 1856, 'because he placed loyalty to his principles over loyalty to individuals'.[204]

Peel was not a man of 1848, but his posthumous fame marked him out *in retrospect* as a trailblazer of the new politics. There were Peels everywhere after 1848, leaders who depended more on consultation and information than on vision, flair and charisma and were prepared to mix politics in new combinations. The 'mind of Peel' may have been less interesting than the romantic mind of Byron, but it was unquestionably better adapted to a world that longed for technical, managerial solutions to the most divisive questions.

And just as Peel's career had been punctuated by frequent political 'conversions' that angered his friends and puzzled his enemies, so many of those who inherited power after 1848 made long journeys across the political spectrum. When Urbano Rattazzi was elected to the Chamber of Deputies in Turin in 1848, he sat with the democrats. But he later moved to the moderate liberals and formed a new group on the centre-left, which in turn entered the coalition (*connubio*) with the centre-right party around Cavour, who had made a similar journey in the other direction. The French lawyer Pierre Marie Pietri had taken part in the insurrection of 1832 and joined the clandestine Society of the Rights of Man. He supported the February Revolution and was sent as one of Ledru-Rollin's revolutionary commissars to Corsica, where he was elected to a seat in the Constituent National Assembly – here he sat on the left. But when Louis Napoleon Bonaparte emerged as a candidate for the presidency in the late autumn of 1848, Pietri swung away to the right and affiliated himself with the prince. On 27 January 1852, after Bonaparte's coup d'état, he succeeded to the prefecture of the Paris police, a post he held until 1858. Alexander Bach, the former democrat who later presided over the modernizing Austrian neo-absolutist regime of the 1850s, was an unusually dramatic example, but there are countless cases of men who surfed the waves of revolution and were still surfing after the counter-revolution set in.[205] The prominence of former democrats in the post-revolutionary police structures is particularly noteworthy.[206]

This mass mobility across the political spectrum is itself a fascinating and important phenomenon. Sometimes it was the people who were on the move, adjusting their thinking and action to changing circumstances. For the individuals involved, this was nothing new; most Europeans of their generation had been navigating an archipelago of ideas and arguments throughout their adult lives; they were practised improvisers. Sometimes, on the other hand, the ideas themselves were in transit. Arguments and practices that had initially flourished on the fringes of the political culture later reappeared near the centre. And ideational change could happen when concepts or arguments remained stable, but their emotional texture changed, as happened, for example, around the cluster of key words associated with 'material progress' after 1848. The words were not new, but the charisma and promise that attached to them were.

It has sometimes been suggested that the revolutions, in opening the Pandora's box of nationalism, divided the continent against itself. But the panorama of administrative change after 1848 suggests revolutions also had a homogenizing, or 'Europeanizing', impact. The archives of the French government in the 1850s are full of correspondence and circulars insisting on the importance of collating foreign examples of every conceivable form of technical process, from cotton manufacture to the construction of tunnels, railway branch lines, sugar refinement and the adoption of an adhesive commercial stamp for bills of exchange.[207] The statistical movement was from its beginnings a transnational affair, involving the exchange of ideas and techniques, first across an informal network of enthusiasts and later through the International Congresses of Statistics that began meeting in 1851.[208] These capacious conduits for knowledge transfer encouraged policy-makers to think of their tasks in comparative/competitive, transnational terms.[209] The weekly *Scientific Review* published by the Ministry of Development in Madrid printed numerous articles bristling with statistics on 'industrial progress in Belgium', 'English industry and the expansion of London', 'revenues of the English and French railways' and 'wool imports to England'.[210]

Ministers and other senior politicians rarely acknowledged the impact of transnational models; they usually preferred to claim responsibility for innovations themselves. But their middle-tier subordinates were a

The face of the 1850s. Sensible and practical administrative men set the tone for the reforms of the 1850s. With his buttoned-down appearance and professional demeanour, the Prussian Minister President, Otto von Manteuffel, exemplified a new type of political leadership.

different matter, because, unlike their bosses, they drew prestige and professional credibility from these horizontal linkages. Police Chief Hinckeldey founded his own Berlin Statistical Office to supply him with data on the city and regularly sent a representative to the International Statistical Congress, with a view to staying abreast of the latest developments in the field.[211] It was widely believed among progressive liberals and socialists after 1848 that the revolutions were the moment when 'political metaphysics, mysticism and revolutionary illuminism' made way for the ascendancy of a 'positive and useful social science'.[212] We have seen that Lorenz Stein captured the same transition when he spoke of the transition from an 'age of constitution' to 'an age of administration'. We are accustomed to thinking of nineteenth-century Europe as divided into zones of modernity and backwardness. While this may be true in a limited way for processes of societal change, it is less relevant to that educated transnational European 'administrative intelligentsia' whose culture and learning were synchronized and genuinely European.[213]

Lastly, we might ponder on the historical meaning of the synthesis that emerged after 1848. The coalitions that sustained the politics of the 1850s were eventually hollowed out by internal divisions and an increasingly inauspicious economic climate. Credit became more expensive. The hard right and the hard left revived, putting the centrist liberal-conservative consensus under pressure. Protectionism came back into fashion. The Social Question returned in an even more challenging form. The 'end of politics' was not in sight for the people of the post-revolution. But the idea feels familiar, perhaps because its appeal (or threat) has been felt more than once. There are suggestive parallels between the transitions of the 1850s and the authoritarian reformism of the Napoleonic era, another moment in which states were reshaped to absorb the waning energies of a revolution. After 1945 and again after 1989, a similar aspiration emerged in western Europe, animated by the vision of a technocratic, transnational form of politics, capable of lifting the management of contentious resources out of the force fields of partisan and national strife. Both moments were marked by a tendency to place economic policy at the centre of government and to respect public opinion while seeking proactively to manage it. There was that same tiredness with the great slogans and categories of left and right and that same hope that technical solutions would somehow enable us to evade the strife and blockage of politics.

Édouard Baldus, *View of Picquigny Station* (1855). This photograph was
included in an album prepared for Queen Victoria after her visit to France to
attend the Universal Exhibition in 1855. Baldus, a renowned master of
architectural and landscape views, captures something in this nondescript image
that we cannot see: the immense promise and excitement of the new railway
networks, which could connect a drab provincial location like this one directly
to the great Parisian metropolis.

Conclusion

Wir stehen selbst enttäuscht und sehn betroffen
Den Vorhang zu und alle Fragen offen

We, too, are disappointed and uncertain
To see our questions all still open after close of curtain

Bertolt Brecht, *Der gute Mensch von Sezuan*, Epilogue

The revolutions of 1848 broke out in a world that remembered an earlier epoch of transformation. From Phrygian caps and cockades to liberty trees and tricolour flags, revolutionaries across Europe decorated their enterprise with the symbols and customs of the great predecessor. Flickering like old movies in the backs of their heads were scenes from the first French Revolution and its Napoleonic aftermath. When she visited Paris in March 1848, the journalist and writer Fanny Lewald was surprised to see the words 'Liberté, Égalité, Fraternité' scribbled on every surface where space could be found, almost as if the people 'were afraid they might forget them'. She heard groups of workers singing the 'Marseillaise' and other songs from the revolutionary era.[1] Marie d'Agoult marvelled at Napoleon's renewed omnipresence as a symbol, unmatched by any other figure of modern times.[2] 'Committees of Public Safety' sprang up in many revolutionary cities. There was intense discussion of how the once-reviled 'principles of 1789' might be applied to Italy.[3] The anonymous pamphlet *Ce sînt meseriaşii?* (Who are the artisans?), widely read in Bucharest during the summer of 1848, stuck closely to the catechism format of the famous 1789 essay *Qu'est-ce que le tiers-état?* (What is the Third Estate?) by the Abbé Sieyès.[4] We find these rhymes and echoes everywhere.

For some sceptical observers of 1848, these habits of mimicry and self-conscious cross-referencing were marks of emptiness, a sign that revolution had withered into mere spectacle. Observing an invasion of the Chamber of Deputies by a group of armed radicals on 24 February, Tocqueville could not fight off the feeling that 'we had staged a play about the French Revolution'.[5] In the winter of 1851–2, Karl Marx turned his disappointment with the present into the fulcrum of a devastating critique. Epochs of 'revolutionary crisis', he noted in *The Eighteenth Brumaire of Louis Bonaparte*, were especially prone to fall under the spell of history, as humans enlisted the ghosts of the dead as chaperones in uncertain times. But woe betide a revolution that failed to escape the gravitational field of the past. It would remain locked for ever within the logic of mimicry. This, Marx argued, was the fate of the European revolutions of 1848–9, whose chief protagonists were gormless epigons, risible parodies of their revolutionary and Napoleonic antecedents.[6]

But the sense of being dwarfed by the past is not a true or objective reflection of the relationship between one epoch and another. It is a mode of reflexive awareness, a form of felt historicity. There was no single memory of 1789, 1793, 1795, 1799, 1812 or 1815, no single narrative capable of holding sway over future generations, but rather a multitude of examples and myths that political actors drew on selectively or adapted in support of a wide range of interests and objectives. The fact that the seventeenth-century Puritans of the English Civil War drew inspiration and meaning from the personalities and events of Mosaic scripture did not make them into re-enactors of the Bible. Tocqueville intuited this when he went on to nuance his observation about the staged character of 1848: 'The quality of imitativeness was so obvious', he wrote, 'that the terrible originality of the facts remained hidden.'[7] Even Marx's trenchant dismissal of the mid-century revolutions was ultimately ambivalent on this question. *The Eighteenth Brumaire* began by denouncing 1848 as the farcical imitation of 1789, but soon evolved into a more open-ended enquiry into the meaning of 1848's strange failure to conform to expectations.

For generations, the question of whether these revolutions 'succeeded' or 'failed' has haunted historical writing on the subject.[8] The question seems reasonable enough. But what would it mean for a revolution to 'succeed'? Was the French Revolution a success? The revolution of 1789 had a profound transformative effect, but the constitutional monarchy it created was soon swept away. The terrorist regime of the Convention was brought down by the Thermidorian coup, which in turn ushered in the Directory, a regime rocked by political instability until it, too, was swept away by the ascendancy of Napoleon. What would it mean, in the face of this constant iteration of new political forms, to call the French Revolution 'a success'? And by whose criteria should we measure success and failure? Some radicals were already arguing in April 1848 that the revolution had failed – by that they meant that it had not fulfilled their hopes. In many states, the election of parliaments was a success for the liberals but a blow to those radicals who saw that they were unlikely to command a majority, even under an extended suffrage. Some (mainly radicals) argued in the Mazzinian mode that splendid failures were of greater and more lasting historical value than mediocre successes. And, over time, failure could be reminted into success: in 1867, Ferenc Deák and Gyula Andrássy, two defeated 1848ers, would help to craft a new and almost independent Hungarian state within the envelope of a restructured Austrian Empire; the cohort of revolutionaries who fled Wallachia and Moldavia after 1848 used their networks in exile to forge themselves into the 'government in waiting' that would inherit power in an independent Romania.[9] Among those who founded the French Third Republic were many veterans of 1848–1851; their memories of the Second Republic shaped the compromise between pragmatic republicans and moderate monarchists on which the new polity was based. The success of the new republic in garnering rural votes owed much to the remembered experience of 'démoc-soc' mobilization during the 'second-wave' upheavals of 1849 and 1850.[10] Bismarck, a counter-revolutionary, hated the ideas and attitudes behind the tumults of March, but for him the revolution was undoubtedly a success. He acknowledged throughout his life that the revolution was the enabling condition on which his own long career in public life was founded. He recognized that in transforming and opening the structures of political power, the revolution had created new opportunities for someone like himself. He could never, he conceded in the memoirs he wrote after his retirement, have embarked on a political career in 'the time before 1848'.[11]

We don't say of an ocean storm, a solar flare or sixteen days of heavy snowfall that they 'succeeded' or 'failed'; we simply measure their effects. To be sure: a revolution is a political event, not a natural one. A revolution, one might argue, is a thing made of will and intention. If the outcome fails to live up to the intention, then we must be entitled to speak of 'failure'. But here we run into the problem that whereas the people swept up in revolutions do sometimes (though certainly not always) develop a coherent intention, the same cannot be said of the revolutions themselves, which are the sum of many potentially dissonant or even contradictory intentions. We have in our heads a mythical ideal of revolution as the generative moment when actors in pursuit of a new order of things smash the world and make it anew in the image of their vision. But has any actual revolution ever met this exacting standard? The revolutions of 1848 certainly did not. They were marked throughout by polyvocality, lack of coordination and the layering of many cross-cutting vectors of intention and conflict.

But if they were chaotic, the revolutions were also deeply consequential. The people who entered the collision chamber of 1848 were not the same when they came out. Liberals spun into power by urban revolts consolidated their hegemony through new political institutions, most of which outlived the revolutions. In their caucuses and associations and above all in parliamentary debate, liberals, radicals and conservatives underwent a fast-track apprenticeship in the techniques of modern politics. Conservatives learned to live with constitutions and representative chambers and used the techniques of mass mobilization to deepen their social base. Catholics rallied to the papacy, inaugurating a form of confessional politics whose impact would persist into the later twentieth century. A new form of leftist politics emerged that focused more on the provision of social goods than on conspiracy and the seizure of power. Most radicals overcame their ambivalence towards universal suffrage and became its staunchest advocates in the decades after 1848.[12] Liberals learned to coalesce with potential allies on the right and the left and to make intricate trade-offs between power and liberty. The process of advocacy itself generated new networks, ideas and arguments, especially for those women who dared to challenge the gender politics of patriarchy. And the face of government and administration changed as officials and statesmen strove to absorb the ideas and techniques most pertinent to understanding the upheaval, channelling its momentum and preventing further commotions.

The post-revolutionary synthesis that emerged from the upheavals (and their suppression) was founded on the continuing political exclusion of the popular classes whose courage and violence had made the revolutions possible and on the marginalization of the democratic politics that spoke in their name. The promise that 'this time' (unlike in 1830) 'the people' would reap the political rewards of their revolution was not fulfilled. This imbalance in the legacy of the revolutions delayed the arrival of universal suffrage in much of Europe for half a century or more and imprinted the liberal order that achieved hegemony after 1848 with an abiding suspicion of democracy.[13] At the same time, the post-revolutionary synthesis, by digesting just enough of the revolution to proof itself against further upheavals, provided the European states with new ways of using commodities, public communications, money, legal norms and sophisticated policing to fend off threats to the liberal-conservative capitalist order.

For the socialists, 1848 was a grandiose moment of arrival. Scores of new socialist newspapers appeared along with a new cadre of *working-class* socialist leaders and organizers; charismatic socialist thinkers like Étienne Cabet and François-Vincent Raspail became celebrated public figures whose faces were known from portraits and caricature. Socialist orators addressed huge audiences and even the centrist papers debated the merits of socialism.[14] But the suppression of the revolutions and the stabilization that followed also produced a narrowing in the bandwidth of socialist dissent: the highly diverse pre-1848 chorus of speculations on the meaning of a good life and the many paths to human flourishing made way for more inclusive and pragmatic platforms focused on amelioration and welfare. From this moment on, the left would be divided between a reformist majority and a revolutionary minority – Louis Blanc was not wrong when he claimed, in 1876, that the programme his Luxembourg Commission had drawn up in 1848 was 'generally adopted today by republicans'.[15]

In the domain of geopolitics, too, the revolutions had profound effects. The emergence of the Italian and German nation-states in the years 1859–71 was a consequence of 1848, not because the revolutions gave rise to new nationalist movements, but because they taught monarchs a lesson in the potency of nationalism and national activists a lesson in the indispensability of state power. Only when the power of the state was yoked to the cultural heft of nationalist elites would the dreams of the patriots take shape on the political map. But the impact of the revolutions is less apparent in the emergence of the Italian and German nation-states as such, which might well have happened without them, than in their very different political structure. In Germany, where most of the states of the

Confederation embarked on modernizing post-revolutionary state-building projects after 1848, Bismarck had to agree to a federal solution to the German problem. The *Kaiserreich* that emerged from the Wars of Unification was not a unitary state, but a 'League of Princes', whose states retained their own sovereigns and parliaments.

In Italy, by contrast, a gulf opened up between Piedmont and the south. Whereas the Italian political emigrants in earlier years of political turbulence had fled the peninsula altogether, in 1848 they sought refuge in liberal and constitutional Piedmont.[16] While the liberal elites gravitated towards the House of Savoy in the north, the Bourbon administration in Naples remained over-focused on the Church and the army and failed to build robust relationships with the most dynamic elements in southern society. In the years that followed, Piedmont embraced the post-revolutionary synthesis but the Papal States and the Kingdom of the Two Sicilies did not. In 1839, the Bourbons in the south had been the first to open a railway, the Naples–Portici – Piedmont's Turin–Moncalieri line did not open until 1848. But after 1848 the Piedmontese administration threw itself into the task of network expansion, whereas the Bourbon government in the south did not. Railway construction there never became the driving force of economic growth that it was in the north. By 1861, of the just over 1,800 kilometres of rail in the peninsula, 1,372 were in the north.[17] For this and other reasons, the outcome of unification was quite different from the German case: the whole of Italy was simply merged with Piedmont. This uncomfortable solution generated new tensions and asymmetries whose effects are still being felt in Italy today. In Wallachia, too, the post-revolutionary administration under Hospodar Ştirbei pursued a reformist course designed to keep the Principality aligned with the policy of the Ottoman government, thereby opening the way, after the Crimean War, to independence, unification with Moldavia and the first steps towards a Romanian nation-state.[18] Here, as in Italy, it was not (just) the revolution itself that made the difference, but the management of its aftermath.

In more ways than one, the 1848 revolutions deepened the divide between Russia and western Europe. They repelled the champions of tsarist autocracy, but they also alienated those Russian leftists who had previously seen the West as the model for their own efforts. Both turned away from 1848 towards the idea of a specifically Russian path to redemption. A process of auto-critique did begin deep within the tsarist administration that would bear fruit after the Crimean War in the era of the 'Great Reforms' (1861–5), but these were partially reversed after 1865 and there was no transition to constitutional government.[19] The revolutions also stirred the antagonisms that would feed into the Crimean War (1853–6), especially on the shores of the Black Sea, where tension over the Danubian Principalities deepened the distrust between Britain and Russia. In 1849, Austria had been the beneficiary of the Russian intervention in Hungary and of Russian efforts to prevent a Prussian-dominated German union. In the light of that memory, Vienna's decision not to support Russia when Britain, France and Piedmont went to war on the side of the Ottomans in 1854 generated deep bitterness in St Petersburg. And the subsequent Russian decision *not* to intervene in defence of Austria was in turn crucial to the success of the Italians and the Germans in establishing their respective nation-states.

Looking back at the revolutions from the end of the first quarter of the twenty-first century, it is impossible not to be struck by the resonances. The questions they were asking about the right to work, the balancing of labour and capital, the plight of the working poor, the deepening of inequality and urban social crisis, are all still with us. And so are the structural problems they faced. How do you synchronize the slow politics of chambers with the fast politics of demonstrations, Twitter, flash mobs and extra-parliamentary movements? When, if at all, is violence a legitimate form of politics? How should we optimize the functionality of liberal institutions while accommodating the demand for social justice, or for the profound – and potentially unpopular – changes required to meet the challenge of climate change?

At a time when 'liberalism', shorn of its charisma and emptied of its history, is equated on the left with colonial violence, plutocracy and market-driven economics, and on the right with leftist fads and social licence, it is worth remembering what a rich, diverse, risky and vibrant thing liberalism was.[20] The liberal vision of a metapolitics focused on the discursive mediation of interests is as indispensable now as it was then. But liberals were also a constellation of interest groups. The radicals were right to denounce their blind spots and the inconsistencies born of self-interest; radical arguments for democracy and social justice were a crucial corrective to liberal elitism. The radicals were the first to see who was in danger of being left behind by a politics focused on parliaments and constitutions; they were the first to see how extreme inequality would corrode the fabric of a political order that failed to integrate the poorer social strata. The failure of liberals and radicals to listen to each other was one of the central impediments to a deeper political transformation. When liberals denounced democrats as 'communists' and radicals ridiculed the 'parlia-parlia-parlia-parliaments' of the liberals, they enacted one of the central tragedies of 1848. On the other hand, neither radicals nor liberals (with some virtuous exceptions) managed to make much sense of the intractable problems of rural society, a category encompassing the great majority of Europeans. This was a glaring omission, for which they would pay dearly.

It is fascinating to ponder on what might have happened if people had behaved differently. What if the liberals had opened themselves to the social logic of radical politics instead of clinging to the skirts of the traditional powers? What if the radicals had managed to agree a minimal social programme, a platform for a politics of amelioration that might have overcome the objections of the liberals? What if the actors of 1848 had seen and avoided the dangers arising from the entanglement of nationalism with civil strife? What if a united front of liberals and radicals had insisted from the very beginning on full control of the executive agencies of the monarchical states – including the armies? What if all the monarchs of Europe had behaved like their Dutch and Danish colleagues and presided over a peaceful transition to parliamentary constitutional monarchy? As the historian Paul Ginsborg pointed out long ago, counterfactual speculations of this kind are fun but futile.[21] Yet they do matter, because counter-factual scenarios are already embedded in those accounts that attribute the 'failure' of revolution to the erroneous path followed by a specific group of actors, the most common suspect being the liberal bourgeoisie. They also hint at those design flaws in the processes of 1848 that are most pertinent to present-day readers: the loss of cohesion under democratic conditions, the failure of dialogue, the hardening of orthodoxies impervious to argument, the inability to prioritize key objectives and coalesce for the purpose of pursuing them; the difficulty of correcting, within any given system, for the preponderance of certain economic and political elites. Particularly striking is the continuing salience of the politics of emancipation that was so central to 1848: the battles for racial and gender equality continue in our own time and the rise of new and old forms of anti-Semitism suggests that the issues raised in 1848 by the emancipation of the Jews have not melted away.

The revolutions of 1848 seemed as old as ancient Egypt when I learned about them at school. Their complexity was a futile, antiquarian scrawl, unsusceptible to the kind of narrative that replenishes modern people. But something has changed. We are re-emerging from something that they did not yet know. The era of high industrialization; the 'take-off into sustained growth'; the rise of the great ideological party-political formations; the ascendancy of the nation-state and the welfare state; the age of secularization; the rise of the great newspapers and the national television audience. These things, which we used to call 'modernity', are now in flux, their hold on us is waning. The old right vs left trigonometry by which we used to plot our political paths no longer works: in a report presented on 7 July 2022, the German Bundesamt für Verfassungsschutz, the body entrusted with monitoring the activities of groups that represent a threat to the constitutional and political order of the country, announced that it had opened a new observation category for groups and networks that belonged neither to the right nor to the left.[22]

The puzzlement generated by new movements – Trump rallies, Occupy Wall Street, QAnon, the *gilets jaunes*, the anti-vaccination protests of German 'Lateral Thinkers' (*Querdenker*) – is a symptom of this transition. But if we read them against the turmoil of the mid-nineteenth-century revolutions, they seem less unfamiliar. The storming of the Capitol on 6 January 2021 in Washington DC was thick with echoes: the invasion of a chamber by an unruly mob; the rejection of the election process (by 'the right' this time, not 'the left') as a snare and a lie; the improvised theatricality and outlandish outfits; the euphoric posturing coupled with appeals to high principle – 'freedom', 'rights', 'the constitution' – all recalled the tumults of 1848. The 'Freedom Convoy' of truckers that paralysed downtown Ottawa for three weeks in January and February 2022 manifested with its bouncy castles, hog roasts and repudiation of parliamentary democracy a blend of carnivalesque style and insurrectionary logic that recalled the street protests of 1848.[23]

This is emphatically not to equate the painstakingly reasoned reformism of, say, Louis Blanc with the often shallow and incoherent politics of today's pop-up protests. But the unstable leadership structures, the partial fusion of disparate ideologies, and the mobile, protean and improvised quality of much present-day political dissent are reminiscent of 1848, and so are the efforts of intellectuals to make sense of them: Ross Douthat's interpretation of the Freedom Convoy as the latest battle in a new class

Truckers protest against anti-COVID measures on Wellington Street, Ottawa, in front of the Canadian parliament, on 28 January 2022.

A yellow-vest (*gilet jaune*) anti-government march in Toulouse in May 2018.
The woman in the centre has donned the red Phrygian cap of the revolution,
adorned on one side with the tricolour cockade. With their theatricality, their
protean politics and their blend of carnival and popular anger, the protests of
the *gilets jaunes* recalled the popular tumults of 1848.

war between Virtuals (educated elites) and Practicals (people who do stuff with their hands), for example, recalls the opposition between 'idlers' and 'industrials' invoked by the followers of Saint-Simon.[24] George Packard's observation that the 'working class' has become *terra incognita* to the 'smart' cosmopolitan elites of the cities recalls the 'mysteries' literature of the 1840s.[25] In general, the heightened ambient awareness of precarity and the preoccupation with waning social cohesion recall the grim diagnoses of the 1840s.

As we cease to be the creatures of high modernity, new affinities become possible. It becomes engrossing, even instructive, to contemplate the people and situations of 1848: the fissured, multifarious quality of their politics; the churn and change without a settled sense of the direction of travel; the anxieties around inequality and the finiteness of resources; the lethal entanglement of civil tumult with international relations; the irruption of violence, utopia and spirituality into politics. If a revolution is coming (and we seem very far removed from a *non-revolutionary* solution to the 'polycrisis' we currently face), it may look something like 1848: poorly planned, dispersed, patchy and bristling with contradictions. Historians are supposed to resist the temptation to see themselves in the people of the past, but as I wrote this book, I was struck by the feeling that the people of 1848 could see themselves in us.

Acknowledgements

There is something about the revolutions of 1848 that defies synopsis. The endless sprawl of the locations, the swarm of protagonists, the cacophony of conflicting claims and opinions. And around this modern monster-event stretches an oceanic literature seething with national, agrarian, political, social and historiographical questions of every kind. I can't claim to have captured or made sense of all or even most of it – every day I think of things and places and people that or who should be in the book but aren't. As I wrote it, I was often reminded of my late friend and former doctoral supervisor, Jonathan Steinberg. In the late 1980s, Jonathan used to give a set-piece lecture on the 1848 revolutions, in which he presented a cardboard disc with a two-ended arrow pinned to it. Around the circumference of the disc were inscribed the 'options' of 1848: liberalism, radicalism, federalism, unitarism, monarchism, republicanism, absolutism, constitutionalism, nationalism, localism and so on. Twirling the arrow this way and that, he would say: 'I've been teaching this subject for twenty years and I still don't understand it!'

In trying to make sense of this panorama of interlocking upheavals, I have called on the expertise and acumen of many friends and colleagues. Special thanks are due to those friends who read the whole text or parts of the manuscript and offered comments and critique: Michael Ledger-Lomas, Marcus Colla, Glenda Sluga, Fernanda Gallo, Charlotte Johann, James Mackenzie, Adam Tooze, Amitav Ghosh, Marion Kant, Sarah Pearsall, Jon Parry, Kristina Spohr. I owe a special debt to former doctoral students Lisa Niemeyer, Diana Siclovan, Anna Ross, James Morris and Christos Aliprantis, whose work on the literary responses to 1848, the political theorist Lorenz Stein, the governance of Prussia in the 1850s, the Wallachian experience of 1848, and Austrian and Prussian policing before and after the revolutions greatly deepened my understanding of the events and the issues. I learned a huge amount from working with them and I have benefited from their advice on issues where the existing literature is murky. In 2018, on the occasion of the 170th anniversary of 1848, two international symposia in Paris showcased the brilliant work being done by a new generation of scholars. They helped me to navigate the revolutions as connected phenomenona. *Les Acteurs européens du 'printemps des peuples' 1848. Colloque international du cent soixante-dixième anniversaire*, convened by Eric Anceau and Vincent Robert, opened at the end of May 2018 at the Sorbonne, and *Les Mondes de 1848*, organized by Emmanuel Fureix, Quentin Delermuoz and Clément Thibaud, opened in December of the same year at the EHESS. Conversations with Quentin Delermuoz, Catherine Brice, Vincent Robert, Catherine Horel, Samuel Hayat, Eric Anceau, Romy Sanchez, Delphine Diaz, Sylvie Aprile, Heléna Tóth, Jonathan Beecher, Heinrich Best, Fabrice Bensimon, Ignazio Veca and Pierre-Marie Delpu all added new notes to the mix. Vincent Robert, author of a magisterial study of the banqueting movement in France, graciously guided me through the various layers of the French franchise on the eve of 1848. I thank Jonathan Beecher in particular for sending me a manuscript of his brilliant *Writers and Revolution* long before it appeared in print in 2021. I also thank Ignacio García de Paso García for sending me offprints and new work on the revolutions in Spain. Viviana Mellone provided helpful answers to my queries about Naples in 1848. David Laven provided sharp (in both senses) comments on the events and the historiography of the Italian revolutions, Dieter Langewiesche sent the offprints of new and old articles and Ralf Zerback sent me a copy of his gripping biography of Robert Blum. Beatrice de Graaf and Pieter Sterenborg provided valuable advice on the Dutch events, and with her astute comments and translations Valentina Kesić opened up the world of the Croatian 1848; Gosia Wloszycka and Andrzej Jajszczyk guided me through the Polish sources on the Galician events of 1846 and Nailya Shamgunova provided invaluable assistance with the Russian literature. Robert J. W. Evans, Michael Bregnsbo, Richard Drayton, Maria Filomena Mónica, Jose Miguel Sardica and Jyrki Vesikansa helped with advice on the complexities of the Habsburg, Danish, Caribbean, Portuguese and Finnish experiences of 1848 respectively, and Abigail Green sent me two chapters of her forthcoming study, *The*

Children of 1848. Oliver Haardt deepened my awareness of the constitutions of 1848 and James Morris corrected errors on the Wallachian events. Without their generous help, the mistakes in this book would be even more numerous. Gareth Stedman Jones, biographer of Marx and pioneering analyst of the early-nineteenth-century Social Question has been a wonderful conversation partner on 1848 since I began taking an interest in this subject. My debt to Jonathan Sperber, author (among many other fine works) of a powerful synoptic study of 1848 and co-editor of a landmark compilation on the revolutions, will be obvious to readers who know the literature.

Conversation is an indispensable research tool, and I have learned much from exchanges with the late Christopher Bayly, the late Michael O'Brien, John Thompson, Jim Sheehan, Holly Case, Peggy Anderson, Axel Körner, Nina Lübbren, Rauf El Ayoubi, Lavinia El Ayoubi, Miles Taylor, Gary Gerstle, James Retallack, Leigh Shaw-Taylor, Renaud Morieux, Lawrence Cole, Pieter Judson, Helmut Walser Smith, Peter Becker, the late Christopher Duggan, David Barclay, James Brophy, Lucy Riall, Richard Bourke, Niamh Gallagher, Richard Evans, Nadeen Ebrahim and Sujit Sivasundaram. My sons Josef and Alexander helped me through sticky patches in the writing, especially during the COVID lockdowns. I would like to thank Simon Winder, the historian's *beau idéal* of commissioning editors, who helped me to see the book trapped inside the manuscript, and the team at Penguin: Annabel Huxley, Eva Hodgkin, Richard Duguid and Liz Parsons. Thanks also to Neil Gower for his beautiful cartography, Cecilia Mackay for her outstanding work on the illustrations, Mark Handsley for his erudite copy-editing in many languages and Mark Wells for compiling an exemplary index. It is a privilege to be working with the Wylie Agency and I am especially grateful to James Pullman at the London office for his guidance and encouragement. My irreplaceable friend Richard Sanger, poet, playwright and teacher, was still reading and commenting on the manuscript when he died of pancreatic cancer in Toronto in September 2022. The book is dedicated to Kristina Spohr with love and gratitude for her companionship and intellectual fellowship over the years that it took to write.

References

INTRODUCTION

1. Axel Körner, *1848. A European Revolution? International Ideas and National Memories of 1848* (2nd rev. edn, Basingstoke, 2004). 2. Paul Boerner, *Erinnerungen eines Revolutionärs. Skizzen aus dem Jahre 1848* (Leipzig, 1920), vol. 1, p. 73. 3. Karl Marx, 'Financial Failure of Government – Cabs – Ireland – The Russian Question', *New York Daily Tribune*, no. 2844, 12 August 1853, reprinted in *Karl Marx. Friedrich Engels Gesamtausgabe*, vol. 12: *Werke Artikel Entwürfe. Januar bis Dezember 1853* (Berlin, 1984), pp. 254–62, here p. 262. 4. Émile Thomas, *Histoire des Ateliers Nationaux. Considérés sous le double point de vue politique et social, des causes de leur formation et de leur existence, de l'influence qu'ils ont exercée sur les événements des quatre premiers mois de la République, suivi des pièces justificatives* (Paris, 1848), p. 17. 5. Cited in Giovanna Fiume, *La crisi sociale del 1848 in Sicilia* (Messina, 1982), p. 72. 6. Benjamin Vicuña Mackenna, *The Girondins of Chile. Reminiscences of an Eyewitness*, trans. J. H. R. Polt (Oxford, 2003), p. 3.

1. SOCIAL QUESTIONS

1. Ange Guépin and E. Bonamy, *Nantes au XIXe siècle. Statistique topographique, industrielle et morale, faisant suite à l'histoire des progrès de Nantes* (Nantes, 1835), pp. 484–5. 2. François Crouzet, 'Wars, Blockade, and Economic Change in Europe, 1792–1815', *The Journal of Economic History* 24/4 (Dec. 1964), pp. 567–8, 568, 570. 3. Émile Souvestre, 'Nantes', *Revue des Deux Mondes*, 4th series, 9 (Jan.–Mar. 1837), pp. 53–74, here p. 62. 4. Henri Sée, 'La Vie politique et économique de Nantes pendant la Monarchie de Juillet, d'après la correspondance inédite de P.-F. Dubois', *Revue Historique* 163/2 (1930), pp. 297–322, here p. 309. 5. Guépin and Bonamy, *Nantes au XIXe siècle*, pp. 455–7. 6. Ibid., p. 472. 7. Ibid., pp. 472–81. 8. Ibid., p. 484. 9. Ibid., pp. 488–9. 10. James Phillips Kay, *The Moral and Physical Conditions of the Working Classes Employed in the Cotton Manufacture in Manchester* (London, 1832), p. 19. 11. Louis-René Villermé, *Tableau de l'état physique et moral des ouvriers employés dans les manufactures de coton, de laine et de soie* (2 vols., Paris, 1840), vol. I, p. 82. 12. Ibid., vol. 1, p. 26. 13. Ibid., p. 29. 14. Carlo Ilarione Petitti, *Sul lavoro de' fanciulli nelle manifatture* (Turin, 1841), p. 16. 15. Philibert Patissier, *Traité des maladies des artisans et de celles qui résultent des diverses professions* (Paris, 1822), pp. 391–2. 16. Ibid., p. 392. 17. Ibid., p. 395–6. 18. Marie-Claire Hoock-Demarle, 'Les écrits sociaux de Bettina von Arnim ou les débuts de l'enquête sociale dans le Vormärz prussien', *Le Mouvement social*, no. 110 (1980), pp. 5–33, here p. 7. 19. Heinrich Grunholzer, 'Erfahrungen eines jungen Schweizers im Vogtlande', Appendix to Bettina von Arnim, *Dies Buch gehört dem König* (1843), pp. 534–98, here pp. 537–8. Bettina von Arnim's own critical remarks can be found in the essay entitled

'Sokratie der Frau Rat'. 20. Friedrich Engels, *Die Lage der arbeitenden Klasse in England* (Leipzig, 1845), p. 261. 21. Adolphe Quetelet, *Sur l'homme et le développement de ses facultés, ou Essai de physique sociale* (2 vols., Paris, 1835), esp. vol. 1, p. 13. Villermé read and commented on Quetelet's manuscript and drew on it for his own *Tableau*. La Sagra was also friendly with Quetelet and made extensive use of his work. For a brilliant analysis of Quetelet's influence, see Alain Desrosières, *The Politics of Large Numbers. A History of Statistical Reasoning*, trans. Camille Naish (Cambridge, Mass., 1998). The quotation is from p. 74; on Quetelet's influence on contemorary social analysis, see pp. 73–95. 22. Friedrich Wilhelm Wolff, '"Die Kasematten von Breslau", Breslauer Zeitung', in Franz Mehring (ed.), *Gesammelte Schriften von Wilhelm Wolff* (Berlin, 1909), pp. 49–56. For a discussion of Wolff and his work on Breslau, see W. O. Henderson, *The Life of Friedrich Engels* (2 vols., London, 1976), vol. 1, pp. 245–8. 23. On the synaesthetic quality of much social description in this era, see Dominique Kalifa, 'Enquête et "culture de l'enquête" au XIXe siècle', *Romantisme*, no. 149 (2010), pp. 3–23. 24. Eugène Sue, *The Mysteries of Paris*, trans. anon. (London, 1845), p. 2. 25. See, for example, Berry Palmer Chevasco, *Mysterymania. The Reception of Eugène Sue in Britain, 1838–1860* (Oxford, 2003). 26. August Brass, *Mysterien von Berlin* (2nd edn, 2 vols., Berlin, 1844), Foreword to the 1st edn, dated March 1844, [p. 4]. 27. Eugène Buret, *De la misère des classes laborieuses en Angleterre et en France. De la nature de la misère, de son existence, des ses effets, des ses causes, et de l'insuffisance des remèdes qu'on lui a opposés jusqu'ici; avec l'indication des moyens propres à en affranchir les sociétés* (2 vols., Paris, 1840), vol. 1, pp. 132–3. 28. On Arnim's use of generic features of the fairy tale genre to encode social critique, see Helen G. Morris-Keitel, 'The Audience Should be King. Bettina Brentano von Arnim's "Tale of the Lucky Purse"', *Marvels and Tales* 11/1–2 (1997), pp. 48–60; on the 'culture of enquiry': Kalifa, 'Enquête et "culture de l'enquête"'. 29. Engels, *Die Lage der arbeitenden Klasse*, p. 45. 30. Guépin and Bonamy, *Nantes au XIXe siècle*, pp. 5–6. 31. Pamela Pilbeam, *French Socialists before Marx. Workers, Women and the Social Question in France* (Teddington, 2000), p. 143. 32. Ange Guépin, *Philosophie du XIXe siècle. Étude encyclopédique sur le monde et l'humanité* (Paris, 1854), pp. 13, 573–4; on the continuation of Saint-Simon's work, p. 543. 33. Claude Henri de Rouvroy, comte de Saint-Simon, *Catéchisme des Industriels* (Paris, 1823), p. 4. 34. On the morality of the Social Question, see Giovanna Procacci, 'Social Economy and the Government of Poverty', in G. Burchel, C. Gordon and P. Miller (eds.), *The Foucault Effect. Studies in Governmentality* (Chicago, 1991), pp. 151–68, here pp. 157–8. The phrase is borrowed from Jacques Donezelot, *The Policing of Families* (London, 1979). On the 'moralizing' character of Social and other 'Question'-based discourses more generally, see Holly Case, *The Age of Questions* (Princeton, 2018), esp. p. 73. 35. Engels, *Lage der arbeitenden Klasse*, p. 115. 36. Ramón de la Sagra, 'Ideas generales sobre la Beneficiencia publica', in La Sagra, *Discursos pronunciados en el Ateneo Scientifico y Literario de Madrid* (Paris, 1838), p. 4. 37. Honoré Frégier, *Des classes dangereuses de la population dans les grandes villes et des moyens de les rendre meilleures* (Brussels, 1840), pp. 76–7. On the ideological gap between the actual helplessness of the poor and the reproofs issued by middle-class commentators on their condition, compare, in relation to the later nineteenth century, Gareth Stedman Jones, *Outcast London. A Study in the Relationship between Classes in Victorian Society*. 38. Frégier, *Des classes dangereuses*, p. 7. 39. Ibid., pp. 295–6. 40. See, for example, Buret, *De la misère des classes laborieuses*, vol. 1, p. 347. 41. Buret, *De la misère des classes laborieuses*, vol. 1, p. 389. 42. Thus the title of the third chapter of Buret, *De la misère des classes laborieuses*, vol. 1, p. 118. 43. On Sismondi as the 'hero' of political economy, see Buret, *De la misère des classes laborieuses*, vol. 1, p. 38. 44. On the intrusion of unarticulated desires into the representation of women, see Sally Alexander, 'Women, Class and Sexual Differences in the 1830s and 1840s. Some Reflections on the Writing of a Feminist History', *History Workshop* 17/1 (Spring 1984), pp. 125–49, here p. 126; for a powerful analysis of the place of women in the discourse of the Social Question, see Joan Scott, '"L'ouvrière, mot impie, sordide . . .". Women Workers in the Discourse of French Political Economy, 1840–1860', in Scott, *Gender and the Politics of History* (New York, 1988), pp. 139–63. **45.** La Sagra, 'Ideas generales sobre la Beneficiencia publica', p. 4; on La Sagra's interest in female labour, see Mónica Burguera, *Las Damas del Liberalismo Respetable. Los imaginarios sociales del feminismo liberal en España (1834–1850)* (Madrid, 2012), p. 86. **46.** Buret, *De la misère des classes laborieuses*, vol. 1, p. 413. **47.** Scott, 'L'ouvrière, mot impie, sordide', p. 6. **48.** Engels, *Lage der arbeitenden Klassen*, p. 220. **49.** Guépin and Bonamy, *Nantes au XIXe siècle*, pp. 636–7. **50.** Ernst Dronke, *Berlin* (2 vols., Frankfurt/Main, 1846), vol. 1, pp. 50–55, 113. **51.** Anonymous call to revolution, Frankfurt, 1847, in Walter Grab (ed.), *Die Revolution von 1848/49. Eine Dokumentation* (Munich, 1980), pp. 27–8. **52.** Ludwig Wittgenstein, *Tractatus Logico-Philosophicus* (London, 1922), p. 25. **53.** This is one of the central arguments of the monumental study by Maurizio Gribaudi, *Paris ville ouvrière. Une histoire occultée, 1789–1848* (Paris, 2014), p. 74. **54.** David McClellan, 'Introduction', in Friedrich Engels, *The Condition of the Working Class in England* (Oxford, 1993), pp. xix–xx. **55.** Louis Blanc, *Organisation du travail* (Paris, [1840]), pp. 65, 94, 110–15. **56.** Ramón de la Sagra, *Lecciones de economía social* (Madrid, 1840), p. 69; on La Sagra's view of industrial progress, see Alfonso Sánchez Hormiga, 'Saint-Simonism and Economic Thought in Spain (1834–1848), *History of Economic Ideas* 17/2 (2009), pp. 121–54; Ascensión Cambrón Infante, 'Ramón de la Sagra, un Gallego ilustrado', *Anuario da Facultade de Dereito da Universidade da Coruña*, 1998, pp. 215–28; consulted online at https://core.ac.uk/download/pdf/61893609.pdf. **57.** Steven C. Hughes, *Crime, Disorder and the Risorgimento. The Politics of Policing in Bologna* (Cambridge, 2002), p. 17. **58.** Robert Lee, 'Urban Labor Markets, In-Migration, and Demographic Growth. Bremen, 1815–1914', *The Journal of Interdisciplinary History* 30/3 (1999), pp. 437–73, here p. 452. **59.** Neil McAtamney, 'The Great Famine in County Fermanagh', *Clogher Record* 15/1 (1994), pp. 76–89, here p. 81. Samuel Lewis recorded over 9,000 such dwellings in Fermanagh in 1837. Samuel Lewis, *A Topographical Dictionary of Ireland* (2 vols., London, 1837), vol. 1, p. 622. **60.** Samuel Laing, *Notes of a Traveller on the Social and Political State of France, Prussia, Switzerland, Italy and Other Parts of Europe* (London, 1842), p. 473. **61.** Berengo, M., *L'Agricoltura Veneta dalla Caduta della Repubblica all'Unità* (Milano, 1963), p. 223, cited in Paul Ginsborg, 'Peasants and Revolutionaries in Venice and the Veneto, 1848', *The Historical Journal* 17/3 (1974), pp. 503–50, here p. 506. **62.** Brian A'Hearn, 'Anthropometric Evidence on Living Standards in Northern Italy, 1730–1860', *Journal of Economic History* 63/2 (2003), pp. 351–81, here pp. 365–6; for a late-nineteenth-century study of height data covering twelve provinces in Lombardy and Piedmont that reports similar results, see Ridolfo Livi, *Antropometria militare* (2 vols., Rome, 1896 and 1905). **63.** Michela Coppola, 'The Biological Standard of Living in Germany before the Kaiserreich, 1815–1840. Insights from English Army Data', *European Review of Economic History* 14/1 (2010), pp. 71–109. **64.** Blanc, *Organisation du travail*, p. 57. **65.** Germán Rueda Hernanz, *España 1790–1900. Sociedad y condiciones económicas* (= Alfredo Alvar Esquerra (ed.), *Historia de España*, vol. 19) (Madrid, 2006), pp. 206, 196. **66.** Joel Mokyr, *Why Ireland Starved. A Quantitive and Analytical History of the Irish Economy 1800–1850* (London, 1985), p. 282; Stanley Z. Pech, 'The Czech Working Class in 1848', *Canadian Slavonic Papers/Revue Canadienne des Slavistes* 9/1 (1967), pp. 60–73, here p. 61. **67.** For an example of the propagation of low agricultural incomes to industrial wages in a number of French regions, see Michel Hau, 'Pauvreté rurale et dynamisme économique. Le cas de l'Alsace au XIXe siècle', *Histoire, Économie et Société* 6/1 (1987), pp. 113–38, esp. pp. 122–6. **68.** Fernand Rude, *Les Révoltes des Canuts (novembre 1831–avril 1834)* (Paris, 1982), p. 13. **69.** Wilhelm Abel, *Massenarmut und Hungerkrisen im vorindustriellen Europa. Versuch einer Synopsis* (Hamburg, 1974); Joel Mokyr, 'Industrialisation and Poverty in Ireland and the Netherlands', *Journal of*

Interdisciplinary History 10/3 (Winter 1980), pp. 429–58, here pp. 451–7. 70. Giovanni Gozzini, 'The Poor and the Life-Cycle in Nineteenth-Century Florence, 1813–59', *Social History* 18/3 (Oct. 1993), pp. 299–317, here p. 313. 71. Coppola, 'The Biological Standard of Living'. 72. B. R. Mitchell, *European Historical Statistics* (London, 1978), pp. 4–5; on Bologna, see Hughes, *Crime, Disorder and the Risorgimento*, pp. 16–17; on Ireland, see also Kenneth H. Connell, *The Population of Ireland 1750–1845* (Oxford, 1950); for a recent discussion, see Peter M. Solar, 'Why Ireland Starved and the Big Issues in Pre-Famine Irish Economic History', *Irish Economic and Social History* 42 (2015), pp. 62–75, esp. p. 66. 73. Mokyr, *Why Ireland Starved*; for a more concise outline, see Joel Mokyr, 'Malthusian Models and Irish History', *The Journal of Economic History* 40/1 (1980), pp. 159–66. Mokyr's findings are confirmed using different data by Morgan Kelly and Cormac Ó Gráda, 'Why Ireland Starved after Three Decades. The Great Famine in Cross-Section Reconsidered', *Irish Economic and Social History* 42 (2015), pp. 53–61. 74. J. Nadal Oller, *El fracaso de la revolución industrial en España, 1814–1913* (Barcelona, 1975), pp. 21–3. 75. Josef Mooser, *Ländliche Klassengesellschaft 1770–1848. Bauern und Unterschichten, Wirtschaft und Gewerbe im östlichen Westfalen* (Göttingen, 1984), p. 343. 76. Hughes, *Crime, Disorder and the Risorgimento*, p. 17. 77. Michael J. Neufeld, *The Skilled Metalworkers of Nuremberg. Craft and Class in the Industrial Revolution* (New Brunswick, 1989), pp. 36–41. 78. Hughes, *Crime, Disorder and the Risorgimento*, p. 84. 79. Robert Bezucha, *The Lyon Uprising of 1834. Social and Political Conflict in the Early July Monarchy* (Cambridge, Mass., 1974), pp. 43–4. 80. Rueda Hernanz, *España 1790–1900*, p. 206. 81. Henri Sée, 'La Vie politique et économique de Nantes pendant la Monarchie de Juillet, d'après la correspondance inédite de P.-F. Dubois', *Revue Historique* 163/2 (1930), pp. 297–322. 82. A. M. Bernal, *La Lucha por la tierra en la crisis del Antiguo Regimen* (Madrid, 1979), pp. 420–25. 83. Vicente Cendrero Almodóvar, 'Pervivencias feudales y conflicto social en la Mancha. El derecho maestral de Calatrava (c.1819–1855)', *Historia Social*, no. 83 (2015), pp. 19–36, here pp. 21–2, 25–6, 30–32, 34–5. 84. Manuel González de Molina and Antonio Ortega Santos, 'Bienes comunes y conflictos por los recursos en las sociedades rurales, siglos XIX y XX', *Historia Social*, no. 38 (2000), pp. 95–116. 85. Bernal, *La lucha por la tierra*, p. 422; on the role of clergy, p. 423. 86. Lucy Riall, *Sicily and the Unification of Italy* (Oxford, 1998), pp. 47–8. 87. Denis Mack Smith, 'The Latifundia in Modern Sicilian History', *Proceedings of the British Academy* 51 (1965), pp. 85–124, here pp. 95–7. 88. Nadine Vivier, *Propriété collective et identité communale. Les biens communaux en France, 1750–1914* (Paris, 1998). 89. Peter Sahlins, *Forest Rites. The War of the Demoiselles in Nineteenth-Century France* (Cambridge, Mass., 1994). 90. Nadine Vivier, 'Une question délaissée. Les biens communaux aux XVIIIe et XIXe siècles', *Revue Historique* 290/1, no. 587 (1993), pp. 143–60, here p. 146; Vivier, 'Les biens communaux du Briançonnais aux XVIIIe et XIXe siècles', *Études rurales*, no. 117, *L'Architecture rurale. Questions d'esthétique* (1990), pp. 139–58, esp. pp. 151–3. 91. Heinz Monz, 'Der Waldprozeß der Mark Thalfang als Grundlage für Karl Marx' Kritik an den Debatten um das Holzdiebstahlsgesetz', *Jahrbuch für westdeutsche Landesgeschichte* 3 (1977), pp. 395–418, here p. 396. 92. On the non-inevitability of the transition, see Francisco J. Beltrán Tapia, 'Social and Environmental Filters to Market Incentives', *Journal of Agrarian Change*, no. 15/2 (2015), pp. 239–60; Peter McPhee, *Revolution and Environment in Southern France. Peasants, Lords and Murder in the Corbières, 1780–1830* (Oxford, 1999), p. 238; on the 'peasant road', see Florence Gauthier, *La Voie paysanne dans la Révolution française. L'Example de la Picardie* (Paris, 1977). 93. González de Molina and Ortega Santos, 'Bienes comunes y conflictos por los recursos', pp. 103–4, 101, 112; Mónica Bosch, 'La defensa del "sagrado derecho de propiedad". La unió dels hisendats contra les ocupacions de terres durant el Trienni Liberal', in J. J. Busqueta and E. Vicedo (eds.), *Béns Comunals als Països Catalans i a l'Europa Contemporània. Sistemes Agraris, Organització social i poder local als Països Catalans* (Lleida, 1996), pp. 375–400; on the environmental character of some such conflicts, see also Manuel González de Molina,

Antonio Herrera, Antonio Ortega Santos and David Soto, 'Peasant Protest as Environmental Protest. Some Cases from the Eighteenth to the Twentieth Century', *Global Environment* 4 (2009), pp. 48–77, here p. 77. 94. Curtis Sarles, 'The Instatement of Order. State Initiatives and Hegemony in the Modernization of French Forest Policy', *Theory and Society* 35/ 5–6 (2006), pp. 565–85, here p. 580. 95. Stefania Barca, 'Enclosing the River. Industrialisation and the "Property Rights" Discourse in the Liri Valley (South of Italy), 1806–1916', *Environment and History* 13/1 (2007), pp. 3–23, here p. 15. 96. Jiří Radimský, 'Dělnické bouře v Brně roku 1843', *Český lid* 36/1–2 (1949), pp. 9–13, here p. 11, col. 2. 97. Bernal, *La lucha por la tierra*, p. 430. 98. John Davis, *Merchants, Monopolists and Contractors. A Study of Economic Activity and Society in Bourbon Naples 1815–1860* (New York, 1981), pp. 323–9. 99. Paul Gonnet, 'Esquisse de la crise économique en France de 1827– 1832', *Revue d'histoire économique et sociale* 33/3 (1955), pp. 249–92, here pp. 251–2. 100. Louise Tilly, 'The Food Riot as a Form of Political Conflict in France', *Journal of Interdisciplinary History* 2/1 (1971), pp. 23–57, here p. 56. 101. Gonnet, 'Esquisse', p. 255. 102. M. Bergman, 'The Potato Blight in the Netherlands and Its social Consequences (1845–1847)', *International Review of Social History* 12/3 (1967), 390–431, here pp. 393– 4. 103. Joel Mokyr, 'Industrialisation and Poverty in Ireland and the Netherlands', *Journal of Interdisciplinary History* 10/3 (1980), pp. 429–58, here pp. 434–8. 104. For lucid reflections on these issues, see Nadine Vivier, 'Pour un réexamen des crises économiques du XIXe siècle en France', *Histoire & Mesure* 26/1, *Revisiter les crises* (2011), pp. 135–55, here p. 151. 105. Mark Traugott, 'The Mid-Nineteenth-Century Crisis in France and England', *Theory and Society* 12/4 (1983), pp. 455–68. 106. Anthony Rowley, 'Deux crises économiques modernes. 1846 et 1848?', in *1848. Révolutions et mutations au XIXe siècle*, no. 2 (1986), pp. 81–90, here p. 82. 107. Gustav Adolf Bergenroth, 'Verhältnisse des Großherzogthums Luxemburg [. . .] in den Jahren 1844, 1845 und 1846', in *Zeitschrift des Vereins für deutsche Statistik* 2 (1848), p. 445, cited in Dietrich Saalfeld, 'Lebensverhältnisse der Unterschichten Deutschlands im neunzehnten Jahrhundert', *International Review of Social History* 29/2 (1984), pp. 215–53, here p. 250. 108. Bergman, 'Potato Blight', p. 399; Paul Servais, 'La crise des années 1845–1848 dans l'est de la Wallonie. Une approche', *Histoire & Mesure* 26/1, *Revisiter les crises* (2011), pp. 157–86, here p. 171. 109. Saalfeld, 'Lebensverhältnisse', p. 250. 110. Manfred Gailus, 'Food Riots in Germany in the Late 1840s', *Past & Present* 145/1 (1994), pp. 157–93, here pp. 172–3. 111. Report in the *Leydsche Courant*, 14 May 1847, cited in Bergman, 'Blight in the Netherlands', p. 401. 112. Mokyr, 'Industrialization and Poverty', p. 433. 113. Amartya Sen, *Poverty and Famines. An Essay on Entitlement and Deprivation* (Oxford, 1981). 114. José García Cabrera, 'Tiempo de escasez, tiempo de carestía. La crisis de subsistencia de 1847 en Jerez de la Frontera', *Historia Social*, no. 42 (2002), pp. 21–38. 115. Gailus, 'Food Riots', pp. 184–5. 116. Ibid., pp. 187–97. 117. Servais, 'La crise des années 1845–1848', pp. 174– 6. 118. Giovanni Federico, 'The Corn Laws in Continental Perspective', *European Review of Economic History* 16/2 (2012), pp. 166–87. 119. On the propensity of British evangelicals to see paradoxical 'blessings in disguise' in scourges such as famine and pestilence, see Boyd Hilton, *The Age of Atonement. The Influence of Evangelicalism on Social and Economic Thought* (Oxford, 1986), pp. 21–2; on the application of this interpretation to the Irish famine, see Ciarán Ó Murchadha, *Famine. Ireland's Agony, 1845–1852* (London, 2011), pp. 194–5. 120. Fernand Rude, *Les Révoltes des canuts, 1831–1834* (Paris, 1982), p. 27. 121. Ludovic Frobert and George Sheridan, *Le Solitaire du ravin. Pierre Charnier (1795–1857), canut lyonnais et prud'homme tisseur* (Lyons, 2014), p. 87. 122. Rude, *Les Révoltes des canuts*, p. 15; on this and other ways in which the legislative environment was skewed against workers and in favour of employers, see Bezucha, *The Lyon Uprising of 1834*, pp. 21–2. 123. Memorandum by Charnier, cited in Fernand Rude, 'L'insurrection ouvrière de Lyon en 1831 et le rôle de Pierre Charnier', *Revue d'Histoire du XIXe siècle* 13/35 (1938), pp. 26–7; on the evolution of Charnier's mutualism, see Frobert and

Sheridan, *Le Solitaire du ravin*, pp. 85–98. **124.** Villermé, *Tableau de l'état physique et moral des ouvriers*, p. 359. **125.** Marceline Desbordes-Valmore to Jean-Baptiste Gergères, Lyons, 29 November 1831, consulted online at https://www.correspondancedesbordesval-more.com/2018/05/revolte-ouvriers-Lyon-1831.html. **126.** On the place of memory in the political culture of the insurrectionaries in Lyons, see Bruno Benoit, 'Relecture des violences collectives lyonnaises du XIXe siècle', *Revue Historique* 299/2 (1998), pp. 255–85. **127.** Rude, *Les Révoltes des canuts*, p. 24. **128.** 'Lyon, 21 Novembre 1831', *La Glaneuse* 1/47, 25 November 1831, p. 1. **129.** *L'Écho de la Fabrique*, Prospectus, 23 October 1831; consulted online at ENS de Lyon, *L'Écho de la Fabrique et la petite presse ouvrière Lyonnaise des années 1831–1835*, http://echo-fabrique.ens-lyon.fr/sommaire.php?id=61&type=numero. **130.** On the journal's emotional vocabulary and its debt to Fourierism, see Emmanuel Renault, 'Mépris et souffrance dans l'Écho de la Fabrique', and Jonathan Beecher, 'Le fouriérisme des canuts', in Ludovic Frobert (ed.), *L'Écho de la Fabrique. Naissance de la presse ouvrière à Lyon* (Lyons, 2010), pp. 87–110 and 111–39. **131.** Bezucha, *The Lyon Uprising of 1834*, pp. 167–8. **132.** Jean-Baptiste Monfalcon, *Histoire des insurrections de Lyon en 1831 et en 1834* (Paris, 1834), pp. 1–2, also 331–2. **133.** Mary Lynn McDougall, 'Popular Culture, Political Culture. The Case of Lyon, 1830–1850', *Historical Reflections/Réflexions Historiques* 8/2 (1981), pp. 27–41, here p. 28. **134.** André Jardin and André-Jean Tudesq, *Restoration and Reaction 1815–1848*, trans. Elborg Forster (Cambridge, 1984), p. 294. **135.** Bezucha, *The Lyon Uprising of 1834*, pp. 187–8. **136.** Speech to the Court of Peers by the Republican Charles Lagrange, 2 July 1835, cited in Bezucha, *The Lyon Uprising of 1834*, p. 190. **137.** Félicité Robert de Lamennais, *La Liberté trahie (du procès d'avril et de la République)* [1834], ed. Lucien Scheler (Paris, 1946), p. 41. **138.** Jonathan Beecher, *Writers and Revolution. Intellectuals and the French Revolution of 1848* (Cambridge, 2021), p. 84. **139.** Jacques Viard, 'Les origines du socialisme républicain', *Revue d'histoire moderne et contemporaine* 33/1 (1986), pp. 133–47, here p. 134. **140.** On these connections, see Deborah Jenson, 'Myth, History and Witnessing in Marceline Desbordes-Valmore's Caribbean Poetics', *L'Esprit Créateur* 47/4 (2007), pp. 81–92. **141.** Jeremy Popkin, 'Worlds Turned Upside Down. Bourgeois Experience in the Nineteenth-Century Revolutions', *Journal of Social History* 40/4 (Summer 2007), pp. 821–39. **142.** For an evocative account of Brno as a historic centre of textile production and especially of the Offermann works, see Kateřina Tučková, Andrea Březinová and Tomáš Zapletal, *Fabrika. Příběh textilních baronů z moravského Manchesteru* (Brno, 2017). **143.** Radimský, 'Dělnické bouře v Brně roku 1843'. **144.** Eyewitness account, cited in Rudolf Kučera, 'Marginalizing Josefína. Work, Gender, and Protest in Bohemia 1820–1844', *Journal of Social History* 46/2 (Winter 2012), pp. 430–48, here p. 436. The following account of these events is indebted to Kučera's excellent analysis. **145.** On the same phenomenon in Britain, see Anna Clark, *The Struggle for the Breeches. Gender and the Making of the British Working Class* (Berkeley, 1995). **146.** Michael Spehr, *Maschinensturm. Protest und Widerstand gegen technische Neuerungen am Anfang der Industrialisierung* (Münster, 2000). **147.** Kučera, 'Marginalizing Josefína', p. 434. **148.** Anon., 'Das Blutgericht (1844)', song of the weavers in Peterswaldau and Langenbielau, reproduced in Lutz Kroneberg and Rolf Schloesser (eds.), *Weber-Revolte 1844. Der schlesische Weberaufstand im Spiegel der zeitgenössischen Publizistik und Literatur* (Cologne, 1979), pp. 469–72. **149.** This account of the events is based largely on the contemporary report by Wilhelm Wolff, 'Das Elend und der Aufruhr in Schlesien 1844', written in June 1844 and reprinted in Kroneberg and Schloesser, *Weber-Revolte*, pp. 241–64. **150.** 'The Manufacturing Districts of Germany', *The Times*, 18 July 1844, p. 6. *The Times Digital Archive*, http://tinyurl.galegroup.com/tinyurl/BPsLc9. Accessed 22 July 2019. **151.** Kroneberg and Schloesser, *Weber-Revolte*, pp. 24–5. **152.** 'Der "Preuße" stelle sich dagegen auf den richtigen Standpunkt', Karl Marx, 'Kritische Randglossen zu dem Artikel "Der König von Preussen und die Sozialreform"', *Vorwärts!*, no. 63, 7 August 1844, pp. 392–409, here p. 404, consulted online at http://www.mlwerke.de/me/meo1/meo1_392.htm. **153.** Anon. [Leopold von Sacher-Masoch], *Polnische Revolutionen. Erinnerungen aus Galizien* (Prague, 1863), p. 89. **154.** Michael Chvojka, 'Zwischen Konspiration und Revolution. Entstehung und Auswirkungen der Revolution von 1846 in Krakau und Galizien. Wahrnehmung und Aktionsradius der Habsburger Polizei', *Jahrbücher für Geschichte Osteuropas*, new series, 58/4 (2010), pp. 481–507. **155.** Moritz Freiherr von Sala, *Geschichte des polnischen Aufstandes vom Jahre 1846. Nach authentischen Quellen dargestellt* (Vienna, 1867), p. 50. **156.** Arnon Gill, *Die polnische Revolution 1846. Zwischen nationalem Befreiungskampf und antifeudaler Bauernerhebung* (Munich, 1974), pp. 76–8. **157.** Hans Henning Hahn, 'The Polish Nation in the Revolution of 1846–49', in Dieter Dowe, Heinz-Gerhard Haupt, Dieter Langewiesche and Jonathan Sperber (eds.), *Europe in 1848. Revolution und Reform* (New York, 2001), pp. 170–85. **158.** Instructions from Ludwik Mierosławski to the District Officers appointed by the National Committee to each Galician District, cited in [Sacher-Masoch], *Polnische Revolutionen*, p. 50. **159.** Gill, *Die polnische Revolution 1846*, p. 186. **160.** [Sacher-Masoch], *Polnische Revolutionen*, p. 95. **161.** See, for example, the accounts in Ksiądz (Father) Karol Antoniewicz, *Misyjne z roku 1846* (Poznań, 1849), pp. 2, 7–8, 14, 16, 17, 24, 27, 35, 80–81. **162.** [Sacher-Masoch], *Polnische Revolutionen*, p. 105; Sala, *Geschichte des polnischen Aufstandes vom Jahre 1846*, pp. 270–72. **163.** These and other horrors are listed in the letter of supplication submitted to the Emperor on 15 April 1846 by one of the few surviving adult males of the family, Henryk Bogusz, transcribed in Léonard Chodźko, *Les Massacres de Galicie et Krakovie confisquée par l'Autriche en 1846* (Paris, 1861), pp. 67–71. **164.** [Sacher-Masoch], *Polnische Revolutionen*, pp. 182–4; Sala, *Geschichte des polnischen Aufstandes vom Jahre 1846*, pp. 232–4. **165.** [Sacher-Masoch], *Polnische Revolutionen*, pp. 184–5; Sala, *Geschichte des polnischen Aufstandes vom Jahre 1846* , pp. 232–3. According to Sala, the conspirators were confined in one of the estate buildings by the peasants, on the assumption that an Austrian patrol would soon appear to bear off the rebels. When the patrol failed to materialize, the peasants attacked the captives and killed a number of them. **166.** Ludwik Dębicki, *Z dawnich wspomnień* (Cracow, 1903), p. 72. **167.** On the Polish literature on 1846, see Gill, *Die polnische Revolution*, pp. 38–9; Lesya Ivasyuk, *Die polnische Revolution von 1846 in Galizien. Österreichische, ukrainische und polnische Wahrnehmungen* (Vienna, 2014), pp. 15–35. **168.** Alan Sked, 'Austria and the "Galician Massacres" of 1846. Schwarzenberg and the Propaganda War. An Unknown But Key Episode in the Career of the Austrian Statesman', in Lother Höbelt and Thomas G. Otte (eds.), *A Living Anachronism? European Diplomacy and the Habsburg Monarchy. Festschrift für Roy Bridge zum 70. Geburtstag* (Vienna, 2010), pp. 49–118, here pp. 51–2; Chodźko, *Les Massacres*, p. 23. For a nuanced polish assessment, see Antoni Podraza, 'Das Präludium der Revolution des Jahres 1848'. Die poinischen Ereignisse des Jahres 1846', in Heiner Timmermann (ed.), *1848. Revolution in Europa. Verlauf, Politische Programme, Folgen und Wirkungen* (Berlin, 1999), pp. 173–82. **169.** Chodźko, *Les Massacres*, p. 27. **170.** Thus Léonard Chodźko, *Les Massacres de Galicie* (Paris, 1861), pp. 51–3, 58, and Dębicki, *Z dawnich wspomnień*, p. 52. **171.** Gill, *Die polnische Revolution*, p. 17. **172.** '. . . die Welt wäre nicht vielseitig ohne die vielen Einseitigkeiten'. [Karl Marx], 'Debatten über das Holzdiebstahlsgesetz. Von einem Rheinländer', *Rheinische Zeitung*, no. 300, 27 October 1842, pp. 116–24, here p. 118. **173.** Metternich to Radetzky, 16 March 1846, cited in Alan Sked, 'The Nationality Problem in the Habsburg Monarchy and the Revolutions of 1848. A Reassessment', in Douglas Moggach and Gareth Stedman Jones (eds.), *The 1848 Revolutions and European Political Thought* (Cambridge, 2018), pp. 322–44, here p. 330. **174.** Sked, 'Austria and the "Galician Massacres" of 1846 ', and 'The Nationality Problem in the Habsburg Monarchy and the Revolutions of 1848'. **175.** Cited in Édouard Conte, 'Terre et "Pureté ethnique" aux confins polono-ukrainiens', *Études rurales*, no. 138–140, *Paysans au-delà du mur* (1995), pp. 53–85, here p. 60. **176.** Antoniewicz, *Misyjne z roku 1846*, pp. 6, 23, 29. **177.** László Péter, 'Introduction', in László Péter, Martyn Rady and Peter Sherwood (eds.), *Lajos Kossuth Sent Word . . . Papers Delivered on the Occasion of the Bicentenary of*

Kossuth's Birth (London, 2003), pp. 1–14, here p. 5.   **178.** Wolfgang Höpken, 'The Agrarian Question in Southeastern Europe during the Revolution of 1848/49', in Dowe at al. (eds.), *Europe in 1848*, pp. 443–71, here p. 459.   **179.** Ivasyuk, *Die polnische Revolution, passim.*   **180.** Leopold Sacher-Masoch, *Graf Donski. Eine Galizische Geschichte, 1846* (1st edn, 1858, with the title *Eine Galizische Geschichte, 1846*; 2nd edn, Schaffhausen, 1864), pp. 339–51.   **181.** Dębicki, *Z dawnich wspomnień*, p. 60.   **182.** Leopold von Sacher-Masoch, 'Eine Autobiographie', *Deutsche Monatsblätter. Centralorgan für das literarische Leben der Gegenwart* 2/3 (1879), pp. 259–69, here p. 260. The reference to dogs licking up the puddled blood of dead insurgents also occurs in [Sacher-Masoch], *Polnische Revolutionen*, p. 185. The resemblance lends credence to the theory that the author of the latter book was in fact Sacher-Masoch junior, working from notes and documents collected by his father (on this see Ivasyuk, *Die polnische Revolution*).   **183.** Otto Lüning, 'Ein politisches Rundgemälde', in Lüning (ed.), *Dieß Buch gehört dem Volke* (Bielefeld, 1845), pp. 1–86, here p. 30.   **184.** Anon. [Luigi Settembrini], *Protesta del popolo delle due Sicilie* [Naples, 1847], p. 37.   **185.** Michael Spehr, *Maschinensturm. Protest und Widerstand gegen technische Neuerungen am Anfang der Industrialisierung* (Münster, 2000), p. 39.   **186.** Jack Goldstone, 'Population and Security. How Demographic Change Can Lead to Violent Conflict', *Journal of International Affairs* 56/1 (2002), pp. 3–21, here p. 8.   **187.** On the non-linear relationship between social conflict and revolutionary upheaval, see Anna Maria Garcia Rovira, 'Radicalismo liberal, republicanismo y revolución (1835–1837), Ayer, no. 29, *La Política en el reinado de Isabel II* (1998), pp. 63–90.   **188.** [Karl Marx], 'Debatten über das Holzdiebstahlsgesetz' . See also the other articles in the series in *Rheinische Zeitung*, nos. 298, 303, 305 and 307. They can be consulted at http://www.mlwerke.de/me/meo1/meo1_116.htm,   http://www.mlwerke.de/me/meo1/meo1_109.htm,   http://www.mlwerke.de/me/meo1/meo1_124.htm,   http://www.mlwerke.de/me/meo1/meo1_131.htm,   and   http://www.mlwerke.de/me/meo1/meo1_139.htm, respectively.   **189.** Monz, 'Waldprozeß der Mark Thalfang', p. 396.   **190.** Riall, *Sicily and the Unification of Italy*, p. 57; Rosario Romeo, *Il Risorgimento in Sicilia* (Bari, 1950), p. 187; Smith 'The Latifundia', p. 98.   **191.** Ph. Vigier, 'Les troubles forestiers du premier XIX siècle français', *Revue forestière française* 32 (1980), pp. 128–35.   **192.** See Vicente Fernández Benítez, *Carlismo y rebeldía campesina. Un estudio sobre la conflictividad social en Cantabria durante la crisis final del Antiguo Régimen* (Madrid, 1988); R. Vallverdú Martí, *La guerra dels Matiners a Catalunya (1846–1849). Una crisi económica i una revolta popular* (Barcelona, 2002); on the place of the Guerra dels Matiners within the Spanish and larger European context, see Rafael Ruzafa Ortega, 'Movimientos sociales en la España del siglo XIX', *Aula-Historia Social*, 22 (2008), pp. 18–38; Ignacio García de Paso García, 'El 1848 español. ¿Una excepción europea?', *Ayer*, no. 106 (2017) (2), pp. 185–206.   **193.** Ignacio de Paso García, '"Ya no hay Pirineos". La revolución de 1848 en Aragón', *Revista de historia Jerónimo Zurita*, no. 91 (2016), pp. 183–203, here p. 199.   **194.** Gailus, 'Food Riots', p. 190.   **195.** Ibid., p. 172.   **196.** Viscount Ponsonby to Viscount Palmerston, Vienna, 20 November 1848, in Markus Mösslang, Torsten Riotte and Hagen Schulze (eds.), *British Envoys to Germany, 1816–1866* (Cambridge, 2006), vol. 3: *1848–1850*, pp. 423–5, here p. 425.   **197.** Rhys Williams, 'Diary of a Utopia. Looting an Empty Utopia', 23 August 2011; consulted online at https://web.archive.org/web/20210813094529/https://finzionimagazine.it/.

2. CONJECTURES OF ORDER

1. Carl Schmitt to Ernst Jünger, 26 April 1939, in Helmuth Kiesel (ed.), *Ernst Jünger – Carl Schmitt. Briefe 1930–1983* (Stuttgart 1999), p. 84.   **2.** [Zoé] Gatti de Gamond, *Fourier et son système* (2nd edn, Paris, 1839), pp. i–ii.   **3.** Claire Démar, *Ma loi d'avenir. Ouvrage posthume, publié par Suzanne* (Paris, 1834), p. 51.   **4.** Ibid., p. 6.   **5.** Ibid., p. 6.   **6.** Ibid., p. 45.   **7.** Ibid., p. 49.   **8.** Ibid., p. 49.   **9.** Ibid., pp. 38, 53, 55, 56.   **10.** Démar,

'Appel d'une femme au peuple sur l'affranchissement de la femme', p. 67; the editor, Suzanne Voilquin, published this essay as an addendum to *Ma loi d'avenir*. 11. Démar, 'Appel d'une femme au peuple', pp. 67–8. 12. Démar, *Ma loi d'avenir*, pp. 25, 55. 13. Patricia Springborg, *Mary Astell. Theorist of Freedom from Domination* (Cambridge, 2005), pp. 1–26, 32–3, 209–37. 14. Démar, *Ma loi d'avenir*, p. 26. 15. Suzanne Voilquin, 'Notice historique', in ibid., p. 7. 16. Cited from the 'profession of faith' Deroin was asked to write on entering the Saint-Simonian 'church', in Joan Wallach Scott, 'Feminist Family Politics', *French Politics, Culture & Society* 17/3–4 (1999), pp. 20–30, here p. 23. 17. Claire G. Moses, 'Saint-Simonian Men/Saint-Simonian Women. The Transformation of Feminist Thought in 1830s' France', *The Journal of Modern History* 54/2, *Sex, Science, and Society in Modern France* (1982), pp. 240–67, here p. 249. 18. Charles Fourier, *Théorie des quatre mouvements et des destinées générales, suivi du Nouveau monde amoureux*, p. 29 (consulted online at https://inventin.lautre.net/livres/Fourier-Theorie-des-4-mouvements. pdf). 19. On residual sexual discrimination in Fourier, see Leslie F. Goldstein , 'Early Feminist Themes in French Utopian Socialism. The Saint-Simonians and Fourier', *Journal of the History of Ideas* 43/1 (1982), pp. 91–108, esp. pp. 102–7. 20. Démar, *Ma loi d'avenir*, p. 37. 21. Fourier, *Théorie des quatre mouvements*, p. 300 (consulted online at https://inventin.lautre.net/livres/Fourier-Theorie-des-4-mouvements.pdf). 22. Démar, *Ma loi d'avenir*, p. 24. 23. Suzanne Voilquin, *Souvenirs d'une fille du peuple, ou La Saint-Simonienne en Égypte, 1834–1836* (Paris, 1865), p. 78. 24. Voilquin, *Souvenirs d'une fille du peuple*, p. 77. 25. Jeanne Deroin, 'Profession de foi', cited in Françoise F. Laot, 'Jeanne Deroin and Mutual Education of Women and Workers'. Pionnières de l'éducation des adultes. Perspectives internationales, 2018, consulted online at https://hal.archives-ouvertes.fr/hal-02315376/ document. 26. Laot, 'Jeanne Deroin', [p. 4]. 27. Bonnie S. Anderson, '*Frauenemancipation* and Beyond. The Use of the Concept of Emancipation by Early European Feminists', in Katherine Kish Sklar and James Brewer Stewart (eds.)' *Women's Rights and Transatlantic Antislavery in the Era of Emancipation* (New Haven, 2007), pp. 82–97, here pp. 89–90; on the limits of Saint-Simonian feminism, see also Goldstein, 'Early Feminist Themes in French Utopian Socialism', pp. 95–7. 28. *Gazette des Femmes* 1/2 (1 August 1836), pp. 33–8. 29. 'Pétition au Roi, à messieurs les députés des départements, et à mm. les pairs du royaume de France, pour l'abolition des Peines contre l'adultère et la suppression entière et complète des articles suivants du Code pénal', ibid. 1/4 (1 October 1836), pp. 97–107, here p. 99. 30. 'Tonibreh de Mauchamps' (= Herbinot de Mauchamps), 'De la prostitution dans la ville de Paris', ibid. 3/3 (1 March 1838) pp. 40–43. 31. Ibid. 1/6 (1 December 1836), pp. 161–5. 32. Ibid. 2/1 (1 January 1837), pp. 12–16. 33. Ibid. 2/2 (1 Febuary 1837), pp. 33–6. 34. Ibid. 3/4 (1 January 1838), pp. 1–5. 35. Marie-Louise Puech, 'Une supercherie littéraire. Le véritable rédacteur de la Gazette des Femmes, 1836–1838', *La Révolution de 1848 et les révolutions du XIXe siècle* 32, no. 153 (June–July–August 1935), pp. 303–12; on male feminism under the July Monarchy, see Karen Offen, 'Ernest Legouvé and the Doctrine of "Equality in Difference" for Women. A Case Study of Male Feminism in Nineteenth-Century French Thought', *The Journal of Modern History* 58/2 (1986), pp. 452–84. 36. Guépin and Bonamy, *Nantes au XIXe siècle*, p. 477. 37. Alfonso Sánchez Hormiga, 'Saint-Simonism and economic thought in Spain (1834–1848)', *History of Economic Ideas* 17/2 (2009), pp. 121–54, here p. 126. 38. The quotation is from Michael Levin, 'John Stuart Mill. A Liberal Looks at Utopian Socialism in the Years of Revolution 1848–9', *Utopian Studies* 14/2 (2003), pp. 68–82, p. 75; J. R. Hainds, 'John Stuart Mill and the Saint Simonians', *Journal of the History of Ideas* 7/1 (1946), pp. 103–12; 39. Cited in Stanley Z. Pech, *The Czech Revolution of 1848* (Chapel Hill, 1969), p. 327. 40. Éliane Gubin, Valérie Piette and Catherine Jacques, 'Les féminismes belges et français de 1830 à 1914. Une approche comparée', *Le Mouvement social*, no. 178 (1997), pp. 36–68, here p. 40. 41. Zoé Gatti de Gamond, *Fourier et son système* (Bordeaux, 1838); Gatti de Gamond, *Fourier y su sistema, principios de la ciencia social* (Bordeaux, 1840); the Catalan edition appeared anonymously: *Fourier, ó sea explanación del sistema societario* (Barcelona, 1841); see also Juan Pro, 'Thinking of a Utopian Future. Fourierism in Nineteenth-Century Spain', *Utopian Studies* 26/2 (2015), pp. 329–48; on Gatti de Gamond's selective reading of Fourier, see Valérie Piette, 'Zoe Gatti de Gamond ou les premières avancées féministes?' *Revue belge de philologie et d'histoire* 77/2 (1999), pp. 402–15, here p. 412.   **42.** Cited in Gisela Bock, *Geschlechtergeschichten der Neuzeit. Ideen, Politik, Praxis* (Göttingen, 2014), p. 111.   **43.** Cited in Joey Horsley, 'A German-American Feminist and Her Female Marriages. Mathilde Franziska Anneke (1817–1884)', FemBio. Notable Women International, consulted at https://www.fembio.org/english/biography.php/woman/ biography_extra/mathilde-franziska-anneke/#_ftn1.   **44.** Flora Tristan, *Pérégrinations d'une Paria (1833–1834)* (Paris, 1838), p. xxiv; on the parallels between Europe and Peru, p. 298.   **45.** Ibid., p. xxxiv.   **46.** Ibid.   **47.** Stéphane Michaud, 'Flora Tristan. Trente-cinq lettres', *International Review of Social History* 24/1 (1979), pp. 80–125, here p. 82.   **48.** Jules Janin, 'George Sand', *Gazette des Femmes* 1/4 (1 October 1836), pp. 113–15. Janin was an eclectic theatre critic and author of *L'Âne mort et la femme guillotinée*.   **49.** Alexander Herzen, *My Past and Thoughts. The Memoirs of Alexander Herzen*, trans. Constance Garnett, rev. Humphrey Higgins, with an introduction by Isaiah Berlin (4 vols., London, 1968), vol. 1, pp. xxiii (introduction) and 345, vol. 2, pp. 903, 972.   **50.** Voilquin, 'Notice historique', in Démar, *Ma loi d'avenir*, pp. 13–14; this passage is discussed in Caroline Arni, '"Moi seule" 1833. Feminist Subjectivity, Temporality, and Historical Interpretation', *History of the Present* 2/2 (2012), pp. 107–21, here p. 108.   **51.** Herbinot de Mauchamps, review of *Pérégrinations d'une paria (1833–1834)*, by Flora Tristan, in *Gazette des Femmes* 3/4 (1 January 1838), pp. 10–11.   **52.** Aurélie de Soubiran, *Virginia* (2 vols., Paris, 1845); see also the hostile review in *Bibliographie Catholique. Revue critique des Ouvrages de Religion, de Philosophie, d'Histoire, de Littérature, d'Éducation etc.* 5 (1845–6), p. 536.   **53.** On Mühlbach's early novels, which are now difficult to find, see Renate Möhrmann, *Die andere Frau. Emanzipationsansätze deutscher Schriftstellerinnen im Vorfeld der Achtundvierziger-Revolution* (Stuttgart, 1977), pp. 73, 106; the citation from Mühlbach's *Bunte Welt* is at p. 76.   **54.** Helynne Hollstein Hansen, *Hortense Allart. The Woman and the Novelist* (Lanham, 1998), *passim*.   **55.** See Margarita López Morla's addendum to Jean Czinski, *Porvenir de las mujeres* (Cadiz, 1841), pp. 32–3.   **56.** Ida Frick, *Der Frauen Sclaventhum und Freiheit. Ein Traum am Hans-Heiling-Felsen. Allen deutschen Frauen und Jungfreuen gewidmet* (Dresden and Leipzig, 1845), p. 15.   **57.** Louise Aston, *Meine Emancipation, Verweisung und Rechtfertigung* (Brussels, 1846), p. 7.   **58.** Ibid., pp. 46–9.   **59.** Thus the title of Saidiya Hartman's study of African American women in the early-twentieth-century black ghettos of the American cities; Saidiya Hartman, *Wayward Lives and Beautiful Experiments. Intimate Histories of Social Upheaval* (New York, 2019), which explores precisely this relationship between oppressive macrostructures and individual efforts to achieve autonomy.   **60.** *Tribune des Femmes*, 1 October 1833, pp. 180–84, here p. 183, consulted online at https://gallica.bnf.fr/ark:/12148/bpt6k855277/f247.item.   **61.** Jörn Leonhard, *Liberalismus. Zur historischen Semantik eines Deutungsmusters* (Munich, 2001), esp. pp. 505–69.   **62.** Maurizio Isabella, *Risorgimento in Exile. Italian Émigrés and the Liberal International in the Post-Napoleonic Era* (Oxford, 2009).   **63.** On this phase in the history of liberal politics, see Helene Rosenblatt, *The Lost History of Liberalism. From Ancient Rome to the Twenty-First Century* (Princeton, 2018), pp. 41–87.   **64.** Comments by Daniel Gordon on Rosenblatt, *Lost History*, in H-Diplo Roundtable XXI-4, viewed online at https://networks.h-net.org/node/28443/discussions/4689724/h-diplo-roundtable-xxi-4-lost-history-liberalism%C2%A0-ancient-rome.   **65.** Germaine de Staël, *A Treatise on the Influence of the Passions upon the Happiness of Individuals and of Nations*, trans. anon. (London, 1798), pp. 17, 196.   **66.** Michael Freeden and Javier Fernández Sebastián, 'European Liberal Discourses. Conceptual Affinities and Disparities', in Michael Freeden, Javier Fernández Sebastián and Jörn Leonhard (eds.), *In Search of European*

Liberalisms. Concepts, Languages, Ideologies (New York, 2019), pp. 1–35, here p. 1; on the positive dimension of a 'situated and thick liberalism' that was 'not sealed but open, not uniform but confidently heterogeneous', see Andreas Kalyvas and Ira Katznelson, *Liberal Beginnings. Making a Republic for the Moderns* (Cambridge, 2008), p. 17.   67. M. Lorenzo de Vidaurre, 'Justificación motivada por las acusaciones en torno a la conducta seguida en Cuzco' (1814), cited in Javier Fernández Sebastián, 'Liberalismos nacientes en el Atlántico iberoamericano. "Liberal" como concepto y como identidad política, 1750–1850', *Jahrbuch für Geschichte Lateinamerikas* 45 (2008), pp. 149–96, here p. 172.   68. Benjamin Constant, *The Liberty of Ancients Compared with That of Moderns* (unknown, 1819), viewed online at https://oll.libertyfund.org/titles/constant-the-liberty-of-ancients-compared-with-that-of-moderns-1819.   69. David Barreira, 'El gran mito del liberalismo. Ni surgió in Inglaterra ni lo inventó John Locke', *El Español*, 21 May 2020.   70. 'La représentation n'est pas le calcul de réduction . . . qui donne en petit l'image du peuple'; Germaine de Staël, *Des circonstances actuelles qui peuvent terminer la Révolution et des principes qui doivent fonder la République en France*, ed. John Viénot (Paris, 1906), p. 18.   71. [Francisco Martínez de la Rosa], 'Exposición', *Estatuto Real para la Convocación de las Cortes Generales del Reino* (Madrid 1834), pp. 5–31, here p. 10.   72. Francisco Martínez de la Rosa, *El Espiritu del Siglo*, vol. 1 (Madrid, 1835), pp. 22–5.   73. Gabriel Paquette, 'Romantic Liberalism in Spain and Portugal, c. 1825–1850', *The Historical Journal* 58/2 (2015), pp. 481–511, here pp. 496–7, 499–502.   74. Massimo d'Azeglio, 'Risposta alla Lettera del Dottore Luigi Carlo Farini intitolata Dei nobili in Italia e dell'attuale indirizzo delle opinoni italiane', in Marco Tabarrini (ed.), *Scritti politici e letterari di Massimo d'Azeglio* (2 vols., Florence, 1872), vol. 1, pp. 197–217, here pp. 199–200, 215.   75. Dieter Langewiesche, *Liberalismus in Deutschland* (Frankfurt, 1988), pp. 7–11, 63.   76. On anticlericalism as a form of 'gender war', see Michael B. Gross, *The War against Catholicism. Liberalism and the Anti-Catholic Imagination in Nineteenth-Century Germany* (Ann Arbor, 2005); Helena Rosenblatt, 'The Rise and Fall of "Liberalism" in France', in Freeden, Fernández Sebastián and Leonhard (eds.), *In Search of European Liberalisms*, pp. 161–84; on the fate of the liberal Catholics, see Francesco Traniello, 'Le origini del cattolicesimo liberale', in Traniello, *Da Gioberti a Moro. Percorsi di una cultura politica* (Milan, 1990), pp. 11–24.   77. The classical exposition of this nexus is Pierre Rosenvallon, *Le Capitalisme utopique. Histoire de l'idée de marché* (Paris, 1979).   78. Dieter Langewiesche, 'Liberalismus und Region', *Historische Zeitschrift. Beihefte*, new series, vol. 19: *Liberalismus und Region. Zur Geschichte des deutschen Liberalismus im 19. Jahrhundert* (1995), pp. 1–18.   79. Antonella Rancan, 'A Study in the Economic Culture of a "Strong People". The Italian Remodelling of Classical Trade Theory (1830–1860)', *History of Economic Ideas* 13/2 (2005), pp. 29–49, here p. 39.   80. Gábor Vermes, *Hungarian Culture and Politics in the Habsburg Monarchy 1711–1848* (Budapest, 2014), p. 316.   81. The classic study of these fluctuations is now David Todd, *Free Trade and Its Enemies in France* (Cambridge, 2015); see also David Todd, 'John Bowring and the Global Dissemination of Free Trade', *The Historical Journal* 51/2 (2008), pp. 373–97.   82. Todd, *Free Trade and Its Enemies*, p. 4.   83. *El Turia*, 3 August 1835, cited in Isabel Burdiel, 'Myths of Failure, Myths of Success. New Perspectives on Nineteenth-Century Spanish Liberalism', *The Journal of Modern History* 70/4 (1998), pp. 892–912, here p. 906.   84. Louis Blanc, *Organisation du travail* (Paris, [1840]), pp. 65, 94, 110–15.   85. Flora Tristan, *L'Union ouvrière* (Paris and Lyons, 1844), pp. 5, 71.   86. Transcribed in Walter Grab (ed.), *Die Revolution von 1848/49. Eine Dokumentation* (Munich, 1980), pp. 27–8.   87. August Becker, *Was wollen die Kommunisten? Eine Rede, im Auszug vorgetragen vor einer am 4. August 1844 im Lokal des s.g. Kommunisten Vereins zu Lausanne, von Mitgliedern verschiedener Arbeiter-Vereine abgehaltenen Versammlung* (Lausanne, 1844), pp. 4, 34.   88. Viviana Mellone, *Napoli 1848. Il movimento radicale e la rivoluzione* (Milan, 2017), p. 40.   89. Wilhelm Weitling, *Garantien der Harmonie und Freiheit* (Vivis, 1842).   90. Christopher H. Johnson, *Utopian Communism in France*.

Cabet and the Icarians, 1839–1851 (Ithaca, 1974). **91.** See Fourier's reflections on 'universal harmony' in Jonathan Beecher and Richard Bienvenu (eds. and trans.), *The Utopian Vision of Charles Fourier. Selected Texts on Work, Love, and Passionate Attraction* (New York, 1972), pp. 81–2, 257–64, 271–328. **92.** Martin Malia, *Alexander Herzen and the Birth of Russian Socialism, 1812–1855* (Cambridge, 1961), pp. 118, 326. **93.** Blanc, *Organisation du travail*, pp. 14, 108, 110, 113–15. **94.** Alphonse de Lamartine, 'Du droit au travail et de l'organsisation du travail' (1844), article published in *La Presse*, excerpted in Émile Thomas, *Histoire des Ateliers Nationaux. Considérés sous le double point de vue politique et social, des causes de leur formation et de leur existence, de l'influence qu'ils on exercée sur les événements des quatre premiers mois de la République, suivi des pièces justificatives* (Paris, 1848), pp. 22–6. **95.** Lorenz Stein, *Der Socialismus und Communismus des heutigen Frankreichs* (Leipzig, 1842), p. 129. The following discussion of Stein is indebted to the powerful analysis in Diana Siclovan, 'Lorenz Stein and German Socialism 1835–1872', PhD thesis, University of Cambridge, 2014, pp. 57–78, viewed online at https://www.repository.cam.ac.uk. **96.** Comments by Daniel Gordon on Rosenblatt, *Lost History*, in H-Diplo Roundtable XXI-4, viewed online at https://networks.h-net.org/node/28443/discussions/4689724/h-diplo-roundtable-xxi-4-lost-history-liberalism%C2%Ao-ancient-rome. **97.** Weitling, *Garantien der Harmonie und Freiheit*, p. 185. **98.** Cited in Vermes, *Hungarian Culture and Politics*, p. 330. **99.** Blanc, *Organisation du travail*, p. 105. **100.** Ludovic Frobert, 'Politique et économie politique chez Pierre et Jules Leroux', *Revue d'histoire du XIXe siècle*, no. 40 (2010(1)), pp. 77–94. **101.** Weitling, *Garantien der Harmonie und Freiheit*, pp. 227–8. **102.** J. Poisson, *Le Romantisme social de Lamennais. Essai sur la métaphysique des deux sociétés: 1833–1854* (Paris, 1932), p. 303. **103.** Roger Picard, 'Un Saint-Simonien démocrate. Ange Guépin', *Revue d'histoire économique et sociale* 13/4 (1925), pp. 456–94, here p. 486. **104.** Stein, *Der Socialismus und Communismus*, pp. iii, viii, iv, 10. **105.** Siclovan, 'Lorenz Stein', pp. 72–6. **106.** Friedrich Carl von Savigny, *Vom Beruf unserer Zeit für Gesetzgebung und Rechtswissenschaft* (Heidelberg, 1814), pp. 10–11. On the significance of this claim, see Charlotte Johann, 'Sovereignty and the Legal Legacies of Empire in Early Nineteenth-Century Prussia', PhD thesis, University of Cambridge, 2021, p. 46. **107.** '... una monarquía sin iglesia preponderante, sin nobleza, poco puede diferenciarse de la república', *La Esperanza*, 28 February 1848. **108.** Karl Ludwig von Haller, *Restauration der Staats-Wissenschaft, oder Theorie des natürlich-geselligen Zustands, der Chimäre des künstlich-bügerlichen entgegengesetzt* (Winterthur, 1816), esp. the Vorrede, pp. iii–lxxii; on the political consequences of the contract theory, pp. 21–34, 218–68; on the persistence of the state of nature, 327–9; on 'natural superiority', 342–6. On Haller's arguments in the context of early conservatism, see the two vintage classics Fritz Valjavec, *Die Entstehung der politischen Strömungen in Deutschland, 1770–1815* (Munich, 1951), and Klaus Epstein, *The Genesis of German Conservatism* (Princeton, 1966); for a detailed analysis of the resonance of his ideas in European political thought and opinion: Ronald Roggen, '*Restauration*' – *Kampfruf und Schimpfwort. Eine Kommunikationsanalyse zum Hauptwerk des Staatstheoretikers Karl Ludwig von Haller* (Freiburg/Schweiz, 1999). **109.** Friedrich Christoph Dahlmann, *Die Politik, auf den Grund und das Maß der gegebenen Zustände zurückgeführt* (Leipzig, 1847), p. 3. **110.** Joseph de Maistre, *Considérations sur la France* ([orig. Lausanne, 1796] 2nd edn, Paris, 1814), here esp. pp. 2–4, 73–4. **111.** Adam Müller, *Von der Nothwendigkeit einer theologischen Grundlage der gesammten Staatswissenschaften und der Staatswirtschaft insbesondere* (Leipzig, 1819), esp. pp. 9–10. **112.** Diary entry, Leopold von Gerlach, Gerlach, 1 May 1816, BA Potsdam, NL von Gerlach, 90 Ge 2, Bl. 9. **113.** Iván Zoltán Dénes, 'The Value Systems of Liberals and Conservatives in Hungary, 1830–1848', *The Historical Journal* 36/4 (1993), pp. 825–50, here p. 828. **114.** Enrico Francia, *1848. La rivoluzione del Risorgimento* (Bologna, 2012), p. 18. **115.** Karl Wilhelm von Lancizolle, *Über Ursachen, Character und Folgen der Julitage* (Berlin, 1831), pp. 66, 73. **116.** Ibid., p. 66. **117.** Ibid., pp. 48–9. **118.** José

A. Piqueras Arenas, 'La revolución burguesa española. De la burguesía sin revolución a la revolución sin burguesía', *Historia Social*, no. 24 (1996), pp. 95–132, here p. 102; on the proliferation of this dichotomy in Germany and Europe after 1830, see Reinhart Koselleck, 'Revolution, Rebellion, Aufruhr, Bürgerkrieg', in Otto Brunner, Werner Conze and Koselleck (eds.), *Geschichtliche Grundbegriffe. Historisches Lexikon zur politisch-sozialen Sprache in Deutschland* (8 vols., Stuttgart, 1972–97), vol. 5 (1984), pp. 653–788, here p. 766; on its importance to conservative understandings of revolution, see Ernst Wolfgang Becker, *Zeit der Revolution! – Revolution der Zeit? Zeiterfahrungen in Deutschland in der Ära der Revolutionen* (Göttingen, 1999), pp. 153–5. **119.** Lancizolle, *Über Ursachen, Character und Folgen*, p. 73. **120.** Thus one of the interlocutors in a fictional conversation noted by Lepold von Gerlach in a diary composed while he was staying in The Hague in 1830, Staatsarchiv Bundesarchiv Potsdam 90 Ge 7, fols. 2–44, here fols. 24–5. **121.** Stanley G. Payne, 'Spanish Conservatism, 1834–1923', *Journal of Contemporary History* 13/4 (1978), pp. 765–89, here p. 775. **122.** Adam Mickiewicz, 'The Books of the Polish Nation. From the Beginning of the World to the "Crucifixion" of the Polish Nation', in Mickiewicz, *The Books and the Pilgrimage of the Polish Nation*, trans. anon. (London, 1833). **123.** Adam Mickiewicz, 'The Book of Polish Pilgrimage' in ibid., p. 93. **124.** Adam Mickiewicz, *Livre des pèlerins polonais*, trans. Count Ch. de Montalembert (Paris, 1833), p. x (from Montalembert's introduction). (Curiously, the French text uses the misspelling *pélerin*.) **125.** Weitling, *Garantien der Harmonie und Freiheit*, p. 260. **126.** Harold Bloom, *The American Religion. The Emergence of the Post-Christian Nation* (New York, 1993), p. 80. **127.** Mickiewicz, *Livre des pèlerins polonais*, p. vi (from Montalembert's introduction). **128.** Félicité de Lamennais, *De la religion, considérée dans ses rapports avec l'ordre civil et politique* (Paris, 1826); for a hostile Gallican commentary, see Anon., *Sur les libertés gallicanes; réponse à l'ouvrage de M. de La Mennais* (Paris, 1826). **129.** Manfred Kridl, 'Two Champions of a New Christianity. Lamennais and Mickiewicz', *Comparative Literature* 4/3 (1952), pp. 239–67, here pp. 240, 252–3. **130.** Félicité de Lamennais, *Words of a Believer*, trans. anon. (New York, 1834), pp. 13, 15, 16, 20–21, 46, 124, 125 and *passim*. **131.** *Singulari nos*, Encyclical of Pope Gregory XVI promulgated on 25 June 1834, viewed online at https://www.catholicculture.org/culture/library/view.cfm?recnum=3885. **132.** Nicholas V. Riasanovsky, 'On Lamennais, Chaadaev, and the Romantic Revolt in France and Russia', *The American Historical Review* 82/5 (1977), pp. 1165–86, here p. 1166; Alec Vidler, *Prophecy and Papacy. A Study of Lamennais, the Church, and the Revolution. The Birkbeck Lectures 1952–1953* (London, 1954), p. 244. **133.** Sylvain Milbach, 'Lamennais: "une vie qui sera donc à refaire plus d'une fois encore". Parcours posthumes', *Le Mouvement social*, no. 246 (2014), pp. 75–96, here p. 77–8; on the perplexing quality of Lamennais and the difficulty of making sense of him, despite an immense body of commentary, see also Victor Giraud, 'Le "Cas" de Lamennais', in *Revue des Deux Mondes*, 6th period, 50/1 (1 March 1919), pp. 112–49. **134.** Charles Sainte-Beuve, 'Review of "Paroles d'un croyant"', *Revue des Deux Mondes*, 3rd series, 2/3 (1 April 1834), pp. 346–56, here p. 351. **135.** Jonathan Beecher, 'Fourierism and Christianity', *Nineteenth-Century French Studies* 22/3–4 (1994), pp. 391–403, here p. 394. **136.** Cited in Edward Berenson, *Populist Religion and Left-Wing Politics in France, 1830–1852* (Princeton, 1984), pp. 41, 45, 48. **137.** Ibid., p. 58. **138.** 'A free government needs religion, because it needs disinterestedness; and incredulity, even with the purest intentions, reduces everything – and must reduce everything – to an enlightened self-interest in the cause of freedom; but one needs to know how to sacrifice one's life: and for a man who sees nothing in the beyond but nothingness, what can be more important than life?' Benjamin Constant, *Du polythéisme romain, considéré dans ses rapports avec la philosophie grecque et la religion chrétienne* (2 vols., Paris, 1833), vol. 2, p. 92; on the absence of religion as favouring the pretensions of tyranny, see Benjamin Constant, *De la religion, considérée dans sa source, ses formes et ses développements* (4 vols., Paris, 1824), vol. 1, p. 88. **139.** Norbert Campagna, 'Politique et religion chez Benjamin Constant', *Revue de Théologie et de Philosophie*, 3rd series, 130/3 (1998), pp. 285–300, esp. pp. 290–92. **140.** Maurizio Viroli, *As If God Existed. Religion and Liberty in the History of Italy* (Princeton, 2012), pp. 146–7. Viroli's powerful study of the 'religion of liberty', a term he borrows from Croce, not from Constant, traces this dimension of *Risorgimento* spirituality back to Macchiavelli, exploring it as an unrealized option in Italian cultural and political history, though it is not always clear whether the book is acclaiming and expounding the concept or offering a history of it. **141.** Giuseppe Mazzini, *Scritti editi e inediti* (94 vols., Imola, 1906–43), vol. 36, pp. 225–33, here pp. 227, 228, 229. **142.** Christopher Duggan, *The Force of Destiny. A History of Italy since 1796* (Boston, 2008), p. 128. **143.** Christopher Clark, 'The Politics of Revival. Pietists, Aristocrats and the State Church in Early Nineteenth-Century Prussia', in Larry Eugene Jones (ed.), *Between Reform, Reaction and Resistance. Studies in the History of German Conservatism from 1789 to 1945* (Providence, 1993), pp. 31–60. **144.** Jonathan Sperber, *Popular Catholicism in Nineteenth-Century Germany* (Princeton, 1984), pp. 55–7, 70–71; still insightful and important: Wolfgang Schieder, 'Kirche und Revolution. Sozialgeschichtliche Aspekte der Trierer Wallfahrt von 1844', *Archiv für Sozialgeschichte* 14 (1974), pp. 419–54. **145.** Joseph von Görres, *Die Wallfahrt nach Trier* (Regensburg, 1845), pp. 3–7, 17, 123. **146.** Jorn Brederlow, *'Lichtfreunde' und 'Freie Gemeinden'. Religioser Protest und Freiheitsbewegung im Vormarz und in der Revolution von 1848/49* (Munich, 1976). **147.** Vermes, *Hungarian Culture and Politics*, p. 324. **148.** Francisco Simón Segura, *La desamortización Española en el siglo XIX* (Madrid, 1973); Francisco Colom González, 'El hispanismo reaccionario. Catolicismo y nacionalismo en la tradición antiliberal española', in Francisco Colom González and Ángel Rivera (eds.), *El altar y el trono. Ensayos sobre el Catolicismo político iberoamericano* (Barcelona, 2006), pp. 43–82. **149.** George Barany, 'The Hungarian Diet of 1839–40 and the Fate of Szechenyi's Middle Course', *Slavic Review* 22/2 (1963), pp. 285–303, here p. 293. **150.** Christopher Clark, 'From 1848 to Christian Democracy', in Ira Katznelson and Gareth Stedman Jones (ed.), *Religion and the Political Imagination* (Cambridge, 2010), pp. 190–213, esp. pp. 205–8. **151.** Boyd Hilton, *The Age of Atonement. The Influence of Evangelicalism on Social and Economic Thought, 1795–1865* (Oxford, 1988). **152.** Mihail Kogălniceanu, words for the opening of the history course at the Mihailean Academy, in Kogălniceanu, *Cuvânt pentru deschiderea cursului de istorie națională* (Iași, 1843), pp. 5–11. **153.** Leopold von Ranke, *Die serbische Revolution, aus serbischen Papieren und Mitteilungen* (Hamburg, 1829), p. 40. **154.** See the prefatory essay by Latour in Silvio Pellico, *Mes Prisons. Mémoires de Silvio Pellico de Saluces*, ed. and trans. A. de Latour (2nd edn, Brussels, 1834); the comments on Venice are in Ilario Rinieri (ed.), *Della Vita e delle Opere di Silvio Pellico. Da lettere e documenti inediti* (3 vols., Turin, 1898–1901), vol. 1, p. 400. **155.** In George Szirtes's more resonant translation: 'Slaves we have been to this hour, / Our forefathers who fell from power / Fell free and lived as free men will, / On land that was their own to till', viewed at https://www.babelmatrix.org/works/hu/Petőfi_Sándor-1823/Nemzeti_dal/en/2086-National_Song. **156.** Preface to the edition of 1843, in Michele Amari, *History of the War of the Sicilian Vespers*, ed. The Earl of Ellesmere (3 vols., London, 1850), vol. 1, p. iii. **157.** Michele Amari, *La Guerra del Vespro Siciliano* (4th edn, 1st Florentine edn, 1851), p. viii; see also Ellesmere's preface to Amari, *History of the War of the Sicilian Vespers*, p. xviii; Roberto Dainotto, *Europe (in Theory)* (Durham, NC, and London, 2007), p. 189. **158.** Bianca Marcolongo, 'Le idee politiche di Michele Amari', in Andrea Borruso, Rosa D'Angelo and Rosa Scaglione Guccione (eds.), *Studi Amariani* (Palermo, 1991), pp. 63–106, here p. 68. **159.** Amari, *La Guerra del Vespro Siciliano*, pp. v, vi, ix. **160.** See Axel Körner, *Politics of Culture in Liberal Italy* (London, 2009); Antonino de Francesco, *The Antiquity of the Italian Nation. The Cultural Origins of a Political Myth in Modern Italy, 1796–1943* (Oxford, 2013). **161.** Attacking the Phanariots was a canny move, since the Greek revolution had ruptured the relation of trust between the Ottoman authorities and the traditional

Greek elites who dominated much of the western Ottoman Empire; Mihail Kogălniceanu [named on the title page as Michel Kogalnitchan], *Histoire de la Valachie, de la Moldovie et des Valaques transdanubiens* (Berlin, 1837), pp. xi, 113 n.1, 260, 369, 371-2, 373, 374. **162.** Guðmundur Hálfdanarson, 'Iceland. A Peaceful Secession', *Scandinavian Journal of History* 25/1-2 (2000), pp. 87-100, here p. 95. **163.** Joseph Remenyi, 'Mihály Vörösmarty, Hungarian Poet, Playwright and Critic', *The Slavonic and East European Review* 31/77 (1953), pp. 352-63. **164.** Katalin Földi-Dósza, 'How the Hungarian National Costume Evolved', in Metropolitian Museum of Art New York (ed.), *The Imperial Style. Fashions of the Hapsburg Era* (New York, 1980), pp. 75-88. **165.** Mark Hewitson, *Absolute War. Violence and Mass Warfare in the German Lands* (Oxford, 2017), pp. 211, 219-20. **166.** Čeněk Zíbrt, 'Svérázný český kroj národní z roku 1848', *Český Lid* 31 (1931), pp. 41-4, here pp. 42-3. **167.** Wolf D. Gruner, 'Der Deutsche Bund, die deutschen Verfassungsstaaten und die Rheinkrise von 1840. Überlegungen zur deutschen Dimension einer europäischen Krise', *Zeitschrift für bayerische Landesgeschichte* 53 (1990), p. 51-78. **168.** Nikolaus Becker, 'Der deutsche Rhein (Patriotisches Lied) 1840', viewed online at https://www.oxfordlieder.co.uk/song/348. The translation is mine. **169.** Alfred de Musset, 'Le Rhin Allemand', viewed online at https://www.bonjourpoesie.fr/lesgrandsclassiques/poemes/alfred_de_musset/le_rhin_allemand. The translation is mine. **170.** Ivan Turgenev, *On the Eve*, trans. Constance Garnett (London, 1973), p. 137. **171.** Francesca Kaucisvili Melzi d'Eril, 'Montalembert e Pellico', *Aevum* 50 (September-December 1976), pp. 613-24, here p. 614. **172.** Giovanni Dotoli, 'L'Italianisme et traduction en France au XIXe siècle', in Jean Balsamo, Vito Castiglione Minischetti and Giovanni Dotoli, *Les Traductions de l'italien en français au XIXe siècle* (Paris, 2004), pp. 7-112, here p. 61. **173.** Ibid., p. 615; Lamennais's comment on the book: F. de Lamennais, *Lettres inédites à la Baronne Cottu* (Paris, 1910), p. 246. **174.** Diary entries 20 and 21 July 1833, in Dragojla Jarnević, *Dnevnik*, ed. Irena Lukšić (Karlovac, 2000), p. 37. **175.** This is one of the central themes of Alberto Banti, *La nazione del Risorgimento. Parentela, santità e onore alle origini dell'Italia unita* (Turin, 2000); and Banti, *Il Risorgimento italiano* (Roma, 2004), esp. pp. v-vi. **176.** '. . . moralnice avuţii, prin carea o naţie se face puternică şi fericită . . .', Gheorghe Asachi, *Albina Românească* 1, 1 June 1829; viewed online at https://tiparituriromanesti.wordpress.com/2011/10/30/albina-romaneasca-primul-ziar-in-limba-romana-din-moldova/. **177.** Chad Bryant, 'Zap's Prague. The City, the Nation and Czech Elites before 1848', *Urban History* 40/2 (2013), pp. 181-201. **178.** 'Die Sprache also macht die rechte Gränze der Völker', Ernst Moritz Arndt, *Der Rhein, Teutschlands Strom aber nicht Teutschlands Gränze* (Leipzig, 1813), p. 10. **179.** Johann Friedrich Ludwig Jahn, *Bereicherung des hochdeutschen Sprachschatzes, versucht im Gebiethe der Sinnverwandtschaft, ein Nachtrag zu Adelung's und eine Nachlese zu Eberhard's Wörterbuch* (Leipzig, 1806). After this publication, Jahn dropped the Johann from his professional name. **180.** Anon., *Dacia literară*, 1 (January-June 1840), p. 1. **181.** Eva Maria Ossadník, 'Neue Denotate im kroatischen Zivilisationswortschatz. Die Revolution von 1848 und die Gesellschaft im Spiegel der zeitgenössischen Presse', *Wiener Slavistisches Jahrbuch* 57 (2011), pp. 159-64. **182.** Thus Kossuth's demands in his newspaper *Pesti Hírlap* in 1842, cited in Istvan Deak, *The Lawful Revolution. Louis Kossuth and the Hungarians, 1848-1849* (New York, 1979), p. 45. **183.** On republican citizenship, see Rogers Brubaker, *Ethnicity Without Groups* (Cambridge, Mass., 2004), p. 139; David A. Bell, 'Lingua Populi, Lingua Dei. Language, Religion, and the Origins of French Revolutionary Nationalism', *The American Historical Review* 100/5 (1995), pp. 1403-37, here pp. 1405-6. On the potentially inclusive implications of the linguistic criterion, see Benedict Anderson, *Imagined Communities. Reflections on the Origin and Spread of Nationalism* (London and New York, 2006), p. 145. **184.** Pieter Judson, *The Habsburg Empire. A New History* (Cambridge, Mass., 2016), p. 209. **185.** Jenny Brumme and Beatrice Schmid, 'Una lengua, una visión. El pensamiento liberal sobre la educación lingüística en España durante el Trienio Constitucional. El Nuevo plan de enseñanza mútua (Barcelona, 1821)', *Revista Internacional de Lingüística Iberoamericana* 15/2 (2017), pp. 99–115, esp. pp. 109–10. **186.** Gary Cohen, *The Politics of Ethnic Survival. Germans in Prague, 1861–1914* (West Lafayette, 2006), p. 25. **187.** Description by János Arany of the work of the Academy in the first decade of its existence. **188.** On the struggle against Latin in Hungary, see István Margócsy, 'When Language Became Ideology. Hungary in the Eighteenth Century', in Gábor Almási and Lav Šubarić (eds.), *Latin at the Crossroads of Identity. The Evolution of Linguistic Nationalism in the Kingdom of Hungary* (Leiden, 2015), pp. 25–34. **189.** Judson, *The Habsburg Empire* , pp. 127–49. **190.** Daniel Rapant, 'Slovak Politics in 1848–1849', *Slavonic and East European Review* 27/68 (1948), pp. 67–90, here p. 70. **191.** Friedrich Ludwig Jahn, *Deutsches Volkstum* (Lübeck, 1810), pp. 7–8, 21. **192.** Kogălniceanu, 'Cuvânt pentru deschiderea cursului de istorie națională', p. 10. **193.** Friedrich Christoph Dahlmann, *Die Politik, auf den Grund und das Maß der gegebenen Zustände zurückgeführt* ([1835] 2nd edn, Leipzig, 1847), p. 5. **194.** Dainotto, *Europe (in Theory)*, p. 6. **195.** Laszlo Deme, 'Writers and Essayists and the Rise of Magyar Nationalism in the 1820s and 1830s', *Slavic Review* 43/4 (1984), pp. 624–40, here p. 627. **196.** Robert Nemes, 'The Politics of the Dance Floor. Culture and Civil Society in Nineteenth-Century Hungary', *Slavic Review* 60/4 (2001), p. 812. **197.** Irena Štěpánová, 'Obrazy a zrcadla. Etnografika a slavika v díle manželů Zapových', *Český lid* 93/2 (2006), pp. 137–51. **198.** Diary entry, 24 February 1843, in Jarnević, *Dnevnik*, p. 213. **199.** For a brilliant discussion of this episode, see Nemes, 'The Politics of the Dance Floor, pp. 802–23. **200.** Miroslav Hroch, 'The Social Composition of the Czech Patriots in Bohemia', in Peter Brock and H. Gordon Skilling (eds.), *The Czech National Renascence of the Nineteenth Century* (Toronto, 1970), pp. 33–52, here pp. 36–9. **201.** Stanley Z. Pech, *The Czech Revolution of 1848* (Chapel Hill, 1969), p. 27–9, 34. **202.** Jarnević, *Dnevnik*, p. 11. **203.** Diary entry, 26 April 1836, in ibid., p. 72. **204.** Diary entry, 4 November 1836, in ibid., p. 79. **205.** Diary entry 26 October 1836, in ibid., p. 97. **206.** Diary entries 13 and 14 July 1839, in ibid., pp. 120–21; Jelena Lakuš and Anita Bajić, 'Interpreting Diaries. History of Reading and the Diary of the Nineteenth-Century Croatian Female Writer Dragojla Jarnević', *Information & Culture* 52/2 (2017), pp. 163–85, here p. 171. **207.** Diary entry, 12 June 1839, in Jarnević, Dnevnik p. 118. **208.** Diary entries, 3 August 1839, 31 March and 30 December 1841, 5 June 1842, 22 January and 3 April 1843, in ibid., pp. 124, 180, 184, 196, 211, 216. **209.** Diary entry, 8 April 1843, in ibid., p. 217; see also the diary entry of 24 February 1843: 'Oh how I will endeavour to benefit my dear homeland; she is my mother, sister, husband and child; let all my strength be consecrated to her; she has all my treasure', ibid., p. 213. **210.** Diary entry, 6 July 1840, in ibid., p. 157. **211.** Friedrich Ludwig Jahn, *Merke zum Deutschen Volksthum* (Hildburghausen, 1833), p. 112. I am grateful to Marion Kant for drawing my attention to this passage. **212.** Jakob Friedrich Fries, *Von Deutschem Bund und deutscher Staatsverfassung* (Heidelberg, 1816), p. 6. **213.** Joseph Eötvös, *The Village Notary. A Romance of Hungarian Life*, trans. Otto Wenckstern (3 vols., London, 1850 (Hungarian orig. Pest, 1845)), vol. 1, pp. 245–6. **214.** Judson, *The Habsburg Empire*, pp. 127–9. **215.** Vermes, *Hungarian Culture and Politics*, p. 292. **216.** Cited in Robert Nemes, *Another Hungary. The Nineteenth-Century Provinces in Eight Lives* (Palo Alto, 2016), p. 98. **217.** Anna Millo, 'Trieste, 1830–1870. From Cosmopolitanism to the Nation', and Eva Cecchinato, 'Searching for a Role. Austrian Rule, National Perspectives and Memories of the "Serenissima" in Venice', in Lawrence Cole (ed.), *Different Paths to the Nation. Regional and National Identities in Central Europe and Italy, 1830–1870* (Houndsmills, 2007), pp. 60–81 and 122–43; Kent R. Greenfield, *Economics and Liberalism in the Risorgimento. A Study of Nationalism in Lombardy, 1814–1848* (Baltimore, 1965). **218.** Dainotto, *Europe (in Theory)*, p. 182. **219.** Zdravko Blažeković, 'György (Đuro) Arnold (1781–1848), the Musician with Two Homelands', *Studia Musicologica Academiae Scientiarum Hungaricae*, 44/1–2 (2003), pp. 69–89, here p. 81. **220.** On this tendency in general, see Karen Offen, 'How (and Why) the Analogy of Marriage with Slavery

Provided the Springboard for Women's Rights Demands in France, 1640–1848', in Kathryn Kish Sklar and James Brewer Stewart (eds.), *Women's Rights and Transatlantic Antislavery in the Era of Emancipation* (Yale University Press, 2007), pp. 57–81. **221.** Fourier, *Théorie des quatre mouvements*, pp. 50–51. **222.** Cited in W. D. Howells, 'Niccolini's Anti-Papal Tragedy', *The North American Review* 115 (1872), pp. 333–66, here p. 340. **223.** [Anon.], 'Italy', *Morning Chronicle* (London), no. 19188, Friday, 25 February 1831, p. 4, col. 1. **224.** Letter of 7 February 1832, in Ludwig Börne, *Briefe aus Paris* (6 vols., Offenbach, 1833–4), vol. 4, letter no. 26, pp. 131–55, here pp. 140–41. **225.** Mickiewicz, *The Books and the Pilgrimage of the Polish Nation*, p. 39. **226.** Rude, *Les Révoltes des canuts*, p. 97. **227.** Pierre Leroux, 'De la philosophie et du christianisme', *Revue encyclopédique* (August 1832), pp. 281–340, here p. 306. **228.** David Brion Davis, *The Problem of Slavery in the Age of Revolution 1770–1823* (Ithaca, 1975), p. 263. **229.** Weitling, *Garantien der Harmonie und Freiheit*, pp. 33, 42–4. **230.** Thus the Hegel scholar Karl Heinz Ilting, commenting on Wannenmann's notes on Hegel's lectures, cited in Susan Buck-Morss, *Hegel, Haiti, and Universal History* (Pittsburgh, 2009), p. 61. **231.** Buck-Morss, *Hegel, Haiti, and Universal History*, pp. 42–5, 48, 52, 59. **232.** An excellent overview: Joel Quirk and David Richardson, 'Anti-Slavery, European Identity and International Society', *Journal of Modern European History/ Zeitschrift für moderne europäische Geschichte/Revue d'histoire européenne contemporaine* 7/1 (2009), pp. 68–92, here pp. 78–9. **233.** John F. Quinn, '"Three Cheers for the Abolitionist Pope!". American Reaction to Gregory XVI's Condemnation of the Slave Trade, 1840–1860', *The Catholic Historical Review* 90/1 (2004), pp. 67–93, here p. 70. **234.** Valentim Alexandre, 'Portugal e a abolição do tráfico de escravos (1834–51)', *Análise Social*, 4th series, 26/111 (1991), pp. 293–333; see also Roquinaldo Ferreira, 'The Suppression of the Slave Trade and Slave Departures from Angola, 1830s–1860s', *História Unisinos* 15/1 (2011), pp. 3–13. **235.** João Pedro Marques, 'Resistência ou adesão à "causa da humanidade"? Os setembristas e a supressão do tráfico de escravos (1836–1842)' *Análise Social*, 4th series, 30/131-2 (1995), pp. 375–402. **236.** S. Drescher, *Capitalism and Antislavery. British Mobilization in Comparative Perspective* (Oxford, 1987), 50–66. **237.** Victor Schoelcher, *De l'esclavage des noirs, et de la législation coloniale* (Paris, 1833), pp. 8–10. **238.** Ibid., pp. 11–52, 72–81, 90–94. **239.** Ibid., pp. 123–31. **240.** Sara E. Johnson, *The Fear of French Negroes. Transcolonial Collaboration in the Revolutionary Americas* (Berkeley and Los Angeles, 2012), p. 137. **241.** See, for example, [Anon.], 'L'Espagne, sa révolution. Son influence sur l'abolition de l'esclavage colonial', *Revue des colonies* 3/2 (August 1836), pp. 49–54; ['Un Haïtien'], 'Haiti. Principe de sa constitution', *Revue des colonies* 3/3 (September 1836), pp. 97–100; [Anon.], 'Portugal. L'Abolition de la traite des noirs', *Revue des colonies* 3/6 (December 1836), pp. 239–41; [Anon.], 'Colonies françaises. Martinique. Pétition des hommes de couleur en faveur de l'abolition de l'esclavage', ibid., pp. 243–4; Ad. Gatine, 'Affaire Parfait – Liberté confisquée', ibid., pp. 225–32; [Anon.], Esquisses de moeurs créoles. Par un créole de Cayenne', ibid., pp. 253–61. **242.** Johnson, *Fear of French Negroes*, p. 183 n.21. **243.** ['Un Haïtien'], 'Haiti. Principe de sa constitution', p. 99; the preface to the inaugural issue is discussed in Kelly Duke Bryant, 'Black But Not African. Francophone Black Diaspora and the "Revue des colonies", 1834–1842', *The International Journal of African Historical Studies* 40/2 (2007), pp. 251–82, here p. 252. **244.** Preface to Gatine, 'Affaire Parfait – Liberté confisquée', p. 225. **245.** Seymour Drescher, 'British Way, French Way. Opinion Building and Revolution in the Second French Slave Emancipation', *The American Historical Review* 96/3 (1991), pp. 709–34, here pp. 713–20; Sue Peabody, 'France's Two Emancipations in Comparative Context', in Hideaki Suzuki (ed.), *Abolitions as a Global Experience* (Singapore, 2016), pp. 25–49, here p. 31. **246.** Drescher, 'British Way, French Way', pp. 709–34, here pp. 715–23. **247.** Lawrence C. Jennings, 'L'abolition de l'esclavage par la IIe République et ses effets en Louisiane 1848–1858', *Revue française d'outre-mer* 56/205 (1969), pp. 375–97, here p. 375; many of Schoelcher's essays are gathered in Victor Schoelcher, *Histoire* *de l'esclavage pendant les deux dernières années* (Paris, 1847). **248.** See the conclusion to Schoelcher, *Histoire de l'esclavage*, pp. 541–8, here p. 541. **249.** Démar, *Ma loi d'avenir*, p. 42. **250.** Martin Bernard, *Dix ans de prison au Mont Saint-Michel et à la Citadelle de Doullens. 1838 à 1848* (Paris, 1861), p. 101. **251.** Franco della Peruta, 'La Révolution française dans la pensée des démocrates italiens du Risorgimento', *Annales historiques de la Révolution française* 49/230 (1977), pp. 664–76, here pp. 664–5. **252.** Cited in George T. Bujarski, '1815–1823. The Question of Cosmopolitanism and National Identity', *The Polish Review* 17/2 (Spring 1972), pp. 23–4. **253.** Almeida discussed this feature of the 1820s revolutions in his essay of 1830 'Portugal na Balança da Europa', discussed in Gabriel Paquette: 'An Itinerant Liberal. Almeida Garrett's Exilic Itineraries and Political Ideas in the Age of Southern European Revolutions (1820–1834)', in Maurizio Isabella and Konstantina Zanou (eds.), *Mediterranean Diasporas. Politics and Ideas in the Long 19th Century* (London, 2015), p. 50. **254.** All three cited in Kôbô Seigan, 'L'influence de la mémoire de la Révolution française et de l'Empire Napoléonien dans l'opinion publique française face à la guerre d'Espagne de 1823', *Annales historiques de la Révolution française*, no. 335 (January/March 2004), pp. 159–81, here p. 174. **255.** Leopold von Gerlach, diary entry, 28 and 29 October 1843, Abschriften aus den Tagebüchern Leopold von Gerlach, Staatsarchiv Bundesarchiv Potsdam 90 Ge 6, fol. 98. **256.** Bujarski, '1815–1823. The Question of Cosmopolitanism and National Identity', pp. 17–18. **257.** Martínez de la Rosa, *El Espíritu del siglo*, pp. xi, xiii, 30. **258.** Cited in Wolfgang Mommsen, 'Die Julirevolution von 1830 und die europäische Staatenwelt', in Mommsen, *1848. Die ungewollte Revolution. Die revolutionären Bewegungen in Europa 1830–1849* (Frankfurt/Main, 1998), pp. 42–67, here p. 58. **259.** Bernard, *Dix ans de prison*, p. 196. **260.** Robert A. Nisbet, 'The Politics of Social Pluralism. Some Reflections on Lamennais', *The Journal of Politics* 10 (1948), pp. 764–86; Louis le Guillou, 'Lamennais, ses amis et la Révolution française', *Revue d'histoire littéraire de la France* 90/4–5 (1990), pp. 715–24. **261.** Della Peruta, 'La Révolution française dans la pensée des démocrates italiens du Risorgimento', pp. 670–73. **262.** Cited in James Sheehan, *German History, 1770–1866* (Oxford, 1989), p. 568. **263.** On Marx as a creative cannibalizer of ideas, see Jonathan Sperber, *Karl Marx. A Nineteenth-Century Life* (New York, 2013), *passim*. **264.** Maria de Fátima Bonifácio, 'Costa Cabral no contexto do liberalismo doutrinário', *Análise Social*, 4th series, 28/123–4 (1993), pp. 1043–91, here pp. 1076–7. **265.** Johan Rudolf Thorbecke, *Ueber das Wesen und den organischen Charakter der Geschichte. Ein Schreiben an Herrn Hofrath K. F. Eichhorn in Göttingen* (Göttingen, 1824), p. 7; on the transformation, see Izaak Johannes Brugmans, *Thorbecke* (Haarlem, 1932), pp. 17–36 and 53–84; Remieg Aerts, *Thorbecke wil het. Biografie van een staatsman* (Amsterdam, 2018), pp. 262–315. **266.** Roger Boesche, 'Tocqueville and *Le Commerce*. A Newspaper Expressing His Unusual Liberalism', *Journal of the History of Ideas* 44/2 (1983), pp. 277–92. **267.** Cited in Georges Navet, 'De l'Aventin à la Croix Rousse. Pierre-Simon Ballanche et le héros plébéien', *Le Cahier* (Collège international de philosophie), no. 5 (1988), pp. 29–41, here p. 29.

3. CONFRONTATION

1. Diary entry of 26 July 1830, in Juste Olivier, *Paris en 1830. Journal*, ed. André Delattre and Marc Denkinger (Chapel Hill, 1951), p. 235. **2.** Diary entry, 10.30 p.m., 27 July 1830, in ibid., p. 239–43. **3.** Diary entry, 6 p.m. 28 July 1830, in ibid., pp. 248, 252, 255–6. **4.** Diary entry, 9.30 p.m., 29 July 1830, in ibid., p. 272. **5.** David H. Pinkney, 'The Revolution of 1830 Seen by a Combatant', *French Historical Studies* 2/2 (1961), pp. 242–6. **6.** Ibid., p. 245. **7.** Ibid., pp. 242–6. **8.** Daniel Stern [Marie d'Agoult], *Mes souvenirs, 1806–1833* (3rd edn, Paris, 1880), p. 327. **9.** Ibid., pp. 328, 330. **10.** Ibid., pp. 330–32. **11.** Mark Traugott, *The Insurgent Barricade* (Berkeley, 2010), p. 105. **12.** Arthur

Asseraf, 'La mer immédiate. Nouvelles, télégraphe et impérialisme en Méditérranée, 1798–1882', *monde(s)*, no. 16 (November 2019), pp. 46–66, here p. 57; the elections lasted from 23 June to 19 July, so the news became known when there was just over a week of voting to go. **13.** David H. Pinkney, *The French Revolution of 1830* (Princeton, 1972), p. 85. **14.** The text of the joint declaration is in Anon., *Événements de Paris, des 26, 27, 28, 29 et 30 juillet; par plusieurs témoins oculaires* (6th edn, Paris, 1830), pp. 11–15. **15.** Edgar Newman, 'The Blouse and Frock Coat. The Alliance of the Common People of Paris with the Liberal Leadership of the Middle Classes during the Last Year of the Bourbon Restoration', *Journal of Modern History* 49/1 (1974), pp. 26–59, here p. 35. **16.** Louis Blanc, *Révolution française. Histoire de dix ans 1830–1840* (11th edn, Paris, 1845), p. 188. **17.** Vincent Robert, *Le Temps des banquets. Politique et symbolique d'une génération, 1818–1848* (Paris, 2010), p. 236. **18.** These examples are drawn from Newman, 'The Blouse and Frock Coat', pp. 35, 37, 42, 43, 44, 48, 52–3. **19.** Louise-Eléonore-Charlotte-Adélaide d'Osmond, comtesse de Boigne, *Récits d'une tante* (4 vols., Paris, 1922), vol. 3, chapter XXI, n.p., consulted online at the Project Gutenberg EBook of *Récits d'une tante*, https://www.gutenberg.org/files/32349/32349-h/32349-h.htm, last consulted on 13 April 2020. **20.** Traugott, *Insurgent Barricade*, p. 107. **21.** 'Le Peuple', *Le Constitutionnel*, 31 July 1830, p. 2. **22.** *Le Corsaire. Journal des spectacles, de la littérature, des arts, des moeurs et des modes*, 1 August 1830. **23.** Diary entry 30 July 1830, in Olivier, *Paris en 1830*, p. 275. **24.** 'Le Peuple', *Le Constitutionnel*, 31 July 1830, p. 2. **25.** Michael Marrinan, *Painting Politics for Louis-Philippe. Art and Ideology in Orléanist France, 1830–1848* (New Haven, 1988), pp. 35–6. **26.** Law of 13 December 1830, in *Album des Décorés de Juillet* (Paris, 1831), pp. 12–16; viewable online at https://gallica.bnf.fr/ark:/12148/bpt6k5530375s/f6.image.texteImage. **27.** M. Giraud-Mangin, 'Nantes en 1830 et les journées de juillet', *Revue d'histoire moderne* 6/36 (1931), pp. 455–68'. **28.** Julia A. Schmidt-Funke, 'The Revolution of 1830 as a European Media Event', European History Online (EGO), published by the Leibniz Institute of European History (IEG), Mainz 2017-08-16. URL: http://www.ieg-ego.eu/schmidtfunkej-2011-en, last consulted on 14 April 2020. My account of the diffusion of the news of 1830 is drawn from Schmidt-Funke's analysis. **29.** Heinrich Heine, *Heinrich Heine über Ludwig Börne* (Hamburg, 1840), pp. 126–7. There is some doubt as to whether this rendering of the letter is authentically contemporary with the events, hence my reference to 'recollections'; see Jeffrey L. Sammons, *Heinrich Heine. A Modern Biography* (Princeton, 1979), p. 153. **30.** Schmidt-Funke, 'The Revolution of 1830'. **31.** 'Histoire d'un pavé', *La Glaneuse*, Sunday, 29 November 1831, p. 2. **32.** Eugène de Pradel, 'L'histoire d'un pavé', *Paris. Ou le livre des cent et un* (15 vols., Frankfurt/Main, 1833), vol. 11, pp. 113–24. On Pradel's prowess and renown as a Spoken Word rhymester, see Adrien Heurpé, *Eugène de Pradel, l'mprovisateur en vers français à Hombourg-ès-Monts* (Hombourg, n.d. [1828]). **33.** 'Mémoires d'une glace', *La Glaneuse*, 29 September 1831, p. 2. **34.** Bezucha, *The Lyon Uprising of 1834*, pp. 74–5. **35.** Georges Weill, *Histoire du parti républicain en France de 1814 à 1870* (Paris, 1900). **36.** Jean-Claude Caron, 'La Société des Amis du peuple', *Romantisme*, no. 28–9 (1980), pp. 169–79, here p. 174. **37.** M. Gisquet, *Mémoires de M. Gisquet, ancien Préfet de Police* (Paris, 1840), vol. 2, p. 4. **38.** This is the estimate offered in Traugott, *Insurgent Barricade*, p. 21. The losses on the government side were seventy dead and more than 290 wounded. **39.** Pamela Pilbeam, *Republicanism in Nineteenth-Century France* (New York 1995). **40.** Jill Harsin, *Barricades. The War of the Streets in Revolutionary Paris, 1830–1848* (London, 2002), pp. 124–38. **41.** Cour de Pairs (ed.), *Rapport fait à la Cour les 11 et 12 Juin 1839 par M. Mérilhou comprenant les faits généraux et la prémière série des faits particuliers* (Paris, 1839), p. 7. **42.** Ibid., pp. 6–8. **43.** Biliana Kassabova, 'Thoughts on Louis-Auguste Blanqui', Stanford History of Political Thought Workshop, 4 December 2017, consulted at https://sites.stanford.edu/history-political-thought/sites/default/files/blanqui_hpt_o.pdf. **44.** See R. F. Leslie, 'Left-Wing Political Tactics in Poland,

1831–1846', *The Slavonic and East European Review* 33/80 (1954), pp. 120–39; M. K. Dziewanowski, 'The Beginnings of Socialism in Poland', ibid., 29/73 (1951), pp. 510–31. 45. Heinrich Heine, notes dated Paris, 5 June, 'Französische Zustände', in Heinrich Heine, *Sämtliche Werke* (12 vols., Stuttgart, n.d.), vol. 1, pp. 5–174, here p. 140. 46. Handwritten notes by the insurgent tailor Louis Quignot, seized by the police and cited in Cour des Pairs (ed.), *Attentats des 12 et 13 Mai 1839. Réquisitoire de Franck Carré, Procureur Général, dans les débats ouverts le 13 janvier 1840* (Paris, 1840), p. 19. 47. Thus the argument set out in a document found, among packets of gunpoweder and bombs, in the apartment of a certain Béro, arrested after the insurrection of 1839, transcribed in Cour des Pairs (ed.), *Attentat des 12 et 13 Mai 1839. Rapport fait à la Cour par M. Mérilhou, comprenant la seconde série des faits particuliers* (Paris, 1839), pp. 119–22. 48. The Saint-Simonian leader Prosper Enfantin had tried to do the same thing in 1832. Martin Bernard, *Dix ans de prison au Mont Saint-Michel et à la Citadelle de Doullens. 1838 à 1848* (Paris, 1861), p. 200; on the use of this tactic, see Bezucha, *The Lyon Uprising of 1834*, pp. 187–8. 49. 'Défense du Citoyen Louis-Auguste Blanqui devant la Cour d'Assises', in Auguste Blanqui, *Textes Choisis*, with a preface and notes by V. P. Volguine (Paris, 1971), consulted at https://www.marxists.org/francais/blanqui/1832/defense.htm. 50. Cour des Pairs (ed.), *Attentat des 12 et 13 Mai 1839. Interrogatoires des Accusés* (Paris, 1839), pp. 1–3 and *passim*. 51. Silvio Pellico. *Le mie prigioni. Memorie* (Turin, 1832), pp. 20, 31–2 and *passim*. 52. Charles Klopp, 'Inklings and Effacements in Silvio Pellico's *Le mie prigioni*', *Italica*, 68/2 (Summer 1991), pp. 195–203. 53. Anonymous review of *Le mie prigioni*, *Foreign Quarterly Review* 11 (January and April 1833), pp. 473–502, here p. 476. 54. Bernard, *Dix ans de prison*, p. 194. Bernard had initially intended to publish the book in 1851, but the project was temporarily abandoned when he was obliged to flee into exile. 55. Ibid., p. 202. 56. Ibid., p. ix. 57. Ibid., p. 47. 58. Ibid., pp. 83, x. 59. See, for example, the report on the German press coverage of the release of the communist Karl Blind from prison in Brussels in *La Réforme*, 25 January 1848, p. 2: 'La Gazette de Cologne dénonçait M. Blind comme un *radical* et un *communiste*, d'autant plus dangereux que ce n'est pas un *exalté*, mais au contraire un homme *froid et tranquille* et allant droit au but.' 60. Bernard, *Dix ans de prison*, pp. 87–9. 61. The classic reception study is Alessandro Galante Garrone, *Filippo Buonarroti e i rivoluzionari dell'Ottocento* (Milan, 1951). 62. Philippe Buonarroti, *Buonarroti's History of Babeuf's Conspiracy for Equality, with the Author's Reflections on the Causes and Character of the French Revolution and His Estimation of the Leading Men and Events of That Epoch. Also, His Views of Democratic Government, Community of Property and Political and Social Equality*, trans. Bronterre (London, 1836), p. xviii. 63. Fragment of an undated manuscript by Buonarroti, cited in Marc Vuilleumier and L. Fazy, 'Buonarroti et ses sociétés secrètes à Genève', *Annales historiques de la Révolution française* 42/201 (1970), pp. 473–505, here p. 495. 64. Arthur Lehning, 'Buonarroti and His International Secret Societies', *International Review of Social History* 1/1 (1956), pp. 112–40, here pp. 120–24. 65. Andryane's arrest and imprisonment are narrated in Alexandre Andryane, *Memoirs of a Prisoner of State in the Fortress of Spielberg*, trans. Fortunato Prandi (London, 1838). 66. Lehning, 'Buonarroti and His International Secret Societies', p. 140. 67. Ethel Matala de Mazza, 'Geschichte und Revolution', in Roland Borgards and Harald Neumeyer (eds.), *Büchner-Handbuch* (Stuttgart, 2009), pp. 168–75, here p. 173; Gideon Stiening, *Literatur und Wissen im Werk Georg Büchners. Studien zu seinen wissenschaftlichen, politischen und literarischen Texten* (Berlin, 2019), p. 60; Thomas Michael Mayer, 'Büchner und Weidig – Frühkommunismus und revolutionäre Demokratie. Zur Textverteilung des Hessischen Landboten', in Heinz Ludwig Arnold (ed.), *Georg Büchner I/II* (Munich, 1979, *Text + Kritik. Sonderband*, pp. 16–298, here pp. 43–5. 68. [Georg Büchner and Friedrich Ludwig Weidig], *Der Hessische Landbote* ([Offenbach/Main,] 1834; repr. Stuttgart, 2016), pp. 7, 20, consulted online at htps://www.reclam.de/data/media/978-3-15-019242-9.pdf. 69.

On Weidig's death, see Sven Hanuschek, '"Es muß endlich aufgeklärt werden." Weidig, Büchner und der *Hessische Landbote* im Werk von Jürg Amann', in Markus May, Udo Roth and Gideon Stiening (eds.), *'Friede den Hütten! Krieg den Pallästen!' Der Hessische Landbote in interdisziplinärer Perspektive* (Heidelberg, 2016), pp. 231–41. 70. Terence M. Holmes, 'Die "Absolutisten" in der Revolution', in Thomas Michael Mayer and Sebastian Wohlfeil (eds.), *Georg Büchner Jahrbuch 8, 1990–1994* (Tübingen, 1995), pp. 241–53. 71. Benjamin Seifert, '"...das Volk aber liegt vor ihnen wie Dünger auf dem Acker." Der "Hessische Landbote" als politisches Manifest des 19. und 20. Jahrhunderts', in Johanna Klatt and Robert Lorenz (eds.), *Manifeste. Geschichte und Gegenwart des politischen Appells* (Göttingen, 2010), pp. 47–71, esp. pp. 59–62. 72. Anon. (ed.), *Défense du citoyen Louis Auguste Blanqui devant la Cour d'Assises, 1832* (Paris, 1832), p. 14. 73. On Blanqui's 'hatred' of Robespierre, see Albert Mathiez, 'Notes inédites de Blanqui sur Robespierre', *Annales historiques de la Révolution française*, 5, No. 28 (July–August 1928), pp. 305–21, esp. pp. 310–11. 74. See Biliana Kassabova, 'Blanqui between Myth and Archives. Revolution, Dictatorship and Education', Stanford History of Political Thought Workshop, 4 December 2017, consulted online at https://sites.stanford.edu/history-political-thought/sites/default/files/blanqui_hpt_0.pdf, esp. pp. 6–8. 75. Patrick H. Hutton, 'Legends of a Revolutionary. Nostalgia in the Imagined Lives of Auguste Blanqui', *Historical Reflections/Réflexions Historiques* 39/3 (2013), pp. 41–54. 76. Cited in Peter Reichel, *Robert Blum. Ein deutscher Revolutionär* (Göttingen, 2007), pp. 33–4. 77. On Mazzini as a proto-'Wilsonian' exponent of democratic peace theory, see the introduction by the editors in Stefano Recchia and Nadia Urbinati (ed.), *A Cosmopolitanism of Nations. Giuseppe Mazzini's writings on Democracy, Nation-Building and International Relations*, trans. Stefano Recchia (Princeton, 2009), pp. 1–30, here pp. 3, 17–18. 78. On Mazzini's iconic global status, see Christopher A. Bayly and Eugenio Biagini, Introduction, in Bayly and Biagini (eds.), *Giuseppe Mazzini and the Globalisation of Democratic Nationalism 1830–1920* (Oxford, 2008), pp. 1–7, here p. 5. 79. Cited in Moncure Daniel Conway, *Thomas Carlyle* (New York, 1881), pp. 123–4. 80. Leona Rostenberg, 'Mazzini to Margaret Fuller, 1847–1849', *The American Historical Review* 47/1 (1941), pp. 73–80, here p. 73. 81. On 'coterie charisma', see Roger Eatwell, 'The Concept and Theory of Charismatic Leadership', *Totalitarian Movements and Political Religions* 7/2 (2006), pp. 141–56. 82. Simon Levis Sullam, 'The Moses of Italian Unity. Mazzini and Nationalism as Political Religion' in Bayly and Biagini (eds.), *Giuseppe Mazzini*, pp. 107–24. 83. Mazzini to Ippolito Benelli, Paris, [Marseilles] 8 October 1831, cited in Levis Sullam, 'The Moses of Italian Unity', p. 115. 84. Franco della Peruta, 'Mazzini dalla letteratura militante all'impegno politico', *Studi Storici* 14/3 (1973), pp. 499–556, here pp. 527–8. 85. Buonarroti, *History of Babeuf's Conspiracy for Equality*, pp. 37–8 n. 86. Mazzini to Pietro Olivero, [January–July 1833], in Giuseppe Mazzini, *Scritti Editi ed Inediti di Giuseppe Mazzini* (Imola, 1909), vol. 5: *Epistolario*, pp. 353–8, here p. 354. 87. For a thoughtful discussion of these issues see the review by Sergio Romagnoli of Gastone Manacorda (ed. and trans.), *Congiura per l'eguaglianza o di Babeuf* – the Italian translation of Buonarroti's French text, *Belfagor* 2/1 (15 Jan. 1947), pp. 123–7. 88. Anon., *Letter-Opening at the Post-Office. The Article on this subject from No. LXXXII of the Westminster Review, September 1844. Entitled Mazzini and the Ethics of Politicians, to which is added Some Account of the Brothers Bandiera by J. Mazzini* (London, 1844), p. 28. 89. 'Manifesto for Young Italy' (1831), in William Lloyd Garrison (ed.), *Joseph Mazzini. His Life, Writings and Political Principles* (New York, 1872), pp. 62, 69, 71–4. 90. Carlo Bianco di St Jorioz, *Della guerra nazionale d'insurrezione per bande applicata all'Italia* (2 vols., Marseilles, 1830). 91. Bianco de St Jorioz, 'Discorso preliminare', in *Della guerra nazionale d'insurrezione*, pp. xvii–c, here pp. xcvii, c. 92. Cited in Nunzio Pernicone and Fraser M. Ottanelli, *Assassins against the Old Order. Italian Anarchist Violence in Fin-de-Siècle Europe* (Champagne, 2018), p. 14. 93. Franco Della Peruta, *Mazzini e i rivoluzionari italiani. Il "Partito d'azione' 1830–1845* (Milan, 1974), p. 160. **94.** Cited in Christopher Duggan, 'Giuseppe Mazzini in Britain and Italy. Divergent Legacies, 1837–1915', *The Italianist* 27/2 (2007), pp. 263–81, here p. 263. **95.** Christopher Duggan, *The Force of Destiny. A History of Italy since 1796* (London, 2007), p. 134. **96.** Della Peruta, *Mazzini e i rivoluzionari italiani*, p. 174. **97.** See the powerful discussion in Lucy Riall, 'The Politics of Italian Romanticism. Mazzini and the Making of a Nationalist Culture', in Bayly and Biagini (eds.), *Giuseppe Mazzini*, pp. 167–86; also Lucy Riall, *Garibaldi. Invention of a Hero* (New Haven, 2007), esp. pp. 29–31. **98.** Giuseppe Mazzini, 'Faith and the Future' (1835), in Mazzini, *The Duties of Men and Other Essays by Joseph Mazzini*, introd. T. Jones (London, 1936), pp. 56–7. On these themes in Mazzini's nationalism, see Maurizio Viroli, *For Love of Country. An Essay on Patriotism and Nationalism* (Oxford, 1995), pp. 146–56. **99.** Della Peruta, *Mazzini e i rivoluzionari italiani*, p. 36. **100.** C. R. Badger, 'A Study in Italian Nationalism. Giuseppe Mazzini', *The Australian Quarterly* 8/31 (Sep. 1936), pp. 70–80. **101.** Riall, *Garibaldi: Invention of a Hero*; see also the excellent discussion 'Garibaldi and the Risorgimento', BBC Radio 4, 'In Our Time', broadcast on Thursday, 1 December 2016, consulted at https://www.bbc.co.uk/programmes/b083qx9j. **102.** See Walter Bruyère Ostells, *La Grande Armée de la Liberté* (Paris, 2009). **103.** Alfred de Musset, *La Confession d'un enfant du siècle* ([1836] London and Paris, 1912), pp. 3, 5. **104.** Cited in J. J. Sheehan, *German History 1770–1866* (Oxford, 1989), p. 613. **105.** Ewald Grothe, *Verfassungsgebung und Verfassungskonflikt. Das Kurfürstentum Hessen in der ersten Ära Hassenpflug 1830–1837* (Berlin, 1996), p. 35. **106.** Ibid, p. 38. **107.** Wolfram Siemann, *Metternich. Strategist and Visionary* (Cambridge, Mass., and London, 2019), p.668. **108.** The use of clandestine agents is one of the central themes of Christos Aliprantis, 'Transnational Political Policing in Nineteenth-Century Europe. Prussia and Austria in Comparison, 1830–1870', PhD thesis, University of Cambridge, 2020. **109.** Grothe, *Verfassungsgebung und Verfassungskonflikt*, pp. 528–9. **110.** Jonathan Sperber, *Rhineland Radicals. The Democratic Movement and the Revolution of 1848–1849* (Princeton, 1991), pp. 39–40. **111.** Wolfgang Neugebauer, *Politischer Wandel im Osten. Ost- und Westpreußen von den alten Ständen zum Konstitutionalismus* (Stuttgart, 1992), pp. 174, 179, 390. **112.** Ibid., pp. 430–31. **113.** James Brophy, *Popular Culture and the Public Sphere in the Rhineland, 1800–1850* (Cambridge, 2007), pp. 162–5. **114.** On the character and reception of these calendars, see Brophy, *Popular Culture and the Public Sphere*, pp. 18–53. **115.** Nils Freytag, *Aberglauben im 19. Jahrhundert. Preußen und die Rheinprovinz zwischen Tradition und Moderne (1815–1918)* (Berlin, 2003), pp. 179–82. **116.** James M. Brophy, 'Carnival and Citizenship. The Politics of Carnival Culture in the Prussian Rhineland, 1823–1848', *Journal of Social History* 30/4 (Summer 1997), pp. 873–904; Brophy, 'The Politicization of Traditional Festivals in Germany, 1815–1848', in Karin Friedrich (ed.), *Festival Culture in Germany and Europe from the Sixteenth to the Twentieth Century* (Lampeter, 2000), pp. 73–106. **117.** Brophy, *Popular Culture and the Public Sphere in the Rhineland*, pp. 54–104; Ann Mary Townsend, *Forbidden Laughter. Popular Humour and the Limits of Repression in Nineteenth-Century Prussia* (Ann Arbor, 1992), pp. 24–5, 27, 48–9, 93, 137; for the same technique, practised by 'smooth-talkers', see the opening scene of Aimé Césaire, *A Season in the Congo*, trans. Gayatri Chakravorty Spivak (London, 2010), pp. 5–6. **118.** Heinrich Best and Wilhelm Weege, *Biographisches Handbuch der Abgeordneten der Frankfurter Nationalversammlung 1848/49* (Düsseldorf, 1969), pp. 188–90. **119.** Sheehan, *German History*, p. 625. **120.** Karl Obermann, 'Die Volksbewegung in Deutschland von 1844 bis 1846', *Zeitschrift für Geschichte* 5/3 (1957), pp. 503–25; James Sheehan, *German Liberalism in the Nineteenth Century* (Chicago, 1978), pp. 12–14. **121.** 'Offenburger Programme of the Southwest German democrats', in Walter Grab (ed.), *Die Revolution von 1848/49. Eine Dokumentation* (Munich, 1980), pp. 28–9. **122.** Kurt Düwell, 'David Hansemann als rheinpreußischer Liberaler in Heppenheim 1847', *Geschichte und Gesellschaft*, special issue 9, *Liberalismus in der*

Gesellschaft des deutschen Vormärz (1983), pp. 295–311, here p. 309. **123.** This summary was composed by Karl Mathy and published in the *Deutsche Zeitung* (Heidelberg), 15 October 1847. The full text is in Ernst Rudolf Huber (ed.), *Deutsche Verfassungsdokumente 1803–1850* [*German Constitutional Documents 1803–1850*], vol. 1: *Dokumente zur deutschen Verfassungsgeschichte* [*Documents on German Constitutional History*] (3rd edn, Stuttgart, 1978), pp. 324–6. This translation is from the German History Documents website of the German Historical Institute, Washington DC, viewed online at http://germanhistorydocs.ghi-dc.org/docpage.cfm?docpage_id=429. **124.** Anon., *Selbstbiographie von Robert Blum und dessen Ermordung in Wien am 9. November 1848, herausgegeben von einem seiner Freunde* (Leipzig and Meißen, [1848]), p. 6. **125.** Robert Blum, entry on 'Beredsamkeit' in Robert Blum, K. Herloßsohn and H. Marggraf (eds.), *Allgemeines Theater-Lexikon oder Encyklopädie alles Wissenswerthen für Bühnenkünstler, Dilettanten und Theaterfreunde. Unter Mitwirkung der sachkundigsten Schriftsteller Deutschlands* (7 vols., 1839–42), vol. 1 (2nd edn), p. 283. **126.** Richard J. Bazillion, 'Urban Violence and the Modernization Process in Pre-March Saxony 1830–1831 and 1845', *Historical Reflections/ Réflexions Historiques* 12/2 (Summer 1985), pp. 279–303, here p. 296. **127.** Robert Blum, entry on 'Einheit' in Anon. (ed.), *Volksthümliches Handbuch der Staatswissenschaften und Politik. Ein Staatslexicon für das Volk, begründet von Robert Blum* (Leipzig, 1852), pp. 306–7, here p. 307. On the broader salience of this idea among liberals, see John Breuilly, *The Formation of the First German Nation-State 1800–1871* (Basingstoke, 1996), p. 32. **128.** Cited in Ralf Zerback, *Robert Blum. Eine Biografie* (Leipzig, 2007), p. 181. **129.** Bazillion, 'Urban Violence and the Modernization Process in Pre-March Saxony', pp. 300–301. **130.** Report of 16 August 1845, cited in Zerback, *Robert Blum*, pp. 182–3. **131.** Blum to Johann Jacoby, 3 November 1845, cited in Zerback, *Robert Blum*, pp. 187–8. **132.** Louise Otto Peters, 'Über Robert Blum', *Frauenzeitung*, 2/21, 25 May 1850, pp. 259–61, here p. 259, cited in Zerback, *Robert Blum* , p. 181. **133.** Robert Blum (ed.), *Fortschrittsmänner der Gegenwart. Eine Weihnachtsgabe für Deutschlands freisinnige Männer und Frauen* (Leipzig, 1847). Blum himself was the author of the entry on Arndt; the Mannheim radical Friedrich Hecker supplied the chapter on Itzstein, convenor of the Hallgarten Circle. **134.** Michael Ledger-Lomas, 'Strauß and the *Life of Jesus* Controversy', in Grant Kaplan and Kevin van der Schei (eds.), *The Oxford Handbook to German Theology* (OUP, 2023), forthcoming. I am grateful to Michael for letting me see a copy of this essay before publication. **135.** Adolf Hausrath, *David Friedrich Strauss und die Theologie seiner Zeit* (Heidelberg, 1876), pp. 379–82. **136.** Ibid., pp. 395–7. **137.** Hegetschweiler was the author of *Beyträge zur einer kritischen Aufzählung der Schweizerpflanzen und eine Ableitung der helvetischen Pflanzenformen von den Einflüssen der Außenwelt* (Zurich, 1831); after his death, the Swiss naturalist Oswald Heer edited and published his *Flora der Schweiz* (Zurich, 1840). For an account of these events, see Heer's introduction, pp. xxi–xxiv. **138.** On these events, see Erik Linstrum, 'Strauss's "Life of Jesus". Publication and the Politics of the German Public Sphere', *Journal of the History of Ideas* 71/4 (2010), pp. 593–616; Marc H. Lerner, *A Laboratory of Liberty. The Transformation of Political Culture in Republican Switzerland, 1750–1848* (Leiden and Boston, 2012), esp. ch. 5, 'Popular Sovereignty in the Züriputsch', pp. 221–64. **139.** On the conflict in the Valais, see Sandro Guzzi-Heeb, *Passions alpines. Sexualité et pouvoirs dans las montagnes suisses (1700–1900)* (Rennes, 2014), pp. 127–41; Anne-Lise Head-König, 'Religion Mattered. Religious Differences in Switzerland and Their Impact on Demographic Behaviour (End of the 18th Century to the Middle of the 20th Century)', *Historical Social Research/Historische Sozialforschung* 42/2 (2017), pp. 23–58, here p. 28. **140.** Stefan Széchenyi, *Kreditwesen*, trans. Michael von Paziazi (Pest, 1830), pp. viii, 30. **141.** Ibid., p. 118. **142.** Ibid., pp. 147–8, 272. For discussions of the book, see Peter F. Sugar and Péter Hanák, *A History of Hungary* (Bloomington, 1990), pp. 191–3; the quotation is in Gábor Vermes, *Hungarian Culture and Politics in the Habsburg Monarchy 1711–1848* (Budapest, 2014), p. 253; see also Istvan Deak, *The Lawful Revolution. Louis*

Kossuth and the Hungarians 1848–1849 (New York, 1979), pp. 26–7. **143.** This is the argument made in R. J. W. Evans, 'The Habsburgs and the Hungarian Problem, 1790–1848', *Transactions of the Royal Historical Society* 39 (1989), pp. 41–62, here p. 59. **144.** John Paget, *Hungary and Transylvania, with Remarks on Their Condition, Social, Political and Economical* (London, 1850), p. 208; on Wesselényi's Anglophilia, see Gál István, 'Wesselényi Miklós angliai levelei', *Angol Filológiai Tanulmányok* 5/6 (1944), pp. 180–88; on the lithographic press, see Ambrus Miskolczy and Katalin Vargyas, 'Questions de société, nationalité, opposition dans le mouvement réformiste hongrois en Transylvanie (1830–1843) (Luttes de l'opposition libérale hongroise pour l'évolution bourgeoise en Transylvanie)', *Acta Historica Academiae Scientiarum Hungaricae* 33/1 (1987), pp. 1–34, here p. 21. **145.** Auguste de Gerando, 'Hungary and Austria', *The Christian Examiner and Religious Miscellany*, 47 (July–September–November 1849), pp. 444–98, here pp. 482–3. This is a translation by 'M.L.P.' of an article published in French in 1848. **146.** Vermes, *Hungarian Culture*, p. 265. **147.** Miskolczy and Vargyas, 'Questions de société', p. 4. **148.** Vermes, *Hungarian Culture*, p. 287. **149.** Andrew C. Janos, *The Politics of Backwardness in Hungary, 1825–1945* (Princeton, 1982), pp. 39–42. **150.** Ibid., pp. 64–5. **151.** Deak, *Lawful Revolution*, p. 29–31. **152.** On the divisions around Kossuth's style and politics, see P. Sándor, 'Sur la conception politique de Deák (Une de ses lettres inédites de 1842)', *Acta Historica Academiae Scientiarum Hungaricae* 26/1–2 (1980), pp. 179–204, here p. 197; on Metternich's reasoning, see Deak, *Lawful Revolution*, p. 35. **153.** George Barany, 'The Hungarian Diet of 1839–40 and the Fate of Szechenyi's Middle Course', *Slavic Review* 22/2 (1963), pp. 285–303, here pp. 300–301. **154.** Vermes, *Hungarian Culture*, p. 290. **155.** Janos, *Hungarian Backwardness*, p. 74; Vermes, *Hungarian Culture*, p. 290. **156.** Iván Zoltán Dénes, *Conservative Ideology in the Making* (Budapest, 2009), p. 42. **157.** Janos, *Hungarian Backwardness*, pp. 58–9. **158.** Deak, *Lawful Revolution*, pp. 56–8. **159.** On Guizot's place among 'the men of 1814' who came of age during and after the French Revolution, see Pierre Rosenvallon, *Le Moment Guizot* (Paris, 1985), p. 21; also Laurence Jacobs, ' "Le moment libéral". The Distinctive Character of Restoration Liberalism', *The Historical Journal* 31/2 (1988), pp. 479–91. **160.** On these themes in Guizot's work, see Lucien Jaume, *Tocqueville. The Aristocratic Sources of Liberty* (Princeton, 2013), pp. 251–90. **161.** Rebecca McCoy, 'Protestant and Catholic Tensions after the French Revolution. The Religious Nature of the White Terror in Languedoc, 1815', *Journal of the Western Society for French History* 43 (2015), consulted at https://quod.lib. umich.edu/w/wsfh/0642292.0043.012?view=text;rgn=main; A. Cosson, '1830 et 1848. La Révolution de 1830 à Nîmes', *Annales historiques de la Révolution française* 65/258 (October–December 1984), pp. 528–40. **162.** François Guizot, address to the Chamber of Deputies, session of 1 March 1843, in Guizot (ed.), *Histoire parlementaire de France. Recueil complet des discours prononcés dans les Chambres de 1819 à 1848 par M. Guizot* (4 vols., Paris, 1864), vol. 4, p. 68. **163.** Stanley Mellon, 'The July Monarchy and the Napoleonic Myth', *Yale French Studies*, no. 26 (1960), pp. 70–78, here p. 71. **164.** Sudhir Hazareesingh, 'Napoleonic Memory in Nineteenth-Century France. The Making of a Liberal Legend', *MLN* 120/4 (2005), pp. 747–73, here p. 771. **165.** Cited in Avner Ben-Amos, *Funerals, Politics and Memory in Modern France 1789–1996* (Oxford, 2000), p. 77. **166.** Adrien Dansette, 'L'Échauffourée de Boulogne 6 août 1840. I & II', *Revue des Deux Mondes* 2nd period (15 April 1958), pp. 609–27 and 275–86. **167.** Ibid., p. 275. **168.** How effectively this could be done became clear in the elections of summer 1846, when the government bumped its mandates up to 290, more than half of whom were civil servants or hailed from tiny constituencies where 'you can nominate a horse if we get a railway'; see Robert Tombs, *France 1814–1914* (London, 1996), p. 370. **169.** Dominique Kalifa, Philippe Régnier, Marie-Ève Thérenty and Alain Vaillant, *La Civilisation du journal. Histoire culturelle et littéraire de la presse française au XIXᵉ siècle* (Paris, 2011). **170.** See Michele Hannoosh, *Baudelaire and Caricature. From the Comic to an Art of Modernity*

(University Park, 1992), p. 118. **171.** William Reddy, *The Invisible Code. Honor and Sentiment in Postrevolutionary France, 1814–1848* (Berkeley, 1997), p. 184. **172.** Hannoosh, *Baudelaire and Caricature*, p. 119. **173.** Gabriel P. Weisberg, 'In Deep Shit. The Coded Images of Traviès in the July Monarchy', *Art Journal* 52/3, *Scatological Art* (Autumn 1993), pp. 36–40; Dorothy Johnson, 'Food for Thought. Consuming and Digesting as Political Metaphor in French Satirical Prints', in Manon Mathias and Alison M. Moore (eds.), *Gut Feeling and Digestive Health in Nineteenth-Century Literature, History and Culture* (Basingstoke, 2018), pp. 85–108, here p. 105. **174.** Irene Collins, 'The Government and the Press in France during the Reign of Louis-Philippe', *The English Historical Review* 69/271 (1954), pp. 262–82, here pp. 262, 265, 269–70, 276, 279–80. **175.** Amy Wiese Forbes, 'The Lithographic Conspiracy. How Satire Framed Liberal Political Debate in Nineteenth-Century France', *French Politics, Culture & Society* 26/2 (2008), pp. 16–50, here p. 33. **176.** Sandy Petrey, *In the Court of the Pear King. French Culture and the Rise of Realism* (Ithaca, 2005), p. 137. **177.** Jo Burr Margadant, 'Representing Queen Marie-Amélie in a "Bourgeois" Monarchy', *Historical Reflections/Réflexions Historiques* 32/2 (Summer 2006), pp. 421–51, esp. pp. 421–3, 449. **178.** Cited in Collins, 'The Government and the Press in France', p. 282. **179.** This account of the banquets is drawn from the classic study by Vincent Robert, *Le Temps des banquets. Politique et symbolique d'une génération (1818–1848)* (Paris, 2010), *passim*. **180.** John J. Baughman, 'The French Banquet Campaign of 1847–48', *The Journal of Modern History* 31/1 (1959), pp. 1–15, here p. 6. **181.** Jacqueline Lalouette, 'Les femmes dans les banquets politiques en France (vers 1848)', *Clio. Femmes, Genre, Histoire*, no. 14 (2001), *Festins de femmes*, pp. 71–91, here pp. 74–5, 89–90. **182.** Charles de Mazade, 'Lamartine, sa vie littéraire et politique', *Revue des Deux Mondes*, 2nd period, part one, 'Introduction' 88 (July and Aug. 1870), pp. 563–82; part two, 'Sa vie politique, I. Lamartine sous le gouvernement de 1830' 89 (Sep. and Aug. 1870), pp. 585–601; part three, 'Lamartine et la Republique de 1848' 90 (Nov. and Dec. 1870), pp. 38–57, here part three, p. 40. **183.** Baughman, 'The French Banquet Campaign', p. 13. **184.** Marco Minghetti, *Miei Ricordi* (3 vols., 2nd edn, Turin, 1888), vol. 1, pp. 115–16. **185.** Vincenzo Gioberti, *Del primato morale e civile degli italiani* (1st Neapolitan edn, Naples, 1848), p. 37. **186.** Ibid., p. 54. **187.** Ibid., p. 44. **188.** Ibid., pp. 88, 91, 99, 151. **189.** The key words: ibid., *passim*. On anarchy and despotism, see ibid., p. 103. On analogous developments in Sicily, where the new bourgeoisie gravitated away from democratic radicalism and towards a traditionalist reformism focused on the 'aristocratic' and 'English' Sicilian constitution of 1812, see Rosario Romeo, *Il Risorgimento in Sicilia* (Rome, 1982), pp. 285–90. **190.** Thus the argument of Enrico Francia, *1848. La rivoluzione del Risorgimento* (Bologna, 2012), pp. 20–21. **191.** Bruce Haddock, 'Political Union without Social Revolution. Vincenzo Gioberti's *Primato*', *The Historical Journal* 41/3 (1998), pp. 705–23, here pp. 706, 708, 711–12. **192.** See the 'Avvertenza per la Seconda Edizione', written in reply to the critics of the first edition, in Gioberti, *Del primato*, vol. 1, p. 37; ibid., pp. ccclxix–cclxxiv. **193.** Fernanda Gallo, *Dalla patria allo Stato. Bertrando Spaventa, una biografia intellettuale* (Rome, 2012), pp. 17, 28–9, 67, 87–90; Luca Mannori, 'Le consulte di stato', *Rassegna storica toscana* 45/2 (1999), pp. 347–79, here p. 350. **194.** Roberto Romani, 'Reluctant Revolutionaries. Moderate Liberalism in the Kingdom of Sardinia, 1849–1859', *The Historical Journal* 55/1 (2012), pp. 45–73, here p. 47. **195.** Maurizio Isabella, 'Aristocratic Liberalism and Risorgimento. Cesare Balbo and Piedmontese Political Thought after 1848', *History of European Ideas*, DOI:10.1080/01916599.2012.762621, pp. 5–7. **196.** Romani, 'Reluctant Revolutionaries', p. 47. **197.** Steven C. Hughes, *Crime, Disorder and the Risorgimento. The Politics of Policing in Bologna* (Cambridge, 2002), pp. 155–8. **198.** Piero Del Negro, 'Il 1848 e dopo', in Mario Isnenghi and Stuart Woolf (eds.), *Storia di Venezia. L'Ottocento e il Novecento* (3 vols., Rome, 2002), vol. 1, pp. 107–68. **199.** Beatrice de Graaf, Ido de Haan and B. Vick, 'Vienna 1815. Introducing a European Security Culture', in Graaf, Hahn and Vick (eds.), *Securing Europe after Napoleon. 1815 and the New*

European Security Culture (Cambridge, 2019), pp. 1–18; Cornel Zwierlein and Beatrice de Graaf, 'Security and Conspiracy in Modern History', *Historical Social Research* 38/1 (2013), pp. 7–45; Christos Aliprantis, 'Transnational Political Policing in Nineteenth-Century Europe. Prussia and Austria in Comparison, 1830–1870', PhD thesis, University of Cambridge, 2020, ch. 2.   **200.** Rüdiger Hachtmann, *Berlin 1848. Eine Politik- und Gesellschaftsgeschichte der Revolution* (Bonn, 1997), p. 175.   **201.** Jonathan House, *Controlling Paris. Armed Forces and Counter-Revolution, 1789–1848* (New York, 2014), pp. 45–51.   **202.** Cited in Siemann, *Metternich*, p. 130.   **203.** Siemann, *Metternich*, p. 137.   **204.** Ibid., pp. 741–2.   **205.** Henry Kissinger, 'The Conservative Dilemma. Reflections on the Political Thought of Metternich', *The American Political Science Review* 48/4 (Dec. 1954), pp. 1017–30.   **206.** Siemann, *Metternich*, p. 616.   **207.** Ibid., p. 602.   **208.** Cited in Wolfgang Mommsen, 'Die Julirevolution von 1830 und die europäische Staatenwelt', in Mommsen, *1848. Die ungewollte Revolution. Die revolutionären Bewegungen in Europe 1830–1849* (Frankfurt/Main, 1998), pp. 42–67, here p. 58.   **209.** D. Biagini, *Ragguaglio storico di quanto è avvenuto in Roma è in tutte le provincie dello Stato Pontificio in sequito del perdono accordato dalla Santità di N.S. Papa Pio IX come dal suo Editto del 16 Luglio 1846* (Rome, 1846), p. 4.   **210.** Margaret Fuller, diary entry, Rome, 17 December 1847, in Fuller, *At Home and Abroad; Or Things and Thoughts in America and Europe*, ed. Arthur B. Fuller (London, 1856; repr. Forgotten Books, London, 2013), p. 263.   **211.** Carlo Curci, *La nuova Italia ed i vecchi zelanti. Studii utili ancora all'ordinamento dei partiti parlamentari* (Florence, 1881), p. 50.   **212.** Hughes, *Crime, Disorder and the Risorgimento*, p. 159.   **213.** Stefano Tomassini, *Storia avventurosa della rivoluzione romana* (Milan, 2008), pp. 41–2.   **214.** Metternich to Apponyi, Vienna, 6 August 1847, in K. von Metternich, *Mémoires, documents et écrits divers laissés par le prince de Metternich*, ed. Prince R. de Metternich (Paris, 1883), vol. 7, pp. 414–16.   **215.** Margaret Fuller, 'Art, Politics and the Hope of Rome', dispatch to the *Tribune*, Rome, May 1847, in Fuller, *These Sad But Glorious Days. Dispatches from Europe, 1846–1850*, ed. Larry J. Reynolds and Susan Belasco Smith (New Haven, 1991), Dispatch 14, pp. 131–9, here p. 136.   **216.** Hughes, *Crime, Disorder and the Risorgimento*, p. 170.   **217.** *Il Popolo*, 5 September 1847, cited in Francia, *1848*, p. 43.   **218.** Francia, *1848*, p. 49.   **219.** [Luigi Settembrini], *Protesta del Popolo delle Due Sicilie* [Naples, 1847], pp. 3, 4, 21, 22, 35, 36, 37.   **220.** Martino Beltrani-Scalia, *Memorie storiche della rivoluzione di Sicilia, 1848–1849* (2 vols., Palermo, 1932), vol. 1, p. 249.   **221.** Francesco Michitelli, *Storia degli ultimi fatti di Napoli fino a tutto il 15 maggio 1848* (Naples, 1849), pp. 41–3.   **222.** Eric Dorn Brose, *The Politics of Technological Change in Prussia. Out of the Shadow of Antiquity, 1809–1848* (Princeton, 1993), pp. 223–4, 235–9; D. Barclay, *Friedrich Wilhelm IV and the Prussian Monarchy 1840–1861* (Oxford, 1995), p. 120.   **223.** Heinrich Simon, *Annehmen oder Ablehnen? Die Verfassung vom 3. Februar 1847, beleuchtet vom Standpunkte des bestehenden Rechts* (Leipzig, 1847), p. 5. The 'stone' Simon refers to in this text was the royal Patent of 3 February 1847 (Patent die ständischen Einrichtungen betreffend) stipulating the conditions under which the king proposed to convene the United Diet. The text of the patent can be consulted at http://www.verfassungen.de/preussen/plandtag47-index.htm.   **224.** For the text of the speech, see Eduard Bleich (ed.), *Der erste vereinigte Landtag* (4 vols., Berlin, 1847), vol. 1, pp. 22, 25–6.   **225.** H. Obenaus, *Anfänge des Parlamentarismus in Preussen bis 1848* (Düsseldorf, 1984), pp. 704–5; Huber, *Verfassungsgeschichte*, vol. 2, p. 494; on the formation of a reformist 'party', see also Johannes Gerhardt, *Der Erste Vereinigte Landtag in Preußen von 1847. Untersuchungen zu einer ständischen Körperschaft im Vorfeld der Revolution von 1848/49* (Berlin, 2007), although I do not share his view that the reformist deputies in the United Diet should be characterized as 'reform-conservatives'.   **226.** On the use of the term 'conservative' in the 1840s, see Rudolf Vierhaus, 'Konservatismus', in Otto Brunner, Werner Conze and Reinhard Koselleck (eds.), *Geschichtliche Grundbegriffe. Historisches Lexikon zu politisch-sozialer Sprache in Deutschland* (Stuttgart, 1972), pp. 531–65, esp. pp. 540–51; Alfred von Martin, 'Weltanschauliche Motive im altkonservativen Denken', in Gerd-Klaus

Kaltenbrunner, *Rekonstruktion des Konservatismus* (Freiburg, 1972), pp. 139–80. **227.** L. von Gerlach, *Denkwürdigkeiten aus dem Leben Leopold von Gerlachs, Generals der Infanterie und General Adjutanten König Friedrich Wilhelms IV* (Berlin, 1891), vol. 1, p. 118. **228.** Letter of 19 February 1848, transcribed in [Isaac Jacob] Adolphe Crémieux, *En 1848. Discours et lettres de M. Ad. Crémieux, Membre du Gouvernement Provisoire* (Paris, 1883), pp. 165–77, here p. 166. **229.** J. M. Rudolf, *Der Freischaarenzug gegen Luzern am 31. März, 1. u. 2. April 1845 und seine nächsten Folgen mit besonderer Rücksicht auf den zweiten Ochsenbein'schen Bericht geschichtlich-militairisch dargestellt* (Zurich, 1846), p. 4. **230.** Ellen Lovell Evans, *The Cross and the Ballot. Catholic Political Parties in Germany, Switzerland, Austria, Belgium and the Netherlands, 1785–1985* (Boston, 1999), p. 47. **231.** W. B. Duffield, 'The War of the Sonderbund', *The English Historical Review* 10/40 (1895), pp. 675–98, here pp. 684–5. **232.** Joachim Remak, *A Very Civil War. The Swiss Sonderbund War of 1847* (Boulder, 1993). **233.** Rudolf, *Der Freischaarenzug nach Luzern*, p. 193. **234.** Dalmatie to Guizot, 23 October 1846, cited in Roger Bullen, 'Guizot and the "Sonderbund" Crisis, 1846–1848', *The English Historical Review* 86/340 (1971), pp. 497–526, here p. 505. **235.** Thomas Brendel, *Zukunft Europa? Das Europabild und die Idee der internationalen Solidarität bei den deutschen Liberalen und Demokraten im Vormärz (1815–1848)* (Bochum, 2005), pp. 380–82; Harald Müller, 'Der Widerhall auf den schweizer Sonderbundskrieg 1847 in den Staaten des deutschen Bundes', *Jahrbuch für Geschichte* 7 (1972), pp. 211–41. **236.** Ferdinand Freiligrath, 'Im Hochland fiel der erste Schuß', in Freiligrath, *Neuere politische und sociale Gedichte* (Cologne, 1849), pp. 36–40. The poem is signed: 'London, 25 February 1848', but the content of the poem suggests that it may have been completed somewhat later in that year. **237.** Thomas Maissen, 'Fighting for Faith? Experiences of the Sonderbund campaign', in Joy Charnley and Malcolm Pender (eds.), *Switzerland and War*, Occasional Papers in Swiss Studies, vol. 2 (Bern, 1999), pp. 9–42, here pp. 13–14, 17–18, 28.

4. DETONATIONS

1. Giuseppe La Farina, *Istoria documentata della Rivoluzione Siciliana e delle sue relazioni co' governi italiani e stranieri (1848–1849)* (Milan, 1860), pp. 25–6; Martino Beltrani-Scalia, *Memorie storiche della Rivoluzione di Sicilia* (2 vols., Palermo, 1932), pp. 242–3. **2.** Transcription of a statement by Francesco Bagnasco, in 'L'Autore dei Proclami di Gennaro 1848', Francesco Ferrara (ed.), *Memorie sulla rivoluzione siciliana del 1847 e 1848*, no. 8 (Palermo, 1848), pp. 130–33. **3.** The Earl of Mount Edgcumbe, *Extracts from a Journal Kept during the Commencement of the Revolution at Palermo in the Year 1848* (London, 1849), p. 6. **4.** Alphonse de Lamartine, *Histoire de la Révolution de 1848* (2 vols., Paris, 1849), vol. 1, pp. 64–5. **5.** Anon., *Storia militare della rivoluzione avvenuta in Palermo nel Gennaio del 1848* (Venice, 1848), p. 7. **6.** Alfonso Scirocco, 'Il 1847 a Napoli. Ferdinando II e il movimento italiano per le riforme', *Rassegna Storica Toscana* 45 (1999), pp. 271–304, here p. 280. See also Angelantonio Spagnoletti, *Storia del Regno delle Due Sicilie* (Bologna, 1997), pp. 274–6. **7.** Giuseppe Restifo, 'L'insorgenza messinese del 1847', *Humanities* 6/11 (2017), pp. 13–26, here p. 17. **8.** Ibid., p. 22; Anon., *Storia militare della rivoluzione*, p. 7. **9.** Alfio Crimi, 'L'istruzione popolare nell'epoca borbonica in Sicilia', in *Nuovi quaderni del Meridione* 11 (1973), pp. 63–9. **10.** Schwarzenberg to Metternich, Naples, 7 September 1847, in Giovanni Schininà, *La Rivoluzione siciliana del 1848 nei documenti diplomatici austriaci* (Catania, 2011), p. 98. **11.** Edgcumbe, *Extracts from a Journal*, p. 1. **12.** Stefan Lippert, *Felix Fürst zu Schwarzenberg. Eine politische Biografie* (Stuttgart, 1998), p. 109. **13.** Anon., *Storia militare della rivoluzione*, pp. 9–10. **14.** Transcription of the proclamation of 9 January in 'L'Autore dei Proclami di Gennaro 1848', Ferrara (ed.), *Memorie sulla rivoluzione siciliana del 1847 e 1848*, p. 131. **15.** Edgcumbe, *Extracts from a Journal*, p. 18. **16.** Schwarzenberg to Metternich, 13 January 1848, in

Schininà (ed.), *La Rivoluzione siciliana*, p. 102.   17. Edgcumbe, *Extracts from a Journal*, p. 24.   18. Anon., *Storia militare della rivoluzione*, p. 18.   19. For a highly critical appraisal, see Giacinto De'Sivo, *Storia delle Due Sicilie dal 1847 al 1861* (2 vols., Rome, 1863), vol. 1, pp. 187–99; also Anon., *Storia militare della rivoluzione*, pp. 14–17, 26 and *passim*.   20. Schwarzenberg to Metternich, 21 January 1848, in Schininà (ed.), *La Rivoluzione siciliana*, p. 105.   21. Anon., *Storia militare della rivoluzione*, p. 23.   22. Matthew Drake Babington, *Messina 1848. Diario inedito*, ed. and trans. Rosario Portale (Moncalieri, 2012), p. 149.   23. Ibid., p. 163.   24. Ibid., p. 149.   25. Ibid., pp. 181, 183.   26. Babington, *Messina 1848* p. 237.   27. Government notice, Palermo, 18 January 1848, signed Ruggiero Settimo, Chairman of the Fourth Committee, in [Elpidio Micciarelli], ed., *Ruggiero Settimo e la Sicilia. Documenti sulla Insurrezione Siciliana del 1848* (Italy, March 1848), p. 10.   28. Anon., *Storia militare della rivoluzione*, p. 12.   29. Lord Napier to Viscount Palmerston, Naples, 14 February 1848, *Correspondence Respecting the Affairs of Naples and Sicily. Presented to Both Houses of Parliament by Command of Her Majesty* (London, 1849), doc. 82, p. 127. The constitution of 1812 is very frequently invoked in the British official correspondence.   30. Earl of Minto (Foreign Secretary Palmerston's special envoy to the Kingdom of the Two Sicilies) to Lord Napier (British Chargé d'Affaires at Naples), Palermo, 21 March 1848, *Correspondence Respecting the Affairs of Naples and Sicily*, enclosure in doc. 139, p. 252.   31. Viscount Palmerston to the Hon. W. Temple, Foreign Office, 3 November 1848, ibid., doc. 341, pp. 558–63; here p. 561.   32. Paola Gemme, 'Imperial Designs of Political Philanthropy. A Study of Antebellum Accounts of Italian Liberalism', *American Studies International* 39/1 (2001), pp. 19–51, here pp. 33, 48–9.   33. Schwarzenberg to Metternich, Naples, 24 January 1848, in Schininà, *La Rivoluzione siciliana del 1848*, pp. 111–12.   34. Schwarzenberg to Metternich, Naples, 3 February 1848, in ibid., p. 114.   35. Metternich to Schwarzenberg, Vienna, 6 February 1848, in ibid., p. 116.   36. Babington, *Messina 1848*, p. 131.   37. Ibid., p. 145.   38. Edgcumbe, *Extracts from a Journal*, p. 39.   39. Cited in A. Blando, 'La guerra rivoluzionaria di Sicilia. Costituzione, controrivlouzione, nazione 1789–1848', *Meridiana*, no. 81 (2014), pp. 67–84, here p. 80. To my knowledge, Scinà's 'Documenti raccolti per scrivere l'istoria della rivoluzione del 1820 in Sicilia' remain unpublished.   40. Cited in Giovanna Fiume, *La crisi sociale del 1848 in Sicilia* (Messina, 1982), p. 72.   41. Salvatore Lupo, 'Tra Centro e Periferia. Sui modi dell' aggregazione politica nel Mezzogiorno contemporaneo', *Meridiana*, no. 2 (1988), pp. 13–50, here pp. 18–19; Lucy Riall, 'Elites in Search of Authority. Political Power and Social Order in Nineteenth-Century Sicily', *History Workshop Journal*, no. 55 (Spring 2003), pp. 25–46, here pp. 35–7.   42. Babington, *Messina 1848*, pp. 152–3.   43. Edgcumbe, *Extracts from a Journal*, p. 39.   44. Francesco Crispi, *Ultimi casi della rivoluzione siciliana esposti con documenti da un testimone oculare* (Turin, 1850), p. 10.   45. Anon., *Storia militare della rivoluzione*, p. 18.   46. Anon., *Storia militare della rivoluzione*, p. 31.   47. Mark Traugott, *The Insurgent Barricade* (Berkeley, 2010), pp. 292–4.   48. For illuminating thoughts on how multilevel interactions at many levels complicate the analysis of revolutionary 'waves', see Colin J. Beck, 'Reflections on the Revolutionary Wave in 2011', *Theory and Society* 43/2 (2014), pp. 197–223.   49. 'L'insurrection en Sicile', 'L'Italie', 'Nouvelles Diverses', 'Dernière nouvelles de l'Italie', in *La Réforme*, 23 January 1848, pp. 1–3. Page 4 is usually reserved for advertisements, financial news and court reporting.   50. 'Le soulèvement en Sicile', 'Nouvelles diverses', in *La Réforme*, 26 January 1848, pp. 1–2.   51. Leader article, *La Réforme*, 1 February 1848, p. 1.   52. Translation of a report from the *Vossische Zeitung* [Berlin], ibid., 5 February 1848, p. 1.   53. 'La Suisse', ibid.   54. Philippe Faure, *Journal d'un combattant de février* (Jersey, 1859), pp. 75–6.   55. 'Discussion de l'Addresse', *La Réforme*, 30 January 1848, p. 1.   56. Alexis de Tocqueville, speech to the chamber of 27 January 1848, excerpted in Tocqueville, *The Recollections of Alexis de Tocqueville*, trans. Alexander Teixeira de Mattos (New York, 1896), pp. 15–16. This speech was all the more remarkable for the fact that it seemed to abandon the argument Tocqueville had advanced in the twenty-first chapter of the third section of the 1840 volume of *Democracy in America*, namely that 'great revolutions' were likely to become rarer in countries, like France and the United States, the majority of whose inhabitants were property-owners; on the contrast, see Seymour Drescher, ' "Why Great Revolutions Will Become Rare". Tocqueville's Most Neglected Prognosis', *The Journal of Modern History* 64/3 (1992), pp. 429–54. 57. 'Discussion de l'addresse', *La Réforme*, 28 January 1848, p. 1. 58. See the discussion of connectedness in John Breuilly, '1848. Connected or Comparable Revolutions?', in Axel Körner (ed.), *1848. A European Revolution? International Ideas and National Memories of 1848* (2nd rev. edn, Basingstoke, 2004), pp. 31–49. 59. *El Clamor público*, 20, 22, 23, 24, 25, 26, 27 February 1848. Citation 27 February 1848: 'Los sucesos de París son una lección muy severa y elocuente para los Reyes y los gobiernos, que con desprecio de la opinión contrarían las exigencias legítimas de las Naciones, anteponiendo sus intereses privados á los intereses públicos.' 60. 'Los pueblos y sus opresores', leader article, *El Eco del Comercio*, 22 February 1848, p. 2. 61. *El Siglo*, 25 and 26 February 1848. 62. See the coverage under the rubric 'Correo estranjero', in *El Heraldo*, 1, 2, 4, 5, 6 January, 18, 19, 20, 21 February 1848, and *passim*. 63. *Algemeen Handelsblad*, 12 Feb. 1848 in Siep Stuurman, '1848. Revolutionary Reform in the Netherlands', *European History Quarterly* 21/4 (1991), pp. 445–80, here p. 454. 64. Rüdiger Hachtmann, ' "... ein gerechtes Gericht Gottes". Der Protestantismus und die Revolution von 1848 – das Berliner Beispiel', *Archiv für Sozialgeschichte* 36 (1996), pp. 205–55; see also Rüdiger Hachtmann, *Berlin 1848. Eine Politik- und Gesellschaftsgeschichte der Revolution* (Bonn, 1997), p. 117. 65. *Vossische Zeitung*, 17 January 1848, pp. 5–8. 66. Ibid., 25 January 1848, pp. 7, 9, 10; 25 January, pp. 5, 6. 67. See Jyrki Vesikansa, *Sinivalkoiseen Suomeen. Uuden Suomen ja sen edeltäjien historia (1847–1939)* (2 vols., Keuruu, 1997), vol. 1, pp. 38–9. 68. 'Chronica straina', *Curierul Românesc*, 29 January 1848 (OS), p. 1. 69. Ibid., 5 February 1848 (OS), p. 2. 70. Ibid., 19 February 1848 (OS), p. 2. 71. See, for example, the 'Chronica Straina' section in *Gazeta de Transilvania*, 19 January 1848, pp. 23–4 (the issues are cumulatively paginated). 72. Le comte de [Joseph Alexander, Graf von] Hübner, *Une année de ma vie. 1848–1849* (Paris, 1891), p. 5. 73. On the post-Napoleonic 'security culture', see Beatrice de Graaf, Ido de Hahn and B.Vick (eds.), *Securing Europe after Napoleon*, esp. pp. 1–18, and Graaf, *Fighting Terror after Napoleon: How Europe Became Secure after 1815* (Cambridge, 2020), *passim*. 74. The outstanding analysis of these events, from which this account is drawn, is Vincent Robert, *Le Temps des banquets. Politique et symbolique d'une génération (1818–1848)* (Paris, 2010), here pp. 373–4. 75. 'Paris, 8 February 1848', in *La Réforme*, 9 February 1848, p. 1; see also *La Réforme*, 10 February 1848, p. 1. 76. Robert, *Le Temps des banquets*, here p. 368. 77. The speech is excerpted in 'Chambre des députés. Séance du 9. Février', *La Réforme*, 10 February 1834, p. 3. 78. Jonathan Beecher, *Victor Considerant and the Rise and Fall of French Romantic Socialism* (Berkeley, 2001), pp. 108–9. 79. Cited in 'Discussion de l'addresse. Les banquets réformistes', *La Réforme*, 12 February 1848, p. 1. 80. 'Les devoirs de l'opposition', *La Réforme*, 14 February 1848, p. 1. 81. *La Réforme*, 21 February 1848, p. 1. 82. On the stockpiling, see Jonathan House, *Controlling Paris. Armed Forces and Counter-Revolution, 1789–1848* (New York, 2014), p. 54; *La Réforme*, 14 February 1848, p. 1. 83. Madame Crémieux [née Louise Amélie Silny], letter, Paris, 23 February [1848], transcribed in [Isaac Jacob] Adolphe Crémieux, *En 1848. Discours et lettres de M. Ad. Crémieux, Membre du Gouvernement Provisoire* (Paris, 1883), pp. 177–82, here p. 178. 84. Diary notes on 22 February 1848 in Faure, *Journal d'un combattant de février*, p. 137. 85. House, *Controlling Paris*, p. 59. 86. Pierre Rosanvallon, *Le Moment Guizot* (Paris, 1985), p. 350. 87. Diary notes on 23 February 1848 in Faure, *Journal d'un combattant de Février*, pp. 138, 141. 88. Madame Crémieux, letter, Paris, 24 February [1848], transcribed in Crémieux, *En 1848*, pp. 185–90, here pp. 187–8. 89. Leader article, *La Réforme*, 24 February 1848, p. 1; 'Nouvelles diverses', ibid., 23 February 1848, p. 2; leader article, ibid., 25 February 1848, p. 1. 90. Ibid., 16 February 1848, p. 1. 91. Robert, *Le Temps des banquets*, p. 385. 92. Radowitz to his wife, 28 February 1848, in Hans Fenske (ed.), *Vormärz und Revolution. Quellen zur deutschen Revolution 1840–1849* (Darmstadt, 1996), pp. 44–5. 93. On the challenge posed by simultaneity and the importance of 'meanwhile', see R. J. W. Evans, '1848–1849 in the Habsburg Monarchy', in Evans and Hartmut Pogge von Strandmann (eds.), *The Revolutions in Europe 1848–1849. From Reform to Reaction* (Oxford, 2000), pp. 181–206, here p. 183. 94. 'Nicht-amtlicher Theil', *Wiener Zeitung*, no. 70, 10 March 1848, pp. 317–18 (p. 317 is the title page of this issue). 95. Herwig Knaus and Wilhelm Sinkowicz, *Wien 1848. Reportage einer Revolution* (Vienna, 1998), pp. 27–8. 96. The public impact of the manifesto was negligible; most of the copies mailed to newspaper offices were opened and seized by the police. One copy made it to and was published in the Brunswick-based liberal journal *Der Leuchtturm*. Heinrich Reschauer, *Das Jahr 1848. Geschichte der Wiener Revolution* (2 vols., Vienna, 1872), vol. 1, p. 122. 97. See, for example, J. J. Freiberger to Chief Minister Kolowrat, 7 March 1848, cited in Reschauer, *Das Jahr 1848*, vol. 1, pp. 128–9. 98. Memorandum from thirty-three members of the Lower Austrian Estates to the College of Representatives (Verordneten-Kollegium) of the Lower Austrian Diet, 3 March 1848, cited in ibid., pp. 131–2. 99. Ibid., p. 143. 100. Istvan Deak, *The Lawful Revolution. Louis Kossuth and the Hungarians 1848–1849* (New York, 1979), p. 67; Mike Rapport, *1848 Year of Revolution* (London, 2008), p. 60. 101. Theresa Pulszky, *Memoirs of a Hungarian Lady* (2 vols., Philadelphia, 1850), vol. 1, p. 144. 102. On the meaning of this moment for Fischhof and his friends, see the treatment in Abigail Green, *The Children of 1848*, chapter 2. I am grateful to Abigail for letting me see this text before publication. 103. William Henry Stiles (former Chargé d'Affaires of the United States at the Court of Vienna), *Austria in 1848–1849. Being a History of the Late Political Movements in Vienna, Milan, Venice and Prague, with Details of the Campaigns of Lombardy and Novara; a Full Account of the Revolution in Hungary and Historical Sketches of the Austrian Government and the Provinces of the Austrian Empire* (2 vols., New York, 1852), vol. 1, p. 105. 104. Peter Frank-Döfering, *Die Donner der Revolution über Wien. Ein Student aus Czernowitz erlebt 1848* (Vienna, 1988), pp. 32–3. 105. Knaus and Sinkowicz, *Wien 1848*, pp. 35–6. 106. For a detailed description of these events, see Matthias Kneisel, *Unvergeßlicher Frühling des österreichischen Kaiserstaates im Jahre 1848* (Iglau, [1848]), pp. 65–6. 107. Gabriella Hauch, *Frau Biedermeyer auf den Barrikaden. Frauenleben in der Wiener Revolution* (Vienna, 1990), pp. 173–4. 108. Anon., 'Verzeichnis der bisher erkannten Gefallenen', *Der Humorist* 12/69, 21 March 1848, p. 274. 109. Frank-Döfering, *Die Donner der Revolution*, p. 39. 110. Kneisel, *Unvergeßlicher Frühling*, pp. 65–6. 111. Ibid., pp. 77–7. 112. Wolfram Siemann, *Metternich. Strategist and Visionary* (Cambridge, Mass., and London, 2019), p. 833. 113. Hübner, *Une année de ma vie*, p. 10. 114. Ibid., p. 16. 115. Cited in Alan Palmer, *Councillor of Europe* (London, 1972), p. 311. 116. Moritz Saphir in *Der Humorist* 12/64, 15 March 1848, transcribed in Knaus and Sinkowicz, *Wien 1848*, p. 44. 117. Cited in *Wiener Zeitung*, no. 77, 17 March 1848, p. 1. This issue of the paper contains a summary of the events of the preceding few days from which this account is drawn. 118. Alice Freifeld, *Nationalism and the Crowd in Liberal Hungary* (Washington DC, 2000), pp. 47–9. 119. Cited in Deak, *Lawful Revolution*, p. 73. 120. György Spira, *A Hungarian Count in the Revolution of 1848* (Budapest, 1974), p. 25. 121. Text of a statement posted in the city on the afternoon of 15 March, cited in Frank-Döfering, *Die Donner der Revolution*, p. 40. 122. *Wiener Zeitung*, no. 77, 17 March 1848, reporting on the events of the previous three days. 123. Frank-Döfering, *Die Donner der Revolution*, p. 40. 124. Spira, *A Hungarian Count*, pp. 28–9. My account of the Hungarian negotiations on 15–17 March is drawn from Spira's analysis. 125. The quotations from the letter to his secretary, Antal Tasner, and the reference to Széchenyi's diary are from ibid., pp. 31–2. 126. Freifeld, *Nationalism and the Crowd*, p. 47. 127. Ibid., p. 50. 128. Spira, *A Hungarian Count*, p.

16. 129. Robert Nemes, 'Women in the 1848–49 Hungarian Revolution', *Journal of Women's History* 13/3 (2001), pp. 193–207, here p. 194. 130. Frank-Döfering, *Die Donner der Revolution*, pp. 39–40. 131. Carl Schurz, *The Reminiscences of Carl Schurz*, trans. Eleonora Kinnicutt, vol. 1, ch. 6, 'Uprising in Germany', unpaginated, consulted online at https://en.wikisource.org/wiki/The_Reminiscences_of_Carl_Schurz/Volume_One/Chapter_06. 132. Diary entry, Karlovac, 24 March 1848, Dragojla Jarnević, *Dnevnik*, ed. Irena Lukšić (Karlovac, 2000), p. 337. 133. Enrico Francia, *1848. La rivoluzione del Risorgimento* (Bologna, 2012), p. 247. 134. Paul Boerner, *Erinnerungen eines Revolutionärs. Skizzen aus dem Jahre 1848* (Leipzig, 1920), vol. 2, p. 49. 135. *Vossische Zeitung (Extrablatt)*, 28 February 1848, accessed online at http://www.zlb.de/projekte/1848/vorgeschichte_image. htm; last accessed 11 June 2004. 136. Muzio (pseud.), 'Physiognomie Berlins im Februar und März 1848', in [Albert Schwegler (ed.)], *Jahrbücher der Gegenwart. 1848*, no. 27 (April 1848), pp. 106–7, here p. 106. 137. Boerner, *Erinnerungen eines Revolutionärs*, vol. 1, p. 73. 138. Karl August Varnhagen von Ense, 'Darstellung des Jahres 1848' (written in the autumn of 1848), in Konrad Feilchenfeld (ed.), *Karl August Varnhagen von Ense. Tageblätter* (5 vols., Frankfurt/Main, 1994), vol. 4: *Biographien, Aufsätze, Skizzen, Fragmente*, pp. 685–734, here p. 724. 139. Hachtmann, *Berlin 1848*, pp. 107–8. 140. Wolfram Siemann, 'Public Meeting Democracy in 1848', in Dieter Dowe, Heinz-Gerhard Haupt, Dieter Langewiesche and Jonathan Sperber (eds.), *Europe in 1848. Revolution und Reform* (New York, 2001), pp. 767–76; Hagen Schulze, *Der Weg zum Nationalstaat. Die deutsche Nationalbewegung vom 18. Jahrhundert bis zur Reichsgründung* (Munich, 1992), pp. 3–48. 141. Boerner, *Erinnerungen eines Revolutionärs*, vol. 1, pp. 81–2. 142. Ibid., pp. 106–7, 109. 143. Alessandro Manzoni, *The Betrothed*, trans. Archibald Colquhoun (orig. 1827; London, 1956), pp. 188–9. 144. See the description of events in the schlossplatz on 15 March in Karl Ludwig von Prittwitz, *Berlin 1848. Das Erinnerungswerk des Generalleutnants Karl Ludwig von Prittwitz und andere Quellen zur Berliner Märzrevolution und zur Geschichte Preußens um die Mitte des 19. Jahrhunderts*, ed. Gerd Heinrich (Berlin, 1985), pp. 71–3. 145. Karl August Varnhagen von Ense, diary entry, 15 March 1848, in Feilchenfeld (ed.), *Varnhagen von Ense*, vol. 5: *Tageblätter*, pp. 429–30. 146. Prittwitz, *Berlin 1848*, p. 116. 147. Cited in Prittwitz, *Berlin 1848*, p. 120. 148. On the composition of the crowd and the variation in mood, see Hachtmann, *Berlin 1848*, pp. 154–5; on the workers at the edge of the crowd, see Wilhelm Angerstein, *Die Berliner März-Ereignisse im Jahre 1848* (Leipzig, 1864), p. 31. 149. Prittwitz, *Berlin 1848*, pp. 129–30. 150. Boerner, *Erinnerungen eines Revolutionärs*, vol. 1, pp. 135–6. 151. Feilchenfeld (ed.), *Varnhagen von Ense*, vol. 5: *Tageblätter*, 18 March 1848, p. 433. 152. Hachtmann, *Berlin 1848*, p. 158. 153. Boerner, *Erinnerungen eines Revolutionärs*, vol. 1, pp. 137–8. 154. Cited in Prittwitz, *Berlin, 1848*, p. 174. 155. Boerner, *Erinnerungen eines Revolutionärs*, vol. 1, pp. 144–5. 156. Annex to the deposition (*protokollarische Aussage*) of the barber's assistant Louis Bergener in Adalbert Roerdansz, *Ein Freiheits-Martyrium. Gefangene Berliner auf dem Transport nach Spandau am Morgen des 19. März 1848* (Berlin, 1848), pp. 178–81, here p. 179. 157. Prittwitz, *Berlin 1848*, p. 232. 158. Text of the address given in ibid., p. 259. 159. For divergent accounts of the role of the military and Frederick William IV in the withdrawal from Berlin, see Felix Rachfahl, *Deutschland. König Friedrich Wilhelm IV. und die Berliner Märzrevolution von 1848* (Halle, 1901); Friedrich Thimme, 'König Friedrich Wilhelm IV., General von Prittwitz und die Berliner Märzrevolution', *Forschungen zur Brandenburg-Preußischen Geschichte* 16 (1903), pp. 201–38; Friedrich Meinecke, 'Friedrich Wilhelm IV. und Deutschland', *Historische Zeitschrift* 89/1 (1902), pp. 17–53, here pp. 47–9. 160. Heinrich, *Geschichte Preußens*, p. 364. 161. David Blackbourn, *History of Germany 1780–1918. The Long Nineteenth Century* (2nd edn, Oxford, 2003), p. 107. 162. On the continuing loyalty of a substantial part of the Berlin population to the monarch, see Hachtmann, *Berlin 1848*, p. 116. 163. Wolfgang Heinrich Riehl, *Nassauische Chronik des Jahres 1848* (initially

published in instalments in the *Nassauische Allgemeine Zeitung* in 1849), ed. Winfried Schüler and Guntram Müller Schellenberg (reprint: Idstein/Wiesbaden, 1979), p. 14. **164.** Hübner, *Une année de ma vie*, p. 11. **165.** Ibid., p. 23. Maximilian Karl Lamoral Count O'Donnell von Tyrconnell was an officer and civil servant in Austrian service and the descendant of an Irish noble dynasty. In 1853, after protecting the emperor from an assassination attempt by a Hungarian nationalist, O'Donnell was elevated from *Graf* to *Reichsgraf*. Since the letters patent awarding the title misspelt his name, the Austrian O'Donnells have since then been known as 'O'Donell'. **166.** Ibid., p. 25. **167.** Ibid., pp. 26, 48-9. **168.** Ibid., pp. 54, 56-7. **169.** Enrico Dandolo, *The Italian Volunteers and the Lombard Rifle Brigade. Being an Authentic Narrative of the Organization, Adventures and Final Disbanding of These Corps, in 1848-49* (London, 1851), p. 36. **170.** Carlo Osio, *Alcuni Fatti delle Cinque Gloriose Giornate* (Milan, 1848), pp. 11-12. **171.** Carlo Cattaneo, *L'Insurrection de Milan* (Paris, 1848), p. 1. **172.** Ibid., pp. 17-18. **173.** Ibid., p. 21. **174.** Ibid., pp. 36, 39-40. **175.** Ibid., pp. 69-70. **176.** Hübner, *Une année de ma vie*, pp. 61-2. **177.** Cattaneo, *L'insurrection de Milan*, pp. 72-4. **178.** Dandolo, *The Italian Volunteers and the Lombard Rifle Brigade*, p. 38. **179.** Piet de Rooy, *A Tiny Spot on the Earth: The Political Culture of the Netherlands in the Nineteenth and Twentieth Century* (Amsterdam, 2015), p. 84. **180.** Remieg Aerts, *Thorbecke wil het. Biografie van een staatsman* (Amsterdam, 2018), pp. 262-315. **181.** Gerlof D. Homan, 'Constitutional Reform in the Netherlands in 1848', *The Historian* 28/3 (1966), pp. 405-25, here pp. 405-12. **182.** Jeroen van Zanten, *Koning Willem II, 1792-1849* (Amsterdam, 2013), p. 530. **183.** Zanten, *Koning Willem II*, p. 544. **184.** Homan, 'Constitutional Reform', p. 414 **185.** Zanten, *Koning Willem II*, pp. 545-54; Aerts, *Thorbecke wil het*, pp. 348-9; Johan Christiaan Boogman, *Rondom 1848. De politieke ontwikkeling van Nederland 1840-1858* (Haarlem, 1978); on the radical movement, see M. J. F. Robijns, *Radicalen en het Nederland (1840-1851)* (Leiden, 1967). **186.** *Handelingen*, Tweede Kamer, 17 August 1848, p. 674. For a recent account emphasizing the effect of Dutch 'consensus culture' in muting the effect of political dissent, see Geerten Waling and Niels Ottenheim, 'Waarom Nederland in 1848 geen revolutie kende', *Tijdschrift voor Geschiedenis*, 133/1 (2020), pp. 5-29, esp. p. 16. **187.** *Handelingen*, Tweede Kamer, 28 March 1848, p. 277. **188.** Johannes Kneppelhout, *Landgenooten!* (Utrecht, 1848), pp. 3-5. **189.** Rooy, *A Tiny Spot*, p. 85. **190.** Aerts, *Thorbecke wil het*, pp. 367-8; Boogman, *Rondom 1848*, p. 53. **191.** Stuurman, 'Revolutionary Reform in the Netherlands', p. 455. **192.** Brecht Deseure, 'From Pragmatic Conservatism to Formal Continuity. Nineteenth-Century Views on the Old-Regime Origins of the Belgian Constitution', *Journal of Constitutional History* 32/2 (2016), pp. 257-77. **193.** Els Witte, *Belgische republikeinen. Radicalen tussen twee revoluties (1830-1850)* (Antwerp, 2020), pp. 280-81. **194.** Ibid., pp. 282-3. **195.** Editorial, *The Times*, 21 March 1848, p. 5, cols. 3-5. **196.** Leslie Mitchell, 'Britain's Reaction to the Revolutions', in Evans and Strandmann (eds.), *The Revolutions in Europe*, pp. 83-98. **197.** Gareth Stedman Jones, *Languages of Class. Studies in English Working-Class History 1832-1982* (Cambridge, 1984), pp. 44, 57, 94-6. **198.** Fabrice Bensimon, 'British Workers in France', *Past & Present* 213/1 (2011), pp. 147-89, esp. pp. 171-3; Arthur Lehning, *From Buonarroti to Bakunin: Studies in International Socialism* (Leiden, 1970), ch. 6; Henry Weisser, *British Working-Class Movements and Europe, 1815-48* (Manchester, 1975), pp. 134-71; Salvo Mastellone, 'Northern Star, Fraternal Democrats e Manifest der Kommunistischen Partei', *Il pensiero politico* 37 (2004), pp. 32-59; Roland Quinault, '1848 and Parliamentary Reform', *The Historical Journal* 31/4 (1988), pp. 831-51. **199.** Boyd Hilton, *A Mad, Bad and Dangerous People? England, 1763-1846* (Oxford, 2006), pp. 618-19. **200.** Mitchell, 'Britain's Reaction', p. 92. **201.** Cited in ibid. **202.** Hilton, *A Mad, Bad and Dangerous People?*, p. 613. **203.** For an analysis of Minutoli's journey to Britain and the correspondence with the administration in Berlin, see Christos Aliprantis,

'The Origins of Transnational Political Policing in Europe, 1830–1870', PhD thesis, University of Cambridge, ch. 2. 204. Miles Taylor, 'The 1848 Revolutions and the British Empire', *Past & Present* 166/1 (2000), pp. 146–80. 205. Cited in Raymond Carr, *Spain: A History* (New York, 2000), p. 431. 206. Ignacio García de Paso García, 'El 1848 español. ¿Una excepción europea?', *Ayer*, no. 106 (2017(2)), pp. 185–206, here p. 191. 207. The secret society known as the 'Tertulia of 18 June' and the Academia del Porvenir, a society dedicated to the teaching of science, literature and the fine arts, both served for a time as arms depots; see Manuel Morales Muñoz, 'La oposición democrática en la génesis revolucionaria (1848–1868)', *Bulletin d'Histoire Contemporaine de l'Espagne*, 55 (2020), paragraphs 3, 10; consulted online at http://journals.openedition.org/bhce/1497. 208. Cited in Florencia Peyrou, '1848 et le Parti démocratique espagnol', *Le Mouvement social*, no. 234 (2011), pp. 17–32; consulted online at https://www.cairn.info/revue-le-mouvement-social1-2011-1-page-17.htm. 209. Clara E. Lida: 'Los ecos de la República democrática y social en España. Trabajo y ciudadanía en 1848', *Semata. Ciencias Sociais e Humanidades*, no. 12 (2000), pp. 323–38, here p. 331. 210. These observations stem from the university professor Jerónimo Borao y Clemente, *Historia del alzamiento de Zaragoza en 1854* (Zaragoza, 1855), pp. 26–8, and are cited in Ignacio García de Paso García, '"Ya no hay Pirineos". La revolución de 1848 en Aragón', *Revista de historia Jerónimo Zurita*, no. 91 (2016), pp. 183–203, here p. 193. My account of the events in provincial Spain is indebted to García's insightful analysis. 211. García de Paso García, 'El 1848 español', p. 193. 212. Edgcumbe, *Extracts from a Journal*, pp. 35–6, 37. 213. Ibid., p. 44.

5. REGIME CHANGE

1. The text and music are by Amir Eid; the singers are Amir Eid and Aida El-Ayoubi; for the Arabic text and a translation, see https://lyricstranslate.com/en/%D9%8A%D8%A7-%D8%A7%D9%84%D9%85%D9%8A%D8%AF%D8%A7%D9%86-0-you-square-tahrir-square.html. 2. On the area in front of the Pilvax as a space where crowds tended to gather in moments of uncertainty, see 'Österreichische Monarchie', *Siebenbürger Wochenblatt*, Kronstadt, 19 September 1848, no. 76, p. 468. 3. Paul Boerner, *Erinnerungen eines Revolutionärs. Skizzen aus dem Jahre 1848* (Leipzig, 1920), vol. 1, p. 74. 4. Fanny Lewald, diary entry, Paris, 12 March 1848, in Hanna Ballin Lewis, *A Year of Revolutions. Fanny Lewald's Recollections of 1848* [1870], ed. and trans. Hanna Ballin Lewis (Oxford, 1998), pp. 41–2. 5. Anon., 'Tagesgeschichte. Die Erhebung von Pesth', *Illustrierte Zeitung*, no. 254, 13 May 1848, p. 313, col. 2. 6. Heinrich Brockhaus, diary entry of 6 April 1848, in [Heinrich Brockhaus], *Aus den Tagebüchern von Heinrich Brockhaus* (5 vols., Leipzig, 1884), vol. 2, p. 179. 7. Francesco Michitelli, *Storia degli ultimi fatti di Napoli fino a tutto il 15 maggio 1848* (Naples, 1849), p. 139. 8. Anon., 'Tagesgeschichte. Die Erhebung von Pesth', *Illustrierte Zeitung*, no. 254, 13 May 1848, p. 313, col. 2. 9. Peter A. Schoenborn, *Adalbert Stifter. Sein Leben und Werk* (Bern, 1992), p. 358. 10. Heinrich König, *Ein Stilleben. Erinnerungen und Bekenntnisse* (2 vols., Leipzig, 1861), vol. 2, pp. 344–5. 11. Alexis de Tocqueville, *Recollections*, trans. George Lawrence, ed. J. P. Meyer and A. P. Kerr (London, 1970), pp. 71–2. 12. Lewald, diary entry, Paris, 15 March 1848, in *A Year of Revolutions*, pp. 42–3. 13. Gabriella Hauch, *Frau Biedermeier auf den Barrikaden. Frauenleben in der Wiener Revolution* (Vienna, 1990), pp. 177–9. 14. Anon., 'Tagesgeschichte. Die Erhebung von Pesth', *Illustrierte Zeitung*, nr. 254, 13 May 1848, p. 313, col. 2. 15. Einheitsplatz, Freiheitsgasse, Märzstraße, Studentenstraße, Versöhnungsstraße and Volksplatz; see 'Straßennamen', Wien Geschichtewiki, consulted online at: https://www.geschichtewiki.wien.gv.at/Stra%C3%9Fennamen. 16. 'Designazione della sede del Monumento commemorativo dei Martiri della Patria, a nuova denominazione

della Porta Tosa in Milano', 6 April 1848, transcribed in Emmanuele Bollati (ed.), *Fasti legislativi e parlamentari delle rivoluzioni italiane nel secolo XIX*, vol. 1: *1800–1849* (Milan, 1863), doc. 131, p. 262. 17. Marie-Éve Thérenty, 'Les "Boutiques d'esprit". Sociabilités journalistiques et production littéraire (1830–1870)', *Revue d'histoire littéraire de la France* 110/3 (2010), pp. 589–604, esp. pp. 592–3. 18. Boerner, *Erinnerungen eines Revolutionärs*, vol. 1, pp. 71–2, 75. 19. W. Scott Haine, *The World of the Paris Café. Sociability among the French Working Class, 1789–1914* (Baltimore, 1996), pp. 61, 142–3; on the political importance of cafés more generally, see also Susanna Barrows, '"Parliaments of the People". The Political Culture of Cafés in the Early Third Republic', in Susanna Barrows and Robin Room (eds.), *Drinking, Behaviour and Belief in Modern History* (Berkeley, 1991), pp. 87–97. 20. Viviana Mellone, 'La rivoluzione napoletana del 1848. Fonti e metodi per lo studio della partecipazione politica', *Meridiana*, no. 78 (2013), pp. 31–51, here pp. 37–9. 21. Giovanni La Cecilia, *Memorie storico-politiche dal 1820 al 1876* (5 vols., Rome, 1877), vol. 4, pp. 164–5. 22. Mellone, 'La rivoluzione napoletana del 1848', pp. 37–9. 23. Fernanda Gallo, *Dalla patria allo Stato. Bertrano Spaventa, una biografia intellettuale* (Rome, 2012), p. 9. 24. Mellone, 'La rivoluzione napoletana del 1848', pp. 37–9. 25. La Cecilia, *Memorie storico-politiche*, vol. 4, p. 165. 26. Karl Schlögel, 'Horror Vacui. The Terrors of Simultaneity', in Schlögel, *In Space We Read Time: On the History of Civilization and Geopolitics*, trans. Gerrit Jackson (New York, 2016), pp. 28–38, here p. 28. 27. Maurizio Gribaudi, 'Ruptures et continuités dans l'évolution de l'espace parisien. L'îlot de la Trinité entre les XVIIIe et XIXe siècles', *Histoire & Mesure*, 24/2 (2009), pp. 181–220, here p. 214; David P. Jordan, 'Baron Haussmann and Modern Paris', *The American Scholar*, 61/1 (1992), pp. 99–106, here p. 100. 28. Rüdiger Hachtmann, *Berlin 1848. Eine Politik- und Gesellschaftsgeschichte der Revolution* (Bonn, 1997), pp. 851–2. 29. See Aiden Lewis and Nadeen Ebrahim, 'Cairo's Tahrir Square gets a contested makeover', *Reuters World News*, 10 August 2020, 4.51 pm, accessed online at: https://www.reuters.com/article/us-egypt-tahrir-square-idUSKCN25620A 30. 'Funérailles des victimes des 22, 23 et 24 février', *La Réforme*, 5 March 1848, p. 1. 31. In fact, the 1840 procession departed from Saint-Germain l'Auxerrois, where the religious service took place (the Madeleine was not yet a consecrated church), reached the place Louis XV via the quai du Louvre, and then traced a path from the Madeleine along the great boulevards to the place de la Bastille. 32. Pierre Karila-Cohen, 'Charles de Rémusat et l'impossible refondation du régime de juillet', *Revue d'histoire moderne et contemporaine* 44/3 (1997), pp. 404–23, here p. 417. 33. On this dimension of public mourning, see Emmanuel Fureix, 'La construction rituelle de la souveraineté populaire. Deuils protestataires (Paris, 1815–1840)', *Revue d'histoire du XIXe siècle*, no. 42 (2011(1)), pp. 21–39, here p. 24. 34. On the symbolism of the lance, see Stefan Gasparri, 'Kingship Rituals and Ideology in Lombard Italy', in Frank Theuws and Janet L. Nelson (eds.), *Rituals of Power, From Late Antiquity to the Early Middle Ages* (Leiden, 2000), pp. 95–114, here pp. 99–100. 35. Details of the ceremony, monument, inscriptions, the texts of speeches, etc. are in 'Notizie interne', *Gazzetta di Milano*, 6 April 1848, pp. 1–3. 36. Wilhelm Angerstein, *Die Berliner März-Ereignisse im Jahre 1848. Nebst einem vollständigen Revolutionskalender, mit und nach Actenstücken sowie Berichten von Augenzeugen. Zur Feststellung der Wahrheit und als Entgegnung wider die Angriffe der reactionären Presse* (Leipzig, 1864), p. 55. 37. Boerner, *Erinnerungen eines Revolutionärs*, vol. 1, p. 174. 38. Angerstein, *Die Berliner März-Ereignisse*, p. 56. 39. Boerner, *Erinnerungen eines Revolutionärs*, pp. 174–7. 40. Eyewitness report by Berlin's Mayor Krausnick, cited in Karl Ludwig von Prittwitz, *Berlin 1848. Das Erinnerungswerk des Generalleutnants Karl Ludwig von Prittwitz und andere Quellen zur Berliner Märzrevolution und zur Geschichte Preußens um die Mitte des 19. Jahrhunderts*, ed. Gerd Heinrich (Berlin, 1985), pp. 229–30; D. Barclay, *Friedrich Wilhelm IV and the Prussian Monarchy 1840–1861* (Oxford, 1995), p. 145; tears of pity: an unnamed witness cited in Adolf Wolff, *Berliner Revolutions-Chronik. Darstellung der Berliner Bewegungen im Jahre*

1848 nach politischen, socialen und literarischen Bezeihungen (3 vols., Berlin, 1851–4), vol. 1, p. 250. **41.** Boerner, *Erinnerungen eines Revolutionärs*, pp. 178–9. **42.** Cited in Wolff, *Revolutions-Chronik*, vol. 1, p. 250. **43.** Dirk Blasius, *Friedrich Wilhelm IV.: 1795–1861. Psychopathologie und Geschichte* (Göttingen, 1992), pp. 116–28; there is an excellent discussion of the events of 19 March 1848 in Hachtmann, *Berlin 1848*, pp. 204–7. **44.** Hachtmann, *Berlin 1848*, p. 215. **45.** Cited in Wolff, *Berliner Revolutions-Chronik*, vol. 1, p. 321. **46.** Wolff, *Berliner Revolutionschronik*, vol. 1, p. 322. **47.** Giambattista Cremonesi, review of Ignazio Cantù, *Gli ultimi cinque giorni degli Austriaci in Milano. Relazioni e reminiscenze* (Milan, 1848), in 'Appendice', *Gazzetta di Milano*, 1 April 1848, pp. 1–2. We shouldn't be too impressed by Cantù's book: it was only eighty-four pages long and contained numerous transcriptions of official announcements! **48.** Wolff, *Berliner Revolutions-Chronik*, vol. 1, p. 324. **49.** Ibid., vol. 1, pp. 326–7; there is an insightful discussion of the two speeches in Hachtmann, *Berlin 1848*, pp. 217–19. **50.** Anon., 'Der Leichenzug der für die Freiheit gefallenen, am 17. März 1848', *Österreichisches Morgenblatt. Zeitschrift für Vaterland, Natur und Leben*, 20 March 1848, pp. 2–3. **51.** Anon., 'Leichenbegängniß der am 13. März Gefallenen', *Wiener Zeitschrift*, 20 March 1848, p. 3; Anon., 'Der Leichenzug der für die Freiheit gefallenen', *Österreichisches Morgenblatt*, 20 March 1848, p. 2. **52.** For the full text of Mannheimer's speech, see I. N. Mannheimer, 'Am Grabe der Gefallenen', *Sonntagsblätter*, 19 March 1848, pp. 11–12. **53.** Anton Füster, *Memoiren vom März 1848 bis Juli 1849. Beitrag zur Geschichte der Wiener Revolution* (2 vols., Frankfurt/Main, 1850), vol. 1, pp. 59–62. **54.** Ibid., vol. 1, pp. 54–6. **55.** Ignazio Veca, 'Bénir, prêcher, s'engager. L'acteur ecclésiastique du printemps des peuples en France et en Italie', and Pierre-Marie Delpu, 'Des passeurs locaux de la révolution. Les prêtres libéraux du royaume des Deux-Siciles (1847–1849)', papers presented at the colloquium *Les Acteurs européens du 'printemps des peuples' 1848. Colloque international du cent soixante-dixième anniversaire*, Sorbonne, Paris, 31 May–2 June 2018; on the Wallachian clergy: comment by Nicolae Mihai of the Romanian Academy, C. S. Nicolăescu-Plopşor Institute for Research in Social Sciences and Humanities. **56.** 'Falke', 'Die Leichenfeier der Gefallenen', *Die Gegenwart. Politisch-Literarisches Tagblatt*, 20 March 1848, p. 3. After taking part as a far-left radical in the October Revolution, 'Falke', whose real name was Georg Peter, would flee the country for London and later the United States. He only returned to Austria after a general amnesty in 1867, having in the meanwhile adopted his pseudonym as his legal name. **57.** On the inadequacy of the metaphor of 'transition', see Samuel Hayat, *1848. Quand la République était révolutionnaire. Citoyenneté et représentation* (Paris, 2014), pp. 71–4. **58.** See the statements by those who took part in these events among the 'pièces justicatives' appended to the first volume of Léonard Gallois, *Histoire de la révolution de 1848* (2 vols., Paris, 1851), vol. 2, pp. 455–9. **59.** Élias Regnault, *Histoire du Gouvernement provisoire* (2nd edn, Paris, 1850), p. 65. **60.** Stern [d'Agoult], *Histoire de la révolution de 1848*, vol. 1, pp. 314–15. **61.** Hayat, *1848. Quand la République était révolutionnaire*, pp. 75–6. **62.** Stern [d'Agoult], *Histoire de la révolution de 1848*, vol. 1, p. 316; Regnault, *Histoire du Gouvernement provisoire*, p. 117. **63.** Hayat, *1848. Quand la République était révolutionnaire*, p. 80. **64.** 'Parte Ufficiale', *Gazzetta di Milano*, no. 1, 23 March 1848. **65.** Christine Trivulce de Belgiojoso [Cristina Trivulzio di Belgiojoso], 'L'Italie et la révolution italienne de 1848', *Revue des Deux Mondes*, new series, 23 (July–Sep. 1848), pp. 785–813, here p. 792. **66.** Giovanna Fiume, *La crisi sociale del 1848 in Sicilia* (Messina, 1982), pp. 224–31. **67.** Paul Ginsborg, *Daniele Manin and the Venetian Revolution* (Cambridge, 1979), pp. 93–4. Ginsborg's is still the best account of these events. **68.** Ibid., p. 98. **69.** Thus a report published in the *Journal des Débats* and reprinted in *The Times*: see 'The Popular Movement in Sicily', *The Times*, no. 19776, 3 February 1848, p. 5, cols. 3–4. **70.** See the announcements dated Palermo, 14 January 1848, and Palermo, 15 January 1848, in [Elpidio Micciarelli, (ed.)], *Ruggiero Settimo e la Sicilia. Documenti sulla Insurrezione Siciliana del 1848* ('Italia', 1848), pp. 1–6. **71.** Until that point he had identified himself as 'President of the Fourth Committee'; 'Il Comitato generale di difesa e sicurezza pubblica riunito nel palazzo pretorio in Palermo a tutti i Siciliani', Palermo 25 January 1848, in ibid., pp. 21–4; on his election as General President and on diplomatic business, see the timeline in section 1 of Giovanni Mulè Bertòlo, *La Rivoluzione del 1848 e la Provincia di Caltanisetta* (Caltanissetta, 1898), n.p. 72. 'Il Comitato generale di difesa e sicurezza pubblica riunito nel palazzo pretorio in Palelmo a tutti i Siciliani', Palermo, 25 January 1848, in [Micciarelli, (ed.)], *Ruggiero Settimo e la Sicilia*, p. 23. 73. Ibid., pp. 22–3. 74. Hachtmann, *Berlin 1848*, p. 290. 75. Cited in Erich Hahn, 'Ministerial Responsibility and Impeachment in Prussia 1848–63', *Central European History* 10/1 (1977), pp. 3–27, here p. 5. 76. James Morris, 'The European Revolutions of 1848 and the Danubian Principality of Wallachia', PhD thesis, University of Cambridge, 2019, p. 57. 77. Doré de Nion, to Alphonse de Lamartine, Bucharest, 26 March 1848, in Arhivele Naţionale ale României (ed.), *Revoluţia Româna de la 1848 în Context European* (Bucharest, 1998), pp. 75–8. 78. Morris, 'The European Revolutions of 1848', p. 52. 79. Emil von Richthofen to Prussian Foreign Minister Canitz, 17 March 1848, in Arhivele Naţionale ale României (ed.*), Revoluţia Româna de la 1848*, pp. 69–71. 80. Apostol Stan, 'Revolution and Legality in the Romanian Principalities in 1848', *Revue Roumaine d'Histoire* 37 (1998), pp. 105–11, here p. 107. My account draws here on the analysis in Morris, 'The European Revolutions of 1848', pp. 60–61. 81. Regnault, *Histoire du Gouvernement provisoire*, p. 6. 82. Giovanna Procacci, 'To Survive the Revolution or to Anticipate It?', in Dieter Dowe, Heinz-Gerhard Haupt, Dieter Langewiesche and Jonathan Sperber (eds), *Europe in 1848. Revolution and Reform*, trans. David Higgins (New York and Oxford, 2001), pp. 507–27, here p. 511; Hayat, *1848. Quand la République était révolutionnaire*, p. 120. 83. Giuseppe La Farina, *Storia della Rivoluzione Siciliana e delle sue relazioni coi governi Italiane e stranieri 1848–49* (Milan, 1860), pp. 156–9. 84. Wilhelm Ribhegge, *Das Parlament als Nation. Die Frankfurter Nationalversammlung 1848/49* (Düsseldorf, 1998), p. 24. 85. Jiří Kořalka, 'Revolutions in the Habsburg Monarchy', in Dowe et al. (eds.), *Europe in 1848* , pp. 145–69, here pp. 149–50. 86. Franz Schuselka, *Das Revolutionsjahr März 1848–März 1849* (2nd edn, Vienna, 1850), p. 229. 87. Stanley Z. Pech, *The Czech Revolution of 1848* (Chapel Hill, 1969), pp. 72–3. 88. Andreas Gottsmann, 'Der Reichstag 1848/49 und der Reichsrat 1861 bis 1865', in Helmut Rumpler and Peter Urbanitsch (eds.), *Die Habsburgermonarchie* (12 vols., Vienna, 1973–), vol. VII/1: *Verfassung und Parlamentarismus. Verfassungsrecht, Verfassungswirklichkeit, zentrale Repräsentativkörperschaften* (Vienna, 2000), pp. 569–665, here p. 573. 89. František Palacký to the Frankfurt parliament's 'Committee of Fifty,' 11 April 1848, in Palacký (ed.), *Gedenkblatter* (Prague, 1874), pp. 149–51. 90. Jiří Kořalka, 'Revolutions in the Habsburg Monarchy', in Dowe et al. (eds.), *Europe in 1848*, pp. 145–69, here p. 152, 91. Schuselka, *Das Revolutionsjahr*, p. 229. The journey was necessary because the emperor had fled the capital. 92. Gottsmann, 'Der Reichstag 1848/49', p. 574. 93. Kořalka, 'Revolutions', p. 151. 94. Schuselka, *Das Revolutionsjahr*, p. 151. Reichstag members were paid, in addition to their travel costs, 200 fl per month as compensation at a time when a senior official was paid between 300 and 500 fl per annum, see Gottsmann, 'Der Reichstag 1848/49', p. 592. 95. Daniel Stern [Marie d'Agoult], *Histoire de la révolution de 1848* (2nd edn, Paris, 1862) vol. 2, p. 210. 96. Schuselka, *Das Revolutionsjahr*, pp. 83–6. 97. Ralf Zerback, *Robert Blum. Eine Biografie* (Leipzig, 2007), p. 220. 98. Hans Kudlich, *Rückblicke und Erinnerungen* (3 vols., Vienna, Pest and Leipzig, 1873), vol. 2, p. 6. 99. Schuselka, *Das Revolutionsjahr*, p. 170. 100. Antonio Zobi, *Catechismo costituzionale, preceduto da un' avvertenza storica* (Florence, 1848), pp. 26, 69. On the quasi-religious dignity of Italian parliamentary elections in 1848, see Enrico Francia, *1848. La Rivoluzione del Risorgimento* (Bologna, 2012), pp. 207–8. 101. Schuselka, *Das Revolutionsjahr*, p. 170. 102. Ibid., p. 147. 103. Kudlich, *Rückblicke und Erinnerungen*, vol. 2, p. 88. 104. Ibid., pp. 82, 88. On the ineffectiveness of presidents, see pp. 83, 85. 105. Schuselka, *Das*

Revolutionsjahr, p. 90. **106.** Ibid., pp. 94–6. **107.** Stern [d'Agoult], *Histoire de la révolution de 1848*, vol. 3 (1853), p. 2. **108.** Heinrich Best, 'Structures of Parliamentary Representation in the Revolutions of 1848', in Dowe et al. (eds.), *Europe in 1848*, pp. 475–505, here pp. 483–4. **109.** Gottsmann, 'Der Reichstag 1848/49', p. 573. **110.** Ibid., pp. 581–2. **111.** Best, 'Structures of Parliamentary Representation', p. 483. **112.** Tocqueville, *Recollections*, p. 95. **113.** Schuselka, *Das Revolutionsjahr*, p. 194. **114.** Laszlo Deme, 'The Society for Equality in the Hungarian Revolution of 1848', *Slavic Review* 31/1 (1972), pp. 71–88, here p. 72 n.3. **115.** Stern [d'Agoult], *Histoire de la révolution de 1848*, vol. 3, p. 4. **116.** Schuselka, *Das Revolutionsjahr*, p. 97. On the conservative outlook of the dominant liberal group in the Frankfurt parliament, see Gunther Hildebrandt, *Politik und Taktik der Gagern-Liberalen in der Frankfurter Nationalversammlung, 1848/1849* (Berlin, 1989). **117.** Charles de Mazade, 'Le Roi Ferdinand II et le Royaume des Deux-Siciles, II: Les Révolutions de 1848, la Réaction à Naples et le nouveau roi', *Revue des Deux Mondes*, 2nd period, 22/4 (15 August 1859), pp. 797–830, here p. 812. **118.** Stern [d'Agoult], *Histoire de la révolution de 1848*, vol. 2, p. 500. **119.** Diary entry, Berlin, 6 June 1848, in Lewald, *A Year of Revolutions*, p. 100. **120.** On this episode (including the quotations) see Hachtmann, *Berlin 1848*, pp. 561–2. On the same tendency in the earlier United Diet see p. 293. **121.** [George Sand], Bulletin de la République No. 16, Paris, 15 April 1848, in *Bulletins de la République émanés du Ministère de l'Intérieur du 13 Mars au 6 Mai 1848. Collection complète* (Paris, 1848), pp. 68–70, here pp. 68–9. For an excellent discussion of Sand's bulletins, see Jonathan Beecher, *Writers and Revolution. Intellectuals and the French Revolution of 1848* (Cambridge, 2021), pp. 98–100. **122.** George Fasel, 'The Wrong Revolution. French Republicanism in 1848', *French Historical Studies* 8/4 (1974), pp. 654–77, here p. 662. **123.** Stern [d'Agoult], *Histoire de la révolution de 1848*, vol. 3, p. 4. **124.** Pierre-Joseph Proudhon, 'La réaction', *Le Représentant du Peuple*, no. 28, 29 April 1848, pp. 1–2; Proudhon, 'Les mystifications du suffrage universel', ibid., no. 29, 30 April 1848, p. 1. **125.** Proudhon, 'Les mystifications du suffrage universel', ibid., no. 29, 30 April 1848, p. 1. **126.** Fasel, 'The Wrong Revolution', p. 662. **127.** Hachtmann, *Berlin, 1848*, p. 561. **128.** Pech, *Czech Revolution*, p. 169. **129.** Francia, *1848. La rivoluzione del Risorgimento*, p. 209. **130.** Best, 'Structures of Parliamentary Representation', p. 487. **131.** Karl Biedermann, *Erinnerungen aus der Paulskirche* (Leipzig, 1849), p. 3. **132.** Best, 'Structures of Parliamentary Representation', p. 487; Biedermann, *Erinnerungen aus der Paulskirche*, p. 5. **133.** Biedermann, *Erinnerungen aus der Paulskirche*, pp. 8, 9, 170–72. **134.** Ibid., pp. 15–19. **135.** Stern [d'Agoult], *Histoire de la révolution de 1848*, vol. 2, p. 230. **136.** This comes from an excerpt from Malvica's unpublished manuscript, the *Storia della rivoluzione di Sicilia negli'anni 1848 e '49* transcribed in Fiume, *La crisi sociale*, p. 233. **137.** Ribhegge, *Das Parlament als Nation*, p. 142. **138.** Flysheet published by the Comitato de' Circoli Italiani di Popoli dello Stato Romano, cited in Gian Luca Fruci, 'L'abito della festa dei candidate. Professioni di fede, lettere e programmi elettorali in Italia (e Francia) nel 1848–49', *Quaderni Storici* 39/117 (2004(3)), pp. 647–72, here pp. 659–60. **139.** Ibid., p. 667. **140.** Dieter Langewiesche, 'Die Anfänge der deutschen Parteien. Partei, Fraktion und Verein in der Revolution von 1848/49', *Geschichte und Gesellschaft*, 4/3 (1978), pp. 324–61, here p. 335. **141.** M. Hewitson, '"The old forms are breaking up, . . . our new Germany is rebuilding itself": Constitutionalism, Nationalism and the Creation of a German Polity during the Revolutions of 1848–49', *The English Historical Review* 125/516 (2010), pp. 1173–1214, here p. 1214. **142.** Jean-Michel Johnston, *Networks of Modernity. Germany in the Age of the Telegraph, 1830–1880* (Oxford, 2021), pp. 96–7. **143.** Delphine Gardey, 'Scriptes de la démocratie. Les sténographes et rédacteurs des débats (1848–2005)', *Sociologie du travail*, 52/2 (2010), pp. 195–211, here pp. 196, 197, 200. **144.** On this problem, see the historical appendix in Hyppolite Prévost, *Nouveau manuel complet de sténographie, ou art de suivre la parole en écrivant* (Paris, 1855), p. 84. **145.** Ludovic Marionneau and Josephine

Hoegaerts, 'Throwing One's Voice and Speaking for others. Performative Vocality and Transcription in the Assemblées of the Long Nineteenth Century', *Journal of Interdisciplinary Voice Studies* 6/1 (2021), pp. 91–108. Franz Wigard, sometime chief stenographer of the Saxon Parliament in Dresden and later a deputy to the Frankfurt National Assembly, was more insistent than Prévost on word-for-word fidelity, but also demanded that the skilful stenographer must possess a lively intelligence in order to convey the 'sense' of what was said and filter out unnecessary material; see Franz Wigard, *Lehrbuch der Redezeichenkunst. Nach Gabelsbergischem Lehrgebäude als Leitfaden für Lehrer wie zum Selbstunterricht* (2 vols., Dessau, 1853), vol. 2, pp. 388–94. **146.** On Groen van Prinsterer, see 'De Stenografie Groent', at Parlement.com, consulted at https://www.parlement.com/id/vhnnmt7i83xj/de_stenografie_groent; on the Dutch stenography service, see Wt. J. Bastiaan, *Gedenkschrift ter gelegenheid van het honderdjarig bestaan van de Stenographische Inrichting van de beide kamers der Staten-Generaal – 1849–1949* ('s-Gravenhage, 1949). **147.** Best, 'Structures of Parliamentary Representation', pp. 487–8. **148.** Langewiesche, 'Die Anfänge der deutschen Parteien', pp. 330–31. **149.** Ibid., p. 335. **150.** Stanley Z. Pech, 'Czech Political Parties', *Canadian Slavonic Papers/Revue Canadienne des Slavistes* 15/4 (1973), pp. 462–87, here p. 485. **151.** Michael Wettengel, 'Party Formation in Germany. Political Formations in the Revolution of 1848', in Dowe et al. (ed.), *Europe in 1848*, pp. 529–58, here p. 553. **152.** On the classification of constitutional types, see Jörg-Detlev Kühne, 'Verfassungsstiftungen in Europa 1848/49. Zwischen Volk und Erfolg', in Dieter Langewiesche (ed.), *Demokratiebewegung und Revolution 1847 bis 1849* (Karlsruhe, 1998), pp. 52–69, esp. p. 59; Kühne, 'Revolution und Rechtskultur. Die Bedeutung der Revolutionen von 1848 für die Rechtsentwicklung in Europa', in Dieter Langewiesche (ed.), *Die Revolutionen von 1848 in der europäischen Geschichte. Ergebnisse und Nachwirkungen* (Munich, 2000), pp. 57–72; Martin Kirsch, 'Verfassungswandel um 1848 – Aspekte der Rezeption und des Vergleichs zwischen den europäischen Staaten', in Martin Kirsch and Pierangelo Schiera (eds.), *Verfassungswandel um 1848 im europäischen Vergleich* (Berlin, 2001), pp. 31–62, esp. p. 38. **153.** Cited in Giorgio Rebuffa, *Lo Statuto albertino* (Bologna, 2003), p. 52. **154.** Ibid., p. 54. **155.** Odilon Barrot, *Mémoires posthumes de Odilon Barrot* (2nd edn, 3 vols., Paris, 1875), vol. 2, p. 321. **156.** Procacci, 'To Survive the Revolution or to Anticipate It?', p. 516. **157.** Stern [d'Agoult], *Histoire de la révolution de 1848*, vol. 2, pp. 500–501. **158.** Article 4 of the preamble states: 'Elle a pour principe la Liberté, l'Egalité et la Fraternité. Elle a pour base la Famille, le Travail, la Propriété, l'Ordre public'; full text: Constitution de 1848, IIe République, consulted at https://www.conseil-constitutionnel.fr/les-constitutions-dans-l-histoire/constitution-de-1848-iie-republique. **159.** J. C. Boogman, *Rondom 1848. De politieke ontwikkeling van Nederland 1840–1858* (Bussum, 1978), p. 62. For a full breakdown of the differences between the new and the old constitution, see https://www.denederlandsegrondwet.nl/id/vi7aaw43p5mk/grondwet_van_1848_ministeriele. **160.** Ron de Jong, 'Hooggespannen verwachtingen. Verkiezingen en de grondwetsherziening van 1848', *De Moderne Tijd* 3/4 (2019), pp. 324–35, here p. 324. **161.** Cited in in N. C. F. van Sas, *De metamorfose van Nederland. Van oude orde naar moderniteit, 1750–1900* (Amsterdam, 2004), p. 460. **162.** Jeroen van Zanten, 'De electorale negentiende eeuw in vogelvlucht, 1814–1917', *De Moderne Tijd* 1/3–4 (2017), pp. 236–46, here p. 237. **163.** Zanten, 'De electorale negentiende eeuw', p. 239. **164.** The total number of electors went from c.90,000 to c.80,000; on this aspect of the transition, see Piet de Rooy, *Republiek van rivaliteiten. Nederland sinds 1813* (Amsterdam, 2002), p. 55. **165.** Remieg Aerts, *Thorbecke wil het. Biografie van een staatsman* (Amsterdam, 2018), pp. 394–5. **166.** *Handelingen*, Tweede Kamer, 14 February 1849, p. 1. **167.** Jens Peter Christensen, 'The Constitutional Act as the Framework for Danish Democracy', in Peter Munk Christiansen, Jørgen Elklit and Peter Nedergaard (eds.), *The Oxford Handbook of Danish Politics* (Oxford, 2020), pp. 9–27, here pp. 10–11. On the new Danish constitution as a transformation shaped by war and the fear of social unrest, see also Michael Bregnsbo, 'Dänemark and 1848. Systemwechsel,

Bürgerkrieg and Kansensus-Tradition', in Heiner Timmermann (ed.), *1848. Revolution in Europa. Verlauf, Politische Programme, Folgen und Wirkungen* (Berlin, 1999), pp. 173–82.   **168.** Ferenc Hörcher, 'Reforming or Replacing the Historical Constitution? Lajos Kossuth and the April Laws of 1848', in Ferenc Hörcher and Thomas Lorman, *A History of the Hungarian Constitution. Law, Government and Political Culture in Central Europe* (London, 2020), pp. 92–121.   **169.** The definitive collection is Horst Dippel (ed.), *Constitutions of the World from the late 18th Century to the Middle of the 19th Century: Sources on the Rise of Modern Constitutionalism* (Berlin and New York, 2010). This extraordinary resource includes about 1,600 constitutions, amendments, human rights declarations, and draughts of constitutions that never came into force.   **170.** Georg-Christopher von Unruh, 'Die demokratischen Grundgesetze für Schleswig-Holstein und Lauenburg von 1848 und 1849', *Der Staat* 27/4 (1988), pp. 610–24, here pp. 611–12.   **171.** On the versatility of constitutions as instruments of political power in a British imperial context, see Linda Colley, *The Gun, the Ship and the Pen. War, Constitutions and the Making of the Modern World* (London, 2021).   **172.** Full text: https://www.jku.at/fileadmin/gruppen/142/pillersdorfsche_Verfassung.pdf. Last consulted on 25 July 2021.   **173.** Preamble to the Statuto del Regno, 4 March 1848, full text at https://it.wikisource.org/wiki/Italia,_Regno_-_Statuto_albertino.   **174.** Morris, 'The European Revolutions of 1848', p. 24.   **175.** Proclamation of Islaz, paragraphs 1 and 13, consulted at https://ro.wikisource.org/wiki/Proclamația_de_la_Islaz.   **176.** Constitution of the Second Republic, art. 1 of the preamble, consulted at https://www.conseil-constitutionnel.fr/les-constitutions-dans-l-histoire/constitution-de-1848-iie-republique.   **177.** On this theme in Stein's work, see Diana Siclovan, 'Lorenz Stein and German Socialism 1835–1872', PhD thesis, University of Cambridge, 2014, pp. 131–78, esp. p. 132.

6. EMANCIPATIONS

1. Heinrich Heine, *Werke und Briefe in zehn Bänden* (10 vols., Berlin and Weimar, 1972), vol. 3, p. 193 (first published in Hamburg, 1830).   **2.** Karl Hermann Scheidler, 'Emancipation', in Johann Samuel Ersch and Johann Gottfried Gruber (eds.), *Allgemeine Encyclopädie der Wissenschaften und Künste* (167 vols., Leipzig, 1830–89), vol. 34 (1840), pp. 2–12; Karl Martin Grass and Reinhard Koselleck, 'Emanzipation', in Otto Brunner, Werner Conze and Reinhard Koselleck (eds.), *Geschichtliche Grundbegriffe: Historisches Lexikon zur politisch-sozialen Sprache in Deutschland* (8 vols., Stuttgart, 2004) vol. 2, pp. 153–97.   **3.** See, for example, 'Pétition à la chambre des députés sur l'inexécution des nouvelles lois, Paris, 20 January 1846', 'Ordonnances du 18 mai, 4 et 5 juin 1846 relative à l'instruction religieuse et élémentaire, au regime disciplinaire, à la nourriture et à l'entretien des esclaves', 'Une femme, nourrice, frappée à coups de baton et blessée par un géreur. Condamnation à 100 francs d'amende par les juges sans assesseurs', 'Supplice dont l'antiquité même ne fournit pas d'exemple. Peine de 15 jours de prison prononcée par les juges sans assesseurs', 'Les colons sont cruels parce qu'ils sont maîtres', 'Suicides d'esclaves', Victor Schoelcher, *Histoire de l'esclavage*, pp. 43–6, 59–75, 331–4, 410–13, 413–17, 455–68.   **4.** Guillaume Suréna, 'Schoelcher/Césaire et le destin des people noirs', *Le Coq-Héron*, no. 195 (2008), pp. 57–65.   **5.** Ibid.   **6.** Henri Wallon, *Histoire de l'esclavage dans l'antiquité* (3 vols., Paris, 1847). The final volume of this work ended with an exhortation: 'it is time to bring our words and our acts into harmony and, by means of a complete reparation of the crime and the example of our fathers, to re-establish among us the sacred rights of humanity and to work for their universal recognition' (vol. 3, p. 469). Wallon's abolitionism is even more plainly expressed in the separately published 'introduction' to this work: Henri Wallon, *De l'esclavage dans les colonies. Pour servir d'introduction à l'Histoire de l'esclavage dans l'antiquité* (Paris, 1847).   **7.** Jacques Adélaïde-Merlande, 'La Commission d'abolition de l'esclavage', *Bulletin de la Société d'histoire de la Guadeloupe*, nos. 53–4 (1982), pp. 3–34, here p. 16.   8. Ibid., p. 16.   9. Ibid., p. 21.   10. Ibid., pp. 20, 21, 17.   11. Ibid., p. 15.   12. Nelly Schmidt, '1848. Liberté et peurs sociales aux Caraïbes. La citoyenneté républicaine face aux réalités coloniales', in Jean-Claude Caron, Philippe Bourdin, Lisa Bogani and Julien Bouchet (eds.), *La République à l'épreuve des peurs. De la Révolution à nos jours* (Rennes, 2016), pp. 119–35, here paragraph 10, consulted online at https://books.openedition.org/pur/47370; quotation: Adélaïde-Merlande, 'La Commission', p. 19.   13. Jean-Pierre Sainton, 'De l'état d'esclave à "l'état de citoyen". Modalités du passage de l'esclavage à la citoyenneté aux Antilles françaises sous la Seconde République (1848–1850)', *Outre-mers*, 90/338–9 (2003), pp. 47–82, here p. 64.   14. Adélaïde-Merlande, 'La Commission', pp. 5, 27.   15. Sainton, 'De l'état d'esclave à "l'état de citoyen"', p. 52; on the long-term destruction of the system, see Oruno D. Lara and Iñez Fischer Blanchet, 'Abolition ou destruction du système esclavagiste?', and Nelly Schmidt, 'L'élaboration des décrets de 1848. Application immédiate et consequences à long terme', in *Les Abolitions de l'esclavage, de L. F. Sonthonaux à V. Schoelcher, 1793, 1794, 1848. Actes du colloque international tenu à l'Université de Paris VIII, les 3, 4, 5 février 1994* (Vincennes, 1995), pp. 335–44 and 345–54.   16. 'Aimé Césaire sur l'abolition de l'esclavage', Ina Histoire, 22 April 2020, viewed at https://www.facebook.com/InaHistoire/videos/aimé-césaire-sur-labolition-de-lesclavage/533912767317934/; last viewed on 6 August 2021.   17. Édouard de Lépine, *Dix semaines qui ébranlèrent la Martinique* (Paris, 1999), p. 158.   18. See Adolphe Gatine's account of the 'Affaire Parfait', relating to a man whose emancipation by his deceased owner was repudiated by the owner's heir. Adolphe Gatine, 'Affaire Parfait – Liberté confisquée', *Revue des colonies* 3/6 (1836), pp. 225–32; on similar struggles in other locations, see Mariana P. Candido, 'African Freedom Suits and Portuguese Vassal Status. Legal Mechanisms for Fighting Enslavement in Benguela, Angola, 1800–1830', *Slavery and Abolition* 32/3 (2011), pp. 447–59.   19. Johnson, *The Fear of French Negroes*, p. 145.   20. Anon., *Courrier de la Martinique*, 27 March 1848, cited in Lépine, *Dix semaines qui ébranlèrent la Martinique*, p. 19.   21. Lépine, *Dix semaines qui ébranlèrent la Martinique*, p. 26.   22. Ibid., pp. 42–4.   23. Ibid., p. 34; Tyler Stovall, 'The Myth of the Liberatory Republic and the Political Culture of Freedom in Imperial France', *Yale French Studies*, no. 111 (2007), pp. 89–103, here p. 99.   24. David Rigoulet-Roze, 'À propos d'une commémoration. L'abolition de l'esclavage en 1848', *L'Homme*, 145, *De l'esclavage* (1998), pp. 127–36, here p. 133; see also Roger Botte, 'L'esclavage africain après l'abolition de 1848. Servitude et droit du sol', *Annales. Histoire, Sciences Sociales*, 55/5 (2000), pp. 1009–37, here pp. 1009–11.   25. These developments are described in detail in Minister van Kolonien (ed.), *Tweede Rapport der Staatscommissie, benoemd bij koninklijk besluit van 29 November 1853, no. 66, tot het voorstellen van maatregelen ten aanzien van de slaven in de Nederlandsche Kolonien* (s'-Gravenhage, 1856), pp. 53–68; a powerful recent analysis is Jessica Vance Roitman, '"A mass of mestiezen, castiezen, and mulatten". Contending with Color in the Netherlands Antilles, 1750–1850', *Atlantic Studies* 14/3 (2017), pp. 399–417.   26. Robin Blackburn, *The Overthrow of Colonial Slavery, 1776–1848* (London, 1988), pp. 507–8; Neville A. T. Hall, *Slave Society in the Danish West Indies: St. Thomas, St. John, and St. Croix*, ed. B. W. Higman (Baltimore, 1992), p. 208; Wim Klooster, 'Slave Revolts, Royal Justice, and a Ubiquitous Rumor in the Age of Revolutions', *The William and Mary Quarterly*, 3rd series, 71/3 (2014), pp. 401–24.   27. M. Kuitenbrouwer, 'De Nederlandse afschaffing van de slavernij in vergelijkend perspectief', *Low Countries Historical Review* 93/1 (1978), pp. 69–100, here pp. 77–8.   28. Cited in Benjamin Claude Brower, 'Rethinking Abolition in Algeria. Slavery and the "Indigenous Question"', *Cahiers d'Études africaines*, no. 195 (2009), pp. 805–28, here p. 808. Bugeaud is commenting on an earlier abolition proposal of 1844.   29. Botte, 'L'Esclavage africain après l'abolition de 1848', p. 1020; Jenna Nigro, 'The Revolution of 1848 in Senegal. Emancipation and Representation', at https://ageofrevolutions.com/2018/04/30/the-revolution-of-1848-in-senegal-emancipation-and-representation/, last viewed on 7 August 2021. **30.** Adélaïde-Merlande, 'La Commission', p. 18. **31.** Mamadou Badji, 'L'abolition de l'esclavage au Sénégal. Entre plasticité du droit colonial et respect de l'Etat de droit', *Droit et Cultures*, no. 52 (2006(2)), pp. 239–74, consulted online at https://journals.openedition.org/droitcultures/729, para. 24. **32.** Martin A. Klein, 'Slaves, Gum and Peanuts: Adaptation to the End of the Slave Trade in Senegal, 1817–48', *The William and Mary Quarterly*, 3rd series, 66/4 (2009), pp. 895–914, here p. 912. **33.** Cited in Lawrence C. Jennings, 'L'abolition de l'esclavage par la IIe République et ses effets en Louisiane 1848–1858', *Revue française d'outre-mer* 56/205 (1969), pp. 375–97, here p. 380. The discussion that follows of the impact of the article on the French citizens of Louisiana is based on this excellent article. **34.** Ibid., pp. 382, 378. **35.** Jennings, 'L'abolition de l'esclavage'. **36.** Oruno D. Lara, *La Liberté assassinée. Guadeloupe, Guyane, Martinique et La Réunion en 1848–1856* (Paris, 2005), p. 184. **37.** Dale Tomich, 'Visions of Liberty: Martinique in 1848', *Proceedings of the Meeting of the French Colonial Historical Society* 19 (1994), pp. 164–72, *passim*; Ulrike Schmieder, 'Martinique and Cuba Grande: Commonalities and Differences during the Periods of Slavery, Abolition, and Post-Emancipation', *Review (Fernand Braudel Center)* 36/1 (2013), pp. 217–42, here p. 233; Lara, 'La Liberté assassinée', pp. 175–92. **38.** Hamelin to Faidherbe, 21 June 1855, cited in Botte, 'L'Esclavage africain après l'abolition de 1848', p. 1021. **39.** Serge Daget, 'A Model of the French Abolitionist Movement and Its Variations', in Christine Bolt and Seymour Drescher (eds.), *Anti-Slavery, Religion, and Reform. Essays in Memory of Roger Anstey* (Folkestone, 1980), pp. 64–79, here p. 77. **40.** Tim Roberts, 'The Role of French Second Republic's Incorporation of Algeria in American Proslavery Territorial Expansion', paper presented at the international colloquium *Les Mondes de 1848*, 12–14 December 2018, Paris, EHESS, organized by Emmanuel Fureix, Quentin Delermuoz and Clément Thibaud. **41.** Brower, 'Rethinking Abolition', p. 806. **42.** Ulrike Schmieder, 'Martinique and Cuba Grande', pp. 89, 93–4; Romy Sanchez, 'Indices de 1848 à Cuba. Échos révolutionnaires dans l'Île Très Fidèle et dans son exil séparatiste', paper presented at the international colloquium *Les Mondes de 1848*, 12–14 December 2018, Paris, EHESS, organized by Emmanuel Fureix, Quentin Delermuoz and Clément Thibaud. I thank Romy Sanchez for sending me the text of this paper. **43.** Vanessa S. Oliveira, *Slave Trade and Abolition: Gender, Commerce and Economic Transition in Luanda* (Madison, 2021), p. 102. **44.** Silyane Larcher, 'L'égalité divisée. La race au cœur de la ségrégation juridique entre citoyens de la métropole et citoyens des "vieilles colonies" après 1848', *Le Mouvement social*, no. 252 (2015), pp. 137–58; on the stickiness of racist colour distinctions, even in formally emancipated societies, see also Roitman, 'Contending with Color'. On Algeria, see Thomas C. Jones, 'French Republicanism after 1848', in Douglas Moggach and Gareth Stedman Jones (eds.), *The 1848 Revolutions and European Political Thought* (Cambridge, 2018), pp. 70–93, here pp. 80–81. **45.** Emily Musil Church, 'In Search of Seven Sisters. A Biography of the Nardal Sisters of Martinique', *Callaloo* 36/2 (2013), pp. 375–90, here p. 377. **46.** On this image, see Thomas Gaehtgens, 'Die Revolution von 1848 in der europäischen Kunst', in Dieter Langewiesche (ed.), *Die Revolutionen von 1848 in der europäischen Geschichte. Ergebnisse und Nachwirkungen* (Munich, 2000), pp. 91–122, here pp. 96–7; cf. 'Kugelgießer hinter einer Barrikade', an engraving by R. Kretschmer, which depicts the same activity, *Wiener Illustrierte Zeitung*, Saturday, 15 April 1848, p. 8. In this image, a woman is seen pulling the lead from a casement window, while four young boys pour the shot. On the left, a man armed with a hatchet – their father? – is seen tightening the bindings on his scythe. **47.** 'Extrablatt der Freude', *Königlich Privilegirte Berlinische Zeitung von Staats- und gelehrten Sachen*, 20 March 1848, p. 3. **48.** Rüdiger Hachtmann, *Berlin 1848. Eine Politik- und Gesellschaftsgeschichte der Revolution* (Bonn, 1997), p. 181. **49.** David Barry, *Women and Political Insurgency. France in the Mid-Nineteenth Century* (New York, 1996), p. 51. **50.** Gabriele Clemens, 'Des femmes sur les barricades? Engagement révolutionnaire en Italie et en Allemagne', paper presented at the colloquium *Les Acteurs européens du* 'printemps des peuples' 1848. Colloque international du cent soixante-dixième anniversaire, Sorbonne, Paris, 31 May-2 June 2018. **51.** Stanley Z. Pech, The Czech Revolution of 1848 (Chapel Hill, 1969), p. 149. **52.** Gerlinde Hummel-Haasis, Schwestern, zerreißt eure Ketten. Zeugnisse zur Geschichte der Frauen in der Revolution von 1848/49 (Munich, 1982), pp. 185-239. **53.** Laura Strumingher, 'The Vésuviennes. Images of Women Warriors in 1848 and Their Significance for French History', History of European Ideas 8/4-5 (1987), pp. 451-88; on the folkloric background, see David Hopkin, 'Female Soldiers and the Battle of the Sexes in France. The Mobilization of a Folk Motif', History Workshop Journal, no. 56 (Autumn 2003), pp. 78-104. **54.** [Anon., no title], Der Humorist 12/94, 19 April 1848, p. 382. **55.** [Eugénie Niboyet], 'Profession de foi', La Voix des Femmes 1/1, 20 March 1848, p. 1. **56.** On the manifesto of 16 March, unpublished at the time, see Michèle Riot-Sarcey, 'Émancipation des femmes, 1848', Genèses, no. 7, Lieux du travail (1992), pp. 194-200, esp. pp. 197-200. **57.** See the excellent discussion of this document in Robert Nemes, 'Women in the 1848-1849 Hungarian Revolution', Journal of Women's Studies 13/3 (2001), pp. 193-207. **58.** Riot-Sarcey, 'Émancipation des femmes, 1848', pp. 194-6. **59.** Jeanne Marie, 'Ce que veulent les socialistes', La Voix des Femmes 1/20 (1848), 11 April 1848, p. 2. On the context and authorship of this piece, see Karen Offen, 'A Nineteenth-Century Feminist Rediscovered: Jenny P. d'Héricourt, 1809-1875', Signs. Journal of Women in Culture and Society 13/1 (1987), pp. 144-58, esp. p. 153 n.23. **60.** Nemes, 'Women in the 1849-1849 Hungarian Revolution'. **61.** George Sand to the editors of La Réforme, 8 April 1848, La Réforme, 9 April 1848, p. 3. **62.** Jonathan Beecher, Writers and Revolution. Intellectuals and the French Revolution of 1848 (Cambridge, 2021), p. 99. **63.** Daniel Stern [Marie d'Agoult], Histoire de la révolution de 1848 (2nd edn, Paris, 1862), vol. 2, p. 31. **64.** On the nineteenth century as an age of questions, see Holly Case, The Age of Questions, or, A First Attempt at an Aggregate History of the Eastern, Social, Woman, American, Jewish, Polish, Bullion, Tuberculosis, and Many Other Questions over the Nineteenth Century, and Beyond (Princeton, 2018). **65.** [M. G. Saphir], Der Humorist 12/66, 17 March 1848, p. 264. **66.** Beecher, Writers and Revolution, p. 34. **67.** Cited in Vicki de Fries, 'Silencing La Voix des Femmes', The French Review 89/1 (2015), pp. 82-97, here p. 88. **68.** Diary entry, 16 April 1848, in Dragojla Jarnević, Dnevnik, ed. Irena Lukšić (Karlovac, 2000), p. 339. **69.** Hachtmann, Berlin 1848, p. 514. **70.** Henning Türk, '"Ich gehe täglich in die Sitzungen und kann die Politik nicht lassen". Frauen als Parlamentszuschauerinnen und ihre Wahrnehmung in der politischen Öffentlichkeit der Märzrevolution 1848/49', Geschichte und Gesellschaft 43/4 (2017), pp. 497-525, here p. 509. **71.** Cited in Türk, 'Frauen als Parlamentszuschauerinnen', p. 515. **72.** Judith A. DeGroat, 'The Public Nature of Women's Work: Definitions and Debates during the Revolution of 1848', French Historical Studies 20/1 (1997), pp. 31-47, here pp. 39-40. **73.** Alexis de Tocqueville, Souvenirs (Paris, 1964), p. 145, cited in DeGroat, 'The Public Nature of Women's Work', p. 45. **74.** J. Palgrave Simpson, Pictures from Revolutionary Paris. Sketched during the First Phases of the Revolution of 1848 (Edinburgh, 1849), p. 214, cited in DeGroat, 'The Public Nature of Women's Work', p. 44. **75.** Gabriele Clemens, 'Des femmes sur les barricades?' **76.** Ruth Whittle, '"Die neue Frau", in the Correspondence of Johanna Kinkel, Malwida von Meysenbug, and Fanny Lewald', German Life and Letters 57/3 (2004), pp. 256-67, here p. 257. On the self-imposed constraints that impeded women's progress, see Helen Morris-Keitel, 'Not "until Earth Is Paradise": Louise Otto's Refracted Feminine Ideal', Women in German Yearbook 12 (1996), pp. 87-100, esp. p. 96. **77.** The classic account is Ute Frevert, 'Mann und Weib, Weib und Mann'. Geschlechter-Differenzen in der Moderne (Munich, 1995). **78.** Ann Taylor Allen, 'Spiritual Motherhood: German Feminists and the Kindergarten Movement, 1848-1911', History of Education Quarterly 22/3 (1982), pp. 319-39 – the discussion of the kindergarten movement that follows is drawn from Allen's excellent study. **79.** Malwida von Meysenbug, Memoiren einer Idealistin (2 vols., Stuttgart, 1922), vol. 1, p.

194. 80. Mary Lyschinska, *Henriette Schrader-Breymann: Ihr Leben aus Briefen und Tagebüchern zusammengestellt* (2 vols., Berlin and Leipzig, 1922), vol. 1, pp. 64, 86; vol. 2, p. 238. 81. Meysenbug, *Memoiren einer Idealistin*, vol. 1, p. 224. 82. Allen, 'Spiritual Motherhood', pp. 327–37; Patrick Harrigan, 'Women Teachers and the Schooling of Girls in France: Recent Historiographical Trends', *French Historical Studies* 21/4 (1998), pp. 593–610. 83. Direção-Geral da Segurança Social. Nucleo de Documentação e Divulgação (ed.), *A mulher em Portugal. Alguns aspetos do evoluir da situação feminine na legislação nacional e comunitária* (Lisbon, 2014), p. 29, consulted at https://www.seg-social.pt/docu ments/10152/18931/A+mulher+em+Portugal+volume+I.pdf/6f6bd84c-e3db-45dc-969d-abf8a318b151/6f6bd84c-e3db-45dc-969d-abf8a318b151. 84. 'Mi lira' (My Lyre) is discussed in Susan Kirkpatrick, 'La tradición femenina de poesía romantica', in Iris M. Zavala (ed.), *Breve historia feminista de la literatura Española (en lengua Castellana)*, vol. 5: *La literatura escrita por mujer. Desde el siglo XIX hasta la actualidad* (Barcelona, 1998), pp. 39–74, here p. 55. 85. Christina Arkinstall, 'No Shrinking Violets But Tall Poppies: Ambition, Glory, and Women Writing in Spain's Mid-Nineteenth Century', in Casa-Museo Emilia Pardo Bazán (ed.), *La Tribuna. Cadernos de Estudios da Casa-Museo Emilia Pardo Bazán*, no. 14 (2019), pp. 58–86; Gloria Espigado Tocino, 'Mujeres "radicales": utópicas, republicanas e internacionalistas en España (1848–1874)', *Ayer*, no. 60 (2005), pp. 15–43, emphasizes the influence of Fourier and Cabet on the networks of radical women in Spain. 86. An example is the friendship between Lydia and Alice in Louise Aston's *Revolution und Contrerevolution* (2 vols., Mannheim, 1849). For a discussion of this theme, see Ruth-Ellen Boetcher Joeres, '1848 from a Distance: German Women Writers on the Revolution', *MLN* 97/3 (1982), pp. 590–614. 87. Kathinka Zitz-Halein, 'Vorwärts und Rückwarts', read at Brigham Young University ScholarsArchive, https://scholarsarchive.byu.edu/sophpm_ poetry/3469. The translation is mine. The poem consists of eight strophes of which I have cited 1, 2, 3 and 7. 88. On d'Agoult as a historian, see Beecher, *Writers and Revolution,* pp. 146–66. 89. Barbara Becker-Cantarino (ed.), *Bettina von Arnim Handbuch* (Berlin, 2019), pp. 324–5. 90. It is interesting to note that d'Agoult was less detached and less insightful in her observations about the prominent women of her time. The account in her *Histoire de le Révolution de 1848* of the history of the debate over women's condition, in which she dismissed the radicals of the 1830s as hyperventilating fantasists, is one of the book's weaker passages. 91. [Jeanne Deroin], 'Qu'est-ce que l'opinion des femmes?', *L'Opinion des femmes*, 21 August 1848, p. 1. 92. See Reimund Leicht, Gad Freudenthal and Rachel Heuberger (eds.), *Studies on Steinschneider. Moritz Steinschneider and the Emergence of the Science of Judaism in Nineteenth-Century Germany* (Leiden, 2011), esp. the essay by Ismar Schorsch, 'Moritz Steinschneider: The Vision beyond the Books', pp. 3–36. 93. Gerhard Endress, 'Kulturtransfer und Lehrüberlieferung. Moritz Steinschneider (1816–1907) und "die Juden als Dolmetscher"', *Oriens* 39/1 (2011), pp. 59–74, here p. 60. 94. Letter of Moritz Steinschneider to Auguste Auerbach [his fiancée] in Prague, Berlin, 20 March 1848, transcribed in Adolf Kober, 'Jews in the Revolution of 1848 in Germany', *Jewish Social Studies* 10/2 (1948), pp. 135–64, here pp. 163–4. 95. Mario Rossi, 'Emancipation of the Jews in Italy', *Jewish Social Studies* 15/2 (1953), pp. 113–34, here pp. 128–9. 96. Tobias Grill, 'Ein Märtyrer für Licht und Wahrheit? Das Wirken Rabbiner Abraham Kohns in Lemberg (1844–1848)', *Jahrbücher für Geschichte Osteuropas*, new series, 56/2 (2008), pp. 178–220. 97. Elena Bacchin, 'Per i diritti degli ebrei: 'percorsi dell'emancipazione a Venezia nel 1848', *Annali della Scuola Normale Superiore di Pisa. Classe di Lettere e Filosofia*, 2013, series 5, 5/1 (2013), pp. 91–128. 98. Marsha L. Rozenblit, 'Jews, German Culture, and the Dilemma of National Identity: The Case of Moravia, 1848–1938', *Jewish Social Studies* 20/1 (2013), pp. 77–120. 99. L. Scott Lerner, 'Narrative over the Ghetto of Rome', *Jewish Social Studies*, 8/2–3 (2002), pp. 1–38, here p. 14. 100. Giancarlo Spizzichino, 'Pio IX e l'Università degli Ebrei di Roma: Speranze e delusioni (1846–1850)', in Claudio Procaccia (ed.), *Ebrei a Roma tra Risorgimento ed*

emancipazione (1814–1914) (Rome, 2014), pp. 263–338, here p. 281. 101. Istvan Deak, *The Lawful Revolution. Louis Kossuth and the Hungarians 1848–1849* (New York, 1979), p. 51. 102. Paul Bernard, 'The Jews in the Habsburg Monarchy before the Revolutions of 1848', *Shofar* 5/3 (1987), pp. 1–8, here p. 5. 103. V. Eichler (ed.), *Nassauische Parlamentsdebatten*, vol. 1: *Restauration und Vormärz, 1818–1847* (Wiesbaden, 1985), pp. 333–7. 104. Stefi Jersch-Wenzel, 'Legal Status and Emancipation', in Michael A. Meyer and Michael Brenner (eds.), *Jewish-German History in Modern Times*, vol. 2: *Emancipation and Acculturation 1780–1871* (New York, 1997), pp. 5–49. 105. Christopher Clark, *The Politics of Conversion. Missionary Protestantism and the Jews in Prussia 1728–1941* (Oxford, 1995), p. 99; Nathan Samter, *Judentaufen im neunzehnten Jahrhundert. Mit besonderer Berücksichtigung Berlins dargestellt* (Berlin, 1906), p. 19. Burg eventually got his promotion, at a point when it became impossible to keep him in the service without loss of honour, see [Gabriel Riesser], 'Die Rechte der Juden in Preußen', *Preußische Jahrbücher* 5 (1860), p. 141. 106. Miklós Konrád, 'Entre émancipation et conversion. Dilemmes juifs en Hongrie dans la première moitié du XIXe siècle', *Histoire, Économie et Société* 33/4 (2014), pp. 58–74, here p. 61. 107. Jersch-Wenzel, 'Legal Status and Emancipation', pp. 5–49, here p. 47. 108. Michael Anthony Riff, 'The Anti-Jewish Aspects of the Revolutionary Unrest in Baden and Its Impact on Emancipation', *Leo Baeck Institute Yearbook* 21 (1976), pp. 27–40, here p. 27. 109. Massimo d'Azeglio, *Dell'Emancipazione civile degl'Israeliti* (Florence, 1848). 110. [Julius Fürst], 'Unser Programm auf das Jahr 1848', *Der Orient. Berichte, Studien und Kritiken für jüdische Geschichte und Literatur* 8, 1 January 1848, p. 1. 111. J. [Ignác] Einhorn, *Die Revolution und die Juden in Ungarn nebst einem Rückblick auf die Geschichte der Letzteren* (Leipzig, 1851), p. 53; Konrád, 'Entre émancipation et conversion', p. 61. 112. Gerhard Hentsch, *Gewerbeordnung und Emanzipation der Juden im Kurfürstentum Hessen* (Wiesbaden, 1979), pp. 68–9; on the exclusion of Jews from guild-controlled crafts in Hamburg, see M. Zimmermann, *Hamburgischer Patriotismus und deutscher Nationalismus. Die Emanzipation der Juden in Hamburg* (Hamburg, 1979), pp. 25–6, 59. 113. Reinhard Rürup, 'Die Emanzipation der Juden in Baden' in Rürup. (ed.), *Emanzipation und Antisemitismus*, pp. 58–9. 114. Bernard, 'The Jews in the Habsburg Monarchy', p. 5. 115. Hentsch, *Gewerbeordnung und Emanzipation*, pp. 43–4. 116. Reinhard Rürup, 'The Tortuous and Thorny Path to Legal Equality: Jew Laws and Emancipatory Legislation in Germany from the Late Eighteenth Century', *Leo Baeck Institute Yearbook* 31 (1986), pp. 3–33; on emancipation as a plurality of 'paths', see Pierre Birnbaum and Ira Katznelson (eds.), *Paths of Emancipation. Jews, States and Citizenship* (Princeton, 1995), esp. p. 11. 117. [Anon.], 'Berlin, 12 March', *Der Orient. Berichte, Studien und Kritiken für jüdische Geschichte und Literatur* 9/13, 25 March 1848, pp. 97–9, here p. 98. 118. Magistrate Neumann to Provincial Government in Frankfurt an der Oder, Department of the Interior, Landsberg, 27 April 1847, in Gebhard Falk (ed.), *Die Revolution 1848/49 in Brandenburg. Eine Quellensammlung* (Frankfurt, 1998), pp. 52–4. 119. Cited in Manfred Gailus, 'Food Riots in Germany in the Late 1840s', *Past & Present* 145/1 (1994), pp. 157–93, here p. 177. 120. Riff, 'Anti-Jewish Aspects', p. 28. 121. Daniel Gerson, 'Die Ausschreitungen gegen die Juden im Elsass 1848', *Bulletin des Leo Baeck Instituts* 87 (1990), pp. 29–44. 122. Cited in ibid., pp. 32, 33. 123. Ibid., p. 34. 124. Ibid., pp. 38–9. 125. Stefan Rohrbacher, *Gewalt im Biedermeier. Antijüdische Ausschreitungen in Vormärz und Revolution (1815–1848/49)* (Frankfurt, 1993), p. 182. 126. 'Preßburg, 18. März', *Der Orient* 9/15, 8 April 1848, p. 118. 127. 'Stuhlweißenburg [the German name for Székesfehérvár], 14 April 1848', ibid. 9/18, 29 April 1848, p. 144. 128 Deak, *The Lawful Revolution*, p. 113; 'Grätz, 17 April 1848', *Der Orient* 9/18, 29 April 1848, p. 140. 129. 'Von der Werra, 7. Mai', *Der Orient* 9/21, 20 May 1848, p. 162. 130. Riff, 'Anti-Jewish Aspects', pp. 29–35. 131. Ibid. 132. On the meaning and impact of Toussenel's work, see Jean-Philippe Schreiber, 'Les Juifs, rois de l'époque d'Alphonse Toussenel, et ses avatars. Le spéculation vue comme anti-travail au

XIXe siècle', *Revue belge de philologie et d'histoire* 79/2 (2001), pp. 533–46; Emil Lehouck, 'Utopie et antisémitisme. Le cas d'Alphonse Toussenel', in Société de l'histoire de la révolution de 1848 et des revolutions du XIXe siècle (ed.), *1848, les utopismes sociaux. Utopie et action à la veille des journées de Février* (Paris, 1981), pp. 151–60.   **133.** Oliver Schulz, 'Der "jüdische Kapitalist". Anmerkungen zu Ursprung und Entwicklung eines antisemitischen Stereotyps im Frankreich der 1840er-Jahre', in Mareike König and Oliver Schulz (eds.), *Antisemitismus im 19. Jahrhundert aus internationaler Perspektive* (Göttingen, 2019), pp. 41–58.   **134.** On this effect, see Rainer Erb and Werner Bergmann, *Die Nachtseite der Judenemanzipation. Der Widerstand gegen die Integration der Juden in Deutschland, 1780–1860* (Berlin, 1989), pp. 38–9.   **135.** On Baden, see Riff, 'Anti-Jewish Aspects', p. 29; 'Preßburg, 13 April 1848', *Der Orient* 9/18, 29 April 1848, p. 143.   **136.** Deak, *The Lawful Revolution*, pp. 85–6.   **137.** 'Gleiwitz, 3. Mai', *Der Orient* 9/23, 3 June 1848, p. 180.   **138.** For an insightful analysis of these efforts at conciliation, see Ignazio Veca, 'La strana emancipazione: Pio IX e gli ebrei nel lungo Quarantotto', *Contemporanea* 17/1 (2014), pp. 3–30, here p. 21   **139.** Ibid., p. 22.   **140.** Luigi Vincenzi, *Alcuni pensieri sopra gli atti di beneficenza del Sommo Pontefice Papa Pio IX. felicemente regnante verso gli Ebrei di Roma, e sopra vari commenti manifestati al pubblico su questo proposito ovvero L'Ebraismo in Roma e nell'Impero innanzi e dopo l'era volgare* (Rome, 1848), p. vi.   **141.** Ibid., p. 102.   **142.** Veca, 'La strana emancipazione', p. 17.   **143.** Spizzichino, 'Pio IX e l'Università degli Ebrei di Roma', pp. 301–6; Salo W. Baron, 'The Impact of the Revolution of 1848 on Jewish Emancipation', *Jewish Social Studies* 11/3 (1949), pp. 195–248, here p. 227.   **144.** Anton Bettelheim, *Berthold Auerbach. Der Mann, Sein Werk, Sein Nachlaß* (Stuttgart and Berlin, 1907), pp. 211–12.   **145.** Cited in Reinhard Rürup, 'Progress and Its Limits. The Revolution of 1848 and European Jewry', in Dieter Dowe, Heinz-Gerhard Haupt, Dieter Langewiesche and Jonathan Sperber (eds), *Europe in 1848. Revolution und Reform*, trans. David Higgins (New York and Oxford, 2001), pp. 749–64, here p. 753.   **146.** Anon., 'Judenverfolgung und die Judensache', *Österreichisches Central-Organ für Glaubensfreiheit, Cultur, Geschichte und Literatur der Juden*, 24 March 1848, pp. 78–80.   **147.** Deak, *The Lawful Revolution*, pp. 314–15.   **148.** Ibid., pp. 113–14.   **149.** 'Miskolz, 20. April', *Der Orient* 9/21, 20 May 1848, pp. 165–6.   **150.** Reinhard Rürup, 'Die "Judenfrage" im 19. Jahrhundert', in Hans-Ulrich Wehler, *Sozialgeschichte heute. Festschrift für Hans Rosenberg zum 70. Geburtstag* (Göttingen, 1974), pp. 388–415, here p. 398.   **151.** The 'tacit alliance' between progressive Jews and pre-1848 liberal leaders is one of the central themes of Catherine Horel, 'Les Juifs de Hongrie 1825–1849. Problèmes d'assimilation et d'émancipation', doctoral thesis, Paris, 1993.   **152.** Richard Wagner, *Das Judentum in der Musik* ([1850] Leipzig, 1869), p. 11.   **153.** Thomas Nipperdey and Reinhard Rürup, *Emanzipation und Antisemitismus. Studien zur 'Judenfrage' der bürgerlichen Gesellschaft* (Frankfurt/Main, 1987); Olaf Blaschke, 'Wider die "Herrschaft des modern-jüdischen Geistes". Der Katholizismus zwischen traditionellem Antijudaismus und modernem Antisemitismus', in Wilfried Loth (ed.), *Deutscher Katholizismus im Umbruch zur Moderne* (Stuttgart, 1991), pp. 236–65; Michal Frankl, *'Emancipace od židů'* [Emancipation from the Jews]. *Český antisemitismus na konci 19. Století* (Prague, 2007).   **154.** Victor Tissot, *Chez les Tziganes* (Paris, 1899), p. 26; discussion in Moses Gaster, 'Bill of Sale of Gypsy Slaves in Moldavia', *Journal of the Gypsy Lore Society*, 3rd series, 2/2 (1923), pp. 68–81, here p. 68.   **155.** Venera Achim, 'Emanciparea țiganilor și programul legislativ al guvernului provizoriu din 1848', *Revista istorică* 20/1–2 (2009), pp. 63–72, here pp. 63–4.   **156.** Elena Marushiakova and Vesselin Popov, 'Gypsy slavery in Wallachia and Moldavia', 2013, p. 6, consulted online at https://www.researchgate.net/publication/235698657_Gypsy_Slavery_in_Wallachia_and_Moldavia.   **157.** Mihail Kogălniceanu [his name is given as 'Michel de Kogalnitchan'], *Esquisse sur l'histoire des moeurs et la langue des Cigains, connus en France sous le nom de Bohémiens, suivie d'un receuil de sept cents mots cigains* (Berlin, 1837), p. iv.   **158.** Raluca Tomi, 'Aboliționismul românesc la 1848. Influențe, trăsături', *Revista istorică* 20/1–2 (2009), pp. 47–61, here p. 54.   **159.** Ibid., p. 59.   **160.** *Anul 1848 în Principatele Române. Acte și documente*, vol. 2 (Bucharest, 1902), doc. no. 578, pp. 105–6, discussed in Achim, 'Emanciparea țiganilor', p. 64.   **161.** Achim, 'Emanciparea țiganilor', pp. 68–9.   **162.** Ibid., p. 70.   **163.** The oration was subsequently published: Gioacchino Ventura, *Elogio funebre di Daniello O'Connell membro del Parlamento Britannico, recitato nei solenni funerali celebratigli nei giorni 28 e 30 giugno dal Rmo. P. D. Gioacchino Ventura ex Generale de' Chierici Regolari. Consultore della Sacra Congregazione de' Riti ed Esaminatore dei Vescovi e del Clero Romano* (Rome, 1847). For discussions of the oration and its impact, see E. Costa, 'Da O'Connell a Pio IX. Un capitolo del cristianesimo sociale del P. Gioacchino Ventura' (1847) in L. Morabito (ed.), *Daniel O'Connell. Atti del Convegno di Studi nel 140° Anniversario della Morte* (Savona, 1990), pp. 93–115; Alberto Belletti, 'Daniel O'Connell's Funeral Oration by Father Gioacchino Ventura, 1847. An Attempted Conciliation between Catholicism and Liberalism as Well as Democracy in Italy', *Nuova Rivista Storica* 100/1 (2016), pp. 219–42.   **164.** Zauli-Sajani's speech is discussed in Veca, 'La strana emancipazione', pp. 18–19.   **165.** Oliver Friggieri, 'L'attività di autori esuli italiani a Malta durante il Risorgimento', *Forum Italicum* 50/3 (2016), pp. 1070–98, doi:10.1177/0014585816678846.   **166.** Hugo Dezius, *Lessing's Nathan der Weise auf der Berliner Bühne* (Berlin, 1843), esp. p. 10.   **167.** I am grateful to the dance historian Dr Marion Kant for drawing these works to my attention.   **168.** This is just a small selection from the bibliography compiled by Marlene L. Daut and posted at https://www.haitianrevolutionaryfictions.com. On the presence of the Haitian example in nineteenth-century political rhetoric, see also Francis Arzalier, 'Exemplarité de la révolution haïtienne', *Présence Africaine*, new series, no. 169 (2004), pp. 33–40.   **169.** Tomi, 'Aboliționismul românesc', p. 55.   **170.** See Fürst's introduction to Einhorn, *Die Revolution und die Juden in Ungarn*, p. iii.   **171.** Thomas C. Jones, 'French Republicanism after 1848', in Moggach and Stedman Jones (eds.), *The 1848 Revolutions and European Political Thought*, pp. 70–93, here pp. 79–80.   **172.** Nelly Schmidt, '1848 et les colonies. Dimensions françaises, perspectives internationales', in Jean-Luc Mayaud (ed.), *1848. Actes du colloque international du cent cinquantenaire, tenu à l'Assemblée nationale à Paris, les 23–25 février 1998* (Paris, 2002), pp. 373–88; on the contingent character of the link between slavery and the revolution in Paris, see Shelby T. McCloy, *The Negro in the French West Indies* (Westport, 1974), p. 147.   **173.** Myriam Cottias, 'Gender and Republican Citizenship in the French West Indies, 1848–1945', *Slavery & Abolition* 26/2 (2005), pp. 233–45.   **174.** Benjamin Fagan, '"The North Star" and the Atlantic 1848', *African American Review* 47/1 (2014), pp. 51–67, here p. 60.

7. ENTROPY

1. For a near-contemporary interpretation of the painting that identifies the people depicted and fills in the narrative detail, see the notes by C. L. Derby in Pennsylvania Academy of the Fine Arts (ed.), *Catalogue of the Thirty-Fifth Annual Exhibition of the Pennsylvania Academy of the Fine Arts, 1858* (Philadelphia, 1858), p. 14; also (with further details) Anon., 'Scene in the French Revolution of 1848', in Buffalo Fine Arts Academy (ed.), *Catalogue of the Permanent Collection of Sculpture and Paintings, with Some Additions* (Buffalo, 1907), pp. 39–40.   **2.** Cited in Maurice Agulhon, *The Republican Experiment 1848–1852*, trans. Janet Lloyd (Cambridge, 1983), p. 40.   **3.** Thus Charles Robin, cited in Maurice Dommanget, *Auguste Blanqui et la révolution de 1848* (Paris, 1972), p. 34.   **4.** *Le Peuple, Le Représentant du peuple, L'Ami du peuple, La Sentinelle du peuple, La Souveraineté du peuple, La Presse du peuple, Le Réveil du peuple, Le Peuple souverain, Le Peuple constituant*. On the claim to representativeness implicit in these titles, see Samuel Hayat, *1848. Quand la République était révolutionnaire. Citoyenneté et représentation* (Paris, 2014), pp. 97–8.   **5.** Daniel

Stern [Marie d'Agoult], *Histoire de la révolution de 1848* (2nd edn, Paris, 1862), vol. 2, p. 38; Rémi Gossez, *Les Ouvriers de Paris* (Paris, 1967), pp. 10–14. **6.** Stern [d'Agoult], *Histoire de la révolution de 1848*, vol. 2, pp. 4–6. **7.** This is the central argument of Hayat, *1848. Quand la République était révolutionnaire.* **8.** This was the reading of Élias Regnault, who saw the commission as a means devised by the moderate liberal ministers to deprive Louis Blanc of political leverage while using him to appease the radical movement; see Élias Regnault, *Histoire du Gouvernement provisoire* (2nd edn, Paris, 1850), p. 126. **9.** Cited in Hayat, *1848. Quand la République était révolutionnaire*, pp. 93–4, 95. My account of these issues follows closely the argument advanced by Hayat. **10.** Marc Caussidière, *Mémoires de Caussidière. Ex-préfet de police et représentant du peuple* (Bruxelles, 1848), p. 64. **11.** Rüdiger Hachtmann, *Berlin 1848. Eine Politik- und Gesellschaftsgeschichte der Revolution* (Bonn, 1997), p. 291. **12.** Cited in ibid., pp. 27, 24. **13.** Paul Boerner, *Erinnerungen eines Revolutionärs. Skizzen aus dem Jahre 1848* (Leipzig, 1920), vol. 2, p. 48. **14.** Hachtmann, *Berlin 1848*, pp. 275–7. **15.** Ibid., p. 278. **16.** Boerner, *Erinnerungen eines Revolutionärs*, vol. 2, pp. 56–9. **17.** Hachtmann, *Berlin 1848*, pp. 251–4. **18.** Peter Amann, 'A "Journée" in the Making: May 15, 1848', *The Journal of Modern History* 42/1 (1970), pp. 42–69, here p. 51. **19.** Stern [d'Agoult], *Histoire de la révolution de 1848*, vol. 2, p. 121. **20.** Louis Blanc, *Pages d'histoire de la révolution de février 1848* (Paris, 1850), p. 109. **21.** Ibid., p. 114. **22.** See esp. 'Paris, 17 Avril', *La Réforme*, 17 April 1848, p. 1. **23.** Blanc, *Pages d'histoire*, pp. 115–16. **24.** 'Manifeste de M. Ledru-Rollin' and 'Encore une conspiration', *L'Assemblée Nationale*, 16 April 1848, no. 47, p. 1. **25.** Stern [d'Agoult], *Histoire de la révolution de 1848*, vol. 2, pp. 182–3. **26.** Aurélien Lignereux, *La France rébellionnaire. Les résistances à la gendarmerie (1800–1859)*, (Rennes, 2008). **27.** Thomas R. Christofferson, 'The French National Workshops of 1848. The View from the Provinces', *French Historical Studies* 11/4 (1980), pp. 505–20. **28.** On the electoral violence of April 1848, see Olivier Ihl, 'The Ballot Box and the Shotgun. Electoral Violence during the 1848 French Constituent Assembly Election', trans. Jennifer Fredette, *Revue française de science politique (English)* 60/1 (2010), pp. 1–29, esp. pp. 1–2, 5–11 DOI: 10.3917/rfspe.601.0001. **29.** George Fasel, 'Urban Workers in Provincial France, February–June 1848', *International Review of Social History* 17/2 (1972), pp. 661–74, here pp. 669–71. **30.** André Dubuc, 'Les émeutes de Rouen et d'Elbeuf (27, 28 et 29 avril 1848)', *Etudes d'histoire moderne et contemporaine* 2 (1948), pp. 243–75, here pp. 262–4; see also John M. Merriman, 'Social Conflict in France and the Limoges Revolution of April 27, 1848', *Societas. A Review of Social History*, 4 (1974), pp. 21–38. **31.** Dubuc, 'Les émeutes de Rouen', p. 274. **32.** Karl Haenchen, 'Flucht und Rückkehr des Prinzen von Preußen im Jahre 1848', *Historische Zeitschrift* 154/1 (1936), pp. 32–95, here pp. 40–41. **33.** Boerner, *Erinnerungen eines Revolutionärs*, vol. 2, p. 173. **34.** Ibid., vol. 2, p. 182. **35.** The text of this notice is provided by the editor, E. Menke-Glückert, in ibid., vol. 2, p. 300 n.189. **36.** Ibid., vol. 2, p. 212. **37.** Ibid., vol. 2, p. 173. **38.** Hachtmann, *Berlin 1848*, p. 343. **39.** Boerner, *Erinnerungen eines Revolutionärs*, vol. 2, p. 212. **40.** Karl Griewank, 'Friedrich Wilhelm Held und der vulgäre Liberalismus und Radikalismus in Leipzig und Berlin 1842–49', PhD thesis (Rostock, 1922), cited in Wilmont Haacke, 'Johann Friedrich Wilhelm Franz Held', *Neue Deutsche Biographie* 8 (1969), pp. 462–3, https://www.deutsche-biographie.de/pnd116681896.html#ndbcontent. **41.** See, for example, 'Auch die Tischlergesellen', 'Die Marqueurs und Feuerburschen', 'Eine Deputation von Buchdrucker- und Schiftgießergehilfen', *Wiener Abendzeitung. Tägliches Ergänzungsblatt der "Sonntagsblätter"*, nos. 13 and 14, Monday, 10 April 1848, and Tuesday, 11 April 1848, pp. 56 and 59. **42.** 'Neuigkeits-Courier', *Allgemeine Theaterzeitung*, no. 81, Tuesday, 4 April 1848, p. 327. **43.** Herwig Knaus and Wilhelm Sinkovicz, *Wien 1848. Reportage einer Revolution* (Vienna, 1998), pp. 82–3. **44.** 'Anonyme Drohbriefe', *Wiener Abendzeitung*, no. 15, Wednesday, 12 April 1848, p. 63. **45.** 'Die Liguorianerinnen!', ibid., no. 12, Saturday, 8 April 1848, p. 52. **46.** Peter Frank-Döfering, *Die Donner der Revolution über Wien. Ein Student aus Czernowitz erlebt*

1848 (Vienna, 1988), pp. 67–8. On cat-concerts and other related forms of 'musical' protest, see Wolfgang Häusler, 'Marseillaise, Katzenmusik und Fuchslied als Mittel sozialen und politischen Protests in der Wiener Revolution 1848', in Barbara Boisits (ed.), *Musik und Revolution. Die Produktion von Identität und Raum durch Musik in Zentraleuropa 1848/49* (Vienna, 2013), pp. 37–80. 47. Frank-Döfering, *Die Donner der Revolution über Wien*, pp. 69–70. 48. Anton Füster, *Memoiren vom März 1848 bis Juli 1849. Beitrag zur Geschichte der Wiener Revolution* (2 vols., Frankfurt/Main, 1850), vol. 1, pp. 90, 98–9. 49. Ibid., vol. 1, p. 108; on the radicalization of the city, see R. John Rath, 'The Failure of an Ideal. The Viennese Revolution of 1848', *The Southwestern Social Science Quarterly* 34/2 (1953), pp. 3–20. 50. 'Ein Nationalgardist der bis um 12 Uhr am Josefsplatz war', *Die Sturmpetition in der Burg* (Vienna, 1848), pamphlet viewed online at Wienbibliothek im Rathaus, https:// www.digital.wienbibliothek.at/wbrobv/content/pageview/1980040, pp. 3–4. 51. Borkowski to his parents, 4 June 1848, in Frank-Döfering, *Die Donner der Revolution über Wien*, pp. 75–87, here pp. 78–9. 52. Paul Ginsborg, *Daniele Manin and the Venetian Revolution* (Cambridge, 1979), p. 183. 53. 'Adresse der Mannheimer Volksversammlung an die badische Kammer (27.2.1848)', in Hans Fenske (ed.), *Vormärz und Revolution. Quellen zur deutschen Revolution 1840–1849* (Darmstadt, 1996), pp. 264–5. 54. Frank Möller, 'Die lokale Einheit der bürgerlichen Bewegung bis 1848', *Historische Zeitschrift. Beihefte*, new series, 16, *Stadt und Bürgertum im Übergang von der traditionalen zur modernen Gesellschaft* (1993), pp. 391–412, here p. 398. 55. Hans Blum, *Robert Blum. Ein Zeit- und Charakterbild* (Leipzig, 1878), p. 213; Ralf Zerback, *Robert Blum. Eine Biografie* (Leipzig, 2007), pp. 112, 187. 56. Karl Biedermann, *Mein Leben und ein Stück Zeitgeschichte* (2 vols., Breslau, 1886), vol. 1, p. 327. 57. Ludwig Häusser, *Denkwürdigkeiten zur Geschichte der badischen Revolution* (Heidelberg, 1851), p. 115. 58. Jan Randák, 'Symbolické chování v revoluci 1848: Revoluční Móda', *Český lid* 93/1 (2006), pp. 49–69, here pp. 58–9; on the nexus between fashion and revolution in Germany, see also Isabella Belting, *Mode und Revolution. Deutschland 1848/49* (Hildesheim, 1997). 59. Hans Blum, *Robert Blum* , p. 259. 60. Häusser, *Denkwürdigkeiten*, p. 121. 61. Friedrich Hecker, *Die Erhebung des Volkes in Baden für die deutsche Republik im Frühjahr 1848* (Basel, 1848), pp. 30, 34, 41, 45. 62. Amalie Struve, *Erinnerungen aus den badischen Freiheitskämpfen. Den deutschen Frauen gewidmet* (Hamburg, 1850), pp. 31–2. 63. Hecker, *Die Erhebung des Volkes in Baden*, pp. 35, 46. 64. Hecker, *Die Erhebung des Volkes in Baden*, p. 1. 65. Struve, *Erinnerungen aus den badischen Freiheitskämpfen*, pp. 33–4. 66. Friedrich Hecker, 'Weiblichkeit und Weiberrechtelei', in Hecker, *Reden & Vorlesungen von Friedrich Hecker* (St Louis and Neustadt an der Haardt, 1872), pp. 92–119; Sabine Freitag, '"Rasende Männer und weinende Weiber". Friedrich Hecker und die Frauenbewegung', *Österreichische Zeitschrift für Geschichtswissenschaften* 9/4 (1998), pp. 568–75; on Struve's involvement in the transport of ammunition see Struve, *Erinnerungen aus den badischen Freiheitskämpfen*, p. 33. 67. Struve, *Erinnerungen aus den badischen Freiheitskämpfen*, p. 36. 68. Hecker, *Die Erhebung des Volkes in Baden*, pp. 1,2, 8. 69. For an analysis of the mutations of this song, which dates back to a radical song of the 1830s, see Michael Kohlstruck and Simone Scheffler, 'Das "Heckerlied" und seine antisemitische Variante. Zu Geschichte und Bedeutungswandel eines Liedes', in Michael Kohlstruck and Andreas Klärner, *Ausschluss und Feindschaft. Studien zu Antisemitismus und Rechtsextremismus. Festschrift für Rainer Erb* (Berlin, 2011), pp. 135–58. 70. Cited in Hans Blum, *Robert Blum*, p. 306. 71. George Fasel, 'The Wrong Revolution. French Republicanism in 1848', *French Historical Studies* 8/4 (1974), pp. 654–77, here p. 655. 72. D. B. Grigg, 'The World's Agricultural Labour Force 1800–1970', *Geography* 60/3 (1975), pp. 194–202. 73. Hans Kudlich, *Rückblicke und Erinnerungen* (3 vols., Vienna, Pest and Leipzig, 1873), vol. 1, p. 65. 74. Paul Ginsborg, 'Peasants and Revolutionaries in Venice and the Veneto, 1848', *The Historical Journal* 17/3 (1974), pp. 503–50, here pp. 516–17, 521 (quotation). 75. Christof Dipper, 'Rural Revolutionary Movements. Germany, France, Italy', in Dieter Dowe,

Heinz-Gerhard Haupt, Dieter Langewiesche and Jonathan Sperber (eds), *Europe in 1848. Revolution und Reform*, trans. David Higgins (New York and Oxford, 2001), pp. 416–40, here p. 420.　76. Report of the estate administration in Gusow to Magistrate Karbe of Lebus District, 26 March 1848, transcribed in Gebhard Falk (ed.), *Die Revolution 1848/1849 in Brandenburg. Eine Quellensammlung* (Frankfurt, 1998), pp. 80–82.　77. Louis Clarenc, 'Les Troubles de La Barousse en 1848', *Annales du Midi* 63 (1951), pp. 329–48.　78. Robert von Friedeburg, 'Dörfliche Gesellschaft und die Integration sozialen Protests durch Liberale und Konservative im 19. Jahrhundert. Desiderate und Perspektiven der Forschung im deutsch-englischen Vergleich', *Geschichte und Gesellschaft* 17/3, *Neue Aspekte der reichsdeutschen Sozialgeschichte 1871–1918* (1991), pp. 311–43, here p. 336.　79. 'Votice po r. 1848', consulted at: https://www.mesto-votice.cz/votice-po-r-1848/d-4527.　80. On the journey from the city to the country as a journey through time, see Nina Lübbren, *Rural Artists' Colonies in Europe, 1870–1910* (Manchester, 2001), pp. 145–7.　81. Josef Mooser, *Ländliche Klassengesellschaft 1770–1848. Bauern und Unterschichten, Wirtschaft und Gewerbe im östlichen Westfalen* (Göttingen, 1984), pp. 247–8.　82. Giovanni Cantoni, 'Sulle condizioni economico-morali del contadino in Lombardia', *L'Italia del popolo*, published in three parts: (1) no. 60, 20 July 1848, p. 1, col. 4–p. 2, col. 2; (2) no. 61, 21 July 1848, p. 1, col. 3–p. 2, col. 2; (3) no. 65, 25 July 1848, p. 1, col. 2–p. 2, col. 1, here part 1, p. 2, col. 1.　83. Dipper, 'Rural Revolutionary Movements', pp. 419, 422.　84. Ginsborg, *Daniele Manin and the Venetian Revolution*, p. 174.　85. On the tendency of mid-nineteenth-century Ottoman peasants to align themselves with the central authorities and against oppressive local grandees, see E. Attila Aytekin, 'Peasant Protest in the Late Ottoman Empire: Moral Economy, Revolt, and the Tanzimat Reforms', *International Review of Social History* 57/2 (2012), pp. 191–227, here pp. 219–20.　86. Giovanni Cantoni, 'Sulle condizioni economico-morali', part 1, p. 2, col. 1.　87. Ibid., part 2, p. 1, col. 3.　88. Ibid., part 1, p. 2, col. 1.　89. Ibid., part 3, p. 2, col. 1.　90. Ibid., part 3, p. 2, col. 1.　91. Fasel, 'The Wrong Revolution', pp. 654, 667–8.　92. Nicolas Stoskopf, 'La fondation du comptoir national d'escompte de Paris, banque révolutionnaire (1848)' in *Histoire, économie et société* 21/3 (2002), pp. 395–411, here pp. 396, 397, 401, 409.　93. Els Witte, *Belgische republikeinen. Radicalen tussen twee revoluties (1830–1850)* (Antwerpen, 2020), pp. 282–3.　94. Rémi Gossez, 'La résistance à l'impôt. Les quarante-cinq centimes', *Bibliothèque de la Révolution de 1848* 15 (1953), pp. 89–132, here p. 92.　95. Claudio Zanier, 'Freschi, Gherardo', *Dizionario biografico degli Italiani* 50 (1998), consulted at https://www.treccani.it/enciclopedia/gherardo-freschi_(Dizionario-Biografico)/.　96. Ginsborg, *Daniele Manin and the Venetian Revolution*, p. 167.　97. Ginsborg, 'Peasants and Revolutionaries', pp. 535–6; Ginsborg, *Daniele Manin and the Venetian Revolution*, pp. 14–15, 21, 177, 302.　98. On the 'crisis of neo-serfdom', see Béla K. Király, 'Neo-Serfdom in Hungary', *Slavic Review* 34/2 (1975), pp. 269–78, esp. pp. 272–3 and 278.　99. Gábor Pajkossy, 'Kossuth and the Emancipation of the Serfs', in Péter, Martyn Rady and Peter Sherwood (eds.), *Lajos Kossuth Sent Word . . . Papers Delivered on the Occasion of the Bicentenary of Kossuth's Birth* (London, 2003), pp. 71–80, here p. 71.　100. Lászlo Péter, 'Introduction', in ibid., pp. 1–14, here p. 5.　101. Wolfgang Höpken, 'The Agrarian Question in Southeastern Europe', in Dowe et al., *Europe in 1848*, pp. 443–71, here p. 447.　102. Róbert Hermann, 'Kossuth, Parliamentary Dictator', in Péter et al. (eds.), *Lajos Kossuth Sent Word*, pp. 41–69, here p. 58; Höpken, 'The Agrarian Question', pp. 449–50.　103. Robert W. Gray, 'Bringing the Law Back In. Land, Law and the Hungarian Peasantry before 1848', *The Slavonic and East European Review* 91/3 (2013), pp. 511–34.　104. Höpken, 'The Agrarian Question', pp. 455–6.　105. Cited in Coloman Benda, 'La question paysanne et la révolution hongroise en 1848', *Études d'histoire moderne et contemporaine* 2 (1948), pp. 221–30, here p. 223.　106. Benda, 'La question paysanne', p. 225.　107. Istvan Deak, *The Lawful Revolution. Louis Kossuth and the Hungarians 1848–1849* (New York, 1979), pp. 116–17.　108. Nicolae Bălcescu, 'Despre starea socială a muncitorilor plugari în Principatele române în deosebite timpuri' (On the social status of ploughmen in Danubian Principalities at different times), *Magazinu istoricu pentru Dacia* 2 (1846) pp. 229–46; on forced seizures, see pp. 235–6. **109.** James Morris, 'The European Revolutions of 1848 and the Danubian Principality of Wallachia', PhD thesis, University of Cambridge, 2019, p. 24. **110.** Nicolae Bălcescu, 'Discurs despre împroprietărirea țăranului' [1848], cited in Alex Drace-Francis, *The Traditions of Invention. Romanian Ethnic and Social Stereotypes in Historical Context* (Leiden, 2013), p. 51. **111.** The full text (in Romanian) can be consulted at 'Proclamația de la Islaz', Wikisource, https:// ro.wikisource.org/wiki/Proclamația_de_la_Islaz; last consulted 27 November 2021. **112.** Cited in Morris, *The European Revolutions of 1848*, p. 111. **113.** Ionescu de la Brad was vice-president, but he played a more active shaping role than the titular president, the land-owner Alexandru Racoviță. **114.** Morris, *The European Revolutions of 1848*, p. 115. **115.** Ibid., p. 7. **116.** Cited in ibid., p. 116. **117.** Morris, *The European Revolutions*, p. 115. **118.** Ibid., p. 120. **119.** In the Austrian Empire, for example, notwithstanding the legislation drafted by Kudlich and passed by the Constituent Assembly, it was the neo-absolutist regime that put in place the compensation arrangements necessary to separate peasant and domanial land. See E. Niederhauser, 'La emancipación de los siervos in Hungría en Europa Oriental', in Jacques Godechot (ed.), *La abolición del feudalismo en el mundo occidental*, trans. Pilar López Máñez (Madrid, 1971), pp. 194–200. Also W. von Hippel, 'El régimen feudal en Alemania en el siglo XVIII y su disolución', in ibid., pp. 102–15; Rainer Koch, 'Die Agrarrevolution in Deutschland 1848. Ursachen – Verlauf – Ergebnisse', in Dieter Langewiesche (ed.), *Die Deutsche Revolution von 1848/49* (Darmstadt, 1983), pp. 362–94. **120.** V. Léoutre, Rapport au Citoyen Ministre de l'Intérieur sur la situation politique et matérielle du département de la Meuse, Bar-sur-Ornain, 25 May 1848, transcribed in Pierre Braun, 'Le département de la Meuse en 1848', *La Révolution de 1848. Bulletin de la Société d'histoire de la Révolution de 1848* 6/36 (1910), pp. 391–404. **121.** Morris, *The European Revolutions of 1848*, p. 99. **122.** Léoutre, Rapport au Citoyen Ministre de l'Intérieur, p. 401. **123.** Thus Jean Baudrillard's formulation expressing an analogous post-Marxian puzzlement at the opacity and passivity of 'the masses': Jean Baudrillard, *In the Shadow of the Silent Majorities, or The End of the Social and Other Essays*, trans. Paul Foss, Paul Patton and John Johnston (New York, 1983). Like many humanities undergraduates of my generation, I was enthralled by Baudrillard in my early twenties. Later I tired of a mode of exposition that seemed more interested in mystification than elucidation. But this essay remains a powerful symptomatic articulation of the disconnect between political analysis and the aspirations and behaviour of most of the people who supposedly make up 'the social'. **124.** Kudlich, *Rückblicke und Erinnerungen*, vol. 1, p. 285. **125.** Ibid., vol. 2, pp. 106–7. On the failure of liberals to understand the problems of the peasantry, see also Ernst Brückmüller, 'Das Agrarproblem in den europäischen Revolution von 1848', in Helgard Frohlich, Margarete Grandner and Michael Weinzierl (eds.), *1848 in europäischen Kontext (Vienna, 1999), pp.35–59.* **126.** 'Tessete, o donzelle, / bandiere e cocarde, / fa l'alme gagliarde / l'invito d'amor!' Mauro Stramacci, *Goffredo Mameli, tra un inno e una battaglia* (Rome, 1991), p. 57. **127.** Michele Calabrese, 'Il Canto degli Italiani: genesi e peripezie di un inno', *Quaderni del 'Bobbio'. Rivista di approfondimento culturale dell'I.I.S. "Norberto Bobbio" di Carignano* 3 (2011), p. 105–40, here pp. 108–9. **128.** Cited in Benedict Anderson, *Imagined Communities. Reflections on the Origin and Spread of Nationalism* (London and New York, 2006), p. 103. **129.** Axel Körner, *1848. A European Revolution? International Ideas and National Memories of 1848*, 2nd rev. edn (Basingstoke, 2004). **130.** On the 'Slavo-Dalmatian' amalgam that attracted many intellectuals in the region, see Konrad Clewing, *Staatlichkeit und nationale Identitätsbildung. Dalmatien in Vormärz und Revolution* (Munich, 2001). **131.** Cited in ibid., p. 324. **132.** Dominique Kirchner Reill, *Nationalists Who Feared the Nation. Adriatic Multi-Nationalism in Habsburg Dalmatia, Trieste, and Venice* (Stanford, 2012), p. 184. **133.** Cited in Hugh LeCaine Agnew, 'Noble *Natio* and Modern Nation. The Czech Case', *Austrian History Yearbook* 23 (1992), pp. 50–71, here p.

71. 134. Rita Krueger, *Czech, German and Noble. Status and National identity in Habsburg Bohemia* (Oxford, 2009), p. 31. 135. Clewing, *Staatlichkeit und nationale Identitätsbildung*, p. 223. 136. Jonathan Sperber, 'Festivals of National Unity in the German Revolution of 1848–1849', *Past & Present* 136/1 (1992), pp. 114–38. 137. Lawrence Cole and Hans Heiss, 'Unity Versus Difference. The Politics of Region-Building and National Identities in Tyrol, 1830–1867', in Lawrence Cole (ed.), *Different Paths to the Nation. Regional and National Identities in Central Europe and Italy, 1830–1870* (Houndsmills, 2007), pp. 37–59. 138. Ginsborg, *Daniele Manin and the Venetian Revolution*, p. 253. 139. Peter Judson, *The Habsburg Empire. A New History* (Cambridge, Mass., 2016), p. 201. 140. 'Ulkomaalta', *Suometar*, 22 April 1848, p. 4. 141. Enrico Francia, *1848. La rivoluzione del Risorgimento* (Bologna, 2012), pp. 142–3. 142. Ibid., p. 144. 143. Report of 9 April, cited in Ginsborg, *Daniele Manin and the Venetian Revolution*, p. 165. 144. Cited in Francia, *1848. La rivoluzione del Risorgimento*, p. 145. 145. Camillo Cavour, *Il Risorgimento*, no. 74, 23 March 1848, p. 1, excerpted in Giuseppe Talamo, *Cavour. Con una nota introduttiva di Giuliano Amato* (Rome, 2010), pp. 152–5, here p. 152. 146. For the terms, see '3.1140 Secret Protocol between Austria and Sardinia against France', in Douglas A. Gibler (ed.), *International Military Alliances 1648–2008* (2 vols., Washington DC, 2009), vol. 1, p. 127. 147. At the end of May, for example, before the order to depart had reached them, a small force of Neapolitan and Tuscan regulars and volunteers held off an assault by a numerically superior Austrian army under Radetzky for long enough to give the Piedmontese forces at Goito time to prepare for the coming Austrian assault on their positions; see Ginsborg, *Daniele Manin and the Venetian Revolution*, p. 172. 148. There is an excellent interpretative summary of these events in Christopher Duggan, *The Force of Destiny. The History of Italy since 1796* (London, 2007), p. 171. 149. Harry Stearns, *1848: The Revolutionary Tide in Europe* (New York, 1974), p. 137. 150. Ibid., pp. 138–9. 151. Enrico Dandolo, *The Italian Volunteers and the Lombard Rifle Brigade. Being an Authentic Narrative of the Organisation, Adventures and Final Disbanding of These Corps, in 1848–49* (London, 1851), pp. 56, 77–8, 93, 133–4. 152. Ibid., pp. 148 (Croats), 45 (129 men), 89–90 (municipal rivalries), 41 (watchword). 153. See the preface to the expanded Italian edition of 1849: Carlo Cattaneo, *Dell'insurrezione di Milano nel 1848 e della successiva Guerra. Memorie* (Lugano, 1849), pp. iii–iv. 154. Cattaneo, *Dell'insurrezione di Milano*, p. 289. 155. Axel Körner, 'National Movements against Nation States. Bohemia and Lombardy between the Habsburg Monarchy, the German Confederation and Piedmont-Sardinia', in Moggach and Stedman Jones (eds.), *The 1848 Revolutions and European Political Thought*, pp. 345–82, here p. 375. 156. Carlo Cattaneo, 'La città considerata come principio ideale delle istorie italiane'; this essay was serially published in the journal *Crepuscolo*, nos. 42 (pp. 657–9), 44 (pp. 689–93), 50 (pp. 785–90) and 52 (pp. 817–21), dated 17 and 31 October and 12 and 16 December 1858 respectively; the quotation is from *Crepuscolo*, 42, p. 657. 157. Franz Schuselka, *Das Revolutionsjahr März 1848–März 1849* (2nd edn, Vienna, 1850), pp. 83–6. 158. Daniel Rapant, 'Slovak Politics in 1848–1849', *The Slavonic and East European Review* 27/68 (1948), pp. 67–90, here p. 82. 159. Vlasta Švoger, 'Political Rights and Freedoms in the Croatian National Revival and the Croatian Political Movement of 1848–1849: Re-establishing Continuity', *The Hungarian Historical Review* 5/1 (2016), pp. 73–104, here pp. 76–7. On the complex political structure of the areas of croat settlement, see Wolfgang Häuser, 'Der kroatisch-cenarische konflikt von, 1848 und die Krise der Habsburger Monarchie', in Heiner Timmermann (ed.), *1848. Revolution in Europa. Verlauf, Folgen und wirkungen* (Berlin, 1999), pp. 209–30, esp. pp. 214–16. 160. Jarnević, diary entry, 12 April 1843, in Irena Lukšić (ed.), *Dnevnik* (Karlovac, 2000), pp. 217–18. 161. Paul Lendvai, *The Hungarians. A Thousand Years of Victory in Defeat*, trans. Ann Major (London, 2021), p. 229. 162. Aleksandra Kolarić, 'Ivan Kukuljević i narodna zahtijevanja 1848. godine', *Papers of the Institute for Scientific Research of the Croatian Academy of Sciences and Arts* 6–7 (1994), pp. 117–21, here pp. 117–19. 163. Kolarić,

'Ivan Kukuljević i narodna zahtijevanja'; the full text of the demands (in Croatian only) can be found at https://hr.wikisource.org/wiki/Zahtijevanja_naroda. **164.** Mijat Stojanović, *Sgode i nesgode moga života*, ed. Dinko Župan, Stanko Andrić and Damir Matanović (Slavonski Brod and Zagreb, 2015), p. 66. **165.** Ibid., p. 66. **166.** Ibid., p. 67. **167.** Ibid., p. 78. **168.** Diary entries 24 and 27 March, in Jarnević, *Dnevnik*, ed. Lukšić et al., pp. 337–8. **169.** Vlasta Švoger, 'Political Rights and Freedoms in the Croatian National Revival and the Croatian Political Movement of 1848–1849. Reestablishing Continuity', *The Hungarian Historical Review* 5/1 (2016), pp. 73–104, here p. 76. **170.** Diary entries 18 March and 16 April 1848, in Jarnević, *Dnevnik*, ed. Lukšić et al., pp. 337, 339. **171.** On Palacký as a patriotically engaged historian, see Monika Baar, *Historians and Nationalism. East-Central Europe in the Nineteenth Century* (Oxford, 2010), pp. 29–35, 241. **172.** František Palacký to the Frankfurt parliament's 'Committee of Fifty', 11 April 1848, in František Palacký (ed.), *Gedenkblatter* (Prague, 1874), pp. 149–51. **173.** Maria Wawrykowa, 'Der Slavenkongreß 1848 und die Polen', *Jahrbücher für Geschichte Osteuropas*, new series, 27/1 (1979), pp. 100–108. **174.** On Polish Panslavism at the Congress, see Alexander Maxwell, 'Walerjan Krasínski, Panslavism and Germanism (1848): Polish Goals in a Panslav Context', *New Zealand Slavonic Journal* 42 (2008), pp. 101–20. **175.** Thus the recollection of the polonized Ukrainian nobleman Prince Leon Sapieha, cited in Lawrence D. Orton, 'Did the Slavs Speak German at Their First Congress?', *Slavic Review* 33/3 (1974), pp. 515–21, here p. 517. **176.** Robert E. Alvis, *Religion and the Rise of Nationalism. A Profile of an East-Central European City* (Syracuse, NY, 2005), p. 163. **177.** Salo W. Baron, 'The Impact of the Revolution of 1848 on Jewish Emancipation', *Jewish Social Studies* 11/3 (1949), p. 236. **178.** For a nationalist but archivally based account of the efforts to mobilize the German-speakers in Posen against the Polish National Committee, see Wolfgang Kohte, *Deutsche Bewegung und preussische Politik im Posener Lande 1848–49* (Posen, 1931), pp. 19–45, esp. pp. 35–6. **179.** Otto Holzapfel, 'Deutsch-dänische Grenz- und Abgrenzungsschwierigkeiten. Patriotismus und Nationalismus im Spiegel einiger schleswig-holsteinischer Liederbücher von 1802 bis 1864', *Jahrbuch für Volksliedforschung* 27/28 (1982/1983), pp. 225–34, here p. 232. **180.** On the role and impact of volunteers, see Anne-Claire Ignace, 'Le volontaire international, acteur du printemps des peuple', paper presented at the colloquium *Les Acteurs européens du 'printemps des peuples' 1848. Colloque international du cent soixante-dixième anniversaire*, Sorbonne, Paris, 31 May–2 June 2018. **181.** Kohte, *Deutsche Bewegung und preussische Politik*, pp. 39, 40, 65, 70, 84–5, 100, 108; on the role of individual 'extremists' in stirring escalatory spirals, see Körner, 'National Movements against Nation States', p. 361. **182.** 'Petition by the Ukrainian people of Galicia, which has been passed to His Majesty through the hands of His Excellency the Governor of Galicia, Franz Count Stadion', in Rudolf Wagner (ed.), *Die Revolutionsjahre 1848/49 im Königreich Galizien-Lodomerien (einschließlich Bukowina). Dokumente aus österreichischer Zeit* (Munich, 1983), pp. 26–8. **183.** Memorandum on the Ukrainians in Galicia for the clarification of their current situation, issued by the Ruthenian Main Assembly, Lemberg (Lviv), 31 July 1848, in ibid., pp. 34–43. **184.** Memorandum from the [Polish] Galicians to the Ministers [of the Austrian Empire in Vienna] concerning the Partition of Galicia, 27 November 1848, in ibid., pp. 61–73. **185.** Wilhelm Jordan at the 46th session of the German Constituent National Assembly, 24 July 1848, in Franz Wigard (ed.), *Stenographischer Bericht über die Verhandlungen der deutschen constituirenden Nationalversammlung zu Frankfurt am Main* (2 vols., Frankfurt/Main, 1848), pp. 1144–5. **186.** Ibid., p. 1144. On the background and impact of the 'parish debate', see Wolfgang Wippermana, '"Gesunder Volksegoismus". Vorgeschichte, Verlauf und Folgen dar Polendebatte in der Paulskirche', in Timmermann (ed.), *1848*, pp. 351–65. **187.** Lawrence C. Jennings, 'French Diplomacy and the First Schleswig-Holstein Crisis', *French Historical Studies* 7/2 (1971), pp. 204–25, here pp. 209, 210, 216, 219–25. **188.** On the pressure from other European states, Winfried Baumgart, *Europäisches Konzert und nationale Bewegung.*

Internationale Beziehungen 1830–1878 (Paderborn, 1999), pp. 324–5; W. E. Mosse, *The European Powers and the German Question, 1848–1871. With Special Reference to England and Russia* (Cambridge, 1958), pp. 18–19. **189.** For details, see Historisches Museum Frankfurt, at https://www.historisches-museum-frankfurt.de/de/node/33850. **190.** Robert Blum to Jenny Blum (née Günther), 4 October 1848, cited in Hans Blum, *Robert Blum* , p. 449. **191.** Metternich to Radetzky, Vienna, 22 August 1847, in Richard de Metternich and M. A. de Klinkowstrœm (eds.), *Mémoires. Documents et écrits divers laissés par le prince de Metternich* (8 vols., Vienna, 1880–84), vol. 7 (1883), doc. no. 1632, p. 476. **192.** Schuselka, *Das Revolutionsjahr*, vol. 1, p. 185. **193.** Priscilla Robertson, *Revolutions of 1848. A Social History* (Princeton, 1952), p. 115. On the liberal and radical criticism of revolutionaries who confounded constitutional and national rights, see also Georgios Varoufakis, '1848 and British Political Thought on the Principle of Nationality', in Moggach and Stedman Jones (eds.), *The 1848 Revolutions and European Political Thought*, pp. 140-161, here p. 158; on conservative critiques, see Richard Smittenaar, 'Feelings of Alarm. Conservative Criticism of the Principle of Nationality in Mid-Victorian Britain', *Modern Intellectual History* 14/2 (2017), pp. 365–91. **194.** Stanley Z. Pech, *The Czech Revolution of 1848* (Chapel Hill, 1969), p. 185. On the disruptive effects of Nationalism in the German case, see Matthew Levinger, *Enlightened Nationalism: The Transformation of Prussian Political Culture 1806–1848* (Oxford, 2000), p. 225. On Czech–German tensions in the Habsburg Empire during and after 1848, see Jeremy King, *Budweisers into Czechs and Germans: A Local History of Bohemian Politics 1848–1948* (Princeton, 2005), pp. 22–30. **195.** Alphonse de Lamartine, *Histoire de la Révolution de 1848* (2 vols., Paris, 1849), vol. 2, p. 123. **196.** Agulhon, *The Republican Experiment*, pp. 36–7. **197.** Émile Thomas, *Histoire des Ateliers Nationaux. Considérés sous le double point de vue politique et social, des causes de leur formation et de leur existence, de l'influence qu'ils ont exercée sur les événements des quatre premiers mois de la République, suivi des pièces justificatives* (Paris, 1848), p. 31, but the perils of 'laziness' were a recurring theme, see also pp. 89, 93, 141, 207. **198.** Donald Cope McKay, *The National Workshops: A Study of the French Revolution of 1848* (Cambridge, Mass., 1933), p. 40. **199.** Thomas, *Histoire des Ateliers Nationaux*, p. 88. **200.** Ibid., p. 31. **201.** Amann, 'A "Journée" in the Making', pp. 48–50. **202.** Ibid., pp. 51–2. **203.** Alexis de Tocqueville, *Recollections*, trans. George Lawrence, ed. J. P. Meyer and A. P. Kerr (London, 1970), p. 117. **204.** Ibid., p. 118. **205.** Jill Harsin, *Barricades: The War of the Streets in Revolutionary Paris, 1830–1848* (London, 2002), p. 289. **206.** Estienne Hennet de Goutel (ed.), *Mémoires du général marquis Alphonse d'Hautpoul, pair de France (1789–1865)* (Paris, 1906), p. 310. **207.** On the fear of communism in 1848, even in settings where it was virtually non-existent, see Bertel Nygaard, 'The Specter of Communism. Denmark 1848', *Contributions to the History of Concepts*, 11/1 (2016), pp. 1–23. **208.** Report of the Paris Prefect of Police, 29 May 1848, excerpted in Roger Price (ed.), *Documents on the French Revolution of 1848* (Basingstoke, 1996), pp. 79–81. **209.** On this scene, see Jonathan Beecher, *Writers and Revolution. Intellectuals and the French Revolution of 1848* (Cambridge, 2021), p. 67. The quotation is from Maurice Toesca, *Lamartine ou l'amour de la vie* (Paris, 1969), p. 451. **210.** George Sand to Étienne Arago, 16 May 1848, cited in Beecher, *Writers and Revolution*, p. 104. **211.** Agulhon, *The Republican Experiment*, p. 55. **212.** Cited in Christopher Guyver, *The French Second Republic, 1848–1852: A Political Reinterpretation* (New York, 2016), p. 117. **213.** Guyver, *The French Second Republic*, p. 119. **214.** Thomas, *Histoire des Ateliers Nationaux*, p. 285. **215.** This is reported in an essay on Trélat in the remarkable compendium produced in 1848 on the deputies of the National Assembly, Anon. (ed.), *Biographie impartiale des représentants du peuple à l'Assemblée Nationale* (Paris, 1848), pp. 464–5. **216.** Cited in 'Pujol, Louis, Ferdinand', *Le Maitron. Dictionnaire biographique. Mouvement ouvrier. Mouvement social*, consulted at https://maitron.fr/spip.php?article36644. **217.** Hippolyte Monin, 'Notice sur Louis Pujol', and Louis Pujol, 'Prophéties des jours sanglants', *La Révolution de 1848. Bulletin de la*

Société d'histoire de la Révolution de 1848 1/4 (1904), pp. 132–5 and 135–7. **218.** My attention was drawn to the barricade as an 'appeal for negotiation' and the decision not to allow this to happen in June 1848 by Alexandre Frondizi, 'Le pronunciamento en contexte républicain. Une pratique révolutionnaire intercontinentale?', paper presented at the international colloquium *Les Mondes de 1848*, 12–14 December 2018, Paris, EHESS. **219.** For a foundational analysis of these issues, on which my account draws, see Jennifer E. Sessions, 'Colonizing Revolutionary Politics: Algeria and the French Revolution of 1848', *French Politics, Culture & Society* 33/1 (2015), pp. 75–100, here p. 86. **220.** Ibid., 'Colonizing Revolutionary Politics'; also Allyson Jaye Delnore, 'Empire by Example?: Deportees in France and Algeria and the Re-Making of a Modern Empire, 1846–1854', *French Politics, Culture & Society* 33/1 (2015), pp. 33–54. But it should be noted that although a number of deportees were sent to a penal colony in Algeria, the great majority of new *colons* encouraged to emigrate there by the Provisional Government in 1848 were poor working-class volunteers with experience of agriculture who hoped to make a new start in Africa; see Yvette Katan, 'Les colons de 1848 en Algérie. Mythes et réalités', *Revue d'histoire moderne et contemporaine* 31/2 (1984), pp. 177–202. **221.** For a forensic analysis of the circumstances of the archbishop's death, see R. Limouzin-Lamothe and J. Leflon, *Mgr Denys-Auguste Affre, archevêque de Paris (1793–1848)* (Paris, 1971), pp. 350–54. **222.** Mike Rapport, *1848, Year of Revolution* (London, 2008), p. 202. **223.** Cited in ibid., p. 184. **224.** Alexander Herzen, *My Past and Thoughts. The Memoirs of Alexander Herzen*, trans. Constance Garnett, rev. Humphrey Higgins, with an introduction by Isaiah Berlin (4 vols., London, 1968), vol. 3, pp. 22–3. **225.** Ibid., vol. 3, p. 24. **226.** Marc Caussidière, *Memoirs of Citizen Caussidière, Ex-Prefect of Police, and Representative of the People* (2 vols., London, 1848), vol. 2, p. 243. **227.** See Beecher, *Writers and Revolution*, pp. 214–16, 239, with source references for the quotations. My understanding of how intellectuals processed the events of 1848 in Paris is deeply indebted to Beecher's brilliant account. **228.** Ibid., pp. 185–93, with a source reference for the quotation. **229.** Sand to Marc Dufraisse, 4 July 1848, and Charlotte Marliani, mid July 1848, both cited in ibid., pp. 107–8. **230.** [Karl Marx], 'Französische Republik', *Neue Rheinische Zeitung*, Thursday, 29 June 1848, p. 1. **231.** The classic treatment of this problem is Mark Traugott, 'Determinants of Political Orientation: Class and Organization in the Parisian Insurrection of June 1848', *American Journal of Sociology* 86/1 (1980), pp. 32–49. **232.** Beecher, *Writers and Revolution*, cited at p. 107. **233.** R. H. Thurston (ed.), *Reflections on the Motive Power of Heat, from the Original French of N.-L.-S. Carnot, Accompanied by an Account of Carnot's Theory by Sir William Thomson (Lord Kelvin)* (2nd edn, New York, 1897), p. 125. **234.** Stephen G. Brush, 'The Development of the Kinetic Theory of Gases. VIII: Randomness and Irreversibility', *Archive for History of Exact Sciences* 12/1 (1974), pp. 1–88, here pp. 19–32; Anon., 'Rudolf Julius Emanuel Clausius', *Proceedings of the American Academy of Arts and Sciences* 24 (May 1888–May 1889), pp. 458–65. **235.** R[udolf] Clausius, 'Ueber die bewegende Kraft der Wärme und die Gesetze, welche sich daraus für die Wärmelehre selbst ableiten lassen', *Annalen der Physik* 155/3 (1850), pp. 368–97; on Clausius and entropy: Brush, 'Kinetic Theory', pp. 29–30; Anon., 'Rudolf Julius Emanuel Clausius', p. 460. **236.** Józef Bem, *O Machinach Parowych* (Lviv, 1829); on the 'citizen-scientists' of 1848, Jonathan Barbier presented a paper, 'Les savants-citoyens en 1848', at the colloquium *Les Acteurs européens du 'printemps des peuples' 1848. Colloque international du cent soixante-dixième anniversaire*, Sorbonne, Paris, 31 May–2 June 2018. **237.** Diana Siclovan, '1848 and German Socialism', in Moggach and Stedman Jones, *The 1848 Revolutions and European Political Thought*, pp. 254–75, here pp. 266–7. **238.** On Helmholtz and organic delay, see Henning Schmidgen, 'Brain-Time Experiments: Acute Acceleration, Intensified Synchronization and the Belatedness of the Modern Subject', in Dan Edelstein, Stefanos Geroulanos and Natasha Wheatley (eds.), *Power and Time* (Chicago, 2020), pp. 223–48; K. M. Olesko and F. L. Holmes, 'Experiment, Quantification and Discovery: Helmholtz's Early Physiological

Researches, 1843–50', in D. Cahan (ed.), *Hermann von Helmholtz and the Foundations of Nineteenth-Century Science* (Berkeley, 1993), pp. 50–108; on the metaphorical nexus connecting the natural sciences with the language of social description, see Laura Otis, *Networking: Communicating with Bodies and Machines in the Nineteenth Century* (Ann Arbor, 2001), esp. pp. 49–80 and 120–46; on the cultural (and specifically Proustian) resonance of this notion of 'lost time', see Marco Piccolino, 'A "Lost Time" between Science and Literature. The "Temps Perdu" from Hermann von Helmholtz to Marcel Proust', *Audiological Medicine* 1/4 (2003), pp. 261–70. **239.** I draw here on the discussion in Jean-Michel Johnston, *Networks of Modernity. Germany in the Age of the Telegraph, 1830–1880* (Oxford, 2021), pp. 185–6. **240.** This is the argument advanced by Traian Ionescu, 'Misiunea lui Al. Gh. Golescu la Paris în 1848', *Revista de Istorie* 27 (1974), pp. 1727–46. My thanks to James Morris for drawing my attention to this article.

8. COUNTER-REVOLUTION

1. Francesco Michitelli, *Storia degli ultimi fatti di Napoli fino a tutto il 15 maggio 1848* (Napoli, 1849), p. 120. **2.** Ibid., pp. 120, 132, 139–40. **3.** My attention was drawn to released political prisoners as emblematic figures in the revolutionary cities of 1848 by Elena Bacchin in 'Political Prisoners and 1848', a paper presented at the at the colloquium *Les Acteurs européens du 'printemps des peuples' 1848. Colloque international du cent soixante-dixième anniversaire, Sorbonne, Paris,* 31 May–2 June 2018; see also Elene Bacchin, 'Political Prisoners of the Italian Mezzogiorno. A Transnational Question of the Nineteenth Century', *European History Quarterly* 50/4 (2020), pp. 625–49. **4.** Michitelli, *Storia degli ultimi fatti di Napoli*, p. 171. **5.** Viviana Mellone, *Napoli 1848. Il movimento radicale e la rivoluzione* (Milan, 2017), pp. 100, 123, 124–5, 142. **6.** Charles de Mazade, 'Le Roi Ferdinand II et le Royaume des Deux-Siciles. II: Les Révolutions de 1848, la réaction à Naples et le nouveau roi', *Revue des Deux Mondes*, 2nd period, 22/4 (15 August 1859), pp. 797–830, here p. 809. **7.** Mellone, *Napoli 1848*, p. 193. **8.** Mazade, 'Le Roi Ferdinand II et le Royaume des Deux-Siciles', p. 806. **9.** Michitelli, *Storia degli ultimi fatti di Napoli*, p. 180. **10.** Ibid., pp. 182–3. **11.** Jules Michelet, *Des jésuites* (Paris, 1843), p. 9. **12.** Eugène Sue, *The Wandering Jew*, trans. anon. (3 vols., London, 1889), Book III, chaps. 15, 16, 53. **13.** Marco Meriggi, *La nazione populista. Il Mezzogiorno e i Borboni dal 1848 all'Unità* (Bologna, 2021), p. 222. **14.** Ignazio Veca, 'Bénir, prêcher, s'engager. L'acteur ecclésiastique du printemps des peuples en France et en Italie', paper presented at the colloquium *Les Acteurs européens du 'printemps des peuples' 1848*. **15.** Mellone, *Napoli 1848*, p. 253. **16.** Cited in ibid., p. 254. **17.** Lord Napier to Viscount Palmerston, Naples, 16 May 1848, in British Government (ed.), *Correspondence Respecting the Affairs of Italy* (London, 1849), vol. 2: *From January to June 30, 1848*, p. 495. **18.** Giuseppe Massari, *I casi di Napoli dal 29 gennaio 1848 in poi: Lettere politiche* (Turin, 1849), pp. 148–9. **19.** For the text of the programme, see the enclosure in Lord Napier to Viscount Palmerston, Naples, 14 May 1848, in British Government (ed.), *Correspondence Respecting the Affairs of Italy* (London, 1849), vol. 2 (January–30 June 1848), p. 494. **20.** Lord Napier to Viscount Palmerston, Naples, 18 May 1848, in *Correspondence Respecting the Affairs of Italy*, vol. 2, p. 512; Ferdinand appears to have told Napier that he had agreed to rephrase the contentious passage of the oath as follows: 'I promise and swear to be faithful to the Constitution, as it shall be developed and modified by the two Chambers together with the King.' Napier duly reported this to Palmerston. But this version of events is not supported by the other Neapolitan sources and may have been part of an effort on the part of the monarch to keep the British on side by burnishing his credentials as a 'constitutional monarch'. I am grateful to Professor Viviana Mellone for her illuminating replies to my queries on this detail. **21.** Mellone, *Napoli 1848*, p. 226. **22.** Lord Napier to Viscount Palmerston, Naples, 18 May 1848, *Correspondence Respecting the Affairs of Italy*, vol. 2, p. 512. 23. Mellone, *Napoli 1848*, p. 226. 24. Massari, *I casi di Napoli*, pp. 161–2. 25. Ibid., p. 164. 26. Cited in Mazade, 'Le Roi Ferdinand II et le Royaume des Deux-Siciles', p. 817. 27. Massari, *I casi di Napoli*, p. 193. 28. Mazade, 'Le Roi Ferdinand II et le Royaume des Deux-Siciles', pp. 818–19; Massari, *I casi di Napoli*, p. 190. 29. Massari, *I casi di Napoli*, p. 190. 30. Denis Mack Smith, 'The Revolutions of 1848–1849 in Italy', in Robert Evans and Hartmut Pogge von Strandmann (eds.), *The Revolutions in Europe 1848–1849. From Reform to Reaction* (Oxford, 2000), pp. 55–81, here p. 68. 31. General Schoenhals, *Campagnes d'Italie de 1848 et 1849*, trans. Théophile Gautier fils (Paris, 1859), p. 182. 32. Sir George Hamilton to Viscount Palmerston, Florence, 6 June 1848, in British Government (ed.), *Correspondence Respecting the Affairs of Italy*, vol. 2, p. 577. 33. Provisional Government of the Venetian Republic to the Neapolitan envoy, Venice, 25 May 1848, signed Manin, Pincherle, Zennari, enclosure in Consul-General Dawkins to Viscount Palmerston, Venice, 28 May 1848, in ibid., vol. 2, pp. 547–8; Paul Ginsborg, *Daniele Manin and the Venetian Revolution* (Cambridge, 1979), p. 300. 34. Mazade, 'Le Roi Ferdinand II et le Royaume des Deux-Siciles', p. 815. 35. This observation is cited by Giuseppe Massari from an article in the Ligurian journal *Corriere Mercantile*, but Massari does not name the author and I have been unable to track down this issue of the journal; see Massari, *I casi di Napoli*, p. 163. On the contagiousness of counter-revolutionary confidence, see Kurt Weyland, 'Crafting Counterrevolution. How Reactionaries Learned to Combat Change in 1848', *The American Political Science Review* 110/2 (2016), pp. 215–31, here p. 221. 36. Lord Napier to Viscount Palmerston, Naples, 16 May 1848, *Correspondence Respecting the Affairs of Italy*, vol. 2, pp. 495–7, here p. 497. 37. Massari, *I casi di Napoli*, pp. 161–2. 38. Meriggi, *La nazione populista*, pp. 197–203. 39. Ibid., pp. 97–100, 187, 197–203. 40. Ibid., pp. 256–8. 41. James Harris, *Let the People Speak! Anti-Semitism and Emancipation in Nineteenth-Century Bavaria* (Ann Arbor, 1994), esp. pp. 132, 114. 42. Wolfgang Schwentker, *Konservative Vereine und Revolution in Preussen, 1848/49. Die Konstituierung des Konservativismus als Partei* (Düsseldorf, 1988), pp. 142, 156–74, 176, 336–8. 43. Friedrich Engels, 'Die neueste Heldentat des Hauses Bourbon', in *Neue Rheinische Zeitung*, no. 1, 1 June 1848, reprinted in Jürgen Herres and François Mélis, *Karl Marx Friedrich Engels. Artikel, Entwürfe, Februar bis Oktober 1848* [= MEGA, section 1, vol. 7] (Berlin, 2016), pp. 40–42. 44. On Sanfedist atrocities, see Tommaso Pedìo, *Giacobini e sanfedisti in Italia meridionale. Terra di Bari, Basilica e Terra d'Otranto nelle cronache del 1799* (Bari, 1974); for a much older account, see Benedetto Maresca, *Il Cavaliere Antonio Micheroux nella Reazione Napoletana del 1799* (Naples, 1895), pp. 240–41; Michael Broers, *The Politics of Religion in Napoleonic Italy. The War against God (1801–1814)*; on the violence of many local bands, see John A. Davis, *Naples and Napoleon. Southern Italy and the European Revolutions (1780–1860)*, pp. 109–10. 45. Metternich to Radetzky, 16 March 1846, cited in Alan Sked, 'The Nationality Problem in the Habsburg Monarchy and the Revolutions of 1848. A Reassessment', in Douglas Moggach and Gareth Stedman Jones (eds.), *The 1848 Revolutions and European Political Thought* (Cambridge, 2018), pp. 322–44, here p. 330. 46. Anne-Sophie Chambost, 'Socialist Visions of Direct Democracy. The Mid-Century Crisis of Popular Sovereignty and the Constitutional Legacy of the Jacobins', in Moggach and Stedman Jones (eds.), *The 1848 Revolutions and European Political Thought*, pp. 94–119, here p. 103. 47. Otto von Bismarck, *Gedanken und Erinnerungen* (2 vols., Stuttgart, 1898), vol. 1, p. 20. 48. On the strength of radical networks among rural people in the German Rhineland, see Michael Wettengel, *Die Revolution von 1848/49 im Rhein-Main-Raum. Politische Vereine und Revolutionsalltag im Großherzogtum Hessen, Herzogtum Nassau und in der Freien Stadt Frankfurt* (Wiesbaden, 1989); for two classic studies of rural radicalization in France, see Philippe Vigier, *La Seconde République dans la Région Alpine. Étude politique et sociale* (2 vols., Paris, 1963), vol. 2: *Les Paysans*, and Maurice Agulhon, *La République au village. Les Populations du Var de la Révolution à la Seconde République* (Paris, 1970); also John Merriman, 'Radicalisation and Repression. A Study of the Demobilisation of the 'Démoc-Socs' during the

Second French Republic', in Roger Price, *Revolution and Reaction. 1848 and the Second French Republic* (London, 1975), pp. 210–35; Roger William Magraw, 'Pierre Joigneaux and Socialist Propaganda in the French Countryside, 1849–1851', *French Historical Studies* 10/4 (1978), pp. 599–640. On the rural insurrection of 1851, which bears out the soare observation, see Ted W. Margadant, *French Peasants in Revolt. The Insurrection of 1851* Clinceton, 1979). **49.** Paul Raphaël, 'La loi du 31 mai 1850', *Revue d'histoire moderne et contemporaine* 14/3 (1910), pp. 296–331; Thomas Kühne, *Dreiklassenwahlrecht und Wahlkultur in Preußen, 1867–1914. Landtagswahlen zwischen korporativer Tradition und politischem Massenmarkt* (Düsseldorf, 1994); for a more positive view of the three-class franchise system, see Hedwig Richter, *Moderne Wahlen. Eine Geschichte der Demokratie in Preußen und den USA im 19. Jahrhundert* (Hamburg, 2017), esp. pp. 252–63. **50.** Cited in Erich Eyck, *Bismarck and the German Empire* (3rd edn, London, 1968), p. 116. **51.** Alfred Meißner, *Ich traf auch Heine in Paris. Unter Künstlern und Revolutionären in den Metropolen Europas*, consulted online at Projekt Gutenberg, unpaginated, see the chapter 'Revolutionstage in Prag' at https://www.projekt-gutenberg.org/meissner/heinepar/chap010.html. **52.** Stanley Z. Pech, *The Czech Revolution of 1848* (Chapel Hill, 1969), pp. 47–52. **53.** Josef Polišenský, *Aristocrats and the Crowd in the Revolutionary Year 1848. A Contribution to the History of Revolution and Counter-Revolution in Austria* (New York, 1980), p. 111. **54.** Pech, *The Czech Revolution*, p. 51. **55.** Mirjam Moravcová, 'Sociální složení členů pražského sboru "Svornost" v roce 1848', *Český Lid* 68/1 (1981), pp. 34–42. **56.** Meißner, *Ich traf auch Heine in Paris*. **57.** Ibid. **58.** Michael Michner, 'Revoluce 1848 v Českých Budějovicích', Magisterská diplomová práce/Master's thesis (Olomouc, 2020). **59.** Anon., *Alfred, Fürst zu Windischgrätz, k.k. Feldmarschall-Leutnant und kommandirender General in Böhmen. Eine treue, unpartheiische Darstellung der letzten Prager Ereignisse, nach authentischen Quellen bearbeitet, nebst zwei Original-Aktenstücken und einer biographischen Lebensskizze des Fürsten* (2nd edn, Vienna, 1848) pp. 16–17. **60.** 'Zprávy z Prahy', *Pražský wečerní list*, no. 1 (1 June 1848), pp. 1–2. **61.** Franz Schuselka, *Das Revolutionsjahr März 1848–März 1849* (2nd edn, Vienna, 1850), p. 108. **62.** Anon., *Alfred, Fürst zu Windischgrätz*, p. 20. **63.** Pech, *The Czech Revolution*, p. 148. **64.** 'Votice po r. 1848', consulted at https://www.mesto-votice.cz/votice-po-r-1848/d-4527. **65.** *Pražský wečerní list*, 17 August 1848, p. 1. **66.** Pech, *The Czech Revolution*, pp. 160, 162–3, 165, 223. **67.** Carlo Zucchi, *Memorie del Generale Carlo Zucchi*, ed. Nicomede Bianchi (Milan, Turin, 1861), p. 127. Zucchi also expressed admiration for the conduct of some volunteer contingents, but most of his references are not complimentary, see pp. 109, 128, 164. **68.** On Radetzky's hold over his officers and men, see Le comte de [Joseph Alexander, Graf von] Hübner, *Une année de ma vie. 1848–1849* (Paris, 1891), pp. 35, 65. **69.** Ginsborg, *Daniele Manin and the Venetian Revolution*, pp. 190–91. **70.** Ibid., pp. 183, 242–3. **71.** Ibid., p. 206. **72.** Ibid., p. 192. **73.** D. Laven, 'The Age of Restoration', in J. A. Davis (ed.), *Italy in the Nineteenth Century* (Oxford, 2000), pp. 51–73, here pp. 67–9. **74.** Ernst Fischer, *Österreich 1848. Probleme der demokratischen Revolution in Oesterreich* (Vienna, 1946), p. 89. **75.** Gabriella Hauch, *Frau Biedermeier auf den Barrikaden. Frauenleben in der Wiener Revolution* (Vienna, 1990), p. 206. **76.** Anton Füster, *Memoiren vom März 1848 bis Juli 1849. Beitrag zur Geschichte der Wiener Revolution* (2 vols., Frankfurt am Main, 1850), vol. 2, p. 101. **77.** Hauch, *Frau Biedermeier auf den Barrikaden*, p. 207. **78.** Albert Rosenfeld, *Das Studenten-Comité in Wien im Jahre 1848. Zum Besten deutscher Flüchtlinge in der Schweiz* (Bern, 1849), p. 108. **79.** Hauch, *Frau Biedermeier auf den Barrikaden*, p. 208. **80.** Rosenfeld, *Das Studenten-Comité in Wien*, pp. 109–10. **81.** Fischer, *Österreich 1848*, p. 91. **82.** Thus the argument of Rosenfeld, *Das Studenten-Comité in Wien* , p. 110. **83.** Rosenfeld, *Das Studenten-Comité in Wien*, p. 110. **84.** 'Der Herr Minister Schwarzer und die 5 Kreuzer', *Wiener Gassenzeitung*, no. 79, 25 August 1848, p. 1. **85.** Kulmer to Jelačić, Vienna, 27 August 1848, cited in G. E. Rothenberg, 'Jelačić, the Croatian Military Border and the Intervention against Hungary', *Austrian History Yearbook* 1 (1965), p. 59. **86.** Benjamin Kewall, diary entry of 12 September 1848, in Wolfgang Gasser (ed.), *Erlebte Revolution 1848/49. Das Wiener Tagebuch des jüdischen Journalisten Benjamin Kewall* (Vienna and Munich, 2010), p. 182. 87. Alexander Maxwell, 'Hungaro-German Dual Nationality. Germans, Slavs, and Magyars during the 1848 Revolution', *German Studies Review* 39/1 (2016), pp. 17–39. 88. Hans Kudlich, *Rückblicke und Erinnerungen* (3 vols., Vienna, Pest and Leipzig, 1873), vol. 3, pp. 4–5. 89. Ibid., vol. 3, p. 8. 90. Ibid., vol. 3, pp. 9–11. 91. Ibid., vol. 3, pp. 12–14. 92. Ibid., vol. 3, p. 17. 93. Priscilla Robertson, *Revolutions of 1848. A Social History* (Princeton, 1952), pp. 238–9. 94. Rosenfeld, *Das Studenten-Comité in Wien*, p. 154. 95. Robertson, *Revolutions of 1848*, p. 239. Anton Füster recalled that it was Fischhof, not Goldmark, who held the general in his arms as he was killed: Füster, *Memoiren vom März 1848 bis Juli 1849*, vol. 2, p. 181. 96. Füster, *Memoiren vom März 1848 bis Juli 1849*, vol. 2, pp. 180–81. 97. Rosenfeld, *Das Studenten-Comité in Wien*, p. 155. 98. Kudlich, *Rückblicke und Erinnerungen*, vol. 3, p. 24. 99. Rosenfeld, *Das Studenten-Comité in Wien*, pp. 156–7. 100. Leopold Auspitz (ed.), *Das Infanterie-Regiment Freiherr von Heß Nr. 49. Eine Chronik* (Telchen, 1889), p. 71. 101. Rosenfeld, *Das Studenten-Comité in Wien*, pp. 169–71. 102. Cited in ibid., pp. 173–4. 103. Bertrand Michael Buchmann, 'Politik und Verwaltung', in Peter Csendes and Ferdinand Opll (eds.), *Wien. Geschichte einer Stadt* (3 vols., Vienna, 2006), vol. 3: *Von 1790 bis zur Gegenwart*, pp. 85–128, here p. 116. 104. Rosenfeld, *Das Studenten-Comité in Wien*, p. 185. 105. C. A. Ritter, *Tagebuch der letzten Oktober- und ersten November-Tage Wiens. Herausgegeben von dem Redakteur des Wiener-Postillons* (2 vols., Vienna, 1848), vol. 1, p. 17. 106. Blum to Eugenie Blum, 17 October 1848, cited in Ralf Zerback, *Robert Blum. Eine Biografie* (Leipzig, 2007), p. 269. The account that follows of the last days in Blum's life is drawn from Zerback's excellent biography. 107. Blum to party comrades in Frankfurt, 17 October 1848, cited in ibid., p. 270. 108. Ibid., p. 271. 109. Hübner to Metternich, Leipzig, 20 August 1845, cited in Zerback, *Robert Blum*, pp. 285–6. 110. Hübner, *Une année de ma vie*, pp. 314, 317. 111. Ibid., p. 421. 112. Ibid., p. 427. 113. Zerback, *Robert Blum*, pp. 289–90. 114. Robert Blum, entry on 'Der Held', in Robert Blum, K. Herloßsohn and H. Marggraf (eds.), *Allgemeines Theater-Lexikon oder Encyklopädie alles Wissenswerthen für Bühnenkünstler, Dilettanten und Theaterfreunde. Unter Mitwirkung der sachkundigsten Schriftsteller Deutschlands* (7 vols., 1839–42), vol. 4 (1841), pp. 208–9. 115. Steven Beller, *Francis Joseph* (London, 1996), p. 49. 116. Maurice Agulhon, *The Republican Experiment 1848–1852*, trans. Janet Lloyd (Cambridge, 1983), p. 62. 117. Cited in Samuel Hayat, 'Se présenter pour protester. La candidature impossible de François-Vincent Raspail en décembre 1848', *Revue française de science politique* 64/5 (2014), pp. 869–903, here p. 878. 118. Karl Marx, *The Eighteenth Brumaire of Louis Bonaparte*, chap. VII ('Summary'), translated by Saul K. Padover from the German edition of 1869, consulted online at https://www.marxists.org/archive/marx/works/1852/18th-brumaire/. 119. D. Barclay, *Friedrich Wilhelm IV and the Prussian Monarchy 1840–1861* (Oxford, 1995), p. 164. 120. Manfred Botzenhart, *Deutscher Parlamentarismus in der Revolutionszeit, 1848–1850* (Düsseldorf, 1977), pp. 538–41; Ernst Rudolf Huber, *Deutsche Verfassungsgeschichte seit 1789* (8 vols., Stuttgart, 1957–90), vol. 2: *Der Kampf um Einheit und Freiheit 1830 bis 1850* (1988), pp. 730–32. 121. Diary entry, 16 October 1848, in Karl August Varnhagen von Ense, *Tagebücher. Aus dem Nachlaß Varnhagen's von Ense* (Leipzig, 1862), vol. 5, pp. 238–9. 122. Ibid., vol. 5, p. 260. 123. Gerlach to Brandenburg, 2 November 1848, cited in Barclay, *Friedrich Wilhelm IV*, p. 179. 124. Rüdiger Hachtmann, *Berlin 1848. Eine Politik- und Gesellschaftsgeschichte der Revolution* (Bonn, 1997), pp. 749–52; Botzenhart, *Deutscher Parlamentarismus*, pp. 545–50; Barclay, *Friedrich Wilhelm IV*, pp. 179–81; Sabrina Müller, *Soldaten in der deutschen Revolution von 1848/49* (Paderborn, 1999), p. 299. 125. Jonathan Sperber, *Rhineland Radicals. The Democratic Movement and the Revolution of 1848–1849* (Princeton, 1991), pp. 314–36. 126. Fanny Lewald, *A Year of Revolutions. Fanny Lewald's Recollections of 1848* [1870], ed. and trans. Hanna Ballin Lewis (Oxford, 1998), p. 146. 127. Bruce Knox, 'British Policy and the Ionian Islands, 1847–1864.

Nationalism and Imperial Administration', *The English Historical Review* 99/392 (1984), pp. 503–29, here pp. 504–5. **128.** David Hannell, 'The Ionian Islands under the British Protectorate. Social and Economic Problems', *Journal of Modern Greek Studies* 7/1 (1989), pp. 105–32, here p. 107. **129.** Knox, 'British Policy and the Ionian Islands', p. 505. **130.** [George Ferguson Bowen], *The Ionian Islands under British Protection* (London, 1851), p. 49. **131.** Hannell, 'The Ionian Islands', pp. 111, 114. **132.** Cited in J. J. Tumelty, 'The Ionian Islands under British Administration, 1815–1864', PhD thesis, University of Cambridge, 1953, p. 125. **133.** Letter from a native of Zante to *The Times*, 11 January 1823, cited in Maris Paschalidi, 'Constructing Ionian Identities. The Ionian Islands in British Official Discourses, 1815–1864', PhD thesis, University College London, 2009, p. 141. **134.** Eleni Calligas, '"The Rizospastai" (Radicals–Unionists). Politics and Nationalism in the British Protectorate of the Ionian Islands, 1815–1864', PhD thesis, University of London, 1994. **135.** Eleni Calligas, 'Lord Seaton's Reforms in the Ionian Islands, 1843–8. A Race with Time', *European History Quarterly*, 24/1 (1994), pp. 2–29, here p. 15. **136.** [Bowen], *The Ionian Islands*, p. 147. **137.** Ibid., p. 52. **138.** Hannell, 'The Ionian Islands', p. 127. **139.** Viscount Kirkwall, *Four Years in the Ionian Islands. Their Political and Social Condition, with a History of the British Protectorate* (2 vols., London, 1864), vol. 1, pp. 186, 188, 192. **140.** [An Ionian], *The Ionian Islands: what they have lost and suffered under the thirty-five years' administration of the Lord High Commissioners sent to govern them; in reply to a pamphlet entitled 'The Ionian Islands under British protection'* [by G. F. Bowen] (London, 1851), p. 108. **141.** [Bowen], *The Ionian Islands*, p. 91. **142.** [An Ionian], *The Ionian Islands*, p. 7. **143.** Paschalidi, 'Constructing Ionian Identities', p. 234. **144.** François Lenormant, *Le Gouvernement des Îles Ioniennes. Lettre à Lord John Russel* [sic] (Paris, 1861), pp. 63, 64, 65–6. **145.** Cited in [Bowen], *The Ionian Islands*, p. 93. **146.** Cited in [An Ionian], *The Ionian Islands*, pp. xv, xviii, xix. **147.** Calligas, 'Constructing Ionian Identities', p. 49 and passim. **148.** Ward to Sir John Russell, 8 December 1849, cited in Paschalidi, 'Constructing Ionian Identities', p. 237. **149.** The letter is discussed in D. Hannell, 'A Case of Bad Publicity. Britain and the Ionian Islands, 1848–51', *European History Quarterly* 17/2 (1987), p. 139. **150.** Enrico Francia, *1848. La rivoluzione del Risorgimento* (Bologna, 2012), p. 142. **151.** A brilliant study of the myth is Ignazio Veca, *Il mito di Pio IX. Storia di un papa liberale e nazionale* (Rome, 2018). The best of the older studies is the classic biography by Giacomo Martina, *Pio IX (1846–1850)* (Rome, 1974), which explains contemporary perceptions of the Pope in terms of his own indecisive behaviour and political manoeuvring. **152.** Pius IX, Allocution of 29 April 1848, transcribed in J. F. Maclear, *Church and State in the Modern Age. A Documentary History* (New York, 1995), pp. 145–7. **153.** Cited in E. E. Y. Hales, *Pio Nono. A Study in European Politics and Religion in the Nineteenth Century* (New York, 1954), p. 79. **154.** Margaret Fuller, letter XXIV, addendum of 7 May to a letter dated Rome, 19 April 1848, in Margaret Fuller, *At Home and Abroad; Or Things and Thoughts in America and Europe*, ed. Arthur B. Fuller (London, 1856; repr. Forgotten Books, London, 2013). **155.** David I. Kertzer, *The Pope Who Would be King. The Exile of Pius IX and the Emergence of Modern Europe* (Oxford, 2018), p. 78. **156.** Fuller to Elizabeth de Windt Cranch, Rome, 14 May 1848, in Robert N. Hudspeth (ed.), *The Letters of Margaret Fuller* (5 vols., Ithaca, 1988), vol. 5: *1848–49*, pp. 64–5. **157.** Giuseppe Monsagrati, *Roma senza il Papa. La Repubblica del 1849* (Rome, 2015), pp. 3–4. **158.** Luigi Carlo Farini, *Lo stato romano dall'anno 1815 al 1850* (2 vols., Florence, 1853), vol. 2, p. 379. **159.** Charles Osborne, *The Complete Operas of Verdi* (New York, 1985), p. 192. **160.** Cited in Christopher Duggan, *The Force of Destiny. The History of Italy since 1796* (London, 2007), p. 132. **161.** Kertzer, *The Pope Who Would be King*, pp. 183–4. **162.** Cristina Giorcelli, 'A Humbug, a Bounder and a Dabbler. Margaret Fuller, Cristina di Belgioioso and Christina Casamassima', in Charles Capper and Cristina Giorcelli (eds.), *Margaret Fuller. Transatlantic Crossings in a Revolutionary Age* (London, 2007), pp. 195–220, here p. 197. **163.** See for example Farini, *Lo stato romano*, vol. 2, p. 29. **164.** Margaret Fuller, letter XXX, Rome, 27

May 1849, in Fuller, *At Home and Abroad*, p. 385. **165.** Thus the claim advanced in Eckart Pankoke, *Sociale Bewegung – Sociale Frage – Sociale Politik. Grundfragen der deutschen 'Socialwissenschaft' im 19. Jahrhundert* (Stuttgart, 1970), p. 176. **166.** Lamartine, 'Du droit au travail et de l'organisation du travail' (1844), in Alphonse de Lamartine, *La Politique de Lamartine. Choix de discours et écrits politiques. Précédé d'une étude sur la vie politique de Lamartine* (2 vols., Paris, 1878), vol. 2, pp. 145–65, here p. 165. Lamartine returned to this theme in an interesting speech he delivered to the National Assembly on 14 September 1848, in which he identified property as the 'invincible fact' on which patriarchal social order was based and insisted that the social question would only be resolved by the gradual recruitment of all classes to a perfected form of proprietary order; see 'Le Droit au Travail', in ibid., pp. 365–84. **167.** Ludwig Häusser, *Denkwürdigkeiten zur Geschichte der badischen Revolution* (Heidelberg, 1851), pp. 168 and 215, but see also p. 152, where the author speaks of an 'anti-government of clubs and party leaders' animated by the 'remorseless Jesuitism' of 'revolutionary morality'. **168.** Dieter Langewiesche, 'Die Anfänge der deutschen Parteien. Partei, Fraktion und Verein in der Revolution von 1848/49', *Geschichte und Gesellschaft* 4/3 (1978), p. 352. **169.** Cited in ibid., p. 350. **170.** Hans-Josef Rupieper, 'Sachsen', in Christof Dipper and Ulrich Speck (eds.), *1848. Revolution in Deutschland* (Frankfurt am Main, 1998), pp. 69–81, here p. 79. **171.** Norbert Waszek, 'David Friedrich Strauss in 1848', in Moggach and Stedman Jones (eds.), *The 1848 Revolutions and European Political Thought*, pp. 236–53. **172.** Jonathan Sperber, *The European Revolutions, 1848–1951* (2nd edn, Cambridge, 2012), pp. 204–5. **173.** Sigismund Stern, *Geschichte des deutschen Volkes in den Jahren 1848 und 1849. In zwölf Vorträgen (gehalten in Berlin)* (Berlin, 1850), pp. 253–4. **174.** Huber, *Deutsche Verfassungsgeschichte seit 1789*, vol. 2, pp. 821–33. **175.** Frank Lorenz Müller, *Die Revolution von 1848/49* (3rd edn, Darmstadt, 2009), pp. 131–2. **176.** The text and a brief commentary can be consulted at https://de.wikipedia.org/wiki/Das_Reden_nimmt_kein_End%E2%80%99%99. **177.** Christoph Klessmann, 'Zur Sozialgeschichte der Reichsverfassungskampagne von 1849', *Historische Zeitschrift* 218/2 (1974), pp. 283–337, p. 330. **178.** Hewitson, '"The old forms are breaking up, . . . our new Germany is rebuilding itself". Constitutionalism, Nationalism and the Creation of a German Polity during the Revolutions of 1848–49', *The English Historical Review* 125/516 (2010), pp. 1204–6. **179.** W. Hoffmann and A. F. Meissner, *Romantisch-geographische Gemälde des Königreichs Preußen. Nach den besten Quellen als Haus- und Reisebuch bearbeitet* (Nordhausen, 1847), p. 630. **180.** Julius Köster, *Die Iserlohner Revolution und die Unruhen in der Grafschaft Mark Mai 1849. Nach amtlichen Akten und Berichten von Zeitgenossen dargestellt* (Berlin, 1899), pp. 71–5. **181.** Ibid., pp. 112–13. **182.** See Tzschirner et al. 'Bericht der Außerordentlichen Deputation zur Prüfung der Robert Blum's Tödtung betreffenden Fragen', in *Landtags-Acten vom Jahre 1849. Dritte Abtheilung, die von den Ausschüssen der zweiten Kammer erstatteten Berichte enthaltend*, vol. 1 (Dresden, 1849), pp. 19–21. **183.** Richard Wagner, 'Die Revolution', *Die Volksblätter*, no. 14, Dresden, Sunday, 8 April 1849; translation cited in E. Michael Jones, *Dionysos Rising. The Birth of Cultural Revolution out of the Spirit of Music* (San Francisco, 1994), pp. 8–9. **184.** Müller, *Die Revolution von 1848/49*, p. 134. **185.** Jones, *Dionysos Rising*, p. 12. **186.** Ibid., p. 13. **187.** Albert Förderer, *Erinnerungen aus Rastatt 1849* (Lahr, 1899), p. 126. Förderer miswrites the name as 'Bönnig'. **188.** Müller, *Soldaten in der deutschen Revolution*, p. 124 and passim. **189.** Sperber, *The European Revolutions*, p. 207. **190.** George Macaulay Trevelyan, *Garibaldi's Defence of the Roman Republic* (London, 1921), p. 107. **191.** Thomas C. Jones, 'French Republicanism after 1848', in Douglas Moggach and Gareth Stedman Jones (eds.), *The 1848 Revolutions and European Political Thought* (Cambridge, 2018), pp. 76–7; on this transition, see also Sudhir Hazareesingh, *From Subject to Citizen. The Second Empire and the Emergence of Modern French Democracy* (Princeton, 1998), and Edward Berenson, *Populist Religion and Left-Wing Politics in France* (Princeton, 1984), pp. 97–126. **192.** On the enmeshed, partially constitutional character of the settlement as one of the keys to its stability and flexibility, see Wolf D. Gruner, 'Was There a Reformed Balance of Power System or Cooperative Great Power Hegemony?', *The American Historical Review* 97/3 (1992), pp. 725-32.   193. Mariano Barbato, 'A State, a Diplomat and a Transnational Church. The Multi-Layered Actorness of the Holy See', *Perspectives* 21/2, *The Changing Role of Diplomacy in the 21st Century* (2013), pp. 27-48.   194. Kertzer, *The Pope Who Would be King*, p. 225.   195. Farini, *Lo stato romano*, vol. 4, pp. 3-4, 5.   196. Kertzer, *The Pope Who Would be King*, pp. 188-9.   197. Cited in ibid., p. 243.   198. Walter Bussmann, *Zwischen Preußen und Deutschland. Friedrich Wilhelm IV.* (Berlin, 1990), p. 319.   199. Keith Hitchins, *A Concise History of Romania* (Cambridge, 2014), p. 92.   200. James Morris, *The European Revolutions of 1848 and the Danubian Principalities of Wallachia*, PhD thesis, University of Cambridge, 2019, p. 140.   201. British consul Colquhoun to Lord Palmerston, 6 April 1848, cited in ibid., pp. 138-9.   202. Cited in ibid., p. 142.   203. For the full text, in the form of a circular to the Russian envoys in Europe, see 'Circulaire addressée par le Comte de Nesselrode, ministre des affaires étrangères de l'Empéreur de toutes les Russies, aux Missions de Russie près les cours d'Europe. En date de St Petersbourg, 1 August 1848', in Georg Friedrich Martens, Friedrich Saalfeld and Frédéric Murhard (eds.), *Archives diplomatiques générales des années 1848 et suivantes, faisant suite au receuil-général et nouveau receuil-général de traités, conventions et autres actes remarquables etc.* (2 vols., Göttingen, 1855), vol. 2, pp. 564-9.   204. Morris, *The European Revolutions of 1848*, p. 68.   205. Cited in ibid. Morris provides an excellent account of these events, to which my own is deeply indebted.   206. Ibid., p. 153.   207. Angela Jianu, *A Circle of Friends. Romanian Revolutionaries and Political Exile, 1840-1859* (Leiden, 2011), p. 131.   208. On the disagreement and subsequent compromise between Görgei and Kossuth, see Arthur Görgei, *My Life and Acts in Hungary in the Years 1848 and 1849* (2 vols., London, 1852), pp. 315-19.   209. Paul Lendvai, *The Hungarians. A Thousand Years of Victory in Defeat* (London, 2021), pp. 239-40.   210. On the significance of the Transylvanian intervention for the later outbreak of the Crimean War, see Eugene Horváth, *Origins of the Crimean War. Documents Relative to the Russian Intervention in Hungary and Transylvania 1848-1849* (Budapest, 1937).   211. See Simon Sarlin, 'The Anti-Risorgimento as a Transnational Experience,' *Modern Italy* 19/1 (2016), pp. 81-92.   212. Anne-Claire Ignace, 'Le volontaire international. Acteur du printemps des peuples'. On foreign volunteers on the Parisian barricades in 1848, see also Delphine Diaz, 'J'ai fait mon service comme un brave citoyen français'. Parcours et récits de combattants étrangers sur les barricades parisiennes en février et juin 1848', paper presented at the colloquium *Les Acteurs européens du 'printemps des peuples' 1848*.   213. Karl Marx and Friedrich Engels, *The Class Struggles in France*, part IV: 'The Abolition of Universal Suffrage in 1850', consulted online at https://www.marxists.org/archive/marx/works/1850/class-struggles-france/ch04.htm.   214. Ibid., part I: 'The Defeat of June', consulted online at https://www.marxists.org/archive/marx/works/1850/class-struggles-france/ch01.htm.   215. Karl Marx and Friedrich Engels, 'Review. May-October 1850' (first published in *Neue Rheinische Zeitung. Politisch-ökonomische Revue*), consulted online at https://www.marxists.org/archive/marx/works/1850/11/01.htm.   216. Heinrich von Sybel, *Die Begründung des Deutschen Reiches durch Wilhelm I.* (6 vols., 3rd edn, Munich and Berlin, 1913), vol. 2, pp. 48-9.   217. Cited in Bismarck, *Gedanken und Erinnerungen*, vol. 1, p. 95.   218. Cited in Felix Gilbert, *Johan Gustav Droysen und die preussisch-deutsche Frage* (Munich and Berlin, 1931), p. 122.   219. Massimo d'Azeglio, *Timori e speranze* (Turin, 1848), p. 29. On the realist turn in Italian political commentary, see Miroslav Šedivý, *Si vis pacem, para bellum. The Italian Response to International Insecurity 1830-1848* (Vienna, 2021), pp. 241-2, 259-60.   220. Ludwig Rochau, *Grundsätze der Realpolitik, angewendet auf die staatlichen Zustände* (2 vols., 2nd edn, Stuttgart, 1859), vol. 1, p. 1. On the importance of this idea for German liberals more generally, see James Sheehan, *German Liberalism in the Nineteenth Century* (London, 1982), pp. 108-13.   221. Ibid., vol. 1, p. 2.   222. Ibid., vol. 1, p. 11. On Rochau, see Duncan Kelly, 'August Ludwig von Rochau and Realpolitik as Historical Political

Theory', *Global Intellectual History* 3/2 (2018), pp. 301–30. **223.** Luigi Angeloni Frusinate, *Della forza nelle cose politiche. Ragionamenti quattro* (London, 1826), p. xv. For discussions of Angeloni, see Maurizio Isabella, *Risorgimento in Exile. Italian Émigrés and the Liberal International in the Post-Napoleonic Era* (Oxford, 2009), pp. 58–9, 100, 128, 136–7; James H. Billington, *Fire in the Minds of Men. Origins of the Revolutionary Faith*, pp. 114–17, 168–72. **224.** Angeloni, *Della forza nelle cose politiche*, pp. 118, 168–70, 171–4. **225.** Cour des Pairs (ed.), *Attentat des 12 et 13 Mai 1839. Interrogatoires des accusés* (Paris, 1839), pp. 1–3, see above, chap. 3. **226.** Enrico Dandolo, *The Italian Volunteers and the Lombard Rifle Brigade. Being an Authentic Narrative of the Organisation, Adventures and Final Disbanding of These Corps, in 1848–49* (London, 1851), p. 260. **227.** Monsagrati, *Roma senza il Papa*, p. 184. **228.** Carlotta Sorba, *Il melodramma della nazione. Politica e sentimenti nell'età del Risorgimento* (Rome and Bari, 2015; 2nd edn, 2021), passim. **229.** 'Er schlinget sich die Binde / Wohl um der Auge Licht / "Oh mein Deutschland, für das ich gestritten / Für das ich im Leben gelitten / Verlass die Freiheit nicht!"' – the translation is mine. **230.** Förderer, *Erinnerungen aus Rastatt*, pp. 121–2. **231.** Richard J. Evans, 'Epidemics and Revolutions. Cholera in Nineteenth-Century Europe', *Past & Present* 120/1 (1988), pp. 123–46, here p. 135.

9. AFTER 1848

1. James Morris, *The European Revolutions and the Danubian Principalities of Wallachia*, PhD thesis, University of Cambridge, 2019, p. 115. **2.** György Csorba, 'Hungarian Emigrants of 1848–1849 in the Ottoman Empire', in Hasan Celal Güzel, Cem Oğuz and Osman Karatay (eds.), *The Turks* (6 vols., Ankara, 2002), vol. 4: *The Ottomans*, pp. 224–32, here pp. 224–5. **3.** Memorandum submitted to the Grand Vizirate, dated 14 September 1849, Grand Vizirate Correspondence Important Documents Chamber, Başbakanlık Osmanlı Arşivleri (BOA = The Prime Minister's Ottoman Archives) A.MKT.MHM.17/16 1 1. I am grateful to Banu Turnaoğlu for her help translating this document. **4.** M. Şükrü Hanioğlu, *A Brief History of the Late Ottoman Empire* (Princeton, 2008), p. 77. **5.** Lawrence Douglas Taylor Hansen, 'Voluntarios extranjeros en los ejércitos liberales mexicanos, 1854–1867', *Historia Mexicana* 37/2 (1987), pp. 405–34, here pp. 407, 408–9, 414–15, 428. **6.** Gian Biagio Furiozzi, *L'emigrazione politica in Piemonte nel decennio preunitario* (Florence, 1979), p. 17. **7.** Marianne Walle, '"Le pain amer de l'exil". L'émigration des Allemands révolutionnaires (1848–1850) vers les Etats-Unis', in *Themenportal Europäische Geschichte*, 2007, www.europa.clio-online.de/essay/id/fdae-1397. **8.** For an overview, see Sylvia Aprile, Delphine Diaz and Antonin Durand, 'Times of Exile', in Delphine Diaz and Sylvia Aprile (eds.), *Banished. Travelling the Roads of Exile in Nineteenth-Century Europe* (Berlin, 2022), pp. 11–39, here pp. 29–30. **9.** Heléna Tóth, 'The Historian's Scales. Families in Exile in the Aftermath of the Revolutions of 1848', *The Hungarian Historical Review* 1/3–4 (2012), pp. 294–314, here p. 303; see also for the standard reference account of the issue, Heléna Tóth, *An Exiled Generation. German and Hungarian Refugees of Revolution, 1848–1871* (Cambridge, 2014), p. 58. **10.** Walle, '"Le pain amer de l'exil"'. **11.** The reference study of this phenomenon is Tóth, *An Exiled Generation*. **12.** Peter MacFie, 'Tasmania – Home for Ireland's Forgotten Rebels of 1848 Who Became Settlers', viewed at https://petermacfiehistorian.net.au/wp-content/uploads/Forgotten-Rebels-2017-04-03.pdf. **13.** Over 500 deportees to the Philippines are recorded for the period August–September 1848; see Juan Luis Bachero Bachero, 'La deportación en las revueltas españolas de 1848', *Historia Social*, no. 86 (2016), pp. 109–31, here pp. 114–15, 119. **14.** Charles Pridham, *Kossuth and Magyar Land. Personal Adventures during the War in Hungary* (London, 1851), p. 200. **15.** These examples are from Tóth, 'The Historian's Scales', pp. 297–8, 299, 305, 306. **16.** Bachero Bachero, 'La deportación en las revueltas españolas', p. 115. **17.** Tóth, *An Exiled Generation*, p. 110. **18.**

Angela Jianu, *A Circle of Friends. Romanian Revolutionaries and Political Exile, 1840–1859* (Leiden, 2011), p. 359. **19.** Cited in Csorba, 'Hungarian Emigrants', p. 226. **20.** Fabrice Bensimon, '1848, les chartistes et le monde', paper presented at the international colloquium *Les Mondes de 1848*, 12–14 December 2018, Paris. **21.** Casimir [sic] Batthyany, 'The Hungarian Revolution', Paris, 10 December 1851, *The Times*, 30 December 1851, no. 20998, p. 5, cols. 3–6. **22.** Bartholomäus Szemere, *Graf Ludwig Batthyány, Arthur Görgei, Ludwig Kossuth. Politische Charakterskizzen aus dem ungarischen Freiheitskriege* (Hamburg, 1853), part 3: *Ludwig Kossuth*, p. 4. Szemere's account of Kossuth aroused indignation within the Hungarian emigration but influenced the early historiography of the Hungarian independence war, especially Mihály Horváth's three-volume *Magyarország függetlenségi harczának története 1848 és 1849-ben* (History of Hungary's Struggle for Independence in 1848 and 1849), published in Geneva in 1865. Marx's understanding of the Hungarian revolution was also shaped by it; see Ruszoly József, 'Az Örök Második' [review of a reprint of Szemere's Politische Charakterskizzen], *Aetas* 7/1 (1992), pp. 242–6. **23.** Jonathan Beecher, 'Lamartine, the Girondins and 1848', in Douglas Moggach and Gareth Stedman Jones (eds.), *The 1848 Revolutions and European Political Thought* (Cambridge, 2018), pp. 14–38, here p. 36. **24.** Edward Castleton, 'The Many Revolutions of Pierre-Joseph Proudhon', in Moggach and Stedman Jones (eds.), *The 1848 Revolutions and European Political Thought*, pp. 39–69, here pp. 39–40, 54, 64. **25.** Cristina Trivulzio di Belgioioso, *Ricordi dell'esilio*, ed. and trans. Luigi Severgnini (Rome, 1978), p. 45. The letters were serialized in twenty-three issues of *Le National*. For the details, see Maurice Gasnier, 'Je privé Je politique dans les *Souvenirs dans l'exil* de la princesse Christine Trivulce de Belgiojoso', in Guillaume Pinson (ed.), *La Lettre et la presse. Poétique de l'intime et culture médiatique*, published online at Médias on 14 September 2021, consulted at https://www.medias19.org/publications/la-lettre-et-la-presse-poetique-de-lintime-et-culture-mediatique/je-prive-je-politique-dans-les-souvenirs-dans-lexil-de-la-princesse-christine-trivulce-de-belgiojoso. **26.** Belgioioso, *Ricordi dell'esilio*, pp. 49–50. **27.** *Nostis et Nobiscum. On the Church in the Pontifical States*, given at Naples on 8 December 1849, consulted online at https://www.papalencyclicals.net/pius09/p9nostis. htm. **28.** Cited in David I. Kertzer, *The Pope Who Would be King. The Exile of Pius IX and the Emergence of Modern Europe* (Oxford, 2018), p. 310. **29.** Ibid., p. 50. **30.** Barbara Spackman, 'Hygiene in the Harem. The Orientalism of Cristina di Belgioioso', *MLN* 124/1 (2009), pp. 158–76. **31.** Lara Michelacci, 'Cristina Trivulzio di Belgioioso allo specchio dell'oriente', *Lettere Italiane* 66/4 (2014), pp. 580–95. **32.** Cristina Trivulzio di Belgioioso, 'Della presente condizione delle donne e del loro avvenire', in *Nuova antologia di scienze, lettere ed arti* 1 (1866), pp. 96–113. **33.** [István Széchenyi], *Ein Blick auf den anonymen 'Rückblick' welcher für einen vertrauten Kreis, in verhältnismässig wenigen Exemplaren im Monate Oktober 1857, in Wien, erschien* (London, 1859). **34.** Anton Füster, *Memoiren vom März 1848 bis Juli 1849. Beitrag zur Geschichte der Wiener Revolution* (2 vols., Frankfurt am Main, 1850), vol. 2, pp. 180–81. **35.** Ibid., vol. 2, p. 302. **36.** See 'Utóhang a "Politikai Divatok"-hoz', in Mór Jókai, *Politikai Divatok* [= *Összes Művei* [Collected Works] vol. 17] (Budapest, 1894), pp. 445–52, here pp. 445–6. **37.** Jókai, *Politikai Divatok*, pp. 140–41. **38.** Ibid., pp. 422–3. **39.** This was the suggestion advanced by Catherine Horel in 'La mémoire de 1848 en Hongrie. Lajos Kossuth et István Széchenyi', a paper presented at the colloquium *Les Acteurs européens du 'printemps des peuples' 1848. Colloque international du cent soixante-dixième anniversaire*, Sorbonne, Paris, 31 May–2 June 2018. I am grateful to Professor Horel for first drawing my attention to Jokai's remarkable novel. **40.** Jókai, *Politikai Divatok*, pp. 428–9. **41.** Miles Taylor, 'The 1848 Revolutions and the British Empire', *Past & Present* 166/1 (2000), pp. 146–80, here p. 172. **42.** Anon., *New York Herald*, 20 March 1848 (Editorial). **43.** Anon., *El Mercurio*, 30 May 1848, cited in Cristián Gazmuri, *El '48' Chileño. Igualitarios, reformistas radicales, masones y bomberos* (Santiago de Chile, 1999), p. 64. **44.** Anon., *Courrier de la Martinique*, 27 March 1848, cited in Édouard de Lépine, *Dix semaines qui ébranlèrent la Martinique, 25 mars–4 juin 1848* (Paris, 1999), p.

19.   45. Robin Blackburn, *The Overthrow of Colonial Slavery, 1776–1848* (London, 1988), p. 509.   46. Matthew Norman, 'Abraham Lincoln, Stephen A. Douglas, the Model Republic and the Right of Revolution, 1848–61', in Daniel McDonough and Kenneth W. Noe (eds.), *Politics and Culture of the Civil War Era. Essays in Honor of Robert W. Johannsen* (Selinsgrove, 2006), pp. 154–77, here pp. 158–9.   47. William Lloyd Garrison, 'Letter to Louis Kossuth', *The Liberator*, 20 February 1852, p. 1.   48. Timothy M. Roberts and W. Howe, 'The United States and the Revolutions of 1848', in R. J. W. Evans and Hartmut Pogge von Strandmann (eds.), *The Revolutions in Europe 1848–1849. From Reform to Reaction* (Oxford, 2000), pp. 157–79, here p. 169.   49. Francis Bowen, 'The War of Races in Hungary', *North American Review* 70 (1850), pp. 78–136, here p. 82. The views expressed in this article were not uncontroversial: in the same year (1850), Bowen was blocked by the board of overseers at Harvard from taking up the McLean Professorship in History there on account of them; see Bruce Kuklick, *The Rise of American Philosophy. Cambridge, Massachusetts, 1860–1930* (New Haven, 1979), p. 29; on the impact of Kossuth, see also Donald S. Spencer, *Kossuth and Young America. A Study of Sectionalism and Foreign Policy, 1848–1852* (Columbia, 1977); see also Tibor Frank, 'Lajos Kossuth and the Hungarian Exiles in London', and Sabine Freitag, '"The Begging Bowl of Revolution". The Fundraising Tours of German and Hungarian Exiles to North America, 1851–1852', both in Freitag (ed.), *Exiles from European Revolutions. Refugees in Mid-Victorian England* (New York and Oxford), pp. 121–43 and 164–86.   50. Cited in Bonnie S. Anderson, 'The Lid Comes Off. International Radical Feminism and the Revolutions of 1848', *NWSA Journal* 10/2 (1998), pp. 1–12, here p. 6.   51. Larry J. Reynolds, *European Revolutions and the American Literary Renaissance* (New Haven, 1988), pp. 15–20.   52. Roberts and Howe, 'The United States and the Revolutions of 1848', p. 169.   53. Timothy Mason Roberts, *Distant Revolutions. 1848 and the Challenge to American Exceptionalism* (Charlottesville, 2009); see also Richard C. Rohrs, 'American Critics of the French Revolution of 1848', *Journal of the Early Republic* 14/3 (1994), pp. 359–77.   54. Bruce Levine, *The Spirit of 1848. German Immigrants, Labor Conflict, and the Coming of the Civil War* (Urbana, 1992), esp. pp. 111–45.   55. Fatih Yeşil, 'European Revolutionaries and Istanbul', at *History of Istanbul*, https://istanbultarihi.ist/431-european-revolutionaries-and-istanbul.   56. Margot Finn, *After Chartism. Class and Nation in English Radical Politics, 1848–1874* (Cambridge, 1993), pp. 60–105; Gregory Claeys, 'Mazzini, Kossuth and British Radicalism, 1848–1854', *Journal of British Studies* 28/3 (1989), pp. 225–61; Miles Taylor, *The Decline of British Radicalism, 1847–1860* (Oxford, 1993), pp. 197, 211, 214.   57. On Anneke's activism in the United States, see Mischa Honeck, *We are the Revolutionists. German-Speaking Immigrants and American Abolitionists after 1848* (Athens, Ga., 2011), pp. 104–36.   58. Taylor, 'The 1848 Revolutions and the British Empire', pp. 146–80.   59. Indrani Munasinghe, 'The Road Ordinance of 1848 and the Kandyan Peasantry', *Journal of the Royal Asiatic Society Sri Lanka Branch*, new series, 28 (1983/84), pp. 25–44, here p. 26.   60. Philip D. Curtin, 'The Environment beyond Europe and the European Theory of Empire', *Journal of World History* 1/2 (1990), pp. 131–50, here p. 149.   61. Munasinghe, 'The Road Ordinance of 1848'.   62. Taylor, 'The 1848 Revolutions and the British Empire', p. 150.   63. Robert Livingston Schuyler, 'The Abolition of British Imperial Preference, 1846–1860', *Political Science Quarterly* 33/1 (1918), pp. 77–92; Schuyler suggests that these adjustments 'came near to dissolving the British empire', here p. 92.   64. Taylor, 'The 1848 Revolutions and the British Empire', p. 171.   65. Leader article, *Sydney Morning Herald*, Wednesday, 11 October 1848, p. 2.   66. Ibid., Thursday, 7 December 1848, p. 2.   67. Ibid., Monday, 18 December 1854, p. 2.   68. Raffaello Carboni, *The Eureka Stockade* [1855] (Carlton, 2004).   69. Jerome O. Steffen, 'The Mining Frontiers of California and Australia. A Study in Comparative Political Change and Continuity', *Pacific Historical Review* 52/4 (1983), pp. 428–40, here p. 434.   70. *El Comercio*, 2 January 1849, cited in Claudia Rosas Lauro and José Ragas Rojas, 'Las revoluciones francesas en el Perú. Una reinterpretación (1789–1848)', *Bulletin de l'Institut Français d'Études Andines*, 36/1

(2007), pp. 51–65, here p. 59. 71. Cited in José Frank Ragas Rojas, 'Ciudadanía, cultura política y representación en el Perú. La campaña electoral de 1850', thesis for the Licenciado en Historia at the Pontificia Universidad Católica del Perú, Lima, 2003, p. 128; viewed online at http://tesis.pucp.edu.pe/repositorio/bitstream/handle/123456789/5828/RAGAS_ROJAS_JOSE_%20CIUDADANIA.pdf?sequence=1&isAllowed=y. 72. Lauro and Ragas Rojas, 'Las revoluciones francesas en el Perú', p. 56. 73. Lastarria became Brissot; Bilbao became Vergniaud; Domingo Santa María became Louvet and so on. Eusebio Lillo, a poet-musician who would later be the chief writer for the paper *El Amigo del Pueblo*, adopted the pseudonym Rouget de Lisle. Santiago Arcos became Marat – as this selection makes clear, Lamartine's book was not just about the Girondins; see Benjamin Vicuña Mackenna, *The Girondins of Chile*, trans. J. H. R. Polt (Oxford, 2003), pp. xxix, xxxviii, xl (introduction by Cristián Gazmuri), 9. 74. Clara A. Lida, 'The Democratic and Social Republic of 1848 and Its Repercussions in the Hispanic World', in Guy Thomson (ed.), *The European Revolutions of 1848 and the Americas* (London, 2002), pp. 46–75, here p. 64; Gazmuri, *El '48' Chileño*, pp. 71, 205. 75. Edward Blumenthal, 'Impérialisme, circulations politiques et exil en Amérique Latine. Autour de Francisco Bilbao', paper presented at the international colloquium *Les Mondes de 1848*. 76. David Rock, 'The European Revolutions in the Rio de la Plata', in Thomson (ed.), *The European Revolutions of 1848 and the Americas*, pp. 125–41, here p. 136. 77. Jorge Myers, '"Una revolución en las ideas". Intellectual Repercussions of 1848 in Latin America', paper presented at the international colloquium *Les Mondes de 1848*. 78. Nancy Priscilla Naro, 'Brazil's 1848. The Praieira Revolt in Pernambuco, Brazil', in Thomson (ed.), *The European Revolutions of 1848 and the Americas*, pp. 100–124, here p. 111. 79. On these debates, see Banu Turnaoğlu, *The Formation of Turkish Republicanism* (Princeton, 2017), esp. pp. 50–85; on contemporary Ottoman interest in the revolutions, see Levent Düzcü, 'Korku ile Tedbir Arasinda Bir Ihtilâli Izlemek. 1848 Ihtilâli ve Osmanli Hükümeti' [Observing a Revolution with Caution and Fear. The 1848 Revolution and the Ottoman State], in *Tokat Gaziosmanpaşa Üniversitesi Sosyal Bilimler Araştırmaları Dergisi* 38 (2016), pp. 51–78. 80. Michael Geyer and Charles Bright, 'Global Violence and Nationalizing Wars in Eurasia and America. The Geopolitics of War in the Mid-Nineteenth Century', *Comparative Studies in Society and History* 38/4 (1996), pp. 619–57, here pp. 629–30. 81. Jonathan Spence, *God's Chinese Son. The Taiping Heavenly Kingdom of Hong Xiuquan* (New York, 1996), pp. 30–32. 82. Jürgen Osterhammel, *The Transformation of the World. A Global History of the Nineteenth Century*, trans. Patrick Camiller (Princeton, 2014), p. 547. 83. For a reflection on this difference, see David A. Bell, 'This is What Happens When Historians Overuse the Idea of the Network', *The New Republic*, 26 October 2013. 84. On the new constitution as a 'milestone', see J. C. Boogman, *Rondom 1848. De politieke ontwikkeling van Nederland 1840–1858* (Bussum, 1978), p. 197; on the relations between the sovereign and parliament, see Ron de Jong, 'Hooggespannen verwachtingen. Verkiezingen en de grondwetsherziening van 1848', *De Moderne Tijd* 3/4 (2019), pp. 324–35, here p. 324; Gerlof D. Homan, 'Constitutional Reform in the Netherlands', *The Historian* 28/3 (1966), p. 425; on the press, H. L. van Kranenberg, Franz C. Palm and Gerard A. Pfann, 'The Life Cycle of Daily Newspapers in the Netherlands', *De Economist* 146/3 (1998), pp. 475–94. 85. D. Barclay, *Friedrich Wilhelm IV and the Prussian Monarchy 1840–1861* (Oxford, 1995), p. 183; H. Wegge, *Die Stellung der Öffentlichkeit zur oktroyierten Verfassung und die preußische Parteibildung 1848/49* (Berlin, 1932), pp. 45–8; G. Grünthal, *Parlamentarismus in Preußen 1848/49–1857/58* (Düsseldorf, 1982), p. 185. 86. 'Kaiserliches Patent vom 31. December 1851', *Allgemeines Reichs-Gesetz und Regierungsblatt für das Kaiserthum Oesterreich*, consulted online at ALEX. Historische Reichts- und Gesetzestexte online, https://alex.onb.ac.at/cgi-content/alex?aid=rgb&datum=1852&page=111&size=45. 87. See 'French Constitution of 1852' at https://en.wikisource.org/wiki/French_Constitution_of_1852. 88. Rosario Romeo, *Vita di Cavour* (Rome, 1984), p. 181. 89. Cited in ibid., p. 182. 90. Alberto Carraciolo, 'Storia economica', pp. 612–17; Denis Mack Smith, *Victor Emanuel, Cavour and the*

Risorgimento (Oxford, 1971), pp. 56–76; Denis Mack Smith, *Cavour* (London, 1985), pp. 94–106; Giacomo Perticone, *Il regime parlamentare nella storia dello Statuto Albertino* (Rome, 1960); Romeo, *Vita di Cavour*; Rosario Romeo, *Dal Piemonte sabaudo all'Italia liberale* (Turin, 1963); Stefano Merlini, 'Il governo costituzionale', in Raffaele Romanelli (ed.), *Storia dello Stato Italiano* (Rome, 1995), pp. 3–72, here pp. 3–10, 13–15, 17–19. 91. Romeo, *Vita di Cavour*, p. 186. 92. See Christopher Clark and Wolfram Kaiser (eds.), *Culture Wars. Secular–Catholic Conflict in Nineteenth-Century Europe* (Cambridge, 2003). For a suggestive discussion – focused on the 1990s – of culture war as a form of conflictual stability that paradoxically affirms an underlying consensus, see Gary Gerstle, *The Rise and Fall of the Neo-Liberal Order. America and the World in the Free Market Era* (New York, 2022). On secular–clerical tensions in Portugal during the Regeneration, see Maria Fátima Bonifacio, *O século XIX português* (Lisbon, 2002), pp. 65–71; on the Netherlands, see Hans Knippenberg, 'The Changing Relationship between State and Church/Religion in the Netherlands', *GeoJournal* 67 (2006), pp. 317–30, here pp. 321–3. 93. Andreas Neemann, *Landtag und Politik in der Reaktionszeit. Sachsen 1849/50–1866* (Düsseldorf, 2000). 94. Bernard Ménager, *Les Napoléon du peuple* (Aubier, 1988), pp. 355–7. 95. Robert J. W. Evans, 'From Confederation to Compromise. The Austrian Experiment, 1849–1867', *Proceedings of the British Academy*, 87 (1994), pp. 135–67, here p. 137. 96. John Deak, *Forging a Multinational State. State Making in Imperial Austria from the Enlightenment to the First World War* (Stanford, 2015), pp. 99–136. 97. Manuel Espadas Burgos, 'Madrid, centro de poder político', in Luis Enrique Otero Carvajal and Ángel Bahamonde Magro (eds.), *Madrid en la sociedad del siglo XIX* (Madrid, 1986), pp. 179–92, here p. 188. 98. Maria Cruz Seoane, *Historia del periodismo en España*, 3 vols., vol. 2: *El siglo XIX* (Madrid, 1983), pp. 241–2; Victor G. Kiernan, *The Revolution of 1854 in Spanish History* (Oxford, 1966), p. 6; José Ramón Urquijo Goitia, 'Las contradicciones políticas del Bienio Progresista', *Hispania*, 57/195 (1997), pp. 267–302; Charles J. Esdaile, *Spain in the Liberal Age. From Constitution to Civil War, 1808–1939* (Oxford, 2000), pp. 109–22; José Ramón de Urquijo y Goitia, *La revolución de 1854 en Madrid* (Madrid, 1984). 99. *La Época*, 25 March 1856, leader article; see also the leader of 31 March 1856, which discusses the attacks on the Unión from left and right. 100. For contemporary British comment on Saldanha's 'strange coalition', which seemed to fly in the face of Portuguese political tradition, see *The Times*, 31 May 1851, p. 4, col. f; also 11 June 1851, p. 4, col. b. On the Patuleia and the Maria da Fonte insurrection, see Maria de Fátima Bonifácio, *História da Guerra Civil da Patuleia, 1846–47* (Lisbon, 1993); Padre Casimiro, *Apontamentos para a história da revolução do Minho em 1846 ou da Maria da Fonte*, ed. José Teixeira da Silva (Lisbon, 1981); José Brissos, *A insurreição miguelista nas resistências a Costa Cabral (1842–1847)* (Lisbon, 1997). For a brilliant synoptic study of the Regeneração, see José Miguel Sardica, *A Regeneração sob o signo do Consenso. A política e os partidos entre 1851 e 1861* (Lisbon, 2001); José Miguel Sardica, 'A Regeneração na política portuguesa do século xix', in Sardica (ed.), *Portugal Contemporâneo. Estudos de História* (Lisbon, 2013), pp. 157–84, here pp. 158–9; also Bonifacio, *O século XIX português*, pp. 61–83. On Costa Cabral's vain efforts to inaugurate a centrist politics before the new regime, see Maria Fátima Bonifácio, 'Segunda ascensão de Costa Cabral (1847–1851)', *Análise Social* 32/142 (1997), pp. 537–56, esp. p. 541. 101. João Luís César das Neves, *The Portuguese Economy. A Picture in Figures. XIX and XX Centuries* (Lisbon, 1994), p. 45. 102. Nelson Durán de la Rua, *La Unión Liberal y la modernazión de la España isabelina. Una convivencia frustrada 1854–1868*, pp. 345–6; for interesting reflections on the parallels between Spanish and Portuguese developments, see Ignacio Chato Gonzalo, 'Portugal e Espanha em 1856. A dispar evolução política do liberalismo peninsular', *Análise Social*, 42/182 (2007), pp. 55–75. 103. For an excellent comparative discussion of 'conservative–liberal modernization' in Prussia and Austria, see Arthur Schlegelmilch, 'Das Projekt der konservativ-liberalen Modernisierung und die Einführung konstitutioneller Systeme in Preußen und Österreich, 1848/49', in Martin Kisch and Pierangelo Schiera (eds.), *Verfassungswandel um 1848 im europäischen*

Vergleich (Berlin, 2001), pp. 155–77. 104. Seoane, *Historia del periodismo en España*, vol. 2, p. 244; Kiernan, *The Revolution of 1854*, p. 5. 105. Howard C. Payne and Henry Gross-hans, 'The Exiled Revolutionaries and the French Political Police in the 1850s', *The American Historical Review* 68/4 (1963), pp. 954–73. 106. Kiernan, *The Revolution of 1854*, p. 5. 107. Grünthal, *Parlamentarismus*, p. 476. 108. Süheyla Yenidünya Gürgen, '1848 İhtilali'nden Sonra Eflak'ın Yeniden Yapılanmasına Dair Bir Değerlendirme. Ştirbei'in Müesses Nizam Arayışları (1849-1851)' [An Evaluation of the Restructuring of Wallachia after the Revolution of 1848. Ştirbei's Quest for Institutional Order (1849–1851)], *Tokat Gaziosmanpaşa Üniversitesi Sosyal Bilimler Araştırmaları Dergisi* 15/1 (2020), pp. 11–23, here pp. 20–21. 109. Clive Trebilcock, *The Industrialization of the Continental Powers* (Harlow, 1981), p. 152; Roger Price, *The French Second Empire. An Anatomy of Political Power* (Cambridge, 2001), p. 228; on Spain, Pablo Martin Aceña, 'Development and Mod-ernization of the Financial System, 1844–1935', in Nicolás Sánchez-Albornoz, *The Economic Modernization of Spain*, trans. Karen Powers and Manuel Sañudo (New York, 1987), pp. 107–27, here p. 110; Durán de la Rua, *Unión Liberal*, pp. 162–3; on Germany and Austria, James J. Sheehan, *German History 1770–1866* (Oxford, 1989), p. 734; Harm-Hinrich Brandt, *Der österreichische Neoabsolutismus. Staatsfinanzen und Politik 1848-1860* (Göt-tingen, 1978), pp. 231–438. 110. Romeo, *Vita di Cavour*, pp. 193–4. 111. Thorvaldur Gylfason, 'The Anatomy of Constitution Making. From Denmark in 1849 to Iceland in 2017', paper presented at the conference *Constitution Making in Democratic Constitutional Orders* at CIDE (Center for Research and Teaching of Economics), Mexico City, 11–12 August 2016, consulted online at https://notendur.hi.is/gylfason/Mexico%20Paper%20 The%20Anatomy%20of%20Constitution%20Making%20Revised%20Black.pdf. 112. Durán de la Rua, *Unión Liberal*, p. 345; Maria Filomena Mónica, *Fontes Pereira de Melo* (Lisbon, 1998). 113. Royal Decree of 20 October 1851, cited in José María García Madaria, *Estructura de la Administración Central (1808-1931)* (Madrid, 1982), p. 129. 114. 'Circu-lar de la Dirección general de 5 de Marzo de 1857 dictando las reglas para el servicio de las obras de reparación', Archivo Histórico Nacional Madrid, FC OP, leg. 51, Expt 14. 115. Royal decree of 10 December 1858, cited in Durán de la Rua, *Unión Liberal*, pp. 137–8; on economic reforms of the Bienio, see Urquijo Goitia, 'Las contradicciones políticas'. 116. Luis Enrique Otero Carvajal, 'El telégrafo en el sistema de comunicaciones Español 1800–1900', in Javier María Donézar and Manuel Perez Ledesma (eds.), *Antiguo Regimen y liberalismo. Homenaje a Miguel Artola* (3 vols., Madrid, 1994), vol. 2, pp. 587–98, here p. 593. 117. Albert Carreras de Odriozola, 'Gasto nacional bruto y formación de capital en España, 1849–1958. Primar ensayo de estimación', in Pablo Martin Aceña and Leandro Pra-dos de la Escosura (eds.), *La nueva historia económica en España* (Madrid, 1985), pp. 32–3. 118. Durán de la Rua, *Unión Liberal*, p. 151. 119. Antonio Gomez Mendoza, 'Los ferrocarriles en la economía española, 1855–1913', in Martin Aceña and Prados de la Esco-sura (eds.), *La nueva historia económica*, pp. 101–16, here p. 113. Gomez Mendoza estimates that national income (excluding earnings that reverted to foreign investors) would have been between 6.5 and 12 per cent lower by 1878 without the infrastructural programme launched in the 1850s. This conclusion is broadly supported in Nicolás Sánchez-Albornoz, 'Introduc-tion. The Economic Modernization of Spain', in Sánchez-Albornoz (ed.), *Economic Modernization*, pp. 1–9, here p. 5. The contrary view is set out in Gabriel Tortella Casares, *Los orígenes del capital financiero en España. Banca, industria y ferrocarriles en el sigli XIX* (Madrid, 1972), esp. chaps. 5–6; see also Esdaile, *Spain in the Liberal Age*, pp. 113–14; there is a broadly analogous debate on France; see Allan Mitchell, 'Private Enterprise or Public Service? The Eastern Railway Company and the French State in the Nineteenth Century', *The Journal of Modern History* 69/1 (1997), pp. 18–41, esp. pp. 18–21. 120. Trebilcock, *Indus-trialization*, p. 152; Price, *The French Second Empire*, p. 211; Alain Plessis, *The Rise and Fall of the Second Empire*, trans. Jonathan Mandelbaum (Cambridge, 1985), p. 62; Éric Anceau, *Napoléon III. Un Saint-Simon à cheval* (Paris, 2008), pp. 343–66; Pierre Milza, *Napoléon III*

(Paris, 2004), pp. 464–99; Antoine Olivesi and André Nouschi, *La France de 1848 à 1914* (Paris, 1997), pp. 49–70; Dominique Barjot, Jean-Pierre Chaline and André Encrevé, *La France au XIXe siècle 1814–1914* (Paris, 1995), pp. 377–405. **121.** On the emperor as a Saint-Simonian technocrat, see especially Anceau, *Napoléon III*. **122.** Franck Yonnet, 'Claude-Henri de Saint-Simon, l'industrialisme et les banquiers', *Cahiers d'économie politique* 46/1 (2004), pp. 147–74; Franck Yonnet, 'La structuration de l'économie et de la banque sous le Second Empire. Le rôle du Crédit Mobilier des Pereire', in Nathalie Coilly et Philippe Régnier (eds.), *Le Siècle des saint-simoniens. Du Nouveau christianisme au canal de Suez* (Paris, 2006), pp. 124–9. **123.** Charles Tilly, 'The Political Economy of Public Finance and the Industrialization of Prussia 1815–1866', *The Journal of Economic History* 26/4 (1966), pp. 484–97, here p. 492; Grünthal, *Parlamentarismus*, p. 476. **124.** Harald Winkel, *Die deutsche Nationalökonomie im 19. Jahrhundert* (Darmstadt, 1977), pp. 86–7, 95; on this view as an instance of the German engagement with 'Smithianism', see Emma Rothschild, '"Smithianismus" and Enlightenment in Nineteenth-Century Europe', King's College Cambridge: Centre for History and Economics, October 1998. **125.** Rondo E. Cameron, 'French Finance and Italian Unity. The Cavourian Decade', *The American Historical Review* 62/3 (1957), pp. 552–69, here pp. 556–61; Romeo, *Vita di Cavour*, pp. 199–205. **126.** On infrastructural investment in Hanover, Saxony and Württemberg, see Abigail Green, *Fatherlands. State-Building and Nationhood in Nineteenth-Century Germany* (Cambridge, 2001), pp. 223–66. **127.** R. J. W. Evans, 'From Confederation to Compromise', pp. 138–9. **128.** Romeo, *Vita di Cavour*, p. 203. **129.** Ministry of Justice, 'Instrucción para llenar con exactitud las hojas de la estadistica civil creada por Real decreto de Diciembre de 1855', 30 January 1856, in *Colección legislativa de España, 1st Term 1856*, vol. 67 (Madrid, 1856), p. 109. See also the bundle of newly devised forms for expenses and receipting attached to 'Real decreto creando en cada Provincia una Junta economica de obras publicas', 15 November 1854, in Archivo Histórico Nacional Madrid, FC Fomento (OO.PP.), Leg. 41, Expt 29. **130.** Cited in Green, *Fatherlands*, p. 251. **131.** M. Blanchard, 'The Railway Policy of the Second Empire', trans. J. Godfrey, in François Crouzet, William Henry Chaloner and Walter Marcel Stern (eds.), *Essays in European Economic History 1789–1914* (London, 1969), pp. 98–111, here p. 104; on Saint-Simonianism and the railways, see M. Wallon, *Les Saint-Simoniens et le chemins de fer* (Paris, 1908); Georges Ribeill, 'Des saint-simoniens à Léon Lalanne. Projets, thèses et controverses à propos de la réorganisation des réseaux ferroviaires, *Revue d'histoire des chemins de fer* 2 (1990), pp. 47–80. **132.** David Hansemann, cited in James M. Brophy, *Capitalism, Politics and Railroads in Prussia, 1830–1870* (Columbus, 1998), p. 50. **133.** Brophy, *Capitalism, Politics and Railroads*, p. 56. The quotation (from David Hansemann) is on p. 50. Von der Heydt's policy of nationalization was reversed in the 1860s. **134.** Cited in Plessis, *Second Empire*, p. 62. **135.** Paul Nolte, *Die Ordnung der Gesellschaft* (Munich, 2000), pp. 52–3. **136.** Jorge Borges de Macedo, 'O aparecimento em Portugal do conceito de programa político', *Revista Portuguesa de História* 13 (1971), pp. 396–423. **137.** On efforts to unify the structure of government in Spain, see García Madaria, *Estructura de la Administración Central*, p. 128; Royal decree of 29 February 1856, cited in ibid., p. 142; cf. the 'Instrucción para promover y ejecutar las obras públicas de caminos, canales, puertos y demas análogos; aprobada por Real decreto de 10 de Octobre de 1845', Archivo Histórico Nacional Madrid, FC OP, leg. 2; on Austria, R. J. W. Evans, 'From Confederation to Compromise', p. 138; George Barany, 'Ungarns Verwaltung 1848–1918', in *Die Habsburgermonarchie 1848–1918*, vol. 2: Adam Wandruszka and Peter Urbanitsch (eds.), *Verwaltung und Rechtswesen* (Vienna, 1975), pp. 329–62. **138.** Plessis, *Second Empire*, p. 62, stresses the influence of Saint-Simonianism on the emperor; James F. McMillan, *Napoleon III* (Routledge, 2014), pp. 138–9, is sceptical. On the Orleanist sympathies of the old financial establishment, see Plessis, *Second Empire*, p. 76. **139.** Tilly, 'Political Economy of Public Finance', p. 490. **140.** Ibid., p. 494. **141.** Romeo, *Vita di Cavour*, p. 204. **142.** Urquijo Goitia, 'Las contradicciones políticas del Bienio Progresista', pp. 282–3; César das Neves, *Portuguese Economy*, pp. 46–7;

in general, see the important study by Mónica, *Fontes Pereira de Melo*. **143.** On the use of developmentalist arguments in relation to canal-building before the advent of the railways, see Telesforo Marcial Herníndez and Javier Vidal Olivares, 'Infraestructura viaria y ferrocar-riles en la articulación del espacio económico valenciano, 1750–1914', *Hispania* 51/177 (1991), pp. 205–43, here p. 225; on continuity in public infrastructural planning in France, with specific reference to the dirigiste tradition of the Corps des Ponts et Chaussées, see Cecil O. Smith, 'The Longest Run. Public Engineers and Planning in France', *The American Historical Review* 95/3 (1990), pp. 657–92; Smith stresses long-term continuity of statist construction projects in France, but also notes that the early 1850s saw a restructuring of railway develop-ment marked firstly by the consolidation of the twenty-eight French railway companies into six regional monopolies, and secondly by highly successful government stimulation of private investment (p. 677). **144.** McMillan, *Napoleon III*, pp. 137–41. **145.** Acta del Consejo of 19 December 1854, cited in Urquijo Goitia, 'Las contradicciones políticas del Bienio Pro-gresista', p. 270. **146.** Conseil Général du Département du Nord, session de 1858, Rapport par M. F. Kuhlmann, Archives Nationales, F/12/6848/B, p. 14. **147.** Leader articles in *A Revolução de Setembro*, 16 September, 21 November and 27 December 1851 and 23 October 1852, cited in Mónica, *Fontes Pereira de Melo*, p. 20. **148.** Ministerio de Fomento, 'Real decreto, creando una comisión para que proponga los medios de armonizar los intereses recíprocos de los fabricantes y trabajadores de Barcelona', 10 January 1851, in *Colección legislativa de España (Primer cuatrimestre de 1851)*, vol. 64 (Madrid, 1855). **149.** Cited in [J. A. Smith], Conde da Carnota (ed.), *Memoirs of Field-Marshal The Duke of Saldanha with Selections from His Correspondence* (2 vols., London, 1880), pp. 315, 326. **150.** Ministry of Agriculture, Commerce and Public Works, Report to the Emperor, Paris, 30 November 1856, Archives Nationales Paris F/14/8508A. **151.** Charles Tilly, 'German Industrialization', in Mikuláš Teich and Roy Porter, *The Industrial Revolution in National Context. Europe and the USA* (Cambridge, 1996), pp. 95–125, here p. 103. **152.** Sheehan, *German History*, p. 734. **153.** Preamble to the Royal Decree of 30 March 1852, cited in Mónica, *Fontes Pereira de Melo*, pp. 29–30. **154.** McMillan, *Napoleon III*, p. 136; Price, *The French Second Empire*, p. 250. **155.** Ian Hacking, *The Taming of Chance* (Cambridge, 1990), pp. 33–4; T. Huertas, *Economic Growth and Economic Policy in a Multinational Setting. The Habs-burg Monarchy, 1841–65* (New York, 1977); W. Goldinger, 'Die Zentralverwaltung in Cisleithanien – Die Zivile Gemeinsame Zentralverwaltung', in Wandruszka and Urbanitsch (eds.), *Verwaltung und Rechtswesen*, pp. 100–189, here pp. 135, 177; Richard J. Bazillion, *Modernizing Germany. Karl Biedermann's Career in the Kingdom of Saxony, 1835–1901* (New York, 1990), p. 268. **156.** This process is well known for Britain, thanks to Lawrence Goldman's work on the early and mid-Victorian statistical movement and its increasingly intimate relationship with government; L. Goldman, 'Statistics and the Science of Society in Early Victorian Britain. An Intellectual Context for the General Register Office', *Social History of Medicine* 4/3 (1991), pp. 415–34; Lawrence Goldman, 'The Social Science Association 1857–1886. A Context for Mid-Victorian Liberalism', *The English Historical Review* 101/398 (1986), pp. 95–134. This kind of work is yet to be done for most of the continental states. **157.** Bazillion, *Modernizing Germany*, p. 268. **158.** Presidency of the Council of Ministers, preamble to royal decree founding a statistical commission, 3 November 1856, in *Colección legislativa de España (Segundo trimestre de 1856)*, vol. 68 (Madrid, 1856), pp. 194–6. **159.** Juan Pro Ruiz, 'Statistics and State Formation in Spain (1840–1870)', working paper produced as part of the research project PB97-0056 of the Dirección General de Inves-tigación Científica y Técnica of Spain, viewed online at citeseerx.ist.psu.edu/viewdoc/download?doi=10.1.1.202. For a good example of the *moderado* view of growth and devel-opment, which acknowledged the need for state intervention but defined the task of the state in terms of the need to contain and minimize the impact of change, see the 1848 *prospecto* of the Ministry of Commerce, Education and Public Works in *Boletín Oficial del Ministerio de Comercio, Instrucción y Obras Públicas*, vol. 1 (1848), pp. 1–3. **160.** Alain Desrosières,

'Official Statistics and Medicine in Nineteenth-Century France. The Statistique Générale de la France as a Case Study', *Social History of Medicine* 4/3 (1991), pp. 515–37. **161.** On the statistical movement, see Silvana Patriarca, *Numbers and Nationhood. Writing Statistics in Nineteenth-Century Italy* (Cambridge, 1996); Lawrence Goldman, 'The Origins of British "Social Science". Political Economy, Natural Science and Statistics, 1830–1835', *The Historical Journal* 26/3 (1983), pp. 587–616; M. J. Cullen, *The Statistical Movement in Early Victorian Britain. The Foundations of Empirical Social Research* (Hassocks, 1975); for an anthology of contemporary treatises, see Richard Wall (ed.), *Comparative Statistics in the Nineteenth Century* (Farnborough, 1973), cited in Emma Rothschild, 'The Age of Insubordination', *Foreign Policy*, no. 119 (Summer 2000), pp. 46–9. **162.** Wolfgang Göderle, 'State-Building, Imperial Science, and Bourgeois Careers in the Habsburg Monarchy in the 1848 Generation', *The Hungarian Historical Review* 7/2 (2018), pp. 222–49, here pp. 227–34. **163.** Nicholas Papayanis, *Horse-Drawn Cabs and Omnibuses in Paris. The Idea of Circulation and the Business of Public Transit* (Baton Rouge, 1997), pp. 92–5. On the same obsession in a British context, see Martin Daunton, 'Introduction', in Daunton (ed.), *Cambridge Urban History of Britain*, vol. 3: *1840–1950* (Cambridge, 2001), pp. 1–56, esp. pp. 1–13. There is now a vast literature on the restructuring of Paris under Haussmann; among those studies I found most useful are David H. Pinkney, *Napoleon and the Rebuilding of Paris* (Princeton, 1958), and Ann-Louise Shapiro, *Housing the Poor of Paris, 1850–1902* (Madison, 1985). **164.** Santos Juliá, David Ringrose and Cristina Segura, *Madrid. Historia de una capital* (Madrid, 1994), pp. 288–313. **165.** Fernando Roch, 'Reflexiones sobre le reordenación urbanistica en el Madrid de mediados del siglo XIX', in Otero Carvajal and Bahamonde Magro (eds.), *Madrid*, pp. 89–96, here pp. 92–3. **166.** Françoise Choay, 'Pensées sur la ville, arts de la ville', in M. Agulhon (ed.), *La Ville de l'âge industriel. Le Cycle haussmannien* (Paris, 1983), pp. 159–271, here p. 168; Jeanne Gaillard, *Paris, la ville 1852–1870. L'Urbanisme parisien à l'heure d'Haussmann* (Paris, 1976). **167.** Anna Ross, *Beyond the Barricades. Government and State-Building in Post-Revolutionary Prussia, 1848–1858* (Oxford, 2019), p. 142. **168.** The best interpretation of these events, on which I draw here, is Barclay, *Friedrich Wilhelm IV*, pp. 75, 237–8, on Hinckeldey, pp. 237–44, 273–5; Frank J. Thomason, 'The Prussian Police State in Berlin 1848–1871', PhD Thesis, University of Baltimore, 1978, p. 185. Although it is formulated within the framework of the older 'decade of reaction' school, this study remains useful. See also B. Schulze, 'Polizeipräsident Carl von Hinckeldey', *Jahrbuch für die Geschichte Mittel- und Ostdeutschlands* 4 (1955), pp. 81–108; Heinrich von Sybel, 'Carl Ludwig von Hinckeldey 1852 bis 1856', *Historische Zeitschrift* 189/1 (1959), pp. 108–23. **169.** M. Masanz and M. Nagl, *Ringstraße. Von der Freiheit zur Ordnung vor den Toren Wiens* (Vienna, 1996), p. 66. **170.** Walter Wagner, 'Die Stellungnahmen der Militärbehörden zur Wiener Stadterweiterung in den Jahren 1848–1857', *Jahrbuch des Vereins für die Geschichte der Stadt Wien* 17–18 (1961/2), pp. 216–85, here p. 223; Masanz and Nagl, *Ringstraße*, pp. 65–71. **171.** Clementina Díez de Baldeón García, 'Barrios obreros en el Madrid del siglo XIX. Solución o amenaza para el orden burgués?', in Otero Carvajal and Bahamonde Magro (eds.), *Madrid*, pp. 117–34; Roger-Henri Guerrand, *Propriétaires et locataires. Les Origines du logement social (1850–1914)* (Paris, 1967). On the association of disease with political unrest, see Richard J. Evans, *Death in Hamburg. Society and Politics in the Cholera Years* (Oxford, 1987), pp. 118–19. **172.** Shapiro, *Housing the Poor of Paris*, pp. 16–28. **173.** See, for example, the Barcelona-based *Boletín enciclopédico de nobles artes. Redactado por una reunión de arquitectos* (1846–7), which discussed and propagated Fourierist and Saint-Simonian ideas and influenced the planning for the transformation of Barcelona; these connections are discussed in Ferran Sagarra i Trias, *Barcelona, ciutat de transició (1848–1868). El projecte urbà a través dels treballs de l'arquitecte Miquel Garriga i Roca* (Barcelona, 1996), esp. pp. 106–19. On the nexus between post-revolutionary political adjustment and urban planning more generally, see Anna Ross, 'Down with the Walls! The Politics of Place in Spanish and German Urban Extension Planning, 1848–1914', viewed online at https://ora.ox.ac.uk/catalog/uuid:719b05c8-217b-41fe-8f9c-8780f190c8ae/download_file?file_format=application%2Fpdf&safe_filename=JMH%2Brevised%2BII.pdf. **174.** Papayanis, *Horse-Drawn Cabs*, pp. 96–7; Elfi Bendikat, *Öffentliche Nahverkehrspolitik in Berlin und Paris 1890–1914. Strukturbedingungen, politische Konzeptionen und Realisierungsprobleme* (Berlin, 1999), pp. 66–70; Juliá, Ringrose and Segura, *Madrid*, pp. 288–313; on the same phenomenon in Berlin, Schulze, 'Polizeipräsident Carl von Hinckeldey', pp. 93–4. **175.** Ross, *Beyond the Barricades*, pp. 143–4. **176.** Cited in Philipp Heckmann-Umhau, 'A Tale of New Cities. Urban Planning in Strasbourg and Sarajevo, 1848–1918', PhD thesis, University of Cambridge, 2022. On the effort to eliminate insalubrious housing in Strasbourg, see Alexander Dominicus, *Die Thätigkeit der Kommission gegen die ungesunden Wohnungen in Strassburg* (Strasbourg, 1901); Leonardo Benevolo, *Die sozialen Ursprünge des modernen Städtebaus. Lehren von gestern – Forderungen für morgen* (Gütersloh, 1971), pp. 108–9; Jeanne Hugueney, 'Un centenaire oublié. La première loi d'urbanisme, 13 avril 1850', *La Vie urbaine* 58 (1950), pp. 241–9. **177.** Heinz Dietrich Fischer, *Handbuch der politischen Presse in Deutschland, 1480–1980. Synopse rechtlicher, struktureller und wirtschaftlicher Grundlagen der Tendenzpublizistik im Kommunikationsfeld* (Düsseldorf, 1981), pp. 60–61, 65; Kurt Koszyk, *Deutsche Presse im 19. Jahrhundert* (Berlin, 1966), p. 123; Franz Schneider, *Pressefreiheit und politische Öffentlichkeit* (Neuwied, 1966), p. 310. **178.** Klaus Wappler, *Regierung und Presse in Preußen. Geschichte der amtlichen Pressestellen, 1848–62* (Leipzig, 1935), p. 94; Richard Kohnen, *Pressepolitik des deutschen Bundes. Methoden staatlicher Pressepolitik nach der Revolution von 1848* (Tübingen, 1995), p. 174; Seoane, *Historia del Periodismo en España*, vol. 2, p. 228. **179.** Pierre Guiral, 'La Presse de 1848 à 1871', in Claude Bellanger, Jacques Godechot, Pierre Guiral and Fernand Terrou, *Histoire générale de la Presse française* (Paris, 1969), pp. 207–382, here p. 242. **180.** Wappler, *Regierung und Presse*, p. 94. **181.** Guiral, 'La Presse', p. 252; Roger Bellet, *Presse et journalisme sous le Second Empire* (Paris, 1967), p. 11. **182.** Bellet, *Presse et journalisme*, pp. 284–5. **183.** Van Kranenberg, Palm and Pfann, 'The Life Cycle of Daily Newspapers in the Netherlands', *De Economist*, pp. 475–94; Manfred Kossok and Mauricio Pérez Saravia, 'Prensa liberal y revolución burguesa. Las revoluciones en Francia y Alemania en 1848 y en España en 1854', in Alberto Gil Novales (ed.), *La Prensa en la revolución liberal. España, Portugal y América Latina* (Madrid, 1983), pp. 390–444, here pp. 433–4. **184.** Wappler, *Regierung und Presse*, pp. 16–17, 5. **185.** Cited in Natalie Isser, *The Second Empire and the Press* (The Hague, 1974) pp. 15–16. **186.** Cited in Price, *The French Second Empire*, p. 172. **187.** Green, *Fatherlands*, pp. 148–88; Guiral, *La Presse*, p. 250; Isser, *The Second Empire and the Press*, p. 16. For an account of the 'offiziöse Presse' in the German states that comes to less sanguine (but also in my view less persuasive) conclusions on the success of such journals, see Eberhard Naujoks, 'Die offiziöse Presse und die Gesellschaft (1848/1900)', in Elger Blühm (ed.), *Presse und Geschichte. Beiträge zur historischen Kommunikationsforschung* (Munich, 1977), pp. 157–70. **188.** Kohnen, *Pressepolitik des deutschen Bundes*, p. 150. **189.** Angelo Majo, *La stampa cattolica in Italia. Storia e documentazione* (Milan, 1992), p. 49; Roger Aubert, *Le Pontificat de Pie IX (1846–1878)* (Paris, 1963), p. 39; Francesco Dante, *Storia della 'Civiltà Cattolica' (1850–1891). Il laboratorio del Papa* (Rome, 1990), pp. 57–63, 141–52. **190.** [Anon.], 'Un nuovo tributo a S. Pietro', *Civiltà Cattolica*, series 6, vol. X (1867), pp. 641–51; Klaus Schatz, *Vaticanum I, 1869–1870* (3 vols., Paderborn, 1992–4), vol. 1, pp. 201–2. **191.** For the last decade or so, a debate has raged in Italian historical writing over the question of why the Kingdom of the Two Sicilies collapsed as it did in 1860. Classic Risorgimento studies conclude that the kingdom expired under the weight of its own inadequacies; 'neo-Bourbonist' accounts argue that the kingdom was a flourishing and well-managed state that fell victim to Piedmontese conquest and international conspiracy. For a good overview focused on the years 1848–60, see Renata de Lorenzo, *Borbonia Felix. Il Regno delle Due Sicilie alla vigilia del crollo* (Rome, 2013). **192.** Simon Sarlin,

'The Anti-Risorgimento as a Transnational Experience' *Modern Italy* 19/1 (2016), p. 84. **193.** Daniel Balmuth, 'The Origins of the Tsarist Epoch of Censorship Terror', *The American Slavic and East European Review* 19/4 (1960), pp. 497-520. **194.** Aleksandr Sergeevich Nifontov, *1848 god v Rossii. Ocherki po istorii 40-kh godov* (Moscow, 1931), pp. 110-11. **195.** Ibid., pp. 178, 179, 186, 190, 193, 199-200. **196.** Gleb Ivanovich Uspensii, *Polnoe Sobranie Sochinenii* (6 vols., St Petersburg, 1908), vol. 1, pp. 175-6, cited in Isaiah Berlin, 'Russia and 1848', *The Slavonic and East European Review* 26/67 (1948), pp. 341-60, here p. 353. **197.** D. V. Dolgushin, 'Rossiya i revolutsia v istorisofskikh interpretatsiakh V. A. Zhukovskogo i F. I. Tiutcheva' [Russia and revolution in the historico-philosophical interpretations of Vladimir Zhukovsky and Fedor Tyutchev], in *Vestnik Tomskogo gosudarstvennogo universiteta*, no. 431 (2018), pp. 29-37, DOI: 10.17223/15617793/431/4, viewed online at http://journals.tsu.ru/uploads/import/1730/files/431_029.pdf; Anna Mesheryakova, 'Russkiye conservatory i evropeyskiye revolyutsii 1848-1849' [Russian conservatives and the European revolutions of 1848-1849], in *Tetradi po konservatizmu. Almanakh*, no. 2 (2017), pp. 61-7; A. P. Dmitriev, 'S. T. Aksakov o religioznom smyslie supruzheskoi liubvi i spasitelnykh urokakh Frantsiskoi revoliutsii 1848 g.' [On the religious meaning of family love and the redemptive lessons of the French revolution of 1848], *Sfera Kultury* 1/3 (2021), pp. 194-200. **198.** Frederick C. Barghoorn, 'Russian Radicals and the West European Revolutions of 1848', *The Review of Politics* 11/3 (1949), pp. 338-54, here p. 348. Herzen quotation, Frederick C. Barghoorn, *Byloe i Dumy* (Leningrad, 1946), esp. pp. 465-7; Lenin citation, Frederick C. Barghoorn, *Sochineniya*, (2nd edn, Moscow, 1949), vol. XV, pp. 464-9; both cited in Barghoorn, 'Russian Radicals', pp. 348, 354. **199.** Walter Bagehot, 'The Character of Sir Robert Peel (1856)', in Mrs Russell Barrington (ed.), *The Works and Life of Walter Bagehot* (9 vols., London, 1915), vol. 2, pp. 177-214, here pp. 191, 192, 208, 211, 212, 213. For a classic discussion of contemporary and historical views of Peel, see Boyd Hilton, 'Peel. A Reappraisal', *The Historical Journal* 22/3 (1979), pp. 585-614. **209.** François Guizot, *Sir Robert Peel. Étude d'histoire contemporaine* (Paris, 1856), p. 2. **201.** Count Camillo Benso di Cavour, speech of 7 March 1850, in Cavour, *Discorsi parlamentari del Conte di Cavour, raccolti e pubblicati per ordine della Camera dei Deputati* (11 vols., Turin, 1863-72), vol. 1 (1863), pp. 395-409, here pp. 408-9. On Peel as Cavour's 'hero', see Adolfo Omodeo, *L'opera politica del Conte di Cavour 1848-1857* (Florence, 1945), p. 63. **202.** Count Camillo Benso di Cavour, *Risorgimento* 3/780 (8 July 1850). **203.** Gaminde, speech of 20 December 1854, *Diario de las sesiones de las Cortes Constituyentes de 1854 a 1855* (Madrid, 1855), p. 529. There exists no systematic study of what Peel meant to his continental European contemporaries, but this would be an interesting project to pursue. **204.** Pedro V to Prince Albert, Lisbon, 5 October 1856, in Maria Filomena Mónica (ed.), *Correspondência entre D. Pedro V e seu tio, o príncipe Alberto* (Lisbon, 2000), pp. 140-53, here p. 145. **205.** R. J. W. Evans, 'From Confederation to Compromise', pp. 146-7; Durán de la Rua, *Unión Liberal*, p. 345. **206.** Ménager, *Les Napoléon du peuple*, pp. 128-9. **207.** Ministry of Public Works, First Division, Central Office of Statistics, 'Demande de renseignements statistiques sur la construction des tunnels', 26 May 1853, Ministry of Agriculture, Commerce and Public Works, Archives Nationales Paris F/14/8508A; for adhesive stamps, see the letter from the French consul in Antwerp, 12 December 1856, in Archives Nationales Paris F/12/2480 (Douanes: Projet de loi portant retrait des prohibitions (1856); dossier de la Commission du Corps législatif; pétitions pour et contre le retrait; précédents (1855-1856); voeux des conseils généraux, voeux des chambres de Commerce (1855-1856); on sugar refinement and consumption, with a strong emphasis on international comparison, see the files in F/12/2483 (Douanes: réforme douanière de 1860 à rapports et mémoires, travaux préparatoires, 1857-1860). **208.** Goldman, 'The Origins of British "Social Science"', esp. pp. 594-5. **209.** On the 'transfer function' of international exhibitions and the paucity of work in this area, see Wolfram

Kaiser, 'Inszenierung des Freihandels als weltgesellschaftliche Entwicklungsstrategie. Die "Great Exhibition" 1851 und der politische Kulturtransfer nach Kontinentaleuropa', in Franz Bosbach and John R. Davis (eds.), *Die Weltausstellung von 1851 und ihre Folgen* (Munich, 2002), pp. 163–80; M. H. Geyer and J. Paulmann (eds.), *The Mechanics of Internationalism* (Oxford, 2001), esp. the introductory essay by the editors, pp. 1–25. 210. 'El progreso industrial en Bélgica', 'Importación de lanas en Inglaterra', 'La industria inglesa y la expansión de Londres', 'La industria algodonera en Alemania', 'Ingresos de los ferro-carriles ingleses y franceses', in Revista Científica del Ministero de Fomento 2 (1863), pp. 28–9, 50–55. 60–61, 193–211, 225–34, 250–51. 211. Ross, *Beyond the Barricades*, p. 145. It is important not to overstate the case: in the files of the Ministry of Development in Madrid, I found copies of the *Mittheilungen aus dem Gebiet der Statistik* issued by the Directorship of Administrative Statistics in the Austrian Empire's Ministry of Commerce and dutifully forwarded to Madrid by the Spanish embassy in Vienna. Closer inspection revealed that the pages were uncut. Primera Secretaria de Estado, subsecretario Antonio Caballero, to Ministro de Fomento, Madrid, 7 August 1854, Archivo Histórico Nacional, Madrid, FC OP (Fomento) leg. 2361. 212. Widukind de Ridder, 'The Legacy of the Abstinence from Revolution in Belgium', in Moggach and Stedman Jones (eds.), *The 1848 Revolutions and European Political Thought*, pp. 185–215, here p. 214. Even Marx and Engels tagged 1848 as the moment when 'utopian' socialism made way for 'a superior, more "scientific" variety'; see Diana Siclovan, '1848 and German Socialism', in ibid., pp. 254–75, here p. 255. 213. I borrow the term 'administrative intelligentsia' from Goldman, 'The Social Science Association', p. 100.

CONCLUSION

1. Fanny Lewald, *A Year of Revolutions. Fanny Lewald's Recollections of 1848* [1870], ed. and trans. Hanna Ballin Lewis (Oxford, 1998), pp. 41–2. 2. Daniel Stern [Marie d'Agoult], *Histoire de la révolution de 1848* (Paris, 1850), vol. 3, p. 86; on Napoleon's presence in revolutionary awareness, see A. Tudesq, 'La Légende napoléonienne en France en 1848', *Revue Historique* 218/1 (1957), pp. 64–85. 3. Simonetta Soldani, 'Approaching Europe in the Name of the Nation. The Italian Revolution, 1846/49', in Dieter Dowe, Heinz-Gerhard Haupt, Dieter Langewiesche and Jonathan Sperber (eds.), *Europe in 1848. Revolution and Reform*, trans. David Higgins (New York and Oxford, 2001), pp. 59–90, here p. 62. 4. Keith Hitchens, *The Romanians, 1774–1866* (Oxford, 1996), pp. 238–9; for the full text, see Ioan C. Brătianu (ed.), *Anul 1848 în Principatele române. Acte şi documente publicate cu ajutorul Comitetului pentru rădicarea monumentului* (6 vols., Bucharest, 1902–10), pp. 460–67, here p. 460. 5. Alexis de Tocqueville, *Recollections*, ed. J. P. Mayer and A. P. Kerr, trans. George Lawrence (London, 1970), p. 53. 6. Karl Marx, *Der achtzehnte Brumaire des Louis Bonaparte*, ed. Hauke Brunkhorst (Frankfurt am Main, 2007). 7. Tocqueville, *Recollections*, p. 53. 8. On the memory of 1848 as a 'failed revolution', see Heinz-Gerhard Haupt and Dieter Langewiesche, 'The European Revolution of 1848. Its Political and Social Reforms, Its Politics of Nationalism, and Its Short- and Long-Term Consequences', in Dowe et al. (eds.), *Europe in 1848*, pp. 1–24, here p. 13. 9. Angela Jianu, *A Circle of Friends. Romanian Revolutionaries and Political Exile, 1840–1859* (Leiden, 2011), p. 360; Silvia Marton, 'Les acteurs de 1848 après 1848. Vies et survie du républicanisme roumain au XIXe siècle', paper presented at the colloquium *Les Acteurs européens du 'printemps des peuples' 1848. Colloque international du cent soixante-dixième anniversaire*, Sorbonne, Paris, 31 May–2 June 2018. 10. Thomas C. Jones, 'French Republicanism after 1848', in Douglas Moggach and Gareth Stedman Jones (eds.), *The 1848 Revolutions and European Political Thought* (Cambridge, 2018), p. 92. 11. Otto von Bismarck, *Gedanken und Erinnerungen* (2 vols., Stuttgart, 1898), vol. 1, p. 2. 12. Anne-Sophie Chambost, 'Socialist Visions of

Direct Democracy. The Mid-Century Crisis of Popular Sovereignty and the Constitutional Legacy of the Jacobins', in Moggach and Stedman Jones (eds.), *The 1848 Revolutions and European Political Thought*, p. 108.   13. Annelien de Dijn, *Freedom. An Unruly History* (Cambridge, Mass., 2020), esp. pp. 277–310 and 344–5. Samuel Hayat, 'The Revolution of 1848 in the History of French Republicanism', *History of Political Thought* 36 (2015), pp. 331–53.   14. Samuel Hayat, 'Working-Class Socialism in 1848 in France', in Moggach and Stedman Jones (eds.), *The 1848 Revolutions and European Political Thought*, pp. 120–139, here p. 128.   15. Louis Blanc, 'A mes électeurs', in Blanc, *Questions d'aujourd'hui et de demain. Troisième série. Politique* (Paris, 1880), pp. 503–517, here p. 505. On the longer-term success of the 'democratic-pluralistic order', see Hannelore Horn, 'Zum Wander des Revolutions begriff (1848–1998)', in Heiner Timmermann (ed.), *1848. Revolution in Europa. Verlauf, politische Programme, Folgen und Wirkungen* (Berlin, 1999), pp. 39–68.   16. Gian Biagio Furiozzi, *L'emigrazione politica in Piemonte nel decennio preunitario* (Florence, 1979), p. 7; Renata de Lorenzo, *Borbonia Felix. Il Regno delle Due Sicilie alla vigilia del crollo* (Rome, 2013), pp. 74–101.   17. De Lorenzo, *Borbonia Felix*, p. 17.   18. Süheyla Yenidünya Gürgen, '1848 İhtilali'nden Sonra Eflak'ın Yeniden Yapılanmasına Dair Bir Değerlendirme. Ştirbei'in Müesses Nizam Arayışları (1849–1851)' [An Evaluation of the Restructuring of Wallachia after the Revolution of 1848. Ştirbei's Quest for Institutional Order (1849–1851)], *Tokat Gaziosmanpaşa Üniversitesi Sosyal Bilimler Araştırmaları Dergisi* 15/1 (2020), pp. 11–23, here p. 21. Imanuel Geiss, 'Die europäische Revolution 1848–1998. Markro und welthistorische Perspoktiven', in Timmermann (ed.), *1848. Revolution in Europa*, pp. 69–94.   20. A good case is made for remembering the 'triumph' of constitutional liberalism in Ángel Rivero, 'Dos Conceptos de liberalismo. Constant, España y el bautizo del liberalismo', *Cuadernos de Pensamiento Político* 49 (January–March 2016), pp. 203–18. An important recent reappraisal of liberalism that pushes in this direction is Helena Rosenblatt, *The Lost History of Liberalism. From Ancient Rome to the Twenty-First Century* (Princeton, 2018).   21. Paul Ginsborg, *Daniele Manin and the Venetian Revolution* (Cambridge, 1979), p. 367.   22. 'Extremismus wird vielfältiger', *Badische Zeitung*, 8 June 2022, p. 1.   23. For a brilliant analysis of the Ottawa protests, see Richard Sanger, 'Diary', *London Review of Books* 44/8 (21 April 2022), pp. 40–41.   24. Ross Douthat, 'A New Class War Comes to Canada', *The New York Times*, 19 February 2022, viewed online at https://www.nytimes.com/2022/02/19/opinion/class-war-canada-truckers-protest. html.   25. George Packard, 'How America Fractured into Four Parts', *The Atlantic*, July/ August 2021, viewed online at https://www.theatlantic.com/magazine/archive/2021/07/ george-packer-four-americas/619012/.

Index

Aargau, Swiss canton of,
227–8, 261
Abel, Wilhelm, 35
Aberdeen, Lord, 635
Academy of Moral and
Political Sciences, Paris,
21, 30
Adam, Victor, 553
Adrianople, Treaty of
(1829), 666, 667
Affre, Monsignor,
Archbishop of Paris, 559
Agoult, Countess Marie d',
364–5, 383, 433–4, 442,
443, 479, 743; on
Constituent Assembly in
Paris, 385, 387, 389,
392; and July Revolution
(1830), 174–6; writes
best contemporary
history of Revolution, 1,
174, 441
agriculture: agrarian reform
in Wallachia, 513–16,
669; food supplies and
natural catastrophes, 37,
38, 44–5, 47–8; Freschi's
L'Amico del Contadino,
510; growth in the food
supply, 36–7; harvest
failures of 1846–7,
48–50, 255–6, 267, 452;
in Hungary, 233, 511–13;
on Ionian Islands, 630;
labour force in France,
503; and 'liberal' model
of private property,
39–42, 44, 276–7, 423–4,
506, 507–8; potato and
grain shocks (1846–7),
44–51, 87, 267, 295,

335, 451–2, 453–5;
repeal of the Corn Laws
in Britain (1846), 338,
737; and rural poverty,
34, 74–5, 507–8;
sharecropping
(*mezzadria*), 34, 37, 247;
smallholding peasants,
34, 37, 42, 513–16;
traditional
'agrosilvopastoral'
system, 39–42, 89–90,
405, 407, 423–4, 506
Aguyar, Andrea, 644–5,
664
'Albert the worker', 364–5,
370, 470, 475, 480, 554,
622
Alecsandri, Vasile, 467
Alejo de Gaminde, Benito,
737–8
Algeciras, 341
Algeria, 176, 420–21, 425,
558–9,
560, 625
Allart, Hortense, 108
Allen, William, 700
Alonso Martínez, Manuel,
721
Alsace, 451, 452–4
Amari, Michele, 140–41,
149–50
Ambrosoli, Ambrogio,
457
American War of
Independence, 708
Ampt, Abraham, 332
Amsterdam, 331, 332
anarchism, 689–90
Ancona, 582
Andalusia, 39, 43, 47

Andrássy, Gyula, 745
Andringa de Kempenaer,
Regnerus van, 332–3
Andryane, Alexandre,
195–6
Angeloni, Luigi, *On Force
in Political Affairs*,
679–80
Angola, 160, 425
Anneke, Mathilde, 106,
107, 109, 702
Annenkov, P. V., 560–61
anti-vaccination protests,
751
Antonelli, Cardinal, 662
Antoniewicz, Karol, 77, 83
Anzani, Francesco, 210
'Arab Spring', 7, 344–5,
352
Arago, Emmanuel, 443
Arago, Étienne, 280, 366
Arago, François, 365, 412,
415, 470, 551
Aristotle, 247
Arndt, Ernst Moritz, 147,
225, 694–5
Arnim, Bettina von, 23,
443
Arnold, Đuro (György),
156
Arnout, Louis-Jules, 553
Asachi, Gheorghe, 146
Astell, Mary, *Reflections
Upon Marriage* (1696),
97
Aston, Louise, 108
Auerbach, Berthold, 458
Auerswald, Hans von,
546–7, 619, 626
Auerswald, Rudolf von,
626–7

833

counter-revolution in,
407, 429, 570, 580, 651,
652–3, 656–8, 676, 712;
death rates in 1845–7
crisis, 48; demographic
growth in, 36;
development of
parliamentary politics in,
211, 214–15; economic
liberalism in, 115, 116;
and Erfurt Union, 666,
677–8; growth of social
activism, 215–16;
Hambacher Fest, 211;
Holstein's membership
of, 543–6; illiberal
crackdowns in late-
1830s, 213–14;
increasingly polarized
mandates in, 648;
intensification of
opposition (1847), 294;
and mental maps of
nationalism, 149;
Metternich's intelligence
bureau, 213, 250;
Metternich's repressive
measures (1834), 166,
212–13, 252–3; mutiny
among miners at
Neustadt, 281; peasant
involvement in
revolution, 504, 505,
506, 549; post-
revolutionary
state-building projects,
747–8; poverty in
pre-1848 period, 34–5,
37, 47, 48, 210–11, 212;
press policies in, 731,
732; protracted political
crisis after July
Revolution, 182, 210–14,
216–18; 'public meeting
democracy' during
Revolutions, 315–16;
Punctation of Olmütz
(November 1850), 678;
regional histories of land
management, 506;
second-wave revolts in,
3–4, 588, 647, 649,
651–8; size of rural
population, 503; status
of Jews in, 446, 449–50,
456, 460; and Swiss crisis

(1845–7), 263, 492;
thickening of dissident
networks in 1840s,
216–18, 219–21; and
Vienna treaties, 127, 250,
659; violence against
Jews during revolution,
451, 452, 454–5
German nationalism:
Blum's tear, 10–11; and
carnivals/traditional
festivities, 211, 212,
215–16; complexity of
'national question',
522–3; and the Czechs,
536–7, 538, 548–9, 590,
593, 596, 649;
Dahlmann's 'mixed
people', 149; desire for
ethnic 'purity', 149;
different visions of the
German nation, 549;
emergence of German
nation-state, 747–8; first
'German elections'
(1848), 394; 'German
Democratic Legion', 497,
498; German gymnastics
movement, 142, 147,
149, 150; and German
language, 147, 531;
German republicanism,
495–501, 503, 647;
'greater-German' and
'lesser-German'
solutions, 649–50, 665;
and the Hungarians, 605,
675; Leipzig crisis
(August 1845), 221–5,
223, 227, 313, 493,
618–19; Märzverein
clubs in south and west,
647; 'old-German
costume', 142, 312, 428;
and Polish question,
539–41, 543, 547–8;
post-1848 exiles, 694–5,
702, 705; as preserve of
cultural elite, 154;
Prussia seizes de facto
control of national
question, 568, 649–50,
665–6, 675, 677–8 ;
Punctation seen as
humiliation, 678; radical
religious movements,

138, 220, 221, 224, 314;
realist reorientation after
counter-revolution,
676–8; Reich
constitution campaign,
650–53; 'Rhine Crisis'
(1840), 143–4;
'Schleswig-Holstein
question', 543–6, 547–8,
665, 678; and second-
wave revolts, 3–4, 588,
647, 649, 651–8; and
Slavic Congress (June
1848), 538; *Sonderweg*
('special path'), 2;
see also Blum, Robert;
Frankfurt National
Assembly
Germany (outside 1815–70
period): Basic Law of the
Federal Republic (1949),
407; German Empire
founded (1871), 460;
Nazi era, 2, 468, 501;
revolutionary destruction
of Holy Roman Empire,
250–51; Weimar
Constitution (1919), 407
Gervinus, Georg Gottfried,
214
Ghica, Ion, 667
Ghilardi, Luigi, 686
gilets jaunes, 751, 753
Ginsborg, Paul, 750
Gioberti, Vincenzo, 126–7,
245–8, 257, 523
Gisikon, Battle of (1847),
262
Gladstone, William, 635
Goldmark, Joseph, 608,
610–12
Golescu, Ștefan, 376
Görgey, Arthur, 673–4
Görres, Joseph, 137–8
Göttingen, university town
of, 214
governments,
revolutionary:
Committee of Safety in
Vienna, 489–91,
600–602, 614;
commonality of political
problems for, 342–3,
344; complexity of the
agrarian question,
505–6, 507–17;

Hemingway, Ernest, *The Sun Also Rises*, 305
Henry, Anne-Marie, 429
Henry, Louis, 467
Heppenheim (Hesse), 217–18
Herbinot de Mauchamps, Frédéric, 104–5
Héricourt, Jenny d', 432, 433
Herschmann, Bernard, 360
Herwegh, Emma, 497, 500
Herwegh, Georg, 497, 498, 651
Herzen, Alexander, 107, 119, 560–61, 736
Hess, Moses, 689
Hesse, Electorate of (Hesse-Kassel), 210, 211–12, 213, 284, 399, 449, 450, 460
Hesse-Darmstadt, 196–9, 210, 214, 217, 257, 314
Heubner, Otto, 653
Heyden, Julius von, *Dessalines*, 467
Heydt, August von der, 720
Hilton, Boyd, 338
Hinckeldey, Karl Ludwig von, 726–8, 729, 741
history, concept of: conservative view of, 165; Europe as a conflicted society, 282; and the French Revolution (1789), 13–14, 164, 743–4; Hegelian idealism, 166–7; intellectual/political journeys of 1830s/40s, 166–8; liberal view of, 164–6; Louis Napoleon on, 717; Marx's materialism, 167; patriotic histories, 139–42; self-historicizing temperament of 1848, 358–9, 493, 502; semantic weight of in 1848, 13–14, 409, 524; sense of irreversible motion, 163–8
Hitler, Adolf, 2
Hobbes, Thomas, 123, 124
Hodshon, Joan, 332
Hoffer, Carl, 606

Holy Roman Empire, 250–51
Hrabowsky von Hrabova, John, 603–4
Huber, Aloysius, 551, 552
Hübner, Carl Wilhelm, 68
Hübner, Count Joseph Alexander, 251, 304, 324–7, 329, 618–19
Hugo, Victor, 172, 186, 467, 560, 563
Humania Association, 440
Hungary: and 1848 electoral franchises, 386; agrarian policy, 233, 511–13; 'April Laws' (1848), 404, 405; Batthyány appointed Prime Minister (17 March), 310; capitulation to Russians at Világos (August 1849), 674, 695; complex geopolitics of revolution/war, 603–6, 615–16, 671–5; conservative political circles, 126, 138, 234–5; cosmopolitan nature of war effort, 675; and Croatian nationalism, 382, 532–6, 603–6; delegation to Vienna (15–17 March 1848), 308–12; Demands of the Radical Hungarian Women, 430–32; the Diet (old body), 7, 230–31, 232, 233, 234, 236, 281, 283, 294–5, 297–8, 306, 381, 404; dissension within revolutionary leadership, 673–4; events of 15 March, 307–8; Galician 'lessons' for opposition leaders, 83, 511; growth of political dissent in, 231–6, 252, 281, 283, 294–5; Hungarian Academy of the Sciences, 148; 'imposed' Austrian constitution (4 March 1849), 673; independence war, 538–9, 548, 604–8,

672–5, 683, 695, 749; Jelačić invades, 603–5, 606, 671; Jewish population, 446, 449, 454, 459, 460–62, 531; liberalism in, 115–16, 232–6; Mór Jókai's novels, 695–8; as multi-ethnic state, 531–2, 673; murder of Lamberg in Buda, 606, 612; national costume, 142, 150, 312, 431; new Diet (1848), 7, 381, 382, 511, 673; new state (1867), 745; and October rising in Vienna, 615–16, 618; Party of Opposition, 231–6, 281, 283, 294–5, 306; Petőfi's national song, 2, 140, 307, 520–21, 682; Protestant minority in, 139; refugees from in Ottoman Empire, 684–5; Royal Hungarian Army, 672–3, 674, 685, 696; rural unrest (1848), 512–13; Russian intervention (summer 1849), 4, 674–5, 683, 695, 749; 'Society for equality' in, 524; South Slav borderlands of, 156, 603–6; Védegylet (Defence Association), 116; Vice-Regal Council in Buda, 308, 313; Vörösmarty's *The Flight of Zalan*, 142; women and patriotism, 150, 155; *see also* Kossuth, Lajos; Magyar nationalism
Hunger, August, 226

Icarian movement, 119, 623–4
Iceland, 142, 715
industrial capitalism/industrialism: in 1830s Nantes, 16, 18; agrarian and industrial crisis (1845–7), 44–51, 87, 267, 295, 331, 335, 451–2, 453–5; Engels's view of, 26–7, 33, 35;

July Revolution (1830), 27,
54, 132, 506–7; awards
of pensions after, 180;
cascading of upheaval to
other countries, 181–2;
casualty figures in Paris,
176; Charles X flees
Paris, 174, 176, 179;
conservative view of,
127–8, 131; as
constitutional event, 116,
169, 176–9;
disturbances/fighting in
Paris (27–29 July),
169–76, 175, 179–80,
182, 183, 185, 210;
economic impact of,
52–3; as 'European
media event', 181; and
gender order, 95, 96,
102, 103–4; inspires
German political crisis,
210–14, 216–18; and
liberalism, 112, 116,
127–8, 169, 170,
176–80, 183–4; in
Nantes, 180–81; official
decorations, 180–81; and
press/newspapers, 170,
177–8, 179–80, 240–41,
365; provincial
government announced
(29 July), 172; public
ceremony honouring the
dead (1840), 354; radical
disappointment at, 102,
183–4, 185, 192; as
sacred moment for
monarchy and liberals,
294; 'story of a paving
stone', 182–3, 184; and
Swiss Guards, 172, 174,
179; worker
participation in, 116,
171, 172–6, 175,
178–81
Jung, Dr Georg, 359

Kamieński, Henryk, 83
Kandern, Battle of (April
1848), 496, 497
Karlsruhe (Baden), 284,
492, 496, 656
Kassel, 211–12, 346
Kay, James, 20
Kemény, Dénes, 232

kindergarten movement,
438–9
Kingdom of the Two
Sicilies: aid for Italian
struggle against Austria,
525, 571–2, 579, 582;
Bandiera brothers fiasco
(1844), 204–5, 240, 499;
Catholic Church in, 362;
conservative resurgence
in, 584–7; constitution
issued in Naples (1848),
3, 278, 283, 296, 346,
372, 381, 399, 569,
570–71, 575–6, 579,
581; counter-revolution,
527, 569–70, 574–84,
578; disappearance of
(1861), 585; elections in
(April/June 1848), 381,
387, 390; Ferdinand II
strikes against Naples
(May 1848), 527, 570,
576–80, 578, 581–4,
586–7; land privatization
in, 42, 506; peasant
uprising in Cilento, 278;
Pius IX flees to
(November 1848),
635–7, 640, 641–2,
661–2; political prisoners
in, 635; reactionary
politics in post-
revolutionary period,
711, 734, 748;
revolution as liberal
opportunity, 278, 372;
revolution in (1820–21),
164, 176, 257, 265, 266,
270–72, 276, 371;
revolution in (1848),
258, 265–8, 268–74,
283–5, 343, 721;
Settembrini's *Protesta del
Popolo delle Due Sicilie*,
257–8, 280, 501; *see also*
Ferdinand II, King of the
Two Sicilies; Naples;
Palermo; Sicily
Kinkel, Gottfried, 688
Kisfaludy, Károly, 150
Kissinger, Henry, 251–2
Kleist, Heinrich von, 467,
627
Kneisel, Matthias, 302,
303

Kneppelhout, Johannes,
334
Kogălniceanu, Mihail, 139,
141, 149, 463
Kohn, Abraham, 445
Kolbe von Schreeb,
Eberhard Freiherr, 541
Kollwitz, Käthe, 70
Kolowrat, Count, 304
König, Heinrich, 346
Königsberg, 216, 220, 373,
449
Könneritz, Julius Traugott
von, 221, 224
Körber, Philip, *Der
Negeraufstand in Hayti*,
467
Kossuth, Lajos, 1, *311*, 454;
address to Hungarian
Diet (3 March 1848),
297–8, 306; anti-socialist
views, 702; character of,
234–5, 310–12, 689,
694; declaration (June
1847), 235–6; elected to
the Diet (October 1847),
236; family of
imprisoned, 687; in
Hungarian delegation to
Vienna (15 March 1848),
309–10; Hungarian war
effort managed by,
672–3, 674; and Jewish
emancipation, 459, 460;
journalism of, 234, 235;
liberal Mexican coverage
of, 707; Magyar
nationalism of, 147, 235,
474, 671–2;
Parliamentary and
Municipal Reports, 234;
peasantry emancipation
proposal, 83, 511–13;
and *Pesti Hirlap*, 235,
695; protectionism of,
116; as refugee in Turkey,
684, 688, 689; tension
with Széchenyi, 235,
310–12; in USA,
700–701
Kotarski, Count Karol, 72
Kotzebue, August von,
murder of (1819), 213,
215, 252
Krafft-Ebing, Richard
von, 84

leftist politics – *cont'd.*
Donnersberg (Thunder
Mountain), 391; efforts
to shut down after June
Days, 622–5; French
Workers' Party (Parti
Ouvrier Français), 60;
Jacobin symbology
during revolutions, 658;
Left Hegelians, 69; and
Lyonnais weavers' trials
in Paris (1834), 59, 60;
Lyons in historical
imaginary of, 60;
marginalized in
post-revolutionary era,
711, 712, 713, 714;
Montagne in 1848
assembly, 401–2; move
towards mixed and
moderate programme,
614, 658–9, 702, 745,
746; and plight of rural
poor, 35; producer and
non-producer binary,
118–19; retrospective
views on revolutions,
741; shrinkage as
political force in Second
Republic, 624, 625; and
Silesian revolt (1844),
69–70; and 'Social
Question', 26–7, 28, 33;
Solidarité républicaine
in France, 648; spectre
of communism, 282,
555, 659; *see also*
socialism
Legnano, Battle of (1176),
520, 643
Lehmann, Henri, 442, 691
Leipzig, 138, 216, 217,
219, 220, 324, 383; crisis
in (August 1845), 221–5,
223, 227, 313, 493,
618–19
Leipzig Society for the
Cultivation of Oratory
(*Redeübungsverein*), 220
Leo XII, Pope, 132
Leopardi, Giacomo, 725
Leopardi, Pietro, 582
Leopold II of Tuscany, 255,
256, 268–9, 334
Léoutre, Commissaire, 517
Leroux, Jules, 121

Leroux, Pierre, 121, 157,
455, 554, 623
Lesser Antilles, 418
Lessing, Gotthold Ephraim,
Nathan the Wise, 467
Lewald, Fanny, 9, 345, 347,
388, 628, 743
Lewicki, Jan Nepomucen,
Galician Massacre,
80, 81
liberalism: in 1840s
Netherlands, 331–2,
333–4; 1848 as apogee
of certain kind of liberal
politics, 407, 646; and
anti-clericalism, 114–15,
131, 178–9, 184; in
Baden, 492–4, 495;
cascade of revolutions in
early 1820s, 164–5, 176;
and 'centralization' of
power, 126–7; crushing
of radicals in name of
revolution, 473, 557–65,
648–9; and economic
competition, 117; in
France during 1848–9,
365, 370, 372, 373,
474–6, 550–52, 555–65;
and French Revolution
(1789), 110, 111, 112;
gravitation towards
forces of order, 10, 92,
237–8, 277–8, 473,
557–65, 648–9, 750;
history of term, 93–4,
109, 111; in Hungary,
115–16, 232–6; idea of
liberty, 111, 179, 423,
646; ignorance of rural
life, 13, 508–11, 518,
519, 613–14, 615, 750;
and inescapability of
conflict, 119, 246–7; and
July Revolution (1830),
112, 116, 127–8, 169,
170, 176–80, 183–4;
laissez-faire principles,
50, 51, 646; liberal
vernacular of nineteenth-
century Europe, 342;
Martínez de la Rosa in
Spain, 112–14;
metapolitical claims of,
110, 113, 115, 749; as of
the 'middle way',

110–14, 116–17, 119,
646–7, 648; model of
private property, 39–42,
44, 50, 53, 69, 70,
89–90, 110, 111, 423–4,
507–8; *moderados* in
Spain, 91, 248, 283,
339–42, 398–9, 700,
713, 716; multiplicity of
'liberalisms', 109–11,
113, 114–15; as *not*
supporting democracy,
110, 112–13, 237–8;
pervasive fear of the
lower orders, 10, 92,
212, 237, 277–8, 294,
648–9; and Pius IX,
253–5, 256–7, 267,
268–9, 295; political
banquets in France, 243,
256, 263, 284, 286–7,
288–9, 294; in post-1830
Belgium, 334–5, 336; in
Prague, 590–92;
prioritizing of political
over social solutions,
110, 113, 114, 646; and
privilege of wealth, 110,
117–18; and problem of
inequality, 5, 114,
117–18, 749–50;
protectionist liberals,
114, 115, 116; in Prussia,
214–17, 484, 485; realist
reorientation after
counter-revolution, 679;
relationship with
national identity, 549;
reverence for
parliaments/
constitutions, 8, 111–12,
114, 116, 119, 164–5,
176–9, 381, 398, 407,
745; rule of law, 111–12,
114, 177; and second-
wave revolts, 647–8; and
state of nature notion,
124; strong regional
variations in, 115–16; in
Switzerland, 227–9,
261–4; thickening of
dissident networks in
German states, 216–18,
219–21; turbulence/
unrest antagonistic to,
90–91, 110–11, 113–14,